READING IN THE BYZANTINE EMPIRE AND BEYOND

Offering a comprehensive introduction to the history of books, readers and reading in the Byzantine Empire and its sphere of influence, this volume addresses a paradox. Advanced literacy was rare among imperial citizens, being restricted by gender and class. Yet the state's economic, religious and political institutions insisted on the fundamental importance of the written record. Starting from the materiality of codices, documents and inscriptions, the volume's contributors draw attention to the evidence for a range of interactions with texts. They examine the role of authors, compilers and scribes. They look at practices such as the close perusal of texts in order to produce excerpts, notes, commentaries and editions. But they also analyse the social implications of the constant intersection of writing with both image and speech. Showcasing current methodological approaches, this collection of essays aims to place a discussion of Byzantium within the mainstream of medieval textual studies.

TERESA SHAWCROSS is Associate Professor of History and Hellenic Studies at Princeton University. Interested in the pre-modern book, she has studied the materiality of manuscripts, the role of authors, translators and scribes, and the interplay between literacy and orality. Publications include: *The Chronicle of Morea: Historiography in Crusader Greece* (2009).

IDA TOTH is Senior Instructor and Lecturer, and Research Fellow at Oxford University. She convenes graduate courses in Medieval Latin, Byzantine Greek and Byzantine Epigraphy. She has published on inscriptional culture and court rhetoric, and on the transmission of the *Life of Aesop* and the *Book of Syntipas the Philosopher*.

Fig. 0.1 Elizabeth and Michael Jeffreys about to join family and friends to celebrate their Golden Wedding in the hall of Exeter College, July 2015 (photograph by © Katharine Jeffreys)

READING IN THE BYZANTINE EMPIRE AND BEYOND

EDITED BY

TERESA SHAWCROSS
Princeton University

IDA TOTH
University of Oxford

CAMBRIDGE
UNIVERSITY PRESS

University Printing House, Cambridge CB2 8BS, United Kingdom

One Liberty Plaza, 20th Floor, New York, NY 10006, USA

477 Williamstown Road, Port Melbourne, VIC 3207, Australia

314–321, 3rd Floor, Plot 3, Splendor Forum, Jasola District Centre, New Delhi – 110025, India

79 Anson Road, #06–04/06, Singapore 079906

Cambridge University Press is part of the University of Cambridge.

It furthers the University's mission by disseminating knowledge in the pursuit of education, learning, and research at the highest international levels of excellence.

www.cambridge.org
Information on this title: www.cambridge.org/9781108418416
DOI: 10.1017/9781108289993

© Cambridge University Press 2018

This publication is in copyright. Subject to statutory exception and to the provisions of relevant collective licensing agreements, no reproduction of any part may take place without the written permission of Cambridge University Press.

First published 2018

Printed and bound in Great Britain by Clays Ltd, Elcograf S.p.A.

A catalogue record for this publication is available from the British Library.

Library of Congress Cataloging-in-Publication Data
NAMES: Shawcross, Clare Teresa M., 1975– editor. | Toth, Ida, 1968– editor.
TITLE: Reading in the Byzantine Empire and Beyond / edited by Teresa Shawcross, Ida Toth.
DESCRIPTION: Cambridge, UK ; New York : Cambridge University Press, 2018. | Includes bibliographical references and index.
IDENTIFIERS: LCCN 2017055930 | ISBN 9781108418416 (hardcover)
SUBJECTS: LCSH: Books–Byzantine Empire. | Books and reading–Byzantine Empire. | Transmission of texts–Byzantine Empire. | Written communication–Byzantine Empire. | Manuscripts, Medieval–Byzantine Empire–History. | Byzantine literature–History and criticism. | Byzantine Empire–Intellectual life.
CLASSIFICATION: LCC Z8.B9 R43 2018 | DDC 028.09495–dc23
LC record available at https://lccn.loc.gov/2017055930

ISBN 978-1-108-41841-6 Hardback

Cambridge University Press has no responsibility for the persistence or accuracy of URLs for external or third-party internet websites referred to in this publication and does not guarantee that any content on such websites is, or will remain, accurate or appropriate.

To Elizabeth and Michael Jeffreys

Contents

List of Figures	*page* xi
List of Contributors	xiii
Preface	xix
List of Abbreviations	xxii

INTRODUCTION TO BOOKS, READERS AND READING	1
Byzantium: a Bookish World *Teresa Shawcross*	3
Modern Encounters with Byzantine Texts and their Reading Publics *Ida Toth*	37
PART I LOVE FOR THE WRITTEN WORD	51
THE EMOTIONS OF READING	53
1 John Mauropous and the Benefits of Reading *Marina Bazzani*	55
2 The Autobiographies of the Patriarch Gennadios II Scholarios *Michael Angold*	68
CENTRE AND MARGINS	91
3 The Role of the Speeches of John the Oxite in Komnenian Court Politics *Judith R. Ryder*	93
4 The Liturgical Poetics of an Elite Religious Confraternity *Paul Magdalino*	116

5 Manuscript Notes and the Black Death in Rural Cyprus 133
Tassos Papacostas

PART II CONTACT WITH A LIVING CULTURE 155

THE POWER OF RHETORIC 157

6 Ancient Greek Rhetorical Theory and Byzantine
Discursive Politics: John Sikeliotes on Hermogenes 159
Panagiotis Roilos

7 Memoirs as Manifesto: the Rhetoric of
Katakalon Kekaumenos 185
Jonathan Shepard

8 Performative Reading in the Late Byzantine *Theatron* 215
Niels Gaul

RELIGIOUS TEXTS 235

9 The Religious World of John Malalas 237
David M. Gwynn

10 *Oikonomia* in the Hymns of Romanos the Melode 255
Johannes Koder

11 Quotation and Allusion in Symeon the New Theologian 271
Manolis S. Patedakis

12 Scriptural Citation in Andronikos Kamateros 296
Alessandra Bucossi

SECULAR TEXTS 315

13 Aristocratic Family Narratives in Twelfth-century Byzantium 317
Peter Frankopan

14 Historiography, Epic and the Textual Transmission
of Imperial Values: Liudprand's *Antapodosis*
and *Digenes Akrites* 336
Günter Prinzing

15 Intertextuality in the Late Byzantine Romance *Tale of Troy* 351
Ulrich Moennig

Contents

PART III COMMUNICATION AND INFLUENCE — 373

EDUCATIONAL PRACTICES — 375

16 Late Byzantine School Teaching Through the *Iambic Canons* and their *Paraphrase* — 377
   Dimitrios Skrekas

TEXT AND IMAGE — 395

17 Eros, Literature and the Veroli Casket — 397
   Liz James

18 Object, Text and Performance in Four Komnenian Tent Poems — 414
   Margaret Mullett

19 Textual and Visual Representations of the Antipodes from Byzantium and the Latin West — 430
   Maja Kominko

INTERLINGUAL CIRCULATION AND TRANSMISSION — 445

20 Basil I, Constantine VII and Armenian Literary Tradition in Byzantium — 447
   Tim Greenwood

21 Bilingual Reading, the *Alexiad* and the *Gesta Roberti Wiscardi* — 467
   James Howard-Johnston

22 Transplanting Culture: from Greek Novel to Medieval Romance — 499
   Roderick Beaton

PART IV MODERN READING AS TEXTUAL ARCHAEOLOGY — 515

TRACES OF AUTHORSHIP — 517

23 Anonymous Textual Survivals from Late Antiquity — 519
   Fiona K. Haarer

24 Authorship and the *Letters* of Theodore Daphnopates — 547
   John Duffy

25	Authorship Revisited: Language and Metre in the *Ptochoprodromika* *Marjolijne C. Janssen and Marc D. Lauxtermann*	558

RECOVERED LANGUAGES 585

26	The Lexicon of Horses' Colours in Learned and Vernacular Texts *Erich Trapp*	587
27	Multilingualism and Translation in the Edition of Vernacular Texts *Manolis Papathomopoulos*	595

Afterword: Reading and Hearing in Byzantium 626
Elizabeth Jeffreys and Michael Jeffreys

Bibliography 638
Index 708

Figures

0.1 Elizabeth and Michael Jeffreys about to join family and friends to celebrate their Golden Wedding in the hall of Exeter College, July 2015 (photograph by © Katharine Jeffreys) *page* ii

1.1 Miniature depicting Alexios Komnenos offering Christ the *Dogmatic Panoply* he commissioned from Euthemios Zigabenos. Vaticanus gr. 666, fol. 2v, twelfth century (© Biblioteca Apostolica Vaticana) 19

1.2 Miniature from the *Romance of Alexander* in which the Amazons are depicted receiving a letter from Alexander the Great. Istituto ellenico di studi bizantini e post bizantini 5, fol. 168r., fourteenth century (© Istituto ellenico di studi bizantini e postbizantini, Venezia) 20

1.3 Miniature from the *Romance of Alexander* in which the Amazons are depicted writing a letter of reply to Alexander the Great. Istituto ellenico di studi bizantini e postbizantini 5, fol. 168v., fourteenth century. (© Istituto ellenico di studi bizantini e postbizantini, Venezia) 21

1.4 Girl reading. Symeon Axentis, Donor panel from the Church of the Archangel (Theotokos) at Galata, Cyprus (1514). Courtesy of: Department of Antiquities, Cyprus, the Bishopric of Morphou, and Stella Frigerio-Zeniou (photograph by © Vassos Stylianou) 22

5.1 Map of the area around the monastery of Hiereon, Cyprus (© Tassos Papacostas, based on the *Topographical Map of Cyprus* 1:50,000 series K.717, Department of Lands and Surveys, Cyprus) 140

5.2 Chart showing deaths per decade recorded in the margins of the Par. gr. 1588 (© Tassos Papacostas) 143

5.3	Chart showing donations and deaths per decade recorded in the margins of the Par. gr. 1588 (© Tassos Papacostas)	145
17.1	The Veroli Casket, lid and rear, Victoria and Albert Museum, London (photograph by © Simon Lane)	398
17.2	The Veroli casket, front, Victoria and Albert Museum, London (photograph by © Simon Lane)	398
18.1	Table showing the basic structure of the poem (© Margaret Mullett)	418
18.2	Analytical diagram of the poem (© Margaret Mullett)	418
24.1	Table showing the percentage share of the total number of clausulae (© John Duffy)	556
25.1	Table showing instances of synizesis and hiatus in samples of one hundred lines from the five poems (© Marjolijne C. Janssen and Marc D. Lauxtermann)	581

Contributors

MICHAEL ANGOLD is Professor Emeritus of Byzantine History at the University of Edinburgh.

MARINA BAZZANI is Lector in Greek and Latin at Oxford University. Her main interest is Byzantine literature, especially poetry of the middle and late periods. Her research has focused on the presence of autobiographical elements in poetic texts, and on textual and linguistic analysis. She is currently working on the poems of Manuel Philes.

RODERICK BEATON is Koraes Professor of Modern Greek and Byzantine History, Language and Literature at King's College London. He has published widely on Greek literature and culture from the twelfth century to the present. His books include *The Medieval Greek Romance* (1989, 2nd edition. 1996).

ALESSANDRA BUCOSSI is Research and Teaching Fellow and Principal Investigator of the research project *The Eleventh and Twelfth Centuries as Forerunners of a United and Divided Europe* at Università Ca' Foscari, Venice. She is the editor of the *editio princeps* of the *Sacrum Armamentarium* by Andronikos Kamateros for the *Corpus Christianorum Series Graeca* (2014).

JOHN DUFFY is the Emeritus Dumbarton Oaks Professor of Byzantine Philology and Literature at Harvard University. His revised text and English translation of the homilies of Sophronius of Jerusalem is forthcoming in the *Dumbarton Oaks Medieval Library* series.

PETER FRANKOPAN is Director of the Oxford Centre for Byzantine Research at Oxford University and Senior Research Fellow at Worcester College, Oxford. He works on the history of the Byzantine Empire, Russia, the Middle East, Iran and Central Asia. His most recent book is *The Silk Roads: A New History of the World* (2015).

NIELS GAUL is A. G. Leventis Professor of Byzantine Studies at the University of Edinburgh. His publications include *Thomas Magistros und die spätbyzantinische Sophistik. Studien zum Humanismus urbaner Eliten in der frühen Palaiologenzeit* (2011) and, edited jointly with Averil Cameron, *Dialogues and Debates from Late Antiquity to Late Byzantium* (2017).

TIM GREENWOOD is Senior Lecturer in the Department of Mediaeval History at the University of St Andrews. He has published widely on the political, social and cultural history of late antique and medieval Armenia. He has recently completed a translation and commentary on the eleventh-century *Universal History* by Stepʻanos Tarōnecʻi' (Stephen of Tarōn) (2017).

DAVID M. GWYNN is Reader in Ancient and Late Antique History at Royal Holloway, University of London. He is the author of a number of recent books, including *Athanasius of Alexandria: Bishop, Theologian, Ascetic, Father* (2012) and *Christianity in the Later Roman Empire: A Sourcebook* (2014).

FIONA K. HAARER teaches at King's College London. Her work covers the history, literature, and culture of the fifth–sixth centuries and she has published a monograph, *The Emperor Anastasius I: Politics and Empire in the late Roman World* (2006).

JAMES HOWARD-JOHNSTON was University Lecturer in Byzantine Studies at the University of Oxford (1971–2009). He is an emeritus fellow of Corpus Christi College, Oxford. His publications include *Witnesses to a World Crisis: Historians and Histories of the Middle East in the Seventh Century* (2010).

LIZ JAMES is Professor of Art History at the University of Sussex.

MARJOLIJNE C. JANSSEN is Research Associate at the Grammar of Medieval Greek Project at Cambridge University.

ELIZABETH JEFFREYS is Emeritus Bywater and Sotheby Professor of Byzantine and Modern Greek Language and Literature in the University of Oxford and Emeritus Fellow of Exeter College.

MICHAEL JEFFREYS was successively Lecturer, Senior Lecturer and Sir Nicholas Laurantus Professor of Modern Greek in Sydney University from 1976 to 2000.

JOHANNES KODER is Professor Emeritus of the University of Vienna and a Member of the Austrian Academy of Sciences. His fields of research include: Byzantine monasticism and ecclesiastical hymnography, issues surrounding historical geography and identity, and the culture of everyday life. His last publication was *Die Byzantiner: Kultur und Alltag im Mittelalter* (2016).

MAJA KOMINKO works for the philanthropic foundation Arcadia and is an independent scholar. Her publications include *The World of Kosmas: Illustrated Byzantine Codices of the Christian Topography* (2013).

MARC D. LAUXTERMANN is Bywater and Sotheby Professor of Byzantine and Modern Greek Language and Literature in the University of Oxford and Fellow of Exeter College.

PAUL MAGDALINO is Emeritus Professor of Byzantine History at the University of St Andrews. He has published on many aspects of Byzantine history and literature from the sixth to the fourteenth centuries. His special interests have included the twelfth century, the city of Constantinople, prophecy and astrology. He recently edited, with Nevra Necipoğlu, *Trade in Byzantium* (2016).

ULRICH MOENNIG is Professor for Byzantine Studies and Modern Greek Philology at the University of Hamburg. He wrote a monograph on a late Byzantine version of the *Alexander Romance* (1992) and is the editor of two late Byzantine fictional texts: *The Tale of Alexander and Semiramis* (2004) and *The Tale of the Hero Donkey* (2009).

MARGARET MULLETT is Professor emerita of Byzantine Studies at Queen's University Belfast and Director of Byzantine Studies emerita at Dumbarton Oaks. She is currently Visiting Professor of Byzantine Greek at the University of Uppsala.

TASSOS PAPACOSTAS is Lecturer in Byzantine material culture at King's College London. His current work focuses on archaeology and architecture from late antiquity to the early modern period, primarily on Cyprus. Recent publications include *Identity/Identities in Late Medieval Cyprus. Papers Given at the ICS Byzantine Colloquium, London 13–14 June 2011* (2014), edited with Guillaume Saint-Guillain.

MANOLIS PAPATHOMOPOULOS (1930–2011) was Professor of Classical Philology at Ioannina University. He was the editor of many classical and Byzantine texts, including Antoninus Liberalis' *Metamorphoses*, the *Life of Aesop*, Oppian's *Cynegetica*, Planudes' translations of Augustine, *On the Trinity* and Boethius, *Consolation of Philosophy*, as well as the anonymous *War of Troy* (with Elizabeth Jeffreys).

MANOLIS S. PATEDAKIS is Assistant Professor in Byzantine Philology at the University of Crete. His special interests focus on epigraphy and manuscript culture from medieval and early modern Crete, and Symeon the New Theologian. His publications include several editions of Greek literary texts and inscriptions, including of the writings of Patriarch Athanasios of Constantinople.

GÜNTER PRINZING is Emeritus Professor für Byzantinistik am Historischen Seminar at the University of Mainz. His publications include the edition of *Demetrii Chomateni Ponemata Diaphora* (2002).

PANAGIOTIS ROILOS is the George Seferis Professor of Modern Greek Studies and of Comparative Literature at Harvard. His publications include *Towards a Ritual Poetics* (with Dimitrios Yatromanolakis); *Amphoteroglossia: A Poetics of the Twelfth-century Medieval Greek Novel*; and *C. P. Cavafy: The Economics of Metonymy*. He is currently completing a book entitled *Byzantine Imaginaries: A Cognitive Anthropology of Medieval Greek Phantasia*.

JUDITH R. RYDER is General Editor of the Liverpool University Press series *Translated Texts for Byzantinists*. After a degree in theology and postgraduate work leading to a doctorate in Byzantine Studies in Oxford, she was a researcher on the Prosopography of the Byzantine World and Junior Research Fellow at Wolfson College, Oxford.

TERESA SHAWCROSS is Associate Professor of History and Hellenic Studies at Princeton University. Interested in the pre-modern book, she has written on the materiality of manuscripts, on the role of authors, translators and scribes, and on the interplay between literacy and orality. Her publications include *The Chronicle of Morea: Historiography in Crusader Greece* (2009). She is currently completing a study of the ideas and practices of empire – and its alternatives – during the late medieval period.

JONATHAN SHEPARD was University Lecturer in Russian History at the University of Cambridge. Co-author with Simon Franklin of *The Emergence of Rus* (1996), his edited volumes include *The Cambridge History of the Byzantine Empire* (2008) and *Byzantium and the Viking World* (co-edited with Fedir Androshchuk and Monica White, 2016).

DIMITRIOS SKREKAS is Research Associate at the University of Oxford, where he is completing a catalogue of the Holkham Hall Collection of Greek Manuscripts at the Bodleian Library. He has published on

Byzantine prosopography and hymnography. His doctoral dissertation on the *Three Iambic Canons* attributed to John of Damascus is under revision for publication.

IDA TOTH holds the post of Senior Instructor and Lecturer and Research Fellow at Oxford University, where she convenes graduate courses in Medieval Latin, Byzantine Greek, and Byzantine Epigraphy. She has published on late Byzantine imperial orations, on the medieval Greek and Slavonic transmission of wisdom literature, and on Byzantine inscriptional traditions in the seventh, eleventh and thirteenth centuries.

ERICH TRAPP pursued classical and Byzantine studies at the University of Vienna and obtained his doctorate with a dissertation on Manuel II Palaiologos' *Dialogue with a Persian*. He was Lecturer for Byzantine Studies at the University of Vienna, and subsequently Professor at the University of Bonn. Now emeritus, he continues his lexicographical work as an honorary member of the Institute for Medieval Studies at the Austrian Academy.

Preface

If you desire to hear of the deeds of good soldiers,
to learn and be instructed, perhaps you will make progress.
If you know letters, start reading;
if, on the other hand, you are illiterate, sit down by me and listen.
And I hope, if you are sensible, that you will profit,
since many of those who have come after them have made great progress
because of the stories of those great men of old.[1]

With these lines at the end of his preface, a fourteenth-century chronicler imagines the fate of his work. There will be those who will pick up the book for themselves and peruse it. But also those who will gather together to listen to its contents, which will be read either by the author himself or by another reader who assumes the authorial voice. At the heart of this dual reception lies a paradox. As was true throughout the pre-modern world, possession of an advanced level of literacy was extremely rare in the Byzantine Empire. Only a handful of people were expected to attain higher education. Books, due to the materials and labour involved, were prohibitively expensive. Moreover, deciphering texts from handwritten manuscripts, despite the aid provided by the transition to the codex and presence of rubrics and marginal symbols, remained a demanding business. Even so, this was a society that laid great store by the written word.

It might be objected that ours is a distorted image of the past. After all, our sources reflect the truth of the aphorism *scripta manent*. Yet it is clear that medieval religion, government, and the economy all demanded of imperial citizens that they participate to the best of their ability –and according to the expectations of their class and gender – in a literate culture. Their Christian faith was based on the authority of revealed

---

[1] Translated in E. Jeffreys and M. Jeffreys, 'The Oral Background of Byzantine Popular Poetry', *Oral Tradition*, 1 (1986), 504–47, at 507; for the original, see J. J. Schmitt, ed., *The Chronicle of Morea, A History in Political Verse* (London, 1904), 93–4 (vv.1349–55).

Scripture. The grant of land, assessment of taxes, and deliberation of court cases all involved the issuing of documents. The value of coins was meant to be guaranteed by their inscriptions. In these and other contexts, the written word was always a living thing: generative and transactional, it shaped individuals and bound them together in communities. Texts were authored, of course. But they were also copied and modified, as well as translated and transposed across languages and into other media. And above all they were read – frequently although by no means exclusively aloud, whether in a private or public setting. Imperial orations, where a complex relationship exists between what was delivered at court and what has been transmitted in manuscript form, are a case in point; so too are vernacular epic and romance. If we are to understand how Byzantines interacted with writing, we need to address questions of materiality and look for traces of transmission and circulation with the performative aspect of textuality kept firmly in mind.

The present volume showcases a range of critical approaches to the study of books, readers and reading. A work of this size and scope represents a protracted endeavour that accumulates many debts. The editors are deeply beholden to the contributors for their commitment to the project, and their willingness to bring to bear their collective expertise on the topic it treats. We are also grateful to Joshua Birk, Emmanuel Bourbouhakis, Lorenzo Calvelli, Averil Cameron, Surekha Davies, Charalambos Dendrinos, Lawrence Douglas, Joe Ellis and Ellen Wilkins-Ellis, Stella Frigerio-Zeniou, Sharon Gerstel, Dimitris Gondicas, Tony Grafton, Geoffrey Greatrex, Molly Greene, David Gwynn, John Haldon, Judith Herrin, David Holton, Ruth Macrides, Fred McGinness, Leonora Neville, Paolo Odorico, Georgios Ploumidis, Charlotte Roueché, Carole Straw, and Christopher van den Berg for their help and encouragement, as well as to the anonymous readers and peer reviewers of both the individual chapters and the complete manuscript for their careful feedback. Sheila Marie Flaherty-Jones, Jonathan Martin, Hollis Shaul, Douglas Whalin, and most especially Randall Pippenger gave vital technical assistance. Amherst College, Mount Holyoke College, Oxford University, and Princeton University provided us with institutional homes and financial support. Our particular thanks go to Michael Sharp and Cambridge University Press for making publication possible. And, as always, to our families – for being there.

Finally, we should like to dedicate this book to two scholars who have made an unparalleled contribution to our knowledge of Byzantium's literary culture: Elizabeth and Michael Jeffreys. Drawing our attention to the interplay between the written and the oral, the Jeffreys have shone a spotlight on previously ignored figures: the folk singer, the preacher, the begging poet, the foreigner and the female patron. They have been staunch advocates for the adoption of editorial practices and the creation of databases that harness the potential of evolving technological platforms and allow us better to visualise the multiple layers of our evidence. In retirement, they continue to be trailblazers, with recent publications including: E. M. Jeffreys, trans., *Four Byzantine Novels, Translated with Notes* (2012) and M. J. Jeffreys and M. D. Lauxtermann, *The Letters of Michael Psellos: Cultural Networks and Historical Realities* (2017).

A *Festschrift* has already been published in the Southern Hemisphere: *Basileia: Essays on Imperium and Culture in Honour of E. M. and M. J. Jeffreys*, ed. G. Nathan and L. Garland (2011). Our new volume brings together a number of colleagues and students of the Jeffreys' from the Northern Hemisphere, notably from Great Britain. With it, the editors and contributors together offer a token of their deep gratitude for the intellectual guidance and personal friendship they have been so unstintingly given.

Finished on 27th December: Feast day of the patron saint of authors, publishers, and parchment makers.

Abbreviations

AHR	*American Historical Review*
AJA	*American Journal of Archaeology*
AnzWien	*Anzeiger der Österreichischen Akademie der Wissenschaften in Wien*
ArtBull	*Art Bulletin*
BacBelg	*Bulletin de la Classe des lettres et des sciences morales et politiques*
BalkSt	*Balkan Studies*
BCH	*Bulletin de correspondance hellénique*
BMGS	*Byzantine and Modern Greek Studies*
BSl	*Byzantinoslavica*
BullBudé	*Bulletin de l'Association Guillaume Budé*
BullJRylandsLib	*Bulletin of the John Rylands Library*
ByzSym	Βυζαντινά Σύμμεικτα
ByzF	*Byzantinische Forschungen*
BZ	*Byzantinische Zeitschrift*
CahCM	*Cahiers de civilisation médiévale (xe–xiie siècles)*
ClMed	*Classica et Mediaevalia*
ClRev	*Classical Review*
CSCO	*Corpus scriptorum Christianorum orientalium*
DChAE	Δελτίον τῆς Χριστιανικῆς Ἀρχαιολογικῆς Ἑταιρείας
DOP	*Dumbarton Oaks Papers*
DTC	*Dictionnaire de théologie catholique*
EHR	*English Historical Review*
ΕΕΒΣ	Ἐπετηρὶς Ἑταιρείας Βυζαντινῶν Σπουδῶν
EKEE	Ἐπετηρίδα Κέντρου Ἐπιστημονικῶν Ἐρευνῶν
EO	*Échos d'Orient*
FHG	*Fragmenta historicorum graecorum*, ed. K. Müller
FM	*Fontes minores*
GRBS	*Greek, Roman and Byzantine Studies*

HA	Հանդէս Ամսօրեայ (Handēs Amsōrya)
ICS	Illinois Classical Studies
IRAIK	Известия Русского археологического института в Константинополе (Izvestiia Russkogo arkheologicheskogo instituta v Konstantinopole)
IstMitt	Istanbuler Mitteilungen
JDAI	Jahrbuch des Deutschen Archäologischen Insituts
JHS	Journal of Hellenic Studies
JMedHist	Journal of Medieval History
JÖB	Jahrbuch der Österreichischen Byzantinistik
JThSt	Journal of Theological Studies
JWalt	Journal of the Walters Art Gallery
JWarb	Journal of the Warburg and Courtauld Institutes
Letopis'	Летопись историко-филологического общества при Императорском Новороссийском Университете (Letopis' Istoriko-filologicheskogo obshchestva pri Imperatorskom Novorossiiskom Universitete: Vizantiiskoe otdelenie)
LSJ	H. G. Liddell, R. Scott and H. S. Jones, *A Greek–English Lexicon*
MEFRA	Mélanges de l'École française de Rome: Antiquité
MEFRM	Mélanges de l'École française de Rome: Moyen âge–Temps modernes
MGH AA	Monumenta Germaniae Historica. Auctores antiquissimi
MusHelv	Museum helveticum
NAMSL	Nouvelles archives des missions scientifiques et littéraires
NE	Νέος Ἑλληνομνήμων
ODB	Oxford Dictionary of Byzantium
OrChr	Oriens christianus
OrChrP	Orientalia christiana periodica
PBE	Prosopography of the Byzantine Empire
PBW	Prosopography of the Byzantine World
PG	Patrologiae cursus completus, Series graeca, ed. J.-P. Migne
PL	Patrologiae cursus completus, Series latina, ed. J.-P. Migne
PLP	Prosopographisches Lexikon der Palaiologenzeit, ed. E. Trapp et al.
PO	Patrologia orientalis

RA	Revue archéologique
RAC	Reallexikon für Antike und Christentum
RBK	Reallexikon zur byzantinischen Kunst
RE	Paulys Real-Encyclopädie der classischen Altertumswissenschaft, new rev. ed. by G. Wissowa and W. Kroll
REArm	Revue des études arméniennes
REB	Revue des études byzantines
REGr	Revue des études grecques
RESEE	Revue des études sud-est européennes
RhM	Rheinisches Museum für Philologie
RHE	Revue d'histoire ecclésiastique
RömHistMitt	Römische historische Mitteilungen
RSBN	Rivista di studi bizantini e neoellenici
SBN	Studi bizantini e neoellenici
SC	Sources chrétiennes
SicGym	Siculorum gymnasium
SIFC	Studi italiani di filologia classica
SOsl	Symbolae Osloenses
StP	Studia patristica
SVThQ	St Vladimir's Theological Quarterly
TAPhS	Transactions of the American Philosophical Society
TLG	Thesaurus linguae graecae
TLS	Times Literary Supplement
TM	Travaux et mémoires
VigChr	Vigiliae Christianae
VizVrem	Византийский Временник (Vizantijskij Vremennik)
YCS	Yale Classical Studies
ZPE	Zeitschrift für Papyrologie und Epigraphik
ZRVI	Зборник радова Византолошког института (Zbornik radova Vizantološkog Instituta)

Introduction to Books, Readers and Reading

INTRODUCTION I

Byzantium: a Bookish World

Teresa Shawcross

Among the works composed by Photios – the captain of the guard, ambassador and chief imperial secretary who served two terms as patriarch under the emperors Michael III and Basil I – is one known as the *Myriobiblos* (the 'Myriad Books') or *Bibliotheca* (the 'Library').[1] A huge endeavour, it consisted of around 279 reviews of varying length that summarised the content of a text or group of texts, and provided remarks on the style as well as biographical details of the authors. Assuming knowledge of works that were considered canonical and therefore used as textbooks, Photios explicitly excluded these from discussion. Instead, his reviews represented forays further afield, pointing to the voracious breadth of his interests. Theological writings dominated, as one would expect of an ecclesiastic, but secular works of greater or lesser antiquity, including a number of considerable rarity, were not neglected: alongside reviews of philosophical disquisitions, histories, biographies, novels, and poems there are ones of scientific compendia such as lexica, medical treatises, herbals, and agricultural manuals. The quality of the collections to which Photios had access is evident from the fact that he often constitutes our fullest or indeed only source for an ancient text. In many instances, he consulted multiple versions, making an effort to seek out reliable, old manuscripts. Where he could secure access to only a fragmentary copy of a particular work, or had to abandon reading it before he had finished, he would leave space at the end of his draft review in the hope he could return to the task later. There were occasions, too, when he appears to have produced a preliminary evaluation based solely on others' excerpts and summaries. In some cases at least, he explicitly acknowledged that he had not yet managed to find or read the text in question.[2]

---

[1] Unless otherwise indicated, all translations from the Greek are the work of the author of this chapter.
[2] R. Henry, ed., *Photius. Bibliothèque* (Paris, 1959–91); W. Treadgold, *The Nature of the Bibliotheca of Photios* (Washington, D. C., 1980); N. G. Wilson, *Scholars of Byzantium* (London, 1996), 89–111;

To be sure, Photios' is a striking work that offers an unrivalled insight into the books available to one individual as well as the approach he took when reading them. The familiarity and engagement with books to which it attests should be considered an extreme, but nonetheless representative, example of a broader tendency among those within the Byzantine Empire's sphere of influence. Institutional and personal libraries played a significant role in the accumulation of knowledge and information within society. Inventories produced during surveys of property together with other records (such as notes of shelfmarks) provide us with snapshots of the contents of particular manuscript collections at specific moments, while monograms and other marks of ownership allow us to reconstruct these collections' materiality.[3] Outside Constantinople, some 960 and 330 books respectively have so far been associated with the monastic libraries of the Great Lavra on Mount Athos and of St John on Patmos, and some 150 with the private library of Constantine Laskaris in Messenia.[4] When Nikephoros Moschopoulos, the titular metropolitan of Crete, moved to Mistra, he may have decided to take with him as many as a couple of hundred volumes, for he travelled with four horseloads of books.[5] Eustathios Boilas, a retired military commander who had received a land grant in the remote and recently annexed province of Tayk, assembled 80 books, which he then housed in the monastery he founded on his estate, while Gregory Pakourianos donated 30 books to his monastic foundation near Plovdiv in Bulgaria.[6]

These numbers are likely to be the tip of the iceberg: anecdotal evidence indicates that the collections attached to the palace, patriarchate, institutions of higher learning and monasteries in the imperial capital were far larger, although today their holdings cannot be reconstructed with any

---

C. Mango, 'The Availability of Books in the Byzantine Empire, A.D. 750–850' in W. C. Loerke et al., eds., *Byzantine Books and Bookmen: A Dumbarton Oaks Colloquium* (Washington, D. C., 1975), 39–43.

[3] N. G. Wilson, 'Books and Readers in Byzantium' in Loerke et al., eds., *Byzantine Books*, 4–8; N. G. Wilson, 'The Libraries of the Byzantine World', *GRBS*, 8 (1967), 66–8, and N. G. Wilson, 'Libraries' in E. M. Jeffreys, J. Haldon and R. Cormack, eds., *The Oxford Handbook of Byzantine Studies* (Oxford, 2008), 823; E. K. Litsas, 'Palaeographical Researches in the Lavra Library on Mount Athos', Ἑλληνικά, 50 (2000), 217–30; F. D'Aiuto, 'Note ai manoscritti del Menologio imperiale', *RSBN*, 32 (2002), 189–214; G. Cavallo, *Lire à Byzance*, P. Odorico and A. Segonds, trans. (Paris, 2006), 3, 86–7. Information on Byzantine libraries is collected together in K. P. Staikos, *The History of the Library in Western Civilisation* (New Castle, DE, 2007), vol. III.

[4] Wilson, 'Libraries', 822–4.

[5] I. Levi, 'Cinque lettere inedite di Manuele Moscopulo', *SIFC*, 10 (1902): 57–8.

[6] P. Lemerle, *Cinq études sur le XIe siècle byzantin* (Paris, 1977), 25; P. Gautier, 'Le typikon du sébaste Grégoire Pakourianos', *REB*, 42 (1984), 121–2.

degree of accuracy. Describing the library he had refounded at the Chora Monastery, Theodore Metochites claimed he had made it 'a treasury' of 'countless books' of various sorts, including not only books 'of our Wisdom / most Divine, which are greatly useful', but also books 'of the Hellenic wisdom that is beyond the gates, / almost as numerous'.[7] While the declaration that in 1453 there had been 120,000 tomes in Constantinople must be an exaggeration, it reflects the sense of one contemporary collector and dealer that very substantial libraries had been in existence prior to the city's sack by the Ottomans.[8] Some 60,000 manuscripts in Greek alone have survived down to our day, to which should be added those in Armenian, Arabic, Syriac, Georgian, Latin, and other languages current in the empire.[9]

Although particular books might be kept under lock and key, their perusal strictly forbidden, most were not merely collected and deposited, but also consumed. One visitor described a small space at the entrance to the imperial palace in such a way as to suggest that manuscripts were considered part of the ordinary contents of the complex. The space, which was a kind of *loggia*, roofed but open on the sides to the elements, was located on the ground floor and was easily accessible. It was furnished with stone tables and benches and had 'many books and ancient writings and histories and, next to them, gaming boards – for the emperor's dwelling is always well supplied'. The founding abbot of the Stoudios monastery, Theodore, similarly indicated in the rule for his community that reading was a normal occupation: 'on days when we perform no physical labour the librarian bangs a gong once, the brothers gather at the place where books are kept and each takes one, reading it until late'.[10] In addition to being available for consultation like this on site, volumes could also circulate, sometimes widely. They might be lost as a result of private theft, shipwreck, or even the plundering activities of a local mob or – as was the case with the library of the metropolitan of Athens, Michael Choniates – a foreign army. To discourage this, notices of ownership placed in books

---

[7] I. Polemis, ed., *Theodori Metochitae carmina* (Turnhout, 2015), 44–6.1106–74; translation adapted from J. M. Featherstone, 'Metochites's Poems and the Chora' in H. A. Klein et al., eds., *The Kariye Camii Reconsidered* (Istanbul, 2011), 221, 225–6.
[8] A. Pertusi, 'Le epistole storiche di Lauro Quirini sulla caduta di Costantinopoli' in K. Krautter et al., eds., *Lauro Quirini umanista* (Florence, 1977), 182–3.
[9] M. Richard and R. Olivier, eds., *Répertoire des bibliothèques et des catalogues de manuscrits grecs* (Turnhout, 1995); J. Waring, 'Byzantine Book Culture' in L. James, ed., *A Companion to Byzantium* (Chichester, 2010), 276.
[10] M.-A. Pérez, ed., *Andanças é viajes de Pero Tafur* (Seville, 2009), 100; *PG* 99, 1713; Wilson, 'Byzantine World', 54, 63.

were frequently accompanied by curses against those contemplating theft or vandalism, while the depredations that still occurred were followed by attempts to seek redress and recover the property.[11] More often, however, collections were disseminated because people actively decided to share the material in their possession with others. The monastery of Patmos, for example, made a list of loans to institutions (fifteen items) as well as to individual monks and laypeople (nineteen items) located across a radius of several hundred miles.[12]

This introductory chapter explores the relationship those who lived within the Byzantine Empire – or came within its ambit – had with books and other objects inscribed with the written word. Tempering the evidence from prescriptive sources with that gleaned from surviving examples of practice, it seeks to identify some of the defining characteristics of textual production, collection, circulation, and, above all, consumption. In addition to reconstructing the ways in which individuals could engage with and experience the process of reading, it considers the institutional framework that rendered possible the formation of a readership in the first place. And it draws attention to the extent and composition of that readership. As we shall see, the acquisition of the skill of literacy remained the prerogative of a minority whose boundaries were defined by gender, class and location. This does not mean, however, that we should ignore the tremendous potency of literate culture in determining forms of solidarity that cut across social stratification. Interactions of a religious and political nature habitually emphasised the inclusionary role of texts, whose message was rendered accessible to the illiterate and transmitted to them through visual representation and oral performance.

How Should One Read?

Books, of course, could cause disappointment and frustration. The teacher John Tzetzes, who had a rather high opinion of his own interpretative capabilities, frequently disagreed with the views expressed in the scholia that accompanied the works he was studying, and in the margins scribbled

---

[11] F. Kolovou, ed., *Michaelis Choniatae epistulae* (Berlin, 2001), 156, 166, 168, 190, 196, 206; J.-F. Boissonade, ed., *Anecdota nova* (Paris, 1844), 3; M. Grünbart, 'Byzantium: a Bibliophile Society?', *Basilissa*, 1 (2004), 120.

[12] C. Astruc, 'Les listes des prêts figurants au verso de l'inventaire du trésor et de la bibliothèque de Patmos dressé en septembre 1200', *TM*, 12 (1994), 495–9; J. Waring, 'Literacies of Lists: Reading Byzantine Monastic Inventories' in C. Holmes and J. Waring, eds., *Literacy, Education and Manuscript Transmission in Byzantium and Beyond* (Leiden, 2002), 265–86.

insults against the 'ignorant buffoons' who had added 'dross' to what was valuable; at times, he even railed against the content of the works themselves.[13] One late medieval reader of a late antique illustrated manuscript of a herbal struggled to make out the old-fashioned majuscule script employed in the labels of the plants and decided for ease of reference to write the names again at the tops of pages in his own hand. Another took a history to task for having promised a narrative written in simple prose yet gone on to use so convoluted a style it gave the reader vertigo and hindered comprehension.[14] An even more acute cry of despair was penned by the mathematician John Chortasmenos next to a specific number problem in a copy of Diophantus' *Arithmetica*: 'Diophantus, may your soul rot in Hell because of the difficulty of the other theorems of yours, and in particular of the present theorem!'. We should feel some measure of sympathy, for the passage that elicited this exclamation was almost certainly the very one from which is derived the theorem, formulated by Pierre de Fermat in 1637 but not proven until 1994 by Andrew Wiles, that is considered to represent the most difficult mathematical problem of all, attracting the largest number of unsuccessful proofs.[15]

Mostly, however, books were seen as a source of gratification. If epistolographic exchanges allowed people in different locations to stay in contact with one another, books were the means by which an even more pronounced form of separation, caused by time, could be surmounted. They made it possible to commune not only with the living, but also with those long dead.[16] Bishop Basil the Lesser related that in reading the homilies of Gregory of Nazianzos he felt it was as if he were in the presence of the man himself and could benefit from his personal companionship.[17] The courtier Michael Psellos expressed his reaction to Gregory's work in even less moderate language, describing himself as having undergone a process of seduction after which he was overcome by an ecstasy similar to the

---

[13] M. J. Luzzato, *Tzetzes lettore di Tucidide: note autografe al codice Heidelberg Palatino Greco 252* (Bari, 1999), 18–20, 49–53; W. B. Standford, 'Tzetzes' Farewell to Thucydides', *Greece & Rome*, 11 (1941), 40–1; A. Kaldellis, *Byzantine Readings of Ancient History: Texts in Translation, with Introductions and Notes* (London, 2015), 65–79.

[14] J.-L. van Dieten, ed., *Nicetae Choniatae Historia* (Berlin, 1975), I: xxxii.

[15] Wilson, *Scholars*, 233; P. Tannery, 'Les manuscrits de Diophante à l'Escorial', *NAMSL*, 1 (1891), 393; J. Herrin, 'Mathematical Mysteries in Byzantium: the Transmission of Fermat's Last Theorem', *Dialogos*, 6 (1999), 22–44, reprinted with some modifications in J. Herrin, *Margins and Metropolis: Authority across the Byzantine Empire* (Princeton, NJ, 2013), 312–34; but see J. Acerbi, 'Why Chortasmenos Sent Diophantus to the Devil', *BMGS*, 53 (2013), 379–89.

[16] E. Boulgares and T. Mandakase, eds., Ἰωσὴφ μοναχοῦ τοῦ Βρυεννίου τὰ παραλειπόμενα (Leipzig, 1784), 179; Cavallo, *Lire*, 53–4.

[17] R. Cantarella, 'Basilio minimo II. Scolii inediti con introduzione et note', *BZ*, 26 (1926), 3–4.

transports produced during an act of love-making to which one has willingly surrendered oneself: 'I am taken over, in an inexpressible way, by the beauty and grace of his [Gregory's] eloquence ... I feel vanquished by the rosaries of the burgeoning terms and abase myself to the sensations they create in me ... I embrace and kiss the one who has ravished me in this way.'[18] Again and again, individuals commenting on the effect the writings of a particular author had scribbled expressions of delight in the margins, such as: 'Oh! Libanius, what a pleasure to read you!'[19]

Reading was considered capable of having an effect resembling that of the coolness of water or the sweetness of honey on a parched or sick palate.[20] But for it to comfort and sustain in this way, the act needed to be carried out in an appropriate fashion. On the most basic level, readers were enjoined to concentrate fully on the text in front of them, denying themselves the diversion of glancing up or speaking to others while reading.[21] A lazy person, it was explained, is easily distracted and turns his gaze 'away from the book and fixes it on the ceiling' or, flicking through 'to see how much is left for him to finish', counts the pages and – assessing the ampleness of the images and other decoration, and the size of the writing – even calculates the lines. A fellow of this sort, who is bored and given to yawning, believes in his heart of hearts that the best use for a volume is as a pillow on which he can lay his head as he nods off; consequently, the profit he draws from texts is less than that of someone who exercises proper self-discipline.[22] But a more subtle though equally detrimental kind of behaviour was that of approaching texts with an eye to style over substance.[23] Those who do not know how to read in order to gain serious knowledge 'of places, nations, and actions' and thus attain familiarity with the 'treasures of learned writings of all types' are to be pitied as having been duped by the educational methods of charlatans who, though they pretend to impart learning, fail to do so and instead

---

[18] A. Mayer, 'Psellos' Rede über den rhetorischen Charakter des Gregorios von Nazianz', *BZ*, 20 (1911), 49.

[19] Wilson, *Scholars*, 232–3.

[20] F. J. G. La Porte-du Theil, 'Notices et extraits d'un volume de la Bibliothèque nationale, côté MCCIX parmi les manuscrits grecs, et contentant les opuscules et les lettres anecdotes de Théodore l'Hirtacènien', *Notices et extraits des manuscrits de la Bibliothèque nationale et autres bibliothèques*, 6 (1800), 42; J. Darrouzès, ed., *Épistoliers byzantins du xe siècle* (Paris, 1960), 150; E. Kurtz and F. Drexl, eds., *Michaelis Pselli Scripta Minora* (Milan, 1941), vol. II, 135; L. M. Leone, ed., *Joannis Tzetzae Epistulae* (Leipzig, 1972), 34; Cavallo, *Lire*, 52–4.

[21] G. Gorce, ed., *Vie de Sainte Mélanie* (Paris, 1962), 178, 180, 188; A. Giardina, 'Melania, la santa' in A. Frachetti, ed., *Roma al femminile* (Rome, 1994), 277–83; Cavallo, *Lire*, 12.

[22] *PG* 79, 1160B; Cavallo, *Lire*, 103. [23] Mayer, 'Psellos' Rede', 49.

peddle figures and tropes in such a way as to lose their students in 'a tortuous labyrinth' of rhetoric.[24]

True readers, resisting the gratuitous immersion in linguistic pyrotechnics that accompanies 'reading for its own sake', should turn to books in order to sharpen and train the intellect, and attain the ability not only to think perceptively and profoundly but also to express their thoughts adequately and communicate them clearly and effectively to others.[25] To this end, they needed to undertake a combination of an intensive (*epimeles*) reading – what we would call close reading – of each text during which they paid careful attention to the glosses and other apparatus that accompanied it, with an extensive (*entribes*) reading of a range of texts through which they covered a large amount of ground in order to 'learn a lot'.[26] The pages of manuscripts allow us to trace how actual individuals approached this double task. Arethas, bishop of Caesarea, crammed the margins of his copy of Aristotle's *Organon* with jottings of various types, while Tzetzes added a copious series of notes in his copy of the *History of the Peloponnesian War* of Thucydides, addressing questions of orthography, grammar, syntax, as well as clarifying chronology and commentating on ancient culture and customs.[27] Some readers, of course, went beyond mere annotation, copying out excerpts or indeed whole works.[28] Manuscripts written in a rapid, idiosyncratic hand with abundant abbreviations, and combining a main text with a heavy apparatus of notes, represent the working copies of scholars who intended to use them as part of a programme of private study, or as preparation for teaching. Sometimes readers worked in groups and divided the labour between them. Seventeen different hands, for example, contributed to the copying and interpretation of a miscellany of astronomical, geographical, and mathematical texts.[29]

---

[24] P. L. M. Leone, ed., *Ioannis Tzetzae Historiae* (Naples, 1968), 372.
[25] M. D. Spadaro, ed., *Kekaumenos. Raccomandazioni e consigli di un galantuomo* (Alessandria, 1998), 190, 198; C. M. Mazzucchi, 'Ambrosianus C 222 inf. (Graecus 886): Il codice e il suo autore', *Aevum*, 78 (2004), 416–17.
[26] Cavallo, *Lire*, 7, 18; B. Wassiliewsky and V. Jernstedt, eds., *Cecaumeni Strategicon et incerti scriptoris de officiis regiis libellus* (St Petersburg, 1896), 158–9.
[27] P. Lemerle, *Le premier humanisme byzantin. Notes et remarques sur enseignement et culture à Byzance des origines au xe siècle* (Paris, 1971), 204–37; Luzzato, *Tzetzes*, 21–139.
[28] A. Markopoulos, 'La critique des textes au xe siècle. Le témoignage du Professeur anonyme', *JÖB*, 32 (1982), 31–7; G. Cortassa, 'Un filologo di Bisanzio e il suo committente: la lettera 88 dell'Anonimo di Londra', *Medioevo greco*, 1 (2001), 97–138.
[29] G. Cavallo, 'Sodalizi eruditi e pratiche di scrittura a Bisanzio' in J. Hamesse, ed., *Bilan et perspectives des études médiévales (1993–1998)* (Turnhout, 2004), 645–65; D. Bianconi, 'Eracle e Iolao: aspetti della collaborazione tra copisti nell'età dei Paleologi', *BZ*, 97 (2004), 521–56; D. Bianconi, 'Libri e mani. Sulla formazione di alcune miscellanee dell'età dei Paleologi', *Signo e testo*, 2 (2004), 311–63; P. Canart, 'Quelques exemples de division du travail chez les copistes byzantins' in P. Hoffmann,

More active intervention on the part of the readers resulted in editions aiming to restore or improve upon an original through the collation of multiple sources; or paraphrases or adaptations; or even wholly new works.[30]

In the case of the philosopher George Gemistos Plethon, it is possible to trace the complete range of these activities, from his marginal notes in manuscripts, to his excerpts and summaries of material, to his editions and commentaries, and, finally, his own original compositions, some of which, such as the *Book of Laws*, were considerable in extent. A detailed picture can be reconstructed not only of Plethon's own working method, but also of the extent of its influence on students of his such as Laonikos Chalkokondyles.[31] In most instances, however, the evidence is more indirect. Much of what is known about the reading habits of Byzantines comes from their output as authors who, in discussing, quoting or even tacitly including in their own writings elements from works that had in some way affected their cast of thought or style, reveal the existence of sometimes very elaborate intertextual relationships.[32] While the abbess Kassia has – unlike her contemporary, Photios – left us no autobiographical notes of her readings, the allusions in her poems suggest knowledge of a wide range of texts.[33]

---

ed., *Recherches de codicologie comparée. La composition du codex au moyen âge en orient et en occident* (Paris, 1998), 49–67; on the relationship between scholars who copied out texts for personal use and professional scribes, Wilson, 'Books and Readers', 9–11 and J. Irigoin, 'Centres de copie et bibliothèques' in Loerke et al., eds., *Byzantine Books*, 17–27; on scholarly collaboration, S. Steckel, N. Gaul and M. Grünbart, eds., *Networks of Learning: Perspectives on Scholars in Byzantine East and Latin West, c. 1000–1200* (Zurich, 2014).

[30] P. Maas, 'Sorti della letteratura antica a Bisanzio' in G. Pasquali, ed., *Storia della tradizione e critica del testo* (Florence, 1962), 490–1; Wilson, 'Books and Readers', 11–14.

[31] A. Diller, 'The Autographs of Georgius Gemistus Plethon', *Scriptorium*, 10 (1956), 27–8; D. Dedes, 'Die Handschriften und das Werk des Georgios Gemistos (Plethon): Forschungen und Funde in Venedig', Ἑλληνικά, 33 (1981), 66–83; F. Pagani, 'Un nuovo testimone della recensio pletoniana al testo di Platone: il Marc. Gr. 188 (K)', *Res publica literarum*, 29 (2006), 5–125; F. Pagani, 'Damnata verba: censure di Pletone in alcuni codici platonici', *BZ*, 10 (2009), 167–202; for a general survey of Plethon's writings and their circumstances of composition, see C. M. Woodhouse, *Gemistos Plethon: The Last of the Hellenes* (Oxford, 1986). For Chalkokondyles, see A. Kaldellis, *A New Herodotus: Laonikos Chalkokondyles on the Ottoman Empire, the Fall of Byzantium, and the Emergence of the West* (Washington, D. C., 2014), 45–8, 259–62.

[32] Cavallo, *Lire*, 3, 133. For example, for Iakovos the Monk's assembly of quotations and other compositional practices, see C. Laga, 'Entering the Library of Jacobus Monachus. The Exemplar of Jacobus' Quotations from the Commentary on the Song of Songs by Gregory of Nyssa' in K. Demoen and J. Vereecken, eds., *La spiritualité de l'univers byzantin dans le verbe et l'image* (Turnhout, 1997), 151–61, and E. M. Jeffreys, 'The Sevastokratorissa Eirene as a Literary Patroness: the Monk Iakovos', *JÖB*, 32 (1982), 63–71.

[33] E. V. Maltese, 'Lettura di Cassia' in F. de Martino, ed., *Rose di Pieria* (Bari, 1991), 339–61; E. V. Maltese, 'Una contemporanea di Fozio, Cassia: osservazioni sui versi profani' in M. Salvador, ed., *La poesia tardoantica e medievale* (Alessandria, 2001), 71–83.

Some readers who turned their hand to writing can be shown to have conceived of their intellectual projects on a notably grand scale. They arranged for copies of the great canonical works, which they claimed had acted as their inspiration, to be purchased and rebranded or, even better, to be produced from scratch according to a set design with regard to format and layout.[34] They also arranged for their own compositions to be issued according to the same specifications, doubtless hoping that this uniformity in outward garb would mean that some of the credentials of more august writings would rub off, aiding the transmission of what was contemporary alongside what was classic. Such was the case with Theodore Metochites, who entrusted the entire contents of his library, including not only the copies of others' works he had assembled but also his own original writings, to a favourite student, Nikephoros Gregoras, whom he appointed as his literary executor.[35] Explaining that the careful curating of the collection as a whole had as its underlying objective the preservation of its creator's compositions, Metochites indicated that these 'offspring' of his 'soul' needed most particularly to survive so that they could constitute his 'monument' for subsequent 'generations of mortals', providing him posthumously with 'immortal glory' and 'renown'. He urged the younger man to dedicate himself to the preservation of his teacher's finished works and drafts from 'all harm' so as to ensure that they stood the greatest chance of remaining intact until 'the end of time'.[36]

Acquiring Literacy

To become educated was to go 'dancing with rhetoricians in the gardens of the Muses'.[37] Instructors at all levels acted as cultural guardians and

---

[34] J. Irigoin, 'Centres de copie', 19–22.
[35] To be fair, it is not clear how much was ordered by Metochites himself, and how much was decided upon by his pupil and friend Gregoras on his behalf. See I. Ševčenko and M. Featherstone, 'Two Poems by Theodore Metochites', *GOTR*, 26 (1981), 28; E. Bianconi, 'La biblioteca di Cora tra Massimo Planude e Niceforo Gregora: una questione di mani', *Segno e testo*, 3 (2005): 41–430; I. Ševčenko, 'Some Autographs of Nicephorus Gregoras', *ZRVI*, 8 (1964), 435–50; I. Pérez Martín, 'El scriptorium de Cora: un modelo de acercamiento à los centros de copia bizantinos' in P. Bádenas et al., eds., Ἐπίγειος οὐρανός. *El cielo en la tierra. Estudios sobre el monasterio bizantino* (Madrid, 1997), 203–23; C. Förstel, 'Metochites and his Books Between the Chora and the Renaissance' in Klein et al., eds., *The Kariye Camii Reconsidered*, 241–66. For the material form of Byzantine books and aspects of their production: H. Hunger, *Schreiben und Lesen in Byzanz: Die byzantinische Buchkultur* (Munich, 1989), 23–124.
[36] Polemis, *Theodori Metochitae carmina*, 95–7.285–361; translation adapted from Featherstone, 'Metochites's Poems', 221–2, 235–6.
[37] G. T. Dennis, ed., *The Letters of Manuel II Palaeologus: Text, Translation and Notes* (Washington, D. C., 1977), 37–9.

facilitators. 'I am prepared to answer all your questions', Psellos told his class, 'and I have opened doors to the sciences and all the arts'.[38] Under professional guidance, students would be exposed to a variety of texts. During these encounters, they could not but become aware of the weight of tradition. It was a humbling experience, but not necessarily one meant to discourage them to the extent that they would give up on the possibility of developing a voice of their own. Though Manuel Palaiologos acknowledged 'if it could be made a law that because there are superior authors the inferior authors should remain silent, why then there should not be one person among the present generation who would dare open his mouth in view of the clear pre-eminence of the ancients', he nonetheless went on to claim that such muteness would in fact 'be a supremely bad thing' (*kakiston*).[39] Of course, students were to delve deep into vocabulary and syntax in order to understand the writings they had inherited from the past; but, beyond that, they were to seek out models that they could then imitate not mechanically, but for a purpose. Ultimately, their aim was to achieve a fluent familiarity with literary antecedents that would enrich their own command of language, allowing them to deploy a range of registers: from the refined Atticism or the more stolid *koine* gleaned from books, to the pungent colloquialisms of their own times – depending upon the context and desired effect. This meant communicating by using an allusive style while at the same time, to the best of their capacity, making it new.[40]

When their offspring were sufficiently grown, good parents were supposed to discourage them from the behaviour associated with toddlers – described as chanting nursery rhymes in a singsong voice and running about naked – and send them to 'pedagogues' or 'if you prefer, teachers'.[41] While an exceptionally gifted child might be entrusted to a schoolmaster at the tender age of five, and prefer studying over playing, most would begin when they were between six and eight years old. For those whose families were able to afford it, personal tuition was available; at the other end of the

---

[38] M. J. Kariakis, 'Student Life in Eleventh-Century Constantinople', *Byzantina*, 7 (1975), 383.
[39] K. N. Sathas, ed., Μεσαιωνική βιβλιοθήκη (Venice, 1872–94), vol. v, 60; Dennis, *Letters of Manuel II*, 149.
[40] For these issues, see H. Hunger, 'On the Imitation (Mimesis) of Antiquity in Byzantine Literature', *DOP*, 23–4 (1969–70), 17–38; M. E. Mullett and R. Scott, eds., *Byzantium and the Classical Tradition* (Birmingham, 1981); A. R. Littlewood, ed., *Originality in Byzantine Literature, Art and Music* (Oxford, 1995).
[41] F. Halkin, ed., 'La vie de saint Nicéphore fondateur de Médikion en Bithynie (†813)', *AB*, 78 (1960), 406; A. Moffat, 'Schooling in the Iconoclast Centuries' in A. Bryer and J. Herrin, eds., *Iconoclasm* (Birmingham, 1977), 89.

spectrum, impecunious orphans might receive instruction from charitable institutions. The majority, however, attended elementary schools as fee-paying pupils. Privately run and directed by a *grammatistes*, these taught the introductory skills of literacy. Beginning with the recitation of the name of all the letters in alphabetical order, pupils would first learn to recognise the shape of each letter, and then to pronounce and copy it out on a wooden tablet. From there, they would progress to syllables, words, and eventually whole phrases.[42]

After this stage, which typically took four to six years, lasting until the age of ten or twelve, pupils might continue with a *grammatikos* who taught the *enkyklios paideia* or liberal arts with a focus on grammar. Here, lessons took the form of line-by-line reading and commentary (*epimerismoi*), supplemented by word-puzzles with deliberate errors which the student had to correct, and by the drafting of short analytical notes (*schediographia*).[43] In some schools, where both advanced elementary and intermediate education were carried out under the same roof, the possibility existed for the study under the *grammatikos* of rhetoric in the form of the practice of 'preliminary exercises' (*progymnasmata*) on a variety of themes that encouraged pupils to use their knowledge and imagination to tell stories, express opinions, and moralise (e.g. 'The history of Atlantis'; 'What words might Pasiphaë have said when in love with the bull'; 'What words might Hades have said upon witnessing Lazarus rise from the dead after four days'; 'Doing good always gives rise to gratitude'). Alternatively, teenagers might come under the more expert instruction of a *rhetor* in order to learn composition and oratory.[44]

Some schoolteachers had the expertise to round off their instruction by inducting their more advanced pupils into the basics of philosophy, mathematics and the sciences. For the most part, however, these disciplines were pursued at centres of higher learning and were the preserve of

---

[42] U. Criscuolo, ed., *Michele Psello. Autobiografia: encomio per la madre* (Naples, 1989), 95; E. V Maltese, *École et enseignement à Byzance* (Paris, 1987), 21, 28–9; D. R. Reinsch and A. Kambylis, eds., *Annae Comnenae Alexias* (Berlin, 2001), vol. 1, 482–5; T. S. Miller, *The Orphans of Byzantium: Child Welfare in the Christian Empire* (Washington, D. C., 2003), 209–46; A. Markopoulos, 'De la structure de l'école byzantine: Le maître, les livres et le processus éducatif' in B. Mondrain, ed., *Lire et écrire à Byzance* (Paris, 2006), 85–96; A. Markopoulos,'L'épistolaire du "professeur anonyme" de Londres: Contribution prosopographique', Αφιέρωμα στον Νίκο Σβορώνο (Rethymno, 1986), vol. 1, 139–44.

[43] Maltese, *École*, 28–9.

[44] C. Roueché, 'The Rhetoric of Kekaumenos' in E. M. Jeffreys, ed., *Rhetoric in Byzantium* (Oxford, 2001), 23–37; for the tradition, see R. J. Penella, 'The Progymnasmata and Progymnastic Theory in Imperial Education' in W. M. Bloomer, ed., *A Companion to Ancient Education* (Malden, MA, 2015), 160–71.

students who had already attained their late teens or were in their early twenties.[45] The Patriarchal School, while providing grounding in influential ancient authors, mainly focused on the forms of exegesis and religious reasoning considered to have superseded pagan learning.[46] The Imperial School of Philosophy – organised around charismatic members of the faculty who disputed with one another and lectured until the members of the audience 'stopped taking notes and were so overwhelmed with fatigue they could not concentrate' – was characterised by a ferocious climate of intellectual competition that encouraged individual professors to issue statements to their students in which they disparaged the instruction provided by opponents and insisted on the superiority of their own classes: 'Should there have been anyone able to give a better explanation than I of any of the things I have discussed, you might have directed yourselves to him. But, until such an individual should present himself, you are to pay attention to my teaching!'[47] Despite a partial reliance on debate as a means of instruction, the Imperial School of Law offered rather more sober training in jurisprudence and legal practice.[48]

The emergence of such institutions notwithstanding, we should imagine higher education for the most part not as conforming to a rigid framework, but rather as a more fluid set-up, in which those avid for learning were attracted by the reputation of scholars, in turn creating a demand for classes. Because there was room for experimentation with the curriculum and also because some professors offered courses in more than one speciality, disciplinary boundaries often became blurred. Nor, for that matter, should every person who was described as a 'teacher' (*didaskalos*) be assumed to have been a professor, since individuals granted a remit to

---

[45] Lemerle, *Premier humanisme*, 261–6; P. Speck, *Die kaiserliche Universität von Konstantinopel* (Munich, 1974); for the issue of the official nature and continuity of these arrangements, see A. Markopoulos, 'Education', in Jeffreys, Haldon and Cormack, eds., *Oxford Handbook of Byzantine Studies*, 790–1.

[46] R. Browning, 'The Patriarchal School at Constantinople in the Twelfth Century', *Byzantion*, 32 (1962), 167–202.

[47] P. Gautier, ed., *Michaelis Pselli Theologica* (Leipzig, 1989), vol. 1, 73; Lemerle, *Cinq études*, 193–248; W. Wolska-Conus, 'Les écoles de Psellos et de Xiphilin sous Constantin IX Monomaque', *TM*, 6 (1976), 223–43; E. V. Maltese, 'Michele Psello commentatore di Gregorio di Nazianzo: note per una lettura dei Theologica', *Syndesmos. Studi in onore di Rosario Anastasi* (Catania, 1994), 289–309.

[48] W. Wolska-Conus, 'L'école de droit et l'enseignement du droit à Byzance au xɪe siècle: Xiphilin et Psellos', *TM*, 7 (1979), 1–103.

interpret and preach religious dogma, as well as to perform specific pastoral duties, were sometimes also designated in this fashion.[49]

Educational Asymmetries

Describing the instructional programme at the School of the Holy Apostles in Constantinople, the deacon Nicholas Mesarites noted that teachers referring to 'books spread open' explained the 'preparatory steps' to beginners who could not themselves yet read. As these beginners acquired skill in reading, he added, they would pore over their lessons continuously and pace 'up and down through the porticoed enclosure' in order to memorise them; having succeeded, they would then carry 'their papers under their arms' and recite 'what is written in them'. Those who were more advanced studied the rudiments of composition by attempting to rehearse 'problems completely from the beginning'. The most qualified of all employed the full resources of their training in order to weave with ease 'webs of phrases'.[50]

The question, however, was not just that of progressing through the curriculum, but also of being granted entry to it in the first place. Access did not depend on ability, but was unevenly distributed according to an individual's location, social background, and, above all, gender. Girls were utterly excluded from the classroom. This bias was underscored in the twelfth century by Tzetzes' scathing attack on a woman who, eager to accede to the study of grammar, was trying her hand at a series of literary exercises ('Instead of weaving you take up a tome, / A quill instead of a shuttle!'). The poet declared that the fairer sex should realise its feebler capacities could not cope with the challenges posed by books and restrict itself to the role traditionally assigned to it of homemaker and childbearer:

> O, woman!
> What do you think you are up to? I am amazed at these books!
> You should return to your distaff and to the drawing of thread!
> Go ply the spindle! Knit together your warps and wefts!
> Letters and learning are appropriate to men.

And he concluded by condescendingly quoting a tag, which he explained, was taken from no less an authority than one of the main representatives of the male literary canon: "*It is for man, and woman should not want it.*"

---

[49] See P. Gautier, 'L'édit d'Alexis Ier Comnène sur la réforme du clergé', *REB* 31, (1973), 172–3.
[50] G. Downey, 'Nikolaos Mesarites: Description of the Church of the Holy Apostles at Constantinople', *TAPhS*, 6 (1957), 899.

/ Speaking thus the good Aeschylus persuades you.' His point was that women should not have the temerity to wish to learn to read, but rather should unquestioningly accept the authority of men who had the twin prerogative of interpreting the classics and applying their precepts.[51]

The occasional female did not surrender to such admonishments and acquired an education in defiance of society's behavioural norms. Examples included Tzetzes' own contemporaries Anna Komnene and Eirene the *Sebastokratorissa*: the one was Emperor John II's elder sister, who penned the *Alexiad*, a notable historical work produced within the empire, and the other was his sister-in-law, who studied grammar and rhetoric, and whose knowledge of epic, history, oratory and other genres made her a leading intellectual light.[52] But these princesses were very much the exception. The author of Komnene's funeral elegy noted that she had been allowed to have tutors and study rhetoric, philosophy and all the sciences, including medicine; but he added that, despite her passion for reading from a young age, she had been granted access to such instruction only after a long period, during which – because her parents were worried about the danger of exposing her to books – she had had to read the texts she was attracted to secretly, like a young maiden looking 'with furtive eyes' through a keyhole at the man intended to be betrothed to her.[53] The metaphor reflects the fact aristocratic girls were groomed as future wives and, if they were permitted to learn letters at all, generally were taught in the confines of their homes by their mothers, who themselves could pass on only the rudiments.

Despite having had a predisposition for learning, the mother and daughter of one the most prominent Byzantine intellectuals, Psellos, were limited to the acquisition of sufficient letters to read the psalter and parse a few other simple religious texts. The elder, Theodote, was said to have suffered 'anguish' because as a woman she could not study freely: trained in the 'working of the loom', she had to acquire the 'basic principles of letters' on her own and 'in secret'. Brought up more liberally, the younger,

---

[51] S. G. Mercati, 'Giambi di Giovanni Tzetzes contro una donna schedografa' in A. Acconcia Longo, ed., *Collectanea Byzantina* (Bari, 1970), vol. 1, 555–6.

[52] Komnene, *Alexias*, ed. Reinsch and Kambylis, vol. 1, 5–6; Choniates, *Historia*, ed. van Dieten, vol. 1, 10; S. P. Lampros, "Ο μαρκιανὸς κῶδιξ 524', *NE*, 8 (1911), 24–5; Jeffreys, 'Sevastokratorissa Eirene'; D. R. Reinsch, 'Women's Literature in Byzantium? The Case of Anna Komnene' in T. Gouma-Peterson, ed., *Anna Komnene and Her Times* (New York, NY, 2000), 83–105, and J. C. Anderson, 'Anna Komnene, Learned Women and the Book in Byzantine Art' in ibid., 125–56; E. V. Maltese, 'Donne e letteratura a Bisanzio: per una storia della cultura femminile' in Francesco de Martino, ed., *Rose di Pieria* (Bari, 1991), 362–93.

[53] J. Darrouzès, ed., *George et Dèmètrios Tornikès. Lettres et discours* (Paris, 1970), 243–5.

Styliane, was allowed to divide her days between practising 'the careful labours of the loom' and learning 'her letters' with teachers, but even so her father's plans for her do not appear to have included the continuation of her lessons after she had reached the marriageable age of puberty.[54] Indeed, the almost total illiteracy of women appears to have been the norm across all social strata: an analysis of women who wrote their names in contrast to those who made their mark in an indicative sample of documents relating to urban centres in Asia Minor shows that the latter represented 84 per cent in the thirteenth and 98 per cent in the fourteenth centuries.[55]

A large proportion of Byzantine boys, especially in the countryside, were also unschooled. Of the different educational establishments available within the empire, the most advanced were found uniquely in the imperial capital, while even elementary schools rarely existed outside major provincial cities and towns. There were almost no village schools. These inequalities in the distribution of opportunities for schooling resulted in the creation of a vast gulf between those men who knew how to read and write fluently enough to be able to compose in a suitably elevated style texts of an elaborately technical nature, and those who were merely able to draw their names in laborious fashion. Most did not even possess the latter skill. It is true that, according to a sample of documents mainly involving those belonging to the monastic profession, illiteracy in Macedonia decreased between the tenth and the fifteenth centuries from 36 per cent to 0 per cent. But a more mixed sample of ecclesiastics and laymen from Asia Minor indicates that during the thirteenth century 38 per cent in Smyrna and 77 per cent in Mantaia still could not sign their names.[56] When men were called upon to act as witnesses, clerics, monks, local landed gentry, soldiers and burghers relatively often penned their own signature, while craftsmen and especially peasants were almost never able to do so.[57]

Portraits of emperors, dignitaries, and other males of substantial social status, fairly often showed their subjects holding books, scrolls or other

---

[54] Psellos, *Autobiografia*, ed. Criscuolo, 89–90; Sathas, Μεσαιωνική, vol. v, 65–6.
[55] A. E. Laiou, 'The Role of Women in Byzantine Society', *JÖB*, 31 (1981), 253–7.
[56] N. Oikonomides, 'Mount Athos: Levels of Literacy', *DOP*, 42 (1988), 167–78; N. Oikonomides, 'Literacy in Thirteenth-century Byzantium: an Example from Western Asia Minor' in J. S. Langdon et al., eds., Τὸ ἑλληνικόν. *Studies in Honor of Speros Vryonis Jr.* (New Rochelle, NY 1993), 253–65.
[57] J. Bompaire, ed., *Actes de Xéropotamou: édition diplomatique* (Paris, 1964), 79; F. Miklosich and J. Müller, eds., *Acta et diplomata graeca medii aevi sacra et profana* (Vienna, 1860–90), vol. IV, 225 and 233–5; R. Browning, 'Literacy in the Byzantine World', *BMGS*, 4 (1978), 50; Oikonomides, 'Literacy in Thirteenth-century Byzantium', 262; M. J. Jeffreys, 'Literacy', in Jeffreys, Haldon and Cormack, *Oxford Handbook*, 796–802.

texts. In the double frontispiece accompanying one theological work, the *Dogmatic Panoply,* Alexios I Komnenos, his hands covered by a liturgical cloth, was painted receiving a scroll containing Christian doctrine from the Church Fathers, and then offering up the exegetical text he commissioned to Christ, who blesses both him and it (Fig. 1.1); similarly, in the frontispiece to his *History* the chancellor Niketas Choniates was drawn scribbling away furiously, his hat pushed back from his brow.[58] By contrast, the women shown perusing or creating texts tended to be outsiders and deviants, such as barbarian women of various stripes, including the queens not only of the Persians and Indians, but also of the mythical Amazons, who were portrayed in a copy of the *Romance of Alexander* receiving and sending letters (Figs 1.2–1.3).[59] While a monumental palatine mosaic in Constantinople – of the emperor Basil I and his family – depicted not only the princes but also the princesses 'holding books', the image was considered unusual enough to require justification. The artist was said to have represented all the emperor's offspring as educated in order to compensate for the fact their sire bore the stigma of having been raised illiterate.[60] One has to wait until the early modern period to find a portrait of a well-nurtured young girl from the Greek-speaking world reading (Fig. 1.4).[61] And certainly no 'digger' or 'washerwoman' was ever depicted taking respite from his or her labours, and finding solace in a book.[62] It should be emphasised that manuscripts, because of the materials and labour involved in their production, were a commodity that was prohibitively expensive for the majority of the population. Ownership of, for example, a copy of the works of Plato that cost

---

[58] Vaticanus gr. 666, fol. 1v., 2r-v; Vienna, Hist. gr. 53, fol. 1v.

[59] Istituto ellenico di studi bizantini e postbizantini di Venezia 5, fols 168r–v, 171r.-v., etc. Even the female figure Byzantine artists most frequently depicted accompanied by books and scrolls, the Mother of God, can be considered transgressive in the sense that many attributes associated with her, such as martial ones, were not considered appropriate for most women. In any case, while she holds texts she is not shown actually engaged in the acts of reading or writing. See, for example, the cycles of illuminations in Vaticanus gr. 1162 and Bibliothèque nationale de France, 1208 and, for analysis, Anderson, 'Anna Komnene, Learned Women'; M. Evangelatou, 'Pursuing Salvation Through a Body of Parchment: Books and their Significance in the Illustrated Homilies of Iakobos of Kokkinobaphos', *Medieval Studies* 68 (2006), 239–84; K. Linardou, 'Mary and her Books in the Kokkinobaphos Manuscripts: Female Literacy or Visual Strategies of Narration?', Δελτίον της Χριστιανικής Αρχαιολογικής Εταιρείας, 29 (2008), 35–48.

[60] I. Ševčenko, ed., *Chronographiae quae Theophanis Continuati nomine fertur liber quo vita Basilii imperatoris amplectitur* (Berlin, 2011), 292 (89).

[61] Symeon Axentis, Donor panel from the Church of the Archangel (Theotokos) at Galata, Cyprus (1514); reproduced in S. Frigerio Zeniou, *Luxe et humilité: se vêtir à Chypre au XVIe siècle* (Limassol, 2012), 47.

[62] van Dieten, ed., *Nicetae Choniatae Historia*, xxxii.

Fig. 1.1 Miniature depicting Alexios Komnenos offering Christ the *Dogmatic Panoply* he commissioned from Euthemios Zigabenos. Vaticanus gr. 666, fol. 2v, twelfth century (© Biblioteca Apostolica Vaticana)

Fig. 1.2 Miniature from the *Romance of Alexander* in which the Amazons are depicted receiving a letter from Alexander the Great. Istituto ellenico di studi bizantini e postbizantini 5, fol. 168r., fourteenth century (© Istituto ellenico di studi bizantini e postbizantini, Venezia)

Fig. 1.3 Miniature from the *Romance of Alexander* in which the Amazons are depicted writing a letter of reply to Alexander the Great. Istituto ellenico di studi bizantini e postbizantini 5, fol. 168v., fourteenth century. (© Istituto ellenico di studi bizantini e postbizantini, Venezia)

Fig. 1.4 Girl reading. Symeon Axentis, Donor panel from the Church of the Archangel (Theotokos) at Galata, Cyprus (1514). Courtesy of: Department of Antiquities, Cyprus, the Bishopric of Morphou, and Stella Frigerio-Zeniou (photograph by © Vassos Stylianou)

8 gold *nomismata* for its parchment and 13 for its transcription, while well within the reach of someone of elevated rank who received an annual court stipend of 3,500 nomismata, was not easily contemplated by an entry-level administrator whose basic remuneration was set at 72 nomismata. It was inconceivable for a manual labourer earning 6–10 nomismata.[63]

Yet even those without the advantages of a formal education or the financial means of purchasing books could have had contact with the written word. Seeking to define textuality, John Mauropous, bishop of Euchaita, described it as a bird whose hybrid nature combined the outward appearance of the swallow – in so far as 'on the white of the parchment the black of the letters stood out' – with the sound of a nightingale able to sing out with a 'melodious voice' that 'enchants my ear'.[64] Although silent reading was known, the oral rendition of texts remained widespread.[65] Accustomed to reading particular types of works aloud even in solitude, the literate expected, through performances that involved declamation and improvisation, to transform the written into the spoken, facilitating reception by others.[66] Thus, a verse chronicler envisaging the fate of his poem after publication emphasised its communication by aural means. He enjoined those who knew letters to take up the manuscript and read it, and those who were unlettered to form an audience:

> if you are educated . . .
> and are knowledgeable in matters of writing
> . . . then take this and read it,
> and if, again, you are illiterate, then sit . . . and listen.[67]

---

[63] Wilson, 'Books and Readers', 2–3; Mango, 'The Availability of Books', 39.

[64] A. Karpozilos, ed., *The Letters of Ioannes Mauropous Metropolitan of Euchaita* (Thessalonike, 1990), 43; G. Karlsson, *Idéologie et cérémoniale dans l'épistolographie byzantine. Textes du xe siècle analysés et commentés* (Uppsala, 1962), Psellos, *Scripta Minora*, ed. Kurtz and Drexl, vol. II, 135, 311; Tzetzes, *Epistolae*, ed. Leone, 34.

[65] P. Saenger, 'Silent Reading: its Impact on Late Medieval Script and Society,' *Viator*, 13 (1982), 367–414.

[66] G. Cavallo, 'Le rossignol et l'hirondelle: Lire et écrire à Byzance, en occident', *Annales*, 56 (2001), 849–61 and Cavallo, *Lire*, 49, 62; C. Cupane, 'Leggere e/o ascoltare. Note sulla ricezione primaria e sul pubblico della letteratura greca medievale' in A. Pioletti and F. Rizzo Nervo, eds., *Medioevo romanzo e orientale. Oralità, scrittura, modelli narrativi* (Naples, 1994), 83–105.

[67] P. Gautier, ed., *Michel Italikos. Lettres et discours* (Paris, 1972), 145–51; Schmitt, ed., *The Chronicle of Morea*, 92–3.1351–2; T. Shawcross, *The Chronicle of Morea: Historiography in Crusader Greece* (Oxford, 2009), 150–65; T. Shawcross, '"Listen, All of You, Both Franks and Romans": the Narrator in the Chronicle of Morea' in R. Macrides, ed., *History as Literature in Byzantium. Papers from the Fortieth Spring Symposium of Byzantine Studies, University of Birmingham, April 2007* (Farnham, 2010), 91–111; H.-G. Beck, 'Der Leserkreis der byzantinischen Volksliteratur im Licht der handschriftlichen Überlieferung' in Loerke et al., eds., *Byzantine Books*, 47–67.

The reception of texts could be further supplemented by the recourse to visual representation.[68] A foreign princess, probably to be identified with the daughter of Louis VII of France, Agnès-Eirene, was the recipient of a manuscript consisting of only a few lines of text composed in the vernacular and copied using simple calligraphy, accompanied by a series of very large illustrations. Essentially a picture book, it was intended to introduce the young girl – who had recently been betrothed to Alexios II Komnenos, the heir to the imperial throne, and needed to be taught to fulfil the role of consort – to the world of court etiquette and ceremonial inhabited by her in-laws.[69] Outside the confines of the palace, ordinary citizens who viewed the depictions of emperors on banners, boards and walls in the streets of the capital were expected to engage with formal iconographic features, interpreting the message correctly despite being unable to decipher the accompanying explanatory inscriptions. In the case of Andronikos I, who murdered Agnès-Eirene's husband of a few months and took his place, they refused to play along and expressly offered alternative interpretations.[70] More banally, even if the peasants working the fields could not themselves puzzle out the letters of the word 'Limit' (*horos*) on a cylindrical boundary marker on Patmos, they were expected to understand the significance of the inscription and modify their conduct accordingly.[71]

These complementary modes of communication through sound and image allowed the illiterate to be transformed, almost by proxy, into members of the literate class. Indeed, although the knowledge of how to read and write was distributed across society in a decidedly patchy manner, the insistence that everyone should be integrated – even if only symbolically – within a literate culture was a feature of the empire. It is no coincidence that, on his accession to the throne, the emperor Basil I, a former stable-hand, demonstrated his prowess as a ruler not only by setting out to rectify his own illiteracy upon obtaining access to the necessary resources, but also by promulgating a decree according to which calculations of taxes that were due – typically written out in fractions of the highest monetary denomination, the gold *hyperpyron* – were to be inscribed

---

[68] K. Weitzmann, 'The Selection of Texts for Cyclic Illustration in Byzantine Manuscripts' in Loerke et al., eds., *Byzantine Books*, 69–109 and plates.

[69] C. J. Hilsdale, 'Constructing a Byzantine Augusta: a Greek Book for a French Bride', *ArtBull*, 87 (2005), 458–83; but see C. Hennessy, 'A Child Bride and her Representation in the Vatican *Epithalamion*, cod. 1851', *BMGS*, 30 (2006), 115–50.

[70] P. Magdalino and R. S. Nelson, 'The Emperor in Byzantine Art of the Twelfth Century', *ByzF*, 8 (1982), 123–83; A. Eastmond, 'An Intentional Error? Imperial Art and "Mis-interpretation under Andronikos I Komnenos', *ArtBull*, 76 (1994), 502–10.

[71] Museum of the Monastery of St John the Divine on Patmos (seen August 2012).

in ledgers in longhand and in capital letters so that everyone, including the simple folk (*agroikoi*), could read them. All those who were expected to fulfil fiscal obligations – and therefore possessed the status of free men and were eligible for imperial citizenship – had to be conceived of, if not as actual readers, at least as potential ones.[72] Indicatively, although Theodore Metochites exhorted the monks of his monastery to have recourse to its library, he explained that the collection of books therein contained was not for them alone, but instead meant to represent a 'great universal work of philanthropy, at the disposition of all mortals'. Acting in conscious imitation of God who, 'rich in bounty, made the air for the common use of all men, as well as the earth and the water', the donor granted use of the entirety of the library's holdings without exception not solely to the 'wealthy', but also to the 'very poor and needy', so that 'inexhaustible' access would be 'common to all' (*pankoinos*).[73] The library was envisaged as a public foundation, irrespective of who actually graced its doors.

The Reader as Imperial Citizen

Reading allowed individuals not only to experience personal growth – as Cyril of Thessalonike put it, 'without letters the soul is blind' – but also to become incorporated into society.[74] On the local level, the sharing of texts reinforced the bonds that organised people into households and other small communities defined by kinship, friendship or profession.[75] At the same time, it served to connect these communities to a broader collective identity that was characterised by its emphasis on the importance of the written word. In the memoirs he composed for the edification of his family, Kekaumenos, a grizzled war veteran turned landowner, considered it appropriate to chastise those who put forward their military or farming professions as justification for having 'no need of reading'. He declared that such excuses were not merely detrimental to those who made them but rebounded on everyone with the result that 'we are all deficient'.[76] Becoming a reader was about contributing to the common good. It was through literacy that one was

---

[72] Theophanis Continuatus, *Chronographia*, ed. Ševčenko, 121–4; Cavallo, *Lire*, 28–9.
[73] Polemis, *Theodori Metochitae carmina*, 44–6.1120–73; translation adapted from Featherstone, 'Metochites's Poems', 220–1, 225–6.
[74] A. Vaillant, ed., *Textes vieux-slaves* (Paris 1968), vol. II, 65–6.
[75] A. Markopoulos, 'Überlegungen zu Leben und Werkes des Alexandros von Nikaia', *JÖB*, 44 (1994), 313–26; P. M. Leone, ed., *Nicephori Gregorae Epistulae* (Matino, 1982–3), vol. II: 180–3; 4; L. Canfora, 'Le cercle de lecteurs autour de Photios: une source contemporaine', *REB*, 56 (1998), 269–73.
[76] Kekaumenos, *Strategicon*, ed. Wassiliewsky and Jerstedt, 83.

thought to transcend the status of a private person (*idiotes*) and became a public citizen (*polites*), with the rights and duties this entailed.

Such attitudes stemmed from the fact that a peculiar kind of bookishness lay at the heart of the empire's perception of itself. The imperial regime claimed that, having at its origins received in Christ the Divine Word Incarnate, it had inherited a mission to disseminate that Word, enshrined in the Old and New Testaments, to humanity through the expansion of its dominion to the furthermost corners of the earth and the end of time.[77] The first texts future citizens would encounter when learning their letters were the psalms, together with passages drawn from scripture, hagiography and other religious writings. Those who had already been fully inducted into the empire's civilisation, and were therefore considered to rank among the citizenry, were expected to continue to '*Examine the Scriptures*, as the Lord commanded' and meditate on them throughout their lives.[78] It is no coincidence that 90 per cent of manuscripts dating from between the ninth and twelfth centuries (including 700 exemplars of Symeon Metaphrastes' compendium of saints' lives) can be shown to have been of biblical, patristic, ascetic, hagiographical and liturgical texts. Members of the elite and more ordinary folk participated in an outpouring of acts of piety in the form of offerings to churches and monasteries of religious manuscripts. Though of uneven quality, these manuscripts were generally intended to give the impression of considerable expenditure through the use of parchment or paper with wide margins, of archaising scripts, and of coloured borders or other decorative elements. Often superfluous to the receiving institutions' immediate catechetical or liturgical requirements, they affirmed by their very existence the donors' desire to be seen as having received illumination and being numbered among those who belonged within the community of believers.[79]

Imperial government was considered to protect the faith by interpreting its message and ensuring the implementation of its basic tenets.

---

[77] D. Nicol, 'Byzantine Political Thought' in J. H. Burns, ed., *The Cambridge History of Medieval Political Thought c. 350–c. 1450* (Cambridge, 1988), 49–80; R. Browning, 'Further Reflections on Literacy in Byzantium', in J. Landon, S. Reinert and J. Allen, eds., *Τὸ ἑλληνικόν: Studies in Honor of Speros Vryonis, Jr.*, vol. 1, *Hellenic Antiquity and Byzantium*, 73–4.

[78] Kekaumenos, *Raccomandazioni e consigli*, ed. Spadaro, 158–9; Maltese, *École*, 25–6; A. Giannouli, 'Education and Literary Language in Byzantium' in M. Hinterberger, ed., *The Language of Byzantine Learned Literature* (Turnhout, 2014), 54.

[79] Wilson, 'Byzantine World', 70; P. Evangelatou-Notara, *Χορηγοί, κτήτορες, δωρητές σε σημειώματα κωδίκων. Παλαιολόγειοι χρόνοι* (Athens, 2000), 17–270; P. Evangelatou-Notara, 'Χορηγοί και δωρητές χειρογράφων τον 11 αιώνα' in V. N. Vlyssidou, ed., *Η αυτοκρατορία σε κρίση; Το Βυζάντιο τον 11ο αιώνα* (Athens, 2003), 483–96; G. Cavallo, 'Il libro come oggetto d'uso nel mondo bizantino', *JÖB*, 31 (1981), 411–5.

Consequently, the aura of sanctity that surrounded scriptural and theological texts rubbed off on the business of the state, providing the impetus for and justification of a model of rulership that was closely associated with bureaucracy. The emperor and his ministers assembled centralised collections of documentation with extreme deliberateness. While only 1,500 documents are known today in their originals, something of the extent of the archival mentality that had existed but whose records are lost to us is hinted at by the survival of more than 60,000 disks of metal that had once been used to seal and guarantee the authenticity of texts of an official nature. The imperial chancery communicated important governmental policy, published new legislation, and, under certain conditions, circumscribed the privileges of institutions and persons. Its personnel followed rigorous guidelines, producing documents in accordance with set formulas. All acts opened with a religious invocation, followed by the name and titles of the issuing authority, and those of the addressee or addressees; they concluded with the date and, at the very end, the various subscriptions. Among the types issued by the imperial chancery in the later medieval period that had legal force were: the *gramma, horismos, prostaxis, prostagma, symbolaion* and *symphonia*. While such acts drew on precedents stretching back to the period when the empire had been pagan, their aspect had evolved in such a way as to emphasise the notion that the Christian God's will was being enacted on earth by his chosen representative. Of them all, the most solemn was the *chrysoboullos logos* ('golden-sealed word'), which ritually repeated the word *logos* three times at its end and was then signed in autograph by the 'most faithful ruler and emperor in Christ' with ink whose red colour evoked Christ's Blood, which had been spilled at the Crucifixion in order to redeem humanity and which guaranteed the replacement of old Mosaic law by the New Covenant. Ink was conceived of as representing the empire's salvific lifeblood.[80]

The extent to which imperial subjects perceived a connection between appropriation of the written word and possession of citizenship can be seen from a marginal note from southern Italy scrawled in Greek in an inexpert hand. Perhaps reflecting its author's internalisation of frequent dressings-down connected with his ethnic origin, this note, which is located only a

---

[80] N. Oikonomides, 'Le support matériel des documents byzantins' in J. Glénisson et al., eds., *La paléographie grecque et byzantine* (Paris, 1977), 385–415; N. Oikonomides, 'La chancellerie impériale de Byzance du 13e au 15e siècle', *REB*, 43 (1985), 190–3; N. Oikonomides, 'The Usual Lead Seal', *DOP*, 37 (1983), 147–57; T. Shawcross, 'Languages, Record-keeping and Collective Memory in an Imperial Eastern Mediterranean' in A. Law, ed., *Mapping the Medieval Mediterranean, c. 300–1550* (Leiden, forthcoming).

few pages after the beginning of the text, declares: 'On many occasions the desire to study seized me. But I abandoned my studies because I am stupid and above all because I am Calabrian, and the Calabrians are a barbaric race inimical to the truth'.[81] However, others from Calabria together with those from the sister provinces of Lucania and Italia – all of which were territories that at various times were either brought back under imperial control or targeted with that object in mind – did not allow themselves to be discouraged so easily, but chose instead to spell out their identity on documents as best they could in Greek, declaring by this means their yearning to belong within the administrative framework of the empire and share more fully in government.[82]

The behaviour of populations located within the heartlands of empire confirms the legitimising role of writing. Individuals and establishments would petition for formal written recognition of their status and, upon receiving it, take great care to store and preserve the documents in question.[83] The ambition to extend one's share of power was frequently articulated through texts. Secret societies recorded the specifics of their activities and membership in statute books. Rebels and usurpers of various kinds communicated with each other by letter, exchanged mutual guarantees of solidarity in the form of written pledges, and announced their credentials for government by publishing manifestoes.[84] Even more routine were attempts to play the system by producing forged books and documents that copied existing administrative procedures: episcopal sees, monasteries and lay households were all inveterate corruptors of chronicles and fakers of imperial edicts.[85] While these texts might seem to have been criminal in nature, or at the very least to have contained revolutionary or subversive elements, in fact they reinforced the empire's way of governing through paperwork. In their emulation of imperial models, they constituted a tribute of sorts. That the regime itself recognised this was so is

---

[81] P. Canart, 'Gli scriptoria calabresi della conquista normanna alla fine del secolo XIV', *Calabria bizantina. Tradizione di pietà e tradizione scrittoria nella Calabria greca medievale* (Reggio Calabria/Rome, 1983), 158–9.
[82] V. von Falkenhausen, 'A Provincial Aristocracy: the Byzantine Provinces in Southern Italy (9th–11th Century)' in M. Angold, ed., *The Byzantine Aristocracy, IX to XIII Centuries* (Oxford, 1984), 223.
[83] Gautier, 'Typikon', 125–31; C. Holmes, 'Political Literacy' in P. Stephenson, ed., *Byzantine World* (London, 2010), 143.
[84] G. F. L. Tafel, ed., *Eustathii metropolitae Thessalonicensis opuscula* (Frankfurt, 1832), 98; H. Hunger, 'Anonymes Pamphlet gegen eine byzantinische Mafia', *RESEE*, 7 (1969), 95–107; H.-V. Beyer, 'Personale Ermittlungen zu einem spätbyzantinischen Pamphlet', H. Hörander et al., eds., Βυζάντιος. *Festschrift für Herbert Hunger* (Vienna, 1984), 13–26; Holmes, 'Political Literacy', 141–2.
[85] *MGH* 19, 55–98: N. Oikonomidès, 'Temps des faux', Αθωνικά σύμμεικτα, 4 (1997), 69–74.

suggested by the extreme reluctance with which it ordered the dissolution of texts that met with its disapproval: it rarely destroyed documentary records or burned codices even after rejecting their content as invalid or, for that matter, heretical.[86]

This does not mean that the written word was associated exclusively with running the empire. The notaries active in the empire included a large group known as the *taboullarioi*, who – as opposed to their colleagues who served in government departments as secretaries and scribes – administered to a private clientele. Yet even these professionals were organised into guilds that were placed under the supervision of imperial officials. The documents they issued usually underwent a process of registration with the state and could therefore, if necessary, be produced as evidence at an official court that would then arrange the enforcement of their terms. Moreover, since only citizens of good standing were allowed to dispose of their property, decisions by testators to bequeath in their last wills and testaments some part of their fortunes for church services or to liberate their household slaves represented political acts in themselves.[87]

The Value of Letters

The Byzantine empire was remarkably long-lived, lasting for over a thousand years and transforming itself significantly during that period. Had a legal student from the era of Justinian been catapulted by some miracle into the school of jurisprudence newly founded (or refounded) under Constantine IX, he might have responded with a spark of recognition, but he would hardly have felt at home. It cannot be denied that centres of learning changed in size, scope and organisation; that new exercises were assigned by teachers; that the literary canon lost and acquired works; that certain genres of writing emerged and certain others fell into abeyance; even, on the most basic material level of all, that parchment and paper replaced papyrus. These shifts in practice affected people's interactions with texts, sometimes in very profound ways. So too did other aspects of life: the frequent presence in manuscripts of accidental or deliberate

---

[86] J. Chabot, ed., *Chronique de Michel le Syrien* (Paris, 1889–1924), vol. III, 166; E. Dulaurier, ed., *La chronique de Matthieu d'Édesse* (Paris, 1858), 71; J. Herrin, 'Book Burning as Purification' in P. Rousseau and M. Papoutsakis, eds., *Transformations of Late Antiquity: Essays for Peter Brown* (Farnham, 2009), 205–22, reprinted with some modifications in Herrin, *Margins*, 335–56.
[87] See, A. Kazhdan, 'Asekretis', *ODB*, vol. I, 204; B. Nerantze-Barbaze, 'Οι βυζαντινοί ταβουλλάριοι', Ελληνικά, 35 (1984), 261–74; H. Saradi-Mendelovici, 'Notes on a Prosopography of the Byzantine Notaries', *Medieval Prosopography*, 9 (1988), 21–49.

damage, as well as of marginalia that have nothing obviously to do with the passages next to which they were written, hints at the disparate physical and psychological conditions under which readers found themselves operating.[88] According to Psellos, something as mundane as damp and overcast weather, or conversely too hot a sun, could be guaranteed to upset his students' attentiveness.[89] Each and every act of reading – representing as it did friction created by contact of a specific mind with a specific text at a specific time and in a specific context – must have been unique in some way.

Still, appreciation of writing as a useful and important skill remained constant. The Byzantines belonged to a fundamentally bibliophile culture. This was in part due to their association of cultural refinement with the ability to read and understand the works they had inherited from the ancient Greeks. But even more important was the state religion's emphasis on Holy Writ. While reading and writing were to some extent a matter of personal intellectual development and personal salvation, they were also seen as connected to notions of citizenship and political liberty. The claim to be 'lettered' was linked to duties and rights: the duty to pay taxes and the right to participate in government. The empire's expansionist project was framed as one not just of military conquest, but also of the dissemination of civilising values through texts.

Actual levels of literacy, of course, depended on a variety of external factors. The majority of the inhabitants of the empire never learned to read or write with any fluency. Even among the most educated members of society, only the smallest handful devoted themselves to the more rarefied intellectual pursuits that earned them the name of scholars (*ellogimoi*).[90] Nonetheless, people who possessed little skill in letters, or none, devoted hard-won resources to the commissioning of psalters and lectionaries. They also endeavoured to sign their name on wills, deeds, charters and other administrative documents as best they could. Those whose position at the periphery of the empire contributed to their precariousness appear to have felt the pressure even more keenly to display accomplishments relating to literacy.

There were always going to be a few cynical individuals who would describe themselves as reaching out for the necessities of life – food and

---

[88] Cavallo, *Lire*, 133–4.
[89] A. R. Littlewood, ed., *Michaelis Pselli Oratoria minora* (Leipzig, 1985), 21–4; A. P. Kazhdan and A. Wharton Epstein, *Change in Byzantine Culture in the Eleventh and Twelfth Centuries* (Berkeley, CA, 1985), 125.
[90] Cavallo, *Lire*, 3, 6, 8; Browning, 'Further Reflections', 68–81.

drink, and a roof over their head – only to find that their hands knocked ineffectually against piles of paper.⁹¹ However, these lamentations exemplified general attitudes less than did the words of a father who, out on a walk with his son in the streets of Constantinople, took pains to point out prosperous government officials and administrators and present their biographies as being worthy of emulation:

> See that man over there, my child? He used to go
> On Shanks's pony and now he has a fat mule with a fine harness.
> This one here, when he was a student, was barefoot
> And see him now in his pointed boots!
> And that one in his student days never had the entrance fee for the bathhouse,
> Whereas now he can bathe himself three times a week:
> Where once his breast was full of lice as big as almonds,
> Now his purse is full of gold coins and bezants.

This sermonising was addressed to a boy for whom learning represented the surest way to achieve success within an imperial framework. The parent framed his stories with repeated injunctions to his child to "'Learn your letters as much as you are able'" so as to "'get on!'" and be "'greatly honoured, and of good fortune'". Education was above all a matter of material profit – and social aspiration.⁹²

The extent to which hopes and anxieties for the future were associated with the acquisition of an education can be gauged from evidence concerning superstitious practices. Horoscopes were cast in order to determine the most propitious date on which to introduce a child to learning. Masses were said that called upon the Holy Spirit to descend 'on this present child so-and-so' and, implanting 'the Holy Letters in his heart', turn him from 'unlettered' into 'lettered'. Prayers were uttered in which saints famous for their scholarship were asked to illuminate a pupil and assist him in acquiring the rudiments of learning. There was even recourse to *graphiphagy*: magical formulas, addressed to angels such as the 'Teaching-One' or the 'Most-Wise-One', were written out on paper then mixed together with consecrated wine and given to a slow learner to swallow so as to assist his progress.⁹³ Appeals of this type to the supernatural continued into more advanced educational contexts: as a young man, the poet and

---

⁹¹ H. Eideneier, ed., *Ptochoprodromos: Einführung, kritische Ausgabe, deutsche Übersetzung, Glossa* (Cologne, 1991), 120–2 (III.81–107).
⁹² Ibid., 119–20 (III.56–77).
⁹³ Browning, 'Literacy', 51–2; A. Vassiliev, ed., *Anecdota graeco-byzantina* (Moscow, 1893), 342.

historian Agathias, desirous of acceding to the final year of the training that would qualify him as a lawyer, made a votive offering to one of the archangels.[94]

The Scope of this Volume

Given that the Byzantine Empire had such an investment in the written word, it is incumbent upon us to investigate how its population engaged with texts and responded to them. How did books and humans interact? What was the effect of the diversity of humanity – its gender, class, language etc. – on these interactions? Why were these interactions important in the medieval period, and why, for that matter, might they still be important today? At a time when we find ourselves increasingly described as belonging to a 'post-Gutenberg' culture, we might wish to ask what we can learn from a civilisation that loved books but flourished not only before the internet but also before the printing press. Though a vast technological distance seems to separate the early twenty-first-century world from the early fifteenth-century one, it is worth pondering the underlying similarities found at either side of the parenthetical era of print.[95] It may not be too much of a stretch to compare the instability of the web with the mutability of manuscript tradition. In both cases, a definition of textuality's essence and limits is demanded that is highly radical.

Recent shifts in the ways in which we maintain records and communicate with one another have highlighted the fact that scholarship, up until the third quarter of the twentieth century, tended to take a print environment for granted and therefore to view the millennium of the Byzantine Empire as representing at best a linking period between, on the one hand, the emergence of modern scholarly editions and scientific philological analysis, and, on the other, the original verve of ancient literary creation.[96] However, following the milestone publication of W. C. Loerke et al., eds., *Byzantine Books and Bookmen: A Dumbarton Oaks Colloquium* (Washington, D. C., 1975), our approach to books, readers and reading has undergone substantial revision. At the forefront of efforts to re-examine

---

[94] A. M. Cameron, *Agathias* (Oxford, 1970), 5.
[95] See Tom Pettitt, 'Before the Gutenberg Parenthesis: Elizabethan–American Compatibilities', originally at http://web.mit.edu/comm-forum/mit5/papers/pettitt_plenary_gutenberg.pdf (accessed May 2016) but now to be found at http://www.academia.edu/2946207/Before_the_Gutenberg_Parenthesis_Elizabethan-American_Compatibilities (accessed 5 December 2017).
[96] See the comments on this matter in Wilson, 'Books and Readers', 14.

the issues surrounding the production and circulation of texts have often been scholars publishing not only in English, but also in German, Italian, French and other languages.[97] Strides have been taken in the study of education.[98] Monographs and edited volumes have drawn attention to the structure of texts, the representation of authorship, and the modalities of reception.[99] They have also explored the interplay of the written word with different media.[100]

Byzantine texts are identifiable as inanimate objects that have the ability to exercise influence over people. But they can also be shown to depend on people's willingness to engage with them and provide them with a semblance of life. And no man or woman has ever been an island. If we are to study the attitudes of the Byzantines towards reading (and, in so doing, perhaps also start to understand our own attitudes a little better), we need to consider the intellectual and emotional responses of individual readers against the contexts in which these readers operated. This requires teasing out the relationship between texts on the one hand and, on the other, the diverse political, social and cultural pressures that defined people's horizons.

How did an individual's degree of access to the written word affect his or her trajectory through life? To what extent did the shared characteristic of literacy, or conversely of illiteracy, generate networks and create communal allegiances? If we are to answer these questions we have to gather evidence regarding not only the formal training through which the Byzantines acquired an education, but also the manner in which they subsequently displayed their literacy and gave it currency in a variety of situations. The spaces one can most straightforwardly identify as performative are those of the classroom and the literary salon, for it is there that the

---

[97] Apart from E. M. and M. J. Jeffreys, *Popular Literature in Late Byzantium* (London, 1983), see, for example: Hunger, *Schreiben und Lesen in Byzanz*; Cavallo, *Lire*; and G. Cavallo, *Leggere a Bisanzio* (Milan, 2007); Mondrain, ed., *Lire et écrire*.

[98] Important studies include: C. N. Constantinides, *Higher Education in Byzantium in the Thirteenth and Early Fourteenth Centuries (ca.1204–ca. 1310)* (Nicosia, 1982); Maltese, *École*; S. Mergiali, *L'enseignement et les lettrés pendant l'époque des Paléologues (1261–1453)* (Athens, 1996); Holmes and Waring, *Literacy, Education and Manuscript Transmission*.

[99] Representative of the range of approaches are: P. Odorico and P. A. Agapitos eds., *Pour une "nouvelle" histoire de la littérature byzantine: problèmes, méthodes, approches, propositions* (Paris, 2002); A. Markopoulos, *History and Literature of Byzantium in the 9th–10th Centuries* (Aldershot, 2004); I. Nilsson, ed., *Plotting with Eros: Essays on the Poetics of Love and the Erotics of Reading* (Copenhagen, 2009); V. Valiavitcharska, *Rhetoric and Rhythm in Byzantium: The Sound of Persuasion* (Cambridge, 2013); A. Pizzone, ed., *The Author in Middle Byzantine Literature. Modes, Functions, Identities* (Boston, MA, 2014); P. Roilos, ed., *Medieval Greek Storytelling: Fictionality and Narrative in Byzantium* (Wiesbaden, 2014).

[100] See, for example: L. James, ed., *Art and Text in Byzantine Culture* (Cambridge, 2007).

vectors of exchange are most readily apparent although they do not lack complexity. However, there is in addition the constant humming of the interplay of the written and the oral – and of the verbal and the non-verbal – in the private study, the public square, the garden, and even on the battlefield. Writing, after all, is only one form of communication among those that human beings can use. It is only one of the many means we have at our disposal in order to store our memories and feed our imagination.

These are the themes the studies collected in this volume set out to explore. Part I, 'For Love of the Written Word', opens with an examination by Marina Bazzani and Michael Angold of the ways in which two individuals – the eleventh-century bishop John Mauropous and the fifteenth-century patriarch Gennadios Scholarios – valued the written word in their roles not merely as readers of others' texts, but also as authors in their own right who left behind autobiographical writings revealing facets of their personalities. Both cases concern prominent ecclesiastics who played significant roles as intermediaries and policymakers. Focusing not just on the individuals themselves, but also on their role within society, Judith Ryder analyses imperial orations in order to look at the relationship of a churchman, John the Oxite, with his ruler, Alexios I, and identify the ideological ground the two men shared, together with that on which they clashed. Paul Magdalino draws our attention away from the imperial court, asking us to think about education and literacy in the context of the activities of a successful religious confraternity; similarly, Tassos Papacostas pieces together from manuscript marginalia the story of a monastery that, under siege from plague, coped and even thrived in the face of the crisis.

A more detailed examination of the formation and circulation of texts within a range of communities is undertaken in Part II, 'Contact with a Living Culture'. These communities included the relatively small – but still by many counts privileged – households of the gentry in the provinces as well as the rather more substantial entourages of magnates, the patriarch, and the emperor in the imperial capital. Starting with an assessment of the type of education available to Byzantines, Panagiotis Roilos and Jonathan Shepard show that rhetorical training drawing on the classical tradition was not merely prized for its own sake, but was also set to work to achieve distinct political goals within a contemporary context, while Niels Gaul indicates how these goals could be achieved at the gatherings referred to as *theatra* through readings and recitations of texts.

These studies emphasise that manuscripts and documents existed within an environment where the non-written generally dwarfed the written. Shedding light on the larger cultural framework, David Gwynn and

Johannes Koder scrutinise the diverse sources that shaped the religious preoccupations of a pair of late antique and early medieval authors, John Malalas and Romanos the Melode, while Manolis Patedakis and Alessandra Bucossi take us on into the middle Byzantine period by looking at strategies of quotation and allusion in Symeon the Theologian and Andronikos Kamateros. Although similarly concerned with intertextuality, Peter Frankopan, Günter Prinzing and Ulrich Moennig choose secular writings as their subject, assessing the impact of oral discourse and texts on the *Alexiad*, *Digenes Akrites* and the *Tale of Troy*. Ultimately, these chapters insist on the formation within Byzantium of both a spiritual lexicon and a worldly lexicon, which, while serving to shape norms in their distinct ways, should be seen as having complemented one another and indeed as having often converged.

Investigating this issue of vocabulary further, Part III, 'Communication and Influence', addresses the challenges to, but also the opportunities for, creativity provided by the barriers erected by language and artistic medium. Dimitrios Skrekas considers the school curriculum's role in disseminating exegetical material such as glosses and paraphrases. Liz James compares the visual and literary depictions of *erotes* or *putti* and Margaret Mullett discusses the ways in which an object (in this case the tent used by the imperial household when on campaign) is represented in ekphrastic poetry; both papers comment on the subversive potential of representation. The relationship between text and image is also probed by Maja Kominko, who looks at how the geographical *antipodes* were presented in the texts and illustrations of Byzantine and Latin manuscripts; in so doing, she touches on two issues, that of conveying the unfamiliar and that of crossing a linguistic divide, which are developed in this section's final three chapters. Here, Tim Greenwood and James Howard-Johnston tackle the transmission of information from Armenian and Norman to Byzantine contexts, while Roderick Beaton looks at a reverse movement from the Greek-speaking to the French-speaking world. As these studies show, inter-linguistic translation can be associated with the transplantation of a particular political culture into a new environment. While Chrétien de Troyes' *Cligès*, as Beaton argues, could not have been written without the prior existence of Byzantine texts such as *Hysmine and Hysminias* by Eumathios Makrembolites, it is also a text that seeks, by reinventing the literary form of the ancient and medieval Greek 'novel', to achieve a transfer of power (*translatio imperii*). In France, the nascent genre of romance articulated a chivalric ethos that would become pre-eminent in western courtly settings of the later medieval period.

Reflecting on the different kinds of methods that have been used to interrogate the traces of medieval textuality, the final section of the volume, Part IV, 'Modern Reading as Textual Archaeology', turns the spotlight on modern scholars, highlighting the ways in which they too, because of their concern with the recovery and revitalisation of Byzantine authors, works and discourses, should also be identified as readers. In their discussions of rhetorical works dedicated to the emperor Anastasios and of epistolographic works associated with John Daphnopates, Fiona Haarer and John Duffy provide us with an exemplary demonstration of the kinds of stylistic and thematic analyses that allow us to identify marks of medieval authorship and correct misattributions. Building on this approach, the concluding series of papers, by Marjolijne Janssen and Marc Lauxtermann, Erich Trapp and Manolis Papathomopoulos, looks at three vernacular texts (the *Ptochoprodromika*, *Digenes Akrites* and the *Theseid*) with a view to showing that linguistic expertise not only makes it possible for us to inch towards more accurate reconstructions of the words of the author, but also teaches us about the reception of texts by highlighting how translators and scribes contributed to the generative corruption of content.

Efforts to excavate the past through work on grammar and lexicography, and, above all, the production of editions, have a long tradition stretching back not just to the early humanists of fourteenth-century Thessalonike, but also to the ecclesiastical fathers of fourth-century Caesarea. As a discipline, philology has a venerable pedigree. And it remains highly relevant today: the backbone of much of what we do. In other respects, however, our love affair with the history of the Byzantine book is only just beginning.

Further Reading

An edition of all of Photios' book reviews can be found in R. Henry, ed., *Photius. Bibliothèque*, 8 vols. (Paris, 1959–91). Introductory studies of books, readers and reading include: W. C. Loerke et al., *Byzantine Books and Bookmen: A Dumbarton Oaks Colloquium* (Washington, D. C., 1975); C. Holmes and J. Waring, eds., *Literacy, Education and Manuscript Transmission in Byzantium and Beyond* (Leiden, 2002); G. Cavallo, *Lire à Byzance*, P. Odorico and A. Segonds, trans. (Paris, 2006); B. Mondrain, *Lire et écrire à Byzance* (Paris, 2006).

INTRODUCTION II

Modern Encounters with Byzantine Texts and their Reading Publics

Ida Toth

Reflections on reading have persisted for as long as the creative use of writing itself. How do readers approach texts? What shapes the context of a given act of reading? What do readers derive from literary works? How should we interpret, discuss, and teach literature in ways that attempt to encompass the full diversity of literary interactions? The significance of these questions for the study of literature reverberates through recurring debates on the practices of literary criticism; and how much more pressing do they seem now, when such debates are being renewed by a generational shift in cognitive styles, with ever-more urgent enquiries into the fate of reading in the digital age![1]

Byzantine literature was both oral and written, and, moreover, like all medieval literatures, it had an oral dimension even when written. The dual aspect of literary culture had a profound effect on Byzantine reading habits, whose extraordinary vitality continues to stimulate modern scholarship, and, auspiciously, to generate significant advances in research. Much of this output has been dedicated to charting chronological, social, cultural and material developments across a millennium-long history. More recently, the scholarly radius has expanded to consider intermittent shifts in educational practices, the status and signification of the written word, and the elaborate hierarchies of reading publics.[2] This has by no

---

[1] I owe a great debt of gratitude to Elizabeth and Michael Jeffreys for their generous help, guidance, and encouragement, and to Niels Gaul, Pelagia Goulimari, Rebecca Gowers, Marc Lauxtermann, and Teresa Shawcross for their feedback on the final draft of this chapter. On paradigm shifts, and a need for new concepts of periodization and taxonomy: P. A. Agapitos, 'Contesting Conceptual Boundaries', *Interfaces – A Journal of Medieval European Literatures*, 1 (2015), 62–91; On the revival of scholarly interest in close reading: A. Federico, *Engagements with Close Reading* (London, 2016).

[2] W. C. Loerke et al., eds., *Byzantine Books and Bookmen: A Dumbarton Oaks Colloquium* (Washington, D. C., 1975); H. Hunger, *Schreiben und Lesen in Byzanz: die byzantinische Buchkultur* (Munich, 1989); G. Cavallo, *Lire à Byzance* (Paris, 2006); B. Mondrain, ed., *Lire et écrire à Byzance* (Paris, 2006); and Teresa Shawcross' contribution to the present volume.

means exhausted the subject nor has it yet equipped it with suitable theoretical models: the vociferous calls for Byzantine readers to be examined with respect to their preferences and their active roles in the processes of literary creation have signposted, and at the same time multiplied, potential avenues of exploration.[3] Against the vastness of the research field, the literary theory employed by the Byzantines themselves provides some grounding and an all-important starting point. Consistent throughout, it conceives of reading as a progression from basic literacy to an ever-deeper comprehension, appreciation, and critical appraisal of literary works. Two influential theoreticians discuss reading in a way that is particularly illuminating and instructive: Dionysios Thrax, the author of the principal Greek grammatical handbook, defines reading as 'the enunciation of verse or prose without faults', which makes it possible to judge the merits of authors, the skills of readers, and the meaning of texts.[4] The act of reading itself is only the first step in this process, to be followed by explanations of literary expressions, particular words, and etymologies, the study of grammatical regularities, and, finally, 'the finest part of all, the critical appreciation of literature' (κρίσις ποιημάτων).[5] Although intended for grammatical education, this handbook was by no means elementary, but rather provided essential tools for learning how to judge literary compositions. Another prominent theoretician, Dionysios of Halicarnassus, similarly describes

---

[3] D. R. Reinsch, 'Der Autor ist tot – es lebe der Leser: Zur Neubewertung der imitatio in der byzantinischen Geschichtsschreibung' in A. Rhoby and E. Schiffer, eds., *Imitatio – Aemulatio – Variatio* (Vienna, 2010), 23–32; K. Bentein and K. Demoen, 'The Reader in Eleventh-century Epigrams' in F. Bernard and K. Demoen, eds., *Poetry and Its Contexts in Eleventh-century Byzantium* (Farnham, 2012), 69–88; F. Bernard, *Writing and Reading Byzantine Secular Poetry, 1025–1081* (Oxford, 2014), 59–124; A. Pizzone, ed., *The Author in Middle Byzantine Literature: Modes, Functions, and Identities* (Boston, MA, 2014), 3–5; M. E. Mullett, 'No Drama, No Poetry, No Fiction, No Readership, No Literature' in L. James, ed., *A Companion to Byzantium* (Chichester, 2010), 227–38; P. A. Agapitos, 'Writing, Reading and Reciting (in) Byzantine Erotic Fiction' in Mondrain, ed., *Lire et écrire*, 125–76. See, also: G. Prince, 'Reader' in P. Hühn et al., eds., *The Living Handbook of Narratology* (Hamburg, 2013), www.lhn.uni-hamburg.de/article/reader (accessed 3 November 2017).

[4] Ἀνάγνωσίς ἐστι ποιημάτων ἢ συγγραμμάτων ἀδιάπτωτος προφορά. Ἀναγνωστέον δὲ καθ' ὑπόκρισιν, κατὰ προσῳδίαν, κατὰ διαστολήν. Ἐκ μὲν γὰρ τῆς ὑποκρίσεως τὴν ἀρετήν, ἐκ δὲ τῆς προσῳδίας τὴν τέχνην, ἐκ δὲ τῆς διαστολῆς τὸν περιεχόμενον νοῦν ὁρῶμεν: G. Uhlig, ed., *Dionysios Thrax, Ars grammatica*, in G. Uhlig and A. Hilgard, eds., *Grammatici Graeci* (Leipzig, 1883, reprint Hildesheim, 1965), vol. I.1, 6 (II.5–8); see V. Valiavitcharska, *Rhetoric and Rhythm in Byzantium: The Sound of Persuasion* (Cambridge 2013), 95: 'Reading is the enunciation of verse or prose without faults. One should read with due regard to dramatic presentation, prosodic features, and punctuation. From these we see, respectively, the merits of [the poet], the skill [of the reader], and the sense [of the text].' Valiavitcharska translates the passage with the additions based on the evidence of Byzantine commentators.

[5] κρίσις ποιημάτων, ὃ δὴ κάλλιστόν ἐστι πάντων τῶν ἐν τῇ τέχνῃ: Dionysios Thrax, *Ars Grammatica*, ed. G. Uhlig, 6 (1.2–3).

reading as a form of advanced literary criticism. In his treatise *On Literary Composition*, he sees a proficient reader as both an experienced performer and a judge of literature, whose skills in delivery depend directly on his or her ability to analyse grammatical, technical, and historical features, to evaluate rhetorical strategies, and critique the style of individual texts and authors.[6]

These passages serve as a reminder that Byzantium produced a marked number of textbooks on how to read and appreciate literature.[7] This legacy was founded on the authority of ancient Greek manuals, but was greatly enhanced by the contributions of Byzantine scholars in their capacity as copyists, grammarians, scholiasts and rhetoricians, who often conveyed a strong sense of pride in their contributions to advanced literary criticism, and, more often than not, found ways to refer to their own linguistic and literary realities.[8] More pertinently, the passages by the two Dionysii make it clear that the Byzantine theory of reading primarily relates to texts that are meant to be read aloud, and, moreover, that the readers of these texts are expected to be both accomplished performers and competent critics, able to present a piece of literature to an audience, and to publicise its merits on the grounds of the formal qualities that it displays.

Thus the expectation of a sophisticated readership lies at the heart of Byzantine literary poetics just as it informs the present chapter, which seeks to explore the many ways in which the modern scholars contributing to this volume read Byzantine texts, and to highlight how their approaches relate to, and differ from, past traditions. Individual chapters in this collection examine a wide variety of topics relating to the processes, effects and products of reading in Byzantine literary culture. They combine analytical practices long known as close reading with historical, sociological and cultural critiques, and show how literary works have been woven into the texture of history and politics, of literary and material culture, and of everyday life. While the chapters display a noticeable methodological

---

[6] W. Rhys Roberts, *Dionysius of Halicarnassus. On Literary Composition Being the Greek Text of the De compositione verborum* (London, 1910), 64–70.
[7] The surviving manuscript evidence of Byzantine literature loosely defined as 'philology' constitutes nearly half of the entire body of the Byzantine literary production such as we know it today but remains woefully underexplored. This was already flagged by K. Krumbacher, *Geschichte der byzantinischen Litteratur von Justinian bis zum Ende des oströmischen Reiches (527–1453)* (Munich, 1897), 449; cf. R. H. Robins, *The Byzantine Grammarians: Their Place in History* (Berlin, 1993), 20.
[8] On Byzantine commentators (among them, Eustathios of Thessaloniki and John Tzetzes), see Valiavitcharska, *Rhetoric and Rhythm*, 91–114; E. Dickey, *Ancient Greek Scholarship: A Guide to Finding, Reading, and Understanding Scholia, Commentaries, Lexica, and Grammatical Treatises, from their Beginnings to the Byzantine Period* (Oxford, 2007), 77–80.

consistency, the thematic scope of the volume as a whole is strikingly broad.[9] Such a range, however, is intentional and, moreover, necessary: by this means alone is it possible to showcase the variety of themes and approaches that Byzantine reading culture has attracted hitherto, and to draw attention to its potential as a future subject of study.

Quest for Meaning

The modern scholars of Byzantine literary culture contributing to this volume, like their Byzantine predecessors, encounter texts directly. They employ the staples of traditional textual scholarship, and focus on the close reading of their primary material arguing that the style of writing – prose rhythm, metre, narrative structure, vocabulary, allusions – can be used as an index of authorial activity and creativity.[10] Some contributors point out that Byzantine authors can themselves be studied as avid and highly responsive readers, who engage in intricate intertextual relationships with their predecessors, and endeavour to rethink and reinterpret texts that they have separately inherited from antiquity.[11] And, in cases where evidence of such connections is less explicit, source criticism and keen textual archaeology supply useful tools for uncovering the hypotextual presence of authors, who might not otherwise be credited for their contributions to the composition of some seminal works of literature.[12]

On the most elementary level, traces of intertextuality provide valuable insights into the processes of transforming raw source material into final texts;[13] and, more often than not, they also reveal purposeful, and carefully

---

[9] The greater emphasis on secular literature in this volume fills the lacuna in the current scholarship, which has paid much closer attention to religious/liturgical reading practices (P. Magdalino and R. S. Nelson, eds., *The Old Testament in Byzantium* (Washington D. C., 2013); R. S. Nelson and D. Krueger, eds., *The New Testament in Byzantium* (Washington D. C., 2016)) and to reading habits in material and inscriptional cultures (L. James, ed., *Art and Text in Byzantine Culture* (Cambridge, 2007); A. Eastmond, ed., *Viewing Inscriptions in the Late Antique and Medieval World* (Cambridge, 2015); M. Lauxtermann and I. Toth, eds., *Inscribing Texts in Byzantium: Continuities and Transformations* (forthcoming).

[10] See in the present volume the contributions by Fiona Haarer, Dimitrios Skrekas, Marjolijne Janssen and Marc Lauxtermann, John Duffy and Margaret Mullett.

[11] On the author as a reader of texts see the contribution by Roderick Beaton.

[12] Authorial presence in meta-narrative passages, and in direct and reported discourse: see in this volume Jonathan Shepard (Katakalon/Skylitzes); Peter Frankopan (George Palaiologos/Anna Komnene); James Howard-Johnston (William of Apulia/Nikephoros Bryennios/Anna Komnene); Tim Greenwood (Leo VI/David the Paphlagonian/Photios/*Vita Basilii*).

[13] Retracing patterns of circulation, orally transmitted knowledge and lived experience in historiographical sources: see in this volume the studies by Jonathan Shepard, Peter Frankopan, James Howard-Johnston and Günter Prinzing.

thought-out, authorial strategies designed to intensify the reading experience. Occasionally, such narrative devices signal inventiveness and innovation.[14] The use of scriptural intertextuality is a vivid case in point: as well as being an effective tool for instilling religious fervour and mystical experiences,[15] it can also become a powerful weapon of invective and criticism[16] – subject to a skilful manipulation of language and quotations matching the character on display, and the audience's expectations of such content.[17]

However, the chapters in this volume move significantly beyond the basic activity of close reading. They tackle the fundamental question of where a work of literature finds its meaning, and deliver a wide range of answers, including:

Social, political, and cultural contexts: Peter Frankopan, Niels Gaul, Paul Magdalino; Tassos Papacostas, and Jonathan Shepard;
Discursive strategies: Michael Angold, John Duffy, Ulrich Moennig and Manolis Patedakis;
Relationship with ideology: Alessandra Bucossi, David Gwynn, Fiona Haarer, Johannes Koder and Judith Ryder;
Visuality and materiality: Liz James, Maja Kominko and Margaret Mullett;
Receptions and transmission: Marina Bazzani and Dimitrios Skrekas;
Cross-cultural encounters and intercultural adaptation: Roderick Beaton, Tim Greenwood, James Howard-Johnston, Manolis Papathomopoulos and Günter Prinzing;
Sociolinguistic systems and socioaesthetic features: Marjolijne Janssen and Marc Lauxtermann, Panagiotis Roilos and Erich Trapp.

This list goes a considerable way towards showcasing the thematic and methodological scope of the volume as a whole, but does little justice to the comprehensive investigations that make up most of its contents. In fact, the real merit of this collection could be easily lost without a reminder that the majority of contributions also show how literary works carry multiple meanings. Consequently, the most insightful results come about from the approaches that combine study of the distinctive literary features

---

[14] As showcased here by Ulrich Moennig in his study of archetypes and intertextuality in Byzantine historical fiction.
[15] See Manolis Patedakis for the case of Symeon the New Theologian's poetry.
[16] See in this volumne Judith Ryder for *Kaiserkritik* in the writings of John the Oxite, and Alessandra Bucossi for invective against the Pope and the Latins in John Kamateros.
[17] See Niels Gaul on the manipulation of language and quotations, and on the intertextual mimesis.

of texts with critiques of their historical, sociological and cultural contexts. A further upshot of such methodological complexity is that it inevitably underscores textual ambiguities, and opens ways to interpreting texts as symbolic, and symptomatic of something latent and even subversive.[18] Some of the source material examined in this volume, such as the memoir, confession and apology, lends itself more easily to uncovering additional layers of meaning, leading, through authorial self-disclosure, to revelations of the authors' emotional bonds, their habits of mind, their personalities and their attitudes towards, not least, reading and literature.[19]

Notwithstanding the perils that readers, and modern readers in particular, may face by over-associating themselves with texts,[20] turning to Byzantine authors who conceptualise their own experiences as readers and critics becomes a source of instructive insight. Their intellectual (and emotional) revelations make it clear that reading mattered primarily because of the effect that it had on the human *ethos* and *psyche*. Enthusing about the benefits of studying the Book of Psalms, one Byzantine reader notes: 'This book is thoroughly rewarding (ὠφέλιμος): read closely, and you will strike pure gold!'[21] Far from being rare or relating to a single text, this understanding of the reward and usefulness (ὠφέλεια) of literature is the core of Byzantine reading poetics, and it needs to be highlighted for the benefit of modern readers where they lack the relevant sensibility to understand it fully.[22] Perhaps more intuitive is the idea that the Byzantines

---

[18] See, for example: Maja Kominko on the inhabitants of the Antipodes as vilified characters; Ulrich Moennig for the *psogos* of a protagonist; Liz James on the subversive use of the motif of *erotes*; Margaret Mullett for tents as places of politically subversive behaviour; Marjolinje Janssen and Marc Lauxtermann on the reversal of norms, and the satirical and carnivalesque features of Ptocho-Prodromic poetry.

[19] See Michael Angold's reading of Gennadios Scholarios' apologetic writings; Marina Bazzani's study of Mauropous' poetry; Jonathan Shepard's analysis of Katakalon passages in Skylitzes' *History*.

[20] See Paul Magdalino on the perils of reading too deeply and making false assumptions about John Geometres' confessional verses as evidence of the poet's monastic profession; Dimitrios Skrekas on the erroneous attribution of the paraphrase of John of Damascus' hymns to Leo Allatius.

[21] Πάνυ πέφυκεν ὠφέλιμος ἡ βίβλος· ταύτην μετελθὼν καλὸν εὑρήσεις πλοῦτον (the Greek text has been downloaded from the *Database of Byzantine Book Epigrams* (accessed 3 November 2017), www.dbbe.ugent.be/typ/4278; the English translation is mine). The database is a vital resource for textual and contextual study of poetic paratexts – material uniquely rich in information on reading and writing culture in Byzantium. See F. Bernard and K. Demoen, 'Byzantine Book Epigrams from Manuscripts to a Digital Database' in C. Clivaz, J. Meizoz, F. Vallotton, et al., eds., *From Ancient Manuscripts to the Digital Era: Readings and Literacies* (Lausanne, 2012), 431–40; F. Bernard and K. Demoen, 'Book Epigrams', in A. Rhoby and N. Zagklas, eds., *The Brill Companion to Byzantine Poetry* (Leiden, forthcoming).

[22] In spite of its centrality, the poetics of didacticism has not received any attention in Byzantine Studies that would match J. Feros Ruys, ed., *What Nature Does Not Teach: Didactic Literature in the Medieval and Early-Modern Periods* (Turnhout, 2008). See for example W. Hörandner, 'The Byzantine Didactic Poem – a Neglected Literary Genre? A Survey with Special Reference to

saw literature as a source of spiritual, moral and intellectual edification: the didactic (and reactive) nature of reading is timeless, and in itself needs no clarification. However, as the present volume clearly illustrates, the values that literature imparts are neither permanent nor universal, and they make the Byzantine form of ethical reading a historical and culture-specific phenomenon that should be measured against its own forms of judgement, and studied accordingly.[23]

Taxonomies of Authorship and Reading Agencies

The potential for discovering the reader's desire for the author (in Barthian terms) is nowhere greater than in a collective exploration of reading practices, just as is found in this volume. This kind of focus – inevitably – offers a more nuanced understanding of the historical author and reader, particularly in terms of class, education, identity, connectivity, and social and political mobility.[24]

This collection also echoes the ever more persistent calls from Byzantine scholars of a post-positivist bent to consider the creative authority behind

---

the Eleventh Century' in Bernard and Demoen, eds., *Poetry and Its Contexts*, 55–68; A. Rigo, 'Le père spirituel de l'empereur Cosmas Tzintziloukès et son opuscule sur les parties de l'âme, les passions et les pensées (xie siècle)' in T. F. Antonopoulou, S. Kotzabassi and M. Loukaki, eds., *Myriobiblos: Essays on Byzantine Literature and Culture* (Boston, MA, 2015), 295–316; I. Toth, 'Fighting with Tales: the Byzantine Book of Syntipas the Philosopher' in C. Cupane and B. Krönung, eds., *Fictional Storytelling in the Medieval Eastern Mediterranean and Beyond (8th–15th Centuries)* (Leiden, 2016), 387–94.

[23] See in the present volume Panagiotis Roilos on John Sikeliotes' understanding of rhetorical virtues as homological to the virtues of the soul; Marina Bazzani on John Mauropous' claims that religious texts impart ethical instruction (ἠθικὰ διδάγματα); Ulrich Moennig on an anonymous author, who uses the structure of his stories to communicate moral content, thus affecting the way his readers perceive the world. For further discussions and methodological pointers on ethical reading, see: P. Roilos, '*Phantasia* and the Ethics of Fictionality in Byzantium: A Cognitive Anthropological Approach' in P. Roilos, ed., *Medieval Greek Storytelling: Fictionality and Narrative in Byzantium* (Wiesbaden, 2014), 9–30; I. Papadogiannakis, 'Dialogical Pedagogy and the Structuring of Emotions in *Liber Asceticus*' in A. D. E. Cameron and N. Gaul, eds., *Dialogues and Debates from Late Antiquity to Late Byzantium* (London, 2017), 94–104; J. Phelan, 'Narrative Ethics' in P. Hühn et al., eds., *The Living Handbook of Narratology* (Hamburg, 2013) www.lhn.uni-hamburg.de/article/narrative-ethics (accessed 3 November 2017).

[24] See in the present volume Niels Gaul: imperial rhetoric entrusted to the second-tier elite of the Palaiologan empire; John Duffy: epistolography indicates individual and group identities, and reading communities; Paul Magdalino: public readings organised by lay confraternities at their local churches; Jonathan Shepard: advice literature authored by a middlebrow military man and a meritocrat; Michael Angold: Gennadios Scholarios' identity as a Byzantine and Orthodox Christian interested in Latin culture; Tassos Papacostas: clergy and monks recording local history for the benefit of the rural community; David Gwynn: apparent eccentricities and emphasis on oracles reflect interests shared by elite readers from the educated classes. For an overview of Byzantine reading practices, see Teresa Shawcross in this volume.

the text more holistically.²⁵ Two themes in particular have emerged as especially relevant to this strand of research: questions of voice and of (self-) representation, and, related to these, the conceptualised synergies between the author and the reader. The contributions in the volume endorse an interactive study of the two.

Complex self-presentation strategies in Byzantine texts are best observed through the rhetorical voices and acting roles that authors themselves assume – at times inhabiting more than one *ethos*, even within the same characters – by means of which they promote values, deliver judgements, and, more generally, interact with their own reading publics.²⁶ The most vivid instances of self-depiction come from the quills of authors who take the guise of narrators, and conjure up convincing accounts of their own experiences in a variety of plausible settings.²⁷ This narrative device provides the authors with suitable opportunities to communicate directly with the intended recipients of their literary compositions. Either by cautioning or urging, they solicit prompt action. To that effect, they give cues for reading, and equip and arm their ideal audience with the skills needed to acquire and impart knowledge. Prompting their readers to read, learn and take action, they aim to ensure that the entire process, in all its stages, is reactivated and re-enacted in perpetuity.²⁸

---

²⁵ On the *ethos* of an orator: N. Gaul, *Thomas Magistros und die spätbyzantinische Sophistik: Studien zum Humanismus urbaner Eliten in der frühen Palaiologenzeit* (Wiesbaden, 2011), 38–52; on first-person intrusions: R. Macrides, 'The Historian in the History' in C. N. Constantinides, N. M. Panagiotakis, E. M. Jeffreys et al., eds., Φιλέλλην *Studies in Honour of Robert Browning* (Venice, 1996), 205–24; on the *ethos* of the narrator: T. Shawcross, '"Listen, All of you, Both Franks and Romans": the Narrator in the Chronicle of Morea' in R. Macrides, ed., *History as Literature in Byzantium* (Farnham, 2010), 93–111; on subjectivity: S. Papaioannou, *Michael Psellos: Rhetoric and Authorship in Byzantium* (Cambridge, 2013), 129–232; on the authorial self-representation in patristic literature: D. Krueger, *Writing and Holiness. The Practice of Authorship in the Early Christian East, Divinations: Rereading Late Ancient Religion* (Philadelphia, PA, 2004).
²⁶ See in the present volume Judith Ryder: the orator as a strong-minded, rebellious churchman bold enough to denounce the emperor to his face, and as more personal and pastoral, less critical of his addressee.
²⁷ See John Duffy for the author as a recipient of imperial gift; the author caught in a sea storm; Manolis Patedakis for Symeon the New Theologian as an author/narrator, pursuing God in a way that recalls the game of chase between a human lover and his beloved.
²⁸ See Manolis Patedakis: Symeon the New Theologian forewarns his readers of his formidable and awe-inspiring subject; Marjolijne Janssen and Marc Lauxtermann: the prefix Ptocho- indicates to the reader/listener that the story unfolds in a topsy-turvy world; Maja Kominko: Kosmas sets out to provide his readers with the tools to refute 'the folly of the myth-makers'; Alessandra Bucossi: Kamateros invites his readers to 'put on the full armour of God', and act as defenders of faith. On the power of the reader to determine the authority of a literary work, also see M. Lauxtermann, 'His, and not His: the Poems of the Late Gregory the Monk' in Pizzone, ed., *The Author in Middle Byzantine Literature*, 77–86. On the viewers and readers of inscriptional poetry: I. Drpić, *Epigram, Art, and Devotion in Later Byzantium* (Cambridge, 2016), 48–66.

By assigning some responsibility for texts to their reading publics, the authors assemble an impressive array of reader taxonomies, very much replicating the striking range of the authorial personae that they themselves assume. The types of readers evoked in this way include:

> *Dissident readers*, upbraided for their ignorance and haughty attitude;[29]
> *Expert, charismatic readers*: celebrity performers with reputations to uphold, creating a spirit of competition, drawing huge crowds and filling their venues of performance to overflowing;[30]
> *Attentive readers and students of didactic literature*, urged to observe precise details of texts they study;[31]
> *Implied readers*, anticipated and preferred by the authors: fellow literati already acquainted with the genre and the subject-matter, or somewhat less knowledgeable, for whom additional sets of instructions may be added to enable their careful and attentive reading.[32]

The present volume as a whole gives plentiful evidence of the poetics of authorship and reading but perhaps most exhaustively in the chapters that deal with fictional storytelling. Descriptions of writing, reading and listening are frequent in narratives of this kind, so that they provide exceptionally fertile ground for the study of the roles of authors, narrators, audiences, and readers in and out of the text.[33] This realm of literature takes many of its cues from rhetoric: authors engage actual readers in hermeneutic games by repeatedly encouraging them to reciprocate, and respond to, the actions of immersive, communal and interactive reading, or to explore their own, subjective experiences by projecting their inner state of mind onto written characters.[34] Moreover, fictional literature tends to evolve gradually, as a result of exchanges between different cultures, or changes within a single culture, and this process requires the readers'

---

[29] See Manolis Patedakis in this volume.
[30] See Paul Magdalino, Johannes Koder, Niels Gaul: a successful performance holds the potential of altering the social standing of the actor/performer/author.
[31] See Dimitrios Skrekas: students instructed on how to translate, paraphrase and interpret the canons under discussion; Panagiotis Roilos: a commentator in communication/dialogue with the reader.
[32] As noted by Jonathan Shepard regarding Skylitzes.
[33] See Roderick Beaton: *Cligés* is a double love story, told by an omniscient narrator. On the roles of authors, narrators, audiences and readers in and out of text, also see M. Paschalis, S. Panayotakis and G. Schmeling, eds., *Readers and Writers in the Ancient Novel* (Groningen, 2009); Agapitos, 'Writing, Reading and Reciting'.
[34] See Ulrich Moennig: new type of erotic romance structured according to the Menandrian scheme for *encomium/psogos*; Roderick Beaton: the *topos* of adventure as a projection of the narrator's inner state of mind in *Hysmine and Hysminias*; the exploration of subjective experience in *Cligés* through dreams and states of illusion.

awareness of the continuing practice of modifying, amplifying, and reusing fictional characters as mouthpieces for diverse, and newly topical, agendas. The range of creativity that imaginative literature embodies is striking, and it deserves our full attention.

Reading Junctures: Delivery, Dissemination, Transmission

Reading involved performance, not only of one's own compositions, but also, and perhaps even more habitually, of the works of others, including the classics and school authors, both sacred and secular. This fundamental point marks the present volume as a whole, but also suggests scope for further consideration regarding the interplay between the oral and the written, the role of reading in public and civic life, and the distribution and transmission of literary works in Byzantium and beyond.

Literature, whether performed or written, could secure presence and influence within the public sphere. The impetus to bring literary pieces to life, therefore, rested primarily with authors themselves, who are indeed often attested as performers and promulgators of their own work.[35] Many testimonies examined in this volume situate public performances within the space of the imperial court, private households, and the schoolroom.[36] They also acknowledge the significance of ecclesiastical and monastic settings as venues for the recitations of religious literature by both new and well-established authors.[37] Presented in more accessible linguistic registers and aided by effective mnemonic devices, these kinds of performances encouraged the active (dialogic) participation of the audience. They could also secure a prompt absorption, and potentially a wide circulation of ideas and messages concerning ecclesiastical and imperial policies.[38]

A significant number of chapters assign performance the central place in their interpretation of literature, but for most of them the questions of the connection, and distinction, between performance and orality are as complex and elusive as they seem to be in Byzantine scholarship as a

---

[35] Among these, emperors and patriarchs seem to have performed literature just as keenly as patronising it: e.g. Gennadios remembered that John VIII Palaiologos had given sermons in his palace (Michael Angold); John the Oxite's speech intended for a deliberative assembly (Judith Ryder).
[36] See Niels Gaul: on late Byzantine 'theatrical' culture; Dimitrios Skrekas: the classroom as a place of performance; Margaret Mullett: tents as places of performance in Komnenian court culture.
[37] See Paul Magdalino: liturgical recitation in the Church of the Kyrou and other sanctuaries of the Theotokos in Constantinople.
[38] On the rhythmical and vocal performance of the cantor (*Melodos*) reciting from the ambo, and a lively use of the dialogic form in liturgical poetry, see Johannes Koder.

whole. Consequently, some of the texts presented in this volume have been interpreted as springing from oral traditions, while allusions to orality in some other cases have been explained by the performative nature of the literary genres to which the texts belong.[39] More tangible traces of performance have been found in references to the use of visual props, such as manuscript illuminations or panel icons. Some of the Byzantine authors considered in this volume reveal much when they encourage readers to consult the images surrounding their texts in specific manuscripts. In other cases, they give instructions as to how their works should be delivered, and even inscribed, in the places of their performance.[40]

It is a much-repeated truism that performative literature loses a great deal of its effectiveness on paper. It is, however, equally important to emphasise that the presentation and in particular the punctuation of a text in a manuscript could serve as a reading aid giving readers directions for oral delivery.[41] In every other sense, however, exploring Byzantine literary works in their written format means exploring their textuality. It requires that we acknowledge that something that has been originally pronounced and performed has also been adjusted to the medium of writing. The beginning of this process is attributable to authors themselves, who chose to create a textual presence by writing down and distributing their literary compositions. Indeed, some authors draw attention to their roles as publishers of their own works, and as editors of ancient and medieval texts:[42] their autograph manuscripts show evidence of redrafting, at times

---

[39] See Ulrich Moenning: the *Life of Judas* has survived only in oral versions, and was written down in post-Byzantine times. Also, on oral transmission see Günter Prinzing and Erich Trapp; on the performative aspects of begging poetry see Marjolijne Janssen and Marc Lauxtermann. In addition, see E. M. Jeffreys and M. J. Jeffreys, 'The Oral Background of Byzantine Popular Poetry' in G. Nagy, ed., *Greek Literature in the Byzantine Period* (New York, NY, 2001), 134–78; C. Cupane, '"Let Me Tell You a Wonderful Tale": Audience and Reception of the Vernacular Romances' in Cupane and Krönung, eds., *Fictional Storytelling*, 479–94.

[40] See in the present volume Niels Gaul: props included in the performance of funerary/commemorative orations and poems; Maja Kominko: the author invites his readers to change the orientation of a drawing in a manuscript, and to look at it from several perspectives; Margaret Mullett: poetry as an expression of gratitude, perhaps sent with a letter, to be performed and then also inscribed.

[41] See on prose rhythm: John Duffy; on metre: Marjolijne Janssen and Marc Lauxtermann. See also D. R. Reinsch, 'Stixis und Hören' in B. Atsalos and N. Tsironi, eds., Πρακτικά του Ϛ' Διεθνούς Συμποσίου Ελληνικής Παλαιογραφίας (Athens, 2008), vol. 1, 259–69; Valiavitcharska, *Rhetoric and Rhythm*, 158–9.

[42] See Marina Bazzani in the present volume: Mauropous as the editor and publisher of his own works, as well as a 'restorer' of ancient texts (he uses the term καταρτίσας to indicate either emendation of a text or its transcription into minuscule).

even of several stages of editorial interventions.[43] On this point, texts that were intended for use in schools are especially noteworthy, because their prolific transmission preserves abundant evidence of the contributions of individual scholars to literary canons, and of the ways in which they adopted, developed and reinvented their source material for educational purposes.[44]

Surviving manuscripts of Byzantine literary material show creative hands at work belonging to authors, translators, scribes and patrons in their distinct roles as writers, teachers and promoters of literature.[45] They provide a wealth of information on literacy, language and the processes of acculturation,[46] on the circulation of literary works, or the paradoxes thereof,[47] and on scholarly networks and reading communities. Taken together, they offer a unique and detailed picture of Byzantine reading culture viewed directly through the prism of its own writing and reading practices.[48]

Towards Some Conclusions

Modern scholars of Byzantine literary culture contributing to this volume associate the reading of literature with literary criticism, and posit that all

---

[43] See Michael Angold in the present volume, who argues that George Scholarios' first apology survives as the author's autograph. It shows evidence of reworking, but it lacks a title, which may mean that it was never delivered.

[44] See Dimitrios Skrekas for a rich history of transmission that testifies to the text's use in schools; Panagiotis Roilos for John Sikeliotes' comprehensive and sophisticated commentary on Hermogenes. For a survey of Byzantine educational practices, see Teresa Shawcross in the volume.

[45] John Mauropous: intellectual, teacher, rhetor, editor, imperial advisor and metropolitan (Marina Bazzani); Liutprand of Cremona: expert linguist and the first author to link Greek and Latin in narrative prose (Günter Prinzing); Kamateros: refers to himself as the compiler of the *Sacred Arsenal* rather than its author, attributing the fatherhood of his work to his imperial patron (Alessandra Buccosi).

[46] See Tassos Papacostas on Paris. gr. 1588, a *synaxarion* filled with notes recording donations, deaths and other important events, mentioning some three hundred individuals, both monks and laymen, as well as some members of the ruling (Latin) aristocracy.

[47] See Johannes Koder, who asserts that papyrus fragments of Romanos' poetry circulated as far as Egypt during the poet's lifetime; and David Gwynn on the curiosities of the transmission of the *Chronicle* of Malalas, which survives in a single defective Greek manuscript, and in numerous manuscripts in other languages, notably Latin, Syriac and Slavonic.

[48] See Dimitrios Skrekas and Manolis Papathomopoulos on using manuscript material to reconstruct the readerships of a literary work. The issue is also addressed in, I. Nilsson and E. Nyström, 'To Compose, Read, and Use a Byzantine Text: Aspects of the Chronicle of Constantine Manasses', *BMGS*, 33 (2009), 42–60; Papaioannou, *Michael Psellos*, 250–67; on the habits of wear and use, private rituals and emotional states of the readers of medieval manuscripts (showcasing a methodology that could be applied to Byzantine manuscript studies), see K. M. Rudy, 'Dirty Books: Quantifying Patterns of Use in Medieval Manuscripts Using a Densitometer', *Journal of Historians of Netherlandish Art*, 2 (2010), www.jhna.org/index.php/past-issues/volume-2-issue-1-2/129-dirty-books (accessed 3 November 2017).

readings are appropriate as long as they are supported by evidence from the text. While acknowledging that the formal and ethical values embedded in the source texts are central to Byzantine poetics, the essays in this collection cast a much wider net in order to recover both authorial assumptions and premises, and the nature of the reader implied by the text. Seeking to understand norms, conventions and contexts, and the text's place in literary history, they inevitably acknowledge literature as a historical, dynamic and changing category. The range of themes that they cover is equally comprehensive: moving beyond a binary relationship between the text and its reader, the studies in this collection consider a wide diapason of author- and reader-related roles reflecting the responsibility of all participants for the creation, presentation, promulgation, reception and study of literary works.

By focusing on the individual stages and distinct agencies in the process of literary reading, the present volume marks a notable departure from the traditional scholarly focus on chronological or generic classification of literature. This can be attributed in part to the unhelpfulness of these categories for any text-and-context based studies, but also, and more importantly, to the current state of flux instigated by comparative literary scholarship, especially as a result of the transition from print to digital technology. Uncertainty about the exact nature of the impact that these methodological shifts will have on our scholarly focus prompts speculation: In what way would digital editions challenge, or supersede, the authority of critical editions in book form? Would a broad focus on medieval European, Mediterranean or, indeed, global literary traditions still support the governing taxonomies and systems of classifications? Would quantitative evidence gathered from texts in an electronic form require a radical overhaul of literary poetics? What effect, and benefit, will the simmering tension between the recently rediscovered interest in close reading and the newly emerging practice of distant reading bring to Byzantine Studies?[49] Finally, would any of these changes assign a different role to the reader? These questions are being repeated by literary scholars across disciplines

---

[49] On methodological and taxonomic shifts, see Agapitos, 'Contesting Conceptual Boundaries'; M. A. Travis, *Reading Cultures: The Construction of Readers in the Twentieth Century* (Carbondale, IL, 1998). For thoughts and considerations on the future of editing, including digital editing, see Elizabeth Jeffreys and Michael Jeffreys in the afterword of this volume. On close reading, see above, note 2. On the recent debates on the merits of distant reading, see S. Ross, 'In Praise of Overstating the Case: a Review of Franco Moretti, *Distant Reading* (London: Verso, 2013)', *Digital Humanities Quarterly*, 8 (2014), www.digitalhumanities.org/dhq/vol/8/1/000171/000171.html (accessed 22 January 2018); on the questions of digital text analysis, see: *Debates in the Digital Humanities* (http://dhdebates.gc.cuny.edu/debates/text/93 (accessed 22 January 2018), with thanks to Tara Andrews for her reading suggestion).

with a shared sense of urgency and anticipation while the ever more productive interface between literature studies and digital humanities suggests that some of the answers could start emerging very soon.

Further Reading

An important source on the Byzantines' theory of reading is G. Uhlig, ed., *Dionysios Thrax, Ars grammatica*, in G. Uhlig and A. Hilgard, eds., *Grammatici Graeci* (Leipzig 1883), vol. 1.1, 5–100. For key studies of reading practices, see P. A. Agapitos, 'Writing, Reading and Reciting (in) Byzantine Erotic Fiction' in B. Mondrain, ed., *Lire et écrire à Byzance* (Paris, 2006), 125–76; K. Bentein and K. Demoen, 'The Reader in Eleventh-century Epigrams' in F. Bernard and K. Demoen, eds., *Poetry and Its Contexts in Eleventh-century Byzantium* (Farnham, 2012), 69–88; D. R. Reinsch, 'Der Autor ist tot – es lebe der Leser; Zur Neubewertung der *imitatio* in der byzantinischen Geschichtsschreibung' in A. Rhoby and E. Schiffer, eds., *Imitatio – Aemulatio – Variatio* (Vienna, 2010), 23–32; and V. Valiavitcharska, *Rhetoric and Rhythm in Byzantium* (Cambridge, 2013).

PART I

Love for the Written Word

The Emotions of Reading

CHAPTER 1

John Mauropous and the Benefits of Reading

Marina Bazzani

John Mauropous (*c*. 990–*c*. 1081) was one of the most prominent figures living in Constantinople in the eleventh century, an intellectual, teacher, rhetor, imperial advisor and metropolitan. During his life he was involved in the political and religious affairs of the empire, often against his will. At a certain point in his career he fell into disgrace, was dismissed from court and appointed Metropolitan of Euchaita on the Hellespont. Eventually, he managed to return to Constantinople where he spent the last years of his life in the monastery of St John the Baptist of Petra.[1] The variety of roles that John played over his life acquainted him with the most influential personalities of the time, and it is because of this that he is widely mentioned in contemporary sources, especially in the works of his most famous pupil, Michael Psellos.[2] However, precise information about some critical episodes of his life and his ecclesiastical career are scarce, so that many of the events that saw him as a protagonist are still enigmatic.[3] Despite his acquaintance with the mighty and the years spent at court, Mauropous was above all an intellectual and teacher who longed to devote his life to the pursuit of learning, and the preservation and dissemination

---

[1] For a detailed account of John's life, see E. Follieri, 'Giovanni Mauropode metropolita di Euchaita, Otto canoni paracletici a N. S. Gesù Cristo', *Archivio italiano per la storia della pietà*, 5 (1967), 1–200, especially 1–19; A. Karpozilos, Συμβολὴ στὴ μελέτη τοῦ βίου καὶ τοῦ ἔργου τοῦ Ἰωάννη Μαυρόποδος (Ioannina, 1982), 23–50; A. Karpozilos, *The Letters of Ioannes Mauropous Metropolitan of Euchaita* (Thessalonike, 1990), 9–27.

[2] For example, K. N. Sathas, Μεσαιωνικὴ Βιβλιοθήκη (Venice, 1872–94), vol. v, 142–67; G. T. Dennis, ed., *Michaelis Pselli Orationes Panegyricae* (Stuttgart, 1994), 143–74, no. 17. The text has also been translated into Italian by R. Anastasi, *Michele Psello: Encomio per Giovanni, piissimo metropolita di Euchaita e protosincello* (Padua, 1968).

[3] The scarcity of precise information and the subsequent uncertainties about the chronology of John's life are reflected in the divergent opinions of several scholars who have studied Mauropous. See, for instance: A. P. Kazhdan, 'Some Problems in the Biography of John Mauropous', *JÖB*, 43 (1993), 87–111; A. P. Kazhdan, 'Some Problems in the Biography of John Mauropous II', *Byzantion*, 65 (1995), 362–87; Karpozilos, *Letters*, 9–27; A. Karpozilos, 'The Biography of John Mauropous Again', Ἑλληνικά, 44 (1994), 51–60; F. D'Aiuto, *Tre canoni di Giovanni Mauropode in onore di santi militari* (Rome, 1994), 11–17; E. De Vries-van der Velden, 'La lune de Psellos', *BSl*, 57 (1996), 239–56.

of knowledge, as is clear from his poems. The contrast between the desire to lead a quiet life of *otium* and the need to be involved in politics characterises several of his epigrams 'to himself', in which John strongly rejects accusations of having wasted his talent because of his decision to follow the principle of λάθε βιώσας (live hidden). On the contrary, he claims to have done his duty by educating the youth, as well as by devoting himself so completely to studying, reading and emending texts that he has damaged his eyesight. It is on this side of Mauropous' activity that the following pages will focus in order to shed light onto the life of a Byzantine scholar.

Mauropous' surviving writings are numerous. Besides the many canons composed while he was a monk, there is a collection of epigrams, letters and speeches that the author himself assembled, as he states in his Πρόγραμμα εἰς τὴν ὅλην βίβλον, by selecting the best and most representative of his works. This probably occurred after the death of Constantine IX and before retiring to the monastery.[4] Due to the character of the writings and to the fact that John himself selected them from his corpus, they are a useful tool to explore aspects of the author's personality and to analyse what sort of literary persona he wished to create for himself.

In this chapter, I would like to focus on Mauropous the poet and scholar, and offer a commentary on poem 29, a short epigram in twelve-syllable verse, composed to celebrate the recovery of some neglected speeches of Gregory of Nazianzos, most probably denoting those speeches that were not recited during the liturgical year in the Orthodox Church.[5] There are several reasons that led me to pick this poem; first of all, the epigram centres

---

[4] The most comprehensive collection of John's writings is preserved in Vat. gr. 676, a parchment codex dated between the end of the eleventh and the beginning of the twelfth century; the manuscript, though not an autograph, may have been compiled during the author's life or soon after his death. It was edited by P. de Lagarde and J. Bollig, eds., *Iohannis Euchaitorum Metropolitae quae in Codice Vaticano Graeco 676 supersunt* (Göttingen, 1882). For a detailed description of John's collection and the way it was assembled, see R. Anastasi, 'Il "Canzoniere" di Giovanni di Euchaita', *SicGym*, 22 (1969), 109–44; N. Wilson, 'Books and Readers in Byzantium' in W. C. Loerke et al., eds., *Byzantine Books and Bookmen: A Dumbarton Oaks Colloquium* (Washington, D. C., 1975), 1–15, in particular 12–13; Karpozilos, Συμβολὴ; M. Lauxtermann, *Byzantine Poetry from Pisides to Geometres: Texts and Contexts* (Vienna, 2003), 62–5; F. Bernard, 'The Circulation of Poetry in 11th-century Byzantium' in S. Neocleous, ed., *Sailing to Byzantium: Papers from the First and Second Postgraduate Forums in Byzantine Studies* (Newcastle-upon-Tyne, 2009), 145–60.

[5] On the Byzantine tradition of manuscript editions of Gregory of Nazianzos and their circulation in two separate collections, see G. Galavaris, *The Illustrations of the Liturgical Homilies of Gregory Nazianzenus* (Princeton, NJ, 1969), 6–12; K. Weitzmann, 'The Selection of Texts for Cyclic Illustration in Byzantine Manuscripts' in W. C. Loerke, ed., *Byzantine Books and Bookmen: A Dumbarton Oaks Colloquium* (Washington, D. C., 1975), 69–109, in particular 93–6; Karpozilos, Συμβολὴ, 82–4; L. Brubaker, *Vision and Meaning in Ninth-century Byzantium* (Cambridge, 1999), 13–14.

on, and exalts the momentous effects of, reading – the *fil conducteur* of the present volume. It also conveys some features of the poet's personality, such as his interest in the use of texts for educational purposes, his lifelong commitment to books and his editorial activity. Finally, I believe that a close analysis of these verses will bring to light the complexity of this text, its wealth of allusions and the subtlety of Mauropous' poetic composition.[6]

The author does not give any detail about the circumstances under which the recovery of Nazianzos' discourses occurred or about their subject. Rather, he focuses mainly on the importance of this re-appropriation, contrasting the benefits derived from their rescue to the loss that would have occurred had the discourses fallen into oblivion.

> Εἰς τοὺς λόγους τοῦ Θεολόγου τοὺς μὴ ἀναγινωσκομένους
> τίς ὁ θρασυνθεὶς πρῶτος εἰπεῖν τοὺς λόγους
> ἥκιστα τούτους ἀναγινωσκομένους;
> τίς κοσμολαμπὲς φῶς καλύπτει γωνίᾳ;
> τίς ἀστέρας λάμποντας ἐγκρύπτει νέφει;
> τίς μαργάρους στίλβοντας εἰς γῆν χωννύει;   5
> φεῦ κλήσεως μὲν βασκάνου ψευδωνύμου,
> εἰ δ' ἔργον εἶχε, ζημίας παγκοσμίου.
> νῦν δ' οὐ γὰρ ἔστιν ἔργον, ἀλλ' ἄλλως λόγος.
> τὸ φῶς ὁράσθω φαῖνον ἐν τῇ λυχνίᾳ·
> πᾶσι προκείσθω, πᾶσι κοινῇ λαμπέτω   10
> ὅσοι βλέπειν ἔχουσι τῶν ἄλλων πλέον·
> ὡς εἴθε πάντες εἶχον εἰδέναι τάδε,
> εἴθε προσεῖχον τοῖσδε πάντες τοῖς λόγοις·
> οὕτω γὰρ ἂν πρόχειρος ἡ σωτηρία
> παρῆν ἅπασιν ἐκ μιᾶς ταύτης βίβλου   15
> ἐῶ γὰρ εἰπεῖν ὡς σοφοὺς ποιεῖ μόνη
> ἀρκοῦσα πρὸς παίδευσιν ἀνθρώποις ὅλην.
> πλήρης μέν ἐστι δογμάτων ἀποκρύφων,
> πλήρης δὲ θείων καὶ σοφῶν μυστηρίων,
> πλήρης δὲ χρηστῶν ἠθικῶν διδαγμάτων,   20
> πλήρης δὲ κομψῶν τεχνικῶν μαθημάτων·
> μουσεῖον αὐτόχρημα, γνῶσιν ἐμπνέον.
> ταύτης ἄμεμπτον τὴν γραφὴν καταρτίσας,
> πολλοῖς τρυφὴν προὔθηκα μὴ κενουμένην.

---

[6] A long-awaited surge of interest in and awareness of eleventh-century poetry and its three major representatives – Michael Psellos, John Mauropus, Christopher Mytilenaios – has occurred over recent years. See the volume by F. Bernard and K Demoen, eds., *Poetry and Its Contexts in Eleventh-Century Byzantium* (Farnham, 2012), in which several of the contributions focus on or touch upon Mauropous' poetry; as well as F. Bernard, *Writing and Reading Byzantine Secular Poetry, 1025–1081* (Oxford, 2014).

On the speeches of the Theologian which are not read
Who was the first to be so bold as to declare that these speeches are the least read? Who hides in a corner the light that enlightens the world? Who conceals these shining stars with a cloud? Who covers these gleaming pearls with a heap of earth? Ah, what a false and envious reputation! If this had been reality, what harm for the whole world! However, this is not reality, but a useless word. Let the light be seen shining on the stand; let it be placed before everyone, let it glow openly to all those who can see more than the others. Ah, if only all could know these things! If only they could turn their mind to these speeches! For thus salvation would be available to all from just this one book. I omit to say how wise it makes people, it alone being sufficient for the complete education of all. For it is full of secret doctrines, it is filled with divine and wise mysteries and with useful moral teachings and it is full of clever practical lessons: a real Museum indeed, which inspires knowledge. By producing a copy of its text without blemish, I have offered a source of infinite delight to many.[7]

vv. 1–5: the poem opens with a series of anaphorical questions, all introduced by the interrogative pronoun τίς. This sequence of four questions with an almost identical structure helps accumulate tension and create expectations in the reader. The poet then, rather than releasing the tension, prolongs the emotional strain even further with an exclamation of horror in lines 6–7 at the thought of what could have happened had the λόγοι been lost for ever; then, only in line 8, does he release the tension that has accumulated so far.

vv. 1–2: these verses are connected by enjambment between τοὺς λόγους, at the end of line 1, and ἀναγινωσκομένους, which forms the whole second half of line 2 and thus acquires special prominence. The participle strikes the reader as outstanding not only for its position, but also because it breaks the metrical rules of the Byzantine twelve-syllable verse with its initial sequence of three short vowels and the anapestic sequence at the end. The use of the participle ἀναγινωσκομένους in place of the perfect participle ἀνεγνωσμένα, which normally carries the meaning of 'edited', seems to suggest that this manuscript had been put aside among the no-longer-read books in the library where John came across it, and that it was bound to become forgotten.[8]

vv. 3–4: the climaxing sequence of questions is characterised by a repeated contrast between brightness and darkness: νέφει and γωνίᾳ at the end of the line strongly oppose the idea of radiance expressed by φῶς

---

[7] Text from Mauropous, *Epigrams*, eds. Lagarde and Bollig, 14 (xxix); translation my own. I am grateful for the insightful suggestions made by the anonymous referee.
[8] R. Anastasi, 'ΛΟΓΟΙ ΜΗ ΑΝΑΓΙΝΩΣΚΟΜΕΝΟΙ', *SicGym*, 23 (1970), 202–4. On this epigram and the reasons for its composition, see also Karpozilos, Συμβολή, 82–4.

and ἀστέρας, and they convey the fear that the discourses, which are bearers of enlightening wisdom, might be concealed in the dark forever. In addition to a similar structure, the first two lines also share linguistic similarity in the use of κοσμολαμπές and λάμποντας, and an affinity between φῶς and ἀστέρας, as both are related to the celestial sphere. The poet also manages to convey irony in line 3 by juxtaposing κοσμολαμπές φῶς and γωνίᾳ: for a light so immense as to brighten up the whole world could hardly be hidden and contained in a corner. By means of such a paradox John stresses once more the substance and the value of these speeches.

v. 5: the poet moves from the metaphor of stars and light to a comparison of the speeches to gleaming pearls. The use of μαργάρους is evocative and slightly ambiguous at the same time. For it originally meant pearl-oyster (Ael. *NA* 15.8) and only later came to signify pearl; in this way John introduces the idea of another natural element – the sea – next to the air and earth just previously mentioned. At the same time he creates a contrast between the opaqueness of the oyster shell and the splendid shine of pearls. In addition, it is interesting to observe how John bestows a sudden descending movement upon the verse by using the expression εἰς γῆν χωννύει and underlines the dive from the celestial dimension, called to mind in the previous lines, to an earthly sphere. Earlier the stars risked being hidden in the sky, whereas now they are in danger of being buried under a heap of soil. Moreover, the imagery of the oyster, which lies in the depth of the sea, seems to allude to the inaccessibility of the speeches before their restitution by John, as well as to anticipate the idea of descent entailed in the second part of the verse.

It is also worthwhile noticing the variety of vocabulary in these lines, as it offers a glimpse of Mauropous' taste for language. The poet uses the compound adjective κοσμολαμπές, a rare word that is attested before John only once in a ninth-century commentary (Komm. Jo. 128).[9] In the following verse, he continues the same line of thought using the verb λάμπω referring to the brightness of light and stars. However, in the case of the μαργάρους, John chooses the verb στίλβω, whose meaning is closely related to polished surfaces such as that of pearls.

vv. 6–7: the tension of the previous questions is channelled into the indignant expression φεῦ κλήσεως βασκάνου ψευδωνύμου, the false belief

---

[9] K. Hansmann, *Ein neuentdeckter Kommentar zum Johannesevangelium* (Paderborn, 1930). The same adjective is used by Theodore Prodromos (see W. Hörandner, ed., *Theodoros Prodromos. Historische Gedichte* (Vienna, 1974), 261 (12.5)).

that these speeches are no longer read. The poet's apprehension is then loosened by the counterfactual at the beginning of verse 7, where the past εἶχε states clearly that such a dreadful event has not occurred.

v. 8: here the poet promptly reassures the reader about the fate of the speeches and dismisses the palpable trepidation of the first part of the epigram. Mauropous dissolves the fear previously raised in the reader both by beginning the line with νῦν δ' οὐ, which leaves no doubt about the state of reality, and also through the concision and the speed of the verse, which is achieved by the use of only monosyllabic and disyllabic words, as well as by the very evident alliteration–ἀλλ' ἄλλως λόγος–in the second hemistich.

vv. 9–11: John reintroduces the theme of light; but this time the light is enabled to perform its active function and to shine freely for the benefit of all men, or at least of those who are capable of seeing better and, therefore, of understanding the value of Gregory's discourses. John powerfully emphasises the importance of these speeches and the urgent need for their widespread dissemination not only by means of the sequence of the imperative forms ὁράσθω, προκείσθω and λαμπέτω in lines 9–10, but more so by alluding to the Gospel of Matthew (5.15). The speeches, like the apostles, are compared to the light of the world, which must not be hidden, but rather must be placed on a stand to enlighten everyone in the house.

vv. 12–15: following the wish that the light propagating from the discourses may become visible to all mankind, John expresses his hope that all men could turn to them, so as to achieve salvation through the teachings of this single book. These verses constitute a sort of watershed within the poem; the first part of the composition, which is dominated by questions, indignation and anxiety over a possible loss of the discourses, is followed up by a second part, which conversely focuses upon the enlightening nature of the discourses themselves and their positive influence on readers. The almost salvific function of the speeches and their immediate accessibility is highlighted by the prominent position of πρόχειρος ἡ σωτηρία in the second half of line 14.

vv. 16–17: the poet further highlights the extraordinary qualities of the newly rediscovered book with an enjambment and through the structure of both verses. The pause after ποιεῖ in line 16 separates the adjective μόνη from the rest of the verse and gives prominence to it. In its turn μόνη is separated from its participle ἀρκοῦσα at the beginning of line 17. In addition to that, the hyperbaton between παίδευσιν, which sits significantly in the very centre of the verse, and ὅλην, also placed in a prominent position at the end of verse 17, helps underline the exceptional action of the discourses, which alone can provide men with wisdom and a complete education.

vv. 18–24: the final part of the poem is the most revealing with regard to personal details concerning the poet. In the last verses John informs the reader of his activity as restorer of manuscripts and, at the same time, shows some traits of his personality through his enthusiasm for this discovery and his judgement on the quality of the speeches.

vv. 18–21: the anaphorical sequence of four verses all introduced by the adjective πλήρης mirrors the opening lines of the composition; once again John adopts this rhetorical device to amplify the resonance of the ideas he wants to express. These verses present the same structure, with just the *variatio* of μέν and δέ and the presence of the verb ἐστί only in line 18. Moreover, the last two lines are even more closely connected through the final rhyme between ἠθικῶν διδαγμάτων and τεχνικῶν μαθημάτων. The juxtaposition of verses with an analogous structure, and the use of anaphora is a recurring stylistic device in several of Mauropous' compositions and not a one-time occurrence.[10] The poet resorts to it in order to express pathos, to increase the reader's expectations and to strengthen ideas. It is plausible that in this case Mauropous resumes the anaphorical succession as a way to reconnect the closing part of the poem to its beginning and to harmonise the two by their shared stylistic features.

It is worthwhile considering the various qualities John assigns to Gregory's discourses as they include a whole range of teachings, which are listed according to their relevance to humankind. First, Mauropous affirms that the discourses contain beliefs and mysteries that are hardly comprehensible to human faculties, by which he probably means the unexplainable mysteries of Christian religion. Then, he acknowledges the presence of valuable moral teachings in the discourses. Finally, and most interestingly, John underlines the value of the speeches from a rhetorical and literary point of view, by stating

---

[10] See Mauropous, *Epigrams*, eds. Lagarde and J. Bollig, 15 (XXX.26–8).:

> ἄτρωτός ἐστι πᾶσιν ὅπλων ὀργάνοις.
> ἄτρεστός ἐστι τοῖς φόβοις τῶν δογμάτων.
> ἄληπτός ἐστι τοῖς βρόχοις τῶν γραμμάτων.

Ibid., 25 (XLVII.20–4):

> σὺ γὰρ τιθηνὸς καὶ τροφός μοι, φιλτάτη,
> σὺ παιδαγωγὸς καὶ διδάσκαλος μόνη·
> ἐν σοὶ πόνους ἤνεγκα μακροὺς καὶ κόπους,
> ἐν σοὶ διῆξα νύκτας ἀγρύπνους ὅλας,
> ἐν σοὶ διημέρευσα κάμνων ἐν λόγοις

Ibid., 43 (XC.5–6):

> ἴσως ἄδοξός ἐστιν, ἀλλ' ἐλευθέρα·
> ἴσως κρότων ἄμοιρος, ἀλλὰ καὶ φθόνων·

that they abound in subtle artistic lessons. Although the literary significance of the discourses is mentioned only at the very end of the composition, it is nonetheless very important, as it reveals what an essential role Mauropous' past practice as a man of letters and a teacher played in his work. John's interest in language and its precise usage, probably a consequence of long years of teaching, also appears in these verses. In particular, the use of διδαγμάτων and μαθημάτων seems to be of particular relevance; for the former expresses something that is taught, while the latter signifies something that is learned. This choice of words seems also to rate the importance of the content over the form of the discourses, as if ἠθικὰ διδάγματα were more meaningful and compelling to teach than τεχνικὰ μαθήματα.

v. 22: in the course of the poem Gregory's discourses slowly acquire a fuller dimension and a life of their own; indeed, after having compared the discourses to light and celestial bodies, John not only describes them as an abode of art and poetry in their very essence – μουσεῖον αὐτόχρημα – but also as a sort of living being that inspires knowledge – γνῶσιν ἐμπνέον. The author's enthusiasm in this concluding sequence is unmistakable, and it is fascinating to observe its almost contradictory nature. The joy and the relief for the rescue of the manuscript initially seems to spring mainly from religious devotion, since these texts alone could readily provide wisdom and deliverance to humankind. More excitedly, in lines 20–1 there appears another, more secular kind of reference that stems from the rhetorical and stylistic skills of the theologian. The idea of the spiritual and artistic value of the discourses is summarised in line 21 by the expression μουσεῖον αὐτόχρημα, γνῶσιν ἐμπνέον, where art and knowledge are indissolubly bound together.

vv. 23–4: the last two lines of the poem are interesting from an autobiographical point of view; in them, the author reveals that he has restored the script of the manuscript to make it perfect in its kind and to provide humanity with never-ending enjoyment, thus confirming his strenuous activity as philologist and restorer of books. It is impossible to determine what John means exactly with καταρτίσας, whether the emendation of the text or its transcription into minuscule.[11] However, keeping in mind the evidence given in several of his poems, one ought certainly to consider these words as a further testimony of Mauropous' love for books, which made him a scholar engaged in the propagation of culture, as well as

---

[11] The verb καταρτίζω has various meanings, among which 'adjust, restore, equip, prepare'; LSJ, 910. The word γραφή can signify either the writing or the copy of a book; see B. Atsalos, *La terminologie du livre-manuscrit à l'époque byzantine* (Thessalonike, 2001), 185–6. It is therefore quite difficult to know what the author means exactly.

in its preservation for posterity. The author's zeal in preserving and emending manuscripts throughout his life and during his stay in Euchaita is attested by several other epigrams, which are relevant and help place epigram 29 within the larger picture of Mauropous' poetry.[12] Two compositions in particular recall the restoration and correction of liturgical books for daily service in the bishopric.[13] In another poem, perhaps written when John was older, he tells of the poor reward gained in return for his care and for the time spent over the books; indeed, he laments that he is very ill and crushed by endless pain.[14]

These short epigrams are revealing of the poet's efforts to emend texts and of his belief that he has done it to the best of his ability.[15] Such a philological zeal blends perfectly with John's interest in linguistic matters and his inclination for teaching, as it emerges from several poems of his collection. Of special note are his poetic manifesto and some poems composed on the occasion of linguistic controversies, and all are worthy of consideration.

In his opening poem John discloses the principles that have guided him in the selection process of his collection. By asserting that he has always been aware of the importance of restraint – μέτρον – in everything, John states that he wants to avoid excess and unpleasantness for his readers by choosing just a small part of his literary works, both in prose and verse.[16] Others, he continues, may well write at great length, but the Day of

---

[12] See Mauropous, *Epigrams*, eds. Lagarde and J. Bollig, 50–1 (XCVII–XCIX).
[13] Ibid., and in particular 50 (XCVII.1–3).:

> ὕμνων ἐπελθὼν ἡμερησίων βίβλους
> πᾶσάν τε τούτων τὴν γραφὴν ἐπιξέσας
> καὶ χεῖρα καὶ νοῦν ὡς ἐνῆν καταρτίσας.

[14] Ibid., 51 (XCIX.1–5):

> καλὴν δεδωκὼς ταῖς βίβλοις ὑπουργίαν,
> αὐτὸς πονηρὰν ἀντιλαμβάνω χάριν·
> τῶν μὲν γὰρ ἤδη τὰς νόσους ἰασάμην,
> ἐγὼ δὲ συντέτηκα καὶ κακῶς ἔχω,
> κόπων τὸ σῶμα συντριβεὶς ἀμετρίᾳ.

[15] Ibid., 51 (XCVIII.1–2):

> οὐ πολλὰ μέν, κράτιστα πάντα δ᾽ ἐνθάδε·
> οὐκ ἂν γὰρ εὕροις ἀλλαχοῦ τὰ βελτίω.

[16] Ibid., 1 (I.1–2):

> πάλαι διδαχθεὶς ὡς ἄριστον πᾶν μέτρον,
> τά τ᾽ ἄλλα πάντα μετριάζω, καὶ λόγους.

John underlines the importance of proportion and restraint also in 19 (XXXIV.11–12):

> ἀμετρία γὰρ πανταχοῦ κακὸν μέγα,
> μάλιστα δ᾽ ἡ φθείρουσα τὴν μέτρου φύσιν.

Judgement will bring justice and their speeches will burn like hay.[17] This statement is relevant as it offers a glimpse into John's literary taste. Such aversion for magniloquent speeches and pedantic linguistic purism comes into sight in various compositions directed against σχεδογράφοι, the authors of σχήδη, short texts initially used in school to illustrate grammatical notions, and that later degenerated into paradoxical compositions used to show one's *ex tempore* rhetorical ability.[18] John's dislike for this kind of abstruse skill and his stance in relation to intellectuals acting in this manner is apparent in several compositions.[19] In an epigram written in response to hostile comments on his usage of the verb πιπράσκω with the preposition ἀντί, the poet reveals himself a bitter polemicist ready to defend the correctness of his choice for the sake of clarity, and on account of his aversion of the obscure word plays that schedographers scatter in their texts.[20] In this case, as the grammatical observation of the critic was essentially correct, John seems to be actually supporting a more contemporary use of Greek. This would be a use in which the meaning of the spoken word corresponded to that of the written word even though it

---

On the question of μέτρον and ἀμετρία see Karpozilos, Συμβολή, 77–8; P. Magdalino, 'Cultural Change? The Context of Byzantine Poetry from Geometres to Prodromos' in Bernard and Demoen, eds., *Poetry and Its Contexts*, 19–36.

[17] Ibid., 2 (1.38–9):

εἰς καῦσιν ἐκδίδωσιν ἀπράκτους λόγους,
ὡς χόρτον, ὡς ἔρημον ἰκμάδος ξύλον.

[18] The bibliography on schedography is immense and what follows is by no means comprehensive. H. Hunger, *Die hochsprachliche profane Literatur der Byzantiner* (Munich, 1978), vol. II, 25–9; A. Garzya, *Storia e interpretazione di testi bizantini* (London, 1974), vii, 1–14; A. P. Kazhdan, 'Schedographia', *ODB*, vol. III, 1849; R. Anastasi, 'Giovanni di Euchaita e gli ΣΚΕΔΙΚΟΙ (sic)', *SicGym*, 24 (1971), 61–9; I. Vassis, 'Graeca Sunt, Non Leguntur', *BZ*, 86/87 (1993–4), 1–19; I. Vassis, 'Τῶν νέων φιλολόγων παλαίσματα: Ἡ συλλογή σχεδῶν τοῦ κώδικα *Vaticanus Palatinus gr.* 92', *Ἑλληνικά*, 52 (2002), 37–68; I. Polemis, 'Προβλήματα τῆς βυζαντινῆς σχεδογραφίας', *Ἑλληνικά*, 45 (1995), 277–302; I. Polemis, 'Γεώργιος μαΐστωρ ἁγιοτεσσαρακοντίτης', *Ἑλληνικά*, 46 (1996), 301–6; I. Polemis, 'Philologische und historische Probleme in der schedographischen Sammlung des *Codex Marcianus GR* XI, 31', *Byzantion*, 67 (1997), 252–63; K. Manaphes and I. Polemis, 'Βασιλείου Πεδιαδίτου ἀνέκδοτα ἔργα', *EEBS*, 49 (1994–8), 1–62; P. A. Agapitos, 'Grammar, Genre and Patronage in the Twelfth Century: a Scientific Paradigm and its Implications', *JÖB*, 64 (2014), 1–22. See also R. H. Robins, *The Byzantine Grammarians: Their Place in History* (Berlin, 1993), 125–48.

[19] R. Anastasi, 'Su Giovanni di Euchaita', *SicGym*, 29 (1976), 19–49; in particular 29–41.

[20] Mauropous, *Epigrams*, eds. Lagarde and J. Bollig, 18 (xxxiii.5–8):

πῶς δ' οἱ λέγοντες καὶ γράφοντες τὴν πρᾶσιν,
ὅπως συνέστη καὶ καθ' ὅντινα τρόπον,
ἔξω φέρονται τοῦ προσήκοντος λόγου,
σκάφην καλοῦντες τὴν ὑμνουμένην σκάφην;

Also ibid., 37 (LXVIII).

might have been in contrast with ancient writers, rather than a purist usage of the language as some of his contemporaries maintained.[21]

This interest in philological disputes formed an integral part of John's teaching activity throughout his life. Mauropous opened a renowned school in Constantinople at the beginning of his career where the young Michael Psellos was among his students. It is possible to gather that lessons took place in his home and that the author was not only devoted to educating, but also to arbitrating literary disagreements among pupils and teachers.[22] However, what is even more interesting and revealing about John's commitment to education is his statement that he offered his knowledge, without charge, to his students and to all those who wished to learn.[23] Such indifference to money suits Mauropous' character and the numerous declarations of contempt for wealth and the Epicurean ideal of λάθε βιώσας by which he longed to live.[24] The genuineness of the poet's commitment to teaching and to a quiet life is further corroborated by the fact that such ambition was felt neither as a renunciation of worldly honours nor as a waste of God-given talents, as John argued forcefully in the last of a series of epigrams εἰς ἑαυτόν.[25] This poem is a reflection on life in the form of a dialogue between the poet and Reason; while Reason objects to John's life choices and his determination to refuse nomination as bishop, Mauropous makes his case by reasserting his contempt for glory

---

[21] Ibid., 18 (XXXIII.30–31):

> τὸ γὰρ σαφές τε καὶ πρόδηλον ἐν λόγοις,
> λογογράφοις ἥδιστον, οὐ σχεδογράφοις.

Anastasi, 'Giovanni di Euchaita', 68–9; Karpozilos, Συμβολή, 91–2.

[22] Ibid., 25 (XLVII.26–8):

> κρίνων μαθηταῖς καὶ διδασκάλοις ἔρις,
> ἕτοιμος ὢν ἅπασιν εἰς ἀποκρίσεις
> καὶ προστετηκὼς ταῖς γραφαῖς καὶ ταῖς βίβλοις.

On Mauropous' school, see P. Lemerle, *Cinq études sur le XIe siècle byzantin* (Paris, 1977), 193–248, especially 197–201, where the author argues that Mauropus was not a regular teacher. Karpozilos, on the other hand, accepts John's teaching career, as well as the fact that his school was located in his house, Karpozilos, *Letters*, 11. See also C. Livanos, 'Exile and Return in John Mauropus, Poem 47', *BMGS*, 32 (2008), 38–49.

[23] Ibid., 25 (XLVII.29–31):

> ἐν σοὶ συνῆξα γνῶσιν ἐκ μαθημάτων,
> ἐν σοὶ δὲ ταύτην τοῖς θέλουσι σκορπίσας
> πολλοὺς σοφοὺς ἔδειξα προῖκα τῶν νέων.

[24] Mauropous, *Letters*, eds. Lagarde and J. Bollig, 51 (v.3–4): 'ἡμᾶς ... τοὺς τὰ μέσα φεύγειν ἐσπουδακότας; τοὺς τὸ λάθε βιώσας, εἴπερ τις ἕτερος, τιμᾶν ἐγνωκότας;'

[25] Mauropous, *Epigrams*, eds. Lagarde and J. Bollig, 46–7 (XCII); on this poem, see also R. Anastasi, 'Note di filologia greca', *SicGym*, 26 (1973), 97–131, in particular 121–4.

and by claiming proudly that he has carried out his duty as long as good health has allowed him[26] through the dedication of his life to the education of youth.[27] Once again it is evident how learning, teaching and preserving knowledge for future generations was an essential component of the poet's beliefs.

It would be possible to continue discussing John's poetry at length, but it is now time to draw some conclusions. The analysis of the text has revealed the many levels of meaning in which this poem can be read and how much information, related to both the style and the poetic self of the author, can be extrapolated from it. It is evident from the text and from what has been argued above that John was a multifaceted intellectual gifted with an extraordinary linguistic talent and a real enthusiasm for books, which he successfully handed down to his pupils through his lifelong commitment to education. It has also been seen how epigram 29 fits within the larger picture of Mauropous' poetry and how many elements recurring in his writings are present in it too. Finally, the way in which John spreads personal evidence in his writings has also been shown. Although this is sparse and often vague, nevertheless it helps shed some light on the personality of the author and seems to anticipate the urge for autobiographical disclosure and the greater craving of poets and writers to assert themselves in their works, which will become apparent in the writings of Michael Psellos and of later Byzantine authors.[28] One might argue that these elements are not truly autobiographical, but rather that they only contribute to the construction of Mauropous' literary persona. Undoubtedly, John wants to convey a certain image of himself throughout the collection of his writing, especially through his personal poems, which are intended to exemplify the various stages of his life and personal

---

[26] Ibid., 46 (XVII.27–9):

> ποῖον λόγου τάλαντον; οὐκ ἔχω λόγον,
> οὕτω καμνόντων (ὡς ὁρᾷς) τῶν ὀργάνων
> ὡς μηδὲ λεπτὸν φθέγμα πέμπειν εὐκόλως.

[27] Ibid., 46 (XCII.41–3):

> καλῶς γεωργήσασα πολλοὺς τῶν νέων-
> πάντας γὰρ οὐ τίθημι, μὴ καὶ κομπάσω·
> πλὴν ἀλλὰ πλείστους-ἦρεν ἐκ μαθημάτων.

[28] Lauxtermann, *Byzantine Poetry*, 36–8. On the rise of autobiographical impulse in the eleventh century, see M. Angold, 'The Autobiographical Impulse in Byzantium', *DOP*, 52 (1998), 52–73; M. Hinterberger, *Autobiographische Traditionen in Byzanz* (Vienna, 1999); M. Hinterberger, 'Autobiography and Hagiography in Byzantium', *Symbolae Osloenses*, 75 (2000), 139–64. On the cultural changes that caused greater self-awareness in Byzantine authors, see A. P. Kazhdan and A. Wharton Epstein, *Change in Byzantine Culture in the Eleventh and Twelfth Centuries* (Berkeley, CA, 1985); and, for a more recent overview, Magdalino, 'Cultural Change?', 23–30.

development. However, I believe it would be wrong to divest John's personal disclosure of all authenticity and spontaneity. For as I have argued elsewhere, behind every autobiographical expression lies a retrospective analysis of one's life carried out to review and, often, justify the outcome of one's existence, but there is also an emotional component, which is deeply rooted in man's need to express himself and to be remembered. Certainly, it is this mix of intellectual sophistication, literary fervour, involvement in the political and cultural events of his epoch and autobiographical disclosure that makes John Mauropous such a remarkable personality and an author worthy of being studied in greater depth.

Further Reading

The key primary sources are: E. Follieri, ed., 'Giovanni Mauropode metropolita di Euchaita, Otto canoni paracletici a N. S. Gesù Cristo', *Archivio italiano per la storia della pietà*, 5 (1967), 1–200; P. de Lagarde and J. Bollig, eds., *Iohannis Euchaitorum Metropolitae quae in Codice Vaticano Graeco 676 supersunt* (Göttingen, 1882). Important studies include: F. Bernard, 'The Circulation of Poetry in 11th-century Byzantium' in S. Neocleous, ed., *Sailing to Byzantium: Papers from the First and Second Postgraduate Forums in Byzantine Studies* (Newcastle-upon-Tyne, 2009), 145–60 and F. Bernard, *Writing and Reading Byzantine Secular Poetry, 1025–1081* (Oxford, 2014); also F. Bernard and K. Demoen, eds., *Poetry and Its Contexts in Eleventh-century Byzantium* (Farnham, 2012).

CHAPTER 2

The Autobiographies of the Patriarch Gennadios II Scholarios

Michael Angold

There are many Byzantine texts that contain long autobiographical passages. Rather than worrying how far these constitute autobiography in any modern sense, we should allow Martin Hinterberger to be our guide. He has not only demonstrated the value of studying these texts for themselves, but has also devised a brilliantly simple solution to the problem of defining autobiography in a Byzantine context by including all first-person narratives, even if occasionally they are couched in the third person![1] This means dealing with an assemblage of very different materials. They range from the detailed autobiographies of Nikephoros Blemmydes to incidental personal information. Hinterberger therefore divides these disparate texts into categories. These include apologetical works, which in the last days of Byzantium seem almost the preferred vehicle for autobiographical reflections.[2] The best known is Demetrios Kydones' apology written around 1363, in which he uses autobiography to explain and defend his Latin sympathies.[3] Rather different, but still entirely autobiographical, is the defence that Paul Tagaris made in 1394 before the patriarchal court, in which he endeavoured to explain how he could be both Latin patriarch of Constantinople and Orthodox patriarch of Jerusalem.[4] It was before the same court, but ten years after the fall of Constantinople, that the *megas chartophylax* Theodore Agallianos delivered two speeches defending himself against charges of corruption and incompetence. His defence is largely autobiographical.[5] Agallianos is

---

[1] M. Hinterberger, *Autobiographische Traditionen in Byzanz* (Vienna, 1999), 97–116.
[2] Ibid., 367–81.
[3] F. Kianka, 'The Apology of Demetrius Cydones', *Études byzantines*, 7 (1980), 57–71.
[4] D. M. Nicol, 'The Confessions of a Bogus Patriarch: Paul Tagaris Palaiologos, Orthodox Patriarch of Jerusalem and Catholic Patriarch of Constantinople in the Fourteenth Century', *JEH*, 21 (1970), 289–99.
[5] M. J. Angold, 'Theodore Agallianos: The Last Byzantine Autobiography' in E. Motos Guirao and M. Morphadakis Philaktos, eds., *Constantinopla: 550 años de su caída* (Granada, 2006), 35–44.

important for our purposes, because he was a close friend and ally of the Patriarch Gennadios II. The charges brought against him were an indirect attack on Gennadios, who had by then resigned the patriarchate, but in retirement remained an influential voice.

At various stages in his life Gennadios produced apologies in order to defend himself against his detractors. Though by no means devoid of interest, his apologies, in the same way as other of his personal writings, provide little autobiographical detail. Gennadios prefers to defend himself by argument and assertion rather than by setting out the facts of his life. His reticence has created an enigma for future generations, so much so that the great Uniate scholar Leo Allatios posited the existence of three men with the name of George Scholarios, as a way of coming to terms with the apparent inconsistencies of Scholarios' career.[6] How was it possible for a man who was an advocate of the union of the Orthodox and Latin churches, to become the leader of the anti-unionists? Joseph Gill, the historian of the Council of Florence, accepted that this was indeed the case, but remained distinctly uncomfortable about it.[7] From an opposite perspective, the Orthodox historian Theodore Zeses had systematically to dismiss the majority of Scholarios' unionist writings as later fabrications, in a misplaced attempt to protect his subject's Orthodoxy.[8]

More recently, Franz Tinnefeld has argued on textual grounds for their authenticity,[9] while C. J. G. Turner has been able to expose the artificiality of the contradiction between Scholarios' apparently pro-Latin views and his later anti-unionist stance.[10] In doing so, they prepared the way for Marie-Hélène Blanchet's superb new biography of George-Gennadios Scholarios. She is able to provide a convincing account of the future patriarch's intellectual and spiritual evolution, which she sees, far from being inconsistent, as an attempt to protect and adapt his core beliefs to the momentous changes occurring in his lifetime. She pays especial attention to what she terms his 'écrits à contenu autobiographique', which are mostly in the form of apologies, and wonders why recent work on

---

[6] M.-H. Blanchet, *Georges-Gennadios Scholarios (vers 1400–vers 1472): un intellectuel orthodoxe face à la disparition de l'empire byzantin* (Paris, 2008), 49–52. On Allatios, see K. Hartnup, *'On the Beliefs of the Greeks': Leo Allatios and Popular Orthodoxy* (Leiden, 2004).
[7] J. Gill, *Personalities of the Council of Florence and Other Essays* (Oxford, 1964), 79–94.
[8] Th. Zeses, Γεννάδιος Β' Σχολάριος: Βίος, συγγράμματα, διδασκαλία (Thessalonike, 1980), 362–405.
[9] F. Tinnefeld, 'Georgios Gennadios Scholarios' in G. Conticello and V. Conticello, eds., *La Théologie Byzantine et sa tradition* (Turnhout, 2002), vol. II, 477–541.
[10] C. J. G. Turner, 'George-Gennadius Scholarius and the Union of Florence', *JThSt*, n.s. 18 (1967), 83–103; C. J. G. Turner, 'The Career of George-Gennadius Scholarius', *Byzantion*, 39 (1969), 420–55.

Byzantine autobiography has overlooked them.[11] The short answer is that where possible Scholarios avoided autobiographical reminiscence. Nevertheless, he could not help but reveal something of the inner man, which gives his apologies a particular interest.

George Scholarios' first apology was a defence of his Latin studies.[12] There is so little concrete detail that the dating is problematic. It survives in the author's autograph. It shows plenty of evidence of reworking, but it lacks any title, which may mean that it was never delivered. It has normally been dated to before the Council of Ferrara/Florence (1438–9) because of the lack of any reference or even allusion to the council. Recently M.-H. Blanchet has suggested that it was composed soon after Scholarios' return from Italy.[13] She does so on the grounds of the similarities of its themes to those of a letter he wrote to his students after his return from the council, but this may only have been a matter of recycling the contents of his apology; for there are strong indications in an opinion Scholarios was asked to give on Bessarion's treatise on the procession of the Holy Spirit – usually referred to as the *Oratio dogmatica* – that Scholarios' apology for his Latin studies dated from before the Council of Florence.[14] Scholarios presented it as a response to criticism sparked off by youthful indiscretions before setting out for the council.[15] An early date for the apology would help explain the declaration it contains that, should he quit his native land, it would not be out of a sense of disillusionment, but in order to obtain proper remuneration.[16] M.-H. Blanchet has shown that in the early 1430s Scholarios was actively considering leaving Constantinople either for the Peloponnese or possibly Rome.[17] By 1437 he had entered imperial service. The question of remuneration was thereafter less relevant.

Scholarios' Latin studies laid him open to the charge that he was a Latin sympathiser. His defence was in three stages. To study Latin did not make you any the less a Byzantine, but what was the purpose of learning Latin if you did not use it to converse with Latins and to acquaint yourself directly with Latin culture? If you consequently found Latins congenial, that did not mean that you were any the less an Orthodox Christian. But some

---

[11] Blanchet, *Scholarios*, 27–31.
[12] L. Petit, K. A. Sideridès and M. Jugie, eds., *Oeuvres complètes de Georges Scholarios* (Paris, 1928–35), vol. I, 376–89.
[13] Blanchet, *Scholarios*, 358–63, 490–3.
[14] Scholarios, *Oeuvres complètes*, eds. Petit, Sideridès and Jugie, vol. III, 100–16.
[15] Ibid., 116.15–33.
[16] Scholarios, *Oeuvres complètes*, eds. Petit, Sideridès and Jugie, vol. I, 387.33–5.
[17] Blanchet, *Scholarios*, 300–6.

might think that Scholarios' own words convict him, for however one reads his apology, it was a eulogy for Latin culture. He reminded his detractors of the many Latins who were studying Greek and the rewards and prestige that this brought them in their native countries. Enthusiasm for study appeared a Latin characteristic, so that 'their peasants seem more learned than students here, while the Hellenic [scholars] among us are such in name only. As for the rest, they can, with two or three exceptions, scarcely be called literate.'[18] He admired those Latin scholars who studied Aristotle and Plato, in contrast to their Byzantine counterparts, who thought them a 'waste of time' (ἄχθος ἐτώσιον).[19] Here he is echoing the opinion of Demetrios Kydones, who applauded the efforts of the Latins to master 'the labyrinths of Plato and Aristotle, for which [the Byzantines] had never ever shown any inclination'.[20] Before the Council of Florence there was only the thinnest of dividing lines separating George Scholarios and Demetrios Kydones in their respective attitudes towards union with the Roman Church. Scholarios was clear that the religious differences with the Latins were trivial (κοῦφα καὶ μέτρια).[21] He makes the naïve assertion that his enemies could not know what he believed and therefore were not in a position to accuse him of deviating from Orthodoxy. This sounds like special pleading. Elsewhere he admitted that at this time out of the devilment of youth he even defended the Latin position, because he was not convinced that the addition of the *filioque* to the creed was strictly speaking unorthodox. He had found support for it in some of the Greek Fathers. He hoped that the council would pronounce definitively on the matter.[22] At the Council of Florence he worked very hard to find a formula that would reconcile Latin and Orthodox differences on the procession of the Holy Spirit.[23]

How was it possible for a proponent of the union of churches, as George Scholarios was both before and during the Council of Florence, to become the leader of opposition to union? This has always been the fascination of George Scholarios. It may also help explain why he is so miserly with autobiographical detail. He was only too aware of his false position and was

---

[18] Scholarios, *Oeuvres complètes*, eds. Petit, Siderides and Jugie, vol. I, 386.31–4.
[19] Ibid., 385.3–386.34.
[20] G. Mercati, *Notizie di Procoro e Demetrio Cidone, Manuele Caleca e Teodoro Meliteniota ed altri appunti per la storia della teologia e della letteratura bizantina del secolo XIV* (Vatican City, 1931), 366.95–6.
[21] Scholarios, *Oeuvres complètes*, eds. Petit, Siderides and Jugie, vol. I, 387.26.
[22] Ibid., vol. III, 115.37–8.
[23] J. Gill, *The Council of Florence* (Cambridge, 1959), 225–6, 241–4, 258–9; Blanchet, *Scholarios*, 316–44.

careful not to supply personal information, which might then be used against him. It was quite otherwise for his friend and ally Theodore Agallianos, who had also originally been a member of the Byzantine delegation to the council, but providentially had been prevented from going by a psychosomatic illness.[24] Unlike those who participated in the council, he had nothing to apologise for in its aftermath. Perhaps this contributed to his greater willingness to lay open to scrutiny the facts of his career.[25]

Scholarios' dilemma was, on the surface, little different from that of most members of the Byzantine delegation to the council. To a greater or lesser degree they anticipated that it would be possible to reach an agreement on the reunion of churches on terms acceptable to the Orthodox Church. George Scholarios did more than most towards achieving this end. This was at the behest of Emperor John VIII Palaiologos, whose advisor he was. The emperor entrusted him with one of the most delicate tasks that arose in the course of the council: drafting a profession of faith in response to the one received from the Latins. He did so, carefully avoiding the most obvious compromise formula, which equated the procession of the Holy Spirit *through the Son*, which was acceptable to the Orthodox, with the Latin teaching of the procession of the Holy Spirit *from the Son*, which was not. When he presented this to the Byzantine delegation, it was approved by twenty-eight votes to twelve against. But the Latins rejected it on grounds of lack of clarity.[26] This was a humiliation, if only because of Scholarios' well-known disparagement of the intellectual standards of Byzantine scholars when compared to their Latin counterparts.[27] He obviously thought that his Latin expertise set him apart from the rest of the Byzantine delegation. It was a blow to discover that the Latins condemned his theology for its lack of clarity. Despite encouraging words from his friend Francesco Filelfo,[28] George Scholarios was beginning to realise that in these surroundings a grasp of Aristotelian thought mediated through Thomas Aquinas was not quite enough.[29] Latins at the council were far more interested in Plato and turned for enlightenment to

[24] C. Patrinelis, Ὁ Θεόδωρος Ἀγαλλιανὸς ταυτιζόμενος πρὸς τὸν Θεοφάνην Μηδείας καὶ οἱ ἀνέκδοτοι λόγοι του (Athens, 1966), 94–5.
[25] See C. J. G. Turner, 'Notes on the Works of Theodore Agallianos Contained in Codex Bodleianus Canonicus Graecus 49', *BZ*, 61 (1968), 27–35.
[26] Gill, *Florence*, 250–2; Blanchet, *Scholarios*, 328–30.
[27] Scholarios, *Oeuvres complètes*, eds. Petit, Sideridès and Jugie, vol. 1, 299.20–9.
[28] E. Legrand, *Cent-dix lettres de François Filelfe* (Paris, 1892), 31–4, no. 12.
[29] S. Ebbesen and J. Pinborg, 'Gennadios and Western Scholasticism: Radulphus Brito's *Ars Vetus* in Greek Translation', *ClMed*, 33 (1981–2), 263–319.

Scholarios' colleague George Gemistos (Plethon). It must have dawned on Scholarios that there would be no great demand for his services in Italy. There was one more humiliation in store. Towards the end of the council the emperor forced him, along with the other lay members of the delegation, to accept in writing the compromise formula on the procession of the Holy Spirit, which would provide the basis for a reunion of the churches. It embraced exactly that equivalence of the Greek *through the Son* and the Latin *from the Son* which Scholarios had earlier been trying to avoid.[30]

As a layman there was no need for Scholarios to sign the act of union. There may therefore be nothing out of the ordinary about his departure from Florence before the end of the council. On the other hand, he left in the company of the emperor's brother Demetrios Palaiologos, for whom departure from the council was an act of defiance directed against the imminent conclusion of a reunion of churches.[31] It also suggests coolness towards Emperor John VIII, whom Scholarios had served faithfully during the council. For example, he can only have drafted his 'Appeal on behalf of Peace and Aid to the Fatherland' on instructions from the emperor. This tract has become notorious because it appears to advocate union of churches on Latin terms in order to obtain aid for Constantinople. It was addressed to the patriarchal synod. The Greek *Acta* of the council suggest that it was read out along with other of Scholarios' pro-unionist tracts on 13 and 14 April 1439 at a meeting of the synod, which was presided over by the emperor with cardinals in attendance.[32] If this was indeed the case, it did not mean that these tracts were specially composed for the occasion. By April 1439 Constantinople was no longer in danger, but it had been in the autumn of 1438, when news reached the Greek delegation that the Turks were preparing to attack Constantinople. This seems the most likely occasion for the original composition of Scholarios' 'Appeal'. The emperor wanted the members of the delegation to the council to provide funds to help with the city's defence, but immediately came up against opposition from the bishops.[33] Scholarios' tract presented them with the alternative, which was to return home with a union concluded very much on Latin terms. This does not mean that it reflected either Scholarios' own point of view, or, for that matter, the emperor's, which was always that union

---

[30] V. Laurent, ed., *Syropoulos. Les 'Mémoires' du Grand Ecclésiarque de l'Église de Constantinople, Sylvestre Syropoulos, sur le concile de Florence (1438–1439)* (Paris, 1971), 426–9; Gill, *Florence*, 258–62; Blanchet, *Scholarios*, 330–2.

[31] Syropoulos, *Mémoires*, ed. Laurent, 460–1.

[32] J. Gill, ed., *Quae supersunt actorum Graecorum Concilii Florentini* (Rome, 1953), 407–8.

[33] Syropoulos, *Mémoires*, ed. Laurent, 272–9.

should only be on the basis of an agreed resolution of the points of dogma separating the two Churches. Scholarios was simply carrying out the task allotted to him by his master. It was a way of bringing home to the bishops the serious implications of their refusal to provide for the defence of Constantinople. He had done much the same in the debates before the Greek delegation set off for Italy, when he had set out two opposing views of the union of churches.[34] There therefore seems to be no good reason to dismiss Scholarios' 'Appeal' as a later falsification; it should be seen, rather, as the product of a particular turn of events.[35]

In his attitude both towards the Latins and Latin culture in general and towards the question of union George Scholarios was remarkably consistent. Down to the end of his life he remained an admirer of Latin culture and of Thomas Aquinas in particular. Thanks to recent work by Hugh Barbour and Christopher Livanos, Scholarios' ability to combine opposition to the union of churches with devotion to the thought of Thomas Aquinas no longer seems a contradiction in terms.[36] Scholarios was an Aristotelian, and like a previous generation of Byzantine scholars he found Thomas Aquinas a particularly illuminating guide to Aristotle's thought. He concentrated on those aspects of Aquinas' work that were in tune with the study of Aristotle at Byzantium. He simply disregarded areas of disagreement, such as dogma. He used Aquinas' philosophical and logical approach the better to understand and elucidate Orthodox positions. As far as he was concerned, it was the mastery of methodology that explained the intellectual superiority of the Latins, not their dogma. The teachings of Thomas Aquinas therefore had little or no relevance to Scholarios' position on the union of churches, which remained an issue to be resolved by an ecumenical council. But in its aftermath Scholarios had to decide whether the union concluded at Florence was legitimate; whether it had been forced or not.

Something of his thinking emerges from the opinion that he gave, after his return from the council, on Bessarion's *Oratio dogmatica*, which to a very large degree provided the reasoned basis on which the Orthodox agreed to the reunion of Church. Scholarios dismisses its argument as specious (κακομηχάνως)[37] and then launches into a bitter personal attack

---

[34] Ibid., 170–1. See Blanchet, *Scholarios*, 310–12.   [35] Blanchet, *Scholarios*, 327–8, 334–41.
[36] H. C. Barbour, *The Byzantine Thomism of Gennadios Scholarios and his Translation of the Commentary of Armandus de Bellovisu on the De ente et essentia of Thomas Aquinas* (Vatican City, 1993); C. Livanos, *Greek Tradition and Latin Influence in the Work of George Scholarios* (Piscataway, NJ, 2006), 27–69.
[37] Scholarios, *Oeuvres complètes*, eds. Petit, Sideridès and Jugie, vol. III, 110.9.

on Bessarion. The two men had been reasonably close in the run-up to the council. They were allies in the early stages of the council. Scholarios provided Bessarion with the materials and arguments for his address to the council on 1 November 1438, in which he refuted the Latin position over the addition of the *filioque*.[38] It was a major triumph for the Orthodox delegation. But Scholarios now accused Bessarion of having the arrogance to believe he was intellectually superior to other men. He reminded him that he was human after all and quite likely to fall into error, especially when he spurned good advice.[39] Scholarios accused Bessarion of preferring to rely on acolytes who did his dirty work. He compared them to a pack of hunting dogs. They fawned over their master and attacked his enemies and even his friends.[40] This accusation comes as a surprise, even as a shock. If true, it places Bessarion's activities at Florence in a new light. Evidence for his deliberate creation of a circle of scholars only comes after his final departure from Constantinople for Rome in 1441,[41] but there is a distinct possibility that he had already begun to build up a following by the time he went to the council. One might think of a man, such as John Argyropoulos, who joined Bessarion later in Italy. The former's invective against Katablattas, which dates to around the time of the council, shows him at work, traducing an opponent.[42]

Scholarios agreed that Bessarion could not have brought about the Orthodox adhesion to the act of union by himself. He knew the kind of people who had helped him: 'nasty, feather-headed little men of no standing, who were full of admiration for your achievements, whatever these may be, in the expectation that the union would bring them honours and bishoprics or, in some cases, large sums of money'.[43] Those more learned than Bessarion were not given a chance to challenge his propositions, because the emperor enjoined silence.[44] This is possibly the only hint of criticism of John VIII Palaiologos that Scholarios ever let drop. Having been instrumental in bringing about the union of churches, Bessarion then abandoned Constantinople for the honours and riches offered by Rome on the pretext of organising aid, but Scholarios could

---

[38] Syropoulos, *Mémoires*, ed. Laurent, 336–7; Gill, *Florence*, 153–5; Blanchet, *Scholarios*, 324–5.
[39] Scholarios, *Oeuvres complètes*, eds. Petit, Sideridès and Jugie, vol. III, 110.32–40.
[40] Ibid., vol. III, 11.3–15.
[41] L. Mohler, *Kardinal Bessarion als Theologe, Humanist und Staatsman* (Paderborn, 1923), vol. I, 283–5, 325–35.
[42] P. Canivet and N. Oikonomidès, '(Jean Argyropoulos), *La Comédie de Katablattas*: Invective Byzantin du xve siècle', *Diptycha*, 3 (1982–3), 1–99.
[43] Scholarios, *Oeuvres complètes*, eds. Petit, Sideridès and Jugie, vol. III, 111.31–5.
[44] Ibid., vol. III, 113.1–4.

see no good coming of this. Bessarion's departure pained him because he had been a dear and wise friend. He claimed to have valued him 'above water, air and life itself'. Now he had departed to become an adornment of Italy, while Scholarios was left behind unappreciated by his fellow citizens.[45]

Scholarios' opinion on Bessarion's *Oratio* may not be a piece of autobiography, but it illuminates a watershed in George Scholarios' career. His decision to oppose the union of Florence rested on his conviction that Bessarion had rigged the union by ensuring that his questionable views on the procession of the Holy Spirit were never subjected to proper scrutiny. But there were more personal considerations. At some point during the council the friendship of the two men came under strain. Scholarios' self-pitying remark about being left behind suggests that the fault may have been more on Bessarion's side than his own. The key moment is likely to have been the failure of the compromise formula presented by Scholarios to the council. Bessarion had initially given it his support, but after the cardinals had rejected it out of hand he realised he would have to work without Scholarios, who seems also to have lost the trust of the emperor. This underlines how humiliating an experience the council was for Scholarios. If he were still uncertain about his stance on the union, when he returned to Constantinople, Bessarion's decision to return to Rome would have decided him. This was the ultimate betrayal of their friendship.

All this nonetheless fails to explain why Scholarios should then have played so active a role in the anti-unionist agitation in Constantinople. At the council he had very largely worked behind the scenes. Only on the occasion of his presentation of his profession of faith had he had a leading role. The humiliation it brought him should have been a lesson. Returning from the council, Scholarios was able to resume his career at court. He may already have been a member of the senate and a *krites katholikos* before he set out for Italy. He certainly held those positions after his return. The high favour in which he now stood is apparent from his role as court preacher. Any coolness between Scholarios and John VIII Palaiologos was soon forgotten, while the emperor came to rely more and more heavily on Scholarios, as his doubts about the advisability of the union increased. At the close of the council, John VIII is supposed to have made the following remark: 'we thought that we were correcting many Latin errors. Now I see that those innovators who have fallen into so many errors are correcting us, even though we have changed nothing.'[46]

---

[45] Ibid., vol. III, 115.1–10.   [46] Syropoulos, *Mémoires*, ed. Laurent, 502.21–4.

This was in response to the pope's refusal to allow a celebration of the Orthodox liturgy.

John VIII showed immense skill in keeping control of the Orthodox delegation during the council. It is often suggested that after his return to Constantinople he lapsed into apathy and allowed matters to take their course.[47] This judgement seems to go against the enormous respect he enjoyed. It also underestimates the difficulties produced by the hostility aroused at Constantinople by the union of Florence. Repression was self-defeating, while the emperor realised that he could use anti-unionist agitation as a way of reminding the papacy of its obligation to bring aid to Constantinople. The emperor's treatment of Mark Eugenikos, the leader of the anti-unionists, reveals his grip on the situation. After forcing him into exile, he allowed him to return, but under conditions of house arrest, which amounted to imperial protection.[48] After Mark's death in 1445, George Scholarios took up the leadership of opposition to the union. He could only have done so with the tacit support of the emperor, for he continued to frequent the court and to hold high office.[49] It was a way in which the emperor was able to exercise a restraining hand on anti-unionist agitation. Down to his death in 1448 John VIII Palaiologos very cleverly maintained a balance between the unionists and the anti-unionists. In this George Scholarios served his master's purpose. He remembered his time at the court of John VIII in his 'Lamentation' of June 1460 as the best days of his life. The height of felicity, as far as he was concerned, was to deliver sermons before the imperial court. There is something like affection in his estimate of John VIII. On occasion Scholarios' judicial duties meant reprimanding the emperor, who took this in good part. It was his belief that the emperor's death signalled the beginning of the terrible end of the Byzantine Empire.[50]

Scholarios' good opinion of the emperor had therefore survived his summary dismissal from court in 1447. He was careful not to blame the emperor, but insisted that it was the work of the unionist patriarch Gregory III Melissenos (1443–50).[51] Nevertheless, it was a decisive moment for Scholarios, because he was able to devote all his energies to the anti-unionist cause without being hobbled by his obligations to the

---

[47] Gill, *Personalities*, 122–3.
[48] M.-H. Blanchet, 'L'Église byzantine à la suite de l'union de Florence (1439–1445): De la contestation à la scission', *ByzF*, 29 (2007), 79–123.
[49] Blanchet, *Scholarios*, 400–5.
[50] Scholarios, *Oeuvres complètes*, eds. Petit, Sidéridès and Jugie, vol. 1, 289.21–2.
[51] Blanchet, *Scholarios*, 414–15.

emperor. To counter the activities of the patriarch he provided the anti-unionists with a solid organisation, in the shape of *Hiera Synaxis*, which was a church within a church. It had its own seal and made its own ordinations.[52] Effectively, it created a schism within the Church of Constantinople. It would have suited Scholarios if the throne had passed to John VIII's brother Demetrios Palaiologos, who had been a leading anti-unionist at the Council of Florence, but the latter waived his claims in the face of opposition led by his mother, Helena Dragaš, who supported the claims of his elder brother, Constantine.[53] The latter's arrival at Constantinople in March 1449 to take up the Byzantine throne was an embarrassment to George Scholarios, because of his close ties with Demetrios Palaiologos. He did his best to defend himself against charges of treasonable support for Demetrios and of dividing the Church, but he found it politic to become a monk. His influence, if anything, increased. He had the satisfaction of seeing the unionist patriarch Gregory III Melissenos – the schismatic patriarch, as Scholarios dubbed him – driven from office and forced to seek refuge in Rome.[54]

The autobiographical pieces Scholarios wrote before the fall of Constantinople do shed light on the conundrum of how a devotee of Latin culture became the leader of anti-unionist opinion in the aftermath of the Council of Florence because they reveal something of the man. His defence of his Latin studies was from a time when he was still striving to make his mark at the Byzantine court. Like most young men in a similar position he was all too aware of rivals and quick to take offence. There is more than a hint of paranoia, but this was a function of a competitive society, where denigration of rivals was the currency of the day. Scholarios was also aware that, given the negotiations over a union of churches, his chances of success in the struggle for preferment lay in his mastery of Latin, which remained an unusual accomplishment for a Byzantine. He was only too willing to bask in the reflected glory of Latin intellectual superiority. But his Latin studies were also his weak spot, for they laid him open to the charge that he was neither a good Byzantine nor a good Orthodox. He realised that earlier conversions to Rome had given Latin studies a bad name at Byzantium.[55] This did not mean, he insisted, that Latin studies were to blame for these conversions, which were entirely a matter

---

[52] Ibid., 427–37.   [53] R. Maisano, ed., *Giorgio Sfranze. Cronaca* (Rome, 1990), 100 (XXIX.12–18).
[54] Scholarios, *Oeuvres complètes*, eds. Petit, Siderides and Jugie, vol. III, 151.1–2.
[55] C. Delacroix-Besnier, 'Conversions constantinopolitaines au XIVe siècle', *MEFRM*, 105 (1993), 715–61.

of the gullibility of the converts. Scholarios was confident that his patriotism and his Orthodoxy would protect him against any such temptation.[56] His claim to be a good Byzantine was entirely genuine. It was reinforced by his experiences at the Council of Florence, which he interpreted in terms of his relationship with Bessarion. While the latter had connived with the Latins and had then abandoned Constantinople for the honours and riches on offer in Rome, Scholarios had done his best to defend the Orthodox position and had then remained in Constantinople, even though his fellow countrymen did not properly appreciate him. Scholarios makes his case with the absolute minimum of personal information. He says nothing about his Latin studies. He says nothing about his friendships with Latins, such as Francesco Filelfo and Cyriacus of Ancona.[57] There is nothing on his family background. His 'autobiographical' pieces from before 1453 offer insights into his personality and his habits of mind, but, on the loosest possible definition of autobiography, these are not autobiographies. That contemporaries or near-contemporaries used their apologies for autobiographical purposes was no reason George Scholarios should do the same. His strength was reasoned argument seasoned with sarcasm. Autobiography would only have exposed his weaknesses. He came from a modest background. Any detailed presentation of his Latin studies – his main claim to distinction – was likely to reveal how close he was to Latins settled in Constantinople.[58] His participation at the Council of Florence ended in humiliation.

His reluctance to indulge in personal reminiscence reflects to a degree his sense of identity. Unlike many of his contemporaries he showed an almost complete indifference to those personal elements of family (γένος) and home (οἶκος) that were so important an element in the late Byzantine identity.[59] He almost never mentions his parents or his relatives. He ignores his childhood and schooling. He prefers to submerge his identity in the mystique of political orthodoxy, in other words in service to a

---

[56] Scholarios, *Oeuvres complètes*, eds. Petit, Sideridès and Jugie, vol. 1, 383.5–24.
[57] Legrand, *Cent-dix lettres de François Filelfe*, 9–12, no. 5 (1 March 1430); 21–3, no. 9 (28 July 1431); 31–4, no.12 (29 March 1439) and, for comments, T. Ganchou, 'Les *ultimae voluntates* de Manuel et Iôannès Chrysolorâs et le séjour de Francesco Filelfo à Constantinople', *Byzantinistica*, 7 (2005), 195–285; E. W. Bodnar and C. Foss, eds., *Cyriac of Ancona. Later Travels* (Cambridge, MA and London, 2003), 94–7.
[58] M.-H. Blanchet and Th. Ganchou, 'Les fréquentations byzantines de Lodisio de Tabriz, dominicain de Péra (†1453): Géôrgios Scholarios, Iôannes Chrysolorâs et Théodore Kalékas', *Byzantion*, 75 (2005), 70–103.
[59] A. Bryer, 'The Late Byzantine Identity', in K. Fledelius and P. Schreiner, eds., *Byzantium: Identity, Image, Influence* (Copenhagen, 1996), 49–50; M. J. Angold, 'Autobiography and Identity: The Case of the Later Byzantine Empire', *BSl*, 60 (1999), 36–59.

greater good represented by the emperor and Orthodoxy and symbolised by the city of Constantinople. The fall of Constantinople in 1453 meant the end of this ideal order, which left the survivors in a state of stupefaction, none more so than George Scholarios. We can follow his attempts to make sense of the new order created by the Ottomans in the three 'autobiographical' pieces that he produced after 1453: his 'Pastoral Letter' of 1454,[60] his *Lament* for his life of 1460,[61] and a personal apology, which was perhaps the last thing he ever wrote and dates to around 1467.[62] The 'Pastoral Letter' contains two short autobiographical passages and the *Lament* one. Otherwise these pieces are as lacking in personal details as his other writings, but they do constitute a meditation on the disintegration of a sense of identity, which was a consequence of the fall of Constantinople. Since autobiography is more usually concerned with the discovery, rather than the destruction, of a sense of self, Gennadios seems to be offering an interesting variant on a major theme of autobiography.

Paradoxically, the destruction of the old order brought him new prominence. Led away into Turkish captivity, in the same way as the great majority of survivors, he was quickly redeemed by the conqueror and appointed patriarch of Constantinople. He was duly installed in office on 6 January 1454. His 'Pastoral Letter' relates these events in some detail. It is worth translating the passage in full, because it is as near as the Patriarch Gennadios, as he now was, comes to an autobiographical narrative:[63]

> Instead of these things [mistreatment by the barbarians], what was saved up for me? While many others were daily being set free, thanks to the work of skilled [negotiators] – not that they would have been called that previously – I remained a useless burden in the hands of the conquerors. I sought the intervention of friends, but they were then unwilling to help me, so I left everything to God. Forgotten as I was, I bewailed [our] common misfortunes along with my sins, [convinced that my friends] were refusing to ransom me over a trifling sum. [I did not know that] they were revealing where I was hidden to the ruler (*despotes*) and were clamouring that I should be given care of the souls of our [people]. They praised me to the skies, being well aware that the essential thing was to rescue me from those

---

[60] Scholarios, *Oeuvres complètes*, eds. Petit, Sideridès and Jugie, vol. IV, 211–31; Blanchet, *Scholarios*, 496–9.
[61] Scholarios, *Oeuvres complètes*, eds. Petit, Sideridès and Jugie, vol. I, 283–94; Blanchet, *Scholarios*, 499–502.
[62] Scholarios, *Oeuvres complètes*, eds. Petit, Sideridès and Jugie, vol. I, 264–74; Blanchet, *Scholarios*, 503–5.
[63] Scholarios, *Oeuvres complètes*, eds. Petit, Sideridès and Jugie, vol. IV, 224.12–25.7.

labyrinths in which I was confined. And straightaway, escorted by the ruler, I was conveyed over a considerable distance so that I could make my entrance into the city, which I found in a far more miserable state than I could describe. I received orders to take charge of a monastery, which had been plundered and stripped bare. I was also expected without any money to ransom those monks, who were to be its future residents. These monks had previously been troublemakers. Now, using as a pretext the misfortunes of the Christians, they gave full rein to their greed and to the satisfaction of their appetites. They perverted a previously sacred order with their impieties, scandalising the souls of onlookers and flooding the whole world with every kind of evil. I had to deal with the crassest of barbarians over redeeming [captives] from slavery and over all kinds of favours and marks of honour they expected from us, while they pretended to [offer in return] the benefits [of their rule], by which they only meant subordination. In practice, their zeal to enslave human souls achieved the exact opposite. I was then compelled to rebuild ruined churches for the Christians gathered there, who – would that it were not so – made little effort either to live according to the ways of their fathers or to worship God according to the law, [a state of affairs] which ought to have been anticipated. Then a synod gathered together, composed of many bishops from both Asia and Europe. By its votes I became first deacon, then priest, and then bishop and patriarch. I shall leave to one side the details of the ceremonies, which were duly performed according to the laws. I shall also pass over my earlier objections, tears and the waste of time, neglecting too all that happened, I mean, after my ordination. I shall have nothing to say about the lack of proper resources to meet my different responsibilities; nor will I now raise the question of the force used to make me act against my better judgement.

At this point specific autobiographical detail peters out, as Gennadios listed the difficulties he faced once he had become patriarch. He closed with the problem of apostasy. Was it, he wondered, worth invoking the full rigour of the law and running the risk of apostasy that this entailed, for this was the path, 'which laymen, monks, and even those dignified with the name of bishop have chosen in preference to traditional [spiritual] remedies, either by deserting to those of a different faith or by threatening to do so'?[64] With a few words Gennadios highlights not only the demoralisation of those who survived the fall of Constantinople, but also their resentment of those whom they held responsible for their plight. These included leaders of the opposition to Emperor Constantine XI Palaiologos – men such as Gennadios. How else can one explain his insertion at this point – completely out of chronological sequence – of a defence of his

---

[64] Scholarios, *Oeuvres complètes*, eds. Petit, Sideridès and Jugie, vol. IV, 225.32–6.

actions on the eve of the siege of Constantinople? Again, it is worthwhile giving the passage in full:[65]

> I cut myself off from everyday life and ceased to attend court, but I did not depart from the city, even though entanglement in its snares necessarily destroys the purpose of repentance. I did not think of quitting the monastery. Neither did I have anything to do with city life. The crowd, which each day flocked to my cell, did so on the perfectly respectable pretext of listening to my words. However, I was forced to ban them from my cell – not that they paid any attention – because I was finding their presence upsetting, whatever spiritual ambitions they may have nursed. I preferred to disappoint friends rather than a soul in thrall to God and to concentrate on communication with the divine. These became my reasons for cutting myself off from [worldly] distractions, though I had little opportunity to enjoy the long sought-after leisure. [This was] because, under equal pressure from all sides and failing to perceive that people make sport of things they should not, I involved myself in ecclesiastical affairs, when it would have been better to remain silent and hidden, like a pearl at the bottom [of the sea]. Once stumbled on (οὗ πατηθέντος), people kept urging those who had given [their support to the union] to mount attacks on us. Otherwise neither by inclination nor by temperament would I have then quarrelled over such matters nor would I have stood up to my opponents. I behaved as I did out of a sense of gratitude rather than expediency, because I hoped that my presence would be of some benefit to my country, while departure elsewhere would seem to those favourable to foreign interests to be a betrayal of the cause of which we were the unwilling leader. [It would mean not only] renouncing my comrades and colleagues, [but also] failing to stand firm in the face of the dangers overtaking my country. I was therefore anxious not to remove myself from harm's way, but [rather] to seek my own safety as best I could. Nevertheless, in a fit of rage the emperor placed me under house arrest, having despaired of winning me over through the good offices of his advisors. Urged so many times to depart, I became his unwilling prisoner.

It is easy to see why the Patriarch Gennadios singled out this brief period of his life for detailed treatment. It was the hinge on which his life turned. It raised him from relative obscurity to the leadership of his Church and people. It is difficult to put into words the enormity of what becoming patriarch meant in the wake of the fall of Constantinople, but Gennadios was fully aware of the weight of responsibility that he now shouldered, if at the same time taken aback by the opposition that he faced. He was confident that he had been specially chosen by God to guide

---

[65] Scholarios, *Oeuvres complètes*, eds. Petit, Sideridès and Jugie, vol. IV, 226.9–35.

his people through *the valley of the shadow of death*. It was therefore necessary to counter criticism that his elevation to the patriarchate was a matter of personal ambition, and to quash suspicions about the nature of his relations with the conqueror.[66] Gennadios presented his actions as motivated by love of his country, and his opposition to Emperor Constantine XI as more the emperor's fault than his own. Enslaved, like so many others, after the fall of Constantinople, he claimed not to have enjoyed any special favours while in captivity. The sultan may have had a role in his liberation, but it was only to allow him to restore a monastery and then to repair churches in Constantinople. Gennadios deliberately covered up the fact that it was Mehmed II who appointed him patriarch. Instead, he emphasised the role of the synod and insisted that his installation as patriarch followed the traditional forms. Like many others, Gennadios was creating a face to suit a critical moment of his life, for the essential thing was to make sense of the catastrophe that had overtaken Byzantium, and to convince his audience that behind his words was divine inspiration.

He explained the fall of Constantinople as divine judgement. He remembered how nobody listened to those, like himself, who were versed in biblical prophecy and the ways of divine providence and predicted what was stored up for Constantinople.[67] So it was that few people anticipated the outcome, despite the overwhelming superiority of the Ottomans, that made their eventual victory more or less inevitable.[68] Gennadios claimed that God gave the Byzantines a whole year to repent, but they remained obdurate.[69] The way they blamed each other was a clear sign that God had removed his protection.[70] The parallels with the fall of Jerusalem were plain to see. After the destruction of Jerusalem, its sanctity passed to Constantinople, the New Jerusalem, which became the centre of a Christian Empire and a model of 'sacred and political virtue'. But God blamed the Byzantines far more than He did the Jews, for they had spurned His greatest gift: salvation offered through His Son. They were left with the hope that, just as God had released the Jews from exile, so He would rescue the Byzantines.[71] A promising sign came in the shape of new martyrs, whose steadfastness was all the more remarkable because unlike

---

[66] See M.-H. Blanchet, 'L'ambiguïté du statut juridique de Gennadios Scholarios après la chute de Constantinople (1453)' in P. Odorico, ed., *Le Patriarcat oecuménique de Constantinople aux xive–xvie siècles: Rupture et continuité* (Paris, 2007), 195–211.
[67] Scholarios, *Oeuvres complètes*, eds. Petit, Siderides and Jugie, vol. iv, 214.4–215.16.
[68] Ibid., vol. iv, 213.37–40.   [69] Ibid., vol. iv, 216.4–15.   [70] Ibid., vol. iv, 216.33–8.
[71] Ibid., vol. iv, 217.4–218.11.

the early martyrs they were living in an age of apostasy. Gennadios was convinced that their sacrifice brought some slight alleviation of their people's sufferings.[72] Another sign was the restoration of the patriarchate, which many understood as a miracle.[73] Gennadios had then to explain why he wished to demit office. Here was another chance to provide some autobiographical detail, but one he refused to take, beyond complaining of the opposition he faced and the actions of the ruler who had given him his liberty so that he could become patriarch, but who had now withdrawn it by not allowing him to return to the monastic estate.[74]

Apart from the two short self-serving passages translated above, there is very little that is autobiographical about the Patriarch Gennadios' 'Pastoral Letter', which more than anything else revealed his inadequacies as patriarch. He was not the Joseph or the Moses that his friend and ally Theodore Agallianos supposed him to be.[75] He preferred to resign his office rather than face its challenges. The parallel he drew with the Jews was not only commonplace; it also offered very little comfort or guidance. He was overwhelmed by the tragedy of the fall of Constantinople and by his responsibilities as patriarch. Two years after taking up office the sultan finally gave him permission to resign. He retired first to the monastery of Vatopedi on Mount Athos, and then around three years later he found a more permanent refuge in the monastery of the Prodromos on Mount Menoikeion, outside Serres. There he composed his *Lament* of 21 June 1460. Although there is only a single autobiographical passage, it is in some ways the most personal of his writings. He starts by invoking his parents. Why did they bring him into the world at such an inauspicious hour? Why did they die and leave him behind to face so many tribulations?[76] He concludes his *Lament* by once again turning to his mother, calling her by her monastic name of Athanasia and begging her to intercede for him.[77] The sentiments seem to have been heartfelt, if sententious. At the very least, they show that Gennadios was not without filial feelings. He also invokes his friends and relatives and, in particular, his students, who had flocked to visit him, as if he were their father and guardian, after he had become a monk. Where were they now? If any had survived the destruction of their city, they would be eking out a miserable and humiliating existence, like so many other survivors. Gennadios stops

---

[72] Ibid., vol. IV, 219.12–27. [73] Ibid., vol. IV, 227.11–19. [74] Ibid., vol. IV, 228.34–29.5.
[75] Patrinelis, Ὁ Θεόδωρος Ἀγαλλιανός, 98.257–9.
[76] Scholarios, *Oeuvres complètes*, eds. Petit, Sideridès and Jugie, vol. I, 284.9–15.
[77] Ibid., vol. I, 293.19–26.

to wonder what had been the point of his teaching them; what had been the point of collecting books for them.[78] He tries to console himself with memories of his life before the fall of Constantinople at the court of John VIII Palaiologos. This is the one autobiographical passage in the *Lament*:[79]

> Alas! How can I remember without tears those audiences made up of the emperor, his brothers, grandees, bishops and clergy, monks, businessmen and citizens, and foreigners, who assembled in the banqueting hall to hear me preach? I was destined to be the last proclaimer of the truth in dogmatics and ethics [i.e. court preacher] appointed for that final generation. I was like some prophet of doom who, wishing to devise a different outcome, saw his words fulfilled in the worst way possible. I told my audience not to hearken to such words. That was the thrust of [my] last sermon, which was delivered in the sixth year before the terrible events that had their beginning at that time. Different people praised different sermons according to the profit that they derived from them, but all were agreed that my skill with words was a God-given gift, for leaving behind the tumult of the law courts and my other responsibilities – the lessons I gave at home, which we offered to assembled Hellenes and Italians, and other cares that protocol imposed – I was always ready to articulate whatever God deemed necessary. O those trials, where presiding [over a tribunal] I sought the truth of the matter, explaining the laws, allowing others room for their own interpretations, preparing the losing party for defeat with a show of clemency and forbearance, and sending all away happy from the trial thanks to the accuracy and precision of my cross-examination, something often judged the most difficult [of tasks]. I only treated harshly those who were violent and had no intention of submitting to due process of law, which frequently meant that my displeasure extended to the emperor himself. This he took in good part; he made no objections when reprimanded, or so it seemed. I am talking about the late John, whose death ushered in the painful demise of our polity. I was not making a show of my abilities, but demonstrating good practice to our successors, for our main concern, when giving judgement, was not so much its immediate application to the case in hand, as the guidance of the many who would come after us. [We wished] in this way to leave some memory of the effort we had made over a point of law, so that those benefiting from its value [would acknowledge that it came from us] and nobody else. It was for this reason that we put ourselves forward as a model for all, not only through the precision of our judgements, but also by reason of the clearness of our conscience, which came from our refusal to take gifts and personal favours or to tolerate any fiscal or

---

[78] Ibid., vol. 1, 287.35–88.24.
[79] Ibid., vol. 1, 288.36–90.2. For the institution of the *theatron*, see Niels Gauls' chapter in the present volume.

property transaction that did not meet with canonical approval. Oh! [How well I remember] those daily discussions with or without the emperor present, in which various propositions would be put forward and, just as in a literary gathering (*theatron*), everybody would be impatient to hear the solution to the problems under discussion. Oh! What good will and marks of honour were we universally accorded! Oh! With what pleasure did people greet us, for they considered as lacklustre any day I was absent from the palace, and on my arrival the next day they embraced me as though I were returning from a long journey. Should I put off any longer taking the path to their door, they rushed in the friendliest way imaginable to my house.

We may doubt whether Gennadios was ever quite that popular. He was idealising his own experience as a way of creating an impression of the felicitous existence enjoyed in Constantinople before its fall, which was in stark contrast to the situation thereafter. His sense of self-worth was tied to his life at the court of John VIII Palaiologos, of which by his own account he was a leading light. He understood his purpose in life was to hand on to future generations essential elements of Byzantine civilisation, whether in his teaching or in his judicial activities. It is easy to see why Gennadios could not come to terms with the demise of this civilisation, which the fall of the city entailed. He mourned the destruction of learning and education, and with them of the most beautiful of languages. People now knew as much about sacred dogma as Gennadios did about dancing and playing the cithern. They preferred to believe in the shades of their ancestors and in old wives' tales. Gennadios conjures up the strangest and most personal of images to illustrate the depths to which Constantinople had sunk. The city was like some highly respected matron who had kicked over the traces and was dancing in the streets to the deep shame of her son, who preferred to leave the scene.[80] It captures one of the deepest fears of the Byzantine – and not only Byzantine – male: the danger that female exuberance, generosity, naïvety or moral weakness will be the undoing of family honour. Gennadios clearly looked on Constantinople as a mother, as many other Byzantines did. The implication is that it had failed him, for he had been forced to abandon the patriarchate, which with God's aid he had restored from nothing.[81] He was prevented from offering his people the guidance they needed; from helping to fashion a new identity to replace the one they had lost. His resignation had left him without bearings. He resented the bonds that still linked him to 'the sorry remnants of his race (*genos*)'.[82] He claimed he had a right to speak like that because

[80] Ibid., vol. 1, 290.30–4. [81] Ibid., vol. 1, 292.18–20. [82] Ibid., vol. 1, 293.7–8.

his birthplace had given him all his sorrows, just as formerly all his joys. He no longer had a homeland. This had to be sought elsewhere, 'which is where our city now is'.[83] The fall of Constantinople shattered Gennadios' sense of identity, which was embedded in the city. It left him with little sense of purpose. His *Lament* is not just about his loss of identity; it is also a reproach directed at Constantinople for failing him. Its fall produced a moral collapse among its people, who rejected Gennadios. Underlying this was the bitterness he felt over the opposition he had encountered to his patriarchate, which, in the end, forced his resignation.

If the autobiographical passages that Gennadios has left behind hardly amount to an autobiography in any modern sense, they do provide insights into his state of mind at crucial moments in his life. In chronological order, these were his role at the court of John VIII Palaiologos, his opposition to Constantine XI on the eve of the fall of Constantinople, and his elevation to the patriarchate. He used the first as a way of illustrating through his own experience exactly what had been lost with the fall of Constantinople. The second was a way of defending himself against the imputations of those who questioned his fitness to be patriarch; and the third explained the stages by which he had become patriarch. They reveal that Gennadios' sense of self, his sense of self-importance, if you like, came from his conviction that he was motivated by the good of his country and guided by his devotion to Orthodoxy. He liked to think that these qualities had recommended him to John VIII Palaiologos and had brought him a position of the highest responsibility. However, his high-mindedness went hand-in-hand with a failure to develop or at least to value personal relationships. It is only in passing that we discover that he had a sister, whose son helped him survive the sack of Constantinople.[84] He is content to do no more than drop hints of his attachment to John VIII Palaiologos and, still more tantalisingly, to Mehmed II.[85] The impression is that Gennadios was a man who functioned best when there was a ruler to defer to. His closest relationship was a symbolic one: with Constantinople, which, he claims, gave him his greatest joys and his greatest sorrows.[86] His devotion to his native city emerged from his passionate evocation of what it was before its fall. Despite a reduced state, when compared with its former glories, it remained free and a focal point of the Christian world.

---

[83] Ibid., vol. 1, 293.8–18. Although Gennadios knew some of St Augustine's works, there is no evidence that he knew *The City of God*. See Livanos, *Greek Tradition*, 33–9.
[84] Blanchet, *Scholarios*, 69–70.
[85] A. Papadakis, 'Gennadius II and Mehmet the Conqueror', *Byzantion*, 42 (1972), 88–106.
[86] Scholarios, *Oeuvres complètes,* eds. Petit, Sideridès and Jugie, vol. I, 293.8–11.

There was no other city, however flourishing, to vie with it. It ensured that its inhabitants continued to prosper, while its marvels continued to astound foreign visitors, who thought that 'they had been snatched up to another heaven'.[87] How was existence possible without it? 'Oh, best of native cities, how can we, your dearest children, survive your loss and how can you bear to be without us? Worse, how can we endure still to be alive, when you are beyond the reach of men? For though apparently still here, you are gone for ever'.[88] With these last words Gennadios was able to catch the irrevocable transition from one dispensation to another. No one else understood or expressed quite so well the meaning of the passing of a great civilisation. It meant a shattering of his identity. Almost always, in one way or another, autobiography is about the search for, the attainment or the affirmation of a sense of identity. Gennadios is dealing in the exact opposite: its destruction. He was never able to rebuild another, beyond being able to say, 'I am a Christian.'[89]

This was an affirmation, which, as Gennadios perhaps hoped, might serve as the core of a new identity. Support for such an idea may be adduced from his final apology written at the end of his life. Though a personal statement, it might serve as the core of a new identity. It comes in the shape of a letter to a friend, the monk Theodore Branas, in which he excuses himself for having failed to keep in touch. Though a personal statement, Gennadios intended it as a codicil to his last will and testament, which underlines its importance to him.[90] His starting point is an assertion that a completely false picture had emerged of events from the second year after the fall of Constantinople.[91] He is, in other words, still distressed by the circumstances of his departure from office. But his tone then changes. He is now resigned to what has happened and takes comfort from two things in particular. The first is the pious fervour of Christians, which suggests that he was softening the harshness of his earlier judgement on the people of Constantinople.[92] The second comes as a surprise: he hails the intelligence and humanity of the sultan, who not only kept bloodshed to a minimum after the storming of Constantinople, but also re-established the Church.[93] Gennadios' narrative of the restoration of the patriarchate has changed.

---

[87] Ibid., vol. 1, 287.6–31.   [88] Ibid., vol. 1, 287.31–4.
[89] A. D. Angelou, '*Who am I?* Scholarios's Answers and the Hellenic Identity', in C. N. Constantinides, N. M. Panagiotakis, E. M. Jeffreys and I. Martin eds., *Φιλέλλην: Studies in Honour of Robert Browning* (Venice, 1996), 1–19.
[90] Scholarios, *Oeuvres complètes*, eds. Petit, Siderides and Jugie, vol. 1, 264.34–5.
[91] Ibid., vol. 1, 265.28–9.   [92] Ibid., vol. 1, 265.34–5.   [93] Ibid., vol. 1, 265.35–66.3.

The inspiration of course came from God, but the implementation was the work of the sultan, who appointed Gennadios patriarch and provided the Church with many gifts. It gave hope that the Church was not entirely undone. Gennadios even wondered whether it was God who had set the Turks over the Christians for their own good. He thought it unlikely, but was unable to reject this possibility out of hand.[94] After thirty years of endeavour for his people – a story, he was confident, that needed many volumes to do it justice[95] – it was time for him to return to monastic seclusion, for he realised, at last, that he could no longer be of any service to the common good.[96] He could only urge Christians to seek consolation in Christ through the Church, which he had helped restore.[97] Gennadios closes on a note of resignation, but he was becoming reconciled to the inevitability of the new order, which had replaced the old.

Further Reading

Important sources are: V. Laurent, ed., *Syropoulos. Les 'Mémoires' du Grand Ecclésiarque de l'Église de Constantinople, Sylvestre Syropoulos, sur le concile de Florence (1438–1439)* (Paris, 1971); L. Petit, K.A. Sidéridès and M. Jugie, eds., *Oeuvres complètes de Georges Scholarios*, 8 vols. (Paris, 1928–35). Key studies include: M.- H. Blanchet, *Georges-Gennadios Scholarios (vers 1400-vers 1472): Un intellectuel Orthodoxe face à la disparition de l'empire byzantin* (Paris, 2008); M. Hinterberger, *Autobiographische Traditionen in Byzanz* (Vienna, 1999); and C. Livanos, *Greek Tradition and Latin Influence in the work of George Scholarios* (Piscataway, NJ, 2006).

---

[94] Ibid., vol. 1, 266.10–17.   [95] Ibid., vol. 1, 266.36–67.1.   [96] Ibid., vol. 1, 272.25–8.
[97] Ibid., vol. 1, 273.8–14.

Centre and Margins

CHAPTER 3

The Role of the Speeches of John the Oxite in Komnenian Court Politics

Judith R. Ryder

When the First Crusade reached Antioch in 1097, the patriarch of that city was John IV or V, otherwise known as Ioannes Oxeites or John the Oxite.[1] Albert of Aachen describes John as *vir Christianissimus*. He relates how John was publicly tortured by the Turks but then, after the crusaders took the city, deservedly reinstated as patriarch.[2] A similar account is given by William of Tyre: having suffered much under the infidel, John was reinstated as patriarch, it being considered canonically unacceptable to elect another. However, William adds that John, two years later, himself decided that his position was of dubious utility, and decided to return to Constantinople.[3] A third account, that of Orderic Vitalis, is rather different: John had been vociferous in opposing Norman proposals to impose Latin rites, and a rumour had spread that he was planning to betray Antioch to the emperor, as a result of which John, whether out of embarrassment or fear, departed his see.[4]

So much for John the Oxite's appearance in western historiography. He appears only fleetingly, but his appearance is of deep significance, given that his was one of the earliest cases of jurisdictional conflict between Latin and Greek hierarchies resulting from the Crusades – something which was

---

[1] Acknowledgement is due to Peter Frankopan, who first introduced me to John the Oxite; to the Leventis Foundation, whose funding for the *Prosopography of the Byzantine World* (www.pbw.kcl.ac.uk) enabled me to work further on John's writings; and to Wolfson College, Oxford, for providing a stimulating and friendly research environment. Thanks also to Jonathan Shepard and Michael Jeffreys for their encouragement and advice during the preparation of this chapter.
  On John's 'numbering', see J. Pahlitzsch, *Graeci und Suriani im Palästina der Kreuzfahrerzeit. Beiträge und Quellen zur Geschichte des griechisch-orthodoxen Patriarchats von Jerusalem* (Berlin, 2001), 34, n. 77. John's 'surname' Oxeites indicates a connection with the island of Oxeia, although his exact connections with the island are unclear. See P. Gautier, 'Jean V l'Oxite, patriarche d'Antioche: notice biographique', *REB*, 22 (1964), 128–9.
[2] S. B. Edgington, ed. and trans., *Albert of Aachen, Historia Ierosolimitana* (Oxford, 2007), 338–9. This and the following two western references to John are cited by Gautier, 'Notice biographique', 131–2.
[3] R. B. C. Huygens, ed., *Guillaume de Tyr: Chronique* (Turnhout, 1986), vol. i, 340.
[4] M. Chibnall, ed. and trans., *The Ecclesiastical History of Orderic Vitalis* (Oxford, 1975), vol. v, 356.

to become such a bitter and complex issue.[5] John is, however, much better known from Byzantine sources, principally from his own writings. Of these there are a number. One is the *On Monasteries*,[6] a piece written against the Byzantine institution of *charistike*, one of the topics with which John's name is particularly connected.[7] Another is his less well-known treatise *On Azymes*, highly critical of the western usage of unleavened bread in the Eucharist.[8] There are also three letters: one concerning John's abdication as patriarch of Antioch; another defending his flight from the Constantinopolitan monastery of the Hodegon, where he experienced difficulties following his abdication; and a third addressing the synod.[9] Finally, there are two pieces addressed to the emperor Alexios I Komnenos,[10] one a speech apparently intended for some kind of deliberative assembly, the second a much shorter piece of less clear context. Within the scope of this chapter, it is not possible to discuss in detail questions of genre, audience, etc., although such questions will be touched upon in the course of the argument. Briefly, the longer address clearly envisages the audience of some kind of assembly, while the shorter piece is specifically submitted in written form.[11] The first has been dated by Gautier to February/March 1091, a point when the empire was under great pressure,[12] while the date of the second is less clear.

These last two pieces, especially the longer speech, will be the focus of this chapter. There are, broadly speaking, two lines of approach to them.

---

[5] See B. Hamilton, *The Latin Church in the Crusader States: The Secular Church* (London, 1980).
[6] Text in P. Gautier, 'Réquisitoire du patriarche Jean d'Antioche contre le charisticariat', *REB*, 33 (1975), 77–132.
[7] *Charistike* was a system, the exact mechanics of which are notoriously difficult to determine, whereby monastic institutions were entrusted to the oversight of individuals, often powerful lay individuals. It was a system which tended – at least in the eyes of its critics – to widespread and detrimental financial exploitation of those institutions. See M. Angold, *Church and Society in Byzantium under the Comneni, 1081–1261* (Cambridge, 1995), 63–9. For a discussion of *charistike* in relation to John himself, see J. P. Thomas, *Private Religious Foundations in the Byzantine Empire* (Washington, D. C., 1987), 186–92.
[8] Greek text in B. Leib, 'Deux inédits byzantins sur les azymes au début du xııe siècle', *OrChr*, ıı/3 (1924), 244–63. John's text on the subject may not be well known, but the controversy surrounding the use of 'azymes' (unleavened bread) in the Eucharist had been central to the 'schism' of 1054. See J. H. Erickson, 'Leavened and Unleavened: Some Theological Implications of the Schism of 1054', *SVThQ*, 14 (1970), 3–24.
[9] Greek text with French translation in Gautier, 'Notice biographique', 128–57.
[10] Greek text with French translation: P. Gautier, 'Diatribes de Jean l'Oxite contre Alexis Ier Comnène', *REB*, 28 (1970), 5–55.
[11] For further discussion of the second piece, see below, pp. 111–14.
[12] For dating, see Gautier, 'Diatribes', 10. For an account of Alexios' rise to power and the early years of his reign, see M. Angold, *The Byzantine Empire, 1025–1204: A Political History*, 2nd edn. (London, 1997), 115–56.

One takes its cue from the French title of Gautier's edition: 'Diatribes ... contre Alexis Ier Comnène', the natural, if possibly misleading, English rendition of which being 'diatribes against'. This line is taken by most commentators, and it is for this, together with his stance against the *charistike*, that John is most well-known amongst Byzantinists: he is regarded as a strong-minded, rebellious churchman, bold enough to denounce the emperor to his face. For example, Alexander Kazhdan states that John 'dared to censure Alexios's entire political program';[13] Joan Hussey describes how John 'unleashed biting invective, hurling against the emperor accusations of widespread ecclesiastical spoliation ... injustice, maladministration, oppression', adding that 'on the moral side he stressed the emperor's lack of genuine repentance ... He also boldly referred to the illegal seizure of the throne';[14] Paul Magdalino describes John as 'Alexios' most outspoken critic';[15] and more recently Jane Baun describes how John 'delivered a scathing critique of Alexios's policies, calling the emperor to solemn repentance',[16] while Peter Frankopan summarises the speech as 'providing a stinging critique of Komnenian rule'.[17] This is to cite but a few of such references, which are standard in secondary works dealing with the period.

However, an alternative view of John's relationship with Alexios has also been advanced, according to which a more careful interpretation needs to be given to John's speech. This viewpoint is found particularly in Margaret Mullett's paper 'The Imperial Vocabulary of Alexios I Komnenos', which discusses the speech at greater length than is the case with most commentators.[18] In particular, Mullett suggests that the contents of the speech should not be regarded as critical of Alexios as they are often considered to be, but may in fact have sat rather well with Alexios' policies at the time.[19] This line is endorsed in the same volume by Michael Angold ('The biting diatribes of John the Oxite against Alexios were almost certainly commissioned by the emperor himself'),[20] and repeated rather

---

[13] A. P. Kazhdan, and A. Wharton Epstein, *Change in Byzantine Culture in the Eleventh and Twelfth Centuries* (Berkeley, CA, 1985), 165.
[14] J. M. Hussey, *The Orthodox Church in the Byzantine Empire* (Oxford, 1990), 147.
[15] P. Magdalino, *The Empire of Manuel I Komnenos, 1143–1180* (Cambridge, 1993), 269.
[16] In J. Harris, ed., *Palgrave Advances in Byzantine History* (Basingstoke, 2005), 110.
[17] P. Frankopan, 'Where Advice Meets Criticism in Eleventh-century Byzantium: Theophylact of Ohrid, John the Oxite and their (Re)presentations to the Emperor', *Al-Masāq*, 20/1 (2008), 71.
[18] M. E. Mullett, 'The Imperial Vocabulary of Alexios I Komnenos', in M. Mullett and D. Smythe, eds., *Alexios I Komnenos. Papers of the Second Belfast Byzantine International Colloquium, 14–16 April 1989. 1. Papers* (Belfast, 1996), 367–70.
[19] Mullett and Smythe, *Alexios I Komnenos*, 390–1.   [20] Ibid., 413.

more tentatively in his *Political History*: 'there is a good chance ... that they [the speeches] were written with the knowledge of the emperor'.[21]

The second approach to John IV, however, has scarcely gained the same level of recognition as the first. Even where it is propounded, moreover, it has not, to my knowledge, been discussed in depth, at least in print. Proponents of this interpretation have so far failed to reconcile the probable imperial commissioning with the letter's content. The aim of this chapter is to deal with some of the problems involved by examining aspects both of the speech itself and of the wider context. By doing so, it will argue in favour of the Mullett/Angold approach to John's 'addresses' to Alexios. However, it is hoped that this discussion may also be of more general use: extensive analysis of a speech often summarised in a phrase or two may also enhance its use in other contexts.

The Structure and Content of the Speech

The speech itself contains elements which can be read as highly useful to Alexios, rather than as necessarily negative. First, let us highlight particular points of interest, in order to give both an idea of structure and development of the text and a sense of the relative weighting of each section.[22]

1a Thanks to God for returning Alexios safely to his people[23] – Alexios, the shepherd and defender of his flock, whose role is to provide comfort in the present struggles. Had Alexios perished, it would have been perilous for his people. The immediate response should be to thank God wholeheartedly (19.1–16).

1b John has serious things to say; he cannot safely keep silent. Even as a private individual (ἐν ἰδιώταις), he had expressed himself directly to Alexios, and been listened to. Now, as priest, 'watchman of the house of Israel', he must fulfil his prophetic duties and instruct people and rulers to turn from their ways and save themselves. John uses language from the Psalms and Ezekiel. Should he neglect his duty, 'the wicked man shall die in his iniquity' (Ezek. 3:18), and John will be held responsible (19.18–21.13).

1c We have *all* sinned; we have *all* departed from the laws of God; we have *all* abandoned his covenant. Therefore God has abandoned us to the nations. But it is impossible to deal with the faults of the many; so instead

---

[21] Angold, *Political History*, 8.
[22] References are to the Greek pages of Gautier's text in Gautier, 'Diatribes'. The divisions used are for convenience rather than reflecting any particular theory of genre or literary composition. In some places, italics have been inserted to highlight particular points brought out in the discussion below.
[23] Alexios had just returned from fighting the Pechenegs. See Gautier, 'Diatribes', 9.

John will focus on Alexios, the 'head of the whole state' (τὴν κεφαλὴν τοῦ τῆς πολιτείας πληρώματος), examining his life, to reveal the 'dispensations of Providence' (τὴν ... τῆς προνοίας οἰκονομίαν) therein. The reason for this, and its benefits, will become clear, to Alexios and those who follow the argument closely (21.13–29).

1d John's personal explanation ('Ηγοῦμαι δέ, ὦ βασιλεῦ) for the current situation: God, seeing the present generation straying, sent punishments – wars etc. – to restrain and correct it. But this failed, and worse still (τὸ δὴ χαλεπώτερον), the relationship between God and Creation/history has been misinterpreted: rather than being understood as punishment for sin, events have been attributed to some kind of chance (κατά τινα ... αὐτοματισμὸν ἢ ἀποκλήρωσιν). John has even heard it said that God was concerned only with the salvation of souls; that the affairs of the world were left to follow their own course (21.30–23.6).

1e God has chosen a particular way to demonstrate his power in the unfolding of events: he has taken one eminent man (Alexios), through that man's successes and failures demonstrating how God gives strength to his people when they act justly, and that it is not the power of the enemy, but the withdrawal of God's protection, which renders God's people vulnerable (23.7–27).

2a Alexios' background and early successes are presented: his noble birth and his exploits against Roussel de Ballieul, Nikephoros Bryennios, Nikephoros Basilakes.[24] A parallel is drawn between Alexios' early victories and biblical accounts of the divinely assisted victories of Gideon, so as to assert that the former also possessed God's favour.[25] Other more recent successes are cited, particularly against the 'Skyths'.[26] Alexios' early days, before his usurpation, are presented as days of great and merited popular acclaim: John speaks of Alexios as the power behind the throne: as 'already reigning' (ἤδη ... βασιλεύων) (23.28–25.32).[27]

2b Situation since Alexios took the throne: entirely different, with war and tumult everywhere; Constantinople is, like Zion, sore pressed. In human terms, Alexios cannot be blamed: far from being indolent, he has gathered armies, fought hard, used all his resources. But divine favour has gone. Why? God is not powerless; God would not forget his people: that is clear from Scripture. So why is this happening to Alexios and his subjects

---

[24] On these, see Angold, *Political History*, 116–17, 124. [25] See esp. Judges 7.
[26] Or Pechenegs. See Angold, *Political History*, 132–4.
[27] This account of Alexios' early days can be seen as an allusion to David, who had a similarly ambiguous relationship to Saul. See esp. 1 Sam. 18.

(σοί τε καὶ τοῖς ὑπηκόοις)? John will explain; and Alexios should not take offence, or suspect ill-will (δύσνοιαν): Alexios has never given John cause to bear a grudge, but has shown him great favour. What John has to say is entirely out of concern for the good of Alexios and of the state (27).

3a (Brief) mention of Alexios' 'unlawful' usurpation (ἔκθεσμος τῆς βασιλείας ἡ κρηπὶς καταβέβληται). War then broke out against Alexios.[28] Alexios should have recognised this as divine punishment for sins committed at the time of his coup: he should have repented, sought reconciliation, entrusted himself to God and *with God's help* gone out against the enemy. Instead, using all human means at his disposal but without reference to God, he went to war with disastrous results. In a further attempt to get the message across, when Alexios was particularly weak God killed Alexios' enemy and dispersed his army;[29] which should have made perfectly clear God's protective powers (29.1–26).

3b But even this did not have the desired effect: *we* should have learnt from this; but *we* did not; and further attempts were made to reverse the situation by relying on human means alone: huge impositions made on all people, places and industries, all sorts of unjust practices employed by all manner of officials in order to exact tribute (29.26–31.15).

3c Criticism of expropriation of church resources and treatment of church buildings and ecclesiastics themselves (31.15–33.16).

3d Description of how vast sectors of the population have been reduced to poverty and famine, even to death; many have been forced into vagrancy, forced to flee to servitude amongst the barbarians (33.16–28).

3e Consequent continuation of divine punishment: Chios, Mytilene, Cyprus and Crete are lost, the Scythians menace the west, scarcely any territory remains in the east. The remaining fragment is in dire straits: but again, there is no attempt to turn to God. The empire of the Romans is reduced nearly to nothing, but we continue to regard as beneficial precisely the things which have brought us to this pass. And now John, having unleashed this tirade, will offer his remedy for the situation (33.28–35.32).

4a What is needed is a change of heart (here, John uses a whole range of Old Testament citations and allusions): a turning to God, who will forgive, as salvation history, the redeeming activity of God in history, has demonstrated so many times. There is a possible catch: surely God has already been much called upon, but has not responded. John cites Isa. 1:15: God

---

[28] Meaning the Norman incursions into the Byzantine Balkans. See Angold, *Political History*, 129–31.
[29] Robert Guiscard, who led the Norman invasion, died on 17 July 1085, leading to the disintegration of the Norman invasion of Byzantine territory. Angold, *Political History*, 133.

has turned away because 'your hands are full of blood'. This too is not irremediable: purification is all that is needed: a restoration of Old Testament standards of justice (Isa. 1:15f.). More specifically, Alexios should stop illegal impositions and activities (ἐκθέσμων εἰσπράξεών τε καὶ πράξεων), amend or promise to amend a number of other matters, and above all turn wholly to God as the sole source of deliverance, who has on so many previous occasions delivered the city (37.1–41.11).

4b The state treasuries (οἱ βασιλικοὶ θησαυροί) are empty, a fact that has been used to justify procurement of resources by all means necessary, just or unjust. But evidence does not support this; clearly a great deal of wealth remains, scattered around the city in numerous palaces. John refers, using New Testament language, to the 'kingdom divided amongst itself, which cannot stand'.[30] He addresses Alexios directly: your family has been a great scourge to the empire, all of them wishing to live imperially, to prosper materially, setting personal gain before the common good. The result of this behaviour of Alexios' family is twofold: it has caused penury to Alexios, forcing him to offend God (i.e. through unjust extortion); and it has brought great harm to the common good (41.12–43.1).[31]

4c Repetition of the requirements of justice: Alexios must do what is fitting for a ruler and what is required by the current situation (ποίει χρηστότητα πᾶσαν τῷ βασιλεῖ πρέπουσαν καὶ ὅσην ὁ καιρὸς νῦν ἀπαιτεῖ); and promise to do the same in the future. He should act in consultation with the army, the church and other groups (μετὰ βουλῆς τοῖς λογάσι τῶν στρατιωτῶν τε καὶ τῶν ὑπὸ τῶν ἐκκλησιαστικῶν τε καὶ τῶν ἄλλων ἀνθρώπων), and be publicly accountable (εἰς μέσον προστιθεὶς τὰ σκέμματα): salvation is to be had through much counsel (σωτηρία ἐν πολλῇ βουλῇ). He should take particular care of the affairs of the church, which is in no less danger than the state (43).

5 It is not just the rulers who have done wrong; it is everyone, even those who have simply tolerated wrongdoing without speaking out. Monks and priests are implicated. They have profaned sacred things, violated the law and transgressed the canons, all of which wrongs Alexios must right. John calls for a collective effort of state and church that will be carried out correctly contrasting these future efforts with the processions that have already occurred, where participation was forced and poverty and

---

[30] Compare with Mark 3:24; Matthew 12:21; Luke 11:17.
[31] πρὸς λύμην μεγίστην καὶ τῇ βασιλείᾳ καὶ ἡμῖν πᾶσι τὸ συγγενές σοι κατέστη· ἕκαστος γὰρ βασιλικῶς ζῆν τε καὶ εὐροπεῖν ἐθέλοντες, τὸ οἰκεῖον κέρδος τοῦ κοινῇ συμφέροντες περὶ πλείονος ἄγοντες, σοὶ μὲν χρημάτων σπάνιν καὶ τὸ πλεονεκτεῖν ἀναγκάζεσθαι καὶ προσκρούειν Θεῷ, τῷ κοινῷ δὲ παντοδαπὰς προύξένησαν ζημίας καὶ θλίψεις. Gautier, 'Diatribes', 41.21–43.1.

disaffection were only magnified. Such processions can achieve nothing because of the spirit in which they are undertaken (45.1–47.25).

6 Conclusion: John has said what he has to say, before the assembly which Alexios had gathered, forced by circumstances to seek advice from everyone present (διὰ τὴν αὐτὴν ... ἀνάγκην ἡμᾶς συγκέκληκας σήμερον, τὴν ἑκάστου περὶ τῶν παρόντων μαθησόμενος γνώμην). He concludes with a prayer: that Christ should lead Alexios to understand and do all this; that he should listen both to Alexios and to '*us*'; that Alexios should have a peaceful reign, having defeated his enemies; and that '*we*' should all be admitted to that other life in Christ (47.26–49.4).

Themes Internal to the Speech

These, then, in summary, are the contents of John's speech to Alexios, designed for a situation in 1091 when the plight of the Byzantines was desperate – a situation particularly starkly expressed in this speech.[32] Although this is a summary, it is reasonably extensive, designed to give a clear sense of the nature of the argument of the speech and the role played within it of the various elements, and to draw out points particularly pertinent to the discussion below. As said earlier, this chapter argues that John's speech itself, regardless of external considerations, contains elements which strongly support the Mullett/Angold thesis that it may not have been particularly unwelcome to Alexios I Komnenos. On the basis of the contents of the text as described above, a number of themes can be drawn out, which combine to give strong support to this thesis. In drawing out these themes, I refer the reader to relevant sections in the summary above, rather than repeating the full references to the edition.

Priority of God

The first such theme is the overriding theological emphasis of John's argument. This appears at the very beginning of the speech: thanks are to be given to God for Alexios' safe return (1a). Alexios appears well here; his survival is of great importance to his people; but the correct response should be to thank God whole-heartedly. Lest this be dismissed as a mere rhetorical *topos*, John drives home the message again later in his introduction, presenting it emphatically as his personal understanding: God has

---

[32] See Gautier, 'Diatribes', 6–15.

tried to correct the present generation, but the repeated response has been a refusal to acknowledge the relationship between God and Creation (1d). This motif of failure to have the correct attitude towards God appears time and time again in the speech: see sections 3a, 3b, 3e, 4a, 5. John's emphasis is overwhelmingly focused on the theological, and this shapes his entire presentation.

Prophet/King

John's theological emphasis links in with both his self-understanding and his understanding of Alexios' role. This too is made clear at the outset: John cannot keep silent because it is his duty to speak out, because he stands in the tradition of the Old Testament Prophet (1b). This is, of course, a standard model, commonly transferred to the Christian priesthood;[33] but it is also not to be dismissed as mere rhetorical *topos*. And the corollary is also highly significant: Alexios, in parallel, stands in the tradition of Old Testament King (as in the description of him as 'shepherd', section 1a). John seems to allude, in the section prior to mention of Alexios' usurpation, to circumstances very similar to King David's rise to power (2a). The motif of David as the type of the Byzantine emperor is also very common, and has wonderful versatility, given that David himself was far from irreproachable.[34] But if Alexios is being compared with David, by extension the special, albeit complex, relationship between God and David also applies to God and Alexios. Alexios' position, despite John mentioning Alexios' usurpation (see below), is secure and divinely sanctioned.

Alexios' Role in Salvation History

Alexios' importance is further emphasised by the way John attributes to Alexios a particular role in what theologians would call 'salvation history': that is, God's direction of human history according to his own plan for salvation. Failure to acknowledge the working of 'salvation history' is, as has been seen above (esp. 4a), a central complaint with John. In connection with this, and as a core theme guiding the whole structure of the

---

[33] For a contemporary comparison, see Niketas of Ankyra's speech *On Ordinations*, where this motif is again used to justify bold speech before Alexios: J. Darrouzès, trans. and ed., *Documents inédits d'ecclésiologie byzantine* (Paris, 1966), 202–3.

[34] A glance at entries for 'David' in the Index to G. Dagron, *Emperor and Priest: The Imperial Office in Byzantium* (Cambridge, 2003) should be enough to indicate its ubiquity.

speech, John represents Alexios as being the means chosen by God to demonstrate the workings of providence (1e). By implication, therefore, while Alexios may have committed certain sins both in the process of making himself emperor and in his attitude to God having done so, John is not thereby arguing against Alexios' leadership. The opposite is true: this is all part of God's plan.

Collective Responsibility: the People of God

Moreover, John places much emphasis on collective responsibility/collective guilt. It is noticeable that John expatiates on this theme at crucial points in the argument. It is introduced at the very beginning of the text (1c), before any mention has been made of Alexios' role. By placing it at this point, John completes the motif, by adding the role of 'People of God' alongside those of 'God', 'Prophet', and 'King', driving home yet again the theological emphasis. Later in the text, a shift is often made at moments of high tension from the singular to the first person plural: this has been highlighted above by use of italics in sections 3b and 3e. Section 5 is entirely structured around this idea, with the additional specific inclusion of church hierarchy and monastics amongst the culpable. John thus begins and ends with collective responsibility, and returns to it at intervals along the way. In weighing up the impact of John's accusations against Alexios, therefore, it is necessary to take into account both the interplay between individual and collective culpability and the vital role of collective culpability in John's overall Old Testament interpretation. These considerations go some way to mitigating John's accusations against Alexios.

The Extent of Alexios' Responsibility

Furthermore, one section of John's text may take the blame yet further away from Alexios, if the argument is followed carefully, as John instructs his audience to do. This is section 4b, a passage often paralleled with Zonaras, who makes a similar criticism: that Alexios treated public funds as private fortune, distributing them to his friends and family.[35] But John makes an interesting distinction: what he seems to be saying is that it is the behaviour of Alexios' family that has injured both Alexios

---

[35] M. Pinder and Büttner-Wobst, T., eds., *Ioannis Zonarae Annales et Epitomae historiarum* (Bonn, 1897), vol. III, 767.

and the people. Although clearly this passage does not excuse Alexios for doing what he was driven to do – he evidently was an actor in the process; and, as John elsewhere makes clear, there are various forms of culpability (see section 5) – nevertheless this continues the mitigating effect introduced by the theme of collective responsibility. The worst offenders are Alexios' family not Alexios, who as an offended party is placed on the same side as the 'people'. Interestingly, this coupling of Alexios and his people has already occurred earlier in the speech, when John asked rhetorically why such terrible things were happening to Alexios and his people (2b).

Actual Criticisms Against Alexios: Potential Scope

As mentioned in the introduction to this chapter, however, John's accusations against Alexios tend to be particularly highlighted in secondary discussions, and they therefore need to be given direct consideration. The most frequently emphasised of John's accusations of wrongdoing are: usurpation, expropriation of church property, and general injustice (unfair taxation, oppression of the poor, corrupt officials failing to deliver justice etc.). Certainly the speech is outspoken in its description both of the parlous nature of the situation and of the wrongs that have been committed, and need to be rectified. However, when the overall structure and theme of John's speech are taken into account, it becomes clear that these criticisms of Alexios have probably been taken out of context and over-emphasised, and need to be interpreted carefully in context.

Usurpation. John does indeed refer to Alexios' accession as unlawful. However, this mention is brief; and John, in line with his emphasis on divine priority, seems to be far more concerned with whether or not Alexios afterwards did proper penance and had the right attitude towards God than with the manner of his accession. Given that imperial succession was a somewhat grey area in Byzantium, based on an interplay of factors in which dynastic succession was far from an enshrined principle, and successful usurpations could be regarded easily enough as divinely sanctioned by the very fact of their success,[36] this is perhaps unsurprising. Moreover, the parallels implied between Alexios and David allow for this; David, like Alexios, was chosen to be king at God's instigation, and indeed exercised

---

[36] See Dagron, *Emperor and Priest*, 13–15; A. Kaldellis, *The Byzantine Republic: People and Power in New Rome* (Cambridge, MA, 2015), 44, 100, 112–15.

power, long before he actually took the throne (see section 2a).[37] John's mention of Alexios' usurpation need not be read purely as critical.

Expropriation of church property. In order to finance his expeditions against the Normans in the early 1080s, Alexios resorted to expropriation of church property, provoking opposition, notably from Leo of Chalcedon.[38] John's speech is often interpreted as a continuation of this opposition.[39] However, although John does describe the expropriations – and other proceedings against parts of the church – vehemently (3c), the precise context and scope of this passage should be noted. Before even getting to the question of the churches, John has expatiated at length on the numerous taxes levied in the secular world (3b). The section on the church is then relatively short and is followed by lengthy descriptions of other ways the general population has suffered (3d). The section on the churches is but a small part of a larger canvas upon which John paints a scene of absolute destruction and desperation. Alexios' expropriation of church property thus is not a central preoccupation for John, but is part of a much wider picture; John the Oxite is not Leo of Chalcedon. Moreover, John's comments regarding expropriation of church property should be read alongside his requests to Alexios elsewhere (4c) to intervene on behalf of the church; and alongside his accusations against the monks and clergy themselves (5).

General injustice. In section 4a, John opens his denunciations of wrongdoing with reference to Isa. 1:15f. This passage summarises the ideal of justice, since Isa. 1:16–17 continues: 'remove the evil of your doings from before my eyes; cease to do evil, learn to do good; seek justice, correct oppression; defend the fatherless, plead for the widow'. John does not give the whole citation, but makes it clear that he intends all of it since a list of accusations of injustice follows immediately afterwards in his text. In section 4c John returns to the theme at more length. But his complaints and demands are, if anything, rather schematic. Alexios is to do what is fitting for a ruler and what is required by the current situation, and to promise to do the same in the future. The specific complaints are few, and the argument returns repeatedly to a general theme of implementation and regulation of justice in all fields. Given the primacy of the theological motif throughout the speech, specific complaints of injustice should also be examined with an eye to Isaiah. John is trying to drive home the

---

[37] The ninth-century story Dagron uses to illustrate his point has St Cyril specifically refer to David as elected by God although not of the family of Saul. Dagron, *Emperor and Priest*, 13–14.
[38] Angold, *Political History*, 137.   [39] Thomas, *Private Religious Foundations*, 202.

message that God directs human affairs. Byzantium is in a desperate situation; this must have something to do with its relationship with God, i.e. God must have withdrawn his protection. There must be a reason for this, and the obvious reason is sin or, in the words of Isaiah, failure of justice. Therefore injustice must be common and so John emphasises injustice. Injustice is easy to find at any time, particularly so in periods of war and civil disorder, so there is little doubt that many of the criticisms would have rung true. But John's reasons for expressing himself as he does may be driven as much by his theological agenda as by any other consideration.

Further Considerations: Useful Elements of Propaganda?

Furthermore, various elements of John's argument could be seen as offering Alexios a very useful tool of propaganda, a way of explaining and justifying changes in policy. With regard to penance and ceremonies of religious propitiation, John himself makes clear that these had already been tried in an attempt to improve the situation – but his speech, by offering an explanation of why they had failed and ways of ensuring that they would succeed in the future, could be interpreted as allowing Alexios to draw a line under these, thereby restoring propagandistic value to new ceremonies.[40] Moreover, John's suggestions for how to improve matters could also be read as giving Alexios justification for making sweeping changes. John's plea for restoration of justice could be used as a validation of widespread purging of the administration, and his attack on Alexios' family could be used as a rationalisation for marginalising those whom Alexios found obstructive. John's call for a change of heart could thus be seen as strong support for reorganisation of the regime to suit Alexios' personal agenda and remove opposition.

External Factors Supporting the Mullett/Angold Thesis

Examination of John's speech to Alexios can thus lead, regardless of external considerations, to some interesting avenues for exploration, which may go some way to addressing the problem of reconciling content with

---

[40] And although John speaks of Alexios having failed to do penance at the beginning of his reign, Anna Komnene tells a different story, in which Alexios undertook heartfelt penance: D. R. Reinsch and A. Kambylis, eds., *Annae Comnenae Alexias* (Berlin, 2001), vol. I, 95–103 (I: III.iv-vi). See also below, p. 110.

possible imperial commissioning. However, can this be supported by other factors? Do external considerations support it, or detract from it? That John apparently departed for Antioch soon after composing the speech could, for example, be interpreted as 'exile', indicating Alexios' displeasure.[41] Are there signs that the relationship between John and Alexios was poor in later years, thus undermining the idea that John's speech was in keeping with Alexios' agenda? Or is it possible to sustain the idea of collaboration and coincidence of interests between John and Alexios on the basis of external considerations?

Indications of Context: John's Career and Relationship with Alexios

John's speech itself suggests both a close relationship between him and Alexios and an imperially sanctioned context for the speech. At 1b, John states that, before John's elevation to ecclesiastical office, he and Alexios had been close enough to indulge in a frank exchange of views without acrimony. Later (2b), John, insisting that what he is saying is not intended to cause offence, says that Alexios has always shown him great favour.

With regard to the specific context of the speech, John (6) states that Alexios called together the consultative assembly for which this speech is intended, wishing to hear a variety of opinions. It is possible that John hijacked this gathering, using it to launch an unexpected attack, as those who view John primarily as Alexios' critic would argue. However, it seems more probable that John's participation was at the very least permitted. Moreover, on the basis of the discussion above of the contents of the speech, it seems quite possible that John's argument was quite compatible with Alexios' interests: that Alexios knew and approved John's approach – perhaps even commissioned it.

It is difficult to provide evidence to substantiate this last possibility, however, particularly since John's career before 1091 is somewhat nebulous. Quite when he became patriarch is unclear, although it has been suggested that he was elected around 1089, and was present as patriarch at a synod in Constantinople in September of that year.[42] Only brief allusions are made to his earlier life.[43] Of his writings, the only one generally seen as earlier than the 'Diatribe' speech[44] is the *De monasteriis*. Gautier

---

[41] Gautier, 'Notice biographique', 129, 131.
[42] V. Grumel, 'Les patriarches grecs d'Antioche du nom de Jean (xie et xiie siècles). Étude littéraire, historique et chronologique', *EO*, 32 (1933), 294.
[43] Gautier, 'Notice biographique', 128.
[44] Although see below regarding the second piece addressing Alexios.

dates this to some time between 1085 and 1092.⁴⁵ It is possible, as Gautier suggests, that it predates the 'Diatribe', and was what recommended him for promotion.⁴⁶ In that case, Alexios would have known, in 1091, the kind of approach to expect from John: the *De monasteriis* is a similar blend of irenic scene-setting narrative and trenchant criticism. If anything, however, it is rather more single-mindedly direct than the speech to Alexios – which may support the idea that the speech is designed to be more than simple criticism. But it is impossible to be certain whether *De monasteriis* pre- or post-dates John's appointment, so the main evidence pointing in the direction of Alexios' knowledge and approval of John's approach are the fact of John's appointment to Antioch and the evidence from the speech itself. Both of these are important considerations, but neither proves 'connivance' between Alexios and John in the 1091 assembly.

However, the indications are that the relationship between John and Alexios remained positive after 1091. There is, admittedly, again only sparse evidence to back this up; but two points can be made. One concerns John's role as patriarch of Antioch. Any idea that John was 'exiled' to Antioch primarily as a sign of imperial displeasure is very difficult to sustain. Recent research into Alexios' role in summoning the Crusades suggests that Alexios had plans for re-conquest and harnessing of western military power from the late 1080s, and as part of this process Antioch would have been of major importance.⁴⁷ The Komnenoi had themselves previously been involved with Antioch, and would have understood its significance: Alexios' brother Isaac had earlier been appointed its governor, prior to Alexios' usurpation and before Antioch fell to the Turks. In this role he had had to struggle – largely unsuccessfully – against both external and internal opposition. Isaac's difficulties had included a dissident patriarch, Aimilianos.⁴⁸ It is therefore unlikely that John's appointment represents the consigning of an unwanted, outspoken opponent to a see where he could do no harm; rather, it is much more likely to represent the placing of a valued associate in a highly sensitive and key strategic position. Of course, this need not rule out the possibility that John's continued presence in the capital was also not entirely desirable. But John's

---

⁴⁵ Gautier, 'Réquisitoire', 86.   ⁴⁶ Gautier, 'Notice biographique', 129.
⁴⁷ See J. Shepard, 'Cross-purposes: Alexius Comnenus and the First Crusade' in J. Phillips, ed., *The First Crusade: Origins and Impact* (Manchester, 1997), 107–29.
⁴⁸ See Angold, *Political History*, 123, 134.

appointment to Antioch implies that Alexios saw a use for him in an important role, rather than simply wanting to dispose of him.

The second indication concerning John's continued relationship with Alexios comes from the piece that John wrote concerning his abdication. Here, John specifically thanks Alexios for the honourable welcome he received on his return from Antioch.[49] John returned to Constantinople in 1100, having, according to the letter he wrote concerning his abdication, been in Antioch for nine years, i.e. since 1091.[50] John's return to Constantinople after the events of the crusade and the subsequent complex of cultural and political clashes which led, in whatever way, to John's abdication, must have been a rather difficult one. That he specifically describes receiving a warm welcome from Alexios suggests a strong underlying relationship.

Alexios and his Family: the Struggle Towards Monarchy

The complexities of Alexios' family relationships add another factor in support of the idea that John's speech may have been helpful to Alexios. Alexios' accession to the throne brought together a complex of dynastic interests; to some extent Alexios can be seen, in the early years, as a useful figure-head for these interests, rather than a leader in his own right.[51] Two particularly prominent examples of the kind of dynamic involved can be seen in the prominence of Anna Dalassene, Alexios' mother-in-law, in the first part of his reign;[52] and in the retention by Alexios of his young wife, Eirene, after he had shown signs of intending to repudiate her.[53] Margaret Mullett describes how in the first decade of Alexios' reign imperial literature tends to be addressed to a plurality of imperial figures. This changes after 1091, when the focus on Alexios himself becomes much clearer.[54] A similar but less positive picture of breakdown of dynastic alliances, even dangerous revolts within Alexios' close family in the 1090s, is presented by Peter Frankopan.[55] While far from constituting proof of any direct relationship with John's speech, this is nevertheless very interesting: at a point where Alexios seems to have, in Mullett's words, 'found a way of making the family support his own style of kingship', John seems to have been talking in terms which could

---

[49] Gautier, 'Notice biographique', 138.25–7.   [50] Ibid., 138.4–6.
[51] Angold, *Political History*, 124–9.   [52] Ibid., 153–4.   [53] Ibid., 127–8.
[54] Mullett, 'The Imperial Vocabulary of Alexios I Komnenos', 384–7.
[55] P. Frankopan, 'Kinship and the Distribution of Power in Byzantium', *EHR*, 122 (2007), 1–34.

have provided justification for Alexios to neutralise or remove obstructive elements of his wider family.[56]

Alexios as 'Champion of Orthodoxy': the Theological Agenda

There is considerable material, primary and secondary, dealing with the relationship between Alexios and the church. Angold describes Alexios' settlement with the church as 'central to his restoration of imperial authority and to the creation of a new synthesis'.[57] Much work has been done attempting to elucidate and evaluate the various elements of the relationship: the complex of interests at stake;[58] Alexios' relationship with the various patriarchs, particularly Nicholas III Grammatikos (patriarch 1084–1111);[59] the hammering-out of imperial versus ecclesiastical rights and responsibilities over questions such as expropriation of church property;[60] the role of the *chartophylax*,[61] monastic *charistike*,[62] patriarchal rights of *stauropegia* and canonical procedures relating to appointment to metropolitan sees;[63] Alexios' use of heresy as a tool of propaganda and his reinvigoration thereby of the *synodikon* of Orthodoxy,[64] together with other positive theological and ecclesiastical initiatives;[65] the extent, nature and purpose of imperial patronage of religious institutions;[66] the relationship between Latin and Greek churches;[67] and more besides. What is generally agreed upon is that Alexios deliberately – indeed, perhaps inevitably – tried to present himself as the champion of orthodoxy and to forge constructive alliances with ecclesiastical elements where and when he

---

[56] This idea, along with a number of others drawn out in this chapter, is touched upon briefly by Margaret Mullett in Mullett, 'The Imperial Vocabulary of Alexios I Komnenos', 390–1.
[57] Angold, *Church and Society*, 7.
[58] See esp. V. Tiftixoglu, 'Gruppenbildungen innerhalb des konstantinopolitanischen Klerus während der Komnenenzeit', *BZ*, 62 (1969), 25–72. Also Angold, *Church and Society*, 54–60.
[59] Angold, *Church and Society*, 49–50.   [60] Ibid., 46–9.   [61] Ibid., 58–9.   [62] Ibid., 63–9.
[63] Ibid., 55–7.
[64] Ibid., 50–4; also D. Smythe, 'Alexios I and the Heretics: The Account of Anna Komnene's Alexiad' in Mullett and Smythe, eds., *Alexios I Komnenos*, 232–59.
[65] Such as his commissioning of the *Dogmatike Panoplia* of Euthymios Zigabenos (see Angold, *Church and Society*, 480–4) and his edict on clerical reform in 1107 (text in P. Gautier, 'L'édit d'Alexis Ier Comnène sur la réforme du clergé', *REB*, 31 (1973), 165–201; see also P. Magdalino, 'The Reform Edict of 1107' in Mullett and Smythe, eds., *Alexios I Komnenos*, 199–218).
[66] See Angold, *Church and Society*, 265–85; also P. Armstrong, 'Alexios I Komnenos, Holy Men and Monasteries' in Mullett and Smythe, eds., *Alexios I Komnenos*, 219–31; and R. Morris, *Monks and Laymen in Byzantium, 843–1118* (Cambridge, 1995).
[67] Texts relating to which being found in W. Holtzmann, 'Die Unionsverhandlungen zwischen Kaiser Alexios I. und Papst Urban II. im Jahre 1089', *BZ*, 28 (1928), 38–67. See also A. Bayer, *Spaltung der Christenheit. Das sogennante Morgenländische Schisma von 1054*, second edition (Cologne, 2004), ch. 9.

could. This could not always work, given the complexity and demands of the situation; but in general it holds true.

The idea that Alexios might have invited and promoted a highly theological interpretation of his reign and role, such as that found in John the Oxite's speech, is therefore perfectly in keeping with what is known otherwise of Alexios' emphasis on ecclesiastical and theological questions. Moreover, John's approach, particularly the way in which he places 'blame' on Alexios, has interesting parallels. One such is Anna Komnene's account of Alexios' penance following his usurpation: Anna's account emphasises Alexios' willing acceptance of sole guilt.[68] Another parallel may be indicated by a passage cited by Bernard Leib, which relates another instance in which Alexios forthrightly accepted dire collective human events as punishment for his own personal sin.[69] Yet another parallel can be found in iconographical representation, described in an *Ekphrasis* of Nicholas Kallikles, of Alexios as a sinner held to account at the Last Judgement.[70] These parallels suggest that Alexios did deliberately apply such ideas to himself, although more consideration would be needed to interpret such passages fully. However, it seems quite possible, even likely, that John's attribution of blame to Alexios, heavily mitigated as it is in his speech, was an important element of Alexios' self-understanding, or at least self-projection.

John's Agenda: Part of a Philosophical Debate?

In his *Political History*, Michael Angold discusses the intellectual currents of the eleventh century, describing a range of elements, from 'humanism', the most prominent proponent of which being Michael Psellos, to 'mysticism', in the tradition of Symeon the New Theologian and his later adherents, including figures such as Niketas Stethatos and, in his own way, Michael Keroularios.[71] A particular consideration highlighted by Angold is the understanding of man's role: to quote Angold, Psellos 'seemed to be coming close to denying the importance of God in human affairs'.[72] It is

---

[68] See above, n. 41.
[69] B. Leib, *Rome, Kiev et Byzance à la fin du XIe siècle: Rapports religieux des Latins et des Gréco-Russes sous le pontificat d'Urbain II (1088–1099)* (New York, NY, 1924, reprint 1968), 7–8. Leib gives as his source 'Ouspenski Porphyre. Histoire de l'Athos, III, p. 239'. According to his bibliography this was published in St Petersburg in 1892. I have not been able to follow up this reference.
[70] See V. Kepetzi, 'Empereur, piété et remission des péchés dans deux *ekphraseis* byzantines. Image et rhétorique', *DChAE*, 20 (1999), 231–44, esp. 235–8. I am grateful to Jonathan Shepard for pointing out this parallel.
[71] Angold, *Political History*, ch. 6.   [72] Ibid., 108.

commonly accepted that there was a significant crisis in intellectual development in Byzantium at the beginning of Alexios' reign, with the trial of John Italos leading to something of a clampdown on philosophical speculation.[73] Can any connections be seen between this and the perspective found in John's speech, or would the hypothesis of such connections be so loose as to serve no useful purpose? It is in any case interesting to note that John in his speech (1d) positions his radical theocentric approach within a range of approaches to the relationship between God, man and human history in a manner which suggests that he sees himself combating a range of influential current intellectual approaches, rather than necessarily voicing a commonly held orthodoxy.

An interesting area for speculation in this regard is whether John the Oxite and his namesake John Italos may have come into direct contact with one another, in Antioch itself. Paul Magdalino argues that John Italos was *chartophylax* in Antioch in the 1090s, and could have been of great use in that context in the run-up to the First Crusade.[74] This would put him in close proximity with John the Oxite. One might wonder what kind of relationship there might have been between them, two men of very different intellectual stamp.

The Second Speech, 'Advice to the Emperor'

Before concluding, however, there is a further matter to be addressed: John's shorter piece addressing Alexios, which has been mentioned but not discussed in detail.[75] This piece (λόγος) opens with John announcing that he is submitting in writing (γραφῇ παραδούς), clearly and in summary (σαφέστατος ἅμα τε καὶ συντομώτατος), making his words as plain as possible for all (τοῖς πᾶσι καταφανῆ δεικνὺς τὰ λαλούμενα), the advice he considers necessary in the present circumstances.[76] John then asks what it is that prevents 'us' from prospering, what it is that makes 'us' weak and our enemies strong, and decides that the cause is not penury, but 'what has been wrongly acquired' (Τὰ κακῶς συναγόμενα) – but despite this, 'we' are again contemplating doing more of the same.[77] Clear reference is made to Alexios' appropriation of church treasures

---

[73] See esp. R. Browning, 'Enlightenment and Repression in Byzantium in the Eleventh and Twelfth Centuries', *Past and Present*, 69 (1975), esp. 13–23.
[74] P. Magdalino, 'Prosopography and Byzantine Identity' in A. M. Cameron, ed., *Fifty Years of Prosopography: The Later Roman Empire, Byzantium and Beyond* (Oxford, 2003), 50–1. I am grateful to Jonathan Shepard for reminding me of Magdalino's thesis concerning Italos' rehabilitation.
[75] Gautier, 'Diatribes', 49–55.   [76] Ibid., 49.1–4.   [77] Ibid., 49.5–22.

(ἄγια ... κειμήλια): 'we' vowed (in 1082) never to resort to this again,[78] yet 'we' are returning to it.[79] As in the longer speech, John's alternative solution is that of a return to a Christian way of life, meaning one of justice. Christ will then restore his protection.[80] Previous pious supplications failed because injustice continued. Once again, John draws on precedents from the Old Testament, according to which the Israelites, although continuing in injustice, expected God's deliverance, while the prophets' task was to call for repentance and restoration of justice.[81] 'We' should learn from this, rather than argue that living in accordance with the gospel, in accordance with justice, is incompatible with present expediency.[82]

The relationship between the two pieces addressed to Alexios is difficult, and probably impossible to resolve definitively. In the original manuscript, as in Gautier's edition, the shorter piece follows the longer, and Gautier regards it as probably later, on the grounds that in the longer speech John says that he has not previously been able to express his opinions on the subject.[83] The scenario Gautier envisages is that John's advice in his first speech had not been followed, and therefore John resubmitted a shorter version in a fresh attempt to put across his arguments. This scenario, however, is speculative, and to a large extent goes hand-in-hand with an assumption that John's longer speech is an unsolicited, aggressive attack on Alexios, rather than something more complex, as the present chapter argues. One internal piece of evidence does argue in favour of Gautier's reading: John's comment in the longer speech that he has not previously been able to express himself on the subject. This, however, is not decisive: the shorter piece is specifically described as being 'in writing', i.e. not envisaged as a 'public' speech in the same way as the longer speech; and its scope is much more limited. The two suggest very different contexts and vary considerably in content, so John may well have regarded the longer speech as something new.

Indeed, it is possible to argue for a reversal of the two texts. Two points in particular support this, although admittedly they are arguments from silence and the more limited scope of the shorter piece may be enough to explain the absence of such material. First, there is no indication in the shorter piece that John was patriarch at the time of writing: where he describes the role of the Old Testament prophet, there is no indication that he applies it to himself, whereas, as has been seen, this

---

[78] See ibid., 16, with n. 63. [79] Ibid., 16.22–5. [80] Ibid., 49.25–51.21.
[81] Ibid., 51.21–53.26. [82] Ibid., 53.26–55.25. [83] Ibid., 16, citing 47.26–8.

self-understanding is important in the longer piece. Second, as has been pointed out, there is no circumstantial evidence in the shorter piece pointing to a particular year for composition: certainly, a situation is envisaged in which Alexios was suffering military defeats and attempting to raise funds through (unjust) measures; but this could apply to many points in the early years of Alexios' reign. Once the possibility is admitted that the shorter text might pre-date the longer, it is possible to suggest an alternative to Gautier's reading of the shorter text. It could be seen as reflecting the state of affairs prior to John's elevation to the patriarchate, described by him in the longer speech (1b), when he gave advice to Alexios and Alexios listened. It could be seen as exactly the kind of submission, perhaps even *the* submission, which recommended him to Alexios and led to his appointment; but in any case, the text implies strongly that John was part of Alexios' 'inner circle'. Reversing the order of the two texts would, of course, support the idea that Alexios expected or commissioned the longer speech, which can then be seen as a development – and, indeed, a more pro-Alexian development – of the earlier theme.

But leaving aside the question of dating and order of composition, it is still the case that elements in the shorter piece are compatible with the interpretation of the longer speech offered in this chapter. First, although in some ways the shorter piece is more hard-hitting than the longer speech (for example, it is more explicit about Alexios' expropriation of church property), in contrast with the longer piece there is *no* accusation of Alexios in the singular: *all* criticisms are of 'us'. Elsewhere in the shorter piece, where blame is not being attributed, John uses first and second person singular respectively to refer to himself and to Alexios, which makes the usage of the third person plural appear once again very deliberate, as it is in the longer speech. Second, the theological framework, so central to John's longer 'speech', is also clearly the core message of this shorter piece: this supports the idea that Old Testament motifs may be crucial to the structure of the longer piece. Third, there is a parallel with the scenario raised in the longer speech: John is giving advice in specific circumstances. In this case there is no mention that the advice is solicited or intended for a particular setting, but there is no indication that John is speaking out of turn. Above all, however, the piece implies, as mentioned above, very close connections between John and Alexios. Not only is there the attribution of blame in the third person plural, but when John explains why previous attempts at pious propitiation have failed, he describes the prayers of city, patriarch, senate, monks and priests as having been against 'us'.[84] If all these are on the 'other side', this implies that John is identifying himself with a small 'inner circle'. The idea therefore that John's approach emanates from within Alexios' entourage rather than constituting an external attack is borne out by the shorter piece, whatever the order of composition.

Conclusion

To some extent, the two different scholarly approaches to John the Oxite's two pieces addressed to Alexios I Komnenos are not mutually exclusive. Both texts are undoubtedly critical: they are based on the idea of sin and repentance; and they emphasise the sin. However, evidence nevertheless stacks heavily in favour of the more subtle Mullett/Angold approach – according to which John's speech coincided with Alexios' agenda and was probably commissioned by Alexios, suggesting that there was more to the relationship between Alexios and John than meets the eye. The situation in 1091, when the longer speech was delivered, was desperate, and Alexios had called a meeting because of this. Anybody speaking at the meeting and offering useful advice would have had to take the existing crisis as their starting point if they were to offer any credible advice. A degree of Kaiserkritik was inevitable. This throws emphasis on other elements in John's speech: its portrait of Alexios as God's chosen player in salvation history, its capacity for being used to justify draconian action in various spheres and reinvigorate efforts to generate religious propaganda. These are probably far more important than John's 'denunciations of Alexios'. The latter could in any case be read as Alexian propaganda in itself: not only being entirely compatible with Alexios' self-projection as imperial penitent taking all blame upon himself, but also, less eschatologically, taking the wind out of the sails of ecclesiastical opposition groups and harnessing support for future initiatives. It may be that John's heavily theological framework, in response to what he sees as misguided ideas prevalent in Byzantine society, is primarily his own, but it can also be seen that it could coincide nicely with Alexios' projects. John thus would appear as Alexios' ideologue, presenting Alexios as the focus of divine plans (at a very interesting point, just before the First Crusade) and providing him with arguments, including theological justifications, which could be employed to allow him to intervene and clamp down almost indiscriminately.

---

[84] Οὐκ ἐλάλουν ἡ πόλις, ὁ πατριάρχης, ἡ σύγκλητος, ἡ τῶν μοναχῶν ἐκείνων καὶ τῶν ἱερέων πληθύς; - Ναὶ ... ἀλλ'ηὔχοντο καθ'ἡμῶν. Gautier, 'Diatribes', 51.27–9.

Further Reading

The key primary source is: P. Gautier, 'Diatribes de Jean l'Oxite contre Alexis Ier Comnène', *REB*, 28 (1970), 5–55. Introductory studies include: M. J. Angold, *Church and Society in Byzantium under the Comneni, 1081–1261* (Cambridge, 1995); M. E. Mullett and D. Smythe, eds., *Alexios I Komnenos: Papers of the Second Belfast Byzantine International Colloquium, 14–16 April 1989, 1: Papers* (Belfast, 1996); J. Shepard, 'Cross-purposes: Alexius Comnenus and the First Crusade' in J. Phillips, ed., *The First Crusade: Origins and Impact* (Manchester, 1997), 107–29; V. Tiftixoglu, 'Gruppenbildungen innerhalb des konstantinopolitanischen Klerus während der Komnenenzeit', *BZ*, 62 (1969), 25–72.

CHAPTER 4

The Liturgical Poetics of an Elite Religious Confraternity

Paul Magdalino

Re-reading Byzantium is always a salutary experience, even when its texts are well edited and appear to be completely transparent. Such texts have often been read on the basis of questionable assumptions about their contextual facts, and only recently have we been concerned to read them as the Byzantines read them: with an eye to the context in which, and the public for whom, they were produced. This chapter starts by revisiting a well-known and much-appreciated author, whose life and work can still yield fresh insights into the context of Byzantine literary production and reception.

Recent studies on the tenth-century poet John Geometres have consolidated and enhanced his reputation as one of the most highly accomplished Byzantine authors.[1] They have also attempted to 'canonise' the facts of his biography. They have correctly cleared up the confusion between him and John, bishop of Melitene; more speculatively, they have affirmed that at the end of his career he became a monk in the monastery of *ta Kyrou* in Constantinople, hence his epithet 'Kyriotes'. In the following pages I shall attempt to demonstrate that this speculation is unfounded. If John Geometres became a monk, which is doubtful, it was not in any monastery of that name; the church of the Theotokos *ta Kyrou* was not monastic, and neither were the people known as the Kyriotai. Their association with the church was of a rather different order, which throws interesting and unexpected light on both lay piety and literary society in Byzantium.

The sole 'evidence' for Geometres' monastic profession is a passage in one of his poetic confessions (poem 289).[2] He writes that he has made commitments (ἐθέμην συνθήκας) and been initiated (τελέσθην) by the prayers of monks (ῥήμασιν οἰοβίων) and by the sacrificial rites – presumably

---

[1] M. D. Lauxtermann, 'John Geometres, Poet and Soldier', *Byzantion*, 68 (1998), 356–80; E. M. van Opstall, ed. and trans., *Jean Géomètre. Poèmes en hexamètres et en distiques élégiaques* (Leiden, 2008), 3–14.
[2] John Geometres, *Poèmes*, ed. van Opstall, 456–66.

Eucharistic celebrations – of priests (μυστιπόλων θυσίαις). As a result, he has learned the dread mysteries of God, seeing, instead of demonic phantoms, a reassuring vision of the Virgin, and he has been momentarily purged of his sins. While the mention of vows and initiation in the context of the Divine Liturgy certainly suggests the office of reception into monastic life, rather than any other religious rite of passage, the poet curiously does not allude to the obvious outward symbols of the monk's status, the tonsure (κουρά) and the habit (σχῆμα). Moreover, it is remarkable that he does not allude, even periphrastically, in this or any other of his works, to any change of personal status. He does not identify with the ranks of the monks (οἰόβιοι) who prayed for him; indeed, in the next poem (290), they figure as just one category – after the martyrs, prophets, saintly bishops and priests – of the holy persons whom he supplicates to intercede for him with the Virgin Mary.[3] The only sacred institution with which he identifies in any way is a church, that of the Theotokos *ta Kyrou*.

Two religious establishments in Constantinople, both dedicated to the Virgin, bore the name of Kyros/Cyrus, the fifth-century poet and city prefect who was later obliged to become a bishop.[4] One was a monastery near the Theodosian Land Walls, the other a church at the centre of the city. While the monastery disappears from the sources after the sixth century, the church continued to function throughout the middle and late Byzantine period. Romanos the Melodist worked and was buried there in the sixth century, and his cult later became associated with an icon of the Virgin Kyriotissa. The church went through several construction phases, including a complete rebuilding after a fire at the end of the twelfth century. This structure of *c.* 1200 has been identified, on the basis of a surviving wall painting, with the mosque now known as the Kalenderhane Camii. Other paintings show that it was used by the Franciscans during the Latin occupation of Constantinople. At some point after its return to Byzantine hands it served a monastery known as the Kyriotissa.[5]

It was clearly this church that John Geometres celebrated in his poem 142, despite the contrary argument of Emilie van Opstall, whose recent

---

[3] Ibid., 468ff.
[4] See A. D. E. Cameron, 'The Empress and the Poet: Paganism and Politics at the Court of Theodosius II', J. J. Winkler and G. Williams, eds., *Later Greek Literature*, YCS 27 (Cambridge, 1982), 217–89.
[5] For the history, identification, and topography of the foundation, see C. L. Striker and Y. Doğan Kuban, eds., *Kalenderhane in Istanbul: The Buildings, their History, Architecture, and Decoration*. (Mainz, 1997–2007), especially the survey by A. Berger, 7–17; see also the very important review by C. Mango, 'Review of C. L. Striker and Y. Doğan Kuban, eds., *Kalenderhane in Istanbul: The Buildings*', in *BZ*, 91 (1998), 586–90, which adds further source references and clears up serious confusions that prevailed in all previous secondary literature.

edition, translation and commentary need revision.[6] The text and translation should read as follows:[7]

> Εἰς τὸν ναὸν τοῦ Κύρου
> Κῦρος μὲν σ'ἐδόμησεν, θῆκε δὲ κῦρος ἁπάντων
> δεσπότις ἡμετέρη τῶν ἐπὶ γῆς θαλάμων,
> ἔνθεν ἐπορνυμένη Βυζαντίδος ἀμφιπολεύει[8]
> κύκλον ὅλον, χαρίτων νάμασι πληθομένη

> On the church of Kyros
> Kyros built you, and Our Lady placed you chief
> Of all her chambers that are on this earth.
> Arising thence, brimming with streams of grace,
> She cares for the whole circuit of Byzantion.

Since there is no reference whatsoever to monastic use, there is no need to identify the church with the ephemeral early Byzantine monastery near the land walls of Constantinople. The reference to the 'circuit' (κύκλον) of the city does not have to mean that the church was close to the perimeter. Indeed, when the poem is understood correctly as saying that the Virgin arising from the church looks after the whole city with her streams of grace, it makes much better sense to envisage a central location for the church from which she arises. The present-day Kalenderhane Camii does indeed stand very close to the geographical centre of the city within the *Constantinian* walls, which even after the construction of the Theodosian land wall continued to define the properly urban area. It was in close proximity to the point (originally a monument?) that marked the navel (*omphalos*, Mesomphalon) of the city. It was also close to the city's main aqueduct, which gives added point to the image of the 'streams of grace' dispensed by the Theotokos.

Geometres' superlative praise for the church of *ta Kyrou* in this and, most probably, the next poem (143),[9] suggests that he had a special regard for it. This suggestion is confirmed by the oblique references that he makes in two other poems. In one, an apparently abusive but possibly bantering

---

[6] Geometres, *Poèmes*, ed. van Opstall, 326–9.
[7] My reading differs from van Opstall's in that I take 'Our Lady' (δεσπότις ἡμετέρη) as the subject of 'placed' (θῆκε). This makes better sense in several ways: (1) it does not require the emendation of the third main verb (see next note); (2) the Virgin, not Kyros, confers authority on the church and she, not the church, looks after the city, according to her traditional role; and (3) if the church were the subject of 'arising', 'cares' and 'brimming' (ἐπορνυμένη ... ἀμφιπολεύει ... πληθομένη), the participles would have to be masculine to agree with ναός or θάλαμος.
[8] As in the manuscript, Par. Suppl gr. 352; van Opstall emends to ἀμφιπολεύεις (Geometres, *Poèmes*, ed. van Opstall, 326).
[9] John Geometres, *Poèmes*, ed. van Opstall, 332–4. This similarly says that the church is first in rank of the Virgin's 'earthly chambers (χθονίων ... θαλάμων)'.

invective, he tells his addressee, a certain Psenas, to 'remove yourself far from *ta Kyrou*, dog';[10] in the other, an extempore appreciation of wine from Prainestos, he signs off as 'the Kyriotes'.[11] Lauxtermann and van Opstall have assumed that in both cases the author is referring to his monastic affiliation, but neither text supports the assumption in the absence of other proof that the monastery existed in the tenth century. In the first case, he is simply warning Psenas to stay away from his neighbourhood, defined by its church, in much the same way that another poet, Christopher Mitylenaios, fifty years later, would tell an unnamed addressee not to come near his home in the vicinity of the church of St Protasios (*ta Protasiou*).[12] That Geometres lived near *ta Kyrou* is clear from a letter in which he describes his house and garden as being close to the navel of the city (μέσον τῆς πόλεως ὀμφαλόν).[13]

In the second poem, Geometres' self-designation as Kyriotes is certainly consistent with the way that monastic surnames were formed: e.g. Lavriotes from Lavra, Ivirites from Iviron, Stoudites from Stoudios, etc. On the other hand, laymen also received surnames derived from religious establishments,[14] so the name Kyriotes cannot be used as evidence that John Geometres was a monk at a monastery of *ta Kyrou*. But if not, what does it signify – the mere fact of residence in the neighbourhood of

---

[10] Reproduced by Lauxtermann, 'John Geometres', 378, from the edition by I. Sajdak, ed., 'Spicilegium Geometreum II', *EOS (Commentarii Societatis Philologae Polonorum)*, 33 (1930-1), 530-1.

[11] J. A. Cramer, ed., *Anecdota Graeca e codd. manuscriptis bibliothecae regiae Parisiensis* (Oxford, 1841; repr. Hildesheim, 1967), 297.

[12] E. Kurtz, ed., *Die Gedichte des Christophoros Mitylenaios* (Leipzig, 1903), 19 (36.12) M. de Groote, ed., *Christophri Mitylenaii Versunm variorum Collectio Cryptensis* (Turnhout, 2012), 30.

[13] The proximity of the church to the Mesomphalon is confirmed by a fourteenth-century document, the *typikon* of the nearby monastery of the Theotokos of Sure Hope (Bebaia Elpidos), which in its boundary description and property list places the church of St Nicholas Mesomphalos to the east of the Kyriotissa monastery: H. Delehaye, ed., *Deux Typica byzantins de l'époque des Paléologues* (Brussels, 1921), 95, 84; A.-M. Talbot, 'Bebaia Elpis: Typikon of Theodora Synadene for the Convent of the Mother of God Bebaia Elpis in Constantinople', trans., in J. Thomas and A. C. Hero, eds., *Byzantine Monastic Foundation Documents: A Complete Translation of the Surviving Founders' Typika and Testaments*, (Washington, D. C., 2000), vol. IV, 1557, 1563; see A. Berger, 'Historical topography in the Roman, Byzantine, Latin, and Ottoman periods, 1. Roman, Byzantine and Latin periods', in C. L. Striker and Y. Doğan Kuban, eds., *Kalenderhane in Istanbul: The Buildings, their History, Architecture, and Decoration. Final Reports on the Archaeological Exploration and Restoration at Kalenderhane Camii, 1966–1978* (Mainz, 1997–2007), vol. I, 13–14. Berger, influenced by the layout of the present street grid, takes 'east' to mean in effect 'north-east' and thus places the Mesomphalon to the north of the third hill of Constantinople, near the Golden Horn. I think it more likely, however, that a Byzantine's idea of east would have been based on the orientation of the churches. This would put the Mesomphalos to the south-east of the Kalenderhane, close to the end of the aqueduct, at the geographical centre of the area within the Constantinian walls.

[14] See A. P. Kazhdan and S. Ronchey, *L'aristocrazia bizantina dal principio dell' XI alla fine del XII secolo* (Palermo, 1997), 325–6.

the church, or some closer, non-monastic association? Ironically, the solution is provided in a text that Lauxtermann has cited in connection with the poem against Psenas, arguing that Geometres wrote this poem in defence of his monastery's interests.[15] Lauxtermann was evidently misled by the editor of the text, Jean Darrouzès, who unhesitatingly introduced it as concerning the abbot and monastery of *ta Kyrou*. However, if the text is read without this erroneous preconception, it yields much more interesting information.

The text is a letter from Nikephoros Ouranos, the well-known writer and military commander under Basil II,[16] to a fellow government official, complaining of the outrage committed in public against the leader of the Kyriotai. I quote and translate the letter as follows:

Ἰωάννῃ ὀστιαρίῳ

Τὸν ἡγεμόνα, τὸν ἱερέα, τὸν φύλακα, τὸν χειρονόμον, τὸν οἰκονόμον ἡμῶν τῶν Κυριωτῶν, ἄνθρωπός τις, ἀνθρώπου τι μᾶλλον παίγνιον καὶ κακὸν Ἀσσύριον (*leg.* ἀσσάριον), εἵλκυσε διὰ μέσης τῆς ἀγορᾶς καὶ ὕβρισε καὶ πληγὰς ἐνέτεινε καὶ εἰς δεσμωτήριον ἔβαλε· καὶ ταῦτα παρ' ἑαυτούς καὶ σὺν οὐδεμίᾳ τῇ αἰτίᾳ, ὡς μήτε νόμων, μήτε δικαστηρίων, μήτε δὲ βασιλείων ἢ αὐτοῦ βασιλέως ὄντος. Αὐτὸς μὲν οὖν μάλιστα ὁ βασιλεὺς ἐνταῦθα ὑβριζόμενος· οὐ γὰρ θεῖος ναὸς μόνον, ἀλλὰ καὶ βασιλικός. Ὁ μὲν οὖν ἔπαρχος μαλακίζεται· ἢν δ' ἂν ὁ μὴ μαλακιζόμενος, ἁπαλὸς ἄλλως ὡς οἶδας πρὸς τὴν ἐκδίκησιν. Ἀλλὰ σὺ δεῖξον τῷ ἀνδραπόδῳ τούτῳ καὶ τριοβολιμαίῳ ὥς εἰσι καὶ νόμοι καὶ δικασταὶ καὶ βασιλεῖαι καὶ πρὸ τούτων οἱ ἐν τοῖς βασιλείοις ἡμεῖς, ἀγαθοὶ μὲν τοῦ Θεοῦ προστάται, πιστοὶ δὲ τοῦ βασιλέως φύλακες καὶ ἰσχυροὶ τιμωροὶ τῶν ἀδικουμένων.

To John the ostiarios[17]

The leader, the priest, the guardian, the choirmaster and steward of us, the Kyriotai, has been dragged through the marketplace, insulted, showered

---

[15] J. Darrouzès, ed., *Épistoliers byzantins du xe siècle* (Paris, 1960), 238.
[16] On his career and writings, see E. McGeer, 'Tradition and Reality in the *Taktika* of Nikephoros Ouranos', *DOP*, 45 (1991), 129–40.
[17] The *ostiarioi* were among the eunuchs who served in the imperial household: N. Oikonomidès, *Les listes de préséance byzantines des ixe et xe siècles* (Paris, 1972), 126–7, 300. Although there were several of them and their function was largely ceremonial, they would have been politically influential through their direct access to the emperor. A number of them functioned as imperial domain administrators: see J.-C. Cheynet, *La société Byzantine: l'apport des sceaux* (Paris, 2008), 242, 267, 281, 506; E. McGeer, J. Nesbitt and N. Oikonomides, eds., *Catalogue of Byzantine Seals at Dumbarton Oaks and in the Fogg Museum of Art* (Washington, D. C., 1991–2009), vol. v, 59, 65, 106. One John, *ostiarios* and *kourator* of the Petrion in the tenth/eleventh century, may have been identical with the correspondent of Nikephoros Ouranos: Cheynet, *La société byzantine*, 242, citing I. Jordanov, *Pečatite ot strategijata v Preslav* (Sofia, 1993), n. 137. John the *ostiarios* was the nephew of another highly placed palace eunuch, the *protovestiarios* Leo, as we learn from other letters addressed to him both by Ouranos (Darrouzès, *Épistoliers*, 226, 229) and Leo of Synada: M. P. Vinson, ed., *The Correspondence of Leo Metropolitan of Synada and Syncellus* (Washington, D. C., 1985), n. 1 and 6.

with blows and thrown into prison by some man, or rather some man's plaything and bad penny.[18] All this was done arbitrarily and with no good cause, as if there were no laws, no law courts, no palace, and not even an emperor. Indeed, the emperor himself is insulted here, for the church (ναὸς) is not only divine but imperial. The eparch has been placated; and even if he were not, he is, as you know, too gentle in making punishment. But you must show that worthless slave that there are laws and judges and authorities, and, above all, that we are in the palace, good defenders of God's interests, the emperor's loyal guards, and powerful avengers of the victims of injustice.

The perpetrator may or may not have been the much-abused Psenas, as Lauxtermann suggests; although he was himself a lowlife, he was apparently in the service of someone with access to prison facilities and the clout to influence the city prefect. But the victim was clearly not an abbot, and the Kyriotai of whom he was the leader (ἡγεμών, not ἡγούμενος) were not a monastic community. The institution to which they were attached is characterised not as a monastery, but as an imperial church, and they included laymen, among whom Nikephoros Ouranos counted himself and possibly also his correspondent.[19] The reference to their leader as 'guardian' (φύλακα), 'choirmaster' (χειρονόμον), and 'steward' (οἰκονόμον) suggests that they were more than merely his 'parishioners'. Thus the Kyriotai seem to have formed a pious association under the direction of one of the priests, conceivably even the *protopapas*, who served the church of the Theotokos *ta Kyrou*. In other words, this was one of the many lay or mixed confraternities that performed various ritual acts of charity and devotion in association with the public churches and certain monasteries, both in Constantinople and in the provinces.[20] The possible existence of a confraternity serving the Theotokos at *ta Kyrou* has recently been deduced from an eighth-century seal, and Ouranos' letter confirms and clarifies this reading of the sigillographic evidence.[21]

---

[18] Reading ἀσσάριον instead of Ἀσσύριον.

[19] The 'us' of the last sentence is inclusive of both, so logically the same should be true of the expression ἡμῶν τῶν Κυριωτῶν in the first sentence. It is plausible that Nikephoros should have addressed his complaint and plea for action to a fellow Kyriotes rather than some other imperial official who was not involved with the group.

[20] See in general J. Baun, *Tales from Another Byzantium: Celestial Journey and Local Community in the Medieval Greek Apocrypha* (Cambridge, 2007), 372ff. and bibliography cited.

[21] McGeer, Nesbitt and Oikonomides, *Seals at Dumbarton Oaks*, vol. v, n. 45.1: Θεοτόκε [ἡ] εἰς τὰ Κύρου βοήθει Τιμοθέῳ [τ]ῷ σῷ οἰκέτι, ἀεί. The editors hesitated between a lay confraternity and a monastic community, presumably because they were influenced by the confusion in the secondary literature.

Beyond what we can deduce from Ouranos' letter, it is difficult to be more specific. But we may be reasonably certain that Ouranos' near-contemporary John Geometres was, as a self-professed Kyriotes, another member of the brotherhood, and we may plausibly conjecture that the initiation to which he refers in his confessional poem was his induction into the confraternity. We may also, on the basis of what we know about Ouranos, Geometres and the history of the *ta Kyrou* church, make some informed guesses about the nature and profile of the association.

Nikephoros Ouranos and John Geometres had striking points in common, apart from the fact that both were Kyriotai at around the same time towards the end of the tenth century. Both combined a high degree of literacy and learning with active military service – a combination that Geometres felt compelled to defend against unnamed critics, but which Ouranos carried off successfully and used to compose treatises on warfare. Both also expressed extreme piety in their writings, and neither is known to have married. In this they resembled Ouranos' friend Symeon the *logothetes* and *magistros* and well-known Metaphrastes ('rewriter') of the corpus of most commonly read saints' lives.[22] After Symeon's death, Ouranos wrote a verse epitaph on his 'companion in myriad toils and cares', lamenting him as a lost Muse and literary critic, and praising his 'flesh that was innocent of fleshly filth, / punishing lifestyle that sought only Christ, / monastic regime in the turmoil of business'.[23]

Ouranos himself was commended by an eminent intellectual churchman, Stephen Metropolitan of Nikomedia and patriarchal *synkellos*, for combining military experience and political affairs with an interest in 'priestly discourses', seasoning his mealtime conversations with the sayings of the Fathers 'like divine salt'. To strengthen his resolve, Stephen compiled for him a little handbook of useful theological advice, which he wrote and gave him in person. As Dirk Krausmüller has pointed out, Stephen seems to have aimed it not only at Nikephoros but also at a wider circle of pious laymen who strove to live virtuous Christian lives in the world.[24]

In these contacts of Nikephoros Ouranos, and by extension in the wider network of his correspondents and the people to whom they wrote, like Leo of Synada, we perhaps begin to glimpse the cultural concerns and the

---

[22] See C. Høgel, *Symeon Metaphrastes: Rewriting and Canonization* (Copenhagen, 2002).
[23] S. G. Mercati, ed., 'Versi di Niceforo Uranos in morte di Simeone Metafraste' in A. Acconcia Longo, ed., *Collectanea Byzantina* (Bari, 1970), vol. 1, 565–73, text: 569–70.
[24] *PG*, 28, cols. 1395–408; D. Krausmüller, 'Religious Instruction for Laypeople in Byzantium: Stephen of Nicomedia, Nicephoros Ouranos, and the Pseudo-Athanasian *Syntagma ad quemdam politicum*', *Byzantion*, 77 (2007), 239–50.

social context that brought Nikephoros and John Geometres together as Kyriotai during the reign of Basil II. Their common membership of the group was despite their very different fortunes at that emperor's hands after Basil took over the government from his eunuch uncle, the *parakoimomenos* Basil, who had been the power behind the imperial throne since 963.[25] While Geometres apparently lost his army appointment when the *parakoimomenos*, his patron, was dismissed and disgraced in 985, Ouranos continued to rise and rise in imperial service. Nevertheless, it is quite possible that he had been initially launched by the patronage of the *parakoimomenos*,[26] and that he was simply more successful than Geometres in gaining the emperor's confidence. It is also very likely that other prominent figures in his cultural circle, notably Symeon Metaphrastes, Stephen of Nikomedia and John the *ostiarios*, had started out as the *parakoimomenos'* protégés. What one cannot fail to notice is that the *parakoimomenos* had been distinguished by the same combination of interests – conspicuous piety and military theory – that became the hallmark of Ouranos. One is thus led to speculate that the powerful, munificent, and cultured *parakoimomenos*, whose monastery of St Basil lay close to the church of *ta Kyrou*,[27] may have been a common factor in the association of the Kyriotai.

Speculation aside, the cultured lay piety of the Kyriotai can also be explained in the context of the traditions associated with the church of the Theotokos *ta Kyrou*. Basic to these was its association with the great hymnographer Romanos the Melodist. According to notices preserved in menologia and synaxaria whose compilation dates from the tenth century, it was at the church of *ta Kyrou* that Romanos settled when he came to Constantinople from Beirut in the reign of Anastasios.[28] Here the Virgin appeared to him in a dream and instructed him to swallow a scroll, which

---

[25] Basil the *parakoimomenos*, the illegitimate (Nothos) son of Romanos I Lekapenos, is commonly but inaccurately referred to in modern literature by his father's surname. For his power and patronage, see Lauxtermann, 'John Geometres', and C. Holmes, *Basil II and the Governance of Empire (976–1025)* (Oxford, 2005), 469–74, with earlier bibliography, and P. Magdalino, '"What We Heard in the Lives of the Saints We Have Seen with our Own Eyes": The Holy Man as Literary Text in Tenth-century Constantinople' in J. Howard-Johnston and P. A. Hayward, eds., *The Cult of Saints in Late Antiquity and the Early Middle Ages: Essays on the Contribution of Peter Brown* (Oxford, 1999), 108–11. For Basil as a patron of the arts, see now also S. Wander, *The Joshua Roll* (Mainz, 2011).

[26] He refers to Basil glowingly in a letter to Stephen of Nikomedia written, evidently, while the *parakoimomenos* was still in favour: Darrouzès, *Épistoliers*, 119–20: τῇ τε θείᾳ καὶ ἱερᾷ ψυχῇ τοῦ θείου ὡς ἀληθῶς ἀνδρὸς τοῦ παρακοιμωμένου.

[27] A. Berger, 'Zur Topographie der Ufergegend am Goldenen Horn in der byzantinischen Zeit', *Istanbuler Mitteilungen*, 43 (1995), 156–7, n. 48.

[28] Sources reproduced and analysed by J. Grosdidier de Matons, *Romanos le Mélode et la poésie réligieuse à Byzance* (Paris, 1977), 160ff., though the identification of the church should be disregarded.

instantly conferred the gift of composing *kontakia*; here too he was buried, and his memory was celebrated on 1 October. It is therefore plausible to suppose that the confraternity of Kyriotai was a continuation of the original choir formed by Romanos in the sixth century, or that it was founded in his memory at some later date, either way with the function of singing his *kontakia*, the verse homilies that he had pioneered. This interpretation is supported, first, by Ouranos' use of the word 'choirmaster' to describe the leader of the Kyriotai, and second, by seventh-century evidence for the existence of such a liturgical association at the nearby church of St John the Baptist in Oxeia. The *Miracles of St Artemios* record the story of a man in the reign of Herakleios 'who used to attend the all-night vigil of the Forerunner and who sang the hymns of the humble Romanos among the saints right up to the present day';[29] the vigil was conducted by a 'society of all-night celebrants (τοῦ φιλικοῦ τῶν τῆς παννυχίδος)', who had their own treasurer (ἀρκάριος) and therefore their own funds.[30] It is significant that the chanter was a layman and single, like both Romanos before him and the tenth-century Kyriotai, John Geometres and Nikephoros Ouranos. It is thus plausible to see the later Kyriotai as perpetuating the traditions that Romanos had inaugurated, and continuing to perform *kontakia* at vigil services, despite the steady encroachment of the monastic rite and the new type of homiletic hymn, the *kanon*, which this popularised. Indeed, the preservation of Romanos' compositions, in the face of increasing liturgical redundancy, in manuscripts of the tenth century and later, may best be explained by their continuing relevance to lay associations, such as the Kyriotai, that were attached to public churches.[31] Choirs of laymen who sang *kontakia* both in and out of church seem to be attested in the twelfth century by the canonist Theodore Balsamon.[32]

---

[29] Miracle n. 18: A. Papadopoulos-Kerameus, ed., *Varia Graeca Sacra* (St Petersburg, 1909; repr. Leipzig, 1975), 20; reproduced with translation and commentary by V. S. Crisafulli and J. W. Nesbitt, *The Miracles of St. Artemios* (Leiden, 1997), 114–15.

[30] This was the moneychanger (τραπεζίτης) Abraamios, who worked near the church: Papadopoulos-Kerameus, *Varia Graeca Sacra*, 21; Crisafulli and Nesbitt, *The Miracles of St. Artemios*, 116–17.

[31] See in general A. Lingas, 'The Liturgical Place of the Kontakion in Constantinople' in C. Akentiev, ed., *Liturgy, Architecture and Art in the Byzantine World: Papers of the XVIII International Byzantine Congress* (St Petersburg, 1995), 50–7. Some *kontakia* attributed to Romanos may actually have been composed as late as the tenth century.

[32] Commentary on canon 15 of the Council of Laodicaea, in G. A. Ralles and M. Potles, eds., Σύνταγμα τῶν θείων καὶ ἱερῶν κανόνων (Athens, 1852–9), vol. III, 185, referring to τοὺς λαϊκούς, τοὺς χοροστάτας τῶν κονδακίων, τοὺς ἐπ' ἐκκλησίας καὶ ἐν ταῖς ἀγοραῖς δομεστικεύοντας.

The liturgical focus of the Kyriotai might have been the tomb of Romanos, wherever this was located within the church.³³ More likely, however, is that it was the icon of the Virgin surnamed Kyriotissa, which is attested from the eleventh century, and which eventually came to figure in the story. Other iconographic types, named after their icons in different churches of Constantinople, appear around the same time – the Hodegetria, the Blachernitissa, the Panagiotissa – and at least one of these icons, the Hodegetria, was associated with a weekly procession conducted by a group of devoted laypeople, including women.³⁴ The procession was joined by other icons and their devotees. From 1048, we have evidence for a similar confraternity in central Greece, devoted to the cult icon of the Virgin Naupaktiotissa.³⁵ The iconographic type of the Virgin labelled Kyriotissa is known from an eleventh-century seal, and from frescoes found in the Kalendarhane Camii: it portrays the Theotokos in a standing position with the Christ-child held frontally.³⁶ Whether the main icon of the Kyriotissa was a mural representation or a portable, processional panel is impossible to tell from either the visual evidence or from the literary allusions in texts of the eleventh and twelfth centuries. An anonymous poetic supplication to the Virgin Kyriotissa does not mention the icon.³⁷ Anna Komnene and Niketas Choniates merely describe people praying to the icon in the church, without being more specific. The most suggestive indication is from silence: in his verse lament on the fire that destroyed the church along with the whole quarter in 1197, Constantine Stilbes mentions that a precious gold and jewelled figure of a dove, 'symbol of the Theotokos', was saved from destruction by being taken to the church of the Forty Martyrs.³⁸ That he does not mention the rescue of the church's cult icon seems to indicate that this could not be removed.

---

³³ No obvious sign of it has come to light in the investigation of the Kalenderhane Camii.
³⁴ For discussion and documentation, see C. Angelidi and T. Papamastorakis, 'The Veneration of the Virgin Hodegetria and the Hodegon Monastery' in M. Vasilaki, ed., *Mother of God. Representations of the Virgin in Byzantine Art* (Athens, 2000), 373–87; B. V. Pentcheva, *Icons and Power: The Mother of God in Byzantium* (University Park, PA, 2006), chapter 4, esp. 129ff. The devotees are explicitly called a confraternity (*diakonia*) in an eleventh-century text about the associated icon of 'Maria the Roman', which was kept at the Chalkoprateia church: E. von Dobschütz, ed., 'Maria Romaia', *BZ*, 12 (1903), 202.
³⁵ J. Nesbitt and J. Wiita, eds., 'A Confraternity of the Comnenian Era', *BZ*, 68 (1975), 360–84.
³⁶ McGeer, Nesbit and Oikonomides, *Byzantine Seals at Dumbarton Oaks*, vol. v, n.45.2; Striker and Kuban, *Kalenderhane*, 124–6, 142–3 and plate 150.
³⁷ S. P. Lampros, ed., "Ὁ μαρκιανὸς κῶδιξ 524', *NE*, 8 (1911), 181, n. 344 (fol. 182r). The text has sometimes been attributed to Psellos, but is not included by L. G. Westerink in his edition of Psellos' poems.
³⁸ J. Diethart and W. Hörandner, eds., *Constantinus Stilbes, Poemata* (Munich, 2005), 28.522ff. In an earlier discussion of this passage, I interpreted it as an allusion to an icon of the Virgin: P. Magdalino,

Though uninformative about the appearance of the icon, the anonymous poem and Anna Komnene nevertheless do give important clues about the nature of the devotion it attracted, and hence about the clientele of the Theotokos Kyriotissa and their activities in her church. Both reveal that the Kyriotissa was cultivated for the gifts of wisdom and eloquence that she had bestowed on the humble Romanos the Melodist. The anonymous verse supplication runs as follows:

> Εἰς τὴν Κυριώτισσαν ὅτε ἀνέγνω
> Καὶ Ῥωμανῷ, δέσποινα, τῷ λάτρει πάλαι
> τόμον φαγεῖν δέδωκας ἐγγεγραμμένον
> ἐμοῦ δὲ τὸν κρατῆρα πλῆσον, παρθένε,
> τῶν τῆς σοφίας γλυκερῶν κερασμάτων.
> Διψῶ γὰρ αὐτοῦ ἐκροφῆσαι πλησμίως
> ὡς ὑγρανεῖ μου τὴν κατάξηρον φρένα.

> *To the Kyriotissa, when he read aloud*
> To Romanos, Lady, your worshipper of old
> You gave a written document to eat,
> Now fill my cup, O Virgin, to the brim
> With the sweet vintage draughts of wisdom
> For I so thirst to drink my fill of them
> That they may irrigate my arid mind.

Anna Komnene writes that Psellos was a self-made intellectual, who owed his extraordinary achievements not so much to his teachers as to his innate talent, 'although God also lent a hand because of the warm entreaties of his mother, who spent many a sleepless night before the revered icon of the Theotokos in the church of Kyros, appealing with hot tears on her son's behalf'.[39] This perhaps implies that she participated in the vigils of the Virgin's feasts.

'Constantinopolitana' in I. Ševčenko and I. Hutter, eds., *AETOS: Studies in honour of Cyril Mango* (Stuttgart and Leipzig, 1998), 229; repr. in P. Magdalino, *Studies on the History and Topography of Byzantine Constantinople* (Aldershot, 2007), n. VIII. It is tempting to identify the dove effigy at *ta Kyrou* with the one that the empress Eirene (d. 1159), wife of Manuel I, offered to the Theotokos in gratitude for her recovery from an illness: W. Hörandner, ed., *Theodoros Prodromos. Historische Gedichte* (Vienna, 1974), n. 34. For a contemporary reference to a similar figure (a lamp?) in the cathedral of Athens (the Parthenon), see A. Kaldellis, *The Christian Parthenon: Classicism and Pilgrimage in Byzantine Athens* (Cambridge, 2009), 155–6, citing Michael Choniates, ed. S. Lampros, Μιχαὴλ Ἀκομινάτου τοῦ Χωνιάτου τὰ σωζόμενα (Athens, 1879–80), vol. I, 40.

[39] D. R. Reinsch and A. Kambylis, eds., *Annae Comnenae Alexias* (Berlin, 2001), vol. I, 162 (v.viii.3). According to Psellos himself, his mother was convinced that he had a literary future by two visions, one of St John Chrysostom, the other of the Theotokos with the Apostles Peter and Paul who appeared to her in the church of the Holy Apostles: John Chrysostom *Encomium for his Mother*, in K. Sathas, ed., Μεσαιωνικὴ Βιβλιοθήκη (Venice, 1872–94), vol. V, 12–13; A. Kaldellis, trans.,

If the Theotokos answered the prayers of those who besought her for wisdom, what did they do for her in return? Did they move on, or did they, like Romanos, contribute to the culture of her house? The clue lies in the reference to 'reading' in the title of the poem. This has been taken, in conjunction with the passage of Anna Komnene, to refer to the author's studies in general. But it can also be taken to refer to the act of reading aloud, in which case the author's plea is not so much for help in revising for his exams, as for inspiration in the recitation, whether improvised or prepared, that he is about to deliver. This interpretation is supported by the evidence of the numerous 'recited metrical prefaces' that have recently been studied by Theodora Antonopoulou.[40] These poems in twelve-syllable verse, dating from the twelfth to fourteenth centuries, were composed to be read aloud by their authors during church services, where they served to introduce the reading of a homily or hagiographical text, usually a well-known composition by an earlier author. Particularly relevant in the present context are works by the anonymous twelfth-century author known to scholarship as 'Manganeios Prodromos', whose massive poetic *oeuvre* preserved in Marc gr. XI.22 is being edited by Michael and Elizabeth Jeffreys.[41] Nine poems (n. 67–74, 103) were, according to their titles, written to be delivered in church; of these five (67–71, all unpublished[42]) were pronounced (67: ἀποστοματισθέντες) or read out (68: ἀναγνωσθέντες) in the church of the Theotokos *ta Kyrou*. The purpose and occasions of their production, which are richly alluded to in the texts, need fuller analysis than can be attempted here. However, some general observations are in order for our discussion of the Kyros church. The poems seem to have been written over more than one year between 1146 and 1149. They consist of lengthy supplications to the Virgin, with extravagant, theologically correct praise for her role as the Mother of God. They beg her favour for the emperor Manuel, in his struggles against the empire's enemies, but mainly they ask her to intercede on behalf of the poet's patron, the *sebastokratorissa* Eirene, Manuel's widowed sister-in-law,

---

Mothers and Sons, Fathers and Daughters: The Byzantine Family of Michael Psellos (Notre Dame, IN, 2006), 60–1.

[40] T. Antonopoulou, 'On the Reception of Homilies and Hagiography in Byzantium: the Recited Metrical Prefaces' in A. Rhoby and E. Schiffer, eds., *Imitatio – Aemulatio – Variatio* (Vienna, 2010), 57–78.

[41] For a list of the poems, see P. Magdalino, *The Empire of Manuel I Komnenos, 1143–1180* (Cambridge, 1993), 494–500.

[42] It was therefore not analysed in depth by Antonopoulou, 'On the Reception', 63–5. I am grateful to Elizabeth and Michael Jeffreys for sharing with me, many years ago, their transcriptions of the unpublished poems.

in her attempt to rehabilitate herself in the emperor's eyes from the unjust accusations that have caused her hardship and distress. The poems were delivered in the context of vigil services that were brightly lit with candles and richly scented with incense and rosewater. They address the clergy of the church. They all end with an invocation to the officiating priest to pronounce the blessing, and two of them clearly allude to a homily by St John Chrysostom that is to follow. More than once, the poet compares the Virgin to a silvered and gilded dove, surely an allusion to the precious effigy that was saved from the fire of 1197 and taken to the church of the Forty Martyrs.

The more than fifty recited metrical prefaces that Theodora Antonopoulou has identified suggest that the delivery of such personal compositions was common practice in the churches of Constantinople from the twelfth century. It was clearly not confined to one church. However, there are some indications that recitation by laymen was most usual in those churches that had particularly strong traditions of lay participation. The list of churches where 'Manganeios' read his poems is suggestive. Apart from the church of *ta Kyrou*, he performed at a private aristocratic chapel (72–4) and at the church of the Hodegetria (103).[43] The private chapel was clearly under the control of its lay owner, the *sebastokratorissa* Eirene, and the church of the Hodegetria, like that of *ta Kyrou*, was served by a lay confraternity. It is no coincidence that both churches are named by the twelfth-century canonist Theodore Balsamon among the sanctuaries where the laity habitually encroached upon the rights and the space of the clergy. Commenting on canon 79 of the Council in Trullo, forbidding laymen to enter the sanctuary, he writes that in the church of Christ at the Chalke, 'anyone who wishes can go in without hindrance', and, in a supplementary note, he adds that, 'I have often tried to prevent laymen from entering the holy sanctuary of the church of my All-holy Lady and Theotokos the Hodegetria, but to no avail, since they say that this is an ancient custom and should not be forbidden.'[44] In his commentary on canon 33 of the Trullanum, Balsamon singles out the church of the Theotokos *ta Kyrou*, along with the church of the Forty Martyrs, as one of the public churches where laymen had clerical functions (κληρικάτα ὀφφίκια) in contravention

---

[43] E. Miller, ed., 'Poésies inédites de Théodore Prodrome', *Annuaire de l'Association pour l'encouragement des études grecques*, 17 (1883), 20–30, 42–4. The poem at the Hodegetria is said to have been delivered on the occasion of the reading of the *Klementia* i.e. the apocryphal Pseudo-Clementine *Recognitions*.

[44] Ralles and Potles, [Again, sps] eds., Σύνταγμα τῶν θείων καὶ ἱερῶν κανόνων, vol. II, 466–7.

of the canon.⁴⁵ It is not known whether the Forty Martyrs also had a confraternity, although this is not unlikely in view of the church's location at the commercial heart of Constantinople and of the secular institutions, the school and notarial offices, which were attached to it.⁴⁶ Finally, one should note that the only other venue which is named for the liturgical recitation of a metrical preface was the Holy Shrine (Ἁγία Σορός) at the church of the Chalkoprateia;⁴⁷ this, like the churches of the Hodegetria and *ta Kyrou*, was a major cult centre of the Virgin Mary, and therefore most probably also the home of a pious lay association. Psellos describes the Friday evening 'readings' at the church of the Chalkoprateia as a major public attraction in the eleventh century.⁴⁸

We may therefore envisage a poet's 'reading' of his pious literary compositions, in conjunction with the works of established sacred authors like the church fathers, as a liturgical activity forming part of the devotions regularly performed by lay confraternities at the churches where they were based. Although the existing recited metrical prefaces appear to be an innovation of the twelfth century, the readings they accompanied were clearly an ancient liturgical institution, and we cannot exclude the possibility that readers before the twelfth century had sometimes added their own words, It is surely indicative that the same notion of reading is applied both to the established text and to the added preface. We should bear this ambiguity in mind when reading the information in the tenth-century *Patria* of Constantinople that many high-ranking men, including Michael Rangabe (the future Michael I) and the Caesar Bardas, had 'read' at the church of the Chalkoprateia.⁴⁹ That the learned laymen associated with the church made their own verbal contributions to its devotional life is clearly implied in a late ninth-century sermon of Euthymios, the future patriarch. Celebrating the feast of the church's *enkainia*, he says: 'Today is inaugurated a church of the unmarried spouse of the unimaginable Father, in which choirs of devout and very-learned men stand on

---

⁴⁵ Ibid., 380–1.
⁴⁶ R. Janin, *La géographie ecclésiastique de l'Empire byzantin*, vol. i, *Le siège de Constantinople et le patriarcat oecuménique, 3: Les églises et les monastères*, second edition (Paris, 1969), 485; Magdalino, *Studies on the History and Topography*, vol. i, 36–9.
⁴⁷ Antonopoulou, 'On the Reception of Homilies and Hagiography in Byzantium', 66.
⁴⁸ A. Littlewood, ed., *Michaelis Pselli Oratoria minora* (Leipzig, 1985), 138–51, no. 37; previously edited by P. Gautier, 'Éloge inédit du lecteur Jean Kroustoulas par Michel Psellos', *RSBN*, 17–19 (1980–2), 119–47; see below.
⁴⁹ T. Preger, ed., *Scriptores originum Constantinopolitanarum* (Leipzig, 1901–7), vol. II, 263.

either side and, providing much benefit to the unlettered, fully receive their recompense from on high.'[50]

Thus it is clear that the church of *ta Kyrou* was not unique as a venue for the devotions of high-status, learned laymen. The social profile of its congregation was equalled if not surpassed by that of the Chalkoprateia. Even so, the Kyros church remains impressive for its literary associations: its foundation by the well-known fifth-century poet Cyrus of Panopolis;[51] its reputation as the home of Byzantium's most famous and prolific hymnographer; the high literary profile of certain Kyriotai at the end of the tenth century; and the cult of the Theotokos Kyriotissa as a source of literary inspiration in the eleventh and twelfth centuries. We may plausibly infer that literature was the hallmark of the church's lay confraternity of the Kyriotai, and that although it surely did not preclude the other pious activities that confraternities performed, such as feeding and bathing the poor, and liturgical devotion to the icon of the Kyriotissa, the Kyriotai gave it priority in their functions and their membership – that they expressed their devotion to the Virgin primarily by chanting the hymns of the humble Romanos, or by composing poems and encomia in her honour. To return to John Geometres, this is surely the context in which to view much of his sacred *oeuvre*, especially his hymns and homilies to the Virgin.[52]

If high-powered literacy was indeed the hallmark of the Kyriotai, they must have constituted something of an elite club. It is true that the Theotokos *ta Kyrou*, being a καθολική ἐκκλησία, welcomed all types of worshippers, as Constantine Stilbes wistfully recalled when lamenting the church's incineration in 1197 – it had been a 'worldly sanctuary ... a haven to those in danger, an ark of salvation for every species'. However, the speed and the sumptuousness with which this imperial church[53] was rebuilt within the next seven years, as the archaeology and the imposing structure of the Kalenderhane bear witness, indicate that its clientele must have been very well-off, or well-connected, or both.

---

[50] M. Jugie, ed., 'Homélies mariales byzantines', *PO*, 16/2 (1922), 89: Σήμερον ναὸς ἐγκαινίζεται τῆς ἀπειρογάμου νύμφης τοῦ ἀκαλήπτου Πατρός, ἐν ᾧ χοροὶ εὐλαβῶν καὶ πολυμαθῶν ἀνδρῶν στοιχηδὸν παρεστείκασιν· καὶ τοῖς ἀγραμμάτοις ὄφελος οὐ μικρῶς γε παρέχοντες, τὴν ἀνωτάτω μισθαποδοσίαν ἄκρως εἰσδέχονται.
[51] On the founder, Cyrus of Panopolis, see Cameron, 'The Empress and the Poet'.
[52] *PPPG*, 106, cols. 812–48, 856–68; A. Wenger, *L'Assomption de la Très-sainte Vierge dans la tradition byzantine, du vie au xe siècle* (Paris, 1955), 185–201, 363–415; compare with Baun, *Tales from Another Byzantium*, 282–3.
[53] As mentioned by Nikephoros Ouranos in his letter (above, 9–11). This means, presumably, that it depended directly on the emperor for its maintenance.

The foregoing foray into the literature surrounding the church of *ta Kyrou* in the Middle Byzantine period has revealed the potential to be found in re-reading well-known Byzantine texts in the context of other texts whose information seems, on first reading, banal. The potential exists not only for a deeper reading of Byzantium but also, especially in the texts examined here, for a new, clear insight into the practice of reading in Byzantium. Thanks not least to the work of Elizabeth and Michael Jeffreys, we are now quite comfortable with the idea that Byzantine literature was, equally and inseparably, both oral and written. Reading was performance, not only of one's own compositions, but also and primarily, of the works of others, including the classics, both sacred and profane.[54] The texts pertaining to liturgical recitation at the church of *ta Kyrou* and other sanctuaries of the Theotokos in Constantinople demonstrate that such performance was not limited to the rhetorical 'theatre' of secular households, the imperial court, or the schoolroom, nor was it confined, in church, to feast days and special occasions; it was additionally, and perhaps even most fundamentally, a part of regular public worship.[55] It is therefore useful to conclude this discussion with a look at a text that positively celebrates the performative aspect of liturgical reading, and in doing so provides some valuable details about the occasion and the milieu. This is Psellos' 'Encomium for the monk John Kroustoulas who read aloud at the Holy Soros', which we have already mentioned as evidence for the popularity of readings at the Chalkoprateia church in the eleventh century.[56] It emerges that the readings took place on Friday evenings, and comprised several texts performed by a succession of readers, each of whom held a candle as he read. The readers mentioned by Psellos included, in addition to the monk John Kroustoulas, a bishop, and an 'intellectual' (λόγιος), presumably a layman, who also performed at the church of *ta Kyrou*. The occasions were open to all, and the audience ranged from bishops and senatorial dignitaries to the poor and needy. A charismatic reader like Kroustoulas could draw huge crowds who filled the church to overflowing. He made the text come alive and brought out the art of its rhetorical construction; like a modern concert soloist, or like an actor, he interpreted the composition that he performed. Readers were celebrities with reputations to uphold, and they created a spirit of

---

[54] See in general G. Cavallo, *Lire à Byzance* (Paris, 2006), especially 35–82.
[55] For rhetorical theatre, see Niels Gauls' chapter in the present volume.
[56] See above, n. 48. For translation and commentary by Stratis Papaioannou, see now C. Barber and S. Papaioannou, eds., *Michael Psellos on Literature and Art: A Byzantine Perspective on Aesthetics* (Notre Dame, IN, 2017), 218–44.

competition among their fans, if not among themselves. There is a hint that the competition extended to the churches in which they performed.[57]

Further Reading

The key primary source is: E. M. van Opstall, ed. and trans., *Jean Géomètre. Poèmes en hexamètres et en distiques élégiaques* (Leiden, 2008). Important studies include: T. Antonopoulou, 'On the Reception of Homilies and Hagiography in Byzantium: the Recited Metrical Prefaces' in A. Rhoby and E. Schiffer, eds., *Imitatio – Aemulatio – Variatio* (Vienna, 2010), 57–78; J. Baun, *Tales from Another Byzantium: Celestial Journey and Local Community on the Medieval Greek Apocrypha* (Cambridge, 2007); J. Koder, 'Romanos Melodos' in C. G. Conticello and V. Conticello, eds., *La théologie byzantine et sa tradition*, 2 vols. (Turnhout, 2002–15), vol. I, 115–94; C. L. Striker and Y. Doğan Kuban, eds., *Kalenderhane in Istanbul: The Buildings* (Mainz, 1997). The dossier of the church of the Theotokos *ta Kyrou* has just been enriched by Georgia Masaouti in her MA thesis at the University of Ioannina (G. Masaouti, Ἀνωνύμου: Λόγος διηγηματικὸς περὶ τῆς ἐν ἀρχῇ παραγωγῆς καὶ οἰκοδομῆς τοῦ πανσέπτου ναοῦ τῆς πανυμνήτου Θεοτόκου τῶν Κύρου (BHG 479i), ἀπὸ τὸ χειρόγραφο, Ἄθως Ἰβήρων 153 (Λάμπρος 4548)', unpublished MA Thesis, University of Ioannina (2017)). Masaouti presents the first critical edition of an anonymous narrative of the church's foundation. She dates this text to the late tenth century and places it in the context of the Kyriotai confraternity.

---

[57] The possibility is raised by a recent study of the cult of the Theotokos at the Chalkoprateia and its rivalry with the church of the Blachernae: D. Krausmüller, 'Making the Most of Mary: The Cult of the Virgin in the Chalkoprateia from Late Antiquity to the Tenth Century' in L. Brubaker and M. Cunningham, eds., *The Cult of the Mother of God in Byzantium: Texts and Images* (Farnham, 2012), 219–45.

CHAPTER 5

Manuscript Notes and the Black Death in Rural Cyprus

Tassos Papacostas

The Black Death swept through Europe and the Mediterranean from 1347 to 1352, wiping out a very large proportion of these regions' population. The aim of this chapter is to look at some neglected evidence from Cyprus.[1] The significance of this material lies primarily in the light it sheds on aspects of the island's little-known rural world in late medieval times. It should be stressed at the outset that it does not contribute to aspects of Black Death studies that are currently being debated, such as the epidemiology of the disease;[2] nor does it easily lend itself to interpretations concerning the long-term economic, social, demographic and other repercussions of the pandemic. Despite these limitations, however, the evidence presented in this chapter does suggest a hitherto unsuspected scenario for the spread of the mid-fourteenth-century outbreak across Cyprus. Equally importantly, it offers invaluable clues about social conditions and the likely impact of the effects of the pandemic on building activity.

The Evidence for the Impact of the Black Death

Discussions of the evidence about and the impact of the Black Death on the island of Cyprus are neither numerous nor lengthy. The earliest are

---

[1] Some of the issues investigated in this chapter were presented at seminars or conferences in the past (Cambridge 2000, Oxford 2001, Kalamazoo 2006). It was on such occasions that I had the opportunity to benefit from relevant comments and discussions with both Elizabeth and Michael Jeffreys, with whom I am fortunate enough to have worked as their student and colleague. With this contribution that is largely based on the interpretation of exiguous written evidence and involves manuscripts and prosopography, two among their numerous scholarly pursuits, I would like to acknowledge in a small way my debt to them.

[2] The long-held view that the Black Death was really a bubonic plague caused by the *Yersinia pestis* bacillus carried by parasitic fleas (*Xenopsylla cheopis*) on rats has been challenged, most notably by G. Twigg, *The Black Death: A Biological Reappraisal* (London, 1984), and more recently and vigorously by S. K. Cohn, *The Black Death Transformed: Disease and Culture in Early Renaissance Europe* (London, 2002) and S. K. Cohn, 'The Black Death: End of a Paradigm', *AHR*, 107 (2002), 703–38.

also the most detailed, starting with the seventeenth-century Venetian Giovanni Francesco Loredano's influential but highly problematic history of the Lusignan kingdom.[3] Writing under the pseudonym Henrico Giblet (the name of a well-known family of medieval Cyprus), he claims that the plague first appeared in early 1348 in the region of Famagusta whence it spread all over the island and lasted for a whole year. Loredano describes in graphic detail the ravages of the pestilence among the population. The king is said to have sought refuge in the 'Castello Dio d'Amore' (Saint Hilarion), taking measures to contain the contagion whose effects subsequently led him to ennoble numerous foreigners who took the names of the (presumably decimated) old noble families.[4] Most of the details provided by Loredano, although not unlikely and indeed reminiscent of descriptions in sources pertaining to affected areas beyond the island's shores, cannot be corroborated by earlier textual evidence. His account formed the basis of that of the eighteenth-century French historian, merchant and landowner in Cyprus Dominique Jauna who often elaborated and added further details, stating for example that the king brought in specialist physicians from abroad to treat the sick, something that again does not find confirmation in earlier sources.[5]

The most comprehensive recent discussion of the Black Death on the island suggests that it reached its shores from Syria by the late summer of 1347.[6] There is, however, some inconclusive evidence which may indicate that this happened somewhat earlier. Permission to bury people other than nuns ('personas estraneas') in the cemetery of the Benedictine nunnery of Saint Anne of Nicosia was granted to the abbess by the pope in July 1347, perhaps suggesting that the pandemic had already claimed its first victims by the early summer of that year (allowing for the request to reach the papal curia at Avignon and the response to be issued).[7] This, however,

---

[3] C. Schabel, 'A Knight's Tale: Giovan Francesco Loredano's Fantastic *Historie de' re Lusignani*' in B. Arbel, E. Chayes and H. Hendrix, eds., *Cyprus and the Renaissance (1450–1650)* (Turnhout, 2012), 357–90.

[4] G. Loredano, *Historie de' re' Lusignani, libri undeci, publicate da Henrico Giblet Cavalier* (Venice, 1660), 330–1.

[5] D. Jauna, *Histoire générale des roïaumes de Chypre, de Jerusalem, d'Arménie, et d'Egypte* (Leiden, 1785), vol. II, 824, 828; on the author, see B. Imhaus, 'Quelques remarques à propos de Dominique Jauna', *EKEE*, 27 (2001), 127–37; and P. Trélat, 'Clio sous le regard d'Hermès: itinéraires et oeuvre de Dominique Jauna, historien de Chypre et des croisades', *Crusades*, 10 (2011), 147–74.

[6] G. Grivaud, *Villages désertés à Chypre (fin XIIe–fin XIXe siècle)* (Nicosia, 1998), 294; the same date was suggested by P. Ziegler, *The Black Death* (London, 1969), 111.

[7] W. H. Rudt de Collenberg, 'Les grâces papales, autres que les dispenses matrimoniales, accordées à Chypre de 1305 à 1378', *EKEE*, 8 (1975–7), 187–252 at 247; C. Schabel and J. Richard, eds., *Bullarium Cyprium* (Nicosia, 2010–12), vol. III, 226, no. t-238.

would date the outbreak on Cyprus too early compared to its spread elsewhere in the eastern Mediterranean, and at about the same time as at Constantinople (early July 1347), where the contagion appears to have been introduced from the Black Sea in the late spring of that year.[8] Much more secure evidence for the chronology of its spread on Cyprus is offered by a series of surviving funerary slabs from Nicosia, hastily carved (often using earlier tombstones) and commemorating the death primarily of nuns and aristocratic patrons of another Benedictine abbey of that city, namely Our Lady of Tortosa. The cause of death is never mentioned in the relevant inscriptions, but the dates on these funerary monuments demonstrate in the most unequivocal manner that mortality rates did not peak until nine months later, in April 1348.[9] This is in accordance with what has been observed elsewhere, with a slowdown during winter and a more vigorous advance in the spring, and provides yet another case of the well-documented effects of the plague on monastic communities.[10] The suggested route of the contagion from Syria to Cyprus also remains to be proved. A parallel is certainly provided by a later outbreak (c. 1449–51), reportedly caused by the arrival at Limassol of two infected Venetian ships from Syria.[11] Egypt, with which there were trade links during this period, is another possible source. In both Syria and Egypt, however, the pandemic did not reach its peak until the winter of 1348–9, more than six months later than on Cyprus, although it is already attested at Alexandria in the autumn of 1347, at Gaza in the late spring of the following year, at Jerusalem in June/July and at Damascus and Aleppo in October (1348).[12] This suggests that it may have been transmitted to the island before reaching the Levantine coastlands, and therefore that it followed a different route, most probably through the Aegean where it is already recorded in

---

[8] O. J. Benedictow, *The Black Death, 1346–1353: The Complete History* (Woodbridge, 2004), 61–93, and M. W. Dols, *The Black Death in the Middle East* (Princeton, 1977), 50–65, on its spread across the Mediterranean.

[9] Ten securely dated cases: B. Imhaus, *Lacrimae Cypriae: Les larmes de Chypre* (Nicosia, 2004), vol. I, 51 (no. 99), 54 (no. 105), 84 (no. 159), 114 (no. 227), 115 (no. 229), 140–2 (nos 268–70), 202 (no. 379), 312 (no. 589); 16 (no. 16) and 337 (no. 660) may also be related to the outbreak); vol. II, 196.

[10] G. Andenna, 'Effetti della peste nera sul reclutamento monastico e sul patrimonio ecclesiastico' in *La peste nera: dati di una realtà ed elementi di una interpretazione. Atti del xxx convegno storico internazionale, Todi 10–13 ottobre 1993* (Spoleto, 1994), 319–47, R. Horrox, *The Black Death* (New York, NY, 1994), 67–70, 253–6, and Dols, *The Black Death*, 167–8, on monastic communities; D. Herlihy, *The Black Death and the Transformation of the West*, ed. S. K. Cohn (Cambridge, MA, 1997), 24, and Benedictow, *The Black Death*, 59–60, on the pattern of spread.

[11] J. Darrouzès, 'Notes pour servir à l'histoire de Chypre (quatrième article)', Κυπριακαί Σπουδαί, 23 (1959), 46.

[12] J.-N. Biraben, *Les hommes et la peste en France et dans les pays européens et méditerranéens* (Paris, 1975–6), vol. I, 74–81; Dols, *Black Death*, 57–62, 155.

the autumn of 1347 following its appearance at Constantinople in the course of the summer.[13]

The evidence for the effects of the Black Death on Cyprus is circumstantial at best. There are no contemporary sources such as those available for Italian cities or the manorial court rolls for England that systematically recorded deaths of tenants. The main narrative texts that cover the period date only from the fifteenth and sixteenth centuries, and in any case their treatment of the subject is extraordinarily brief (chronicles of Leontios Machairas, Florio Bustron, 'Amadi', Diomede Strambali). According to these and depending on the author, the deadly pestilence claimed between one and two thirds of the population.[14] For more evidence we must turn elsewhere. A note in a fourteenth-century Gospel commentary (Par. gr. 1216) puts the daily death toll at an unnamed, presumably urban location (Nicosia? Famagusta?), at 500, while other sources suggest that there was no let-up, as soon thereafter there were earthquakes, an invasion of locusts and a drought that caused severe famine.[15] Although corroborating archaeological evidence is lacking and would in any case be difficult to interpret, the excavation at the site of the old Town Hall in the heart of Nicosia has brought to light next to a church a mass burial containing the remains of at least six infants and a child whose death may be related to the upheavals of this period; further analysis of the skeletal material may offer helpful indications.[16]

In his detailed account of the plague in Egypt and Syria the near-contemporary Arab historian al-Makrizi (1363/4–1442) reports that the Cypriots were expecting the end of the world after witnessing the epidemic

---

[13] Benedictow, *Black Death*, 61, 69.

[14] Grivaud, *Villages désertés*, 275–6 and 439, with bibliography.

[15] Darrouzès, 'Notes (quatrième article)', 40; Grivaud, *Villages désertés*, 431, 435, 437; K. Komodikes, *Οι πληροφορίες των Βραχέων Χρονικών για την Κύπρο. Η κατάταξη και ο σχολιασμός τους* (Nicosia, 2006), 214–15, appendix xxxviii.

[16] Y. Violaris, 'Excavations at the Site of Palaion Demarcheion, Lefkosia', *Cahiers du Centre d'Etudes Chypriotes*, 34 (2004), 70; the outbreak of 1363 is said to have affected children in particular: R. M. Dawkins, ed., *Leontios Makhairas. Recital Concerning the Sweet Land of Cyprus Entitled 'Chronicle'* (Oxford, 1932), vol. II, 60; M. Pieris and A. Nicolaou-Konnari, eds., *Leontios Makhairas. Χρονικό της Κύπρου. Παράλληλη διπλωματική έκδοση των χειρογράφων* (Nicosia, 2003), 101. The evidence from skeletal remains is controversial: in 2000 it was announced that DNA with *Yersinia pestis* was identified among purported Black Death victims in a mass burial at Montpellier, and in 2007 in burials associated with other outbreaks, although it has also been argued that the molecular evidence is inconclusive; see M. Drancourt et al., 'Yersinia pestis Orientalis in Remains of Ancient Plague Patients', *Emerging Infectious Diseases*, 13.2 (2007), available on www.cdc.gov/eid/content/13/2/332.htm (accessed 10 November 2017), with earlier bibliography.

and the violent storms and earthquakes that followed.[17] The chronicle of the Augustinian canon Henry Knighton, writing in the later fourteenth century at Leicester, depicts a similarly apocalyptic and highly imaginative picture, claiming that 'in Cyprus mountains were levelled blocking rivers and causing many citizens to drown and towns to be destroyed'.[18] More recent historians, inspired by the above accounts, have stated that the entire population of the island perished and that Cyprus lay deserted thereafter. This claim, which can be traced back at least to the eighteenth century and the *History of the Huns, Turks and Mongols* by the French orientalist Joseph Deguignes (Paris, 1756–8), was taken up by Justus Friedrich Karl Hecker in *The Black Death in the Fourteenth Century* (Berlin, 1832) and almost became a *topos* in nineteenth-century literature on the plague through the numerous editions of Hecker's English translation (London, 1833).[19]

Needless to say, both the medieval reports and more recent assessments are clearly grossly exaggerated; yet there is no doubt that the impact of the Black Death was severe enough to cause major social and economic upheavals. The island's vulnerable coastline was perhaps left exposed, as suggested by the Turkish attack on the fortress at Kyrenia in December 1347, well after the outbreak but before its peak in the following spring.[20] The severe outbreak of *c.* 1361–3 was similarly accompanied by Turkish raids on the north coast, facilitated, according to Leontios Machairas, by the fact that the island was left empty and defenceless.[21] A certain degree of moral laxity, well documented in other parts of the world during this period, is implied by papal documents of August 1348, although whether it can be associated with conditions at the time of the outbreak cannot be ascertained: one granted the right of absolution to Abbot Guido of Premonstratensian Bellapais (overlooking the island's north coast) for monks who had rebelled against the rules of their order; another two granted the same right to the Latin archbishop Philip of Nicosia, in this case for fifty individuals who had attacked members of the clergy and for another fifty, including monks and priests, who were living in concubinage.[22]

---

[17] G. Wiet, 'La grande peste noire en Syrie et en Égypte' in *Études d'orientalisme dédiées à la mémoire de Lévi-Provençal* (Paris, 1962), vol. I, 370–1.
[18] Horrox, *Black Death*, 76.
[19] For example in F. A. Gasquet, *The Great Pestilence (AD 1348–9), Now Commonly Known as the Black Death* (London, 1893),2; on Hecker, see Herlihy, *Black Death*, 19–20.
[20] P. Schreiner, *Die byzantinischen Kleinchroniken* (Vienna, 1975–9), vol. I, 206.
[21] Makhairas, *Chronicle*, ed. Dawkins, vol. II, 120; *Makhairas*, eds. Pieris and Nicolaou-Konnari, 135.
[22] Rudt de Collenberg, 'Les grâces papales', 249; Schabel and Richard, eds., *Bullarium Cyprium*, vol. III, 242, nos. t-323, t-325.

The decline of the kingdom's old nobility has been at least partly attributed to the Black Death. Residing mainly at Famagusta and Nicosia, this group was particularly vulnerable and remains the only social class about which some detailed information has been preserved. Rudt de Collenberg's meticulous study based on the Vatican archives has shown that out of 105 noble families attested in the thirteenth century, 26 – that is, a quarter – disappeared after the middle of the fourteenth century.[23] Several matrimonial dispensations granted by Pope Clement VI to Cypriots in 1349 cite the lack of other suitable candidates as a result of the plague ('*paucitas nobilium ratione epidemiae*') as the main reason for the need to regularise marriages between couples related within prohibited degrees of consanguinity or affinity; a few months earlier, in September 1348, the same pope had responded favourably to a request from the Latin archbishop of Nicosia to regularise such marriages, although the blame was put on the position of the island among 'infideles' rather than on the epidemic.[24] The archbishop's reaction to mixed marriages between Greeks and Latins and the ensuing measures taken in 1353 may also be related to the demographic effects of the pestilence; two years earlier the same effects were cited as the cause for the cancellation by the pope of the preaching of a new crusade on the island against the Turks of Asia Minor, while the documented doubling of the price of slaves has been attributed to a labour shortage, in all likelihood another result of the pestilence.[25]

Besides its severe demographic impact, the Black Death had of course economic consequences, as elsewhere in both Europe and the Mediterranean. On Cyprus these repercussions were amplified by further outbreaks

---

[23] W. H. Rudt de Collenberg, 'The Fate of Frankish Noble Families Settled in Cyprus' in P. W. Edbury, ed., *Crusade and Settlement* (Cardiff, 1985), 268–72 at 270; Grivaud, *Villages désertés*, 294.

[24] W. H. Rudt de Collenberg, 'Les dispenses matrimoniales accordées à l'Orient Latin selon les registres du Vatican d'Honorius III à Clément VII (1223–1385)', *MEFRM*, 89 (1977), 11–93, nos. 100, 101, 104, 105 (similar formulae are used in later dispensations: nos. 136, 137); Schabel and Richard, eds., *Bullarium Cyprium*, vol. III, 245, no. t-338, and 249–62, nos. t-362, t-377, t-423, t-437; N. Coureas and C. Schabel, eds., *The Cartulary of the Cathedral of Holy Wisdom of Nicosia* (Nicosia, 1997), 300–1.

[25] C. Schabel, trans., *The Synodicum Nicosiense and Other Documents of the Latin Church of Cyprus, 1196–1373* (Nicosia, 2001), 268–70; see also A. Nicolaou-Konnari, 'Greeks' in A. Nicolaou-Konnari and C. Schabel, eds., *Cyprus. Society and Culture 1191–1374* (Leiden, 2005), 59–60; P. Edbury, "Ἡ πολιτικὴ ἱστορία τοῦ μεσαιωνικοῦ βασιλείου ἀπὸ τὴ βασιλεία τοῦ Οὔγου Δ' μέχρι τὴ βασιλεία τοῦ Ἰανοῦ' in T. Papadopoullos, ed., *Ἱστορία τῆς Κύπρου*, vol. IV, *Μεσαιωνικὸν βασίλειον – Ἑνετοκρατία* (Nicosia, 1995), vol. IV.2 90–1 n. 138; N. Coureas, 'Economy' in Nicolaou-Konnari and Schabel, eds., *Cyprus*, 152.

in the early 1360s, in the 1390s and during the first half of the following century.²⁶ Peter Edbury has suggested that the manumission of increasing numbers of serfs during the fourteenth century may be related to economic pressure resulting from the dramatic fall in population. The same author has also argued that, with the subsequent decrease in both production and consumption, the volume of trade in urban centres must have declined, leading to a proportional fall in the state's revenues from taxes and dues at a time when a significant proportion of the country's wealth was generated by commercial activity.²⁷ In the same period a reduction has been observed in the revenues of the Hospitaller Order from its substantial Cypriot estates that, according to Gilles Grivaud, must also be linked to the drop in population.²⁸

Not surprisingly, all discussions of the Black Death in Cyprus which, like those concerning other Byzantine and formerly Byzantine territories, have been few and brief, were until now based on the restricted evidence from the island's urban milieu, where most of the relevant sources originate, and remain unanimous on its dire consequences.²⁹ There is, however, a hitherto unexploited source that sheds, albeit indirectly, some welcome light on the fate of the rural population of a particular region, in the mountainous hinterland of Paphos. It consists of a long series of marginal notes in a manuscript from the monastery of Hiereon (μονὴ τῶν Ἱερέων), today known as Hagia Mone, on the western flank of Mount Panagia (Fig. 5.1).

---

[26] Source bibliography in Grivaud, *Villages désertés*, 439; see also Komodikes, Οι πληροφορίες των Βραχέων Χρονικών, 215–19, and A. Dincer, 'Disease in a Sunny Climate: Effects of the Plague on Family and Wealth in Cyprus in the 1360s' in S. Cavaciocchi, ed., *Le interazioni fra economia e ambiente biologico nell'Europa preindustriale sec. XIII–XVIII* (Florence, 2010), 531–40.

[27] P. W. Edbury, 'Some Cultural Implications of the Latin Conquest of Cyprus' in J. A. Koumoulides, ed., *Cyprus: The Legacy. Historic Landmarks that Influenced the Art of Cyprus, Late Bronze Age to CE 1600* (Bethesda, MD, 1999), 104; Edbury, "Ἡ πολιτικὴ ἱστορία', 91; see also Schabel and Richard, eds., *Bullarium Cyprium*, vol. III, 264, no. t-443 (September 1349).

[28] A. Luttrell, 'The Hospitallers in Cyprus: 1310–1378', Κυπριακαὶ Σπουδαί, 50 (1986), 164–6; Grivaud, *Villages désertés*, 294.

[29] On Byzantium, see C. S. Bartsocas, 'Two Fourteenth-century Greek Descriptions of the "Black Death"', *Journal of the History of Medicine and Allied Sciences*, 21 (1966), 394–400; K. P. Kostes, Στον καιρό της πανώλης. Εικόνες από τις κοινωνίες της ελληνικής χερσονήσου, 1405–1905 αιώνας (Herakleion, 1995); M.-H. Congourdeau, 'Pour une étude de la peste noire à Byzance' in M. Balard et al., eds., Εὐψυχία. *Mélanges offerts à Hélène Ahrweiler* (Paris, 1998), vol. I, 149–63; and M.-H. Congourdeau, 'La Peste Noire à Constantinople de 1348 à 1466', *Medicina nei Secoli*, 11 (1999), 377–90.

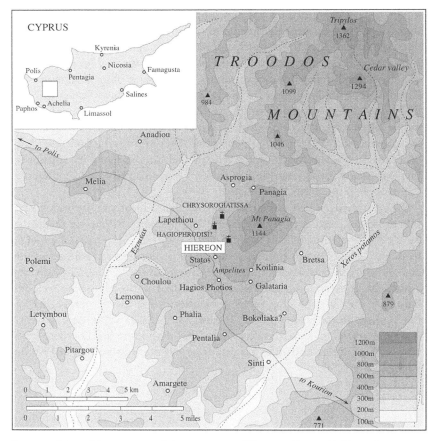

Fig. 5.1 Map of the area around the monastery of Hiereon, Cyprus (© Tassos Papacostas, based on the *Topographical Map of Cyprus* 1:50,000 series K.717, Department of Lands and Surveys, Cyprus)

The Marginal Notes of the Parisinus Graecus 1588

The Par. gr. 1588 contains a standard version of the *Synaxarion* of Constantinople but preserves no colophon, as it is mutilated at the end. It can nevertheless be dated to the early twelfth century and attributed with certainty to the hand of the monk Klemes of the monastery of Hiereon. Klemes is securely attested in 1112, when he copied the Par.gr. 1531, containing saints' lives and homilies, for the abbot Gerasimos of the same monastery. In 1142, by now himself at the head of the community, he restored and rebound the mid-tenth-century Par. gr. 668 (homilies of John Chrysostom). According to the ownership notes, two more manuscripts now in the Bibliothèque Nationale (Par. gr. 648 and 1534) also belonged either to Klemes or to his monastic community.[30] The evidence for this bibliophile monk's activity at a remote monastery in the western Troodos suggests that Hiereon was not an altogether insignificant establishment. It is first attested in 963 and continued functioning after the conquest of Cyprus by Richard the Lionheart in 1191 and the island's purchase by Guy de Lusignan in the following year. It is occasionally mentioned in later sources, both in Lusignan (1192–1473) and Venetian times (1473–1570/71), and eventually became a *metochion* of the much better-known monastery of Kykko, a status it preserves to this day. A late tradition according to which it was founded in early Christian times (by Nicholas of Myra and a certain Eutychios) cannot be verified.[31]

As already mentioned, the Par. gr. 1588 is mutilated: the last days of July and the entire month of August are missing from the *synaxarion*. Nevertheless, the surviving commemorations for the remaining eleven months of the year are accompanied by no fewer than 276 marginal notes, 85 per cent of these bearing a date. These were painstakingly deciphered and published by Jean Darrouzès in 1951 but curiously never attracted the attention they deserve.[32] Although the earliest note appears to belong to the mid-twelfth century and records the death of the aforementioned Klemes (f. 54r), the first dated entry was written in 1203, recording the death of a monk (f. 246v), and the latest in September 1570, recording rather poignantly the fall of Nicosia to the invading Ottoman army (f. 10v). Nothing was added to the manuscript's margins after this date. The vast majority of entries belong to the late thirteenth and the fourteenth centuries: some 90 per cent record donations to Hiereon and deaths of either monks or

---

[30] J. Darrouzès, 'Un obituaire chypriote: le Parisinus graecus 1588', Κυπριακαί Σπουδαί, 15 (1951), 25–62; C. N. Constantinides and R. Browning, *Dated Greek Manuscripts from Cyprus to the Year 1570* (Washington, D. C., 1993), nos. 6, 7, 107*; J. Darrouzès, 'Manuscrits originaires de Chypre à la Bibliothèque Nationale de Paris', *REB*, 8 (1950), 179, 189; the Par. gr. 83 may have also belonged to Hiereon: J. Darrouzès, 'Autres manuscrits originaires de Chypre', *REB*, 15 (1957), 152.

[31] Further details and bibliography on the monastery's history and archaeology in T. Papacostas, 'Byzantine Cyprus: The Testimony of Its Churches, 650–1200', 3 vols, unpublished DPhil thesis, University of Oxford (1999), vol. I, 94–5, 2: 39–40, 97–8; K. Kokkinophtas and I. Theocharides, Μετόχια της Ιεράς Μονής Κύκκου. Μονή των Ιερέων ή Αγία Μονή (Nicosia, 1999); S. Perdikis, 'Le monastère des Hiereôn (des Prêtres) à Paphos. Du paganisme au christianisme', *Cahiers du Centre d'Etudes Chypriotes*, 43 (2013), 227–42.

[32] Darrouzès, 'Un obituaire chypriote'. The conclusions drawn and statistical figures given below take into account only dated or datable notes.

villagers from the neighbouring rural communities. The remaining notes deal with natural disasters, usually in the area of the monastery, and with a small number of events further afield, including the fall of crusader outposts on the mainland in the second half of the thirteenth century. This rather exceptional interest in the fate of mainland strongholds may have something to do with the (unknown) local feudal lord who perhaps maintained links across the sea. More intriguing is the absence of any record of major local events, at least in periods when there was demonstrably an interest in adding to the manuscript's margins. Thus there is no reference to the Genoese invasion of 1373 and the subsequent occupation of Famagusta (the island's major port at the time), nor to the Mameluke raids that culminated with the invasion of 1426, and nothing about the accession or death of Lusignan kings who had dealings with the monastery (only the death of Henry II in 1324 is recorded: f. 179v).[33]

Nevertheless these notes offer novel insights into and shed ample light on a large and varied number of important issues that await further investigation: the fate of Orthodox monasticism under Latin rule; the role and functioning of a monastery within a nexus of families in a remote mountainous region of close-knit rural communities; the agrarian economy and land-ownership pattern of such areas; the processes of acculturation that took place in late medieval Cyprus; and a host of other topics such as toponymy, anthroponymy, prosopography and, most importantly, literacy and language.[34] These notes in fact probably provide the most extensive evidence on which to base a study of rural society in medieval Cyprus, away from the royal court in Nicosia and the mercantile communities of cosmopolitan Famagusta.

The format of the publication by Jean Darrouzès follows the layout of the *synaxarion* itself. Since the latter is a calendar of the ecclesiastical year, the marginal notes appear in a sequence following the day of the month rather than year, month and day. This has obscured a crucial fact that is immediately obvious as soon as the notes are rearranged chronologically: a very uneven distribution of recorded deaths and donations across the decades is thus revealed (Fig. 5.2).[35] The available sample, although not huge, is large enough to allow some valid conclusions. At the same time it should be stressed that what we have is certainly not a complete record of

[33] Peter II, James I, Janus and an unnamed king are mentioned in the context of various grants to the monastery (f. 60r, 76r, 91r, 115v, 227v).
[34] Constantinides and Browning, *Dated Greek Manuscripts*, 75–6.
[35] The uneven chronological distribution is also discernible in the table of dated notes provided by Darrouzès, 'Un obituaire chypriote', 55.

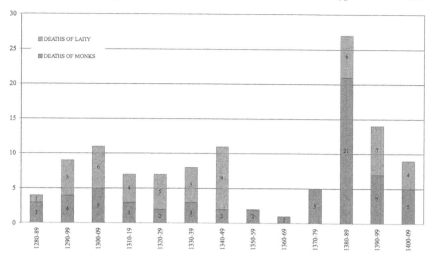

Fig. 5.2 Chart showing deaths per decade recorded in the margins of the Par. gr. 1588 (© Tassos Papacostas)

all the deaths and donations at Hiereon. Although approximately one hundred members of the community are recorded for the Lusignan period, it is clear that a far greater number had joined its ranks and died there throughout these centuries without leaving any trace in the written record. The approximate size of the community may be indicated by an undated (probably fourteenth-century) tax exemption concerning eighteen monks of the monastery (f. 69r), although this number perhaps includes those residing at its dependencies (f. 10v, 71r, 91r, 145r, 175r, 220r). The chart shows clearly a rise in recorded deaths from the 1370s to the end of the century. This period coincides with the hegoumenate of Germanos from the nearby village of Polemi, who was elected on 8 May 1369 and died on 22 July 1396 (f. 213r, 265r). During his time at the helm of the community some sixty notes were added to the manuscript's margins, including seventeen by Germanos himself. It is clear then that the rise in recorded deaths is due not to the ravages of any epidemic or natural disaster in the last decades of the fourteenth century, but to the diligence of the monks in recording events at Hiereon under the guidance of Germanos. The same cannot be said of the recorded donations in the middle of the century, for their rise must surely reflect a real and dramatic increase. As will be shown below, this has to be related to the Black Death.

The Year 1348 at Hiereon

The marginal notes in the Par. gr. 1588 contain no direct reference whatsoever to an outbreak of plague, either in 1347–8 or at any later date. A look at what did make it into the record at the time of the Black Death, however, is both surprising and instructive. First, the number of deaths registered in the late 1340s is not particularly high (Fig. 5.2). That of George the son of Michael tou Lemoneos and his wife Michalou, who bequeathed to the monastery an ox and ten *modioi* of wheat, is recorded on 5 April 1348 (f. 190r) and perhaps represents early and sporadic casualties among the local population. One month later Michael tou Koubara passed away and made an identical bequest to the monastery (f. 210v), although whether he was also a victim of the plague is far from clear. Then the *chartophylax* of the church of Paphos, Gregory, his son Michael and sister Segete, all died within two days in late May 1348 (f. 227r), almost certainly as a result of the epidemic. Gregory's office, however, suggests that he and his family, although presumably hailing from the region of Hiereon, were probably residing at Paphos, on the coast, and not in the vicinity of the monastery, although news of their death reached the community to which they bequeathed an ox. The cause of death of the monk (at Hiereon?) and *anagnostes* Gerasimos on 17 June, on the other hand, is impossible to determine (f. 239v).

These deaths in the spring and early summer of 1348 of course broadly coincide with the peak of mortality at Nicosia, as attested by the funerary inscriptions mentioned above, which show that the pestilence was at its deadliest there during April. Leaving aside the family of the *chartophylax*, only the death of George and Michalou on the same day in early April may be associated with the epidemic in the region of Hiereon. This does not amount to much at a time when the population of the urban centres is thought to have been decimated. Of course there is the possibility that the community cared to register only the demise of the few benefactors who left a bequest, thus explaining the small number of recorded deaths. Yet the number of donations (discussed below) in precisely the same period suggests that the monastery was highly regarded among the local population whose loyalty it commanded and that, had the death toll been greater, it would have certainly benefited from many more legacies.[36]

---

[36] For the willingness of peasant families to make donations see A. Laiou, 'The Peasant as Donor (13th–14th Centuries)' in J.-M. Spieser and E. Yota, eds., *Donation et donateurs dans le monde byzantin. Actes du colloque de l'Université de Fribourg, 13–15 mars 2008* (Paris, 2012), 107–24.

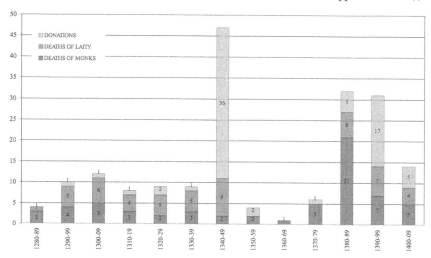

Fig. 5.3 Chart showing donations and deaths per decade recorded in the margins of the Par. gr. 1588 (© Tassos Papacostas)

The evidence presented so far would suggest, rather surprisingly, that Hiereon and its immediate region were hardly affected by the pestilence. That the dearth of registered deaths is definitely not due to the lack of a willing pen, or indeed of an available hand at the monastery, is amply proven by the staggering number of donations recorded for the same period (Fig. 5.3), coming from entire families, couples, but also single individuals including women. Among the sixty-seven fourteenth-century donations almost half are dated between March and June of 1348. Whereas mortality at Nicosia peaked in April, the donations to Hiereon reached their climax in May and June (eleven and ten respectively); the disparity may reflect the time it took for news from the capital and other lowland areas, that must have been affected as badly, to reach the distant monastery.

There can be no doubt that these donations are linked to the outbreak. But they are certainly not the result of a surplus of land and assets that might have arisen following a high mortality rate among the rural population, for this would have presumably occurred slightly later, in the following months or years, something that is not borne out by the evidence. Rather they represent the expression of the piety and fear of some forty individuals who, by offering some of their most valuable assets to their local monastery, sincerely hoped that they might be spared. And indeed, at least some of them were. A few telling examples will suffice to illustrate the point. John tou Boutin, his wife Eirene and his (unnamed) mother offered a cow, a heifer and a copper cauldron to the monastery on 24 June 1348, presumably a couple of weeks after news of the epidemic's ravages reached their region; almost exactly one year later, on 1 July 1349, and well after the end of the pestilence, John and his wife Eirene tou Kourtesi, most probably the same couple, donated a vineyard at Ampelites and four animals (σφακτά); John tou Boutin returned to the monastery at least once more, for on 6 March 1351 he presented the community with another vineyard at Ampelites, three oxen and a copper vessel for the salvation of his and his wife Eirene's souls (f. 243v, 250r, 174r). A second example concerns a family from Pentalia. John Xenos and his wife visited the monastery on 8 April of an unknown year, perhaps 1348, and became *synadelphoi* offering three oxen;[37] on 20 December 1348 the same couple – the wife's name is given as Anna tou Lalouta – gave an ox, while one year later, on 8 December 1349, they offered together another ox (f. 191v, 95r, 78v). The family's attachment to Hiereon did not stop with their donations in the aftermath of the Black Death but continued into the next generation, for John's son Theodoret became a monk at the monastery where he died in 1387, while another individual associated with the family, Joachim, also became a monk and died there in 1378 (f. 112r, 117r). A more distant family member, Theodore the son of George Xenos, joined Hiereon in 1375 as the monk Thomas (f. 76r).

Some families are particularly well represented among the approximately three hundred individuals recorded in the margins of the Par. gr. 1588.[38] A case in point is the Laloutas (Λαλουτᾶς) family, from which the wife of the aforementioned John Xenos issued. No fewer than a dozen Laloutades based in several nearby villages (Phalia, Pentalia, Statos) appear between

---

[37] The precise meaning of the term *synadelphos* in not entirely clear, but it must refer to some kind of association with the monastery, perhaps even a type of confraternity that is also attested elsewhere on Cyprus: J. Darrouzès, 'Notes pour servir à l'histoire de Chypre (troisième article)', *Κυπριακαί Σπουδαί*, 22 (1958), 227–31; F. Evangelatou-Notara, Ἀδελφᾶτον. Ψυχικόν. Evidence from Notes on Manuscripts', *Byzantion*, 75 (2005), 164–70; and G. Grivaud, 'Fortunes and Misfortunes of a Small Byzantine Foundation' in A. Weyl Carr, ed., *Asinou Across Time. Studies in the Architecture and Murals of the Panagia Phorbiotissa, Cyprus* (Washington, D. C., 2012), 26–7. It involved a donation perhaps in exchange for either an annual allowance or more probably prayers and commemoration after death. Nine individuals (including women) and nine couples (including Latins) are thus described in connection with Hiereon.

[38] The vast majority are included in E. Trapp et al., eds., *PLP* (Vienna, 1979–96); also published as CD-ROM (Vienna, 2001).

1336 and 1421 in connection with the monastery as monks, donors and patrons.[39] In late May and early June 1348 two couples and one individual belonging to this family offered between them a donkey, an ox, a cow and a heifer to Hiereon (f. 106v, 118r, 231v, 232r, 261v). It is noteworthy that their donations were restricted to animals and no member of the family is recorded in connection with a land grant, although they are known to have owned at least one property at Ampelites (f. 237r).

The generosity of these patrons and the fact that some owned several properties suggest that they were not altogether unimportant, at least locally. Their legal status, however, is not indicated in the notes. If they were not free peasants (*francomati*) but serfs (*paroikoi*, like most of the rural population), their relatively comfortable situation would be somewhat surprising, although there are indications in the sources of the period suggesting that this social class owned not only movable property but also real estate ('*heritages de terre*' in Philip of Novara's *Livre de forme de plait*).[40]

As a result of the numerous donations, the summer of 1348 found the monastic community considerably wealthier while most of the country was presumably on the brink of economic collapse. One of the largest monetary grants to the monastery ever recorded in these notes, amounting to 76 *nomismata*, was made on 15 May (f. 221v).[41] Although the value and meaning of the term *nomisma* in this context is not clear (one bezant? its half denomination, the *gros grand*? or a generic term referring to coins?), the sum is surely not negligible, considering that most other fourteenth-century monetary gifts do not exceed ten *nomismata* (f. 167v, 194r, 234v, 243r).[42] Within a couple of weeks Hiereon acquired more than fifty

---

[39] A Constantine Laloutas is recorded in 1351 in another manuscript (Par. gr. 97) as its donor to the church of Saint Theodore at Letymbou: J. Darrouzès, 'Notes pour servir à l'histoire de Chypre (premier article)', Κυπριακαί Σπουδαί, 17 (1953), 96.

[40] P. Edbury, 'Philip of Novara and the *Livre de forme de plait*' in Πρακτικά τοὺ Τρίτου Διεθνούς Κυπρολογικού Συνεδρίου (Nicosia, 1996–2001), vol. II, 564–6; see also J. Richard, 'Οἱ πολιτικοὶ καὶ κοινωνικοὶ θεσμοὶ τοῦ μεσαιωνικοῦ βασιλείου' in Papadopoullos, ed., Ἱστορία τῆς Κύπρου, vol. I, at 365–8; N. Svoronos, on the other hand, suggests that they were free peasants: N. Svoronos, 'Ζητήματα σχετικά με την οικονομική, κοινωνική και νομική κατάσταση των Ελληνοκυπρίων στη διάρκεια της φραγκικής κυριαρχίας', Σημείο, 4 (1996), 38; see also Nicolaou-Konnari, 'Greeks', 45.

[41] A donation of 100 *nomismata* on 4 June of an unknown year (perhaps 1348? mid-fourteenth century according to Darrouzès, 'Un obituaire chypriote') is the largest recorded (f. 234r); only a dozen monetary donations are recorded in the whole of the manuscript, their small number being perhaps indicative of the degree of monetization of the rural economy.

[42] In a document of the early fourteenth century a donkey is valued at 40 bezants and a horse was bought for 150, while the annual salary of an ironsmith was 36 bezants, that of a scribe 180, and of a gate-keeper a mere 12 bezants: J. Richard, 'Le casal de Psimilofo et la vie rurale en Chypre au XIVe siècle', *MEFRM*, 59 (1947), 131, 148; for prices later in the century see J. Richard, 'Les comptes du collecteur de la chambre apostolique dans le royaume de Chypre (1357–1363)', *EKEE*, 13–16 (1984–7), 1–47.

animals (including bulls, cows, calves, horses, mares, donkeys, and as many as fifteen oxen), a couple of houses (f. 231r) and a few household items (f. 221v, 243v). In addition eight vineyards were donated, mostly at a nearby locality aptly named Ampelites (Fig. 5.1).[43] The decision to relinquish these vineyards at that particular time, in the late spring or early summer, confirms the exceptional circumstances, as the 'labour des vignes' (ploughing, pruning, layering of runners, etc.) takes place in March/April and a donation soon thereafter, in the wake of so much effort, would make little sense under normal conditions.[44]

It should be stressed that while the number of donations may seem small in absolute numbers, it is rather high considering that the pool from which the monastic community drew its patrons was restricted to half a dozen modest rural settlements in the vicinity of the monastery, within a radius of no more than 6 miles / 9 kilometres (Fig. 5.1).[45] The *timor mortis* that clearly seized the rural population upon hearing the news of the pandemic's ravages in the cities is a reaction well documented elsewhere (the wills from Venetian Crete bear witness to this)[46] and was repeated at Hiereon during the later outbreak of 1394, as the recorded donations suggest. A contemporary marginal note in the Par. gr. 297 illustrates well this type of response: on 27 April 1393 a certain George Xenos (perhaps belonging to the homonymous family from Pentalia mentioned above), having fallen ill, donated a silver buckle to a shrine of the Virgin in the region of Paphos; the note makes clear that this act of piety was due to

---

[43] Ampelites is marked on H. H. Kitchener's *Trigonometrical Survey of the Island of Cyprus* (London, 1885) between Koilinia, Statos and Galataria; it survived as a toponym into modern times in the territory of Statos – Hagios Photios (M. N. Christodoulou and K. Konstantinidis, *A Complete Gazetteer of Cyprus* (Nicosia, 1987), vol. I, 106 [VD 65 60 XLVI 10]) and is the location of a new settlement where the inhabitants of these two villages were transferred in the 1970s. The Par. gr. 1588 contains a dozen references to fourteenth-century landowners at Ampelites from nearby villages.

[44] On the 'labour des vignes', see J. Richard, 'Agriculture in the Kingdom of Cyprus' in K. M. Setton, ed., *A History of the Crusades* (Madison, WI, 1969–89), vol. V, *The Impact of the Crusades on the Near East*, eds. N. P. Zacour and H. W. Hazard, 276.

[45] In the cases where the village from which donors originated is given, this can be easily identified with modern settlements (Koilinia, Lemona, Lapithiou, Statos, Melia, Pentalia, Phalia); others are less easy to identify on the ground but were clearly situated in the same area: Damasida (f. 198v) is mentioned in sixteenth-century documents and marked as 'damasita' on Leonida Attar's map to the east of Statos and north of Galataria: Grivaud, *Villages désertés*, 241, 448; F. Cavazzana Romanelli and G. Grivaud, *Cyprus 1542: The Great Map of the Island by Leonida Attar* (Nicosia, 2006), 105, Fig. 40a, 143.

[46] Out of approximately 670 early fourteenth- to early fifteenth-century wills, 93 were drafted in the spring of 1348: S. McKee, *Wills from Late Medieval Venetian Crete 1312–1420* (Washington, D. C., 1998).

George's fear of imminent death.[47] The same fear prompted the island's surviving nobility in the years immediately following the outbreak of 1348 to apply almost en masse to the papal curia for *absolutiones in articulo mortis* that allowed the beneficiary to be granted unconditional absolution of all sins at the moment of death.[48]

A study of the deserted villages of Cyprus from the end of Byzantine to the end of Ottoman rule (late twelfth to late nineteenth century) by Gilles Grivaud appears to support what the notes from Hiereon suggest. Taking into account the admittedly exiguous evidence that hardly allows a close dating of abandonments, it concludes that there was no increase in such occurrences in the course of the fourteenth century, indicating that most rural areas, especially those in the mountains, must have escaped relatively unscathed.[49] There is one more element leading to the same conclusion. Both Nikephoros Gregoras and al-Makrizi in their description of the ravages of the plague on Cyprus stress its deadly effects on animals, something that the latter author also reports for central Anatolia, Gaza and Egypt with regard to beasts of burden and cattle.[50] Yet the numerous oxen and other domestic animals donated to Hiereon show, on the contrary, that this region's livestock remained unaffected.

Despite the island's relatively small size the plague clearly left at least some mountainous regions untouched, although later outbreaks are known to have reached and devastated other semi-mountainous areas: according to yet another manuscript note the plague of 1437/8, which allegedly killed 20,000 people in Nicosia alone, left 102 dead at the village of Amargete which lies halfway between Hiereon and the coast.[51] The countryside was clearly not always immune to the successive outbreaks. Nevertheless, like the mountains of Paphos in 1348, other remote areas were perhaps also bypassed by the plague. The unverified assertion of Loredano that the royal family fled to Saint Hilarion, considered safe enough because of its isolation on top of an inaccessible peak, was mentioned above. The flight of King James and his court to the remote monastery of Machairas in the eastern Troodos during the outbreak of the

---

[47] Darrouzès, 'Notes (troisième article)', 247.
[48] The peak year was 1350, with sixty-four *absolutiones* for eighty-six individuals: Rudt de Collenberg, 'Les grâces papales', 190–1, 226–31; see also Schabel and Richard, eds.,*Bullarium Cyprium*, vol. III, 270–93.
[49] Grivaud, *Villages désertés*, 256; but see also the remarks of B. Arbel, 'Cypriot Villages from the Byzantine to the British Period: Observations on a Recent book', *EKEE*, 26 (2000), 442–3.
[50] Bartsocas, 'Greek Descriptions of the "Black Death"', 395; Wiet, 'La grande peste', 369–70, 374.
[51] J. Darrouzès, 'Notes pour servir à l'histoire de Chypre (deuxième article)', Κυπριακαί Σπουδαί, 20 (1956), 43–4.

1390s is better documented.⁵² There is no doubt that the lucky escape of the villages around Hiereon was due to their remoteness.⁵³ The area lies at the edge of the inhabited valleys of the western Troodos; beyond stretch the Paphos forest and the central part of the massif. In antiquity a Roman road traversed the region passing not far from the site of Hiereon, in which there was a pagan shrine, and linking the cities of Kourion on the south coast and Arsinoe (Polis) on the north-west coast (Fig. 5.1). There is, however, no evidence that this road either remained in use or was maintained in later centuries, although this is not out of the question considering that the monastery appears to have maintained links with Arsinoe, only a minor episcopal centre by the medieval period.⁵⁴

It is also significant that the monastery is not known to have possessed any famous relic or miracle-working icon that would have attracted pilgrims from other parts of the island.⁵⁵ This also suggests something about the local economy. The trip to the coast and the town of Paphos is not a particularly arduous or long one.⁵⁶ Moreover, there is evidence for imported ceramics used at the monastery such as Byzantine tablewares, glazed coarse sgraffito wares of probable Syrian origin and Islamic glazed wares.⁵⁷ But these surely reached the region as gifts presented to the community and do not represent any substantial commercial exchange, for there seems to have been little contact between Paphos and its mountainous hinterland; had this been the case then the plague would have certainly spread with as much intensity and ferocity as it did in the lowlands. The reason must be that the type of agricultural produce available around Hiereon could presumably be found in the

---

⁵² Makhairas, *Chronicle*, ed. Dawkins, 1: 612 n. 2; *Makhairas*, eds. Pieris and Nicolaou-Konnari, 422.

⁵³ Isolation is also thought to have protected sparsely populated regions of northern Europe: Benedictow, *Black Death*, 109, 146, 216–17.

⁵⁴ T. Bekker-Nielsen, *The Roads of Ancient Cyprus* (Copenhagen, 2004), 215; a bishop of Arsinoe died and was buried at Hiereon in 1320, while an *oikonomos* of the see is mentioned in connection with a donation in 1382 and another as its *hegumen* in 1407 (f. 169r, 167v, 191r).

⁵⁵ The only significant relic at the monastery, a fragment of the *omophorion* of the Virgin which she allegedly gave to Saint Nicholas, is not attested there until the eighteenth century: C. N. Constantinides, Ἡ Διήγησις τῆς θαυματουργῆς εἰκόνας τῆς Θεοτόκου Ἐλεούσας τοῦ Κύκκου (Nicosia, 2002), 270; see also Kokkinophtas and Theocharides, Μονή των Ιερέων, 22.

⁵⁶ In 1736 Vassilij Barskij left Hiereon in the morning and after an overnight stay at Polemi reached the Enkleistra, in the outskirts of Paphos; Richard Pococke in 1738 made the journey from the monastery to the town within a single day: A. D. Grishin, *A Pilgrim's Account of Cyprus: Bars'kyj's Travels in Cyprus* (Altamont, NY, 1996), 52; C. D. Cobham, *Excerpta Cypria: Materials for a History of Cyprus* (Cambridge, 1908), 262–3.

⁵⁷ M.-L. von Wartburg, 'Cypriot Contacts with East and West as Reflected in Medieval Glazed Pottery from the Paphos Region' in C. Bakirtzis, ed., *VIIe congrès international sur la céramique médiévale en Méditerranée, Thessaloniki 11–16 octobre 1999* (Athens, 2003), 153–6.

immediate hinterland of Paphos too, which was anyway no great centre of consumption but merely the only large settlement in western Cyprus in this period.

The Aftermath

A question that immediately arises in view of the circumstances of Hiereon after 1348, as these are revealed by the evidence of the marginal notes in the Par. gr. 1588, is this: How did the monastic community manage its newly acquired wealth and what was the extra revenue invested in? Since the archaeological evidence from the monastery is very restricted, it is impossible to say whether new buildings were put up in the second half of the fourteenth century. A vaulted cruciform structure standing to the north of the *katholikon* may date from this period, although there is no secure evidence for this.[58] Nor is there any information on the purchase of either ecclesiastical furnishings and vessels, or relics in order to enhance the shrine's appeal, which is what happened for example at the hospital of Santa Maria della Scala in Siena. There, the vast sums of money amassed from bequests and donations were used in 1357 to acquire several relics in Venice from an astute Florentine who claimed that he had obtained them at Constantinople and that they had belonged to no less a figure than Emperor Constantine.[59] The monks at Hiereon were perhaps aware that they owed their survival to the lack of crowd-pulling objects of veneration such as those sought out by the Sienese hospital.

One of the most discussed aspects of the Black Death crisis in western Europe is its impact on building activity. This was expressed in two entirely opposed manners. First, during the outbreak itself some building projects were abandoned midway through as a result of the depletion of the labour force. The most frequently cited example comes, once more, from Siena. According to an ambitious plan conceived in the early fourteenth century, the city's old and already large cathedral was going to be incorporated within a vast new church, the *Duomo Nuovo*, becoming its transept. Although work had started by the time of the Black Death, the project was interrupted and never completed. However severe the effects of the plague, it has nevertheless been pointed out that it was only one among

---

[58] Kokkinophtas and Theocharides, Μονή των Ιερέων, 9.
[59] D. Gallavotti Cavallero, *Lo Spedale di Santa Maria della Scala in Siena: Vicenda di una committenza artistica* (Pisa, 1985), 80, 132, n. 117.

several reasons that led to this development.⁶⁰ On Cyprus there is no evidence (or none has been identified) for the abandonment of building projects or the suspension of work on any kind of commission in this period; a claim made for the western end of the Latin cathedral of Saint Sophia in Nicosia, although not unlikely, remains unsubstantiated.⁶¹

The second manner in which the Black Death affected building and artistic activity in the longer term was by causing a surge in commissions. One of its numerous effects on society in Europe was the growth of religious sentiment, and this was partly expressed through the foundation of churches and especially funerary chapels during the third quarter of the fourteenth century.⁶² This was at least partly a result of the same phenomenon of which Hiereon is a witness, namely the enrichment of ecclesiastical foundations through donations by the frightened faithful, but also of the numerous bequests left by victims of the plague. Suffice to mention the often-cited case of Saint Germain l'Auxerrois in Paris: whereas the church received a mere 5 legacies per year on average before 1348, between June 1348 and March 1349 these rose to a staggering 445.⁶³ Needless to say that there are no comparable data from Cyprus. Nor is there any building or work of art surviving today on the island that may be securely dated to the immediate aftermath of the Black Death, and thus be put in direct relation with the pandemic's repercussions. Indeed, establishing the chronology of numerous modest rural churches and their monumental decorations remains a recurrent problem.⁶⁴ If there is, however, one place on the island where evidence might be found, this is surely Famagusta, a flourishing emporium in the first half of the fourteenth century. And it is to Famagusta that the only explicit source reference to a plague-related

---

⁶⁰ The city's economic decline, local problems and also structural difficulties contributed decisively: K. van der Ploeg, *Art, Architecture and Liturgy: Siena Cathedral in the Middle Ages* (Groningen, 1993), 115–16; for other examples, see Ziegler, *Black Death*, 147, 168.

⁶¹ A. Michel, *Histoire de l'art depuis les premiers temps chrétiens jusqu'à nos jours* (Paris, 1905–29), vol. II, 558, where Camille Enlart suggests that the well-documented flood of 1330 (Grivaud, *Villages désertés*, 431) and an alleged plague in the same year (that is not recorded in any source) resulted in the suspension of work on the north tower of Saint Sophia; this assertion may be related to a later papal letter, of September 1347, which granted an indulgence of a hundred days to those who contributed to the completion or repair of the cathedral (Coureas and Schabel, eds., *Cartulary*, 299–300; Schabel and Richard, eds., *Bullarium Cyprium*, vol. III, 236 no. t-295); there is, however, no clear evidence to link the latter with the effects of the epidemic.

⁶² S. K. Cohn, *The Cult of Remembrance and the Black Death: Six Renaissance Cities in Central Italy* (Baltimore, MD, 1992), 140, 160, 252; S. K. Cohn, 'Piété et commande d'oeuvres d'art après la peste noire', *Annales: Histoire, Sciences Sociales*, 51 (1996), 551–73; for evidence from Egypt see Dols, *The Black Death*, 269–70.

⁶³ Biraben, *Les hommes et la peste*, vol. I, 172; Cohn, *Black Death Transformed*, 90.

⁶⁴ A. Weyl Carr, 'Art' in Nicolaou-Konnari and Schabel, eds., *Cyprus*, 325.

foundation on Cyprus pertains: in 1348 a church '*in tempore pestis fundata*' is mentioned outside the walled town.[65]

Although the numerous surviving monuments of the city, like those of the countryside, are not securely dated, two of its most important churches are thought to have been erected in the mid-fourteenth century. The Orthodox cathedral of Saint George of the Greeks and the church of Saints Peter and Paul, perhaps belonging to one of the eastern rites, were both built as rib-vaulted three-aisled basilicas in a Gothic style inspired by the slightly earlier Latin cathedral of Saint Nicholas; they were the largest churches in the city after the latter and among the largest ecclesiastical structures put up on the island in medieval times.[66] Nevertheless, their foundation in the middle decades of the fourteenth century (Saint George was still under construction in 1363) is not easy to account for. The city's golden age, largely a result of the loss of the crusader outposts on the mainland in the later thirteenth century and the translocation of economic activity across the sea to Cyprus, was drawing to a close. As we saw above, the ravages of the Black Death, although not documented in detail, were surely severe and consequently the demographic and economic impact must have been dire. How could these exceptionally large structures have been erected in these far from propitious circumstances? There is no written evidence to suggest that Famagusta's religious foundations benefited from legacies and donations at the time of the pandemic; yet this is not unlikely in view of the evidence from Hiereon, and may at least partly explain the paradox described above. After all, it is probably in these same years that the Latin bishop of Famagusta Léger de Nabinaud, appointed in August 1348, commanded sufficient funds to erect his episcopal palace next to the cathedral of Saint Nicholas.[67]

The construction of the new Greek cathedral at this juncture is significant on another level, for it provides the earliest secure evidence for the establishment of an Orthodox bishop in the city. This development may need to be reassessed within the context of the effects of the Black Death. Famagusta's depleted population of largely Latin and Syrian origin was perhaps subsequently boosted by an indigenous element from rural areas that eventually tilted the demographic balance in favour of the Greeks. The latter asserted their presence in the city and their economic and social

---

[65] Rudt de Collenberg, 'Les grâces papales', 251; Schabel and Richard, eds., *Bullarium Cyprium*, vol. III, 243, no. t-329 (see also nos. v-44 and v-159).
[66] J.-B. de Vaivre and P. Plagnieux, *L'art gothique en Chypre* (Paris, 2006), 271–96.
[67] De Vaivre and Plagnieux, *L'art gothique*, 450–1.

rise through the construction of an ostentatious cathedral to match that of the Latins.[68] Future research on the chronology and circumstances of the foundation of this and other monuments on the island may shed further light on these issues, but it certainly ought to take into account the upheaval of 1348, the response it elicited, and to consider its likely repercussions.

Over the decades the monks of remote Hiereon, at least some of whom were obviously literate, added notes in the margins of one of their monastic library's manuscripts. The codex provided through the nature of its content (a synaxarion) a convenient structure (a calendar) for recording deaths and donations to the community. This investigation has illustrated how this aspect of the monks' writing activity furnishes unintended and hitherto unsuspected indirect yet irrefutable evidence on otherwise undocumented historical developments. That the Black Death did not spread in the western Troodos valleys is perhaps unsurprising, but that it elicited the reaction it did, as these notes amply demonstrate, is surely noteworthy. The likelihood that urban populations which were heavily affected by the pestilence, on the other hand, may have reacted in a similar way, with all the repercussions that this may have had, becomes much stronger in view of this evidence. Had the monks of Hiereon been less forthcoming in their recording practices, we would have never suspected the proposed scenario.

Further Reading

The main primary source is: J. Darrouzès, 'Un obituaire chypriote: le Parisinus graecus 1588', Κυπριακαί Σπουδαί, 15 (1951), 25–62. Key studies include: O. J. Benedictow, *The Black Death, 1346–1353: The Complete History* (Woodbridge, 2004); C. N. Constantinides and R. Browning, *Dated Greek Manuscripts from Cyprus to the Year 1570* (Washington, D. C., 1993); A. Nicolaou-Konnari and C. Schabel, eds., *Cyprus: Society and Culture 1191–1374* (Leiden, 2005); E. Trapp et al., eds., *Prosopographisches Lexikon der Palaiologenzeit (1261–1453)*, 12 vols. (Vienna, 1979–96, 2001).

---

[68] On the ethnic composition of Famagusta's population, see P. W. Edbury, 'The Lusignan Regime in Cyprus and the Indigenous Population' in P. W. Edbury, *Kingdoms of the Crusaders. From Jerusalem to Cyprus* (Aldershot, 1999), article XX, 4; for Saint George and the implications of its architecture, T. Papacostas, 'Byzantine Rite in a Gothic Setting: Aspects of Cultural Appropriation in Late Medieval Cyprus' in P. Ł. Grotowski and S. Skrzyniarz, eds., *Towards Rewriting? New Approaches to Byzantine Archaeology and Art* (Warsaw, 2010), 121–30.

PART II

Contact with a Living Culture

The Power of Rhetoric

CHAPTER 6

Ancient Greek Rhetorical Theory and Byzantine Discursive Politics: John Sikeliotes on Hermogenes

Panagiotis Roilos

In his interesting and as a whole very insightful discussion of post-Platonic western European ideas about rhetoric, Brian Vickers observes:

> Either in the *Greek* version of personal involvement, or in the Roman, with representation through a professional orator, when the decisions of a court or assembly depend on a vote taken or decision passed after hearing speeches on both sides of the case, rhetoric can indeed claim to be a discipline essential to the life of a democracy. When emperors or dictators rule, however, and such issues are decided by edict or by appointed administrators, rhetoric's *role in society* inevitably *declines*.[1]

This predictable verdict – found in Vickers' study *In Defence of Rhetoric* – is pronounced in the preliminary comments on Vickers' analysis of what he calls 'fragmentation of rhetoric' in the European Middle Ages, which he defines in contradistinction to the development of a systematic interest in ancient rhetoric during the Renaissance. Due precisely to its sweeping vehemence, such a truism cannot but be vulnerable to several counter-arguments. In this regard, it should be emphasised that in the Greek Middle Ages, from late antiquity to the fall of Constantinople, literary

---

[1] B. Vickers, *In Defence of Rhetoric* (Oxford, 1988), 214 (my emphasis). Vickers endorses McKeon's overall views about medieval rhetoric and especially his chronological divisions. According to McKeon, the last period of medieval rhetoric (after 1300) was marked by the (re)discovery of ancient rhetorical theory, especially Hermogenes, and it prefigured later developments in the Renaissance: R. McKeon, 'Rhetoric in the Middle Ages' in R. S. Crane, ed., *Critics and Criticism* (Chicago, IL, 1952), 260–96; on the influence of the Hermogenean corpus on Western European Renaissance letters, see A. Patterson, *Hermogenes and the Renaissance: Seven Ideas of Style* (Princeton, NJ, 1970).

This chapter, which was completed in November 2009, is part of a broader study on the work of John Sikeliotes and the defence of rhetoric in eleventh-century Byzantium. I am currently completing a commentary on, and the English translation of, Sikeliotes' treatise. This research project was supported in part by a Fellowship in Byzantine Studies at Dumbarton Oaks in the spring of 2009 and its main aspects were presented at a public lecture at Dumbarton Oaks in May 2009. I would like to thank John Duffy, Paul Magdalino, Teresa Shawcross and Ida Toth for their helpful comments. I owe special thanks to Dimitrios Yatromanolakis for his useful remarks on an earlier version of this chapter.

theory and practice were engaged to varying degrees in a creative dialogue with ancient rhetorical tradition, including the Hermogenean corpus – a fact that is conspicuously and erroneously silenced or neglected in impressionistic, West-centred approaches to what is arbitrarily defined as *the* European Middle Ages. In my brief introductory *anaskeuê* (refutation) of this partial view of rhetoric, which has by and large hegemonised the study of rhetoric in the Greek and Latin Middle Ages – or, rather, in my defence of the importance of rhetoric in the Greek Middle Ages – I would like to focus on two problematic aspects of Vickers' reasoning. First, 'Greek' is employed by him in an amusingly manneristic fashion conveying a stereotypical attitude to Greek culture(s): almost everything produced in the Greek language after the 'glorious' classical period or, in the best cases, after late antiquity is often relegated to the margins of West- (i.e. Latin-) centred approaches to post-classical humanism. In other words, Vickers' use of 'Greek' refers only to a highly marked period of Greek literature, while leaving out its also (but differently) marked later developments. The fact that almost no reference to medieval Greek rhetorical tradition is made in his discussion of rhetoric in the Middle Ages does not come, therefore, as a surprise. If he had taken into account, even very briefly, the case of Greek rhetoric in medieval times, his views about the 'fragmentation' of rhetoric in European literature during the Middle Ages would have been amended accordingly. Second, the 'role in society' of specific discursive and other socioaesthetic institutions, rhetoric included, is subject to change from period to period.[2] 'Modification' rather than 'decline' may thus be a more accurate term to describe such developments, at least as far as the functions of rhetoric in the Greek Middle Ages are concerned.

For rhetoric's (and medieval Greek literature's) own sake my present *anaskeuê* could take the form of an *êthopoiia* ('character study'), which, in accordance with the formulaic rules of the genre, could have the following title: 'What words would a Byzantine author have pronounced in defence of rhetoric against modern scholars' flippant accusations?' Such an *êthopoiia* may have been articulated as follows:

> As has been said a number of times, Demosthenes' discourse was considered excellent by everybody in antiquity. However, since his personal style is not pertinent to our political system (except only for rhetorical exercises), since we do not live in a democracy but are ruled by an emperor it is advisable to turn to the Theologian, who, at any rate, is better than Demosthenes and

---

[2] For the notion of socioaesthetics, see D. Yatromanolakis, *Sappho in the Making: The Early Reception* (Cambridge, MA, 2007).

everybody else; for he developed political rhetoric into a more innovative and divine discourse in such a marvellous manner that no words can capture. This kind of rhetoric was imitated and further developed by many others and, most outstandingly, by the Euphrates or, rather, the Ocean of the Church, Chrysostom – for, as I said, democracy has not been our political system.[3]

This is not a fictional *ēthopoiia* but a passage from John Sikeliotes' early eleventh-century commentary on Hermogenes' *On Ideas*. Far from being a naïve imitation of previous approaches to rhetorical theory and practice in Greek tradition, Sikeliotes' work often bespeaks a considerable degree of self-awareness and sophistication. Commenting on Hermogenes' canonisation of Demosthenes as the supreme model of the ideal mixture of styles in ancient Greek rhetoric, Sikeliotes counteroffers his own (and other Byzantines') paradigm of rhetoric in the new era that succeeded Greek antiquity: 'the Theologian' mentioned in the passage quoted above is none other than Gregory of Nazianzos, who was admired throughout Byzantium as a model of rhetorical forcefulness and theological brilliance.[4] For Sikeliotes, Gregory, along with 'the Ocean' of the Church, John Chrysostom, was the archetype of Byzantine political rhetoric that replaced Demosthenes, the ancient Greek exemplum of this kind of rhetorical discourse. In this chapter, my main aim is to reconstruct some important discursive strategies through which Sikeliotes articulated his systematic Christianisation of ancient Greek rhetorical theory. Homologies between different domains of human knowledge and experience (ranging from ethics to medicine to philosophy to theology) constituted, I argue, the pivotal conceptual foundations on which Sikeliotes constructed his overall cultural political edifice, with a view to adjusting inherited rhetorical ideals to his contemporary, Christian discursive priorities.

But who was the little-known John Sikeliotes? On the basis mainly of his own, as a rule obscure, comments on his work and life, we can say with

---

[3] Κέκριται παρὰ πάντων τῶν παλαιῶν ἄριστος ὁ Δημοσθενικὸς λόγος, ὡς πολλάκις εἴρηται. Ἐπειδὴ δὲ τὸ κατ' αὐτὸν εἶδος ἀσύμφορόν ἐστι τῇ νῦν πολιτείᾳ, εἰ μὴ καὶ ταῖς μελέταις μόνον, ὅτι οὐ δημοκρατούμεθα, ἀλλὰ βασιλευόμεθα, μετιτέον ἐπὶ τὸν θεολόγον, ὡς καὶ Δημοσθένους καὶ τῶν ἄλλων κρείττονα, καθότι τὸν πολιτικὸν λόγον εἰς τὸ καινότερον καὶ θειοειδέστερον μετενεγκὼν θαυμασίως ἢ κατὰ λόγον ἐξειργάσατο, ὃν οἱ μετ' αὐτὸν μιμησάμενοι διεπλάτυναν, ἐξαιρέτως δὲ καὶ τῆς ἐκκλησίας Εὐφράτης, μᾶλλον δὲ ὠκεανός, Χρυσόστομος, διὰ τὸ ὡς ἔφην μὴ δημοκρατεῖσθαι (Sikeliotes, *Commentary*, in C. Walz, ed., *Rhetores Graeci* (Stuttgart, 1832–6), vol. VI, 472.8–19: hereafter, Sikeliotes, *Commentary*).

[4] It would be a tedious task to enumerate the studies that attest to the multifaceted reception of Gregory by later Byzantine authors; here, suffice it to note the old but fundamental work of J. Sajdak, *Historia critica scholiastarum et commentatorum Gregorii Nazianzeni* (Krakow, 1914); see also the studies in J. Mossay, ed., *Symposium Nazianzenum* (Paderborn, 1983).

considerable confidence only that he was active in the late tenth to early eleventh century. His reference to a speech that he delivered at the Monastery of Pikridion (in the presence most probably of Emperor Basil II) offers a *terminus post quem* for the composition of his commentary. The way he refers to Basil II indicates, I argue, that he wrote his work on Hermogenes after that emperor's death, that is, after 1025.[5] Explaining why he decided to refrain from a detailed, systematic, stylistic study of certain rhetorical speeches, Sikeliotes emphasises first that, being rather poor, he does not have the luxury of applying himself to such an arduous but ultimately unrewarding task, and, second, that those who are currently in power do not resemble those old Roman emperors who supported literature.[6] In his discussion of the interaction between rhetoricians and men of power, Sikeliotes singles out Hadrian and Marcus (Aurelius) as models of inspired Roman rulers who sponsored intellectual production and creativity.[7] Sikeliotes' indirect, negative comments on the political situation during the period in which he was writing his own commentary indicate that most probably he wrote or, at least, completed this work after the death of Basil II, with whom he seems to have been on good terms. Earlier in his commentary, in a passage replete with poignant criticisms against the frivolous understanding and practice of rhetoric, Sikeliotes implies that, in the period he was writing his work, mediocre rhetoricians were favoured by the 'first men of the state'.[8] How closely, or for how long Sikeliotes was associated with Basil – an emperor known for his suspicious attitude to intellectuals – cannot be established on the basis of the available material.[9]

---

[5] Sikeliotes, *Commentary*, ed. Walz, 447.24–7–448.1. Sikeliotes quotes a brief passage from the very beginning of his speech, in which he significantly calls his addressee an "emperor" (ὦ βασιλεῦ; ibid.: 447.27). Any speculation concerning the date when Sikeliotes delivered his speech in honor of Basil is, of course, open to debate; see M. Lauxtermann, 'Byzantine Poetry and the Paradox of Basil II's Reign' in P. Magdalino, ed., *Byzantium in the Year 1000* (Leiden, 2003), 214, who suggests that the speech must have been delivered in the early years of Basil's reign. Lauxtermann assumes that Sikeliotes was a contemporary of John Geometres; it may very well have been that Sikeliotes was considerably younger than Geometres, if he composed his commentary after 1025, as I suggest on the basis of his (admittedly obscure) references to his own activities and the political situation (most probably) following Basil's reign.

[6] Sikeliotes, *Commentary*, ed. Walz, 444.31–445.16.

[7] The reference to Marcus Aurelius may be an allusion to Hermogenes' association with this emperor, attested by W. C. Wright, ed., *Philostratos, Lives of the Sophists* (Cambridge, MA, 1921), 204–5 (II.577). I find it worth noting that this is also mentioned by Syrianos in his commentary on Hermogenes' *On Issues*: H. Rabe, ed. *Syriani in Hermogenem Commentaria* (Leipzig, 1892–3), vol. II, 1.9–2.2.

[8] Sikeliotes, *Commentary*, ed. Walz, 83.29–84.2.

[9] For Basil II's attitude to men of letters in general, see the discussion in Lauxtermann, 'Byzantine poetry'.

Although the author of the most wide-ranging medieval Greek commentary on Hermogenes and one of the most intriguing works of Byzantine rhetorical theory in general, Sikeliotes remains almost entirely unexplored.[10] His impact on later authors is indirectly illustrated by a reference to him in a thirteenth-century manuscript (Vat. 105) as: 'ὁ φιλοσοφώτατος καὶ ῥητορικώτατος Σικελιώτης ... ὁ θαυμαστὸς καὶ πολὺς τὴν σοφίαν Σικελιώτης' ('the great philosopher and rhetorician Sikeliotes ... Sikeliotes most wondrous in learning'). John Doxapatres explicitly acknowledges his debt to Sikeliotes, who, however, as Michael Psellos mentions, had attacked John Geometres, another important source of inspiration for Doxapatres, and most probably an older contemporary of Sikeliotes. In the same thirteenth-century manuscript (Vat.105), Doxapatres' borrowings from Sikeliotes were negatively criticised and condemned as a kind of plagiarism, despite the fact that Doxapatres refers to Sikeliotes in his commentary.[11] Although apparently based on a misunderstanding of Doxapatres' intentions and actual practice, perhaps caused by confusion in the tradition of his and Sikeliotes' texts, this judgement is indicative of Sikeliotes' significant reputation as a 'most philosophical and rhetorical' man of letters, which seems to have overshadowed at least Doxapatres' contributions to rhetorical theory.

---

[10] Sikeliotes wrote also some (as yet unpublished and unexplored) comments on Ailios Aristeides, on which see F. W. Lenz, *Aristeidesstudien* (Berlin, 1964), 97–9 and 113–17. I intend to discuss his comments on Ailios Aristeides in a separate study. From his own words we can infer that Sikeliotes composed also a speech 'against the Saracens,' a speech 'on the horse,' and an *anaskeuê* of the myth of Prometheus (Sikeliotes, *Commentary*, ed. Walz, 447.19–24). Apart from sporadic references to Sikeliotes' work on Hermogenes' *On Ideas* and especially George Kustas' brief but insightful discussion of the way Sikeliotes develops the concept of *emphasis* (allusiveness), this author's presence in, and probable important contribution to mid- and late Byzantine rhetoric, has never been the subject of a systematic study before. Kustas observes with regard to this issue: 'a scholar of catholic learning, writing in a style all his own, he has hardly been noticed, partly because he is lost among a long, arid list of commentators and partly because he has traditionally been confused with John Doxapatres': G. Kustas, *Studies in Byzantine Rhetoric* (Thessalonike, 1973), 188; and, I would add, partly also because his language and style make his the most obscure surviving Byzantine rhetorical commentary – a quality that confounded even the formidable Hugo Rabe. Leaving aside its strict and rather biased overtones, I believe that Rabe's judgement of Sikeliotes' convoluted style is to the point; according to him, Sikeliotes' treatise is interspersed with flowery discursive elements, indulges in complicated expressions, and is replete with lines from different authors which are obscure rather than clearly quoted, thus causing considerable difficulties ('sermo floribus conspersus, sententiis implicatis helluans, scriptorum locis ornatus non tam citatis quam obscure adumbratis difficultates affert haud mediocres,' H. Rabe, ed., *Prolegomenon Sylloge* (Leipzig, 1931), cxiii).

[11] Doxapatres, *Rhetorical Discourses*, in Rabe, ed., *Prolegomenon Sylloge*, 422.8.

Psellos also indirectly points to *didaskalos* Sikeliotes' considerable impact,[12] although he deems it worthwhile to criticise his attacks against other authors in some length. If Psellos did not think that Sikeliotes was, or could be, considerably influential, he would not have used his case as a negative example of allegedly unfair criticism in a piece addressed to his own students – a piece that includes just such an unfair attack against that *didaskalos* on Psellos' own part.[13] Psellos' point that Sikeliotes' commentary is a compilation of views previously expressed by Paul (of Caesarea) and Syrianos is, of course, part of his scathing criticism and by no means substantiated by the available material.[14] By referring to Syrianos, Psellos obviously meant the Neoplatonist thinker's two commentaries on Hermogenes' works *On Ideas* and *On Issues*. Although an investigation of Sikeliotes' dependence on Syrianos is beyond the scope of this chapter, it is pertinent to note that, to my mind, the Byzantine commentator made use of both commentaries by Syrianos. However, as far as Syrianos' influence on Sikeliotes is concerned, a comparison of their works leaves no doubt that the latter's creative originality was not obstructed by his familiarity with the work of the former; this fact makes me think that Sikeliotes' supposed debt to Paul, whose commentary on Hermogenes' *On Ideas* has not survived, may similarly also have not been as pervasive as Psellos wants his readers to believe.

Psellos must have been right in his reference to Sikeliotes' vehement criticisms; as his comments on Sikeliotes indicate, he had directly in mind, I believe, the commentary on Hermogenes' *On Ideas* – perhaps among other works now lost. Indeed, in this commentary, Sikeliotes does not spare older or contemporary rhetoricians his sharp criticism and sarcasm. He castigates especially those overconfident practitioners of rhetoric who rely not on *technê* and systematic knowledge but merely on their *physis* and natural talents. In their analyses of rhetorical issues, such men resemble the Bacchae who dismembered Pentheus, thus causing laughter or rather lamentation among educated rhetoricians but deep admiration among

---

[12] A *didaskalos* Sikeliotes is also mentioned as a historiographer in a preface to Skylitzes' *History*: I. Thurn, ed., *Joannis Scylitzae Synopsis Historiarum* (Berlin, 1973), 3–4, preserved in a number of manuscripts; however, the information provided by this preface has been received with considerable skepticism: O. Kresten, 'Phantomgestalten in der byzantinischen Literaturgeschichte', *JÖB*, 25 (1976), 213–17; compare with H. Hunger, *Die hochsprachliche profane Literatur der Byzantiner* (Munich, 1978), vol. I, 476–7; A. Markopoulos, 'Byzantine History Writing at the End of the First Millenium' in Magdalino, ed., *Byzantium in the Year 1000*, 183–93.

[13] P. Gautier, ed., *Michaelis Pselli Theologica* (Leipzig, 1989) 180–1 (47.69–105).

[14] Ibid., 181 (47.97–100). It is worth noting that Sikeliotes refers to Paulos' teacher, John of Caesarea: Sikeliotes, *Commentary*, ed. Walz, 243.11–13.

ignorant people.¹⁵ Unqualified teachers are not spared his vehement castigation either: good instructors, he stresses, should not try to learn the analyses of previous commentators by heart; they rather must acquire systematic knowledge of rhetorical theory so that they may be able to give appropriate explanations and examples to their students.¹⁶ At another point in his commentary, Sikeliotes also compares such sporadic and impressionistic dealing with serious rhetorical problems to the grinding and consumption of hastily mixed seeds during periods of starvation. His condemnation of the injudicious and unsystematic study of rhetoric is also accompanied here by some indirect yet bitter comments on the fact that, in his day, it was just such purported rhetoricians who happened to enjoy recognition.¹⁷

Psellos criticises Sikeliotes also in another brief piece of his on Gregory of Nazianzos' oration on Easter.¹⁸ The fact that Psellos refers here only to Sikeliotes' views is indicative of the latter's status as an established and, most probably, a leading authority in rhetorical theory. Once more, Psellos is not absolutely right in reporting that Sikeliotes did not find any traces of *emphasis* in Gregory of Nazianzos; on the contrary, Sikeliotes, who opposes the view of those who seem to have attributed exaggerated importance to Gregory's use of figures of speech at the expense of the *dianoia* of his orations, stresses that many examples of *emphantikai lexeis* may be found in the works of that Church father.¹⁹ Psellos' own interest in the rhetorical (as well as theological) value of Gregory's work is well-known; suffice it here to mention his short treatise on the 'Theologian Style' – addressed to *bestarches* Pothos²⁰ and his piece on 'The styles of Gregory the Theologian, Basil the Great, Chrysostom, and Gregory of Nyssa'.²¹ Indicative of Psellos' admiration of Gregory is also his explicit comparison of his speeches with the Platonic dialogues, the most important examples of

---

¹⁵ Sikeliotes, *Commentary*, ed. Walz, 85.17–86.21. For Sikeliotes' view on the same issue see also discussion above in n. 5. Other times, he does not refrain from criticising the style of even respected authors such as Prokopios of Gaza, Polemon, Aspasios or Basilikos, and Minucianus (94.3–15 and 111.15–23). Not infrequently, the study of the work of Gregory of Nazianzos gives rise to his passionate disapproving of other rhetoricians (see 109.19–20; 134.7–135.18; 198.7–32; 307.13–308.9; and 439.23–410.30).
¹⁶ Ibid., 308.24–310.21.   ¹⁷ Ibid., 90.9–91.10.
¹⁸ Psellos, *Theologica*, ed. Gautier, 401 (102.19–23).
¹⁹ Ibid., 198.21–7; compare to 408 (103.3–6).
²⁰ Text in A. Mayer, 'Psellos' Rede über den rhetorischen Charakter des Gregor von Nazianz', *BZ*, 20 (1911), 48–60; I have not been able to get access to P. Levy, 'Michaelis Pselli de Gregorii Theologi charactere iudicium: Accedit eiusdem De Ioannis Chrysostomi charactere iudicium ineditum', unpublished PhD dissertation, University of Leipzig (1912).
²¹ J. F. Boissonade, ed., *Michael Psellus: De operatione daemonum* (Nuremberg, 1838), 124–31.

pagan philosophical and rhetorical discourse according to Psellos.[22] It is not unlikely that Sikeliotes – who, as the available sources allow us to conclude, was the only other Byzantine man of letters to have dealt with Gregory's rhetorical work in a systematic, theoretical way in the eleventh century – was judged antagonistically by Psellos, a man not immune to such passionate temptations.

Thanks to its subtle redefinition of the semantic and pragmatic associations of the term 'political', the excerpt from Sikeliotes' commentary that I quoted above is significant for our understanding of Sikeliotes' (and other Byzantine rhetoricians') work as a kind of potential *anaskeuê* of biased views that several modern scholars hold against rhetorical art in the Middle Ages. Already in the *Prolegomena* to his extensive commentary on Hermogenes, Sikeliotes defended rhetoric's functions by exploring, among other issues, its importance for public life. Gregory, Chrysostom, and Basil the Great – three of the most influential Church Fathers[23] – are juxtaposed with important figures of classical Greek political life, like Miltiades, Themistocles and Demosthenes, 'the Nile of the Athenians'.[24] If the latter are praised as the foremost 'political philosophers' of ancient Athens who defended their city-state by means of the 'persuasiveness of their language', their Christian counterparts are commended as orators 'of the same kind' (i.e. 'political philosophers'), whose rhetorical impact transcended the boundaries of a specific state to be felt all over the world. Thanks to the irresistible power of such Christian orators, 'the whole earth is transferred and transported toward a fine order and awareness'.[25]

This rather peculiar – at least for many a modern scholar – juxtaposition of *political* leaders of antiquity to eloquent representatives of Christian rhetoric should be viewed in connection with Sikeliotes' overall cultural and aesthetic reappropriation of one of the most influential texts of ancient Greek rhetorical theory: arguably, Sikeliotes' commentary on Hermogenes as a whole – which has been articulated as a systematic Christianisation of

---

[22] Psellos, *Theologica*, ed. Gautier, 384–6 (98.41–134); see also P. Roilos, *Amphoteroglossia: A Poetics of the Twelfth-century Medieval Greek Novel* (Cambridge, MA, 2005), 46.

[23] I find it significant that most probably in the early 1090s (in 1092), i.e. almost seven decades after Sikeliotes' zealous promulgation of the importance of those three Fathers as exempla of Christian *politikos logos*, John Mauropous would canonise them as the Three Hierarchs of the Church (see A. Karpozilos, Συμβολὴ στὴ μελέτη τοῦ βίου καὶ τοῦ ἔργου τοῦ Ἰωάννη Μαυρόποδος (Ioannina, 1892), 162–6.

[24] Sikeliotes, *Prolegomena*, ed. Rabe, 394.30–95.16.

[25] Ibid., 395.15–16. Once more Sikeliotes employs his favorite aquatic imagery to describe Chrysostom's overwhelming forcefulness: John is 'our golden and sweet ocean,' he stresses (395.10–11).

the venerated ancient rhetorician's prescriptions – constitutes the most methodical *theoretical* attempt throughout Byzantine tradition at an assimilation of ancient Greek literary theory into the principles of Christian ethical and educational discourse.[26] Contrary to the majority of similar Byzantine works that precede or follow it, Sikeliotes' monumental scholarly and pedagogical edifice is based on carefully conceptualised and creatively constructed discursive grounds. In his Christian rewriting of Hermogenes' theory of stylistic 'ideas', he does not confine himself to sporadic references to examples of Christian rhetorical tradition or to a hasty defence of the subject in his introduction, as other Byzantine rhetoricians would have done; instead, he is engaged in a consistent, and more often than not, astute dialogue with the sanctioned prescriptions of his heathen prototype. For instance, although bespeaking a similar propensity to Christianisation, the anonymous (most probably tenth-century) commentator of the same Hermogenean treatise,[27] John Doxapatres in the eleventh century, or Joseph Rhakendytes in the fourteenth century undertake only a partial and unsystematic re-evaluation of inherited literary prescriptions in the light of works of their own religious tradition. For instance, Doxapatres draws on both the ancient and, especially, the Christian tradition in order to establish the divine origin of rhetoric. In addition to pagan myths related to oratory, *Genesis* offers him the best examples of the three kinds of *politikos logos* as performed by God.[28] In this respect, rhetoric deals with things that are 'really divine and marvellous' and help men imitate God.[29] This is an idea explicitly or implicitly endorsed by the majority of the medieval Greek defenders of this art. Doxapatres seems to repeat verbatim Trophonios' formulation of this view which is also employed by another anonymous commentator of the same work by Aphthonios.[30]

Sikeliotes' commentary is an unswerving exploration of the different ways in which ancient Greek stylistic models are adopted, developed, or reinvented in Christian discursive contexts. His discussion abounds in

---

[26] In that respect, his cultural political enterprise could be compared with the Christianisation of aspects of ancient literature and culture in the works of Byzantine allegorists such as Ioannes Diakonos Galenos, on whom see P. Roilos, '*Unshapely Bodies and Beautifying Embellishments*: the Ancient Epics in Byzantium, Allegorical Hermeneutics, and the Case of Ioannes Diakonos Galenos', *JÖB*, 64 (2014), 231–46.
[27] *Rhetores*, ed. Walz, vol. VII, 861–1087.
[28] Doxapatres, *Rhetorical Discourses*, ed. Rabe, 90.16–91.5 and 92.5–93.15; compare to Roilos, *Amphoteroglossia*, 52.
[29] Ibid., 125:2–4.
[30] See Sikeliotes, *Prolegomena*, ed. Rabe, 13.21–4 (Trophonios) and 166.15–18 (anonymous).

allusions or direct references to the Bible or other works of Christian literature; but it is Gregory of Nazianzos, who provides the principal ideological, rhetorical, and structural axis around which Sikeliotes' analysis is articulated. Every single 'idea' of Hermogenes' rhetorical system is illustrated in Sikeliotes' commentary through examples drawn from Gregory, who has replaced Demosthenes as the paradigmatic orator of the new era.[31] The dialectics between the sanctioned, inherited rhetorical principles of the ancients and their innovative exemplification in Christian works is not unidirectional: Hermogenes' stylistic prescriptions are employed to elucidate a number of cases in Christian rhetorical works, and the latter are elevated to the status of discursive and ethical prototypes that surpass all preceding literature and most creatively exemplify the ancient rhetorician's sanctioned prescriptions of eloquence. In this cross-fertilisation of ancient literary theory and Christian rhetorical practice, older rhetorical ideas are reinterpreted, or selected ideals are reactivated with significant diversions from the focus of their original definitions.

This difference in focus constitutes one of the most effective hermeneutic mechanisms that Sikeliotes employs throughout his Christianisation of ancient Greek rhetorical theory. It is within this discursive context that his redefinition of the concept of 'political' discourse should be viewed. Sikeliotes offers the most methodical and original handling of the topic of *politikos logos* in the context of the contemporary Byzantine political system throughout the medieval Greek rhetorical tradition. Previous or later relevant discussions do not go beyond the formulaic tripartite division of political systems as described, for instance, by John of Sardis in his commentary on the *Progymnasmata* of Aphthonios.[32] Despite the fact that Sikeliotes devotes only a relatively limited number of pages to a systematic discussion of this issue, it is there that some of the most forceful aspects of his overall moral and educational reasoning are developed. This is anything but fortuitous. First, in Hermogenes' treatise, the different types of political oratory are given a prominent position; pointedly dealt with especially immediately after the analysis of *deinotês*, they conclude his essay, thus marking its theoretical culmination. At a later point in his *Prolegomena*, Sikeliotes makes it clear that he is deeply aware of the significance that the

---

[31] For some general observations about Sikeliotes' use of Gregory of Nazianzos as a rhetorical model, see: T. M. Conley, 'Demosthenes Dethroned: Gregory Nazianzus in Sikeliotes' Scholia on Hermogenes' Περὶ Ἰδεῶν', *ICS*, 27/28 (2002–3), 145–52. I intend to undertake a systematic analysis of Sikeliotes' application of specific Hermogenean rhetorical 'ideas' to Christian rhetoric in a separate study.

[32] Doxapatres, *Rhetorical Discourses*, ed. Rabe, 145.1–146.24.

ancient theoretician attributed to this type of rhetorical discourse: Hermogenes' aim, Sikeliotes emphasises, is to prescribe the virtues of political oratory and, through it, of rhetorical discourse as a whole.[33] Sikeliotes, abiding by the usual practice of Byzantine commentators, follows the structure of Hermogenes' text and includes his observations about *politikos logos* at the appropriate place at the end of his commentary. However, more interesting than this predictable arrangement of his analysis is Sikeliotes' decision to focus on this kind of rhetorical discourse already in his *Prolegomena*. This kind of ring composition contributes to the discursive and ideological cohesion of his analysis, since the rhetorical and educational principles that are set forth in his introduction, and then reiterated at the end of his discussion, condition also his overall argumentation throughout his commentary. Second, his redefinition of *politikos logos* in the light of Christian rhetorical practice helps him to overcome a major thorny issue in his parallel investigations into the functions and the theoretical validation of rhetoric in antiquity, on the one hand, and in Byzantium, on the other: by forging a strong link between the ancient Greek *politikos logos* – the most prominent rhetorical type both in Hermogenes' theory and in classical oratorical practice in general – and Christian discursive paradigms, Sikeliotes promotes not only the authority of the former but also the importance of the latter and of his own activity as rhetorician and educator.

Therefore, it is not without significance, I would argue, that the words that introduce his defence of rhetoric in his *Prolegomena* are '*politikê epistêmê*', a term subtly alluding to the relevant works of the two most influential philosophers of ancient Greece, Plato and Aristotle, as well as to the prioritisation of *politikos logos* in Hermogenes' paradigmatic rhetorical system. In Sikeliotes' theoretical edifice, '*politikê*' is invested with a moral and intellectual potential that lends itself to a convenient assimilation into Christian ethics: this *epistêmê*, according to this medieval Greek rhetorician, is closely connected to 'magnanimity' (*megalonoia*), which helps people to achieve the purification of the intellectual (*gnôstikon*) part of their soul from its material associations. To such people, as well as to those who desire to discover what is really beneficial and conducive to security in this life – a life to which we have all 'been expelled from the untormented and calm state of perfection' – the 'secret rites and mysteries of the common good of rhetoric and the rituals of its methods' are 'necessary',

---

[33] Sikeliotes, *Prolegomena*, ed. Rabe, 402.4–10.

whereas to 'irreverent' people they are 'inaccessible'.[34] Already this introductory passage sets the ideological and rhetorical tone for the overarching syncretistic orientation of his discussion. The ineluctably conspicuous references to the pagan origins of *politikê* and *rhetorikê* are combined with subtle allusions to the biblical image of man before – and after – the Fall. Especially the metaphorical/homological connection of religious rituals with the 'mysteries' of rhetoric accords Sikeliotes' account a 'dignified' discursive modality, which is not in dissonance with Hermogenes' conceptualisation of rhetoric as a whole and of the stylistic 'idea' of 'dignity' in particular.[35] This homology, formulated dynamically as it is in terms of a ritual poetics,[36] sets into motion a complex, almost anagogical intercrossing not only of discursive but also of conceptual textures of different socioaesthetic origins – pagan and Christian. Sikeliotes' transition from ancient rhetorical theory to transcendental Christian practice is now well underway:

> For it [rhetoric] is undoubtedly the best part of philosophy and the first regulating impress of the superior power, if it imitates God in ordering things in a rational manner, because it takes care of the souls and the bodies and the houses and the cities – every single one of these separately and all of them together – since they have been turned away from the better life as a result of the Fall and driven disorderly and in disarray due to the chaotic powers ... By being a creator of foundations and bases and order, and by organising the elements of our intellectual essence and arranging, and guiding them in every way, it [rhetoric] leads us toward prudent governance.[37]

Sikeliotes dwells on the same topic in more detail at the end of his commentary, where he discusses the different types of *politikos logos*. In a

---

[34] Sikeliotes, *Prolegomena*, ed. Rabe, 393.17–394.14.
[35] On this view of rhetoric in Hermogenes, see Roilos, *Amphoteroglossia*, 141.
[36] 'Homology' refers to analogous deep structures of signification in different epistemological and experiential domains. For this conceptualisation of 'homology', see D. Yatromanolakis and P. Roilos, *Towards a Ritual Poetics* (Athens, 2003), 40 where also the notion of ritual poetics is put forward; 'ritual poetics' refers to the ways in which 'ritual *textures*... interact with and act upon the formation, expression, and manipulation of diverse cultural and sociopolitical discourses'. In this sense, ritual poetics should be defined in terms of interdiscursivity. On aspects of Byzantine rhetoric in terms of ritual poetics, see Roilos, *Amphoteroglossia*, 140–68, 189–96.
[37] Φιλοσοφίας γάρ ἐστι τὸ κάλλιστον ἄντικρυς καὶ χαρακτὴρ ὁ πρῶτος τοῦ κρείττονος τακτικός, εἴπερ θεὸν ὑποκρίνεται λογικῇ φύσει διαταττόμενον, καὶ κοινῇ καὶ καθ' ἕκαστον ψυχῶν τε καὶ σωμάτων οἰκιῶν τε καὶ πόλεων ἐπιμελομένη τῶν ἀμεινόνων τῇ ἐκπτώσει παρατραπέντων καὶ φερομένων ἄτακτα καὶ ἀσύντακτα ταῖς ἀσυναρτήτοις δυνάμεσι ... ἀλλὰ κρηπῖδος οὖσα καὶ βάσεως καὶ κοσμήσεως δημιουργὸς τά τε τῆς νοερᾶς οὐσίας ἡμῶν διαστέλλουσα καὶ παντοίως διεξάγουσα καὶ ἰθύνουσα πρὸς τὸ οἰκονομικὸν ἐφιστᾷ (Sikeliotes, *Prolegomena*, ed. Rabe, 394.14–28-20).

magisterial reorientation of the focus of Hermogenes' treatise – a discursive twist that had been strategically prepared for not only in his *Prolegomena* but also throughout his discussion – he advances a manifesto-like canonisation of new, Christian discursive models at the expense of the old ones. Despite the fact that, as his continuous references to Gregory of Nazianzos indicate, he never neglected the purely rhetorical aspects of these novel prototypes, here it is especially their moral and educational authority that he celebrates; and albeit adopting the categorisations discussed by Hermogenes, he proposes a different conceptualisation of the 'true' (*tô onti*) *politikos logos*. Such, he argues, is that discourse which accords 'the powers of the soul an equality of rights pertaining to the spiritual cities, which directs what is deficient to abundance, which is devoted to undisturbed peace and advances victories at the invisible wars and transfers [us] to that *city* of which we have been robbed'.[38] This type of discourse, he stresses, has been especially practised by the 'Holy Fathers', who help men to communicate and even to be united with God, thus elevating their mortal nature to the state of eternity. Accordingly, the three major categories of *politikos logos* in Hermogenes' theoretical system are adjusted here to the needs of Christian orators: deliberative speech focuses on what is profitable for men's double nature;[39] the panegyric pertains to the glorification of God and his supporters or to the castigation of his enemies; and judicial rhetoric aims at refuting or at restoring to the right path 'those who have been led astray'.

As is well known, more often than not the adjective '*politikos*' was charged with negative associations in medieval Greek moralistic contexts. Relevant examples abound. Here it suffices to mention a telling definition of this term by Basil the Great: '*politikos* we call someone who uses vulgar language'.[40] Contrary to the established derogatory use of this specific word in Christian literature and drawing rather from the spiritual appropriation of the concept of *polis/politeia* in the same tradition, Sikeliotes

---

[38] ... ὁ ἰσονομίαν βραβεύων ταῖς δυνάμεσι τῶν ψυχῶν τῶν νοερῶν πόλεων τό τε ἐνδέον περιττὸν διϊθύνων, εἰρήνην δὲ πραγματευόμενος ἀστασίαστον καὶ νίκας εἰσηγούμενος τῶν ἀφανῶν πολέμων καὶ πρὸς τὴν πολιτείαν μεταβιβάζων ἧσπερ ἀπεσυλήθημεν (Sikeliotes, *Commentary*, ed. Walz, 467.2–7).

[39] Διάφορος is the adjective that is here used to refer to men's nature. A *scholion* by an anonymous reader interprets the meaning of this word as follows: 'Διάφορος, that is [our] essence that has been constituted of body and soul' (Ibid., 467). That this scholiast may be right is supported, in my view, by the fact that earlier in his commentary Sikeliotes had defined rhetoric as an art pertinent to the well-being of both the souls and the bodies of men (449.9–11); the same idea had been also emphasised in his *Prolegomena* (Sikeliotes, *Prolegomena*, ed. Rabe, 394.17–18).

[40] *PG*, vol. XXIX, 476.13.

proposes an innovative reinterpretation of the ancient Greek terminological, ideological and socioaesthetic connotations of the rhetorical genre of *politikos logos*. Although his commentary does not provide references to concrete intertexts of the Christianising appropriation of the notion of *polis/politeia*, hagiography and the works of the Church Fathers are replete with such examples. Intimations of the reformulation of the ancient 'idealised cognitive models' of *polis* may be detected very early in the history of Christian sociopolitical imaginaries – already in the work of St Paul, especially his Letter to the Ephesians (2:12, 19).[41] In the second century, Clement of Alexandria articulated a legitimisation of this anagogical reappropriation of the image of *polis* by adducing parallels from heathen philosophy: 'I wish that Christ's spirit gave me wings to fly to my own Jerusalem; for the Stoics too call the sky the *polis* (city) par excellence ... and we are also aware of Plato's *polis*, which is located as an archetypal paradigm in the sky.'[42] The heavenly 'city above' or the 'spiritual city' is also encountered as a *topos* of desired eternity in the works of Gregory of Nazianzos, Basil the Great, and John Chrysostom. An especially eloquent description of this transcendental space is found in Gregory's funerary oration for his sister Gorgonia: 'our fatherland is the *polis* of Jerusalem above, the *polis* that is not visible but spiritually conceivable, in which we are citizens and toward which we hasten'.[43] Also similar is the idea conveyed in the following words of John Chrysostom: 'so let us take care of our return, let us go back up to the *polis* in the heavens, where we have been registered as citizens (*politeuesthai*)'.[44]

It is this transcendental definition of the concept of *polis* that allows Sikeliotes to identify political philosophers – the most esteemed group of rhetoricians, in his view – with the Church Fathers, who, by practising the

---

[41] For the notion of 'idealised cognitive models' in terms of categorial principles that help men to organise and conceptualise reality, see G. Lakoff, *Women, Fire, and Dangerous Things: What Categories Reveal about the Mind* (Chicago, IL, 1987), esp. 68–90. For a discussion of comparable cognitive schemata in Byzantine culture from a historical, cognitive anthropological perspective, see P. Roilos, '*Phantasia* and the Ethics of Fictionality in Byzantium: A Cognitive Anthropological Perspective' in P. Roilos, ed., *Medieval Greek Storytelling: Fictionality and Narrative in Byzantium* (Wiesbaden, 2014); for important relevant methodological suggestions with regard to the study of ancient Greek socioaesthetic phenomena, see Yatromanolakis, *Sappho in the Making*, esp. 1–49; D. Yatromanolakis, 'Genre Categories and Interdiscursivity in Alkaios and Archaic Greece', *Synkrise/Comparaison*, 19 (2008), 169–87; and D. Yatromanolakis,, 'Symposia, Noses, *Prosôpa*: A Kylix in the Company of Banqueters on the Ground' in D. Yatromanolakis, ed., *An Archaeology of Representations: Ancient Greek Vase-Painting and Contemporary Methodologies* (Athens, 2009), 414–65.
[42] O. Stählin, ed., *Clemens Alexandrinus. Stromata* (Leipzig, 1905–36), vol. IV, 26.172.
[43] *PG*, vol. xxxv, 796.16–19.
[44] J. Dumortier, ed., *Jean Chrysostome. A Théodore* (Paris, 1966), 17.47–9.

'real' *politikos logos*, goad men toward eternity. In his *Prolegomena*, he attempted to establish the relevance of the ancient Greek types of political discourse to Christian imaginaries and their promulgation through rhetoric, by defending also this art's importance for another kind of imagined transcendental community, Plato's idealised *politeia* – a heathen parallel, according to Clement of Alexandria, of the Christian heavenly city. Although elsewhere Sikeliotes refers to Plato in positive terms,[45] he is firm in his refutation of the ancient philosopher's attack against rhetoric. First of all, Sikeliotes counters Plato's refusal to acknowledge rhetoric's contribution to his ideal *politeia* or to the function of real cities. In his polemic, Sikeliotes draws on a tradition that goes back to Isocrates and Aristotle and was most systematically expressed in Ailios Aristeides' essay *In Defence of Rhetoric*.[46] Despite the fact that, true to his habitual obscure allusiveness, the Byzantine commentator refrains from revealing his sources, the focus and the construction of his refutation leave no doubt that here he is engaged in an indirect dialogue with this specific work by Aristeides. In particular, Sikeliotes' insistence on the contradictions in Plato's condemnation of rhetoric points, in my view, to his debt to the ancient sophist. It may be pertinent to note here that John Doxapatres is more open about his own use of the same work in his *Rhetorical Discourses on Aphthonios*.[47]

Sikeliotes' main argument is that rhetoric contributes to the restraining of human passions and to the preservation of equilibrium in society, both of which are important conditions for the existence and peaceful administration even of the Platonic *politeia*. Not unlike Ailios Aristeides,[48] Sikeliotes advocates rhetoric's value as an art and as a proper *epistêmê*, or rather as the most valuable constituent of philosophy itself, since it is

---

[45] For instance, Sikeliotes endorses Plato's use of *semnos* discourse in *Timaeus* (Sikeliotes, *Commentary*, ed. Walz, 318.27–32; 481.15–17). Elsewhere, Sikeliotes calls Plato 'sweet' (210.16–17).

[46] Later, Syrianos, in his commentary on Hermogenes' *On Ideas*, will also draw on *Gorgias* to argue for rhetoric's status as a legitimate and useful art: H. Rabe, ed., *Syriani in Hermogenem commentaria* (Leipzig, 1892–3), vol. II, 4.14–5; 6.13–7.1; 8.22–9.2. It is significant that the Neoplatonist Syrianos bases his defence of rhetoric on sporadic positive references in Plato's own work to rhetoric's potential value as an occupation conducive to moral development (4).

[47] Doxapatres, *Rhetorical Discourses*, ed. Rabe, 121.9–11. Doxapatres quotes a long passage from *Gorgias* (463a–65c) and then, drawing from Ailios Aristeides – an ancient author greatly respected in Byzantium – he embarks on a detailed refutation of Plato's views. For some other debts of Doxapatres to Aristeides as evinced in his commentary on Hermogenes' *On Issues*, see S. Glöckner, *Über den Kommentar des Johannes Doxopatres zu den Staseis des Hermogenes* (Kirchhain, 1908), 15–16.

[48] See especially Aristeides' arguments in: F. W. Lenz and C. A. Behr, eds., *P. Aelii Aristidis Opera quae exstant omnia* (Leiden, 1978), 131–204.

based on systematic reasoning. In a pompous address to Plato, which does not seem to be entirely ironic, he asks the 'divine' ancient thinker how it is possible for philosophy to subsist, if its 'paternal' discipline of rhetoric is abandoned. According to Sikeliotes' zealous but rather circular argumentation, one of the following must be true: either Plato 'philosophises unphilosophically' (at least with regard to this point), or oratory is not a 'shadowy' occupation, as Plato maintains. Sikeliotes' criticism, not unlike Aristeides', focuses on Socrates' views in *Gorgias*. The medieval Greek commentator does not disclose his Platonic interlocutor but informed readers, then and now, would identify him with no major difficulty.[49]

In addition to such implicit but rather easily identifiable intertextual allusions to *Gorgias*, some of Sikeliotes' general arguments and especially metaphoric homologies between rhetoric and other arts or *epistêmai* may be viewed as general, allusive responses to relevant Platonic ideas about rhetoric.[50] Medical imagery and its figurative associations with rhetorical discourse are predominant throughout his commentary. If viewed in the context of his overall argument against Plato, the extent to which Sikeliotes employs this kind of connection – which is unprecedented and arguably unique in the tradition of Byzantine commentaries on the Hermogenean corpus – may be interpreted, I argue, as an attempt to establish a firm epistemological analogy between rhetoric and medicine, the *technê* par excellence that Plato in *Gorgias* opposes to rhetoric, in order to expose the supposed inferior status of rhetoric as a mere knack.[51] To my mind one cannot exclude the possibility that Sikeliotes' use of medical discourse may

---

[49] Allusions to *Gorgias* and to Platonic arguments against rhetoric in general are encountered throughout Sikeliotes' work. Especially in his *Prolegomena*, he refers to Plato's use of mythological exempla in this specific dialogue and to his overall discussion of rhetoric in connection with other humble arts (see *Prolegomena*, ed. Rabe, 395.16–24; 396.6–9, 20–3).

[50] The concept of homology is pertinent to the elucidation of such multilayered discursive associations. By contrast, the notion of 'conflation' can be misleading. The problematic methodological and hermeneutic results to which the idea of conflation may lead are particularly evident in R. Rehm's *Marriage to Death* (Princeton, 1994). Rehm's book offers perhaps the most problematic application of the concept of conflation to ancient Greek literature in recent scholarship. See the authoritative observations of C. Sourvinou-Inwood in 'Review: *Marriage to Death. The Conflation of Wedding and Funeral Rituals in Greek Tragedy* by R. Rehm', *Classical Review*, n.s. 46 (1996), 58–9.

[51] See especially *Gorgias* 462b–66a. Ailios Aristeides was the first to confute Plato's biased comparison of rhetoric with medicine in a systematic way. It is worth noting that later, in his commentary on *Gorgias*, Olympiodoros paralleled the work of a rhetorician to that of a pharmacist who prepares the drugs prescribed by a doctor (the metaphorical equivalent of the political philosopher; see R. Jackson et al., eds., *Olympiodorus: Commentary on Plato's Gorgias* (Leiden, 1998), 40). In this manner, Olympiodoros tried to remedy Plato's vehement disparagement of rhetoric. In Sikeliotes, the role of the rhetor is promoted even further, since it is compared, not to the work of a pharmacist, but to the scientific expertise of a doctor; see below n. 60.

reflect the inchoate and less systematic, but marked appropriation of similar imagery in the anonymous tenth-century commentary on the same Hermogenean treatise. The anonymous author compares the structure of rhetorical discourse with the constitution of human beings: *ennoia* corresponds to the soul, *methodos* to the 'movement' of the soul, *lexis* to the body, the figures of speech to bodily forms, and so on. The anonymous comments also on the relation between the soul and the body in the philosophical systems of the Stoics and the Platonists as well as in Galen's medical theory; the latter, the anonymous notes, agrees with the Stoic idea that the soul does not preexist the body and that all animate beings are rather created through the *kraseis* of the elements; by contrast, the anonymous' own interpretation concurs with the Platonic view that the soul resides in the body from the very beginning and strives to rule over it.[52]

Sikeliotes' appreciation of the scientific authority of medicine and its discourse is evinced early in his commentary: in his discussion of Hermogenes' emphasis on the systematic teaching of rhetoric and its superiority to inherent talents, Sikeliotes offers an interesting explanation of the phenomenon of naturally gifted individuals; his analysis combines scientific knowledge with marked moralistic and theological principles. Natural talents, Sikeliotes asserts, are gifts granted by God to those men whose *kraseis* ('constitutions') are excellent. However, it depends upon men to secure ideal *kraseis* for themselves and their progeny: turning to the authority of Hippocrates and Galen, Sikeliotes stresses that a man's *krasis* is conditioned by his diet and overall way of life.[53] Correct eating habits, healthy nutrition, and a moderate way of life secure an excellent constitution for humans and their children. The opposite happens when men indulge in gluttony and the passions deriving from the *chymoi* of inappropriate food. *Chymos* and *krasis* are, of course, marked terms and concepts in Galen's physiological and medical theory, on which Sikeliotes clearly draws here. In a rather unexpected shift of the focus of his argumentation, Sikeliotes links medical wisdom about the importance of diet and its genetic effects with the production of different modes of rhetorical discourse: 'as intoxicated men', he argues, 'produce drunkards, so, too, the man who is thick at his *êthos* creates analogous discourse; and likewise he

---

[52] *Rhetores*, ed. Walz, vol. VII, 883.15–85.5; for similar ideas in Sikeliotes, see discussion below.
[53] In this part of his commentary, Sikeliotes explicitly refers to the Hippocratic treatise on epidemics and Galen's works on *krasis* and *diaita* (most probably his (Galen's) treatise *On the Properties of Foods* [Sikeliotes, *Commentary*, ed. Walz, 453–553K] and the pseudo-Galenic work *On the Humors* [19.485–96K]).

who is gracious produces gracious speeches, and so does each single individual [according to his own *êthos*]'.⁵⁴

Clearly, this intriguing connection between medical knowledge and discursive *êthos* is based on the underlying idea that rhetoric is closely related (and conducive) to the moral formation of individuals and communities, an idea advocated throughout Sikeliotes' commentary. According to him, as perfect *krasis* results from a combination of both inherent predispositions and medical/biological factors, so rhetorical discourse is the result of both natural talent and personal *êthos*; the last items in each pair of this homology (medical/biological factors and personal *êthos*) are similarly dependent to a great extent on men's free volition and moral choices, and, as such, should be the objects of special care and learning. These correspondences between medicine and rhetoric become even clearer later in Sikeliotes' commentary, when he compares the corrective or rather preventive function of the 'idea' of *eukrineia* ('limpidity') with the effect of prophylactic and therapeutic drugs prescribed by a prudent doctor.⁵⁵

At several other points of his discussion, Sikeliotes, drawing especially on Galen and on ancient psychology, dwells on further figurative homologies between the constitution of the human body and the composition of rhetorical 'ideas'. Rhetorical discourse is thus often compared to an animate entity. As different kinds of living organisms are similar to each other in certain respects but differ in others, so certain rhetorical modes share some discursive features with other 'ideas' while preserving their own charateristic identity. For instance, nutritive force (*threptikê*) is the only function human beings and plants share;⁵⁶ movement, mortality, and 'the ability to reproduce similar organisms' are the characteristic attributes that bring men close to 'irrational' animals; on the other hand, spirituality and the rational (*logikon*) part of the soul link men to angels. Similarly, the rhetorical idea of purity (*katharotês*) and that of forcefulness (*deinotês*), for

---

⁵⁴ καθὰ καὶ ὁ μέθυσος μεθύσους παῖδας προΐησι, καὶ ὁ παχὺς τὸ ἦθος ὁμοίους καὶ τοὺς λόγους ἀπογεννᾷ, καὶ ὁ χαρίεις χαρίεντας, καὶ ἕκαστος παραπλησίους (Sikeliotes, *Commentary*, ed. Walz, 92.2–4).

⁵⁵ Sikeliotes, *Commentary*, ed. Walz, 185.13–16. It is worth noting that the same idea is also expressed in the tenth-century anonymous commentary on Hermogenes' *On Ideas* (*Rhetores*, ed. Walz, vol. VII, 934.7–18).

⁵⁶ Sikeliotes' discussion here reflects aspects of Platonic and Aristotelian psychology, which, it should be noted, were by and large adopted by Galen. In this respect, characteristic is Sikeliotes' reference to the nutritive faculty of the body with a term (*threptikê*) that Aristotle uses to describe the lowest part of the soul (e.g. in *On the Soul*, 415a; 416d; 434a); at the same time, the view that this is a quality that human beings share with plants recalls also Plato's ideas about the lowest kind of the soul (*epithymêtikon*; *Timaeus* 77b3–4; see Aristotle, *On the Generation of Animals*, 740b).

instance, are distinguished on the basis of their respective distinctive subject-matters (*ennoiai*) while occasionally employing the same lexical elements.[57]

The structure and function of rhetorical discourse is further paralleled to the anatomy of a human being: the *ennoiai* (subject-matters) pertinent to an idea correspond to the head – the centre of the soul; and just as the soul needs to be set into motion in order to be active and creative, so an *ennoia* has to be activated through the appropriate rhetorical *methodos* in order to be expressed. *Lexis* (diction) is paralleled to the human body, whose limbs correspond to the *kôla* (parts) of words, its appearance to figures of speech (*schêmata*), the articulation of its different members to *synthêkê* (combination of sounds) in discourse, and the analogies between its parts to rhythm in speech.[58] Sikeliotes' comparison of rhetorical discourse with human physiology should be viewed in light of the other homologies that he employs throughout his commentary to underline the significance of harmonious symmetry, both in rhetoric and in other domains of human experience and the broader world. Although there is nothing in Sikeliotes' description that may help us establish concrete intertextual relations, it is worth noting that, in his treatise *On the Use of Parts*, Galen describes the human body as an example of perfection in nature as a whole.[59] The same homological comparison is further developed in Sikeliotes' explication of the rhetorical 'idea' of *kallos* (beauty). Once more he adduces the example of bodily beauty and harmony – as described, he explicitly adds here, by Galen – in order to illustrate the phenomenon of *kallos* in discourse: as health and beauty in the human body result from the balanced mixture of *chymoi* and *kraseis*, so *kallos* in discourse is also created by means of symmetrical proportions. This symmetry can be achieved only through the *epistêmê* of rhetoric, which dictates the correct use of the different elements

---

[57] Sikeliotes, *Commentary*, ed. Walz, 115.18–116.11.   [58] Ibid., 117.28–118.18.
[59] This Galenic work was particularly influential on Neoplatonic and Christian authors; see O. Temkin, 'Byzantine Medicine: Tradition and Empiricism', *DOP*, 16 (1962), 107. Worth mentioning are also the parallel homological patterns found in the intriguing work *The Constitution of Man* by Meletios, an author of original thought, who remains however a rather obscure figure: J. A. Cramer, *Anecdota Graeca e codd. manuscriptis bibliothecarum Oxoniensium* (Oxford, 1836), 1–157. Temkin, 'Byzantine Medicine', continues to be fundamental for Galen as a philosopher and his influence on later thinkers; see also: R. Todd, 'Galenic Medical Ideas in the Greek Aristotelian Commentators', *Sosl*, 52 (1977), 117–34. On the general interaction of medicine and philosophy in late antiquity/early Byzantium see L. G. Westerink, 'Philosophy and Medicine in Late Antiquity', *Janus*, 51 (1964), 169–77. Informative on medicine in Byzantium are Temkin, 'Byzantine Medicine', and Hunger, *Literatur*, vol. 1, 287–320; also see J. Duffy, 'Byzantine Medicine in the Sixth and Seventh Centuries: Aspects of Teaching and Practice', *DOP*, 38 (1984), 21–7, which addresses the role of medicine in education in early Byzantium.

of speech, despite the fact that the process and the conditions of the final constitution of both discursive and bodily *kallos* resist interpretation.⁶⁰ Sikeliotes is careful not to pursue this analogy beyond the doctrinal principles dictated by theological orthodoxy. Whereas in rhetoric *ennoiai* (the metaphorical equivalent of the centre of the soul) are deduced and 'drawn forth' by diction, the relation between the soul and the body is based, he emphasises, on different dynamics: in human individuals, the soul is the 'mistress' – not a slave (*doulê*) – who by no means is subjugated to the needs and *krasis* of the body. By making this qualification, Sikeliotes firmly differentiates his own Christian 'psychology' from that of his main medical source, Galen, who proposes an agnostic, if not explicitly materialistic, view of the relationship between *psychê* and *sôma*.⁶¹

Sikeliotes indulges in an exceptionally creative appropriation of medical discourse when he explicates the term *symphtharsis*, which Hermogenes employs in his discussion of the ideal mixture of different 'ideas.' In his commentary on the same work, Syrianos had already noted the medical associations of this word, briefly pointing out that it refers to digestion and the production of the nutritional *chymos* ('liquid') after the alteration of

---

⁶⁰ Sikeliotes, *Commentary*, ed. Walz, 321.19–322.23; Sikeliotes' observation about the impossibility of interpreting the phenomenon of aesthetic and bodily beauty as a whole echoes a similar idea expressed in Phoibammon's discussion of the *mixis* of rhetorical styles (*Prolegomenon Sylloge*, ed. Rabe, 382.15–25). Phoibammon's authorship is not unquestioned; see ibid., cvii–cviii; cf. A. Brinkmann, 'Phoibammon Περὶ μιμήσεως', *RhM*, 61 (1906), 117–34. Stegemann's piece on him remains very informative; he makes the interesting point that Phoibammon, in his discussion of rhetorical *mimêsis*, opposed Stoic views on the subject (W. Stegemann, 'Phoibammon', *RE*, 39 (1941), 326–43). It may not be fortuitous that Sikeliotes places special emphasis on the analogy between rhetoric and medicine, to which Plato accords a relatively superior status in *Gorgias*, rather than with painting. Sikeliotes' acceptance of the limitations of both medicine and rhetoric does not undermine their status as *epistêmai*; it seems, rather, to be a variation of the dialectics between *physis* and (controllable and thus teachable) *êthos* that Sikeliotes discussed earlier in his commentary.

⁶¹ Sikeliotes, *Commentary*, ed. Walz, 118.20–5. On Galen's views on the soul see the discussions in L. G. Ballester, 'Soul and Body: Disease of the Soul and Disease of the Body in Galen's Medical Thought' in P. Manuli, M. Vegetti, eds., *Le opere psicologiche di Galeno* (Naples, 1988), 117–52; J. Pigeaud, 'La psychopathologie de Galien' in ibid., 153–83; R. J. Hankinson, 'Greek Medical Models of Mind' in S. Eversen, ed., *Psychology* (Oxford, 1991), 208–17; H. Von Staden, 'Body, Soul, and Nerves: Epicurus, Herophilus, Erasistratus, the Stoics, and Galen' in J. P. Wright and P. Potter, eds., *Psyche and Soma: Physicians and Metaphysicians on the Mind–Body Problem from Antiquity to Enlightenment* (Oxford, 2000), 105–16. For Galen's conceptualisation of the soul as a 'slave' (*doulê*) of the physical needs of the body, see P. De Lacy, 'The Third Part of the Soul' in Manuli and Vegetti, ed., *Le opere psicologiche di Galeno*, 58–9. It is worth noting that Galen dedicated a whole treatise to the relation between the soul and the *kraseis* of the body (*That the Soul's Qualities Follow the Body's Temperaments*; J. Marquardt, I. Müller and G. Helmreich, *Claudii Galeni Pergameni scripta minora* (Leipzig, 1884–93), vol. II, 32–79). Plutarch is also mentioned by Sikeliotes as a thinker whose ideas on the specific matter are close to those of Galen.

different kinds of food in the stomach.[62] Sikeliotes – whose interpretation is reproduced almost verbatim by Gregory Pardos in the twelfth century[63] – mentions the specific physical connotations of the term but, in his meticulous clarifications of Hermogenes' metaphor, he goes beyond any other commentator, earlier or later. At the very beginning he makes it clear that this word does not signify absolute destruction and disintegration. Such complete decomposition occurs, he notes, when an 'irrational' animal dies and its whole entity, that is both its body and the soul, is destroyed. Here, Sikeliotes again finds the opportunity to let his Christian beliefs enter his physiological and psychological discourse: the souls of men, he emphasises, are immortal and therefore, in their case, dissolution concerns only the elements that constitute their bodies. Clearly, this subtle but important distinction derives from an idealistic approach to the soul – one that supports its immortality as opposed, for instance, to Galen's materialistic views on this issue. In addition to its conspicuous Christian origins, the underlying differentiation between perishable matter and eternal, immaterial substance/soul, on which Sikeliotes' observations here are based, finds an intriguing parallel, I argue, in Proklos' commentary on Plato's *Timaeus*, where a comparable distinction is discussed in connection with the idea of *symphtharsis*, which Proklos also views as a process related to matter.[64]

Sikeliotes further clarifies that biological *symphtharsis* is of two kinds: first, it is related to the decomposition of dead bodies, which results in the creation of other organisms such as worms and lice; second, it concerns the function of digestion. From this point on, Sikeliotes' explication takes the form of a short medical exposition of the function of digestion, extensively based on Galen's description of the circulation and distribution of the nutritional *chymoi* in the human body. After digestion, the phlegm is 'drawn' to the head; the yellow bile to the gall bladder; the black bile to the intestines or the spleen; and the blood both to the heart, which 'attracts' the best part of it, and to the liver, which absorbs its less pure kind. All the

---

[62] Syrianos, *Commentary on Hermogenes*, ed. Rabe, vol. II, 66.1–6. Similar is the explication of the term by the tenth-century anonymous commentator of the Hermogenean treatise (*Rhetores*, ed. Walz, vol. VII, 1042.16–21).
[63] *Rhetores*, ed. Walz, vol. VII, 1132.7–20.
[64] E. Diehl, ed., *Procli Diadochi in Platonis Timaeum commentaria* (Leipzig, 1903–6), vol. II, 254; see vol. III, 326, where the co-existence and the simultaneous respective autonomy of the body and the soul are discussed.

remaining useless substances are eliminated from the body through its pores and orifices.[65]

Sikeliotes, focusing on the grammatical details of Hermogenes' original text, stresses that the ancient rhetorician does not mean that the blending of different 'ideas' occurs in the same way as *symphtharsis*. Hermogenes, Sikeliotes explains, says καθάπερ ἐκ συμφθάρσεως, not just ἐκ συμφθάρσεως, thus implying that he does not approach the mixture of different styles in discourse in terms of actual *symphtharsis*, because in that case it would not be possible to discern each individual 'idea' and describe it appropriately.[66]

By associating medical wisdom with rhetoric, and by advocating the importance of firm and systematic distinctions for rhetorical theory, Sikeliotes establishes the status of this art as a legitimate discipline. In one of the most intriguing passages in his commentary, he develops the epistemological principles of his overall method. While commenting on Hermogenes' emphasis on the importance of a systematic learning of the discipline of rhetoric, as opposed to a mere imitation of rhetorical models, Sikeliotes expatiates on the topic in much more detail than Hermogenes' text alone would justify, precisely because his main, but implicit, aim is to refute Plato's condemnation of rhetoric. Sikeliotes asserts that there are four steps and levels of knowledge, which correspond to four different, but complementary, epistemological processes. The first level of knowledge is achieved through the senses, and constitutes the content of empirical perception. The formation of belief or conviction (*doxa*) is the next phase, which is followed by the activation of thinking (*dianoia*). The last and most valuable step in the whole gnosiological process is the acquisition of knowledge through the faculty of *nous*. By means of sensory familiarisation with the world, some awareness/mental simulacrum (*phantasia*) is formed, which is based entirely on material elements. *Phantasia* – the 'passive *nous*' – transfers the basic information that it has collected to the level of *doxa*, which, according to Sikeliotes, represents the 'gnostic power of the soul that receives' – and elaborates, it may be added – 'the impressions shaped through *phantasia*'. In its turn, *doxa* forwards its more advanced

---

[65] Sikeliotes' description here recalls elements from Galen; on Galen's ideas on digestion, see T. Tieleman, *Galen and Chrysippus on the Soul: Argument and Refutation in the De Placitis II–III* (Leiden, 1996), 66–105; O. Powell, trans., *Galen: On the Properties of Foodstuffs* (Cambridge, 2003), 13–18.

[66] Sikeliotes says that the concept of *krasis* would have been equally inaccurate for describing the blending of styles, because it would also indicate the impossibility of differentiating between the various 'ideas'.

perception to *dianoia*, the 'active' epistemological medium that conveys all accumulated information to the intellect (*nous*). Sikeliotes employs a paretymological association to illustrate *dianoia*'s dynamic mediatory role: '*dianoia*', he stresses, 'is [that power of the soul] that traverses (*dianyei*) the territory of the sensory simulacra of conviction (τὰ τῆς αἰσθητῆς φαντασίας τῆς δόξης) and elevates them to *nous*'. In the end, *nous* organises all types of information and achieves the ultimate kind of knowledge, the '*epistêmê* of beings'.[67]

The basic epistemological schema adopted by Sikeliotes does not depart considerably from established gnosiological theories that can be traced back to ancient Greek philosophy and especially to Plato and Aristotle. However, Sikeliotes further demonstrates the climactic development of the gnosiological process with an intriguing homology, in which the four perceptual powers of the soul undertake the role of personified agents/sememes of an inchoate allegorical narrative: *aisthêsis* is paralleled to a gate that receives those who enter an enclosed space; *phantasia* marks a brief stop at the entrance, until *doxa*, a kind of guard, is notified; *dianoia* is compared to a trusted servant; finally, *nous* resembles the master of the house, who administers everything.[68] Sikeliotes' allegorical presentation of this hierarchical epistemological schema finds an intriguing parallel in Synesios of Cyrene's description of the gnosiological process in his astute treatise on dreams.[69] There is no specific evidence for a *direct* intertextual response of Sikeliotes to Synesios' specific work, although the latter's appeal to later Byzantine intellectuals, at least, is evidenced by Nikephoros Gregoras' commentary on it.[70]

The search for possible specific intertexts of Sikeliotes' personifications here cannot but be an idle and unrewarding task. What is of greater significance is that the structure of his compact allegorical description is replete with ritualistic overtones recalling *deep* narrative patterns portraying man's course toward perfection; such *deep* semantic structures, or rather textures – Sikeliotes' passage included – are based on homological relations between different domains of experience and systems of signification. On a first level, Sikeliotes endorses Plato's epistemological premises: *empeiria* is a faulty form of knowledge, based on experience that is random and unable to explain the causes of phenomena. *Epistêmê*, on the other hand, is the highest form of knowledge, based on subtle noetic processes. The

[67] Sikeliotes, *Commentary*, ed. Walz, 88.13. [68] Ibid., 88.14–21.
[69] A. Garzya, ed., *Opere di Sinesio di Cirene: Epistole, Operette, Inni* (Turin, 1999), 5.
[70] P. Pietrosanti, ed., *Nicephori Gregorae explicatio in librum Synesii "De Insomnis"* (Bari, 1999).

important difference lies in the fact that, whereas for Plato rhetoric is entirely dissociated from knowledge and accorded the status of a dubious knack, for Sikeliotes it is a form of true *epistêmê*, like, for instance, medicine. This is also, of course, the view of Hermogenes, who, however, refrains from addressing the ancient philosopher's criticism. As a matter of fact, Sikeliotes approves of Hermogenes' confident stance with regard to this issue, and considers it a feature of the ancient rhetorician's strategic *deinotês*. To Sikeliotes' mind, if Hermogenes had undertaken to defend his art explicitly, he would have placed unnecessary emphasis on the relevant debates.[71] That Sikeliotes does precisely the opposite, especially in his *Prolegomena*, but also at numerous other points throughout his extensive commentary, should be viewed in connection with his overall didactic project and systematic reinterpretation of ancient Greek rhetorical theory. Not surprisingly, for Sikeliotes, flawed knowledge is exemplified not by rhetoric but by other forms of pagan, pseudo-scientific occupations like astrology. These are nonsensical and demonic fabrications, he stresses, that may lead Christians astray and destroy them, as happened with Julian the Apostate. By contrast, in his illustration of the work of a true *epistêmôn*, Sikeliotes focuses on the importance of the accurate use of fundamental rhetorical concepts analysed by Hermogenes: *ennoia*, *lexis*, *methodos*.[72] Echoing the ancient rhetorician, Sikeliotes reaffirms that *epistêmê* is not a matter of personal talent granted to a person by nature (*physis*), but the result of diligent study.

The antithesis between *physis* or simple *empeiria*, on the one hand, and *epistêmê*, on the other – which I would view as an implicit response to Plato's refusal in *Gorgias* (and in *Protagoras*) to accord rhetoric the status of a teachable art or *epistêmê* – is connected to Hermogenes' point about the importance of his theory of ideas for those who want to imitate ancient authors. Later defenders of Hermogenes' analysis go one step further, viewing *mimêsis* not only as a significant application of his rhetorical theory but as an essential condition of rhetoric's function as a teachable *epistêmê*. Sikeliotes draws his relevant argumentation especially from the sixth-century Neoplatonic author Phoibammon, whose discussion he reproduces verbatim in his *Prolegomena*. For Phoibammon, the accurate mastery not only of the different types of styles but also of the terms of '*mimêsis* of the ancients' is an indispensable credential of a (rhetorical) *epistêmôn*.[73] In a detailed analysis, Phoibammon undertakes to challenge those who

---

[71] Sikeliotes, *Commentary*, ed. Walz, 81.7–9.   [72] Ibid., 90.9–14.
[73] Sikeliotes, *Prolegomena*, ed. Rabe, 376.14–16.

hold this kind of imitation impossible. Sikeliotes, who endorses this view and Phoibammon's overall argumentation, provides some further original ideas on the relation between *mimêsis* and *zêlos* ('emulation'), adducing a few examples from Christian literature. *Zêlos* is 'passionate and stagnant' and seems to connote a type of keen eagerness, whereas mimesis is 'calm and capable of improvement'. What Sikeliotes seems to imply here is that the latter, by being open to development, is more closely related to the teachable *epistêmê* of rhetoric than the former.[74]

The concept of imitation of archetypal models, discursive as well as moral, and the related ideas of image and true likeness permeate Sikeliotes' analysis as a whole, since they help him formulate a number of homological relations of rhetoric with other kinds of systematised knowledge (philosophy, music, mathematics, medicine) and anagogical discourses. As a matter of fact, rhetoric encompasses all other disciplines, since its theory and practice presuppose a combination of major aspects of different forms of organised knowledge. According to Sikeliotes, the man who is experienced in rhetoric is also knowledgeable in any other science (τῶν ἐπιστημῶν ἁπασῶν ἴδρις δείκνυται): from arithmetic he draws the principles that govern the symmetry and analogy of sentences and *kôla*; from music, the rhythm and sonority of discourse and the methods of rousing different emotions; from geometry, the arrangement of spaces and dimensions, and the ability to circumscribe meaning within specific *kôla*; from astronomy, several discursive methods and figures, like repetition and *epanaphora*; from philosophy, the processes of provable argumentation; from grammar, the rules of proper Greek.[75]

Sikeliotes' transition from the refutation of Plato's accusations of rhetoric to a strategic Christianisation of inherited rhetorical 'ideas' (in the Hermogenean sense of this term) and mimetic practices is facilitated by his recurrent emphasis on the beneficial impact of rhetoric on human *êthos* and *psychê*: *êthos* is related to the moralistic aspects of his defence of rhetoric, while the focus on *psychê* is related to the theological and anagogical value of this specific art. Rhetorical virtues are thus seen by Sikeliotes as homological to the virtues of the soul: the rhetorical idea of clarity (*katharotês*) is connected with temperance (*sophrosynê*) and resembles a chaste wife; amplitude (*peribolê*) is equivalent to piety and liberty;

---

[74] Teachability is one of the main Platonic criteria for acknowledging an activity as a *technê*. Plato explores this idea in connection with rhetoric especially in *Gorgias* and *Protagoras*; for this criterion in Platonic epistemology, see: R. Woodruff, 'Plato's Early Theory of Knowledge' in S. Everson, ed., *Epistemology* (Cambridge, 1990), 70–1.
[75] Sikeliotes, *Commentary*, ed. Walz, 172.13–173.2.

force (*deinotês*) 'imitates prudence' (*phronêsis*) and aims at perfection, sometimes hiding the things that need to be hidden, and other times communicating things that need to be communicated.[76]

In Sikeliotes' theoretical system, rhetoric is eventually rendered, as he argues, 'the most essential and best part of *politikê*, since it reshapes men by making them milder, precisely like Prometheus in the myth; it is not a mere reflection but the image and likeness of the immovable idea of the One who has commanded order'.[77] Through a series of homological associations that promote this idea of likeness in a number of discursive domains, rhetoric is methodically promoted by the Byzantine commentator to a 'discipline . . . a *divine* and marvellous art, which imitates the first cause that judiciously and harmoniously organises all that has been constituted out of antithetical forces'.[78]

Further Reading

The key source is: C. Walz, ed., "Ἐξήγησις εἰς τὰς Ἰδέας τοῦ Ἑρμογένους ἀπὸ φωνῆς Ἰωάννου φιλοσόφου τοῦ Σικελιώτου' in *Rhetores graeci ex codicibus Florentinis, Mediolanensibus, Monacensibus, Neapolitanis, Parisiensibus, Romanis, Venetis, Taurinensibus et Vindobonensibus* (Stuttgart, 1834), vol. VI, 56–504. Relevant studies include: T. M. Conley, 'Demosthenes Dethroned: Gregory Nazianzus in Sikeliotes' Scholia on Hermogenes' Περὶ Ἰδεῶν', *ICS*, 27/28 (2002–3), 145–52; G. Kustas, *Studies in Byzantine Rhetoric* (Thessalonike, 1973); P. Roilos, *Amphoteroglossia: A Poetics of the Twelfth-century Medieval Greek Novel* (Cambridge, MA, 2005) and '*Phantasia* and the Ethics of Fictionality in Byzantium: A Cognitive Anthropological Perspective' in P. Roilos, ed., *Medieval Greek Storytelling: Fictionality and Narrative in Byzantium* (Wiesbaden, 2014), 9–30.

---

[76] Sikeliotes, *Prolegomena*, ed. Rabe, 399.27–400.23; see similar views in John of Sardis, *Commentary on Aphthonios*, in H. Rabe, ed., *Ioannis Sardiani Commentarium in Aphthonii Progymnasmata* (Leipzig, 1928), 132–5. On these ethical dimensions of rhetorical theory in Byzantium, see Roilos, *Amphoteroglossia*, 144–5; 30–1.

[77] Ἔστι δὲ πολιτικῆς μέρος ἡ ῥητορικὴ τὸ συνεκτικώτατόν τε καὶ κάλλιστον μεταποιοῦσα τοὺς ἀνθρώπους εἰς τὸ πραότερον οὐχ ἧττον ἢ ὡς ὁ <τοῦ> μύθου Προμηθεύς, οὐκ εἴδωλον δήπουθεν ἀλλ᾽ εἰκὼν καὶ ὁμοίωμα μὴ κινουμένης ἰδέας τοῦ εὐταξίαν ὁρίσαντος (Sikeliotes, *Prolegomena*, ed. Rabe, 396.20–5). The Platonic myth to which Sikeliotes refers is commented upon in some detail also by Ailios Aristeides, who employs it as an archetypal fictitious illustration of rhetoric's beneficial effects on society: according to the myth, when the world was created, Hermes – thanks to the mediation of Prometheus – granted this art to the noblest men so that they could create peaceful and safe communities; see Lenz and Behr, eds., *Aristidis Opera*, 394–401.

[78] ἐπιστήμη ἄρα ... τέχνη θεία τε καὶ θαυμασία καὶ τὴν αἰτίαν ἐκμιμουμένη τὴν πρώτην, ἢ τὸ πᾶν διαξάγει εὐφυῶς καὶ ἐναρμονίως τὸ ἐκ τῶν ἐναντίων συνεστηκός Sikeliotes, *Prolegomena*, ed. Rabe, 397.16–20).

CHAPTER 7

Memoirs as Manifesto: the Rhetoric of Katakalon Kekaumenos

Jonathan Shepard

Few beyond the gilded court circle in Middle Byzantium were in sufficient command of Attic Greek and the principles of advanced rhetoric to compose and fluently deliver full-length orations; indeed, the number of grand imperial occasions appropriate for staging them was finite. Yet, as Elizabeth Jeffreys has pointed out, 'effective communication both written and oral continued to be a fundamental requirement, particularly in a society as linguistically conservative as the Byzantine'.[1] Even young persons not raised at the imperial court needed to handle words competently, whether for making speeches of one sort or another or for expressing themselves on paper. To this end, they could be trained with the help of handbooks which contained various forms of preliminary exercises (*progymnasmata*), learning how to hone points and to encapsulate with the help of the saying (*gnome*), moralising fable (*mythos*), tale (*diegema*) and other elements of discourse.[2]

Figures of speech and other such nuts and bolts of rhetoric formed an integral part of Byzantine writing. As Elizabeth Jeffreys notes, even a military man such as the author of the mid-eleventh-century text *Admonitions and Anecdotes* (*Consilia et Narrationes*), showed proficiency in this respect.[3] One practical application for such training emerges from

---

[1] E. M. Jeffreys, 'Rhetoric' in E. M. Jeffreys et al., eds., *The Oxford Handbook of Byzantine Studies* (Oxford, 2008), 828.
[2] Jeffreys, 'Rhetoric', 829–30. See also E. M. Jeffreys, 'Rhetoric in Byzantium' in I. Worthington, ed., *A Companion to Greek Rhetoric* (Oxford, 2007), 170–3, 175–6.
[3] Jeffreys, 'Rhetoric', 832; Jeffreys, 'Rhetoric in Byzantium', 176. The author of *Admonitions and Anecdotes* (G. G. Litavrin, ed. and trans., Советы и рассказы Кекавмена, second edition (St Petersburg, 2003); C. Roueché, ed. and trans., *Kekaumenos, Consilia et Narrationes* (2013), www.ancientwisdoms.ac.uk/library/kekaumenos-consilia-et-narrationes/ (accessed 13 November 2017), who is known only by his family name, Kekaumenos, was on active service in the mid-eleventh century and wrote up his work in, most probably, the earlier to mid-1070s. A large part of his work consists of military advice, and the work was earlier sometimes termed *Strategikon* for this reason. It has been suggested that Kekaumenos and the subject of this article (Katakalon Kekaumenos, author of Skylitzes' supposed source K) were one and the same; but this has not

'Skirmishing', the manual composed a century earlier by a member of Nikephoros II Phokas' entourage. When addressing their troops before combat in mountain passes, commanders are advised to address them 'in eloquent language', steadying them 'with honeyed words' and, on a more practical note, pointing out the advantages that rough terrain has to offer.[4] Such injunctions raise questions as to the role of rhetoric in the course of campaigning and army life in general, whether in the form of 'honeyed words' or simply effective communication.

Some basis for an answer may come from John Skylitzes' coverage of the military and political history of Byzantium in the mid-eleventh century; or rather, the coverage in a source (now lost) that he seems to have used for his chronicle. In earlier publications we have inferred, from the disproportionate place the commander Katakalon Kekaumenos occupies in the *Synopsis of the Histories* (*Synopsis Historion*), that a 'suspected source' close to Katakalon was available to Skylitzes.[5] Katakalon is known to have been active between 1038 and 1057: he first saw service in Sicily under Maniakes; was *archon* of the Danubian cities around 1043; governor of Ani and Iberia around 1050 and *doux* of Antioch c. 1056. A year later, Katakalon played a leading role in the 'Great Rebellion' – the uprising against Michael VI by a group of leading generals which placed Isaac I Komnenos on the throne. Reconstruction of Katakalon's career together with evaluation of his historical importance has been facilitated by the *Prosopography of the Byzantine World*, and full portrayal of Katakalon's

---

been established: C. M. Brand and A. Kazhdan, 'Katakalon Kekaumenos', *ODB*, vol. III, 1113. On the other Kekaumenos, see also below, pp. 206–7.

[4] 'Skirmishing', ch. 23, in G. T. Dennis, ed. and trans., *Three Byzantine Military Treatises* (Washington, D. C., 1985), 230–1; E. McGeer, 'Two Military Orations of Constantine VII' in J. W. Nesbitt, ed., *Byzantine Authors: Literary Activities and Preoccupations* (Leiden, 2003), 114. The value of rhetoric for commanders is axiomatic in the text known as *Rhetorica militaris*, whose first three chapters were edited in H. Köchly and W. Rüstow, *Griechische Kriegsschriftsteller* (Leipzig, 1853–5), vol. II, 15–20; it is now available in a complete edition by I. Eramo, ed., *Siriano. Discorsi di guerra* (Bari, 2010); H. Hunger, *Die hochsprachliche profane Literatur der Byzantiner* (Munich, 1978), vol. II, 328–9. The text seemingly formed part of a much lengthier work by Syrianos, datable to the ninth or tenth century: C. Zuckerman, 'The Military Compendium of Syrianus Magister', *JÖB*, 40 (1990), 210; P. Rance, 'The Date of the Military Compendium of Syrianus Magister (Formerly the Sixth-century Anonymus Byzantinus)', *BZ*, 100 (2007), 703–5, 733–7; Eramo, ed., *Siriano*, 14–15 (introduction). See also Jeffreys, 'Rhetoric in Byzantium', 176

[5] This view is summarised, with references to earlier literature, in J. Shepard, 'A Suspected Source of Scylitzes' *Synopsis Historion*: the Great Catacalon Cecaumenus', *BMGS*, 16 (1992), 171–81. Earlier publications are cited below only where directly relevant. The possibility that Skylitzes used a Katakalon-related source is allowed in A. Kazhdan and A. Cutler, 'Skylitzes, John', *ODB*, vol. III, 1914; M. Angold and M. Whitby, 'Historiography' in Jeffreys et al., eds., *Oxford Handbook*, 843.

achievements would be worthwhile.[6] This larger-than-life figure would, however, require more space than is available here. So, too, would an attempt to reconstitute the full extent of Skylitzes' lost source from his text. Instead, we shall review certain sections of Skylitzes' work that look likeliest to emanate from this hypothetical source and propose that the source's author was making a case.[7]

The persona and the background of John Skylitzes remain open to argument, for want of evidence. But it is overwhelmingly likely that he composed his *Synopsis* while enjoying the trust, and perhaps still the employment, of Alexios I Komnenos. He held senior posts in the early 1090s, as Eparch of the City and *droungarios tes viglas*, and had retired by 1094/5.[8] Skylitzes tailored his materials to suit two kinds of reader: first, he wrote a handbook for those already acquainted with the full-length 'Histories' to carry around with them – on tours of duty, perhaps – and to refresh their memory; second, for those unfamiliar with the subject-matter, he added a handy *Synopsis*, enabling them to follow things up in 'the Histories' themselves.[9] His extensive coverage of military matters and attention to the Balkans corresponds quite closely to the agenda of governing circles in the 1090s, and conditions at the time of writing seem to have guided his choice of source-materials.[10] If, as is most likely, Skylitzes composed his work in two stages, recounting events from 811 to 1057 in the main part, but later continuing the story until 1079,[11] one has grounds for supposing that he tended to follow his sources closely; he selected them according to their fitness for his purposes,

---

[6] *PBW*, 'Katakalon 101' http://pbw2016.kdl.kcl.ac.uk/person/Katakalon/101/ (accessed 3 April 2018).
[7] Besides the works cited above, see E. M. Jeffreys, 'The Attitudes of Byzantine Chroniclers Towards Ancient History', *Byzantion*, 49 (1979), 199–238; E. M. Jeffreys et al., eds., *Studies in John Malalas* (Sydney, 1990); E. M. Jeffreys, M. J. Jeffreys and R. Scott, trans., *The Chronicle of John Malalas* (Melbourne, 1986) (which amounts to 'a kind of edition in translation', rather than just a translation [preface, ix]); *PBW*. See now also below, n. 128. The subject seems fitting for a volume in honour of scholars who have made so important a contribution to the study of rhetoric, chronicle-writing and now also prosopography.
[8] W. Seibt, 'Ioannes Skylitzes: Zur Person des Chronisten', *JÖB*, 25 (1976), 81–3; C. Holmes, *Basil II and the Governance of Empire (976–1025)* (Oxford, 2005), 81–8.
[9] I. Thurn, ed., *Ioannis Scylitzae Synopsis Historiarum* (Berlin, 1973) [hereafter Skylitzes, *Synopsis*, ed. Thurn], 4.51–9 (preface); Holmes, *Basil II*, 89–91, 203, 217.
[10] Holmes, *Basil II*, 183–7, 216–17, 220–4, 228–33, 236–7.
[11] Its modern editor, E. T. Tsolakes argued strongly in favour of John Skylitzes' responsibility for the latter work, conventionally called 'Skylitzes Continuatus': E. T. Tsolakes, ed., Ἡ Συνέχεια τῆς χρονογραφίας τοῦ Ἰωάννου Σκυλίτζη (Thessalonike, 1968), 79–95 (introduction). See also, broadly favouring Skylitzes' authorship of the continuation, Seibt, 'Ioannes Skylitzes', 81; B. Flusin and J.-C. Cheynet, trans., *Jean Skylitzès. Empereurs de Constantinople* (Paris, 2003), vi, xxi–xxii; Holmes, *Basil II*, 67–8, 80, 83, 85, 90–1.

essentially the instruction, edification and entertainment of members of the politico-administrative elite in the first half of Alexios I's reign.[12] This is plain from his paraphrase of Attaleiates' chronicle for emperors' reigns from Isaac I Komnenos' to the start of Nikephoros III Botaneiates'. And his extensive use of Theophanes Continuatus – which he follows very closely – has long been recognised, even if he does not appear to name it among the sources listed in his preface.[13] Besides extensive coverage of campaigning, a certain fascination with conspiracies and the course of military rebellions manifests itself in Skylitzes' use of, for example, Attaleiates' account of the rebellions of Nikephoros Bryennios and Nikephoros Botaneiates.[14] Likewise with his recourse to a text concerning Bardas Skleros' rebellion in the late tenth century.[15] Against this background, it

---

[12] On Skylitzes' purposes, see especially Holmes, *Basil II*, 146–9, 162–70, 181–2, 185–90, 216–17, 223–6, 233, 237–8. See also C. Holmes, 'The Rhetorical Structures of John Skylitzes' *Synopsis Historion*' in E. M. Jeffreys, ed., *Rhetoric in Byzantium* (Aldershot, 2003), 192–9. A rather different assessment of Skylitzes' purposes and of his composition-date is offered by E.-S. Kiapidou, *H σύνοψη ιστοριών του Ιωάννη Σκυλίτζη και οι πηγές της (811–1057)* (Athens, 2010), a work that became known to me only after submission of this chapter to the editors. Kiapidou draws attention to the exceptionally free use of the first-person singular or plural in the section devoted to Michael VI's reign, and argues that this represents the person of Skylitzes himself, 132–3, 461–3. Arguing for a composition-date of 'most probably 1059–1071', and for a likely dating to 'the reign of Isaac I and slightly later', 136, 133, she suggests that Skylitzes may have addressed his work to Katakalon Kekaumenos, drawing on oral informants, 'including perhaps Kekaumenos himself', 132, but that Skylitzes also intended to sing the praises of Isaac I Komnenos; the sudden abdication of Isaac in 1059 caused Skylitzes to stop with the abdication of Michael VI, himself speculating in the first-person singular as to his prospects of gaining 'the heavenly kingdom', 462; Skylitzes would then have been a young man, 'in the circle of Katakalon Kekaumenos and Isaac I Komnenos', 136. Since full treatment of Kiapidou's theses would require a separate study, I shall confine myself to noting the value of her observation about the relative frequency of the first-person in Skylitzes' coverage of Michael VI's reign, while querying whether the first-person need invariably represent Skylitzes himself. As noted below (n. 90), Skylitzes' pruning of details of campaign theatres and operations seems slighter for the mid-eleventh century than for earlier periods, and this light touch could well have extended to other aspects of the written text that, to my mind, still seems by far the likeliest main source for Skylitzes' coverage of Michael VI's reign. This would have been compatible with some authorial intervention by Skylitzes himself, drawing on oral information from the 'old men' cited in his preface (Skylitzes, *Synopsis*, ed. Thurn, 4.49; below, n. 69). The first-person speculation as to Michael's domicile after his death seems to me far likelier to vent Katakalon's spleen in the late 1050s than any views of Skylitzes, whether writing as a young man and shortly after the reign of Isaac, or a generation later. Kiapidou's suggestions do not take account either of the strong vein of unfavourable comparison of Isaac with Katakalon pervading Skylitzes' section on Michael's reign, or of the evidence from Psellos' correspondence of Katakalon's capacity for putting his views forcefully on paper (below, pp. 205–6, 208).

[13] See, Hunger, *Hochsprachliche profane Literatur*, vol. 1, 391; Flusin and Cheynet, *Skylitzès*, xii–xiii; Holmes, *Basil II*, 125 and n. 6. One cannot rule out the possibility that Theodore Daphnopates, whose name features in Skylitzes' list of sources, may have been responsible for part of Theophanes Continuatus: Flusin and Cheynet, *Skylitzès*, x and n. 37; Holmes, *Basil II*, 93–4.

[14] Skylitzes Continuatus, ed. Tsolakes, 172–6, 177–81 (text); 70–1 (table of borrowings from Attaleiates).

[15] For the source, now lost, on Skleros' rising, see below, p. 208.

seems worth reopening the question of whether Skylitzes' main source for the mid-eleventh century may not have contained data in comparable detail not only about foreign wars but also about the Great Rebellion that brought Alexios Komnenos' uncle, Isaac, to the throne in 1057. The latter topic would have been pertinent, given that very many officers seem to have been ill-disposed towards Alexios around the time when Skylitzes probably composed the main part of his *Synopsis*. Widespread antipathy in the army lay behind a plot to assassinate the emperor during his Balkan campaign in 1094.[16]

Our scope here will be fairly narrow. The first section of this study reviews three sets of materials in Skylitzes' chronicle and reaffirms their associations with Katakalon Kekaumenos. Some are blatant, but other associations are oblique. Our thesis is that much of the closing section of the main part of Skylitzes' *Synopsis* comes from a source close enough to Katakalon to make him its likeliest author; and that the other two sets of materials under review have the same origins. This text will be labelled 'K'. The second section of this study draws attention to the officers' culture which these sets of materials bespeak: their debates and speeches entailed construction of arguments and persuasive turns of phrase. Such articulacy is what the prescriptive works of the ninth and tenth century presuppose, even if those works' focus was on morale-boosting speeches. The third section reviews the intellectual training and rhetorical tools likely to have been available to a senior commander. Comparison with other texts written by or about military men provides reason to believe that Katakalon could well have put pen to paper and memorialised his achievements, giving literary form to views often vented through the spoken word. If, as is most likely, the Great Rebellion loomed large in his composition, this tends to suggest that he designed it to be a manifesto. One can only speculate as to what prompted him to take up his pen in anger, but some sort of fall from grace would be a plausible scenario. Finally, the fourth section considers further evidence for the existence of works comparable to that which we have hypothesised in Katakalon's case. Personal histories were of particular use when regimes were in question, as would have been the case if and when he composed K. Yet there is a singularity to Katakalon. He presented himself as a plain-speaking soldier who owed his promotion and honours to sheer talent. In placing himself at the centre

---

[16] D. R. Reinsch and A. Kambylis, eds., *Annae Comnenae. Alexias* (Berlin, 2001), vol. 1, 267–79 (IX.5.1–9.6); P. Frankopan, 'Challenges to Imperial Authority in the Reign of Alexios I Komnenos: the Conspiracy of Nikephoros Diogenes', *BSl*, 64 (2006), 258–62, 270–1.

of the events of 1057, Katakalon's writing strategy was perhaps not unlike that of a younger contemporary so different in other ways and who nonetheless corresponded with him, Michael Psellos.[17]

Katakalon's Fingerprints – Three Sets of Materials in Skylitzes Associated with Katakalon Kekaumenos

Leaving aside episodes in Katakalon's earlier career, such as his command of the Danube towns and districts around 1043,[18] our focus is on the aforementioned sets of materials in Skylitzes. Two of these bear on Katakalon's feats of generalship in Byzantium's borderlands between c. 1045 and 1049: operations against the Pechenegs in the Balkans; and the campaigns against Dvin and the Turks, while he was governor of Ani and Iberia. The third set of materials records Katakalon's participation in the Great Rebellion of 1057, blow by blow. One of our basic propositions is that certain sections in Skylitzes relay Katakalon's vantage-point and also background details on foreign peoples readily available to him, even when these do not recount his own achievements. Accordingly, we shall begin with the set of materials which seems to support this proposition quite clearly: Skylitzes' coverage of operations against the Pechenegs in the Balkans.

Operations Against the Pechenegs

Katakalon was a relatively late arrival on the Balkan scene, assigned there together with other eastern army units only after things had got seriously out of hand and the Pechenegs were driving all before them. Soon, Katakalon was himself a prisoner-of-war. Gravely wounded at the battle of Diakene (1049) and lying among the heaps of dead, Katakalon was found, recognised and nursed back to health by a Pecheneg who had got to know him at the time of his Danubian posting, several years earlier. Convalescence probably took some while, given the severity of the wounds: this would mean that his captivity among the Pechenegs was protracted.[19] The hiatus in Katakalon's career seems to shape Skylitzes' treatment of operations against the Pechenegs in the 1040s and earlier

---

[17] On Psellos' 'notorious self-centredness', see now S. Papaioannou, *Michael Psellos: Rhetoric and Authorship in Byzantium* (Cambridge, 2013), 3.

[18] For Katakalon's command on the lower Danube, see *PBW*, 'Katakalon 101: Narrative; Dignity/ Office; Location'.

[19] Skylitzes, *Synopsis*, ed. Thurn, 469.55–9. See below, p. 191.

1050s. Katakalon's personal role in the Byzantines' dealings with the Pechenegs occupies only a modest proportion of this set of materials.[20] Yet there are grounds for supposing that most, if not all, Skylitzes' coverage of the Pechenegs' migration into the Balkans and the subsequent hostilities derives from K. In other words, K will have contained a disquisition upon the Pechenegs, their warfare and the strategies used against them, and also the background to their mass migration across the Danube in, most probably, mid-winter 1046–7.

Several considerations favour this supposition. First, Skylitzes' coverage of the Pecheneg crisis is weighted towards the earlier stages of their presence on 'Roman' territory up to and including episodes just subsequent to Diakene; and the later stages are recounted from, effectively, a Pecheneg perspective. Even if one allows for the fact that the most spectacular and significant events occurred during the earlier period, the chronicle's treatment of the early 1050s is decidedly sketchy in comparison. And it ends abruptly, somewhat out of key with the Byzantine disaster recounted in the immediately preceding passage, the retreat from Preslav.[21] We are told that the Pechenegs, hearing that Constantine IX was intent on sending yet another expedition against them, sought a peace-treaty, an event datable to 1053.[22] One should further note that Skylitzes' overall treatment of the closing years of Constantine IX's reign is thin, something of a scrapbook of court intrigues, plague and other occurrences in the capital, including criticism of the costly building works at St George of the Mangana. Skylitzes' cursory treatment of Constantine's later years could mirror the absence of Katakalon from imperial circles, assuming that K was Skylitzes' main source for those years.[23] If Katakalon remained in Pecheneg hands until the treaty of 1053 (involving, most likely, a prisoner exchange), he would have been able to follow the Byzantino-Pecheneg wars from the enemy camp, and would have been correspondingly less well-informed about goings-on at Constantinople or in other theatres.

That the later stages of the Pecheneg wars are related from what was, in effect, the Pecheneg vantage-point offers a further clue that K was

---

[20] Ibid., 467.96–469.60.   [21] Ibid., 475.17–476.37.
[22] Ibid., 476.40–1; I. Pérez Martín, ed. and trans., *Miguel Ataliates. Historia* (Madrid, 2002) [hereafter Attaleiates, *Historia*, ed. Pérez Martín], 33 and n. 110 on 251; E. Malamut, 'L'image byzantine des Petchénègues', *BZ*, 88 (1995), 127–8; P. Stephenson, *Byzantium's Balkan Frontier: A Political Study of the Northern Balkans, 900–1204* (Cambridge, 2000), 93.
[23] Skylitzes, *Synopsis*, ed. Thurn, 473.64–474.84; 476.44–477.78. Funding for the monastery of St George came partly from revenues raised after a sizeable unit of Armenian forces – 'the Iberian host' – was disbanded; condemnation of this measure was closely in key with Katakalon's thinking, as of other militarily inclined writers.

Skylitzes' source. Quite full details are given of operations at Adrianople and Preslav,[24] but not the comprehensive battle stations which feature when Katakalon himself was fighting. And while a couple of fatal injuries sustained at Adrianople are described, one was that of a Pecheneg chief, Soultzous, struck down together with his horse by a projectile from a catapult.[25] Moreover, the Pechenegs are said to have learnt 'through a deserter' of Constantine IX's intention to resume the offensive against them in 1053: this detail is much more likely to have been gleaned by someone in the Pecheneg camp than by an observer in Constantinople or with the Byzantine field army.[26] Katakalon, if still in a Pecheneg encampment in 1053, would have been well-placed to do the gleaning. So the later stages of the Pecheneg war are recounted essentially from a Pecheneg perspective.

Our second consideration follows on from this, reflecting upon Katakalon's *curriculum vitae* and unusual opportunity to learn about Pecheneg affairs. That a Pecheneg should have recognised and rescued him from among the corpses at Diakene says something for the personal ties he had forged with the nomads during his first stint on the Danube around 1043. The Pecheneg's name was, according to most manuscripts of Skylitzes, 'Koulinos'. This form closely resembles one given in the dative ('Goulinoi') for a son of the Pecheneg leader Kegen; Skylitzes describes him rallying to his father's aid against assassins, and it is most likely that these slightly variant forms denote one and the same person.[27] Once taken prisoner, Katakalon would have had ample opportunity for learning Pecheneg personal names, names which appear in some profusion in Skylitzes' account of the Pecheneg wars.[28] He could have supplemented what he had already learnt during his first tour of duty on the Danube, around the time when Kegen's grouping of Pechenegs were installed there.[29] Moreover, Katakalon's links with Koulinos could well underlie

---

[24] Ibid., 470.67–471.7; 475.21–476.37.
[25] Ibid., 470.94–471.95. The other casualty described was Constantine Arianites: 470.89.
[26] Ibid., 476.40–1.
[27] Cod. Vindobonensis Hist. gr. 74 names Katakalon's rescuer as 'Galinos' (Skylitzes, *Synopsis*, ed. Thurn, 469.50, *app. crit.*) and also has the (dative) form 'Goulinai' for Kegen's son (465.47, *app. crit.*). This witness, deriving from Michael of Diabolis' interpolated version of Skylitzes, is of high, albeit not overriding, quality: xxvi, xxxv, xlv (introduction). That these slightly variant forms denote one person was the view of G. Moravcsik, *Byzantinoturcica*, second edition (Berlin, 1958), vol. II, 166. See also Malamut, 'L'image byzantine', 125, n. 136; Flusin and Cheynet, *Skylitzès*, 378–9, n. 153; Shepard, 'Suspected Source', 172, n. 5.
[28] See, Moravcsik, *Byzantinoturcica*, vol. II, 86 (Baltzar), 151 (Karamonos), 156 (Kataleim), 272 (Selte), 289 (Soultzous).
[29] Stephenson, *Balkan Frontier*, 89–90.

the survey of recent Pecheneg history provided in Skylitzes. This encompasses the conflict between the Pechenegs and the Uzes in which Kegen proved his mettle, his rivalry with Tyrach, quest for asylum in Byzantium, role as a frontiersman and eventual triggering of Tyrach's invasion.[30] They could also account for the wealth of detail about Kegen and, indeed, for the pro-Kegen slant discernible in Skylitzes' account of Byzantino–Pecheneg relations. The vicissitudes Kegen underwent as a go-between are recounted sympathetically, culminating with his misplaced trust in the Pecheneg insurgents' sworn pledges: he visited them, only to suffer death and dismemberment.[31] Earlier, while sleeping in his encampment outside Constantinople, Kegen had been the target of an assassination attempt by three Pechenegs armed 'with swords'; he suffered wounds, 'but not fatal ones'.[32] There follows what reads like an eyewitness description of the procession that made its way into Constantinople: the wounded Kegen lay in a wagon drawn by his two horses, followed by two of his sons on foot and the would-be assassins in chains.[33] If, as is most likely, one son was the Koulinos who later nursed Katakalon back to health, he is probably the source of the description. Kegen's accomplishments are also underlined sympathetically, being those of a meritocrat: he was of obscure birth, but 'extremely energetic in matters of warfare and strategies'.[34]

This leads to a third consideration. Issues of the 'right' tactics and strategy to employ against the nomads – and the failure of the imperial court to grasp this – loom large in Skylitzes' coverage of the Pechenegs in the mid-eleventh century, reflecting priorities in our hypothetical source, K. It is made clear that Katakalon had strong views on the tactics to be adopted for battle at Diakene: he clashed with the commander-in-chief, the eunuch Nikephoros *raiktor*;[35] and for all Katakalon's 'very loud shouting' to the effect that 'now is the time to join battle!', he was overruled. Katakalon obeyed orders and, in the eventual debacle, made a last stand with his servants and a few kinsmen.[36] To summarise what should ideally be argued through, I suggest that the question of the most effective counterinsurgency strategy to be used against the Pechenegs runs through Skylitzes' text, reflecting a preoccupation originally in K. Both the disaster at Dampolis preceding the battle of Diakene,[37] and the relatively sketchily treated, but generally successful, later operations against the Pechenegs, vindicate the tactics Katakalon had proposed before Diakene

---

[30] Skylitzes, *Synopsis*, ed. Thurn, 455.32–458.46.   [31] Ibid., 472.35–8.   [32] Ibid., 465.39–40.
[33] Ibid., 465.43–8.   [34] Ibid., 455.43–4.   [35] Ibid., 468.22–31.   [36] Ibid., 469.43–5.
[37] Ibid., 466.81–467.89.

(when he had urged his commander-in-chief not to let the Pechenegs form a compact mass, but to attack them at once, while still 'scattered and spread about').[38] The passages recounting the later operations mostly concern small-scale engagements: the Byzantines attack small detachments of Pechenegs, while they are dispersed for plundering, or when they are sleeping off the after-effects of plundering and heavy drinking.[39] This is reminiscent of the stratagem Katakalon had used to break up a Muslim force besieging him in Messina: he sallied out from the city against the carousing besiegers and slew their intoxicated leader, a ruse which caused the Muslims to lift the siege.[40] So while the narrative of the Pecheneg wars illustrates the incompetence of Constantine IX's government and offers information about Pecheneg ways, it is also a disquisition upon the 'right' method of combating these nomads, indicating how Katakalon's strategy would have dealt with them far earlier – a sure sign of Katakalon's 'fingerprints'.

In Ani and Iberia

Our second set of materials in Skylitzes relates to Katakalon's stint as governor of Ani and Iberia, which concluded with his transfer to operations against the Pechenegs. One could usefully demonstrate a correlation between Skylitzes' coverage of Caucasian affairs and Katakalon's physical presence there, a pattern of coverage comparable to that for the Pechenegs. Here, however, we shall merely note that Katakalon was governor from c. 1045 until 1049, and it is essentially in those years that Skylitzes' account of affairs in the Caucasus is anchored.[41] Katakalon's 'fingerprints' are detectable in the full accounts of campaigns he conducted, the operations against Dvin in 1046–7 and the battles against the Turks in the following year. The inclination to praise Katakalon's strategies is obvious, to the point where the battle of Kaputru is depicted as virtually a victory. This contrasts with all our other sources, including Michael Attaleiates, which are unanimous that Kaputru was really a Byzantine defeat.[42] While the

---

[38] Ibid., 468.24. [39] Ibid., 472.32–3, 46; 473.58–60. [40] Ibid., 407.23–38.
[41] Skylitzes, *Synopsis*, ed. Thurn, 435.72–439.5; 448.48–454.29; 464.11–28. On Katakalon's posting to Ani: *PBW*, 'Katakalon 101: Narrative; Description; Dignity/Office; Location'; Flusin and Cheynet, *Skylitzès*, 364, n. 80. K. N. Iuzbashian argued for dating Katakalon's appointment to 1046: K. N. Iuzbashian, 'Скилица о захвате Анийского царства в 1045г.', *VizVrem*, 40 (1979), 87, n. 77.
[42] Skylitzes, *Synopsis*, ed. Thurn, 452.60–453.96; Attaleiates, *Historia*, ed. Pérez Martín, 34; J. Shepard, 'Scylitzes on Armenia in the 1040s and the Role of Catacalon Cecaumenos', *REArm*, n. s. 11 (1975–6), 277–8.

origins of the Byzantine claim to the realm of Ani are related fairly briefly and simplistically,[43] extensive coverage is given to the enlistment of the emir of Dvin to seize strongholds belonging to King Gagik II of Ani, and to the despatch of an expedition against Dvin upon the emir's refusal to give up these strongholds to the emperor in 1045.[44] It was the ensuing disaster which led to the appointment of Katakalon as governor of Ani and Iberia. Coverage is given both to the disaster and to Katakalon's systematic reduction of Emir Abul Aswar's strongholds, culminating in the blockade of 'the fortress called Chelidonion, built on a precipitous mountain, not far from Dvin'.[45] The starving inhabitants would have surrendered before long 'had not ... Leo Tornikios' revolt broken out suddenly in the west'.[46]

Thus, drastic foreshortening of complex and protracted events allows for fuller coverage of those campaigns when Katakalon is in command, as also of operations immediately preceding them, notably the expedition against Dvin of 1045. The latter provides a foil for Katakalon's successes. Military affairs have pride of place, and external potentates, even adversaries, receive their due. Abul Aswar is a 'man most versed in generalship, if ever there was one'.[47] The Georgian magnate Liparit is 'renowned for intelligence and courage',[48] and he joins forces with Katakalon only to suffer capture at the battle of Kaputru after falling from his horse. We hear something of Liparit's spell in Turkish captivity, and also of a further expedition against Abul Aswar on which Katakalon does not seem to have served.[49] This regard for soldierly qualities, whether in a comrade-in-arms such as Liparit, or a worthy opponent such as Abul Aswar, is consistent with the positive line taken towards Kegen and the presentation of Pecheneg affairs for roughly the same period. The focus on Katakalon's activities, refracted through Skylitzes, would explain why, as it were, the light goes out on the east not long after Katakalon's redeployment to the Balkans to try and quash the Pecheneg uprising in 1049. One should also note the silence in Skylitzes – and thus presumably in K – concerning a drastic step taken by

---

[43] Skylitzes, *Synopsis*, ed. Thurn, 435.72–436.10; Shepard, 'Scylitzes on Armenia', 305.
[44] Skylitzes, *Synopsis*, ed. Thurn, 436.10–437.38.   [45] Ibid., 438.73–4.   [46] Ibid., 438.75–9.
[47] Ibid, 437.39; *PBW*, 'Aplesphares 101: Description' http://pbw2016.kdl.kcl.ac.uk/person/Aplesphares/101/ (accessed 3 April 2018); M. Canard, 'Dwin' in P. Bearman, T. Bianquis, C. E. Bosworth et al., eds., *Encyclopaedia of Islam*, second edition (Leiden, 2009) http://dx.doi.org/10.1163/1573-3912_islam_SIM_2165 (accessed 1 December 2017).
[48] Skylitzes, *Synopsis*, ed. Thurn, 447.27–8; *PBW*, 'Liparites 101: Description' http://pbw2016.kdl.kcl.ac.uk/person/Liparites/101/ (accessed 3 April 2018).
[49] Skylitzes, *Synopsis*, ed. Thurn, 454.10–19, 464.11–28. On the expedition to Dvin led by Nikephoros *raiktor*, see W. Felix, *Byzanz und die islamische Welt im früheren 11. Jahrhundert* (Vienna, 1981), 171.

Katakalon not long after arriving in Ani. In effect he purged the influential *katholikos* Peter, who had been instrumental in the handover of the city to the Byzantines in 1045. According to Aristakes of Lastivert, *Kamenas* (Katakalon Kekaumenos) 'proceeded to malign him in letters to the emperor, and in a deceptive way expelled him from the town'.[50] Whether Katakalon acted on his own initiative (as Aristakes avers), or carried out a plan pre-concerted with Constantine IX is hard to determine. Equally hard to fathom is why this episode is missing from Skylitzes' account. It could be that K omitted all mention of such political intriguing as disreputable and out of keeping with its presentation of Katakalon. Viewing the omission of this episode in isolation, one might indeed put this down to a preoccupation with straightforwardly soldierly virtues. These are, after all, foremost in the image of Katakalon that K seems to have sought to convey. Consideration of another part of Skylitzes may, however, show this image to be not so much simple suppression as literary artifice. Words, phrasing and sentiments were orchestrated to specific effect, and to make a case. We are, in other words, dealing with an exercise in rhetoric.

The Great Rebellion and the Reign of Michael VI

Our third set of materials in Skylitzes suggests that the agenda of his hypothetical source – K – did not stop at commemoration of Katakalon's military feats and his competence as governor of Ani and Iberia. It seems to me that Skylitzes drew very heavily on K for the last section of the main part of his chronicle, devoted to the reign of Michael VI. Likewise, perhaps, for such little as he relates of the reign of Michael's predecessor, Theodora. The imbalances in Skylitzes' treatment of the two reigns are striking. Fewer than two full pages of Thurn's edition of Skylitzes are devoted to Theodora's reign, recounting her appointment of eunuchs to senior posts, and changes of top commands and troop movements of the eastern forces; these would have been of direct concern to Katakalon, who was then *doux* of Antioch and thus partly responsible for eastern defences.[51] Still more strikingly, the first six months of Michael VI's reign

---

[50] M. Canard and H. Berbérian, trans., *Aristakès de Lastivert. Récit des malheurs de la nation arménienne* (Brussels, 1973), 56.

[51] Skylitzes, *Synopsis*, ed. Thurn, 479–80. Katakalon held office at Antioch some time between 1054 and late 1056: J.-C. Cheynet, 'Les ducs d'Antioche sous Michel IV et Constantin IX', repr. in J.-C. Cheynet, *La société byzantine: l'apport des sceaux* (Paris, 2008), vol. I, 204, 206; *PBW*, 'Katakalon 101: Narrative; Dignity/Office; Location'. On Theodora's reign, see K.-P. Todt, 'Die Frau als Selbstherrscher: Kaiserin Theodora, die letzte Angehörige der Makedonischen Dynastie', *JÖB*, 50 (2000), 139–71.

receive little more than two pages, whereas the final six months or so score almost eighteen.⁵² The caesura comes with the reception at court at Eastertide 1057,⁵³ when the senior commanders were denied their requests for higher titles and stipends and began to hatch a plot to overthrow the emperor – the 'Great Rebellion'. It is no exaggeration to say that Skylitzes offers not so much an account of Michael's reign as a narrative of the Great Rebellion – the first outright military *coup* to meet with success for some 250 years. There seems no need to postulate any significant source for Skylitzes' account of the reign of Michael VI other than K.

To make such a sweeping claim for K's importance as a source of Michael VI's reign requires justification. Katakalon Kekaumenos is not, after all, named in every episode of Skylitzes' account of the reign or of the Rebellion's fortunes. But there is consistency, in that some of those episodes which do not feature Katakalon himself revolve around themes close to his heart: they focus on the meanness and churlish demeanour of Michael and his counsellors towards the army commanders; or they highlight the iniquitousness of a situation in which civilians continued to receive imperial dignities, 'neither having manned the ramparts nor ever fought it out with the enemy', whereas 'those who had been defenders of their country since boyhood and had spent sleepless nights that these might sleep securely [in their beds] were overlooked'.⁵⁴ Thus the episodes recounting Michael's brusque refusal of back pay to the general, Bryennios, and his ridicule of the request for the title of *magistros* put by Hervé Frankopoulos, a commander of Frankish mercenaries, parallel the confrontation between the other commanders and Michael at the Eastertide reception. Each leads to rebellion – an individual one, in Hervé's case,⁵⁵ while Bryennios' thirst for vengeance makes him amenable to the plot which the other rebellious generals have already begun to hatch.⁵⁶

One can discern a common thread running through these episodes and the main revolt. Both the commanders had associations with Katakalon. Hervé, we are told, had served with Maniakes on Sicily,⁵⁷ as had Katakalon; and Hervé and Katakalon alike commanded a wing at Diakene.⁵⁸

---

⁵² Skylitzes, *Synopsis*, ed. Thurn, 481.42–483.91; 483.94–500.93.
⁵³ Easter Sunday fell on 30 March that year. ⁵⁴ Skylitzes, *Synopsis*, ed. Thurn, 486.7–10.
⁵⁵ Ibid., 484.44–485.54. ⁵⁶ Ibid., 484.38–40.
⁵⁷ Ibid., 484.42–3; *PBW*, 'Hervé 101: Narrative' http://pbw2016.kdl.kcl.ac.uk/person/Hervé/101/; 'Anonymus 195: Narrative' http://pbw2016.kdl.kcl.ac.uk/person/Anonymus/195/ (accessed 3 April 2018).
⁵⁸ Skylitzes, *Synopsis*, ed. Thurn, 468.39–40; *PBW*, 'Chronology: 1049' http://pbw2016.kdl.kcl.ac.uk/chronology/?current_year=1049 (accessed 3 April 2018).

As for Bryennios, it was none other than Katakalon who approached him to join in the projected Rebellion, a proposal he accepted 'readily'. Thus incidents at first sight unrelated to Katakalon involve persons quite closely associated with him, and they dovetail into the account of the principal Rebellion. They serve to illustrate both the meanness of the emperor and the justice of the rebels' cause. And they give Katakalon's quarrel with the emperor a much broader context, embracing not only Isaac Komnenos but also other top commanders. Moreover, they raise an issue of principle: lifelong 'defenders of their country' are no less deserving of reward than are those who have never 'fought it out'.

Cohesiveness and consistency of themes characterise Skylitzes' account of Michael VI's reign. It climaxes with the attainment of the title *kouropalates* by Katakalon, having virtually begun with the Eastertide reception and the emperor's refusal to grant him the title of *proedros*. This story of Katakalon's advancement to befitting honours offers a familiar refrain, highlighting as it does his outstanding qualities of leadership and courage already seen from his dealings with the Pechenegs and in the east. The battle near Nicaea fared badly for the rebels at first: the government forces would have 'won outright victory' had not Katakalon broken through on his wing and charged ahead to the enemy camp, which was prominently placed. The sight of Katakalon hacking down their tents with his sword induced panic among enemy troops while reviving morale on his own side, and victory was theirs.[59]

There are, however, additional themes in Skylitzes' account of the Great Rebellion that are far less pronounced in episodes from Katakalon's earlier career. Attention is paid not only to Katakalon's deeds but also to his deliberations during the Rebellion's earlier stages. His dilemma upon withdrawing to his country seat in Koloneia is stated sympathetically, and his apparent vacillation explained. Reportedly, Katakalon became anxious that he had declared his readiness to rebel precipitately, and would now be abandoned to his fate by his fellow conspirators: 'he pondered and sought out how and in what manner he might provide for his own security'.[60] He was particularly apprehensive about three *tagmata* of foreign-born soldiers stationed nearby, fearing lest they arrest and send him to the emperor.[61] Katakalon's method of suborning the army officers of the district is expounded: each morning, while 'pretending to be taking a muster',[62] he would call aside the commander of a *tagma* and confidentially offer him the choice of participation in the rising, or decapitation.

---

[59] Skylitzes, *Synopsis*, ed. Thurn, 495.43–52 [60] Ibid., 490.9–10. [61] Ibid., 490.14–18.
[62] Ibid., 491.30–1.

Katakalon's apprehensions are further elucidated in justification of his delay in joining forces with Isaac Komnenos, the general whom other commanders and their forces had already publicly acclaimed as emperor at Gounaria on 8 June 1057.[63]

Isaac Komnenos' inadequacies are underlined, unfavourable comparisons being drawn, directly or indirectly, with Katakalon. In fact, this is another theme of Skylitzes' account of Michael VI's reign. Katakalon's merits were recognised by the aggrieved generals when they swore oaths of mutual fidelity after enduring Michael VI's insults at the Eastertide reception in 1057. The claim is even made that Katakalon's fellow generals would have opted for him as emperor had he not 'cut the cackle with a pithy word';[64] standing up and immediately proclaiming Isaac 'emperor of the Romans', 'he caused the others to do the same'; he had, allegedly, appeared to 'all' of them to be outstandingly suitable for the throne, on account of his 'advanced age, courage and experience'.[65] Isaac's timidity is a recurrent motif, with indications that Katakalon was the mainstay of the Rebellion, despite his initial hesitation. It was, we are told, the news of Katakalon's winning over of large numbers of troops in eastern Asia Minor that raised the spirits of Isaac Komnenos, who had hitherto been 'utterly craven and cowering from fear'.[66] Likewise during the subsequent battle against government forces, Isaac was 'shaken' by the enemy's initial success and 'looking to flight into Nicaea'. It was Katakalon's breakthrough that 'inspired courage in those around Komnenos'.[67] Katakalon's political judgement, too, proves incomparably superior to the hapless Isaac's. After their victory at Nicaea, 'Komnenos and all the commanders with him' were willing to accept Michael VI's offer of co-emperorship for Komnenos and other concessions. 'Only [Katakalon] Kekaumenos' insisted on Michael's outright abdication, warning his comrades of what awaited them once they laid down their arms: poisoning for Komnenos and blinding for the rest of them, one by one. Michael's envoys proceeded secretly to approach Katakalon, urging him to stand firm 'and never give in': Isaac had only to approach Constantinople for 'the entire City populace' to drive out Michael and welcome Isaac 'with victory chants and hymns'.[68] And this – broadly speaking – is what happened. Skylitzes' account

---

[63] For this ceremonial acclamation before rank-and-file soldiery, see ibid., 489.74–8.
[64] Ibid., 487.28–31. On the oath-taking of the generals in Hagia Sophia, see J.-C. Cheynet, 'Foi et conjuration à Byzance' in M.-F. Auzépy and G. Saint-Guillain, eds., *Oralité et lien social au Moyen Âge* (Paris, 2008), 276.
[65] Skylitzes, *Synopsis*, ed. Thurn, 487.26–7. [66] Ibid., 491.44–5. [67] Ibid., 495.46–7, 51–2.
[68] Ibid., 497.1–17.

concludes with the old emperor's abdication, the arrival by *dromon* at the palace of Katakalon, now titled *kouropalates* and joined towards evening by Isaac, and the patriarch's crowning of Isaac in Hagia Sophia the following day, 1 September 1057.[69]

The three sets of materials in Skylitzes reviewed above feature Katakalon Kekaumenos prominently, while setting his activities in a broader perspective. Their techniques in projecting both the importance of his role and the rationale behind his conduct are not unsubtle. The section covering the months of the Great Rebellion is, from this aspect, particularly well-crafted. The passages purporting to describe Katakalon's forebodings amount to an apologia, a riposte to potential criticism of certain of his actions or apparent inaction. Indeed, the account of the coup contains more than a hint of polemic. Isaac Komnenos comes within the author's sights, as being by nature timorous and ill-fitted for the imperial office that was virtually thrust upon him. One is left in no doubt as to the true hero, who had seen the Rebellion through from hesitant beginnings to sage rejection of Michael VI's offer of co-emperorship for Isaac.

All this would suggest that our hypothetical written text – K – was composed while issues of court-titles and appropriate recognition for services rendered during the Rebellion still rankled. Heavy-handed reminders of Isaac's indebtedness to Katakalon would have lost their edge after Isaac's abdication on 21/22 November 1059, and consequent inability to make amends. One would anyway expect a text composed after that date to have made more fulsome reference to Constantine Doukas' participation in the events of 1057.[70] By far the likeliest author of a text detailing Katakalon's distinguished military record and role in Michael VI's downfall is the man himself.[71] There is no pressing need to postulate a

---

[69] Ibid., 500.86–93. According to Skylitzes Continuatus, ed. Tsolakes, 103.17–18, once installed in the City, Isaac formally bestowed the title of *kouropalates* on his own brother John and on Katakalon. These supplementary details, which were taken from a source other than Attaleiates (see table of borrowings: ibid., 64), and on our reckoning, were not in K either, could have been taken from some other source. A possible candidate is one of the 'old men' whom Skylitzes cites as reliable oral informants in his preface (Skylitzes, *Synopsis*, ed. Thurn, 4.49).

[70] In Skylitzes' account of Michael VI's reign, Constantine features only once, listed with his brother John and 'the other army commanders' at the Eastertide reception: Skylitzes, *Synopsis*, ed. Thurn, 483.8–9; Flusin and Cheynet, *Skylitzès*, 399, n. 12.

[71] A further hint of K's composition soon after the events of spring and summer 1057 is the seeming implication that Michael VI is still on earth: Skylitzes, *Synopsis*, ed. Thurn, 500.82–3. According to Michael Psellos (É. Renauld, ed. and trans., *Michel Psellos. Chronographie, ou Histoire d'un siècle de Byzance (976–1077)* (Paris, 1926–8) [hereafter Psellos, *Chronographie*, ed. Renauld], vol. II, 110), he lived on as a monk 'for a short time' after abdicating; in any case, he seems to have died before 1 September 1059: J. Shepard, 'Isaac Comnenus' Coronation Day', *BSl*, 38 (1977), 24; Holmes, *Basil II*, 91; *PBW*, 'Michael 6: Death' http://pbw2016.kdl.kcl.ac.uk/person/Michael/6/ (accessed 3 April 2018).

third party, some biographer relying on Katakalon's testimony for his materials. It is just conceivable that Katakalon could have narrated his deeds in the third person, replete with the details of court-titles and commands that Skylitzes reproduces.[72] At any rate, although Katakalon's talents and achievements are to the fore, they are presented in terms of factual historical accuracy rather than of outright encomium, a distinction Byzantine writers drew, even while finessing it.[73]

An Articulate Officers' Culture, and Michael VI's Downfall as a Moralising Tale

In support of this identification of authorship of K for Katakalon Kekaumenos, one can bring internal and external evidence to bear. First, one should note the frequency with which commanders' discussions on tactics are reported. To judge from K, arguing a case replete with factual examples and vivid phrases was not unusual among Byzantium's high command. This is consistent with the 'honeyed words' by which field-commanders were expected to inspire their men on the point of combat. Besides signalling correct, and incorrect, ways of attacking Dvin, K records the strategy Katakalon had proposed for the battle of Diakene. Reportedly, the eunuch commander-in-chief Nikephoros rebuffed him: 'Stop, o general! And do not countermand me when I am the commander!'[74] Yet this apparently followed discussion of what should be done, everyone else present taking the same line as Nikephoros.[75]

Overall strategy could likewise be open to debate. Thus Katakalon put successive proposals to his fellow-general, Aaron, on how they should cope

---

[72] See, for example, specifics of Katakalon's title, command and troops for the defence of Messina: Skylitzes, *Synopsis*, ed. Thurn, 406.17–19. Well-informed persons, 'men incapable of lying', 'assured' that Michael VI's envoys had secretly urged Katakalon to hold fast against Michael's terms (497.12–14). This could suggest the work's composition in the third person, citing additional persons for corroboration, a politic move seeing that the treacherous envoys numbered Psellos among them (Shepard, 'Suspected Source', 176). However, one cannot rule out authorial intervention by Skylitzes here, perhaps invoking the testimony of the 'old men' mentioned in his preface (Skylitzes, *Synopsis*, ed. Thurn, 4.49) and himself vouching for their trustworthiness. In general, he could have turned K's first person singular into the third person while occasionally leaving it unaltered, as with the first-person speculation as to Michael VI's heavenly reward (ibid., 500.82). Thus we lack clinching evidence that K itself referred to Katakalon in the third person. See also Kiapidou, *Η σύνοψη ιστοριών*, 131–3, 461–3.
[73] Hunger, *Hochsprachliche profane Literatur*, vol. 1, 379; C. Chamberlain, 'The Theory and Practice of Imperial Panegyric in Michael Psellus', *Byzantion*, 56 (1986), 23–7; E. Pietsch, *Die Chronographia des Michael Psellos: Kaisergeschichte, Autobiographie und Apologie* (Wiesbaden, 2005), 75–7, 80; Angold and Whitby, 'Historiography', 843; Jeffreys, 'Rhetoric in Byzantium', 175–6.
[74] Skylitzes, *Synopsis*, ed. Thurn, 468.26–7.   [75] Ibid., 468.15, 25–6.

with Turkish raids in the course of 1048. His advice was taken when a host of Turks led by Hasan 'the Deaf' streamed into Byzantine Armenia: the Turks were lured into a deserted-looking camp and massacred after they had dispersed to plunder it.[76] However, Katakalon's counsel was disregarded when another large Turkish force made for Byzantium's borderlands some months later. Katakalon was now all for 'meeting the Turks outside the Roman borders ... when the enemy were mostly without horses and the rest of them were weary from much travelling', and 'they lacked the iron tools with which they shoe their horses' hooves'.[77] Katakalon, despite his apparent expertise in the Turks' customs and movements, was overruled by his fellow-general. Aaron insisted on relying on fortifications and 'not fighting such a host of barbarians with so small a force (of one's own) except with the emperor's knowledge'. In the event, the Turks managed to capture the huge and wealthy city of Artze, and Katakalon was powerless to prevent them. He had urged Aaron to take action 'and not pointlessly sit still and waste time'.[78] Aaron refused 'saying that nothing could be done against the wishes of the emperor'.[79] We are further told that, in sacking the city, the Turks gained money, weapons, iron tools, horses and beasts of burden.[80] Katakalon's strategic judgement was, by implication, vindicated twice over.

This episode shows the limitations to Katakalon's powers of persuasion, but it presupposes that he routinely exercised them while on campaign. And shortly afterwards, reprising his counsel to Aaron, Katakalon sought to impress upon Liparit the merits of attacking the Turks while they were dispersed and unorganised.[81] Reasoned argument is grist to the mill of generalship. Katakalon's ability to argue a case features during the Great Rebellion, too. For example, when warning commanders against accepting Michael VI's terms, he cited not only practical pitfalls but also divine dangers: they had declared Michael deposed by means of fearsome oaths; to let him now remain as emperor would be to commit perjury and to risk incurring God's wrath.[82]

If Katakalon Kekaumenos' capacity for marshalling arguments and making a case emerges from K, internal evidence also points towards his authorship of the actual text. Katakalon's manner of speaking, in so far as it is refracted through K, resembles the manner in which our three sets of materials are written: preference for the 'pithy word' (συντόμῳ λόγῳ) as

---

[76] Ibid., 449.60–76.   [77] Ibid., 450.85–92; Shepard, 'Scylitzes on Armenia', 274.
[78] Skylitzes, *Synopsis*, ed. Thurn, 451.40–1.   [79] Ibid., 451.43–4.   [80] Ibid., 452.55–8.
[81] Ibid., 452.63–4.   [82] Ibid., 497.5–11; Cheynet, 'Foi et conjuration', 276.

against 'cackle' (τὰς πολυλογίας), delineation of military detail, and brief synopses of situations. A few examples may illustrate the terse style and 'no-nonsense' approach. Battle-stations are stated and the fortunes of each wing summarised. At Kaputru, for instance, Katakalon was opposite Ibrahim Inal, Aaron faced Chorosantes, and Liparit faced Ibrahim's half-brother, Aspan Salarios.[83] Terrain of military significance is noted, for example the ample cover from the vineyards near Dvin that Abul Aswar exploited to ambush the Byzantine army.[84] Katakalon's injuries at Diakene are listed clinically. He was 'speechless', with 'the bare skull' cut 'from the crown to the eyebrows after his helmet had fallen off'; another wound ran 'from the throat, just where the tongue is rooted, cutting across the throat and finishing at the mouth'.[85] He also sustained blood-loss. The characteristics of individuals are stated concisely, and we have already noted K's positive remarks about Abul Aswar, Liparit and Kegen (above, pp. 193, 195) as well as the sideswipes at Isaac Komnenos (p. 199).

K specifically notes Katakalon's ability to 'cut the cackle' and to apply verbal – if not physical – pressure, as when acclaiming Isaac emperor in 1057, or when he gave individuals a choice between joining in the rising and decapitation.[86] Katakalon also appreciated quips and sayings, judging by a 'maxim, barbarian indeed yet full of sense' that Kegen proffered to the Byzantines by way of advice after his enemy Tyrach and other invading Pechenegs had surrendered: 'kill the snake while winter holds, and it cannot stir its tail: once warmed by the sun, it will bring us toil and trouble'.[87] Given the indications that Katakalon got to know Koulinos well and was perhaps well acquainted with Kegen himself, K most probably conveys a Pecheneg saying – or *gnome* – that Katakalon had heard. A passage in our third set of materials shows similar mordant humour, while neatly rounding off the story of the Great Rebellion. The story nears its end with an exchange between Michael VI and the churchmen sent by Patriarch Michael Keroularios, urging him to abdicate at once: 'What will the patriarch provide for me instead of the kingdom (βασιλεία)?' asks Michael. 'The heavenly kingdom!' reply the churchmen, and 'even as they spoke he abdicated'.[88] The text speculates on how Michael might have fared had he abdicated sooner, thereby averting the bloodshed: 'I do

---

[83] Skylitzes, *Synopsis*, ed. Thurn, 452.72–453.77.
[84] Ibid., 437.45–53. Mention is also made of Abul Aswar's flooding of the ground so as to embog the cavalry.
[85] Ibid., 469.55–8; Shepard, 'Suspected Source', 172.
[86] Skylitzes, *Synopsis*, ed. Thurn, 487.28–9; 491.32–4.   [87] Ibid., 459.68–70
[88] Ibid., 499.74–500.76.

not know whether he will receive the heavenly kingdom in compensation. But this will be as God sees fit.'[89]

Gloating over Michael's ignominious departure from office, an exercise in pure *Schadenfreude*, characterises this mixture of direct speech and authorial speculation. Doubts as to the nature of Michael VI's reward in heaven counterbalance his dismissal of the generals' request for stipends at Easter, with which the account of the Rebellion begins. Tight deployment of materials and heavy irony bring a moral to the story. Some of these traits might reasonably be attributed to John Skylitzes, rather than to Katakalon himself, for quite similar literary qualities and choice of subject-matter characterise his chronicle in general. Soldierly virtues are at a premium and Skylitzes' style is generally unvarnished. He shows a penchant for compression, studding his narrative with colourful episodes and aphorisms.[90] However, in respect of Michael VI's Eastertide reception at least, Skylitzes' redacting of K was fairly light, and he did not collate it with an alternative version of the reception, provided by Psellos' *Chronographia*. Skylitzes has the emperor refusing the generals' requests, yet showering praise upon them 'and especially [Katakalon] Kekaumenos', who owed his rank 'not to his forefathers or some patronage, but to his own exploits alone'.[91] On the contrary, Michael VI gave the generals short shrift, according to Psellos. He insulted them all and singled out '[Katakalon] Kekaumenos from Koloneia' for personal abuse, accusing him of incompetence and of nearly losing Antioch. Katakalon was stunned, having expected high honours.[92] Psellos' version has the merit of internal consistency, making the indignation of so many of the commanders comprehensible, and it is surely preferable to what is on offer in Skylitzes. And Michael's alleged encomium for Katakalon's meritocratic career corresponds with what one can infer from elsewhere in K about Katakalon's self-image, a soldier of modest origins but of talent, one of the 'defenders of their country since boyhood'.[93] Katakalon could hardly have put it better himself – and indeed, if

---

[89] Ibid., 500.78–83.
[90] See Holmes, 'Rhetorical Structures', 191–4; Holmes, *Basil II*, 103–9, 128–36, 147–58, 162–7, 454–5. Holmes observes in Skylitzes' treatment of earlier tenth-century episodes (for which we have Theophanes Continuatus as a control) a tendency to omit geographical data and full details of military operations, Holmes, *Basil II*, 102–7, 145–52, 163–8. If these tendencies are largely absent from his mid-eleventh-century coverage, this could reflect the details' greater topicality and readier comprehensibility to readers in Skylitzes' own time.
[91] Skylitzes, *Synopsis*, ed. Thurn, 483.15–17.
[92] Psellos, *Chronographie*, ed. Renauld, vol. II, 84. Skylitzes cites Psellos' historical work in his preface, albeit critically and probably with reference to his *Historia syntomos*, not to the *Chronographia*: Skylitzes, *Synopsis*, ed. Thurn, 3.
[93] Ibid., 486.8–9. See above, p. 197.

he composed the moralising tale that begins with the Eastertide reception and ends with Michael VI's downfall, he did.

Military Memoirs as Manifesto?

The encomium of Katakalon Kekaumenos that Michael VI allegedly delivered in 1057 was, then, most probably concocted by Katakalon himself. It suggests that Skylitzes followed K's account closely, without much alteration to the wording, and that the stylistic traits noted above are attributable to K, rather than to systematic reworking on Skylitzes' part. We have already noted other distortions or omissions in K, the misrepresentation of the battle of Kaputru and the silence about the removal of the *katholikos* Peter from Ani. The extolling of Katakalon's exploits attributed to Michael VI is of a different order, not merely because it seems to invert historical reality, but because it seems to be the key to understanding our hypothetical text, K. This text abounded in recollections of Katakalon's years as a soldier, the stratagems, acts of heroism and grand strategy. But it seems to have been weighted towards the reign of Michael VI, more precisely, its second half, concluding with Michael's conversation with the churchmen about compensation and the entry of Katakalon and Isaac into the Great Palace. This set-piece surely constitutes a riposte to insults from the emperor that, according to Psellos, had left Katakalon stunned, even if the abuse is, in K's version of the Eastertide reception, transmuted into compliments.[94] If the text places a particular construction upon recent events,[95] it would seem designed to influence those now in the corridors of power.

That Katakalon Kekaumenos should have been capable not merely of putting thoughts to paper but of coherent arguments, too, is hardly surprising. Besides Katakalon's self-representation as a robust debater, we have independent evidence that he could present a case complaining of injustices and demanding remedial action. His correspondence with Michael Psellos after retiring to live near Koloneia around 1060 attests confidence in his own penmanship and judgement. Psellos notes how Katakalon had 'often in your letters to me' extolled the virtues of the metropolitan of Koloneia.[96] Moreover the intimations of rewards denied

---

[94] Skylitzes, *Synopsis*, ed. Thurn, 486.7–8. The generals' complaint about honours going to those who had never 'manned the ramparts' whereas heroes went unrewarded surely expresses Katakalon's personal position.
[95] On the date of composition of K, see above, n. 71.
[96] E. Kurtz and F. Drexl, eds., *Michaelis Pselli Scripta minora* (Milan, 1936–41) [hereafter Psellos, *Scripta minora*, ed. Kurtz and Drexl], vol. II, 44.19–22.

and of disappointment resounding throughout Psellos' three extant letters to him echo the tone of K. Although now a monk, Katakalon agitates incessantly over non-payment of the (substantial) stipend due to him as holder of the dignity of *kouropalates*; judging by Psellos' first letter to him, Katakalon has already complained about the 'meanness' of the emperor, Constantine X.[97] According to Psellos' second letter, Katakalon's agent in the capital had made every effort to get the payment resumed, badgering the patriarch and the emperor, 'and me before all'. But his efforts have been to no avail. Somewhat unctuously, Psellos consoles Katakalon: if he fails to receive his due from the emperor of this world, he will be repaid many times over by the heavenly sovereign, in the bliss laid up for the just.[98]

Katakalon's literary competence was far from unique among persons holding military commands in Middle Byzantium, even if Katakalon himself was, in some senses, a special case. This emerges from the text composed by his namesake and probable kinsman, Kekaumenos, likewise a senior army commander. This product of soldierly sense and worldly wisdom defies precise labelling. The title *Admonitions and Anecdotes* given by its Russian discoverer is apt enough for a miscellany involving military tactics, household management and careerist tips, spiced with anecdotes.[99] As Elizabeth Jeffreys has observed, the 'seemingly artless' story-telling of Kekaumenos' work and his disavowal of literary knowledge cloaks compositional competence.[100] Kekaumenos seems to have been well-drilled in *progymnasmata* in rhetoric.[101] These techniques serve to convey home-truths, moral guidelines and advice on tactics, addressing a readership of individuals in the army, but not exclusively so. When offering advice based on experience, Kekaumenos – unlike Katakalon – does not present his actions in particularly heroic mode. Yet the unadorned style interspersed

---

[97] Psellos, *Scripta minora*, ed. Kurtz and Drexl, vol. II, 92.19–20. For dating of the first extant letter to 1060 and identification of the emperor as Constantine X, see *PBW*, 'Katakalon 101: Narrative (1060)'. A slightly later dating was proposed by G. G. Litavrin, 'Три письма Михаила Пселла Катакалону Кекавмену', *RESEE*, 7 (1969), 464–5.

[98] Psellos, *Scripta minora*, ed. Kurtz and Drexl, vol. II, 168.22–4.

[99] One by-product of *PBW*'s overview of Katakalon's career is to highlight the implausibility of his authorship of the *Admonitions and Anecdotes*. The two writers may well have belonged to the same family and had similar backgrounds, but they were not identical. By the time the *Admonitions and Anecdotes* was nearing completion in (most probably) the mid-1070s, Katakalon would have been a monk for over ten years and, having been the oldest of the disaffected generals at the Eastertide reception of 1057, he may well now have been dead. See also Litavrin, *Советы и рассказы*, 54–5; n. 858 on 563; n. 922 on 576; below, n. 114.

[100] Jeffreys, 'Rhetoric', 834.

[101] Jeffreys, 'Rhetoric', 830–1; C. Roueché, 'The Rhetoric of Kekaumenos' in Jeffreys, ed., *Rhetoric in Byzantium* (Aldershot, 2003), 29–34.

with moralising resembles what we have seen in K; both works contain cautionary tales, and 'reminiscence' (*apomnemoneuma*) was an exercise close-related to the *chreia* and the *gnome*.[102] Furthermore, the zeal to instruct shown by the *Admonitions and Anecdotes* and so characteristic of Byzantine military manuals is discernible in K, as elsewhere in Skylitzes.[103] A vein of didacticism, alongside self-advertisement, runs through K's reflections upon tactics: the efficacy of pouncing on enemy forces which are not in battle-order is a recurrent theme.[104]

Thus Katakalon seems to have been drawing on essentially the same literary techniques as his namesake and rough contemporary. Both his subject-matter and his style subsequently recommended his text – K – to a chronicler of a later generation. Skylitzes himself, while a lawyer and senior administrator rather than a military man, seems to have had cultural horizons comparable with those of the two Kekaumenoi.[105] Katakalon presumably received secondary-level education, but he could have gleaned something of rhetorical techniques directly from reading textbooks, an ambitious young soldier resorting to self-help.[106] Katakalon was, indeed, putting his compositional skills to fresh uses with his tract. For the final section, covering events from Easter 1057 onwards, he aimed at something more than military reminiscence. It amounted to a 'History of the Great Rebellion' and would have been recognisable as such to Lord Clarendon.[107] Whether Katakalon sought to dignify his text explicitly as 'History' can scarcely be determined in the absence of K's original title or full contents, and the question is not central to our purpose here. Our point

---

[102] Roueché, 'Rhetoric', 32. For definitions of 'reminiscence' in *progymnasmata*, see G. A. Kennedy, trans., *Progymnasmata: Greek Textbooks of Prose Composition and Rhetoric* (Leiden, 2003), 15 (Theon), 176–7 (Hermogenes). See also C. Roueché, 'The Literary Background of Kekaumenos' in C. Holmes and J. Waring, eds., *Literacy, Education and Manuscript Transmission in Byzantium and Beyond* (Leiden, 2002), 114–17.

[103] Holmes, 'Rhetorical Structures', 194–9; Roueché, 'Literary Background', 117–23.

[104] Skylitzes, *Synopsis*, ed. Thurn, 407, 433, 449, 450, 468.

[105] Holmes, 'Rhetorical Structures', 187–93; Holmes, *Basil II*, 86–9.

[106] K's stress on Katakalon's lack of family connections and of patronage (Skylitzes, *Synopsis*, ed. Thurn, 483.15–17) bespeaks the self-made man, and students needed money to advance far along the curriculum: Roueché, 'Rhetoric', 28. Noteworthy are Katakalon's reportedly awkward relations in 1057 with the Armeniakoi, the thematic unit encompassing Koloneia in which he had (most probably) first seen action as a young officer: Skylitzes, *Synopsis*, ed. Thurn, 491.46–492.49; Flusin and Cheynet, *Skylitzès*, 404, n. 29; Litavrin, 'Три письма', 466. Suggestive, if not wholly conclusive, is K's highly sympathetic portrayal of the talented Pecheneg Kegen: he owed his rise to military feats that made the untalented hereditary chieftain Tyrach regard him as a threat: Skylitzes, *Synopsis*, ed. Thurn, 544.40–51.

[107] Although differing in many ways, K shares with Clarendon's *History* insight into the self-preservation instincts of both ruler and rebels: B. H. G. Wormald, *Clarendon: Politics, History and Religion, 1640–1660* (Cambridge, 1951), 156–7.

is that Katakalon was presenting a case. If he had taken study of the *progymnasmata* to heart, he would not have found the task of composition especially daunting. As it was, he felt equal to sustaining an epistolary dialogue with Psellos. And he was quite capable of forging 'imperial letters' to place five *tagmata* of foreign soldiers and Romans under his command for a (fictitious) campaign against a Turkish emir; nor did he baulk at recording this.[108]

Katakalon would not have been the only military man to get his own campaigns or those of his family recorded in a positive light, whether writing them up himself, employing a ghostwriter, or commissioning an author to recount them in the third person. The composition of a narrative history of John Kourkouas' 'works and deeds' by a judge, Manuel *protospatharios*, is well attested;[109] and the existence of 'a sort of secular biography of Nikephoros Phokas has been deduced by modern scholars.[110] There are strong grounds for supposing the composition of a kind of manifesto eulogistically recording Bardas Skleros' military feats and revolt against Basil II, and for inferring use of this work by Psellos and Skylitzes.[111] If the manifesto was available to these writers, its contents could very well have been known to Katakalon, too. One may also surmise that a manifesto celebrating the feats of George Maniakes was composed soon after his rebellion against Constantine IX and subsequent defeat and death.[112]

Through collating the three sets of materials in Skylitzes derived from K with the character of Katakalon that emerges from them and from Psellos' correspondence with him, one may surmise that Katakalon was a disappointed man by the later stages of Isaac Komnenos' reign. In such circumstances, Katakalon would have had cause to bring out a kind of *curriculum vitae*, climaxing with his part in the recent Rebellion. The incentive would have been the greater if other military leaders had inspired manifestos for their feats and virtues in the wake of their fall from imperial grace or failure to gain the throne. Judging by the sets of materials traceable

---

[108] Skylitzes, *Synopsis*, ed. Thurn, 491.26–7.
[109] I. Bekker, ed., *Theophanes Continuatus, Ioannes Cameniata, Symeon Magister, Georgius Monachus* (Bonn, 1838), 427–8; A. Kazhdan, 'Kourkouas, John', *ODB*, vol. II, 1157.
[110] I. N. Liubarskii, 'Nikephoros Phokas in Byzantine Historical Writings', *BSl*, 54 (1993), 253; Flusin and Cheynet, *Skylitzès*, xiii–xiv.
[111] Holmes, *Basil II*, 255–68, 272–3, 278–92.
[112] J. Shepard, 'Byzantium's Last Sicilian Expedition: Scylitzes' Testimony', *RSBN*, n.s. 14–16 (1977–9), 148–54. On the profusion of private narratives in this period, often written in 'the language of heroes', see C. Roueché, 'Byzantine Writers and Readers: Storytelling in the Eleventh Century' in R. Beaton, ed., *The Greek Novel AD 1–1985* (London, 1988), 127–9.

to K, Katakalon recounted his military career, offering information on the campaign theatres where he had had extensive experience. And he laid emphasis on his personal worthiness for the throne and on the consensus in 1057 that he deserved it. The exchanges between Michael VI and the clergymen, and Katakalon's entry into the palace and Isaac's coronation, could fittingly have concluded the account of the Rebellion, and indeed the entire work. If our inference from this passage that Michael was still alive at the time of writing holds good, Katakalon completed his work during the reign of Isaac Komnenos: Michael seems to have died before Isaac's reign ended on 21/22 November 1059.[113] Katakalon, who was older than Isaac and the other generals and thus probably nearing his sixties,[114] can scarcely have still harboured imperial ambitions. But he might well have asserted his moral right to the title and stipend of *kouropalates*, through circulating his version of the Rebellion, integrated with his military memoirs. Katakalon may have hoped that his manifesto would remind Isaac – and opinion in Constantinople and military circles – of the emperor's indebtedness, and of his duty to bestow largesse, if not office, on the retired commander.

Katakalon and His Text as *sui generis*

The later phases of Isaac's reign were fraught, not least because of the discontent his attempts at retrenchment aroused in the capital, while a sizeable portion of the army had fought against him at Nicaea in 1057.[115] Screeds such as K or manifestos singing the praises of contenders for the throne like Bardas Skleros and George Maniakes seem to have proliferated in eras of political instability.[116] They gave talented individuals of sometimes obscure origins recognition, and could commemorate them in failure or in death. Equally, ambitious members of leading families had their own agendas, whether aspiring to the throne or simply reminding current rulers

---

[113] See above, n. 71; Skylitzes, *Synopsis*, ed. Thurn, 500.82–3.
[114] Katakalon's 'advanced age' (*gera*) was one of the reasons why they had reportedly looked to him as the best candidate for the throne: ibid., 487.26. One may believe the indication that he was old, while doubting whether this really counted in his favour.
[115] Attaleiates, *Historia*, ed. Pérez Martín, 47–8, 53; Skylitzes Continuatus, ed. Tsolakes, 104, 109, 110; J.-C. Cheynet, *Pouvoir et contestations à Byzance (963–1210)* (Paris, 1990), 339–44.
[116] For this phenomenon in Byzantine and other cultures, see J. Shepard, 'History as Propaganda, Proto-foundation-myth and "Tract for the Times" in the Long Eleventh Century (*c.* 1000–*c.* 1130)' in T. N. Jackson, ed., *Old Rus' and Medieval Europe: The Origin of States* (Moscow, 2016).

of their distinction and links with past emperors.[117] Elaborate commemorations in writing and overt manifestos alike could serve as counters in the political board-game, with the aim of blocking one's elimination from the game rather than invariably celebrating arrival on the throne itself.

Several texts – some extant, others reasonably surmised – are the product of the political flux of the later eleventh century. They purport to offer conspectuses of the recent past or focus explicitly on an individual's feats, and they vary in accordance with his character and political context. Nikephoros Botaneiates may well have imparted details of his early military exploits to Attaleiates by word of mouth, rather than writing, for incorporation in his *History*. Botaneiates' spelling skills seem to have been weak. This could well signal other cultural limitations. Perhaps Attaleiates insisted on his love of reading and nocturnal study so as to compensate for what many would consider a deficiency in a general, let alone an emperor.[118] At any rate, Attaleiates' *History* offers ruminations on and celebrations of a veteran's pathway to the throne, most probably composed while Nikephoros III Botaneiates (1078–81) was on the throne and in hopes of securing his tenure there.[119]

From a different, indeed rival, perspective, John Doukas seems to have written up his own military and political accomplishments during the 1070s; he was an influential figure at the court of his nephew Michael VII Doukas, although eventually sidelined.[120] John's (non-extant) work contained intimations that his qualities enjoyed general recognition, and 'he would easily have gained the imperial sceptre, had not divine opposition manifested itself'.[121] Nikephoros Bryennios drew upon this work of John when he put together an account of his homonymous grandfather's military feats and the rebellion he mounted during the 1070s. Nikephoros

---

[117] Holmes, *Basil II*, 186–7, 202–16, 235–6, 297.

[118] Attaleiates, *Historia*, ed. Pérez Martín, 222.26–7; O. Karagiorgiou, 'On the Way to the Throne: the Career of Nikephoros III Botaneiates Before 1078' in C. Stavrakos, A.-K. Wassiliou and M. K. Krikorian, eds., *Hypermachos. Studien zur Byzantinistik, Armenologie und Georgistik, Festschrift für Werner Seibt zum 65. Geburtstag* (Wiesbaden, 2008), 113. Attaleiates' very full account of Botaneiates' leadership of his men back from the debacle at Preslav to Adrianople on an eleven-day *Anabasis* can only derive from the hero himself: Attaleiates, *Historia*, ed. Pérez Martín, 30–3, and n. 103 on 251.

[119] Attaleiates, *Historia*, ed. Pérez Martín, xxxvi–xlii (introduction); Karageorgiou, 'Way to the Throne', 127–32.

[120] See L. Neville, 'A History of the Caesar John Doukas in Nikephoros Bryennios' *Material for History?' BMGS*, 32 (2008), 170–2, 174, 186–7.

[121] P. Gautier, ed. and trans., *Nicéphore Bryennios. Histoire. Introduction, texte, traduction et notes* (Brussels, 1975), 176–9; Neville, 'John Doukas', 178. See now L. Neville, *Heroes and Romans in Twelfth-century Byzantium: The Material for History of Nikephoros Bryennios* (Cambridge, 2012).

highlighted his family's ties with the Komnenoi and imperial credentials, alongside Alexios Komnenos' youthful exploits. Nikephoros could have worked on this compilation during the 'enforced leisure' that his own abortive bid for the throne after Alexios' death brought him.[122] Alexios' route to the throne and the first two decades of his reign loom large in the work of Alexios' daughter, Anna, registering her own imperial aspirations and credentials as well as the pattern of written materials available to her.[123]

Katakalon Kekaumenos was writing from a lowlier, rather lonely, standpoint, differing from the likes of Anna Komnene or, indeed, Nikephoros Bryennios and the other well-connected authors noted above. If our considerations hold true, K's prose was unvarnished, whereas John Doukas' style seems to have been deliberately archaising, signalling his literary attainments.[124] Katakalon was presenting himself in apposition to these comfortably placed members of the imperial establishment as well as to fairly 'soft targets', court eunuchs in command of armies such as Nikephoros at Diakene. Katakalon seems to have written with an eye to self-vindication, as if battling verbally against overwhelming odds by means of records of his campaigning and a battery of *progymnasmata*.

One might even suggest that Katakalon, in playing up and offering verbal proof of his singularity, had objectives more akin to those of Michael Psellos in writing his *Chronographia*: each was intent on writing himself into the script of a grand narrative. Setting aside the glaring differences in their levels of prose-style and literary polish and Psellos' matchless talent for encomia, one may note that neither inherited advantages of wealth or lineage. And Psellos, like Katakalon, 'draws attention to his role in making history'.[125] Each, while flexing his ego, was demonstrating his proficiency in matters of grave import to the state, with strong undertones of apologia. Prominent among the motifs in Psellos' *Chronographia* is his critique of Constantine IX's regime: he was clearly trying to distance himself politically from his former patron.[126] By presenting

---

[122] E. M. Jeffreys, 'Nikephoros Bryennios Reconsidered' in V. N. Vlysidou, ed., *The Empire in Crisis? Byzantium in the Eleventh Century (1025–1081)* (Athens, 2003), 211–14.
[123] For the question of Anna's sources and ambitions see, e.g., contributions to T. Gouma-Peterson, ed., *Anna Komnene and Her Times* (New York, NY, 2000); V. Stanković, 'Nikephoros Bryennios, Anna Komnene and Konstantinos Doukas', *BZ*, 100 (2007), 169–75; Angold and Whitby, 'Historiography', 844.
[124] Neville, 'John Doukas', 184–5, 187.
[125] R. Macrides, 'The Historian in the History' in C. N. Constantinides et al., eds., Φιλέλλην: *Studies in Honour of Robert Browning* (Venice, 1996), 216.
[126] Pietsch, *Die Chronographia*, 66, 75–6.

himself in statesmanlike guise, the trusted counsellor of flawed rulers and an orator who seeded even the ritual compliments of encomia with immanent truths,[127] Psellos dignified the fact that his initial advancement was due to Constantine's patronage. Reanimating the characters and courts of recent rulers with high-style Greek and rhetorical imagery, Psellos was playing some of his strongest cards in a political game that continued as he jockeyed for position at Constantine X's court in, apparently, the early 1060s.[128] His *Chronographia* demonstrated the facility with which he could outshine any other re-constructor of the recent past, without much recourse to names or details.[129] We have already noted Psellos' reference, in a letter, to Katakalon's recouping many times over in heavenly bliss the money due to him from the earthly emperor (Constantine X). One should not rule out the possibility that Psellos was, maliciously, echoing the theme that seems to conclude the text of K.[130] One may, indeed, wonder whether it is fortuitous that Psellos' *Chronographia* specifies that Michael VI singled out Katakalon for vilification at the Eastertide reception, deriding his pursuit of lucre at Antioch.[131] Psellos, having urged Katakalon in private correspondence to be content with his lot on earth, could have been drawing attention in his *Chronographia* to past slurs against his record of public service.

The differences between Katakalon's literary workmanship and earthly priorities and Psellos' are, for all this comparability of objectives of K and the *Chronographia*, vast; they were writing from very different

---

[127] The contrast between Psellos' public utterances while Constantine was emperor and what he was now writing prompted his disquisition in the *Chronographia*: Psellos, *Chronographie*, ed. Renauld, vol. I, 128–9; Chamberlain, 'Panegyric in Michael Psellus', 16–19; Pietsch, *Die Chronographia*, 77–83.

[128] Seemingly, Psellos drafted the main part of the *Chronographia* in the opening years of Constantine X's reign: Hunger, *Hochsprachliche profane Literatur*, vol. I, 378; Pietsch, *Die Chronographia*, 5–6. On Psellos' stance as moral arbiter, see ibid. 83–7, 109–11, 130; A. Kaldellis, *The Argument of Psellos' Chronographia* (Leiden, 1999), 152–4, 169–72, 178–85; see now M. J. Jeffreys, 'Psellos and "His Emperors": Fact, Fiction and Genre' in R. Macrides, ed., *History as Literature in Byzantium* (Farnham, 2010), 73–91. Significantly, Psellos' relations with Constantine X cooled quite soon after Constantine's accession, thus around the time when he was writing the main part of the *Chronographia*: Jeffreys, 'Psellos', 81–3.

[129] Macrides, 'The Historian', 215, 217. For the fictitious nature of his self-portrayal as close confidant of successive rulers, most blatantly in the case of Isaac I Komnenos, see now Jeffreys, 'Psellos', 78–81, 90.

[130] Psellos, *Scripta minora*, ed. Kurtz and Drexl, vol. II, 168.22–169.2.

[131] Psellos, *Chronographie*, ed. Renauld, vol. II, 84. One might further speculate whether Psellos' elaborate account of his own embassies to Isaac Komnenos and the negotiations he conducted on behalf of the still-reigning emperor may in part serve to rebut K's portrayal of Psellos and his fellow envoys as secretly urging Katakalon to reject the terms: ibid. vol. II, 98–105; Skylitzes, *Synopsis*, ed. Thurn, 496–7.

vantage-points and with different specific goals. Katakalon would surely have numbered Psellos – with his armchair strategy and fitful personal participation in campaigning[132] – among the gentlemen of Byzantium now abed rather than being one of the true 'defenders of their country'. Katakalon was, by his own estimation, *sui generis* and proudly so, and this presumably fortified him in retelling the recent past, to show the superiority of his judgement and how events served to vindicate it. Thus K records him as being in a minority of one in opposing the decision to wait until the Pechenegs had massed at Diakene; likewise his was the one voice raised against accepting Michael VI's offer of terms.[133]

After a lifetime of making a case by word of mouth, drafting reports from the field and even, in 1057, forging 'imperial letters', Katakalon could feel confident in enlisting the written word to his cause. He most probably wrote in hopes of safeguarding his title, stipend and standing at the court of Isaac I Komnenos. Katakalon's courage and judgement had seen Isaac through the travails of 1057, piloting him to a throne that Katakalon had renounced for himself. His manifesto proved, however, even less effective in political terms than the dazzling tableaus conjured up by Psellos some years later.[134] It failed to rally his fortunes. Katakalon's withdrawal to Koloneia and assumption of the monk's habit were most probably involuntary, as the stopping of his stipend certainly was.[135]

Katakalon Kekaumenos and the work that we have attributed to him are at once characteristic of senior commanders and *sui generis*. Katakalon seems to have drawn freely on basic *progymnasmata* for oral use in the course of campaigning, while K itself is testimony to his ability to put them into literary form, an extensive argument couched in narrative. To an extent, then, Katakalon's case exemplifies the part that rhetoric, in the sense of tools for 'effective communication', played in Byzantine writing and military life. Yet Katakalon seems to have composed his work at speed, in political and personal circumstances at once insecure and without recent

---

[132] See Hunger, *Hochsprachliche profane Literatur*, vol. II, 338; E. de Vries-van der Velden, 'Psellos, Romain IV Diogènès et Mantzikert', *BSl*, 58 (1997), 287–91, 300–4, 306; Kaldellis, *Argument*, 182–3.
[133] Katakalon 'alone' advocated total rejection: Skylitzes, *Synopsis*, ed. Thurn, 497.3.
[134] Composing the first, main part of the *Chronographia* does not seem to have ensured for Psellos lasting intimacy with Constantine X: Jeffreys, 'Psellos', 82–3.
[135] Judging by Katakalon's denunciation of Constantine X's meanness in a letter to Psellos (above, p. 206), one may suppose him to have been responsible for the stopping of Katakalon's stipend as *kouropalates*. One may surmise that Katakalon's retirement and assumption of the monk's habit occurred after the abdication of Isaac (who thereupon became a monk himself), but evidence for reconstructing a precise chronology is lacking.

precedent. Judging by the three sets of materials traceable to K reviewed above, especially the section on Michael VI's reign, Katakalon played up his own individualism alongside his contribution to the Great Rebellion's success. In light of the idiosyncrasy which K seems almost to celebrate, and in the absence of the complete text, one hesitates to categorise it in terms of literary genre. Perhaps the genre in which Katakalon's text sits most comfortably is that of the annals of heroic failure.

Further Reading

The key primary source is: B. Flusin and J.-C. Cheynet, trans., *Jean Skylitzès. Empereurs de Constantinople* (Paris, 2003). Relevant studies include: C. Roueché, 'The Rhetoric of Kekaumenos' in E. M. Jeffreys, ed., *Rhetoric in Byzantium* (Aldershot, 2003), 23–37; E. M. Jeffreys, 'Rhetoric in Byzantium' in I. Worthington, ed., *A Companion to Greek Rhetoric* (Oxford, 2007), 166–84; M. J. Jeffreys, 'Psellos and "His Emperors": Fact, Fiction and Genre' in R. Macrides, ed., *History as Literature in Byzantium* (Farnham, 2010), 73–91; J. Shepard, 'A Suspected Source of Scylitzes' *Synopsis Historion*: the Great Catacalon Cecaumenus', *BMGS*, 16 (1992), 171–81.

CHAPTER 8

Performative Reading in the Late Byzantine Theatron

Niels Gaul

The Byzantines regularly either referred to or implicitly conceptionalised the physical and social space in which rhetoric was read or performed as a *theatron*.[1] Derived from ancient theatre, the term is first attested, in this specific meaning, in late antiquity.[2] From the eleventh century at the latest, *theatron* described a circle of learned men who gathered around a patron, patroness or host either to listen to letters or texts that the latter had received, selected, or written, or to perform their own compositions.[3] For official occasions that involved the performance of rhetoric, such as the *synodos endemousa* or deliberations of the emperor's council, the sources seem to prefer the largely synonymous term *syllogos* over *theatron*,[4] and for a reading circle of learned friends, *kyklos* or *choros*.[5] Regardless of the context, expressions such as stepping 'into the middle' (εἰς τὸ μέσον) or

---

[1] I am very grateful to the editors of this volume as well as Anna Adashinskaya, Florin Leonte, Divna Manolova, Andrea Mattiello, Mihail Mitrea, and the late Anna Christidou for their pertinent remarks on various draft versions of this chapter.
For present purposes, 'reading' includes performance of rhetorical compositions from memory. On the *theatron*, see I. Medvedev, 'The So-called *Theatra* as a Form of Communication of the Byzantine Intellectuals in the 14th and 15th Centuries' in N. G. Moschonas, ed., Πρακτικά τοῦ Β´ Διεθνοῦς Συμποσίου «Η' ἐπικοινωνία στὸ Βυζάντιο» (Athens, 1993), 227–35; P. Marciniak, 'Byzantine *Theatron* – a Place of Performance?' in M. Grünbart, ed., *Theatron: Rhetorische Kultur in Spätantike und Mittelalter* (Berlin, 2007), 277–85; I. Toth, 'Rhetorical *Theatron* in Late Byzantium: the Example of Palaiologan Imperial Orations' in ibid., 429–48; G. Cavallo, *Lire à Byzance* (Paris, 2006), 57–66.
[2] See N. Gaul, 'The Letter in the *Theatron*: Epistolary Voice, Character, Soul and their Audience' in A. Riehle, ed., *A Companion to Byzantine Epistolography* (Leiden, forthcoming) with further bibliography.
[3] Rhetoric in this sense includes compositions in learned and presumably also vernacular verse.
[4] N. Gaul, *Thomas Magistros und die spätbyzantinische Sophistik: Studien zum Humanismus urbaner Eliten in der frühen Palaiologenzeit* (Wiesbaden, 2011), 17 n. 1, 19 and 27.
[5] Especially in the Komnenian period: M. Mullett, 'Aristocracy and Patronage in the Literary Circles of Comnenian Constantinople' in M. Angold, ed., *The Byzantine Aristocracy, IX–XIII Centuries* (Oxford, 1984), 176.

placing oneself 'in the middle' (ἐν τῷ μέσῳ) often denoted a 'theatrical' setting.⁶ Such performance indicators suggest that a *theatron* was a somewhat fluid affair whose occurrence may be assumed even when the term itself, or any of its near-synonyms, is absent from a source. In analysing the performative elements that made up such occasions of 'theatrical' reading, this chapter draws, *inter alia*, on approaches advanced by performance studies: even if not fully, dramatically acted out, 'theatrical' readings of rhetoric were certainly staged occasions whose performative – and consequently, also political and social – ramifications are all too easily ignored by the modern scholar.⁷

Of course, the *theatron* was merely one ritualised practice among the many social performances that structured Byzantine society, particularly in the late period.⁸ In Palaiologan Constantinople, performances clustered around the imperial court as well as the numerous religious foundations, many of which were restored or revivified in the late thirteenth and early fourteenth centuries.⁹ By this time, mechanical wonderworks (famously described by Liudprand of Cremona), imperial triumphs and appearances in the hippodrome had given way to the radiant ceremony of *prokypsis*. The urban liturgies established by the late antique emperors, and practised in a modified form in the tenth century, still existed in the fourteenth although the destinations of imperial processions had undergone significant changes.¹⁰ Oaths of allegiance to the senior emperor in

---

⁶ Such as Andronikos II stepping forward to defend his patriarch, Athanasios I: 'When he had positioned himself in the middle (οὗ δὴ καὶ ἐς μέσον τεθέντος), he delivered a loud and far-sounding harangue' (A. Failler, ed., *Georges Pachymérès. Relations historiques* (Paris, 1984–2000), vol. IV, 569.27–9 (XII.21)). The present chapter uses the adjective 'theatrical', in quotation marks, in the meaning of '(Byzantine) *theatron*-style'.

⁷ But see recently E. C. Bourbouhakis, 'Rhetoric and Performance' in P. Stephenson, *The Byzantine World* (London, 2010), 175–87 and E. C. Bourbouhakis, 'The End of ἐπίδειξις. Authorial Identity and Authorial Intention in Michael Choniates' Πρὸς τοὺς αἰτιωμένους τὸ ἀφιλένδεικτον' in A. Pizzone, ed., *The Author in Middle Byzantine Literature. Modes, Functions, Identities* (Boston, MA, 2014), 201–24.

⁸ Evoking associations with Geertz' concept of the 'theatre state': P. Roilos, 'The Sacred and the Profane: Re-enacting Ritual in the Medieval Greek Novel' in D. Yatromanolakis and P. Roilos, eds., *Greek Ritual Poetics* (Cambridge, MA, 2004), 213.

⁹ V. Kidonopoulos, 'The Urban Physiognomy of Constantinople from the Latin Conquest Through the Palaiologan Era' in S. T. Brooks, ed., *Byzantium: Faith and Power (1261–1557)* (New York, NY, 2006), 105–9.

¹⁰ R. Macrides, 'Ceremonies and the City: the Court in Fourteenth-century Constantinople' in J. Duindam, T. Artan and M. Kunt, eds., *Royal Courts in Dynastic States and Empires: A Global Perspective* (Leiden, 2011), 217–35; P. Magdalino, 'Pseudo-Kodinos' Constantinople' in P. Magdalino, *Studies on the History and Topography of Byzantine Constantinople* (Aldershot, 2007), Item XII, 1–14, and A. Berger, 'Imperial and Ecclesiastical Processions in Constantinople' in N. Necipoğlu, ed., *Byzantine Constantinople: Monuments, Topography and Everyday Life* (Leiden, 2001), 73–88.

Constantinople were sworn on the gospels, while intrigues against him took the form of written prophecies placed on his empty throne.[11] As was the case elsewhere into the Renaissance and beyond, the performance of the miraculous had political power: carefully staged processions of relics and icons through the imperial city sought to avert God's wrath, or visually resolve theological schisms and controversies.[12] Churches and monasteries in Constantinople and across the empire gave structure and meaning to days, months and years through a recurrent cycle of liturgies that were fixed in writing and brought to life by regular and unchanging performances.[13] Just as was true of the medieval West, diplomatic exchanges, the delivery of justice and many other events depended on ritualised communications, as did performances that were more occasionally staged.[14]

By analysing readings in the *theatron*, the following paragraphs seek to highlight the highly interconnected elements that were characteristic of performance. Borrowing terminology from Jeffrey C. Alexander's recent work on social performances in the public and political spheres, this chapter looks in turn at: the script and its cultural background; the actors or rather, in the context of the *theatron*, the actor (performer) in the singular; the audience; the means of symbolic production and *mise-en-scène*; and, finally, the distribution of social power.[15] Adapting Austin's well-known analysis of speech-acts,[16] Alexander suggests that social performances are judged as either successful or unsuccessful (infelicitous). Success comes when the audience experiences an authentic re-fusion – or even flow – of the 'increasingly disentangled' elements of performance: '[i]n a fused performance, audiences identify with actors, and cultural

---

[11] A. Failler, ed., *Georges Pachymérès. Relations historiques* (Paris, 1984–2000). vol. IV, 599 (XII.31), 629–31 (XIII.5).

[12] Niccolò Machiavelli, *Discorsi sopra la prima deca di Tito Livio*, in F. Bausi, ed., *Edizione nazionale delle opere di Niccolò Machiavelli* (Rome, 2001), vol. I, 84–5 (I.12); trans. in E. Crick, ed., *Niccolò Machiavelli: The Discourses* (London, 2003), 143. Patriarch Athanasios I gained a reputation for ever-multiplying processions, see Pachymeres, *Relations historiques*, ed. Failler, vol. IV, 675.30–1 (XIII.23) and 689.14–15 (XIII.27). For prominent cases of relic translations see the cases of Arsenios Autoreianos (discussed in Pachymeres, *Relations historiques*, ed. Failler, vol. III, 94–9 (VII.31); L. Schopen and I. Bekker, eds., *Nicephori Gregorae Historiae Byzantinae* (Bonn, 1829–55), vol. I, 167) and Athanasios I (discussed in A.-M. Talbot, *Faith Healing in Late Byzantium* (Brookline, MA, 1983),12–20).

[13] A. W. White, *Performing Orthodox Ritual in Byzantium* (Cambridge, 2015); R. Nelson, 'Emphatic Vision: Looking at and with a Performative Byzantine Miniature', *Art History*, 30 (2007), 489–502.

[14] G. Althoff, *Die Macht der Rituale. Symbolik und Herrschaft im Mittelalter*, second edition (Darmstadt, 2012).

[15] I adopt the system and terminology proposed by J. C. Alexander, 'Cultural Pragmatics: Social Performance Between Ritual and Strategy' in J. C. Alexander, B. Giesen and J. L. Mast, eds., *Social Performance: Symbolic Action, Cultural Pragmatics, and Ritual* (Cambridge, 2006), 32–7. More recently, J. C. Alexander, *Performance and Power* (Cambridge, 2011).

[16] J. L. Austin, *How to Do Things With Words* (Cambridge, MA, 1962), 12–24.

scripts achieve verisimilitude through effective *mise-en-scène*'.[17] Certain axioms facilitating successful performances highlighted by Alexander certainly coincide with the rules of rhetoric, such as cognitive simplification and moral agonism.[18] However, as the sources at our disposal provide few certain answers to the types of questions modern literary criticism raises, some of the conclusions put forward in the present chapter must remain to some extent speculative.

Scripts and Background Symbols

For a performance to be successful, its script must ring true, or authentic, to the receiving culture – or, according to Alexander, to that culture's symbols and collective representations.[19] Defined as 'meaning primed to performance',[20] a script – more often than not unwritten – was brought to life by an actor invested with props and placed in a certain setting (*mise-en-scène*). The late Byzantine *theatron* actualised two intertwined background symbols in particular: a longstanding tradition of public performances on the one hand and adherence to the rules of classicising rhetoric and Atticising grammar on the other. In a wider sense and depending on the content of the text performed it is worth noting that virtually all discourses circulating in late Byzantium could potentially contribute symbols that informed the text and captivated the audience.[21]

By the early fourteenth century rhetorical 'theatre' had enjoyed a long history. The basic script of *theatron*-style performance ran as follows: the audience gathered, either at a prearranged time or in a more *ad hoc* fashion; the performer stepped 'into the middle'; he read, or improvised, a rhetorical (philosophical, theological) text, which may occasionally have required multiple sittings; the audience was expected to pass judgement, usually applause (clapping and stamping of the feet); the *theatron* dissolved.[22] A successful performance became the topic of conversations, just as an unsuccessful one was subjected to gossip. In the context of the

---

[17] See Alexander, 'Cultural Pragmatics', 54–76, quote at 29.
[18] Alexander, 'Cultural Pragmatics', 59–60. On repetitiveness and predictability, see below p. 223 and n. 49; H. Hunger, 'Die Antithese. Zur Verbreitung einer Denkschablone in der byzantinischen Literatur', *ZRVI*, 23 (1984), 9–29.
[19] Alexander, 'Cultural Pragmatics', 33; also see R. Schechner, *Performance Theory*, second edition (New York, NY, 1988), 66–111.
[20] Alexander, 'Cultural Pragmatics', 58.
[21] Compare S. Greenblatt, *Shakespearean Negotiations* (Berkeley, CA, 1988).
[22] The technical term is διαλύω, see P. L. M. Leone, ed., *Niceforo Gregora. Fiorenzo o Intorno alla sapienza* (Naples, 1975), 126.1672: ἐντεῦθεν ὁ σύλλογος καὶ τὸ θέατρον διελύετο.

theatron, the core of the performative script, i.e., the actual performative reading of rhetoric, was often fixed in written form;[23] however, it is not always clear whether the extant version – on which we have to base our analysis – was finalised before or after performance and thus, to what degree it reflects the script actually performed in the *theatron*. Either way, it is important to keep in mind that in terms of performance theory, the text read did not constitute the whole performative script but merely its central part. The fact that such *theatra* were intricately connected to networks of learning and therefore closely tied to literary practices privileged the *theatron*'s chances of leaving traces to posterity.

The rules of grammar of the predominantly 'Attic' or Atticising sociolect, and of ancient rhetoric, constituted the second symbol.[24] As was true of the concept of the *theatron* itself, the purposeful and adjustable traditionality – as opposed to unreflected tradition – of grammatical and rhetorical *paideia* created a link of every present performance to the past, fusing by means of multilayered, complex *mimēsis* the voices of past rhetors with those of the present.[25] 'Attic' Greek, rather than distorting reality,[26] thus emerges as a feature instrumental in creating Byzantine reality and authenticity: *mimēsis* not necessarily evoking and imitating an extratextual reality, however defined, but rather a linguistically eclectic past adding rhetorical verisimilitude to the present. The Byzantine focus on rhetorical traditions that to the modern ear sound decidedly unoriginal, and thus inauthentic, thus merely emphasises that authenticity is a culturally determined quality. It was with regard to these two symbols that each new 'theatrical' script positioned itself.

Actor(s)

It fell to the actor (performer) – 'literature that walks and talks before the [audience's] eyes' – to bring any script to life.[27] For the most part, the learned actors in the late Byzantine *theatron* were members of the

---

[23] Alexander, 'Cultural Pragmatics', 58: 'meaning sketched out beforehand'.
[24] For a rare imitation of the Ionian dialect see Gregoras' oration dedicated to Emperor Andronikos II: P. L. M. Leone, ed., 'Nicephori Gregorae ad imperatorem Andronicum II Palaeologum orationes', *Byzantion*, 41 (1971), 510–15. The 'theatrical' performance of vernacular texts is a case apart.
[25] For concepts of *mimēsis* see D. A. Russell, 'De Imitatione' in D. West and A. J. Woodman, eds., *Creative Imitation and Latin Literature* (Cambridge, 1979), 1–16; S. Halliwell, *The Aesthetics of Mimesis: Ancient Texts and Modern Problems* (Princeton, 2002); H. Hunger, 'On the Imitation (μίμησις) of Antiquity in Byzantine Literature', *DOP*, 23/24 (1969/70), 15–38 and the contributions in A. Rhoby and E. Schiffer, eds., *Imitatio – Aemulatio – Variatio* (Vienna, 2010). For the Latin side C. M. Chin, *Grammar and Christianity in the Late Roman World* (Philadelphia, PA, 2008).
[26] See the famously insightful C. Mango, *Byzantine Literature as a Distorting Mirror* (Oxford, 1975).
[27] M. Boulton, *The Anatomy of Drama* (London, 1960), 3.

somewhat blurry second-tier elite that emerged during the tenth and flourished in the eleventh, twelfth, late thirteenth, and early fourteenth centuries. Best understood to have belonged below the high aristocracy but on a level with or indeed above the upper middlemen – *mesoi*, in late Byzantine sources – this class was affluent enough to afford proper *paideia* for their sons. In the Palaiologan period, its members were often scions of the Constantinopolitan, Thessalonian, or provincial urban elites, to whom *paideia* provided a means of participating in public discourse, securing one's social status and advancing one's career.[28] Thus access to the *theatra*, and accordingly to late Byzantine public discourse, was by and large limited to the upper strata of urban society.[29] To acquire the *paideia* necessary to participate or compete successfully in the *theatron*, the designated sons of aspiring families accumulated years of grammatical and rhetorical training first in the house of a schoolmaster, such as Theodore Hyrtakenos, Hyaleas, Chalkomatopoulos, and Maximos, and later possibly the circle of a gentleman scholar, such as Maximos Planoudes in Constantinople or Thomas Magistros in Thessalonike.[30] A few talented boys of petty means were also singled out, for reasons unknown to us, to acquire grammatical and rhetorical education, occasionally by working in a gentleman scholar's household, as young Philotheos Kokkinos in the *oikos* of Magistros; but they constitute the exception that proves the rule.[31] By contrast, members of the imperial aristocracy by birth could choose to display learned as well as aristocratic behaviour.[32]

In order to perform successfully, the actor needed to fuse the audience's hopes, fears, and expectations with his own, or rather, with those which he alleged to be his own. While the toolbox of rhetoric provided the perfect means for engaging the audience, one aspect of *paideia* that came under

---

[28] For *pepaideumenoi* who were genuine members of the urban, semi-aristocratic elite (i.e., not dependent on teaching for their livelihood), I adopt Browning's term of 'gentlemen scholars', see R. Browning, 'Teachers' in G. Cavallo, ed., *The Byzantines* (Chicago, IL, 1997), 105.

[29] In contrast to competing legitimate competences, such as emerging *hesychasm*.

[30] Following D. Bianconi, *Tessalonica nell'età dei Paleologi: Le pratiche intellettuali nel riflesso della cultura scritta* (Paris, 2005), 92, I am reluctant to use the term 'school'. On Hyrtakenos, who is the only source of information on Hyaleas and Chalkomatopoulos, see A. Karpozilos, 'The Correspondence of Theodore Hyrtakenos', *JÖB*, 40 (1990), 275–84. Insights into Neamonites' letters now offered by M. Mitrea, 'A Late Byzantine πεπαιδευμένος: Maximos Neamonites and his Letter Collection', *JÖB*, 64 (2014), 197–223. On the circle around Planoudes, C. N. Constantinides, *Higher Education in Byzantium in the Thirteenth and Early Fourteenth Centuries (1204–ca. 1310)* (Nicosia, 1982), 66–89; on Magistros, Gaul, *Thomas Magistros*, 230–71.

[31] Gaul, *Thomas Magistros*, 237–39; A.-M. Talbot, 'The *Miracles of Gregory Palamas* by Philotheos Kokkinos' in Stephenson, ed., *Byzantine World*, 237.

[32] Such as Andronikos II, John Kantakouzenos and Manuel II in the Palaiologan period; or along different trajectories Isaac Komnenos and Anna Komnene in the twelfth century.

particular scrutiny was the actor's rhetorically construed *ethos* ('character'). Its significance can be easily glimpsed in a number of sources, including the following passage from Nikephoros Choumnos' correspondence:[33]

> What else? I have received the letter that you have sent to us, who had asked for it, and which you have sent not so much for reasons of necessity as of ambition [i.e., in order to show off]. For it knew to show forth every aspect of beauty. I for one didn't know which features to praise first, or rather, which one above all the others. The easy flow of thoughts that were so cleverly organised and all appeared equally admirable? The harmony and precision of expression? The (prose) rhythm? Or composition before rhythm? Or, above all the rest, that which caught me more than everything, *the beauty of your character,* creating the letter with your soul, as it were, so that you did not seem to lead the conversation with paper and ink but in person, communicating with your living voice.[34]

Choumnos' long list of positive attributes pays due attention to formal aspects but culminates in the concept of a 'character' that shines forth from the letter – an evocation of the well-known epistolary concept of the letter as an 'icon of the soul'.[35] Late Byzantine rhetors-in-training learnt to fashion their *ethos* through memorising, and occasionally composing, progymnasmatic *ethopoiiai*, which had enjoyed renewed popularity from the tenth century onward (expanding on the stock transmitted from late antiquity). Not accidentally, their repeated rise to prominence coincided with the reappearance of the *theatron* as a performative practice. The production of new progymnasmatic materials reached a peak in the twelfth century (Basilakes) and continued through the early (Hexapterygos) and late thirteenth century (George of Cyprus, George Pachymeres).[36] Studying *ethopoiiai* provided the perfect means of learning how to add rhetorical and emotional colour to one's 'own' *ethos* for the purpose of 'theatrical'

---

[33] See Gaul, *Thomas Magistros,* 38–50.
[34] J. F. Boissonade, ed., *Anecdota Nova* (Paris, 1844), 94–5 (Nikephoros Choumnos, *ep.* LXXVIII): πῶς πλέον· τὴν ἐπιστολὴν δεξάμενος, ἣν οὐ κατὰ χρείαν μᾶλλον ἢ φιλοτιμίαν αἰτησαμένοις ἡμῖν ἔπεμψας. εἶχε γὰρ, ὡς ἐν βραχεῖ φάναι, καλῶν εἶδος ἅπαν ἐν ἑαυτῇ δεικνῦσα· κἀγὼ δ' οὐκ εἶχον ὅτι πρῶτον ἢ μάλιστα τῶν αὐτῆς ἐπαινέσομαι, πότερον τὴν τῶν νοημάτων εὐπορίαν οὕτω πυκνῶν καὶ θαυμαστῶν πάντων ὁμοίως φαινομένων, ἢ τὴν ἁρμονίαν ἢ τὴν ἀκρίβειαν τῶν ὀνομάτων, ἢ τὸν ῥυθμόν, ἢ πρὸ τοῦ ῥυθμοῦ τὴν συνθήκην, ἢ πρὸ τῶν ἄλλων πάντων, ὅ με καὶ πλέον τῶν ἄλλων εἶλε, τὸ τοῦ ἤθους καλόν, ἔμπνουν, ὡς εἰπεῖν, τὴν ἐπιστολὴν ἐργαζόμενον, ὡς μηδ' ἐν χάρτῃ σε δοκεῖν μᾶλλον καὶ μέλανι τὴν ὁμιλίαν, ἀλλ' αὐτοπρόσωπον ποιεῖσθαι, ζώσῃ φωνῇ προσδιαλεγόμενον.
[35] A. R. Littlewood, 'An "Icon of the Soul": the Byzantine Letter', *Visible Language,* 10 (1976), 197–226.
[36] See N. Gaul, 'Rising Elites and Institutionalization – Ethos/Mores – 'Debts' and Drafts' in S. Steckel, N. Gaul, M. Grünbart, eds., *Networks of Learning: Perspectives on Scholars in Byzantine East and Latin West, c. 1000–1200,* (Zurich, 2014), 259–69. Generally, E. Amato and J. Schamp, eds., *Ethopoiia: la représentation de caractères entre fiction scolaire et réalité vivante à l'époque impériale et tardive* (Salerno, 2005).

performance; indeed one can be certain that language and quotations (intertextual *mimesis*) were adjusted, and occasionally gendered, to match both the character on display as well as to meet the audience's expectations.

A rhetor's rhetorical *ethos* was composed of many facets including musical voice modulation (*euglottia*), gestures, posture, appearance, in short, of the elements that constituted the actor's demeanour.[37] While nothing comparable to ancient instructions on voice training survives from the Byzantine period, a skilled rhetor's voice was expected to sound just as sweet as music.[38] Manuscript interpunctuation (*stixis*) can help us recover the vocal mode of Byzantine performances and reveal the rhythm of performance.[39] When performing a dialogical piece or dialogue, more elaborate acting may have been involved, in the sense of giving a distinct 'voice' to each *prosopon*,[40] but probably without props such as costumes, masks, or panels.[41] Excessive gestural behaviour could be turned against the one whose texts were performed.[42] With actors largely sharing the same social background and *paideia*, and thus level of (political) insight and information, any dispute seemed to have been about details even though on occasion the tone could get fierce, reflecting growing insecurity among the learned stratum.[43] Ambition (*philotimia*) was often thought to drive 'theatrical' performances.[44]

---

[37] M. W. Gleason, *Making Men: Sophists and Self-Presentation in Ancient Rome* (Princeton, 1995) and A. L. Boegehold, *When a Gesture Was Expected* (Princeton, 1999) await Byzantine companions.
[38] Cavallo, *Lire*, 50–1. C. Gastgeber, 'Manuel Meligalas. Eine biographisch-paläographische Studie' in C. Gastgeber, ed., *Miscellanea Codicum Graecorum Vindobonensium*, vol. 1 (Vienna, 2009), 71–4. M. Grünbart is preparing a study on middle Byzantine *euglottia*, a term that seems absent from Palaiologan epistolography.
[39] D. R. Reinsch, 'Stixis und Hören' in B. Atsalos and N. Tsironi, eds., Πρακτικά του ΣΤ' Διεθνούς Συμποσίου Ελληνικής Παλαιογραφίας, (Athens, 2008), vol. 1, 259–69; V. Valiavitcharska, *Rhetoric and Rhythm in Byzantium: The Sound of Persuasion* (Cambridge, 2013); and the contributions in A. Giannouli and E. Schiffer, eds., *From Manuscripts to Books* (Vienna, 2011).
[40] Many late Byzantine dialogues contain linguistic markers indicating a change of speaker; when delivered orally, a mild modulation of the voice would have sufficed to transmit any change to the audience.
[41] In all cases of late Byzantine dialogical writing I have studied to date, there seems to have been a single actor as was the case in deuterosophistic rhetoric. See N. Gaul, 'Embedded Dialogues and Dialogical Voices in Palaiologan Prose and Verse' in A. Cameron and N. Gaul, eds., *Dialogues and Debates from Late Antiquity to Late Byzantium* (New York, NY, 2017).
[42] I. Ševčenko, ed., *Études sur la polémique entre Théodore Métochite et Nicéphore Choumnos* (Brussels, 1962), 253 (Theodore Metochites, *Or.* 14.27.1–11).
[43] See I. Polemis, 'The Treatise *On Those who Unjustly Accuse Wise Men, of the Past and Present*: a New Work by Theodore Metochites?', *BZ*, 102 (2009), 203–17 and Ševčenko, *Études*, 276–96.
[44] Gaul, *Thomas Magistros*, 23–5; fundamental on the role of *philotimia* in connecting ruling and cultural elites is P. Magdalino, 'Byzantine Snobbery' in Angold, *Byzantine Aristocracy*, 173–201.

Audience

The success of any performance depended on the degree to which the actor managed to fuse his act with the audience's expectations, or – a more delicate business – the degree to which he succeeded in pushing the audience's boundaries.[45] In turn, the audience drew on those symbols (described above) that created, as it were, a 'horizon of expectation'.[46]

Regarding the audience's social background, there is little to add to the preceding remarks about the actor. Members of the late Byzantine literate elite – coinciding to a fair degree with courtiers and ecclesial officials in Constantinople and the urban elites, members of the *gerousia* as well as upper middlemen, in other places such as Thessalonike – are likely to have constituted the largest part of it, led by members of the (educated) higher aristocracy. Frequently, the audience must have been composed of those who performed on another occasion. One aspect that does not yet seem to have received sufficient attention is the differentiation between active and passive command of the Atticist sociolect.[47] Judging from the correspondence of schoolmasters such as Hyrtakenos and Neamonites, the sons of courtly and urban elites were expected to master the basics of grammar and rhetoric. Accordingly, they must have been able to follow a performance passively (and to converse pleasantly, with a modest stock of archaising phrases and quotations memorised from Homer and Euripides, the two first authors of the grammatical curriculum), without necessarily themselves having the ability to actively compose rhetorical set-pieces.[48] The repetitiveness and 'lacking originality' of learned rhetoric allowed especially the group with limited exposure to Atticism to pass judgement on a performance: 'People inured to stereotype are highly receptive to' – stylistic and generic – 'variation'.[49] How much the common populace (*demos*), when present, would have understood remains an open question.

---

[45] Emotional responses to rhetorical performances were one core aspect of the new Edinburgh-based network on 'Emotions through Time: From Antiquity through Byzantium'; http://emotions.shca.ed.ac.uk (accessed 1 December 2017).

[46] Borrowed from H. R. Jauss, 'Literary Theory as a Challenge to Literary History', *New Literary History*, 2 (1967), 11–19.

[47] Gaul, *Thomas Magistros*, 163–8.

[48] C. Holmes, 'Political Literacy' in Stephenson, *Byzantine World*, 137–48; for an eleventh-century example, C. Roueché, 'The Literary Background of Kekaumenos' in C. Holmes and J. Waring, eds., *Literacy, Education and Manuscript Transmission in Byzantium and Beyond* (Leiden, 2002), 111–38; C. Roueché, 'The Rhetoric of Kekaumenos' in E. M. Jeffreys, ed., *Rhetoric in Byzantium* (Aldershot, 2003), 23–37; see also the chapter by Jonathan Shepard in the present volume.

[49] T. Schmitz, *Bildung und Macht: Zur sozialen und politischen Funktion der zweiten Sophistik in der griechischen Welt der Kaiserzeit* (Munich, 1997), 160–75 and 220–31 emphasizes this for the second

Reminiscent of ancient and Renaissance theatre, the audience was fully visible and, indeed, encouraged to participate by constantly displaying reactions to the text performed. The means of expressing satisfaction were collective cheering, clapping and stamping of the feet, while an infelicitous performance might be jeered at and was subjected to scorn and ridicule afterwards.[50] Generally, though: the more engaged the audience, the more successful the performance.[51]

Means of Symbolic Production and *Mise-en-Scène*

Bringing a script to the 'stage' (*scène*) required temporal sequencing and spatial choreography, yet comparatively little attention has been paid to the means of symbolic production, i.e., the props of 'theatrical' performances, and *mise-en-scène*.

Different genres of texts (scripts) prompted different venues, whose specific architectural configuration in turn influenced the *mise-en-scène* and regulated the spatial movements of both actor and audience.[52] The reading of a philosophical treatise took place in a circle of literati and friends or, at least under Andronikos II, in a court setting: occasionally the emperor himself expounded his – controversial – ideas.[53] Funeral orations or poems were presumably performed next to the tomb of the deceased in the *katholikon* of an aristocratic monastic foundation, with relatives, monks, or nuns in attendance: as specified in *typika*, they could involve splendid lighting arrangements as well as other visual, and perhaps musical, effects.[54] Widows and exiles – such as Theodora Raoulaina, Andronikos II as monk Antonios, George of Cyprus, Maximos Planoudes or Nikephoros

---

sophistic; P. Magdalino, *The Empire of Manuel I Komnenos (1143–1180)* (Cambridge, 1993), 353–4 (quotation ibid. 353) for the Komnenian period.

[50] Gaul, *Thomas Magistros,* 32–34; it is difficult to arrive at reliable data as any instance of failure in the *theatron* is usually reported in the context of overall criticism of a certain individual. See also below, p. 229.

[51] See G. A. Karla, 'Rhetorische Kommunikation in den Kaiserreden des 12. Jhs.: Der Kontakt zum Publikum', *JÖB*, 57 (2007), 83–94 and Toth, 'Rhetorical *Theatron*', 445–6; for the second sophistic, M. Korenjak, *Publikum und Redner: Ihre Interaktion in der sophistischen Rhetorik der Kaiserzeit* (Munich, 2000).

[52] Compare Magdalino, *Empire of Manuel I*, 353: 'verbal recitation was only part of a total orchestration, in which architecture, décor, dress, music and choreography also played a part'.

[53] R. Romano, ed., *Costantino Acropolita: Epistole* (Naples, 1991), 257–66 (195.51–2); Nikephoros Choumnos, *Anecdota Nova*, ed. Boissonade, 13–14 (IX.4–5).

[54] S. T. Brooks, 'Poetry and Female Patronage in Late Byzantine Tomb Decoration: Two Epigrams by Manuel Philes', *DOP*, 60 (2006), 223–48.

Gregoras – received literati and convened gatherings in their monastic lodgings.⁵⁵ Occasionally, gardens or other outdoor venues may have been preferred.⁵⁶ Actors must have been accustomed to changing venue frequently.

The staging of 'theatrical' state occasions required especially careful choreography, for which venues as different as the various *triklinoi* of the palaces, the Church of Hagia Sophia, or the hippodrome could be used.⁵⁷ An imperial oration was integrated into court ceremonial, presupposing an altogether more formal *mise-en-scène*. The partially surviving great halls of Tekfur Saray in Istanbul, the Laskarid-period palace at Nymphaion, or the Mystras palace offer an idea of the possible setting.⁵⁸ A feastday homily in Hagia Sophia, whose vocal and ceremonial elements were acted out in the vast space of the church, was tied to the liturgical calendar – again with ramifications for the script – as well as subordinate to the ritual of the liturgy. When used for the ongoing theological or juridical debates of the tumultuous fourteenth century, Hagia Sophia was frequently referred to as a *theatron*. On such occasions, the cathedral seems to have been teeming with emperors, courtiers, bishops, clergy and common folk, providing the background for a '*theatron* of state' perhaps not too far removed from Nikephoros Choumnos' hyperbolic description thereof.⁵⁹ The image of John Kantakouzenos presiding, in full imperial regalia, over the council of 1351 surrounded by bishops, abbots and, in the background, courtiers, comes close to offering us a visualisation of such a setting.⁶⁰

---

⁵⁵ George of Cyprus and Planoudes taught at Christ Akataleptos, and Gregoras at Christ in Chora where Emperor Andronikos II spent the last years of his life.
⁵⁶ M.-L. Dolezal and M. Mavroudi, 'Theodore Hyrtakenos' Description of the Garden of St. Anna and the Ekphrasis of Gardens' in A. Littlewood, H. Maguire and J. Wolschke-Bulhmann, eds., *Byzantine Garden Culture* (Washington, D. C., 2002), 105–58.
⁵⁷ Magdalino, *Empire of Manuel I*, 352, hints at the possibility of performances on the galleries of Hagia Sophia in the twelfth century.
⁵⁸ Toth, 'Rhetorical *Theatron*', 436–40.
⁵⁹ For example Magistros describes Patriarch Niphon performing before Emperor Andronikos II (*PG*, 145:392A–B). See Toth, 'Rhetorical *Theatron*', 440 on Choumnos' detailed description of a truly universal *theatron* (*or.* 19.52.14–53.2).
⁶⁰ Preserved on fol. 5v of ms. Paris. gr. 1242, this image was produced in the 1370s under the ex-emperor's close supervision. See I. Spatharakis, *The Portrait in Byzantine Illuminated Manuscripts* (Leiden, 1976), 148–51 and figures 96–7, and C. Förstel, *Trésors de Byzance: manuscrits grecs de la Bibliothèque nationale de France* (Paris, 2001), 28 (no. 42) and 30 (plate 42). Although the setting was the Theotokos church at Blachernai, no architectural details are rendered. For a Trapezuntine '*theatron* of state' see J. O. Rosenqvist, ed., *The Hagiographic Dossier of St. Eugenios of Trebizond in Codex Athous Dionysiou 154* (Uppsala, 1996), 308–35 (John Lazaropoulos, *Synopsis*, ll.1141–599).

Public assemblies (*ekklesiai*) featured performances of deliberative oratory in the ruins of the Constantinopolitan hippodrome.⁶¹ Andronikos II's harangue following the devastating earthquake of June 1296 must have been a memorable event, and was seemingly successful in averting potential unrest: the emperor led the patriarch and his bishops, many lords and the whole populace of Constantinople in a huge procession (λιτανεία) to the hippodrome, where there was enough room for everyone (μέχρι καὶ τοῦ ἱπποδρομίου ... ὡς χωρήσαντος ἅπαντας); facing an icon of the Theotokos he intoned a loud and far-sounding impromptu harangue to the people, which befitted the occasion (σχεδιάσας δημηγορίαν [μακρὰν καὶ διωλύγιον] πρέπουσαν τῷ καιρῷ), explained the earthquake as evidence of 'God's wrath' (μήνιμα θεῖον), and, finally, promised and immediately enacted judicial reforms.⁶²

Architectural and decorative features, as well as lighting, are likely to have influenced the audience's experience of the scene, and in particular of the actor's position in relation to these elements. In locations such as the Blachernai palace, the imperial palace of Trebizond, and possibly even the Pammakaristos church, marble incrustations could provide a splendid background, as could frescoes or mosaics showing religious or worldly motifs that were sometimes accompanied by epigrams – all of which served to reinforce a certain message, and perhaps even lend additional emphasis to the tropes of an encomium.⁶³ Brad Hostetler's thought-provoking work on the interaction of epigraphical, visual, and architectural elements (e.g. in the Theotokos Pammakaristos church) suggests that late Byzantine master builders, poets and mosaic-makers may well have paid attention to

---

⁶¹ C. N. Tsirpanlis, 'Byzantine Parliaments and Representative Assemblies from 1081 to 1351', *Byzantion*, 43 (1973), 432–81.

⁶² Pachymeres, *Relations historiques*, ed. Failler, vol. III, 261.15–63.14 (IX.15–16). The question arises as to what degree this event would have been perceived as 'theatrical'. In Gaul, *Thomas Magistros*, 22, I maintained that the venue of a *theatron* ought to be closed, i.e., fitting a limited number of people; this idea has rightly been questioned by A. Riehle, 'Review: Niels Gaul, *Thomas Magistros und die spätbyzantinische Sophistik*', *Bryn Mawr Classical Review*, 2012.05.37 (http://bmcr.brynmawr.edu/2012/2012-05-37.html, accessed 1 December 2017). As every so often, boundaries may have been somewhat blurred.

⁶³ On Blachernai, F. Tinnefeld, 'Der Blachernenpalast in Schriftquellen der Palaiologenzeit' in B. Borkopp and T. Steppan, eds., Λιθόστρωτον. *Studien zur byzantinischen Kunst und Geschichte* (Stuttgart, 2000), 277–85; compare C. Mango, *The Art of the Byzantine Empire, 312–1453* (Toronto, 1986), 247–8; on Trebizond, ibid., 252–3; on Pammakaristos, H. Belting, D. Mouriki and C. Mango, *Mosaics and Frescoes of St. Mary Pammakaristos (Fethiye Cami Istanbul)* (Washington, D. C., 1978), 12. A.-M. Talbot, 'Epigrams in Context: Metrical Inscriptions on Art and Architecture of the Palaiologan era', *DOP*, 53 (1999), 75–90 especially at 77–9 provides a useful reminder of how much the reading of an epigram *in situ* differed from listening to the same poem in a 'theatrical' setting, a not unlikely scenario.

such detail.⁶⁴ Lighting – sun-lit venues, or spaces illuminated by flickering candles, candelabras, or torches – was used to create specific impressions. Current work on acoustics certainly suggests that venues were designed to maximise the effect.⁶⁵

While there is no evidence for 'costumes' proper, one may contemplate to what degree court and ecclesial costumes gave a distinctive aspect to performances. Many actors and members of the audience pursued a career at court or in the church, and Maria Parani has aptly described ceremonial costume as 'principally rhetorical in function'.⁶⁶ Not by chance, the re-codification of dress and colour codes under Michael VIII and Andronikos II – as evidenced by pseudo-Kodinos – coincided with the peak of late Byzantine 'theatrical' performances:⁶⁷ both testify to the early Palaiologan effort of restructuring and controlling Byzantine public discourse. Depending on the numbers assembled and lighting available, these costumes must have created a splendid scene, as is suggested by the miniature of John Kantakouzenos mentioned above. For its part, the audience would have been impressed by the actor's outfit and regalia – such as a staff of office, which could have potentially played a role in the performance, by lending additional emphasis to gestures. The surviving images of Theodore Metochites in the esonarthex of the Kariye Camii or Alexios Apokaukos in the Paris. gr. 2144, fol. 11r – depicted as the *ktetor* of the codex – are indicative.⁶⁸

Finally, the role of manuscripts – whether these were full codices on display or '(manu)scripts of speeches' – must be considered briefly.⁶⁹ This has an immediate bearing on the question of the nature of a complex text's

---

⁶⁴ Hostetler's paper was presented at the 49th Spring Symposium of Byzantine Studies at Exeter College, Oxford, in March 2016.
⁶⁵ See, for example, L. James, *Light and Colour in Byzantine Art* (Oxford, 1996); R. Franses, 'When All That is Gold Does Not Glitter' in A. Eastmond and L. James, eds., *Icon and Word: The Power of Images in Byzantium* (Aldershot, 2003), 13–24. With regard to sound, see Sharon Gerstel's current work on the acoustics of late Byzantine churches (http://newsroom.ucla.edu/stories/measuring-the-sound-of-angels-singing, accessed 14 November 2017).
⁶⁶ M. Parani, 'Cultural Identity and Dress: the Case of Late Byzantine Ceremonial Costume', *JÖB*, 57 (2007), 95–134 at 95 and M. Parani, *Reconstructing the Reality of Images: Byzantine Material Culture and Religious Iconography (11th–15th Centuries)* (Leiden, 2003), 54–71; W. Woodfin, *The Embodied Icon: Liturgical Vestments and Sacramental Power in Byzantium* (Oxford, 2012), 133–63; R. Macrides, J. Munitiz and D. Angelov, eds., *Pseudo-Kodinos and the Constantinopolitan Court: Offices and Ceremonies* (Farnham, 2013), 319–58.
⁶⁷ Macrides, Munitiz and Angelov, eds., *Pseudo-Kodinos*, 34–69.
⁶⁸ See Spatharakis, *Portrait*, 129–39 and figures 86–91 and Spatharakis, *Trésors de Byzance*, 25–8 (no. 41) and 27 (plate 41).
⁶⁹ See Cavallo, *Lire*, 47–55 and 139–58.

performance: surely often it would have been either impromptu, or by heart. One imagines that on festive occasions, sermons or pieces of epideictic rhetoric, such as encomia, were memorised before performance.[70] In yet other cases the existence of a 'script' can be surmised like the few autograph folia from the quill of John Katrarios surviving in the composite Paris. Suppl. gr. 1284, fols. 7v–9v.[71] Remarkably, the folia carry autograph revisions: above all, Katrarios added quotations from ancient authors spicing up, as it were, his original composition.[72] However, we cannot know whether he – or someone else – actually held these sheets in hand while performing, as a modern orator would; whether he performed from memory on the basis of this draft, and then subsequently revised it; or whether he jotted down the whole draft only after a first impromptu performance, and embellished it at a later stage. When Theodore Metochites criticised Nikephoros Choumnos' *theatron* in the 1320s, he implied the presence of a 'script' that was perhaps already in the form of the codex. Philosophical and astronomical treatises of considerable complexity are likely to have been read out from parchment or paper rather than recited from memory, while letters, at least on first performance in the addressee's circle, must have been declaimed from the very sheet of paper or parchment on which they had been received.

Related to these matters is the question of illuminated manuscripts, of which a fair number survive from the late Byzantine as well as earlier periods, though the content of very few of these is 'worldly'. Were their images displayed in any way during performance, or were they merely intended to regale an individual reader? In a Trapezuntine context, Trahoulia suggests that the former may have been the case with the Venice codex of the *Alexander Romance* (Istituto Ellenico, MS gr. 5), arguing that the images, large enough to be visible when displayed on a bookstand, were 'most effective if viewed while' the intended audience, composed of Emperor Alexios III (r. 1349–90) and possibly his *theatron*, was 'listening to an oral recitation of the narrative'.[73] Beyond manuscripts, panel icons

---

[70] Due to the silence of sources, Byzantine studies are lacking an equivalent of M. Carruthers' *The Book of Memory: A Study of Memory in Medieval Culture* (Cambridge, 2008).

[71] For the publication of the text and a facsimile of fol. 7v see A. Sideras, *Eine byzantinische Invektive gegen die Verfasser von Grabreden: Ἀνωνύμου μονῳδία εἰς μονοδοῦντας* (Vienna, 2002), 48–61, but compare my review, N. Gaul, 'Review: Alexander Sideras, Eine byzantinische Invektive gegen die Verfasser von Grabreden', *BZ*, 100 (2007), 257–61.

[72] D. Bianconi, 'Qualcosa di nuovo su Giovanni Catrario', *Medioevo Greco*, 6 (2006), 69–91.

[73] N. S. Trahoulia, 'The Venice Alexander Romance: Pictorial Narrative and the Art of Telling Stories' in R. Macrides, ed., *History as Literature in Byzantium* (Farnham, 2010), 148–9 and 161. The argument of size excludes other late Byzantine illuminated manuscripts, such as the 'pocket'

are likely to have been included in the performance of certain literary genres, such as funerary or commemorative orations or poems.[74] Yet whether texts of other genres would have been supported by illustrative material, as was the case with late medieval mendicant preaching in the west, cannot be known for certain.

Social Power

Social power, at the most fundamental level, determined not only who had access to a *theatron*, but also which venue and which props were available for the *mise-en-scène*. Hierarchy controlled, or attempted to control, whether a performance was successful or not, as well as the amount of prestige (social capital) an actor gained from it or lost in its wake. At the same time it defined the very parameters within which a performance could be judged: the importance of the highest-ranking attendee or patron (the two were not always identical) and the formality of the occasion determined what other members of the ruling elite would be present and, therefore, affected the magnitude of the potential gains or losses of symbolic capital an actor might incur. Significantly, in many cases the presiding member, patron or patroness of the *theatron* controlled access to it. Convening '*theatra* of state' was at the discretion of the emperor, his ministers, or the patriarch; such as Gregoras' encounter with Barlaam of Calabria in the palace of John Kantakouzenos, which Gregoras himself subsequently dialogised in the *Phlorentios*.[75]

Equally, an actor's standing within society would have exerted an influence over the judgement that was inversely proportional to the audience's power, and occasionally even pre-empted any open criticism. When a performer commanded a large amount of cultural or economic capital, was of high social standing, or backed by a power beyond the reach of the presiding member or any other member of the audience, the audience had little choice but to 'judge' the performance publicly to have been a success

---

menologion commissioned by the *despotes* Demetrios Palaiologos, Andronikos II's youngest son (MS Oxford, Bodleian Library, gr. th. f. 1); see I. Hutter, 'Der *despotes* Demetrios Palaiologos und sein "Bildmenologion" in Oxford', *JÖB*, 57 (2007), 188–214 with further bibliography.

[74] Brooks, 'Poetry and Female Patronage'. A *caveat* arises regarding the degree to which such commemorative performances were perceived as *theatra*.

[75] S. Mergiali, *L'enseignement et les lettrés pendant l'époque des Paléologues (1261–1453)* (Athens, 1996), 73–83; D. Manolova, 'Nikephoros Gregoras' *Philomathes* and *Phlorentios*' in Cameron and Gaul, eds., *Dialogues and Debates*, 203–19.

regardless of its actual achievement. An actor's social power was certainly capable of forcing an audience to award praise.

The success of a performance was thus rarely decided by a majority vote. The correspondence of Manuel II Palaiologos preserves a striking example of how judgement fell to the highest-ranking person present.[76] Overall, the possibility for participants of exercising control over the distribution of symbolic or social power turned the *theatron* into an efficient political tool. Every performance, for reasons justified or fabricated, had the potential of altering an actor's social standing. In certain instances, the display of rhetoric was a façade (a mandatory and superficial ritual) behind which politics was negotiated. However, even high up the social ladder, one was never entirely secure, and this was especially true when there was an opponent of equal standing, as happened during the controversy between Choumnos and Metochites.[77] Although a hierarchical aspect had been inherent in the *theatron* from its reappearance in the eleventh and twelfth centuries, the early Palaiologan emperors – especially Andronikos II and his ministers – seem to have perfected a pecking order of *theatra* that permeated the entire learned stratum of society. That is, different *theatra* were assigned different levels of prestige: those convened in a gentleman scholar's *oikos* ranked lowest, those in the imperial palace highest; and fully public ones higher than more private occasions. Especially in a political climate increasingly critical of imperial prerogatives, steering public opinion mattered:[78] the rewards awaiting expressions of loyalty – as in the well-known cases of Choumnos and Metochites, and many others, who transformed the symbolic power of 'theatrical' careers into political power and whose offspring married into the Palaiologos clan – may have induced others to follow the examples they set.[79] Perhaps not purely by chance, both Michael VIII and Andronikos II

---

[76] See G. T. Dennis, ed., *The Letters of Manuel II Palaeologus. Text, Translation and Notes* (Washington, D. C., 1977), 24–5 (IX.11–19) for a well-known example from the correspondence of Emperor Manuel II Palaiologos.

[77] Ševčenko, *Études* and now A. Riehle's convincing reinterpretation, A. Riehle, 'Literatur, Politik und Gesellschaft unter Andronikos II. Palaiologos: Untersuchungen zu den Briefen des Nikephoros Chumnos', unpublished doctoral thesis, LMU Munich (2011).

[78] D. G. Angelov, *Imperial Ideology and Political Thought in Byzantium 1204–1330* (Cambridge, 2007), 161–80; T. Shawcross, 'In the Name of the True Emperor: Politics of Resistance after the Palaiologan Usurpation', *BSl*, 66 (2008), 203–27.

[79] N. Gaul, 'All the Emperor's Men (and his Nephews): *Paideia* and Networking Strategies at the Court of Andronikos II Palaiologos, 1290–1320', *DOP*, 70 (2016).

emerge as apt, and frequent, performers of public harangues (δημηγορίαι), as is clear from Pachymeres' account.[80]

If one scrutinises references to the 'informal' and 'classless' atmosphere that allegedly prevailed in late Byzantine *theatra*,[81] one discovers that the sources where these references occur in fact acknowledge and reaffirm existing social hierarchies by following rhetorical formalities. Usually a socially inferior participant congratulates his social superior on the success of the latter's composition in a *theatron*, as in the following example by Hyrtakenos, who praises Choumnos. The sentiment it conveys has very little to do with 'classlessness' as Hyrtakenos hastens to confirm Choumnos' success in the *theatron*, and thus implicitly acknowledges the latter's higher standing:[82]

> The treatise was performed. We enjoyed listening and were enthused from our focusing on the text declaimed with a ready mind. When we left the *syllogos* and made our way home, there was only one topic of conversation: this was entirely, without exception, your treatise's achievement in not accomplishing the same [as earlier writings; i.e. it was new and stimulating]. For there was none who did not applaud, offer praise, or was full of joy and enthusiasm.[83]

Conclusion: Felicitous and Infelicitous Performances

Examples of felicitous and, more rarely, infelicitous performances can be found in late Byzantine sources. A well-known example of a successful performance is provided by Philotheos Kokkinos in his *Life of St Gregory Palamas*. After interrogating young Palamas, Theodore Metochites was

---

[80] Pachymeres, *Relations historiques*, ed. Failler, vol. I, 72–9 (I.17); 142–7 (II.8); 208–15 (II.30); vol. II, 328–33 (IV.1); vol. IV, 508–27 (XII.2). Pachymeres frequently employs the phrase 'loud and far-sounding' (μακρὰν καὶ διωλύγιον κατέτεινε τὴν δημηγορίαν), as in vol. IV, 533.21–2 (XII.5), and compare with nn. 6 and 62 above).
[81] Medvedev, 'So-called Theatra'.
[82] In similar terms, Gregory Akindynos, ed. A. C. Hero, *Letters of Gregory Akindynos* (Washington, D. C., 1983), 66–9 (XVIII) congratulated Gregoras on the success of his *Life of St. Constantine* in Thessalonian *theatra*; tellingly, both Hyrtakenos and Akindynos preserved in their collections the letters they wrote to doyens of *paideia* and power (Choumnos, Gregoras), while Choumnos chose not to include any letters sent to Hyrtakenos: hardly an accident of transmission.
[83] F. J. G. La Porte-du Theil, 'Lettres de Théodôre l'Hyrtacènien', *Notices et Extraits*, 5 (1798), 709–44 at 727 (V): ἀνεγινώσκετο μὲν ὁ λόγος· ἡδόμεθα δ᾽ ἡμεῖς ἀκροώμενοι καὶ ἦμεν ἐκθειάζοντες, ὅσοις ἦν ἔργον τοῖς ἀναγινωσκομένοις συννοίᾳ προσέχειν, ἐξιοῦσι δὲ τοῦ συλλόγου καὶ προϊοῦσιν οἴκαδε οὐκ ἔσθ᾽ ὅπως οὐκ ἦν κοινὴ πεποιημένοις τὴν ὁμιλίαν· ἥδ᾽ ἦν ἅπασα περὶ τοῦ λόγου, μὴ ταὐτὰ δρᾶν τοῖς προτέροις· οὐδεὶς γὰρ ἦν ὃς οὐκ ἐκρότει καὶ ἐπῄνει καὶ ἐνεθουσία ὑφ᾽ ἡδονῆς.

allegedly so impressed that he could not restrain himself and could not conceal his wonder but, turning to the emperor, said, full of marvel:

> 'Even Aristotle himself, I believe, if he had been seated here in our presence listening to this young man, would have bestowed more than moderate praise on him . . .' Therefore the emperor took, as it were, pride in the noble young man, and was full of joy and imagined great things for the youth, and formed plans on his behalf. The young lad, however, having his gaze fixed on the Heavenly Emperor and His kingdom and the imperishable and undecaying Senate [of angels], and being completely filled with that purpose and matter, declined the emperor's offer to join the court hierarchy.[84]

Late Byzantine hagiography also provides a striking example of an unsuccessful performance:

> That Andronikos [II] Palaiologos was great among the emperors, who was later [as a monk] renamed Anthony. Therefore, after he had invited the holy man [St Maximos] to the palace, the emperor began to converse with him in the midst of many. The holy man, as was his custom, answered by quoting words from the Theologian [St John the Evangelist] in response to the emperor's words, and he made the rhetors marvel at how he declaimed by heart the words of the Theologian and the whole Holy Bible. As this holy man had not been trained in grammar, however, he was considered to be lacking in rhetorical skills: Therefore, after he had heard from the *megas logothetes* [Metochites] [and/or?] the *epi tou kanikleiou* [Choumnos] "*his voice is Jacob's voice, but the hands are the hands of Esau* [Gen 27.22]", he [the holy man] left the palace in a hurry, calling those men weak-minded and foolish. And he was never to enter the imperial palace again.[85]

---

[84] D. G. Tsames, ed., Φιλοθέου Κωνσταντινουπόλεως τοῦ Κοκκίνου ἁγιολογικὰ ἔργα, Α΄· Θεσσαλονικεῖς ἅγιοι (Thessalonike, 1985), vol. 1, 438 (§ 11): ὡς μηδὲ παρ' ἑαυτῷ κατασχεῖν μηδὲ κρύψαι δυνηθῆναι τὸ θαῦμα, ἀλλὰ τὸν λόγον εὐθὺς μετ' ἐκπλήξεως τρέψαντα πρὸς τὸν βασιλέα, 'καὶ αὐτὸς Ἀριστοτέλης', εἰπεῖν, 'εἰ παρὼν ἀκροατὴς καθίστατο τούτου, ἐπῄνεσεν ἂν οὐ μετρίως, ὥς γε ἐγὼ νομίζω . . .' διὰ ταῦτα καὶ βασιλεὺς ἐγκαλλωπιζόμενος ἦν ὡσανεὶ τῷ γενναίῳ καὶ χαίρων καὶ μεγάλα τινὰ περὶ αὐτοῦ καὶ φανταζόμενος ἅμα καὶ βουλευόμενος, ἀλλ' ἐκεῖνος πρὸς τὸν ἄνω βασιλέα καὶ τὰ βασίλεια καὶ τὴν σύγκλητον τὸν ἄφθαρτον καὶ ἀγήρω βλέπων ἐκείνην καὶ ὅλος τοῦ κατ' ἐκεῖνα σκοποῦ γιγνόμενος καὶ τοῦ πράγματος.

[85] F. Halkin, 'Deux vies de s. Maxime le kausokalybe, ermite au Mont Athos (XIVe s.)', *AB*, 54 (1936), 38–112 at 71 (Theophanes of Peritheorion, *Life of Maximos Kausokalybes*): Ἀνδρόνικος ἦν ἐκεῖνος ὁ μέγας ἐν βασιλεῦσιν ὁ Παλαιολόγος, ὁ καὶ μετονομαστεὶς Ἀντώνιος . . . ὅθεν καὶ προσκαλεσάμενος εἰς τὰ βασίλεια τοῦτον ὁ βασιλεὺς ἤρξατο ὁμιλεῖν τὸν ὅσιον μέσον πολλῶν. αὐτὸς δ', ὡς ἔθος εἶχεν, ἐκ τοῦ Θεολόγου πρὸς τὸν λόγον τοῦ ἄνακτος λόγους φέρων ἀνταπεκρίνετο· καὶ τοῖς ῥήτορσιν ἔπληττεν, πῶς ἀπὸ στήθους τὰ τοῦ Θεολόγου ἀναφωνεῖ καὶ πᾶσαν θείαν γραφήν. ἐπεὶ δὲ γραμματικὴν οὐ μεμάθηκεν οὗτος ὁ ὅσιος, ἐν τοῖς ῥήμασιν ἀδαὴς ἐνοεῖτο· διὰ τοῦτο καὶ παρὰ τοῦ μεγάλου λογοθέτου ἐκείνου ἀκούσας τοῦ κανικλείου τό· "ἡ μὲν φωνὴ φωνὴ Ἰακώβ, αἱ δὲ χεῖρες χεῖρες Ἠσαύ" ἀπελθὼν ᾤχετο, ματαιόφρονας καλέσας ἐκείνους καὶ ἄφρονας· καὶ πλεῖον εἰς τὰ βασίλεια οὐκ ἐγένετο.

While it is true that examples of infelicitous performances are both difficult to find and also usually a feature of sources unsympathetic to the actor(s), there cannot be any doubt that the system allowed for both success and failure.

In conclusion, the *theatron* emerges as a seminal social performance of the early Palaiologan period. On the one hand, *theatra*, as social spaces, connected literati with each other. On the other, they linked the learned stratum with the aristocracy by means of patronage and social inclusion. The learned orbited around the nucleus formed by the ruling elites, the Palaiologoi, Kantakouzenoi and their associates – as had been the case in the twelfth century with the Doukai, Komnenoi and Angeloi –, who played their roles as patrons, members of the audience, and, occasionally, as performers. 'Theatrical' acts of public reading, in all their complexity and with all their social ramifications as outlined in this chapter, no doubt contributed to efforts to keep the early Palaiologan polity together.

Further Reading

Key studies include: J. C. Alexander, 'Cultural Pragmatics: Social Performance Between Ritual and Strategy' in J. C. Alexander, B. Giesen and J. L. Mast, eds., *Social Performance: Symbolic Action, Cultural Pragmatics, and Ritual* (Cambridge, 2006), 29–90; E. C. Bourbouhakis, 'Rhetoric and Performance' in P. Stephenson, *The Byzantine World* (London, 2010), 175–87 and E. C. Bourbouhakis, 'The End of ἐπίδειξις. Authorial Identity and Authorial Intention in Michael Choniates' Πρὸς τοὺς αἰτιωμένους τὸ ἀφιλένδεικτον' in A. Pizzone, ed., *The Author in Middle Byzantine Literature. Modes, Functions, Identities* (Berlin, 2014), 201–24; N. Gaul, 'The Letter in the *Theatron*: Epistolary Voice, Character, Soul and their Audience' in A. Riehle, ed., *A Companion to Byzantine Epistolography* (Leiden, forthcoming); I. Toth, 'Rhetorical *Theatron* in Late Byzantium: the Example of Palaiologan Imperial Orations' in M. Grünbart, ed., *Theatron: Rhetorische Kultur in Spätantike und Mittelalter* (Berlin, 2007), 429–48.

Religious Texts

CHAPTER 9

The Religious World of John Malalas
David M. Gwynn

The *Chronicle* of John Malalas (*c.* 490s–*c.* 570s) will always hold a unique place in Byzantine historiography. The oldest extant Byzantine universal history, the eighteen books of the *Chronicle* cover from Creation down to the author's own time in the age of Justinian I (emperor 527–65). The identity and motives of the author and the editions and language of the text raise complex questions. Yet the *Chronicle* remains an essential source for the social, political and religious world of late antiquity and particularly for the dramatic reign of Justinian that forms the subject of the eighteenth and last book of the work. The purpose of this chapter is to make a small contribution to our understanding of Malalas and his *Chronicle* through a reassessment of his approach to religion and religious history, of the reading on which he drew and of his place within the religious world in which he lived.

It is perhaps not fair to say that Malalas was neglected in older Byzantine scholarship, for the importance of the *Chronicle* as a literary and historical text has long been recognised. Yet only in recent decades has the *Chronicle* begun to receive the detailed assessment its importance merits. For this 'rediscovery' of Malalas the majority of the credit must go to Elizabeth Jeffreys and her Australian colleagues in the 1980s. In 1986 Elizabeth and Michael Jeffreys and Roger Scott published the first translation of the full text of Malalas in any modern European language.[1] This was followed in 1990 by a collection of *Studies in John Malalas*, edited by Elizabeth Jeffreys, with Brian Croke and Roger Scott.[2] All subsequent scholarship

---

[1] E. M. Jeffreys, M. J. Jeffreys, R. Scott, eds., *The Chronicle of John Malalas: A Translation* (Melbourne, 1986). All translations from Malalas henceforth come from this volume, while for the new standard edition of Malalas' *Chronicle*, see I. Thurn, ed., *Ioannis Malalae. Chronographia* (Berlin, 2000).

[2] E. M. Jeffreys, ed., with B. Croke and R. Scott, *Studies in John Malalas* (Sydney, 1990). See also E. M. Jeffreys, 'The Beginning of Byzantine Chronography: John Malalas' in G. Marasco, ed., *Greek*

on Malalas and his *Chronicle* has necessarily built upon the foundations laid by these two publications.[3]

The Australian translation of Malalas into English and the *Studies* that formed a companion to that translation shed new light upon a number of the most difficult problems that the *Chronicle* raises for modern scholars. The *Chronicle* survives at length in Greek in only a single defective eleventh- or twelfth-century manuscript (Oxford Baroccianus 182), but the work was originally widely read and was translated into numerous other languages, notably Latin, Syriac and Slavonic.[4] Several articles in the *Studies* volume assess these different linguistic versions and their significance, and place Malalas within the wider tradition of Byzantine chronicle writing. Such analysis is made more complex by the vexed question of authorship, for the identity of the *Chronicle*'s compiler and the unity of the text itself remain subjects of debate. The final sections of Book xviii, from the year 532 onwards, reveal a Constantinopolitan focus not shared by the earlier books whose author was evidently an Antiochene. This led to the belief that the *Chronicle* originally ended in 532 and was continued to 565 or possibly to 574 by a different author. Elizabeth Jeffreys and her colleagues have argued strongly in favour of a single author who wrote the first edition of his *Chronicle* while serving under the *comes Orientis* in Antioch. The author then continued his text after he moved from Antioch to Constantinople, perhaps in 535 when the office of the *comes Orientis* was virtually abolished.[5] They have not convinced all their critics,[6] but it is this conclusion that has been cautiously adopted here. At the very least, the Australian project did succeed in bringing out the literary merits of the author, who had frequently been dismissed as 'childish' or 'incompetent' by earlier scholars. The appellation 'Malalas' derives from *mll*, the Syriac root for 'rhetor' or 'scholastikos', and the author deserves credit for his

---

and Roman Historiography in Late Antiquity, Fourth to Sixth Century A.D. (Leiden, 2003), 497–527, which summarises much of the material from the *Studies*.

[3] Including, of course, the present chapter, which I hope makes this an appropriate contribution to a volume celebrating the work of Elizabeth and Michael Jeffreys.

[4] Even the name John Malalas must be reconstructed from the Slavonic translation of the *Chronicle*. For a recent restatement of the problematic transmission of Malalas and its implications, see G. Greatrex, 'Malalas and Procopius' in M. Meier, C. Radtki and F. Schulz, eds., *Die Weltchronik des Johannes Malalas: Autor – Werk – Überlieferung* (Stuttgart, 2016), 169–85.

[5] For Malalas' connection to Antioch and the *comes Orientis*, see B. Croke, 'Malalas: The Man and his Work' in E. M. Jeffreys et al., eds., *Studies in John Malalas*, 6–11. Croke proposes that 'the most likely terminus' (19) for the first edition of the *Chronicle* is after the signing of the Endless Peace with Persia in 532, Malalas, *Chronographia*, ed. Thurn, 401 (xviii.76); trans., Jeffreys et al., *Chronicle*, 282.

[6] See, for example, M. Whitby, '*Malalas Continuatus*: Review of E. M. Jeffreys ed. with B. Croke and R. Scott, *Studies in John Malalas* (Sydney 1990)', *ClRev*, 41 (1991), 326.

research and for his simplified linguistic style that made his work accessible and helps explain the popularity of the *Chronicle* for later generations.

The wide-ranging articles in *Studies in John Malalas* also include contributions on Malalas' sources, his records of buildings and his use of chronological structures. Yet there is one subject that receives relatively little attention, and that concerns the religious attitudes of the author. This is not to suggest that this important question was ignored. In his introduction to Malalas' life and work, Brian Croke explores the religious function and structure of the *Chronicle* and provides a short survey of the major evidence for Malalas' approach to religion.[7] Elizabeth Jeffreys' reconstruction of Malalas' worldview further highlights his interest in talismans, rituals and mystical and philosophical figures and his strong views on Christian millenarianism,[8] all themes to which I will return below. In a volume that devotes over one hundred pages to the *Chronicle*'s language and manuscript history, however, it is striking that just twelve pages divided between two contributors are dedicated explicitly to Malalas' religious beliefs and the religious context within which he wrote.

There are good reasons for this choice of emphasis. The complex problems raised by Malalas' unclassical vocabulary, manuscript transmission and numerous translations have bedevilled scholarship on the *Chronicle*. It was the great achievement of the Australian project to see the way past these problems and make further research possible. There also appears to have been a conscious intention to step away from the older scholarly debates over Malalas' religion, particularly in the late nineteenth century, which focused to an excessive degree on the author's possible adherence to particular Christian doctrines.[9] We must not exaggerate the religious content of the *Chronicle*. Malalas was not an ecclesiastical historian.[10] He exhibits very little interest in Christian doctrine and the great councils and fathers of the Church, which figure so prominently in other Byzantine

---

[7] Croke, 'Malalas', 11–17.
[8] E. M. Jeffreys, 'Malalas' World View' in Jeffreys et al., eds., *Studies in John Malalas*, 63–6. These arguments are repeated and expanded in E. M. Jeffreys, 'Literary Genre or Religious Apathy? The Presence or Absence of Theology and Religious Thought in Secular Writing in the Late Antique East' in D. M. Gwynn and S. Bangert, eds., *Religious Diversity in Late Antiquity* (Leiden, 2010), 511–22.
[9] These older debates, which will be discussed further below, are conveniently summarised in B. Croke, 'Modern Study of Malalas' in E. M. Jeffreys et al., eds., *Studies in John Malalas*, 332–7.
[10] See now A. Martin, 'L'histoire ecclésiastique intéresse-t-elle Malalas?' in J. Beaucamp, ed., *Recherches sur la chronique de Jean Malalas 1* (Paris, 2004), 85–102.

chronicles such as the *Chronicon Paschale* and the *Chronographia* of Theophanes,[11] and religious concerns take up relatively little of the overall text. This caution needs to be remembered as a counterbalance to the argument that follows.

Nevertheless, it is the fundamental premise of this chapter that close analysis of the religious context of the *Chronicle* of Malalas is essential both for our understanding of the author and for how we approach his text as a historical source. Malalas' personal religious background and beliefs are not easy to define. To quote from the Conclusion to the *Studies in John Malalas*, 'his religious interests were not those of a dedicated theologian but he was open to religious speculation of the widest sort, on the edges of orthodox Christian belief'.[12] Yet in the final words of that Conclusion, it is maintained that 'we can, however, look to find in his chronicle a reflection of attitudes, beliefs and historical perspectives that were widespread throughout the sixth-century Byzantine world'.[13] Only by examining again the evidence for Malalas' own religious views and how they are expressed through his *Chronicle* can we learn if it is possible to reconcile these two potentially, although by no means necessarily, contradictory claims.[14]

Malalas was a Christian: this at least is beyond any possible doubt. As Brian Croke declares in the opening paper of the *Studies in John Malalas*, Byzantine chronicles 'fulfilled a religious function ... they explained the pattern of God's providence for mankind in a complete and organised chronological framework'.[15] That framework is explicitly Christian. Malalas states in his preface that he will follow the model of sacred history laid down by the Christian chronographic tradition led by Sextus Julius

---

[11] Unlike the authors of those later chronicles, Malalas was a secular official not a cleric or a monk, despite the older argument of Haury, which incorrectly identified John Malalas as John Scholastikos, patriarch of Constantinople 565–77. See J. Haury, 'Johannes Malalas identisch mit dem Patriarchen Johannes Scholastikos?', *BZ*, 9 (1900), 337–56.

[12] Jeffreys et al., 'Conclusion', in Jeffreys et al., *Studies in John Malalas*, 340.

[13] Ibid. Michael Maas draws the same judgement when he asserts that the *Chronicle* of Malalas is 'far more representative of widely held beliefs in the sixth century than the classicising history of Procopius': M. Maas, 'Roman Questions, Byzantine Answers: Contours of the Age of Justinian' in M. Maas, ed., *The Cambridge Companion to the Age of Justinian* (Cambridge, 2005), 18.

[14] I am by no means the first to propose that further study of the religious dimensions of Malalas' *Chronicle* is required if we are to advance on the foundations laid by the Australian Malalas project. Three important volumes of papers on Malalas have been published in the last few years that include a number of contributions on religious themes: Beaucamp, ed., *Recherches sur la chronique de Jean Malalas I*; S. Agusta-Boularot, J. Beaucamp, A.-M. Bernardi, E. Caire, eds., *Recherches sur la chronique de Jean Malalas II* (Paris, 2006); and Meier, Radtki and Schulz, eds., *Die Weltchronik des Johannes Malalas*.

[15] Croke, 'Malalas', 11. On the chronicle tradition before Malalas, see B. Croke, 'The Early Development of Byzantine Chronicles' in E. M. Jeffreys et al., eds., *Studies in John Malalas*, 27–38.

Africanus and Eusebios of Caesarea. World history begins with Adam (1.1), and the passage of time is shaped by biblical and Christian chronology, which provides the structure into which secular events are inserted.[16]

The pagan past is therefore subordinated to the Christian vision of history. Following a rational euhemerist approach, Zeus (1.8–10, 1.13), Aphrodite (1.9) and the other Olympian deities are presented in the *Chronicle* as human beings rather than gods, and Zeus indeed is described as a member of the tribe of Shem and so incorporated into the Judaeo-Christian tradition (1.8).[17] The majority of Malalas' early material on ancient Greece and Rome in Books I–VI is drawn from myth rather than classical historiography, notably the long account of the Trojan War in Book V, while Books VII–IX trace Roman and Hellenistic history very briefly down to Augustus.[18] Marginalising the period before the reign of the first Roman emperor places the focus on the Incarnation of Christ, which spans Books IX–X. Books X–XII then cover the rulers of Rome from Augustus to Constantine, the first Christian emperor, whose conversion begins Book XIII. After the death of Julian 'the Apostate' (XIII.23–5), the last pagan emperor, the Christian Empire then endured down to the reigns of the emperors under whom Malalas lived: Anastasios (Book XVI), Justin (Book XVII) and Justinian (Book XVIII, the last and longest book of the *Chronicle*).

Until the final few books, when he could also draw upon oral accounts and his own experiences, Malalas' construction of the past derived almost exclusively from his use of written sources.[19] It has therefore been argued that the interpretation of that earlier material likewise depends on previous writers and so can reveal little of Malalas himself.[20] As the Australian

---

[16] For further discussion of Malalas' approach to chronological structure and his place within the chronicle tradition, see M. Whitby, 'The Biblical Past in John Malalas and the Paschal Chronicle' in H. Amirav and B. Ter Haar Romney, eds., *From Rome to Constantinople: Studies in Honour of Averil Cameron* (Leuven, 2007), 279–302.

[17] On Malalas' euhemerism, see E. Hörling, *Mythos und Pisitis: Zur Deutung heidnischer Mythen in der christlichen Weltchronik des Johannes Malalas* (Lund, 1980), esp. 43–77.

[18] See further R. Scott, 'Malalas' View of the Classical Past' in G. Clarke, ed., *Reading the Past in Late Antiquity* (Canberra, 1990), 147–64.

[19] E. M. Jeffreys, 'Malalas' Sources' in Jeffreys et al., eds., *Studies in John Malalas*, 167–216.

[20] For an extreme statement of this view, see W. Treadgold, 'The Byzantine World Histories of John Malalas and Eustathius of Epiphania', *International History Review*, 29 (2007), 709–45; and Treadgold, *The Early Byzantine Historians* (Basingstoke, 2007), 235–56. Treadgold rejects Malalas' references to the sources he consulted as fictitious and asserts that Malalas derived almost his entire work from one source, Eustathios of Epiphania, whose text he plagiarised and then published under his own name.

Malalas project has demonstrated once again, however, in his selection of material for inclusion and in the structure of that material it is possible to trace Malalas' own interests and emphases. The placement of the Incarnation at the exact centre of the work is too perfect, with the Annunciation at the conclusion of Book IX and the birth of Christ in the opening lines of Book X. More complex structural plans have been proposed, including dividing the *Chronicle* into three hexads representing Old Testament times (Books I–VI), Rome (Books VII–XII) and the Christian Empire (Books XIII–XVIII), a scheme that further emphasises the place in the divine plan of the conversion of Constantine at the beginning of the final hexad.[21] But the central event, as we would expect in a Christian chronicle, is the Incarnation of Christ, and the chronology of Christ's birth and death is very important to Malalas, a theme to which I will return later in this chapter.

The Christianity of Malalas is also visible in his unquestioning conception of divine providence acting in the world. It is the Christian God who oversees the course of history, His will is expressed most frequently through the earthquakes that recur throughout the later books of the *Chronicle* and are recorded by Malalas as expressions of *theomēnia*, the 'wrath of God'.[22] The fire that damaged Antioch in the early 520s 'foretold God's coming displeasure' (XVII.14), and is followed by the great earthquake that struck the city in 526. 'Great was the fear of God that occurred then, in that those caught in the earth beneath the buildings were incinerated and sparks of fire appeared out of the air and burned anyone they struck like lightning' (XVII.16). Christians were not spared, and 'no holy chapel nor monastery nor any other holy place remained which had not been torn apart' (XVII.16). The toll is said to have approached a quarter of a million dead. 'For this was the great festival of the Ascension of Christ our God and a great throng of visitors had come to town' (XVII.16).

Malalas offers no explanation for what caused Antioch to suffer God's wrath on one of the holiest days of the Christian year.[23] Yet he also offers no protest or complaint, and even amid the destruction he can find

---

[21] Scott, 'Malalas' View', 159–60.
[22] In the later sections of the *Chronicle* (Malalas, *Chronographia* ed. Thurn, 370–1 (XVIII.28), trans. Jeffreys et al., *Chronicle*, 258; and from Thurn 384 (XVIII.55); trans. Jeffreys et al., 268, onwards), *theomēnia* is replaced by the more prosaic *seismos*.
[23] It is tempting to seek to impose a religious interpretation here and elsewhere in the *Chronicle* (see for example Malalas, *Chronographia*, ed. Thurn, 265 (XIII.35); trans. Jeffreys et al., *Chronicle*, 186, when Nicaea, the site of the first ecumenical council in 325, is first struck by an earthquake under Valens, an emperor whom Malalas describes as an 'Arian'). But Malalas himself draws no explicit implications.

evidence of God's care for His people. 'For pregnant women who had been buried for twenty or even thirty days were brought up from the rubble in good health, many, who gave birth underground beneath the rubble, were brought up unharmed with their babies and survived' (XVII.16). God further revealed His love through a sign. 'On the third day after the collapse the Holy Cross appeared in the sky in the clouds above the northern district of the city, and all who saw it stayed weeping and praying for an hour' (XVII.16).

At first sight this might appear to modern eyes as a simplistic and perhaps even laughable expression of superstition and blind faith. Yet Malalas reveals a trust in God's providence and grace that had the strength to survive even the devastation of his beloved city. Nor is his conception of providence always so straightforward. In Antioch in 526 all faced destruction, protected neither by religion nor morality. Two years later, the earthquake that shook Laodicea in 528 destroyed half the city, 'including the Jewish synagogues', and the 7,500 people killed included 'a large number of Hebrews and a few Christians' (XVIII.28). However, 'the churches of the city remained intact, being preserved by God' (XVIII.28).[24] God was less merciful to Christians when He unleashed the great plague in 542, but in this instance at least His motives are explained. 'The Lord God saw that man's transgressions had multiplied and he caused the overthrow of man on the earth, leading to his destruction in all cities and lands. The plague lasted a while, so that there were not enough people to bury the dead' (XVIII.92). For Malalas, as for many of his contemporaries, the world could be a very dangerous place, and the wrath of God inspired fear and required supplication. Not even the recurring disasters that he described, however, could shake his confidence in the love of God for His people.

From the structure of the *Chronicle* and the actions of God within its text, we can accept without further argument that Malalas was Christian. Rather more difficult is the task of defining just what being Christian meant to Malalas. It has often been said that Malalas shows little interest in doctrine or heresy and this is largely true, although the evidence merits further analysis. Yet Malalas does have strong religious interests. He was apparently fascinated by the mystical knowledge possessed by

---

[24] In Constantinople slightly later Hagia Sophia was less fortunate, for in 558 'the dome of the Great Church was being restored, for it had cracked in several places because of the shocks that had occurred through God's benevolence'. Malalas, *Chronographia*, ed. Thurn, 297 (XVIII.128); trans. Jeffreys et al., *Chronicle*, 297.

philosophers, oracles and holy men and women, and by the rituals and talismans of what we might describe as magic. He also had committed views on Christian millenarianism and the possible Second Coming of Christ, which may have motivated his decision to write the *Chronicle* in the first place. All these themes are discussed further below, for they raise two fundamental questions. First, what do Malalas' interests reveal regarding the nature of his own Christianity? Is it accurate to describe his *Chronicle*, in the words of Elizabeth Jeffreys, as revealing 'a whole series of strands of barely Christian beliefs and superstitions, which had him, the chronicler of an apparently Christian society, in thrall, whilst Christian doctrines and heresies left him unmoved'?[25] Second, in light of the often idiosyncratic values that Malalas upholds, to what extent are we justified in speaking of him as in any way representative of the religious world in which he lived?

Malalas says almost nothing regarding the doctrinal controversies that divided the Christian Roman Empire. He is aware of the 'Arian' Controversy in the fourth century, for he follows the orthodox tradition in condemning Constantius II (XIII.17) and Valens (XIII.34) as 'Exakionites' ('Arians'),[26] and he refers to the confiscation of 'Arian' churches in his own time under Justinian (XVIII.84).[27] None of these passages make any reference to doctrine, and neither does Malalas' very brief account of Nicaea in 325, when 'the Council of 318 Bishops took place against Arius, concerning the Christian faith' (XIII.11). There is no allusion to the Nicene Creed and the debates over the true divinity of the Son and the relationship between the Persons of the Trinity, or to the struggles of Athanasios of Alexandria against the 'Arian heresy', the themes that dominate our ecclesiastical records for the fourth century. The only hint that Malalas knew the issues at stake occurs in his brief description of the Council of Constantinople in 381, which met 'concerning the consubstantiality of the Holy Spirit' (XIII.40). Malalas is also the earliest extant Greek source to record the legend that Constantine was baptised by

---

[25] Jeffreys, 'Literary Genre', 521.
[26] This traditional characterisation of these two emperors as 'Arian' likewise occurs in passages attributed to the chronicler John of Antioch (S. Mariev, ed., *Ioannis Antiocheni fragmenta quae supersunt omnia* (Berlin, 2008), fragments 201 and 207–9), whose relationship to Malalas remains a subject for debate.
[27] Malalas also records the earlier expulsion of the 'Arians' from their churches by Theodosios I (Thurn ed., *Chronographia* 187 (XIII.37); trans. Jeffreys et al., *Chronicle* 266) and Leo I (295 (XIV.41); trans. Jeffreys et al., *Chronicle* 205), although he reports that Justinian originally expelled other heresies but left 'Arian' churches alone (Thurn ed., *Chronographia* 357 (XVIII.7); trans. Jeffreys et al., *Chronicle*, 247).

Sylvester of Rome (XIII.2) rather than by the 'Arian' Eusebios of Nikomedia. This legend was to become central to later Byzantine polemic over the orthodoxy of Constantine, as we see from Theophanes, who denounces Constantine's historical baptism by Eusebios of Nikomedia as an 'Arian forgery' (*Annus Mundi* 5814).[28] Malalas appears unaware of any such debate, omitting Eusebios entirely and preferring to emphasise the simple fact that 'the Emperor Constantine became a Christian'.[29]

Concerning the Christological controversies of the fifth and sixth centuries that continued unabated during his own lifetime, Malalas is only slightly more forthcoming. After the preaching of Nestorios in Constantinople inspired a riot, the Council of Ephesus in 431 was summoned 'against Nestorios, to depose him from his see. The Council was led by Cyril, bishop of Alexandria the Great' (XIV.25). Nestorios' teachings are omitted, as are the debates that followed his expulsion, and even the great Council of Chalcedon in 451 merits no more than the briefest passing description as 'the Council of 630 bishops' (XIV.30). One could scarcely realise from those few words that the ecclesiastical and doctrinal decisions of Chalcedon were to cause divisions within Eastern Christianity that have not healed to this day.

The ongoing conflicts play little role in the later books of Malalas' *Chronicle*. A number of bishops are said to have been deposed because they were 'Nestorian', including three bishops of Antioch (Stephen (XV.6), Kalandion (XV.6), Flavian (XVI.11)) and two bishops of Constantinople (Euphemios (XVI.11) and Makedonios (XVI.11)). Most significantly, in the year 512, 'a civic insurrection took place among the Byzantines in Constantinople over Christian belief, because the emperor [Anastasios, 491–518] wanted to add to the *Trisagion* the phrase they use in the eastern cities, "he who was crucified for us, have mercy on us". The population of the city crowded together and rioted violently on the grounds that something alien had been added to the Christian faith' (XVI.19). The rioters burned the house of the ex-prefect Marinos the Syrian, possibly Malalas' source, who they believed had inspired Anastasios' action.[30] 'They found

---

[28] C. de Boor, ed., *Theophanis Chronographia* (Leipzig, 1883–5), vol. 1, 25.

[29] For a detailed comparison between the accounts of Constantine in Malalas and Theophanes, see R. Scott, 'The Image of Constantine in Malalas and Theophanes' in P. Magdalino, ed., *New Constantines: The Rhythm of Imperial Renewal in Byzantium, 4th – 13th Centuries* (Aldershot, 1994), 57–71.

[30] Earlier in 512 Marinos had defeated a naval attack by the rebel Vitalian. Malalas makes no reference to Vitalian's claims to defend Chalcedonian orthodoxy against Anastasios, merely declaring that 'Christ the Saviour and the emperor's *tyche* had won the victory'. Thurn, ed., *Chronographia* 332 (XVI.16); trans. Jeffreys et al., *Chronicle* 227.

an eastern monk in the house whom they seized and killed and then, carrying his head on a pole, they chanted "Here is the enemy of the Trinity"' (XVI.19). Finally Anastasios quieted the rioters and then took steps to eliminate the ring-leaders, and so, to Malalas' approval, 'excellent order and no little fear prevailed in Constantinople and in every city of the Roman state' (XVI.19).[31]

Anastasios died in 518, and in the first year of Justin I (518–27) the bishop Severos of Antioch fled his see, to be replaced by Paul. The new bishop 'included in the diptychs of the churches of each city the 630 bishops of the Council of Chalcedon. As a result there was a great schism and many broke communion with him, stating that those who followed the Council supported the doctrines of Nestorios' (XVII.6). Later in Justin's reign Paul's successor, Euphrasios, 'carried out a great persecution of those known as Orthodox, and put many to death' (XVII.11). The 'Orthodox' here are those who rejected the Council of Chalcedon, usually identified in modern scholarship as the 'Monophysites' or 'Miaphysites'. The unavailing measures to secure Christian unity culminate in the first edition of Malalas' *Chronicle* with a rescript of Justinian sent to the cities in 530/1,

> saying that those who did not take communion in the holy churches should be sent into exile, for they were excusing themselves by citing the Council of Chalcedon, that is, the Council of 630 Bishops. A riot broke out in Antioch, and the mob burst into the bishop's residence, throwing stones and chanting insults. Those who were in the patriarchate came out, together with the *comes Orientis*, and resisted them with missiles and stones and killed many of the rioters. (XVIII.64)[32]

All the passages cited above are embedded within a text dominated by military and political events and civic affairs, and so are far less prominent in the overall scheme of the *Chronicle* than their presentation here might suggest. It was on the basis of this very limited evidence that Brian Croke understandably concludes that unlike a number of his contemporaries, 'Malalas was not inclined to dwell on contemporary theological

---

[31] On the events of 512, see further M. Meier, 'Σταυρωθεὶς δι' ἡμᾶς – Der Aufstand gegen Anastasios im Jahr 512', *Millennium*, 4 (2007) 157–237.

[32] Slightly later in Book XVIII there is another brief reference to an edict of Justinian 'concerning the orthodox faith and against impious heretics'. Malalas, *Chronographia* ed. Thurn, 402 (XVIII.78); trans. Jeffreys et al., *Chronicle*, 282–3. This edict of 533 is quoted in full in the entry for that year in the *Chronicon paschale* and possibly stood at the end of the edition of Malalas that the *Chronicon paschale*'s author used (Treadgold, *Early Byzantine Historians*, 240, n. 59), although this cannot be proven.

developments and ecclesiastical discord'.[33] Yet in rejecting the older scholars who had sought to identify a Miaphysite influence on the *Chronicle*,[34] Croke also asserts that despite his reticence Malalas was 'clearly orthodox'.[35] This claim is supported by Elizabeth Jeffreys, who declares that Malalas 'must have been an orthodox Chalcedonian'.[36] He may employ the term 'Nestorian' as an insult and refer to the Miaphysites as 'those known as Orthodox' (XVII.11), but this is explained as Malalas' reflection of contemporary Antiochene language and not an indication of his own theological views.[37] There is no expression of support for Miaphysite heroes such as Severos of Antioch, and although his account of the *Trisagion* riot in 512 does not condemn the added clause that was believed to express Miaphysite views, he may have been influenced by his probable source, the Miaphysite Marinos the Syrian.[38]

It is apparent from the preceding paragraphs that Malalas was far less influenced by the doctrinal debates of his time than the ecclesiastical writers whose views dominate so much of our evidence. This relative lack of interest in theology, which Malalas shared with his contemporaries Prokopios and John Lydos,[39] is a strong indication that these doctrinal debates were not perhaps so all-pervasive in the age of Justinian as is sometimes assumed. Nevertheless, even a man like Malalas who tried to step back from the debates was still influenced by them. There are theological views visible in the *Chronicle*, and those views cannot easily be described as 'orthodox Chalcedonian'. What polemical emphasis appears in Malalas is directed against those who persecuted the opponents of Chalcedon, and the term of abuse he uses, 'Nestorian', was traditionally

---

[33] Croke, 'Malalas', 17.
[34] The arguments are surveyed in Croke, 'Modern Study', 332–7: see in particular C. E. Gleye, 'Beiträge zur Johannesfrage', *BZ*, 5 (1896), 422–64; E. Chernousov, 'Études sur Malalas', *Byzantion*, 3 (1926), 65–72; and the brief references in K. Krumbacher, *Geschichte der byzantinischen Litteratur von Justinian bis zum Ende des oströmischen Reiches (527–1453)* (Munich, 1897), 331; and H. Hunger, *Die hochsprachliche profane Literatur der Byzantiner* (Munich, 1978), vol. I, 320 (who argues that the text down to 532 is Miaphysite and Antiochene, from 532 on Chalcedonian and Constantinopolitan. Croke is particularly influenced by E. Patzig, 'Der angebliche Monophysitismus des Malalas', *BZ*, 7 (1898), 111–28, in which Patzig sets out to counter Gleye's arguments in favour of Malalas' Miaphysite influences, although Croke rightly rejects Patzig's own conclusion that Malalas was in fact a 'Nestorian'.
[35] Croke, 'Malalas', 16.   [36] Jeffreys, 'Malalas' World View', 63.   [37] Croke, 'Malalas', 15.
[38] Ibid., 16; E. M. Jeffreys, 'Chronological Structures in the Chronicle' in Jeffreys et al., eds., *Studies in John Malalas*, 164.
[39] This was noted in R. Scott, 'Malalas and his Contemporaries' in Jeffreys et al., *Studies in John Malalas*, 67–85, although with little analysis. On recent debates over the religious views of Prokopius, see M. Whitby, 'Religious Views of Procopius and Agathias', *Electrum*, 13 (2007), 73–93.

directed against the adherents of the Council of 451. Malalas' approach to Church history was certainly shaped by his Antiochene background,[40] but neither this nor the sources on which he drew are sufficient to explain away those rare episodes in the *Chronicle* where a theological bias does come through. It would seem more natural to regard Malalas as a moderate opponent of Chalcedon,[41] but not openly polemical, and more concerned with the rhythms of civic and imperial society than with doctrinal debates.

A couple of further observations need to be made here. When scholars speak of Malalas as 'Chalcedonian' or 'Miaphysite', we must remember that when he composed the original text of his *Chronicle* in the 530s these categories did not have the force they would later acquire. The separate Miaphysite Church in Syria only began to emerge as an independent entity through the activities of Jacob Baradeus from the 540s onwards. In the 520s and 530s many still sought reconciliation between the supporters and opponents of Chalcedon, and Malalas' use of the term 'Nestorian' is highly appropriate in this context, for it was through their shared hostility to alleged followers of Nestorios that Justinian would seek to find common ground between these groups through his condemnation of the Three Chapters in *c*. 544. Malalas, one suspects, would have supported such reconciliation. However, he says little of Justinian's efforts to achieve ecclesiastical unity beyond a reference to an 'edict concerning the orthodox faith and against impious heretics' (XVIII.78), a council of Constantinople of uncertain date (XVIII.83), and several short notices on the varying fortunes of Vigilius of Rome (XVIII.97–8, 107, 111).[42] It was in part due to his lack of an obvious doctrinal allegiance that Malalas would prove an acceptable source to later writers whose religious attitudes varied widely. His *Chronicle* was exploited with little expression of hostility to its author by men as diverse as John of Ephesus, Evagrios, John of Antioch and the compiler of the *Chronicon Paschale*.[43]

---

[40] This is particularly true of the attention he pays to the succession of Patriarchs of Antioch: see Jeffreys, 'Chronological Structures', 162–4.

[41] Here, although on rather different grounds, I agree with Treadgold, *Early Byzantine Historians*, 236. For a more neutral conclusion, see V. H. Drecoll, 'Miaphysitische Tendenzen bei Malalas?' in Meier, Radtki and Schulz, eds., *Die Weltchronik des Johannes Malalas*, 45–57.

[42] Given the very limited detail Malalas offers on Justinian's ecclesiastical policy, whose importance to the emperor cannot be in doubt, it is uncertain how far R. Scott ('Malalas, the Secret History, and Justinian's Propaganda', *DOP*, 39 (1985), 99–109) is correct to argue that Malalas drew to a significant degree on court propaganda in constructing his account of Justinian's reign.

[43] See E. M. Jeffreys, 'Malalas in Greek' in Jeffreys et al., eds. *Studies in John Malalas*, 249–54; and W. Witakowski, 'Malalas in Syriac' in Jeffreys et al., eds, *Studies in John Malalas*, 299–310. One exception is the Egyptian chronicler John of Nikiu who, according to Patzig ('Der angebliche Monophysitismus', 128), described Malalas as a 'heretic'.

For the present enquiry into the religious elements that shape the *Chronicle* of Malalas, Christian theology and heresy are less significant than other themes that appear to have attracted Malalas' more personal attention. Most notably, Malalas reveals a fascination for what Elizabeth Jeffreys has described as 'the underbelly of the Byzantine Christianised society'.[44] This category includes rituals and talismans, mystics and wonder-workers, and oracles. Much of the material that Malalas presents on these subjects might once have been described as 'pagan superstition' and has been presented as challenging or conflicting with his Christian beliefs. Yet as we have already seen, Malalas in his *Chronicle* seeks to incorporate pagan myth and history into a vision of the world that is explicitly Christian. The same model underlies his approach to pagan religion, which he traces from the past into the Christian present to reinforce the providential role of God in the events of his own time.

Malalas places particular emphasis on rituals and the use of talismans, from Greco-Roman antiquity through to the Christian Empire. The wonder-worker Apollonios of Tyana created numerous talismans during the reign of Domitian (x.51): talismans against storks, the river Lykos, tortoises and horses in Byzantium, and against the North Wind, scorpions and mosquitoes in Antioch (the latter also required a ritual procession in which busts of Ares with suspended shields and daggers were carried to chants of 'Out with the mosquitoes'). The greatest talismans and rituals relate to the foundation of cities. According to Malalas, when a new city was founded in antiquity a maiden was sacrificed and her image preserved as a statue, the *tyche* of the city.[45] Alexander the Great sacrificed a girl he named Macedonia when he founded Alexandria in Egypt (VIII.1), Aimathe was sacrificed by Seleucus Nicator for Antioch (VIII.13). This tradition culminated for Malalas with Constantine at Constantinople, who named the *tyche* of his new city Anthousa but who rejected the maiden sacrifice and instead 'made a bloodless sacrifice to God' (XIII.7). The first Christian emperor also placed in his city the most famous of all urban protective talismans: the Palladion. Stolen from Troy by Odysseus and Diomedes (V.43), it was given by Diomedes to Aeneas (VI.24), whose descendants Romulus and Remus brought it to Rome (VII.1). There it remained, until 'Constantine took secretly from Rome the wooden statue

---

[44] Jeffreys, 'Literary Genre', 517.
[45] A. Moffatt, 'A Record of Public Buildings and Monuments' in Jeffreys et al., eds., *Studies in John Malalas*, 105–7; Jeffreys, 'Malalas' World View', 57–8.

known as the Palladion and placed it in the forum he built, beneath the column which supported his statue' (XIII.7).[46]

Constantine's translation of the Palladion to his new city represented the continuity from the ancient past to the Christian Empire. But the reign of Constantine likewise saw the rediscovery of the greatest of all Christian talismans to bless the new age. 'The emperor Constantine sent his mother, lady Helena, to Jerusalem to seek for the precious Cross. She found the precious Cross, with the five nails, and brought it back. From that time Christianity prospered in every way' (XIII.5). Yet Malalas' tone is not one of naked Christian triumphalism. Some pagan temples were destroyed, including the Serapeum (XIII.48), wrongly attributed to Honorius rather than Theodosios I, and others were reused in Constantinople (XIII.39) and elsewhere (XIII.37). But equally, ancient monuments could be reinterpreted as Christian (IV.13), and the only explicit reference to the destruction of pagan books and the 'pictures and statues of their loathsome gods' (XVIII.136) occurs near the end of Book XVIII in the section added in the second edition of the *Chronicle*.[47] Malalas' vision is one of Christian completion of the past not rejection of it, as we see again in his attitude towards miracle workers and oracles.

Malalas reveals a recurring interest in *mystikoi*, individuals who possessed superior wisdom and/or were capable of magic or the working of miracles.[48] Once again, these individuals form a chain that unites Greek and Roman mythology (Hephaistos (I.15), Perseus (II.13), Dionysios (II.24)) with Old Testament and Roman history (Joshua (IV.3), Sampson (IV.17), Augustus (X.6)), and connect that past to Malalas' present. After Augustus, 'a high priest with mystic knowledge, and emperor' (X.6), there is a long gap until the last-named *mystikos*, Maurianus (XV.16), who lived under Zeno and may have been Malalas' source. However, the mystical tradition does not fail in the intervening centuries, but passes into the hands of the followers of Christ. The supremacy of the Christian inheritance is confirmed by the victory of the apostle Peter over Simon Magus,

---

[46] On the movement of the Palladion and the *tyche* of Constantinople, see further C. Ando, 'The Palladium and the Pentateuch: Towards a Sacred Topography of the Later Roman Empire', *Phoenix*, 55 (2001), 397–404.

[47] Moffatt, 'Record of Public Buildings', 102. When a statue of Julian 'the Apostate' in Constantinople fell down, a cross was erected in its place, but the original destruction was not apparently deliberate. Malalas, *Chronographia*, ed. Thurn, 404 (XVIII.82); trans. Jeffreys et al., *Chronicle*, 284).

[48] On the different categories of *mystikoi* in Malalas, see A.-M. Bernardi, 'Les mystikoi dans la chronique de Jean Malalas' in Beaucamp, ed., *Recherches sur la chronique de Jean Malalas I*, 53–64.

a man capable of powerful magic and who claimed falsely to be Christ (x.32–4),[49] and by the glory of the martyrs.[50] Visions and powers of healing are now held by the Christian heirs of the ancients, just as Christian relics have taken over the roles of older talismans, for it was the Christian God who inspired all such knowledge when he first gave wisdom to Adam and his son Seth (1.1).

Malalas' vision of the Greco-Roman past prefiguring the Christian present is perhaps most explicit in his approach to pagan oracles. Several major pre-Christian figures are said to have recognised the Trinity and predicted the coming of Christ (Hermes Trismegistos (II.5); Orpheus (IV.8–10); Plato (VII.15) and the Pythian oracles at Memphis (III.13) and on the Hellespont (IV.12)). The oracles culminate again with Augustus, who when he asked who his successor would be was informed by the Pythia that 'a Hebrew child ruling as god over the blessed ones bids me abandon this abode and return to Hades' (x.5). This and other oracles are known to have been in circulation in the sixth century, particularly through the collection usually described as the Tübingen Theosophy, and so were certainly not unique to Malalas.[51] But set alongside his wider approach to pagan history and religion throughout his *Chronicle*, the oracles form part of a coherent vision that saw Christianity as the natural continuation of wisdom and beliefs held by the most learned of mankind from the beginning of Creation.

The final religious element that shapes Malalas' conception of his *Chronicle* is perhaps the most important for understanding his original aims. But I will treat this dimension of his thought only briefly, for here we are again indebted to Elizabeth Jeffreys, who in a series of important articles has revealed the significance of Malalas' almost unique

---

[49] For the ancient tradition of Simon Magus, see M. J. Edwards, 'Simon Magus, the Bad Samaritan' in M. J. Edwards and S. Swain, eds., *Portraits: Biographical Representation in the Greek and Latin Literature of the Roman Empire* (Oxford, 1997), 69–91.

[50] Malalas predictably placed particular emphasis on martyrs with Antiochene connections whose cults remained influential in his day, including Ignatios (Malalas, *Chronographia*, ed. Thurn, 208–9 (XI.10); trans. Jeffreys et al., *Chronicle*, 146), Babylas (233–4 (XII.35); trans. Jeffreys et al., *Chronicle*, 165–6), and Kosmas and Damianos (234–5 (XII.36); trans. Jeffreys et al., *Chronicle*, 166–7). On Malalas' use of hagiography and his knowledge of Christian saints and martyrs, see P. Boulhol, 'La geste des saints et l'histoire du monde: À propos des sources hagiographiques de Malalas' in Beaucamp, *Recherches sur la chronique de Jean Malalas I*, 103–16.

[51] On the Theosophy, see further P. F. Beatrice, *Anonymi Monophysitae Theosophia: An Attempt at Reconstruction* (Leiden, 2001).

interpretation of the chronology of the birth and death of Christ.[52] Immediately following the announcement of Christ's birth, placed as we have already seen in the opening section of Book X at the precise centre of the *Chronicle*, Malalas declares that Christ was born in year 5967 from Creation and crucified in year 6000 (X.2). The same calculation is then repeated in a digression within Malalas' account of the years CE 528/9 near the beginning of the reign of Justinian (XVIII.8). Yet in traditional Byzantine Christian chronography, the birth of Christ was placed in the year 5500. According to the principle of chiliasm, Christian world history was organised into blocks of one thousand years that each corresponded to one of the seven days of Creation,[53] and so the year 6000 potentially heralded the Second Coming of Christ. Fundamental to Malalas is his insistence that the year 6000 is already in the past, and so could not be reached either in 491 (the year 6000 in the Alexandrian calendar)[54] or in 528/9, despite the recurring natural disasters of his times. For Elizabeth Jeffreys, Malalas' aim 'was to demonstrate that mankind could live unperturbed by fears of God's "benevolent chastisement" since the millennium in which they were living was that ushered in at the moment of Christ's resurrection, and atonement for man's sins: this, indeed, was his motive for writing the chronicle'.[55]

Jeffreys' argument is highly compelling. The period on either side of AD 500 saw considerable agitation in both Greek and Syriac writers that the year 6000 was approaching,[56] and Malalas must be seen within the context of this wider debate. As Jeffreys has again observed, however, Malalas' own views were highly idiosyncratic. The only roughly contemporary source that appears to share Malalas' conviction that Christ's crucifixion fell in the year 6000 is a fragment from a sermon of Hesychios of Miletus.[57] Hesychios' relationship to Malalas is uncertain and it is equally conceivable

---

[52] For the argument summarised here, see in particular Jeffreys, 'Chronological Structures', 111–20; and E. M. Jeffreys, 'Malalas' Use of the Past' in G. Clarke, ed., *Reading the Past in Late Antiquity* (Canberra, 1990), 121–46, restated in Jeffreys, 'Literary Genre', 519–21.

[53] One thousand years corresponds to a single day in the eyes of God, 'for a thousand years in your sight are like yesterday when it is past, or like a watch in the night' (Psalms 90:4 NRSV).

[54] Malalas' entry for AD 491 has been abridged by the editor of our extant Greek manuscript, but appears to indicate that there was originally another temporal digression here on the question of when six thousand years from Creation would fall. Malalas, *Chronographia* ed. Thurn, 317–18 (XV.16); trans., Jeffreys et al., *Chronicle*, 219.

[55] Jeffreys, 'Malalas' Use of the Past', 137.

[56] See W. Brandes, 'Anastasios O ΔΙΚΟΡΟΣ: Endzeiterwartung und Kaiserkritik in Byzanz um 500 n. Chr.', *BZ*, 90 (1997), 24–63.

[57] The relevant passage is given in L. Dindorf, ed., *Ioannis Malalae Chronographia* (Bonn, 1831), lii–liii.

that Hesychios could have derived his argument from Malalas or conversely that he was Malalas' source.[58] Malalas' emphasis on the year 528/9, on the other hand, is entirely unique. Possibly his temporal digression in the entry for that year was addressed to the Antiochenes, to reassure those who feared that recent calamities, particularly the great earthquake of 526, heralded the coming of the end.[59] Yet no other evidence suggests that this was a major issue at the time,[60] and it is notable that Malalas' highly personalised chronology left no mark on Byzantine millennial debates, despite the apparent popularity of his *Chronicle* for later writers. Here as elsewhere, Malalas' interest in millenarianism reflects the climate of his age, but his approach is very much his own.[61]

All the elements considered in this limited analysis of the religious interests of Malalas and his *Chronicle* have pointed towards the same twin conclusions. Malalas was shaped by the sixth-century world in which he lived. That world was never as black and white as a number of contemporary ecclesiastical writers would like to suggest, never rigidly divided between Chalcedonian and Miaphysite, Christian and pagan. There were divisions, as Malalas too attests, over doctrine, practices and concepts of religious time and space. But Malalas' essential vision is one of continuity rather than conflict, the Christian present emerging from the pagan past that was itself under the providence of the Christian God. Through his construction of that vision, Malalas emerges as a witness to how a reasonably well-read sixth-century man could interpret his world and its history. In many respects he is perhaps more typical than the highly educated elite writers such as Prokopios or the ecclesiastical historians such as Evagrios on whom we so often focus, and he exerted considerable influence on later chroniclers and historians. As Elizabeth Jeffreys has repeatedly emphasised, Malalas offers 'a fascinating example of the Byzantine *mentalité*' of his world.[62]

Yet the *Chronicle* of Malalas is at the same time one of the most deeply idiosyncratic works of Byzantine literature. Some of Malalas' apparent

---

[58] Jeffreys, 'Malalas in Greek', 255, n. 18.
[59] Jeffreys, 'Chronological Structures', 118. This seems more plausible than the other interpretation proposed by Jeffreys (118–19), concerning the date of Easter Sunday in 528.
[60] There is no contemporary support for Croke's claim (Croke, 'Malalas', 12) that Malalas' cosmic chronology 'was considered very important' in the 530s, or that millenarian ideas influenced Justinian and his presentation of his reign (Scott, 'Secret History', 108–9).
[61] The closest parallel to Malalas' contemporary yet idiosyncratic approach is perhaps Kosmas Indikopleustes (Scott, 'Malalas and his Contemporaries', 78–9), although Malalas' *Chronicle* attained a popularity that Kosmas' *Christian Topography* would never achieve.
[62] Jeffreys, 'Beginning of Byzantine Chronography', 525.

eccentricities may reflect his Antiochene and Syriac background, including his interest in pagan oracles and in millenarianism.[63] It has also been argued that Malalas' emphasis on rituals and oracles rather than theology makes him in some sense a representative of sixth-century popular religion, just as his simpler and less classicising style made him more accessible than the ornate rhetoric of Prokopios. But limited attention to doctrine and a knowledge of religion that transcends the narrow canon of patristic Christianity does not necessarily equate to 'popular'. Malalas' interest in the continuity of pagan and Christian history is shared by a number of his elite contemporaries; and while he is not always either a clear or polished writer, he does derive from the educated classes. Even within the elite, moreover, some of Malalas' beliefs appear to remain unique. No other extant author compares to his diverse yet selective spectrum of religious interests. This is perhaps best attested by the millenarian views that may have provided his original motivation, but which, like other peculiarities of his work, were to be ignored by the later writers who otherwise so valued his *Chronicle*. In the field of religious studies, as in other fields of Late Antique and Byzantine history and historiography, Malalas thus remains a puzzle and a challenge. He composed a work that both reflected the fears and convictions of his age and expressed his own at times highly personal beliefs and values. If we are to exploit fully that text as a source for earlier history and as a window into the period in which it was written, we must remain aware of these two at times contradictory elements that characterise the *Chronicle* of Malalas.

Further Reading

The key primary source is: I. Thurn, ed., *Ioannis Malalae. Chronographia* (Berlin, 2000); E. M. Jeffreys, M. J. Jeffreys and R. Scott, eds. and trans., *The Chronicle of John Malalas* (Melbourne, 1986). Studies include: E. M. Jeffreys, with B. Croke and R. Scott, eds., *Studies in John Malalas* (Sydney, 1990); M. Meier, C. Radtki and F. Schulz, eds., *Die Weltchronik des Johannes Malalas: Autor – Werk – Überlieferung* (Stuttgart, 2016).

---

[63] On this question, which merits further analysis but which I have not had the opportunity to examine in detail here, see Croke, 'Malalas', 12–14, and in particular Jeffreys, 'Malalas' World View'.

CHAPTER 10

Oikonomia *in the Hymns of Romanos the Melode*

Johannes Koder

In his role as a poet and creator of hymns or sermons in the form of hymns, which he himself sang or recited, Romanos the Melode (*c.* 485 – after 562) sought above all else to impart the faith.[1] According to popular belief, he authored more than a thousand hymns.[2] Of the approximately ninety hymns transmitted under his name, around sixty should, in the opinion of his twentieth-century editors, be regarded as authentic.[3] Seen from the perspective of literary history, these are to be classified as liturgical hymnography. However, they also reflect the theological disputes of the fifth and sixth centuries. Indeed, Romanos attempted in his hymns to impart the content of these theological issues to the faithful present at the liturgy, albeit often in a somewhat simplified manner. Rather than by means of reading, his audience thus received Romanos' compositions through listening, a means of transmission more typical of liturgical poetry than of any other genre in Byzantine literature. Two factors in particular allowed for an enhanced reception of the hymns' message: the rhythmical and vocal performance of the cantor

---

[1] I would like to thank Leena Mari Peltomaa of Vienna, for her valuable suggestions for improving and expanding this chapter. My gratitude also goes to the anonymous readers for their suggestions. This chapter was translated into English by Jonathan Martin, Judith Ryder and Teresa Shawcross.
[2] See the Synaxar for October 1st, section 3, in H. Delehaye, ed., *Synaxarium Ecclesiae Constantinopolitanae* (Brussels, 1902), 95–184.
[3] Editions: J. Grosdidier de Matons, ed., *Romanos le Mélode. Hymnes*, 5 vols. (Paris, 1964–81), with French translation; P. Maas and C. A. Trypanis, eds., *Sancti Romani melodi cantica: Cantica genuina* (Oxford, 1963) and *Sancti Romani melodi cantica: Cantica dubia* (Berlin, 1970); R. Maisano, ed., *Romano il melode. Cantici*, 2 vols. (Turin, 2002), with Italian translation. See also J. Koder, *Romanos Melodos. Die Hymnen, übersetzt und erläutert*, 2 vols. (Stuttgart, 2005–6), with German translation. In what follows, I use the edition and numbering of Grosdidier de Matons; in the case of the few hymns not included in that edition, I follow the edition and numbering of P. Maas and C. A. Trypanis. In his recent work, J. H. Barkhuizen has translated thirteen hymns into English: J. H. Barkhuizen, *Romanos the Melodist: Poet and Preacher: Introduction with Annotated Translation of Selected Poetic Homilies* (Durbanville, 2012). Of particular relevance are the observations found in his introduction (5–15) concerning the linguistic and literary background of Romanos the Melode.

(*melodos*) reciting from the ambo, and the active involvement of the audience, who sang the refrain.[4]

Romanos paid special attention to the dogmatic teachings regarded as orthodox during the reign of Justinian I, taking heed of the position of the emperor on such matters.[5] Although he himself was not a theologian in the modern sense of the word, his work nevertheless provides evidence of his familiarity with, and promotion of, the prevailing theological positions in Constantinople at the time.[6]

In his *oeuvre* as a whole, Romanos gives central ideological importance to the redemption of humanity as an integral aspect of the Christian doctrine of salvation. God's will to redeem finds its expression in the divine *oikonomia*. Because the notion of *oikonomia* plays such an important role in Romanos' poetry, it forms the focus of this chapter, which begins with those texts in which the word is explicitly used. The term itself, a Greek compound noun, presents difficulties in translation, because of the diversity of its theological significance and application. Its original, pre-Christian meaning is 'management of a household or family', hence: 'husbandry, thrift'. Further meanings include 'arrangement, regulation, plan, administration, stewardship, principles of government' etc.[7] *Oikonomia* develops into a more complex concept in early Christian and early Byzantine ecclesiastical literature. For the purposes of this chapter, the following *lemmata* given by Lampe, supported by numerous textual references, should be especially noted:

---

[4] J. Koder, 'Romanos Melodos und sein Publikum: Zur Einbeziehung und Beeinflussung der Zuhörer durch das Kontakion', *AnzWien*, 134 (1999), 63–94, and Koder, 'Imperial Propaganda in the Kontakia of Romanos the Melode', *DOP*, 62 (2008 [2010]), 275–91.

[5] On this, see P. T. R. Gray, 'The Legacy of Chalcedon: Christological Problems and their Significance' in M. Maas, ed., *The Cambridge Companion to the Age of Justinian* (Cambridge, 2005), 215–38, esp. 227–35; J. van Oort and O. Hesse, eds., *Christentum und Politik in der Alten Kirche* (Leuven, 2009); K.-H. Uthemann, 'Kaiser Justinian als Kirchenpolitiker und Theologe', *Augustinianum*, 39 (1999), 5–83. On Justinian's ecclesiastical policies (until 536): J. Speigl, 'Formula Iustiniani, Kircheneinigung mit kaiserlichen Glaubensbekenntnissen (Cod. Iust. I,1,5–8)', *Ostkirchliche Studien*, 44 (1995), 105–34; H. Leppin, *Justinian: das christliche Experiment* (Stuttgart, 2011), 92–106, 181–91, 293–315.

[6] See J. Koder, 'Positionen der Theologie des Romanos Melodos', *AnzWien*, 143 (2008), 25–56; J. Koder, 'Romanos Melodos' in C.-G. Conticello and V. Conticello, eds., *La théologie byzantine et sa tradition* I/1 (VI–VIII s.) (Turnhout, 2015), 115–96 (with further bibliography).

[7] LSJ, 1204b. A detailed treatment can be found in G. Richter, *Oikonomia: Der Gebrauch des Wortes Oikonomia im Neuen Testament, bei den Kirchenvätern und in der theologischen Literatur bis ins 20. Jahrhundert* (Berlin, 2005), esp. 6–31 on the pseudo-Aristotelian *Oikonomika* and the Septuagint, and 33–48 on the New Testament and the early Christian community.

'dispensation, arrangement, government, adaption of a means to an end, prudent handling of a situation'.[8]

The semantic development of *oikonomia* in Christian theology has long been a central topic in scholarly investigations.[9] This term has been shown from the early patristic period onward to have been used to designate the activity of God and of the Trinity, and of heavenly beings and powers, but also to designate human activity, particularly that of the holders of ecclesiastic office. For the purposes of this chapter, two connotations of *oikonomia* need to be emphasised. The first of these was associated with the manner in which God works upon his creation, specifically through his son's relationship to humanity: Christ's incarnation, his death on the cross, and his resurrection. This exegetical approach to the doctrine of salvation finds its fullest expression in the teachings of Irenaeus of Lyons, which have been studied in detail by Gerhard Richter.[10] Of special interest for this chapter is the role in divine *oikonomia* that Irenaeus – as early as the second century – attributes to the Virgin Mary. In the context of Christ's death on the cross, Irenaeus depicts the Mother of God as the 'paraclete', who, as a married virgin, counteracts through her 'virgin obedience' (*parthenike hypakoe*) to God the 'virgin disobedience' (*parthenike parakoe*) of that other married virgin, Eve.[11] Her preeminent role is then confirmed in Proklos' famous Marian sermon, in which the author speaks of the connection between Eve ('the door of sin') and Mary ('the gate of salvation').[12] In the same vein,

---

[8] G. W. H. Lampe, *A Patristic Greek Lexicon* (Oxford, 1961), 940b–43a, C & D; no addition to these meanings in E. Trapp, W. Hörandner, J. Diethart et al., *Lexikon zur byzantinischen Gräzität, besonders des 9.-12. Jahrhunderts* (Vienna, 1994–2011), 1108a. A detailed presentation of the semantic development of the term in the period under consideration is given in H. Thurn's thesis, *Oikonomia von der frühbyzantinischen Zeit bis zum Bilderstreit: semantologische Untersuchungen zur Wortfamilie* (Munich, 1961).

[9] Of seminal importance in this regard: Richter, *Oikonomia*, and F. Schuppe, *Die pastorale Herausforderung: Orthodoxes Leben zwischen Akribeia und Oikonomia: theologische Grundlagen, Praxis und ökumenische Perspektiven* (Würzburg, 2006). See further H. Karpp, *Textbuch zur altkirchlichen Christologie: Theologia und Oikonomia* (Neukirchen–Vluyn, 1972); esp. on Gregory of Nyssa: R. J. Kees, *Die Lehre von der oikonomia Gottes in der Oratio catechetica Gregors von Nyssa* (Leiden, 1995).

[10] Richter, *Oikonomia*, 116–35.

[11] τοῦ Κυρίου . . . ἀνακεφαλαίωσιν τῆς ἐν τῷ ξύλῳ γενομένης παρακοῆς διὰ τῆς ἐν τῷ ξύλῳ ὑπακοῆς ποιησαμένου, καὶ τῆς ἐξαπατήσεως ἐκείνης λυθείσης ἣν ἐξηπατήθη κακῶς ἡ ὕπανδρος παρθένος Εὔα διὰ τῆς ἀληθείας ἣν εὐηγγελίσθη καλῶς ὑπὸ τοῦ ἀγγέλου ἡ ὕπανδρος παρθένος Μαρία. L. Doutreleau, B. C. Mercier and A. Rousseau, eds., *Irénée de Lyon. Contre les hérésies, livre 5* (Paris, 1969), vol. II, 249–51 (5.19.1).

[12] καὶ πύλην σωτηρίας ὁ τεχθεὶς τὴν πάλαι τῆς ἁμαρτίας ἔδειξεν θύραν ὅπου γὰρ ὁ ὄφις διὰ τῆς παρακοῆς τὸν ἰὸν ἐνέχεεν, ἐκεῖ ὁ λόγος διὰ τῆς ἀκοῆς εἰσελθὼν τὸν ναὸν ἐζωοπλάστησεν. E. Schwartz, ed., *Acta conciliorum oecumenicorum* (Strasbourg, 1914), 103 (1.1.1), also 107; compare to L. M. Peltomaa, 'Die berühmteste Marien-Predigt der Antike: Zur chronologischen und mariologischen Einordnung der Predigt des Proklos', *JÖB*, 54 (2004), 77–96, and Peltomaa, 'Towards the Origins of the History of the Cult of Mary', *StP*, 40 (2006), 75–86.

in the *Akathistos Hymn* Mary is greeted as the 'restoration of the fallen Adam' and 'redemption of the tears of Eve'.[13]

Rather than show any uniform linear semantic development, these writings of the various Church Fathers emphasize, to varying degrees, the two opposing terms *theologia* and *oikonomia*.[14] While the Cappadocian Fathers do not make any connection between *theologia* (i.e. their explanation of the relationship between the divine persons of the Trinity) and God's *oikonomia* (the way in which God works in the world in the concrete form of his son),[15] John Chrysostom uses the two terms frequently and sees no need for an explanation of their dogmatic significance, perhaps because he regards it as self-evident. He relates Christ's *oikonomia* principally to Christ's 'earthly life, in which humility is emphasised'.[16] He also identifies it 'in the actions of the apostles', explaining it as 'the close engagement and care which becomes, as *synkatabasis*, the central theme in ecclesiastical *oikonomia*'.[17] Cyril of Alexandria (378–444), a theologian in the tradition of the Cappadocians, is noteworthy because he strictly adheres to the terminology of the 'incarnation' (*sarkosis, sarx*) of the *logos*, and avoids speaking of Christ as 'human' (*anthropos*).[18] Romanos, in contrast, uses both expressions.[19] Cyril differs from earlier writers, however, in that he defines 'becoming flesh' as *henosis* or *henosis oikonomike*, a definition subsequently adopted by other fifth-century

---

[13] χαῖρε, τοῦ πεσόντος Ἀδὰμ ἡ ἀνάκλησις·/ χαῖρε, τῶν δακρύων τῆς Εὔας ἡ λύτρωσις, *Akathistos Hymnos*, in C. A. Trypanis, ed., *Fourteen Early Byzantine Cantica* (Vienna, 1968), 30 (1.8–9). See also Romanos, *Hymns*, ed. Grosdidier de Matons, vol. II, 90–2, 100 and 110 (XI.3, 10 and 18); vol. IV, 450 (XLI.20).

[14] Richter, *Oikonomia*, 215ff., esp. 311, which summarises the development of the meaning of the two terms; also 450–2.

[15] Ibid., 323–35.

[16] Ibid., 358. See also T. N. Zeses, Ἄνθρωπος και κόσμος εν τη οικονομία του θεού κατά τον ιερόν Χρυσόστομον (Thessalonike, 1971).

[17] Richter, *Oikonomia*, 359.

[18] For more on this: Richter, *Oikonomia*, 359–425, esp. the summary: 417ff. On *oikonomia* 'suited to the flesh', or 'suited to humanity' in Markellos of Ankyra, who lived only a few generations earlier, see the summary in A. Grillmeier, *Jesus der Christus im Glauben der Kirche*, vol. I, *Von der Apostolischen Zeit bis zum Konzil von Chalcedon* (Vienna, 1979), 422ff.

[19]
Χριστὸς γὰρ ἐκ Παρθένου σωματοῦται ὡς ἄνθρωπος,
ὃς καὶ τὸν Ἀδὰμ ἀνακαλέσας εἷλε τὴν ἀρὰν ἐκ τῆς παρθένου. (Romanos, *Hymns*, ed. Grosdidier de Matons, vol. II, 154 (XIII.23.3–4)).
Μήτις οὖν τοῦ Χριστοῦ τὴν πλευρὰν εἴπῃ ψιλοῦ ἀνθρώπου
ἄνθρωπος γὰρ ὁ Χριστὸς καὶ Θεὸς ἦν. (Ibid., vol. IV, 226 (XXXVI.19.1–2)).
Τὸν αὐτὸν οὖν Χριστὸν ἐπιστάμεθα υἱὸν ἕνα,
ἅμα Θεόν τε καὶ ἄνθρωπον,
τῇ ἀνάρχῳ μὲν φύσει ἀθάνατον,
ὑπομείναντα δὲ θάνατον τῇ σαρκί. (Ibid., 504 (XLIII.4.1–3)).
See also below, ibid., 502 and 520 (XLIII.1 and 16); vol. v, 138 (XLVIII.Pro.1).

theological authors.[20] Of these, Theodoret of Cyrrhus (c. 393–466) should be singled out as an innovator: Theodoret not only connects *oikonomia* with the divine plan of salvation, he also regards it as having already existed *before* the Creation, and therefore as the foundation of the Creation itself.[21]

In addition to having these connotations, the word *oikonomia* is employed by clerics and monks in Byzantine theological texts in opposition to *akribeia* ('exactness', 'discipline', 'precision').[22] Florian Schuppe shows that evidence of this meaning is attested as early as the third and fourth centuries. Patristic texts testify to this use of *oikonomia* in the sense of departure from the normal treatment of the weak that is associated with *akribeia*. From the fifth century at the latest, the term begins to denote limited and exceptional accommodation of particular persons who have fallen away from the Church, in cases where such an accommodation could serve the well-being of the Church as a whole.[23] This meaning of *oikonomia* is increasingly obvious in the context of monastic penitential practices, taking the meaning of a loving relaxation of monastic discipline (*synkatabasis*) that enables the return of someone who has gone astray; this easing up imitates God's love of humanity (*philanthropia*).[24] This second connotation of *oikonomia* is only of minor significance for Romanos.[25] The Justinianic Code itself does not yet use the term *oikonomia* in this meaning, although the expressions *epieikeia* and *philanthropia* are to be found,[26] which could be regarded as corresponding to *oikonomia* in imperial and ecclesiastical legal terminology.[27]

---

[20] For example, Theodoret of Cyrrhus, '*Quaestiones et responsiones ad orthodoxos*' in J. C. T. Otto, ed. *Corpus Apologetarum Christianorum* (Jena, 1880), III/IV, 2–3 (1.7) and 22–3 (17.7), and Justinian, 'Edictum rectae fidei' in R. Albertella, M. Amelotti, L. Migliardi and E. Schwartz, eds., *Drei dogmatische Schriften Iustinians*, second edition, reprinted as *Legum Iustiniani imperatoris vocabularium* (Milan, 1973), 146; see Richter, *Oikonomia*, 377–81 and 419–20.

[21] Richter, *Oikonomia*, 433–5; see P. B. Clayton, Jr., *The Christology of Theodoret of Cyrus: Antiochene Christology from the Council of Ephesus (431) to the Council of Chalcedon (451)* (Oxford, 2007). On the attitude of Ephraim the Syrian (c. 300–73) towards the concept of the economy of salvation, see Grillmeier, *Jesus der Christus*, 519–27.

[22] LSJ, 55a; less helpful is Lampe, *Patristic Greek Lexicon*, 64b.

[23] Schuppe, *Pastorale Herausforderung*, 111ff., esp. 140–1.   [24] Ibid., 142.

[25] The term *akribeia* occurs only once (and its appearance is not certain, on textual grounds), in the Second Hymn to the Forty Martyrs, where the following is said (Maas and Trypanis, eds., *Cantica genuina* 496 (58.2.6)): οὗτοι ἀμφιβόλων †ἀκριβείας διδάσκαλοι†, οὗτοι νοσοῦντας ἀεὶ ἰῶνται. J. Grosdidier de Matons, *Romanos le Mélode et les origines de la poésie religieuse à Byzance* (Paris, 1977), 241–2, considers this hymn authentic, although it should be observed that his assessment of the authenticity of the hagiographical hymns (217–42) is based primarily on form rather than content.

[26] R. Schoell and G. Kroll, eds., *Justinian, Novellae, in Corpus Iuris Civilis*, vol. III (Berlin, 1954), 711–14 (CXLV). Prooimion et passim: 'forbearance, gentleness' and 'love towards men', 'clemency, mercy'. See Lampe, *Patristic Greek Lexicon*, 523a and 1475b–6b.

[27] As in Richter, *Oikonomia*, 515–23. See also H. S. Alivizatos, *Die Oikonomia: Die Oikonomia nach dem kanonischen Recht der Orthodoxen Kirche* (Frankfurt, 1998).

An attempt to find an English equivalent for Romanos' use of the term *oikonomia* that is uniform and yet does justice to the various contexts in which it appears in his hymns leads to a compromise translation as 'plan of salvation'.[28] When Romanos uses the word *oikonomia* explicitly, he does so with an emphasis on its first group of associative meanings. This occurs in the following hymns: 'On the Samaritan Woman' (H.19), the first and fourth hymns 'On the Resurrection' (H.40 and 43), 'On the Ascension' (H.48), 'On Earthquakes and Fires' (H. 54) and 'On the Beheading of the Forerunner' (H. 38M.-Tr.).[29] Romanos foregrounds Christ, the second person of the Holy Trinity, in his hymns by means of the ever-present idea of *oikonomia* as 'plan of salvation', an understanding which he sometimes states expressly, sometimes merely implies.[30] This may be explained by the fact that, during Romanos' lifetime, Christological, rather than the earlier Trinitarian, themes dominated theological discussion. In Romanos, therefore, the dominant second divine person often speaks expressly in the name of the Trinity, and by doing so, he expresses the salvific activity of the Trinity as a whole, which is made manifest in the activity of Jesus Christ in the here and now.

This is clearly stated in the prooimion and the first four verses of the fourth hymn 'On the Resurrection' (H.43), which include Romanos' lengthiest exposition of dogma.[31] At the beginning, the faithful ('we') confess that they have found eternal life in Christ's voluntary death on the cross. This is also the central theme of the hymn:

> In your free death we found eternal life,
> almighty, sole God of all things!
> For through your holy awakening
> you summoned all things back, merciful one.[32]

---

[28] For the discussion of the full range of meaning, see: Richter, *Oikonomia*, 684ff.

[29] To this can be added the (probably falsely attributed to Romanos) H.80, 'On the Martyr Stephen', Maas and Trypanis, eds., *Cantica dubia* 143 (80.12.4–5):

> παρέστησας Χριστοῦ πᾶσαν οἰκονομίαν
> ἐν σώματι αὐτὸν ἄνω ἀναληφθέντα.

> You bore witness to Christ's entire plan of salvation,
> how he was received bodily above.

[30] In a number of hymns based on the Old Testament, however, a certain reticence is observable in this respect.

[31] See the commentary of Grosdidier de Matons, *Romanos le Mélode. Hymnes*, vol. IV, 501ff.

[32]
> Τὸν σὸν ἑκούσιον θάνατον ζωὴν ἀθάνατον εὕρομεν,
> παντοδύναμε καὶ μόνε τῶν ὅλων Θεέ
> σὺ γὰρ ἐν τῇ σεπτῇ σου ἐγέρσει
> πάντας ἀνεκαλέσω, οἰκτίρμων. (Romanos, *Hymnes*, ed. Grosdidier de Matons, vol. IV, 500 (XLIII.Pr.1–4)).

The faithful recognise (H.43.1) the ineffability and the incomprehensibility of the mystery of *oikonomia*, and that the saviour 'remains consubstantial with the Father and with us'. They recognise him as 'one from both', who *remained what he was and became what he was not*, having taken flesh from the immaculate Virgin. Truly both God and man – rather than merely these in appearance – he, one and the same, took suffering upon himself in his *oikonomia*:

> O our saviour, the mystery of your plan of salvation,
> is ineffable and incomprehensible...
> Both God and Man in truth, not in fantasy,
> one and the same, you took suffering upon yourself,
>   according to the plan of salvation
> in order to give freedom from suffering to mortals.[33]

Romanos' dogmatic position as expressed in the first four stanzas of H.43 corresponds to the edicts of Emperor Justinian published in 533 and 551.[34] For this reason, it has been assumed that the poem dates to shortly after 551 – that is to say, to the period around the Council of Constantinople of 553.[35] Later in the poem – as in the earlier hymn 'On the Presentation in the Temple'[36] –

---

[33] Τὸ μυστήριον τῆς σῆς οἰκονομίας, ὦ σωτὴρ ἡμῶν, ἄφραστόν ἐστιν, ἀκατάληπτον...
καὶ Θεὸς ὢν ἀληθείᾳ καὶ ἄνθρωπος οὐ φαντασίᾳ
εἷς ὁ αὐτὸς κατεδέξω τὸ πάθος οἰκονομίᾳ,
ἵνα τῶν παθῶν δώσῃς τοῖς βροτοῖς ἐλευθερίαν. (Romanos, *Hymnes*, ed. Grosdidier de Matons, vol. IV, 502 (XLIII.1.1–2, 7–9))

[34] L. Dindorf, L. M. and M. Whitby, eds. and trans., *Chronicon Paschale* (Liverpool, 1989), 635ff. Details and further evidence can be found in Maisano, *Cantici*, vol. I, 577–9, notes 4–10. See Uthemann, 'Kaiser Justinian', 34ff.

[35] Grosdidier de Matons, *Romanos, origines de la poésie religieuse*, 243. There are striking parallels with the Justinianic hymn 'The Only-Begotten Son', composed in 535–6, i.e. immediately following the final separation from the Miaphysites. On this, see Uthemann, 'Kaiser Justinian', 38–48, edition in W. Christ and M. Paranikas, *Anthologia Graeca carminum Christianorum* (Leipzig, 1871), 52. Lines 1–5 of the Justinianic hymn in particular bear comparison with Romanos, *Hymnes*, ed. Grosdidier de Matons, vol. IV, 500–41 (XLIII), esp. with stanzas 1 and 3.

[36] The feast of the *hypapante*, or 'meeting', celebrated forty days after the birth of Christ, when the Holy Family encountered Symeon in the Temple. The elderly Symeon spoke these words to Mary (Romanos, *Hymnes*, ed. Grosdidier de Matons, vol. II, 188–90 (XIV.12.5–9)):

τὸν σταυρούμενον ἄλλοι Θεὸν μὲν κηρύξουσιν, ἄλλοι δὲ πάλιν ἄνθρωπον,
καὶ ἀσεβείας καὶ εὐσεβείας τὰ δόγματα κινοῦνται·
καὶ οὐράνιόν τινες μὲν ὑποπτεύσουσι τὸ σῶμα,
ἄλλοι φαντασίαν· ἕτεροι δὲ πάλιν ἐκ σοῦ τὴν σάρκα ἄψυχον
καὶ ἕτεροι ἔμψυχον...

Some will proclaim the Crucified One as God, others as man.
The teachings of impiety and of piety will come into conflict.
Some will hold his body to be heavenly, others an illusion.
Others again that he received flesh without a soul from you,
and others (flesh) with a soul.

Romanos refutes heretics who interpret Paul incorrectly,[37] claiming that Christ did not take on flesh from his mother: 'In the manner of what is heavenly, they claim, / so too are all heavenly things.'[38] This corresponds to the accusation that the heretics have denied the 'true incarnation of the divine Logos from the holy ever-virgin mother of God Mary',[39] an accusation that Justinian levelled at Eutyches (CJ I 1.6.8), and, more generally, at the 'enemies of the truth', in 533; he repeated it more strongly in the *Edictum rectae fidei* of 551.[40] Justinian's edict reproaches those who had strayed from the true faith because they had excluded, even rejected, *oikonomia*, and denied the incarnation.[41]

The fourth hymn 'On the Resurrection' makes it clear that Romanos' Christology is based fundamentally on the concept of divine *oikonomia*.[42] Further evidence of this can be found in all his Christological hymns whose subject-matter are the Crucifixion, the Descent into Hades and the Resurrection. The idea is particularly prominent in the hymn 'On the Triumph of the Cross' (H.38), although it is not made explicit. Even his first hymn 'On the Resurrection', which may have been composed as early as 526, deals with the idea of *oikonomia*. In this hymn, the 'other' Mary explains gently to the apostles Peter and John why it was not they but the women at the tomb who were first permitted to learn of the resurrection:

---

[37] 'As was the man of dust, so are those who are of the dust; and as is the man of heaven, so are those who are of the heaven.' 1 Corinthians 15:48. Translation, RSV.

[38] Οἷος γάρ, φησίν, ἔστιν ὁ ἐπουράνιος, / τοιοῦτοί εἰσιν οἱ ἐπουράνιοι πάντες (Romanos, *Hymnes*, ed. Grosdidier de Matons, vol. IV, 520 (XLIII.16.4–5)).

[39] τὴν ἐκ τῆς ἁγίας ἀειπαρθένου θεοτόκου Μαρίας ἀληθινὴν σάρκωσιν τοῦ θεοῦ λόγου, B. W. Frier, S. Connolly, S. Corcoran et al., eds., *The Codex of Justinian: A New Annotated Translation*, trans. F. H. Blume (Cambridge, 2016), vol. I, 28–9 (1.1.7.11).

[40] ἐπειδὴ δὲ καὶ ἡ ἐν ἀνθρωπότητι τελειότης καὶ τῆς καθ' ἡμᾶς οὐσίας ἡ δήλωσις εἰσκεκόμισται διὰ τοῦ λέγειν 'σεσαρκωμένην', παυσάσθωσαν καλαμίνην ῥάβδον ἑαυτοῖς ὑποστήσαντες. τοῦ γὰρ ἐκβάλλοντος τὴν οἰκονομίαν καὶ ἀρνουμένου τὴν σάρκωσιν ἦν τὸ ἐγκαλεῖσθαι δικαίως, ἀφαιρουμένου τὸν υἱὸν τῆς τελείας ἀνθρωπότητος. Justinian, *Edictum rectae fidei*, 136 (78).27–33. See Grosdidier de Matons, *Romanos le Mélode. Hymnes*, vol. IV, 520–1 (n. 1). In the second hymn 'On the Epiphany', Romanos returns to this theme (*Hymnes*, ed. Grosdidier de Matons, vol. II, 280–2 (XVII.9)): οὐκ οὐράνιον σῶμα), referring indirectly, through his choice of words, to the 'Phantasists' (οὐ φανταζόμεθα ὡς πολλοί) and Docetists (ὁ δοκῶν γὰρ εἰδέναι) as enemies of the faith. The former denied that Christ's body was created, and were often associated with Arians by their opponents. A range of different groups can be brought together under the term 'docetist'; what they have in common is that, in part influenced by dualism, they regard the incarnation and suffering of the Lord as only appearing to have taken place.

[41] The terms σάρκωσις and σεσαρκωμένη are found in Justinian only in the *Contra monophysitas*, in Albertella, Amelotti, Migliardi and Schwartz), eds., *Drei dogmatische Schriften Iustinians*, second edition, 6–78, and in *Edictum rectae fidei*, 130–68, esp. 136.

[42] Grosdidier de Matons, *Romanos, origines de la poésie réligieuse*, 263–4, 271–7; A. de Halleux, 'Hellénisme et syrianité de Romanos le Mélode: A propos d'un ouvrage récent', *RHE*, 73 (1978), 632–41, esp. 638; see also A. Korakides, Ἡ περὶ τοῦ λόγου θεολογία τῶν κοντακίων Ῥωμανοῦ τοῦ Μελωδοῦ (Athens, 1973).

> You initiates of the Lord, truly passionate lovers!
> It is not as you suspect,
> so persevere and do not lose heart!
> What happened was part of the divine plan of salvation,
> by which the women, who were the first to fall,
> should be the first to see the Resurrected One.[43]

The 'Hymn on the Ascension' (*analepsis*) is another instance of the use of the term *oikonomia*. As in the case of the fourth hymn 'On the Resurrection', this hymn too begins with a programmatic prayer:

> You have completed your plan of salvation for us
> and united the things of the earth with the things of heaven.
> You have been raised to glory,[44] Christ, God,
> but in no wise through separation; rather, you remain,
> calling to those who love you:
> I am with you, and no one is against you![45]

This passage emphasises that *oikonomia* is the basis of the union between the heavenly and earthly, as it was earlier during the incarnation and is now during the ascension (*analepsis*). Later in the text, *oikonomia* is connected specifically with the birth of Christ from the Virgin:

> He rules over the angels, and through the angels,
> He who came from the Virgin proclaims his loving plan of salvation.[46]

---

[43] Μύσται τοῦ Κυρίου καὶ ὄντως θερμοὶ ἐρασταί,
μὴ ὡς ὑπολαμβάνητε,
ἀλλ' ὑπομείνατε, μὴ ἀθυμεῖτε
τὸ γὰρ γενόμενον οἰκονομία ἦν
ἵνα αἱ γυναῖκες ὡς πρῶται πεσοῦσαι
ἴδωσι πρῶται τὸν ἀναστάντα. (Romanos, *Hymnes*, ed. Grosdidier de Matons, vol. ιν, 490 (XL.6.6–11))

[44] See the hymn to Christ in 1 Tim. 3:16.

[45] Τὴν ὑπὲρ ἡμῶν πληρώσας οἰκονομίαν
καὶ τὰ ἐπὶ γῆς ἑνώσας τοῖς οὐρανίοις
ἀνελήφθης ἐν δόξῃ, Χριστὲ ὁ Θεός,
οὐδαμόθεν χωριζόμενος, ἀλλὰ μένων ἀδιάστατος
καὶ βοῶν τοῖς ἀγαπῶσί σε
Ἐγώ εἰμι μεθ' ὑμῶν καὶ οὐδεὶς καθ' ὑμῶν. (Romanos, *Hymnes*, ed. Grosdidier de Matons, vol. v, 138 (XLVIII.Pro.1))

[46] ἀγγέλων δεσπόζει καὶ δι' ἀγγέλων γνωρίζει / τὰς φιλανθρώπους οἰκονομίας ὁ ἀνατείλας ἐκ τῆς παρθένου (Ibid., 164 (XLVIII.15.7–8)). The connection of 'loving *oikonomia*' (literally, 'philanthropic') with Christ's birth from the virgin Mary can also be found in Gregory of Nazianzos, *Apologetica*, PG 35.433A: καὶ γέγονε καινὸν μυστήριον ἡ περὶ τὸν πεσόντα δι' ἀπείθειαν ἐκ φιλανθρωπίας οἰκονομία. Διὰ τοῦτο γέννησις καὶ Παρθένος· διὰ τοῦτο φάτνη καὶ Βηθλεέμ …

This expression corresponds to an interesting sequence in the hymn 'On the Samaritan Woman', which was recited on the fourth Sunday after Easter – that is, ten days before the Ascension of Christ: 'They found him in conversation with the woman, he who had come and had been born on earth from the Virgin, in accordance with the plan of salvation.'[47] In this text, Romanos relates his understanding of *oikonomia* to the idea of the integration of the *Theotokos* into the plan of salvation, which had become particularly prominent since the Council of Ephesus (431).[48] It is unsurprising that, in Romanos' conceptualisation of salvation, John the Baptist is assigned a key role alongside Mary. It is his task, as the 'one who comes before' (*prodromos*, 'forerunner'), to proclaim after his death the imminence of salvation to those who have been waiting in the underworld since the fall and the expulsion from paradise. This proclamation can be read in the hymn 'On the Decapitation of the Forerunner', the text whose content marks the transition from the Old to the New Covenant: 'The awe-inspiring beheading of the forerunner was in accordance with the divine plan of salvation, so that even to those in Hades he might preach the coming of the Saviour.'[49]

From these examples, we may deduce that the first meaning of *oikonomia* – God's will to save humans – takes obvious precedence in the hymns. Indeed, Romanos often expresses God's will using the lexical field of *boule* (*boulema*, *boulesis*, *boulomai*), which combines the meanings 'deliberation', 'plan', 'counsel', 'purpose', 'decision' and 'will'.[50] This becomes particularly clear in the second 'Christmas Hymn', in which Romanos gives the Mother of God a prominent intercessory role. The relevant stanzas are presented as a dialogue between Mary and her newborn child, to whom she pleads for the salvation of Adam and Eve and their descendants:

---

[47] συνόμιλον εὗρον τῷ γυναίῳ τὸν ἐλθόντα
καὶ τεχθέντα ἐκ παρθένου ἐπὶ γῆς οἰκονομίᾳ. (Ibid., vol. II, 350 (XIX.21.2–3)).
[48] On Mariology in Romanos, see F. Migliori, 'La figura di Maria Vergine e Madre di Dio negli Inni di Romano il Melode', *Theotokos*, 15 (2007), 37–76.
[49] Ἡ τοῦ Προδρόμου ἔνδοξος ἀποτομὴ οἰκονομία γέγονέ τις θεϊκή, / ἵνα καὶ τοῖς ἐν Ἅιδῃ τοῦ σωτῆρος κηρύξῃ τὴν ἔλευσιν (Romanos, *Hymnes*, eds. Maas and Trypanis, vol. I, *Cantica genuina*, 294 (2Pr.1–2)). This report corresponds to what is said about the Prophet John, τὸ τέλος τῶν προφητῶν, in chapter 2f. of the *Descensus Christi ad inferos* in the *Acts of Pilate*, ed. C. V. Tischendorf, *Evangelia apocrypha*, second edition (Leipzig, 1876), 324–6.
[50] See, Lampe, *Patristic Greek Lexicon*, 302a–3b. Romanos uses the noun *thelema* less frequently, and almost always in connection with human actions, including their negative aspects (620b–21a); this is the case with an internal monologue in the 'Second Hymn to the Ten Virgins', into which a dialogue between Christ and his soul is embedded (Romanos, *Hymnes*, ed. Grosdidier de Matons, vol. V, 314–16 (LI.13)).

When the unblemished one brought these prayers
before God who lay in the manger, he granted them forthwith.
He explained in the following way:
'O mother, both for your sake and through you I save them.
Had I not wished to save them, I would not have dwelt in you,
would not have shone from you; nor would you have heard "my mother"!'[51]

In response to Christ's words regarding the perfection of his incarnation, Mary reiterates:

What you are going to accomplish, that I wish now to learn.
Do not hide from me the plan you have had from eternity![52]

In response, the Lord prophesies his death on the cross and resurrection:

I am defeated by the love which I have for mankind...
Hanging on the cross, you will weep [for me] as one dead,
but you will greet me when I rise,
O full of grace![53]

Christ responds in turn:

All these things will happen to me according to my will;
and the cause of all these things will be the favourable disposition
which from of old until this day
I have, as God, shown towards humans, seeking to save them.[54]

---

[51]   Ὡς δὲ τοιαύτας δεήσεις προσήγαγεν ἡ ἄμωμος
Θεῷ κειμένῳ ἐν φάτνῃ, λαβὼν εὐθὺς ὑπέγραφεν
ἑρμηνεύων τὰ ἐσχάτως, φησίν
Ὦ μῆτερ, καὶ διὰ σὲ καὶ διὰ σοῦ σῴζω αὐτούς.
Εἰ μὴ σῶσαι τούτους ἠθέλησα, οὐκ ἂν ἐν σοὶ ᾤκησα,
οὐκ ἂν ἐκ σοῦ ἔλαμψα, οὐκ ἂν μήτηρ μου ἤκουσας.
(Romanos, *Hymnes*, ed. Grosdidier de Matons,
vol. II, 104 (XI.13.1–6))

This is an interpretation of John 10:7ff., in which Isaiah 7:2 is cited. On the unusual dialogue form included in the internal monologue, see H. Hunger, 'Das "Enthymem" in der liturgischen Dichtung des frühen Byzanz' in T. Schirren and G. Ueding, eds., *Topik und Rhetorik* (Tübingen, 2000), 93–101.

[52]   Ὃ μέλλεις τελεῖν τί ἐστι θέλω νῦν μαθεῖν
μὴ κρύψῃς ἐμοὶ τὴν ἀπ' αἰῶνός σου βουλήν.
(Romanos, *Hymnes*, ed. Grosdidier de Matons,
vol. II, 106 (XI.15.7–8))

[53]   Νικῶμαι διὰ τὸν πόθον ὃν ἔχω πρὸς τὸν ἄνθρωπον...
κρεμάμενον ἐν σταυρῷ καὶ δακρύσεις ὡς θανόντα,
ἀλλ' ἀσπάσει με ἀναστάντα, ἡ κεχαριτωμένη.
(Ibid., 108 (XI.16.1, 9–11))

[54]   Ὅλων δὲ τούτων ἐν πείρᾳ βουλήσει μου γενήσομαι,
καὶ πάντων τούτων αἰτία διάθεσις γενήσεται
ἣν ἐκ πάλαι ἕως ἄρτι
πρὸς τοὺς ἀνθρώπους ἐπεδειξάμην ὡς Θεός, σῶσαι ζητῶν.
(Ibid., 108 (XI.17.1–4))

In this way, Romanos understands the plan for the salvation of humanity to have been a part of the plan of creation from the very beginning; the process of salvation is completed in the incarnation of Christ, the second divine person of the Trinity. The plan of salvation is an integral element of Romanos' hymns even when he does not use the term *oikonomia* to explicitly refer to this idea.[55]

It would appear from this that the second patristic usage of *oikonomia*, as a term placed in opposition to *akribeia*, is relatively unimportant for Romanos. Indeed, this meaning of *oikonomia* is barely mentioned or can be identified only indirectly in his hymns.[56] At this point, however, the hymn 'On Earthquakes and Fires' must be discussed, for it includes both meanings of *oikonomia* mentioned at the beginning of this chapter. In this poem, Romanos attempts to situate a historically documented list of catastrophes within God's plan of salvation, drawing clear parallels between, as well as harmonising, divine and imperial power.[57] The hymn was composed on the occasion of the rebuilding of St Sophia in Constantinople, which had been destroyed by fire during the Nika Riots of 532. The new church was consecrated on 27 December 537.

At the beginning of the poem, Romanos elucidates the ways in which God, as a healing physician, seeks lovingly to bring sinners to repentance, but at the same time requires a willing and receptive disposition from them:

> He, the good ruler, gives to all
> great gifts of grace;
> But he wants those gifts to be requested, in order to accustom
> his servants to bring their requests to him, the ruler.[58]

---

[55] Similar examples can be found in the hymns 'On the Holy Lights' (ibid., vol. II, 238 (XVI.2)), 'On the Marriage at Cana' (vol. II, 314 (XVIII.15)), 'On the Lepers' (vol. II, 362 (XX.1)), 'On the Suffering of the Lord' (vol. IV, 180 (XXXV.14) and 222 (XXXVI.16)), 'On the Great Canon' (vol. IV, 260 (XXXVII.23)) and 'On the Resurrection' (vol. IV, 514–16 (XLIII.12)).

[56] The second connotation of *oikonomia* is indirectly implied only in the 'Hymn to the Prophet Elijah', in which Romanos describes the 're-education' of Elijah, who is stubbornly insistent on the punishment of sinners, but is brought by God from *akribeia* to *oikonomia* when God sends the hungry prophet to the widow in Sarephtha, who is starving together with her children, to ask her for food. When the prophet then witnesses the death of the widow's son, he relents (thereby giving *oikonomia* precedence over *akribeia*), praying to God (ibid., vol. I, 334 (VII.26.3–8)).

[57] On the content of this, see J. Koder, 'Climatic Change in the Fifth and Sixth Centuries?' in P. Allen and E. M. Jeffreys, eds., *The Sixth Century: End or Beginning?* (Brisbane, 1996), 270–85.

[58]
> Πᾶσι μὲν δωρεῖται ὡς δεσπότης ἀγαθὸς
> μεγάλα τὰ χαρίσματα
> θέλει δὲ αἰτεῖσθαι τὰς χάριτας ἵνα συνεθίσῃ
> τοὺς οἰκέτας τοῦ προσφέρειν τὴν δέησιν τούτῳ ὡς δεσπότῃ.
> (Romanos, *Hymnes*, ed. Grosdidier de Matons,
> vol. V, 472 (LIV.2.3–6))

Romanos next refers to an event in the Old Testament as an example of God's plan and design – the punishment of the Israelites for their worship of the Golden Calf while Moses was receiving the Ten Commandments (H.54.3–4: Exodus 32) – and then he adds a further example from the New Testament:

> It was certainly also in accordance with the plan of salvation,
> what the Canaanite woman experienced:
> that the Creator refused to heal her daughter.
> Inwardly the Lord is loving; outwardly he is angry.[59]

After these examples from the Old and New Testaments, the hymn of repentance continues by listing further attempts by God to educate humankind through catastrophe, including the Nika Riots, which resulted in countless dead and the burning of St Sophia, at which point, however, God's mercy prevails. Here, Romanos does not use the word *oikonomia* since the point does not need to be laboured further:

> Those who feared God stretched out their hands to him
> pleading for mercy from him
> and an end to the evils.
> With them, as is fitting, the emperor also prayed ...
> When God heard the voice of those who cried out and of the emperors,
> he granted the city his loving mercies.[60]

Justinian and Theodora began immediately to rebuild the new church of St Sophia, and Justinian is said to have exclaimed on the occasion of

---

[59] Since the text of Codex P, ἐπείγετο, does not seem to make sense in this context, the current translation is based on the reading of Grosdidier de Matons, who suggests a more more plausable ἀπείπετο, Grosdidier de Matons, *Romanos le Mélode. Hymnes*, vol. v, 476, app. crit. and n. 1:

> Ἄγαν ἦν οἰκονομικὸν
> καὶ τὸ τῆς Χαναναίας,
> ὅτιπερ θεραπεύειν
> ἀπείπετο ὁ κτίστης τὴν θυγατέρα τὴν αὐτῆς· [Matthew 15:21–8] ...
> Ἔνδοθεν ὁ δεσπότης φιλάνθρωπος, ἔξωθεν ὀργίλος.
> (Romanos, *Hymnes*, ed. Grosdidier de Matons, vol. v, 476 (LIV.5.1–2, 5))

The adjective *oikonomikon* is used for metrical and syntactical reasons, and not to indicate any meaning divergent from that of *oikonomia*.

[60]
> Θεὸν οἱ δεδιότες χεῖρας ἐξέτεινον αὐτῷ
> ἐλεημοσύνην ἐξαιτοῦντες παρ' αὐτοῦ
> καὶ τῶν κακῶν κατάπαυσιν.
> Σὺν τούτοις δὲ εἰκότως ἐπεύχετο καὶ ὁ βασιλεύων.
> (Ibid., 490 (LIV.18.2–5))
> Ὅτε δὲ ἤκουσε Θεὸς φωνῆς τῆς τῶν κραζόντων καὶ τῶν βασιλευόντων,
> καὶ ἔδωκε τῷ ἄστει τοὺς φιλανθρώπους οἰκτιρμούς. (Ibid., 490 (LIV.19.1–2))

the dedication ceremony: *Praise God, who found me worthy to accomplish such a work. I have surpassed you, Solomon!*[61] Then, from stanza 18 onwards, divine and earthly *oikonomia* are brought together: the divine plan of salvation and the earthly renunciation of *akribeia* correspond to the *philanthropia* of God in heaven and that of the imperial couple on earth. The hymn contains an exhortation to all the faithful to pray for the emperor, for the citizens of Constantinople and for the clergy, which is then followed by Romanos' own closing prayer. Generally, alongside the specific reference to 'earthly' *oikonomia* discussed above, Romanos' hymns feature other uses that are not explicit but are nevertheless significant: these are connected with particular circumstances that prompt the renunciation of *akribeia*.[62] This leads to a continuous – but often implicit – presence of both meanings of *oikonomia*: that is, of those denoting both God's activity in relation to Creation, and human departure from *akribeia*.

Rather than through the written word, Romanos' hymns transmitted their ideological and religious propaganda predominantly through recitation, thereby making no demands on the reading ability of the audience. The use of vocal and rhythmical methods conveyed with particular effectiveness matters that were, both formally and stylistically, also communicated by a lively use of the dialogic form. Papyrus fragments demonstrate how far-reaching this form of ecclesiastical and imperial propaganda was: dated to the second half of the sixth century/beginning of the seventh century, they can possibly be placed within the lifetime

---

[61] Δόξα τῷ θεῷ τῷ καταξιώσαντί με τοιοῦτον ἔργον ἀποτελέσαι Ἐνίκησά σε, Σολομών, *Diegesis peri tes Hagias Sophias*, c. 27, in T. Preger, ed., *Scriptores originum Constantinopolitanarum* (Leipzig, 1901), vol. I, 105; see G. Prinzing, 'Das Bild Justinians I. in der Überlieferung der Byzantiner vom 7. bis 15. Jahrhundert', *Fontes Minores*, 7 (1986), 89–92; A. Berger, *Untersuchungen zu den Patria Konstantinupoleos* (Bonn, 1988), 421; and J. Koder, 'Justinians Sieg über Salomon', in L. Bratziotes, ed., Θυμίαμα στη μνήμη της Λασκαρίνας Μπούρα (Athens, 1994), 135–42.

[62] An expression typical of this use can be found in the 'First Hymn to the Ten Virgins', in which Christ uses two examples in support of his request that not too high a value be given to *akribeia* (Romanos, *Hymnes*, ed. Grosdidier de Matons, vol. III, 356 (XXXI.24.5–8)):

> I reject those who keep the fast without compassion,
> and accept rather those who eat, but with compassion.
> I hate those virgins who are inhumane,
> and honour the married who love their fellow humans.
>
> ἀρνοῦμαι τοὺς νηστείαν φυλάττοντας μετὰ ἀσπλαγχνίας,
> καὶ προσδέχομαι δὲ μᾶλλον τοὺς ἔσθοντας μετὰ εὐσπλαγχνίας
> παρθένους δὲ μισῶ ὄντας ἀπανθρώπους,
> φιλανθρώπους δὲ τιμῶ γεγαμηκότας.

of Romanos himself. They certainly confirm that Romanos' hymns circulated as far as Egypt.[63]

Oikonomia and the complex of ideas surrounding this term expressed one of the core values of Byzantine society. Romanos the Melode employed the word in his hymns to bring the faithful closer to understanding two fundamental concepts: the divine 'plan of salvation' and the related doctrinal judgements of the emperor and the church of Constantinople. Romanos, almost inevitably, dealt with the former meaning of *oikonomia* far more than with the latter, especially when following the Church's liturgical year, and in particular in relation to the High Feasts.

Romanos' hymns cited in this chapter also clearly demonstrate that Mary, as the *Theotokos*, had come to play a central role as an intercessor no later than the conciliar decisions of Ephesus (431) and Chalcedon (451). In this context, mention should be made of the *stichera* 'On the Birth of Christ' (H. 83), which appear under the name of Romanos the Melode in the manuscripts, and are associated either with the Feast of the Birth of Christ or with its prefeast (25 or 24 December).[64] These works can be attributed to Romanos the Melode with a high probability;[65] regardless of the question of their authorship, these *stichera* can be taken as a very early example of liturgical

---

[63] See J. Koder, 'Anmerkungen zu dem Romanos-Papyrus Vindob. G 26225', *JÖB*, 53 (2003), 23–6, and Koder, 'Romanos der Melode: Der Dichter hymnischer Bibelpredigten in Dokumenten seiner Zeit' in H. Froschauer, ed., *Ein Buch verändert die Welt: Älteste Zeugnisse der Heiligen Schrift aus der Zeit des frühen Christentums in Ägypten* (Vienna, 2003), 59–71.

[64] Rainer Stichel proceeds on the assumption that Romanos composed this 'zum Vortrag während der Weihnachtsprozession von Jerusalem nach Bethlehem' (for use during the Christmas procession from Jerusalem to Bethlehem'; see R. Stichel, 'Die musizierenden Hirten von Bethlehem: Die Bedeutung der mittelalterlichen slavischen Übersetzungsliteratur für die byzantinische Lexikographie' in W. Hörandner and E. Trapp, eds., *Lexicographica Byzantina* (Vienna, 1991), 249–82, esp. 267.

[65] Romanos, *Hymnes*, eds. Maas and Trypanis, vol. II, *Cantica dubia*, 164–71 (no. 83) regard the attribution of this hymn to Romanos as spurious (p. xiii), since it does not follow the form of a *kontakion* (hence the description *Stichera* in the manuscripts: that is, verses inserted into the recitation of the psalms). It has come down to us only in the 'Western' manuscript tradition – a weak argument, as I demonstrated some years ago. Grosdidier de Matons, however, has included it among the authentic hymns (Grosdidier de Matons, *Romanos le Mélode. Hymnes*, vol. II, 131–61. (no. 13)), for the reason that the *akrostichis* (ΑΙΝΟΣ ΤΑΠΕΙΝΟΥ ΡΩΜΑΝΟΥ ΕΙΣ ΤΑ ΓΕΝΕΘΛΙΑ, 'Praise by the humble Romanos on the Birth') attributes the work to Romanos. The resonances with the *Akathistos Hymn* and the evident internal parallels with Christmas Hymns 10 and 11 are in any case noteworthy.

hymnography in which the idea of *oikonomia*, without being made explicit, permeates the entire text.[66]

Further Reading

The key editions are: J. Grosdidier de Matons, ed., *Romanos le Mélode. Hymnes*, 5 vols. (Paris, 1964–81); P. Maas and C. A. Trypanis, eds., *Sancti Romani melodi cantica: Cantica genuina* (Oxford, 1963) and *Sancti Romani melodi cantica: Cantica dubia* (Berlin, 1970). Studies include: G. Richter, *Oikonomia: Der Gebrauch des Wortes Oikonomia im Neuen Testament, bei den Kirchenvätern und in der theologischen Literatur bis ins 20. Jahrhundert* (Berlin, 2005); J. Koder, 'Romanos Melodos und sein Publikum: Zur Einbeziehung und Beeinflussung der Zuhörer durch das Kontakion', *AnzWien*, 134 (1999), 63–94.

---

[66] Passages where the sense of 'plan of salvation' is particularly clearly expressed are Romanos, *Hymnes*, ed. Grosdidier de Matons, vol. II, 150 (XIII.19.3–4); vol. III, 86–90 (XXIII.1–4), 110–14 (XXIV.1–4); vol. IV, 32–6 (XXXII.2–4) and 72–4 (XXXIII.3–4).

CHAPTER 11

Quotation and Allusion in Symeon the New Theologian

Manolis S. Patedakis

Symeon the New Theologian (*c.* 949–1022) was born, according to his hagiographer Niketas Stethatos, to noble parents in Galate, a village of Byzantine Paphlagonia.[1] At a 'tender age', probably between six and eight years old, his parents sent him to Constantinople into the care of his grandparents who held a position in the palace. There, he was entrusted to an elementary schoolmaster (γραμματιστής) and received his primary education (προπαιδεία). In accordance with the hagiographical topos, the future saint devoted himself to his studies without behaving in a childish way and made good progress. In later years, he trained as a shorthand scribe and a calligrapher. However, as he had not received a secular education (θύραθεν) nor studied rhetoric (λόγου ῥητορικοῦ), he lacked a 'Hellenised tongue' (ἐξελληνισθῆναι τὴν γλῶτταν). Material that was not Christian (ἔξωθεν) and therefore harmful he had only 'touched with the tips of his fingers', as he had restricted his studies to the safer subject of grammar (γραμματική).[2] Since Symeon had moved to Constantinople as a child, he certainly would have had the opportunity

---

[1] This paper is written in honour of Professors Elizabeth and Michael Jeffreys. No words can express my gratitude to them. Elizabeth, as a supervisor, always patiently and willingly supported my work at Oxford. They kept their office and home open, were the kindest and wisest organizers of our weekly seminar, and shared generously their time and knowledge. They remain a source of inspiration, especially when writing on an author, who partly expressed himself in political verses – the topic to which Michael and Elizabeth themselves have also greatly contributed.

For Symeon's *Vita*, see: I. Hausherr, ed., G. Horn, trans., *Un grand mystique byzantin. Vie de Syméon le Nouveau Théologien (949–1022) par Nicétas Stéthatos* (Rome, 1928). See also the recent edition based on more manuscripts, and the translation into Modern Greek and English, in: S. P. Koutsas, Νικήτα τοῦ Στηθάτου βίος καὶ πολιτεία τοῦ ἐν ἁγίοις πατρὸς ἡμῶν Συμεὼν τοῦ Νέου Θεολόγου (Athens, 2005) and P. H. Greenfield, *The Life of Saint Symeon the New Theologian* (Cambridge, MA, 2013). For a brief modern account of Symeon's life, see: H. J. M. Turner, *The Epistles of St. Symeon the New Theologian* (Oxford, 2009), 1–6 and J. Koder, 'Ὁ Συμεὼν ὁ Νέος Θεολόγος καὶ οἱ ὕμνοι του' in A. Markopoulos, ed., *Τέσσερα κείμενα γιὰ τὴν ποίηση τοῦ Συμεὼν τοῦ Νέου Θεολόγου* (Athens, 2008), 2–7; on Symeon's literary production see: J. Koder, 'Γιατί ὁ Συμεὼν ὁ Νέος Θεολόγος ἔγραφε τοὺς ὕμνους του', *Nea Estia*, 160 (2006), 806–19.

[2] All the above details are narrated in Stethatos, *Vie*, eds. Hausherr and Horn, 2–5 (1–2).

to continue studies at an advanced level had this been felt to be appropriate.[3] However, after primary school, his paternal uncle (who was also a high official in the imperial chamber), seeing that Symeon 'excelled most people in beauty',[4] attempted to introduce him to the emperor and into the palace. Symeon was unwilling but he yielded under his uncle's pressure: he embarked on a professional career in the palace, was honoured with the office of *spatharokoubikoularios*, and became a member of the senate.[5] After the abrupt death of his uncle in 963, Symeon apparently persisted in his new career for several years, until he retired from public life to Stoudios monastery, probably for political reasons.[6] These would explain Symeon's withdrawal from school in order to assume an office in the palace, while later he seems to have abandoned his education together with his political career to enter Stoudios monastery.[7]

The hagiographer Niketas Stethatos is quite explicit in his narration as to the levels of learning Symeon achieved in school, as well as to the point

---

[3] For a discussion on the structure of education in Symeon's times, see: A. Markopoulos, 'De la structure de l'école byzantine. Le maître, les livres et le processus éducatif' in B. Mondrain, ed., *Lire et écrire à Byzance* (Paris, 2006), 85–96. On the levels of Byzantine education, from the primary (προπαιδεία) to the secondary encyclical stage (ἐγκύκλια), see, also: A. Markopoulos, 'Education' in E. M. Jeffreys, J. Haldon and R. Cormack, eds., *The Oxford Handbook of Byzantine Studies* (Oxford, 2008), 785–95.

[4] Stethatos, *Vie*, eds. Hausherr and Horn, 4 (3.1–6): Ὁ τοίνυν πρὸς πατρὸς αὐτοῦ θεῖος ὡς ἑώρα κάλλει σώματος καὶ ὡραιότητι τῶν πολλῶν αὐτὸν διαφέροντα... see with the autobiographical reference by Symeon himself to the youngster Georgios in: B. Krivochéine, ed., J. Paramelle, trans., *Syméon le Nouveau Théologien. Catéchèses*, (Paris, 1963–5), vol. II, 366 (XXII.24–8): ὡραῖος τῷ εἴδει καὶ φαντασιώδες τό τε σχῆμα καὶ τὸ ἦθος καὶ τὸ βάδισμα κεκτημένος, ὡς ἐκ τούτων καὶ ὑπολήψεις πονηρὰς ἔχειν τινὰς εἰς αὐτόν, τοὺς τὸ ἔξωθεν μόνον βλέποντας περικάλυμμα καὶ κακῶς κρίνοντας τὰ ἀλλότρια.

[5] Stethatos, *Vie*, eds. Hausherr and Horn, 4 (3.9–11), also in p. LXXXIX and Symeon, *Catecheses*, eds. Krivochéine and Paramelle, vol. II, 370 (XXII.70–2): Τὴν γὰρ ἡμέραν οἴκου προΐστατο τῶν πατρικίων τινὸς καὶ ἐν τῷ παλατίῳ καθ' ἑκάστην προήρχετο, φροντίζων τῶν τῷ βίῳ ἁρμοζόντων..., where Symeon refers to himself as having held another post, probably held after his uncle's death, as 'a supervisor in the house of one of the patricians'.

[6] J. A. McGuckin, 'Symeon the New Theologian (d. 1022) and Byzantine Monasticism' in A. Bryer and M. Cunningham, eds., *Mount Athos and Byzantine Monasticism* (Aldershot, 1996), 18–20; see M. Bazzani, 'Autobiographical Elements in Symeon the New Theologian: Modes and Causes of Self-disclosure in the Writings of the New Theologian', *BSl*, 64 (2006), 222–4.

[7] The narration in A. Kambylis, ed., *Symeon Neos Theologos. Hymnen* (Berlin, 1976), 148–51 (XVIII.133–225) on Symeon's resistance to the evil Pharaoh might refer to such a set of circumstances after he had abandoned his office to enter monastic life. A further insight is offered in: Turner, *The Epistles*, 2, who comments on the possibility that Symeon in the above passage refers to his deliverance by God from the sexual immorality in the court of the emperor Romanos II; see Symeon, *Catecheses*, eds. Krivochéine and Paramelle, vol. III, 332 (XXXVI.28–39/Euch. II).

An alternate edition of the hymns of Symeon is by J. Koder, eds., J. Paramelle and L. Neyrand, trans., *Syméon le Nouveau Théologien. Hymnes*, 3 vols. (Paris, 1969–73); however, I use Kambylis' text for this article.

at which that formal education ended. Symeon had just started in the secondary level when he was forced to relinquish it for a provisional career in the palace, which he temporarily accepted. However, the description of the early years of Symeon's life accords well with Niketas' intention to conform with the hagiographical *locus communis* that the saint did not have any schooling experience beyond the primary stage, and that he did not receive any secular education. It is important to be aware of these supposed limits to his education before examining any aspect of his technique as an author that reveals his knowledge, literary training and inspiration. In this chapter, after presenting Symeon's education and study experience, I will focus on one of the merits of his literary production – which continued right up until his death in 1022, in both poetry and prose: that is, the technique by which he incorporates sources of inspiration from other texts in his own writings.[8]

Monastic and Divine Knowledge

All major studies based on Niketas' narrative in the *Vita* and Symeon's own autobiographical references agree that his educational background and learning experience were the fruit of a so-called 'monastic education'.[9] This term implies an education in biblical and patristic texts, as well as other independent study that would be possible within the intellectual and liturgical milieu of a monastery. In the case of Symeon, at just fourteen years of age, after the sudden death of his uncle,[10] and having already embarked on a state career, Symeon attempted for the first time to enter Stoudios monastery. This was the milieu that played a significant and formative role in his learning.

---

[8] The manuscript tradition of Symeon's works is very wide. His edited works consist of fifty-eight hymns, thirty-four instructive sermons (κατηχήσεις), fifteen theological and ethical treatises, about three hundred short theological chapters (ἑκατοντάδες), twenty-four alphabetical chapters, and four letters.

[9] H. J. M. Turner, *St. Symeon the New Theologian and Spiritual Fatherhood* (Leiden, 1990), 37–9; H. Alfeyev, *St. Symeon the New Theologian and Orthodox Tradition* (Oxford, 2000), 13–42; F. M. Fernández Jiménez, *El humanismo bizantino en San Simeón el Nuevo Teólogo: la renovación de la mística bizantina* (Madrid, 1999), 5–12. A useful, up-to-date account of secondary literature on Symeon can be found in: A. Markopoulos, 'Vergöttlichung und Erlösung. Versuch einer Lektüre des Hymnos Nr. 13 von Symeon Neos Theologos' in K. Belke, E. Kislinger, A. Külzer and M. A. Stassinopoulou, eds., *Byzantina Mediterranea, Festschrift für Johannes Koder zum 65. Geburtstag* (Vienna, 2007), 435–6, n. 2–6. See also the modern Greek translation of the same article with some changes: A. Markopoulos, 'Θέωση και σωτηρία. Απόπειρα ανάγνωσης του ύμνου αρ. 13 του Συμεὼν του Νέου Θεολόγου' in Markopoulos, ed., *Τέσσερα κείμενα*, 62–4, n. 3–4.

[10] Stethatos, *Vie*, eds. Hausherr and Horn, 4–6 (3.13–4.12).

As already mentioned, Symeon soon became a proficient shorthand writer and a calligrapher, who would 'write very finely and would please anyone seeing his letters'.[11] He had undertaken this task as his main handiwork as a monk (ἐργόχειρον) in the Stoudios monastery, home of one of the richest monastic libraries in Constantinople, as well as of a well-run and well-known scriptorium. Therefore, it is reasonable to think that he subsequently gained significant writing and reading experience by using and copying codices.[12]

According to the *Vita*, Symeon also dedicated himself to conversing (ὡμίλει) with the divine Scriptures and reading lives of famous past ascetics.[13] As is clear from his writings, he had certainly read hagiographical works such as the *Vitae* of Anthony, Sabbas, Euthymios and Arsenios as well as of holy women such as Pelagia, Mary of Egypt, Theodora, Euphrosyne and Xene.[14] There are numerous further concrete examples of Symeon's diverse readings. In a passage acknowledged to be autobiographical,[15] he narrates (in the third person singular) how the youngster Georgios was guided in his ascetic readings by his spiritual father, Symeon Eulabes (Εὐλαβής),[16] who gave the novice a book of the *Spiritual Law* by Mark the Hermit. Further in the same passage, Symeon points out the three chapters that he, as a young man, gleaned from that book and

---

[11] Ibid., 4 (2.17–19): ὅθεν καὶ κάλλιστα τὰ τῶν ταχυγράφων ἐν βραχεῖ τῷ χρόνῳ κατορθωκὼς ὡραῖα γράφειν λίαν μεμάθηκεν, ὡς τὰ ὑπ' ἐκείνου γραφέντα βιβλία πιστοῦται σαφῶς τὸ λεγόμενον; see 38 (27.1–3): Μετὰ δὲ τὴν ἀνάγνωσιν ἥπτετο τοῦ ἐργοχείρου γράφων τὰς δέλτους τῶν θεοπνεύστων γραφῶν· ἦν γὰρ ἄγαν εὐφυῶς γράφων, ὡς ἡδονῆς πληροῦσθαι πάντα τὸν τὰ ἐκείνου βλέποντα γράμματα. All English translations of quoted passages are mine.

[12] The studies mentioned in note 8 describe the intellectual and educational milieu of the Monastery of Saint John the Forerunner at Stoudios, and make some interesting remarks on its organisation, Alfeyev, *St. Symeon*, 13–16, esp. 15: 'Be that as it may, the rule indicates that monks could borrow at least one book each at the same time: if there were seven hundred or a thousand monks in the monastery, how many books must there have been in the library?' For an attempt to reconstruct the library of the Stoudios, see: N. Eleopoulos, *Ἡ βιβλιοθήκη καὶ τὸ βιβλιογραφικὸν ἐργαστήριον τῆς Μονῆς τῶν Στουδίου* (Athens, 1967), and the older study by O. O. Volk, 'Die byzantinischen Klosterbibliotheken von Konstantinopel, Thessalonika und Kleinasien', unpublished PhD thesis, Munich (1955), 80–91. As a rule, general studies on Byzantine libraries mention only briefly the library of the Stoudios. See, for example, the most recent: N. G. Wilson, 'Libraries' in Jeffreys, Haldon, and Cormack, eds., *Oxford Handbook*, 820–7.

[13] Stethatos, *Vie*, eds. Hausherr and Horn, 36–8 (26.20–2); compare to 34 (24.9–10) and 84 (62.11–13).

[14] Symeon, *Catecheses*, eds. Krivochéine and Paramelle, vol. I, 422–4 (v.559–72); vol. II, 16, 18, 20 and 22 (VI.40, 71, 90, 96 and 102–3); vol. III, 170 and 216 (XXIX.75–7 and XXX.271–2). See Turner, *St. Symeon*, 51; Alfeyev, *St. Symeon*, 132–5.

[15] Krivochéine and Paramelle, *Syméon le Nouveau*, vol. II, 366, n. 1; M. Hinterberger, *Autobiographische Traditionen in Byzanz* (Vienna, 1999), 234–7 and the detailed article by Bazzani, 'Autobiographical Elements', 221–42. However, evidence on his education is not evaluated in either study.

[16] Symeon, *Catecheses*, eds. Krivochéine and Paramelle, vol. II, 366 (XXII.29–38).

planted deep into his own heart.[17] His hagiographer Niketas Stethatos mentions the same episode, adding that this volume also included the work of Diadochos of Photike.[18] Another book mentioned in the *Vita* is the 'classical' ascetic work called the *Klimax* by John Sinaites, which Symeon found while searching in his ancestors' library, during a short visit to his homeland.[19] He embraced it and memorised the following passage: 'the detachment from senses is the mortification of soul and the death of mind before the death of body'.[20] Other scholars have traced cross-references from patristic texts (or their exegetical tradition), ascetic writings, canonical literature and *florilegia*. Influences from Gregory of Nazianzos, John Chrysostom, Gregory of Nyssa, Maximos the Confessor, pseudo-Makarios and pseudo-Dionysios have been attested in the titles, quotations and ideas of Symeon's works.[21]

Apart from contact with Christian literature through reading, Symeon was further educated by the rich aural experience as a regular listener of church services. This is clearly attested in the scant information that Stethatos provides for us: 'he would never sit when the Holy Writ was read, but after entering one of the chapels of the church he would stay unmoved listening to readings and shedding a flood of tears on the ground'.[22] The importance of the liturgical ritual for Symeon should not be underestimated, although, to the writer's present knowledge, it has not been directly addressed before.

As Stethatos summarises, all who knew him were impressed by Symeon's judgement and rhetorical skills (συνέσει καὶ τοῖς λόγοις), for he surpassed everyone in wisdom and knowledge (σοφίας καὶ γνώσεως). Concurrently, Symeon's contemporaries wondered 'how could he be so

---

[17] Ibid., 366 (XXII.38–51). The first chapter dealt with the attention paid to one's conscience. The other two are based on a similitude and a passage from the gospels (Luke 18.38): 'The one who yearns for the divine operation of the Holy Spirit before fulfilling the orders is similar to a slave who asks for his freedom immediately after being bought for a bargain with silver. The one who prays in bodily form without yet having spiritual knowledge resembles the blind man, who was calling "Son of David, have mercy upon me".'
[18] Stethatos, *Vie*, eds. Hausherr and Horn, 6–7 (4.15–19).   [19] Ibid., 12–13 (6.21–4).
[20] Ibid., 12–13 (6.32–4). The passage is the heading of ch. XVIII of Sinaites' edition (*PG*, 88.932B). About the influence of John Sinaites on Symeon's texts, see: Turner, *St. Symeon*, 45–6.
[21] Turner, *St. Symeon*, 39–51; Alfeyev, *St. Symeon*, 52–63, 127–32; M. Scorsone, 'Gli Ἔρωτες θεῖοι di Simeone il Nuovo Teologo: ermeneutica di un'intitolazione apocrifa', *Medioevo Greco*, 0 (2000), 191–6; I. Afentoulidou, 'Οἱ ὕμνοι τοῦ Συμεὼν τοῦ Νέου Θεολόγου. Σχέσεις τῶν ἐπιγραφῶν με τους ὕμνους', *Byzantina*, 22 (2001), 130–1; J. Koder, 'Der Titel der Hymnensammlung des Symeon Neos Theologos', *Palaeoslavica*, 10 (2002), 215–21.
[22] Stethatos, *Vie*, eds. Hausherr and Horn, 38–9 (28.5–7): οὐδὲ γὰρ ἐκάθητο τῶν θείων ἀναγινωσκομένων γραφῶν, ἀλλ' εἰς ἓν τῶν τοῦ ναοῦ εἰσερχόμενος εὐκτηρίων ἵστατο ἀσάλευτος τῆς ἀναγνώσεως ἀκροώμενος καὶ τοῖς δάκρυσιν καταρραίνων τὸ ἔδαφος.

wise and knowledgeable and a teacher of the others, when he had received no secular education?'[23] Stethatos argues rhetorically that 'inasmuch as God wrought His disciples and apostles wiser than all the wise men and rhetors, so Symeon, by virtue of his intense ascetic life, became the teacher, even for those who spent a long life struggling to attain virtue; the astounding responses in his epistles are a proof of that fact'.[24] According to another opaque passage from his *Vita*,[25] Symeon was raised to the rank of *didaskalos* when he was ordained a priest. Thus he was promoted to a higher ecclesiastical dignity, possibly due to the outstanding level of his Christian education.

Indeed, Symeon was highly esteemed for his erudition amongst his contemporaries. A case in point illustrating this was his heated dispute with Stephen of Nikomedia, which was revealed to be a debate about real Christian knowledge and sanctity, in both written and spoken word.[26] As revealed in Symeon's fourth epistle, an educational dimension certainly existed in their discussion on true wisdom;[27] that is the argument partly was on whether education can lead to wisdom. The nature of wisdom had been one of Symeon's constant concerns, for in his writings, and on many occasions, he castigated the 'wise' men of the lay world and expressed his

---

[23] Ibid., 30–1 (20.4–7): ἐδόθη αὐτῷ καὶ λόγος ἐκεῖθεν σοφίας καὶ γνώσεως, ὡς πάντας θαυμάζειν ἐπὶ τῇ συνέσει καὶ τοῖς λόγοις αὐτοῦ καὶ οὕτω λέγειν ἐκπληττομένους· "πόθεν ἡ τοιαύτη τούτῳ σοφία καὶ γνῶσις παιδείαν μὴ μεμαθηκότι τὴν θύραθεν;"; 144–5 (105.7–8). See the self-assessment of Symeon in *Hymns*, 448 (LVIII.3–4): σὺ γὰρ οἶδας μου τὸ ἀσθενὲς τοῦ λόγου / καὶ ἀμέτοχον μαθήσεως τῆς ἔξω, as well as 59 (III.15–16): Ὁ ἔχων ὦτα ἀκούειν ἀκουέτω, νοῶν ἀληθῶς ῥήματα ἀγραμμάτου.

[24] Ibid., 30–1 (20.12–18): εἰς τοσοῦτον γὰρ ὕψος αὐτὸν ἡ σύντονος ἄσκησις δι' ὀλίγου ἀναδραμεῖν ἀπειργάσατο, ὡς ὑπερελάσαι καὶ αὐτοὺς τοὺς ἐγχρονίσαντας ἐν τοῖς ἀγῶσι τῆς ἀρετῆς καὶ γενέσθαι τούτων ἐκείνων διδάσκαλον κατὰ τὸν μέγαν Δανιὴλ τὸν προφήτην, καὶ τοῦτο γνώσεται πᾶς ὁ βουλόμενος ἐξ ὧν παρ' ἐκείνων ἐρωτώμενος ἀντέγραφεν αὐτοῖς καὶ ταῖς ἐπιστολαῖς κατέπληττεν ὑπερβαλλόντως αὐτούς. For two short letters of Symeon, see his *Vie* in 132–5 (Stethatos, *Vie*, eds. Hausherr and Horn, 96) and 136–9 (99). See also the recent edition: Symeon, *The Epistles* ed. Turner.

[25] Ibid., 40–1 (30.3–6): ψήφῳ τοίνυν Νικολάου τοῦ Χρυσοβέργη τοῦ πατριάρχου καὶ τῶν μοναχῶν τοῦ ἁγίου Μάμαντος εἰς τὸν θρόνον ἀνάγεται διδασκαλικὸν καὶ ἱερεὺς χειροτονεῖται ὁ συλλειτουργὸς τῶν ἄνω δυνάμεων.

[26] We can infer the existence of a debate from several relevant texts. These include Symeon, *Hymnen*, ed. Kambylis, 168–86 (XXI) (in the form of a letter on 'how you separate the Son from the Father'), and the Fourth Epistle of Symeon 'about the self-appointed teachers' (Symeon, *The Epistles*, ed. Turner, 138–81). In addition, there are several passages from Stethatos, *Vie*, ed. Hausherr and Horn, 102–9 (75.1–78.20), where the debate and all of Symeon's responses are described; at 108–33 (79.1–95.23), the debate continues after Symeon is accused of worshipping his spiritual father, Symeon Eulabes, as a saint; at 144–51 (105.1–7.27), and finally Symeon's apology to the second accusation in front of the patriarch.

[27] Alfeyev, *St. Symeon*, 39–40.

opinion with regard to real wisdom.²⁸ Stephen, a highly ranked and well-educated prelate, considered it a provocation to receive criticism from a monk, especially on theological and canonical matters, or issues regarding learning. However, he was compelled to respect Symeon's education as being sufficiently advanced to get involved in a theoretical debate with him.

Although Symeon is depicted as not having an advanced secondary (encyclical) education, there are numerous references that confirm his liturgical reading, copying and rhetorical activities. The discrepancy between presentation and evidence accords well with traditional hagiographical topoi that Niketas was promoting: namely, that the saint imitated the model of Christ in the process of acquiring knowledge.²⁹ The audience is expected to react with wonderment as to how a man ignorant of secular learning could be competent in matters of theology; wisdom in this case is attributed to Symeon's overwhelming mystical experience of the Divine Grace.³⁰ Niketas certainly intended to extol the main character in the *Vita*, and to show that his hero, through *imitatio Christi*, fulfils the paradox of being capable in rhetorical attainments despite his lack of a formal education.

The present chapter begins by approaching the issue of Symeon's learning. As has so far been pointed out, this complex issue has been perplexing and leaves plenty of room for interpretation in sources and modern scholarship. McGuckin, in a paper on Symeon's luminous visions, justifiably sees in him 'a man who was trained rhetorically (despite Niketas Stethatos' fumbling attempts in the *Vita* to underplay this aspect of Symeon's skill) and who uses his technique and his knowledge (particularly of the scriptures) to telling effect in the process of constructing his religious autobiography'.³¹ This particular modern scholar leaves open the

---

[28] See the elaborate simile likening knowledge to a treasure chest in: Symeon, *Catecheses*, eds. Krivochéine and Paramelle, vol. III, 34–48 (XXIV.1–186). For a further insight on the subject, see: Koutsas, Νικήτα τοῦ Στηθάτου, 50, n. 1; 122, n. 23.

[29] Niketas' phrasing (see above note 23) resembles the passage from John 7.15: ἐθαύμαζον οὖν οἱ Ἰουδαῖοι λέγοντες· πῶς οὗτος γράμματα οἶδεν μὴ μεμαθηκώς. See the interpretation in Alfeyev, *St. Symeon*, 16: 'Even when a certain hagiographical source mentions an "unlettered" monk, it does not usually mean that he was not able to read: the author only wishes to emphasize that his hero did not obtain his wisdom from books, but directly from God.'

[30] Stethatos, *Vie*, eds. Hausherr and Horn, 48–9 (36.11–14).

[31] J. A. McGuckin, 'The Luminous Vision in Eleventh-century Byzantium: Interpreting the Biblical and Theological Paradigms of St. Symeon the New Theologian' in M. Mullett and A. Kirby, eds., *Work and Worship at the Theotokos Evergetis 1050–1200* (Belfast, 1997), 121–2. Likewise, for a higher rhetorical esteem of Symeon's writings, see the analysis of the employment of metaphors and imagery in: A. P. Kazhdan, 'Das System der Bilder und Metaphern in den Werken Symeons des

possibility that Symeon had at least begun professional training and even obtained a higher education before becoming a monk.

Arguing in the same direction, the question of whether Symeon obtained a greater amount of education than Niketas attributes to him remains open. Moreover, it is evident that prior to his monastic training, Symeon was certainly familiar with the works of the 'Hellenes', or classical pagan authors, even if only on an introductory level. Although he is aware of their authority, their works were not in his scope of knowledge and wisdom. In his *First Ethical Discourse*, a work in which he examines the nature of the heavenly mysteries, he says that 'Hellenic speech' is on sensible things, namely, that pagan treatises can be understood because their content is conceived through human senses, but their narrations are futile, and they also talk about futile things.[32] Real wisdom emanates neither from the sensual world nor from texts which relate to it.[33] Despite his rhetorically attested deficiency in secular learning, Symeon wrote with efficiency, productivity and originality, although not according to profane literary conventions, but rather those of one educated in the Christian textual tradition.

The Text Behind the Text: Originality in Symeon's Writing

A good idea of the intertextual content in Symeon's works can be gauged from the indices of allusions included in all critical editions of his writings.[34] They demonstrate that he primarily uses passages from the Scriptures and from patristic literature, and less often also references from ascetical and hagiographical texts, canons, church services, and hymnography. This paints a picture which accords with Symeon's reading and learning experience as already described. In only a few cases have

---

"Neuen" Theologen' in P. Hauptmann, ed., *Unser ganzes Leben Christus unserem Gott Überantworten* (Göttingen, 1982), 221–39, reprinted in A. P. Kazhdan, *Authors and Texts in Byzantium* (Aldershot, 1993), XIII. For a literary analysis of Hymns XIII and XVII, see: Markopoulos, 'Vergöttlichung und Erlösung', 439–41 = Markopoulos, 'Θέωση και σωτηρία', 72–6, and F. Conca, 'L'inno 17 di Simeone il Nuovo Teologo', *Atti della Accademia Pontaniana*, 49 (2000), 139–50.

[32] J. Darrouzès, ed. and trans., *Syméon le Nouveau Théologien. Traités théologiques et éthiques* (Paris, 1966–7), vol. I, 278–80 (1.94–103).

[33] See the sections below, which refer to 'the myth of the prisoner' and *apatheia* (impassibility).

[34] Symeon, *Traités théologiques et éthiques*, ed. Darrouzès, vol. II, 461–76; Krivochéine and Paramelle, eds., *Syméon le Nouveau*, vol. III, 359–83; Koder, Paramelle, and Neyrand, eds., *Syméon le Nouveau*, vol. III, 313–28; Kambylis, ed., *Symeon Neos*, 550–68; J. Darrouzès, ed. and trans., *Chapitres théologiques, gnostiques et pratiques* (Paris, 1996), 213–16.

Quotation and Allusion in Symeon the New Theologian   279

editors discerned allusions to classical texts.[35] However, originality in Symeon's use of other sources does not lie in the mere citation of or allusion to a passage from another author. Interpreting Symeon's literary production and writing technique according to his own definition of wisdom, it will become clear that the author selected influential passages from other sources (the Bible, hymnography, even classical texts), inserted and expanded them into his poetry and prose.

Let us begin by describing the main patterns by which Symeon quotes passages from other texts. In some cases he clearly denotes a single passage by naming the author of the source he uses (i.e. Paul, Peter, or Gregory of Nazianzos).[36] In most other cases, he does not mention the author's name, but he simply cites one or more consecutive passages, a common way for quoting throughout his writings. The citation of continuous quotations can function as a launch pad for the idea that he is about to expound.[37] In another instance, he composes a metrical version of a scriptural passage.[38] However, the above techniques occur when the connections with his readings are straightforward, and it is easy to define and identify their provenance.

In the more advanced level of Symeon's originality in using his sources, he draws his original idea from a passage, usually the Scriptures, and then he further develops and enriches it. On occasion, he may expand upon an idea, image or allegory so as to develop further what the initial source has already established. A good example of this technique comes from Symeon's allegorical description of escape, likening it to that from the biblical Pharaoh. It is found in a hymn where an autobiographical detail about Symeon's own life is presented as a token of the acts of Divine Love, or the light of the Holy Spirit.[39] Similarly, the Gospel parable of the merchant of the precious pearl is extended into a long narrative, depicting the real search for the Kingdom of God (Hymn XVII.537–84, 702, 825). The symbol of the precious pearl corresponds with the main idea in this

---

[35] Turner, *St. Symeon*, 39, n. 11 and A. Alexakis, 'Μορφολογικὲς παρατηρήσεις στὴν Εὐχὴ Μυστική, δι' ἧς ἐπικαλεῖται τὸ Πνεῦμα τὸ Ἅγιον ὁ αὐτὸ προορῶν τοῦ Συμεὼν τοῦ Νέου Θεολόγου', in Markopoulos, ed., *Τέσσερα κείμενα*, 39.

[36] Symeon, *Hymnen*, ed. Kambylis, 122 (XVII.294); 345 (XLII.29); 92 (XIII.21); Symeon, *Ethical Discourses*, ed. Darrouzès, vol. I, 204 (I.129), 206 (I.12) and 208 (I.28); vol. II, 20 (IV.185) and 308 (X.687–8); and Symeon, *Catecheses*, eds. Krivochéine and Paramelle, vol. I, 370 (IV.686); vol. II, 378 (XXII.179); vol. III, 182 (XXIX.214–5).

[37] Symeon, *Hymnen*, ed. Kambylis, 102–3 (XV.22–43); 156–7 (XIX.111–45); 165–6 (XX.198–211); 315–17 (XXXVI.1–52).

[38] Ibid., 122–3 (XVII.292–310) on the well-known passage about love from I. Cor. 13.

[39] Ibid., 148–51 (XVIII.140–222). See, above, n. 7 and Bazzani, 'Autobiographical Elements', 230.

hymn that only the Divine is desirable. In another case, based on a phrase from St Paul (Eph. 5.16, ἐξαγοραζόμενοι τὸν καιρόν)[40] quoted both in the title and the main text of his oration, Symeon structures a prolonged allegorical discussion about the successful merchant who takes advantage of his 'chance' and gains profit (Symeon, *Ethical Discourses*, vol. 1, 384 (XII.1–2 and 14–5): 386–8 (XII.24–80)). This image is compared in the latter part of the work with spiritual life.

From the above first group of examples, it is clear that Symeon is not innovative in his technique of quoting from the Scriptures. He merely adheres to the patterns found in the patristic, exegetical and ascetical traditions.[41] Nonetheless, his 'bright individuality' lies in the specific textual choices he employs, and in the way in which he combines them with further quotations. He develops them into images, finally expanding the passages in new metaphorical and allegorical contexts.[42] Therefore, while his allegorical register may begin with a symbolic interpretation of biblical passages, it extends up to connecting them as examples with certain aspects of his mystical experience of the Divine Light, as will be further explained in the course of this chapter.[43]

Seen from this viewpoint, not all citations have the same value in Symeon's works. Some simply support the idea or ideas conveyed in a small passage, while others inspire the idea(s) of longer passages, of a whole work, or of the core of the author's mystical experience, the presence of Divine Light. Hence, a chosen passage can underpin a whole poem or prose work, and the main idea of this work will depend on that parallel textual usage and the technique involved. In the main body of this chapter, an analysis of selected extensive parallel usages will attempt to verify Symeon's allusive technique concerning texts that functioned as inspiration for his writings, but which are not clearly identified.

---

[40] See the relevant discussion in: Kazhdan, 'Das System', 229.
[41] Alfeyev, *St. Symeon*, 52–3, 55–61. As an example of such an approach concerning Gregory of Nazianzos, see: K. Demoen, *Pagan and Biblical Exempla in Gregory Nazianzen: a Study in Rhetorics and Hermeneutics* (Turnhout, 1996), esp. 233–88.
[42] Alfeyev, *St. Symeon*, 61; Kazhdan, 'Das System', 223.
[43] This is made quite clear through the main biblical paradigms with which McGuckin connects Symeon's visions of God: McGuckin, 'The Luminous Vision', 100–4. See, also: Alfeyev, *St. Symeon*, 63–72, and the analysis in D. Krueger, 'Homoerotic Spectacle and the Monastic Body in Symeon the New Theologian' in V. Burrus and C. Keller, eds., *Toward a Theology of Eros: Transfiguring Passion at the Limits of Discipline* (New York, NY, 2006), 103–6. For the notion of the rhetorical term παράδειγμα / exemplum in Gregory, see, also: Demoen, *Pagan and Biblical*, 35–206.

Hymnography

The mystical prayer of Symeon,[44] which was placed at the front of the collection of his hymns, is an invocation to God and to the Holy Spirit,[45] as the title declares (l.1–2). In the first paragraph God is continuously invoked in a repetitive sequence of more than twenty-five imperatives in the form ἐλθέ ('come').[46] This is not a mere coincidence: the same imperative to the Holy Spirit appears once in a much briefer invocation, the prayer Βασιλεῦ οὐράνιε (*O Heavenly King*), recited by a priest at the beginning of every church service.[47] In addition to this, other sections of Symeon's mystical prayer find analogies in the same common service prayer, such as the phrasing alluding to a royal context at the end of the first chapter (l.14–17), which corresponds to the notion of the address, *O Heavenly King*. In Symeon's invocation, God is named as the 'nameless treasure' (ἀκατονόμαστος θησαυρός, l.4), while in the prayer He is called 'the treasure of the good' (ὁ θησαυρὸς τῶν ἀγαθῶν). Moreover, Symeon's 'true light' (τὸ φῶς τὸ ἀληθινόν, l.3) corresponds to the phrase 'the spirit of truth' (τὸ πνεῦμα τῆς ἀληθείας). However, most striking is the similarity in wording between the beginning of the third paragraph in Symeon's prayer, 'Lord, encamp in myself' (ἐνσκήνωσον, δέσποτα, ἐν ἐμοί, l.37–8) and the phrase 'camp in ourselves' (σκήνωσον ἐν ἡμῖν) of the Βασιλεῦ οὐράνιε prayer. It is thus evident that Symeon does not compose his invocation by literally following the brief service prayer, but that he bears it in mind when he develops his own, more elaborate rendering.[48]

---

[44] Symeon, *Hymnen*, ed. Kambylis, 42.4–44.56; J. Koder, ed., J. Paramelle and L. Neyrand, trans., *Syméon le Nouveau Théologien. Hymnes*, vol. 1, 150.1–154.56.

[45] McGuckin, 'Symeon the New Theologian', 188.

[46] For the origin of this imperative from ancient Greek hymns and prayers, as well as from Syriac texts of the third century CE, see: Alexakis, 'Μορφολογικὲς παρατηρήσεις', 51–2.

[47] D. Apostolike, ed., Ὡρολόγιον τὸ Μέγα (Athens, 1977), 4, 27, 39, 45, 100, 136, 158: Βασιλεῦ οὐράνιε, Παράκλητε, τὸ Πνεῦμα τῆς ἀληθείας, ὁ πανταχοῦ παρὼν καὶ τὰ πάντα πληρῶν, ὁ θησαυρὸς τῶν ἀγαθῶν καὶ ζωῆς χορηγός, ἐλθὲ καὶ σκήνωσον ἐν ἡμῖν καὶ καθάρισον ἡμᾶς ἀπὸ πάσης κηλίδος· καὶ σῶσον, Ἀγαθέ, τὰς ψυχὰς ἡμῶν. This prayer opens all services of day and night, the *mesonyktikon* (midnight service), the matins, the hours, the vespers, and the *apodeipnon*. It is also significant that the invocation of the Βασιλεῦ οὐράνιε is sung as an *idiomelon* at the beginning of the canon during the Sunday Pentecost service, when the church celebrates the visitation of the Holy Spirit, as well as a *doxastikon* in the vespers of Pentecostal Monday, when several invocation prayers to the Holy Spirit are also read; see: D. Apostolike, ed., Πεντηκοστάριον (Athens, 1959), 103, 210–3.

[48] A. Alexakis has recently analysed the structure and content of this very elaborate prayer and has convincingly grounded its possible relation with ancient prayers and hymns, rhetorical theory, as well as early Christian fathers such as Gregory of Nazianzos. See Alexakis, 'Μορφολογικὲς παρατηρήσεις', 37–60.

The next passage concerning the creation of the world and Adam, in Symeon's *First Ethical Discourse*, can be aptly labelled the *Negation of Creation*, as it relates the reaction of Nature against Adam after he committed the Original Sin:

> Therefore, after he (Adam) was expelled from paradise, all the creation created by God from non-existence,[49] upon seeing [this], was not willing to submit to the transgressor anymore; the sun did not want to shine, the moon did not bear to light, the stars did not choose to appear to him, the springs would not burst forth anymore; the rivers did not want to flow, and the air thought in secret to retract itself and not give breath to anyone whom it [the air] would fall on; the beasts and all the animals on earth, as they would see him [Adam], deprived of the previous glory, having despised him, all together immediately went rough against him; the sky as if justly was somehow moving to fall down over him and earth did not bear him on her back anymore.[50]

The editor of the text admits difficulty in identifying a textual source for this passage.[51] It may be argued, however, that the answer to this matter lies with hymnography. Specifically, several hymns sung on Holy Friday refer to all creation, which reacts in a similarly negative way at the sight of the Passion of Christ.[52] In addition to the Holy Friday Hymns, the hymnographical focus of the *Tyrophagos* Sunday services (on the last day before Lent) lies mainly upon the Original Sin and the Expulsion from Paradise. Here the *troparia* describe the reaction of Nature after Adam's disobedience in a manner that resembles Symeon's narration above.[53]

---

[49] Compare the phrasing in the original with the phrase in the prayer of the *Anaphora* (ἄξιον καὶ δίκαιον) from John Chrysostom's liturgy, σὺ ἐκ τοῦ μὴ ὄντος εἰς τὸ εἶναι ἡμᾶς παρήγαγες: in F. E. Brightman, ed., *Liturgies, Eastern and Western* (Oxford, 1894), 384.

[50] Symeon, *Ethical Discourses*, ed. Darrouzès, vol. 1, 190 (1.66–77): Τοιγαροῦν καὶ ἐξελθόντα τοῦ παραδείσου αὐτὸν πᾶσα ἡ κτίσις, ἡ ὑπὸ Θεοῦ παραχθεῖσα ἐκ τοῦ μὴ ὄντος, θεασαμένη, οὐκέτι ὑποταγῆναι τῷ παραβάντι ἐβούλετο· ὁ ἥλιος λάμψαι οὐκ ἤθελεν, ἡ σελήνη φᾶναι οὐκ ἔφερε, τὰ ἄστρα ὀφθῆναι τούτῳ οὐχ εἵλοντο, αἱ πηγαὶ βρύειν οὐκ ἔμελλον· οὐκ ἐβούλοντο ῥέειν οἱ ποταμοί, ἐφ' ἑαυτοῦ ἐμελέτα ὁ ἀὴρ συσταλῆναι καὶ μὴ δοῦναι τῷ προσκεκρουκότι ἀναπνοήν· τὰ θηρία καὶ πάντα τὰ ζῷα τῆς γῆς, γυμνωθέντα τοῦτον τῆς πρῴην θεασάμενα δόξης, καταφρονήσαντα αὐτοῦ, ἐτραχύνθησαν ἅπαντα εὐθὺς κατ' αὐτοῦ· ὁ οὐρανὸς καταπεσεῖν δικαίως ἐπ' αὐτὸν οἱονεί πως κεκίνητο καὶ ἡ γῆ ἐπὶ τοῦ νώτου φέρειν τοῦτον οὐκ ἔστεγε.

[51] Ibid., n. 1.

[52] *Τριῴδιον* (Athens, 1960), 427: see the *oikos* from the matins of Holy Saturday: Ὁ συνέχων τὰ πάντα ἐπὶ Σταυροῦ ἀνυψώθη, καὶ θρηνεῖ πᾶσα ἡ Κτίσις, τοῦτον βλέπουσα κρεμάμενον γυμνὸν ἐπὶ τοῦ ξύλου, ὁ ἥλιος τὰς ἀκτίνας ἀπέκρυψε, καὶ τὸ φέγγος οἱ ἀστέρες ἀπεβάλοντο, ἡ γῆ δὲ σὺν πολλῷ τῷ φόβῳ συνεκλονεῖτο· ἡ θάλασσα ἔφυγε, καὶ αἱ πέτραι διερρήγνυντο· μνημεῖα δὲ πολλὰ ἠνεῴχθησαν καὶ σώματα ἠγέρθησαν... This passage follows the less vivid description from the Gospels: Luke 23.44–5; Mathew 24.29; Mark 13.24–5.

[53] Ibid., 65, see in the vespers the *doxastikon*: (Εἰς τὴν λιτήν): Ἥλιος ἀκτίνας ἔκρυψεν, ἡ σελήνη σὺν τοῖς ἄστροις εἰς αἷμα μετετράπη, ὄρη ἔφριξαν, βουνοὶ ἐτρόμαξαν, ὅτε Παράδεισος ἐκλείσθη...

The common subject between the passage from the *First Ethical Discourse* and its hymnographical equivalent, that is the Negation of Creation in reaction to the Expulsion from Paradise, supports the interpretation that Symeon could have drawn the original idea from a hymnographical context and subsequently expounded it into his allegorical prose-version. Hymnography gives to Symeon short individual structural ideas which he develops into a prose passage and a unified long allegory about the Negation of Creation.

In addition to the examples stated above, which show the rich hymnographical production of the Orthodox Church as a direct source of inspiration for Symeon, in other cases images in Symeon's passages come from the Scriptures or through sources which themselves are based on scriptural narrative. Hymn XXIX describes in 270 verses the mystical experience of the Divine Light, which is God's appearance to His beloved and His departure which causes pain to man, who strives to regain the unique unification with Him. God appears to Symeon in his locked cell and calls him to repentance (v.1–53). The narrator's heart basks in the overwhelming experience of the Divine Light in front of God Himself. When he realises that God is running away, he starts chasing Him, as a hound would chase a hare. When finally God draws away and hides Himself (v.54–65), Symeon sits and mourns his loss: ἀλλ' ἐν ᾧ εὑρέθην τόπῳ / καθεζόμενος ἐθρήνουν (v.63–4, 'I sat and mourned at the place where I was').

If the reader searches for antecedents of this mourning, two biblical passages present themselves: the aftermath of the eviction of the first-formed from paradise in Genesis, and the psalmic lament of the deported Jews by the banks of the rivers of Babylon. In both cases, the feeling is similar to that of Symeon who is deprived of something precious, the light and sight of God.

Since Genesis (8.7–24) does not include any lament of Adam and Eve after their expulsion, it is reasonable to surmise that Symeon draws this image from the exegetical tradition.[54] It is worth mentioning here that both Symeon and his hagiographer, Niketas Stethatos, have employed the same phrasing (derivatives from καθεζόμενος ἐθρήνουν) in two other passages, where the expulsion of Adam and Eve from paradise is mentioned.[55] As already noted, hymnography of the *Tyrophagos* Sunday

---

[54] Alfeyev, *St. Symeon*, 56, n. 66–7.
[55] Symeon, *Catecheses*, eds. Krivochéine and Paramelle, vol. I, 400 (v.281–4): ἔξω οὖν τοῦ παραδείσου περιπατοῦντες καὶ καθεζόμενοι, μετεμέλοντο, ἔκλαιον, ἐθρήνουν, τὸ πρόσωπον ἔτυπτον, ἔτιλλον σύροντες ἑαυτῶν τὰς τρίχας, τὴν ἑαυτῶν σκληροκαρδίαν ἀποκλαιόμενοι; J. Darrouzès, ed., *Nicétas Stéthatos, Opuscules et Lettres* (Paris, 1961), 172.6–9: καὶ ὡς ἐκεῖνος γυμνὸν τῆς τοῦ Θεοῦ χάριτος

revolves around the broader theme of the expulsion from paradise,[56] where the specific theme of Adam's mourning is a *locus communis*.[57] Thus this mourning of Adam, which is absent in other texts, may be more clearly interpreted when compared to its hymnographical alternatives.

In yet another reference to Adam's mourning (from a prose text on the virtues of ascetic life), Symeon says: 'And still, if you have seen Christ but he has not yet offered you to drink of his cup, prostrate yourself. Wail, importune, lament, beat your face, as Adam did once, and pluck the hair of your head'.[58] Here Symeon associates the mourning of Adam upon being denied paradise with the lament of the man who has seen Christ but was later deprived of the view of Him. This strengthens the connection between the motifs of mourning Adam and the lamenting person who is deprived of God in Hymn XXIX (v.63).

The lamentation scene in Hymn XXIX also has a second biblical analogy referenced above, the psalmic mourning of the exiled Jews by the rivers of Babylon. Psalm 136.1 is narrated in a similar way: 'By the waters of Babylon, there we sat down and there we wept, when we remembered Zion.' It is worth mentioning here that this psalm is sung in the matins each Sunday during the *Triodion* period (that is, the period of three weeks before the beginning of Lent) to which *Tyrophagos* Sunday belongs.[59] The Psalmic text exhorts Jews to repentance and lamentation for what has been taken away from them. It is sung during the particular period of the *Triodion* which predates the major period of contrition, that is, Lent, standing as a reminder to repenting Christians, who should lament their sins like the Jews of the Old Testament.

Therefore, although it appears to be difficult to pinpoint the exact provenance of the overall mourning theme in Hymn XXIX,

---

ἑαυτὸν ὄψεται καὶ τῆς ἀθανάτου τρυφῆς τοῦ Θεοῦ ἐξόριστον καὶ τοῦ παραδείσου τούτου ἀπέναντι καθεζόμενον καὶ θρηνοῦντα εὑρήσει . . .

[56] Mother Mary, ed., F. K. Ware, trans., *The Lenten Triodion* (London, 1978), 39.

[57] Apostolike *Τριῴδιον*, 65 (*doxastikon* in the vespers) Ἐκάθισεν Ἀδάμ, ἀπέναντι τοῦ Παραδείσου, καὶ τὴν ἰδίαν γύμνωσιν θρηνῶν ὠδύρετο; 66 (*Aposticha, Doxastikon*) Ἐξεβλήθη Ἀδὰμ τοῦ Παραδείσου, διὰ τῆς βρώσεως· διὸ καὶ καθεζόμενος ἀπέναντι τούτου ὠδύρετο ὀλολύζων, ἐλεεινῇ τῇ φωνῇ; 68 (*oikos* in the matins) ἐκάθισεν Ἀδὰμ τότε καὶ ἔκλαυσε ἀπέναντι τῆς τρυφῆς τοῦ Παραδείσου, χερσὶ τύπτων τὰς ὄψεις, καὶ ἔλεγεν; 69 (in the *Synaxarion* of the day) ὁ δὲ ἀπέναντι καθήμενος ἔκλαιε, ὅσων ἀγαθῶν ἐστέρηται . . .

[58] Symeon, *Ethical Discourses*, ed. Darrouzès, vol. II, 182–4 (VII.385–8).

[59] The psalm, in an elaborate and slow melismatic genre of the *polyeleos*, is sung after the second stance of *kathismata* in the matins. See Mother Mary and Ware, *The Lenten Triodion*, 153. It is also important to stress that the structure of the hymns for the whole period of *Triodion* owes its formation to the Studite tradition of the ninth century; see 41–3, and E. Wellesz, *A History of Byzantine Music and Hymnography* (Oxford, 1961), 141.

verse 763 in particular conveys a call to repentance which echoes the above-mentioned sources – the hymnographical and biblical narratives about mourning and loss.

Bible

In the same Hymn XXIX, the deprivation of the sight of God proves short, as the Lord appears again before the prostrating and bewailing man. Then a vivid scene of chase develops between the two (v.66–118), with imagery unfolding in a striking fashion. Now, the narrator proceeds to pursue Him in order to catch Him again. When he succeeds, he leaps to embrace Him (v.69–70), and tries to reach Him and grasp the edges of His clothes (v.74–5), yet the Beloved departs once more. Verbal and adverbial words referring to eager motion are abundant in the twenty-octosyllable verses throughout this scene: ἀνεπήδων ... ὥρμων δράξασθαι ... ἔφευγεν ... τάχος, ἔτρεχον ... εὐτόνως· ἐδρασσόμην ... φθάνων· ἵστατο ... ἀφίπτατο ... κατεδίωκον ... ἀπιόντος ἐρχομένου, κρυπτομένου, φαινομένου ... οὐκ ἐστράφην εἰς τοὐπίσω· ... οὐκ ἐνέδωκα τοῦ τρέχειν ... πάσῃ μου ἰσχύϊ ... πάσῃ μου δυνάμει ... ἐζήτουν ... περιεσκόπουν (v.69–89) (I was jumping ... urging to grasp ... He was departing ... in haste, I was running ... vigorously; I was grasping ... catching; He was standing ... He was flying ... I was pursuing ... while He was leaving, He was coming, He was hiding, He was appearing ... I did not turn back; ... I did not give up running ... with all my might ... with my strength ... I was asking ... seeking around). This major scene in the poem describes in detail a hide-and-seek struggle between the two persons; man pursues God in a way that recalls two human beings chasing each other. Therefore, probably an analogous intertextual context recalls this scene in Symeon's hymn.

To continue with the hymn's syllogism: as despair overwhelms the human lover, he does not know what to do or whom to address; he is seeking in the narrows and crossroads, asking everyone for information (v.89–92).[60] At this point, the hymnical context recalls the scene of the search for the Beloved in the biblical *Song of Songs* (3.1–3), with this underlying reference to love as a motivation for the chase. In the next few verses the narrator discards the possibility that any logic or knowledge could assist in the search for his beloved (v.96–104; compare to v.107–8).

---

[60] τὰς ὁδοὺς περιεσκόπουν / καὶ φραγμούς, τὸ ποῦ φανεῖται· / ἐπληρούμην τε δακρύων / καὶ τοὺς πάντας ἐπηρώτων; Luke 14.23.

The passage from then on deals with the idea of the loss of the lover, and transfers man's longing for union with God to an amatory context.[61] Verses like καὶ σφοδροῦ καρδίας πόνου (v.106, with a vehement pain of heart), ὅθεν βλέπων μου τὸν πόθον (v.115, whence seeing my longing), ὅλος ὅλῳ μοι ὡράθη, ὅλος ὅλῳ μοι ἡνώθη (v.128–9, He entirely appeared to all of myself, He was all unified to all of myself), lead to the final stage of Divine Love, the climax of the hymn. The majority of the remaining verses read more like an interpretation than a hymn to God, on the paradox of how this mystical unification with Symeon has become possible (v.130–314). This is a paradox that will have no explanation in logical (sensual) terms.

The hallmark of Divine Love, only implicit in the first section of the hymn (where the reference to the canticles has been identified), culminates in the last section: 'desire kindles desire and fire feeds flame; still, with me it is not like this, but (it is difficult to say) the excess of my love extinguishes my love; for, I do not love as much as I want, and I consider myself as having no love of God at all; as I demand incessantly to be loved, as much as I want, I even lose the love of God that I had, what a wonder!'[62] Derivatives from ἔρως, ἀγάπη and especially πόθος are used nineteen times in this hymn's final section (v.312–69), thus transforming it into a pure love poem. A transformation into a hymn of Divine Love is evident throughout this highly original passage, which commences with the key quotation from the amatory book of the Canticles (3.1–3). Even if we were to judge only from the number of cross-references in Symeon's works to the *Song of the Songs*,[63] Hymn XXIX is unquestionably deeply inspired by this book of the Bible.

Hymn XV narrates in 264 verses how the incarnation of Christ from the root of David has given grace to the human body, down to the last of its members. In the first section, Symeon admits his contemptible and lowly state through many quotations taken from St Paul (v.1–44). In the extended passage which follows (v.45–107), he extols the attributes of the Godhead and the role of the divine dispensation which raised a man from the house of David to an adopted son of God (v.108–34). Up to this point, the hymn develops merely introductory ideas, in comparison with the more innovative elements that come hereafter.

---

[61] For the connection between the running of lovers in Symeon with the *Song of the Songs* and its exegetical tradition see, also: McGuckin, 'Symeon the New Theologian', 195–6.
[62] πόθος γὰρ πόθον ἀνάπτει / καὶ τὸ πῦρ τρέφει τὴν φλόγα· / ἐν ἐμοὶ δ' οὐκ ἔστιν οὕτως, / ἀλλὰ (πῶς, εἰπεῖν οὐκ ἔχω) / ἔρωτος τὸ ὑπερβάλλον / σβέννυσι τὸν ἔρωτά μου· / οὐκ ἐρῶ γὰρ ὅσον θέλω, / καὶ λογίζομαι μηδ' ὅλως / ἔρωτα θεοῦ κεκτῆσθαι· / ἐκζητῶν δὲ ἀκορέστως / τοῦ ἐρᾶν με, ὅσον θέλω, / προσαπόλλω καὶ ὃν εἶχον / ἔρωτα θεοῦ, ὢ θαῦμα ... Symeon, *Hymnen*, ed. Kambylis, 263 (XXIX.316–28).
[63] Alfeyev, *St. Symeon*, 54; Turner, *St. Symeon*, 41.

In the following sections, Symeon repeatedly forewarns his readers that he is going to tell them about things that are fearsome and awe-inspiring (φρικτά ... φρικτά ... ὑπὲρ ἔκπληξιν ... φρικτότερα, v.138–41). He proceeds by asserting that all parts of the human body become Christ-like, even the foot and the hand (v.142–7). To his mind, this is a reality and not a blasphemy: 'thus the bodily parts of any of us will become members of Christ and Christ will become our members and He will make all the disgraceful members graceful by adorning them with the beauty and glory of His divinity' (v.151–4).[64] The reference to disgraceful (ἀσχήμονα) and graceful (εὐσχήμονα) parts (μέλη) of the human body certainly alludes to the relevant passage from St Paul (1 Cor. 12.22–5).[65] This concept can already be found at the beginning of the hymn.[66]

Deification of all parts of the human body is explained in great detail in the following verses (v.155–205) in a plain yet provocative way. Accordingly, all bodily parts, both graceful and disgraceful, even a man's glands, become Christ-like;[67] whereby they partake of a veritable divine intercourse and wedding, as the choice of wording declares: σπέρμα ... ἐν συνουσίᾳ θείᾳ ... συνενοῦται ... γάμος ... μίγνυται ... ὑφ' ἡδονῆς ... ἑνοῦται (v.172–8, 'semen ...in a divine intercourse ... wedding ... copulates ... under pleasure ... is united). Symeon defends these radical concepts by the following rhetorical argument: 'I also tell you; see Christ in the womb; and consider that (He was) in the womb and He slipped out of the womb from whence my God passed through and came out' (v.196–8). Borrowing his ideas from St Paul, who says that 'we honour more the dishonoured members of the body and that the disgraceful members have more grace', Symeon describes here the union between man and God in purely erotic terms. It is obvious that in the present hymn he had adopted St Paul's concept and applied it to his own context.[68]

---

[64] καὶ οὕτω μέλη ἅπαντα ἑνὸς ἡμῶν ἑκάστου / μέλη Χριστοῦ γενήσονται καὶ Χριστὸς ἡμῶν μέλη / καὶ πάντα τὰ ἀσχήμονα εὐσχήμονα ποιήσει / κάλλει θεότητος αὐτὰ κατακοσμῶν καὶ δόξῃ.
[65] 1 Cor. 12.22–5: ἀλλὰ πολλῷ μᾶλλον τὰ δοκοῦντα μέλη τοῦ σώματος ἀσθενέστερα ὑπάρχειν ἀναγκαῖά ἐστιν καὶ ἃ δοκοῦμεν ἀτιμότερα εἶναι τοῦ σώματος, τούτοις τιμὴν περισσοτέραν περιτίθεμεν, καὶ τὰ ἀσχήμονα ἡμῶν εὐσχημοσύνην περισσοτέραν ἔχει, τὰ δ' εὐσχήμονα ἡμῶν οὐ χρείαν ἔχει. ἀλλὰ ὁ θεὸς συνεκέρασεν τὸ σῶμα, τῷ ὑστερουμένῳ περισσοτέραν δοὺς τιμήν, ἵνα μὴ ᾖ σχίσμα ἐν τῷ σώματι, ἀλλὰ τὸ αὐτὸ ὑπὲρ ἀλλήλων μεριμνῶσιν τὰ μέλη.
[66] τοῦ σώματος πολλὴν ἀσχημοσύνην (Symeon, *Hymnen*, ed. Kambylis, 102 (xv.19).
[67] εἰς γὰρ πολλὰ γινόμενος εἷς ἀμέριστος μένει, / μερὶς ἑκάστη δὲ αὐτὸς ὅλος Χριστὸς ὑπάρχει· / πάντως οὖν οὕτως ἔγνωκας †καὶ δάκτυλόν μου Χριστὸν† / καὶ βάλανον· (ibid., 106–7 (xv.159–62)).
[68] In his *Fourth Ethical Discourse* on dispassion, in an extended section (Symeon, *Ethical Discourses*, ed. Darrouzès, vol. II, 34–52 (IV.369–615)) Symeon likened the complete spiritual stature of Christ with the members of the human body. Amongst them, he grants a special honour to genitals: 'members and genitals that should be covered are the unceasing prayer of mind, the inner pleasure

Having elaborated upon the notion of the disgraceful parts of the human body, Symeon substantiates his radical argumentation by presenting the example of his spiritual father, Symeon Eulabes. 'Saint Symeon the Pious, the Stoudite; he felt no shame (οὐκ ἐπῃσχύνετο) in seeing the bodily parts of any man, either to see somebody naked or to be seen naked by anybody' (v.207–10).[69] This passage can be fully understood as a word-for-word reference to *Genesis* (2.25). Before the fall, Adam and Eve 'were both naked and they were not ashamed'.[70] In two further instances in his prose works, Symeon refers to the nudity of the first-formed, although there he focuses on the situation in which they found themselves after they were aware of their nakedness. In the first case, Symeon says that Adam 'tasted the (fruit from the) tree and obtained a sensible way of seeing, and having realised and seen passionately the nakedness of his body, he was justly deprived of all good things';[71] whilst in the second, which is a comment on the same incident, he says that Adam and Eve were not ashamed until 'after the (original) sin and the transgression and after being out of paradise and being deprived of God and having dropped their divine glory, then as it was written "Adam knew his wife and she conceived"'.[72]

In these two passages, the reader encounters four derivatives from the same root as the word for passion (πάθος), i.e. ἐμπαθῶς ... ἐμπαθῶς ... ἐμπαθῆ; πάθους. Using similar terminology, Symeon also refers to his spiritual father, Symeon Eulabes, in Hymn xv: he claims that Symeon was not ashamed of nudity because he had attained the state of impassibility (ἀπάθειαν), the same word found in v.220 of the hymn which

---

that is born by the shedding of tears, the joy of heart and her ineffable consolation': Μέλη καὶ μόρια ἃ ἐγκαλύπτεσθαι χρεών, ἡ ἀδιάλειπτος εὐχὴ κατὰ νοῦν, ἡ ἐκ τῆς χύσεως τῶν δακρύων ἐγγινομένη ἡδύτης, ἡ χαρὰ τῆς καρδίας καὶ ἡ ἄφατος ταύτης παράκλησις (34 (IV.375–8)). For a further analysis and interpretation of Hymn xv as 'a sexed image of the glorious body of the monk', see: Krueger, 'Homoerotic Spectacle', 106–12.

[69] οὕτως ἐγένετο καὶ νῦν ἐν τοῖς ἐσχάτοις χρόνοις / ὁ Συμεὼν ὁ ἅγιος Εὐλαβὴς ὁ Στουδίτης· / οὗτος οὐκ ἐπῃσχύνετο μέλη παντὸς ἀνθρώπου / οὐδὲ γυμνούς τινας ὁρᾶν οὐδὲ γυμνὸς ὁρᾶσθαι· (Symeon, *Hymnen*, ed. Kambylis, 108 (xv.206–9). Alfeyev, *St. Symeon*, 24–7; the author compares Symeon Eulabes with holy fools, who would also not mind being seen naked, however without equating him with a holy fool. Turner, *St. Symeon*, 62–4 and Bazzani, 'Autobiographical Elements', 229, n. 35.

[70] Gen. 2.25: καὶ ἦσαν οἱ δύο γυμνοί, καὶ οὐκ ᾐσχύνοντο.

[71] Symeon, *Ethical Discourses*, ed. Darrouzès, vol. II, 404 (XIII.49–52): ... τοῦ ξύλου ἐγεύσατο καί, αἰσθητῶς ἀναβλέψας, ἐμπαθῶς τε τὴν γύμνωσιν τοῦ σώματος αὐτοῦ θεασάμενος καὶ ἰδών, ἁπάντων ἐστερήθη δικαίως τῶν ἀγαθῶν ...

[72] Symeon, *Catecheses*, eds. Krivochéine and Paramelle, vol. III, 58 (xxv.104–8): ἀλλὰ μετὰ τὴν ἁμαρτίαν καὶ τὴν παράβασιν καὶ μετὰ τὸ ἔξω γενέσθαι τοῦ παραδείσου καὶ τοῦ Θεοῦ γυμνωθῆναι καὶ τῆς αὐτοῦ θείας δόξης ἀποπεσεῖν, τότε, ὡς γέγραπται, «ἔγνω Ἀδὰμ τὴν γυναῖκα αὐτοῦ καὶ συλλαβοῦσα ἔτεκε».

characterised Adam and Eve while still in Paradise.[73] This is why Symeon the New Theologian, when referring to Symeon Eulabes, employs an indirect allusion to *Genesis* (2.25).

Classics and Patristics

Allusions to hymnography and the Bible motivate us to look for similar equivalents from classical literature. While this source material is not readily noticeable in Symeon's texts, in a few of his allegories well-known examples from classical texts can be recognised.

In Symeon's *First Ethical Discourse* there is an extended description of how man experiences God. This metaphorical narration can be named 'the Allegory of the Prisoner'.[74] The author commences by addressing the following question to his virtual dissidents: 'how do you not blush to inquire about and teach those matters, which you do not know, as if you have already become rich in things beyond ourselves and you have been appointed as our teachers from the heavens?'[75] Subsequently, he proceeds by arguing on the issues, such as the divine knowledge and the union with God experienced by saints, when their mind is altered and snatched away from the world of the senses (l.319–39).

The allegory of the prisoner is developed into four parallel pairs of comparison:

Ὡς γὰρ ὁ (l.339) ... οὕτω καὶ ὁ (l.445) ... (For like the one who ... such is also the one who ...)

Καὶ καθάπερ ἐκεῖνος (l.351) ... οὕτω δὴ καὶ ὁ (l.358) ... (Exactly as that man who ... so is also the one who ...)

Καὶ ὥσπερ πάλιν (l.363) ... τὸν αὐτὸν τρόπον (l.373) ... (Likewise again ... in like manner ...)

---

[73] Alfeyev, *St. Symeon*, 253–4. For the meaning of ἀπάθεια and that of 'spiritual senses' in the writings of Symeon see the philosophical approach in S. Ramphos, 'Αἴσθησις ὀξύμωρος. Θεογνωσία ποιητικὴ στὸν τρίτο ὕμνο τοῦ ἁγίου Συμεὼν τοὐπίκλην Νέου Θεολόγου' in Markopoulos, ed., *Τέσσερα κείμενα*, 92–3, 95–9.

[74] Symeon, *Ethical Discourses*, ed. Darrouzès, vol. 1, 296–302 (1.319–415). In addition to the translation in French by the editor, see the English translation of this passage in: A. Golitzin, trans., *St. Symeon the New Theologian. On the Mystical Life: The Ethical Discourses*. vol. 1: *The Church and the Last Things* (Crestwood, NY, 1995), 74–7. On the same allegory see also: S. Ramphos, Ἡ πολιτεία τοῦ Νέου Θεολόγου: Προϊστορία καὶ ἀγωνία τοῦ Νέου Ἑλληνισμοῦ (Athens, 1981), 55–7 and C. Barber, 'Symeon The New Theologian: Seeing Beyond Painting' in C. Barber, *Contesting the Logic of Painting: Art and Understanding in Eleventh-Century Byzantium* (Leiden, 2007), 35–43. A more detailed analysis of this allegory is prepared by the writer of this text in order to be published soon in a separate article.

[75] Symeon, *Ethical Discourses*, ed. Darrouzès, vol. 1, 294 (1.304–7).

Καὶ καθάπερ αὖθις (l.378) ... οὕτω μοι νόει καὶ (l.384–5) ... (Moreover by the very same way ... likewise think also ...).

A prisoner from birth (ὁ ἀπὸ γεννήσεως, l.339) is bound in a dark and gloomy prison, illuminated only by the flickering light of an oil lamp. He remains unaware of all things that exist outside the prison, that is, the visible world and the creatures of God. Hence, he is likened to the man who is bound in the dark prison of worldly senses (l.339–50). But when a hole is opened on the prison's roof, he can suddenly see the ether of the sky, and becomes stunned by the brilliant light, unknown to him before. In like manner, the one who suddenly beholds the spiritual light, feels as if he has been set free from the shackles of passions and senses (l.351–63). As the prisoner gazes often at the opening above, he becomes familiar with the sight of light, and is no longer surprised by it; a man's soul undergoes a similar change after being initiated into the spiritual light, when his astonishment disappears, and he considers that something more perfect and sublime exists beyond (l.363–77). The prisoner becomes aware of his incarceration and the existence of wonderful things beyond his confinement because of this light, even when he is not fully able to understand this. Only after he is cast out of the prison can he see the full light, as well as all things and everyone imbued by it; likewise, the one who has detached himself from the needs of flesh leaves behind all worldly matters and beholds the Divine Light (l.378–87).

Symeon's allegory of the prisoner has already been connected to Plato's 'Allegory of the Cave' (*Rep.* 514a–20a), although modern scholars would only credit an indirect debt to the classical text,[76] as they do not adequately ascertain to what extent Symeon was aware of Plato's passage. In my opinion, there is strong evidence that Symeon was not ignorant of the famous passage from Plato's *Republic*. First, we can link Symeon's allegory to a passage by Gregory of Nazianzos, according to which the soul rejoices and moves propitiously to her Lord, having abandoned the current life as if it were a grievous jail.[77] Notably, a further metaphor referring to the sun

---

[76] Darrouzès, *Traités théologiques*, 296, n. 1; Golitzin, *St. Symeon*, 74, n. 5; see B. Krivochéine, *Dans la lumière du Christ: Saint Syméon le nouveau théologien, 949–1022, vie, spiritualité, doctrine* (Chevetogne, 1980), 183–4, 369–71; Ramphos, Ἡ πολιτεία τοῦ Νέου Θεολόγου, 58: on the contrary Ramphos states that Symeon's 'Allegory of the Prisoner' is an ironic version of Plato's 'Allegory of the Cave', – maybe overturning it? – thus in a polemical tone Symeon judges similar intellectual attempts by his adversaries.

[77] F. Boulenger, ed., *Grégoire de Nazianze. Discours funèbres en l'honneur de son frère Césaire et de Basile de Césarée* (Paris, 1908), 46–7 (XXI.2): θαυμασίαν τινὰ ἡδονὴν ἥδεται καὶ ἀγάλλεται καὶ ἵλεως χωρεῖ πρὸς τὸν ἑαυτῆς δεσπότην, ὥσπερ τι δεσμωτήριον χαλεπὸν τὸν ἐνταῦθα βίον ἀποφυγοῦσα ...

(l.342, 369–73, 389–90) is incorporated in Symeon's wider allegory. The metaphor of the soul's incarceration in the mortal body and the allegorical equation of the sun to God are also encountered in Symeon's Hymn XXVII. 95–102.[78] Of course, this metaphor of the sun was first employed by Plato (*Rep.* 507b–509c).[79] According to Gregory of Nazianzos, 'sun is for the sensible, what God is for the spiritual, one of the strangers (pagans) said',[80] a passage which is quoted verbatim by Symeon in yet another work.[81] In this context, it is clear that Gregory alludes to the Platonic metaphor of the sun and to Plato himself by stressing the phrase, 'one of the strangers said'. Furthermore, Symeon shows that he is aware of the allusion from Gregory of Nazianzos by stating 'and Gregory the Theologian says so'. Symeon in his turn has further built upon the mediated knowledge of Plato that Gregory of Nazianzos offers.

However, Symeon has added two unprecedented details to his allegory of the prisoner. First, the notion of the sun acquires a novel significance through the introduction of a negative element, thereby giving the sun a double meaning. Whilst positively, as in Plato, the bright allegorical sun beyond the prison is likened to the light of God,[82] the real-world sun, marked in a negative way, is likened to the illusionary oil-lamp of the dark prison.[83] Second, Symeon refers to an imprisonment from the man's birth.[84] By this, he probably means that we are born in our flesh, thus we remain in our bodies as congenital prisoners.

Despite these minor differences or additions, Symeon's concept of the soul's torment in the dark prison of the flesh is a close parallel to Gregory's allegory which, in turn, in all likelihood has a Platonic origin. It is rather

---

[78] τούτῳ νυνὶ δὲ λείπονται μόνῳ, ὅτι κρατοῦνται / τῷ σώματι καὶ σκέπονται καὶ καλύπτονται, οἴμοι, / ὡς δέσμιοι ἐν φυλακῇ τὸν ἥλιον ὁρῶντες / καὶ τὰς ἀκτῖνας τὰς αὐτοῦ δι' ὀπῆς εἰσιούσας, / καὶ μὴ δυνάμενοι αὐτὸν ὅλον κατανοῆσαι / ἢ κατιδεῖν τῆς φυλακῆς ἔξωθεν γεγονότες / ἢ παρακύψαντες τρανῶς ἀπιδεῖν εἰς ἀέρα. For the connection between the *First Ethical Discourse* and Hymn XXVII as well as for the wider use of the metaphor of the sun in Symeon's works, see: Kazhdan, 'Das System', 224, 237.

[79] For a further connection between Plato's 'metaphor of the sun' and the usage by Symeon, see: Ramphos, 'Αἴσθησις ὀξύμωρος', 98–9, 118.

[80] J. Barbel, ed., *Gregor von Nazianz. Die fünf theologischen Reden* (Düsseldorf, 1963), 122 (30.1–2): Τοῦτο ἐν αἰσθητοῖς ἥλιος, ὅπερ ἐν νοητοῖς θεός, ἔφη τις τῶν ἀλλοτρίων. It is worth mentioning that Gregory also employs the same allegory in other works of his: *PG*, 35.1084A; *PG*, 36.364B.

[81] Symeon, *Ethical Discourses*, ed. Darrouzès, vol. II, 308 (x.688–90): Περὶ τούτου γὰρ καὶ ὁ θεολόγος οὕτω λέγει Γρηγόριος· «Ὅπερ ἐστὶ τοῖς αἰσθητοῖς ἥλιος, τοῦτο τοῖς νοητοῖς Θεός.»

[82] Ibid., vol. I, 296 (1.342)1: μὴ εἰδὼς ὅτι φῶς ἡλιακόν ἐστιν ἔξωθεν; 298 (I.369): ὃν τρόπον καὶ ἐπὶ τοῦ ἡλίου γέγονεν ἐφ' ἡμᾶς.

[83] Ibid., vol. I, 300 (1.389–90): λυχνιαῖον δὲ φῶς τὸ τοῦ ἡλίου λογίζου μοι φῶς, ἔξωθεν δὲ τούτου τὸ ἀνεκλάλητον.

[84] Ibid., vol. I, 296 (1.339): ὁ ἀπὸ γεννήσεως ἐν σκοτεινῇ καὶ ζοφωτάτῃ ὢν φυλακῇ; 379: ἀπὸ γεννήσεως αὐτοῦ κάθειρξις.

likely that Symeon is aware of both the Platonic allegories, namely, that of the Sun and that of the Cave. Yet, it is also clear that Gregory of Nazianzos acts as an additional medium, and it is interesting to see how Symeon grafts them in his writings.

Some other allusions support the idea that Symeon is probably aware of classical texts. In a chapter of his *Centuriae*, he regards the consecutive generations of saints as a golden chain, in which each saint is bound as a single link to an unbroken sequence: 'Saints coming after the preceding saints, generation after generation, and getting attached to them through the work of God's orders, are equally enlightened by them, having received the grace of God by participation, and they become exactly as a golden chain (χρυσῇ ἅλυσις), each of them being joined with the previous one, being bound together by their faith and their acts and their love, so that they are and they have become one chain, as God is one, that cannot be easily broken.'[85] This simile possibly alludes to the well-known passage in the *Iliad* (Il. Θ.19–27), where Zeus addresses the gods and goddesses using the reference to a golden chain. This pair of words (σειρὴν χρυσείην, Il. Θ.19) has been used both in classical and in Christian literature, by Lucian and Gregory of Nazianzos among others, so that it has become a *locus communis* through the centuries.[86]

Another instance can be found in the rather long Hymn xxx, which analyses the purification of the soul by the fire of the Divine Spirit. In three different passages of this hymn (v.368–72, 391–5, 420–4), Symeon says that after he had been deprived of the vision of God, he remained like a being enclosed in a large earthenware jar. More specifically, in the first passage he relates that 'sitting in the middle of my tent, as being confined in a basket or a jar, I was crying, I was lamenting greatly without seeing outside'.[87] Consequently, after he has recovered the vision of God, he says: 'having seen Him I was stunned, being confined in the house and enclosed

---

[85] Symeon, *Centuriae*, in Darrouzès, ed., *Chapitres théologiques*, 122 (III.11–19): Ἀπὸ γὰρ τῶν προλαβόντων ἁγίων οἱ κατὰ γενεὰν καὶ γενεὰν διὰ τῆς τῶν ἐντολῶν τοῦ Θεοῦ ἐργασίας ἐρχόμενοι ἅγιοι, τούτοις κολλώμενοι, ὁμοίως ἐκείνοις ἐλλάμπονται, τὴν τοῦ Θεοῦ χάριν λαμβάνοντες κατὰ μέθεξιν, καὶ ὥσπερ τις γίνονται χρυσῆ ἅλυσις, καθεὶς τούτων ὄντες γονάτιον ἐν ἑκάτερος τῷ προλαβόντι τῇ πίστει καὶ τοῖς ἔργοις καὶ τῇ ἀγάπῃ συνδούμενος, ὡς εἶναι μίαν αὐτοὺς καὶ γίνεσθαι σειρὰν ἐν ἑνὶ τῷ Θεῷ μὴ δυναμένην ταχέως διαρραγῆναι. See P. McGuckin, trans., *Symeon the New Theologian: The Practical and Theological Chapters and the Three Theological Discourses* (Kalamazoo, 1982), 73, n. 3. The same idea of the saints' union without a reference to a golden chain is analysed in Symeon, *Ethical Discourses*, ed. Darrouzès, vol. I, 224–36 (I.1–102); McGuckin, 'Symeon the New Theologian', 183, n. 11.

[86] Revelations 45:18; Gregory of Nazianzus, *Poemata histórica*, II. De se ipso, *PG* 37.979A.

[87] καὶ καθήμενος ἐν μέσῳ / τῆς σκηνῆς ὥσπερ ἐν θήβῃ / ἢ ἐν πίθῳ κεκλεισμένος / ἔκλαιον, ἐθρήνουν σφόδρα / ἔξωθεν ὅλως μὴ βλέπων· Symeon, *Hymnen*, ed. Kambylis, 278–9 (xxx.368–72).

in the jar and being in the middle of the darkness, I mean, in between heaven and earth'.[88] Nonetheless, he could not understand how it was possible 'to see Him, and to be seen by Him; I have seen Him again having suddenly entered inside the house and the jar and being united ineffably'.[89] The motif of the enclosure in a jar is repeated several times, and it might be a reminiscence of the famous story about the philosopher Diogenes.[90] Another possible allusion could be the 'earthen vessels' referred to by St Paul (2. Cor. 4:7).

Lastly, from the beginning of Hymn XXVIII (on the revelation of the operation of the Divine Light to those who practise the virtuous life), Symeon expresses a will to remain enclosed in his cell, having no contact whatsoever with the outside world (v.1–15), so that he would be able to fulfil his insatiable appetite to behold his Lord (v.16–64). The profundity and the tangibility of this mystical experience – both in his cell and in his soul – makes him liken it to a treasure that he keeps hidden in his bosom (v.62–4). Nobody, not even a robber, can either pull it out or snatch it away, even if he kills its bearer (v.66–7). And even if a robber searches the bearer's purse and garments or loosens his belt, the search will be in vain; even if the robber cuts his belly open and gropes around within it, he will not be able to find or catch Him (v.69–72). For He is invisible and intangible and untouchable (v.73–4). And God, the very object of Symeon's ardent desire is finally named, 'the something, o wonder, the nothing (οὔ τι), for it does not have any name'.[91] This last verse recalls the answer of Odysseus to the Cyclops after he blinded him (Od.1,364–7): 'my name is nobody' (οὖτις). Similarly God in Symeon has no name; He can be called 'something', and in a wonderful way, also, 'nothing'.

Be this as it may, the reader notices again that Symeon prefers to employ his allusions in a cryptic way, rather than pointing explicitly to a textual context that he had in mind. Thus we are usually left puzzled about the provenance of several images that seem to have come from other textual contexts.

---

[88] ὃν ἰδὼν ἐξεθαμβήθην / ἐν οἰκίᾳ καθειργμένος / καὶ ἐν πίθῳ κεκλεισμένος / καὶ τοῦ σκότους ὢν ἐν μέσῳ, / οὐρανοῦ καὶ γῆς σοὶ λέγω· Ibid., 279 (xxx.391–5).
[89] πῶς ὃν βλέπω, πῶς με βλέπει· εἶδον πάλιν τοῦτον ἔνδον / τῆς οἰκίας καὶ τοῦ πίθου / ὅλον ἀφνης γεγονότα / ἑνωθέντα τε ἀφράστως (ibid., 280 (xxx.420–4). L.260, 279); McGuckin, 'Symeon the New Theologian', 194, n. 52.
[90] For the presence of the philosopher in the early Christian fathers, see: D. Krueger, 'Diogenes the Cynic Among the Fourth Century Fathers', *VigChr*, 47 (1993), 29–49. For the reference to the abiding of Diogenes in the jar, see: H. S. Long, ed., *Diogenis Laertii Vitae philosophorum* (Oxford, 1964; repr. 1966), 6.23.19–21.
[91] τὸ τί, ὦ θαῦμα, τὸ οὐ τί· ὄνομα γὰρ οὐκ ἔχει Symeon, *Hymnen*, ed. Kambylis, 246 (xxviii.77).

While not exhaustive, this chapter has studied representative allusive techniques in Symeon the New Theologian's works. It begins with an examination of his primary, encyclical and monastic education in order to get some idea about his rhetorical and literary training. The degree of his familiarity with wider textual traditions is difficult to prove and not easily revealed, yet his ability as an author cannot be disregarded. Although we find little evidence to support the notion that Symeon was well-versed in classical literature, he certainly was well-read in the Christian classics, that is, the Scriptures, patristic and ascetic literature, hymnography and hagiography.

The main body of the chapter contains a number of examples studying the techniques by which Symeon refers to other texts. He often declares his learnedness in the Scriptures, making references by verbatim quotation or naming the source and/or its author. References to non-verbatim sources of inspiration are less easy to discern, for he employs a concept or an idea rather than a specific passage in order to build it into a new allegorical scene or narrative. Using this technique, his allusions do not appear in the form of mere quotations. They usually comprise the central expanded idea, an inspiration or a concept around which a section or a whole work will revolve.

Regardless of the origin of his allusions, Symeon principally intends to share his mystical experience.[92] He feels compelled to explain to his reader the spiritual (νοητός) presence of God and His Light in sensual (αἰσθητός) terms, thus he employs examples from the real world for this purpose. Many of these examples, which are allegorical and rich in their imagery, are inspired from other texts, as shown above, and their initial ideas are expanded by the author into a much longer allegory or scene which is Symeon's own original contribution. Very often their source is difficult to discern. In an analogous 'mystical' technique, Symeon allows his reader, contemporary or modern, only to suspect the alluded text, without permitting him to read the exact reference from the more recent or more antique textual past. His images are so vivid and his narration so artful that the original idea is always further underlined through the new creation of the author.[93]

---

[92] Primarily, Symeon's mystical experience motivated him to write. Secondarily he felt the necessity to describe it to his brothers. See, Koder: 'Γιατί ὁ Συμεών', 815–18 and Koder, 'Ὁ Συμεών ὁ Νέος', 9–11.

[93] Special thanks to the anonymous reviewers and Vangelis Zournatzis for their suggestions during the composition and revision of this article.

Further Reading

The key texts are: P. H. Greenfield, *The Life of Saint Symeon the New Theologian* (Cambridge, MA, 2013) and A. Kambylis, ed., *Symeon Neos Theologos. Hymnen* (Berlin, 1976). Important studies include: C. Barber, 'Symeon the New Theologian: Seeing Beyond Painting' in C. Barber, *Contesting the Logic of Painting: Art and Understanding in Eleventh-century Byzantium* (Leiden, 2007), 23–59 and A. Markopoulos, ed., Τέσσερα κείμενα για την ποίηση του Συμεών του Νέου Θεολόγου (Athens, 2008).

CHAPTER 12

Scriptural Citation in Andronikos Kamateros

Alessandra Bucossi

In 1982, Northrop Frye described the Bible as 'The Great Code' for the decryption of western literature and culture.[1] It is a truism to say that the same 'Great Code' is the key also to understanding much of Byzantine literature.[2] However, when we approach a complex piece of medieval Greek writing, we should remember that contemporary readers were certainly expected to be able to decipher encoded texts or, better, to display familiarity with a code that could allow them to fully understand a text and its concealed implications. In this context, the *Sacred Arsenal*[3] by Andronikos Kamateros is a good example of how the Bible can function as

---

[1] N. Frye, *The Great Code: The Bible and Literature* (London, 1982).

[2] Some valuable contributions, particularly on the usage of biblical quotations: R. Maisano, 'La funzione letteraria della Bibbia nei testi bizantini' in xxe *Congrès International des études byzantines-Pré-Actes* (Paris, 2001), vol. 1, 38–46; R. Maisano, 'Funzione letteraria delle citazioni bibliche nelle preghiere dei contaci di Romano il Melodo' in N. Grisanti, ed., *Ad contemplandam sapientiam: Studi di filologia letteratura e storia in memoria di Sandro Leanza* (Catanzaro, 2004), 369–77; R. Maisano, 'La funzione letteraria della Bibbia in Niceta Coniata' in A. Garzya, ed., *Spirito e forme nella letteratura bizantina* (Naples, 2006), 47–64. In the wake of the seminal article by Riccardo Picchio, 'The Function of Biblical Thematic Clues in the Literary Code of "Slavia Orthodoxa"', *Slavica Hierosolymitana*, 1 (1977), 1–31, a number of publications of great interest have appeared in recent years by Slavist scholars on the literary function of biblical quotations, for example M. Garzaniti, 'Bible and Liturgy in Church Slavonic Literature. A New Perspective for Research in Medieval Slavonic Studies' in J. A. Álvarez-Pedrosa and S. Torres Prieto, eds., *Medieval Slavonic Studies. New Perspectives for Research. Études slaves médiévales. Nouvelles perspectives de recherche* (Paris, 2009), 127–48; M. Garzaniti, 'Sacre scritture ed esegesi patristica nella Vita di Metodio' in A. Bartolomei Romagnoli, U. Paoli and P. Piatti, eds., *Hagiologica. Studi per Réginald Grégoire* (Fabriano, 2012), 385–92; M. Garzaniti and F. Romoli, 'Le funzioni delle citazioni bibliche nella letteratura della Slavia ortodossa' in M. Garzaniti, A. Alberti, M. Perotto and B. Sulpasso, eds., *Contributi italiani al xv Congresso Internazionale degli Slavisti (Minsk, 20–27 settembre 2013)* (Florence, 2013), 121–56; C. Diddi, 'Le "chiavi tematiche bibliche" nel contesto della tradizione retorica e letteraria europea', *Studia Ceranea*, 3 (2013), 11–28; F. Romoli, 'Le citazioni bibliche nell'omiletica e nella letteratura di direzione spirituale del medioevo slavo orientale (xii–xiii sec.)', *Mediaevistik*, 27 (2014), 119–40.

[3] *ODB* translates the Greek title *Hiera Hoplotheke* (Ἱερὰ ὁπλοθήκη) with 'Sacred Panoply' (see s.v. 'Kamateros'), however since this translation can be confused with the title of the well-known text by Euthymios Zygabenos, 'Dogmatic Panoply', I prefer to encourage the usage of the title 'Sacred Arsenal', or even better the Latin translation 'Sacrum Armamentarium'.

a code that veils and mystifies an open polemic. Moreover, it shows how biblical quotations could be used as a rhetorical tool to extol the role of the Byzantine emperor in the church and, therefore, be a powerful expedient in boosting imperial propaganda.[4]

Andronikos Kamateros was neither an orator nor a preacher, or at least our sources do not describe him as such. Rather, he was a nobleman active at the Constantinopolitan court during the second half of the twelfth century,[5] and, most certainly, an eminent man – he had the dignity of *sebastos*[6] as well as the senior offices of *epi ton deeseon* (1155),[7] *eparchos* of Constantinople (1157–61)[8] and *megas droungarios tes viglas* (1166).[9] In all probability, he had at least a general understanding of rhetoric – Tzetzes, while discussing Hermogenes' and Aphthonius' *Progymnasmata* in his *Chiliads*,[10] refers to some '*démêlés littéraires*'[11] he had with Andronikos – but, as far as we know, he did not write orations or homilies. If he had not composed, by imperial order, the voluminous *Sacred Arsenal*,[12] he would be a little-known twelfth-century *megas droungarios*, despite the fact that his noble origin had made him a second cousin to emperor Manuel Komnenos on his maternal side and the father of the future empress Euphrosyne Doukaina Kamatera (*floruit* 1169–1210), who married

---

[4] My argument in this chapter is essentially based on my DPhil thesis ('Prolegomena to the critical edition of *Hiera Hoplotheke* – *Sacred Arsenal* by Andronikos Kamateros', University of Oxford (2006) and, therefore, reflects that stage of my studies and maturity. If I had to write the same chapter today, it would certainly be different; what would be exactly the same would be my gratitude for my DPhil supervisor Elizabeth Mary Jeffreys. For a more extended study, see my *editio princeps* of the *Sacred Arsenal*: A. Bucossi, ed., *Andronici Camateri Sacrum Armamentarium: Pars prima* (Turnhout, 2014).

[5] J. Darrouzès, 'Les documents byzantins du XIIe siècle sur la primauté romaine', *REB*, 23 (1965), 72–8; J. Spiteris, *La critica Bizantina del primato romano nel secolo XII* (Rome, 1979), 177–94; A. C. Cataldi Palau, 'L'*Arsenale Sacro* di Andronico Camatero: Il proemio ed il dialogo dell'imperatore con i cardinali latini: Originale, imitazioni, arrangiamenti', *REB*, 51 (1993), 5–62.

[6] On the appellations used to address Kamateros, see M. Grünbart, *Formen der Anrede im byzantinischen Brief vom 6. bis zum 12. Jahrhundert* (Vienna, 2005), 195.

[7] J. Darrouzès, ed., *George et Dèmètrios Tornikès: Lettres et discours* (Paris, 1970), 140–1, no. 16. (henceforward Darrouzès, *Tornikès*).

[8] A. Meineke, ed., *Ioannis Cinnami Epitome rerum ab Ioanne et Alexio Comnenis gestarum* (Bonn, 1836), 210 (henceforward *Kinnamos, Epitome*); I. Sakkelion, ed., Πατμιακὴ βιβλιοθήκη (Athens, 1890), 316.

[9] S. N. Sakkos, Ὁ Πατήρ μου μείζων μού ἐστι: ἔριδες καὶ σύνοδοι κατὰ τὸν ιβ' αἰῶνα (Thessalonike, 1968), vol. I, 154 (henceforward Sakkos, *Ekthesis*).

[10] P. M. Leone, ed., *Ioannis Tzetzae Historiae* (Naples, 1968), 370 (IX.656); 438 (XI.211).

[11] Darrouzès, *Tornikès*, 44, n. 70.

[12] On the dating of the *Sacred Arsenal*, see A. Bucossi, 'New Historical Evidence for the Dating of the *Sacred Arsenal* by Andronikos Kamateros', *REB*, 67 (2009), 111–30.

Alexios III Angelos around 1169.[13] The *Sacred Arsenal*, on the contrary, remained a very influential theological compilation until the fifteenth century.[14] It was read, copied, and refuted by the most famous Byzantine theologians, amongst them Blemmydes,[15] Bekkos,[16] Bessarion,[17] and Mark Eugenikos.[18]

Since a critical edition of the *Sacred Arsenal* has only recently appeared,[19] it is useful to present the structure of the text briefly.[20] Kamateros' literary monument is a theological compilation made up of two dialogues between the emperor and the Latin and Armenian envoys that are reported to be *verbatim* transcriptions of the events, and of two voluminous anthologies. The text is introduced by an epigram composed by George Skylitzes,[21] followed by a prologue and a proem. The first half of the *Sacred Arsenal* is dedicated to the Latin church and contains a dialogue on papal primacy and the procession of the Holy Spirit, a prefatory exhortation 'addressed to those who say that the all-holy Spirit proceeds from the Father and the Son', two vast anthologies – the first one

---

[13] K. N. Sathas, ed., *Bibliotheca Graeca Medii Aevi* (Venice, 1872–94; reprint 1972), vol. VII, 414; E. L. Vranouse, Πρόσταξις τοῦ αὐτοκράτορος Μανουὴλ Α' Κομνηνοῦ ὑπὲρ τῆς ἐν Πάτμῳ μονῆς Ἰωάννου τοῦ Θεολόγου, in Χαριστήριον εἰς Ἀναστάσιον Κ. Ὀρλάνδον (Athens, 1965–8), vol. II, 95–6; D. I. Polemis, *The Doukai: A Contribution to Byzantine Prosopography* (London, 1968), 131; J.-L. van Dieten, ed., *Nicetae Choniatae Historia* (Berlin, 1975), 455; K. Varzos, Ἡ γενεαλογία τῶν Κομνηνῶν (Thessalonike, 1984), vol. II, 727. For prosopographical notes, see Polemis and Varzos.

[14] See A. Bucossi, 'The *Sacred Arsenal* by Andronikos Kamateros, a Forgotten Treasure' in A. Rigo and P. Ermilov, eds., *Byzantine Theologians. The Systematization of their Own Doctrine and their Perception of Foreign Doctrines* (Rome, 2009), 33–50.

[15] M. Stavrou, ed., 'Le premier traité sur la procession du Saint-Esprit de Nicéphore Blemmydès: présentation, édition critique et traduction annotée', *OrChrP*, 67 (2001), 80–4.

[16] John Bekkos, *Refutationes adversus Andronici Camateri, viglae drungarii, super scripto traditis testimoniis de Spiritu Sancto animadversiones*, PG 141, 396–613.

[17] Bessarion possessed a copy of the *Sacred Arsenal*, today *Venetus Marcianus Graecus* 158 (coll. 515). E. Mioni, *Bibliothecae Divi Marci Venetiarum codices graeci manuscripti*, (Rome, 1981), vol. I, *Thesaurus Antiquus, codices 1–299*, 230–1.

[18] John Plousiadenos, *Josephi Methonensis Episcopi Responsio ad libellum domini Marci Eugenici metropolitae Ephesi, in quo Marcus quid de sacrosanta Florentina sentiret exponit*, PG 159, 1092; and John Plousiadenos, *Disceptatio de differentiis inter Graecos et Latinos. Et, De Sacrosanta Synodo Florentina*, PG 159, 967–8.

[19] The fullest version of the text is preserved in two manuscripts: M = *Monacensis graecus* 229, thirteenth century; and V = *Venetus Marcianus graecus* Z. 158 (coll. 515), first quarter of the fourteenth century.

[20] A more detailed description and analysis of the contents of the *Sacred Arsenal* can be found in A. Bucossi, 'Dialogues and Anthologies of the *Sacred Arsenal* by Andronikos Kamateros: Sources, Arrangements, Purposes' in C. Macé and P. Van Deun, eds., *Encyclopaedic Trends in Byzantium: Proceedings of the International Conference held in Leuven, 6–8 May 2009* (Leuven, 2011), 269–84.

[21] Full text and translation in A. Bucossi, 'George Skylitzes' Dedicatory Verses for the *Sacred Arsenal* by Andronikos Kamateros and the *Codex Marcianus graecus* 524', *JÖB*, 59 (2009), 37–50. See also A. Rhoby, 'Zur Identifizierung von bekannten Autoren im Codex Marcianus graecus 524', *Medioevo Greco*, 10 (2010), 167–204.

is a compilation of patristic passages and the second of syllogisms – an allocution that follows the patristic anthology and a final epilogue. The second half of the text, dedicated to the Armenian church, broadly follows the same pattern.

In the prologue, Andronikos Kamateros refers to himself as the compiler of the *Sacred Arsenal* rather than its author. He in fact describes the role he played in the composition with these words:

> The emperor laid the care and solicitude for these upon the aforementioned *sebastos*, because this [*sebastos*] was near him at that time and attended the dialogues, but after having enjoined him initially to note down the dialogues, to compile the [anthology of] quotations, to set forth notes after each quotation, of which the greater and the more obscure part he himself virtually dictated to him in his own words, and to prepare the syllogisms, this [*sebastos*] [at the end] was only useful for the composition of the proems, addresses and epilogues.[22]

From this passage it is clear that Kamateros does not ascribe paternity of the *Sacred Arsenal* to himself and that he wants to pay homage to his emperor by denying his own intervention. However, the very last sentence of the passage states clearly that at least some sections of the *Sacred Arsenal* – proems, addresses and epilogues – were composed by him.

This contribution analyses some of those parts of the text that the *megas droungarios* Kamateros claims are his own work in order to explore how he uses biblical quotations as a rhetorical tool that extols his emperor, Manuel Komnenos. Indeed the following analysis explores how Andronikos embellishes the canvas of his text with endless biblical allusions; he links one biblical reference to another, one passage to another, hinting at the original context from which these passages have been excerpted. Key, and unmistakably recognisable, words of the Bible are modified and adapted to the new context, but also, and even more interestingly, these same words modify and adapt the text to fit into a context that is suspended between the reality of the twelfth-century reign of Manuel Komnenos, the Gospel events and teachings, and the order of the eternal Christendom. This

---

[22] The English translation is mine and will appear in the Liverpool University Press series *Translated Texts for Byzantinists*. Kamateros, *Sacred Arsenal*, 14.31–40, Τῷ δηλωθέντι σεβαστῷ τὴν περὶ τούτων ἀνέθετο φροντίδα καὶ μέριμναν ὡς παρισταμένῳ τηνικαῦτα τούτῳ καὶ ἀκροωμένῳ τῶν διαλέξεων· ὑποθέμενος αὐτῷ πρότερον τήν τε τῶν διαλέξεων συγγραφήν, τὴν τῶν χρήσεων παρεκβολήν, τὴν τῆς ἐφ᾽ ἑκάστῃ τῶν χρήσεων ἐπιστασίας ἔκθεσιν, ὧν τὰς πλείους καὶ γριφωδεστέρας αὐτὸς αὐτολεξεὶ σχεδὸν πρὸς τοῦτον ἀπεστομάτισε, καὶ τὴν τῶν συλλογισμῶν μεταχείρισιν· τούτου πρὸς μόνην τὴν τῶν προοιμίων, τῶν προσφωνημάτων καὶ τῶν ἐπιλόγων γραφὴν χρησιμεύσαντος.

procedure is a kind of Proustian madeleine: every quotation summons up a new quotation and the complete picture becomes clear only once the reader recognises every single allusion. To take another metaphor, this contribution follows Ariadne's thread through the labyrinth of Kamateros' thoughts and the biblical quotations or allusions that he inserts. Through this analysis of two sections of the texts: the Proem and the Prefatory Exhortation, I attempt to unveil the multifaceted message that the *Sacred Arsenal* is intended to convey.

The Proem of the *Sacred Arsenal*

The proem of the *Sacred Arsenal* is composed of two main sections. The first extols the emperor's orthodoxy, the second reports how after numerous meetings with representatives of other churches and faiths, Manuel Komnenos asked Andronikos Kamateros to compile an 'arsenal' of biblical and patristic passages in support of the Greek interpretation of some Christian doctrines. The first, eulogistic, section is of course the most interesting for our analysis and, therefore, the only one analysed in this contribution; indeed it is in this section precisely that Kamateros uses the Bible as a code to encrypt his anti-papal message most extensively.[23]

'A lion will roar and who will not be frightened?'[24] This biblical quotation from the Book of Amos introduces immediately the main reason for which Kamateros wrote his vast work: the emperor had issued an order. The command is sacred because it regards God, and furthermore it is significant because it was given by the great emperor Manuel Komnenos. The beginning of the proem compares the emperor with Peter. His heart is enflamed with love for God like that of the coryphaeus of the apostles;[25] his heart is upset like that of Peter when he draws his sword against the guards of the chief priest.[26] These are the first images of the praise of Manuel, an emperor so great to be described not only as an apostle, but even as the chief of the apostles. As Paul Magdalino has already pointed out by highlighting the resemblance between the images inserted in the *Sacred Arsenal* and in the opening of the Edict of 1166, the references to Peter are particularly characteristic of the imperial propaganda of Manuel Komnenos.[27] The emperor in fact, Magdalino states, 'was ultimately

---

[23] Kamateros, *Sacred Arsenal*, 16.1–18.63.   [24] Ibid., 16.1 = Am. 3:8.   [25] Ibid., 16.8–10.
[26] Ibid., 16.10–16
[27] C. Mango, 'The Conciliar Edict of 1166', *DOP*, 17 (1963), 317–30; J. Gouillard, 'Le synodikon de l'Orthodoxie: Edition et commentaire', *TM*, 2 (1967), 216–26; P. Magdalino, *The Empire of Manuel I Komnenos, 1143–1180* (Cambridge, 1993), 287–8. Sakkos, *Ekthesis*, 167–73.

Scriptural Citation in Andronikos Kamateros 301

concerned to impress the Christian world, and especially the Latin world, as the ruler of Christian unity'.[28] Therefore, as we shall see with the rest of the text, Kamateros chooses Petrine and Pauline images, typical also of the papal rhetoric, to exalt the role of the emperor as the supreme protector of the universal Church.

Coming back to the proem, if attention is paid to the parallelism between Peter and the emperor, the content of the first part of *Sacred Arsenal* can be found *in nuce*. One sentence is particularly meaningful: 'drawing the sword of the Spirit, that is to say, the words of God emanating from his lips'.[29] The image of the emperor drawing the 'sword of the Spirit' is used because the *Filioque* question, that is the discussion on the procession of the Holy Spirit, is the main subject of the first dialogue. Even more interestingly, the verb used by Kamateros in the sentence 'the words of his lips emanated from God' is not chosen by chance; indeed ἐκπορ- εύεσθαι (to 'proceed' or 'emanate') is the technical term used in theology to describe the procession of the Holy Spirit.[30] As the Spirit proceeds from the Father, so the words of God proceed from the emperor; therefore, Kamateros inserts right at the beginning of the proem the best justification for Manuel's intervention in the definition of dogmas.

There is, however, another noteworthy point to be added. The quotation from the Letter to the Ephesians is revealing of the nature of *Sacred Arsenal* because in that same letter Paul invites his readers to 'put on the full armour of God'.[31] This is the passage that inspires the titles of the *Dogmatic Panoply* (*Panoplia dogmatike*) written by Zigabenos for Alexios Komnenos and, although in a synonymous form, of the *Sacred Arsenal*;[32] therefore, it is clear that the series of references to spiritual 'weapons' are also allusions to the titles of these Komnenian masterpieces.

The description of the emperor's enemies that follows could represent more than a general description: each of these sentences arguably contains a very particular reference. Kamateros writes:

---

[28] Magdalino, *Empire of Manuel I*, 291.
[29] Kamateros, *Sacred Arsenal*, 17.10–12, κἀντεῦθεν ἕλκοντος τὴν τοῦ Πνεύματος μάχαιραν, τὰ τῶν αὐτοῦ δηλονότι χειλέων ἐκπορευόμενα τοῦ Θεοῦ ῥήματα. Cf. Eph. 6:17, καὶ τὴν μάχαιραν τοῦ πνεύματος, ὅ ἐστιν ῥῆμα Θεοῦ. It must be noted here that the same reference is found in the Edict of 1166 in Sakkos, *Ekthesis*, 168.3–4.
[30] John 15:26.   [31] Eph. 6:1, ἐνδύσασθε τὴν πανοπλίαν τοῦ Θεοῦ.
[32] For a comparison between the *Dogmatic Panoply* and the *Sacred Arsenal* see A. Bucossi, 'Andronico Camatero e la zizzania: sulla politica ecclesiastica bizantina in età comnena' in F. Burgarella, F. D'Aiuto and V. Ruggieri, eds., *Ortodossia ed eresia a Bisanzio (sec. IX–XII): atti della IX Giornata di studio dell'Associazione Italiana di Studi Bizantini, Pontificio Istituto Orientale, Roma, 5–6/12/2008* = *RSBN*, 47 (2010), 357–71. The text of the Πανοπλία δογματική can be found in *PG* 130.

[The emperor] whose heart is inflamed with love for God and with zeal for Him and through Him, like Peter the chief of the apostles, and therefore drawing the sword of the Spirit, that is to say, the words of God emanating from his lips, smiting the hearing of the people who serve the chief priest of shame, Satan, and who are so proud of vain [words] against Christ, and who are walking in the depth of error and in the darkness of falsehood, and who are coming, as against a thief, against the one who on the same day opened Paradise to the thief, and with the swords of the heresies that cut off these people from the universal Church, and using the cudgels of dogmas that are completely without fruits and are dry because of impiety, [and] are useful only for the rightful sevenfold lighting of the eternal fire against them.[33]

In the parallel with Peter discussed above, it is possible to detect an allusion to the polemic about the primacy of Rome, since Kamateros seems to imply that it is the emperor and not the pope who is the guarantor of the Faith, and it is the emperor that now must be seen as the chief of the apostles. Although perhaps a more problematic reading, one could even identify the 'chief priest of shame, Satan'[34] in this passage as the pope himself. Indeed, a closer reading of the metaphor seems to suggest that for Kamateros it was the pope, as chief priest, who sent his guards (the cardinals) with all their arsenal of wrong dogmas against Christ (the Orthodox faith). When then Andronikos refers to those 'who are so proud of vain [words] against Christ',[35] he may well be referring to the Armenians, because they are more concerned with Christological issues than the Latins, while those 'who are walking in the depth of error and in the darkness of falsehood' could be Muslims.[36] In fact, in a later passage, Kamateros, praising the successes of Manuel in convincing representatives of other faiths, refers to the latter as 'those who are extremely practised in the deceptive superstition of the Ishmaelites and Persians and who are known as those who guide these peoples towards destruction'.[37] In the light of this interpretation, the sentence 'who are coming, as against a thief, against the one who, on the same day, opened Paradise to the thief' probably sums up the situation,[38] whereby the thief represents all the enemies of the Orthodox church (Latins, Armenians and Muslims), while

---

[33] Kamateros, *Sacred Arsenal*, 16.8–22.   [34] Ibid., 16.13–14, τῷ τῆς αἰσχύνης ἀρχιερεῖ Σατάν.
[35] Ibid., 16.14–15, κενὰ κατὰ Χριστοῦ φρυαττομένων.
[36] Ibid., 16.15–16, κἂν τῷ βαθεῖ τῆς πλάνης καὶ τοῦ ψεύδους σκότῳ πορευομένων.
[37] Ibid., 19.88–90, τοῖς τὴν τῶν Ἰσμαηλιτῶν καὶ Περσῶν λαοπλάνον θρησκείαν ἄκρως ἐξησκηκόσι, κἀκείνων ὁδηγοῖς εἰς ἀπώλειαν χρηματίζουσιν; cf. B. Kotter, ed., *Die Schriften des Johannes von Damaskos*, IV, *Liber de haeresibus. Opera Polemica* (Berlin, 1981), 60.1
[38] Ibid., 16.16–17, κἀπὶ τὸν αὐθήμερον ἀνοίξαντα τῷ λῃστῇ τὸν παράδεισον ὡς ἐπὶ λῃστὴν ἐρχομένων.

Scriptural Citation in Andronikos Kamateros 303

the Greek church is the only true body of Christ, which, as Christ, forgives sinners who recognise their error.

The passage continues with another reference to weapons, but this time the impious weapons of the heretics. The weapons are 'the swords of the heresies that cut off these people from the universal Church'.[39] Does Kamateros intend here to refer to the Latins, against whom this kind of accusation is usually made? And he says 'the cudgels of dogmas that are completely without fruits and are dry because of impiety [and] are useful only for the rightful sevenfold lighting of the eternal fire against them',[40] is he talking about the Armenians and the Muslims, who will be condemned for not having accepted the Truth? The syntax of the entire passage is highly complicated. The entire following long laudatory sentence depends on the phrase 'when the order is about God and is sacred, and it is [given] by such a great emperor':[41] the genitive βασιλέως ('of the emperor') will be repeated again and again, creating a long passage without a full stop, a long anaphora: 'such a great emperor ... emperor to whom, as to the chosen instrument ... an emperor by whom through his fear ... an emperor to whom, because of his manifold virtues...'[42]

The description of the opponents depends on a series of plural genitive participles: 'of the people who serve the chief priest of shame, Satan, and who are so proud of vain [words] ...[43] who are walking in the depth of error and in the darkness of falsehood ...[44] who are coming, as against a thief,[45] followed by another series of plural genitives, this time depending on the passage 'with the swords ... and using the cudgels',[46] 'of the heresies that cut off these people from the universal Church ...[47] of dogmas that are completely without fruits and are dry because of impiety[48] [and] are useful only for the rightful sevenfold lighting of the eternal fire against them'.[49] This usage of plural genitives one after the other creates a

---

[39] Ibid., 16.17–19, μετὰ μαχαιρῶν τῶν τῆς καθολικῆς ἐκκλησίας ἀποτεμνουσῶν τούτους αἱρέσεων.
[40] Ibid., 16.19–22, καὶ ξύλων τῶν ἀκάρπων πάντη καὶ κραύρων τῆς ἀσεβείας δογμάτων τῶν εἰς οὐδὲν ἄλλο χρησιμευόντων τούτοις, ἀλλ' ἢ πρὸς μόνην τὴν δικαίαν κατ' αὐτῶν τοῦ αἰωνίου πυρὸς ἑπταπλάσιον ἔκκαυσιν.
[41] Ibid., 16.7, ὅτε περὶ Θεοῦ καὶ θεῖον τὸ κέλευσμα καὶ βασιλέως τηλίκου.
[42] Ibid., 16, βασιλέως τηλίκου [l.8] ... βασιλέως ᾧ κατὰ τὸ τῆς ἐκλογῆς σκεῦος [l.23] ... ᾧ διὰ τοῦ θείου φόβου [l.26] ... βασιλέως ᾧ διὰ τὰς ποικίλας ἀρετάς [l.32].
[43] Ibid., 16, τῶν τῷ τῆς αἰσχύνης ἀρχιερεῖ Σατὰν δουλουμένων [ll.13–14] ... κενὰ φρυαττομένων [ll.14–15].
[44] Ibid., 16.15–16, κἂν τῷ βαθεῖ τῆς πλάνης καὶ τοῦ ψεύδους σκότῳ πορευομένων.
[45] Ibid., 16.17, ἐπὶ λῃστὴν ἐρχομένων.   [46] Ibid., 16.17 and 19, μετὰ μαχαιρῶν and ξύλων.
[47] Ibid., 16.18–19, τῶν τῆς καθολικῆς ἐκκλησίας ἀποτεμνουσῶν τούτους αἱρέσεων.
[48] Ibid., 16.19–20, τῶν ἀκάρπων πάντη καὶ κραύρων τῆς ἀσεβείας δογμάτων.
[49] Ibid., 16.20–1, τῶν εἰς οὐδὲν ἄλλο χρησιμευόντων.

deliberate confusion between the opponents and their weapons, so in the end the final impression is that the real enemies are the heresies and the wrong dogmas that lead to eternal damnation.

The second parallel adduced in the proem gives a clear explanation of why the emperor has to fight as Peter: it is because he, as Paul, is concerned with the fortunes of the Church, and with its unity, '[And also this order is from] an emperor to whom – as to the 'chosen instrument',[50] the mouth of the Lord, the herald of God, Paul – belong continuous 'solicitude for all the churches[51] and anxiety for their union'.[52] But Kamateros adds a further Pauline parallel:

> And moreover [an emperor] by whom words unheard by ears and that do not enter the hearts of men were heard, because he was lifted up, through his fear and his desire of God, to the height of all virtues and thus drew near God. Wherefore the mysteries of God were often proclaimed by him to us in many unwritten public speeches no less than in private audiences.[53]

Here Kamateros recalls a passage from 1 Corinthians, 'However, as it is written: "What no eye has seen, what no ear has heard, and what did not enter the heart of a man", these are the things God has prepared for those who love him.'[54] If we continue reading the First Epistle to the Corinthians, we can understand better the meaning of the entire passage. The 'things that God has prepared' and that 'no eye has seen...' are the 'mysteries of God' that He reveals by his Spirit. Consequently, it is clear that the emperor, when he proclaims the 'mysteries of God',[55] is inspired by the Holy Spirit and, therefore, that his doctrinal interpretations are absolutely orthodox.

To sum up what has been said so far, the emperor, when he is metaphorically described as Peter, has the characteristics of a holy warrior, the ability to prepare a *Sacred Arsenal* and the readiness to fight; but in the parallel made with Paul, the central characteristics are his care and his concern for the Church and his inspiration by the Holy Spirit. If my

---

[50] Acts. 9:15.   [51] 2 Cor. 11:28.
[52] Kamateros, *Sacred Arsenal*, 16.23–17.25, βασιλέως ᾧ κατὰ τὸ τῆς ἐκλογῆς σκεῦος, τὸ τοῦ Κυρίου στόμα, τὸν θεοκήρυκα Παῦλον, διηνεκὴς ἡ *τῶν ἐκκλησιῶν πασῶν μέριμνα* καὶ ἡ φροντὶς τῆς τούτων ἑνώσεως.
[53] Ibid., 17.26–31, μᾶλλον μὲν οὖν ᾧ διὰ τοῦ θείου φόβου καὶ πόθου πρὸς ὕψος ἀρθέντι πασῶν ἀρετῶν, οὕτω τε Θεῷ πλησιάσαντι, ἀνήκουστα μὲν τοῖς ὠσὶν ἀνθρωπίναις τε καρδίαις μὴ ἀναβαίνοντα ἠκούσθησαν ῥήματα· διὸ καὶ παρ' αὐτοῦ πολλάκις ἡμῖν συχναῖς μὲν ἀγράφοις δημηγορίαις, οὐχ ἧττον δὲ κἂν σιλεντίοις, Θεοῦ κατηγγέλθη μυστήρια.
[54] 1 Cor. 2:9, Ἀλλὰ καθὼς γέγραπται· Ἃ ὀφθαλμὸς οὐκ εἶδεν καὶ οὖς οὐκ ἤκουσεν καὶ ἐπὶ καρδίαν ἀνθρώπου οὐκ ἀνέβη, ἃ ἡτοίμασεν ὁ Θεὸς τοῖς ἀγαπῶσιν αὐτόν.
[55] 1 Cor. 2:1, καταγγέλλων ὑμῖν τὸ μυστήριον τοῦ Θεοῦ.

interpretation is correct, what could be more clearly anti-papal than this proem? The Roman argumentations are completely reversed. The pope is described as the 'chief priest of shame, Satan' and the emperor is the successor of Peter and Paul.

The third time the noun βασιλεύς ('emperor') occurs, the emperor is likened to 'the son of thunder':[56] '[And also this order is from] an emperor to whom the wisdom of God granted an appropriate heart because of his manifold virtues and the purity of mind, soul and body, and allowed him to draw on an abundance of wisdom to satiety, as indeed [he did], like the son of the thunder, he himself often thundered dogmas of theology and orthodoxy.'[57] John, the beloved disciple of Jesus, identified with John the Evangelist, John the Theologian, is by antonomasia the 'son of thunder', and therefore the emperor is compared here with the highest authority in matter of procession of the Holy Spirit. However, this is not the only identification of this section. The passage in fact opens with a very brief, but unmistakably direct, reference to Solomon; the words χύμα σοφίας ('abundance of wisdom') indeed recall immediately the χύμα καρδίας ('largeness of heart') that God gave to Solomon.[58] From these two references it is clear that Kamateros is insisting on Manuel's theological wisdom, representing it through the allusions to Solomon, the wisest of kings, and John, who was not only the theologian *par excellence*, but also the Evangelist who wrote most extensively on the Holy Spirit.

Peter, Paul and John – the fighter, the preacher, the theologian; the chief of the apostles, the trumpet of God, the son of thunder – the opening of the *Sacred Arsenal* could not have been more complete. The description of the emperor through these parallels cannot leave any doubt about the role that Kamateros ascribes to him and the impact that imperial power has on the Church. The conclusion of the long praise of the emperor represents its highest point:[59]

---

[56] Kamateros, *Sacred Arsenal*, 17.36, βροντῆς υἱόν; Mc. 3:17.
[57] Ibid., 17.32–37, βασιλέως, ᾧ διὰ τὰς ποικίλας ἀρετὰς καὶ τὴν τοῦ νοῦ καὶ τῆς ψυχῆς καὶ τοῦ σώματος καθαρότητα τὸ οἰκεῖον στῆθος ἀνῆκεν ἡ τοῦ Θεοῦ σοφία, καὶ χύμα σοφίας εἰς κόρον ἀπαρύσασθαι δέδωκε· καὶ μέντοι καὶ ἀπηρύσατο, καὶ κατὰ τὸν τῆς βροντῆς υἱόν, θεολογίας καὶ αὐτὸς καὶ ὀρθοδοξίας πολλάκις ἐβρόντησε δόγματα.
[58] Cf. 1 Regnorum (Masoretic text) [1 Kings] 5:12, καὶ σοφίαν πολλὴν σφόδρα καὶ χύμα καρδίας ὡς ἡ ἄμμος ἡ παρὰ τὴν θάλασσαν; III Reg. 5:9. Same quotation in Sakkos, *Ekthesis*, 161.
[59] Kamateros, *Sacred Arsenal*, 17.38–47, Αἱ κατὰ τὰς χρυσᾶς ἡμέρας τῆς αὐτοκράτορος ἀρχῆς τούτου συγκροτηθεῖσαι, καὶ ἄλλαι μὲν δύο δὲ τέως μέγισται σύνοδοι, καὶ τοῦτον μὲν τῆς ὀρθοδοξίας ὑπερασπιστὴν καὶ πρόμαχον ἔχουσαι, τὴν δ' ἐκκλησίαν δεινῶς σαλευθεῖσαν ἑδράσασαι καὶ στηρίξασαι, τῶν λεγομένων μάρτυρες ἀπαράγραπτοι· οὐ γάρ εἰσι λαλιαὶ οὐδὲ λόγοι τούτου, ὧν οὐχὶ αἱ φωναὶ ὡς θεῖαι ἠκούσθησαν καὶ ἐδέχθησαν. Ὅθεν καὶ πρὸς πᾶσαν τὴν γῆν ἐξῆλθεν ὁ φθόγγος αὐτοῦ, τὰ δὲ ῥήματα πρὸς τῆς οἰκουμένης τὰ πέρατα.

The [synods] assembled during the golden days of the reign of this emperor and [especially] the other two great synods [assembled] up to this time, because they had him as defender of orthodoxy and champion, and because they soothed and settled the Church that was dreadfully storm-tossed, are witnesses not to be missed of what has been said: for *there are not speeches or words* of this [man] *of which the sound is not heard* and accepted as holy. Whence *his voice spread all over the earth, [his] words to the ends of the world*.[60]

I strongly believe that the two synods Kamateros mentions here are the one concerning the sacrifice of Christ, which ended in 1157, and the other dealing with the sentence from the Gospel of John, 'The Father is greater than I', which ended in 1170.[61] These two synods in fact resolved the most important theological quarrels of Manuel's reign, 'they soothed and settled the Church that was dreadfully storm-tossed'. However, there is another point to add: if I am right and the two synods are 1157 and 1170, it means that Kamateros suggests here that his text should be interpreted as a kind of apologetic writing in response to the charges of heresy raised against Manuel. In fact, Manuel was blamed for exactly these synods,[62] and it is exactly for these synods that Kamateros praises him, as 'defender and champion of orthodoxy'.[63] In addition, it must be noted that this is the first passage in which Kamateros inserts, although with forms slightly adapted to the context, a long biblical quotation (Psalm 19:3–4). Indeed, until this point there have been only allusions, parallels, metaphors and

---

[60] Ps. 19:3–4.
[61] The identification of the synods is not certain. Jean Darrouzès, in his article published in 1965 (Darrouzès, *Les documents byzantins*, 73–4), states: 'Andronikos gives us important information which reduces the margin for the dating; in fact when he composed his preface the emperor had just presided over two important synods. They are the two assemblies of 30 January and 18 February 1170 (V. Grumel and V. Laurent, *Les Regestes des actes du patriarcat de Constantinople, 1: Les actes des patriarches, fasc. 11 et 111: Les regestes de 715 à 1206*, 2nd edn. revised and corrected by J. Darrouzès (Paris, 1989), nos. 1109–10.); because in no other near circumstances, since 1166, are there two synods presided over by the emperor.' Personally, I do not see any reason why we should suppose that Kamateros refers to these assemblies. The passage quoted before does not allow us to identify those two synods with two assemblies of the same synod. It could also be possible that Kamateros was referring to the two major synods summoned by Manuel during his reign: the one concerning the sacrifice of Christ, which ended in 1157, and the other dealing with the sentence from the Gospel of John 'The Father is greater than I', which ended in 1170. On the other hand, it could even be that Kamateros did not consider at all the synods held in 1170, because the great synod on the passage from Saint John could be considered concluded with the Edict of 1166.
[62] It must be recalled that, according to Kinnamos, the deacons of Saint Sophia were so upset by Manuel's pro-Latin interpretation of the passage from the Gospel of John 14:28 'The Father is greater than I' that they even stated that they were sure that 'if not now, later, after his death, the emperor will surely be subjected to anathema'. Kinnamos, *Epitome*, ed. Meineke, 254–5.
[63] Kamateros, *Sacred Arsenal*, 17.40–1, τῆς ὀρθοδοξίας ὑπερασπιστὴν καὶ πρόμαχον. Cf. Ps. 30:3; 70:3.

key words but not fully developed sentences. Therefore, we could say that a kind of climax develops through the praise of the emperor: playing Peter's role, he fights against the heresies; playing Paul's role, he cares for the Church unity; and, as 'son of the thunder', he himself intervenes in the life of the Church, even clarifying theological matters during the last two great synods. In this way the justification of Manuel's behaviour as *epistemonarches*[64] is complete. Manuel is called by God and he has the right to intervene. Moreover, because he learns directly from God, he can also bypass the tradition and the authority of the Church and proclaim his own interpretation of orthodox theology.

I use the word *epistemonarches* here with the 'theological' connotations that the term acquired during the reign of Manuel Komnenos.[65] Examples of this evolution can be found in Eustathios of Thessalonike and Theodore Balsamon,[66] who seem to have linked the role of *epistemonarches* very closely to that of *didaskalos*, connecting the imperial duty of maintaining the ecclesiastical order (discipline) with theological expertise (knowledge of God). It is clear that in Kamateros' text ἐπιστήμη indicates the imperial duty of defending the internal order of the Church as well as incorporating what Job Iasites, a century later, defines as 'the manly nourishment' that is 'the full initiation into the dogmas'.[67] Thus Manuel is presented as having

---

[64] It must be noted that this term does not appear in the *Sacred Arsenal*. The best contributions on the term and its meaning during the eleventh and twelfth centuries are R. Macrides, 'Nomos and Kanon, on Paper and in Court' in R. Morris, ed., *Church and People in Byzantium* (Birmingham, 1990), 61–85, especially 63–4; and Magdalino, *Empire of Manuel I*, 248–55. In addition, Paul Magdalino argues also that 'since the monastic context was without direct relevance or resonance for her subject, her [Anna Komnene] usage can be seen primarily as a reaction to the church's flattering reference to Manuel's "artful and epistemonarchic wisdom" – a reference which, like Anna's, applied to an emperor, and exploited the non technical, literal sense of the word by playing on the association of τέχνη and ἐπιστήμη', P. Magdalino, 'The Pen of the Aunt: Echoes of the Mid-twelfth Century in the *Alexiad*' in T. Gouma-Peterson, ed., *Anna Komnene and Her Times* (New York, NY, 2000), 32.

[65] Compare to the sentence 'ἐντέχνῳ καὶ ἐπιστημοναρχικῷ σοφίᾳ' in G. A. Ralles and A. Potles, eds., Σύνταγμα τῶν Θείων καὶ ἱερῶν κανόνων (Athens, 1852–9; repr. 1966), vol. v, 309, 'With artful and epistemonarchic wisdom' used to describe Manuel's behaviour at the synod that deposed the patriarch Kosmas II in 1147, trans. from Magdalino, 'Pen of the Aunt', 32.

[66] G. Dagron, *Emperor and Priest: The Imperial Office in Byzantium* (Cambridge, 2003), 254–5 and 265–6.

[67] See Job Iasites' explanation of the role of *epistemonarches* from the *Reply* written to the imperial *Tomos* of Michael VIII: 'This role of *epistemonarches* is given to him because he is recognised as pious and most Christian: it is his duty, therefore, to repay to his mother the church the cost of his education, to protect her and support her with great gratitude in exchange not only for the milk she gave him, the basic institution in piety, but for the bread he has eaten, that of piety, in full initiation into the dogmas, the manly nourishment. But the very great Pope, not being pious, how is he going to guide us with the required science (knowledge)?', this translation is taken from Dagron, *Emperor and Priest*, 255.

a full theological knowledge that allows him not only to be protector of the Church, guide, good shepherd, new Moses, new Peter, but also to have a full theological knowledge that forces him to be a theologian, *didaskalos*, 'guardian of orthodoxy'.[68] We could say, therefore, that Manuel possessed and exercised the full power of imposing over the Church not only an epistemonarchic guidance (traditionally the power of managing church leaders and transforming canonical decrees into imperial laws), but also that particular epistemonarchic guidance that is theological and dogmatic and through which he could impose his own interpretation of dogma.

The laudatory part of the proem concludes by recalling the emperor's piety, orthodoxy and care for the reunion of the two divided branches of the universal Church:

> [But] before everything and above all, his apostolic and pious zeal for the orthodoxy and concord and union of the churches and the combination and healing up and complete cicatrisation of the limbs and the portions that have been divided for a long time from the one head of the Saviour, I mean Christ, with Him [again].[69]

The Prefatory Exhortation of the *Sacred Arsenal*

If the proem can – with some restrictions – be interpreted as an anti-papal tirade, on the grounds that the references to Peter and the 'chief priest of shame, Satan' sound quite outspoken, the exhortation 'addressed to those who say that the all-Holy Spirit proceeds from the Father and the Son' expresses Kamateros' ideas quite clearly. This exhortatory speech is addressed to the cardinals, or better, to the Roman Church in general, and is designed to introduce the anthology of patristic quotations that follows the dialogue. Kamateros invites the opponents of the Greek Church to abandon the *Filioque* and to trust the guidance of the emperor. He starts again by describing the voice of the emperor as a 'thunderclap', as the God-inspired trumpet recalling the images used in the proem: 'You have heard a grandiloquent imperial dialogue which has resonated from the Heaven like a thunder-clap ... You know the holy power that has came from the imperial mind of the ruler ... through the golden and God-inspired trumpet, I mean, through the most charming

---

[68] Definition from Magdalino, *Empire of Manuel I*, 316.
[69] Kamateros, *Sacred Arsenal*, 18.57–63, πρὸ πάντων καὶ ὑπὲρ πάντα, τὸν ὑπὲρ τῆς ὀρθοδοξίας καὶ τῆς τῶν ἐκκλησιῶν ὁμονοίας τε καὶ ἑνώσεως, καὶ τῆς τῶν τῆς μιᾶς κεφαλῆς τοῦ Σωτῆρος, λέγω Χριστοῦ, διαστάντων ἔκπαλαι μερῶν καὶ μελῶν πρὸς αὐτὴν συναρμογῆς καὶ συμφυΐας καὶ συνουλώσεως, ἀποστολικὸν τούτου ζῆλον καὶ ἔνθεον.

tongue of the ruler.'⁷⁰ He then goes on, saying, 'Nevertheless, if you have the ears of those who hear, so that you become conveyors of the blessing to those who speak to you'.⁷¹ Here Kamateros recalls Matthew 13:16–17, 'But blessed are your eyes because they see, and your ears because they hear. For I tell you the truth, many prophets and righteous men longed to see what you see but did not see it, and to hear what you hear but did not hear it.'⁷² He is promising the cardinals that, after having listened to the teaching of the emperor, they can become new apostles and bring blessings and salvation to the world. It is only the emperor, in fact, who can announce 'the mysteries of God'; the passage of the proem analysed above, which describes the emperor as the only one 'by whom words unheard by ears and that do not enter the hearts of men were heard', can also be recalled here.⁷³ Therefore, the underlying message remains the same: only the emperor has the right understanding, and only he is the source of Truth for the Church.

The next section recalls again a passage from the Gospels (Matthew 7:7 and Luke 11:9–13), where Jesus assures his disciples, 'Ask and it will be given to you; seek and you will find; knock and the door will be opened to you.' But Kamateros' version is slightly different; he says, 'And if asking you really wanted to receive, and enquiring to find, and if you pray that doors be opened when you knock'.⁷⁴ Therefore, it is clear that Kamateros is insisting on the fact that the cardinals, having received a clear explanation of the right dogma from the emperor, should now follow the Truth. In my view, this is a complaint about the behaviour of the Roman church; Kamateros indeed sounds surprised by the fact that even a clear demonstration does not convince the cardinals to correct their theological mistakes.

---

[70] Ibid., 79.1–10, Ἠκούσατε τῆς οἷα βροντῆς οὐρανόθεν καταρραγείσης καὶ τὰς ὑμετέρας μὴ μόνον ἀκοὰς ἀλλὰ καὶ διανοίας περικτυπησάσης μεγαλοφώνου βασιλικῆς διαλέξεως, ὧ μὴ μόνον ἐκ τοῦ Πατρὸς ὡς παρελάβετε, ἀλλ᾽ αὐθαιρέτως κἀκ τοῦ Υἱοῦ τὴν τοῦ παναγίου Πνεύματος ἐκπόρευσιν δογματίζοντες· ἔγνωτε θείαν δύναμιν ἐξελθοῦσαν τοῦ τῶν ὅλων ἀνθρωπίνων νόων αὐτοκράτορος βασιλικοῦ νοὸς διὰ τῆς χρυσηλάτου καὶ θεοπνεύστου σάλπιγγος τῆς λαμπρωτάτης, φημί, γλώττης τοῦ αὐτοκράτορος.

[71] Ibid., 79.17–18, Ὅμως ἐὰν ἀκουόντων ὦτα κέκτησθε, ἵν᾽ οὕτω καὶ μακαρισμοῦ τοῖς πρὸς ὑμᾶς λέγουσι γίνησθε πρόξενοι. Compare to μακαρισμοῦ προξένοις in B. Pruche, ed., *Basile de Césarée: Sur le Saint-Esprit*, second edition, revised and augmented (Paris, 1968), 286.11 (VI.13.11).

[72] Mt. 13:16–17, Μακάριοι οἱ ὀφθαλμοὶ ὅτι βλέπουσιν, καὶ τὰ ὦτα ὑμῶν ὅτι ἀκούουσιν. Ἀμὴν γὰρ λέγω ὑμῖν ὅτι πολλοὶ προφῆται καὶ δίκαιοι ἐπεθύμησαν ἰδεῖν ἃ βλέπετε καὶ οὐκ εἶδαν, καὶ ἀκοῦσαι ἃ ἀκούετε καὶ οὐκ ἤκουσαν.

[73] 1 Cor. 2:9.

[74] Kamateros, *Sacred Arsenal*, 79.19–80.20, αἰτοῦντές τε λαβεῖν ἀληθῶς ἐθέλητε, καὶ ζητοῦντες εὑρεῖν, ἀνοιγῆναί τε κρούουσιν ὑμῖν ἀξιοῦτε.

Then he continues in his usual way of connecting sentences as he follows the thread of his thought. He connects the image of the door that will be opened to those who knock[75] with that of the door of salvation of John 10:1–16. These are the key sentences of John's passage:

> I tell you, one who does not enter by the door into the sheepfold, but climbs up some other way, the same is a thief and a robber. But one who enters in by the door is the shepherd of the sheep. The gatekeeper opens the gate for him, and the sheep listen to his voice . . . I am the door. If anyone enters in by me, he will be saved, and will go in and go out, and will find pasture. The thief only comes to steal, kill, and destroy . . . I am the good shepherd. I lay down my life for the sheep . . . I have other sheep, which are not of this fold. I must bring them also, and they will hear my voice. They will become one flock with one shepherd.

Kamateros writes:

> Behold the rhetor[76] and star of the holy churches of God, the great emperor, wise defender of orthodoxy who has opened many doors to you, and especially that of salvation, through which he who enters will be saved, instructs you to enter through these doors and having found and received painlessly what is sought, to cease clambering through the other gate[77] that is the addition to the Holy Creed.[78]

The interpretation here is as follows: the cardinals must be sure of what they want; they had the chance to understand the right belief about the procession of the Holy Spirit, since the emperor, answering their questions, showed them the Truth: the door of salvation. What is striking here is that the emperor is being depicted as the gatekeeper mentioned by Jesus. We cannot avoid connecting this gatekeeper with the most famous Gatekeeper: Saint Peter, to whom Jesus said: 'I will give you the keys of the Kingdom of Heaven.'[79] Therefore, if the emperor is identified with

---

[75] Mt. 7:6–8; Lc. 11:8–10.
[76] Cf. Ἄκουε, Παῦλε, τῶν ἐκκλησιῶν μεγαλοφωνότατε ῥῆτορ in B. Flusin, ed., *Saint Anastase le Perse et l'histoire de la Palestine au début du VIIe siècle*, (Paris, 1992), vol. 1, section 7, line 19; Παῦλος ὁ τῶν ἐθνῶν διδάσκαλος καὶ ῥήτωρ τῶν ἐκκλησιῶν διαπρύσιος in J.-L. van Dieten, ed., *Nicetae Choniatae Orationes et epistulae* (Berlin, 1972), Oration 17, 182.22.
[77] Joh. 10:1, Ἀμὴν ἀμὴν λέγω ὑμῖν, ὁ μὴ εἰσερχόμενος διὰ τῆς θύρας εἰς τὴν αὐλὴν τῶν προβάτων ἀλλὰ ἀναβαίνων ἀλλαχόθεν ἐκεῖνος κλέπτης ἐστὶν καὶ λῃστής. Same passage quoted in the Edict of 1166, in Sakkos, *Ekthesis*, 167.20.
[78] Kamateros, *Sacred Arsenal*, 80.20–8, πολλὰς ὑμῖν ἰδοὺ θύρας, πρὸ δ' αὐτῶν τὴν σωτήριον δι' ἧς εἴ τις εἰσελεύσεται σωθήσεται, διανοίξας ὁ τῶν ἁγίων ἐκκλησιῶν τοῦ Θεοῦ ῥήτωρ καὶ φωστήρ, ὁ μέγας τῆς ὀρθοδοξίας ὑπέρμαχος θεόσοφος ἡμῶν βασιλεὺς εἰσελθεῖν διὰ τούτων προτρέπεται καὶ τὸ ζητούμενον ἀπόνως εὑρόντας καὶ λαβόντας παύσασθαί ποτε τοῦ δι' ἄλλης ἀναβαίνειν τῆς τῷ θείῳ δηλαδὴ συμβόλῳ παρεντεθείσης προσθήκης.
[79] Mt. 16:17–19.

Peter, what is this if not anti-papalism on the part of Kamateros? The emperor has the power to open the door of salvation. The role traditionally attributed to Peter (in the Byzantine as well as in the Latin tradition) of being the way to salvation, because he was the first to recognise Jesus as God, is here attributed to Manuel. Furthermore, Kamateros writes, 'cease clambering through the other gate, that is, the addition to the Holy Creed'.[80] For some cardinals who certainly knew the Gospel by heart this sentence would not have been a compliment. Jesus in fact says, 'One who does not enter by the door into the sheepfold, but climbs up some other way, the same is a thief and a robber.' So, if my interpretation is correct, it is as if Kamateros is here challenging the reader with some rhetorical questions: who is this robber if not the pope who abuses his role in the Church by occupying a place that was supposed to belong to the emperor? Who is this robber and thief if not the Roman church that wants to have primacy over the Constantinopolitan church? However, Kamateros does not stop here; let us examine the following and concluding part. The final judgement concludes the section dedicated to the Latin church: Kamateros recalls Matthew 25:31–3: 'When the Son of Man comes in his Glory, he will sit on his throne in heavenly Glory. All the nations will be gathered before him, and he will separate the people one from another as a shepherd separates the sheep from the goats. He will put the sheep on his right and the goats on his left.' Kamateros writes:

> Because you will not be followed by the sheep worthy of a place on the right hand, sheep who have a good shepherd, the emperor, [who] goes before them and guides [them] to the pasture of salvation; be yourselves ready to enter through these gates into the sheepfold, and becoming one flock under one great shepherd, listen to his voice, and directed by the pastoral pipe of his words, feed yourselves with pleasure on the dogmas of salvation and drink the rightness of the Faith.[81]

This is the highest point of the praise for the emperor, depicting the emperor as Jesus. Indeed this description reaches an exceptionally high point: not only is the emperor the guide, and the protector of the Church – a role normally attributed to him by the Byzantine church, and to the pope by the Latin

---

[80] Kamateros, *Sacred Arsenal*, 80.26–8.
[81] Ibid., 80.28–37, ὅτι μὴ δ' ἀκολουθήσουσιν ὑμῖν τὰ τῆς δεξιᾶς στάσεως ἀξιούμενα πρόβατα, καλὸν ἔχοντα ποιμένα τὸν αὐτοκράτορα· καὶ τούτων ἔμπροσθεν πορευόμενον καὶ πρὸς νομὴν ὁδηγοῦντα σωτήριον, διὰ τῶν τοιούτων τοίνυν θυρῶν εἰς τὴν τῶν προβάτων αὐλὴν εἰσελθεῖν καὶ αὐτοὶ προθυμήθητε καὶ μία ποίμνη γενόμενοι ὑφ' ἑνὶ τηλίκῳ ποιμένι, τῆς αὐτοῦ φωνῆς ἀκούετε· καὶ τῇ ποιμαντικῇ τῶν λόγων τούτου τρεπόμενοι σύριγγι, τρέφεσθε μεθ' ἡδονῆς τὰ σωτήρια δόγματα καὶ πίνετε καὶ τὴν ὀρθοτομίαν τῆς πίστεως.

church – not only is he a shepherd, a father of the Church and the vicar of Christ – again, these terms are customarily used to describe both the pope and the emperor – he is also the reincarnation of Jesus. He is described by the words that Jesus applied to himself: 'the good shepherd', the 'one great shepherd' who guides the sheepfold with his voice and feeds them with his body and blood. Indeed Kamateros' words are chosen carefully: 'feed yourselves with pleasure on the dogmas of salvation and drink the rightness of the Faith.'[82] We surely cannot be wrong to recognise here a reference to the Last Supper.

Kamateros then concludes with a final harsh invitation: 'And, indeed, remaining faithful to the things transmitted by these great divinely inspired heralds and, before these, by the Saviour himself, do not wish to alter the eternal rules that our Fathers set out;[83] consider in fact what you have been taught directly from the Saviour himself about the procession and the mission of the all-holy Spirit!'[84]

Conclusions

The passages we have analysed are not homiletic, or at least not in a strict sense. We can certainly state that Kamateros was more influenced by religious writings than by the high-level rhetoric of, for example, Eustathios of Thessalonike; yet we cannot define the *Sacred Arsenal* as a homily. It is clear that Kamateros was familiar with the Fathers of the Church – or at least he had to become familiar with them because of the *Sacred Arsenal* – but the passages analysed are still distant from Patristics. However, we can try to define these passages, to say something more about his way of composing his text and the tradition and the environment by which this text is influenced. As Magdalino pointed out in his study of Manuel, there is a close similarity between the rhetorical register of the *Sacred Arsenal* and the official documents of the Church redacted under Manuel's reign. The points of contact between the official

---

[82] Ibid., 80.36–7.
[83] Prov. 22:28, μὴ μέταιρε ὅρια αἰώνια, ἃ ἔθεντο οἱ πατέρες σου. It is interesting to note that the same allusion to the Book of Proverbs is reported by Choniates to be part of a reply by the emperor to the Pope written around 1167–8, "μὴ δώσεις ἑτέρῳ τὴν δόξαν σου" γράφων τῷ πάπα, "μηδὲ πατέρων ὅρια μέταιρε, μή πως τὸ ἀπρομήθευτον ὕστερον ἔργοις αὐτοῖς ὁποῖόν ἐστιν ἐπιγνοὺς τηνικαῦτα πλήττῃ τὴν ψυχὴν μεταμέλῳ διὰ τὴν τοῦ εἰκότος ὀλιγωρίαν, ὁπότε τὸ κακὸν παντάπασιν ἀθεράπευτον" (Choniates, *Historia*, 200); Maisano, 'La funzione letteraria della Bibbia in Niceta Coniata', 59.
[84] Kamateros, *Sacred Arsenal*, 80.37–43, ναὶ μὴν καὶ τοῖς παρὰ τόσων θεοφόρων κηρύκων, πρὸ δ' αὐτῶν παρὰ τοῦ Σωτῆρος αὐτοῦ, παραδοθεῖσιν ἐμμένοντες μὴ θέλετε μεταίρειν ἃ οἱ πατέρες ἡμῶν ἔθεντο αἰώνια ὅρια· ὁρᾶτε γὰρ τί παρ' αὐτοῦ τοῦ Σωτῆρος εὐθὺς περὶ τῆς τοῦ παναγίου Πνεύματος ἐκπορεύσεως καὶ τῆς ἀποστολῆς ἐκδιδάσκεσθε.

synodal records of the 'Father is greater than I' controversy, especially the *Edict* of 1166, and the text of Kamateros highlighted throughout this contribution certainly confirm Magdalino's notes:

> In its combination of official documentation, patristic *florilegium*, and imperial encomium, the *Sacred Arsenal* clearly belongs to the same tradition as the *Ekthesis* of 1166. It may provide the clue to the concerns which led Manuel to take such a strong stand in the 'Father is greater than I' controversy. It raises the suspicion that in his dealings with his own clergy, as in his dealings with foreign theologians, Manuel was ultimately concerned to impress the Christian world, and especially the Latin world, as the ruler of Christian unity ... Certain features of the *Edict* – the claim to Constantine's inheritance in the *intitulatio*, and the flattering reference to Saint Peter in the opening lines of the *prooemium* – were undoubtedly made for western consumption.[85]

Having recalled Magdalino's words about the common milieu, I would conclude with some further considerations. Kamateros' text is an example of a kind of imperial/ecclesiastical rhetoric, which is perhaps best defined as 'epistemonarchic rhetoric', chosen and promoted by Manuel at a time when his intervention in the life of the Byzantine church became stronger, but also at a time when the universal role claimed by the papacy risked collision with Manuel's understanding of his own role as emperor. Magdalino rightly called attention to Manuel's intention 'to impress the Christian world, and especially the Latin world', but I would suggest enriching his explanation with an interpretation that also takes into account Manuel's concern with Byzantine 'domestic affairs'. I would say that his imperial propaganda is certainly designed to impress the West, with its continuous references to Petrine and Pauline passages for example, but it is also designed to impress the internal opponents of Manuel, who did not favour his pro-Latin attitude, through the more or less veiled antipapal message of the writings that he commissioned. Indeed, it seems to be highly likely that the insistence on Manuel's orthodoxy, especially against the Latins, and the choice of the topics themselves – against Roman theology and the Christological heresies – are signs that the *Sacred Arsenal* can be understood as an apologetic writing to excuse Manuel's behaviour in the 'Father is greater than I' affair. The analysis of the passages presented, read against the background of the contemporary situation in Constantinople, prompts one to consider also the possibility that the whole text was written to demonstrate and defend Manuel's orthodoxy,

---

[85] Magdalino, *Empire of Manuel I*, 291.

especially from the accusation of being too openly pro-Latin. The church of Constantinople was demonstrating her uneasiness with the approval of a Latin interpretation of Christological dogmas and the imperial imposition of them; therefore, it was entirely to Manuel's benefit to show himself to be very orthodox on the questions of papal primacy, procession of the Holy Spirit, and Christology. In this context, Kamateros' rhetoric and his shrewd ability to embroider his text with biblical quotations were certainly an effective tool to boost the imperial propaganda of Manuel Komnenos.

Further Reading

The main text is: A. Bucossi, ed., *Andronici Camateri Sacrum armamentarium: Pars prima* (Turnhout, 2014). Introductory scholarship includes: G. Dagron, *Emperor and Priest: The Imperial Office in Byzantium* (Cambridge, 2003); P. Magdalino, The *Empire of Manuel I Komnenos, 1143–1180* (Cambridge, 1993); J. Spiteris, *La critica Bizantina del primato romano nel secolo xii* (Rome, 1979).

Secular Texts

CHAPTER 13

Aristocratic Family Narratives in Twelfth-century Byzantium

Peter Frankopan

The *Alexiad* of Anna Komnene is one of the most interesting and enigmatic of Byzantine sources. The text provides a detailed narrative commentary on the reign of Emperor Alexios I Komnenos, from just before his accession to the throne in 1081, up to his death thirty-seven years later, in 1118. The account poses a great many questions, from the bias of the author (the daughter of the eponymous hero) to the scope of the work, which sees some topics covered in exhaustive length, but others entirely ignored.

Perhaps the most important question, however, concerns the provenance of the material that makes up the *Alexiad*. Where did Anna Komnene get her information? What primary sources were available to her, and how did she use them? Is it possible to detect individual accounts that the author used or relied on in detail, or filleted for facts, details and information? The sheer length and scale of the text suggests that Anna was able to draw on a substantial archive. If so, what conclusions can we make about how this was assembled? Given the prominence and significance of the *Alexiad*, it is surprising that there have been so few attempts to examine the composition of the text or to identify the blocks on which it was built. Jakov Liubarskii wrote an excellent article on the sources of Anna Komnene's history, in which he sought to address precisely this question, but this is one of only a very small handful of efforts to explore what kind of material Anna had at her disposal and where it came from. That Liubarskii's essay still provides the most useful guide to the architecture of the *Alexiad* is telling about the state of modern approaches to this text.[1] What Liubarskii did not address was how Anna gathered her evidence, or whence she gathered it; rather, he was primarily concerned with detecting references in the *Alexiad* and suggesting different types and forms of

---

[1] I. Liubarskii, 'Why is the *Alexiad* a Masterpiece of Byzantine Literature?' in R. O. Rosenqvist, ed., Λειμών: *Studies Presented to Lennart Rydén on his Sixty-Fifth Birthday* (Uppsala, 1996), 127–41.

evidence that the author was able to use, from chrysobulls to letters and other official documents. The Russian scholar either thought this question of provenance unimportant, or felt he could provide no useful answer to it.

The issue of the origins of the information in the *Alexiad* finally entered mainstream scholarly debate following a provocative paper given by James Howard-Johnston at the Belfast symposium in 1989 which was subsequently published some years later. Howard-Johnston does not look at the issue of the constituent elements of Anna's history apart from in the broadest terms, but rather focuses on developing a crucial hypothesis that the author relied heavily on her husband, Nikephoros Bryennios, not only as a gatherer of information, but as an editor for a good deal of the material that appears in the text.[2] Howard-Johnston's argument is important not just for considering whether Bryennios really was a significant contributor to the *Alexiad*, but also for opening up the issue of where Anna – or, for that matter, Bryennios – found the material that makes up the account of the reign of Emperor Alexios I Komnenos. Neither Anna nor Bryennios can surely have been useful witnesses, at least for the first years of Alexios' rule: Anna, we know, was born in 1083, and therefore she can be ruled out as an eye-witness for at least the first decade of her father's emperorship;[3] while we do not know when Bryennios was born, the fact that Anna repeatedly refers to her husband's death in 1138 as premature suggests that he too was born around the start of Alexios' reign in 1081, and not much earlier.[4]

In other words, then, regardless of whether Howard-Johnston is right to see Bryennios playing a key role in the composition of the *Alexiad*, there is a long way to go in identifying the provenance of the facts, stories and details that appear in the text. As Liubarskii noted elsewhere, there are several documents that are reproduced in full – a letter sent by Alexios to Henry IV of Germany; a chrysobull extending executive powers to Anna Dalassene, the emperor's mother; and the Treaty of Devol of 1108, that marked the agreement between Alexios and the Norman leader

---

[2] J. Howard-Johnston, 'Anna Komnene and the *Alexiad*' in M. Mullett and D. Smythe, eds., *Alexios I Komnenos – Papers of the Second Belfast Byzantine International Colloquium, 14–16 April 1989* (Belfast, 1996), 260–302; see also his chapter in the present volume for a discussion of the sources used in the *Alexiad*.
[3] For Anna's birth, see D. Reinsch and A. Kambylis, eds., *Annae Comnenae Alexias* (Berlin, 2001), vol. I, 183–4 (VI.viii.1–2), and A. Kazhdan, 'Die Liste der Kinder des Alexios I in einer Moskauer Handschrift (GIM 53/147)' in R. Stiehl and H. Stier, eds., *Beiträge zur Alten Geschichte und deren Nachleben* (Berlin, 1970), vol. II, 234.
[4] For biographical details for Nikephoros Bryennios, see B. Skoulatos, *Les personnages byzantins de l'Alexiade: analyse prosopographique et synthèse* (Louvain, 1980), 224–32.

Bohemond, following the latter's assault on Epiros; there are also references to decrees and letters in the *Alexiad*, some of which are drawn on extensively enough to assume that the author had sight of the original documents. These would all appear to be 'official' documents of one kind or another, which Anna (or perhaps her husband) had been able to procure, copy or borrow from an archive of some sort that had retained them for one reason or another.[5]

The purpose of this chapter is to look at a possible undetected narrative source for the *Alexiad*, and to suggest that the author of the text was able to draw on a history of the Palaiologos family that focused specifically on the figure of George Palaiologos. Palaiologos was a leading figure during the reign of Alexios I, holding important positions, such as that of *doux* of Dyrrachion during the Norman attacks of the 1080s on Byzantium's western flank.[6] The hypothesis is made difficult by the fact that no such source survives. However, it will argue that a narrative centred on George was written and that this was used in the composition of the *Alexiad*. Furthermore, the chapter will try to show how this source was used by Anna Komnene, thereby providing some insights into the editorial process behind the *Alexiad* itself. A by-product here will be to reach some conclusions about the likely shape and scope of the Palaiologan source by considering what elements of this hypothetical source appear in the *Alexiad*. Narrative history writing in Byzantium is dominated by the imperial rather than the aristocratic – that is to say, by history written about the emperor (positive or negative), but rarely, if ever, focusing on the great families of the empire. By identifying a history about George Palaiologos, and not about the emperor, therefore, we will be laying some preliminary groundwork to re-evaluate the canon of Byzantine secular literature, at least in the Komnenian era.

Suspicions that Anna had had access to a source centred on the figure of George Palaiologos are raised in the first instance by the comment made by the author that this individual had made a singularly important contribution to the *Alexiad*. In a passage setting out the reliability of her account as a whole, Anna Komnene explains her own diligence in gathering material and editing it in a way that was both even-handed and faithful to her father's deeds. The sources that she cites are generic, not literary in

---

[5] Grant of powers to Dalassene: Komnene, *Alexias*, ed. Reinsch and Kambylis, vol. 1, 101ff. (III.vi.4–8.44–95). Letter to Henry IV: ibid., 112ff. (III.x.3–8.66–34). Treaty of Devol: ibid., 413–23 (XIII.xii). I. Liubarskii, 'Об источниках "Алексиады" Анны Комниной', *VizVrem*, 25 (1964), 99–120; also Howard-Johnston, 'Anna Komnene and the Alexiad', 278f.

[6] On George Palaiologos generally, see Skoulatos, *Les personnages byzantins*, 99–105.

aspiration or execution; rather, she says, she drew on simple accounts by soldiers who had served with the emperor.⁷

She does, however, single out one individual: George Palaiologos. According to Anna, she had personally heard her uncle, George, discussing the past with her father, the emperor, on many occasions. Anna states that her recollections of these conversations formed, if not the backbone of her text, then at least an important part of it.⁸ As the author goes on to say shortly after, in addition to the humble musings of war veterans, conversations which she had had with her maternal and paternal uncles (τοὐμοῦ πατρὸς καὶ τῶν πρὸς πατρὸς καὶ μητρὸς ἐμοὶ θείων ἠκηκόειν πολλάκις) were central to the composition of the text.⁹ Anna's comments about her sources need to be taken with a pinch of salt, for there is plenty of material whose provenance is not acknowledged. For example, she says nothing about the official documents that can be identified in the text, many cited in full. Nor does she mention her debt to Psellos, even though the borrowings from this text are substantial – including one lengthy passage that is lifted *verbatim*.¹⁰ Nor does she note her use of Bryennios' writings in this section of the text, even though she refers to his works on several occasions, and indeed borrows from her husband heavily in her accounts of the revolts of Roussel de Bailleul, Nikephoros Bryennios (the elder) and Nikephoros Basilakes.¹¹

The explanation, surely, is that Anna avoids noting the use of other materials here as her main motivation in this passage is not to provide a comprehensive list of sources, but to underline her credentials as a reliable guide to her father's reign. Anna's is a trustworthy source, is the implication, because the author was personally acquainted with, and related to, the protagonists, and furthermore was familiar with the honest, nuts-and-bolts testimony of good, decent soldiers. In this context then, it is curious that Palaiologos – and no one else – is singled out by the author.¹²

The reference to George is not enough alone to develop a hypothesis about a Palaiologan family source. Nevertheless, the attribution of a key role to this individual is significant because of the profile that he enjoys

---

⁷ Komnene, *Alexias*, ed. Reinsch and Kambylis, vol. 1, 452 (XIV.vii.7.64–74).
⁸ Ibid., 451 (XIV.vii.5.45ff.). ⁹ Ibid., 425f. (XIV.vii.7.77ff.).
¹⁰ Ibid., 107ff. (III.viii.6–10), with footnotes. For details of these parallels and other passages corresponding to Psellos, see also *Alexias*, vol. II, 266ff.
¹¹ For Roussel de Bailleul, see ibid., 11–17 (I.i–iii); for Nikephoros Bryennios, ibid., 18–27 (I.iv–vi); for Nikephoros Basilakes, ibid., 27–34 (I.vii–ix) (all with footnotes giving the parallel passages). See also Howard-Johnston's chapter in this volume.
¹² Anna also notes the contribution of her maternal and paternal uncles, without naming them, Ibid., 452–3 (XIV.vii.7.75–8).

Aristocratic Family Narratives in Twelfth-century 321

throughout the text, where he is one of the substantial supporting cast of characters who appear alongside the eponymous hero Alexios I. Anna Komnene regularly lists the names of Byzantine military commanders, confidants and rivals of the emperor in her account. Individual acts of valour – such as in the case of Kamytzes, whose bravery is recorded at length – likewise also appear regularly in the course of the text.[13]

Inevitably, some figures enjoy greater profiles than others. These can be essentially divided into characters with primary and secondary importance. While the latter feature in brief, for example usually simply being listed as being present at a key moment, those in the former category have rather more developed roles. Figures such as Tatikios, the *caesar* John Doukas, Manuel Boutoumites, Constantine Katakalon Euphorbenos and others too feature at the heart of one or more episodes – leading the knights of the First Crusade across Asia Minor, regaining the western coast of Asia Minor or dealing with the troublesome Latins following the establishment of the Crusader states.[14]

George Palaiologos is certainly to be included in the first rank of characters in the *Alexiad*. Indeed, he is perhaps the figure who enjoys the highest profile of all in the text. We learn of his dispatch to Dyrrachion in 1081.[15] We are told about the role he played in the defence of that town against the Normans of Robert Guiscard.[16] His command of troops against the Pechenegs in the 1080s is described, as is his narrow escape following the disastrous assault on Dristra.[17] We find him protecting a key town during a Cuman invasion in the mid-1090s.[18] We find him giving advice to the emperor about tactics.[19] And we see him fiercely defending Alexios against an ambitious and arrogant crusader soon after the spectacular recovery of Nicaea.[20]

Taken together, then, the careful singling out and acknowledgement of Palaiologos by Anna, and the visibility of this individual in the text are significant. At the very least, we can conclude that the author was well-supplied with information about her uncle's life – although how she knew so much about Palaiologos is unclear. It is possible, of course, that Anna had listened attentively to George's musings as she was growing up, and in

---

[13] For Kamytzes, see ibid., 444ff. (XIV.v.4–7.24–71); 448–9 (XIV.vi.3–6.29–75).
[14] On Constantine Katakalon Euphorbenos, John Doukas, Manuel Boutoumites and Tatikios, see Skoulatos, *Les personnages byzantins*, 62–5, 138–45, 181–5 and 287–92.
[15] Komnene, *Alexias*, ed. Reinsch and Kambylis, vol. I, 111 (III.ix.4.34–9).
[16] Ibid., 120–36 (IV.i–vi).   [17] Ibid., 215f. (VII.iv).   [18] Ibid., 286 (X.ii.6.43–7).
[19] Ibid., 129 (IV.v.3.8ff.); 205 (VII.ii.3.64–7); 210 (VII.iii.4.11–31).
[20] Ibid., 329f. (XI.iii.2.54–64).

the first decade of the twelfth century when we know Palaiologos was alive.[21] However, a more logical and plausible explanation is that Anna had access to written material which either focused on George, or in which this individual had a prominent role.

We can take this further too, by stretching out what we learn about Palaiologos in the *Alexiad*. George is particularly prominent in Anna's coverage of the Norman attacks on Epiros in the early 1080s, a time when pressure on the empire was acute – and when Palaiologos' bravery played a vital role in repelling the fearsome attacks of Robert Guiscard. He also features extensively during the wars against the Pechenegs, most notably during the ill-fated expedition against the Danube. As the campaign turned into a fiasco, George becomes the focus of a lengthy passage relating his flight from Dristra in the mid-1080s. The dream sequence that follows would neither seem to be part of a military record, nor an episode which would have been recorded in archives of letters, correspondence and official documents which were presumably kept in Constantinople.[22]

Moreover, while the fact that George plays an important role in Anna's coverage of the Norman attacks may be consistent with the quality of her sources for Guiscard's assault on Byzantium, what the author actually says about her uncle should prompt us to question exactly where she had drawn her information. It is less that Anna notes the counter-measures which Palaiologos took in defending Dyrrachion and the surrounding area that is striking here, and more that she records thoughts he is supposed to have had and things he is supposed to have done,[23] especially instances of his personal bravery,[24] and specific advice he gave to

---

[21] Regarding George's survival into the twelfth century, see Skoulatos, *Les personnages byzantins*, 104, where the date of his death is given as between 1119 and 1136. George is mentioned in the *Life* of Cyril Phileotes, E. Sargologos, ed., *La vie de Saint Cyrille le Philéote, moine byzantin* (Brussels, 1964), 237. Skoulatos gives 'around 1110' as the date of this episode (*Les personnages byzantins*, 104). The nature of the text makes such dating in any case schematic, but the indications are that the episode should in fact be dated somewhat earlier. Phileotes died in 1110. In the text, the episode with George precedes the second visit of Alexios to Phileotes, which Sargologos dates to 1105 (*La vie de Saint Cyrille*, 40). In any case, rather clearer evidence for placing George's death some time into the twelfth century is cited: George is not listed amongst the deceased in the *typikon* of the monastery of Kecharitomene (1119), but is found in the obituary of the Pantokrator (1136) (P. Gautier, 'L'obituaire du typikon du Pantocrator', *REB*, 27 (1969), 235).

[22] Komnene, *Alexias*, ed. Reinsch and Kambylis, vol. I, 215–16 (VII.iv.1–3).

[23] Palaiologos not only reinforced the town's defences, but visited these constantly, during the day and at night, ibid., 120 (IV.i.1.16–19); George's initiatives to thwart the Norman assault on the walls are reported in detail in ibid., 128 (IV.iv.6–8.49–75).

[24] George worked tirelessly to frustrate the Normans from within Dyrrachion and indeed led at least one sortie from the town. He had shown exceptional bravery, and been wounded in the clashes, continuing fighting even after an operation which left part of an arrow still embedded in his head, ibid., 127 (IV.iv.31–40).

the emperor.²⁵ We can draw one of two conclusions from this: either Anna was using reports which went into detail about these matters and which commented on Palaiologos' valour and his cunning; or alternatively, the author of the *Alexiad* invented these in order to add colour to her narrative. While superficially it might seem plausible that the flourishes about Palaiologos are *topoi*, stylised episodes or short rhetorical exercises, this in fact raises other awkward questions. Why did George's courage need to be underlined at specific points in the text, and not elsewhere, and why was the heroism of other figures not similarly noted?

The logical answer here is that the details on Palaiologos' bravery are not made up, or based on hazy conversations she had overheard, but rather that she had been able to draw on a source that recorded George's achievements at Dyrrachion. This in itself would be consistent with the profile of the *Alexiad* as a whole, and with the coverage of the Norman attacks on Epiros specifically, where there is ample and obvious evidence that Anna Komnene had been able to draw on a wide range of written material, from official documents (in the form of letters to Henry IV and perhaps from Leo Kephalas, and of a summary of privileges granted to Venice), to narrative sources from southern Italy – including those of Geoffrey Malaterra and William of Apulia.²⁶ The fact that this section of the *Alexiad* is clearly based on a rich tapestry of written accounts means that identifying another source, albeit previously unknown, focusing on the achievements of George Palaiologos, would not come as a surprise.

There are a further two reasons to suspect the existence of an account centred on Palaiologos and to establish use of this by the author of the *Alexiad*. These come from two other sections of the text where attention is fixed firmly on this individual. Anna provides a detailed account of the disastrous expedition against the Danube region in the mid-1080s when the Byzantine army was routed by Pecheneg steppe nomads after launching an ill-judged attack on Dristra. The assault descended into chaos. The imperial forces scattered, with the emperor barely managing to escape with his life, reaching safety with great difficulty before ransoming soldiers who had been captured by the Pechenegs.²⁷

---

²⁵ Reports from or about Palaiologos appear at ibid., 122 (IV.ii.1.65–72); 127–8 (IV.iv.4.48–9). He gave sanguine advice to the Emperor, ibid., 129 (IV.v.2–3.95–10).
²⁶ P. Frankopan, 'Turning Latin into Greek: Anna Komnene and the *Gesta Roberti Wiscardi*', *JMedHist*, 39 (2013), 80–99; P. Brown, 'The Gesta Roberti Wiscardi: A "Byzantine" History?' *JMedHist*, 37 (2011), 162–79.
²⁷ Komnene, *Alexias*, ed. Reinsch and Kambylis, vol. I, 208–14 (VII.iii.1–10).

The author then suddenly shifts her attention to George Palaiologos, and reports how he too had found safety in the wake of the flawed attack on the nomads.[28] Palaiologos is the only character whose fate is recorded at any length. This passage contains a dream-sequence – of which there are no other examples in the *Alexiad*. Under the intense pressure of pursuit, Palaiologos had a vision that is reported at length: George imagined himself in the company of Leo, bishop of Chalcedon. This figure, dressed in priestly robes, appeared from nowhere, offered Palaiologos his horse, and promptly disappeared. George then made good his escape.[29] It is not just the vision that is highly unusual, for we also can pick out editorial intervention in this passage. The bishop in question had been a thorn in the emperor's side, complaining bitterly about the expropriation of church treasure which had helped fund Byzantine resistance against the Normans and which had been done again, in contravention of a solemn agreement not to do so, by Alexios in the mid-1080s.[30] Leo's criticisms had been a profound embarrassment for the emperor, who eventually silenced the cleric by having him tried and then exiled.[31] Perhaps not surprisingly, therefore, Anna notes in this part of the *Alexiad* that Leo was an ignorant man, with a worrying lack of knowledge of religious affairs. According to Anna, Leo had not the slightest grasp of basic Christian doctrine.[32] The barbed comments about Leo of Chalcedon in the passage on George's escape are therefore not entirely unexpected. However, they are problematic in so far as they contrast sharply with what else we learn in the passage dealing with Palaiologos' escape from the Pechenegs. After all, vision or no vision, Leo is given credit for saving George's life by offering him a horse on which to escape.[33] More telling still is that it is noted here that George viewed the clergyman with affection and considered he was a man of outstanding virtue ('ἐξείχειτο δὲ τοῦ ἀνδρὸς ὁ Παλαιολόγος ἀεὶ καὶ διαφερόντως ἐτίμα διὰ τὸ περιὸν αὐτῷ τῆς ἀρετῆς').[34] The contradictions here in the attitudes to Leo are best explained, therefore, as a manifestation

[28] Ibid., 215–16 (VII.iv.1–4).   [29] Ibid., 215 (VII.iv.1.57–62).
[30] On Leo in the *Alexiad*, see ibid., 144ff. (V.ii.4–6.16–58). For the text of Alexius' chrysobull, detailing the restoration of confiscated ecclesiastical property and promising to refrain from such actions in the future, see V. Grumel, 'L'affaire de Léon de Chalcédoine. Le chrysobulle d'Alexis Ier sur les objets sacrés', *Études Byzantines*, 2 (1944), 126–33.
[31] Ibid., 145 (V.ii.6.50–4); See also I. Sakellion, 'Documents inédits tirés de la bibliothèque de Patmos. 1: Décret d'Alexis Comnène portant déposition de Léon, métropolitain de Chalcédoine', *BCH*, 2 (1878), 113.
[32] In Book V, Anna criticises particularly Leo's inability to engage in logical argument (ibid., 145 (V.ii.5.40f.)), while in Book VII she emphasises his lack of understanding of religious matters (ibid., 215 (VII.iv.1.62–5)).
[33] Ibid., 215 (VII.iv.59ff.).   [34] Ibid., 215 (VII.iv.1.66ff.).

of two hands at work: one, Anna's, providing negative comments about Leo of Chalcedon; the other, praising the cleric for his virtue.

The hypothesis that Anna is drawing on a source relating Palaiologos' achievements is consistent with other elements from this passage in the text. The author goes on to note the outstanding leadership that George displayed on finding a contingent of one hundred and fifty Byzantine soldiers, who were exposed to danger; he showed enormous courage leading them into battle with Pechenegs, showing no regard to his own safety; his sealed his men's support by the solemn giving of oaths, underlining their solidarity; and he persevered against overwhelming odds, and in spite of the fact that both he and his horse were wounded. All these are events, descriptions and metaphors which we would expect to find in an encomiastic account centred on George Palaiologos – including the way he finally reached safety, where he was nursed back to health by a kindly widow.[35]

Even the way this passage is brought to a close shows Anna putting her source to one side. Thus, having reported how her uncle found safety, the author says that these were the things that had happened to Palaiologos ('ἀλλὰ τοιαῦτα μὲν τὰ τῷ Παλαιολόγῳ συμπεσόντα').[36] It was time, in other words, to change the subject. This serves as a good indication that Anna had set to one side one slab of material which she had been working from, in order to turn to another.

The same editorial process is at work in a second passage in the text, where the focus once again rests unerringly on George Palaiologos. On this occasion, the narrative even goes so far as to quote Palaiologos, and, moreover, to do so in direct, rather than reported speech. Again, then, this would be consistent with a source written with George as the central character. Palaiologos plays a prominent role in the *Alexiad*'s coverage of the build-up to the Komnenoi coup of 1081, which brought Alexios to the throne. It was Palaiologos who took the women of the family to safety;[37] it was Palaiologos who intercepted an envoy from Emperor Nikephoros III Botaneiates to Nikephoros Melissenos at a crucial moment during the Komnenoi's preparations;[38] it was Palaiologos who gave the signal for the storming of the Kharisian Gate, which allowed the Komnenoi and their supporters to get into Constantinople;[39] and it was Palaiologos who spoke

---

[35] Ibid., 215f. (VII.iv.2–3.70–92). [36] Ibid., 215 (VII.iv.4.92f.).
[37] Ibid., 69f. (II.vi.1–3.30–55). [38] Ibid., 82f. (II.xi.1–5.12–65). [39] Ibid., 81 (II.x.3.90–2).

up decisively for Eirene Doukaina, Alexios' wife, after the young general had taken the imperial capital.[40]

The ubiquity of George Palaiologos is a striking feature of Anna's coverage of her father's usurpation. But what is most telling here, at least with regard to the identification of a Palaiologan source, is what we learn from these passages beyond noting George's presence at key events, which might of course have been known to Anna from elsewhere. It is that the content of the passages where George appears corresponds closely with what we would expect to find in an *encomium* dedicated to this individual.

It is not just that the account of the Komnenoi coup makes great play at the steadfast loyalty shown by George Palaiologos. Nor even that George's bravery is noted on more than one occasion. Most revealing is the use of speech in this section. Time and again, Anna purports to quote her uncle.[41] This may be a device on the part of the author. However, it should be noted that while direct speech is used occasionally by the author of the *Alexiad* in the history of Alexios' reign, it is not used with anything like the regularity with which it is deployed in this part of the text. Crucially too, the fact that it is only Palaiologos' comments that are quoted, and not those of any other figure, should cause us to pay close attention here to the question of what Anna's source or sources must have been.

If the close focus on George is suggestive of a source that had this individual as its central character, then so too is the type of information about him which appears in this part of the *Alexiad*. Palaiologos is prominent in the account of Alexios' entry to Constantinople and his seizure of power. Moreover, he repeatedly appears playing a decisive role. It was George who ordered the entry into the imperial capital; it was George who intercepted the envoy who had been sent to the Komnenoi's principal rival at the time, Nikephoros Melissenos; it was George who commanded the fleet during the coup, with his contribution, once again, being crucial to the success of the coup; and it was George who assured the coronation of Eirene Doukaina alongside Alexios, when this had seemed in doubt.

Indeed, Palaiologos emerges from the account of the putsch of 1081 with a role more prominent than that of any other figure, certainly greater than the emperor's elder brother, Isaac Komnenos, and greater even than Alexios himself. According to the *Alexiad*, George took the Komnenoi women and their relatives to safety, himself deciding on the

---

[40] Ibid., 89 (III.ii.1.78–84).   [41] Ibid., 70 (II.vi.3.55f.); 82f. (II.xi.3.38–50); 89 (III.ii.1.82f.).

appropriate location where they would be sufficiently protected in case the insurrection went wrong.[42] Palaiologos too was responsible for gathering funds and protecting these for the duration of the coup – and presumably disbursing it to the auxiliaries, mercenaries, troops and supporters who had cast their lot with Alexios and his brother.[43]

George's visibility in the account of Alexios' seizure of the throne, the fact that his interventions during the coup were not only timely but decisive, and the extensive use of direct speech attributed to Palaiologos, all point to the fact that Anna Komnene was well supplied with information about this figure, and was not just relying on memories of conversations which her uncle had had with her father or other family members many years after the events in question. The level of detail provided makes any hypothesis that Anna's coverage relied purely on memory difficult to sustain. Moreover, the passages relating to Palaiologos have a different feel to the rest of the narrative; had she depended on the recollection of stories, there would have been rather parallels across the text since she could be expected to draw on conversations in other contexts also.

What makes the argument about the existence of and Anna's dependence on a non-extant Palaiologan source more credible still is the treatment accorded to Nikephoros Palaiologos, George's father, in this part of the text. According to the *Alexiad*, Nikephoros had been a supporter of Emperor Nikephoros III Botaneiates and had been entrusted by the latter with an important command position in the eastern part of Asia Minor.[44] In each occasion of his appearance in the account of the Komnenoi coup, the portrayal of George's father is extremely flattering – one which would not be out of place in a family history.

On the first occasion, Anna does little more than mention that there were fears amongst Alexios' family about whether George himself could be trusted. After all, it was noted, his father Nikephoros was close to Nikephoros III Botaneiates.[45] At face value, this reference may seem innocuous, if not counter-productive: bearing in mind that any work focused on George would have been written towards the end of that individual's life – more likely in the twelfth rather than the eleventh century, and certainly well after Alexios' usurpation – the comment of the elder Palaiologos' allegiance to Botaneiates (and therefore not to the Komnenoi) is surprising. However, as the Komnenoi emperors were

---

[42] Ibid., 69f. (II.vi.3.49–52).   [43] Ibid., 70 (II.vi.3.55–8).
[44] P. Gautier, ed., *Nicéphore Bryennios. Histoire* (Brussels, 1975), 239 (III.15.12–13).
[45] Komnene, *Alexias*, ed. Reinsch and Kambylis, vol. 1, 69 (II.vi.2.35–8).

shortly to learn, loyalty to the sovereign was a quality that could not be relied on – even from the closest members of the imperial family itself, to say nothing of other members of the Byzantine aristocracy.[46] In other words, Nikephoros' allegiance to Botaneiates – described in fact as intense devotion – may mask a nuanced praise of George's father which was designed to show the steadfastness, resolve and reliability of the Palaiologos family to the ruler, in contrast, that is to say, with other aristocrats of this period.

The comment about Nikephoros' loyalty is repeated shortly afterwards in the *Alexiad*. According to Anna's account, even until the last moment, Nikephoros Palaiologos was rallying troops with which to oppose the usurper.[47] Indeed, the elder Palaiologos sought to continue his opposition to Alexios and his followers even after Nikephoros III himself had given up hope. It was with a heavy heart, then, that George's father laid down his arms ('ὁ δὲ δυσανασχετῶν ὅμως ἀπῄει').[48]

The emphasis and stress laid on Nikephoros Palaiologos' personal qualities would naturally be more consistent with a family source, where his resolute support of the doomed regime reflects well on this individual, showing him as a man who was not prepared to put his own interests first and to be an opportunist at a time of crisis. And this observation can be extended further by closely following what else the *Alexiad* has to say here. For in addition to the underlining of Nikephoros' steadfastness comes praise too of his ability and generalship. Thus, Anna reports him as urging the doomed Botaneiates to let him lead Varangian troops ('τοὺς ἀπὸ τῆς Θούλης νήσου βαρβάρους') against the usurpers. With these alongside him, the elder Palaiologos felt that he would have no difficulty in resisting the Komnenoi attacks and, moreover, would succeed in expelling them from Constantinople altogether.[49] It is difficult not to be astonished by this comment. What the author of the *Alexiad* is saying, in effect, is that Nikephoros Palaiologos was a superior commander to Alexios Komnenos; that the barbarians from Thule would and could have outclassed the military support gathered by Alexios and his brothers; and that the success of the Komnenoi required little to de-rail it. It is not the eponymous hero of the *Alexiad* who is well-served by this passage, therefore, but Nikephoros Palaiologos himself.

---

[46] See P. Frankopan, 'Kinship and the Distribution of Power in Komnenian Byzantium', *EHR*, 72 (2007), 1–34.
[47] Komnene, *Alexias*, ed. Reinsch and Kambylis, vol. I, 84 (II.xi.7.80–4). [48] Ibid., 84 (II.xi.7.88).
[49] Ibid., 84 (II.xi.7.82ff.).

There is one final reason to suspect that Anna had had access to and drawn from a source that focused on the Palaiologoi. We learn from the *Alexiad* of the final effort made by Botaneiates to save face before he was deposed. The Emperor Nikephoros approached the Komnenoi, offering to adopt Alexios as his son, invest him with the imperial dignity and not only share power with him, but hand over full power to him, retaining only ceremonial duties.[50] This offer was flatly opposed by the *caesar*, John Doukas.[51] It is significant that the offer to the Komnenoi is recorded at length, suggesting that the source of this evidence must have been closely involved either in the transmission or the reception of the message and offer to Alexios. Indeed, not only are the detailed terms of Botaneiates' offer set out in full, but they are recorded in direct speech. It comes as little surprise, then, to find that the conveyor of the proposal to the Komnenoi, and the individual who is quoted at length, is none other than Nikephoros Palaiologos.[52]

There are good grounds then to suspect that Anna Komnene was able to use an account centred on the Palaiologos family. And in fact, Anna's editorial technique allows us to speculate about the form that it took: the author either lifted passages uncritically and in bloc, as in the case of the comment about Nikephoros' prowess in 1081 where a section has presumably been copied word for word; or more clumsily, such as when the author intervenes to add a barbed comment about Leo of Chalcedon's ignorance, which jars with the praise this figure had received only a few lines earlier in the text. In this instance, the author opened the seam of her material to interject a personal opinion.

In turn, this provides the outline of what Anna was working from. The account at her disposal evidently focused on more than one member of the family, rather than a work solely praising George Palaiologos and recording his deeds – suggesting that the author was likely using history that focused on the wider Palaiologos clan. The role of the work seems to have been to stress the service that the family played in Byzantium in the late eleventh century, both under the Komnenoi and under the previous regime of Nikephoros III Botaneiates. It sought to stress that the family did not only have responsibilities and duties in the imperial capital, but across Byzantium as a whole. This can be seen from the passing reference to Nikephoros Palaiologos' role in Mesopotamia, but above all from the careful record of his son, George, serving in every major military arena in

---

[50] Ibid., 84f. (II.xii.2.96–09) and 85 (II.xii.3.18–23).   [51] Ibid., 85 (II.xii.3.23–8).
[52] Ibid., 84 (II.xii.1.95f.) and 85 (II.xii.3.13ff.).

the first two decades of Alexios' reign — fighting the Normans, the Pechenegs, and the Cumans, as well as being present in Asia Minor during the passage of the First Crusade on its way to Jerusalem.

Anna borrowed liberally from this account, selecting episodes and details she deemed useful, and rejecting the rest. This is why there is nothing in the *Alexiad* about other aspects about the Palaiologoi, such as their estates, family, or legendary piety, recorded so vividly in the life of St Cyril Phileotes: the author was not interested in showing the qualities, characteristics or generosity of the family as this was secondary to her focus on her father, his exploits and his reign.[53] Such was the tightness of Anna's attention that key events from Alexios' reign are ignored altogether: a very major victory scored over the Pechenegs in the early 1080s, for example, is not even mentioned in the *Alexiad*. The reason for this was almost certainly because it had been gained not by the emperor, but by Gregory Pakourianos.[54]

We can see the author using precisely the same technique elsewhere in the *Alexiad*, where she cannibalises a text, keeping what she wants and discarding what she does not. This is how she treats Michael Psellos' *Chronographia*, extracting its account of Isaac I Komnenos' campaign against the Pechenegs in the 1050s word-for-word, but leaving aside everything else as superfluous to her portrayal of Komnenian rule.[55]

There is, then, a further observation to make here concerning Anna's use of her Palaiologan source, for it is of some importance that we understand why the author chose to include this material in the first place. It is possible to detect a pattern here, a method and a way in which the author used the material that was available, for none of the borrowings are coincidental. Rather, they are selective and carefully chosen. In the case of the passage from Psellos, Anna's borrowing allowed her to stress that her father had an imperial pedigree, because his uncle had held the throne; it also allowed Anna to establish that emperors in general, and Komnenian emperors in particular, had a track record of taking the threat posed by the steppe nomads seriously, an important observation given criticisms of Alexios' handling of the northern frontier which lay behind the massive

---

[53] See above, note 21.
[54] P. Frankopan, 'A Victory of Gregory Pakourianos Against the Pechenegs', *BSl*, 57 (1996), no. 2, 278–81.
[55] Komnene, *Alexias*, ed. Reinsch and Kambylis, vol. 1, 107ff. (III.viii.6–10). See also above, note 9.

rebellion of the aristocracy immediately before the First Crusade.[56] And using the work of the polymath Michael Psellos was a subtle way of suggesting that great authors wrote about great emperors – a neat way to showcase Alexios as well as the *Alexiad*.

So why did Anna draw on her Palaiologan source? Again, Anna's borrowings are not coincidental. In the case of the account of the defence of Dyrrachion during the Norman attack of the early 1080s, Anna includes details of George's bravery for good reason: to deflect blame from Alexios for one of the biggest military fiascos of his reign. In 1081, faced with the Norman invasion, Alexios had decided to launch an all-out attack on Robert Guiscard, with catastrophic results. Soundly defeated in battle, he then saw Dyrrachion itself surrender to the enemy force. Little wonder, then, that he was roundly criticised in Constantinople afterwards, and his reputation suffered a shattering blow.[57] Palaiologos' prominence in Anna's coverage of the Norman assault is to be explained as part of the author's wider aims here: that is, to defend Alexios by showing that Dyrrachion had been adequately reinforced, well-protected and well-led during the Norman assault, and, furthermore, that George Palaiologos had done all in his power to save the town, sustaining near life-threatening injuries in the process.[58]

The conspicuous reference to Palaiologos' bravery following the doomed assault on Dristra has the same intention. It shows that in spite of the repulse from the Danube region, the Byzantines did not retreat ignominiously. Rather, Anna uses the example of her uncle to highlight his heroism, and, by extension, to salvage some pride for the imperial military generally and for her father in particular from an otherwise embarrassing episode that had seen the emperor confidently march north, assuming an easy victory was his for the taking. It is no surprise, then, that Anna notes that the emperor himself was wounded on both occasions – in the retreats from Dyrrachion in 1081 and from Dristra a few years later.[59] It is in this context that she turned to her Palaiologan source: to draw out a better picture of two crushing setbacks that reflected poorly on Alexios. Having

---

[56] P. Frankopan, 'Expeditions Against the Serbs in the 1090s: the *Alexiad* and Byzantium's Northwest Frontier on the Eve of the First Crusade', *Bulgaria Medievalis*, 3 (2012), 385–97.
[57] Komnene, *Alexias*, ed. Reinsch and Kambylis, vol. 1, 183 (VI.vii.7.67–74); also 143 (v.i.5.55–60).
[58] This is particularly emphasised: see ibid., 127 (IV.iii.4.31–40).
[59] For Alexios' exploits towards the end of the battle and during the retreat from Dyrrachion, ibid., 135–8 (IV.vi.8.64–IV.vii.5.71). Anna describes Alexios being slightly wounded in the battle, 135 (IV.vi.8.75–8), but repeatedly emphasises how close Alexios came to danger. For Alexios' injury on the retreat from Dristra, see 214 (VII.iii.12.47–50).

extracted what she needed from this material, she abandoned the source, as what else it said was of limited value for the task at hand, namely showing Emperor Alexios I Komnenos in the best possible light.

Explaining why the author drew on the source so heavily for her coverage of the coup of 1081 is more complicated. It may well be that Anna simply had less information to hand for the backdrop to the Komnenoi seizure of power, and therefore took the opportunity to rely on an account dealing with her uncle and his family. After all, Anna raided the writings of her husband, Nikephoros Bryennios, for the build-up to Alexios' entry to Constantinople: although Bryennios' history does not go as far as the usurpation of the Komnenoi, he does outline negotiations between the rivals seeking to take the throne from Nikephoros III Botaneiates.[60] That Anna borrows extensively from her husband's account and also on our Palaiologan source might be taken to suggest the profile of the sources that she had at her disposal.[61] Quite why Anna may have had limited information for her father's coup and relied heavily on a narrative account focusing not on Alexios or his brother Isaac, but on George and Nikephoros Palaiologos, is not clear. However, the wanton destruction caused by the Komnenoi's supporters provides one possible explanation as to why there were no other accounts for Anna to use: it is not hard to suppose why records of the troops' behaviour in 1081 might have been suppressed or destroyed, not least given the embarrassing submission of and appearance by Alexios before the Synod soon afterwards to atone for the behaviour of his troops.[62] An obvious alternative, of course, is that the carnage which accompanied Alexios' entry to Constantinople was such that the author had to find material with which to pad her account, thereby allowing her to devote appropriate space in the text to her father's accession while eschewing further detail about the accompanying scenes.

It is of some significance too, then, that a careful reading of the *Alexiad* would appear to confirm not only that the author was well informed about the Palaiologoi and had a dossier of information centred on George and Nikephoros, but that this material took the form of a written

---

[60] Book IV of Bryennios deals with the activities of Alexios, Nikephoros Bryennios, Nikephoros Melissenos, Basilakes, George Palaiologos and others. See Bryennios, *Histoire*, ed. Gautier, 258–311.
[61] For Anna's borrowing from Bryennios, see above, note 10.
[62] Anna Komnene comments specifically on the appalling scenes which accompanied the entry of the Komnenoi into Constantinople in 1081, and on her father's subsequent penance, Komnene, *Alexias*, ed. Reinsch and Kambylis, vol. I, 98–100 (III.v.2–6.52–9). John Zonaras also stresses the carnage caused by Alexios' supporters; M. Pinder and T. Büttner-Wobst, eds., *Ioannis Zonarae Annales et Epitome Historiarum* (Bonn, 1841–97), vol. III, 741–2 (XVIII.23).

account – likely a history specific to this family. Having outlined the preliminary stages of the assault on the capital by the Komnenoi and their allies, Anna explains that the rebels reached the city walls before riding on to the monastery of the Kosmidion. At this point, declares Anna, the narrative will be broken so that she can clarify matters ('καὶ γάρ, ἵνα μεταξύ πως ἐπιδιηγησαίμην καὶ σαφέστερος ἡμῖν ὁ λόγος προΐη').[63]

The coverage then breaks off to provide two lengthy anecdotes. The second takes the form of a detailed explanation of how John Doukas came to join the Komnenoi, bringing with him a quantity of gold that he had expropriated from a tax collector.[64] The first, however, centres on George Palaiologos. The fact that it contains direct speech is a useful pointer that it is based on a written source, as is the fact that the quoted speech is that of George Palaiologos – setting him as subject and principal, rather than object or agent.[65] It is worth noting too that while comments attributed to George are provided here, no other individual is quoted in this passage, directly or indirectly – which might again be taken as a useful indicator of material that was Palaiologos-centric.

The frictions between George Palaiologos and his father are even recorded, with doubts, feelings and concerns referred to and elaborated on. Personal exchanges between father and son are reported in indirect speech, with the differences of opinion between the two men also noted.[66] Even the views of George's mother-in-law are mentioned in this part of the *Alexiad*, as is an elegant account of her beauty, while Palaiologos' concerns for her and for his own wife are also recorded.[67] Finally, the advice of where the best place for the womenfolk to seek refuge is reported, as it is stressed that it was the elder Palaiologos' advice that turned out to be crucial.[68]

It seems likely that this close focus on the Palaiologoi is the result of Anna's access to a written source. The high level of detail and the nature of the information – complimentary, insightful and always informative – lifted by the author of the *Alexiad* points to a now-lost account of the exploits of one of the great aristocratic families of the middle Byzantine period. Moreover, the fact that it is not just George Palaiologos who is mentioned, but other family members too, including leading female

---

[63] Komnene, *Alexias*, ed. Reinsch and Kambylis, vol. 1, 69 (II.vi.1.30f.).
[64] Ibid., 70ff. (II.vi.3–9.54–29).   [65] Ibid., 70 (II.vi.3.55f.).
[66] Ibid., 83f. (II.xi.6.65–80), records the sea-borne exchange between Nikephoros and his son at the time of the Komnenoi coup.
[67] Ibid., 60 (II.vi.2–3.38–49).   [68] Ibid., 70 (II.vi.3.51f.).

figures, suggests that the focus of the account was on the Palaiologoi more generally – rather than on the figure of George alone.

Family histories were surely commissioned in the middle Byzantine period by aristocratic patrons, recording the lives and deeds of illustrious ancestors in the eleventh and twelfth centuries, to be read out and performed at family and social gatherings, though examples of these are few and far between.[69] In many ways, this is the missing link in Byzantine literature from this period: while we are rich with accounts of the reigns of emperors and those of saints, there are almost no surviving histories that showcase aristocratic (rather than imperial) patronage, though there are other ghost accounts, like the Palaiologos source, that can be identified through patient detective work.[70]

That individuals such as George Palaiologos – who served empire and emperor with distinction, and who stood at the summit of Byzantine society through his close kinship with Alexios, and at the apex of the imperial military by virtue of his command positions – would have recorded their achievements would hardly be surprising; if anything, it would be more surprising if they had not done so.

The fact then that accounts such as these have not survived is not in itself a surprise, given the differential both in importance with saints' lives and accounts of imperial reigns. It was highly likely that family histories would be lost over time. For one thing, they would not have been preserved in those great archives that weathered centuries of change, namely the monastic archives, which meant that their chances of survival were slim. Additionally, accounts about previous generations, even in very illustrious families, would eventually have become less relevant. Documents about forefathers generations past would have been curios but no more, unless of course the individuals in question were emperors, absolutely at the heart of government rather than immediately next to it, as the Palaiologoi were.

Nevertheless, magnates in Byzantium evidently did have an eye on preserving their names for posterity – as is clear from the number of non-imperial monastic foundations established in the empire. That the

---

[69] M. Mullett, 'Aristocracy and Patronage in the Literary Circles of Comnenian Constantinople' in M. Angold, ed., *The Byzantine Aristocracy, IX–XIII Centuries* (Oxford, 1984), 173–201; P. Magdalino, *The Empire of Manuel I Komnenos, 1143–1180* (Cambridge, 1993), 339–53; A. Kaldellis, *Hellenism in Byzantium. The Transformation of Greek Identity and the Reception of the Classical Tradition* (Cambridge, 2007), 235–7. Also see Frankopan, 'Turning Latin into Greek', 12.

[70] L. Neville, 'A History of Caesar John Doukas in Nikephoros Bryennios's *Material for History*?', *BMGS*, 32 (2008), 168–88.

typika of at least some of these institutions make a point of recording the achievements of the settlor is therefore significant – in other words, underlining both the desire for, and the act of, record-making.[71]

The aim here has been to unstitch a small seam in Anna's narrative account. By arguing that the author was able to rely on a Palaiologan account relating to this period, not only has it been possible to explain one element of the historiography of the *Alexiad*, but also to provide some insights into the detail and accuracy of Anna's account. As such, then, it can perhaps serve as a useful blueprint for how we might try to approach this source in other ways – to identify other written accounts and other sources, and to learn more about the editorial process behind Anna's great history. It brings implications too about aristocratic patronage and image within Byzantium, about the ways in which magnates wished to portray themselves, the sort of qualities and characteristics that were highly valued, and the ways in which *kudos* could be won.

In this sense, therefore, we might profitably look to sources like *Digenis Akritis*, so brilliantly edited and translated by Elizabeth Jeffreys, for other ideas about non-imperial secular writing in Byzantium.[72] When it comes to medieval Greek literature, there is still much to be done if we are to understand complex sources properly.

Further Reading

The key sources are: D. R. Reinsch and A. Kambylis, eds., *Annae Comnenae. Alexias*, 2 vols. (Berlin, 2001); P. Gautier, ed. and trans., *Nicéphore Bryennios. Histoire. Introduction, texte, traduction et notes* (Brussels, 1975); M. Pinder and T. Büttner-Wobst, eds., *Ioannis Zonarae Annales et Epitomae historiarum*, 3 vols. (Bonn, 1841–97). Study: J. Howard-Johnston, 'Anna Komnene and the Alexiad' in M. Mullett and D. Smythe, eds., *Alexios I Komnenos – Papers of the Second Belfast Byzantine International Colloquium, 14–16 April 1989* (Belfast, 1996), 260–302.

---

[71] The *Typika* of Michael Attaleiates, Gregory Pakourianos and George the Cappadocian provide three examples of prominent individuals recording their achievements alongside their donations to endow monastic foundation: J. Thomas and A. Constantinides Hero, eds., *Byzantine Monastic Foundation Documents: A Complete Translation of the Surviving Founders' Typika and Testaments*, (Washington, D. C., 2000), esp. vol. I, 333–7; vol. II, 522–7; vol. III, 991–3.
[72] E. M. Jeffreys, ed. and trans., *Digenis Akritis: The Grottaferrata and Escorial Versions* (Cambridge, 1998).

CHAPTER 14

Historiography, Epic and the Textual Transmission of Imperial Values: Liudprand's Antapodosis *and* Digenes Akrites

Günter Prinzing

One of the open questions in research on the middle Byzantine epic of *Digenes Akrites* is that concerning the identity and historicity of the emperor who paid a memorable visit to young Digenes on the eastern frontier of the empire.[1] This question appears to have little connection with issues of the interface between oral and written traditions, unless we think more carefully about the nature of the sources that need to be examined in order to answer it. The initial textual recording of history occurs at the point of transition from the purely oral form of transmission to the stage when a story is first set down in writing. Once written down, however, the text does not stop mutating, since it can still be read in various ways, not merely by silent reading to oneself (which could be accompanied by a process of copying or note-taking), but also by reading aloud in front of an audience (which would allow listeners to make a mental note of the contents, which can then be recounted from memory). From there, the text can be transmitted still further, whether orally or in writing, whether abridged or expanded, perhaps as a transcript or a paraphrase of the version that has been received.[2] That medieval sources come down to us with such a complicated, stratified past becomes clear

---

[1] I would like to express my gratitude to the editors, Teresa Shawcross and Ida Toth, for their kind support, their many suggestions for improving the text, but also their forbearance. Once more I am obliged to John M. Deasy (Mainz) for the translation.
 Still useful as a general introduction to the subject is H.-G. Beck, *Geschichte der byzantinischen Volksliteratur* (Munich, 1971), 63–97, 81–2. For a more recent overview of the research about the *Digenes* epic, see E. Trapp, 'Digenēs Akritēs' in H. L. Arnold, ed., *Kindlers Literatur Lexikon*, (Stuttgart, 2009), vol. VI, 603–4 and C. Cupane and B. Krönung, 'Geschichten von der Grenze', in F. Daim, ed., *Das Goldene Byzanz und der Orient* (Schallaburg, 2012), 155–69, especially 164–8.

[2] See also H. Hunger, *Schreiben und Lesen in Byzanz. Die byzantinische Buchkultur* (Munich, 1989), 90–2 and 124–7; C. Holmes, 'Written Culture in Byzantium and Beyond: Contexts, Contents and Intepretations' in C. Holmes and J. Waring, eds., *Literacy, Education and Manuscript Transmission in Byzantium and Beyond* (Leiden, 2002), 1–31; M. Mullett, 'No Drama, No Poetry, No Fiction, No Readership, No Literature' in L. James, ed., *A Companion to Byzantium* (Malden, MA, 2010),

from the first of the main sources considered in this chapter, a passage from the *Antapodosis* of Liudprand of Cremona, the well-known cleric, statesman and historian.[3] Written around 960, it reports a legend from the early life of the later Emperor Romanos I Lekapenos (920–944) that was circulating in Constantinople,[4] probably in a written rather than an oral form, and was then picked up by Liudprand during his first visit to Constantinople which he undertook in 949/50 in his capacity as an ambassador of Margrave Berengar II of Ivrea.[5] The second passage to be examined comes from the intricate verse epic *Digenes Akrites*, whose anonymous compiler(s) (*fl. c.* twelfth century) also seem(s) to have relied on information coming, at least partly, from tenth-century chronicles and works of historiography from Byzantium.

Of the main Greek versions of the Digenes epic contained in manuscripts G (Grottaferrata: Cod. Cryptoferrat. Z.α.XLIV, late thirteenth or early fourteenth century) and E (Escorial: Cod. Scorial. gr. 496 [Ψ-IV-22], late fifteenth century), only the former reports in Book Four, the section known as the 'romance' of Digenes Akrites, details about the emperor's visit.[6] In addition, allusions to the encounter are also to be found in the

---

229–38, here: 'Readership' 233–8; and E. Bourbouhakis, 'Rhetoric and Performance' in P. Stephenson, ed., *The Byzantine World* (London, 2010), 175–87.

[3] On Liudprand (and his works) see: E. Karpf, 'L(iutprand) v. Cremona' in *Lexikon des Mittelalters*, vol. V (1991), col. 2041–2; P. Chiesa, 'Liutprando', in *Dizionario Biografico degli Italiani* 65 (2005), 298–303; R.-J. Lilie et al., eds., *Prosopographie der mittelbyzantinischen Zeit, Zweite Abteilung (867–1025)*, (Berlin, 2013), vol. IV: *Landenolfus (# 24269) – Niketas (# 225701)*, 'Liudprand', # 24745, 240–2 [hereafter *PmbZ II*]. Most recently on the *Antapodosis*, R.-J. Lilie et al., *PmbZ. Prolegomena* (Berlin, 2009), 173–5; T. Haye, 'Liutprand von Cremona' in Arnold, ed., *Kindlers Literatur-Lexikon*, vol. X, 221; and S. Penn, 'Liutprand of Cremona' in G. Dunphy and C. Bratu, eds., *The Encyclopedia of the Medieval Chronicle* (Leiden, 2010), 1034.

[4] On Romanos I and his reign see J. Shepard, 'Equilibrium to Expansion (886–1025)' in J. Shepard, ed., *The Cambridge History of the Byzantine Empire, c. 500–1492* (Cambridge, 2008), 505–11; Lilie et al., *PmbZ II (867–1025)*, vol. V: *Niketas (# 25702) – Sinapes (# 27088)*, 'Romanos I. Lakapenos', # 26833, 578–93, see also below footnote 25.

[5] M. McCormick, 'Liutprand of Cremona' in A. Kazhdan et al., eds., *ODB*, vol. II, 1241–2, stating with regard to the content of the *Antapodosis*: 'Despite muddled chronology, its anecdotal account is rich in Byz. data. Descriptions of events before Liutprand's lifetime derive from oral sources – possibly in Constantine VII's milieu – or lost written sources shared with surviving Byz. historians'. On the legend reported by Liudprand, see the text referring to footnote 27 below.

[6] E. M. Jeffreys, ed., *Digenis Akritis: The Grottaferrata and Escorial Versions* (Cambridge, 1998), 124–33 (G IV.971–1089); on the manuscripts, xviii–xxiii; on the textual tradition, xxiii–xxvi; on the relationship between G and E, xxvi–xxx. See also E. Trapp, ed., *Digenes Akrites. Synoptische Ausgabe der ältesten Versionen* (Vienna, 1971), 228, 230, 232, 234, 236 (G IV.971–1089); on the Grottaferrata version, 33–7; and on the Escorial version, 37–41. On the 'Romance of Digenes Akrites' as part of the whole epic, see Beck, *Geschichte*, 79–85, and Jeffreys, ed., *Digenis Akritis*, xvii–xxvii.

tradition of manuscripts A (Athens: Nat. Library 1074, produced on Andros in the mid-seventeenth century), T (a lost Trapezuntine manuscript of the sixteenth century) and P (Thessalonike: University Library 27, produced on Chios in 1632): these manuscripts form the basis on which E. Trapp, after excluding manuscript O (Oxford: Lincoln College 24, produced on Chios 1674), which also belongs to this group, has reconstructed version Z by means of compilation.[7] The above-mentioned problem of the emperor's identity arises because the manuscripts mentioning the emperor's visit give him different names. In G, he is Basil,[8] in Z, Romanos.[9] This has led to a difference of opinion in scholarship of whether the historical emperor to whom reference is made should be identified as Basil I or II, or (perhaps more likely) Romanos I or IV.[10]

According to version G, the following incident took place at the end of the emperor's visit:

Ὑποχωρεῖν βουλόμενος, λέων τις ἐκ τοῦ ἄλσους
ἐξελθὼν διεπτόησε τοὺς μετ' αὐτοῦ παρόντας
(πολλοὶ γὰρ λέοντες εἰσὶν ἐν ἐκείνῳ τῷ τόπῳ)
καὶ πρὸς φυγὴν δὲ καὶ αὐτὸς ὁ βασιλεὺς ἐτράπη.
Ὁ δὲ παῖς πρὸς τὸν λέοντα ὑποδραμὼν εὐθέως,
ποδὸς αὐτοῦ δραξάμενος ἑνὸς τῶν ὀπισθίων,
ἀποτινάξας ἰσχυρῶς καὶ τῇ γῇ καταρράξας
νεκρὸν αὐτὸν ἀπέδειξε πάντων ὁμοῦ βλεπόντων.
Τοῦτον κρατῶν ἐν τῇ χειρί, καθάπερ τις τὸν πτῶκα,

---

[7] *Digenes Akrites*, ed. Trapp, 229, 231, 233, 235 (Z v.2301–77, especially 2334–77) and on the various versions; 13–15 (Oxford version); 16–22 (P-version); 22–3 (Trebizond-version); 24–6 (Andros [-Athens]-version); 26–33 (version Z). On the passage with the emperor's visit, see 30 and (more detailed) 58–62. Concerning Z, see Jeffreys, ed., *Digenis Akritis*, xv–xvi, xxi, xxiv, but also the reviews of Trapp's work by H. Eideneier, 'Review of E. Trapp, *Digenes Akrites*', *Südost-Forschungen*, 31 (1972), 515–19 and, in more detail, by M. J. Jeffreys, 'Digenis Akritas Manuscript Z', *Dodone*, 4 (1975), 163–204.

[8] *Digenis Akritis*, ed. Jeffreys, 124 (G IV.972–7): 'Ταῦτα τὰ κατορθώματα ὁ βασιλεὺς ἀκούσας / ὁ τηνικαῦτα τὴν ἀρχὴν τοῖς ῥωμαίοις διέπων / Βασίλειος ὁ εὐτυχὴς καὶ μέγας τροπαιοῦχος, / ὁ καὶ συνθάψας μεθ' ἑαυτοῦ τὴν βασίλειον δόξαν / (ἔτυχε γὰρ κατὰ Περσῶν ποιῶν τὴν ἐκστρατείαν / ἐν ἐκείνοις τοῖς μέρεσιν ἐν οἷς ὁ παῖς διῆγεν), καὶ μαθών...', and 125: 'When the emperor heard of these achievements, / the emperor who at that time exercised authority over the Romans, / Basil the fortunate and the great winner of victories, / who interred the imperial glory with himself, / (for he happened to be on campaign against the Persians / in the regions where the boy was living) / – when he learnt ...'

[9] *Digenes Akrites*, ed. Trapp, 229 (Z V.2301–03): 'Ὡσαύτως καὶ ὁ βασιλεὺς ὁ μέγας τῶν Ῥωμαίων, / Ῥωμανὸς ὁ πανευτυχὴς κ' ἄριστος τροπαιοῦχος, ἀκούων τὰ' ('Likewise also the great emperor of the Romans, Romanos, the most fortunate and best winner of victories, when he heard...').

[10] N. Oikonomidès, 'L' 'épopée' de Digénis et la frontière orientale de Byzance aux xe et xie siècles', *TM*, 7 (1979), 387, and P. Magdalino, '*Digenes Akrites* and Byzantine Literature: the Twelfth-Century Background to the Grottaferrata Version' in R. Beaton and D. Ricks, eds., *Digenes Akrites: New Approaches to Byzantine Heroic Poetry* (Aldershot, 1993), 6, 10–12, 14.

πρὸς βασιλέα ἤνεγκε «Δέξαι,» λέγων, «κυνῆγιν
τοῦ σοῦ οἰκέτου, δέσποτα, διὰ σοῦ θηρευθέντα.»
Καὶ πάντες ἐξεπλάγησαν ἔντρομοι γεγονότες,
Τὴν ὑπεράνθρωπον αὐτοῦ ἰσχὺν κατανοοῦντες.
Καὶ τὰς χεῖρας ὁ βασιλεὺς πρὸς οὐρανὸν ἐκτείνας,
«Δόξα σοι,» ἔφη, «δέσποτα, ποιητὰ τῶν ἁπάντων,
ὅτι με κατηξίωσας τοιοῦτον ἄνδρα βλέψαι
ἐν τῇ παρούσῃ γενεᾷ ἰσχυρὸν παρὰ πάντας.»
Καὶ τὴν δορὰν τοῦ λέοντος ἐπαρθῆναι κελεύσας
Καὶ πλείστας πρὸς τὸν θαυμαστὸν ἐποίει ὑποσχέσεις·
ἀλλήλους ἀσπαζόμενοι, ὑπεχώρουν εὐθέως
πρὸς τὸν στρατὸν ὁ βασιλεύς, ὁ δὲ παῖς πρὸς τὴν κόρην.

> While he was wanting to withdraw, a lion came out of the grove
> and terrified those who were present with him
> (for there are many lions in that place),
> and even the emperor himself turned in flight.
> But the boy immediately ran up to the lion
>   and seized one of its back legs;
> he shook it vigorously, dashed it to the ground
> and showed that it was dead as everyone watched.
> Holding it in his hand as you would a hare,
> he took it to the emperor. 'Accept,' he said,
> 'your servant's prey, lord, hunted for you.'
> And all were amazed and terrified
> as they became aware of his superhuman strength.
> The emperor lifted his hands to heaven,
> 'Thanks be to you,' he said, 'Lord, Maker of all things,
> because you have found me worthy of seeing
> in this present generation a man of this sort, whose strength surpasses
>   all others.'
> And ordering the skin to be stripped from the lion,
> he made very many promises to the marvellous youth.
> They embraced each other and immediately withdrew,
> the emperor to the army and the boy to the girl.[11]

In this context, it is important that Digenes, just before killing the lion, had also succeeded in taming a wild horse, thus accomplishing two tremendous, if not superhuman, heroic feats during his meeting with the emperor.[12] This is significant because quite similar deeds, the taming of a horse or, in one variant of the story, of a wolf, were also attributed to

---

[11] *Digenis Akritis*, ed. Jeffreys, 130–1 (G IV.1066–86); *Digenes Akrites*, ed. Trapp, 234 (G IV.2017/1066–2037/1086).

[12] *Digenis Akritis*, ed. Jeffreys, 130–1 (G IV.1054–65); or *Digenes Akrites*, ed. Trapp, 234 (G IV.2005/1054–2016/1065).

Emperor Basil I. Henri Grégoire (d. 1964) once drew the conclusion from this similarity that 'the legends surrounding Basil served the compiler of the *Digenes* epic, who worked between 928 and 944, as his model'.[13]

Two of the four relevant passages come from the *Vita Basilii*, the emperor's biography, most probably commissioned by Constantine VII's anonymous 'ghost writer' and incorporated in Book Five of this pro-Macedonian historical work, the so-called *Theophanes continuatus*. This section reports that Basil (who would later rule as Basil I) was the only member of the entourage of Emperor Michael III to succeed in recapturing the emperor's horse, which had fled during a hunt, by leaping fearlessly onto the animal.[14] Greatly impressed by this performance as well as by Basil's other outstanding qualities, the emperor soon appointed him *protostrator*.[15] A further episode recounts that when, during a hunting party with the emperor at the so-called Philopation (near Constantinople), a huge wolf appeared, throwing nearly all into a state of panic, Basil made a rush at it, hurled the emperor's battle mace at the beast, and split its head open. To quote the episode's central passage: 'While the attendants of the hunt were noisily scaring up the game, a wolf of truly prodigious dimensions leaped out of the thicket, sending nearly everyone into a state of panic and confusion. Basil rushed forward against the beast, hurled the imperial *bardoukion* <at it> from behind, struck the animal's head in middle and split it in two.'[16]

The third and fourth passages come from Book Four of the so-called *Genesios*, which also dates from the time of Constantine VII, and was written on his orders. The passage from chapter 26, describes how Basil, the newly appointed groom of the imperial stables, broke in one of Michael III's horses. He leapt onto the wild animal, as Alexander had

---

[13] P. Schreiner, 'Das Herrscherbild in der byzantinischen Literatur des 9. bis 11. Jahrhunderts', *Saeculum*, 35 (1984), 141 and 146 (summarising here Grégoire's results in one sentence). See in H. Grégoire, *Autour de l'épopée Byzantine* (London, 1975), 487 and 495 (II), 300 (IV), and 425 (VI).

[14] I. Ševčenko ed., *Chronographiae quae Theophanis continuati nomine fertur Liber quo Vita Basilii imperatoris amplectitur* (Berlin, 2011), 13* and 50–3 (XIII.1–23); I. Bekker, ed., *Theophanes Continuatus, Ioannes Cameniata, Symeon Magister, Georgius Monachus* (Bonn, 1838), 230–1. (C. Mango convincingly commented on the question of Constantine VII's authorship, which was most recently also treated by P. Magdalino, 'Knowledge in Authority and Authorised History: the Imperial Intellectual Programme of Leo VI and Constantine VII' in P. Armstrong, ed., *Authority in Byzantium* (Farnham, 2013), 200–7.

[15] *Chronographiae quae Theophanis continuati*^, ed. I. Ševčenko 52–3 (XIII.23–9); *Theophanes Continuatus*, ed. Bekker, 231.

[16] *Chronographiae quae Theophanis continuati*^, ed. I. Ševčenko 54–5 (XIV.1–10); *Theophanes Continuatus*, ed. Bekker, 232. The quoted passage: 54.5–10: 'θορύβου δὲ κ<ι>νουμένου ἀπὸ τῶν συμπληρούντων τὸ κυνηγέσιον, ἐξέθορεν ἐκ τῆς ὕλης λύκος παμμεγεθέστατος, ὥστε σχεδὸν πάντας διαπτοηθῆναι καὶ εἰς ταραχὴν ἐμπεσεῖν. ὁρμήσας δὲ κατ' αὐτοῦ ὁ Βασίλειος, καὶ ῥίψας ἐξόπισθεν τὸ βασιλικὸν βαρδούκιον, ἔτυχεν τοῦ θηρίου κατὰ τὸ μέσον τῆς κεφαλῆς καὶ ταύτην ἐδιχοτόμησεν.'

once onto Bucephalus, and reined it in to the astonishment (and alarm) of the bystanders. He then enjoyed numerous marks of favour, was consequently appointed *patrikios*, adopted by the emperor, and finally made co-emperor.[17] But according to the fourth passage, contained in chapter 40, Basil, after becoming emperor, allegedly killed on the hunt a giant deer, and another time a wolf.[18]

All this is well known to Digenes research: previous attempts to explain the origin of the text with a plausible but inadequate analysis of the historical facts have been met with justified scepticism over the years. This applies especially to the answers put forward to the questions as to how and in what circumstances the text that has come down to us in its multiple versions was originally constructed.[19] Yet, this does not imply that all proposed solutions are misleading or that they *a priori* have to come to nothing; often enough, in fact, they have stimulated further research, by revealing and advancing new horizons of knowledge.[20]

One such attempt, which has not yet received adequate attention, is Trapp's argument for giving priority to Romanos I as the identity of the emperor who is supposed to have encountered Digenes.[21] Trapp has based his argument on a number of chronological and historical considerations that include the following:

(1) the identification of several central characters in Books One to Three of version G,[22] including those of Digenes' paternal grandfather, Chrysoherpes or Chrysoberges and of Ambron, the emir's

---

[17] A. Lesmueller-Werner and I. Thurn, eds., *Iosephi Genesii Regum libri quattuor* (Berlin, 1978), 78–9 (IV.26.42–52). A. Kaldellis, trans., *Genesios. On the Reigns of the Emperors. Translation and Commentary* (Canberra, 1998), 97–8. German translation: A. Lesmüller-Werner, ed., *Byzanz am Vorabend neuer Grösse ... Die vier Bücher der Kaisergeschichte des Ioseph Genesios. Übersetzt, eingeleitet und erklärt* (Vienna, 1989), 116. See A. Kazhdan and A. Cutler, s.v. Basil I, in *ODB*, vol. 1, 260, and R.-J. Lilie et al., eds., *PmbZ. Erste Abteilung (641–867). 1. Band: Aaron (# 1) – Georgios (# 2182)* (Berlin, 1999), 'Basileios I,' # 832, at 278.

[18] Lesmüller-Werner and Thurn, eds., *Iosephus Genesii*, 89 (IV.89–92); Kaldellis, trans., *Genesios*, 111; Lesmüller-Werner, trans., *Byzanz am Vorabend*, 129.

[19] *Digenis Akritis*, ed. Jeffreys, xvi–xvii, xxxi and xxxviii.

[20] See Beck, *Geschichte*, 68–9 and 74–8, and Jeffreys, ed., *Digenis Akritis*, xvii–xviii, xviii, and xxx–xli, especially at xxx–xxxii, xxxvii–xxxviii and xli.

[21] Trapp, ed., *Digenes Akrites*, 59 and especially 60–1, where he states (61): 'Accordingly it is clear that Digenes' encounter with the emperor occurred already in the period of Romanos I, as Kyriakides had previously pointed out' (in S. P. Kyriakides, 'Grégoire Henri. Inscriptions historiques byzantines. Ancyre et les Arabes sous Michel le Ivrogne (Byzantion iv 437–468)', Λαογραφία, 10 (1929), specifically 652–4).

[22] Therefore in the so-called 'Lay of the Emir' (see Beck, *Geschichte*, 71–9; Jeffreys, ed., *Digenis Akritis*, xxvii), whose prototype one should probably date to shortly before 944, according to Beck, *Geschichte*, 78.

grandfather – the former with 'Chrysocheir, the leader of the Paulicians', and the latter 'with Omar of Melitene who died in battle against the Byzantines in 863';

(2) the 'hero's theoretical date of birth after 900';

(3) the 'fact that Andronikos Doukas, who had fallen out of favour with Leo VI in 907, has been recognised as Digenes' grandfather on his mother's side';

(4) according to G IV, vv. 56 and 1050, 'the emperor, who ... had banished Digenes' grandfather ... can no longer here [sc. in 1050, G.P.] even be considered as being the emperor who restituted the confiscated estates'.[23]

Based on these findings, Trapp arrives at an important conclusion:

> A further indication of the misrepresentation of the emperor's name [i.e. from Romanos to Basil, G.P.] to be found in G is provided by the fact that this version is also subject to a literary influence of which nothing is to be found in Z. It concerns the description of the taming of a wild horse, which, as Grégoire has established, was borrowed from *Theophanes cont.* 230–1, where Constantine VII reports it with regard to the later Emperor Basil. *But Digenes' second deed as well, namely the slaying of a lion of which all persons present were terrified, probably has its model in the account found in the same historical work* [230–1, my emphasis], which reports that while hunting Basil had brought down a huge wolf of which everyone was similarly terrified. One clearly recognises how easily the reference to this historical report could also bring about a change in the emperor's name from Romanos to Basil.[24]

Although until now no relevant source has been identified that expressly refers to Romanos I rather than to Basil I, the aforementioned text by Liudprand of Cremona may fill that lacuna.[25] In Book Three, chapters 24 and 25 of his famous *Antapodosis* ('Retribution' or 'Tit for Tat'), Liudprand gives an account of an anecdote (or tale) about Romanos I Lekapenos and his fight with a lion.[26]

---

[23] Trapp, ed., *Digenes Akrites*, 60 (with all quotations). However, the identification of Digenes' maternal grandfather, called Antakinos in G 54 (or Andronikos in Z 1317) with Andronikos Doukas, is not absolutely proved, see Beck, *Geschichte*, 72 (with footnote 3) and Jeffreys, ed., *Digenis Akritis*, 388 (name index): her comment on Antakinos ('exiled by the emperor Basil'), given here, but also on 125 (footnote to LL.971–1086) on the identification of the emperor in this section with Basil (i.e. Basil I or II, see 389) does not take Trapp's remarks into account. (The same applies to Trapp's following observations, see Jeffreys, ed., *Digenis Akritis*, xxxvii–xxxviii and xlvii).

[24] Trapp, ed., *Digenes Akrites*, 61.   [25] See footnote 5 and the text, to which it refers.

[26] The most important studies on this text with regard to our topic are: J. Koder, 'Liutprand von Cremona und die griechische Sprache' in J. Koder and T. Weber, eds., *Liutprand von Cremona in*

Liudprand's Antapodosis *and* Digenes Akrites

In Paolo Chiesa's edition of Liudprand's *Opera omnia*, the original text of this passage extending from chapter 24 to 25 reads as follows:

(77) **24**, Nunc autem quoniam imperatoris Ρομανοῦ mentio facta est, quis fuerit qualiterve ad /380 imperii culmen pervenerit, hic non absurdum mihi videtur inserere. **25:** Imperante Leone, Constantini huius genitore, Ρομανος imperator iste, quamquam πτοχος, ab omnibus tamen χρησιμος habebatur. Erat autem ex mediocribus ipsis qui navali pugna /385 stipendia ab imperatore acceperant; qui cum saepius et iterum εις την μαχην nonnulla χρησιμοτατα faceret, a sibi praeposito adeo ετημιθη, ὁπως προτοκαραβος fieri mereretur. Quadam autem nocte dum exploratum Saracenos abiret, essetque eodem in loco palus atque arundinetum non modicum, contigit leonem /390 ferocissimum ex arundineto prosilire cervorumque multitudinem in paludem dimergere unumque eorum capere sibique ventris rabiem mitigare. Ρομανος δὲ τὸν ἀυτων ψοφον ακουων εδειλίασεν σφοδρα: putavit enim Saracenorum multitudinem esse, qui se conspectum fraude aliqua vellent perhimere. Ορθρου /(78) 395 δὲ βαθεως exurgens, cum diligentissime cuncta consideraret, conspectis vestigiis εὐθέως quid hoc esset agnovit. Leone itaque in arundineto commorante, Ρομανος Grecum ignem, qui nullo praeter aceti liquore extinguitur, undique per arundinetum iactare praecepit. Erat autem in arundineto acervus arundinibus /400 plenus, in quem leo confugiens illo est ab igne salvatus: ventus quippe contraria ex parte flans ignem, ne ad acervum usque perveniret, amovit. Romanós praeterea post ignis extinctionem uno tantum cum assecula, ensem solum dextra, sinistra autem pallium gestans, locum omnem peragrans lustrat, si forte os /405 ex eo vel signum aliquod repperiret. Iam vero cum in eo esset, ut nichil inveniens repedaret, quid hoc monstri esset, quod acervus ille sit ab igne salvatus, studuit visere. Cumque duo propter assisterent secumque rebus ex nonnullis confabularent, leo eos tantum audivit, quoniam quidem ob caligantes oculos /410 παρα τῶ καπνω videre non potuit. Volens igitur leo animi sui furorem, quem ab igne conceperat, in hos evomere, saltu rapidissimo, qua illorum voces audierat, eos inter prosiliit. Romanós vero, non ut suus assecula pavitans, sed ea potius mente consistens, ut, etsi fractus

---

Konstantinopel. Untersuchungen zum griechischen Sprachschatz und zu realienkundlichen Aussagen in seinen Werken (Vienna, 1980), 1–70, and W. Berschin, *Greek Letters and the Latin Middle Ages: From Jerome to Nicholas of Cusa*, revised and expanded edition, trans. J. C. Frakes (Washington, D. C., 1988), 174–82, especially 180, where Berschin writes among other things: 'Liudprand was ... the first and only medieval author to link Latin and Greek in narrative prose.' In addition Schreiner, 'Das Herrscherbild', 146, H. Hunger, 'Liudprand von Cremona und die byzantinische Trivialliteratur' in E. Konstantinou, ed., *Byzanz und das Abendland im 10. und 11. Jahrhundert* (Cologne, Weimar and Bonn, 1997), 203, A. Kazhdan, 'Romanos I Lekapenos' in *ODB*, 1806 (stating there: 'A legend attributes his rise to a successful single combat with a lion') and Lilie et al., eds., *PmbZ* II, vol. v, 'Romanos I Lakapenos', # 26833, 588, with the following remark on Romanos' fight with the lion: 'In Byzantium, it looks as if it later resulted in the formation of legends about the early stages of his career. Thus Liudprand, Antapodosis III 25, reports on a spectacular lion hunt, in which R. was believed to have put a huge lion to death just with a sword.'

caderet orbis, inpavidum /415 ruinae ferirent, pallium quod manu gestabat leonis inter brachia misit. Quod dum pro homine leo discerperet, Romanós totis hunc a tergo viribus inter clunium iuncturas ense percussit; qui dissotiatis divisisque cruribus quia stare non potuit, poenitus cecidit. Leone igitur interfecto, Romanos seminecem assecculam /420 suum solo stratum eminus vidit, quem et vocare voce praecipua coepit; sed cum nullum daret omnino responsum, isdem Romanos /(79) propter eum adstitit pedeque pulsans 'ἔγειρε, ειπεν, ἄθλιε κα᾿ ταλεπορε, μὴ φοβοῦ!' Qui consurgens prae admiratione, dum leonis immanitatem conspiceret, non habuit ultra spiritum./425 Ἐξεπλίσσοντο δὲ πάντες πέρι τοῦ Ρομανοῦ τάυτα ακουσαντες; unde factum est ut, tam pro caeteris quamque pro praeclaro praesenti hoc facinore, non multo post a Leone imperatore tanto donaretur honore, ὅπως πάντα τὰ πλοῖα in manibus suis essent eiusque iussionibus oboedirent.[27]

This is how Paolo Squatriti renders this passage in his recent translation based on Chiesa's edition:

> Now, however, since the emperor Ρομανος was mentioned, it does not seem senseless to me to insert something here about who he was and how he reached the imperial office. In the reign of Leo, father of the present emperor Constantine, that emperor Ρομανος, although πτοχος, was considered χρησιμος by all. He came from one of those lowly families that took pay from the emperor for naval battles; since he often and repeatedly εις την μαχην rendered several χρησιμοτατα, at length he deserved to be made ετημιθη ὁπως πρωτοκαραβος by his commanding officer. On a certain night, when he went to spy on the Saracens and in that place there was quite a big swamp and reed bed, it happened that a very ferocious lion leapt from the reeds and mired a multitude of deer in the swamp and seized one of them and with it mitigated the ravenous rage of its stomach. Ρομανος δὲ τὸν ἀυτων ψοφον ακουων εδειλίασεν σφοδρα, for he thought it was a horde of Saracens who, having noted him, wanted to kill him off by some trick. Arising ορθρου δὲ βαθεως when he very carefully thought through everything, having studied the remains he recognized ἐυθέως what it had been. Since the lion was hiding in the reed bed, Ρομανος ordered that Greek fire be shot throughout the reed bed, which cannot be extinguished by any liquid except vinegar. Within the reed bed, however, there was a hillock full of reeds, and by escaping onto it the lion was saved from the fire. In fact, the

---

[27] P. Chiesa, ed., *Liudprandi Cremonensis Antapodosis, Homelia paschalis, Historia Ottonis, Relatio de legatione Constantinopolitana* (Turnhout, 1998), 77–9 (III.24–5.378–429). But see Koder, 'Liutprand', 61, and tables 2–5, with excellent illustrations of the most accurate manuscript *Cod. lat. monac.* 6388: This is Chiesa's *Leithandschrift* and basis of his spelling of the Greek words interspersed in *Ant.* III, 25, see Chiesa, ed., *Liudprandi*, xcix. With regard to his (Koder's) correct rendering of the Greek words and passages in *Antapodosis* III.25, one should correct the following misspellings of them in the above quotation 77.383, χρησιμος (read χρήσιμος), 77.386: χρησιμοτατα (χρησιμότατα), 77.392 ψοφον (ψόφον), 77.393 σφοδρα (σφόδρα) and 79.422–23, ἄθλιε κα᾿ ταλεπορε (ἄθλιε καὶ ταλέπορε).

wind, spreading the fire in the opposite direction, removed it from the area, preventing it from reaching as far as this hillock. So after the fire was out, Ρομανος, criss-crossing the whole site with only one servant, holding only a sword in his right hand and in his left hand a cloak, checked to see if by chance he might find a bone of the lion or any trace of it. Indeed, as he was at the point when he could go back, as he had found nothing, he decided to see by what prodigy it happened that the hillock had been spared by the fire. And when the two fellows sat down nearby and were chatting about many things among themselves, the lion only heard them, as it could not see because of its watering eyes παρα τῶ καπνω. And as the lion desired to spew forth onto them the rage of its spirit, which it had conceived because of the fire, with a very quick leap toward where it heard their voices, it appeared in their midst. Romanos was not quaking like his servant, but rather evaluating the situation in his mind, so that, even if the world should fall apart, the wreckage would leave him fearless; he cast the cloak that he held in his left hand between the paws of the lion. And while the lion tore it to shreds as if it were a person, Romanos struck it from behind with his sword with all his strength, between the joints of his hindquarters; and since the lion could not stand with disjointed and divided legs, it slowly fell. Once the lion was dead, Romanos saw his servant prostrate on the ground, half dead, and he began to call him with a loud voice; but as he gave no response at all, the same Romanos stood next to him, and, kicking him with his foot, 'Εγειρε,' ειπεν, 'ἀθλιε κᾀ ταλεπορε, μη φοβοῦ!' Upon rising, when he saw the immensity of the lion, he was breathless with admiration. Εξεπλισσοντο δὲ πάντες πέρι τοῦ Ρομανοῦ τάυτα ακουσαντες; whence a little afterwards it came about that, both for other deeds and this outstanding deed, very great honor was accorded to him by the emperor Leo, οπως παντα τὰ πλοια were entrusted to Romanos' hands and obeyed his orders.[28]

It is very likely that this text, for which there is no parallel in Greco-Byzantine literature, especially not in the historiographic and chronicle literature about Romanos I Lekapenos, was, despite its preservation only in Liudprand's *Antapodosis*, in fact Byzantine in origin. The story undoubtedly represents an anecdote from the biography of Emperor Romanos I that Liudprand may himself have read in Constantinople during his first journey to the city, probably in the environs of the palace. Alternatively, this tale could have been related to him orally by his father or even his

---

[28] P. Squatriti, trans., *The Complete Works of Liudprand of Cremona. Translated with an introduction and notes* (Washington, D. C., 2007), 120–2; concerning the *Graeca* here, see n. 26. Squatriti's translation of the text's Greek passages, given in footnotes, is in two places incomplete: in 120 n. 27 'very' should be inserted before 'terrified' and n. 36 should be 'honored by being appointed captain' to render also the words ὅπως προτοκαραβος; at the same time the superfluous word 'made' before ετημιθη in the main text should be deleted.

step-father, who for their part had also undertaken missions to Byzantium during the reign of Emperor Romanos I, in 927 and 942 respectively, on behalf of King Hugh of Italy (927–47). But even in this case they might have brought it back from the Byzantine court in written form. Be that as it may, the original version of the Romanos anecdote, as Koder has conclusively shown, had been written in Greek and therefore it very probably reached Liudprand (and possibly before that, his father or step-father) in this format rather than by word of mouth during his (or their) stay in Constantinople.[29]

Even if this anecdote has gone almost entirely unnoticed in the debate concerning the identity of the emperor who visited Digenes, it must nevertheless be pointed out that, in addition to Schreiner, Hunger, Kazhdan and Berschin, Évelyne Patlagean has also referred to Liudprand's text in her article 'De la chasse et du souverain'. Here, Patlagean mentions Digenes' successes at hunting (or rather, at slaying beasts), but does not make any link between the Romanos anecdote as transmitted by Liudprand and the text concerning Digenes.[30] It therefore has to be stressed that the documentary evidence from Liudprand forms the missing link between Trapp's thesis (based on the material from his version Z of the Digenes epic) and the historiographical Greek tradition, which is otherwise silent about any successes at hunting by Romanos Lekapenos. As a result, Trapp's thesis on the priority and authenticity of the name Romanos in the context of the emperor's visit gains in probability, even if it cannot be regarded as definitive.[31]

---

[29] See n. 5 above. With regard to the use of Greek in the *Antapodosis* Koder, 'Liutprand', is very instructive: his chapters 'Glossary', 40–51 and 'Summary', 58–61, show that *Antapodosis* III.25 (but also *Antapodosis* I.10–11) is not only especially rich in individual Greek words, but also in Greek sentences or sequences of words, because only the *Antapodosis* chapters just mentioned contain lengthier narrative passages about emperors Basil I, Leo VI and Romanos I. This observation leads him to the following important conclusion: 'There would therefore have been pieces of information which Liudprand had at his disposal in writing, that may be less representative of the spoken language of the tenth century, but are rather closer to the historiography (chronicles) of this epoch' (61). This was accepted by Hunger, 'Liudprand', 197–8. With regard to the appearance, function and use of Greek in Liudprand's work, especially in the *Antapodosis* see also: Berschin, *Greek Letters*, 180; Chiesa, ed., *Liudprandi Cremonensis*, xvi–xvii, xlvii, liv–lvi, lxii–lxiv, lxxii–lxxiii, lxxviii, xcv, xcix, and Squatriti, trans., *Complete Works of Liudprand of Cremona*, 16–17.

[30] E. Patlagean, 'De la chasse et du souverain', *DOP* 46 (1992), 258–9. Also A. R. Littlewood, 'Gardens of the Palaces' in H. Maguire, ed., *Byzantine Court Culture from 829 to 1204* (Washington, D. C., 1997), 28. Also Schreiner, 'Das Herrscherbild', 146, Hunger, 'Liudprand', 203, and for Kazhdan and Berschin above n. 22 and 23.

[31] In addition, one may here point out the structural similarity of the anecdote in Liudprand's text to the accounts in the *Vita Basilii* or in *Genesios*: the description of the special achievement of the 'hero' precedes a reference to the reward by the commander or the emperor.

At this juncture it is tempting and perhaps not entirely inappropriate to enter the field of speculation, and to propose the following hypothetical scenario: if Romanos I had succeeded in establishing his own dynasty,[32] and in the aftermath an author comparable to Constantine VII had written a version of *Vita Romani I*, not only would the story of the vanquished lion have been included in this biography, but it would have possibly also found its place in Byzantine court historiography. Had this happened, we would probably find the name of Romanos instead of that of Basil in the passage about the emperor's visit in Book Four of version G of *Digenes*.

In this chapter, we have examined two stories, the first of which, that of Digenes' fight with the lion during the emperor's visit as given in G IV, shows a close textual relationship to the *Vita Basilii*, the history of the so-called *Genesios*, and also to Liudprand's anecdote. However, the issue becomes more complex when the textual evidence from this group is compared with the episode of the taming of the wild horse and Digenes' fight with the lion from version G IV. In the first instance, Basil is said to have accomplished his great feats at court. He not only tames the wild horse in the presence of the grooms, but also vanquishes the giant wolf and kills it in the presence of Emperor Michael III and his entourage while hunting. Romanos, on the other hand, allegedly fights the lion somewhere along the Byzantine–Arab frontier, perhaps in south-east Asia Minor, apparently in a territory controlled by the navy. This follows from both Romanos I's promotion to the rank of the admiral of the fleet (as intimated at the end), and from the episode about Romanos, the lion, the reed bed, and the Greek Fire.[33] Romanos is accompanied by just one man who proves to be timorous; in other words, Romanos could not expect much help from him. Despite the obvious differences, these accounts have some features in common: they show both Basil and Romanos occupying relatively humble positions at the time of their feats, and being rewarded with immediate boosts to their careers in the aftermath of their great accomplishments, which eventually resulted in their elevation to the Byzantine throne. If one compares the character of Basil as depicted in the *Vita Basilii* and Genesios with that of Romanos as he appears in Liudprand's anecdote, one can see that the spectacular hunting or taming successes of both future emperors are basically interchangeable. Both men's great deeds ultimately

---

[32] See O. Kresten and A. E. Müller, *Samtherrschaft. Legitimationsprinzip und kaiserlicher Urkundentitel in Byzanz in der ersten Hälfte des 10. Jahrhunderts* (Vienna, 1995), 77 and H. Hunger, 'Zum Dynastieproblem in Byzanz', *AnzWien*, 131 (1994), 276.

[33] On the Greek fire, see most recently J. H. Pryor and E. M. Jeffreys, *The Age of ΔΡΟΜΩΝ. The Byzantine Navy ca 500–1204* (Leiden, 2006), 607–31.

meet with the same success, and become equally important as core elements of the staged imperial representation of hunting: as such, they all, but especially the slaying of the lion, point significantly to both men's special power, courage and boldness. Moreover, since the days of David and Saul (cf. 1 Samuel, 17:34–7) such a deed, all the more so if it is followed by a further similar one, could be understood as qualifying each man who proves capable of performing it (or them) to become ruler (or emperor respectively).[34] This finding is vividly illustrated by the tenth- or eleventh-century Byzantine ivory casket from Troyes, which is kept in the treasury of the cathedral there, and is regularly shown in exhibitions. In the catalogues of the most recent exhibitions, it is described as a 'casket with emperors and hunters' (New York 1997) or 'carved box with emperors riding and hunting' (London 2008).[35] Particularly interesting for us is the iconography of the imperial hunting scenes on the two side panels: one shows the killing of a boar with a lance by a hunter accompanied by three hounds; the other depicts two hunters on horseback, one of whom is clearly an emperor slaying a lion with his bow and arrows, while the other hunter raises his sword to defend against the beast. Owing to the lack of additional clues (such as, for instance, inscriptions), it is impossible to identify the emperors depicted here more closely solely from the iconography.[36]

However, things are somewhat different in the case of the ivory 'Casket with Warriors and "Mythological Figures"' from the Metropolitan Museum, New York, that has moved increasingly into the focus of research because of the exhibition *The Glory of Byzantium: Art and Culture of the Middle Byzantine Era, AD 843–1261*.[37] Thus, recently Helen Evans in a well-founded, convincing contribution reached the interesting

---

[34] I wish to thank Teresa Shawcross for kindly drawing my attention to this passage in the OT. See A. Stamatios and A. Weckwerth, 'Löwe' in *RAC*, 23 (2010), col. 257–86, in part B. II. c. ('Heidnisch. In der Kunst. Löwenkampf u.-jagd als Herrscherpropaganda'), col. 265, and in part C. I. b.a. ('Jüdisch. b. Symbolik. 1. Altes Testament. A. Positiv'), col. 269 (the author is Stamatios alone in both cases)

[35] See H. C. Evans and W. D. Wixom, eds., *The Glory of Byzantium: Art and Culture of the Middle Byzantine Era AD 843–1261* (New York, NY, 1997), 204–6, no. 141; R. Cormack and M. Vassilaki, eds., *Byzantium, 330–1453* (London, 2008), 125 and 397, no. 67 (E. Dauterman Maguire), each with further references; the following references may also be added: K. Wessel, 'Kaiserbild' in *RBK*, 3 (1978), col. 805–6, C. Jolivet-Lévy, 'L'image du pouvoir dans l'art byzantin à l'époque de la dynastie macédonienne (867–1056)', *Byzantion*, 57 (1987), 455, and H. Maguire, 'Art and Text' in E. M. Jeffreys, J. Haldon, R. Cormack, eds., *The Oxford Handbook of Byzantine Studies* (Oxford, 2008), 725.

[36] Evans and Wixom, eds., *Glory of Byzantium*, 204–6, no. 141; Cormack and Vassilake, eds., *Byzantium, 330–1453*, 125 and 397, no. 67.

[37] Evans and Wixom, eds., *Glory of Byzantium*, 232–33, no.155.

conclusion that, as regards the figurative decoration on the casket, the content of all those panels mounted on the top and on both long sides refer to various sections of the Digenes Epic.[38] Only the image of the enthroned emperor in the 'far left panel on the left side' refers directly to our topic. With reference to the opening part of the scene with the emperor (that has not been dealt with in more detail here above), Evans sees in the emperor depicted 'not a generic depiction of imperial authority, but the emperor Basil, whose visit to Digenis is described at the end of Book IV'.[39]

It is possible to agree with this conclusion insofar as the panel with the enthroned figure here should indeed probably refer to precisely the emperor visiting Digenes. However, the results of this present study now suggest that when trying to identify this figure more closely, one should not restrict oneself to the Emperor Basil (I or II) mentioned in the text, but in this case also take an emperor by the name of 'Romanos', in particular Romanos I, into consideration.[40]

A comparison of texts about emperors' successes at hunting with the text about the emperor's visit to Digenes shows that the latter puts such propagandistic imperial displays of hunting ability into question and therefore carries a different message: Because Digenes had effortlessly parried the lion's attack and rescued the emperor, who did not know how to defend himself and wanted to flee in terror, he, the hero, had outperformed the emperor. As a result, the emperor not only appeared just as powerless and feeble as he had proved to be against the lion, but also his prestige as a hunter was, so to speak, transferred to Digenes. He was now effectively confirmed in his authority as unchallenged lord of the empire's borderland district which the emperor had granted him by a chrysobull to rule over just shortly before the lion appeared.[41] Interestingly enough, Digenes, who was himself endowed with the gift of ruling, as follows from his victorious fight with the lion and other heroic deeds (see above, p. 338), did not even think of taking advantage of the emperor's current

---

[38] H. C. Evans, 'Digenis Akritis and a Middle Byzantine Rosette Casket in the Metropolitan Museum of Art' in G. Bühl, A. Cutler and A. Effenberger, eds., *Spätantike und byzantinische Elfenbeinwerke im Diskurs* (Wiesbaden, 2008), 97–109 (with Fig. 6). I would like to thank Ida Toth for kindly drawing my attention to this article.
[39] Evans, 'Digenis Akritis', 102.   [40] Ibid.
[41] I. Ševčenko, 'Constantinople Viewed from the Eastern Provinces in the Middle Byzantine Period', *Ukrainian Studies*, 3–4 (1979–80), 712–47 (repr. in I. Ševčenko, *Ideology, Letters and Culture in the Byzantine World* (London, 1982), 734: 'Finally, toward the end of the encounter, a lion appears. The emperor takes flight, Digenis Akritas does not. Intrepid, he kills the beast and offers it to the emperor, who must have felt sheepish indeed. In this game of one-upmanship Digenis wins hands down.' See also P. Magdalino, 'Honour Among Romaioi: the Framework of Social Values in the World of Digenis Akrites and Kekaumenos', *BMGS*, 13 (1989) 183–218, especially 190–1.

weakness in order, for instance, to play the role of a rebel or a usurper. On the contrary: being just as proud and self-confident as prudent and modest, he preferred to remain content with this privilege, evidently because he still felt himself bound by ties of loyalty towards the 'holy emperor'.[42] Thus the compiler of version G presents Digenes to readers as a kind of idealised but powerful aristocratic figure on the periphery of the empire: As a man who also was able to address a piece of exhortative advice to the emperor Basil during his visit. Provided the latter would 'love his subjects' and exercise his rule in justice, Digenes, his 'servant' (or even 'slave'),[43] expressed his wish always to acknowledge or to take into account the emperor's sovereignty,[44] regardless of whether his name was Basil (I/II) or (originally) Romanos (I).

Further Reading

The key texts are: E. M. Jeffreys, ed., *Digenis Akritis: The Grottaferrata and Escorial Versions* (Cambridge, 1998); E. Trapp, ed., *Digenes Akrites. Synoptische Ausgabe der ältesten Versionen* (Vienna, 1971); P. Chiesa, ed., *Liudprandi Cremonensis Antapodosis, Homelia paschalis, Historia Ottonis, Relatio de legatione Constantinopolitana* (Turnhout, 1998). For an introduction, see: C. Cupane, and B. Krönung, 'Geschichten von der Grenze' in F. Daim, ed., *Das Goldene Byzanz und der Orient* (Schallaburg, 2012), 155–69; C. Jouanno, 'Shared Spaces: 1 Digenis Akritis, the Two-blood Border Lord' in C. Cupane and B. Krönung, eds., *Fictional Storytelling in the Medieval Eastern Mediterranean and Beyond* (Leiden, 2016), 260–84.

---

[42] Jeffreys, ed., *Digenis Akritis*, 126 (G IV.995) (*despota agie*).
[43] Ibid. (G IV.993) (*ton son oiketen*), translated here as 'your servant'. On the metaphorical use of the term 'doulos/slave', see Y. Rotman, *Byzantine Slavery and the Mediterranean World*, trans. J. M. Todd (Cambridge, MA, 2009), 183–8.
[44] See Jeffreys, ed., *Digenis Akritis*, 128 (G IV.1033–41), with the editor's comment 129 (on vv. 1028 [- 1041]: 'This speech may be seen as a statement of the self-confidence of the magnates of Asia Minor, expressing a feeling of both material and ethical superiority over Constantinople and the emperor; compare the advice, in the tradition of a 'Mirror of Princes' ... At another level, the speech shows the heroic dominance of the epic hero over even the most powerful figure in the 'historical' world.' See also G. Prinzing, 'Beobachtungen zu "integrierten" Fürstenspiegeln der Byzantiner', *JÖB*, 38 (1986), 1–31, especially 22–4 and D. R. Reinsch, 'Bemerkungen zu einigen byzantinischen Fürstenspiegeln des 11. und 12. Jahrhunderts' in H. Seng and L. M. Hoffmann, eds., *Synesios von Kyrene: Politik – Literatur – Philosophie* (Turnhout, 2013), 410.

CHAPTER 15

Intertextuality in the Late Byzantine *Romance* Tale of Troy

Ulrich Moennig

The challenge of understanding Byzantium lies in reading it on its own terms.[1] Byzantium, on its own terms, claimed to be the Roman Empire. Going back to the early Christian exegetic tradition of the Book of Daniel, this claim became the medieval Christian equivalent of what modern secular societies call ideology. In Chapter 7 of the Book of Daniel, Daniel sees a vision of four beasts. Christian exegetic tradition linked this vision to the ancient scheme of four world empires. It was the Creator's plan that the fourth and the last was the Roman Empire. The Last Judgement was expected to come after the fall of the Roman Empire.[2] The present chapter takes as its starting point the assumption that Byzantine narratives about the past refer – explicitly or implicitly – to Chapter 7 of the Book of Daniel and to the eschatological expectation that the Roman Empire was the final period in the history of the world. Given that Byzantine chronicles form a narrative, which draws the line from God's Creation to the present state of the Roman Empire, all chapters in a chronicle are related to the Roman Empire. This chapter presents an early stage of more systematic research in Byzantine self-understanding within the frame of Byzantine historical fiction. Given that history, according to the Byzantines, was part of God's Creation, could it be a subject of fictional writing? I will attempt to give a preliminary answer to this question by analysing a late Byzantine piece of historical story-telling, the *Tale of Troy*, and will focus on what the author might have read as reflected in this work.

---

[1] I am grateful to a number of colleagues for giving me the opportunity to discuss the questions examined in this chapter, among them to Charalambos Messis and Filippo Ronconi (both École des hautes études en sciences sociales, Paris) and Kostas Yiavis (Humboldt fellow at the University of Hamburg in 2011–13). Kostas Yiavis also made useful suggestions on the English style.
[2] G. Podskalsky, *Byzantinische Reichseschatologie. Die Periodisierung der Weltgeschichte in den vier Großreichen (Daniel 2 und 7) und dem Tausendjährigen Friedensreiche (Apok. 20). Eine motivgeschichtliche Untersuchung* (Munich, 1972); E. M. Jeffreys, 'The Attitudes of Byzantine Chroniclers Towards Ancient History', *Byzantion*, 49 (1979), 199–238, esp. 206.

The authorial poetics of a text can be studied in many ways. One major way involves examining the usage of certain 'sources' of narrative content, especially material such as topics and themes; this material from the *Tale of Troy* requires more detailed research than I have done so far. Another possible line of investigation considers the study of literary models as witnessed in the archetypal features of a text, like genre, structure and narrative coherence. This chapter explores the archetypal variety of intertextuality and the concept of innovation in literary writing, both of which constitute seminal features of Byzantine historical fiction.[3] The underlying question, thus, is not only: which texts did the author read; but also: which kinds of texts and literature did the author read?

Late Byzantine Romance

In 1261, under Emperor Michael VIII Palaiologos, the Byzantines succeeded in recapturing Constantinople, after the city had been lost to the Latins in 1204. The dynasty of the Palaiologoi was to reign for almost two hundred years, until 1453, when the Ottomans conquered Constantinople and brought an end to the Byzantine Empire. Despite the weakness of the empire, which prompted humiliating diplomatic alliances and also caused a number of civil wars, Byzantine art and literature flourished during these centuries. The impetus for innovation regained strength both in factual and fictional writing, harking back to the late eleventh and especially the twelfth centuries.[4] Literature written in the vernacular was especially prone

---

[3] G. Genette, *Palimpsests. Literature in the Second Degree* (Lincoln, NE, 1997), 1.
[4] On late eleventh- and twelfth-century Byzantine fiction, see R. Beaton, *The Medieval Greek Romance*, second edition (London, 1996), 70–88; E. M. Jeffreys, 'The Novels of Mid-twelfth Century Constantinople: the Literary and Social Context' in I. Ševčenko and I. Hutter, eds., *AETOS: Studies in Honour of Cyril Mango* (Stuttgart, 1998), 191–9; E. M. Jeffreys, 'A Date for Rhodanthe and Dosikles?' in P. A. Agapitos and D. R. Reinsch, eds., *Der Roman im Byzanz in der Komnenenzeit* (Frankfurt am Main, 2000), 127–36; I. Nilsson, *Erotic Pathos, Rhetorical Pleasure: Narrative Technique and Mimesis in Eumathios Makrembolites' Hysmine and Hysminias* (Uppsala, 2001); P. Roilos, *Amphoteroglossia: A Poetics of the Twelfth-century Medieval Greek Novel* (Cambridge, MA, 2005); P. A. Agapitos, 'In Rhomaian, Frankish and Persian Lands: Fiction and Fictionality in Byzantium and Beyond' in P. A. Agapitos and L. B. Mortensen, eds., *Medieval Narratives Between History and Fiction. From the Centre to the Periphery of Europe, c. 1100–1400* (Copenhagen, 2012), 235–367; A. Kaldellis, 'The *Timarion*: Toward a Literary Interpretation' in P. Odorico, ed., *La face cachée de la littérature byzantine: Le texte en tant que message immédiat* (Paris, 2012), 275–88; A. Kaldellis, 'The Emergence of Literary Fiction in Byzantium and the Paradox of Plausibility' in P. Roilos, ed., *Medieval Greek Storytelling. Fictionality and Narrative in Byzantium* (Wiesbaden, 2014), 115–29.

to develop in directions that were both experimental and innovative.[5] At the very centre of this evolution stands the genre of romance.[6] This genre had been revived in the twelfth century and flourished from the time around the turn of the thirteenth to fourteenth centuries onwards in the vernacular.

The genre of romance was subject to constant change, with only a few features remaining unaltered. Romance was a genre-in-progress; each new text explored the limits of what was acceptable to its readers. The evolution of romance in Byzantium's later centuries was characterised by some novel combinations of generic features.[7] Some of these features were relevant for style, such as a characteristic verse, the *versus politicus*, and a system of 'repeated phrases'.[8] Obviously, romances were written in a way that they were recognisable as such to their readers. And once readers identified a text as a romance, they had gained the (implied) information that they were reading a piece of fiction. In the course of the fourteenth century there was a new development: the anonymous author of the *Tale of Achilles* cast his story as a biography,[9] a device which up until then was employed in a variety of texts outside the realm of fictional writing, among which the most prevalent were saints' lives.[10] The *Tale of Achilles* is written as a fictional biography, and its biographical arrangement closely resembles the structure of an encomium. The *Tale of Achilles* thus reads as an encomium

---

[5] Generally on late Byzantine vernacular literature, see H.-G. Beck, *Geschichte der byzantinischen Volksliteratur* (Munich, 1971); E. M. Jeffreys and M. J. Jeffreys, *Popular Literature in Late Byzantium* (London, 1983).

[6] For a recent full bibliography on the late Byzantine Romance, see P. A. Agapitos, 'SO Debate: Genre, Structure and Poetics in the Byzantine Vernacular Romances of Love', *SOsl*, 79 (2004), 7–101, especially 90–101.

[7] U. Moennig, 'Literary Genres and Mixture of Generic Features in Late Byzantine Fictional Writing' in Roilos, ed., *Medieval Greek Storytelling*, 163–82.

[8] 'The reasons for this are not fully understood': E. M. Jeffreys, ed., *Digenis Akritis: The Grottaferrata and Escorial Versions* (Cambridge, 1998), liv. For a discussion, see: M. J. Jeffreys, 'Formulas in the *Chronicle of the Morea*', *DOP*, 27 (1973), 163–95; E. M. Jeffreys and M. J. Jeffreys, 'The Traditional Style of Early Demotic Verse', *BMGS*, 5 (1979), 113–39; E. M. Jeffreys, 'The Later Greek Verse Romances: a Survey' in E. M. Jeffreys, M. J. Jeffreys and A. Moffatt, eds., *Byzantine Papers: Proceedings of the First Australian Studies Conference Canberra, 17–19 May 1978* (Canberra, 1981), 116–27; E. M. Jeffreys and M. J. Jeffreys, 'The Style of Byzantine Popular Poetry: Recent Work' in C. Mango and O. Pritsak, eds., *Okeanos: Essays Presented to Ihor Ševčenko* (Cambridge, MA, 1984), 309–43; E. M. Jeffreys and M. J. Jeffreys, 'The Oral Background of Byzantine Popular Poetry', *Oral Tradition*, 1 (1986), 504–47; M. J. Jeffreys, 'Ἡ γλώσσα τοῦ Χρονικοῦ τοῦ Μορέως – γλώσσα μιας προφορικῆς παράδοσης;' in H. Eideneier, ed., *Neograeca Medii Aevi: Text und Ausgabe. Akten zum Symposion Köln 1986* (Cologne, 1987), 139–63.

[9] The text is usually referred to as the *Achilleid*, which is arbitrary; the title *Tale of Achilles* is used by Beaton, *Medieval Greek Romance*, 102–4.

[10] U. Moennig, 'Biographical Arrangement as a Generic Feature and its Multiple Use in Late Byzantine Narratives. An Exploration of the Field', *Phrasis*, 51 (2010), 103–47.

of a fictional protagonist.[11] This text also paves the way for another innovative feature of the Byzantine romance: its protagonist is the first fictional hero named after a historical person – Achilles – to whom he then becomes linked by intertextuality.[12]

Historical Topics in Late Byzantine Romance

In this chapter I define a historical person as a person referred to in Byzantine chronicles. I define as a historical topic in a narrative text material familiar to Byzantine readers from chronicles. The most widely read chronicle in the Palaiologan centuries was Manasses' *Synopsis chronike*, a text which features an affinity to romance-like writing (see below, pp. 356–7).[13]

It is still not clear which text first introduced topics of world history into a piece of narrative literature that was consciously written and understood as fiction. This raises the question of the generic marker of romance (and, implicitly, of fiction): what were the signals for Byzantine readers that they were reading a fictional and not a factual text? There is a clear contender for the text that may have been the first of this kind: the *War of Troy*.[14] Dealing with a historical topic within a fictional framework, this piece was composed in the thirteenth century.[15] The Greek *War of Troy* is based on a French original, a romance from twelfth-century France.[16] It was translated into Greek in Frankish Morea.[17] If the criterion for classifying a late Byzantine narrative text as a romance is that it was recognised as one within a series of generic romances, then the *War of Troy* cannot easily be labelled in this way. After all, the story was not organised as the love story

---

[11] Ibid., 123–5.
[12] U. Moennig, ed., *Die Erzählung von Alexander und Semiramis. Kritische Ausgabe mit einer Einleitung, Übersetzung und einem Wörterverzeichnis* (Berlin, 2004), 49–50; U. Moennig, 'Romeo und Julia in Byzanz. Oder: Worum geht es eigentlich in der *Byzantinischen Achilleis*' in U. Moennig, ed., *. . . ὡς ἀθύρματα παῖδας. Festschrift für Hans Eideneier* (Berlin, 2016), 121–33.
[13] The *Synopsis chronike* is edited by O. Lampsidis, ed., *Constantini Manassis Breviarium chronicum* (Athens, 1996).
[14] E. M. Jeffreys and M. Papathomopulos, eds., *Ὁ Πόλεμος τῆς Τρωάδος (The War of Troy)* (Athens, 1996).
[15] E. M. Jeffreys, 'Byzantine Romances: Eastern or Western?' in M. Brownlee and D. Gondicas, eds., *Renaissance Encounters: Greek East and Latin West* (Princeton, NJ, 2013), 221–37.
[16] E. M. Jeffreys, 'The Comnenian Background to the *Romans d'Antiquité*', *Byzantion*, 50 (1980), 455–86.
[17] E. M. Jeffreys, 'Place of Composition as a Factor in the Edition of Early Demotic Texts' in N. M. Panayotakis, ed., *Origini della letteratura neogreca: Atti del secondo Congresso Internazionale 'Neograeca Medii Aevi' (Venezia, 7–10 novembre 1991)* (Venice, 1993), vol. I, 310–24.

of a central couple. Nevertheless, it displays a high affinity to this genre.[18] Given that the background of the *War of Troy* is Frankish, one could even doubt that it is truly Byzantine at all (in the sense that it was not a product of Byzantine society). On the other hand, the *War of Troy* was obviously read in fourteenth-century Constantinople – one could argue that it was 'Byzantinised' within the process of reception. Some of the late Byzantine romances featuring a link to history by topics or motifs show similarities to this text.[19] This is clearly the case with the *Tale of Achilles* and the *Tale of Alexander and Semiramis*, and one may ask if these were also known to, and used by, the author of the *Tale of Troy*.[20]

The *Tale of Achilles* was the first in a new series of texts, which were most probably products of Byzantine society (if not Constantinople itself) and *recognisably* inscribed into the genre of romances, and which introduced a historical topic into this genre. This sub-series consists of the following texts known to us today:

Tale of Achilles, first half of the fourteenth century[21]
Tale of Troy, second half of the fourteenth century (approximately)
Tale of Alexander and Semiramis, second half of the fourteenth century
Tale of Achilles, Naples version, later than the *Tale of Troy*[22]
Tale of Belisarius, c. 1395[23]

Novelisation

A society that considered the course of the world to be predetermined by Divine Providence introduced topics of world history into a genre of fictional writing, romance. What were the processes that led to this result? First, we will have to establish the importance of romance as a genre in the fourteenth century. In a stimulating article, Margaret Mullett introduced

---

[18] For romance-like elements see E. M. Jeffreys' comment in Agapitos, 'SO Debate', 61–3.
[19] Jeffreys, 'Byzantine Romances: Eastern or Western?', 226.
[20] G. Spadaro, 'L'inedito Polemos tis Troados e l'Achilleide', *BZ*, 71 (1978), 1–9; Beaton, *Medieval Greek Romance*, 170–4; U. Moennig, 'Κοινοί τόποι του υστεροβυζαντινού μυθιστορήματος στη Διήγηση Αλεξάνδρου και Σεμίραμης' in E. M. Jeffreys and M. J. Jeffreys, eds., *Neograeca Medii Aevi: Αναδρομικά και προδρομικά: Approaches to texts in Early Modern Greek* (Oxford, 2005), 259–69.
[21] The original version of the Tale of Achilles dates later than Kallimachos and Chrysorrhoe: Moennig, ed., *Alexander und Semiramis*, 53.
[22] Beaton, *Medieval Greek Romance*, 104.
[23] For the date of composition see W. F. Bakker and A. F. van Gemert, Ἱστορία τοῦ Βελισαρίου. Κριτικὴ ἔκδοση τῶν τεσσάρων διασκευῶν μὲ εἰσαγωγή, σχόλια καὶ γλωσσάριο, second edition (Athens, 2007), 42.

the Bakhtinian term 'novelisation' into the discussion of Byzantine narrative writing: 'In an era when the novel reigns supreme, almost all the remaining genres are to a greater or lesser extent "novelised."'[24]

If we recognise 'novelisation' in a number of texts, we can take this as an indicator that the genre of romance 'reigned supreme' in the period under consideration. A number of late Byzantine narrative texts feature an affinity to the genre of romance: they were novelised (as, for example, the *Consolation concerning Bad Fortune and Good Fortune*, Meliteniotes' *Poem to Sophrosyne*, the *Entertaining Tale of the Quadrupeds*, the *Tale of the Hero Donkey*). This indicates that romance 'reigned supreme' after some time in the fourteenth century, if not earlier.

A second question: were there any precursors to Byzantine historical romances – narrative texts which dealt with historical topics? Two novelised texts of the mid-fourteenth century are thematically linked to God's Creation and its history: Meliteniotes' *Poem to Sophrosyne* and the late Byzantine *Life of Alexander*, recension *ζ (= zeta).[25] Thus, a link between romance-like writing and historical topics can be recognised at the latest by some point in the fourteenth century (Constantine Hermoniakos' *Iliad* was obviously not written as a romance, because it does not feature any of the characteristics of the genre, which were established when the text was produced 'in Epiros around 1320').[26]

The first link between historical story-telling and the genre of romance might have been established much earlier than the fourteenth century. A twelfth-century text that had an affinity to romance (is it a twelfth-century example of 'novelisation'?) was Manasses' *Synopsis chronike*, the manual for world history *par excellence* in the last centuries of Byzantium.[27] The literariness of this text has been pointed out by

---

[24] M. Mullett, 'Novelisation in Byzantium: Narrative After the Revival of Fiction' in J. Burke, ed., *Byzantine Narrative: Papers in Honour of Roger Scott* (Melbourne, 2006), 1–28, esp. 4–5.

[25] For the relation of the *Poem to Sophrosyne* to the genre of romance see P. A. Agapitos, Ἀφήγησις Λιβίστρου καὶ Ροδάμνης. Κριτικὴ ἔκδοση τῆς διασκευῆς α (Athens, 2006), 191–8; for a date of composition of the poem, see S. Schönauer, ed., *Untersuchungen zum Steinkatalog des Sophrosyne-Gedichtes des Meliteniotes: mit kritischer Edition der Verse 1107–1247* (Wiesbaden, 1996). See also the following remark of E. M. Jeffreys, *Digenis Akritis*, xlvi: 'Melitiniotis, Εἰς τὴν Σωφροσύνην is a difficult case, where dating evidence is partly contradicted by literary analysis'.

[26] On this text see E. M. Jeffreys, 'Constantine Hermoniakos and Byzantine Education', Δωδώνη, 4 (1975), 79–109; E. M. Jeffreys, 'The Judgement of Paris in Later Byzantine Literature', *Byzantium*, 48 (1978), 112–31 (the quotation is at p. 130).

[27] For the (rich) manuscript tradition, both Byzantine and early modern, of Manasses' *Synopsis chronike* see Lampsidis, ed., *Constantini Manassis Breviarium chronicum*, vol. I, lxxvi–cxlii.

D. Reinsch and I. Nilsson.[28] Is it by chance that some of the romances or romance-like texts that deal with a historical topic quote Manasses?[29] It is noteworthy that in vv. 1153–5, which refer to the love story of Paris and Helen as a cause of the Trojan War, Manasses addresses the personification of Eros (as if the text were a romance). He refers to fire in a literal way (announcing the coming end of Troy), bringing to mind at the same time the metaphorical fire of love (the metaphor of the fire of love is very common in Byzantine romances):

> ἐνταῦθά σου τὸ παίγνιον, τύραννε πάντων Ἔρως, ἐνταῦθά σου τὸ παίγνιον καὶ τὸ τῆς ἔχθρας σπέρμα, ὅθεν ἀνῆψας λιπαρὰν κάμινον τοῦ πολέμου.
>
> This is the result of your game, tyrant Eros, this is the result of your game and the seed of discord, from which you incensed a huge fire of war.

Clearly, in the twelfth century a relationship between historical topics and novel-like writing had already been established. The process of literary evolution in the course of the thirteenth and fourteenth centuries prepared the ground for late Byzantine historical romances.

The *Tale Of Troy*

A further step towards linking historical topics to the fictional genre of the romance was made by the anonymous author of the *Tale of Troy*. The text is known under a variety of titles, which may cause some confusion as to its identity. The title in the *codex unicus*, the Parisinus Suppl. graec. 926,[30] reads as follows: 'Διήγησις γεναμένη ἐν Τροίᾳ: Ἅπας ὁ ἀφανισμὸς ἔνθε ἐγίνη' (freely translated: 'Narration about what happened in Troy: The whole catastrophe which took place there').

---

[28] On romance-like elements in Manasses' chronicle, see D. R. Reinsch, 'Historia ancilla litterarum? Zum literarischen Geschmack in der Komnenenzeit: Das Beispiel der *Synopsis chronike* des Konstantinos Manasses' in P. Odorico and P. A. Agapitos, *Pour une "nouvelle" histoire de la littérature Byzantine: Problèmes, méthodes, approches, propositions* (Paris, 2002), 81–94, and esp. 88: 'Der "Romandichter" ... hat jedenfalls in diesem Punkt die Grenzen seines Genos "Chronik" überschritten'; I. Nilsson, 'Narrating Images in Byzantine Literature: the *Ekphraseis* of Konstantinos Manasses', *JÖB*, 55 (2005), 121–46.
[29] See e.g. E. M. Jeffreys in Jeffreys and Papathomopoulos, eds., *War of Troy*, lxiv–lxv; Beaton, *Medieval Greek Romance*, 168.
[30] This manuscript belonged to the Saibante collection. See E. M. Jeffreys, 'The Greek Manuscripts of the Saibante Collection' in K. Treu et al., eds., *Studia Codicologica* (Berlin, 1977), 249–62.

Lars Nørgaard and Ole Smith have given it the arbitrary title *A Byzantine Iliad* in their *editio princeps*.[31] Demetrios Dedes has named the text Διήγησις τῆς Τρωάδος, i.e. *Tale of Troy* in his unpublished doctoral thesis, a title derived from the subscription 'τέλος τῆς Τρωάδος' (literally: 'end of Troy') in the manuscript.[32] Elizabeth Jeffreys refers to this text as *Troas*;[33] Roderick Beaton calls the text the *Tale of Troy* (obviously after Dedes).[34] For reasons of convenience, I too will refer to it as the *Tale of Troy*.

The *Tale of Troy* was written by an anonymous author. Strictly speaking, for the time being there is no evidence for a date of composition except that it was written after the *Tale of Achilles* (given that it adopts the feature of biographical arrangement)[35] and before the Naples version of the *Tale of Achilles* (given that this version quotes the *Tale of Troy*).[36] Within the context of late Byzantine narratives that combine historical topics with romance-like writing, the *Tale of Troy* marks a new stage of development. The outline of its story is based on a historical source, a chapter in the *Synopsis chronike* of Constantine Manasses (verses 1108–451);[37] at the same time it is inscribed into the genre of romance, making it a historical romance. The romance has a central protagonist, Paris, whose life is presented from the *omina* before his birth until his dramatic death at the hands of Neoptolemos, Achilles' son. The *Tale of Troy* differs considerably from other texts of its kind, and marks an innovative step in the evolution of the genre. In Byzantine romances, protagonists are presented as 'good' heroes. The *Tale of Achilles*, an immediate precursor, is even an encomium of its protagonist. Contrary to this generic expectation, in the *Tale of Troy* Paris is presented as a negative protagonist, a villain who causes harm and destruction. Thus, the *Tale of Troy* is a *psogos* of its protagonist.

---

[31] L. Nørgaard and O. L. Smith, eds., *A Byzantine Iliad: The Text of Par. suppl. gr. 926. Edited with Critical Apparatus, Introduction and Indexes* (Copenhagen, 1975).

[32] D. Dedes, 'An Edition of a Medieval Greek Poem on the Trojan War (Διήγησις τῆς Τρωάδος)', unpublished PhD thesis, University of London (1971); cf. R. Lavagnini, *I fatti di Troia. L'Iliade bizantina del cod. Paris. Suppl. Gr. 926* (Palermo, 1988).

[33] See Jeffreys and Papathomopoulos, eds., *War of Troy*, lxvi.

[34] Beaton, *Medieval Greek Romance*, 107.

[35] For a full discussion on the relative chronology of the *Tale of Achilles* and the *Tale of Troy* see Moennig, ed., *Alexander und Semiramis*, 49–61.

[36] For a new attempt to establish a date of composition see below, pp. 369–70.

[37] Nørgaard and Smith, eds., *A Byzantine Iliad*, 10; on Manasses' account of the Trojan War see Jeffreys, 'The Attitudes of Byzantine Chroniclers', 204.

Synopsis of the *Tale Of Troy*

While the queen of Troy (anonymous in this romance) is pregnant, King Priam sees the same dream three times. His wife will give birth to a burning torch. Due to the repetition of the dreams and some other signs, Priam decides to discuss his dream with the royal council. According to the court's vaticinators, the dream is a prophecy: the unborn child will destroy Troy. This is why the counsellors insist that the baby must be killed upon birth. But when the boy is born, the king refuses to murder him. The royal couple builds a tower to separate the newborn from the world around him. The counsellors again insist that the infant must be killed. Priam and his wife are forced to put him into a basket, and bring it to the shore. The waves of the sea carry the basket to the island of Lesbos, where a shepherd finds the boy and raises him. He names him Paris. Very early Paris proves to be a gifted boy both at school and in martial arts. He becomes a handsome young man. His beauty rivals that of Aphrodite. Boys of his age elect Paris as their leader. One day, while playing, he cuts the ear of another boy whose parents insist that the case must be examined by the king of Troy. On this occasion, Priam and his wife recognise their son. But again, signs point to the inevitable doom. The people of Troy understand this and demand that Paris be murdered. The queen and the king arrange that their son is not killed but locked away in the company of twelve other young men in the same tower, which they had built when the boy was born.

But destiny cannot be avoided. In the tower, Paris kills a young companion. Again there are signs, and the vaticinators confirm their interpretation that Paris will destroy Troy, and that he needs to be eliminated. He has to flee from Troy in a boat, and that is how – after a number of adventures – he comes to Menelaus' court.

At this point (v.463), the narrator changes the focus to Helen. She is the most beautiful woman the world has ever seen. The kings of Greece fight for her hand. In order to avoid a war, her future husband, Menelaus, is selected by lot. Menelaus believes that he cannot protect his marital rights. That is why all kings must take an oath: if somebody seduces Helen, they all will support Menelaus against the perpetrator. The focus here turns again to Paris (vv.579–80). Paris and Helen meet, they fall in love and they leave Greece for Troy. Prophetic signs accompany their arrival in Troy. The statues shout out that fate cannot be changed: 'Priam, do not kill your son Paris, for what will happen is determined, time is the servant of fate' (vv.772–5).

The abduction of Helen is the cause of the Trojan War: the kings of Greece are obliged to support Menelaus. One of those who arrive at the Trojan shore is Achilles, who becomes the focus of vv.795–877, but thereafter and until the end in verse 1166 the emphasis will keep changing. The Trojan War lasts for more than nine years (vv.878–96). Both sides now think that it should be decided by a duel between Menelaus and Paris. Paris is no longer the bright hero he was at the beginning of the tale. Menelaus, who previously declared himself to be weak, prevails, and it is only with the help 'of the goddess' (i.e. Aphrodite) that Paris manages to escape (vv.938–46):

> Paris thrust at Menelaus with his lance onto his breast,
> but Menelaus took no harm from the steel,
> and Menelaus strikes his lance on Paris;
> the lance passes through Paris' shield, and damages his armour.
> Menelaus struck Paris with his sword on his helmet,
> but the sword broke into three pieces.
> Menelaus grabs Paris by his helmet, drags him by the helmet's strap,
> in order to drag him to the Greek ships with great joy.
> But the goddess helped Paris, and the strap snapped.

In the next scene, Achilles kills Hector with treachery. Priam and his sons Paris and Deiphobus think of revenge: they offer Polyxene's hand to Achilles. With treachery, too, Paris and Deiphobus assassinate Achilles (vv.983–6). Now follows the well-known episode with the Trojan horse and the fall of Troy (verses 987–1052). In order to tell the story of Paris' death, the narrator starts with an excursus on the funeral and the grave of Achilles (vv.1080–104). The ghost of the murdered Achilles demands the assassination of the family of Priam, including Paris (vv.1105–32). Neoptolemus, Achilles' son, kills Priam, Paris, Polyxene and the rest of the royal family of Troy on the grave of his father (vv.1133–6). Only now can the Greeks return to their homeland (vv.1137–9). The romance ends with a lament of Achilles' death (vv.1140–56) and of the vanity of life (vv.1157–66).[38]

Sources of the Motifs

The text raises questions about its literary sources – sources both in the more conventional sense of 'the origin of the narrative motifs' and in the

---

[38] The basis for this summary is my own edition of the text, which I am preparing; verse numbers follow the edition of Nørgaard and Smith, eds., *A Byzantine Iliad*.

Intertextuality in the Romance Tale of Troy   361

more abstract sense of archetypal intertextuality. The principal source, Manasses' *Synopsis chronike* (*Syn*), is not followed consistently. The anonymous author used additional sources related to the topic of the Trojan War and treated his material in a rather free way.[39] According to the *Tale of Troy* Priam (vv.24–5), not Hecuba (*Syn*, vv.1122–6), has the premonitory dream. In Manasses' account, the reason for Achilles' wrath is the assassination of Palamedes (*Syn.*, vv.1277–341), while in the *Tale of Troy* it is the abduction of Briseis (whom the anonymous author confuses with Chryseis) from him (vv.800–45). The *Tale of Troy* introduces the story of Achilles disguised as a girl (vv.846–77), elements of which recall not only ancient accounts of how Odysseus revealed Achilles' identity on Skyros but also Manasses' version (vv.1376–411) of how Palamedes revealed Odysseus' sanity on Ithaca during recruitment for the war. In the *Tale of Troy*, during the years of the war Helen is in Troy (e.g. vv.908–24), while Manasses tells the version of the Egyptian Helen (*Syn.*, vv.1175–208; 1452–65). The author of the *Tale of Troy* also integrates the scene about the duel between Paris and Menelaus, treated in Book 3 of the *Iliad*, into his story. He also makes use of the version that refers to Neoptolemus' revenge and the death of Polyxene on Achilles' tomb (vv.1070–9, 1108–32, 1031–8, 1135–7), which circulated in a number of texts in the fourteenth century, including the *War of Troy* (ed. Jeffreys and Papathomopoulos, vv.12361–479). The author also introduces narrative units originating from other romances of love, especially the *Tale of Apollonios*.[40] Paris' shipwreck (vv.419–52), his arrival in Menelaus' place and the evolution of the love story between Paris and Helen (verses 583–685) are a reworking of the analogous scenes from the *Tale of Apollonios* (cf. ed. Kechagioglou, vv.135–248).[41] Obviously, the author of the *Tale of Troy* felt free to use his material in quite a creative way (the following variants of the traditional narrative material are likely to be

---

[39] R. Lavagnini gives a detailed analysis of the additional sources and of how the author treated them: Lavagnini, *I fatti di Troia*, 36–57; see also Dedes, 'An Edition', 33–4 and, recently, R. Lavagnini, 'Tales of the Trojan War: Achilles and Paris in Medieval Greek Literature' in C. Cupane and B. Krönung, eds., *Fictional Storytelling in the Medieval Eastern Mediterrenian and Beyond* (Leiden, 2016), 253: '[H]is [i.e. the anonymous author's] consciousness in belonging to an ancient, glorious tradition cannot be denied.'

[40] According to G. Kechagioglou, Ἀπολλώνιος τῆς Τύρου. Υστερομεσαιωνικές και νεότερες ελληνικές μορφές (Thessalonike, 2004), the extant *Tale of Apollonios* was composed in fourteenth-century Cyprus (vol. I, 334–49). The author of course could also have had access to a version of the *Apollonios*, which is not identical to the *Tale of Apollonios* published by Kechagioglou (cf. Kechagioglou, Ἀπολλώνιος τῆς Τύρου, vol. I, 354).

[41] Dedes, 'An Edition', 42–4; Lavagnini, *I fatti di Troia*, 31–2; Kechagioglou, Ἀπολλώνιος τῆς Τύρου, 352–4.

inventions of the author of the *Tale of Troy*: Priam himself sees the dream about Paris' devastating future; the scene 'Achilles disguised as a girl' is part of the narrative on Achilles' wrath; Achilles' appearance *post mortem* is part of the story of Paris' death). It is this free treatment of his material that makes it difficult to identify the exact sources that the author might have used. At this point in my research, I believe that the narrative material on the Trojan War is in keeping with the (post-Homeric) versions of the story circulating in the Komnenian and Palaiologan centuries, represented by Tzetzes' *Allegoriai*, the anonymous *War of Troy* and Hermoniakos' *Iliad*, and at some points it comes close to the *Iliad* itself and, supposedly, to the *paraphraseis* of the *Iliad*.[42]

In some parts, the free treatment of the narrative material in the *Tale of Troy* follows set *topoi*: the infant Paris' exposure, his seclusion in a tower in order to avoid harm and the frequent triple repetition of fatal signs is modelled on the 'tale of fate';[43] the parallels between the stories of Paris and Apollonios and the duel between Paris and Menelaus show features common to the late Byzantine romance of love; the episode of Paris' death also serves as a *topos* illustrating how a wicked person deserves a dramatic death. Faithfulness, thus, to his sources and their exact narrative content is not a major concern of the anonymous author of the *Tale of Troy*. What encourages him to modify the pre-existing narrative material are needs of archetypal intertextuality. The author of the *Tale of Troy* quotes a number of texts, or *kinds* of texts, not necessarily only with reference to their narrative contents, but also to their more abstract generic features, such as elements of structuring, the claim that the story really happened in history, and the claim that the story is fictitious.

Archetypal References and Models

Since the *Tale of Troy* was first published in 1975, a number of questions have arisen about formal aspects of the text. The title refers to a historical event – the sack of Troy was understood to be history by Byzantine audiences, given that it was a subject in chronicles such as the *Synopsis chronike* – but the content is centred on a single protagonist, Paris, until, in

---

[42] On this kind of text, see I. Vassis, *Die handschriftliche Überlieferung der sogenannten Psellos-Paraphrase der Ilias* (Hamburg, 1991), 1–32.

[43] For more details, see below p. 368.

the course of the tale, Achilles appears as a 'rival' protagonist.[44] In a previous paper, I tried to give some answers to questions regarding the topics of love, destiny, history and death.[45] Here, my focus is on archetypal intertextuality – on what texts the author read in the sense of 'What *kinds* of texts did he read?'

Previously, I referred to the *Synopsis chronike* as a source for narrative content. Here I refer to the presence of the *Synopsis chronike* in the *Tale of Troy* as a reference to a genre. The subject of this genre is history. The 'claim' of this genre is the representation of what happened in the real world.

That the author of the *Tale of Troy* was also a reader of texts that belonged to the genre of romance is visible both in 'content' (see the nod to the *Tale of Apollonios* quoted above) and at the abstract level of generic features, which include the following:

(1) in part, the story is organised as the love story of a young and beautiful couple;
(2) the traditional imagery of love, including the metaphor of love as paradise, which is a characteristic feature (although not an exclusive one) of Byzantine romance;
(3) the *ekphrasis* of the young girl in her palace;
(4) the young man fighting for his love, including the duel with his counterpart (Paris and Menelaus);
(5) the biographical arrangement first introduced into romance by the author of the *Tale of Achilles*.

The elements of romance in the *Tale of Troy* are dominant to such an extent that we can reasonably assume that it was composed as a piece of fiction, and that it met the expectations regarding the genre of romance, as they were created in the course of the fourteenth century.

At this point we face the following situation: one genre strongly present in the *Tale of Troy* points towards a genre of factual writing (chronicle), the other genre points towards fiction.

A third archetypal model for the *Tale of Troy* is the so-called 'tale of fate'. This refers to its narrative thrust. A 'tale of fate' is a story that starts

---

[44] Especially Lavagnini, *I fatti di Troia*, 13–14, observes an organisation in two parts, the first being the coherent story of Paris and the second being a sequence of events 'con particolare rilievo' on Achilles.
[45] U. Moennig, "Έρως, μοίρα, ιστορία, θάνατος. Διαπλεκόμενοι θεματικοί άξονες στη Βυζαντινή Ιλιάδα' in S. Kaklamanes and M. Paschales, eds., *Η πρόσληψη της αρχαιότητας στο Βυζαντινό και νεοελληνικό μυθιστόρημα* (Athens, 2005), 73–85.

with a dreadful prophecy. Repeated attempts are made to avoid fate, which not only fail, but even contribute to the fulfilment of the initial prophecy. The story of Moses in the Old Testament, for example, is a well-known instance of a 'tale of fate'.

Thus, the anonymous author of the *Tale of Troy* had a broad reading experience, which is expressed in various features of intertextuality and is reflected on various levels of the text. But what was his educational background?

The Innovative Move: the *Tale Of Troy* as a *Psogos* of its Protagonist

As I have already written, the *Tale of Troy* is structured as a biography of its protagonist.[46] In that, it follows the model of the *Tale of Achilles*. Therefore, the question is whether there is any archetypal difference between the *Tale of Achilles* and the *Tale of Troy* that can be considered a conscious innovative step in the evolution of romance.

Byzantine rhetoric provided definitive rules for creative writing with a biographical pattern in Menander Rhetor's treatise *On Epideictic Speeches*, more precisely in the chapters entitled 'Imperial Oration' and 'Funeral Speech'. Originally, the chapter 'Imperial Oration' related only to encomiastic writing about rulers: 'The imperial oration is an encomium of the emperor.'[47] In the Byzantine period, the rules of both treatises were applied to a large number of saints' lives,[48] and to some pieces of historical writing,[49] as well as to a number of texts that describe the lives of historical persons (or persons perceived as historical). Texts of this latter kind are the various anonymous redactions of the *Life of Alexander* and the versions of the anonymous *Digenes Akrites*, particularly the twelfth-century Grottaferrata version and the later version Z.[50]

The author of the *Tale of Troy* intended to 'construct' a negative protagonist. Thus, the rules of *encomium* would not have been of any use to him. What he needed were the rules of *psogos*. But was there any

---

[46] For a full discussion, see Moennig, 'Biographical Arrangement'.
[47] D. A. Russell and N. G. Wilson, eds. and trans., *Menander Rhetor* (Oxford, 1981), 76–95 (368–77, esp. 368) and 170–9 (418–22).
[48] T. Pratsch, *Der hagiographische Topos: Griechische Heiligenviten in mittelbyzantinischer Zeit* (Berlin, 2005), 402–4.
[49] Cf. A. Markopoulos, 'From Narrative Historiography to Historical Biography: New Trends in Byzantine Historical Writing in the 10th–11th centuries', *BZ*, 102 (2009), 697–715.
[50] On the date of Z, see M. J. Jeffreys, 'Digenis Akritas Manuscript Z', *Dodone*, 4 (1975), 163–201.

theory for writing a *psogos*? The advice of the rhetors Hermogenes and Aphthonios proved to be useful for our author:

> μὴ ἀγνόει δέ, ὅτι καὶ τοὺς ψόγους τοῖς ἐγκωμίοις προσνέμουσιν, ἤτοι κατ' εὐφημισμὸν ὀνομάζοντες ἢ ὅτι τοῖς αὐτοῖς τόποις ἀμφότερα προάγεται.

> Do not overlook the fact that they include *psogoi* (invectives) with encomia, either naming it euphemistically or because both use the same topics.[51]

> διαιρεῖται δὲ (i.e. ὁ ψόγος) τοῖς αὐτοῖς κεφαλαίοις, οἷσπερ καὶ τὸ ἐγκώμιον.

> It is divided into the same headings.[52]

There is no doubt that the *Tale of Troy* features the conventional *topoi* of biography, but they function in quite different ways. The following analysis, which illustrates this point more clearly, is structured by reference to Menander:[53]

After a brief *prooimion* (vv.1–3), the narrator talks about Paris' *native country*, Troy, his *family* (vv. 4–18; Paris will cause its extinction through his *praxeis*), his *birth* and the numerous ominous signs and prophecies related to his mother's pregnancy (vv.20–9; 36–7; 85–7). Consequently, the Trojans attempt to pre-empt what is foreseen in a number of prophecies, the destruction of Troy caused by Paris. Paris' *nature* anticipates his future deeds in the service of Aphrodite (vv.175–80):

> Like the flower in its best moment, the finest day of a rose,
> that is how everybody sees and admires him.
> Painters' hands could not create a more beautiful picture.[54]
> His brightness rivals the Sun and Venus' star.
> Which words are appropriate to write about him, how to praise him,
> his beauty, his grace, his manners and his handsomeness?

There is reference to his *nurture* in a shepherd's house (vv.154–8), and to his *education* (vv.165–74). His *accomplishments* as a young man and an

---

[51] H. Rabe, ed., *Hermogenis opera* (Leipzig, 1913), 15.8–11; G. A. Kennedy, trans., *Progymnasmata. Greek Textbooks of Prose Composition and Rhetoric* (Leiden, 2003), 81.
[52] H. Rabe, ed., *Aphthonii progymnasmata* (Leipzig, 1926), 27.17–18; Kennedy, trans., *Progymnasmata*, 111.
[53] For a definition of the term *topos* and its validity in Byzantine biographical writing, see Pratsch, *Der hagiographische Topos*, 11–12. I refer to Menander, because his treatises go into the most detail. I do not have any evidence that the author of the *Tale of Troy* referred directly to Menander. (Cf. Moennig, 'Biographical arrangement', 112–14: 'Once the standard structure was established, the biographical pattern could also be transferred without direct reference to Menander's treatise').
[54] I translate this verse as emended in Dedes' edition.

adult are repeatedly mentioned (vv. 191–200; 612–26; 641–5; 646–53; 682–4). Paris turns out to be a person of numerous virtues: just as in Menander 373.5–8, they are ἀνδρεία (courage), δικαιοσύνη (justice), σωφροσύνη (temperance), φρόνησις (wisdom). Unfortunately he uses them primarily to cause harm, as indeed his *actions* show. His *justice* is only noteworthy due to its absence (vv.213–16):[55]

> A boy caused an offence, one of his company,
> and the others give report to Paris.
> He summarily decided to have his ear cut,
> they completely cut off his ear, so that there is no deception.

His mistress is Helen, the most beautiful woman in the world, but she is already married to another man; this may serve as a proof of Paris' lack of *temperance* (vv.698–724):[56]

> Menelaus, Helen's marvellous husband, wanted
> to leave his city, to visit another place,
> a beautiful fortified place in his possession
> and, as all rulers tended to do,
> to inspect their castles and make provisions.
> He prepared his vessel, so that he embarks and leaves,
> and he ordered Paris to substitute him during his absence,
> to make all provisions needed for his place
> and to be a judge in case of a legal suit, so that nobody is wronged.
> And then he left to inspect his castles.
> This was the occasion Paris had been looking for,
> this was the opportune moment Paris had waited for,
> what he had been looking for in the sky, and asking for from the clouds,
> and had with sighs phrased to the moon at night.
> He started a sexual relationship with Helen,
> he fulfilled the demands of dreadful Eros ...
> Four months he had joy together with Helen,
> the sweetness of desire, beauty and light.
> Then Helen was pregnant by Paris,
> Paris had made her pregnant, the wife of Menelaus.

As to *courage*, it was Aphrodite who saved his neck in a duel against Menelaus, and his greatest *praxis*, Achilles' death, was an act of treachery and assassination rather than the result of Paris' martial virtue (vv.977–86):

---

[55] *Menander Rhetor*, ed. Russell and Wilson, *Treatises*, 88 (375.8–10): 'under "justice" you should commend mildness towards subjects'.

[56] Ibid., 90 (376.4–6): 'because of the emperor, marriages are chaste, fathers have legitimate offspring'.

> And Paris stands at Achilles' right side,
> and Deiphobos at his left, the wicked brothers.
> Achilles was about to embrace them with love,
> Paris and Deiphobos, as his brothers-in-law.
> Achilles had confidence in their great oath,
> he did not know, nor did he expect, their wickedness.
> A deceitful double-edged knife he takes from his belt,
> from the side he rammed into Achilles,
> Paris and Deiphobos assassinated Achilles,
> the marvellous Achilles, the glory of the Greeks.

By way of a *syncrisis*, a story about Achilles is inserted into the story of Paris' life, and of his death, which is also directly related to this addendum. Achilles is not a perfect protagonist either: he seduced Briseis/Chryseis against her will, and took her from her family without their consent (v.807). He then assassinated Hector with treachery (v.960) instead of killing him in a duel. Nonetheless, he is depicted in a much more positive light than Paris. Finally, as a result of Paris' actions, the city of Troy is destroyed. Lamentation follows, not for the death of Paris but for that of Achilles.

According to Hermogenes and Aphthonius, *encomion* and *psogos* follow the same rules. Following this, our anonymous writer modified the newly created subtype of biographical-encomiastic romance, and converted it into a biographical *psogos*.[57] Most probably, the fact that there was a hagiographical model for a negative protagonist, too – a model that employed the same inversion of the *topoi* of *encomion* into *psogos* – was helpful for the author of the *Tale of Troy*.[58] This model was the apocryphal *Life of Judas*.

In his article on the role of Byzantine rhetoric as a theory of creative writing, Vasilis Katsaros writes: 'Rhetorics . . . clearly break the boundaries imposed by genre.'[59] This mechanism allowed the rules of biographic-encomiastic writing to be applied to fictitious narrative writing – this might have already been the case in the twelfth century with the *Digenes Akrites* (I hesitate to be absolute about *Digenes Akrites*, because I think that there is no criterion for us to judge if this text was composed and perceived as

---

[57] I agree with Lavagnini, 'Tales of the Trojan War', 246 n. 49, who states (with reference to U. Moennig, "Ἔρως, μοῖρα, ἱστορία, θάνατος'): 'the portrayal [i.e. the portrayal of Paris in the Tale of Troy] is ... far more nuanced and sympathetic, Paris actually appearing both as a victim of fate, worthy to be commiserated with, and an adventurous young man and passionate lover'.

[58] A. Kazhdan, 'Invective' in A. Kazhdan et al., *ODB* (Oxford, 1991), vol. II, 1004–5: 'Elements of invective could penetrate even hagiography' (Kazhdan quotes Niketas David Paphlogons vita of Patriarch Ignatios as an example).

[59] B. Katsaros, 'Ἡ ῥητορική ὡς "Θεωρία Λογοτεχνίας" τῶν Βυζαντινῶν' in Odorico and Agapitos, *Pour une "nouvelle" histoire de la littérature Byzantine*, 95–106, esp. 104.

fictional), and in the fourteenth century with the *Tale of Achilles*. The *Tale of Troy* is a text written in the tradition of the *Tale of Achilles*, but featuring one major difference: in this text, the rules of encomiastic writing have been 'inverted', with the result that they function as the *topoi* of *psogos*. It is this employment of the *topoi* of *encomion* that convinces me that the author of the *Tale of Troy* was well acquainted with rhetorical practice. He mastered the rules of both *encomion* and *psogos*, because he was trained to do so: he had passed through Byzantine education in rhetoric.

Two Byzantine *Psogoi* with Considerable Resemblances to the *Tale Of Troy*

A text of a different genre, also organised as a *psogos* and featuring a striking resemblance to the *Tale of Troy*, is the middle Byzantine *Life of Judas*.[60] This text, unfortunately, has survived only in a number of oral versions, written down in post-Byzantine manuscripts. Here is a summary of the *Life*:

Judas originates from Ischara. His father is Rovel. The night Judas is conceived, his mother sees a dreadful dream: the unborn child will destroy their tribe. Judas is born, and his mother makes a box, and exposes the newborn in the sea. Shepherds find the box and raise the baby. After some time, the shepherds bring the child Judas to Ischara where he grows up, unrecognised, in his parents' house. His mother gives birth to a second boy, whom Judas kills out of avarice. Judas leaves Ischara for Jerusalem. After many years, Judas meets his parents in Jerusalem. They do not recognise him, and he does not recognise them. In a fight, Judas kills his father. Later, he marries the widow – his mother. His wife and mother tells him the story of her life. Now recognition takes place. Judas leaves their house and joins the company of Christ. The fatal end of the story is well known.

It becomes obvious, both from similarities in narrative material about the exposure of the newborn and structural resemblances, that the author of the *Tale of Troy* knew the *Life of Judas*, and that the middle Byzantine *Life of Judas* was one of the archetypal models of the late Byzantine romance: it was the model for structuring the *Tale of Troy* as a 'tale of fate'.

---

[60] All information about the *Life of Judas* is drawn from W. Puchner, 'Europäische Ödipustradition und griechisches Schicksalsmärchen', *BalkSt*, 26 (1987), 321–49; W. Puchner, *Studien zum Kulturkontext der liturgischen Szene: Lazarus und Judas als religiöse Volksfiguren in Brauch, Lied und Legende Südosteuropas* (Vienna, 1991); W. Puchner, 'Byzantinische und westliche Einflüsse auf die religiöse Dichtung Kretas zur Zeit der venetianischen Herrschaft: Das Beispiel der apokryphen Judasvita in dem Gedicht Altes und Neues Testament' in Panayotakis, ed., *Origini della letteratura neogreca*, vol. II, 278–312.

Both *encomium* and *psogos* were subjects in Byzantine education in rhetoric. The relevant exercises are part of the *Progymnasmata*. The most important late Byzantine collection of *Progymnasmata* is by Georgios Pachymeres (1242–1308/10).[61] Surprisingly, the *psogos* in Pachymeres' collection is a *psogos* of Paris, titled Ψόγος τοῦ Πάριδος Ἀλεξάνδρου ('Invective on Paris, or Alexandros').[62] The narrative of the *psogos* can be summarised as follows:

Paris originated from Hellespontine Phrygia. His native city was Troy. His grandfather was Laomedon, his father Priam. While she was pregnant with Paris, his mother saw ominous dreams. That is why the baby Paris was given away to shepherds and grew up in bad company. As a young man, he cared too much about his appearance. As an adult, he seduced Helen from her husband, to whom he was indebted. This was the cause of the Trojan War. During the war, Menelaus asked him for a duel. Paris was so dreadful that he cannot be compared to any other dreadful person.

Reading the *Tale of Troy* as a *psogos* also gives a solution to the formal problem of the introduction of the story and the character of Achilles, who becomes a rival protagonist to the central figure of Paris: this is achieved by drawing on the heading of *syncrisis*, which is an integral part of a *psogos*.

The resemblance between Paris in the *Tale of Troy* and his counterpart in Pachymeres' *Invective on Paris* does not necessarily mean that the anonymous author was familiar with this collection of rhetorical exercises. But still, the coincidence is striking. It can be taken as proof of how closely related Byzantine creative writing was to the practice of rhetorical education – regardless of whether this writing was in learned or vernacular Greek.

A Proposal for a Date (and Context) of Composition for the *Tale Of Troy*

Until now there has been no satisfactory proposal for a date of composition for the *Tale of Troy*. Given that the *Tale of Troy* represents a stage of literary evolution beyond the *Tale of Achilles*, which provides a *terminus post quem*, is there any text which represents a further step in the development of late Byzantine literature, thus providing a *terminus ante quem*?

---

[61] On Pachymeres, see the monograph of S. Lampakes, ed., Γεώργιος Παχυμέρης: Πρωτέκδικος και Δικαιοφύλαξ (Athens, 2004).
[62] C. Walz, ed., *Rhetores graeci ex codicibus Florentinis, Mediolanensibus, Monacensibus, Neapolitanis, Parisiensibus, Romanis, Venetis, Taurinensibus et Vindobonensibus* (Stuttgart, 1832), vol. 1, 551–96: 568–72.

In the previous sections, focus was on the innovative step from the *encomion* of the (fictional) protagonist' to the *psogos* of the (fictional) protagonist'. Now I will focus on the combination of the fictional genre of romance and historical topics. The *Tale of Achilles* features a strong link to the topic of the Trojan War, but still it is mainly a romance of love. The *Tale of Troy* marks a further step in a line of progress towards the evolution of a late Byzantine historical romance, given that the love story and the story of a historical event are completely interwoven. The expected next step in this evolution would be a proper historical romance. What could reasonably be the generic features of a proper late Byzantine historical romance? Most importantly, the story would probably correspond to an incident known from chronicles. And, given that it would not be organised as the love story of a central couple, it probably would lack the rhetoric of love, which had been a generic feature of Greek romance since Antiquity. There is such a text: the *Tale of Belisarius*. The story corresponds recognisably to a chapter in Byzantine chronicles (see especially *Syn.*, vv.3145–212). At the same time, the narrative material taken from various sources is reshaped in a quite free manner.[63] As a consequence, I argue that the *Tale of Belisarius*, which dates to ±1395, postdates the *Tale of Troy*.

In her review of my edition of the *Tale of Alexander and Semiramis* Elizabeth Jeffreys remarks that I give very little information about the context of the composition of this text, which is an adaptation of narrative material which originates in Persian literature.[64] There is no concrete information about this context, and that is why one has to argue on the basis of a line of literary development. The *Tale of Alexander* follows, in some (archetypal) respects, the model of the *Tale of Achilles*, as the *Tale of Troy* does. *Treachery* is the only significant topic shared by both stories: in the *Tale of Troy* more explicitly towards the end, in the *Tale of Alexander and Semiramis*, in its main part. Both works could have been composed in similar contexts.

This leads me to another question: If we accept that *treachery* is a topic dealt with both in the *Tale of Troy* and the *Tale of Alexander and Semiramis*, are there any other late Byzantine texts which deal with abstract topics of human behaviour within a frame of fiction? The *Tale of Belisarius*, for instance, deals with *envy* (φθόνος). Other fictional texts come to mind,

---

[63] Cf. the recent analysis by M. Hinterberger, *Pthonos. Mißgunst, Neid und Eifersucht in der byzantinischen Literatur* (Wiesbaden, 2013), 442–55.

[64] E. M. Jeffreys, 'Review of Ulrich Moennig, *Die Erzählung von Alexander und Semiramis*', BZ, 100 (2008), 870–2.

like the satiric *Tale of the Hero Donkey*, which deals with *hypocrisy*, or the, also satiric, *Entertaining Tale of the Quadrupeds*, which deals with wickedness (πονηρία) (although this needs further consideration). It seems to me that, while late Byzantine fiction of the earlier decades of the fourteenth century deals more generally with the conditions of human existence, with an appreciation of both an ideal life and transcendentalism, the fictional texts of the later decades of the century deal with the undesirable features of human character and their dreadful results. The turning point is the *Tale of Achilles*, and more precisely verses 1275–7 in the Naples version. Achilles, in breaking the wall of the paradise of love, upsets a literary *topos*. The paradise of love may have appealed to people who preferred to flee from reality rather than face it (perhaps an appealing idea during the reign of Andronikos II), but it could not stand against the experience of the empire in decline. Valid for the texts I link to the *Tale of Troy* and for the *Tale of Troy* itself are the following two facts: they all mirror Byzantine education, and the authors of the later texts were readers of the previous ones.

Conclusions and an Outlook for Further Research

One conclusion of this chapter – that the author of the *Tale of Troy* was an educated Byzantine – does not come unexpectedly, given that reading vernacular literature in terms of literariness and as just another type of learned literature ('a conscious choice for stylistic reasons') has become a tradition within modern scholarship in Byzantine Studies.[65]

More important is the conclusion that the linkage of historical topics and a Byzantine genre clearly marked as fiction is a product of a complex evolution within the genre of romance. This evolution took place in the course of the second half of the fourteenth century and obviously in the very centre of Byzantium or, at least, not far away from it.

A question for future research is what this evolution of romance may tell us about the attitude of the Byzantines towards their own history. Did the thirteenth-century Peloponnesian *War of Troy*, which was widely read by

---

[65] A number of those who take part in the discussion about literariness in Byzantine vernacular literature contribute to Agapitos, 'SO Debate', 7–101. With a focus on linguistic features: E. Trapp, 'Learned and Vernacular Literature in Byzantium: Dichotomy or Symbiosis?', *DOP*, 47 (1993), 115–29; M. Hinterberger, 'Δημώδης και λόγια λογοτεχνία: διαχωριστικές γραμμές και συνδετικοί κρίκοι' in Odorico and Agapitos, *Pour une "nouvelle" histoire de la littérature byzantine*, 153–65. The original quotation is in French ('un choix conscient pour des raisons stylistiques') and is taken from Hinterberger's résumé, p. 165.

the authors of fourteenth-century literature – and perhaps also the epirotic *Iliad*, translated into vernacular Greek by Constantine Hermoniakos – intrigue the Byzantines so much that they chose to propagate their own narratives about *Romanitas* using the vehicle of romance, which in the fourteenth century 'reigned supreme'?[66] If the latter conclusion is valid, then is the subject of late Byzantine historical fiction Byzantium itself and its self-perception as the Roman Empire?

Further Reading

The main text is: L. Nørgaard and O. L. Smith, eds., *A Byzantine Iliad: The Text of Par. suppl. gr. 926. Edited with Critical Apparatus, Introduction and Indexes* (Copenhagen, 1975). For an introduction, see: R. Beaton, *The Medieval Greek Romance*, second edition, revised and expanded (London, 1996); E. M. Jeffreys, 'Byzantine Romances: Eastern or Western?' in M. Brownlee and D. Gondicas, eds., *Renaissance Encounters: Greek East and Latin West* (Princeton, NJ, 2013), 221–37; U. Moennig, ''Ερως, μοίρα, ιστορία, θάνατος. Διαπλεκόμενοι θεματικοί άξονες στη Βυζαντινή Ιλιάδα' in S. Kaklamanes and M. Paschales, eds., *Η πρόσληψη της αρχαιότητας στο Βυζαντινό και νεοελληνικό μυθιστόρημα* (Athens, 2005), 73–85 U. Moennig, 'Biographical Arrangement as a Generic Feature and its Multiple Use in Late Byzantine Narratives: an Exploration of the Field', Phrasis, 51 (2010), 103–47 and R. Lavagnini, 'Tales of the Trojan War: Achilles and Paris in Medieval Greek Literature' in C. Cupane and B. Krönung, eds., *Fictional Storytelling in the Medieval Eastern Meditterraean and Beyond* (Leiden, 2016), 234–59.

---

[66] Jeffreys, 'Byzantine Romances: Eastern or Western?', 231–3.

PART III

Communication and Influence

Educational Practices

CHAPTER 16

Late Byzantine School Teaching Through the Iambic Canons *and their* Paraphrase

Dimitrios Skrekas

This study aims to offer insights into the texts that provided students in the Byzantine world with advanced lexical and rhetorical training.[1] Three hymns, the iambic canons attributed to John of Damascus, were among the texts that had a prominent place in schoolrooms.[2] In this chapter, three hitherto unnoticed manuscripts with a paraphrase (*Paraphrasis* or Παρά-φρασις – hereafter *Paraphrasis*) of these canons are brought to the fore in order to shed light on the history of the text's transmission, while a portion is edited for the first time and presented in the appendix.

In Byzantium, the curriculum at the secondary educational level consisted of a combination of the *trivium* of grammar, rhetoric and philosophy, and the *quadrivium* of mathematics, music, geometry and astronomy.[3] In the middle Byzantine period, alongside Homer, ancient Greek tragedies, comedies, and texts of historians and philosophers, some emphasis was also put on ecclesiastical texts.[4] Students were exposed to the poems of Gregory

---

[1] I wish to express my gratitude to the anonymous readers, as well as to S. Antonopoulos, T. Antonopoulou, Fr. M. Constas, A. Giannouli, G. Papagiannis, S. Papaioannou and R. Stefec for their useful comments and support. The chapter is dedicated to Professors E. M. and M. J. Jeffreys, and especially to Elizabeth who acted as my supervisor. In 2003, I first noticed the importance of one of the manuscripts (the *Oxoniensis* D'Orville 113, see below). When I reported this to Elizabeth, she immediately rushed off to the Bodleian Library, consulted the codex, and then sent me a message with her thoughts. This moment signified a turning point in my studies at Oxford. Elizabeth's support has been and continues to be of special importance. For this, I remain profoundly grateful.

[2] On these three iambic canons (which celebrate three Feasts of the Lord: Christmas, the Theophany, and Pentecost) see D. Skrekas, 'Studies in the Iambic Canons Attributed to John of Damascus: a Critical Edition with Introduction and Commentary', unpublished DPhil thesis, University of Oxford (2008), forthcoming in a revised form.

[3] A. Markopoulos, 'Education' in E. M. Jeffreys, J. Haldon and R. Cormack, eds., *The Oxford Handbook of Byzantine Studies* (Oxford, 2008), 788–9; A. Markopoulos, 'Teachers and Textbooks in Byzantium Ninth to Eleventh Centuries' in S. Steckel, N. Gaul and M. Grünbart, eds., *Networks of Learning. Perspectives on Scholars in Byzantine East and Latin West, c. 1000–1200* (Zürich, 2014), 3–15.

[4] See S. Papaioannou, *Michael Psellos: Rhetoric and Authorship in Byzantium* (Cambridge, 2013), 56–63 (on specifically the Homilies of Gregory of Nazianzos, the most important such text).

of Nazianzos,[5] as well as other poetry, including hymns, among which were the iambic canons. Especially during, but also to some extent before, the Komnenian period, these canons were taught in schools, and they even retained their place in the curriculum under the Ottoman Empire.[6] The canons' inclusion in curricula spanning centuries was not arbitrary, but due rather to their theological acuteness and especially to their formal stylistic qualities: their linguistic and metrical complexities. They were used primarily to teach students the doctrines of the Church, as well as grammar, syntax and language.

Thus, although the canons were composed in order to be chanted during church services (as indeed they are to this day), their use in schools as theological and literary models gave them a 'textbook' character that in the Byzantine and post-Byzantine periods attracted a considerable amount of exegetical activity in the form of special lexica, various paraphrases, and detailed commentaries.[7] Indeed, among all hymnographic texts, it is the asmatic canons (rather than other hymnographic genres, such as the *kontakion, idiomela* etc.) that dominated the commentary tradition.

Within the Byzantine hermeneutical tradition of the three iambic canons, the *Paraphrasis* associated with Mark Eugenikos, the fourteenth-century Bishop of Ephesus, are perhaps the least well known. Leo Allatius (*c.* 1586–1669), the scholar who first made use of a few sentences from this *Paraphrasis*, probably from a codex in the Vatican Library, attributed the *Paraphrasis* to Eugenikos, following his source.

---

[5] See C. Simelidis, ed., *Selected Poems of Gregory of Nazianzus* (Göttingen, 2009), 75–9.
[6] See P. Demetracopoulos, 'The Exegeses of the Canons in the Twelfth Century as School Texts', *Diptycha*, 1 (1979), 143–57.
[7] See L. de Stefani, 'Il Lessico ai Canoni giambici di Giovanni Damasceno secondo un ms. Romano', *BZ*, 21 (1912), 431–5; also F. Montana, 'Dal glossario all'esegesi. L'apparato ermeneutico al canone pentecostale attribuito a Giovanni Damasceno nel ms. Ottob. Gr. 248', *Studi classici e orientali*, 42 (1992), 147–64 for one glossary and an anonymous paraphrasis of the iambic canon on Pentecost from Ottob. gr. 248. F. Montana, 'Tre parafrasi anonime bizantine del canone giambico pentecostale attribuito a Giovanni Damasceno', *Koinonia*, 17 (1993), 61–79 for three anonymous paraphrases of the same canon. F. Montana, 'I canoni giambici di Giovanni Damasceno per le feste di Natale, Teofania e Pentecoste nelle esegesi di Gregorio di Corinto', *Koinonia*, 13 (1989), 31–49; F. Montana, ed., *Gregorio di Corinto. Esegesi al canone giambico per la Pentecoste attribuito a Giovanni Damasceno* (Pisa, 1995), l–lv; A. Giannouli, *Die beiden byzantinischen Kommentare zum Großen Kanon des Andreas von Kreta* (Vienna, 2007), 14–24; and more recently P. Cesaretti and S. Ronchey eds., *Eustathii Thessalonicensis exegesis in canonem iambicum pentecostalem: Recensuerunt indicibusque instruxerunt* (Berlin, 2014), 48*–72*. A. Kominis, Γρηγόριος Πάρδος, Μητροπολίτης Κορίνθου καὶ τὸ ἔργον αὐτοῦ (Athens, 1960), 100–23 gives a detailed list and description of commentaries on various hymnographical texts. A rather far-fetched reading of the Byzantine *Paraphrasis* as a 'philosophical statement' is presented in F. Lauritzen, 'Paraphrasis as Interpretation. Psellos and a Canon of Cosmas the Melodist (Poem 24 Westerink)', *Byzantina*, 33 (2014), 61–74 on Psellos' paraphrasis of the Canon on the Holy Thursday.

School Teaching Through the Iambic Canons and Paraphrase 379

Since Allatius' time no one has fully investigated the manuscript tradition or the question of authorship of the text. The result has been a confusion regarding the text's attribution that continues to repeat itself in the secondary literature.[8] Allatius referred in his *De libris apocryphis* to the problem of the authorship of the iambic canon on Pentecost with these words: 'Gregory Pardos ... and Mark Eugenikos in the commentary on the aforementioned canon (on Pentecost) (wrote): "Another similar canon, as some people say, by John of Damascus; some others though, by John Arklas the monk, and I concur with them".'[9]

Allatius attributed this phrase to Eugenikos, and this ascription has never been questioned. This last phrase has been cited, for instance, by both Nikodemos the Hagiorite (1749–1809) – the compiler of the *Heortodromion* (Ἑορτοδρόμιον), which is the main commentary on the canons for the great feasts – and Bartholomaios Koutloumousianos (1772–1851), the editor of Greek Orthodox liturgical books such as the *Menaia* (Μηναῖα) and the *Pentekostarion* (Πεντηκοστάριον).[10] Nikodemos and Bartholomaios took for granted that the *Paraphrasis* was written by Eugenikos.[11] In fact, the identity of the author is far from resolved.

---

[8] In discussing the epithet μητροπάρθενον in the ninth ode of the iambic canon on Pentecost, 121, Allatius cited the following from the *Paraphrasis*: 'Also Mark Eugenikos in the Paraphrase (wrote) "hail O queen, glory and utterance"' (Necnon Marcus Eugenius (sic) in Paraphrasi, χαίροις ὦ δέσποινα κλέος καὶ ἄκουσμα). See L. Allatius, *De libris Ecclesiasticis Graecorum: dissertationes duae* (Paris, 1645), 280 (reprinted also in: L. Allatius, *De libris Ecclesiasticis Graecorum, dissertationes et observationes variae* (Paris, 1646, 280 and 1712, vii)).

[9] 'Gregorius Pardus ... et Marcus Eugenicus in Expositione in dictum Canonem: Ἕτερος κανὼν ὅμοιος, ὥς τινες λέγουσι, τοῦ ἁγίου Ἰωάννου τοῦ Δαμασκηνοῦ· ἕτεροι δέ, Ἰωάννου μοναχοῦ τοῦ Ἀρκλᾶ, οἷς καὶ ἐγὼ συντίθεμαι' in M. Le Quien, ed., *Johannis Damasceni Opera omnia* (Paris, 1712), vol. I, section lxxix; reprinted also in *PG* 94, xciv, 185–6. Kominis, Γρηγόριος Πάρδος, 119 argued convincingly that the phrase 'and I concur with them', and others similar to it that appear in many manuscripts which transmit the commentaries of both Gregory Pardos and Eugenikos (Kominis attributes our *Paraphrasis* to Eugenikos), is but a scribal comment which was never uttered by the commentators themselves. Indeed, it is apparent from their works that none of them ever expressed any opinion regarding the matter of the canon's authorship. On Gregory Pardos, see Montana, ed., *Gregorio di Corinto*, 2 in the apparatus for variants.

[10] B. Kralides and P. Philippides, eds., Nikodemos the Hagiorite, Ἑορτοδρόμιον, ἤτοι ἑρμηνεία εἰς τοὺς ἀσματικοὺς κανόνας τῶν δεσποτικῶν καὶ θεομητορικῶν ἑορτῶν (Venice, 1836). On Nikodemos, see R. A. Klostermann, 'Heortodromion, ein Alterswerk des Nikodemos Hagiorites', *OrChrP*, 46 (1980), 446–62 and E. Criterio, 'Nicodemo Agiorita' in C. G. Conticello and V. Conticello, eds., *La théologie byzantine et sa tradition* (Turnhout, 2002), II: 938 with relevant bibliography on Nikodemos, 973–8. On Bartholomaios and his work on the edition of the *Pentekostarion*, see D. Stratis, Βαρθολομαῖος Κουτλουμουσιανός (1772–1851) Βιογραφία–Ἐργογραφία (Mt. Athos, 2002), 344–50.

[11] Nikodemos, by mentioning the Greek–Latin volume as his source (in Nikodemos the Hagiorite, Ἑορτοδρόμιον, eds. Kralides and Philippides, 553, n. 1), hints at Allatius' Prolegomena: 'Regarding this iambic canon, we note here all these that we have found in the preface of the Greek–Latin first volume of John of Damascus' (Σημειοῦμεν ἐνταῦθα περὶ τοῦ Ἰαμβικοῦ τούτου Κανόνος ἐκεῖνα ὁποῦ

Medieval Interpretations of the Three Iambic Canons

If we are to understand the *Paraphrasis* and the context in which it operated, we need first to review Byzantine interpretations of the three iambic canons. The earliest instances of direct quotation are to be found in George Choiroboskos' Ἐπιμερισμοί (*Epimerismoi*) on the Psalms as well as in the anonymous Ἐπιμερισμοί on Homer.[12] Within the Byzantine tradition of teaching, such Ἐπιμερισμοί aimed to offer both grammatical and syntactical analysis of almost all the words in a given text.[13] At the end of the ninth century, a certain Theodosios penned glosses on the three iambic canons under the title 'Words that occur in the canons of Christmas, Theophany and Pentecost given in alphabetical order' (Λέξεις ἐγκείμεναι τοῖς κανόσι κατὰ στοιχεῖον τῆς Χριστοῦ Γεννήσεως, τῶν Φώτων καὶ τῆς Πεντηκοστῆς).[14] Around the tenth century, some of these glosses were

---

εὕρομεν εἰς τὰ προλεγόμενα τοῦ Γραικολατίνου Πρώτου Τόμου Ἰωάννου τοῦ Δαμασκηνοῦ). See also B. Koutloumousianos, ed., Πεντηκοστάριον χαρμόσυνον (Venice, 1837), δ΄: 'others (attribute this (i.e. the iambic canon on Pentecost)) to John the monk Arklas, with whom I concur' (ἕτεροι δὲ Ἰω(άνν)ου μοναχοῦ τοῦ Ἀρκλᾶ, οἷς καὶ ἐγὼ συντίθεμαι). In all probability both Bartholomaios and Nikodemos copied their information from Allatius but they did not reference any more than the text cited by Allatius. The *Paraphrasis* is mentioned by L. Petit, 'Marc Eugénicos' in *DTC*, 9, 1973. With the exception of I. Bulović, M. Pilavakis and N. Constas, who compiled lists of manuscripts transmitting Eugenikos' works (I. Bulović, Τὸ μυστήριον τῆς ἐν τῇ ἁγίᾳ Τριάδι διακρίσεως τῆς θείας οὐσίας καὶ ἐνεργείας κατὰ τὸν ἅγιον Μάρκον Ἐφέσου τὸν Εὐγενικόν (Thessalonike, 1983), 507; M. Pilavakis, 'Markos Eugenikos's First Antirrhetic against Manuel Calecas' *On Essence and Energy*: Editio Princeps with Introduction and Commentary', unpublished PhD thesis, University of London (1987), 122–3; N. Constas, 'Mark Eugenikos' in Conticello and Conticello, eds., *La théologie byzantine et sa tradition* II, 438), recent scholarship has not made use of the text of the *Paraphrasis* under discussion. See also E. Mineva, Τὸ υμνογραφικό έργο του Μάρκου Ευγενικού (Athens, 2004), 201. On the life and work of Eugenikos, see *DTC*, 9, 1968–86; K. Mamone, Μᾶρκος ὁ Εὐγενικός, Βίος καὶ ἔργον (Athens, 1954); K. Mamone, Ἐπὶ τοῦ βίου καὶ τοῦ ἔργου Μάρκου τοῦ Εὐγενικοῦ', *Ἀθηνᾶ*, 59 (1955), 198–221; C. N. Tsirpanlis, *Mark Eugenicus and the Council of Florence: A Historical Re-evaluation of his Personality* (Thessalonike, 1974), esp. 109–18; *PLP*, no. 6193, 'Εὐγενικὸς Μάρκος (Eugenikos, Markos)'.

[12] See W. Bühler and C. Theodoridis, 'Johannes von Damaskos *terminus post quem* für Choiroboskos', *BZ*, 69 (1976), 397–401. The grammar of George Choiroboskos was 'highly popular' in Byzantine education. C. Theodoridis, 'Die Abfassungszeit der Epimerismen zu Homer', *BZ*, 72 (1979), 1–5. Markopoulos, 'Education', 789 and A. Giannouli, 'Education and Literary Language in Byzantium' in M. Hinterberger, ed., *The Language of Byzantine Learned Literature* (Turnhout, 2014), 56, n. 17 for further bibliography. For a recent discussion of Choiroboskos and his dates, see D. D. Resh, 'Toward a Byzantine Definition of Metaphrasis', *GRBS*, 55 (2015), 754–87.

[13] For the *Epimerismi Homerici* and their history, see A. R. Dyck, ed., *Epimerismi Homerici* (Berlin, 1983), 3–16. For a general introduction, see E. Dickey, *Ancient Greek Scholarship, A Guide to Finding, Reading, and Understanding Scholia, Commentaries, Lexica, and Grammatical Treatises, from Their Beginnings to the Byzantine Period* (Oxford, 2007), 27–8, Giannouli, 'Education', 61–2, esp. n. 46, and A. Borovilou-Genakou, 'Οἱ ἐπιμερισμοὶ κατὰ στοιχεῖον Γραφικά: παρατηρήσεις στὴ δομὴ καὶ στὸν τρόπο σύνθεσής τους', *Βυζαντινά*, 28 (2008), 21–50.

[14] See Montana, *Gregorio di Corinto*, li. The name is transmitted as 'Theodoros' in some manuscripts. See de Stefani, 'Il Lessico', 57. Editions of the Lexicon: L. Bachmann, ed., *Anecdota Graeca* (Leipzig,

added to various lexica, including the *Souda* and also the *Gudianum*, *Genuinum* and *Magnum*.[15]

The three main commentators on the canons were, however, the twelfth-century authors Gregory Pardos, Theodore Prodromos, and Eustathios of Thessalonike. In all probability, all three worked as *grammatikoi*, teaching grammar in the schools of the capital.[16] A close reading of their work on the canons sheds light on how the systematic exegetical tradition on these texts developed, originating with the short commentaries by Gregory Pardos on a large number of canons (twenty-three in total), which were then overshadowed by Theodore's highly significant *scholia* on a smaller number of canons (seventeen in total), and culminating in Eustathios' work, a *tour de force* focused on only one canon.[17] Whereas Gregory's work shows the inexperience of a youthful author, Theodore's commentaries give the impression of an experienced scholar who carefully marshals convincing arguments, while that of Eustathios, written in the scholar's seventies, exhibits the wisdom – and idiosyncrasies – of an old man.

Of the three works, the commentaries by Gregory Pardos are the most concise and least analytical. Gregory avoids using either long *prooimia*

1828), vol. I, 450–9 (from the manuscript Coisl. 345); J. A. Cramer, ed., *Anecdota Graeca e codd. Manuscriptis bibliothecarum Oxoniensium* (Oxford, 1835), vol. II, 473, 25–474, 34 (from the manuscript Baroc. gr. 50); L. de Stefani, 'Per le fonti dell' Etimologico Gudiano', *BZ*, 16 (1907), 52–68 (from Coisl. 345, Baroc. gr. 50, Laur. 57. 26); de Stefani, 'Il Lessico', 431–5 (L. de Stefani records here variants from Rom. Angel. B. 5.11); G. de Andrés, ed., 'Carta de Teodosio el Grammatico (s. ix) sobre el lexico de los canones de san Juan Damasceno, según el codice Complutense "Villamil No 30"', *Emerita*, 41 (1973), 377–95 (from the manuscript Complut. Villamil 30); F. Montana, 'L'Inizio del lessico di Teodosio Grammatico ai canoni liturgici nel Laur. 57.48', *Rivista di filologia e di instruzione classica*, 123 (1995), 193–200 (from the manuscript Laur. 57.48 Montana edits the text from Α-Γ); A. Borovilou-Genakou, 'Baroccianus gr. 50: Ἐπιμερισμοί κατὰ στοιχεῖον Γραφικά. Terminus ante quem pour le lexique de Théodose le grammairien (ixe s.)' *Byzantion*, 72 (2002), 265–9 (edition of the text from Baroc. gr. 50), JSTOR, www.jstor.org/stable/44172754); A. Borovilou-Genakou, 'Ἐπιμερισμοί κατὰ στοιχεῖον γραφικά καὶ Ἰαμβικοί Κανόνες Χριστουγέννων, Φώτων καὶ Πεντηκοστῆς', *ByzSym*, 19 (2009), 83–97.
[15] Montana, *Gregorio di Corinto*, li. See A. Nauck, ed., 'Iohannis Damasceni canones iambici cum commentario et indice verborum' *Mélanges gréco-romains, Bulletin de l'Académie impériale des sciences de Saint-Pétersbourg*, 6 (1893), 199–223. See also Demetracopoulos, 'The Exegeses', 145.
[16] See R. Browning, 'The Patriarchal School at Constantinople in the Twelfth Century', *Byzantion*, 32 (1962), 186–93 and R. Browning, 'The Patriarchal School at Constantinople in the Twelfth Century', *Byzantion*, 33 (1963), 19–20, 22–3, as well as Demetracopoulos, 'The Exegeses', 149. It is still unclear whether the so-called 'Patriarchal School' existed as such. On this see B. Katsaros, *Ιωάννης Κασταμονίτης. Συμβολή στη μελέτη του βίου, του έργου και της εποχής του* (Thessalonike, 1988), 163–207, with extensive bibliography; I owe this reference to A. Giannouli. See also I. Nesseris, 'Η Παιδεία στην Κωνσταντινούπολη κατά τον 12ο αιώνα', unpublished PhD thesis, University of Ioannina (2014), 17–53.
[17] See Montana, *Gregorio di Corinto*, lii–liii.

before each canon's commentary, or *erotapokriseis* (ἐρωταποκρίσεις, ἀπορία-λύσις)– pairs of questions and answers – preferring instead to dwell on the syntactical order of the words in each text, and providing a word-by-word paraphrasis of each *heirmos* and *troparion*. He tries to offer reliable *lectiones* as well as to locate the *testimonia* from biblical and patristic texts that provided the basis for the composition of the canons. He also mentions the dogmatic and historical aspects of each of the texts he examines.

While there are many manuscripts containing Gregory's work, those of his successor, Theodore Prodromos, are even more numerous, suggesting that the latter work made the earlier one redundant and replaced it. The distinctive style of Theodore – who had a reputation a century later for being 'the first commentator of the canons' as Nikephoros Blemmydes writes – is apparent throughout his work.[18] Thus, before offering up his interpretation, which tends to view theological matters allegorically, Theodore customarily writes a long *prooimion* about the canon and the feast it accompanies and also uses paired questions and answers in order to clarify difficult and obscure phrases, as well as to foster a better reading.[19] He employs many neologisms – most notably long compound words – and in some cases the text has its own prose metre. Specific references against interpretations proposed 'by some people who stupidly and ridiculously interpret and approach' certain phrases in a different way from himself suggest that he was not unaware of his predecessors and indeed was referring here to Gregory Pardos, whose commentaries he may have used.[20]

[18] 'τῶν ἱερῶν κανόνων πρῶτος σαφηνιστής' (*PG* 142, 541D). There is uncertainty regarding Theodore Prodromos' identification (see *ODB*). On Theodore's commentaries see W. Hörandner, ed., *Theodoros Prodromos. Historische Gedichte* (Vienna, 1974), 44–5. A very poor edition, based only on one manuscript (the Roman Angelicus B. 5.11), was begun in 1888 by Stevenson and Pitra, but never completed. Theodore's commentary is dedicated to a certain *Orphanotrophos* who encouraged him to interpret the canons. This is Alexios Aristenos, Theodore's famous patron, to whom he dedicated a series of poems as well as some letters (PG 133, 1239–92; Theodore Prodromos, 56a.1, 56 b. 7, 56 d. 28, 56 t. 2). See also Kominis, Γρηγόριος Πάρδος, 114, esp. n. 2. On the history and function of the Orphanotropheion, its school and Aristenos' pivotal role there, see T. S. Miller, *The Orphans of Byzantium: Child Welfare in the Christian Empire* (Washington, D. C., 2003), esp. 186–8, 193, 200, 205–6, 244–5.

[19] See e.g. H. Stevenson, ed., *Theodori Prodromi Commentarios in Carmina Sacra Melodorum Cosmae Hierosolymitani et Ioannis Damasceni* (Rome, 1888), 62, where Theodore Prodromos puts ἀπορία with its λύσις in support of the reading πρωτόκτιτον instead of πρωτόκτιστον/πρωτόπλαστον.

[20] Kominis, Γρηγόριος Πάρδος, 112. See Theodore Prodromos' commentary on Kosmas' canon for Christmas, 32: 'some have interpreted this in a most foolish and stupid manner, and, to say the truth, they have completely misinterpreted it' (γελαιότατα (leg. γελοιότατα) καὶ ἀνοήτατά (leg. ἀνοητότατά) τινες ἐξηγήσαντο, καὶ ἀληθέστερον δὲ φάναι, παρεξηγήσαντο).

School Teaching Through the Iambic Canons and Paraphrase

The third of these commentators, Eustathios, wrote his *Exegesis* ('Εξήγησις, or explanation) of the iambic canon of Pentecost after he had left his position as a teacher in Constantinople and assumed the office of bishop of Thessalonike.[21] His was the most extensive treatise ever written that focuses on a single canon.[22] Indicating that the interpretation of the canon was 'a formidable task' ('πρᾶγμα δύσεργον'), Eustathios adds that this work has been neglected by 'all those who very carefully deal with similar texts' ('παρεωραμένου τοῖς τὰ τοιαῦτα μετελθοῦσιν ἐπιμελέστερον'). Yet at the same time he engages with his predecessors' work, opening his *prooimion* with an imitation of the preface of Theodore's commentary: where Theodore writes, 'You seem, O man of God' ("Εοικας, ἄνθρωπε τοῦ θεοῦ'), Eustathios uses, 'You seem, O brother' ("Εοικας, ὦ ἀδελφέ'). In all probability the 'brother' being referred to here was not a fictitious person – despite the author's use of a classic *recusatio* topos – but rather someone who had need of a commentary on this very difficult iambic canon.[23]

Eustathios examines the canon from a number of perspectives using a methodology not dissimilar to that which he employs elsewhere for his Homeric *Parekvolai* (Παρεκβολαί).[24] He edits the text, discussing various readings and selecting the one he believes to be the most appropriate. He provides literal paraphrases of the canon's text. He also emphasises the theological doctrine of the Holy Spirit as well as of the Holy Trinity.[25] Finally, he is the first to initiate a discussion of the iambic canons' authorship, introducing the name of John Arklas as an alternative to

---

[21] S. Ronchey, 'Those "Whose Writings Were Exchanged": John of Damascus, George Choeroboscus and John "Arklas" According to the Prooimion of Eustathius's *Exegesis in Canonem Iambicum de Pentecoste*' in C. Sode and S. Takács, eds., *Novum Millennium, Studies on Byzantine History and Culture, dedicated to Paul Speck* (Aldershot, 2000), 327.

[22] S. Ronchey, 'An Introduction to Eustathios' "Exegesis in Canonem Iambicum"', *DOP*, 45 (1991), 149.

[23] Demetracopoulos, 'The Exegeses', 145. This practice did not cease even after the fall of Constantinople, but remained in use up to the late nineteenth century. Several *Mathemataria* exist which contain asmatic canons with various epimerisms and paraphrases. See A. Skarveli-Nikolopoulou, Τὰ Μαθηματάρια τῶν Ἑλληνικῶν Σχολείων τῆς Τουρκοκρατίας. Διδασκόμενα κείμενα, σχολικὰ προγράμματα, διδακτικὲς μέθοδοι. Συμβολὴ στὴν ἱστορία τῆς νεοελληνικῆς παιδείας (Athens, 1993), 21–31.

[24] Long available only in Mai's edition, A. Mai, ed., *Spicilegium Romanum* (Rome 1841), vol. v, 161–338 (reprinted in *PG* 136, 501–754), based on a single manuscript, Vat. gr. 1409 (thirteenth–fourteenth century), it may now be read in: Eustathios of Thessaloniki, *Exegesis*, eds. Cesaretti and Ronchey.

[25] Ronchey, 'An Introduction', 157. See P. Cesaretti, 'Eustathios' Commentary on the Pentecostal Hymn Ascribed to St. John Damascene: a New Critical Edition', *Svenska Kommittén för Byzantinska Studier Bulletin*, 5 (1987), 19–22; Ronchey, 'An Introduction', 149–58; Ronchey, 'Those "Whose Writings Were Exchanged"', 327–9.

John of Damascus.²⁶ However, Eustathios' position on the matter is somewhat convoluted: there is a *volte-face*, since, despite advancing philological arguments in support of Arklas' and not the Damascene's authorship, Eustathios suggests to his readers that they should continue to treat the canon as if it were written by the Damascene.²⁷ This is indeed what Eustathios himself goes on to do in the body of the commentary proper.

The didactic character of these commentaries is apparent when we observe the phraseology used throughout. Theodore addresses his commentary to a group of listeners: 'You, the listeners who are the most attentive, would have complained to the melodist.'²⁸ Gregory is more explicit, writing: 'May we be worthy of illumination, we all who teach these texts according to our strength and those who study them for the love of God.'²⁹ Eustathios' intention in writing a commentary appears to have been of a similarly pedagogic nature, since the work was intended for a 'friend' ('φίλος') who was also a teacher and who, in all probability, required assistance in teaching others the meaning of the obscure Pentecost iambic canon. It seems likely that these exegetical texts were first delivered as lectures in schools and then, in order to be published, underwent various changes in their style.³⁰ As their rich history of transmission testifies, these texts were widely disseminated for use in schools, with manuscripts often taking the form of interlinear glosses above the canons' text. Students were instructed on how to translate, paraphrase and interpret the canons under discussion.

The Manuscripts of the *Paraphrasis*

Returning to the *Paraphrasis*, we note that Kominis was the first scholar who presented the incipits and desinits of the *Paraphrasis*. In so doing, he followed Vat. gr. 952 (first half of the fifteenth century).³¹ Yet the same corpus of scholia is preserved in at least three other codices: Vindobonensis

---

²⁶ See Eustathios of Thessalonike, *Exegesis*, ed. Cesaretti and Ronchey, 12–13 (proem 125ff).
²⁷ Ibid., 18–19 (prooem 259–80).
²⁸ Τάχα δὲ διεμεμψιμοιρήσασθε τῷ μελῳδῷ οἱ νουνεχέστατοι τῶν ἀκροατῶν. (Prodromos, *Commentarios*, ed. Stevenson, 77).
²⁹ Ἧς καταξιωθείημεν τῆς ἐλλάμψεως, οἵ τε κατὰ δύναμιν ταῦτα διδάσκοντες καὶ οἱ σκοπῷ φιλοθέῳ μανθάνοντες. (Pardos, *Commentary*, ed. Montana, 84.4).
³⁰ Demetracopoulos, 'The Exegeses', 144.
³¹ Kominis in fact followed L. Petit in *DTC*, 9 (1926), 1973. Kominis acknowledges Petit's reference to Ambr. M 15 sup, yet – based on the date of the MS according to A. Martini and D. Bassi, *Catalogus codicum Graecorum Bibliothecae Ambrosianae* (Milan, 1906), vol. I, col. 420–1 (eleventh century) – excludes any possibility of this commentary being identical to the one in Vaticanus gr. 238, which he, therefore, regards as *codex unicus* for the transmission of the Eugenikos

School Teaching Through the Iambic Canons *and* Paraphrase 385

Phil. gr. 183 (fourteenth–fifteenth century), Vindobonensis Phil. gr. 34 (d. 1430) and Oxoniensis D'Orville 113 (sixteenth century).

Below is a description of these codices:

Wa Vindobonensis Phil. gr. 183, fourteenth and fifteenth century; 213/220 × 143/150 mm; ff. 274; paper.[32] The codex transmits miscellaneous texts by numerous authors, such as Maximos Planoudes, Synesios, Gregory of Nazianzos, John Glykys, Manuel Moschopoulos, Philostratos, Leo Choirosphaktes, Michael Synkellos, Makarios Makres, Diodoros, Mark Eugenikos, John Eugenikos, and Bessarion.

The *Paraphrasis of the Three Iambic Canons* is given with interlinear glosses and notes in the margins in the following order:

ff. 234^r–238^r: Christmas canon
ff. 238^r–242^r: Theophany canon
ff. 242^r–246^r: Pentecost canon

Wb Vindobonensis Hist. gr. 34, 1430; 295 × 210/215 mm; ff. 397; paper.[33] Collection of ecclesiastical canons. Matthew Blastares, Anonymous, John IV the Nesteutes, Niketas of Herakleia, Nikephoros, patriarch of Constantinople, John of Kitros, Leo VI, Constantine Doukas, Constantine Harmenopoulos, Philotheos, patriarch of Constantinople, Andronikos II Palaiologos, Petros Chartophylax, Sisinios II, Theodore Balsamon, Athanasios of Alexandria, Photios, Theodore of Stoudios, Neilos Diasorenos, John Phournes, and Nicholas Kabasilas.

The *Paraphrasis* is transmitted with anonymous interlinear glosses and marginal scholia as follows:

ff. 361^{v}v–365^r: Christmas canon
ff. 365^r–368^r: Theophany canon
ff. 368^r–371^r: Pentecost canon

V Vaticanus gr. 952; first half of the fifteenth century; 215 × 140 mm; ff. 194; paper.[34] Miscellaneous texts by various authors such as Maximos

---

commentary. Kominis did not check the text in Ambr. M. 15 sup., which in any case does not transmit the same text.

[32] H. Hunger, *Katalog der griechischen Handschriften der Österreichischen Nationalbibliothek*, (Vienna, 1961–94), vol. 1, 291–3. See also R. S. Stefec, 'Zwischen Urkundenpaläographie und Handschriftenforschung: Kopisten am Patriarchat von Konstantinopel im späten 15. und frühen 16. Jahrhundert', *RSBN*, 50 (2013), 321.

[33] Hunger, *Katalog*, vol. 1, 35–8.

[34] Kominis, Γρηγόριος Πάρδος, 118–19. On the dating of the MS see G. Stickler, *Manuel Philes und seine Psalmenmetaphrase* (Vienna, 1992), 103 and 169. For a description of the MS see also P. Schreiner, 'Appendix: bemerkungen zum Vaticanus gr. 952', *BZ*, 96 (2003), 56–7.

Planoudes; translations of Cato's *Gnomai*; Manuel Philes' poetical paraphrasis on the Psalms. The three iambic canons are accompanied by the *Paraphrasis*, which is attributed to Mark Eugenikos. The *Paraphrasis* is transmitted in the margins and the copyist notes its brevity by adding the following remark: 'it has been explained and commented upon in detail by various authors, but as it is seen here (not in such detail) it has been interpreted by the holiest amongst the monks, Mark, the one truly *Eugenikos* (i.e. noble) in his soul'.[35] It is not clear why and how the name of Eugenikos is given by the copyist.

The *Paraphrasis* is listed as follows:

ff. 18ʳ–23ʳ Christmas canon
ff. 23ʳ–27ᵛ Theophany canon
ff. 28ʳ–33ʳ Pentecost canon

It is the copyist alone (and not the compiler) who attributes the Pentecost canon to John Arklas, 'as some people say', acknowledging that he disagrees with the attribution to the Damascene: 'as some people say (that it is composed) by John of Damascus, while some others by John monk Arklas, and I concur with them'.[36]

O Oxoniensis D'Orville 113; sixteenth century; 140 × 195 mm; ff. 319 [plus 4 blank]; paper.[37] The three iambic canons, various patristic texts by John of Damascus, Ps-Dionysios the Areopagite, as well as the dogmatic

---

[35] ἐξηγηθεὶς μὲν παρὰ διαφόρων πλατύτερον, ὡς ὁρᾶται δὲ ἐνταῦθα, παρὰ τοῦ τιμιωτάτου ἐν μοναχοῖς κυρ(οῦ) Μάρκου τοῦ καὶ κατὰ ψυχὴν τῷ ὄντι εὐγενικοῦ

[36] ὡς τινὲς μὲν λέγουσιν τοῦ ἁγίου Ἰωάννου τοῦ Δαμασκηνοῦ, ἕτεροι δὲ Ἰωάννου μοναχοῦ τοῦ Ἀρκλᾶ, οἷς καὶ ἐγὼ συντίθεμαι.

[37] In 1804 the Bodleian Library purchased in an auction a large collection of Greek and Latin Manuscripts from the library of Jacques Philippe D'Orville (1696–1751). D'Orville came from Amsterdam and taught as Professor of History, Eloquence and Greek there from 1730 to 1742. He collected material in order to edit Greek poetry, especially Theokritos and the *Greek Anthology*. His collection after his death passed to his son, and was then taken to London, sold to J. Cleaver Banks, and finally was bought from him almost intact by the Bodleian Library. For MS D'Orville 113, see also *Catalogue Des Livres De La Bibliotheque De S.A.S. Frédéric-Henri, Prince D'Orange, &c. &c. &c.* (The Hague, 1749), 225.7; F. Madan, et al., *A Summary Catalogue of Western Manuscripts in the Bodleian Library at Oxford which Have Not Hitherto Been Catalogued in the Quarto Series* (Oxford, 1895–1953); reprinted, with corrections in vols. I and VII (Munich, 1980), vol. IV, 37–150 (nos. 16879–17496), esp. 64–5 (no. 16991), and A. D. Renting and J. T. C. Renting-Kuijpers, eds., with notes on the manuscripts by A. S. Korteweg, *The Seventeenth-century Orange-Nassau Library: The Catalogue Compiled by Anthonie Smets in 1686, the 1749 Auction Catalogue, and Other Contemporary Sources* (Utrecht, 1993), 193; cat. no. 568.

definition at the Council of Florence. In some of the texts there are interlinear glosses in Latin.

The *Paraphrasis* is given as follows:

ff. 1^r–7^v: the iambic canon on Christmas
ff. 8^r-14^v: the iambic canon on Theophany
ff. 15^r–22^r: the iambic canon on Pentecost

This manuscript provides the texts of the three iambic canons with both Greek and Latin translations. There are selective interlinear Latin glosses followed by: a) something referred to as a *paraphrasis* (παράφρασις) that is found only in the acrostics and *heirmoi* (είρμοί) and not in the remaining *troparia*; b) the main body of the *Paraphrasis*, here called σύνταξις; and c) an *interpretatio* in Latin. Two interesting issues emerge from the study of this codex. First, that while the text of the *Paraphrasis* is similar to that found in V, Wa, and Wb, it is referred to as a *syntaxis* (σύνταξις) and another text is instead named *paraphrasis* (παράφρασις) – a text that is in fact more like a poetic translation rather than a *syntaxis* since the latter is usually understood as a word-by-word paraphrastic translation.[38] Second, the Latin translation is that edited by Aldus Manutius in 1501–2.[39] It is almost certain that the same copyist added the Latin text and selective glosses at the beginning. When compared with Manutius, however, the Greek text has some informative differences. As such, it is likely that the scribe took only the Latin section from the printed book, copying the remainder from another source that transmitted the canon texts. The copyist attributes all three canons to John of Damascus. Although there is no precise date for the production of this manuscript, the use of the Aldine edition makes 1501–2 a *terminus post quem*.

D'Orville 113 is important as the latest witness to the transmission of the *Paraphrasis*. It is likely to have originated in a bilingual environment, and more research on D'Orville's collection may reveal its provenance. It is clear that D'Orville 113 was intended to instruct people on the meaning of the iambic canons.[40]

---

[38] παράφρασις (in margin) Εὐφημίης δι' ἐπῶν μέλεσι τὰ ἐφύμνια ταῦτα ὑμνεῖ τὸν υἱὸν τοῦ Θεοῦ, τῶν ἀνθρώπων ἕνεκα γεννώμενον κατὰ σάρκα ἐν τῇ γῇ καὶ ἀφανίζοντα τὰ πολλῶν στεναγμῶν ἄξια κακὰ τοῦ κόσμου. Ἀλλ', ὦ ἄναξ, τοὺς ὑμνητὰς σῶζε τούτων τῶν ἐν τῷ κόσμῳ θλίψεων.
[39] A. Manutius, ed., *Poetae Christiani veteres (Prudentii Poetae Opera)* (Venice, 1501), unpaginated.
[40] D'Orville 113 comes from the *Illustre School* at Breda in the south of the Netherlands. On this reformed school, which functioned for just twenty-three years (1646–69), see Renting and Renting-Kuijpers, eds., *The Seventeenth-century Orange-Nassau Library*, 32–3; 45–7, and A. Voss, 'Reformed Orthodoxy in the Netherlands' in H. J. Selderhuis, ed., *A Companion to Reformed Orthodoxy: Brill's*

The collation of the four codices under discussion reveals that they all share more or less the same text. Yet, due to the text's character, namely that it is an interpretation of the canons in paraphrastic form, the copyists felt free to modify and alter some parts. This is especially true in the case of the copyist of V, who does not transmit some of the explanatory remarks given in all other codices.

Wb transmits the best text, although some inaccuracies do occur: see e.g. σεβάσμιον ἀσεπτόν: σεπτὸν καὶ σεβάσμιον cett.; (3.14);[41] βιαία: βιαίως cett. (3.85); ἐθῶν: ἐθνῶν cett. (3.115) ὕμνει σε: ὕμνησε cett. (3.181). Wa has affinities with Wb and thus should be placed within the same family – although it gives some idiosyncratic readings, like ἄφωνον: ἄφθονον cett. (3.17). The copyist of Wa consistently omits the σ of the preposition πρός in compound words, like προλαβών: προσλαβὼν cett. (1.40), προκαλοῦμαι: προσκαλοῦμαι cett. (1.73). Usage of προ is not uncommon in Wb: see e.g. προφέρειν: προσφέρει cett. (1.67). Wa not infrequently gives the text in a synoptic way, with omissions of particles, and changes of word order and phraseology: see e.g. ὅπου ἐξήνθησεν ἡ ἁμαρτία: ὅπου καταπολὺ (leg. κατὰ πολὺ) ἐβλάστησεν, ἐπλεόνασεν ἡ ἁμαρτία O: ὅπου ἐξήνθησε καὶ ἐπλεόνασεν ἡ ἁμαρτία V: ὅπου ἐξήνθησε πλεῖστον ἢ ἐπλεόνασεν ἡ ἁμαρτία Wb (1.68–9).

V has also some anomalies in orthography (σκοντινούς, 1.132), uses abbreviations and condenses certain phrases: see τοῖς ὑμνοῦσί σε: τοῖς περὶ τοὺς θείους ὕμνους ἀναστρεφομένοις cett. (3.4). It also omits certain lines: see 1.137–9 ἐν ἄλλοις... ἤτοι τὴν ἑορτὴν τῶν φώτων cett.; 2.49 δυναστῶν καὶ δαιμόνων Wa: καὶ δυναστῶν δαιμόνων cett.; and 3.18–19 Τὸ δὲ σεπτὸν ... ταυτοσήμαντον ὂν cett. If Wa and Wb share common characteristics, O and V also seem closely related in that they both omit certain notes: for instance, at 2.92–4 the scholion on Lycophron's Alexandra is omitted, and at 116–23: Σημ. Ἄριστα ... λέξιν. O treats the *Paraphrasis* in a freer way, almost seeming to re-paraphrase the text (ἐθεάσατο ὁ πρότερον ἐσκοστισμένος: ὁ πρὶν ἐσκοτισμένος εἶδεν cett. (1.66).

Authorship of the *Paraphrasis*

Save for the one witness, Vat. gr. 952, all the remaining codices contain no indication of authorship, but instead each time transmit the work

---

Companions to the Christian Tradition (Leiden, 2013), 139. D'Orville 113 was bought by P. de Hondt, bookseller at the Hague, in 1749 and later owned by D'Orville.

[41] Unless otherwise stated, numbers 1, 2 and 3 indicate the iambic canons for Christmas, Theophany and Pentecost respectively.

anonymously. This cannot be coincidental and should alert the reader to exercise caution in drawing absolute conclusions about the commentary's authorship, since it is not easy to distinguish its writer or indeed writers. Thus, tempting though it is to attribute this paraphrase to Mark Eugenikos, the evidence remains inconclusive and it is more prudent to speak of the *Paraphrasis* as anonymous.[42]

The author of the *Paraphrasis* does not mention Gregory Pardos by name but does seem to be thoroughly familiar with his work, from which the anonymous author draws, but with which he also occasionally disagrees.[43] A comparison of a noteworthy passage in the two texts shows that our compiler almost entirely based his text on Gregory, using the latter's commentary on the Pentecost extensively. Thus the acrostic of the iambic canon on Pentecost:

> **Θ**ειογενὲς λόγε, πνεῦμα παράκλητον πάλιν ἄλλον
> **Ἐ**κ γενέτου κόλπων ἧκας ἐπιχθονίοις
> **Ο**ἷα πυρὸς γλώσσῃσι φέρον θεότητος ἀΰλου
> **Σ**ῆμα τεῆς φύτλης καὶ χάριν ὑμνοπόλοις.

> Only-begotten Logos of God, You sent from the heart of the Father
> Again to those upon earth another Advocate, the Spirit,
> Bringing, in tongues of fire, the immaterial Godhead's
> Sign of Your Nature and Grace for the chanters.

is interpreted in the following way by Gregory:

> 3. Λόγε Θεοῦ καὶ Πατρός, πρὸ πάντων τῶν αἰώνων γεννηθεὶς ἀρεύστως καὶ ἀπαθῶς ὡς ὁ ἡμέτερος λόγος ἐκ νοῦ, τὸ Πνεῦμα τὸ ἅγιον <u>ἔπεμψας ἡμῖν τοῖς ἐπιγείοις ἀνθρώποις πάλιν ἄλλον παράκλητον</u> ... <u>φέρον θεότητος ἀΰλου σημεῖον τῆς ἰδίας φύσεως καὶ χάριν ἡμῖν τοῖς περὶ τοὺς ὕμνους τοὺς θείους ἀναστρεφομένοις</u>.

> Logos of God and Father, you, who have been begotten before all ages with no change and no passion like our logos from the mind, you sent the Holy Spirit to us earthly humans again another advocate ... Bringing, of the pure, immaterial Godhead, a sign of His own nature and grace for those who are occupied with these divine hymns.[44]

---

[42] For Eugenikos' hymnographical work see Mineva, *Το υμνογραφικό έργο*.
[43] See 3.93–95: ὅθεν ὁ μελῳδὸς πατροσθενοξύμμορφον εἶπεν αὐτὸν τὸν παράκλητον, ὡς ἀνωτέρω συντέτακται, καὶ οὐ τὸν λόγον τοῦ Χριστοῦ, καθ' ἃ τινὲς ὑπειλήφασι and Pardos, *Commentary*, ed. Montana, 44.2. The text of Gregory Pardos' commentaries as it currently survives has been identified as the final text, prepared by the author (Kominis, *Γρηγόριος Πάρδος*, 94 and Demetracopoulos, 'The Exegeses', 149). Disagreement between the *Paraphrasis* and Gregory's *Exegesis* makes it impossible to identify the former as a condensed version of the latter.
[44] Pardos, *Commentary*, ed. Montana, 2–4.3–5.

while our compiler gives the following (I underline the borrowed phrases):

> Ὦ Λόγε, ὁ ἐκ Θεοῦ <u>γεννηθείς</u>, <u>ἔπεμψας τοῖς ἐπιγείοις ἀνθρώποις ἐκ τῶν κόλπων τοῦ Πατρὸς</u> <u>πάλιν ἄλλον παράκλητον</u>, τὸ ἅγιον Πνεῦμα, φέρον ὥσπερ ἐν γλώσσαις πυρὸς τῆς ἀΰλου θεότητος σημεῖον τῆς σῆς φύσεως, καὶ χάριν ἡμῖν τοῖς περὶ τοὺς θείους ὕμνους ἀναστρεφομένοις.

> O Logos, who have been begotten from God, you sent to the earthly humans from the bosom of the Father again another advocate, the Holy Spirit ... Bringing, as in flaming tongues of the immaterial Godhead, a sign of your own nature and grace for those who are occupied with these divine hymns.

By contrast, our compiler does not seem to make use of either Theodore Prodromos (in his *Paraphrasis* for Christmas and Theophany canons, since there is no *Paraphrasis* on the Pentecost canon by Prodromos) or Eustathios (for the *Paraphrasis* on the Pentecost canon).

The compiler's method is primarily concerned with providing various *testimonia* from classical, as well as biblical and patristic texts,[45] incorporating these into his *Paraphrasis*. When uncertain, he uses disjunctive conjunctions (ἤ, εἴτε), or appends additional notes (see e.g. 2.144; 3.116: Σημ<είωσις> or Σημ<είωσαι>), thus offering his readers more than one option. Furthermore, he frequently utilises explanatory conjunctions and particles (such as ἤγουν, εἴτ'οὖν).

Conclusions

The *Paraphrasis* seems to be the last Byzantine product in a series of interpretations of the iambic canons. These commentaries go back to the Komnenian and even earlier periods, as has been shown above. Although we cannot be certain as to when the *Paraphrasis* was composed, our manuscript witnesses point to the fourteenth or fifteenth centuries. Both its context and the method of its construction leave no doubt of its textbook character. The commentator's vocabulary, the interlinear glosses above the canons' texts as well as other interpretative notes, which are always found in the manuscripts transmitting the text of the *Paraphrasis*,

---

[45] For an example concerning a classical text, see the end of the *Paraphrasis* of the 1st troparion of the 6th ode on the Theophany: Εἴληπται δὲ τὰ ἐν τοῖς προτέροις δυσὶ στίχοις ἐκ τοῦ Λυκόφρονος περὶ Ἡρακλέους λέγοντος ὃν ἐκάλουν ἐκεῖνοι τριέσπερον (L. Mascialino, ed., *Lycophronis Alexandra* (Leipzig, 1964), 33–5). From one concerning a religious text, see the *Paraphrasis* of the 1st troparion of the 3rd ode on the Theophany canon: Ὁ ἐμφυτεύσας πρότερον τῇ κτίσει τὸν θάνατον, σχηματισθεὶς εἰς φύσιν *κακούργου καὶ πονηροῦ θηρίου*, τοῦ ὄφεως, ἐπισκοτεῖται (Gen. 3.1).

hint at schoolroom usage. Given the primarily theological nature and the high linguistic register of the text of the iambic canons, it is likely that the *Paraphrasis* was written for teachers and/or students. Finally, it is worth noting that despite the fact that the surviving testimony regarding the text of the *Paraphrasis* is rather limited, since it is transmitted in only four extant codices, the work's indirect impact was widespread, largely due to its ascription to Mark Eugenikos and its connection with the thorny issue of the authorship of the iambic canon on Pentecost.

Further Reading

The main texts: P. Cesaretti and S. Ronchey, eds., *Eustathii Thessalonicensis exegesis in canonem iambicum pentecostalem: recensuerunt indicibusque instruxerunt* (Berlin, 2014); D. Skrekas, 'Studies in the iambic canons attributed to John of Damascus: a critical edition with introduction and commentary', unpublished DPhil thesis, University of Oxford (2008). Studies include: C. G. Conticello and V. Conticello, eds., *La théologie byzantine et sa tradition*, 2 vols. (Turnbout, 2002–15); P. Demetracopoulos, 'The Exegeses of the Canons in the Twelfth Century as School Texts', *Diptycha*, 1 (1979), 143–57.

Appendix

It is beyond the scope of this chapter to offer a complete critical edition of the *Paraphrasis* of the three iambic canons. Instead, what is given here is a *proekdosis* of the ninth ode of the iambic canon on Pentecost. The text of the canon comes from Skrekas, 'Studies in the Iambic Canons', 38–9 and the *Conspectus Siglorum* refers to the complete edition of the entire text of the *Paraphrasis*, which I have prepared for publication. Verbatim quotations from the iambic canon are given in italics.

CONSPECTUS SIGLORUM
CODICES

Wa	Vind. Phil. gr. 183	xiv–xv
Wb	Vind. Hist. gr. 34	1430
V	Vat. gr. 952	xv
O	Oxon. D'Orville 113	xvi

Abbreviationes: Apparatus Criticus

acr.	acrostichis
add.	addidit, addiderunt
al.	manus, alia manus
appar.	apparatus
cett.	ceteri
cf.	confer
cod(d).	codex, codices
cont.	contacium
et seq.	et sequuntur
heirm.	heirmus
in marg.	in margine
lin.	linea

om.	omisit, omiserunt
scr.	scripsit
trad.	tradit, tradunt
trop.	troparium

Editionis Selectio

Ὠδὴ θ′
Εἱρμὸς
Χαίροις, ἄνασσα, μητροπάρθενον κλέος·
Ἅπαν γὰρ εὐδίνητον εὔλαλον στόμα
Ῥητρεῦον οὐ σθένει σὲ μέλπειν ἀξίως·
Ἰλιγγιᾷ δὲ νοῦς ἅπας σου τὸν τόκον
Νοεῖν· ὅθεν σε σὺν φόβῳ δοξάζομεν.   125

Ὕδειν ἔοικε τὴν φυσίζωον κόρην·
Μόνη γὰρ ἐν δίνῃσι κεκρύφει λόγον,
Νοσοῦσαν ἀλθαίνοντα τὴν βροτῶν φύσιν,
Ὃς δεξιοῖς κλισμοῖσι νῦν ἱδρυμένος
Πατρὸς πέπομφε τὴν χάριν τοῦ πνεύματος   130

Ὅσοις ἔπνευσεν ἡ θεόρρυτος χάρις,
Λάμποντες ἀστράπτοντες ἠλλοιωμένοι
Ὀθνείαν ἀλλοίωσιν εὐπρεπεστάτην,
Ἰσοσθενοῦσαν τὴν ἄτμητον εἰδότες
Σοφὴν τρίφεγγον οὐσίαν δοξάζομεν.   135

Hinc editur oda nona ex canone iambico in Pentecosten cum paraphrase.
OVWaWb

126 Ὕδειν] ὑδεῖν O 134 εἰδότες] ἰδότες Wa

Ode 9. Heirm. *Χαίροις, ὦ δέσποινα, κλέος* καὶ ἄκουσμα *μητροπάρθενον· ἅπαν γὰρ στόμα* εὔστροφον καὶ *εὔλαλον, ῥητορεῦον οὐ* δύναται ὑμνεῖν σε ἀξίως. *Ἰλιγγιᾷ δὲ* καὶ ἀτονεῖ *ἅπας νοῦς, νοεῖν σου τὸν* ἀπόρρητον *τόκον. Ὅθεν σε δοξάζομεν* καὶ τιμῶμεν σὺν φόβῳ καὶ εὐλαβείᾳ.

trop. 1. Πρέπει ὑμνεῖν τὴν γεννήσασαν τὴν ζωὴν παρθένον· *μόνη γὰρ ἐν* ταῖς λαγόσι καὶ τοῖς σπλάγχνοις αὐτῆς ἔκρυψε, καὶ ἐβάστασε τὸν Θεὸν Λόγον, ἰατρεύοντα *νοσοῦσαν τὴν τῶν* ἀνθρώπων *φύσιν. Ὃς, ἱδρυμένος* καὶ καθεζόμενος *νῦν ἐν τοῖς δεξιοῖς* θρόνοις *τοῦ Πατρός*, ἔπεμψεν ἡμῖν *τὴν χάριν τοῦ* ἁγίου *Πνεύματος*.

trop. 2. Ἡμεῖς, *ὅσοις ἔπνευσεν ἡ* ἀπὸ Θεοῦ ῥυεῖσα καὶ ἐκχυθεῖσα *χάρις* τοῦ ἁγίου *Πνεύματος, λάμποντες, ἀστράπτοντες, ἀλλοιωθέντες* ἀλλοίωσιν ξένην καὶ παράδοξον, ὡραιοτάτην, γινώσκοντες, ἰσοσθενῆ καὶ ὁμοδύναμον οὖσαν τὴν ἀμέριστον *σοφὴν* τρισυπόστατον μίαν φύσιν, *δοξάζομεν* καὶ τιμῶμεν αὐτήν.

1 in marg. Ο σύνταξις **2–5** εὔστροφον καὶ ... εὐλαβείᾳ] τῶν ἀνθρώπων καὶ ἅπας νοῦς οὐ δυνήσονται ὑμνεῖν σε ἀξίως V **6** in marg. Wa trad. Ἰστέον δὲ ὅτι τὸ κλέος ἐπὶ τῶν θαυμασίων ἀκουσμάτων ἐξαιρέτως λέγεται ὡς ἐν τῷ (τροπαρίῳ)· ἡμεῖς δὲ κλέος οἷον ἀκούομεν οὐδέποτε ἴσμεν. Εἴρηται οὖν κἀνταῦθα πρὸς τὴν θεοτόκον τὸ μητροπάρθενον κλέος. Τί γαρ θαυμασιώτερον ἄκουσμα τοῦ μητέρα καὶ παρθένον τὴν αὐτὴν χρηματίσαι;
5 in marg. Ο σύνταξις | πρέπει] πρέπειν V **9–10** Ὅς, ἱδρυμένος ... θρόνοις] ὅς, καθήμενος ἐν τοῖς θρόνοις V **9** νῦν] om. Wa **11** in marg. Ο σύνταξις ἔπνευσεν] ἐνέπνευσεν OWaWb | ἐκχυθεῖσα correxi ex ἐκχεθεῖσα codd.
13–15 ὡραιοτάτην ... αὐτήν] δοξάζομεν καὶ τιμῶμεν τὴν μίαν τρισυπόστατον φύσιν V

Text and Image

CHAPTER 17

Eros, Literature and the Veroli Casket

Liz James

On the lid of the tenth-century Veroli Casket, a group of youths hurl stones at Europa as, chased by two women, she rides off on her bull; to their right, some naked small boys, erotes or putti, skip through the air while a bearded man (Herakles?) plays the lyre, centaurs play the flute and syrinx and three beardless, plump figures stage an ecstatic dance (Fig. 17.1). The Casket is decorated on all four sides with similar classicising figures, dressed in a version of classical costume, depicted in a neo-classical style and ostensibly making up scenes from classical mythology (Fig. 17.2).[1] On the front, in the left-hand plaque, an eros eyes up an unidentified nude woman through a mask, while another pulls a thorn from her foot and her companion, who we think could perhaps be Hippolytos or Kastor, holds a rearing horse; next to him, a male figure takes a winged horse, surely Pegasus, to drink, while, to the right, a female figure, variously identified as Demeter, Persephone, Hekate or Pirene, looks on. The Sacrifice of Iphigeneia is easily recognised on the right-hand panel, but it nevertheless incorporates two irrelevant figures, usually taken to be Asklepios and Hygeia. On one end of the casket, a 'boy in a basket' hovers above Dionysos and his chariot; on the other, an eros lurks on top of an altar garlanded by snakes while another, wearing what appears to be a brassiere, rides a sea-monster, in the style of Europa and her bull.

---

[1] The Veroli Casket (Victoria and Albert Museum, London, 216-1885) is made up of seven ivory plaques with figural carving framed by bone rosette strips on a wooden core, with metal handles and lock. It is 11.2 cm x 40.5 cm x 16 cm. For more details see, see A. Goldschmidt and K. Weitzmann, *Die byzantinischen Elfenbeinskulpturen des X-XIII. Jahrhunderts, I Kästen* (Berlin, 1930), no. 21; J. Beckwith, *The Veroli Casket* (London, 1962); and the catalogue entries by A. Cutler, 'The Veroli Casket' in H. Evans and W. Wixom, eds., *The Glory of Byzantium: Art and Culture of the Middle Byzantine Era AD 843–1261* (New York, NY, 1997), 230–1, no. 153, and A. Eastmond, 'The Veroli Casket' in R. Cormack and M. Vassiliaki, eds., *Byzantium 330–1453* (London, 2008), 124 and 397, no. 66. A. Cutler, 'On Byzantine Boxes', *JWalt*, 42 (1984–5), 32–47 is an important introduction to boxes and their materials, technique, imagery and subversive elements. I regret having discovered P. Chatterjee, 'Vision, Transformation and the Veroli Casket', *Oxford Art Journal*, 36 (2013), 325–44 too late to include in my discussion.

Fig. 17.1 The Veroli Casket, lid and rear, Victoria and Albert Museum, London (photograph by © Simon Lane)

Fig. 17.2 The Veroli casket, front, Victoria and Albert Museum, London (photograph by © Simon Lane)

On the back, in the left panel erotes kiss and suckle at a female panther, another scrambles onto the back of a deer, one more watches on eagle back. Then, in the right plaque, an amorous couple (sometimes said to be Hippolytos and Phaedra, sometimes Ares and Aphrodite) stand next to erotes re-enacting the Rape of Europa, and then, the final image, a little putto performs a vulgar sexual act on a horse while above him another eros, hovering in mid-air, disappears into a basket, leaving only his naked bottom and waving legs visible.

The images on the Veroli Casket are not unique. Indeed, it has been suggested that the artists of ivory and bone caskets worked from a repertoire of images, assembling the boxes in workshops.[2] Thus Europa appears on a single casket panel also in the Victoria and Albert Museum; another fellating eros is depicted on a detached ivory plaque from a casket now in the Louvre; the so-called 'boy in a basket' is known from late antiquity, as well as being used in other media, including bone and ivory caskets and a twelfth-century silver-gilt perfume brazier now in the Treasury of San Marco.[3] As a group, however, these scenes seem to contradict a traditional reading of Byzantine art that perceives it as solemn, devout and sacred; they are lively, overtly secular and apparently pagan. So how did the Byzantines read and understand them? What comment do they make on Byzantium's relationship with its classical past? To discuss these questions, I shall move the figures conventionally identified as putti or as erotes away from the margins of the casket, where they have often been interpreted as offering a mocking or satiric commentary on the action, to centre stage, to see whether these classicising figures can help us 'read Byzantium', what they might say about the interplay between images and texts, and the role of 'stories', whether depicted, written or transmitted orally.

The imagery on the Veroli Casket has rightly been described as 'eclectic'.[4] Scenes and figures do not appear to form any sort of narrative sequence; our expectation that they should is perhaps an irrelevant one, as I will discuss later. The identity of many of the figures is not clear, and

---

[2] On duplicates in ivory and bone and a discussion of the implications for the production of bone and ivory boxes, see Cutler, 'On Byzantine Boxes', and A. Cutler, '"Ehemals Wien": the Pula Casket and the Interpretation of Multiples in Byzantine Bone and Ivory Carving', *RömHistMitt*, 41 (1999), 117–28.

[3] For visual parallels, see Cutler, 'Veroli Casket', 230. The Victoria and Albert Museum panel is A.541–1910 in the collection; the Louvre panel is discussed and illustrated in A. Guillou and J. Durand eds., *Byzance et les images* (Paris, 1994), 242–3, no. 155A (155B shows a 'boy in the basket'); the perfume brazier is described by M. Da Villa Urbani, 'Perfume Brazier in the Form of a Domed Building' in Cormack and Vassilaki, eds., *Byzantium*, 207 and 423, no. 176.

[4] In the first instance by Cutler, 'Veroli Casket', 230.

where they can be recognised, what we may perceive as extraneous or irrelevant iconographic figures and details are also present, most notably in the stoning of Europa. Consequently, we struggle to read and make sense of it. Erika Simon has, with some justification, interpreted the iconography of the Casket in terms of Nonnos' *Dionysiaka*, suggesting that the confusion therefore is part of some Dionysiac celebration of pleasure and chaos.[5] Anthony Cutler has seen a comedic element in the decoration of bone and ivory caskets and on the Veroli Casket specifically in the parodying of ancient coin types in the profile heads on the lid.[6] Eunice and Henry Maguire discussed the humour, irreverence and satiric nature of some of the figures and suggested that the humour and the lack of inscriptions on the Casket served to disarm the pagan, classicising subject-matter, making it palatable for a Christian audience.[7] Antony Eastmond proposed that the images might provide a classical sanction for the more irreverent side of court life.[8] Coupled with the confusing nature of the iconography are issues of function – we do not know what the box was used for – and patronage – we do not know who commissioned or owned it. More information in both these areas would certainly make a difference in our reading of the imagery. As it is, we are left to consider the potential meanings of the iconography in something of a void.

It is, however, an unrealistic expectation that tenth-century Byzantines should either have intended or wished to reproduce classical iconography precisely. We do know that it was easy for the Byzantines to make up good stories explaining the meaning of the images around them.[9] If they could invent stories, then there is no reason that they could not invent images too, and even create stories to go with the made-up images.[10] That the Veroli Casket got the myth of Europa 'wrong' and that the scenes on it cannot be identified may be because the Byzantine audience was not interested in reading the 'true' story as we define it. Instead, the Veroli Casket gives an image of a distant world, peopled with figures doing all

---

[5] E. Simon, 'Nonnos und das Elfenbeinkästchen aus Veroli', *JDAI*, 79 (1964), 279–336.

[6] Cutler, 'On Byzantine Boxes', and Cutler, 'Veroli Casket'.

[7] E. D. Maguire and H. Maguire, *Other Icons: Art and Power in Byzantine Secular Culture* (Princeton, 2007), 160.

[8] Eastmond, 'Veroli Casket', 397.

[9] For examples of these stories, see the *Parastaseis Syntomoi Chronikai*: A. Cameron and J. Herrin, eds., *Constantinople in the Early Eighth Century: The Parasataseis Syntomoi Chronikai* (Leiden, 1984); and the *Patria*: T. Preger, ed., *Scriptores originum Constantinopolitanarum* (Leipzig, 1901–7); A. Berger, *Accounts of Medieval Constantinople. The Patria* (Washington, D. C., 2013).

[10] D. Kinney, 'The King, the Horse and the Cuckoo: Medieval Narrations of the Statue of Marcus Aurelius', *Word and Image*, 18 (2004), 372–98.

Eros, Literature and the Veroli Casket 401

sorts of unlikely things (was Europa being stoned any more unlikely than her riding a bull?), one that bore a tangential relationship to classical mythology, but a classical mythology that had been filtered through centuries of Byzantine Christian culture, in which fidelity to the classical original was not terribly important. It may be that the figures on the Veroli Casket masquerade as characters from classical myth, shown not as the actual characters but playing at being characters.[11] In this context, it is conceivable that the iconography of the Veroli Casket was an invented iconography to fit an invented story, or perhaps no story at all. Why should there be a narrative? Is this our expectation rather than a Byzantine one? Instead of a narrative, is the Casket's imagery developed around a specific theme, one in which the erotes play an intrinsic part?

Small, naked plump boyish figures feature throughout the imagery of the Casket, visible in all but one of the panels.[12] They are generally described in the scholarly literature as 'erotes' or as 'putti'. These labels are confusing. Though the erotes might be expected to be winged and carry bows and arrows, as is the traditional iconography of Eros or Cupid, those identified in this way on the Veroli Casket tend not to have any such attributes. 'Putto' is an even more misleading term. It is clearly anachronistic; it is our tag derived from Renaissance art, and it comes laden with all the baggage of that field of study.[13] Nevertheless, 'erotes' and 'putti' are often used interchangeably, along with more generic phrases such as 'boys' or 'youths', and almost automatically by art historians to describe the nude, chubby lads found in a variety of genres of Byzantine art.[14] The choice of word is very often determined less by the appearance of the figures and more by the wish of the art historian to establish pagan classical models for them. There is a level of vagueness in this: if a classical or classicising scene can be identified, then the figures are taken as representing the protagonists of that scene; if, however, the figures cannot be identified, then, if they are nude and male, they tend to be labelled

---

[11] A. Papagiannaki, 'Aphrodite in Late Antique and Medieval Byzantium' in A. C. Smith and S. Pickup, eds., *Brill's Companion to Aphrodite* (Leiden, 2010), 321–46. Papagiannaki suggests that the putti may have been reminiscent of mimes, though it is unclear what tenth-century theatrical displays were like: R. Webb, *Demons and Dancers: Performance in Late Antiquity* (Cambridge, MA, 2008).
[12] The exception is the plaque with the Sacrifice of Iphigeneia on the front right. For the physical characteristics of these boys as indicating a form of idealised beauty, see M. Hatzaki, *Beauty and the Male Body in Byzantium: Perceptions and Representations in Art and Text* (Basingstoke, 2009), 111.
[13] See C. Dempsey, *Inventing the Renaissance Putto* (Chapel Hill, NC, 2001).
[14] See, for example, the index to Maguire and Maguire, *Other Icons*, where 'boys/youths', 'eros/erotes' and 'putti' are cross-referenced.

'erotes' or 'putti'.[15] 'Eros' tends to be the default position for such images. There is a further measure of circularity here for if a figure is perceived as profane and comedic, it is more likely to be described in the scholarly literature as an eros. As a result, the ways in which and the reasons why certain figures are identified as putti or erotes often say more about art historians than they do about clear-cut definitions. Indeed, in general, the use of the term seems determined less by the appearance of the figure and more by the wish of art historians to establish pagan classical models for Byzantine works of art.

Related to concerns about the art historical labelling of such figures is the question of how to read them. The erotes depicted on the Veroli Casket typify in many ways how these figures have generally been understood in Byzantine art. Erotes are regularly interpreted as figures that both mock and provoke mockery.[16] Their presence in a scene is said to lend an air of travesty or satire, especially when that scene is related to classical myth, as with the stone-throwers in the Europa scene on the Veroli Casket. The presence of figures hurling stones at Europa or performing fellatio on a horse shows an inversion of decorum, and this is perceived as a typical aspect of erotes. In this context of irreverence and mockery, the nudity of the erotes is seen to add to the humour in an almost ribald way, creating a shameful pagan image.[17] Such figures are also seen as undercutting pagan imagery through the use of undignified juxtapositions: the 'boy and the basket' pictured next to the Dionysiac procession at the end of the casket, for example, or the masked eros and the standing woman on its front.[18] In these readings, erotes are perceived as located outside the social order, threatening or creating disorder; they may invert the natural order, but they play out their scenes on the edge of the main drama.[19]

---

[15] For example, K. Weitzmann, *Greek Mythology in Byzantine Art* (Princeton, 1984), 134 and figs. 17 and 18, where figures are identified as from myth if their actions appear identifiable and as putti if not.

[16] In this context, Dempsey, *Renaissance Putto*, sees Renaissance putti as representations of fecklessness and the joy of infancy with no sense of right or wrong; as perfect symbols for uncontrollable sensations and irrational physical and mental alterations that happen unbidden in the body, such as sudden fright or being moved by music.

[17] On nudity as shameful and pagan, see Maguire and Maguire, *Other Icons*, 106; for nudity and mockery, 109–20. Also on nudity, see B. Zeitler, '*Ostentatio Genitalium:* Displays of Nudity in Byzantium' in L. James, ed., *Desire and Denial in Byzantium* (Aldershot, 1999), 185–204; H. Maguire, 'Other Icons: The Classical Nude in Byzantine Bone and Ivory Carvings', *JWalt*, 62 (2004), 9–20.

[18] For inversion of decorum, Maguire and Maguire, *Other Icons*, 145, 149. Papagiannaki, 'Aphrodite', 242–6, suggests that the scene of the masked eros and the woman was part of a theatrical play.

[19] Maguire and Maguire, *Other Icons*, 160.

Interpretations of Byzantine classicism derive from the concept of a tenth-century 'Macedonian Renaissance', the period to which most surviving Byzantine neo-classical art belongs. It has been argued that the tenth century saw a conscious renaissance, perhaps led by Constantine VII Porphyrogennetos, a deliberate revival of classical styles and values by artists and patrons.[20] Although the term 'renaissance' is widely discarded now because of its misleading analogy with fifteenth-century humanistic Italy and its emphasis on ideas of 'genius' and the evolution of art, attitudes to the Byzantine classical tradition in art tend still to be dominated by the legacy of Kurt Weitzmann, who argued that the only good Byzantine art was that which could be traced back to a (usually lost) classical prototype.[21] Classicism in Byzantine art is thus often considered in terms of how it reflects Byzantine fidelity, or otherwise, to its classical heritage, rather than considering what it might have meant in the Byzantines' own terms.

Classicism in tenth-century Byzantine art was not necessarily an indicator of an interest in the classical past or a return to classical artistic values. Rather, as John Hanson has argued, classical style might have been as much about the tenth-century present as about the fifth-century BCE past, if not more.[22] If so, it is possible to come up with a range of possible scenarios in which a classical revival might have served as a way of exoticising art, as was the case with Chinoiserie or Japonaisism in eighteenth- and nineteenth-century Britain, or as a means of making it possible to show unusual or illicit subject-matter in an acceptable fashion, as the Casket does, making it distinct from 'everyday' art. An interest in classical art forms may have reflected issues of education, fashion and taste. In the case of bone and ivory boxes, which may not have been particularly high-status objects, that taste may have been an aspirational taste, the tenth-century equivalent of Josiah Wedgwood's jasperware. Similarly, as Cyril and Marlia Mango have suggested in the context of cameos, Byzantine artists and audiences were concerned with the rich decorative effect of such

---

[20] See K. Weitzmann, *Illustrations in Roll and Codex: A Study in the Origin and Method of Text Illustration* (Princeton, 1947); Weitzmann, *Greek Mythology*.

[21] Weitzmann, *Illustrations in Roll and Codex*. J. Hanson, 'The Rise and Fall of the Macedonian Renaissance' in L. James, ed., *A Companion to Byzantium* (Oxford, 2010), 338–50. Beckwith, *Veroli Casket*, is concerned almost exclusively with the possible classical models for the imagery of the Casket.

[22] J. Hanson, 'Erotic Imagery on Byzantine Ivory Caskets' in James, ed., *Desire and Denial*, 173–84, and Hanson, 'Rise and Fall'; also H. Maguire, 'Epigrams, Art and the "Macedonian Renaissance"', *DOP*, 48 (1994), 105–15.

imagery rather than its iconography.[23] The classicising imagery of the Veroli Casket was perhaps perceived neither as ribald nor pagan, but rather glamorous, fashionable and mysterious, not as a copy of antique models but images in the manner of the classical world read through the filter of Byzantium.

In this tenth-century context, Constantine of Rhodes' poem on the columns and statues of the city is worth considering.[24] In it, Constantine described two classical pagan works of art, the Gigantomachy on the gate of the Senate House and the statue of Athena next to it.[25] He also described the Anemodoulion, a monumental bronze weather-vane that he ascribed to the time of Theodosios I (379–95) depicting erotes and personifications of the winds, classicising and pagan in form, if not actually classical.[26] In Constantine's poem, the gate, brought from the Temple of Artemis in Ephesus where it had been made at 'the time of the dark error of idolatry', displayed the 'errors' of the 'foolish Hellenes' and was brought to the city as 'a plaything for the city/and a toy for children and a butt of men's laughter',[27] while the statue of Athena from Lindos, though beautiful, was a 'deceit' created by 'madmen'.[28] These comments, evoking as they do Eusebios' remarks on the pagan statues brought by Constantine I to Constantinople as 'toys for the laughter and amusement of the spectators', might imply a view of classical art as needing mockery and disparagement.[29] But the Anemodoulion with its nude erotes, potentially just as classical, was described differently. It was a 'wonder' and an 'exceptional' work of sculpture, one greatly admired by the poet.[30] Whether this differentiation represented an awareness of a division

---

[23] C. Mango and M. Mundell Mango, 'Cameos in Byzantium' in M. Henig and M. Vickers, eds., *Cameos in Context* (Oxford, 1993), 57.

[24] See L. James, ed., *Constantine of Rhodes: On Constantinople and the Church of the Holy Apostles* (Farnham, 2012), with a new edition of the Greek text by I. Vassis. For Constantine the Rhodian, also see G. Downey, 'Constantine the Rhodian: his Life and Writings' in K. Weitzmann, ed., *Late Classical and Mediaeval Studies in Honor of A. M. Friend, Jr.* (Princeton, 1955), 212–21.

[25] Constantine of Rhodes, *On Constantinople*, ed. James, 26–31.125–62.

[26] R. Janin, *Constantinople Byzantine: dévelopement urbain et répertoire topographique* (Paris, 1964), 100; A. Berger, *Untersuchungen zu den Patria Konstantinupoleos* (Bonn, 1988), 313–14. A reconstruction of the monument is found at www.byzantium1200.com/tetrapylon.html (accessed 22 December 2017).

[27] Constantine of Rhodes, *On Constantinople*, ed. James, 28–9.151–2.

[28] 'Errors' of the 'foolish' Hellenes is at line 147; 'deceit' is line 156; and 'madmen' line 161.

[29] F. Winkelmann, ed., *Eusebius Werke. Über das Leben des Kaisers Konstantin* (Berlin, 1975), 108 (III.54.3); A. M. Cameron and S. G. Hall, trans., *Eusebius: Life of Constantine* (Oxford, 1999), 143. On disclaimers, see H. Maguire, 'The Profane Aesthetic in Byzantine Art and Literature', *DOP*, 53 (1999), 189–205, esp. 204.

[30] Constantine of Rhodes, *On Constantinople*, ed. James, 30–3.178 and 185–6.

between pieces re-used from the pagan world (the Gigantomachy and the statue) and a piece made for a Christian emperor, whether Constantine was distinguishing between images of the gods and images of personifications cannot be proved. However, his two contrasting accounts suggest it was the ascription of origin for works of art that determined their classical referents in Byzantium, rather than their style. In other words, classicising style – the appearance of a work of art – need not have referred to paganism in Byzantine minds in the tenth century, but a known classical context, such as a supposed original location in a pagan temple, might. If so, the iconography of the Veroli Casket, as the work of a Christian artist for a Christian patron, may not have been perceived as 'pagan' in the same way that the Athena of Lindos was and therefore its classicising iconography may not have needed undermining or excusing through a satiric subtext of erotes.

If the erotes were not necessarily mocking figures, then what were they? There was a long tradition in Hellenic and Roman art of the depiction of the boyish figure of Eros, winged and armed, and of his siblings, Anteros, Pothos and Himeros.[31] Derivatives of these figures, not always winged and not always armed, were portrayed in various media, from stone sculpture, notably sarcophagi, and mosaics and painting to smaller-scale bone and ivory carvings.[32] These nude boys were shown engaged in activities ranging from chariot-racing and gladiatorial combats to fishing, and were used to represent figures as diverse as the Seasons and Herakles.[33] They could be used in scenes as varied as the bacchic and the funerary, and sometimes in both together, as on the fourth-century sarcophagus of Constantina now in the Vatican Museum.[34] They also featured in scenes

---

[31] See D. K. Hill, 'Bacchic Erotes at Tarentum', *Hesperia*, 16 (1947), 248–55, and her remarks at 255 about problems in the written sources. For Roman putti, the key reference is R. Stuveras, *Le putto dans l'art romain* (Brussels, 1969). Otherwise there are various discussions of specific monuments or motifs (W. Deonna, 'Eros jouant avec un masque de Silene', *RA*, 3 (1916), 3–256). I am very grateful to Janet Huskisson for her advice.

[32] See the detailed account of Stuveras, *Le putto*. Mosaics include the third-century example from Antioch depicting erotes fishing, now in the Dumbarton Oaks collection: BZ.1940.64 and *Handbook of the Dumbarton Oaks Collection, Harvard University* (Washington, D. C., 1967), 102, no. 346. Sarcophagi include examples such as the Season sarcophagus, also at Dumbarton Oaks: BZ.1936.65 and G. M. A. Hanfmann, *The Season Sarcophagus in Dumbarton Oaks* (Cambridge, MA, 1951); for bone and ivory carvings, see L. Marangou's catalogue of the Benaki Collection, L. Marangou, *Bone Carvings from Egypt* (Tübingen, 1976).

[33] See the examples in Stuveras, *Le putto*; Marangou, *Bone Carvings*.

[34] Illustrated, among other places, in J. Beckwith, *Early Christian and Byzantine Art* (London, 1970, 2nd edn. 1979), 30, pl. 14.

depicting lovers, both adulterous and faithful, and in company with Aphrodite.[35] Their images continued to appear in late antique and early Christian art, for example in the ambulatory mosaics of Sta Costanza in Rome, where they are depicted harvesting grapes, and in ivory and bone plaques into at least the seventh century.[36] They have even been understood as influencing the depiction of angels in Christian art.[37]

Textual references to erotes stress their appearance in contexts related to love and the experience of love, and this seems to imply that to label the figures as 'erotes', they need to be read in a visual context in which 'love' played a part. In this context of 'love', such figures were not particularly or necessarily transgressive or satirical. Rather, as erotes, they depicted the forces of love/Love, personified as Eros. Love's forces could be destructive and dangerous with the potential to upset the natural order. An epigram in the *Planudean Anthology* concluded, 'What shall men's strength avail when Love (Ἔρως) has stormed heaven and Cypris has despoiled the Immortals of their arms!'[38] and Moschos described the paradoxes of Eros: 'Evil is his heart but sweet his speech ... His hands are tiny but they shoot far ... All about him is savage ... If you catch him, bring him bound and have no mercy on him.'[39] *Digenes Akrites* takes the power of love as a central theme, able to torture lovers and enslave good sense.[40] Love, however, could also be depicted in a paradisiacal, sylvan setting. Philostratos' account of a 'painting' of erotes in his *Imagines* locates them in an orchard gathering apples, wrestling and hunting a hare, all scenes carrying a double meaning in the context of the pursuit of love and creating the image of a playful, unreal world.[41] It seems fair to say that the implications of erotes for their Hellenistic and Roman audiences involved a perception of the forces of love, as the word itself implied.

---

[35] Stuveras, *Le putto*, takes as his subdivisions of categories bacchic, funerary, decorative, genre, Cupid, playing games, with Aphrodite, in the divine world and with the sea, ultimately concluding that erotes are impossible to pin down as motifs.

[36] For Sta Costanza, see W. Oakeshott, *The Mosaics of Rome* (New York, NY, 1967), 61–4; bone plaques discussed in Marangou, *Bone Carvings*.

[37] Hatzaki, *Beauty and the Male Body in Byzantium*, 111–15.

[38] *Planudean Anthology*, no. 214: text and trans. in W. R. Paton, ed., *The Greek Anthology* (London, 1915), vol. v, 286–7

[39] Moschos in the *Greek Anthology*, IX, 440; Paton, ed., *Greek Anthology*, vol. III, 244–7

[40] E. M. Jeffreys, ed. and trans., *Digenis Akritis: The Grottaferrata and Escorial Versions* (Cambridge, 2004), 44–5 (G III.1–8) and 86–7 (G IV.342).

[41] A. Fairbanks, ed., *Philostratus the Elder and the Younger, Imagines; Callistratus, Descriptions* (New York, NY, 1969), 20–9 (*Imagines* 1.6). The translation uses 'cupid' as the translation for eros in this passage, as also at 64–9 (*Imagines* 1.16), reserving Eros for the god of love.

What then of Byzantine views? Constantine of Rhodes' account of the Anemodoulion describes it as

> a four-legged structure full of wonder, fitted with four brazen sides
> adorned on all sides both with carved creatures
> and tendrils bursting with fruits and small pomegranates.
> Naked Erotes entangled in vines
> stand there smiling sweetly
> and laughing from on high at those below;
> in contrast, other youths, kneeling,
> blow out the winds through bronze trumpets,
> one the west wind, and again another the south.
> At the summit of this, a monstrous creature made of bronze
> with bronze wings being blown around
> depicts the sharp blasts of the winds,
> all the gales that blow towards the city.[42]

Constantine, of all tenth-century Byzantine writers, might have had some claim to knowing how the classical world had spoken of Eros and erotes for he was almost certainly Redactor J of the *Palatine Anthology* and thus familiar with many of the epigrams on *eros* contained within it.[43]

The thirteenth-century author Niketas Choniates also described the erotes on the Anemodoulion. It appears first in his *History* as a monument near to which Andronikos I Komnenos erected a statue of himself. Here, it is described as a four-sided bronze monument on which nude erotes were represented pelting one another with apples.[44] Choniates gives a longer

---

[42] Constantine of Rhodes, *On Constantinople*, ed. James, 30–3.185–99.

> ἀγαλματουργῶν ἔργον ἐξῃρημένον,
> τετρασκελὲς τέχνασμα θαύματος πλέον,
> πλευραῖς χαλκαῖς τέτρασι καθηρμοσμένον
> ζῴοις τε πλαστοῖς πάντοθεν κεκασμένον
> βλαστοῖσι καρπῶν καὶ ῥοΐσκων ἐμπλέοις.
> Γυμνοί τ' Ἔρωτες ἐμπλακέντες ἀμπέλοις
> ἑστᾶσιν αὐτοῦ προσγελῶντες ἡμέρως
> καὶ τοῖς κάτωθεν ἐγγελῶντες ὑψόθεν
> ἄλλοι τ' ἐποκλάζοντες ἔμπαλιν νέοι
> σάλπιγξι χαλκαῖς προσφυσῶσιν ἀνέμους,
> ζέφυρον ἄλλος, ἄλλος αὖ πάλιν νότον.
> Ἐφ' οὗπερ ὕψει χαλκοσύνθετον τέρας
> πτέρυξι χαλκαῖς προσφυσώμενον κύκλῳ
> πνοὰς λιγείας ζωγραφεῖ τῶν ἀνέμων,
> ὅσας ἀῇται προσφυσῶσιν εἰς πόλιν.

[43] Downey, 'Constantine the Rhodian'; A. D. E. Cameron, *The Greek Anthology from Meleager to Planudes* (Oxford, 1993); M. D. Lauxtermann, *Byzantine Poetry from Pisides to Geometres: Texts and Contexts* (Vienna, 2003), vol. I, 116–17.

[44] J.-L. van Dieten, ed., *Niketae Choniatae. Historia* (Berlin, 1975), 332–3.

description in his account of the monuments destroyed by the Crusaders after the Sack of Constantinople in 1204:

> Every melodious bird singing its spring songs was carved there, farmers' labours, pipes and milk-pails, bleating sheep and bounding lambs were depicted there. Also the open sea was spread out and schools of fish could be seen, some being caught and some overcoming the nets and dashing free back into the deep sea. Groups of two and three Erotes [were there], armed against each other, naked of clothing, being hit by and throwing apples, and shaking with sweet laughter. This four-sided object, ending in a pointed form like a pyramid, had a female figure suspended from above which turned round with the first stirrings of the winds whence it was called a wind slave [Anemodoulion].[45]

The two accounts share similarities: the Anemodoulion was a pyramid with bronze sides, adorned with carvings and a female figure atop the whole. However, Choniates adds additional details: birds, animals and fish; labouring figures; and erotes pelting each other with apples. Both authors give a picture of naked, laughing erotes, entangled in vines or pelting one another with apples.[46] The nudity of the erotes is not described in a negative, shameful or mocking fashion; there is no sense of slapstick humour or travesty or disorder. These are not transgressive, satiric figures, but joyous and playful ones, like those of Philostratos. Nor do the erotes conspicuously undercut pagan imagery. Indeed, the reverse may be true. Choniates' scene of apple-throwing erotes was one with a respectable classical precedent in Philostratos, a precedent that underlined the erotes as personifications of the forces of love.[47]

For both writers, the Anemodoulion glorified and beautified Constantinople. Constantine's Anemodoulion is one of his seven wonders. Choniates' text is, in part, an elegy for the lost glories of Constantinople, one in which the knowledge and appreciation of the Byzantines for their art is contrasted with the brute ignorance of the Latins, and where images from the past, which are actually a mixture of classical and late antique, are seen

---

[45] Choniates, *Historia*, ed. van Dieten, 648–9, trans. by B. Bjørnholt and used with her permission and my emendments.
[46] See also Maguire and Maguire, *Other Icons*, 119.
[47] Philostratos, ed. Fairbanks, 20–9 (*Imagines*, 1.6). Philostratos explains the relationships between the scenes of erotes that he describes and different types and stages of love, though Choniates does not. The resemblance to Philostratos does not include textual similarities of vocabulary beyond 'erotes' and 'mela'. Another Byzantine source to mention erotes is Nikephoros Basilakes' *prosopoiia* of the gardener and the cypress tree, where the gardener can imagine his apples in a painting being collected by erotes. See A. Pignani, ed., *Niceforo Basilace. Progimnasmi e monodie* (Naples, 1983), 225–8 and 364–6. I am grateful to Ruth Webb for this observation.

as vital parts of the Byzantines' own Roman heritage.[48] The statues described by Choniates serve as manifestations of civilisation, learning and culture against the brutal destructiveness of the uncultured and unlettered barbarian westerners. This art was a symbol of the values and beauties of his world rather than any comment on the classical past. In the context of civic pride and culture that both Constantine and Choniates imply, it seems implausible that the erotes were perceived as harbingers of disorder and chaos.

Later literary texts offer a similar sense of the place of the erotes in Byzantium. In Manganeios Prodromos' twelfth-century poem describing the *sebastokratorissa* Eirene's tent, the tent is said to be decorated with erotes playing music, with satyrs, nereids and muses joining in the dance, and with birds and foxes playing and dancing too.[49] These erotes must be close to the erotes of the Anemodoulion, for the *sebastokratorissa*'s tent was surely not a place for subversive, comedic or even indecorous imagery, especially in the light of what is known of Eirene.[50] It is hard to imagine that the satyrs and erotes were shown seducing horses on the tent; it is easier to conceive of them as involved in the sort of dancing shown to the right of the Rape of Europa on the Veroli Casket. Prodromos' description fits the pattern of erotes 'having a good time' but it also creates a fantasy scene peopled by mythological figures, a setting like that of Philostratos and of the Anemodoulion, a 'looking-glass world' set in a classical landscape.[51] The account of the imagery of the tent also echoes the theme of 'love' in its various manifestations: the erotes are one indication; the satyrs too may have illustrated the power Eros had over gods and humans alike.[52] This imaginary, pseudo-classical world of the Casket and of the tent has a

---

[48] A. Cutler, 'The *De Signis* of Nicetas Choniates: a Reappraisal', *AJA*, 72 (1968), 113–18. For the Byzantines as Romans, see A. Kaldellis, *Hellenism in Byzantium: The Transformation of Greek Identity and the Reception of the Classical Tradition* (Cambridge, 2007).

[49] J. C. Anderson and M. J. Jeffreys, 'The Decoration of the *Sebastokratorissa*'s Tent', *Byzantion*, 64 (1994), 8–18. Anderson and Jeffreys make comparisons between the text and ivory boxes to show similarities in iconography across media, but they do not comment specifically on the presence of the erotes, except to suggest that they represent children (16). See also Margaret Mullett's contribution to this volume.

[50] On Eirene, her piety and personality, see E. M. Jeffreys, 'The *Sevastokratorissa* Eirene as a Literary Patroness: the Monk Iakovos', *JÖB*, 32 (1982), 63–71, and M. J. Jeffreys and E. M. Jeffreys, 'Who was Eirene the Sevastokratorissa?', *Byzantion*, 64 (1994), 40–68.

[51] M. E. Mullett, 'The Classical Tradition in the Byzantine Letter' in M. E. Mullett and R. Scott, eds., *Byzantium and the Classical Tradition* (Birmingham, 1981), 75, uses 'looking-glass world' and 'classical landscape' in the context of Byzantine letters but notes that an artificial classical world should not be confined to epistolography.

[52] Anderson and Jeffreys, '*Sebastokratorissa*'s Tent', 16, citing an image in the eleventh-century copy of the *Cynegetica*, Venice, Marc. gr. 479, fol. 33.

further literary parallel, for the twelfth-century romances set up a very similar sort of perception of a lost classicising past in which Hysmine and Hysminias live in Aulikomis and Eurykomis, and Hysminias can be sent as a herald for the festival of Zeus. Just as the romances created a classicising fantasy, hazily reminiscent of the classical past, so too do the classicising images of the Veroli Casket.[53]

Although no actual images of figures identified as erotes survive from the art of the twelfth century, the romances also reveal that aspect of the erotes apparent in Philostratos and the epigrams of the *Palatine* and *Planudean Anthologies*: the disturbing power of Eros. Eros as god of love was used by Christian writers as an allegory of love, and both *eros* and *agape* could express the positive and negative qualities of love.[54] As Paul Magdalino has shown, King Eros was the ruler of physical love, and *eros* was not a wishy-washy emotion but a physical sexual passion, the love that perhaps dared not speak its name in Byzantium, but which was nevertheless very much alive in the romances.[55] In *Rhodanthe and Dosikles*, Eros shoots his arrows to enflame; in *Drosilla and Charikles*, Eros speaks to love and the burning pains of love; in *Hysmine and Hysminias*, erotes are used most explicitly of all, dancing, sporting and teaching games of love. It is in *Hysmine and Hysminias* that a painting of King Eros is described: naked, with wings instead of feet, holding a torch and a bow, and with a two-edged sword, he seems a composite of a pagan genius and a Christian angel.[56] He is served by Day and Night and surrounded by the months. Eros and the erotes are not comic, mocking figures here. King Eros is all-powerful and needs to be taken very seriously indeed. In the romances, scorning love, or underestimating its power, ends in tears, heartbreak, separation, kidnap and danger. Elsewhere, Elizabeth Jeffreys has

---

[53] As Elizabeth Jeffreys notes in her translation and commentary on *Hysmine and Hysminias*. I am very grateful to her for allowing me to read and use her translations of the three novels, *Rhodanthe and Dosikles, Drosilla and Charikles* and *Hysmine and Hysminias*, now published as *Four Byzantine Novels* (Liverpool, 2012), and for her thoughts on erotes. Cutler, 'On Byzantine Boxes', 46, makes a similar association, as does Hanson, 'Erotic Imagery', 181–2.

[54] 'Love' in A. Kazhdan et al., eds., *ODB* (Oxford, 1991), vol. II, 1254–5; A. M. Cameron, 'Sacred and Profane Love: Thoughts on Byzantine Gender' in L. James, ed., *Women, Men and Eunuchs: Gender in Byzantium* (London, 1997), 1–23, esp. 8–12 on the appropriation of *eros* by Christian authors.

[55] C. Cupane, '*Eros Basileus*: la figura di Eros nel romanzo bizantino d'amore', *Atti dell' Academia di Scienze, Lettere e Arti di Palermo*, 33 (1973–4), 243–97; P. Magdalino, 'Eros the King and the King of Amours: Some Observations on "Hysmine and Hysminias"', *DOP*, 46 (1992), 197–204.

[56] *Hysmine and Hysminias*, ed. Jeffreys, 188–90 (11.7.2–11.3); Hatzaki, *Beauty and the Male Body*, 111–15. On descriptions of art in the novels, see P. Chatterjee, 'Viewing and Description in *Hysmine and Hysminias*: the Fresco of the Virtues', *DOP*, 67 (2013), 209–25.

commented on a poem by Manganeios Prodromos describing the brocade dress as worn by the young granddaughter of the *sebastokratorissa* Eirene with a pattern of archers with arrows pointing to her breast and thigh, and suggested that these archers should be seen as erotes.[57]

It was surely erotes such as these that the twelfth-century canonist Theodore Balsamon fulminated against in his comment on Canon 100 of the Council of Trullo: '[C]ertain persons who were consumed by erotic desires and were indifferent to their manner of life represented erotes and other abominable things on panels and on walls and in other media, so that they might satisfy their carnal desires by the sight of them.'[58] Balsamon's comment suggests that such images existed outside the romances and, as John Hanson has previously argued, there seems no reason not to read eros as passion into the imagery of ivory and bone caskets.[59] Love, as an unbridled sexual force, might very well cause individuals to act in unmannerly ways, just as effectively as Dionysiac excess.

However, erotes also feature in written sources about another facet of love, namely marriage. Menander Rhetor's treatises on rhetoric influenced Byzantine authors of all periods. In his account of the epithalamion, the wedding speech, Menander emphasised the place of erotes: in the prooemion, as a 'pleasing thought appropriate to the subject'; and in the description of the bridal chamber, where they wait, 'their bows drawn, stringing their arrows, the tips ready smeared with the ointment of desire'. Menander also notes that Eros himself should be present throughout the speech.[60] Erotes seem to have been present at Byzantine weddings as diverse as the double wedding of the sons of Anna Komnene and Nikephoros Bryennios, and the *adventus* looking like a wedding procession of the governor of Boleron in the satirical twelfth-century poem, *Timarion*.[61]

Hellenic and Roman sources imply that the term 'erotes' was used in the literal sense as a reference to *eros*, love, and to Eros, the god of love, rather than as a generic iconographic descriptors. When Greek and Byzantine

---

[57] Poem 56: E. M. Jeffreys, 'The Depiction of Female Sensibilities in the Twelfth Century' in C. Angelidi, ed., *Byzantium Matures: Choices, Sensitivities and Modes of Expression (Eleventh to Fifteenth Centuries)* (Athens, 2004), 73–85.
[58] T. Balsamon, ed., *Scholion on Canon 100 of the Quinisext Council*, trans. in C. Mango, *Art of the Byzantine Empire: Sources and Documents* (Toronto, 1974), 234.
[59] This is a key part of the argument of Hanson, 'Erotic Imagery'.
[60] D. A. Russell and N. G. Wilson, eds., *Menander Rhetor* (Oxford, 1981), 135–47 (VI Epithalamium.399.11–405.14). It was Margaret Mullett who pointed out this aspect of the erotes to me.
[61] Theodore Prodromos, 'Epithalamion for the Sons of the Most Blessed Caesar' in P. Gautier, ed., *Nicephore Bryennios. Histoire* (Brussels, 1975), 340–55; R. Romano, ed., *Timarione* (Naples, 1974), 175–85. I am grateful to Margaret Mullett for these references.

sources use the word 'erotes', they do not mean little tubby winged boys. Rather, they invoke the forces of love and the power of Eros. Consequently, should we wish to identify figures as erotes, then they should be explored in a context of love in its various manifestations. Paula Nuttall has suggested that the imagery used on fifteenth-century wood and bone 'gaming' boxes combines and layers different aspects of love, from the courtly and romantic, to the physical and sexual, and marital and procreative, as well as making fun of Western chivalric traditions of love. Her model is one that can be applied to the Veroli Casket.[62] In the case of the Casket, the plump, naked boys can be seen as personifications of *eros*, as erotes, because a narrative of the different aspects of love can be constructed around the imagery of the Casket, from marriage to carnality. Marriage as a theme, as Simon recognised, is clearly suggested by elements of the iconography, ranging from the wreath-bearing eros at the front right, via Iphigeneia (who believed she was brought to the altar to be married), Europa, the amorous couples and the Dionysiac elements.[63] A symbolic interpretation of Europa, her bull and the stone-throwers in this context is not impossible – a suggestion about the dangers of unregulated passion and the risks of unbridled love. Erotic love may be further indicated by the overtly sexual elements of the Casket. As Averil Cameron has suggested, the level of anxiety about sexual activity in Byzantium implied a very high awareness of sex and desire, and of sex as a potential challenge to the social order.[64] Certainly scenes of bestiality, forbidden by canon law, may serve as a warning of the indecent power of love, its transgressive, lurking dangers. But erotic love, which epithalamia recognised as an aspect of marriage, may also be made 'safe' in visual terms through the employment of erotes and animals. In this setting, an eros engaging with a horse might be seen as pure fiction, where the image of a man and a woman involved in physical relations might be impossible to portray because too indecent or indecorous. And this is not to exclude the elements of humour and buffoonery that may be present on the Casket, for they serve to poke fun at love and the disorderly effects of love: marital love

---

[62] P. Nuttall, 'Dancing, Love and the Beautiful Game: a New Interpretation of a Group of Fifteenth-century "Gaming" Boxes', *Renaissance Studies*, 24 (2010), 119–41. My thanks to Michelle O'Malley for this suggestion.

[63] Simon, 'Nonnos'. Whether the stone throwers can be seen as parodying the apple-throwing erotes is an interesting suggestion raised by one of the readers of this chapter.

[64] A. M. Cameron, 'Desire in Byzantium: the Ought and the Is' in L. James, ed., *Desire and Denial in Byzantium* (Aldershot, 1999), 205–14.

may itself be both depicted and parodied in the scenes of Europa and the erotes playing at being Europa, even Eros himself mocked.

Although this may seem to bring us full circle, I would suggest that where the mocking aspects of profane, classicising art in Byzantium have often been stressed as sinister and derogatory, the Veroli Casket, the Anemodoulion and the romances suggest a different reading, one offering more fun and a remarkably anxiety-free approach to enjoying classicism in the Byzantine world. They allow us to see that art could create imaginary worlds and that images did not always need to be grounded in some form of reality, whether of the actual world around the Byzantines or of a set of identifiable classicising scenes. Art could tell 'good stories' as well as literature. But the erotes of the images and texts alike may also offer us an entry to the Byzantine way of love. One thing that Philostratos' text makes clear is the potential significance of love revealed by almost every aspect of the iconography in a scene depicting erotes. If the erotes really did personify love in its various manifestations, then objects such as the Casket which depict them offer us the chance to decipher one of the least-understood facets of the Byzantine world: its view of love, especially human love.

Further Reading

The main textual source is: L. James, ed., *Constantine of Rhodes. On Constantinople and the Church of the Holy Apostles*, including a Greek edition by I. Vassis (Farnham, 2012). Studies include: P. Chatterjee, 'Vision, Transformation and the Veroli Casket', *Oxford Art Journal*, 36 (2013), 325–44; A. Cutler, 'On Byzantine Boxes', *JWalt*, 42/43 (1984–5), 32–47; E. D. Maguire and H. Maguire, *Other Icons: Art and Power in Byzantine Secular Culture* (Princeton, NJ, 2007).

CHAPTER 18

Object, Text and Performance in Four Komnenian Tent Poems

Margaret Mullett

The occasional poetry of the Komnenian era can often appear artisanal: the verses were commissioned at the same time as the icon or veil or goblet they would grace, or the lines were penned to accompany a letter and amuse the recipient. The temptation is to assume they were also banal. Yet few of these poems were either transparent or innocent: repeated readings were necessary to appreciate their full significance. In this reading of four such poems I attempt to show how a structural analysis of a single poem can help complex considerations of what an artefact described in the poem might have looked like, and so cast light on the relationship of text and image. I also attempt to show how the parallelism of two pairs of poems suggest issues of reception (the viewing of inscribed lines, or the performance of others). The poems, which have the unusual subject-matter of courtly campaign tents, may be seen, as a group, to play with, and retreat from, ideas of tents as the potential place of politically subversive behaviour by members of the Byzantine elite.

In 1994, Michael Jeffreys and Jeffrey Anderson published an article entitled 'The Decoration of the *Sebastokratorissa*'s Tent',[1] in which Jeffreys edited two poems of Manganeios Prodromos relating to the time when the *Sebastokratorissa* Eirene forcibly accompanied her brother-in-law Manuel I *eis to taxeidion*,[2] on campaign, and Anderson attempted a

---

[1] J. C. Anderson and M. J. Jeffreys, 'The Decoration of the *Sebastokratorissa*'s Tent', *Byzantion*, 64 (1994), 8–18.

[2] M. J. Jeffreys and E. M. Jeffreys 'Who was Eirene the Sevastokratorissa?', *Byzantion*, 64 (1994), 40–68; E. M. Jeffreys, 'The Sevastokratorissa Eirene as Literary Patroness: the Monk Iakovos', *JÖB*, 32 (1081), 241–56; E. M. Jeffreys, 'The Sebastokratorissa Irene as Patron' in L. Theis et al., eds., *Female Founders in Byzantium and Beyond*, 60 (Vienna, 2014), 177–94; see also K. Barzos, Ἡ γενεαλογία τῶν Κομνηνῶν (Thessalonike, 1984), vol. I, 361–78. On the concept see M. J. Jeffreys, 'Manuel Komnenos' Macedonian Military Camps: a Glamorous Alternative Court?' in J. Burke and R. Scott, eds., *Byzantine Macedonia. Identity, Image and History* (Melbourne, 2000), 184–91. My indebtedness to the work of the honorands of this volume is clear from these first two footnotes – but it goes far beyond that.

reconstruction of her tent, using ivory boxes but also an image from the Marciana *Kynegetika*.[3] Subsequently Anthony Kaldellis discussed the first poem (145) as an example of the Komnenian third sophistic,[4] and I have used it in a piece on muses for a Paris volume on hidden messages and audiences.[5] Kaldellis describes it as 'mentioning graces, cupids and their like in virtually every line with an almost suffocating effect'.[6] In the Paris article I saw it as an important point in Byzantine thinking about literary inspiration, the point when Muse becomes Patroness or Patroness becomes Muse of Muses: in fact she becomes Kalliope, the Muse of heroic poetry, and the Muse of Eirene's relatives Isaac Komnenos and Anna Komnene.[7] Subsequently I have seen it as even more important, with implications for imperial ceremony,[8] for story-telling,[9] and for experiencing the Byzantine text,[10] but perhaps we should start with the poem itself.

145

Εἰς τὴν σεβαστοκρατόρισσαν, ἐπὶ τῇ σκηνῇ αὐτῆς ζῶα διάφορα ἐχούσῃ ἐντετυπωμένα

    Δέσποινα, μοῦσα τῶν μουσῶν, ἀκρόπολις τοῦ κάλλους,
    τὰ πρόθυρά σου τῆς σκηνῆς πεπλήρωνται χαρίτων.

---

[3] Ps-Oppian, *Kynegetika*, Marc gr. Z 139, fol. 2v, in I. Spatharakis, *The Illustrations of the Cynegetica in Venice: Codex Marcianus Graecus Z 139* (Leiden, 2004), Fig. 4.
[4] A. Kaldellis, *Hellenism in Byzantium: The Transformation of Greek Identity and the Reception of the Classical Tradition* (Cambridge, 2007), 245.
[5] M. Mullett, 'Whose Muses? Two Advice Poems Attributed to Alexios I Komnenos' in P. Odorico, ed., *La face cachée de la littérature byzantine. Le texte en tant que message immédiat* (Paris, 2012), 195–220.
[6] Kaldellis, *Hellenism*, 245.
[7] For Anna as tenth muse (but the author of an *Alexiad*) see Theodore Prodromos, 'Epithalamion for the Sons of the Most Blessed Caesar', in P. Gautier, ed., *Nicéphore Bryennios. Histoire* (Brussels, 1975), 341–55; for Isaac and Kalliope, see Theodore Prodromos' poem in W. Hörandner, ed., *Theodoros Prodromos. Historische Gedichte* (Vienna, 1974), 297 (XLII.36–9). Isaac himself claims to have written epic verse in his typikon for the Kosmosoteira, L. Petit, ed., 'Typikon du monastère de la Kosmosotira près d'Aenos (1152)', *IRAIK*, 13 (1908) (ch. 106), 69; K. N. Papazoglou, ed., Τυπικόν Ισαακίου Αλεξίου Κομνηνού τῆς Μονῆς Θεοτόκου τῆς Κοσμοσώτειρας *(1151/52)* (Komotene, 1994); J. P. Thomas and A. C. Hero, eds., *Byzantine Monastic Foundation Documents: A Complete Translation of the Surviving Founders' Typika and Testaments* (Washington, D. C., 2000), vol. II, 801–44.
[8] M. Mullett, 'Tented Ceremony: Ephemeral Performances under the Komnenoi' in A. Beihammer, S. Constantinou and M. Parani, eds., *Court Ceremonies and Rituals of Power in the Medieval Mediterranean* (Leiden, 2013), 487–513.
[9] M. Mullett, 'Performing Court Literature in Medieval Byzantium: Tales Told in Tents' in M. A. Pomerantz and E. Birge Vitz, eds., *In the Presence of Power: Court and Performance in the Pre-Modern Middle East* (New York, NY, 2017), 121–41.
[10] M. Mullett, 'Experiencing the Byzantine Text, Experiencing the Byzantine Tent' in M. Jackson and C. Nesbitt, eds., *Experiencing Byzantium* (Farnham, 2013), 269–91.

Ἔρωτες πλήττουσιν χορδάς, σιγῇ κιθαροδοῦσιν,
δοκοῦσι παίζειν σάτυροι, σκυρτῶσιν ἱπποκράται,
αἱ μοῦσαι συγχωρεύουσι, πηδῶσι νηρηίδες,
ὄρνιθες ὑπερίπτανται, κυνηγετοῦσιν ἄλλοι
τῆς Ἰνδικῆς τὰ χρυσέα πτηνὰ συναναπτάντα.
Ὁ χρυσοπτέρυξ ψιττακός, τοῦ κάλλους ὁ λυχνίτης,
πρὸς τὴν χρυσέαν σμάραγδον ἐρίζει τῶν ταώνων,
καὶ πρὸς τοὺς γαύρους ὄρνιθας καὶ τῶν πτερῶν τὸν κύκλον·
τὴν τοῦ χρυσοῦ χλωρότητα τὴν ἐν τοῖς μεταφρένοις
συναντιπαρατίθησι καὶ συμπαραδεικνύει.
Ἀλώπεκες αἱ πονηραὶ τοὺς δόλους ἐκλιποῦσαι
τῇ λύρᾳ προσανέχουσιν, ὀρχοῦνται πρὸς κιθάραν.
Τίς οὖν εἰς τὸ προτείχισμα καὶ τὴν αὐλαίαν ταύτην
οὐκ ἀπιδὼν καταπλαγῇ καὶ μᾶλλον ἀπορήσει;
Ἂν γὰρ εἰς τὸ προσκήνιον αἱ χάριτες τοσαῦται,
πόσον λοιπὸν ἐν τῇ σκηνῇ τῆς χάριτος τὸ θαῦμα,
τῆς ἀπολύτως καὶ μιᾶς καὶ πρώτης τῶν χαρίτων;
Ἔρωτες ἔξω παίζουσιν, ἔρωτες ἔνδον ἄλλοι,
αὐχένας ὑποκλίνουσι καὶ γόνυ τῇ δεσποίνῃ,
ἐπὶ τὸ δουλικώτερον ὑποσχηματισθέντες.
Καὶ χάρις σου ταῖς χάρισι καὶ ταῖς ὑπεροχαῖς σου
καὶ δόξα ταῖς χάρισι καὶ τοῖς κοσμήμασί σου·
Ἔρως ἐρώτων πέφηνας, χάρις χαρίτων ἔφυς,
σειρὴν σειρήνων γέγονας, μοῦσα μουσῶν ἐφάνης·
οὐκ ἔχεις ἀντεξέτασιν μετὰ θνητῶν γυναίων.
Μετὰ μουσῶν σε προσκυνῶ, τιμῶ μετὰ σειρήνων,
μετὰ χαρίτων σέβομαι, ταῖς ὥραις σε συνάπτω,
μεθ' Ἥρας, μετὰ Θέτιδος, μετὰ τῶν οὐρανίων·
ἔρρωσο, χάρις καὶ σειρὴν καὶ μοῦσα Καλλιόπη.

In Michael Jeffreys' translation, this reads:

> To the *Sebastokratorissa*, on her tent which had different animals depicted on it
>
> My lady, Muse of Muses, akropolis of beauty,
> The porch of your tent is filled with delights.
> Cupids are plucking strings and quietly strumming the kithara,
> Satyrs seem to play, centaurs gambol,
> The muses join in the dance, the nereids are leaping,
> Birds fly above, while others hunt
> the golden birds of India which fly together.
> The gold-feathered parrot, jewel of beauty,
> vies with the golden emerald of the peacocks,
> And with those proud birds and the circle of their feathers
> contrasts and makes comparisons together
> with the freshness of the gold upon their backs.

Object, Text and Performance in Four Komnenian Poems 417

>   Cunning foxes, abandoning their wiles,
>   devote themselves to the lyre, dance to the kithara.
> 15   Who then could look at this porch and curtain
>   and not be amazed, in fact dumbfounded?
>   For if the delights in the entrance are so great,
>   How great must be the marvel of delight inside the tent,
>   She who is absolutely unique and first of the graces?
> 20   Cupids play outside while inside there are other cupids
>   submitting with bent necks on bended knee to their mistress,
>   taking on a more servile aspect.
>   And thanks be to your Graces and your supremacy,
>   And glory to your brilliance and the virtues that adorn you.
> 25   You were born cupid of cupids and grace of graces,
>   you have become siren of sirens, you have proved muse of muses.
>   You cannot be compared with mortal women.
>   I revere you with the muses, I honour you with the sirens,
>   I do reverence to you with the graces, I link you with the hours,
> 30   with Hera, with Thetis, with the immortals.
>   Greetings, grace and siren and muse Kalliope![11]

So is this a poem with a suffocating and indiscriminate scattering of mythological figures and hybrids?[12] I suggest rather that it is a neat and highly structured little poem with sophisticated ring composition – a technique recently made fashionable again by Mary Douglas.[13] The first half deals with the tent, the second with its lady (Fig. 18.1). Each half divides into two: the section on the tent divides into mythological animals dancing, birds and foxes playing and displaying; the section on the lady divides into a tableau of her in state with cupids, and a section demonstrating that she cannot be compared to mortal women, only to muses and hours, graces and sirens and the goddesses Thetis, queen of the Nereids and mother of Achilles, and Hera, queen of the Olympians. The beginning of a section is thrice signalled by the *erotes*, who open 1A, 11A and 11B.

An outer ring opens with the invocation '*Despoina, mousa ton mouson*, Lady, Muse of Muses' and closes with *mousa Kalliope*. And the poem is built on a central chiasmus. The mythological and hybrid musicians of 1A come full circle with the elaborate mythological compliments of 11B; the display of the golden birds of India, the parrots and peacocks in 1B meet the central tableau of the lady in state with cupids falling before her in 11A (20–2) that is at the heart of the poem. The first section, the tent, has its own ring: the strings and kithara of line 3 are picked up again

---

[11] Anderson and Jeffreys, '*Sebastokratorissa*'s Tent', 11–13.   [12] Kaldellis, *Hellenism*, 245.
[13] M. Douglas, *Thinking in Circles: An Essay on Ring Composition* (New Haven, CT, 2007).

Greeting line 1
I The tent of the sebastokratorissa: A mythological animals playing and dancing 2–5
                                        B birds and foxes flying, displaying and dancing 6–14
       Transition: who, having seen the text, would not want to see the lady? 15–19
II The lady of the tent: A tableau of the lady displayed in state 20–24
                           B she can be compared only to immortal women 25–30
       Greeting line 31

Fig. 18.1   Table showing the basic structure of the poem (© Margaret Mullett)

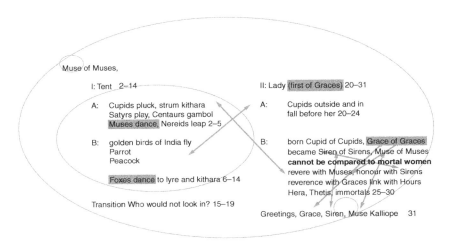

Fig. 18.2   Analytical diagram of the poem (© Margaret Mullett)

in the lyre and kithara of line 14. There is also in the tent section I a refrain of dance: the muses and nereids dancing in the last line of IA at line 5 are picked up by the foxes dancing in the last line of IB, line 14. The second section, that of the Lady, also has its refrain: the graces in the first line of IIA are picked up by the graces in the first line of IIB. And an extended chiasmus in II connects Muse, Siren, Grace to Grace, Siren, Muse, all synonyms for the lady. A smaller chiasmus in IIB, lines 25–7, Siren: Muse:: Muse: Siren includes in line 26 the key message of IIB: she cannot be compared to any mortal woman (Fig. 18.2).

So the poem carefully frames a vision of the Lady in state, attended by immortals and golden birds, by dance and music. She is the lady of love, Thetis, whose celebrity wedding attracted all the immortals, and the mother of a warrior-hero, but she is also Hera, queen of the Olympians, wife of Zeus. It is a very imperial vision, with the tableau of *proskynesis* at its heart. It is a safe vision, in that it is peopled not by plotting courtiers but by the prancing hybrids[14] and scampering cupids,[15] who signal frivolity and lack of seriousness in narrative, rhetorical and satirical texts of the period,[16] but it makes its own claims, perhaps comforting to a lady compelled to accompany the emperor on campaign.[17]

But the poem is one of a pair. And comfort – though perhaps not safeness – disappears if we read the follow-up poem, number 146:

> τοῦ αὐτοῦ εἰς τὸ αὐτὸ
> Ὁπόταν ἴδω τὰς σκηνὰς τὰς πεπηγμένας ταύτας
> κεχαλασμένας ἐπὶ γῆς καὶ μεταπηγνυμένας,
> τὴν πρόσκαιρον λογίζομαι τοῦ βίου παροικίαν
> καὶ τὴν σκηνὴν τοῦ σώματος τὴν μετατιθεμένην.

> *By the same on the same*
> These tents which are now pitched, whenever I see them
> Lying collapsed on the ground and repositioned,
> I think of the temporary sojourn of human life
> And the mutability of the earthly body's tent.[18]

Pomp gives way to a proper appreciation of the temporary nature of earthly life and power. Just as Romanos in his *First Nativity* plays off the eternal and earthly aspects of imperial ceremony, as the Magoi with their *systema* bow at the court of a heavenly and eternal king born in temporary lodgings and utter poverty,[19] so the Mangana poet is able to show totally (politically) orthodox thinking while converting a punitive exile into a claim of queenship.[20] A retinue or reception of mortals would be a far more dangerous matter to represent in such an imperial poem, and at the same time – and ironically – less daring than the comparison with the queenly Hera enabled by the skittish hybrids and frivolous cupids. On the one hand she is the queen of heaven; on the other it is all a frivolous trifle.

---

[14] E. D. Maguire and H. Maguire, *Other Icons: Art and Power in Byzantine Secular Culture* (Princeton, 2007), 11–28.
[15] See Liz James' chapter in this volume.
[16] As in R. Romano, ed., *Timarion* (Naples, 1974), 175–85, on which see M. Mullett, 'The Imperial Vocabulary of Alexios I Komnenos' in M. Mullett and D. Smythe, eds., *Alexios I Komnenos. Papers of the Second Belfast Byzantine International Colloquium, 14–16 April 1989*, vol. I, *Papers* (Belfast, 1996), 392–3.
[17] On the *sebastokratorissa* Eirene's travels see Anderson and Jeffreys, '*Sebastokratorissa*'s Tent', 13.
[18] Anderson and Jeffreys, '*Sebastokratorissa*'s Tent', 12–13.
[19] J. Grosdidier de Matons, ed., *Romanos le Mélode, Hymnes* (Paris, 1965), vol. II, 58 (I Nativity x.9.4).
[20] The clearest presentation of the evidence for the two spells of disfavour into which Eirene fell during her widowhood (1142–ca.1152) including imprisonment and compulsory campaign in Bulgaria is in Jeffreys, 'The *Sebastokratorissa* Eirene as Patron', n. 7. See also my n. 52 below on possible reasons.

But there is another pair of twelfth-century tent poems, which also have dangerous issues to skirt. Theophylaktos' poems 11 and 12 are addressed to a 'most learned Aaron', identified as Rodomir Aaron by Gautier.[21] This descendant of John Vladislav of Bulgaria, a cousin of Eirene Doukaina, *magistros*, *vestarches* and *strategos*, then *proedros* and *doux*, is known to us from three stories in the *Alexiad*. He first appears before the battle of Lebounion in 1091 when he goes off to spy on, and is able to identify, an approaching army as belonging to the Caesar Melissenos rather than a band of Pechenegs.[22] He next appears threatening Alexios' subterfuge at the capture of Nicaea in 1097, when with Monastras he is conducting a group of Turks to the emperor, but is taken prisoner by them and only by offering them in his excellent Turkish freedom with gifts is he able to complete the assignment – to Alexios' extreme annoyance.[23] What may be a final appearance in November 1107,[24] after the landing of Bohemund, when the imperial army en route to Thessalonike is troubled at Psyllos by an assassination attempt by an Aaron and his brother Theodore, which fails and they are reduced to arranging for *libella* to be thrown into Alexios' tent. Both brothers and their mother are exiled, Aaron's place of exile being represented in the manuscript by a lacuna.[25] This is again an imperial relative with a possibly seditious past and/or future, and reception, the reception of a client in a tent, is again the issue.

11

τοῦ Βουλγαρίας εἰς τὸν φιλολογώτατον Ἀαρὼν κεκαθικότα αὐτὸν εἰς τὴν τένταν αὐτοῦ

Σκηνῆς Ἀαρὼν τῆς πάλαι προεστάτει
λειτουργὸς ὢν ἔναιμος ἐκ τῶν θυμάτων.
Σκηνὴν δὲ νῦν ἔπηξεν Ἀαρὼν νέος,

---

[21] P. Gautier, ed., *Théophylacte d'Achrida. Discours, traités, poésies, lettres* (Thessalonike, 1980), vol. I, 124–5, 366–7. See also B. Skoulatos, *Les personnages byzantins de l'Alexiade. Analyse prosopographique et synthèse* (Louvain, 1980), 274–5. V. Laurent, 'Princes bulgares dans la sigillographie byzantine', *EO*, 33 (1934), 424–6; M. Lascaris, 'La prosopographie de l'empire byzantin, Appendix, La famille byzantine des Aaron et les homonymes', *EO*, 33 (1934), 385–95 at 395.

[22] D.R. Reinsch and A. Kambylis, eds., *Annae Comnenae Alexias* (Berlin, 2001), 244–5 (VIII.iv.5); E. Sewter and P. Frankopan, trans., *Anna Komnene. The Alexiad* (London, 2009), 223.

[23] Komnene, *Alexias*, ed. Reinsch and Kambylis, 327–9 (XI.ii.7–10); Sewter and Frankopan, trans., 302–4.

[24] According to Gautier, *Théophylacte d'Achrida*, vol. II, 124–5, and to I. Djurić, 'Théophylacte d'Achrida sous la tente d'Aaron', *ZRVI*, 27–8 (1989), 89–91, but not to B. Skoulatos, *Personnages byzantins de l'Alexiade. Analyse prosopographique et synthèse* (Louvain, 1980), 3–4, or to C. Holmes, *Basil II and the Governance of Empire (976–1025)* (Oxford, 2005), 215.

[25] Komnene, *Alexias*, ed. Reinsch and Kambylis, 385–7 (XIII.i.5–10); Sewter and Frankopan, trans., *The Alexiad*, 358–60.

                εἰς ἣν καλῶν ἅπαντας ἐνδεεῖς στέγους
5   θύει τὸ φιλάνθρωπον, ἁγνὴν θυσίαν,
                ζωοῦσαν, οὐ σφάττουσαν, οὓς ἂν προσλάβοι·
                ὁ γὰρ λόγος δέδωκεν αὐτῷ τὴν χρίσιν·
                οὐ νεκροποιὸς δ' ἐστιν, ὃν χρίει λόγος.

From the archbishop of Bulgaria to the most learned Aaron who sat him down in his tent

> Aaron presided over a tent of old,
> a priest covered in blood from sacrifices
> but now a new Aaron has set up his tent,
> where, summoning all those who need a roof,
> he offers his *philanthropia*, a pure sacrifice,
> which gives life to, rather than killing, those it welcomes.
> For the Word has given him anointing,[26]
> and no one anointed by the Word is a murderer.[27]

12

Ἕτεροι

                Τὴν σαρκικὴν γέννησιν Ἀαρὼν πάλαι
                ἐξ Ἀβραὰμ ἔσχηκε τοῦ φιλοξένου.
                Ὁ νῦν δ' Ἀαρὼν τῷ φιλοξένῳ τρόπῳ
                σκηνῆς ἑαυτοῦ πάντας ἔνδον εἰσάγων
                ἐξ Ἀβραὰμ ἔσχηκε ὁ κρείττω τόπον.

Other verses

> Aaron of old took his fleshly origin
> from Abraham the hospitable.
> Our modern Aaron, who in his own hospitable way
> invites everyone into his tent,
> has obtained from Abraham a better place.[28]

Here the first poem plays with the idea of seditious threat by recalling the biblical priest Aaron as covered in blood but suggests that the modern Aaron has instead chosen *philanthropia*.[29] This choice appears to rule out

---

[26] Or 'learning'. In the *Alexiad* Rodomir comes over as smart and savvy rather than learned or pious. As heir of the conquered Bulgaria he must always have been a potentially suspicious figure.
[27] Theophylaktos of Ohrid, *Poems*, ed. Gautier, vol. 1, 367.
[28] Ibid. Gautier is clear that both poems are by Theophylaktos.
[29] Old Testament names including Aaron recall the Bulgarian Kometopouloi (David, Aaron, Samuel and Moses) under Samuel, a real threat to the empire, I. Thurn, ed., *Ioannis Scylitzae. Synopsis Historiarum* (Berlin, 1973), 328; W. Seibt, 'Untersuchungen zur Vor- und Frühgeschichte der

murder, but may still imply the appropriation of an imperial virtue, which should be exercised by the emperor rather than by a dangerous relative: the suggestion comes with a whiff of treason. The second poem sanitises the picture: there is no blood, no sacrifice, and it emphasises rather *philoxenia*,[30] by recalling the hospitality of Abraham rather than the sacrifices of Aaron, and also praising the modern Aaron who will be rewarded for his hospitality by a place in the bosom of Abraham.[31]

Is it possible to date these poems? And decide whether the sedition of Psyllos was in the past or still in the future? We need to find a time both when Aaron was on campaign in the Balkans and when Theophylaktos was travelling from Ohrid. There are two possibilities when Aaron might have been in the vicinity: the period from September 1105 to November 1106 when Alexios was preparing for Bohemond's invasion, and then during the second Norman war after Bohemond's landing on 9 or 10 October 1107.[32] Of the ten possible journeys of Theophylaktos from his see in Ohrid, one, dating to between 1089–90 and 1094–5, is specifically mentioned as a long journey to see the emperor in an army camp; another is to the vicinity of Thessalonike during 1106 when we know Alexios was organising in the region, another in 1108 to Thessalonike and Constantinople and back, which seems to coincide with the second Norman War. The first sounds promising, but there is no evidence that Aaron was with the emperor in Macedonia at that stage. The second is possible, but though Monastras is mentioned as serving in the preparations, Aaron is not. The third would be after the episode at Psyllos, which happened very early in the campaign after Bohemond's invasion.[33] As there is no way to decide between these occasions, it is impossible to date the encounter. In any case, Aaron remains a potentially dangerous courtier.

"bulgarischen" Kometopulen', *HA*, 89 (1975), 65–100, as well as the descendants of John Vladislav; see the family tree in Lascaris, 'La famille byzantine des Aaron', 413.

[30] *Philanthropia* usually suggests the imperial virtue; the semantic field of *philoxenia* makes room also for the almsgiver saints. For the latter see for example E. Sargologos, ed., *La vie de saint Cyrille le Philéote, moine byzantin* (Brussels, 1964), 77–8 (XI.2), in which Abraham is cited.

[31] The surface meaning of course contrasts pre-Christian religion versus post-Logos piety, παλαί as against νῦν; an anonymous reader of this chapter points out the ambiguity of the figure of Aaron in the Old Testament, both Moses' right hand and a potentially treasonous type. And indeed tents regularly host threats in the Old Testament, most dangerously in the story of Judith and Holofernes (see Mantegna's pink tent in the National Gallery of Art in Washington DC).

[32] Komnene, *Alexias*, ed. Reinsch and Kambylis, 364–70 (XII.iii.1–4.4) and 384–423 (XIII); Sewter and Frankopan, trans., *The Alexiad*, 337–42 and 357–96.

[33] Theophylaktos of Ohrid, *Letters*, ed. Gautier, vol. II, 229–31 (G 30), 407–13 (G 77), 531–3 (G110), 535 (G111), 539 (G113). See M. Mullett, *Theophylact of Ochrid: Reading the Letters of a Byzantine Archbishop* (Aldershot, 1997), table X, 403–7 (G120).

These pairs of poems have much in common: a longer poem that deals with ceremonial reception, and a shorter poem that deals with eternal truths, of transience or hospitality. But they are different, partly in the length of the 'long' poem, but more strikingly in the associated worlds of imagery adduced. The *sebastokratorissa* moves in the world of pagan mythology; Rodomir Aaron in that of the Old Testament. Both are potentially threatening figures at court, but their threat is defused in these poems in different ways: the patroness becomes a muse rather than a plotter; the aristocrat with an Old Testament name attains Old Testament virtues.

The comparison of these two pairs of poems, and the closer analysis of Manganeios' poem 145, may allow us to look again at some of the thickly packed suggestions and puzzles in the classic article of Jeffreys and Anderson. They are clear that the tent as described is plausible: there are Komnenian images of tents, some of them decorated, and nearly all the images may be found either in manuscripts or on ivory boxes of the period. They find it difficult to envisage how the scenes are combined, though they tend to the idea of panels separated by decoration; they find the idea of a porch (προθύρα) even more difficult to envisage, and they are not absolutely sure which images are 'rhetorically' present, and which are physically present on the tent. They are also not sure which figures are represented on the tent and which are inside. They suggest that pictures on tents may match the subject-matter of tents in their surrounding narrative; they suggest that they may be arranged like the panels on boxes to allow a loose association that will not constrain the viewer's imagination, and they suggest that the mythological is combined with the day-to-day to raise the tone of the composition. Most brilliantly of all, they suggest that the technique could be embroidery and that poem 146 could have been embroidered on the tent.

To take their uncertainties in turn, let us consider the porch, the location of figures, their arrangement, and the technique. The porch in the poem draws the reader in; it is 'filled with graces'. The verb πεπλήρωνται at line 2 creates the ambiguity which asks 'are they in the tent or on the tent?' At 15 (in the transition) the ambiguity is resolved: we return to the προτείχισμα and the αὐλαία, which suggests a textile reality and at 17 the προσκήνιον is contrasted with the inside of the tent, cupids outside with cupids inside.[34] The porch then, or whatever is in front of the entrance to the tent, is decorated with what is described in sections 1A and 1B.

---

[34] On αὐλαία, LSJ, http://stephanus.tlg.uci.edu/lsj/#eid=1&context=lsj, sv: 'curtain, esp. in the theatre' (accessed 29 December 2017).

The location of figures becomes easier to understand given the structure of the poem. Section I is about the tent, and section II about the Lady within the tent. We visualize at IA the erotes playing instruments and the mythological figures, the satyrs and centaurs, muses and nereids, dancing. These in some way must figure on the tent. Anderson and Jeffreys suggest that the muses do not, partly because they are not represented in any surviving art of the period,[35] at least not dancing (their natural state in Komnenian and later literature).[36] They are 'the only figures rhetorically motivated'.[37] But it would be hard to differentiate muses and nereids from satyrs and centaurs whom Jeffreys and Anderson are happy to envisage on the tent: lines 4 and 5 show them in parallel, though line 4 ends each half-line with the actors, and line 5 offers a one-line chiasmus of dancers and dancing. Jeffreys and Anderson correctly point out that in IB, at line 6, the form ὑπερίπτανται gives us the only spatial clue: the birds are represented above the musicians and dancers. Already however they have suggested that the birds may not be on the tent: they are 'introduced rhetorically, not in any way that gives evidence of their part in a scene'. The first impulse however seems the better: two registers represent a) music and dance with b) birds flying above. Still in IB, at lines 13 and 14 foxes also associate themselves with the dance, so they appear presumably in the lower register. So we imagine birds above, and below *erotes* and hybrids playing instruments with both mythological figures and foxes dancing. What happens after that in the poem, in the transition, in IIA, and in IIB, does not affect the nature of the tent. In IIA we see the Lady *sebastokratorissa* and her entourage of cupids inside the tent, and in IIB she is first described

---

[35] On the lack of representations see O. Lampsides, 'Die Entblössung der Muse Kalliope in einem byzantinischen Epigramm', *JÖB*, 47 (1997), 107–10, esp. 108. There is a possible representation of Kalliope in Marc. gr. 139, fol. 2r, Spatharakis, ed., *The Illustrations*, Fig. 2; see Mullett, 'Whose Muses?' 212, but sirens, cupids, centaurs, birds and foxes may easily be found. Henry Maguire has proposed that the dancing personifications on the crown of Constantine Monomachos are graces; see H. Maguire, 'Enamel Plaques and Medallions: "The Crown of Constantine IX of Monomachos,"' in H. Evans and W. Wixom, eds., *The Glory of Byzantium: Art and Culture of the Middle Byzantine Era, AD 843–1261* (New York, NY, 1997), 210–12, no. 145. Virtues are regularly to be found in imperial manuscripts of the period as well as in the novel, and, as Foteini Spingou points out, in Marc. gr. 524 where, though they do not dance, they appear in the circle of a round object, like the goblet of no. 236–9/261, S. Lampros, ed., "Ὁ Μαρκιανὸς κῶδιξ 524', *NE*, 8 (1911), 153, or with the graces 30 (no. 61), or surrounding the emperor, κυκλόθεν, in the kouboukleion of Blachernai, 152 (no. 247/269). See F. Spingou, 'Word and Image at the Court of Manuel Komnenos. Epigrams on Works of Art in Marc. gr. 524, Followed by a Description of the Manuscript', unpublished MPhil thesis, Oxford University (2010).

[36] G. T. Dennis, ed., *The Letters of Manuel II Palaeologus. Text, Translation and Notes* (Washington, D. C., 1977), 37–9 (XIV); Mullett, 'Whose Muses?', 211.

[37] Anderson and Jeffreys, '*Sebastokratorissa*'s Tent', 17.

successively as cupid of cupids, grace of graces, siren of sirens, muse of muses, then the poet himself bows (προσκυνῶ) to her surrounded by muses, sirens and graces; he associates with her (συνάπτω) hours, Hera and Thetis and the immortals. Finally he greets her as grace and siren and the family muse Kalliope.[38] I incline to the view that these figures are all adduced in comparison with the Lady, rather than being envisaged as physically present. But if they were present they would be inside the tent like the kneeling cupids rather than on it.

To arrive at the choreography, or arrangement, of the scenes is an impossibility given the fact that we have no surviving described, or even represented, model, a problem that beset Anderson and Jeffreys. The closest parallels are two textual passages and one manuscript illumination. Al-Mutanabbi's tenth-century tent of Sayf al-Dawlah with its gardens and trees, pearls and animals, and the humiliated Byzantine emperor doing *proskynesis*

Better than the lost freshness of youth altogether,
is the water of the lightening cloud in a tent upon which I fix my hopes; [i.e. the patron]

Upon it [i.e. the tent] are gardens which no cloud has woven,
And branches of tree upon which no doves sing;

And upon the margins of every two-sided fabric,
there is a string of pearls which have not been bored by their arranger;

You see pictures of animals that upon it have come to a truce,
an enemy fights his opponent, and makes peace with him;

If the wind strikes it, it undulates,
as if its old horses travel round and its lions stalk prey;

In the picture of the Byzantine with a crown, there is obeisance [lit.=humiliation],
to the one of shining visage who wears no crowns but his turbans; [the patron, Sayf al-Dawlah]

The mouths of kings kiss [the hem of] his shroud,
for his sleeve and fingers are too exalted,[39]

---

[38] Ibid., 15.
[39] Al-Mutanabbi, *Ekphrastic Passage describing the Tent of Sayf al-Dawlah*, trans. M. Pomerantz (unpublished), ll. 18–24, between an opening lament of lost love and youth (ll. 1–18) and a concluding section on praise of the patron (ll. 25–42). For a reading of the poem, 'Your Faithfulness is like the Abode', 'U. Tabbā', ed., *Dīwān al-Mutanabbī* (Beirut, 1994), 256–60, see M. Larkin, *Al-Mutanabbi: Voice of the 'Abbasid Poetic Ideal* (Oxford, 2008), 35–41. I am very grateful to Maurice Pomerantz for his translation, and to him and to Sharon Gerstel for (independently) pointing me in this direction.

prefigures the *Digenes* dowry with its 'multiform shapes of animals' in *synkopas*

> A beautiful tent, very large, embroidered with gold
> Decorated with multiform shapes of animals
> And the ropes were of silk and the poles of silver,[40]

the three tents of the ceiling of the Cappella Palatina,[41] and the pard, deer, falcon and hare in two registers in the *Kynegetika*. The design of the tent in the *Kynegetika* appears to take up the entire vertical surface of the tent, but the emphasis on the 'porch' might suggest something more like the Vienna Ottoman tents.[42] Anderson and Jeffreys suggest that there need not be a logically coherent narrative image, and that the ivory boxes with their discrete panels might be a better parallel. So separate panels of muses and musicians, foxes and birds could be dispersed over the available area. Interestingly they offer an aesthetic judgement on the idea of separate panels: 'the loose compositional bonds ... allowed the carvers to create an atmosphere of celebration free of any strong association with some particular story, which, if identified, would act to constrain the viewer's imagination'.[43] I suspect that this cannot work for our poem, where structure and formality are so important. I also believe that what is on the tent is mirrored to some extent inside the tent, leading up to the formal *proskynesis* of poet to Lady, and acclamation of her as immortal. We are meant to envisage a formal, ceremonial order of things in which animals and hybrids and nymphs have a place. If Anderson and Jeffreys are right about the decoration on tents in narratives mirroring the activity of the narrative, rather than representing more functional concerns (wrestling reflecting the warfare of the *Book of Kings*, rather than showing a conventional image of a 'war-tent') this structured poem about reception and acclamation demands a more structured artistic composition.[44]

---

[40] E. M. Jeffreys, ed., *Digenis Akritis: The Grottaferrata and Escorial Versions* (Cambridge, 1998), 120–1 (G IV.908–10). For discussion of συγκοπή, see Anderson and Jeffreys, '*Sebastokratorissa*'s Tent', though ζώων ἔχουσαν συγκοπάς could also suggest animal combats, as in Maguire and Maguire, *Other Icons*, 58–82; G. W. H. Lampe, *A Patristic Greek Lexicon* (Oxford, 1969), sv 'slaughter', LSJ sv συγκόπτω 'thrash soundly'. Πολυμόρφους ἰδέας might also suggest hybrids.

[41] B. Brenk, ed., *La Cappella Palatina a Palermo* (Modena, 2010), Fig. 889 (which has a hawk flying and a pard, compare with Fig. 891, seated), Fig. 934 (which has hawks in roundels and foxes below), and 935 (which has birds in roundels above and rabbits or hares below). Thanks as ever to Lioba Theis.

[42] Heeresgeschichtliches Museum, Wien, Inv. No. N.I. 4688; see N. Atasoy, *The Ottoman Imperial Tent Complex* (Istanbul, 2000), 272, no. 135.

[43] Anderson and Jeffreys, '*Sebastokratorissa*'s Tent', 15–16.

[44] Ibid., 15; for the book of Kings, Vat. gr. 333, fol.18v, J. Lassus, *L'illustration byzantine du livre des rois* (Paris, 1973), Fig. 31.

The decorative technique is also unclear. The ἐντετυπωμένα of the lemma implies impression or carving, stamping, even printing, while the χρυσοκέντητον of the Digenis wedding gift implies embroidery. The tent(s) of the *Eiseterioi* illustration suggest motifs woven into the panels and roundels of silk or other high-status textiles.[45] Jeffreys' and Anderson's insightful suggestion that poem 146 was short enough to be embroidered on the tent finds its support in the regular use of twelfth-century epigrams for veils, chalice-covers and other textiles.[46] It finds more support in the second pair of poems, similarly unequal in length, and in which the first, longer, poem touches on political aspects of the aristocrat holding court, while the second, shorter poem offers uncontroversial truisms: the tent as a symbol of hospitality in Theophylaktos' poem for Rodomir Aaron matching the tent as symbol of the transience of human life in the Mangana poet's poem for Eirene. It may be, as Anderson and Jeffreys hint, that in each case the second poem is designed to be embroidered on the tent, the first to be delivered in the tent. And if a decoration is required for Aaron's tent, what better image than the hospitality of Abraham to inspire Theophylaktos' shorter poem? In each case the longer poem may act as warning or advice.

In the case of the *sebastokratorissa*, though she is acclaimed implicitly as Queen and immortal mother of an Achilles,[47] the seriousness of the political message is undermined by the personnel of her court. Though Jeffreys and Anderson suggest that the mythological characters were designed to raise the tone of the tent's decoration over a simply animal-decorated one, it is clear that cupids at any rate lower that tone.[48] Muses had been regularly confused with maenads since the time of Nonnos,[49] sirens and satyrs both had pejorative associations,[50] and hybrids in general

---

[45] Vat. gr. 1851, fol. 6r. On the poem see M. J. Jeffreys, 'The Vernacular *Eiseterioi* for Agnes of France' in E. M. Jeffreys, M. J. Jeffreys and A. Moffatt, eds., *Byzantine Papers: Proceedings of the First Australian Byzantine Studies Conference, Canberra* (Canberra, 1981), 101–15; on the manuscript and the illuminations see C.J. Hilsdale, 'Constructing a Byzantine *Augusta*: a Greek Book for a French Bride', *ArtBull*, 87 (2005), 458–83.
[46] Anderson and Jeffreys, '*Sebastokratorissa*'s Tent', 18. See for example V. Nunn,'The Encheirion as Adjunct to the Icon in the Middle Byzantine Period', *BMGS*, 10 (1986), 73–102.
[47] Some recent studies suggest that her difficulties with Manuel arose through her ambitions for her son, Jeffreys and Jeffreys, 'Who Was Eirene?', 42; E. M. Jeffreys and M. J. Jeffreys, eds., *Iacobi Monachi Epistulae* (Turnhout, 2009), xxix. Maria Evangelatou has been pursuing evidence for these ambitions in Eirene's patronage of the Kokkinobaphos manuscripts in M. Evangelatou, 'Threads of Power: Clothing Symbolism, Human Salvation and Female Identity in the Illustrated Homilies by Iakobos of Kokkinobaphos', *DOP*, 68 (2014), 241–324.
[48] See Liz James' chapter in this volume.   [49] M. Mullett, 'Muse into Maenad', in preparation.
[50] Maguire and Maguire, *Other Icons*, 51–5 explores the positive aspect of wit and jesting of sirens, and though, *Digenis Akritis*, ed. Jeffreys, 210–11 (G VII.162) 'a song that surpassed the song of the sirens', their song can be neutral or positive, the threat of their singing could not have been

carried their own connotations, recently explored by Henry and Eunice Maguire.[51] If Henry Maguire is correct about the Monomachos crown as combining imperial ladies with virtues and graces,[52] it provides a precedent for combining imperial ladies with muses, an altogether more worthy resonance for the *sebastokratorissa:* there is mythology and mythology. But we are here a step away from raw political ambition. You are immortal, you are a queen, the Mangana poet is saying, but your sphere is literature. Be content and be a muse. In the case of Rodomir Aaron, Theophylaktos' poem may refer obliquely to the attempted assassination at Psyllos in 1107. By praising Aaron's hospitality (lines 4–5) and learning (φιλολογώτατος in the lemma), and by expressing belief in his innocence (line 8), it urges him to a virtuous life. A learned man is not a murderer. But the shorter poem, in each case, was bland enough to be stamped on the tent itself.

Finally, we may consider the occasional setting of these poems. Theophylaktos specifically speaks of a visit to Rodomir Aaron's tent, flung wide to receive those in need of shelter. This implies a visit of Aaron, with or without the emperor, to Bulgaria or of Theophylaktos to the whereabouts of the *doux*. The poems ask to be read, with the help of the lemma, as poetic thanks, perhaps sent with a letter,[53] to be delivered performed and perhaps then (poem 12) to be inscribed. Manganeios Prodromos gives no such clues of his personal presence, and it is debatable whether he visited the *sebastokratorissa* at all. His poem 145 reads as if the tent is the tent she deserves rather than any actual object, no more realistic than her retinue of *erotes* and (possibly)[54] muses, sirens and graces. His own initial *proskynesis* may be from afar,[55] but poem 145 is perhaps again to be read and enjoyed when it reached her, and its accompanying poem 146 perhaps to be inscribed on the tent itself.

---

forgotten; satyrs were more generally associated with the train of Dionysos but more specifically with shameful conduct, Maguire and Maguire, *Other Icons*, 145.

[51] Ibid., 11–28.   [52] See above n. 36.

[53] That Theophylaktos sent letters with poems is clear from poem 2 and G129 both to Michael Pantechnes the doctor, Theophylaktos of Ohrid, *Letters*, ed. Gautier, vol. 1, 349–51 (II); vol. II, 583 (G129). Accompanying letters are lost for poem 1 to Bryennios who asked for a letter, and for poem 3 to Nicholas Kallikles, thanking him for the Galen requested in G112, vol. 1, 347–9 (I), 351 (III); vol. II, 537 (G 112). Poems can also mimic letters, as here in Manganeios 145.31, ἔρρωσο, and poem 72 of Theodore Prodromos is described as an ἐπιστολή, Prodromos, *Historische Gedichte*, ed. Hörandner (Vienna, 1974), 522. For a model see K. Demoen, 'Gifts of Friendship That Will Remain For Ever: Personae, Addressed Characters and Intended Audience of Gregory Nazianzen's Epistolary Poems', *JÖB*, 47 (1997), 1–11.

[54] See above 415–17.

[55] As in a poem where he imagines himself flying through the air to hover above Philippopolis to be in the emperor's presence (4.16–44, see Jeffreys, 'Glamorous Alternative Court?', 188).

There is no reason to believe that the Mangana poet had access to Theophylaktos' pair of poems, and the poems are sufficiently different to suggest that they were independently composed. The significance of tents in Komnenian court culture has become clear in recent years: tents are places where people above all hold court and receive clients, and if on campaign may be settings for alternative receptions, alternative, that is to an imperial levee.[56] Tents were regarded as temporary, but versatile and resilient, light and capable of infinite reinvention.[57] They inspired, perhaps, not just one but two genres of court poetry: the poem about eternal truths, to be inscribed on a tent, and the poem describing or responding to reception, whether serious or frivolous, to be performed in a tent. Tents were guarantees of imperial authority, symbols of Roman civilisation but also represent an ambivalent space, surrounded by a hostile environment where normal rules do not necessarily apply, and treason could threaten.[58] Reading these tents, and the texts about the tents, required careful appreciation of scrupulously positioned subtexts; the mythological and biblical characters invoked play a studied and illuminating part in the structure and import of the poems.

Further Reading

Studies include: M. J. Jeffreys and E. M. Jeffreys 'Who was Eirene the *Sevastokratorissa?*', *Byzantion*, 64 (1994), 40–68; J. C. Anderson and M. J. Jeffreys, 'The Decoration of the *Sebastokratorissa*'s Tent', *Byzantion*, 64 (1994), 8–18; M. Mullett, 'Tented Ceremony: Ephemeral Performances under the Komnenoi' in A. Beihammer, S. Constantinou and M. Parani, eds., *Court Ceremonies and Rituals of Power in the Medieval Mediterranean* (Leiden, 2013), 487–513 and M. Mullett, 'Experiencing the Byzantine Text, Experiencing the Byzantine Tent' in M. Jackson and C. Nesbitt, eds., *Experiencing Byzantium* (Farnham, 2013), 269–91.

---

[56] Hilsdale, 'Constructing a Byzantine Augusta', 472 and notes; H. Maguire, 'The Philopation as a Setting for Imperial Ceremonial and Display' in C. Bakirtzis, N. Zekos and X. Moniaros, eds., *Byzantine Thrace: Evidence and Remains; Komotini 18–22 April 2007: Proceedings*, ByzF, 30 (2011), 71–82; Mullett, 'Tented Ceremony'.

[57] Mullett, 'Experiencing'.

[58] See for example Geoffrey de Briel's act of betrayal against Prince William before the Battle of Pelagonia in revealing their plan of flight, addressing his tent, τέντα μου ἠγαπημένη, J. J. Schmitt, ed., *The Chronicle of Morea: A History in Political Verse* (London, 1904), 256–7 (ll.3856–72). Many thanks here to the editors.

CHAPTER 19

Textual and Visual Representations of the Antipodes from Byzantium and the Latin West

Maja Kominko

The antipodes, the areas on the opposite side of the globe where people walk with their feet up and heads pointing down, intrigued authors in Antiquity, the Middle Ages and beyond.[1] The concept, rejected on occasion as illogical, also provoked theological controversy. This chapter offers a brief exploration of different views on the antipodes – and traces the transmission of the idea – in Byzantium and the Latin West.

As a corollary of the conception of the spherical universe with a spherical earth at its centre, the term 'antipodes' was originally introduced to illustrate the fact that in such a universe the directions 'up' and 'down' can only be relative. According to Diogenes Laertius, who wrote in the third century, this term had been used already by Pythagoras, who believed that the earth was wholly inhabited, and that there were antipodean peoples on the other side of the earth, who experienced as up that which is down for people in the *oikoumene*.[2] The earliest attested usage of the term can be found in Plato's *Timaeus*, where the author illustrates the relativity of directions in a spherical universe by describing people who stand on opposite sides of the globe, and consequently have their feet opposite to one another.[3] Gradually, however, 'antipodes' became associated with an actual area of the earth situated opposite the known

---

[1] For discussion of images of the antipodes, both written and visual, beyond the Middle Ages see W. L. Eisler, *The Furthest Shore. Images of Terra Australis from the Middle Ages to Capitan Cook* (Cambridge, 1995).

[2] R. D. Hicks, ed. and trans., *Diogenes Laertius. Lives of Eminent Philosophers* (London, 1975), vol. II, 342–3 (VIII.26). For surveys of ancient theories on the antipodes see A. Hiatt, *Terra Incognita: Mapping the Antipodes Before 1600* (London, 2008); A. Rinaud, *Le continent austral: hypothèses et découvertes* (Paris, 1983); J. S. Romm, *The Edges of the Earth in Ancient Thought* (Princeton, 1992), 129–32.

[3] R. G. Bury, trans., *Plato. Timaeus* (Cambridge, MA, 1929), 158–9 (63A). Similar significance is given to this term by Aristotle (W. K. C. Guthrie, trans., *Aristotle. On the Heavens* (Cambridge, MA, 1953), 326–31 (IV.1.308a). See also G. Moretti, 'The Other World and the Antipodes: the Myth of the Unknown Countries Between Antiquity and the Renaissance' in W. Haase, ed., *The Classical Tradition and the Americas* (Berlin, 1993), 241–84; Romm, *The Edges of the Earth*, 124–8.

oikoumene. This theory, probably introduced as early as Parmenides, was largely inspired by the notion that the division of the heavens into five zones corresponded to a similar division of the earth.[4] Consequently, two habitable zones, one in the northern hemisphere and one in the southern, were believed to co-exist: sandwiched between the cold zones around the poles, and the equatorial zone that was inaccessible on account of the heat.[5] On grounds of symmetry rather than science, most classical writers accepted that the southern habitable zone contained another land corresponding to the known *oikoumene*.[6] This southern continent was frequently called *antichthon*, a counter-earth, after the term originally employed by the Pythagoreans to designate the additional planet of the solar universe that was considered to be antithetical to the earth.[7]

This image of the globe was further modified under the influence of Eratosthenes' estimation of the size of the *oikoumene*. Eratosthenes reckoned that the length of the inhabited world was a little less than half of the circumference of the earth. He also believed that the *oikoumene* was twice as long as wide, and that it accordingly measured approximately one quarter of the earth's surface.[8] His estimation was combined with the zonal division of the earth in the terrestrial globe made by Crates of Malos to illustrate the itinerary of Odysseus.[9] Crates imagined four inhabited lands

---

[4] On attribution of this theory to Parmenides, see D. W. Roller, ed. and trans., *The Geography of Strabo* (Cambridge, 2014), 115–16 (II.2.1–2). For the discussion of this theory see, H. D. P. Lee, ed. and trans., *Aristotle. Meteorologica* (Cambridge, MA, 1952), 178–83 (II.5.362b); G. Aujac, ed. and trans., *Géminos. Introduction aux phénomènes* (Paris, 1975), 21–9 (V.1–48), 74–5 (XV.1–4), 80–3 (XVI.25–38); Strabo, *Geography*, ed. Roller, 129–30 (II.5.3); T. E. Page, ed. and trans., *Virgil. Georgics* (Cambridge, MA, 1907), 152–3 (I.237–8); R. Goulet, ed. and trans., *Cléomède. De Motu Circulari* (Paris, 1980), 109 (I.6.6–7), 94 (I.2.1), and 95 (I.2.2). See also Hiatt, *Terra Incognita*, 16–17; G. Aujac, 'Poseidonios et les zones terrestres: les raisons d'un échec', *BullBudé*, 35 (1976), 74–8.

[5] Aristotle, *Meteorology*, ed. Lee 176–9 (II.4.362a35–362b30).

[6] See for example Virgil, *Georgics*, ed. Page, 152–3 (I.237–8); See also A. Peden, 'The Medieval Antipodes', *History Today*, 45 (1995), 28–30.

[7] Philolaus, *Testimonia*, in H. Diels and W. Kranz, eds., *Die Fragmente der Vorsokratiker* (Berlin, 1951–2), vol. I, p. 403 (Fragments 16.7; 17.2–3); H. Tredennick, trans., *Aristotle. Metaphysics* (Cambridge, MA, 1961), 32–5 (I.5.986a8–13); Aristotle, *On the Heavens*, ed. Guthrie, 216–19 (II.13.293a18–293b8). See also D. O'Brien, 'Derived Light and Eclipses in the Fifth Century', *JHS*, 88 (1968), 117; D. R. Dicks, *Early Greek Astronomy to Aristotle* (New York, 1970), 65–8; Moretti, 'The Other World and the Antipodes', 242.

[8] Strabo, *Geography*, ed. Roller, 131–2 (II.5.6). Eratosthenes accepted the existence of the five climatic zones, which he discusses in his poem *Hermes* see J. Powell, ed., *Collectanea Alexandrina* (Oxford, 1925), 58–63; Romm, *The Edges of the Earth*, 128.

[9] As a Stoic, Crates credited Homer with belief in a spherical earth, and commented on his poems accordingly. He took the verse of the *Odyssey* 1.23, 'The Ethiopians who dwell sundered in twain, the farthermost of men', to mean that the Ethiopians lived on either side of the equatorial ocean. On Crates' geographical reading of Homer see Strabo, *Geography*, ed. Roller, 38–40 (I.1.6–7), 61–2 (I.2.24), 123 (II.3.8). For the description of his globe see Strabo, *Geography*, ed. Roller, 134 (II.5.10). See also

on the earth, two in the northern and two in the southern hemisphere, separated by the ocean.[10] This notion became immensely popular among later writers, both Greek and Latin,[11] although it was a matter of controversy whether the additional lands, inaccessible to exploration, were inhabited.[12]

At the same time, the term 'antipodes' continued to be employed in its original sense, that is, as a theoretical concept resting on the belief that the earth is spherical and placed in the centre of the universe.[13] It is also interesting to note that some authors emphasised the relativity of the term antipodes, noting that the known *oikoumene* can be considered antipodal by the inhabitants of the lands south of the equator.[14] However, this notion was not universally accepted. The Epicureans, for example, believed the universe to be infinite and, consequently, without a centre in which the earth would be located.[15] Other authors, most notably Plutarch,

---

B. Harley and D. Woodward, 'Greek Cartography in the Early Roman World' in B. Harley and D. Woodward, eds., *The History of Cartography*, vol. I, *Cartography in Prehistoric, Ancient, and Medieval Europe and Mediterranean* (Chicago, IL, 1987), 163; H. J. Mette, *Sphairopoiia: Untersuchungen zur Kosmologie des Krates von Pergamon* (Munich, 1936); E. L. Stevenson, *Terrestrial and Celestial Globes: Their History and Construction, Including Consideration of their Value as Aids in the Study of Geography and Astronomy* (New Haven, CT, 1921), vol. I, Fig. 5.

[10] Strabo, *Geography*, ed. Roller, 61–2 (1.2.24). See also Hiatt, *Terra Incognita*, 17–18.

[11] Kleomedes, *De Motu Circulari*, ed. Goulet, 95 (1.2.2) and 97 (1.2.6); Geminos, *Phenomena*, ed. Aujac, 75–6 (XVI.1–2), 79–80 (XVI.19–22), and 81 (XVI.26–30); C. W. Keyes, trans., *Cicero. De Re Publica* (Cambridge, MA, 1928), 272–7 (VI.xix–xx); H. Rackham, trans., *Cicero. Academica* (Cambridge, MA, 1979), 624–7 (II.xxxix.123); W. H. Stahl, trans., *Macrobius. Commentary on the Dream of Scipio* (New York, NY, 1990), 206 (II.v.33); D. Adolf, ed., *Martianus Capella. De nuptiis Philologiae et Mercurii* (Stuttgart, 1969), 298 (VI.604); S. A. Barney et al., eds., *The Etymologies of Isidore of Seville, Etymologies* (Cambridge, 2006), 293 (XIV.v.17); J. O. Thomson, *History of Ancient Geography* (Cambridge, 1948), 386; Moretti, 'The Other World and the Antipodes', 243. For a thorough discussion of the antipodes, with a focus on Latin sources, see Hiatt, *Terra Incognita*, 20–32.

[12] Geminos, *Phenomena*, ed. Aujac, 75–6 (XVI.1–2), 79–80 (XVI.19–22), and 81 (XVI.26–30). For the role of this speculation in early geographies see J. K. Wright, 'Terrae Incognitae: the Place of the Imagination in Geography' in J. K. Wright, *Human Nature in Geography: Fourteen Papers 1925–1965* (Cambridge, MA, 1966), 68–88.

[13] In general it seems that authors, especially those writing in Greek, preferred to employ the term *antipodes* when discussing a theoretical concept, illustrating the relativity of directions on the spherical earth. E. Diehl, ed., *Procli Diadochi in Platonis Timaeum commentaria* (Leipzig, 1903–6), vol. I, 119–24 (22E); I. Mueller, trans., *Simplikios. On Aristotle On the Heavens 3.7–4.6* (London, 2009), 70 (4.1.308a17); H. Rackham, trans., *Pliny. Natural History* (Cambridge, MA, 1938), vol. I, 296–7 (II.55.161) and vol. II, 186–9 (IV.12.89–91) and employed the term *antichthon* to designate the southern, habitable zone of the globe. G. J. Toomer, trans., *Ptolemy. Almagest* (London, 1984), 287–94 (VI.6). Pliny, *Natural History*, ed. Rackham, vol. II, 398–9 (VI.81); P. Berry, *Pomponius Mela. Geography or De situ orbis* (Lewiston, NY 1997), 0–2 (I.1–2) and 22–4 (I.12–13); J. D. Duff, trans., *Lucan. The Civil War* (Cambridge, MA, 1958), 448–9 (VIII.160).

[14] Moretti, 'The Other World and the Antipodes', 254.

[15] Epicurus, according to Diogenes Laertius, *Lives of Ancient Philosophers*, ed. Hicks, 574–7 (x.46) and 590–1 (x.60); W. H. D. Rouse, trans., *Lucretius. On the Nature of Things* (Cambridge, MA, 1982),

dismissed the existence of the antipodes on logical grounds, arguing that the idea of an upside-down world was simply absurd.[16]

The coming of Christianity did not, at least initially, have an impact on cosmography. Only a few Christian authors rejected the idea of a spherical universe with a spherical earth in the centre, positing instead a system based on a flat earth.[17] Although it is frequently assumed that such a system was determined by Scriptural indications concerning the shape of heaven and earth, in reality the clues provided by the Bible were mostly presented in the form of poetic allusions rather than pragmatic descriptions. As such, they could be quoted by those who believed the earth was flat, as well as by those who imagined it spherical.[18] Though from the point of view of Christian dogma there was nothing unacceptable in the physical form of the universe as described in classical Greek and Roman sources,[19] the Christian authors who rejected classical cosmography did so on the grounds that this shape of the universe was a pagan notion.[20] Their rejection was grounded in two fundamental issues: the connection between the classical cosmography and astrology,[21] and the ancient perception of

---

78–87 (I.951–1051), 270–5 (II.1048–89) and 540–3 (VI.647–52). See also D. Furley, *The Greek Cosmologists* (Cambridge, 1987), 197; Hiatt, *Terra Incognita*, 18–19.

[16] A. O. Prickard, ed. and trans., *Plutarch. On the Face in the Moon* (Winchester, 1911), 21–2 (VII.924a–c) with a somewhat entertaining analogy to the human body in 924c.

[17] For the most comprehensive discussion of Christian cosmography in late antiquity and the early Middle Ages, see: H. Inglebert, *Interpretatio Christiana. Les mutations des savoirs (cosmographie, géographie, ethnographie, histoire) dans l'Antiquité chrétienne (30–630 après J.C.)* (Paris, 2001). It is important to note that it is not true that the majority of Christians believed the earth to be flat. See J. B. Russel, *Inventing the Flat Earth: Columbus and Modern Historians* (New York, NY, 1991); Inglebert, *Interpretatio Christiana*, 31–6.

[18] For example Isaiah 40:22 is quoted in support of the idea that heaven is shaped like a hemisphere R. Riedinger, ed., *Pseudo-Kaisarios. Die Erotapokriseis. Die griechischen christlichen Schriftsteller der ersten Jahrhunderte* (Berlin, 1989), 97; Severianos, *Gabalorum Episcopi in Mundi Creationem Homiliae*, PG 56, coll. 452; R. M. Grant, trans., *Theophilos of Antioch. Ad Autolycum* (Oxford, 1970), 2.13.22–3, 2.13.25; A. M. Malingrey and R. Flacelière, eds. and trans., *Jean Chrysostom. Homélies sur l'incompréhensibilité de Dieu* (Paris, 1970), vol. II, 223, 476; John Chrysostom, *Homily on the Epistle to Hebrews*, PG 63, 111; Diodoros, in R. Henry, ed., *Photius. Bibliothèque* (Paris, 1959–91), vol. IV, 8–48 (cod. 223), a sphere (C. Scholten, ed., *Johannes Philoponos. De opificio mundi. Über die Erschaffung der Welt* (Freiburg, 1997), vol. I, 132.6–11) or a vault (W. Wolska-Conus, ed., *Cosmas Indicopleustès. Topographie chrétienne* (Paris, 1968–73), vol. I, 325 (II.21) and 539–41 (IV.4).

[19] For a detailed discussion of the classical cosmography, see J. Evans, *The History and Practice of Ancient Astronomy* (Oxford, 1998).

[20] For example, Severianos, *In mundi creationem homiliae*, 452; John Chrysostom, *Homily on the Epistle to Hebrews*, 111. See also Inglebert, *Interpretatio Christiana*, 54–5.

[21] Diodoros, in *Photius. Bibliothèque*, ed. Henry, vol. IV, 8–48 (cod. 223). The incompatibility of the spherical universe with Christian dogma is also discussed by Eznik of Kolb in a treatise which preserves part of the teaching of Antiochene masters. See: C. J. F. Dowsett, 'On Eznik's Refutation of the Chaldean Astrologers', *ReArm*, 6 (1969), 45–65; Inglebert, *Interpretatio Christiana*, 55–6.

the spherical universe as eternal, which contradicted the Christian doctrine of Creation and the Christian hope of Resurrection.[22] This is not to say, however, that all Christians who opposed astrology or the eternity of the universe necessarily rejected the spherical model of the universe.[23]

Christian authors thus approached the idea of the antipodes much as their classical predecessors had done. Some accepted their existence,[24] while others dismissed it on the basis of the arguments employed already by the Epicureans and Plutarch.[25] It was not until Augustine that someone pointed out that an inhabited antipodean region was incompatible with Christian dogma. Since the zone around the equator was impassable on account of heat, the inhabitants of the other hemisphere could not be descendants of Adam through the sons of Noah, and, consequently, could not have been redeemed by Christ.[26] This notion was later taken up by Prokopios of Gaza, who argued that, if there were men on the other side of the earth, Christ must have gone there and suffered to save them. He also posited the existence of an antipodean equivalent to the earthly Paradise, Adam, the serpent and the Flood.[27]

The most systematic and the most complex opposition to the idea of the antipodes from the Greek milieu comes from the sixth-century writer known

---

[22] Prokopios of Gaza, *Commentary on Genesis*, PG 87.1, 39–41; *Chronicon Paschale*, PG 92, 573. On the eternity of the universe see R. R. K. Sorabji, *Time, Creation and the Continuum* (London, 1983).

[23] For the *Hexaemeron* of George of Pisidia, who defended the sphericity and mobility of heaven see G. Bianchi, 'Sulla cultura astronomica di Giorgio di Pisidia', *Aevum*, 40 (1964), 35–51. The most extensive Christian discussions of the classical model of the cosmos as acceptable from a Christian point of view came from John Philoponos. For an excellent discussion see C. Wildberg, 'Prolegomena to Study of Philoponus' Contra Aristotelem' in R. Sorabji, ed., *Philoponus and the Rejection of Aristotelian Science* (London, 1987) 197–209; C. Wildberg, *John Philoponus' Criticism of Aristotle's Theory of Aether* (Berlin, 1988), 13–17; B. Elweskiöld, 'Cosmas Indicopleustes and John Philoponus: a Christian Controversy on the Structure of the World in Sixth-century Alexandria', unpublished doctoral thesis, Lund University (2005).

[24] H. Crouzel and M. Simonetti, eds. and trans., Origen. *Traité des principes, Peri Archôn* (Paris, 1978–84), 264–70 (II.3.6). See also G. Boffito, *Cosmografia primitive classica e patristica* (1903), 53; Moretti, 'The Other World and the Antipodes', 262.

[25] A. Bowen and P. Garnsey, trans., *Lactantius. Divine Institutes* (Liverpool, 2003), 213–4 (III.24). For the derivation of Lactantius' arguments from earlier authors mocking antipodes see Moretti, 'The Other World and the Antipodes', 243–4; Hiatt, *Terra Incognita*, 56–60.

[26] G. E. McCracken et al., trans., *Augustine. The City of God Against the Pagans* (Cambridge, MA, 1957–72), 49–53 (XVI.ix).

[27] Prokopios of Gaza, *Commentary on Genesis*, PG 87.1, 69B–70. On Prokopios' sources see B. ter Haar Romeny, 'Procopius of Gaza and his Library' in H. Amirav and B. ter Haar Romeny, eds., *From Rome to Constantinople. Studies in Honour of Averil Cameron* (Leuven, 2007), 173–90. Prokopios posited a hemispherical model of the universe, arguing that a spherical universe would be by its nature eternal and therefore unacceptable for Christians: Prokopios of Gaza, *Commentary on Genesis*, 39–41. For a more general discussion of the character of Prokopios' commentary on Genesis see K. Metzler, 'Genesiskommentierung bei Origenes und Prokop von Gaza', *Adamantius*, 11 (2005), 114–23.

Textual and Visual Representations of the Antipodes 435

as Kosmas Indikopleustes who, in his treatise *Christian Topography*, dismissed the spherical model of the universe.[28] The treatise originated in Alexandria, where its author is very likely to have resided for most of his life.[29] The original part of the treatise, Books 1–5, was written shortly after 543 CE.[30] The following five books, composed largely as a response to the criticism of the original publication, were added later, probably after 547, although some sections might have circulated earlier as independent publications.[31]

The treatise aims to present a universe whose shape is determined by its function as a setting for the divine plan of salvation. Kosmas believes that the universe, resting on a rectangular earth, is divided by the firmament into two superimposed spaces which correspond to two conditions of human existence: the earthly, which serves to prepare humankind for the future, and the heavenly, which will open at the Second Coming of Christ.[32] This image of the universe is likened to the tabernacle of Moses, which is divided in two by

---

[28] The *Christian Topography* was written anonymously. It is only in the eleventh century that the name Kosmas appears in one of the illustrated manuscripts of the treatise, accompanied by an epithet Indikopleustes in commentaries that quote the work. See Indikopleustes, *Topographie chrétienne*, ed. Wolska-Conus (Paris, 1968), vol. I, 109–16.

[29] M. V. Anastos, 'The Alexandrian Origin of the Christian Topography of Cosmas Indicopleustes', *DOP*, 3 (1946), 73–80.

[30] The *terminus post quem* for the publication of the original corpus is the earthquake that destroyed Corinth in 543 (V. Grumel, *La Chronologie* (Paris, 1958), 478), mentioned in Indikopleustes, *Topographie chrétienne*, ed. Wolska-Conus, vol. I, 293–95 (1.22). The original treatise entitled Χριστιανικὴ Τοπογραφία περιεκτικὴ παντὸς τοῦ κόσμου consists of the following books (λόγοι): Book 1 Πρὸς τοὺς χριστιανίζειν μὲν ἐθέλοντας, κατὰ τοὺς ἔξωθεν δὲ σφαιροειδῆ τὸν οὐρανὸν νομίζοντας εἶναι καὶ δοξάζοντας; Book 2 Ὑποθέσεις χριστιανικαὶ περὶ σχημάτων καὶ τοποθεσίας (παντὸς τοῦ κόσμου ἐκ τῆς θείας Γραφῆς τὰς ἀποδείξεις ἔχουσαι; Book 3 Ὅτι βεβαία ἐστὶ καὶ ἀξιόπιστος ἡ θεία Γραφὴ καὶ συμφώνως αὐτὴ ἑαυτῇ καθ' ἑαυτὴν διηγουμένη, Παλαιά τε καὶ Καινὴ Διαθήκη, σημαίνουσα καὶ τὸ χρήσιμον τῶν σχημάτων τοῦ παντὸς κόσμου; Book 4 Ἀνακεφαλαίωσις σύντομος καὶ διαγραφὴ σχημάτων τοῦ κόσμου κατὰ τὴν θείαν Γραφήν, καὶ τῆς σφαίρας ἀνατροπή; Book 5 Ἐν ᾧ ἐστι τῆς σκηνῆς ἡ διαγραφή, καὶ τῶν προφητῶν καὶ ἀποστόλων ἡ συμφωνία.

[31] The *terminus post quem* for the second publication is provided in Indikopleustes, *Topographie chrétienne*, ed. Wolska-Conus, vol. III, 15–17 (VI.3), where the author refers to two eclipses: that of the sun on the 12th day of Mechir and that of the moon on the 24th day of Mesore, identified with the eclipses of 6 February and 17 August 547. See T. Oppolzer, *Canon of Eclipses* (New York, NY, 1962), 168; Grumel, *Chronologie*, 202. Book 6, identified as συνημμένος (joined, or additional) is entitled Περὶ μεγέθους ἡλίου; Book 7 Πρὸς Ἀναστάσιον ὅτι ἀκατάλυτοί εἰσιν οἱ οὐρανοί and Book 8 Εἰς τὴν ᾠδὴν Ἐζεκίου, καὶ εἰς τὸν ἀναποδισμὸν τοῦ ἡλίου both refer to the *Christian Topography* as a different work by the same author. Book 9 is entitled Καταγραφὴ δρόμου ἄστρων; Book 10 Χρήσεις πατέρων συνᾴδουσαι τῷ ὅλῳ συγγράμματι. Two of the illustrated complete manuscripts of the treatise (Sin. gr. 1186 and Laur. Plut. IX. 28, both dated to the eleventh century) contain two more books, but these are clearly identified as not belonging to the *Christian Topography*.

[32] For the discussion of Kosmas' cosmography see W. Wolska-Conus, *La topographie chrétienne de Cosmas Indicopleustès: théologie et science au VIe siècle* (Paris, 1962) and M. Kominko, *The World of Kosmas: the Byzantine Illustrated Codices of the Christian Topography* (Cambridge, 2013).

the veil just as the universe is divided by the firmament.[33] Moreover, the furnishings of the tabernacle, the table and the menorah, are believed to represent the earth and the heavenly bodies.[34] At the same time, these objects carry a chronological symbolism. Thus, the table of the tabernacle, with the twelve breads placed on it, is not only the image of the earth, but also the image of a calendar year. Its four corners stand for four seasons and the twelve breads represent the twelve months. Likewise, the menorah, in addition to representing the heavenly bodies, symbolises, through its seven branches, the seven days of the week. This symbolism is consistent with the notion that the physical and the temporal aspects of the cosmos are in harmony. It exemplifies Christian opposition to the spherical universe which many authors perceived as necessarily eternal.

The *Christian Topography* combines ancient science with the exegesis of Scripture. This method originated from the Eastern Syrian school of Nisibis, and was ultimately inspired by the teaching of Theodore of Mopsuestia.[35] On these grounds modern scholars have often branded Kosmas as a Nestorian, but there is little in the Christian Topography to support such a view.[36] Kosmas was not primarily concerned with Christology, and he dealt with this subject only inasmuch as it was important for his cosmography. His opponents are first and foremost those Christians who accepted classical theories of the universe, and it is against them that his treatise was written.

In the prologue, Kosmas lays out the scope of his project: to eradicate completely the error of the pagan theories on the universe (ἐκ βάθρων

---

[33] Indikopleustes, *Topographie chrétienne*, ed. Wolska-Conus, vol. I, 267–9 (Hypothesis 6), 307 (II.2), 341 (II.35), 453 (III.16), 491 (III.55); vol. II, 39–41 (V.20), 49–51 (V.27), 63 (V.35), 73 (V.41), 99 (V.64), 169–71 (V.112), 363–5 (V.248); vol. III, 67–9 (VII.11–12), 133 (VII.71), 145 (VII.82) 153–5 (VII.87–8), 219 (IX.11).

[34] The table of the tabernacle as the image of the earth: ibid., vol. I, 323 (II.19), 351 (II.43); vol. II, 59–63 (V.33–4); vol. III, 219 (IX.11); the menorah as the image of the heavenly bodies, vol. II, 59–61 (V.33); vol. III, 205 (IX.1–2).

[35] A. Becker, 'The Dynamic Reception of Theodore of Mopsuestia in the Sixth Century: Greek, Syriac, and Latin' in S. F. Johnson, ed., *Greek Literature in Late Antiquity: Dynamism, Didacticism, Classicism* (Aldershot, 2006), 29–47; R. Devreesse, *Essai sur Théodore de Mopsueste* (Vatican, 1948), 26; Wolska-Conus, *Topographie chrétienne*, 40–61; 65–9.

[36] It is clear that the author did not believe the two natures of Christ to be separate. On the contrary, he asserted that Christ's humanity and divinity were combined within one person, in the same way as the two spaces and the two conditions of existence were joined within one universe. See Indikopleustes, *Topographie chrétienne*, ed. Wolska-Conus, vol. I, 267–9 (Hypothesis 6), 419 (II.99), 421–3 (II.102); vol. II, 97 (V.62), 371 (V.254); vol. III, 125 (VII.65), 289 (X.48). Kosmas describes the union between the two natures as inseparable, vol. II, 135 (V.88), 157 (V.104), 191–3 (V.131) 303–5 (V.202–3), but see also 146–7 (V.98 note), where Kosmas enumerates Christ's attributes according to his divinity (κατὰ τὴν θεότητα) and according to his humanity (κατὰ τὴν ἀνθρωπότητα); Wolska-Conus, *Topographie chrétienne*, 90–8.

ἀνελεῖν τῶν ἑλληνικῶν ὑποθέσεων τὴν πλάνην), to refute 'the folly of the myth-makers' (τῶν μυθολόγων τὴν ἄνοιαν), and to provide his Christian readers with the tools to do the same themselves. He confesses his lack of secular education (τῆς ἔξωθεν ἐγκυκλίου παιδείας), and his ignorance of the art of rhetoric, which does not allow him to compose a discourse in an elaborate style.[37] It should briefly be noted, however, that these self-confessions represent a literary topos in Christian literature across the board. Yet, these shortcomings only serve to stress that the theories he describes are truly Christian, and that what he sets out to do should be seen:

> not as communicating opinions and conjectures of my own devising, but the knowledge obtained from the divine scriptures, and from the living voice of that most divine man and great teacher Patrikios
>
> (οὐκ οἴκοθεν ὁρμηθείς, οὐδ' ἐξ ἐμαυτοῦ πλασάμενος ἢ στοχασάμενος, ἀλλ' ἐκ τῶν θείων Γραφῶν παιδευθείς, καὶ διὰ ζώσης δὲ φωνῆς παραλαβὼν ὑπὸ τοῦ θειοτάτου ἀνδρὸς καὶ μεγάλου διδασκάλου Πατρικίου).[38]

This true knowledge he contrasts with the teachings of the pagans, the outsiders (οἱ ἔξωθεν, οἱ ἔξω) or Hellenes (οἱ Ἕλληνες), who describe the universe as spherical and eternal.[39] In the opening of Book 1, Kosmas outlines three kinds of attitude towards knowledge: first, that of true Christians; second, that of the pagans; and third, that of those who only pretend to be Christian, but in reality profess pagan beliefs concerning the universe. In Kosmas' words, true Christians are guided by the desire for true knowledge (τῆς ἀληθοῦς γνώσεως), hold the Old and New Testament to be truly Divine, believe that God created the universe from nothing, and have faith in the Resurrection of men.[40] The second group, the pagans, are immersed in the wisdom of this world (οἱ δὲ τῇ τοῦ κόσμου τούτου σοφίᾳ κοσμούμενοι). Their theories on the shape of the universe are based on their own reasoning rather than on the Holy Scriptures, which

---

[37] Indikopleustes, *Topographie chrétienne*, ed. Wolska-Conus, vol. 1, 305 (II.1). See also S. Rubenson, 'Philosophy and Simplicity: the Problem of Classical Education in Early Christian Biography' in T. Hägg and P. Rousseau, eds., *Greek Biography and Panegyric in Late Antiquity* (Berkeley, CA, 2000), 110–39.

[38] Indikopleustes, *Topographie chrétienne*, ed. Wolska-Conus, 307 (II.2). Similarly, in 433–5 (II.111), where Kosmas stresses that the Christian opinions are created on the basis of the Holy Scripture and not on 'fictions and conjectures of our belief' (οὐχ ἑαυτοῖς πλασαμένοις ἢ στοχασαμένοις). Mar Aba, who is referred to in this passage as Patrikios, is considered to have been a student and later a teacher in the East Syrian school of Nisibis; see Becker, 'The Dynamic Reception of Theodore of Mopsuestia', 45–52.

[39] Indikopleustes, *Topographie chrétienne*, ed. Wolska-Conus, vol. 1, 527–9 (III.87).

[40] Ibid., 305 (II.1).

they count among the myths. Kosmas declares them to be both deceivers and deceived (πλανῶντες καὶ πλανώμενοι) (2 Timothy 3:13) because they believe heaven to be spherical and rotating.[41] Finally, he describes those who want to be Christians, but at the same time wish to immerse themselves in the wisdom and the multitude of errors of this world (οἱ δὲ χριστιανίζειν μὲν ἐθέλοντες, τοῖς λόγοις δὲ καὶ τῇ σοφίᾳ καὶ τῇ ποικιλίᾳ τῆς πλάνης τοῦ κόσμου τούτου πάλιν θέλοντες κοσμεῖσθαι).[42] It is against this last group that Kosmas directs his discourse, comparing them to those castigated in 2 Kings 17:32-3 as fearing the Lord and at the same time serving foreign gods.[43] Indeed, on this matter he engages in a controversy with a contemporary Alexandrian, John Philoponos, who accepts the classical image of the universe as compatible with the Bible and who in his *On the Making of the World* ridicules Kosmas' theories.[44] It is important to note that their dispute should be read in the context of the Christian–pagan debate on the eternity of the universe, in which both authors participate. While Philoponos accepts the spherical model of the cosmos, at the same time demonstrating that it cannot be eternal, for Kosmas the fact that the universe cannot be eternal precludes any possibility that it may be spherical.[45] For him, a spherical and perpetually rotating universe must necessarily be eternal. Undermining the connection between the temporal and spatial form of the universe is a logical mistake of fable-makers, who invent new theories 'blinded by their excessive need for approval' (τυφλώττουσαν ὑπὸ τῆς ἄγαν φιλοτιμίας).[46]

---

[41] Ibid., 307 (II.2). In Paul's letter these epithets refer to evil-doers: 'But evil men and seducers shall wax worse and worse, deceiving, and being deceived' (πονηροὶ δὲ ἄνθρωποι καὶ γόητες προκόψουσιν ἐπὶ τὸ χεῖρον, πλανῶντες καὶ πλανώμενοι) (2 Tim. 3:13). They are later used by Christian writers, often outside the context of Paul's letter, as for example M. Rauer, ed. *Origenes. Die Homilien zu Lukas in der Übersetzung des Hieronymus und die griechischen Reste der Homilien und des Lukas-Kommentars* (Berlin, 1959), 227–336 (fr. 154:7); John Chrysostom, *De Pseudoprophetis*, PG 59, col. 558 and 564. Invectives against pagans are repeated in Indikopleustes, *Topographie chrétienne*, ed. Wolska-Conus, vol. II, 275–7 (v.178), 363–5 (v.248) and (along with invectives against Jews and heretics) in 369 (v.252); vol. III, 41 (VI.25).

[42] Ibid., vol. I, 307–9 (II.3). The invectives against the Christian followers of pagan doctrines appear again in vol. II, 353–5 (v.243) and (along with the invectives against pagans, Manicheans and Marcionites) in 275–7 (v.178).

[43] Ibid., vol. I, 309 (II.4) and 265 (Hypothesis 4).

[44] On the Kosmas-Philoponos debate see Elweskiöld, 'Cosmas Indicopleustes and John Philoponus'.

[45] Indikopleustes, *Topographie chrétienne*, ed. Wolska-Conus, vol. III, 57–167 (VII). This aspect of the debate has been so far mostly overlooked. For a discussion see Kominko, *World of Kosmas*.

[46] See Indikopleustes, *Topographie chrétienne*, ed. Wolska-Conus, 59–61 (VII.2–3) for invectives against such people.

Textual and Visual Representations of the Antipodes 439

Kosmas strives to disprove ancient Greek and Roman theories of the universe not only by recourse to the Bible, but also by recourse to logic and observation.[47] He repeatedly stresses that his exposition is based on Holy Scripture as well as empirical observation and on the reading of ancient writers.[48] He strives to demonstrate that the image of the universe deriving from biblical exegesis is compatible with that resulting from observation.[49] Throughout the text it is clear that the audience Kosmas addresses were Christians exposed to, and in danger of accepting, the pagan theories of the universe. These were the people who, like the author himself, sought to understand the world surrounding them, and perhaps perceived some difficulties in reconciling the Bible with science and observation.

The *Christian Topography* is richly illustrated. Although the original manuscript is lost, the similarity of the illustrations in all three preserved Byzantine codices, dating to the ninth (Vat. gr. 699) and eleventh centuries (Sin. gr. 1186, Laur. Plut. IX. 28), as well as a very close relationship between their textual content and the images, leaves little doubt that they reflect the sixth-century original. The majority of the illustrations pertaining to cosmography appear in Book 4. This book, which contains very little text, resembles a table of plates for the cosmographic exposition of the preceding books. The last of the cosmographic miniatures depicts the antipodes as four men standing at the cardinal points of the globe. Although the miniature is preserved in only one of the three manuscripts, the eleventh-century codex Laurentianus Plut. IX. 28, and the corresponding folios are missing from the other two codices, it seems fairly clear that this image must have been present in the sixth-century original.[50] Not only is the

---

[47] The arguments based on logic and observation are primarily gathered in Book 1. Arguments on the grounds of logic: if the heavenly bodies move along with the sphere of heaven, it is impossible to account for the irregular movements of planets; if they move alone, they must be cutting through the heavens, consequently making its substance divisible, which is perishable and therefore non-eternal (Indikopleustes, *Topographie chrétienne*, ed. Wolska-Conus, vol. I, 281–5 (I.9–13)); if the sphere of the universe moves, than we should ask what this great space that the universe is located in is, as the movement requires a space (319–21 (II.15–16)). For the in-depth discussion of Kosmas' polemical method see Kominko, *World of Kosmas*. On the incompatibility of the spherical model of the universe with the Christian faith, see in particular Indikopleustes, *Topographie chrétienne*, ed. Wolska-Conus, 417 (II.97), 419–21 (II.100), 493–5 (III.57–8), 561 (IV.17), 565 (IV.20). On the contrast of pagan and Christian science see 433–5 (II.111).

[48] On the ancient authors whose works, according to Kosmas, support his theories see Indikopleustes, *Topographie chrétienne*, ed. Wolska-Conus, 395–9 (II.78–80). On observation of phenomena (here specifically eclipses) supporting his theories on the universe see 383–5 (II.67–8). See also M. V. Anastos, 'Aristotle and Cosmas on the Void: a Note on Theology and Science in the Sixth Century' in M. V. Anastos, *Studies in Byzantine Intellectual History* (London, 1979), 36–50.

[49] See for example his discussion of eclipses: Indikopleustes, *Topographie chrétienne*, ed. Wolska-Conus, vol. I, 265 (Hypothesis 4), 423–5 (II.103), 553 (IV.13); vol. III, 15–17 (VI.3) and 209 (IX.5).

[50] In Vat. gr. 699 there is a lacuna after 4:22. In Sin. gr. 1186 a lacuna after 4:17.

drawing of the antipodes (διαγραφὴν τῶν ἀντιπόδων) referred to in the text,[51] but the author himself also encourages all who have a 'healthy vision and sane mind' to turn the miniature around, and judge whether the antipodes can all be standing upright at the same time (καὶ πᾶς τις ἐν ὑμῖν ἔχων ὄψεῖς ὑγεῖς καὶ λογισμοὺς σώφρονας περιστρέψει ὡς ἂν βούληται τὴν γῆν καὶ εἰπάτω, εἰ πάντες οἱ ἀντίποδες δύνανται ὄρθιοι κατὰ ταὐτὸν εἶναι).[52] Such an invitation to change the orientation of a drawing and look at it from several perspectives is, to the best of my knowledge, unique in late antique and Byzantine art, and strongly suggests that the miniature in the Laurenziana codex was in fact very similar to the original sixth-century illustration of the treatise.[53]

The arguments against the notion of the antipodes are scattered throughout the *Christian Topography*. Like many other authors, Christian and non-Christian alike, Kosmas finds the idea of upside-down people nonsensical.[54] Referring to the original significance of the concept he notes that it is impossible for two people with their feet opposite to each other to be upright.[55] Moreover, in his discussion of the antipodes, Kosmas draws on arguments from the Bible, pointing out that, according to Acts 17:26, one race of humans, descended from one man, inhabits the entire world (ἐπὶ παντὸς προσώπου τῆς γῆς). Rather than develop this quotation into an argument similar to that of Augustine, he claims that Holy Scripture situates the human race only on the face of the earth and not on its opposite side (οὐκ ἐπὶ ἀντιπροσώπου).[56] He also quotes Philippians 2:10, where we read that the name of Jesus should make every knee

---

[51] Indikopleustes, *Topographie chrétienne*, ed. Wolska-Conus, vol. I, 569 (IV.25). See also J. W. McCrindle, *The Christian Topography of Kosmas, an Egyptian Monk* (London, 1897), 137; Wolska-Conus, *Cosmas Indicopleustès*, vol. I, 568.

[52] Indikopleustes, *Topographie chrétienne*, ed. Wolska-Conus, vol. I, 567–9 (IV.23).

[53] Because the illustration in the *Topographie chrétienne* shows figures standing at the four opposite points of the earth, it seems that it takes inspiration from ancient theories on the terrestrial globe ultimately deriving from the globe of Crates. Such an image of the earth was very well known in antiquity, as indicated by numerous descriptions, but no extant representation can be safely identified as illustrating it. It has been suggested that the coins of Lucius Aemilius Buca (c. 44 BCE with a diagonal cross on their surface), show a similar disposition of lands separated by the Ocean (Harley and Woodward, 'Greek Cartography', 164, ill. 10.3). Nevertheless, such a hypothesis is very tenuous, as it is not supported by any written sources. Not only is there no evidence to support such an identification, but also some ancient and late antique representations of globes with a similar diagonal division can be identified as celestial rather than terrestrial globes, either because they are covered with stars, or because they are represented next to Urania, see P. Arnaud, 'L'image du globe dans le monde romain: science, iconographique, symbolique', *MEFRA*, 96 (1984), 80–112; H. G. Gundell, *Zodiakos. Tierkreisbilder im altertum. Kosmische Bezüge und Jenseitsvorstellungen im antike Alltagsleben* (Mainz, 1992), 295 (nos. 316, 319–20).

[54] Indikopleustes, *Topographie chrétienne*, ed. Wolska-Conus, vol. I, 285–7 (I.14).

[55] Ibid., 291–3 (I.20). [56] Ibid., 429 (II.107).

flex – the celestial (ἐπουρανίων), terrestrial (ἐπιγείων) and those under the earth (καταχθονίων). Kosmas seems to imply here a distinction between the καταχθόνιοι and ἐπίγειοι, and the ἀντίχθονες ('those opposite', that is, the antipodes), who cannot be classified as either of those two.[57] Further, Kosmas quotes Luke 10:19, where Jesus gives the apostles power to tread over snakes and scorpions, which in Kosmas' interpretation is impossible to reconcile with the idea of a spherical earth where, according to some, there is no 'up' and no 'down'.[58]

Next to Prokopios of Gaza, Kosmas is the only other late antique author to dispute the existence of the antipodes. They both posit this in the context of their broader rejection of the concept of the spherical earth along with the spherical universe. After the sixth century, the antipodes do not seem to have caused any controversy among Greek authors, who do not discuss them in detail, but only refer to them in a cursory fashion. A letter of Photios of Constantinople suggests that the antipodes were understood as a theoretical concept, a corollary of the conception of the spherical universe with a spherical earth at its centre.[59] In the eleventh century, Psellos expressed his embarrassment at the ignorance of the young prince Andronikos, who did not believe that the antipodes could exist, because if they existed people there would have to walk upside-down.[60] Tzetzes refers to this idea in Plato and pokes fun at the notion of the upside-down people as incomprehensible.[61] Gregory Pachymeres rejects the possibilty of another *oikoumene*, but this is because in his estimation, the whole of the globe, with the exception of the known inhabited earth is covered by water.[62] At no point beyond the sixth century do the antipodes become a theological issue for the Greek authors.

Just how inoffensive the antipodes were to the Byzantines is apparent from their appearance in the illuminated Byzantine Psalters: in the ninth-century Khludov and Paris Psalters, the illustrations show four figures standing at the opposite points of the globe, very much like in the *Christian Topography*; in the eleventh-century Barberini and Theodore

---

[57] Ibid. On the use of the term antichthonians in the sources see Romm, *The Edges of the Earth*, 131–2 and n. 27.
[58] Ibid.
[59] K. Staab, 'Photios. In epistolam ad Romanos, Fragmenta' in *Pauluskommentar aus der griechischen Kirche aus Katenenhandschriften gesammelt* (Münster, 1933), 479.
[60] É. Renauld, ed. and trans., *Michel Psellos. Chronographie, ou histoire d'un siècle de Byzance (976–1077)* (Paris, 1926–8), 179–80 (VII.14).
[61] P. L. M. Leone, *Ioannis Tzetzae Historiae* (Naples, 1968), 275–9 (VII.143).
[62] R. P. E. Stephanou and P. Tannery, *Quadrivium de Georges Pachymère* (Vatican, 1940) 4.12–13.

Psalters, two clusters of figures are depicted, standing on the poles of the earth.[63] In all four manuscripts, the images of the antipodes accompany Psalm 101:25:'At the beginning it was you, O Lord, who founded the earth, and the heavens are works of your hands.' Thus, they serve to illustrate the universe created by God, who, according to another passage of the Psalms 'founded the earth on its stability' (Psalm 103:5) – a notion which the antipodes, as understood by the Greek writers, exemplify.

In contrast to the Greek tradition, the antipodes were very much an object of controversy among Latin authors. Unlike the Byzantines, Latins understood 'antipodes' primarily as denoting not a region of the earth but the actual inhabitants of the southern hemisphere. Among the first to dismiss these mythical inhabitants was Tertullian, who names the antipodes alongside the fabled and absurd races of the dog-faced men and skiapods, whose existence he rejected.[64] A few centuries later, Isidore of Seville (c. 560–636 CE) firmly rejected the idea of the antipodes:

> With regard to those who are called *antipodae* – because they are thought to be opposite us in that, placed beneath the earth, as it were, their footprints oppose our own – it is by no means to be believed. Neither the solidity nor the centre of the earth permits it, nor is it confirmed by any historical evidence, but it is the poets, in a kind of quasi-reasoning, who make such conjectures.[65]

The only antipodes he was prepared to accept were a curious race of men in Libya whose feet, equipped with eight toes, faced backwards.[66] A similar

---

[63] Khludov Psalter (Moscow, Historical Museum, cod.gr.129), fol. 91v; Paris Psalter (Paris, Bibliothèque Nationale, cod. gr. 20), fol. 9r; Barberini Psalter (Rome, Bibliotheca Apostolica Vaticana, cod. gr. 372), fol. 172r; Theodore Psalter (London, British Library, cod. Add. 19352), fol. 135v. See K. Corrigan, *Visual Polemics in the Ninth-century Byzantine Psalters* (Cambridge, 1992), 25 and 68.

[64] Tertullian, *Ad Nationes*, PL 1, 570–1 (1.8.1–13).

[65] Isidore, *Etymologies*, ed. Barney et al., 199 (IX.ii.133): 'Iam vero hi qui Antipodae dicuntur, eo quod contrarii esse vestigiis nostris putantur, ut quasi sub terris positi adversa pedibus nostris calcent vestigia, nulla ratione credendum est, quia nec soliditas patitur, nec centrum terrae; sed neque hoc ulla historiae cognitione firmatur, sed hoc poetae quasi ratiocinando coniectant.' See also Inglebert, *Interpretatio Christiana*, 92; G. Boffito, 'La legenda degli antipodi,' in A. Della Torre, ed., *Miscellanea di studi critici ed. in onore di Arturo Graf* (Bergamo, 1903), 583–601; W. W. McCredy, 'Isidore, the Antipodeans and the Shape of the Earth', *Isis*, 87 (1996), 108–27.

[66] Isidore, *Etymologies*, ed. Barney et al., 245 (XI.iii.24): 'Antipodes in Libya plantas versas habent post crura et octonos digitos in plantis.' This kind of Antipodal race is consistent with the traditional attribution to the southern part of Africa-Ethiopia of people blackened and otherwise deformed by the heat of the sun, an ancient notion reflected, for example, in Pliny's *Natural History*, ed. Rackham, 476–9 (VI.35.187). The Antipodes of Isidore seem to be a mixture of the Indian people whose feet face backwards, described by Megasthenes, and eight-toed people described by Ktesias and Pliny. See V. I. J. Flint, 'Monsters and Antipodes in the Early Middle Ages and Enlightenment', *Viator*, 15 (1984), 70–1; J. B. Friedman, *The Monstrous Races in Medieval Art and*

idea about the identity of the antipodes is illustrated on the maps accompanying eighth-century Beatus of Liebana's *Commentary on the Apocalypse*, where a land to the south of the *oikoumene*, separated from it by the ocean, is identified by a label as the fourth part of the world, unknown on account of the heat of the sun, where the legendary Antipodes are said to live.[67] The text of the label, taken verbatim from the *Etymologies* of Isidore, is accompanied in many other manuscripts by the figure of a skiapod, most probably inspired by Isidore's identification of the antipodes as one of the fantastic races.[68] Whereas it is not clear if Beatus imagined the earth as flat or spherical, Isidore certainly believed it to be a sphere.[69] This indicates that he did not understand the notion of 'antipodes' to be in any way related to the earth's shape, but rather as designating mythical inhabitants of the southern hemisphere, in whose existence he did not believe. Similarly, Bede (672/673– 735 CE), another author who believed that the earth was spherical, decisively rejected, in his discussion of the five climatic zones of the globe, any possibility that the temperate zone in the southern hemisphere was inhabited.[70] In the eighth century, Virgil of Salzburg argued in favour of the existence of the inhabited antipodes, but he was reprimanded, and his teaching was condemned by pope Zacharius.[71] It is important to note, however, that Zacharius did not condemn the theory that the earth was spherical, but merely denied that it was inhabited by peoples who had not descended from Adam, and whom the apostles,

---

Thought (Cambridge, MA, 1981), 12; R. Wittkower, 'Marvels of the East: a Study in the History of Monsters', *JWarb*, 5 (1942), 159–97.

[67] After Isidore, *Etymologies*, ed. Barney et al., 293 (XIV.v.17): 'Extra tres autem partes orbis quarta pars trans oceanum interior est in meridie, quae solis ardore incognita nobis est; in cuius finibus Antipodes fabulose inhabitare produntur.' Although it has been argued that such an interpretation of this land was originally intended by Beatus himself. J. G. Arentzen, *Imago Mundi Cartografica* (Munich, 1984), 108–10; D. von den Brincken, *Fines Terrae. Die Enden der Erde und der vierte Kontinent auf mittelalterlichen Weltkarten* (Hanover, 1992), 51. This has been disputed by scholars who note that this inscription does not appear in the Beatus tradition uniformly, but only in one branch of the stemma, in manuscripts presenting the final stage in the evolution of the *Commentary*, See J. Williams, 'Isidore, Orosius and the Beatus Map', *Imago Mundi*, 49 (1997), 17–21.

[68] M. Destombes, *Mappemondes A.D. 1200–1500* (Amsterdam, 1964), 40–2; 79–80.

[69] Isidore, *Etymologies*, ed. Barney et al., 100 (III.xxxii); C. B. Kendall and F. Wallis, eds., *Isidore of Seville. On the Nature of Things* (Liverpool, 2016), 175–6 (48).

[70] F. Wallis, trans., *Bede. The Reckoning of Time* (Liverpool, 1999), p. 96 (34).

[71] *Epistola XI Zachariae papae ad Bonifacium archiepiscopum*, PL 89, col. 946D. See also J. B. Russel, 'Saint Boniface and the Eccentrics', *Church History*, 33 (1964), 235–47. The papal rejection of the antipodes has been often confused with the rejection of the theory that the earth was spherical. For example Tom Paine (1737–1809) wrote that 'Vigilius (Vergil of Salzburg) was condemned to be burned (sic) for asserting the antipodes, or in other words, that the earth was a globe'. See T. Paine, *The Age of Reason* (London, 1794), 496–4. On the later history of Zacharias' letter, on its use during the trial of Gallileo and on its quotation by Kepler see Flint, 'Monsters and Antipodes', 65–7.

charged with preaching to all nations (Matthew 28:19; Acts 2:4–5), would not have been able to reach.[72] Far from being purely a theological problem, this issue had long-lasting and unfortunate consequences: it was, for example, taken up again by sixteenth-century theologians, who contested the humanity of the Native Americans, arguing that they were not descendants of Adam.[73] While this was a pole apart from Augustine and his discussion of the antipodes, it is something of a paradox that the antipodean people seem to have lived on in the Christian imagination in the West, largely because their existence was so fervently denied.

Further Reading

The key textual sources are: W. Wolska-Conus, ed., *Cosmas Indicopleustès. Topographie chrétienne*, 3 vols. (Paris, 1968–73), and S. A. Barney et al., eds., *The Etymologies of Isidore of Seville. Etymologies* (Cambridge, 2006). Studies include: A. Hiatt, *Terra Incognita: Mapping the Antipodes Before 1600* (London, 2008); H. Inglebert, *Interpretatio Christiana. Les mutations des savoirs (cosmographie, géographie, ethnographie, histoire) dans l'Antiquité chrétienne (30–630 après J.C.)* (Paris, 2001); M. Kominko, *The World of Kosmas. The Byzantine Illustrated Codices of the Christian Topography* (Cambridge, 2013).

---

[72] Russel, *Inventing the Flat Earth*, 20–3; 91–2; Flint, 'Monsters and Antipodes', 75–6.
[73] G. Gliozzi, *Adamo e il Nuovo Mondo. La nascita dell'antropologia come ideologiia coloniale: delle genealogie bibliche alle teorie razziali (1500–1700)* (Florence, 1977), 67–72; I. Hanke, *Aristotle and the American Indians: a Study in Race Prejudice in the Modern World* (London, 1959), 40–8, 76–8.

Interlingual Circulation and Transmission

CHAPTER 20

Basil I, Constantine VII and Armenian Literary Tradition in Byzantium

Tim Greenwood

The relationship between Byzantium and Armenia in the second half of the ninth century has traditionally been plotted along two axes. It has been projected in terms of gradual Byzantine re-engagement with the leading princely houses of historic Armenia after an extended period of exclusion and separation. This formed part of a wider Byzantine strategy of consolidation and then expansion along the eastern frontier that achieved its fullest expression in the following century.[1] At the same time, the relationship has also been studied in terms of the presence of Armenians throughout the institutions of the Byzantine state, with identification usually made on the basis of name or ancestry.[2] This chapter proposes that both axes stand in need of revision. In relation to the first, the model of rupture in the decades before 850 CE and re-engagement thereafter no longer fits the evidence; in relation to the second, it is clear that the Armenian presence in Byzantium was also characterised by literary and intellectual exchanges whose significance has not been fully appreciated hitherto.

The contention that Byzantium had to revive its ties with the local elites in historic Armenia in the second half of the ninth century after a long hiatus depends largely on the absence of evidence to the contrary.[3]

---

[1] M. Whittow, *The Making of Orthodox Byzantium, 600–1025* (London, 1996), 310–57; J. Shepard, 'Constantine VII, Caucasian Openings and the Road to Aleppo' in A. Eastmond, ed., *Eastern Approaches to Byzantium* (Aldershot, 2001), 19–40; T. W. Greenwood, 'Patterns of Contact and Communication: Constantinople and Armenia, 860–976' in R. G. Hovannisian and S. Payaslian, eds., *Armenian Constantinople* (Costa Mesa, CA, 2010), 73–100.

[2] I. Brousselle, 'L'intégration des Arméniens dans l'aristocratie byzantine au ixe siècle' in *L'Arménie et Byzance: histoire et culture* (Paris, 1996), 43–54; N. Garsoïan, 'The Problem of Armenian Integration into the Byzantine Empire' in H. Ahrweiler and A. E. Laiou, eds., *Studies on the Internal Diaspora of the Byzantine Empire* (Washington, D. C., 1998), 53–124.

[3] Most recently, B. Martin-Hisard, 'Domination arabe et libertés arméniennes (viie–ixe siècle)' in G. Dédéyan, ed., *Histoire du peuple arménien* (Paris, 2008), 213–41. For example, at 231: 'Tant que Mélitène, Téphriké et Karin ne seraient pas prises, l'accès au territoire arménien échapperait aux Byzantins.'

Certainly the impression obtained from the Armenian historical tradition is that Byzantium and Armenia were out of contact with one another for long periods across the eighth and ninth centuries, a state of affairs punctuated by occasional raids. It is, however, worth reflecting that the four major Armenian writers whose histories cover this period – Łewond, Thomas Arcruni, John Katholikos and Stephen of Tarōn – were all clerics, that one was a *katholikos* of Armenia and that another was sponsored by the *katholikos* of his day.[4] The operation of Byzantine influence did not sit comfortably with their wider ecclesiastical and literary purposes and it may well be the case that it was deliberately downplayed or ignored. Three of the writers promoted notions of independent action and direction by Armenian Christians, under the headship of the *katholikos*, without recourse to, or direction from, either imperial or patriarchal authorities in Constantinople. The only exception is provided by Thomas Arcruni, whose *History of the House of Arcrunik'* is focused more narrowly upon the deeds of one princely family across several generations.[5] Significantly, it is only through his composition that we can begin to trace Byzantine involvement and attempted intervention in Armenian affairs on a more consistent basis. Unfortunately this is limited to the period after 851 CE, when Bughā's devastating campaigns across Armenia began.[6] The two centuries prior to that date are skated over in barely two pages of Patkanean's edition, comprising a bare list of caliphs without reference to Armenian affairs or interests.[7] This suggests a complete loss of family records and collective memory, although disquiet about Arcruni activities in that period cannot be entirely excluded.[8]

We therefore learn little about Byzantine initiatives across historic Armenia before 851 CE, at least from an Armenian perspective. The value of the isolated references that do survive has not always been appreciated. For example, Stephen of Tarōn records that the first Armenian prince to be accorded an imperial title while remaining in his own district was Ašot

---

[4] John Katholikos (Yovhannēs V Drasxanakertc'i) held office between 897/8 and 924/5 while Stephen of Tarōn (Step'anos Tarōnec'i) was commissioned by the Katholikos Sargis I (992/3–1019).

[5] K'. Patkanean, ed., *Թովմա Արծրունի եւ Անանուն, Պատմութիւն տանն Արծրունեաց* [*Tovma Arcruni and Anonymous, History of the House of Arcrunik'*] (St Petersburg, 1887; repr. Delmar, NY, 1991); R. W. Thomson, trans., *Thomas Artsruni: History of the House of the Artsrunik'* (Detroit, MI, 1985).

[6] Bughā al-Kabīr: see, most recently, P. B. Golden, 'Khazar Turkic Ghulâms in Caliphal Service', *Journal Asiatique* (2004), 301–2 and n. 10.

[7] Thomas Arcruni, *History of the House of Arcrunik'* ed. Patkanean, 104–6; Thomson, *Thomas Artsruni: History*, 170–3.

[8] For discussion of the re-imagination of the Armenian past – and the deliberate downplaying of Byzantine involvement – see T. W. Greenwood, 'A Reassessment of the *History* of Łewond', *Le Muséon*, 125 (2012), 138–40.

Bagratuni, prince of Sper, at some point during the reign of the Emperor Theophilos (829–42).⁹ Since this very remote and mountainous district bordered directly onto Byzantine-held territory – specifically the theme of Chaldia – the choice of the prince of Sper as the earliest recipient of imperial largesse is unsurprising. Stephen of Tarōn also reports campaigns undertaken across Armenian districts during the same emperor's reign. By combining Stephen of Tarōn's record with other, later sources, Laurent proposed that Theophilos undertook a very complicated sequence of actions across Armenia in 837 CE and this analysis has been accepted by most commentators.¹⁰ In fact, it seems far more likely that the campaigns undertaken in Basean, in Xałtik', against Theodosioupolis and in Vanand should be spread across several years rather than condensed into one.¹¹ Conceivably they were intended to exploit, and perhaps even complement, the twenty-year rebellion of Bābak in north-western Iran. After all, Khurramite survivors fled to Byzantine territory after the final defeat of Bābak in 838 and were incorporated into imperial forces under the command of Theophobos, himself a Khurramite leader who had sought refuge with a large body of supporters four years previously.¹² Brief notices such as this one reveal that channels of contact and communication between Byzantium and Armeria were open before 850 CE.

This study, however, is more directly concerned with the reformulation of the second axis. Armenians operating within the Byzantine Empire have generally been identified on the basis of anthroponymy. They have been detected holding senior military commands – and hence participating in the political process – from the middle of the sixth century.¹³ By way of illustration, in 778, four of the five *strategoi* who participated in an expedition against Germanikeia in Cilicia have been identified as Armenian: Artabasdos (Artavazd) of the Anatolikoi; Tatzates (Tačat) of the

---

⁹ G. Manukyan, ed., Ստեփանոս Տարաւնեցի Ասողիկ, Պատմութիւն տիեզերական, [Step'anos Tarōnec'i Asołik, *Universal History*] (Ant'ilias, 2012), 734; T. W. Greenwood, trans., *The Universal History of Step'anos Tarōnec'i* (Oxford, 2017), 205.
¹⁰ J. Laurent, *L'Arménie entre Byzance et l'Islam depuis la conquête arabe jusqu'en 886 (Nouvelle édition revue et mise à jour par M. Canard)* (Lisbon, 1980), 249–52.
¹¹ J. Signes Codoñer, *The Emperor Theophilos and the East 829–842: Court and Frontier in Byzantium during the Last Phase of Iconoclasm* (Farnham, 2014), 4.2 and 4.3 advances the same argument.
¹² M. Rekaya, 'Mise au point sur Théophobe et l'alliance de Bābek avec Théophile (833/4–839/40)', *BZ*, 44 (1974), 43–67; J.-C. Cheynet, 'Théophile, Théophobe et les Perses' in S. Lampakes, ed., *E Byzantine Mikra Asia, 6os–12os ai. [Byzantine Asia Minor 6th–12th Centuries]* (Athens, 1998), 39–50. Theophobos: *PmbZ* 8237; *PBE* 1(2001/2015), Theophobos 1, www.pbe.kcl.ac.uk/person/p8066 (accessed 20 December 2017).
¹³ See, for example, Justinian's commander Narses: A. H. M. Jones, J. R. Martindale and J. Morris, *The Prosopography of the Later Roman Empire.* (Cambridge, 1980), vol. IIIB, Narses 1.

Boukellarioi; Karisterotzes (Varaztiroc') of the Armeniakoi; and Gregory, son of Mousoulakios (Mušeł) of the Opsikion.[14] This pattern, of *strategoi* with apparently strong Armenian affiliations, is repeated throughout the eighth and ninth centuries.

Rather than imposing a modern definition, what exactly did contemporaries understand by the term 'Armenian'? The passage in Theophanes' *Chronographia* recording the four *strategoi* above specifically describes Artabasdos as 'Armenian'. Łewond's *History* records a campaign against Bišan (surely Bahasnā, east of Germanikeia) in the reign of Leo IV in which Artavazd Mamikonean and Tačat Anjewac'i participated as *zōravars* (commanders).[15] This is clearly the same campaign. Unlike Theophanes, Łewond identified the noble families from which the two commanders came.[16] The specific designation of Artavazd as 'Armenian' in Theophanes' *Chronographia* is atypical and may have been used because Artavazd had only recently arrived from historic Armenia. Łewond's *History* records that he had been forced to seek refuge in Byzantium after an abortive rebellion and the murder of a tax-collector in the Armenian district of Širak, probably in 771.[17] On the other hand, following this line of argument, the epithet 'Armenian' should also have been applied to Tačat Anjewac'i, since he too had originally come from historic Armenia. According to Łewond, Tačat enjoyed a career of twenty-two years in the Byzantine army down to 782, and so it could be that his 'Armenian' origin had been quietly forgotten by this time.[18] Since neither Varaztiroc' nor Gregory son of Mušeł were identified as 'Armenian' by Theophanes, the evidence from this passage is far from clear.

It is worth remembering that during these centuries, the districts of historic 'Greater Armenia' all lay beyond the frontiers of the Byzantine Empire. By contrast substantial parts of what had comprised Roman Armenia in late antiquity remained under continuous imperial hegemony,

---

[14] C. de Boor, ed., *Theophanis Chronographia* (Leipzig, 1883–5), vol. I, 451; C. Mango and R. Scott, trans., *The Chronicle of Theophanes Confessor: Byzantine and Near Eastern History, A.D. 284–813* (Oxford, 1997), 623. Artabasdos: *PmbZ* 640; Tatzates: *PmbZ* 7241; Varaztiroc': *PmbZ* 8568; Gregorios: *PmbZ* 2406.

[15] B. Martin-Hisard, trans., and A. Hakobian, ed., *Łewond Vardapet Discours historique* (Paris, 2015), 190–1.

[16] In a subsequent passage, we also learn that Tačat's father was named Grigor: Łewond, *Discours historique*, ed. Martin-Hisard and Hakobian, 198–9.

[17] Ibid., 152–3.

[18] Łewond states that Tačat held the rank of *zōravar*, commanding six thousand men, for twenty-two years: ibid., 198–9. He cannot have held the rank of *strategos* of the Boukellarioi for that period, however, because this theme was only created in 766/7: Theophanes, *Chronographia*, ed. de Boor, 440; Mango and Scott, *Theophanes*, 608 and n. 15.

if not control.¹⁹ Much of what had been the Justinianic province of Armenia I and almost all of Armenia II came to be incorporated within the theme of the Armeniakoi. These territories were then transferred into the new themes of Chaldia and Koloneia, probably in the reign of Theophilos.²⁰ Although the provincial designation may have been abandoned, it is highly likely that these regions continued to reflect Armenian cultural traditions, not least in terms of naming practices. Nor were these the only regions of the empire to contain sizeable Armenian populations. Armenians had been settled in the Balkans at the end of the sixth century by the emperor Maurice and these communities were supplemented periodically thereafter.²¹ Moreover, we can assume that Constantinople had its own Armenian community, even if they are hidden from view; the lack of an Armenian quarter may in fact illustrate the ubiquity of Armenians in the capital.

Straightaway, therefore, a distinction may be drawn between newly arrived Armenians moving westwards into the empire from outside, indigenous Armenians who continued to live in what had previously been Roman Armenia, and transplanted Armenians settled in communities scattered across the empire, notably in Thrace and Macedonia. Members from all three groups could claim to be, or could be defined as, 'Armenian'. An Armenian-sounding name in isolation reveals little about the origins of that individual. We should not assume that it denotes recent migration or settlement. Indeed an Armenian name may not always have served as an indicator of ethnicity, reflecting contemporary fashions or aspirations instead. The name of Bardanes Tourkos, the *strategos* of the Anatolikoi who rebelled against Nikephoros I in 803, highlights his Turkic, perhaps Khazar, ethnicity, but in combination with a typically Armenian name.²² Garsoïan has suggested that by the end of the tenth century, the name

---

[19] For a discussion of the Roman provinces of Armenia and their refashioning over time, see R. H. Hewsen, *The Geography of Ananias of Širak* (Wiesbaden, 1992), 17–27.

[20] N. Oikonomidès, *Les listes de préséance byzantines des IXe et Xe siècles* (Paris, 1972), 349; E. McGeer, J. Nesbitt and N. Oikonomides, eds., *Catalogue of Byzantine Seals at Dumbarton Oaks and the Fogg Museum of Art* (Washington, D. C., 1991–2005), vol. IV, 85 (Chaldia) and 125 (Koloneia).

[21] Initial transfer by Maurice: G. V. Abgaryan, ed., Պատմութիւն Սեբէոսի [*History of Sebēos*] (Erevan, 1979), 86–7 and 90–2; R. W. Thomson and J. D. Howard-Johnston, trans., *The Armenian History Attributed to Sebeos* (Liverpool, 1999), vol. I, 31 and 36–8. Subsequent transfer by Constantine V: Theophanes, *Chronographia*, ed. de Boor, 427 and 429; Mango and Scott, *Theophanes*, 590 and 593, dated to 754/5.

[22] M.-F. Auzépy, 'State of Emergency (700–850)' in J. Shepard, ed., *Cambridge History of the Byzantine Empire c. 500–1492* (Cambridge, 2008), 272; Bardanes: *PmbZ* 766.

Bardas (Vard) had become too common to be taken as a secure indicator of Armenian ancestry; it may have become fashionable long before then.[23]

Although the political consequences of Armenian migration and settlement within the empire have been studied in some detail, its social and cultural impact has not been given as much attention.[24] Those who arrived from outside the empire will have brought their own languages and cultural traditions with them but the prevailing view has been that these prominent signs of 'otherness' were quickly shelved in the race to assimilate. Of course, it is highly likely that some who migrated will have wanted to leave behind their old identities and conform to Byzantine norms as quickly as possible. Yet there will have been others who sought to preserve their old traditions despite their new surroundings. And between these two poles of complete rejection and faithful retention of one's cultural inheritance, there will have been all manner of positions, with individuals preserving some traditions and discarding others.

Furthermore, instead of simply assuming that old identities were compromised or subsumed, it may be more appropriate to envisage not merely the survival of these cultural memories within the Byzantine Empire but also their potential impact upon contemporary Byzantine culture, whose uniformity and immutability tends to be assumed rather than proved. After all, in 732 Leo III married his eldest son, the future Constantine V, to a Khazar princess, and she is thought to have been responsible for the introduction to the imperial court of the *tsitzakion*, a Khazar-style robe, suggesting that imperial fashion at least was not unchanging.[25] Instead of thinking solely in terms of a loss of Armenian identity, we need to consider the possible influence of Armenian tradition upon Byzantine culture and society, a process of cultural fusion rather than simply displacement.

This general proposition needs to be qualified by one final observation. We should be wary of taking for granted that there was a single Armenian identity or cultural tradition. If the number of recognised Armenian dialects in the eighth century is anything to go by – and the contomporary biblical commentator Step'anos Siwnec'i proposed seven, all associated

---

[23] Garsoïan, 'Armenian Integration', 96–9 and n. 170.
[24] For a recent study, and helpful bibliography, see J.-C. Cheynet and G. Dédéyan, 'Vocation impériale ou fatalité diasporique: les Arméniens à Byzance (IVe–XIe siècle)' in G. Dédéyan, ed., *Histoire du peuple arménien* (Paris, 2008), 297–326. Cheynet and Dédéyan usefully address both Armenian artistic influence, at 307–8, and religious and cultural influences, at 320–3. The classic study for artistic and intellectual exchange remains S. Der Nersessian, *Armenia and the Byzantine Empire* (Cambridge, MA, 1945).
[25] Theophanes, *Chronographia*, ed. de Boor, 409–10; Mango and Scott, *Theophanes*, 567–8 and n. 1; Whittow, *Orthodox Byzantium*, 225–6.

with remote, mountainous districts – it may be more helpful to envisage a range of different regional and local traditions and practices.[26] In other words, the cultural inheritance remembered and cherished by one migrant may have been particular and we need to be aware of, and sensitive to, such differentiation.

Bearing these introductory observations in mind, let us now turn to a specific case study exploring the operation of Armenian tradition within a Byzantine context. The origins and ancestry of Basil I continue to be controversial.[27] Although the best-known source, the *Vita Basilii*, supplies the most developed account of Basil's Armenian ancestry and early career, it is also separated from the events it records by over a century.[28] Therefore, rather than starting with the *Vita Basilii*, let us work through those sources advertising an Armenian ancestry for Basil I in chronological order.

The earliest assertion of an Arsacid connection appears in the funeral oration delivered by Leo VI for his father in 888. Basil was descended from the Arsacids 'but as to what they are it is not a subject for us to discuss, for our purpose is not to compose a history but a eulogy ... nevertheless they themselves came from imperial offspring, for the source of their royal blood was Artaxerxes, who for a very long time was a great king and he subdued countless peoples and he was accorded the remarkable surname "Longhand"'.[29] Leo then maintained that this described the extent of his authority rather than the length of his hand. There is no further discussion of the meaning of Arsacid or Artaxerxes, nor precisely how the Arsacids were related back to the Achaemenid Artaxerxes. This suggests that these claims held meaning for contemporaries without further explanation,

---

[26] S. Siwnecʻi, 'Մեկնութիւն քերականին' ['Commentary on Grammar'], in N. Adontz, ed., *Denys de Thrace et les commentateurs arméniens* (Louvain, 1970), 187. For Armenian diversity and differentiation, see T. W. Greenwood, 'Armenian Neighbours 600–1045' in Shepard, *Cambridge History of the Byzantine Empire*, 333–6.

[27] N. Adontz, 'L'âge et l'origine de l'empereur Basile I (867–886)', *Byzantion*, 8 (1933), 475–500, and *Byzantion*, 9 (1934), 223–60, reprinted and repaginated in N. Adontz, *Études arméno-byzantines* (Lisbon, 1985), 47–109; G. Moravcsik, 'Sagen und Legenden über Kaiser Basileios I', *DOP*, 15 (1961), 59–126; A. Markopoulos, 'Constantine the Great in Macedonian Historiography: Models and Approaches' in P. Magdalino, ed., *New Constantines: The Rhythm of Imperial Renewal in Byzantium, 4th–13th Centuries* (Aldershot, 1994), 159–70; A. Schminck, 'The Beginnings and Origins of the "Macedonian" Dynasty' in J. Burke and R. Scott, eds., *Byzantine Macedonia: Identity, Image and History* (Melbourne, 2000), 61–8; N. Tobias, *Basil I: Founder of the Macedonian Dynasty* (Lewiston, NY, 2007), 1–41. See also M. E. Shirinean, 'Armenian Elites in Constantinople: Emperor Basil and Patriarch Photius' in R. G. Hovannisian and S. Payaslian, eds., *Armenian Constantinople* (Costa Mesa, CA, 2010), 53–72.

[28] I. Ševčenko, ed., *Chronographiae quae Theophanis Continuati nomine fertur liber quo vita Basilii imperatoris amplectitur* (Berlin, 2011).

[29] A. Vogt and I. Hausherr, eds. and trans., 'Oraison funèbre de Basil I par son fils Léon le sage', *OrChrP*, 26 (1932), 44–6; author's translation.

supporting the contention that they were current during the lifetime of Basil I. The puzzling feature is why Leo VI should wish to establish descent from either the Arsacids or Artaxerxes in the first place.[30]

The second relevant source is the *Vita Ignatii* composed by Niketas David the Paphlagonian.[31] The dating of this text remains contentious. Tamarkina has recently proposed that it was composed during the late ninth-century polemical debate between two factions of supporters of Ignatios, and more precisely between late 886 and 901/2, when one of the factions was reconciled to the Church.[32] If Tamarkina is correct in challenging the conventional date of 906 suggested previously by Jenkins, the composition of the *Vita Ignatii* becomes more closely associated with attitudes and beliefs circulating at the end of the reign of Basil I and gains in importance for this study.[33]

The evident hostility towards Photios expressed in this text is well-known.[34] One of the many criticisms advanced by Niketas David is that Photios was guilty of using the past to justify the present by inventing an ancestry for Basil I from 'Tiridates, the great Armenian king at the time of the holy martyr Gregorios'.[35] While these details were not lifted from Leo VI's oration, their inclusion in the *Vita Ignatii* strongly suggests that Basil's Armenian ancestry was promoted during his own lifetime. Of particular significance for this study is the central role accorded by Niketas to Photios in devising this Armenian ancestry because it appears that Photios also deployed his knowledge of Armenian historical tradition when negotiating with the Armenian church.[36] If a letter preserved in Armenian from Photios to Zak'aria, the *katholikos* of Armenia, is treated as genuine – and

---

[30] This chapter explores only the Armenian ancestry of Basil I but the claim to Persian descent also merits serious consideration. It is possible to advance parallel arguments to those outlined below, with 'Persian' being equated, or perhaps conflated, in the ninth century with 'Khurramite'. The settlement of large numbers of Khurramites within the empire in the reign of Theophilos and their subsequent military service afforded them a political influence, one that may be reflected in the roles of Apelates and Eulogios, both 'Persians', in the conspiracy to murder Michael III. Adontz, 'L'âge et l'origine', 231, proposed a Persarmenian origin, but this term no longer held any meaning in the ninth century, either in Byzantium or Armenia, and so Adontz's suggestion should be rejected.

[31] *Vita Ignatii*, PG 105, cols. 487–573.

[32] I. Tamarkina, 'The Date of the Life of the Patriarch Ignatius Reconsidered', BZ, 99 (2006), 616–30.

[33] R. J. H. Jenkins, 'A Note on Nicetas David Paphlago and the Vita Ignatii', DOP, 19 (1965), 241–7.

[34] See, for example, H. Ahrweiler, 'Sur la carrière de Photius avant son patriarcat', BZ, 58 (1965), 348–63; Jenkins, 'Note', 247; Tamarkina, 'Ignatius Reconsidered', 616–17 and 622; Shirinean, 'Armenian Elites', 65–7.

[35] *Vita Ignatii*, PG 105, col. 565D 8–10.

[36] See I. Dorfmann-Lazarev, *Arméniens et byzantins à l'époque de Photius: Deux débats théologiques après le triomphe de l'orthodoxie* (Louvain, 2004); for a different interpretation, see T. W. Greenwood, 'Failure of a Mission? Photios and the Armenian Church', *Le Muséon*, 119 (2006), 115–59.

Basil I, Constantine VII and Armenian Literary Tradition 455

there are several separate arguments that collectively support this proposition – the accusations levelled by Niketas David against Photios, of historical invention and creativity, are found to have an ecclesiastical corollary, for the letter contains similar features.[37] A separate text, describing the role of Photios in the alleged discovery of the relics of Gregory the Illuminator in a tomb in Constantinople, also fits this general pattern of the exploitation and further development of Armenian tradition for contemporary political or polemical purposes.[38]

A third source provides a different perspective. Although considerable sections of the *Vita Euthymii* have not been preserved, this text, composed between 920 and 925, nevertheless supplies an important new insight into the ancestry of Basil I.[39] It records that Basil left the following instruction: 'But it was Stylianos called Zaoutzes in the Armenian language, because he was a Macedonian of Armenian descent like himself, whom he left in charge, committing to him the direction of all matters, ecclesiastical and political.'[40] This is the first indication that Basil was of Armenian descent and that he came originally from Macedonia; in other words, he was a Balkan Armenian. The passage also implies that Basil placed such trust in Stylianos precisely because he had the same background.

The longest and best-known source for the ancestry of Basil I is the *Vita Basilii*, which comprises Book V of Theophanes Continuatus. It was almost certainly commissioned, rather than composed, by Basil's grandson, the emperor Constantine VII Porphyrogennetos, soon after 948.[41]

---

[37] For the text of this letter, see N. Akinean and P. Tēr-Połosean, 'Թուղթ Փոտայ պատրիարքի առ Զաքարիա կաթողիկոս Հայոց Մեծաց' ['Letter of Patriarch Photios to Katholikos Zak'aria of Greater Armenia'], *Handēs Amsōreay*, 82 (1968), 65–100 and 129–56. Arguments in favour of its authenticity: see Greenwood, 'Failure of a Mission', 134–42. Adontz, 'L'âge et l'origine', 233–4, argues forcefully that while the accusation of genealogical invention made by Niketas against Photios may have been merited, the character of that invention is a '*fiction puérile* '.

[38] Edited text: see Ł. Ališan, ed., *Հայապատում: Պատմիչք եւ պատմութիւնք* [*Armenian History: Historians and Histories*] (Venice, 1901), vol. II, 263–5; and Anon. '*Պատմութիւն յաղագս գիւտի նշխարաց սրբոյն Գրիգորի Հայոց Մեծաց Լուսաւորչի*' ['*History concerning the discovery of the relics of St Grigor the Illuminator of Greater Armenia*'], *Ararat* 35 (1902), 1178–83]. Translation and commentary: T. W. Greenwood, 'The Discovery of the Relics of St. Grigor and the Development of Armenian Tradition in Ninth-century Byzantium' in E. M. Jeffreys, ed., *Byzantine Style, Religion and Civilization: In Honour of Sir Steven Runciman* (Cambridge, 2006), 177–91.

[39] P. Karlin-Hayter, ed. and trans., *Vita Euthymii Patriarchae CP* (Brussels, 1970), 5 and 10.

[40] *Vita Euthymii*, ed. Karlin-Hayter, 5.23–7.

[41] For arguments against composition by Constantine VII, see I. Ševčenko, 'Re-reading Constantine Porphyrogenitus' in J. Shepard and S. Franklin, eds., *Byzantine Diplomacy* (Aldershot, 1992), 184; for the date, see I. Ševčenko, 'La biographie de l'empereur Basile Ier' in *La civiltà bizantina dal IX all'XI secolo: aspetti e problemi*, II (Bari, 1978), 91–127. In his introduction to Ševčenko's new edition of the text, Mango approved of Ševčenko's contention that the real author was a ghost

It asserts that Basil came from the land of Macedonia and was by race Armenian, from the line of the Arsacids, the Armenian royal house.[42] It confirms that Aršak himself was of Parthian origin and renowned for his bravery.[43] Thereafter it supplies an outline of family history, highlighting key figures and episodes.[44] At the demise of that dynasty, two members of the Arsacid line, named Artabanos and Kleines, fled to Constantinople, where they were welcomed by Leo I and settled in Nikaia in Macedonia in spite of pressure from the king of Persia to return them. Nor was this an end to demands for their restoration. In the time of Herakleios, a request from the caliph was similarly rejected. Herakleios took the added precaution of moving them to Philippopolis, deemed to be even more remote, and hence secure. Subsequently they moved to Adrianople. In the reign of Constantine VI and Eirene, Basil's grandfather Maiktes visited Constantinople where he met another Armenian called Leo and married his daughter.[45] Their son, who curiously is never named, in turn married the daughter of a widow from Adrianople, 'a noble and attractive lady who had led a chaste life of widowhood since the death of her husband and about whom reports, not quite unreliable, circulated that she traced her ancestry back to Constantine the Great'.[46] The genealogical study concludes by noting that 'this imperial root Basil flourished' from the lineages of both his parents, for while his father was from the line of Aršak, his mother was descended from Constantine the Great and Alexander the Great as well.[47]

How should we approach this mass of genealogical detail? As Brubaker has observed, Basil I was an emperor without an imperial past; it should also be noted that he lacked a noble background.[48] Clearly the elaborate ancestry developed in the *Vita Basilii* was intended to address this perceived lack of legitimacy, providing Basil I and his successors with a long and glorious descent from the Armenian royal family as well as Constantine and Alexander. Instead of simply tracing Basil's ancestry from a single individual, the *Vita Basilii* supplies an outline family history, describing how his ancestors had interacted with famous emperors of the past

---

writer, one of the literati who gathered at Constantine's court and preferred a date of c. 950 for its composition: Theophanes Continuatus, *Vita Basilii*, ed. Ševčenko, 3*-11*.
[42] Theophanes Continuatus, *Vita Basilii*, ed. Ševčenko, 2.1–3   [43] Ibid., 2.4–5.
[44] Ibid., 2.8–3.31.
[45] Adontz, 'L'âge et l'origine', 242: Maiktes for either Maikes or Maiakes, the Armenian Hmayak.
[46] Theophanes Continuatus, *Vita Basilii*, ed. Ševčenko, 3.16–20.   [47] Ibid., 3.23–27.
[48] L. Brubaker, 'To Legitimize an Emperor: Constantine and Visual Authority in the Eighth and Ninth Centuries' in Magdalino, ed., *New Constantines*, 151.

including Leo the Great and Herakleios. These multiple imperial connections gave Basil's house an historic pedigree, just as the mass of portents and signs involving the young Basil all predicted his imperial future.[49] Basil therefore had a royal and imperial ancestry, his family had been protected by the greatest emperors of the past and there were numerous proofs pointing to his extraordinary rise to the imperial office.

There can be little doubt that at one level, this detail is highly problematic. For Jenkins, the first section of the *Vita Basilii*, including Basil's descent, the portents that attended his childhood and his arrival in Constantinople are 'historically quite worthless' and, aside from his Armenian stock and his, or his father's, imprisonment in Bulgaria, 'a fairy tale'.[50] It cannot be denied that there is an epic quality to the account. Attempting to sift the account for genuine information about his family history is unlikely to get very far. Indeed it is unclear why Jenkins should have picked out his Armenian background and the temporary imprisonment in Bulgaria as 'certainly true'; without independent corroboration, these are no more likely to be 'true' than any other detail. If, however, the family history provided in the *Vita Basilii* is treated as a reflection of, and response to, attitudes, issues and concerns from the middle of the tenth century, then it can be read in a very different way and gains in historical significance.[51]

Several features of Basil's family history respond well to this approach. As noted above, the *Vita Basilii* established a long, and carefully constructed, tradition of engagement between Basil's ancestors and prominent, legitimate emperors. When Artabanos and Kleines arrived in Constantinople, seeking refuge from the Persian king, they were received by Leo the Great. He protected and rewarded them, despite pressure being applied by the Persian king to return them. Likewise, when the caliph invited their descendants to return, it was the emperor Herakleios who intervened and transferred them to Philippopolis. The Byzantine Empire emerges as a place of refuge and security for members of the Armenian elite compelled to flee from their ancestral lands. Leo I and Herakleios are both portrayed as resisting all attempts to negotiate an Arsacid return. Their actions are consistent with those of an emperor protecting his loyal

---

[49] For a complete study, see Moravscik, 'Sagen und Legenden'; for an analysis of one vision, namely Elijah's appearance to Basil's mother, see P. Magdalino, 'Basil I, Leo VI and the Feast of the Prophet Elijah', *JÖB*, 38 (1988), 193–6.
[50] R. J. H. Jenkins, 'The Classical Background of the *Scriptores post Theophanem*', *DOP*, 8 (1954), 27.
[51] Brubaker makes a similar observation in the final paragraph of her study, Brubaker, 'Constantine and Visual Authority', 158, without further elaboration.

servants, something that Constantine VII would have been keen to promote, given the contested circumstances of his own accession to sole rule in January 945. There is also the distinct sense of self-interest as well, that the Arsacids had something to offer which was of benefit to Roman emperors, Persian kings and Arab caliphs alike. What was it?

One could argue that the Arsacids brought with them their military experience, and conceivably their own troops as well, and that this was what was being eagerly sought.[52] Certainly it is telling that Aršak's principal virtue to be highlighted in the text was his bravery. But this is to look for a plausible historical explanation within what is evidently an elegantly constructed fiction. Buried in the account is what seems to be the actual reason, the unequivocal statement that the Armenian people – a term deliberately undefined – were devoted to the Arsacids and would not hesitate to follow them.[53] In other words, the text asserts that the Arsacid royal line still retained political relevance and meaning for Armenians. Their significance was rooted in Armenian cultural memory, as the enduring popularity and successive reformulation of the so-called *Vision of Sahak* attests.[54] This text confidently predicted the revival of the Armenian kingdom by a member of the Arsacid family and the restoration of the Armenian church by someone descended from the line of Saint Gregory.[55] Indeed the *Vita Basilii* refers specifically to the fulfilment of this prophecy at the accession of Basil I.[56] Just as Basil's ancestors were projected as giving political leadership to Armenians within the Byzantine Empire in the past, by implication Basil's grandson Constantine VII Porphyrogennetos could offer the same leadership. The ancestry of

---

[52] See P. Charanis, *The Armenians in the Byzantine Empire* (Lisbon, 1963), 16–21 and 32–4; Garsoïan, 'Armenian Integration', 61–6. For one remarkable late ninth-century career, see G. Dédéyan, 'Mleh le Grand stratège du Lykandos', *REArm*, 15 (1981), 72–102.

[53] Theophanes Continuatus, *Vita Basilii*, ed. Ševčenko, 2.43–5.

[54] For a study of this intriguing but elusive text, see Adontz, 'L'âge et l'origine', 246–59; G. Garitte, 'La vision de S. Sahak en grec', *Le Muséon*, 71 (1958), 225–78. A version of this text is preserved in the early sixth-century *History* of Łazar P'arpec'i but this may be a later interpolation; see G. Tēr Mkrtč'ean and S. Malxasean, eds., Ղազարայ Փարպեցւոյ Պատմութիւն Հայոց [*Łazar P'arpec'i History of Armenia*] (Tiflis, 1904; reprinted Delmar, NY, 1985), 29–37; English translation by R. W. Thomson, *The History of Łazar P'arpec'i* (Atlanta, GA, 1991), 65–72. It seems to have been in circulation by the seventh century.

[55] The Arsacid (or Aršakuni) house was the Armenian royal line until the deposition of the last king in 428 CE. Gregory the Illuminator was the founder of the Armenian church in the early fourth century. Sahak was the last direct relative of Gregory to occupy the office of *katholikos* and he died in 438 CE.

[56] Theophanes Continuatus, *Vita Basilii*, ed. Ševčenko, 19.35–40; see Adontz, 'L'âge et l'origine', 255, who argues that the *Vision of Sahak* was composed in Constantinople, conceivably by Photios himself, to prove Basil's Arsacid ancestry. This remains highly speculative.

Basil I enabled Constantine to present himself as the direct heir to the Arsacid kings of Armenia and thereby claim the Arsacid political legacy as king of all Armenians. He was in a position to appeal to all who thought of themselves as Armenian, irrespective of which district they came from, when they had arrived within the empire, which family they claimed descent from or what confessional position they espoused. Advertising an Arsacid ancestry therefore had a particular potency.

If one accepts the above, the question of motivation remains. Why did Constantine Porphyrogennetos make these claims to Arsacid ancestry in this manner at this time? Not only did he repeat the Arsacid connection advanced in the two sources discussed above; he developed and amplified that connection. By contrast, the claims to descent from Constantine or Alexander are not promoted. Two possible solutions present themselves, one 'eastern' and the other 'Balkan'.

The first sets this composition in the context of Constantine's wider ambitions along the eastern frontier. These can be deduced from the four so-called 'Armenian chapters' of the *De administrando imperio*, the diplomatic handbook compiled by Constantine for his young son, the future Romanos II, in 952.[57] Although the individual details found in each chapter have been examined and discussed many times, the underlying intent has been overlooked.[58] One of the most striking features to emerge from these chapters is that Constantine was at pains to project the emperor resident in Constantinople as retaining personal responsibility for the conduct of diplomacy. Successive emperors are shown negotiating with Armenian princes through envoys and correspondence and in person; they are also portrayed concluding treaties, interpreting earlier agreements, even deciding upon the exact location of a boundary.[59] It seems that Constantine was trying to emphasize to his young heir the need to maintain direct control along this sector of the frontier, specifically in relation to contacts with Armenian princes. This would ensure that the emperor was not side-lined or excluded through the incorporation of the

---

[57] G. Moravscik, ed., R. J. H. Jenkins, trans., *Constantine VII Porphyrogenitus. De administrando imperio*, second edition (Washington, D. C., 1967), 189–223 (cc. 43–6).

[58] See, for example, Shepard, 'Constantine VII', 22–9; J. D. Howard-Johnston, 'The *De Administrando Imperio*: a Re-examination of the Text and a Re-evaluation of its Evidence about the Rus' in M. Kazanski, A. Nercessian and C. Zuckerman, eds., *Les centres proto-urbains russes entre Scandinavie, Byzance et Orient* (Paris, 2000), 317–18 and 326–7; and Greenwood, 'Patterns of Contact and Communication', 84–95 and 97–9.

[59] *De administrando*, ed. Moravscik and Jenkins, c. 45 analyses the actions and agreements of Leo VI, Romanos I Lecapenos and Constantine VII in respect of the Iberian princes with interests around Theodosioupolis; for the boundary decision, see 46.156–75.

Armenian elite in local networks of power and authority centred upon the great magnate families of the eastern empire.

There is no evidence, from within the *De administrando imperio* or elsewhere, to suggest that Constantine advertised his Arsacid ancestry in order to attract Armenians from outside the empire into imperial service. However, one of the strategies advocated by Constantine in that text involved securing rights over Armenian lands that could be realised in the future. These 'Armenian futures' contemplated a simple exchange, of ancestral territories for security and status within the empire. It is in this context, of recent and ongoing Armenian migration into the empire, that the assertion of an Arsacid ancestry obtains meaning and justification. Accordingly, Constantine stressed his Armenian background and Arsacid credentials in order to attract and secure the loyalty of newly arrived Armenians.

Arguably, this ideological dimension reflects the wider strategy for the eastern frontier in the middle of the tenth century. The creation of a network of small so-called 'Armenian themes' along this frontier at this time expresses the same strategy, albeit in administrative terms. It too implies intent on the part of the emperor and the central administration to retain direct control over military appointments in the East. This offered another means of counterbalancing the regional networks of power and authority then being constructed by the great magnate families of the eastern empire.[60] One can speculate that these families also stressed and promoted their noble ancestry and their heroic achievements through a variety of media, including family history. None of these have been preserved, but we do know that Manuel's biography of John Kourkouas ran to eight books and covered his family background and his own achievements, as well as containing portents pointing to his future greatness.[61] Arguably Constantine advertised his Arsacid origins in the context of rival claims to glorious ancestries and great deeds.

The second solution also has an internal political perspective but is focused more particularly upon the Balkan context to Basil's ancestry supplied by the *Vita Basilii*. Throughout the text, the Arsacid house is

---

[60] See Oikonomides, *Les listes*, 345–6, arguing that this process can be observed in the 940s and 950s, and 355–63. A novel of Nikephoros II Phokas refers specifically to Armenian themes and Armenian *stratiotai*: N. Svonoros, *Les novelles des empereurs macédoniens concernant la terre et les stratiotes* (Athens, 1994), 162–73; trans. E. McGeer, *The Land Legislation of the Macedonian Emperors* (Toronto, 2000), 86–9. See also Greenwood, 'Armenian Neighbours', 352 and 361.

[61] I. Bekker, ed., *Theophanes Continuatus, Ioannes Cameniata, Symeon Magister, Georgius Monachus* (Bonn, 1838), 426.1–28.2 (VI).

associated consistently with the Balkans. This may simply be because Basil I did indeed come from the Balkans, as the *Vita Euthymii* indicates; the strong evidence for substantial Armenian settlement in the Balkans has been noted previously.[62] The *Vita Basilii* contains no hint of any desire on the part of the Arsacid house or the emperor to return to historic Armenia. Such a possibility is articulated only by the Persian king and the caliph and, unsurprisingly, is rejected out of hand.

Accepting the contention that the Arsacid connection is an elaborate fiction, it follows that the sites in the Balkans associated with Arsacid settlement were chosen deliberately and so deserve particular attention. The text records that Leo the Great settled Artabanos and Kleines in Nikaia in Macedonia; that Herakleios arranged for their transfer to Philippopolis in Macedonia; and that they subsequently moved to Adrianople. While Maiktes married the daughter of an Armenian called Leo from Constantinople, Basil's father married the daughter of a widow from Adrianople, thereby reinforcing the Adrianople connection.[63] What was the recent history of each location?

In the middle of the tenth century, Adrianople was firmly under Byzantine rule. Nevertheless it remained uncomfortably close to the frontier. It had twice been captured by Symeon of Bulgaria, in 914 and 922, but on both occasions it had been quickly recovered.[64] In 914 it had been redeemed by the payment of a cash subsidy under a negotiated settlement, while in 922 it had been abandoned by the Bulgars after rumours that a Byzantine relief force was close at hand. The fact that Adrianople changed hands four times in quick succession indicates that it was of great strategic importance to both sides. The particular circumstances of the first episode repay further scrutiny. In 914, Adrianople had been betrayed by its commander, one Pankratoukas, who is described as being of Armenian descent. This may seem incidental, but we find a parallel episode from the end of the tenth century. Skylitzes refers to several *illustrioi* from Adrianople who held the rank of *strategos*, including one Batatzes, who were suspected of treachery and who fled to Samuel

---

[62] See above, n. 21.
[63] Theophanes Continuatus, *Vita Basilii*, ed. Ševčenko, 2.33–4 (Nikaia), 2.45–6 (Philippopolis), 2.47–9 and 3.16–17 (Adrianople). The link with Constantinople, at 3.3–7, appears incidental but has the virtue of providing Basil with kinship ties among the Armenian elite in the capital.
[64] The 914 campaign: Theophanes Continuatus, *Chronographia*, ed. Ševčenko, 387.14–388.4 (VI); Georgius Monachus, ed. Bekker, 880.5–9. The latter contains a much-abridged version of the former, echoing its first and last sentences. The 922 campaign: Theophanes Continuatus, *Chronographia*, ed. Ševčenko, 404.18–5.10 (VI); Georgius Monachus Continuatus, *Chronicon*, 897.3–16. These accounts are closely related to one another.

Kometopoulos, the Bulgar emperor, who was himself of Armenian origin.[65] In both instances, therefore, it seems that local notables of Armenian descent were induced to switch from Byzantine to Bulgar service. Conceivably, it was to address this problem and shore up support for Byzantium that Constantine associated the Arsacid house so closely with Adrianople, in the hope that advertising a royal Armenian ancestry might convince the local elite to remain loyal.

The tenth-century history of Nikaia in Macedonia, south-east of Adrianople, is obscure. Given its proximity to Adrianople, and its location firmly within the boundaries of the Byzantine Empire, its inclusion is likely to have been on the same grounds as Adrianople. Philippopolis, on the other hand, upstream from Adrianople on the river Maritza, was not in Byzantine possession during the sole rule of Constantine Porphyrogennetos. Leo the Deacon confirms that Philippopolis was under Bulgar control when it was captured by the Rus leader Sviatoslav in late 969.[66] After John Tzimiskes had ejected Sviatoslav from Bulgaria in 971, the emperor installed a group of Paulicians around Philippopolis, confirming its recent acquisition.[67] It seems very likely that Philippopolis had been captured by Symeon in 914 and retained thereafter.

Why did Constantine connect the Arsacids to Philippopolis? One possibility is that this fortified centre too had a longstanding Armenian community to whom the *Vita Basilii* was appealing. It is, however, difficult to envisage the circumstances under which they could have encountered the text, unless they had relatives within the empire. In the alternative, by establishing a longstanding Armenian association with a site in Bulgar control, Constantine may have been laying the groundwork for the future annexation of Philippopolis by introducing the notion that it would be a recovery or restoration of Armenian as much as imperial territory. In other words, Constantine was establishing through the *Vita Basilii* a legitimate claim to territory then outside the empire, a claim that was based on an historic link. Significantly this pattern of behaviour on the part of Constantine can also be traced in

---

[65] I. Thurn, ed., *Ioannis Scylitzae Synopsis Historiarum* (Berlin, 1973), 343; B. Flusin and J.-C. Cheynet, trans., *Jean Skylitzès Empereurs de Constantinople* (Paris, 2003), 287.

[66] C. B. Hase, ed., *Leonis Diaconi Caloënsis Historiae libri decem*, in *Historiae libri decem* (Bonn, 1828), 105; A.-M. Talbot and D. F. Sullivan, trans., *The History of Leo the Deacon: Byzantine Military Expansion in the Tenth Century* (Washington, D. C., 2005), 155 and n. 92.

[67] Skylitzes, *Synopsis*, ed. Thurn, 286; Flusin and Cheynet, *Jean Skylitzès*, 241 and n. 17.

the *De administrando imperio* in respect of districts beyond the eastern frontier then under Armenian and Iberian control.[68]

If one accepts this contention, it follows that Constantine VII had ambitions along the Bulgarian as well as the eastern frontier towards the start of his rule as sole emperor.[69] Two other passages in the *Vita Basilii* offer some support. The first describes how the young Basil and his family were carried off into captivity by the Bulgar leader Krum after the fall of Adrianople in 813.[70] Previously this passage has been used in the long-standing debate over the year in which Basil was born. The actions of Manuel, bishop of Adrianople, and his clerical colleagues have therefore been overlooked. According to the text, Manuel and his team undertook missionary activities among the Bulgars, for which they were martyred under Krum's successor, Mutragon.[71] This might seem incidental if it were not for the familiar, and securely attested, subsequent history of the spread of Christianity in Bulgaria and the emergence of an effectively autonomous Bulgar church.[72] The rivalry between Latin and Byzantine missions in Bulgaria in the early 860s is well-known, as is the baptism of the Bulgar leader Boris in 865.[73] Boris became the godson of the emperor Michael III and took his baptismal name. The *Vita Basilii* undermines this tradition by positing that a bishop of Adrianople was actively preaching and teaching in Bulgaria long before the reign of Michael III. The text is constructed in such a way that Basil I is associated with this earlier conversion attempt. It reveals that Basil's own relatives were among those to suffer martyrdom, enabling Basil to share in the honour therefrom.[74] At the same time, the role of Michael III in the conversion process is diminished. Furthermore, by stating that Manuel was martyred at the

---

[68] Greenwood, 'Patterns of Contact and Communication', 90–2 and 97–9. See also Theophanes Continuatus, *Chronographia*, ed. Ševčenko, 387.21–388.1 (VI), where Philippopolis is defined as three days' travel from Adrianople and separated by mountains and rivers. The stress on isolation is consistent with the above proposition.

[69] This runs against the view of Stephenson '[T]he political absorption of Bulgaria ... cannot have been contemplated by Constantine VII and his son Romanos II': see P. Stephenson, *Byzantium's Balkan Frontier: A Political Study of the Northern Balkans 900–1204* (Cambridge, 2000), 46.

[70] Theophanes Continuatus, *Vita Basilii*, ed. Ševčenko, 4.1–11.

[71] Ibid., 4.8–24. Mutragon is a corruption of Omurtag (814/15–c. 831).

[72] J. Shepard, 'Slavs and Bulgars' in R. McKitterick, ed., *The New Cambridge Medieval History*, vol. II: *c. 700–c. 900* (Cambridge, 2008), 239–46; Whittow, *Orthodox Byzantium*, 280–5.

[73] F. Dvornik, *The Photian Schism: History and Legend* (Cambridge, 1948; repr. 1970); G. Dagron, 'L'église et l'état (milieu IXe–fin Xe siècle)' in G. Dagron, P. Riché and A. Vauchez, eds., *Evêques, moines et empereurs (610–1054)*, *Histoire du Christianisme* (Paris, 1993), vol. IV, 169–83, and see also 921–36 for Bulgaria; L. Simeonova, *Diplomacy of the Letter and the Cross: Photios, Bulgaria and the Papacy 860s–880s* (Amsterdam, 1998).

[74] Theophanes Continuatus, *Vita Basilii*, ed. Ševčenko, 4.22–4.

hands of a pagan Bulgar leader, Constantine was able to tarnish the character and Christian pedigree of the current Bulgar leader, Peter. When analysed in these terms, this passage emerges, rather unexpectedly, as an important source for Constantine's view of Bulgaria.

The second passage lends itself to a similar interpretation. It records how Basil challenged and overcame a previously undefeated Bulgar wrestler, pinning his shoulders to a table.[75] Although this story has traditionally been understood as a simple proof of Basil's physical strength, the basis for his rapid advancement, it may also be read metaphorically as a portent, that Byzantium, in the person of one of Basil's descendants, would eventually challenge and overcome Bulgaria. As such, it takes its place alongside a mass of portents – an eagle hovering over the infant Basil, the gift of the apple, his mother's dreams, of the golden vine and then Elijah's prophecy, the untamed horse ridden by Basil – all predicting an imperial future for the young Basil.[76] Several of these employ images and motifs familiar from classical literature and from the Old Testament. This particular episode, however, of single combat with an enemy champion, is found repeatedly in Armenian historical literature and ultimately in Persian epic tradition. For example, in the seventh-century *History* attributed to Sebeos, the Armenian Smbat Bagratuni is described engaging the king of the Kʻushans in single combat between the battle lines, 'both men of gigantic strength and fully covered in armour'.[77] Although incapable of proof, it is possible that this story was intended to appeal to, and resonate with, those aware of equivalent Armenian traditions. Once again, therefore, this passage reflects the mid-tenth-century aspirations of Constantine VII far more closely than any mid-ninth-century historical event. In predicting victory over the Bulgars, Constantine was once more revealing his own ambitions in that theatre, if not for himself, then for his immediate successors. We should not be surprised that Nikephoros II Phokas reopened hostilities against Bulgaria as early as 966 and thereby set the tone for relations between Byzantium and Bulgaria for the next fifty years, decades that were characterised by armed conflict. The *Vita Basilii* suggests that Constantine VII cherished similar dreams.

Having proposed that the *Vita Basilii* reflects the attitudes and concerns of Constantine VII in the middle of the tenth century, let us return finally

---

[75] Ibid., 12.13–35. [76] Moravcsik, 'Sagen und Legenden', 84–9.
[77] Abgaryan, *History of Sebēos*, 102–3; Thomson and Howard-Johnston, *History Attributed to Sebeos*, 52.

to assess the background and formative years of Basil I. On the basis of the *Vita Euthymii*, it seems most probable that Basil did indeed come from Macedonia and that he was of Armenian descent. As for his actual background, an anonymous poem composed between 867 and 872 states that Basil came from simple pious parents and compares him with the Old Testament figure of David who also enjoyed a meteoric rise, from obscurity as a shepherd boy to divinely ordained king of Israel.[78] It seems clear, therefore, that Basil had humble origins. The sequence of patrons recorded in the *Vita Basilii* was therefore a necessary part in his biography, as Tougher has rightly observed.[79] Why was such a claim advanced? There would appear to be little point in claiming a royal Armenian ancestry for Basil unless there was a significant constituency within the political elite who understood the symbolic meaning of this claim and responded to it. In other words, the assertion of an Arsacid ancestry was designed to appeal to those members of the powerful elite in ninth-century Byzantium who were themselves of Armenian descent and who retained sufficient knowledge of their own cultural and historical traditions to be able to understand the significance of this claim. If there was no such constituency, there would seem to be little point in advancing such a claim. Although identifying members of the Armenian elite in ninth-century Byzantium – and the shadowy networks of power, patronage and kinship that Basil exploited – lies outside the remit of this chapter, it is striking that the two leading figures at the death of Basil I on 29 August 886, Stylianos and Photios, both had strong Armenian connections.[80]

In conclusion, claiming a royal Arsacid ancestry held political significance in the ninth century and continued to do so in the middle of the tenth century. Although the evidence is not extensive, it is sufficient to demonstrate that Basil I claimed an Arsacid descent during his lifetime. Whether he did so in the terms outlined by Niketas is impossible to say but it seems very improbable. Yet the very fact that Niketas chose to ridicule Photios through his forged genealogy of Basil I reflects a wider social and political reality: that Armenian connections and traditions held particular significance and meaning at this time.

Basil's Armenian ancestry was retained and developed in the *Vita Basilii* under the oversight of his grandson, Constantine VII Porphyrogennetos.

---

[78] A. Markopoulos, 'An Anonymous Laudatory Poem in Honor of Basil I', *DOP*, 46 (1992), 225–32.
[79] S. Tougher, 'After Iconoclasm (850–886)' in Shepard, *Cambridge History of the Byzantine Empire*, 294.
[80] Photios, see Shirinean, 'Armenian Elites', 62–5; Stylianos Zaoutzes, see *Vita Euthymii*, ed. Karlin-Hayter, 149–52.

Once again, it was intended to resonate with Armenians living and working within the empire, both securing the loyalties of newly arrived Armenians and reconnecting with those Balkan Armenians whose drift towards the great rival of Byzantium in the Balkans, the Bulgar state, needed to be checked. Indeed there are strong grounds for arguing that the *Vita Basilii* anticipated future confrontation with, and eventual victory over, the Bulgars. When viewed in the context of the future strategy for expansion eastwards into historic Armenia, as outlined in the *De administrando imperio* and discussed above, it looks very much as though plans for territorial acquisition and recovery in both the east and the west were never far away from the mind of Constantine VII. It was, however, his grandson Basil II who realised those ambitions.[81]

Further Reading

The key primary sources are: P. Karlin-Hayter, ed. and trans., *Vita Euthymii Patriarchae CP* (Brussels, 1970); I. Ševčenko, ed., *Chronographiae quae Theophanis Continuati nomine fertur liber quo vita Basilii imperatoris amplectitur* (Berlin, 2011); A. Vogt and I. Hausherr, eds. and trans., 'Oraison funèbre de Basil I par son fils Léon le sage', *OrChrP*, 26 (1932), 44–6. Studies include: N. Adontz, 'L'âge et l'origine de l'empereur Basile I (867–886)', *Byzantion*, 8 (1933), 475–500, and *Byzantion*, 9 (1934), 223–60; reprinted in N. Adontz, *Études arméno-byzantines* (Lisbon, 1985), 47–109; G. Moravcsik, 'Sagen und Legenden über Kaiser Basileios I', *DOP*, 15 (1961), 59–126.

---

[81] Stephenson, *Byzantium's Balkan Frontier*, 47–79; see also P. Stephenson, *The Legend of Basil the Bulgar-Slayer* (Cambridge, 2003), 1–48; C. Holmes, *Basil II and the Governance of Empire (976–1025)* (Oxford, 2005), 394–428 and 487–502.

CHAPTER 21

Bilingual Reading, the Alexiad *and the* Gesta Roberti Wiscardi

James Howard-Johnston

The *Alexiad* has few, if any, rivals among the works of history penned in Byzantium. This is true of the scale of its coverage – wide-ranging both in space and time – and of its close observation of particulars, whether it be the portrayal of individuals or narration of episodes, large and small, in war and peace.[1] The writing is on a high stylistic plane, in places emulating and matching the classicism of Psellos' virtuoso account of imperial rule and the court in the eleventh century. It is a magnificent history of a long reign (1081–1118), that of Alexios, founder of the Komnenian dynasty, who is portrayed as champion and saviour of the empire of the latter-day Romans. It has attracted the admiration of readers of all sorts for its author or authors, not least from among scholars eager to laud Anna Komnene as the first female historian known to posterity.[2]

A text composed at the very apex of society cannot, of course, cast light on the general level of literacy in Byzantium in the way that Kekaumenos' tips on life can. Nor can much be inferred about educational attainments outside the high intelligentsia. It is on the processes involved in literary production, within the genre of history, that the *Alexiad* can shed a great deal of light, in particular on the relative importance of oral as against written sources, and, in the sphere of the written, between documentary and literary sources. In addition, it provides a rare example of the use of a Latin source by a Byzantine history. Close scrutiny of the *Alexiad* can thus add something to knowledge and understanding of research and writing in Byzantium.

---

[1] D.R. Reinsch and A. Kambylis, eds., *Annae Comnenae Alexias* (Berlin, 2001); E. R. A. Sewter, trans., *The Alexiad of Anna Comnena*, revised by P. Frankopan (London, 2009).
  This chapter was originally presented to the Oxford Byzantine Studies Seminar in May 1990. It has been retouched in places, and considerably improved thanks to the comments of two anonymous readers. The conclusions tally in general with those of P. Frankopan, 'Turning Latin into Greek: Anna Komnene and the *Gesta Roberti Wiscardi*', *JMedHist*, 39 (2013), 80–99. A different interpretation is offered in P. Brown, 'The *Gesta Roberti Wiscardi*: a "Byzantine" History?' *JMedHist*, 37 (2011): 162–79.
[2] T. Gouma-Peterson, ed., *Anna Komnene and Her Times* (New York, NY, 2000).

The text bears the marks of Anna's learning. There are numerous classical tags. Special interest is shown in intellectual history, above all in show-trials of potentially subversive figures who dissented from Orthodoxy. A daughter's affection for a father is evident. She is protective of his reputation, presenting him as the inheritor of a storm-tossed ship of state, who navigated, like a latter-day Odysseus, past all manner of hazards to bring his people to safety.[3] Rather surprisingly, it is weighted towards warfare, with campaign histories (dating mainly to the first half of the reign) taking up much more space than domestic politics at the centre. Three sets of campaigns are highlighted: the war against the Normans of southern Italy, which began disastrously with a defeat outside Dyrrachion in 1081 and lasted until 1085, when Norman forces withdrew from the Balkans; a series of campaigns against the nomad Pechenegs in the Balkans, between 1086 and 1091; and finally, the passage of the First Crusade through Byzantine territory and into the Levant, the sieges it conducted and the engagements it fought both with and without its Byzantine allies.

Coverage of the first of these major military components of the *Alexiad* is comprehensive but it is broken up into batches of material that are dispersed across the early books of the *Alexiad* (i.10–16, iii.9–10, 12, iv.1–v.7, vi.1, 5–6). It is one of only two subjects dealt with in the *Alexiad* that are well reported in other contemporary or near-contemporary sources (the other is the account of the First Crusade and its aftermath).[4] The other principal independent source for the Norman–Byzantine war, the *Gesta Roberti Wiscardi*, was written in southern Italy, some fifteen years after its end, by William of Apulia.[5] William's account is strikingly similar to parts of the *Alexiad*. It looks as if a body of material has somehow travelled from southern Italy to Constantinople, leaping over the language barrier between Latin and Greek, and has been incorporated into Anna's text.[6]

How on earth did this happen? By what means were the stories conveyed to the imperial court? Were they transmitted orally or in writing? Why were they picked up and reused? Were they available in translation?

---

[3] R. Macrides, 'The Pen and the Sword: Who Wrote the Alexiad?' and J. Liubarskii, 'Why is the Alexiad a Masterpiece of Byzantine Literature?', both in Gouma-Peterson, ed., *Anna Komnene and Her Times*, 63–81 and 169–85.

[4] R.-J. Lilie, *Byzantium and the Crusader States, 1096–1204* (Oxford, 1993).

[5] M. Mathieu, ed. and trans., *Guillaume de Pouille. La Geste de Robert Guiscard* (Palermo, 1961). Latin text cited henceforth as *Gesta Roberti*, Mathieu's commentary as Mathieu, *Guillaume de Pouille*.

[6] P. Frankopan, 'The Foreign Policy of the Emperor Alexios I Komnenos (1081–*c.* 1100)', unpublished DPhil thesis, Oxford (1998), 75–83; also his chapter in this volume.

These and other questions cry out for answers, which can only be obtained by subjecting the two texts to careful scrutiny, in particular by carrying out a meticulous comparison of parallel passages. Such a procedure should be able to establish the precise relationship between them and may also cast light on the process of the *Alexiad*'s composition.

This chapter had its genesis in a small, fruitful colloquium held in Northern Ireland in spring 1989. The topic was the reign of Alexios Komnenos (1081–1118), which had not been subjected to proper scrutiny for nearly a century.[7] Small gatherings of scholars engaged in a common endeavour are exciting affairs, especially for an interloper like myself whose principal fields of interest lie elsewhere. This was particularly true on this occasion, as is made evident in the publication of the proceedings.[8] In the course of the colloquium, Graham Loud presented a paper on the relationship between the *Gesta* of William of Apulia and the *Alexiad* of Anna Komnene, as well as discussing the transfer of mythic mutations of history from Norman oral tradition into the *Alexiad*.[9] He took note of several convergences between the two texts but concluded that these could be explained by the historical realities that both authors were reporting. In adopting this view, he was disagreeing with the firm conclusion reached by Jakov Liubarskii, that the *Gesta* and the *Alexiad* drew a considerable amount of shared material from a common written source.[10] Loud's paper was interesting and provocative for anyone who had, as I had, accepted Liubarskii's thesis without hesitation. Since Liubarskii had merely presented his supporting case in summary form, he had left room for legitimate doubt on the part of Loud and others.

Back in Oxford, I set to work on a general study of the *Alexiad*,[11] in the course of which I struggled to make sense of its account of the Norman–Byzantine war, with its strange juxtaposition of campaign narratives: succinct, lucid, gravid, with detailed information and attentive to key strategic issues, on the one hand; and garbled material, full of geographical

---

[7] The only comprehensive study was F. Chalandon, *Essai sur le règne d'Alexis I Comnène* (Paris, 1900).
[8] M. Mullett and D. Smythe, eds., *Alexios I Komnenos – Papers of the Second Belfast Byzantine International Colloquium, 14–16 April 1989* (Belfast, 1996).
[9] G. A. Loud, 'Anna Komnena and her Sources for the Normans of Southern Italy' in I. Wood and G. A. Loud, eds., *Church and Chronicle in the Middle Ages: Essays Presented to John Taylor* (London, 1991), 41–57.
[10] J. Liubarskii, 'Об источниках "Алексиады" Анны Комниной', *VizVrem*, 25 (1964), 110–17.
[11] J. Howard-Johnston, 'Anna Komnene and the Alexiad' in Mullett and Smythe, eds., *Alexios I Komnenos*, 260–302.

and chronological confusion, on the other.[12] The seminar paper of 1990 which forms the core of this chapter brought together the results of a period of sustained engagement with the relevant sections of the *Alexiad*. The effort, often frustrating, to sort out the confusions in the text and to explain how they were generated was ultimately very rewarding, in that it provided the clearest possible corroboration for the thesis that two hands were at work in the composition of the *Alexiad*.

In the first section, a brief outline is given of events covered by William of Apulia, to provide a context for the investigation into the relationship of his text with the *Alexiad*. In the next two sections, the fourth and fifth books of the *Gesta* are examined in turn, with a view to showing (1) that the *Gesta* contributed a substantial amount of material to the *Alexiad*, and (2) that this material came *directly* from the *Gesta* itself rather than via a common source. This latter conclusion, which is at variance with Liubarskii's, is reached principally on the basis of arguments already deployed by him. In section four, the parts of the *Alexiad*'s account that are not based on the *Gesta* are surveyed and suggestions are put forward as to the character of the sources used. Section five seeks an explanation for the presence and misplacing of a not inconsiderable number of passages that disturb the flow of the narrative and have baffled readers of the *Alexiad*. This involves a speculative probe into the editorial processes that transformed the raw material provided by the sources into the final text left to us by Anna. Finally, consideration is given to the process of transmission of the *Gesta* material to a highly placed literary milieu in Constantinople.

The Norman–Byzantine War According to the *Gesta Roberti*

The *Gesta Roberti Wiscardi* culminates in a clear and surprisingly unpartisan account of the Norman–Byzantine war of 1081–5.[13] It was written on a commission from Roger Borsa, second Norman duke of southern Italy (1085–1111), but was dedicated to Pope Urban II (1088–99) as well as Roger.[14] The poem is testimony to a phase of goodwill both between the Normans and the papacy on the eve of the great military–religious venture in the Near East that the pope was organising, and between Roger and Bohemond, his elder half-brother, who plays a leading role in the history.

---

[12] E. Kislinger, 'Vertauschte Notizen: Anna Komnene und die Chronologie der byzantinisch-normannischen Auseinandersetzung 1081–1085', *JÖB*, 59 (2009), 127–45.

[13] See G. A. Loud, *The Age of Robert Guiscard: Southern Italy and the Norman Conquest* (Harlow, 2000), 209–23 for a modern account of the war.

[14] William of Apulia, *Gesta Roberti*, ed. Mathieu, 98 and 258 (prologue and v.410–14).

It seems likely that William of Apulia, who is otherwise unknown, was either supplied with relevant materials from which to compose his poem or was given access to the ducal library/archives and received general instructions on the political line to follow. There is no evidence that he was a man of standing, in a position to present a personal view.[15] It follows, therefore, that his *Gesta* was a versified official biography of Robert Guiscard that incorporated an authorised version of the history of the Normans in southern Italy. It is highly likely that it was attuned to circumstances at the time of writing. Its completion may be dated between summer 1097 and summer 1099, a period when Norman interests, insofar as they were represented by Bohemond, leader of the Norman contingent of crusaders, were converging on those of Byzantium. The Byzantines were cultivating the Normans as useful allies, even perhaps their chief potential clients in the Crusading forces, and the Normans were responding to this flattering attention. These circumstances help explain the tone of the last two books — the absence of anti-Byzantine rhetoric, the positive attitude to Alexios Komnenos and the candour about the internal opposition to Robert.[16]

Book Four of the *Gesta* describes the pretext for war, Robert Guiscard's preparations, both diplomatic and military, the first campaign (1081–2) and Robert's actions back in Italy (1082–4). It includes several digressions: (1) on the Investiture Controversy, slanted to support the Gregorian party and charging Emperor Henry IV with depravity as well as simony (lines 31–64);[17] (2) on the rise of Alexios Komnenos (77–121), an account that verges on the encomiastic (Alexios is praised as astute, intrepid, noble, undeterred by difficulty, and so forth); (3) on the deposition of Nikephoros Botaneiates (142–53); (4) on Dyrrachion (234–43); and (5) on Venice (277–85).

William does not delve into the ultimate cause of the war, simply noting the context of its outbreak. Robert is presented as exploiting political instability in Byzantium, taking up the cause of a pretender to the imperial throne, an impostor (as William acknowledges) claiming to be the deposed emperor Michael VII Doukas (1071–8), whose son Constantine had been engaged to Robert's daughter Helen (1–5, 162–70). Robert then celebrates the marriages of two other daughters to important noblemen from Spain and France (6–15), and negotiates a political alliance with Pope

---

[15] Mathieu, *Guillaume de Pouille*, 17–25.   [16] Ibid., 11–17.
[17] H. Vollrath, 'The Western Empire under the Salians' in D. Luscombe and J. Riley-Smith, eds., *New Cambridge Medieval History* (Cambridge, 2004), vol. IV.2, 50–65.

Gregory VII: the pope receives Robert, thereby recognising the Norman dukedom, while Robert swears an oath of fealty, thereby implicitly undertaking to provide military assistance whenever requested to do so, in return for papal backing of his bid for the Roman crown (16–32, 66–9). Nothing is said about the less newsworthy negotiations with certain Slav princes in Dalmatia, which resulted in their supplying Robert with shipping (noted at 134–5). After a short notice about the foundation of a church dedicated to St Matthew and a palace at Salerno (70–2), there is an account of the preparations for the planned Balkan expedition, which goes ahead despite Alexios' efforts to appease Robert by honouring his daughter (122–41, 154–70). The local response to Robert's call to arms was initially cool, and much cajoling and inveigling was required to get more enthusiastic backing. The mobilisation is then described: Otranto was the port of embarkation; ships were fitted out; a cavalry force was then sent ahead on the Dalmatian ships to raid Corfu. Robert waited at Otranto for his wife (Sichelgaita) and the counts who were to accompany him. He made an ostentatious show of his respect for the pretender, wrote temporising letters to emperor and pope, who were each requesting his aid against the other, and delegated his ducal authority in Apulia, Calabria and Sicily to Roger Borsa who was declared his heir. Two powerful counts (one a nephew of Robert's) were deputed to advise him, with instructions to provide what assistance they could to the pope. Robert then sailed for Dalmatia with the main body of the army and a fifty-strong fleet (171–201).

The outlines of Norman strategy can be reconstituted from William of Apulia's account of the operations. A bridgehead was established on the Balkan mainland when the advance force captured Butrint. The surrender of Corfu to Robert helped secure it against attack from the sea. Bohemond, Robert's son by his first marriage, was put in command of the land forces, and advanced north. Dyrrachion, which commanded the west end of the main land route across the Balkans, was the chief objective. Disinformation had been spread, as is evident from the *Alexiad*, to deceive the Byzantines into expecting an attack on the Gulf of Corinth, and to distract attention from the secret negotiations under way with Botaneiates' commander at Dyrrachion. While the land forces moved ahead and took Avlona, a storm disrupted the advance of the fleet under Robert. The consequent delay gave Alexios time to replace the unreliable commander at Dyrrachion with George Palaiologos, a trusted supporter (201–34).[18]

---

[18] See also Peter Frankopan's chapter in this volume.

Bilingual Reading, Alexiad, Gesta Roberti Wiscardi   473

The siege began on 17 June – with construction of an impressive siege-tower as a platform for a massive stone-thrower and of permanent barracks in the Norman camps in order to demoralise the defenders by demonstrating the determination of the besiegers to stick at the task through winter, if necessary, until the city fell. A Byzantine attempt to relieve the city failed when the initial Venetian success that led to a naval blockade of the besieging army was followed by the comprehensive defeat of the Byzantine land forces commanded by Alexios. William of Apulia gives a full and apparently reliable account of the public exchanges at the start of the siege, which ended with some of the defenders mocking the pretender sponsored by Robert; of the Venetian naval victory; of an initial probe by a Byzantine detachment against Butrint (which resulted in defeat, the capture of the Byzantine general who was privy to Alexios' plans, and the revelation of those plans to the Normans); and of the decisive Norman victory over the main Byzantine army under Alexios on 18 October outside Dyrrachion (243–76, 286–435). The siege was then pressed until the city was captured on 21 February 1082, William giving a detailed account of negotiations with a disgruntled Venetian magnate who indicated his willingness to betray the city (436–505). Book Four ends with a reference to domestic problems in southern Italy, Robert's return and his later rescue of Pope Gregory VII from Rome where he had been under attack from Emperor Henry IV and his forces for two years (506–70).

Book Five continues the story of the Balkan campaign. Bohemond, deputising for Robert as supreme commander of the expeditionary force, succeeded in breaking through the Pindos mountains into Thessaly in 1082 but was forced to withdraw to the Dalmatian coast by Alexios' patient strategy of carefully targeted harassment in the course of 1083 (1–79). An excursus comes next, to bring the story of the naval war in the Adriatic, left off in spring 1082, up to date. The Venetian fleet returned to the area of Dyrrachion, penned the Norman garrison back into the citadel and itself wintered outside the city (presumably he is referring to the winter of 1083–4) before resuming operations in the following spring. It then sailed down the coast to join the Byzantine fleet off Corfu, thus extending the naval blockade south to cover most of the Norman enclave, including their key bases at Butrint and on Corfu (80–105).

After another excursus on the submission to Robert of Jordan I, Prince of Capua, who in 1082 had gone over to the Byzantine side (106–20) and a note on the consecration by Gregory VII of the church of St Matthew at Salerno (121–4), William begins an excellent account of Robert's naval counteroffensive in autumn 1084. The expeditionary force assembled at

Taranto (chosen presumably for maximum security in case of a preemptive strike by the Venetians), then moved to an advance base of operations at Brindisi. Brindisi was chosen, according to William, because it provided a safer autumn anchorage than Otranto, but also probably because it was the Italian port closest to the intended landfall in the Balkans at Avlona, where the Norman fleet would be able to prevent any Venetian reinforcements reaching the Byzantine task force. Roger Borsa accompanied his father on this campaign, for which large naval forces were mobilised. The figure of 120 warships given by William does not include the transport vessels (127–49). The fleet joined the land forces under Bohemond's command, but the start of operations was delayed for two months by bad weather (150–3). It was therefore late in the autumn of 1084 that the Norman fleet engaged the combined Venetian–Byzantine fleet. William focuses on a Norman victory and the relief of the Norman garrison holding the capital of Corfu. He gives an analysis of Robert's dispositions beforehand and a phase-by-phase account of the battle itself (154–201). The clarity and precision of this narrative are such as to suggest that he was using an official source, most probably a victory dispatch issued by Robert for circulation in his dukedom and beyond.[19]

William then turns to describe the hardships suffered in the course of the following winter, spent in a sheltered basin, away from the coast up the river 'Gliceus' (Glykys in Greek, the ancient Acheron and modern

---

[19] The military dispatch played a vital part in upholding the prestige of rulers and in ensuring accountability on the part of subordinates in antiquity and the Middle Ages. Large numbers can be detected lurking beneath the surface of classical and Byzantine texts, such as Caesar's *Gallic Wars*; Arrian's *Periplus of the Black Sea*; Malchos' dense but lucid narrative about Roman operations and diplomacy in the Balkans in the 470s; Theophylaktos Simokattes' history of Balkan and eastern operations in the reign of Maurice (582–602); the *Chronicon Paschale*, which reproduced the text of Herakleios' victory dispatch of 8 April 628; and, leaping forward to the middle Byzantine period, detailed accounts of Basil I's campaigns in the East presented in the biography commissioned by Constantine Porphyrogennetos; the so-called *Kriegstagebuch*, which supplied the rich material common to Leo the Deacon and John Skylitzes about John Tzimiskes' defeat of the Rus in Bulgaria in 971; and many of Skylitzes' later campaign narratives. References: F. E. Adcock, *Caesar as a Man of Letters* (Cambridge, 1956); P. A. Stadter, *Arrian of Nicomedia* (Chapel Hill, NC, 1980), 32–41; P. Heather, *Goths and Romans 332–489* (Oxford, 1991), 233–7; M. Whitby, *The Emperor Maurice and His Historian: Theophylact Simocatta on Persian and Balkan Warfare* (Oxford, 1988), 94–105, 230–3; J. Howard-Johnston, *Witnesses to a World Crisis: Historians and Histories of the Middle East in the Seventh Century* (Oxford, 2010), 44–54; I. Ševčenko, ed. and trans., *Chronographiae quae Theophanis continuati nomine fertur liber quo vita Basilii imperatoris amplectitur* (Berlin, 2011), 136–59, 162–89; G. Moravcsik, *Byzantinoturcica* (Berlin, 1958), I, 398–9; C. Holmes, *Basil II and the Governance of Empire (976–1025)* (Oxford, 2005), 94–5, 111–14, 272–6; I. Colvin, 'Reporting Battles and Understanding Campaigns in Procopius and Agathias: Classicising Historians' Use of Archived Documents as Sources' in A. Sarantis and N. Christie, eds., *War and Warfare in Late Antiquity* (Leiden, 2013), 571–98.

Mavropotamo), roughly mid-way between Corfu and Kephalenia. A combination of bitter cold and a shortage of supplies spread disease through the Norman forces and left ten thousand dead, including five hundred knights. Bohemond was one of those who fell sick. He was allowed to return to Italy for medical treatment (202–28). In spring 1085, after the death and burial of Pope Gregory VII, who is given a laudatory obituary (255–67), Robert Guiscard and Roger Borsa resumed operations, their objective being to capture Kephalenia, the next island on the sea-route to the Gulf of Corinth. Robert himself had difficulty relaunching the main part of the fleet, since the Gliceus had sunk to a low level in spring. He managed to haul the ships down to the sea after constructing a narrow artificial channel (technical details are supplied by William) and then sailed south to join Roger Borsa on Kephalenia (228–87). It was on the way there that he fell ill and died, despite the prayers of his wife who makes a speech full of apprehension about the future (288–322). Grief-stricken, Roger secures the support of the troops in his father's camp and back on Kephalenia. The main army then panics and hastily evacuates its position, setting fire to the large ships and leaving a majority of the soldiers behind (323–90). A violent storm off the coast of Apulia damages the fleet. Many drown. Robert's corpse is washed overboard and recovered with difficulty. From Otranto, where the heart and entrails are removed and the body is stuffed with aromatic substances, Robert's remains are taken to Venosa for burial (391–409).

The *Alexiad* and *Gesta Roberti* Compared: Background, Preparations and Opening Operations of the 1081 Campaign

Almost all the *Alexiad*'s material on Robert Guiscard's preparations for war and his campaign in 1081 up to and including the start of the siege of Dyrrachion was based on William of Apulia's versified official history of these events (iv.1–271). The dependence of the *Alexiad* on the *Gesta* is evident from striking similarities in substance and in arrangement. The principal divergences occur in passages picked out by Anna for elaboration and embellishment. These deal with the conventional subjects for rhetorical turns in classicing histories, such as actions that cause widespread distress (like those of Robert, when he is recruiting troops for his first expedition (i.14.1–2)) or battles that lead to slaughter on a very large scale (as at the 1080 defeat of the German rebels against Emperor Henry IV (i.13.8)). She is also inclined to slip in comments of her own, as, for example, her claim that primacy in the church was transferred to Constantinople together with secular power in late antiquity (i.13.4).

The parallels between the two narratives can be summed up as follows:

1. The *Alexiad* follows the *Gesta* in integrating items of domestic Norman history into the main history of Robert's diplomatic and military preparations. Thus notices about the weddings of two of his daughters, the initial resistance in southern Italy to his call to arms, the arrival of his wife at Otranto, and the delegation of authority to Roger Borsa during his absence all reappear in the *Alexiad* at the appropriate places in the military–diplomatic narrative, save that the last two are transposed.[20]

2. Both sources describe at the same point the negotiations between Pope Gregory VII and Robert Guiscard that took place in June 1080. Both report that the pope gave his backing to Robert's political ambition, although Anna has him aim merely for the status of king (*rex*) and makes no connection with his campaign against Byzantium (i.13.6). Both attach excursuses on the Investiture Controversy, although here Anna substitutes an anti-papal *psogos* for the anti-imperial tirade in the *Gesta* and rearranges this section by placing the excursus in front of the account of the negotiations. The substance of the account of the war in Germany provoked by the ecclesiastical disagreement, which culminated in the battle of the river Elster in 1080, is very similar in both sources, down to the figure of thirty thousand dead.[21]

3. Once the Norman forces reach Dyrrachion and both narratives become more detailed, the parallels in substance and arrangement within individual episodes of the narrative are yet more striking. Both sources give the same foundation legend for Dyrrachion, describe the initial siege-operations of the Normans in similar terms, and report the public exchanges between the besiegers and the besieged (in which the latter offered to surrender if they were convinced of the purported identity of the pretender, and then mocked him when he was paraded in state in front of the walls).[22]

The *Alexiad* does not reproduce all the material in *Gesta* (iv.1–271). Some excisions are made: details of the foundation of a church of St Matthew

---

[20] William of Apulia, *Gesta Roberti*, ed. Mathieu, 204, 210 and 214 (iv.6–15, 128–32, 185, 186–94); Komnene, *Alexias*, ed. Reinsch and Kambylis, 42–3 and 47–9 (i.12.11, 14.1–2, 15.1, 14.3).

[21] William of Apulia, *Gesta Roberti*, ed. Mathieu, 204–6 (iv.16–70); Komnene, *Alexias*, 43–7 (i.13.1–10).

[22] William of Apulia, *Gesta Roberti*, 216–18 (iv.234–71); Komnene, *Alexias*, ed. Reinsch and Kambylis, 120–2 (iii.12.8–iv.1.4).

and a palace at Salerno (71–2) and of the ceremonial side of the meeting between the pope and Robert in 1080 that were of interest only to westerners (21–3); an account of Alexios' rise to power presented in two passages (77–121, 142–53) that was redundant because the *Alexiad* gives its own rather fuller narrative; and the description of the storm that wrecked the Norman fleet and then delayed the start of the siege of Dyrrachion (218–24) for which the *Alexiad* used a different eyewitness source in the Norman expeditionary force (iii.12.4–7). The *Alexiad* also includes a fair amount of supplementary material, taken from Byzantine sources, which is not to be found in the *Gesta*.

But all in all the parallels are inexplicable save by the hypothesis that the *Alexiad* draws all the shared material from the *Gesta*, which is, of course, much the earlier of the two texts. For we would expect independent, and mutually uncontaminated, Byzantine and Norman histories of the war to diverge substantially. Different observations would be made from the two opposing sides. The spotlight would fall on different episodes. Differences of interpretation would develop under the influence of the political and personal interests of the chief protagonists on each side and these would, in turn, have an impact on the structure and substance of the narrative reconstructions of past events. The longer the period that elapsed between the events and the composition of the histories, the more their narratives would diverge as vagaries of memory and vested interests had more time to play upon and reshape the historical record. I labour the point, obvious though it may seem, because Graham Loud has maintained the contrary view in this case, namely that the reason for the similarities between the two texts lies in their faithful attention to a single set of real events.[23]

Further scrutiny of parallel passages in the two texts should remove any lingering doubts, indeed should demonstrate that the *Alexiad* makes *direct* use of the *Gesta*. Neither chance nor oral transmission can account for the appearance in both texts of demonstrable historical errors (items 1–3 in the list below), let alone for the agility shown by some of William's expressions that have managed to leap over the language barrier and to reappear virtually unchanged in Greek guise (items 3–6 in the list below). There are, as Liubarskii observed, some cases of literal translation of Latin phrases into Greek – as clear an indication as any that the *Gesta* was feeding directly into the *Alexiad*.

1. In both texts, Benevento is the venue for Gregory VII's meeting with Robert (*Gesta*, iv.16–18, 69–70, *Alexiad*, i.13.6). This is a mistake. There

[23] Loud, 'Anna Komnena', 50–2.

can be no doubt that it took place at Ceprano since the two key documents to emerge from the meeting (Gregory's formal investiture of Robert with his dukedom, dated 6 June, and Robert's oath of fealty to the pope, dated 29 June) were both issued at Ceprano. William of Apulia seems to have confused this meeting with an earlier attempt to hold a meeting at Benevento *in August 1073*, and Anna simply follows William.[24]

2. A second error occurs in the same section of the *Gesta* (iv.42–8). Gregory VII, it is clearly implied, instigated the revolt against Henry IV led by Welf IV and Rudolf of Rheinfelden (transmuted into Landolf in the *Alexiad*). The same charge resurfaces at the corresponding place in the *Alexiad*'s excursus on the Investiture Controversy (i.13.7).[25]

3. The *Alexiad* also reproduces a learned fiction in the *Gesta* about the second foundation of Dyrrachion. According to this thoroughly unhistorical account, the legendary founders of Thebes, Zetas and Amphion, travel through time and space to the second century BCE and to Epiros. There they rebuild a city on the site of ancient Epidamnos that had been depopulated after Pyrrhus' wars with Rome. There are some striking similarities (underlined) in phrasing between the two versions of this story.

> Quondam fuit urbs opulenta
> Magnaque praecipue tegulosis obsita muris.
> Rex Epirotarum dicier hanc Epidamnum
> Pyrrhus praecepit, quia fortia ferre Quiritum
> Bella Tarentinis sociatus non dubitavit.
> Inde frequens bellum varios et passa labores
> Evacuata viris fuit ad nihilumque redacta.
> Destructam spatio post composuere minori
> Zetus et Amphion et praecepere vocari
> Dirachium.[26]
>
> (*Gesta*, iv.234–43)

Ἐν ᾗ βασιλεὺς ποτὲ Ἠπειρώτης Πύρρος ... Ταραντίνοις ἑνωθεὶς Ῥωμαίοις ἐν᾽ Ἀουληνίᾳ καρτερὸν τὸν πόλεμον συνεστήσατο ... ἄοικος πάντῃ καταλέλειπται. Ἐν ὑστέροις δὲ χρόνοις, ὥς Ἕλληνές φασι ... ὑπ᾽ Ἀμφίονος καὶ

---

[24] Loud, 'Anna Komnena', 50–1 and *Robert Guiscard*, 197–8, 205–6.
[25] Mathieu, *Guillaume de Pouille*, 317–18.
[26] 'It was once a large opulent city, surrounded by mainly brick walls. Pyrrhus, king of the Epirotes, ordered that it be called Epidamnus, since, allied with the Tarentines, he had no doubt that he could cope with major wars against the Quirites [Romans]. Later, after suffering frequent attack and diverse troubles, it was emptied of men and reduced to nothing. Zetus and Amphion restored it a short time after its destruction and ordered that it be named Dirachium'.

Ζήθου ἀνοικοδομηθεῖσα εἰς ὃ νῦν ὁρᾶται σχῆμα, αὐτίκα καὶ τὴν κλῆσιν μεταμείψασα Δυρράχιον προσηγόρευται.²⁷ (*Alexias*, iii.12.8)²⁸

4. Another case of close linguistic convergence occurs a little earlier. William of Apulia says nothing about the territorial lordship of Ebalus, husband of the younger of Robert's two daughters married in 1080, simply describing him as 'Egregio comiti Francorum stemmate claro' (iv.12: 'distinguished count of the Franks, with a famous lineage'), a phrase that is translated in the *Alexiad* (i.12.11) as 'ἐπιφανεστάτῳ καὶ τούτῳ κόμητι' ('this very distinguished count').²⁹

5. Several close parallels (underlined) exist in the accounts of the preparations made in Dyrrachion to withstand siege:

> ... Ducis hoc circumdatur obsidione.
> Fit pavor obsessae non parvus civibus urbis,
> Et vigiles statuunt; custodia fida per urbem
> Ponitur; imperio factam ducis obsidionem
> Notificant, et opem legatis poscere curant.³⁰
> (*Gesta*, iv.243–7)

Περιστοιχισθέντες οὖν οἱ τοῦ Δυρραχίου ἐντὸς ἐξ ἑκατέρου μέρους ... μεγίστῳ δέει συνείχοντο. Ὁ δέ γε Παλαιολόγος Γεώργιος ... σκοπεῖς δι' ὅλου καταστήσας τοῦ τείχους ... Τηνικαῦτα δὲ καὶ διὰ γραμμάτων τὴν τοῦ Ρομπέρτου ἔφοδον ἐδήλου τῷ αὐτοκράτορι ...³¹ (*Alexias*, iv.1.1)

6. The most striking parallel, however, has been missed by Liubarskii. It appears at the same point in both accounts, when there was a public exchange of views, involving the formal staking and denying of the pretender's claim, before the start of serious siege operations against Dyrrachion:

---

²⁷ 'In which once Pyrrhus, Epirote king ... allied with the Tarantines engaged in a major war against the Romans in Apulia ... It was left entirely uninhabited. Later, as the Greeks recount ... it was rebuilt by Amphion and Zethos in its currently visible form, and immediately changed its name and was called Dyrrachion.'
²⁸ Liubarskii, 'Об источниках [Ob istochnikakh]', 112–13. The *Alexiad* provides an additional piece of information about an inscription that, it claims, recorded the foundation story. Since it is hard to conceive that there was such an inscription and that someone took the trouble to note it down and report it to the historian, this looks like an editorial touch added at a late stage by Anna.
²⁹ In fact he was Ebles de Roucy. Mathieu, *Guillaume de Pouille*, 311.
³⁰ 'The duke besieged it on all sides. There was no little fear among the citizens of the besieged city, and they posted watchmen; security was tightened inside the city; they reported the siege instituted by the duke to the empire, and charged the envoys to ask for help.'
³¹ 'Penned in thus on each side, those inside Dyrrachion ... were seized with the greatest fear. George Palaiologos posted watchmen along the whole wall ... At that time he also reported Robert's attack in a letter to the emperor.'

> Dux venisse refert se, regni sede repulsus
> Immerito Michael ut restituatur honori.³²
> (*Gesta*, iv.260–1)

Κελεύει τοίνυν ὁ Παλαιολόγος ἄνωθεν πυθέσθαι, ὅτου χάριν παραγέγονεν· ὁ δὲ φησίν 'ὥστε τὸν τῆς βασιλείας ἐξωσθέντα Μιχαὴλ τὸν ἐμὸν κηδεστὴν εἰς τὴν ἰδίαν τιμὴν αὖθις ἀποκαταστῆσαι'³³ (*Alexiad*, iv.1.3)

Robert thus claimed that his sole object was to restore the unjustly deposed Michael Doukas to his *honor*. The word *honor* was pregnant with meaning to a westerner, denoting as it did a whole complex of rights associated with lordship. Its literal translation in Greek as τιμή (honour, glory) looks decidedly odd and fails to convey the meaning of the original Latin.³⁴

The *Alexiad* and *Gesta Roberti* Compared: From the Siege Of Dyrrachion (1081) to the Death of Robert Guiscard (1085)

Once the siege begins, the two versions drift apart. There was no shortage of Byzantine sources and it was to these that the *Alexiad* now turned, thus abandoning the *Gesta*. There are major differences in the accounts of the sea-battle between Normans and Venetians, of Alexios' mobilisation and march on Dyrrachion, of his defeat outside the city, of his flight and of the subsequent betrayal of the city.³⁵ The divergence is as great if not greater when the campaigns of the following years are described. Thus, for example, the accounts of Bohemond's westward thrusts and their

---

³² 'The duke said that he had come, in order that Michael, who had been dethroned undeservedly, might be restored to his dignity [*honori*].'

³³ 'Palaiologos then ordered inquiries to be made from above, as to why he had come. He replied, "So as to restore again my kinsman Michael who was driven out from the empire to his own dignity [*timen*]."'

³⁴ Byzantine doubts about this claim are reported in both sources. William singles out their most offensive taunt: 'Iste solebat / Crateras mensis plenos deferre Lieo, / Et de pincernis erat inferioribus unus' (218–19 (iv.269–7)): 'that man used to serve tables with bowls full of wine, and was but one of the lowly cup-bearers'). The charge resurfaces in the *Alexiad*, but, rather surprisingly, its account is much more even-handed. It reports (121–2 (iv.1.4)) that there were conflicting views in the city. Some noised it about that the pretender was the wine-steward of Emperor Michael Doukas, others accepted his claims, others still considered him to be a complete impostor who was merely Robert Guiscard's stooge.

³⁵ William of Apulia, *Gesta Roberti*, ed. Mathieu, 218–30 (iv.272–505); Komnene, *Alexias*, ed. Reinsch and Kambylis, 122–3, 126–40, 141–2 (iv.2, 4–8, v.1.1–2).

containment in 1082–3 are completely independent and much effort is required to extract a coherent common narrative from them,[36] while the *Alexiad* plays down the significance of the Norman naval victory in 1084 by presenting it as merely one – the third – in a series of four naval engagements.[37] Differences such as these were only to be expected when one source was written half a generation, the other two generations, after the events.

Book Five of the *Gesta* opens with the departure of Robert for Italy early in 1082 and Bohemond's attacks on Ioannina and Larissa. William appears to have had difficulty in extracting a clear account of operations from the materials he was using. The *Alexiad* provides a better account, which brings out the overall strategy pursued by both sides and is full of precise detail. There is no connection between the two accounts save their common origin in real events. We seem to face a classic example of the superiority of history written from contemporary documents over history based largely on orally transmitted and somewhat garbled information.

When Robert Guiscard prepares to return to the fray in the Balkans (in autumn 1084, at *Gesta*, v.125 ff.), we can once again observe intermittent convergences between the texts. These suggest that the text of the *Gesta* was to hand and was being quarried, but that it was no longer treated as the main source into which to slip supplementary information. Instead the narrative was based on Byzantine sources, with pieces, large and small, of material from William of Apulia subsequently incorporated.

The first sign of the influence of *Gesta* comes in odd sentences that are scattered over the text of what looks like a pre-existing narrative in the *Alexiad*. Something, however, has gone badly awry, since they are sprinkled over the wrong section of the text, that dealing with the expedition of 1081 rather than that of 1084 (on which more will be said below). These odd sentences convey, more or less accurately, information provided by William of Apulia about the events of 1084:

1. A Byzantine fleet under the command of an admiral, named Maurix, had joined the Venetians in the Adriatic and had established a blockade of the Norman enclave in Dalmatia (iv.3.1), as happened in 1084 (*Gesta*, v.99).

---

[36] William of Apulia, *Gesta Roberti*, ed. Mathieu, 236–40 (v.1–79); Komnene, *Alexias*, ed. Reinsch and Kambylis, 149–61, 168 (v.4–7, vi.1).
[37] William of Apulia, *Gesta Roberti*, ed. Mathieu, 244–6 (v.154–98); Komnene, *Alexias*, ed. Reinsch and Kambylis, 176–9 (vi.5.4–9).

2. Brindisi was the springboard for the expedition (i.15.1, 16.1), as in 1084 (Gesta, v.132–3).
3. Roger Borsa took part (i.16.1), as in 1084 (Gesta, v.143–6).
4. The naval task force numbered 150 ships (i.16.1), a round figure apparently based on William of Apulia's report of the naval strength of the 1084 task force (120 warships plus an unspecified number of transport vessels [Gesta, v.143, 147–9], as against the 50 warships and transport vessels from Dalmatia used in 1081 [Gesta, iv.134–5, 199–201]).
5. The crossing took place late in the year, when storms were to be expected according the Alexiad (i.16.1: winter), which was true of 1084 (Gesta, v.133–5: autumn).
6. Bad weather delayed the start of operations for two months (iv.3.2), as happened in 1084 (Gesta, v.152–3); this is a more excusable error since bad weather also disrupted the Norman advance on Dyrrachion in 1081 (Gesta, iv.218–21).

The accounts of the third naval engagement of 1084, which resulted in a decisive Norman victory, are independent.[38] On this occasion, William of Apulia's version is the better articulated and probably derives directly from an official account, say a victory dispatch written for circulation among Norman leaders back in southern Italy. But two passages in William of Apulia dealing with problems encountered by the Normans in the following winter and spring are reproduced in the Alexiad, although they are misplaced in the winter of 1081–2.

1. The first concerns an epidemic that struck the Norman naval and military forces, with devastating effects (Gesta, v.210–20). The Alexiad understands correctly that the *populus* encamped near the Gliceus River (210) consisted of naval personnel and was for that reason distinguished from *reliquus exercitus* (216), which, as William of Apulia has already reported, was encamped at a certain distance, at Vonitsa (208–9). The Alexiad (iv.3.1–2) attributes the epidemic to starvation, caused by the Byzantine–Venetian blockade, as well as to the bitter winter cold (Gesta, v.210–11), but remains faithful to the original Latin when it comes to the casualty figures and the length of time the epidemic raged: it netted ten thousand sailors in approximately three months, while five hundred counts

---

[38] William of Apulia, *Gesta Roberti*, ed. Mathieu, 244–6 (v.154–98); Komnene, *Alexias*, ed. Reinsch and Kambylis, 177–8 (vi.5.6–7).

and other elite cavalry died as well as innumerable ordinary cavalrymen (a majority of the latter, according to William of Apulia).

2. A description of the measures taken to create a canal inside the bed of the Gliceus River and thereby to refloat the Norman fleet in spring 1085 is reproduced in the *Alexiad*, with many of the same details:

> Dux, qui difficilem facilem facit arte laborem,
> Dum fluvium solitis cognovit egere fluentis,
> Namque meatus aquae brevis arta fauce fluebat,
> Multos afferri palos et ab amnis utraque
> Margine configi connexos vimine iussit,
> Et multis multa praecisis arbore ramis
> Composuit crates, et arenis desuper implet.
> Sic aqua lascive dispersa refertur in unum.
> Alveus altior hinc coepitque capacior esse,
> Cogitur unde viam praebere meabilis unda
> Navibus, illaesaeque maris revehuntur ad undas.[39]
>
> (*Gesta*, v.244–54)

> Ἀλλ' οἷα μηχανικώτατος ὢν καὶ βαθύνους ἀνὴρ πασσάλους ἑκατέρωθεν ἐκέλευε πήγνυσθαι τοῦ ποταμοῦ, συνδεδέσθαι δὲ τούτους διὰ λύγων πυκνῶν, εἶτα δένδρα παμμεγέθη κόπτοντας ῥιζόθεν ὄπισθεν αὐτῶν καταστρωννύειν ψάμμον ἐπιπάττοντας ἄνωθεν, ὡς εἰς ἕνα τὸ ὕδωρ συλλείβεσθαι τόπον ὥσπερ εἰς διώρυχα μίαν τὴν ἐκ τῶν πασσάλων γεγονυῖαν συναθροιζόμενον. Καὶ κατὰ μικρὸν ἀναλιμνάζον τὸ ὕδωρ τὴν κρηπῖδα πᾶσαν ἐπλήρου τοῦ ποταμοῦ καὶ εἰς βάθος ἀξιόλογον ἤρχετο, ἕως τὰς ναῦς ἀνεκούφισε καὶ τὰς τέως ἐρηρεισμένας νῆας τῇ γῇ ἀνέσχε τὲ καὶ ἀκρόπλους ἐποίησε. Καὶ τὸ ἀπὸ τοῦδε εὐπλοίας ἐπιδραξάμενα τὰ πλοῖα εὐκόλως πρὸς τὴν θάλασσαν εἱλκύσθησαν.[40] (*Alexias*, iv.3.3)

The similarities are so close that Mathieu was forced, in this instance, to admit that the whole passage from which this extract has been quoted

---

[39] 'The duke, who could with ingenuity make a difficult task easy, understood that the river lacked its usual flow of water – for a thin stream was flowing down a narrow channel. He ordered many piles to be brought, driven in on either side of the river, and bound together with osiers. He made wattle structures out of many branches previously cut from trees, and covered them with sand. The water which had been spread out wantonly was thereby brought together and united. The channelled water began to rise and increase in volume. Thus the water became passable and was coerced into providing a road for the ships and they were brought back intact to the waves of the sea.'

[40] 'But being a most ingenious and intelligent man, he gave orders for piles to be driven in on either side of the river and for them to be tightly bound together with osiers; they were then to cut down large trees from the roots and lay them out behind the piles, spreading sand over them, so as to confine the water to a single place, that is, gathered into a single channel formed by the piles. Gradually the water level rose until it filled the whole structure in the river and reached a depth great enough to lighten and lift the ships which had been resting on the ground, and make them float. Thereafter, with navigability recovered, they were easily pulled to the sea.'

(on the troubles of winter and spring, *Alexiad*, iv.3.2–3) was based on the corresponding passage in the *Gesta* (v.210–54, minus the lines dealing with Bohemond's illness and departure [223–8] and Roger Borsa's expedition to Kephalenia [228–34]). She envisaged an intermediary oral stage in which the Latin text was translated aloud and taken down in dictation by Anna, before its material was incorporated in the *Alexiad*.[41] When the two passages are examined side by side, the *Alexiad* does indeed seem to have incorporated notes taken by a scrupulous scholar, but surely from the text itself rather than from dictation. The notes have been expanded almost to the level of a full translation when it comes to rendering the technical details of the construction of the man-made channel in Greek.

The main event of 1085 was the death of Robert Guiscard early in the campaigning season. It was to bring about a sudden change in Norman–Byzantine relations. For it resulted almost immediately in the withdrawal of the Norman forces from the Balkans where they were coming under intensifying Byzantine pressure. The deathbed scene provided the occasion for William of Apulia to compose a lament that he puts into the mouth of Robert's wife, Sichelgaita, and to portray his son and heir, Roger Borsa, as overwhelmed by grief. This emotional centrepiece of Book Five is preceded by a brief account of his setting off to join Roger Borsa, who has been sent ahead with a detachment to attack Kephalenia, and is followed by a description of the measures taken by Roger Borsa to secure the allegiance of the expeditionary force and the repatriation of Robert's corpse (284–409).

When we turn from the *Gesta Roberti* back to the *Alexiad* we encounter the same set of episodes – the attack on Kephalenia by a detachment commanded by Roger Borsa, Robert's death just after his arrival with the whole force, the storm that damaged the hearse-ship, and the funeral at Venosa – but this time they are correctly placed in the narrative (vi.6). The chief differences result from the *Alexiad*'s selective use of the *Gesta*.[42] Several episodes are excised: (1) the occasion when apparently irrational panic seizes the Norman forces, downcast after Robert's death, and leads to their hasty evacuation (probably rejected as a distortion introduced for dramatic effect (v.364–90)); (2) the long scene of lamentation by Robert's

---

[41] Mathieu, *Guillaume de Pouille*, 45–6.
[42] There are also some minor discrepancies: Robert appears to set off on his own to join Roger Borsa (Komnene, *Alexias*, ed. Reinsch and Kambylis, 179 (vi.6.1)); Sichelgaita, who arrives just before Robert dies, finds a mysterious, unnamed son weeping over him (180 (vi.6.3)); she then announces Robert's death to his designated heir (180 (vi.6.3)), i.e. Roger Borsa, the implication (quite false) being that he was not at his father's side at the last.

wife (292–336), briefly noted at *Alexiad*, vi.6.3; and (3) details about the preparation of the corpse at Otranto and the disposal there of the putrid inner organs (397–400).

On the whole, the *Alexiad* has successfully integrated William of Apulia's material with information taken from other sources, to form a clear and rather pithier account of the end of Alexios' first great antagonist. There is, it is worth noting, no trace in the *Alexiad* of a canard that was sponsored and spread by Bohemond and that surfaces in Orderic Vitalis and William of Malmesbury against the wife of Robert, Sichelgaita, who was accused of murdering her husband.[43] In this respect it is as discreet as the *Gesta*.

Other Sources, Written and Oral, of the *Alexiad*

The *Gesta* is the only extant written source used by the *Alexiad* for the Norman–Byzantine war. Other contributions, almost all of them Byzantine, can be identified only by the subjective process of analysing the text into constituent parts, on the basis of differences in subject-matter, points of view and degree of detail. The majority of the material in the *Alexiad* derives from these other shadowy sources.

Most of them were, in my view, written and official in character: dispatches of military commanders including Alexios himself, correspondence between Alexios and the Byzantine authorities in the Balkans, diplomatic reports and negotiating documents.[44] The private papers of important protagonists may also have been used. Such official records and private papers provided, alongside the *Gesta*, the basic source material for the *Alexiad*, where it presents a clear, solidly founded military and diplomatic narrative. It should also be noted that, for the most part, the diverse material included on domestic affairs, diplomacy and operations in the field has been successfully blended together.

a. The *Alexiad*'s coverage of events in 1081 is fuller than William of Apulia's. Large *lacunae* in the *Gesta* can be filled in from its pages. The main additions concern (1) a Norman embassy to Constantinople led by Raoul that returned on the eve of war (Raoul insisted that the pretender Michael Doukas was an impostor and attempted in vain to dissuade Robert from his planned expedition [i.15.2–6]); (2) ambivalent behaviour

---

[43] Mathieu, *Guillaume de Pouille*, 335.
[44] Howard-Johnston, 'Anna Komnene', 278–80. *Contra* prolegomena (7*-8*) of Reinsch and Kambylis, *Annae Comnenae. Alexias*; also see Peter Frankopan's contribution to this volume.

on the part of George Monomachatos, immediate predecessor of George Palaiologos as governor of Dyrrachion (i.16.2–8, iii.9.4, 12.1); (3) a diplomatic effort to isolate the Normans in the west (iii.10); (4) negotiations that neutralised the Turks in north-west Asia Minor (iii.11.4–5); (5) the securing of active naval support from Venice and a subsequent Venetian victory over the Norman fleet at Dyrrachion (iv.2.2–6); (6) Alexios' mobilisation of Byzantine forces (a detailed breakdown is given), and march west (iv.4.1–4); (7) news received on the march about the progress of the siege and George Palaiologos' valiant defence (iv.4.4–5.1); (8) rejection of the cautious strategy of blockade recommended by George Palaiologos and others (iv.5.3); and (9) a full history of the land battle outside Dyrrachion that ended disastrously with the rout of the army and the emperor's escape on horseback (iv.6 –7).

b. Similar sources provide material for the account of Balkan operations in 1082–3 (v.4–7, vi.1, 5.1). They bring out the general strategy pursued by each side, as well as supplying a balanced account of the naval warfare in late 1084 and early 1085, which resulted in a decisive shift in the balance of power in the Adriatic in favour of the Venetians and the Byzantines, despite one spectacular Norman victory in the third of the four engagements fought in the waters around Corfu (vi.5.4–9).

Much of what has been said above about the nature of the Byzantine sources used by the *Alexiad* must remain hypothetical. But there are some positive indications in its favour to be found in the text itself. A small number of document-based passages can be identified. The opening sentences are quoted from Robert's fobbing-off letter to Pope Gregory VII in 1081 (i.13.10); there is no reason to doubt their authenticity, since the thrust of the quoted passage parallels the summary of Robert's line of argument given by William of Apulia (iv.179–84). Summaries are given of three other documents: (i) the gist of George Palaiologos' report on the progress of the Norman campaign and their investment of Dyrrachion is presented at iv.2.1; (ii) the terms offered by Alexios to Venice to secure their alliance in 1081 are outlined at iv.2.2: payment in two instalments, the second to be made once the Venetians have mobilised, irrespective of the outcome of the battle, and no restriction to be placed on the Venetians' pursuit of their own interests as long as there is no adverse effect on those of Byzantium; (iii) an accurate résumé is given of the golden bull granting trading and other privileges to Venice, which was issued by Alexios, according to the *Alexiad*, after the fourth and final engagement with Norman fleet, but possibly (as is argued below) several years later, in 1092, when the Byzantines were determined to consolidate the old alliance at a time of increasing dependence on Latin Christendom and of increasing nervousness (vi.5.10).

Another document, of very different character, may underlie the account of Alexios' flight after the battle of Dyrrachion in 1081. Even in defeat, Alexios is portrayed as a heroic figure who possesses physical strength and fighting skills bordering on the superhuman. He is transformed into an invincible warrior in the mould of an akritic hero, who is capable of escaping from the tightest of corners and of winning against overwhelming odds. Propaganda, pumped out after the battle to repair the damage done to the emperor's image by focusing on his valour, is the most likely ultimate source of this unusual, semi-fictional matter (iv.7).

Finally we come to evidence gathered directly from eyewitnesses. The odd vivid detail may have been picked up from the reminiscences of Alexios, George Palaiologos and Anna's uncles or from the memoirs of old soldiers, although how much reliance should have been placed on the anecdotes of even the most distinguished of them in later years is debatable (xiv.7.4–7). However, there is only Anna's general statement to go on, and no Byzantine participant is specifically cited as a source in the course of the narrative. By contrast, two western informants are mentioned. Peter son of Aliphas is cited as the source for an incident in the battle of Dyrrachion where Alexios fought three Normans at once (iv.6.8). The other informant is the unnamed emissary of the Latin archbishop of Bari to Robert, who was with him before and probably after the start of the siege of Dyrrachion (iii.12.8). He was almost certainly the source of the graphic account of the violent storm that wrecked Robert's fleet as it was rounding Cape Glossa and entering the Bay of Avlona (iii.12.4–6), since he is cited immediately afterwards, as well as the informant mentioned a little later as a source for the opening Norman engineering operations against Dyrrachion (iv.5.1).

The description of the storm has the hallmarks of eyewitness testimony and was surely based largely, if not entirely, on the oral testimony of the cited source. Visual, auditory and olfactory impressions are vividly conveyed by the narrative. It was a sudden, violent (and rather unseasonal) snowstorm. Winds from the mountains stir up a raging sea. Oars snap. Sails tear. Spars fall down. The leather cladding on the wooden towers constructed on the large ships becomes waterlogged. The nails holding it in place are loosened, and under the increased weight of the soaked leather the towers collapse and sink the ships carrying them. All this happens to an accompaniment of cries, groans and prayers from the sailors. When the storm abates and the survivors gather on land, they collect the dead who have been washed ashore and give them a decent burial in spite of the stench emanating from the putrid corpses.

There are parallels with William of Apulia's much shorter account (iv.218–29), but they are not close. It appears to be a good example of the divergence of memories that can develop between two accounts, both dependent immediately or ultimately on eyewitness testimony about the same events. William of Apulia provides no detail about the storm and the progressive damage that it did to the ships. He reflects the point of view of Robert and his staff, noting that Robert's ship escaped with difficulty and stressing the scale of the loss of provisions suffered and the consequent delay in the start of the siege of Dyrrachion that was fully exploited by the Byzantine defenders, much to Robert's chagrin.[45] The main point of convergence concerns the stinking human remains that were washed ashore, but William then drops the subject and makes no mention of their burial.

This brief survey of the sources of the *Alexiad*'s account of the Byzantine–Norman war of 1081–5 apart from the *Gesta* accounts for all the additional material that it contains. It also provides negative corroboration for the conclusion already reached, namely that the *Alexiad* draws directly on the *Gesta*. For the search for possible traces of material similar in character to that in William of Apulia but not replicated in the *Gesta* itself, i.e. derived from a putative shared source, draws a blank. Only two passages are candidates – the account of the storm that wrecked the Norman fleet and an extract from Robert's equivocating letter to Gregory VII – and both are much more likely to have come directly from other sources. In general, the correspondences of substance, arrangement and, on occasion, of language between the *Alexiad* and the *Gesta* are so close that direct dependence of the former on the latter provides the only satisfactory explanation. It seems inconceivable that the author or authors first assembled a set of sources that, for a large slice of Norman affairs, so exactly parallelled the dossier used by William of Apulia and then chanced to hit upon expressions in Greek that mirrored the Latin verse into which William of Apulia had reshaped his material. It follows that a relatively small amount of information from the Norman side was acquired orally from Norman informants. The citation of two such eyewitnesses should not be taken as the tip of an iceberg of orally transmitted matter, nor

---

[45] Komnene, *Alexias*, ed. Reinsch and Kambylis, 118 (iii.12.6) mentions the loss of stores but comments that it was mitigated because it was harvest season.

should the information provided by the archbishop of Bari's emissary be supposed to encompass events that occurred well outside the period of his recorded presence in the expeditionary force. Leaving aside the argument developed above, which, in effect, eliminates all but a handful of passages from consideration as orally transmitted, it is, of course, most improbable that the author or authors of the *Alexiad* managed to extract an account so similar to that of the officially sponsored *Gesta* from a single informant who must have suffered from all the usual disabilities of isolated eyewitnesses. The convention of introducing an eyewitness citation into a Byzantine historical text should not be misunderstood. It was not to indicate that the narrative was based upon a mass of directly observed material, but rather to provide touches of immediacy, to remind the reader that the narrative presented was connected with real events, and to label the occasional passages that were, exceptionally, not based on written sources.

Formation of the *Alexiad*: Drafting and Editing

Up to this point I have been building on Liubarskii's work, by elaborating and refining his arguments. In the process, his conclusion that a common written source provided material for the *Gesta* and the *Alexiad* has been jettisoned.

It is *prima facie* unlikely that two sources composed half a century apart and at opposite ends of the Mediterranean drew on the same source and were equally attentive to its contents. The hypothesis of a common source becomes less and less tenable the more parallels of substance, arrangement and phrasing there are. Liubarskii's reluctance to accept that there was a simpler and more direct link between the texts (namely direct use of the *Gesta* by the *Alexiad*) may originate in his awareness of an obvious difficulty, although he does not bring it out into the open. *There is no evidence that Anna knew Latin.* Liubarskii would have had to suppose that the source reached Anna in the form of a specially commissioned translation that otherwise has left no trace in the Byzantine historical tradition.

We now come to the nub of our argument. The *Alexiad*'s account is an odd mixture of excellent history on the one hand, with matter taken from William of Apulia slotted into the Byzantine material at the appropriate places, and, on the other hand, of a number of passages of bewilderingly confused chronology that have long befuddled readers. Thanks to the existence of the *Gesta*, real history can be extracted from the *Alexiad*. It is summarised in section 1 above. But the disturbing, muddled passages have been discarded rather than been analysed. Hands have been raised in despair. Vain attempts have been made to unravel the confusion. No satisfactory explanation has been advanced.

It may be possible to find a solution to this last problem and simultaneously to explain how a historian who knew little or no Latin came to make extensive use of a Latin source, by bringing into play a hypothesis, formulated for quite other reasons. There are two puzzling and disconcerting features of the *Alexiad* – coexistence of matter written in disparate styles, and an extraordinary unevenness in the editorial treatment of the military material that forms almost three-quarters of the contents of the text. The simplest and in my view most satisfactory explanation is to suppose that *two hands* were at work on the *Alexiad*, an earlier one belonging to a clear-headed military historian who was an excellent *raconteur*, and a second one, Anna's, who was concerned rather to shape the narrative into something akin to an epic.[46] The first hand is that of Nikephoros Bryennios, Anna's husband, who was commissioned to write an *Alexiad* by Anna's mother and who, Anna tells us, left her what he had composed (which went only to 1080) on his death in 1138.[47]

Anna says nothing about any research covering the following thirty-eight years of the projected history of Alexios' reign or any other preparatory work that Nikephoros may have carried out. It does not follow, though, from this silence that he had made absolutely no progress on the main part of his commission, that he had not identified and begun to exploit useful sources, that he had not assembled dossiers of relevant materials and begun to organise them by topic. Anna was simply (and accurately) defining what Nikephoros had *composed*, i.e. as a final draft. Since it is unlikely that history emerged fully formed and linguistically burnished from Nikephoros' mind, without passing through one or more drafting stages, Anna's silence probably encompasses drafts as well as research materials acquired on Nikephoros' death. They appear to form well over half the material incorporated in the *Alexiad* as we have it, as it was left by Anna on her death, probably in 1153.

There was one fundamental difference between husband and wife, apart from gender. Nikephoros was a military man and Anna was not. This does not mean that Nikephoros was better, more intelligent, more suited to

---

[46] Howard-Johnston, 'Anna Komnene', 276–88.
[47] Komnene, *Alexias*, ed. Reinsch and Kambylis, 7–8 (proem, 3.2–4).

writing history in general, than his wife.⁴⁸ Far from it. Anna was probably the more intelligent of the two and certainly the better educated and the more intellectual. She was well read and, unlike Nikephoros, could spice what she wrote with apposite quotations from classical texts, above all from Homer. She knew and gained inspiration from the works of recent historians and writers, above all from Michael Psellos. She could paint virtuoso word-pictures of notable contemporaries and conjure up the emotions of past episodes in which she had been involved. But she had not served in the field. She had not held high command. She had not acquired, through direct experience, the knowledge and understanding necessary to make sense of available written and orally transmitted material about specific operations and the campaigns to which they belonged. Intelligible military history can only be written from the perspective of command. That was the great advantage that Nikephoros enjoyed over her. He had also evidently had dealings with Western leaders, during and after the First Crusade, and had gained their trust, in particular that of Bohemond. For when Bohemond was forced to negotiate terms of surrender with Alexios in autumn 1108, with his army trapped and starving outside Dyrrachion, it was Nikephoros who persuaded him to accept most of the humiliating terms on offer.⁴⁹

Nikephoros then, unlike Anna, had the knowledge needed first to identify important sources of information and track them down, and then to interpret them critically. He was thus in a position to piece together, out of disparate primary material, coherent, lucid military narratives, pointed up with plenty of specific detail. Only when this had been done and a basic structure had been formed could the multifarious experiences of individual combatants be brought into play to supply vivid detail. Without a skeleton narrative, attending to strategic and tactical aspects of operations, anecdotal matter deriving from eyewitnesses in the thick of the fray would form a bewildering assemblage of particular incidents. In addition, Nikephoros had both the opportunity and the incentive to learn to communicate directly with Crusade leaders. It was not a matter of book learning, but of picking up, bit by bit, in the course of encounters with Westerners from Italy and France, enough Latinate speech to cope without interpreters, as it appears he did when he met Bohemond in 1108.⁵⁰ Unless he was a gifted

---

⁴⁸ L.A. Neville, *Heroes and Romans in Twelfth-Century Byzantium: The Material for History of Nikephoros Bryennios* (Cambridge, 2012).
⁴⁹ Komnene, *Alexias*, ed. Reinsch and Kambylis, 413 (xiii.11.2). Compare with Lilie, *Byzantium and the Crusader States*, 72–81.
⁵⁰ Komnene, *Alexias*, ed. Reinsch and Kambylis, 413 (xiii.11.2).

linguist – and there is nothing to suggest he was – he would have needed help from a Latin-reader with the *Gesta Roberti*. But he is more likely, than Anna, to have acquired the basic grasp of Latin needed to gather the gist of what William was saying. He is also more likely to have come across a bilingual individual from whom to get help in construing the Latin text.

In this section, I hope to demonstrate that the hypothesis of two hands at work enables us to understand how that part of the *Alexiad* which deals with the Byzantine–Norman war of 1081–5 reached its final unsatisfactory state, by identifying several stages in the editorial process. Inevitably there is much that is conjectural. Assumptions are made about the working-methods of Nikephoros and Anna. The serious errors, which are errors of arrangement, are attributed to Anna who could not make sense of some of the material she inherited. Anna, I argue, was responsible for the tangles in our text, and I shall make a suggestion as to how she was misled into introducing them.

A first and basic assumption is that Nikephoros took notes on the many sources – official documents, private papers and other writings – that he thought would yield useful material for his *Alexiad*. The first stage in the production of a historical work, that of identifying and exploiting useful sources of information, could not be carried out efficiently in the head alone. Notes would help the preliminary digestion of raw primary material and act as useful *aide-mémoire* later. It would be easier and faster to refer to notes rather than the original documents and other writings used when he came to put together a connected narrative. The second assumption is that he organised these notes by reference to the sources from which they were taken. For this, proof is readily available in Book Eleven (7–12) of the *Alexiad*, a wonderfully chaotic account of Byzantine–Crusader relations after the capture of Jerusalem (July 1099) up to the death of Raymond of Saint-Gilles (February 1105). There is a blithe disregard for chronology, which can only be explained by the supposition that the material has been arranged by source rather than by chronology. Anna, it seems, has put in material (mainly documentary) taken from different files and has retained the preliminary grouping of that material by file used.[51]

After completion of the basic research, Nikephoros had to decide which of his sources was to provide the core material for each section of his history. For the opening phase of the Norman–Byzantine war, as far as the start of the siege of Dyrrachion, it was the *Gesta* of William of Apulia. Thereafter he probably relied on an assemblage of Byzantine state papers.

---

[51] Lilie, *Byzantium and the Crusader States*, 259–76; Howard-Johnston, 'Anna Komnene', 292, n. 61.

Next, he probably extracted supplementary material from a variety of other sources, most of them written, and grafted them onto the précis of the main source or sources. In later drafts, a strategic interpretation would be added and would overlay the digested material, while the final version would be enlivened by dramatic scenes and snatches of direct speech.

Most of the material that Nikephoros bequeathed to Anna had not reached the stage of final drafting, although the sections on the Byzantine council of war before the battle of Dyrrachion and on the operations of 1082–3 were not far from it. His drafts probably covered the whole Byzantine–Norman conflict save for Robert's actions in autumn 1084 and the following winter. Anna then incorporated into the *Alexiad* whatever she found in different stages of drafting in Nikephoros' papers, making few modifications apart from stylistic upgrading and rhetorical amplification.

The material extracted from William of Apulia is well integrated into the core of Byzantine-based material. This is true of the 1081 narrative up to the October battles on sea and land outside Dyrrachion and also of the death of Robert Guiscard in spring 1085. These sections of the *Alexiad* seem to consist largely of intermediate drafts of Nikephoros'. But there was a residue of material from William of Apulia that Nikephoros had not yet inserted into the main core of the narrative and which, I suggest, Anna found in the form of raw, undigested notes, filed together but unlabelled and undated. It was her attempts, laudable but disastrous, to complete the job, that produced a remarkable series of confusions and led her to fabricate or distort several episodes.

This residue consisted of full, accurate notes on selected sections of Book Five of William of Apulia's poem. The sections that had attracted Nikephoros' attention were those describing Robert's mobilisation of the second, larger task force in the Adriatic in late summer 1084 and its subsequent actions up to spring 1085. Presumably he had no reliable Byzantine information on the Norman preparations and dispositions for this second Balkan offensive.

Anna made one serious mistake, which then forced her into a series of consequential errors. The mistake was to identify Robert's second naval expedition of 1084 (covered by notes in the hypothetical unlabelled and undated files) with that of 1081. She then attempted to inject the filed material into Nikephoros' draft account of 1081 (at i.16.1 and iv.3.2), which already combined William of Apulia's material with Byzantine material. She added several *scholia*: (1) Robert decides to move his base of operations from Otranto to Brindisi, on the ground that the crossing from Brindisi to Corfu was shorter (quite false); (2) Robert changes his mind and summons (for some inexplicable reason) Roger Borsa to join him, although he has just appointed him his deputy in Italy; (3) the task force is inflated to triple its size of fifty ships as recorded by William of Apulia; and (4) a two-month delay, caused by bad weather, is introduced before the start of operations.

She then reproduced Nikephoros' text without tampering with it, up to and including the start of the siege of Dyrrachion in June 1081 and the Venetian naval attack and victory (early October 1081). This is the point (iv.3) at which she decided to transplant the rest of the material from the unlabelled file in a single block. A Byzantine fleet has appeared and, acting in concert with the Venetians, institutes a blockade of the Norman forces. A naval victory is won over Robert, who hastily retreats and draws his ships ashore, up the Gliceus River. Winter now begins, apparently that of 1081–2 (in fact, that of 1084–5, as we learn from William of Apulia). The Norman forces are laid low by an epidemic; Robert has difficulty in relaunching his fleet in late spring/early summer in the following year, but succeeds after devising and constructing an artificial channel.

Attention now shifts to Constantinople where Alexios mobilises for war, marches on Dyrrachion and suffers defeat (all therefore dated to 1082), with the city finally being betrayed early in 1083.

There are a number of other errors for which Anna should be held responsible.

1. Robert returns to Italy after the fall of Dyrrachion to deal with a threatened invasion by Henry IV (referred to as king of Alamania), which has been instigated by Alexios. He gathers an army together at Salerno, marches up to Rome, joins forces with the pope and sets off north, *against Germany* (v.3.1,6). What a travesty of the dramatic events at the climax of the Investiture Controversy, when Henry IV came south to dispose of Gregory VII, whose pontificate he did not recognise! His target was Rome, not the Norman dukedom. Far from retreating promptly (having heard of Alexios' defeat outside Dyrrachion, v.3.7), Henry established himself early in 1082 in the hills south of Rome, initiating a blockade that was to last over two years until his troops forced their way into the city in March 1084 and besieged Gregory in the Castel Sant'Angelo. He then formally installed his candidate, Guibert, as Pope Clement III in St Peter's, and was crowned emperor by him. It is true that Robert Guiscard did eventually come to Pope Gregory VII's aid late in May 1084 and that the German army had withdrawn by then, but there was no question of Gregory's remaining in the city, as stated in the *Alexiad* (v.3.7). The Norman

expedition was in effect a rescue mission. The pope was escorted out of the city to safety, first in Benevento, then in Salerno where he died a year later.[52]

2. Bohemond, in whose hands the army is left when Robert returns to Italy, is consistently referred to as a younger son and Roger Borsa as the eldest (v.3.3–4), whereas, in reality, Roger, the oldest son by Robert's second marriage to Sichelgaita, was younger than Bohemond, the only son of his first marrriage.[53]

3. The dramatic scene in which Bohemond meets Robert at Salerno, and reports the failure of the 1082–3 campaign, has been embellished by Anna and misplaced immediately before Robert's return to the Balkans in autumn 1084 (vi.5.1–2).

4. Anna introduced a muddle about the sea-route used in 1084 (vi.5.3), probably to distinguish it from that used in 1081 according to her reconstruction. This time Robert moves south from Brindisi to Otranto, supposedly to shorten the sea-crossing to Avlona, whereas, in reality, Brindisi was preferred as the safer autumn anchorage (*Gesta*, v.132–42).

Conclusions

Two conclusions may be drawn from this comparison of the *Gesta* and the *Alexiad*. First, a substantial amount of material in the *Alexiad* was taken *directly* from the Latin text of the *Gesta*, by Nikephoros Bryennios, probably with the help of a translator. And second, despite the clearly ordered narrative of events supplied by the *Gesta*, a considerable amount of confusion was introduced into the *Gesta*-based sections of the *Alexiad*'s narrative of the 1081 campaign by Anna Komnene. The principal reason for this was that Anna was almost entirely dependent, in this section of the *Alexiad*, on the dossier of materials she inherited from her husband and did not have direct access herself to the *Gesta*. Where the dossier was disordered or incomplete, she was inevitably going to have immense difficulty in producing an orderly and accurate narrative.

These are the direct conclusions of this chapter. They, in their turn, suggest a number of others, which are outlined below, some fairly uncontroversial in the light of the evidence that has been presented, others contentious but perhaps worth airing.

---

[52] Loud, *Robert Guiscard*, 219–22.   [53] Ibid., 300.

First there is the question of the strength of the hypothesis advanced above, that the hand principally responsible for the *Alexiad*'s substance was that of Nikephoros Bryennios. This will never be proved beyond all reasonable doubt, both for lack of direct evidence about Nikephoros' progress on his *Alexiad* and because of the paucity of other historical sources for the reign of Alexios Komnenos against which to compare and analyse Anna's *Alexiad*. It has to be treated as a working hypothesis and its truth tested by a series of experiments in which it is applied to different sections of the *Alexiad*. As such experiments yield more satisfactory results – making sense of the text, explaining the errors or muddles that disfigure it – more confidence can be placed in it.

By far the most important of these experiments is the one that has just been completed. For the relative abundance of other sources about the Byzantine–Norman war of 1081–5 and the considerable overlap between the accounts of the *Gesta* and the *Alexiad* have allowed us to probe the exact relationship between the two texts and to examine in detail the formation of the *Alexiad*'s version. The experiment, a long-drawn-out one, appears to have worked. For it does provide an explanation for the particular amalgam of coherent history, on the one hand, and laboured and confused narrative, on the other, that we find in the *Alexiad*'s account.

Second, the application of the hypothesis to this part of the *Alexiad* has enabled us to define the limits of the damaged areas in the text, hence to isolate the work of Nikephoros and, in particular, those sections of his draft that were well advanced and were based in the main on documentary sources. They were put together by someone adept at strategic appreciation and able to make sense of the tactical information supplied by heterogeneous sources. This mass of solid, document-based information lurking in the pages of the *Alexiad* can then be used to supplement and modify William of Apulia's account and thus to construct a rounded, more balanced history of Byzantine–Norman relations.

Third, a small contribution can be made to the vexed question of the date and circumstance of the first grant of substantial commercial concessions to Venice, Byzantium's longstanding client and ally in the central Mediterranean region. If Anna is responsible (and this is perfectly possible, though not certain) for the placing of Nikephoros' summary of the golden bull issued by Alexios – immediately after the fourth naval engagement of 1084 that resulted in a Venetian victory (vi.5.10) – we need not necessarily accept the dating implied by this position. For Anna may well have slipped it in at the wrong point. The way is then open to suggest either an earlier date (the majority view of recent scholarship prefers 1082 to Anna's 1084) or a later one, even as late as 1092. This latter date corresponds to year 6600 after Creation, according to the Byzantine calendar, and year 15 of the contemporary fiscal cycle. This may be conjectured to have been the date given in the original Greek text of the golden bull, which was corrupted in the course of transmission to the two extant copies of two later versions of the lost official Latin translation (probably made in Constantinople) that were included in an early thirteenth-century register of the Venetian chancellery.[54]

If the later date is the correct one, the grant of commercial and other privileges should not be viewed as a reward for services rendered in the war against the Normans. There was no need for Byzantium to provide a special incentive on this occasion. The Venetians were, of course, defending their own interests even more than Byzantium's in 1081–5, since the growth of Norman naval power threatened their own ascendancy in the Adriatic. The grant should perhaps be viewed rather as an inducement offered in order to obtain favours in the future, as a deliberate act of policy aimed at tightening links with the old client and ally at a time when Byzantium's traditional pre-eminence among the Christian powers of the Mediterranean had been undermined by Turkish successes in the East and was about to face a serious challenge from the heartlands of Christendom north of the Alps. On this hypothesis, Byzantium was casting the Venetians in the role of naval police, with the task of securing the western sea approaches to Byzantine territory and in effect escorting the Crusading forces east and minimising any damage, material or political, that they might do in transit. They were therefore to be the seaborne analogues of the recently pacified Pechenegs who shepherded the Crusaders across the Balkans with remarkable success. In the event, the proximity of Venetian naval forces seems to have acted as an effective deterrent and no attempt was made to seize any of the offshore islands in the Adriatic or any territory on the Dalmatian mainland.

Finally, there remains the question of how a copy of the *Gesta* came into Nikephoros' possession. It is possible that the normal processes of private

---

[54] The text of Alexios' golden bull was included in Latin translations of two later documents of confirmation, dating from 1147 and 1187 respectively, which were themselves copied into the Venetian *Liber pactorum I*. By then two minor errors had crept in: year of the world 6600 had become 6200 (692 CE) in the 1147 copy, and the first digit had disappeared from fiscal year 15 (pulling the date ten years back to 1082) in both copies. Full discussion in D. Jacoby, 'The Chrysobull of Alexius I Comnenus to the Venetians: the Date and the Debate', *JMedHist*, 28 (2002), 199–204. See Howard-Johnston, 'Anna Komnene', 295; P. Frankopan, 'Byzantine Trade Privileges to Venice in the Eleventh Century: the Chrysobull of 1092', *JMedHist*, 30 (2004), 135–60.

exchange eventually brought a copy to Constantinople at some point between its composition and Nikephoros' death, hence that there was no involvement by any political authority. This is, however, extremely unlikely since the Byzantine appetite for Western manuscripts was very far from voracious and there is no evidence that the *Gesta* achieved wide circulation, even within the Norman world and its peripheries in the West. There is only one extant medieval manuscript, dating from the late twelfth century and coming from the monastery of Mont Saint Michel in Normandy. The other medieval manuscript of which we have a record is now lost, but it too was lodged in Normandy, in the monastery of Bec-Hellouin, and probably dated from the twelfth century. It is this latter one that served as the basis for the *editio princeps* of 1582.[55]

It is tempting, therefore, to consider an alternative, namely that Nikephoros had heard of the existence of the text and, when he was embarking on his grand historical enterprise, managed to procure a copy from southern Italy. By what means he did so, whether by commissioning someone to make a copy or by using the good offices of a Norman acquaintance or by pure good fortune, is quite unknown. What is undeniable, though, is that he appreciated its value, as soon as he read it, and decided to use it as the principal source for much of his account of the Norman–Byzantine war of 1081–5.

Further Reading

The main sources: D. R. Reinsch and A. Kambylis, eds., *Annae Comnenae. Alexias*, 2 vols. (Berlin, 2001); E. R. A. Sewter, trans., *The Alexiad*, revised by P. Frankopan (London, 2009); M. Mathieu, ed. and trans., *Guillaume de Pouille. La Geste de Robert Guiscard* (Palermo, 1961). Studies include: P. Brown, 'The Gesta Roberti Wiscardi: a "Byzantine" History?' *JMedHist*, 37 (2011): 162–79; P. Frankopan, 'Turning Latin into Greek: Anna Komnene and the *Gesta Roberti Wiscardi*', *JMedHist*, 39 (2013), 80–99.

[55] Mathieu, *Guillaume de Pouille*, 70–5.

CHAPTER 22

Transplanting Culture: from Greek Novel to Medieval Romance

Roderick Beaton

'The scholar who identifies a means by which Chrétien de Troyes might have encountered Greek romance will indeed have found the subject's Holy Grail.' So wrote the medievalist Helen Moore in the *Times Literary Supplement* in 2005.[1] The closest approach yet to that 'grail' was made by Elizabeth Jeffreys in her article 'The Comnenian Background to the *Romans d'Antiquité*', in which she proposed that the passage of the Second Crusade, and particularly of Eleanor of Aquitaine, through Constantinople at the end of 1147, may have served as a catalyst for the development of the vernacular romance in Old French during the following decades.[2]

That article is still regularly cited, but the arguments made back in 1980 have not yet been systematically followed up. There are two routes that might lead to this tantalisingly elusive 'grail', and both are signalled by Jeffreys. One is to follow up the story through the historical record of the Second Crusade and the numerous biographies of Eleanor. To judge from the most recent history of that Crusade, which admittedly has rather little to say on matters of culture or literature, the kind of evidence that would be needed may simply not exist. Perhaps discouragingly, it turns out that the western leader who spent the longest time in the Byzantine capital

---

[1] H. Moore, 'From the Greek', *TLS* (8 July 2005), 5–6. In English the terminology conventionally applied to these texts is confusing. The 'Greek romance' is increasingly known today as the '(ancient) Greek novel', and throughout this chapter I apply the same generic term to its Byzantine successors as well. Although there are good reasons for including the 'romances' of the Middle Ages within the history of fiction, that term, which originally designated the *language* of the texts, not their content or genre, seems here to stay, at least in English. (Most European languages, which follow French practice, are spared this confusion by having just the one term, derived from *roman*.) In what follows, I refer to *Hysmine and Hysminias* and other 'Greek romances' as 'novels', but defer to convention in referring to Chrétien's fictions as 'romances'. The argument that these terms do not distinguish separable genres is most forcefully made in M. A. Doody, *The True Story of the Novel* (London, 1997).

[2] E. M. Jeffreys, 'The Comnenian Background to the *Romans d'Antiquité*', *Byzantion*, 50 (1980), 112–31, and E. M. Jeffreys, '"The Wild Beast from the West": Immediate Literary Reactions in Byzantium to the Second Crusade' in A. Laiou-Thomadakis and R. Mottahedeh, eds., *The Crusades from the Perspective of Byzantium and the Muslim World* (Washington, D. C., 2001), 110–13.

during the winter of 1147–8 was the German king, Conrad, a fact that hardly helps explain literary developments in *French*.[3] In this chapter I have chosen the alternative route, which goes, instead, by way of a close reading of two key fictional texts of the period.

Hysmine and Hysminias by Eumathios (or Eustathios) Makrembolites[4] used to be dismissed, along with the other novels (or 'romances') of the Komnenian period, as mere appendages to the Greek novel of antiquity – 'imitators of other imitators', in the crushing phrase of Adamantios Korais just over two hundred years ago.[5] Rediscovered as a work of real literary interest in the 1970s, largely thanks to a spirited essay by Margaret Alexiou,[6] *Hysmine and Hysminias* has emerged in the last few years as the most sophisticated of a group of fictional experiments in Greek from the mid-twelfth century whose place in the long story of the novel, from its origins in late antiquity to the best-sellers of the early twenty-first century, has yet to be fully evaluated.[7] Of its author nothing is known except that he appears to have enjoyed some official position at the Byzantine court. There is still no agreement on the sequence in which the four novels were written, but all four can now be dated with some confidence between about 1135 and 1160.[8]

---

[3] J. Phillips, *The Second Crusade: Extending the Frontiers of Christendom* (New Haven, CT, 2007), 184, 212 (Conrad); 191–2 (King Louis).

[4] M. Marcovich, ed., *Eustathius Macrembolites. De Hysmines et Hysminiae Amoribus Libri XI* (Munich, 2001); E. M. Jeffreys, ed. and trans., *Four Byzantine Novels* (Liverpool, 2012), 157–269. All references to this text in the notes that follow will be to Marcovich's edition.

[5] 'ἄλλων μιμητῶν μιμητάς': A. Korais, Προλεγόμενα στοὺς ἀρχαίους Ἕλληνες συγγραφεῖς, vol. I (Athens, 1984 [first edition 1804]), 28.

[6] M. Alexiou, 'A Critical Reappraisal of Eustathios Makrembolites' *Hysmine and Hysminias*', BMGS, 3 (1977), 23–43; M. Alexiou, 'Eros and the "Constraints of Desire" in Hysmine and Hysminias' in M. Alexiou, *After Antiquity: Greek Language, Myth, and Metaphor* (Ithaca, NY, and London, 2002), 111–27.

[7] On *Hysmine and Hysminias* specifically, see I. Nilsson, *Erotic Pathos, Rhetorical Pleasure: Narrative Technique and Mimesis in Eumathios Makrembolites' Hysmine and Hysminias* (Uppsala, 2001). On all four Komnenian novels, see R. Beaton, *The Medieval Greek Romance*, second edition (London, 1996); P. Roilos, *Amphoteroglossia: A Poetics of the Twelfth-Century Medieval Greek Novel* (Cambridge, MA, 2005); F. Meunier, *Le Roman byzantin du XIIe siècle: à la découverte d'un nouveau monde?* (Paris, 2007).

[8] A judicious summary of the evidence and recent debate is given by Jeffreys, *Four Byzantine Novels*, 161–5. The evidence for a terminus ante quem of 1138 for at least one of the four was first presented in E. M. Jeffreys, 'A Date for *Rhodanthe and Dosikles*?' in P. A. Agapitos and D. Reinsch, eds., *Der Roman im Byzanz in der Komnenenzeit* (Frankfurt am Main, 2000), 127–36. That *Hysmine and Hysminias* was the first of the Komnenian novels to be written was argued by S. V. Polyakova in articles published in Russian in 1969 and 1971 (for discussion and bibliography, see Beaton, *Medieval Greek Romance*, 80–1, 242) and endorsed in S. MacAlister, *Dreams and Suicides: the Greek Novel from Antiquity to the Byzantine Empire* (New York, NY, 1996). The traditional dating, which places it last, is accepted in Beaton, *Medieval Greek Romance*, 80–1, 211–12, and Meunier, *Le Roman*, 295 n. 296.

Transplanting Culture: Greek Novel to Medieval Romance 501

In *Hysmine and Hysminias*, the hero tells the story of his love for Hysmine for the benefit of a friend, but ends by invoking writing as the only way to immortalise his supreme experience. Sent on a ritual mission from Eurykomis (Broad Town) to Aulikomis (Courtly Town), Hysminias is entertained by a nobleman whose daughter, as she points out to him, has the feminine form of his own name. She flirts with him outrageously, and he, an innocent at this stage of the tale, undergoes a form of initiation through a series of erotic dreams and learned discourses on the paintings that adorn the girl's family home. Finally he declares his love and the pair elope by sea, only just in time to forestall a marriage arranged for Hysmine by her parents. Their ship is overtaken by a storm, and the heroine is consigned to the waves by the captain, as a sacrifice to placate an angry Poseidon. Hysminias is captured by pirates along with the rest of the ship's passengers and crew and finds himself a slave in a noble household in Daphnepolis (Laurel Town, i.e. Apollo's), which seems the mirror image of his own home in Eurykomis. From Daphnepolis, the whole household decamps on a ritual mission to another town, just as Hysminias had done at the story's beginning. Serving his master in his host's household at Artykomis (Artemis' Town), Hysminias is astonished to find among the women there a fellow slave who makes overtures to him, and bears an uncanny resemblance to his lost Hysmine. Soon the mysterious slave-girl reveals that she *is* Hysmine, miraculously saved after being cast into the sea. At last the pair are recognised by their own families, who have come to look for them, are granted their freedom and allowed to marry.

Cligés by Chrétien de Troyes is traditionally dated to the mid-1170s, but may have been written as much as a decade later.[9] This early work by the acknowledged inventor and master of the chivalric romance in the west makes a number of allusions to diplomatic and political realia from the reign of Manuel I, and is generally recognised as the 'odd one out' among Chrétien's five romances because of its relatively precise locations and its apparent derivation from 'Greco-Byzantine material' – material, however, which is never more precisely specified.[10]

---

[9] C. Luttrell and S. Gregory, eds., *Chrétien de Troyes. Cligés* (Cambridge, 1993). All references to the text in the notes that follow will be to this edition. However, the most recent edition is L. Harf-Lancner, ed., *Chrétien de Troyes. Cligès* (Paris, 2006). English translations cited here are from W. W. Kibler, trans., *Chrétien de Troyes. Arthurian Romances* (London, 1991). For a summary of the discussion on dating, see J. Duggan, *The Romances of Chrétien de Troyes* (New Haven, CT, 2001), 13–15.

[10] Chrétien, *Arthurian Romances*, ed. Kibler, 7–8; see further L. Polak, *Chrétien de Troyes: Cligés* (London, 1982), 7–14, drawing on A. Fourrier, *Le Courant réaliste dans le roman courtois en France au moyen âge* (Paris, 1960), 165–73; K. Ciggaar, 'Encore une fois Chrétien de Troyes et la "matière byzantine": La Révolution des femmes au palais de Constantinople', *CahCM*, 38 (1995), 267–74.

Cligés is a double love story, told by a more or less omniscient narrator. Alexander, son of the emperor of Constantinople, determines to be dubbed a knight at the court of Arthur of Britain. There he falls in love with the beautiful Soredamors, who dreams of him at length. Alexander proves his worth in battle by saving Arthur's kingdom from a usurper and is rewarded with the hand of his beloved, with whom he returns to Constantinople to succeed his father as emperor. The result of their union is a son named Cligés. When Alexander dies, he is succeeded by his trusted brother Alis, who has promised never to marry, so that Cligés in due course can inherit the empire. But Alis goes back on his word, and sends the fifteen-year-old Cligés as his proxy to negotiate for him to marry the daughter of the Holy Roman Emperor, Fenice. Cligés does as commanded, but inevitably he and the equally young Fenice fall in love. On their way back from Germany to Constantinople, Cligés has the opportunity to prove his skill at arms in saving his uncle's bride from abduction by German rivals. Back at Constantinople, Fenice is married to the emperor, Alis, but remains a virgin thanks to a potion devised by her Greek nurse. This induces the emperor to believe that he is making love with his bride when in fact he is asleep and only dreaming. Meanwhile, to get over his grief at the loss of Fenice, Cligés follows in his father's footsteps to win renown at Arthur's court in Britain. In this he succeeds, but soon he cannot bear to be parted any longer from Fenice, and returns once more to Constantinople. There, two further Greek-designed stratagems enable Cligés and Fenice to fulfil their love: a second potion fakes her death, while a magic tower provides them shelter without fear of discovery. Discovered nonetheless, the pair face the wrath of the emperor Alis and are forced to flee – to Cligés' friends in Britain. War between the British and the Greeks is averted only by the timely death of the usurper Alis, and Cligés and Fenice live happily ever after.

That *Hysmine and Hysminias* could itself have been the (or a) missing source for *Cligés* is unlikely. The proposal of S. V. Polyakova, made some years ago in Russian, that Makrembolites' novel could have been the

---

For a further allusion, in the name of the hero, to Kilij Arslan II, Sultan of Iconium, see H. Kahane and R. Kahane, 'L'énigme du nom de Cligés', *Romania*, 82 (1961), 113–21. Despite much speculation, there is no way of knowing what the book was that Chrétien says he used in the library of the Bishop of Beauvais (Chrétien, *Cligés*, 1.13–23; Chrétien, *Arthurian Romances*, 123). The proverbial story about Solomon's wife, alluded to in the episode of the fake death of Fenice (Chrétien, *Cligés*, 210.5854–57; Chrétien, *Arthurian Romances*, 195) was thought in the middle ages to have come from Constantinople (Polak, *Chrétien*, 87–8). For the suggestion of a Persian source, perhaps transmitted via Byzantium, for the episode of the potion given to Alis, see L. Polak, '*Tristan* and *Vis and Ramin*', *Romania*, 95 (1974), 216–34 and Polak, *Chrétien*, 60–1.

source for *other* works in the courtly tradition has not, perhaps, been given the attention it deserves. But the only previous attempt to compare these two texts, by Meunier, misses the point by trying to show that Chrétien was not a source for Makrembolites. This is to put the *charrette* before the *chevalier*, since there is no serious possibility that any of the Byzantine novels was written as late as the 1170s.[11] That there are important differences between the two stories, their authors' approaches to narrative, and the distinct thought-worlds of the Christian East and the Christian West to which they respectively belong, is sufficiently apparent from the brief summaries just given. The argument of this chapter is that, despite these manifest differences, both authors explore in their respective fictions new ways of thinking about the representation of time and space, and of the human individual within them, that are characteristic of the twelfth century, and that form part, in turn, of that century's legacy to the subsequent rise of literary fiction as we know it today.

Space and Time

On the face of it, the fictional representation of space and time could not be more different in the two novels. Makrembolites moves his characters through an almost geometric series of alternations among four towns whose names are invented, whose inhabitants, customs, and physical setting are indistinguishable from one another (all four are by the sea, otherwise they have no visible hinterland), and whose location cannot be placed, even relatively to one another, on any map.[12] The only real place named, Syria, is never reached by any of the characters.[13] There can be no more telling example than this of what Mikhail Bakhtin, writing about the ancient novel, termed 'abstract' space; a theoretical potential of the ancient novel, according to one twentieth-century formulation, has here been taken to its extreme.[14] But in the process, to the 'sexual symmetry' that

---

[11] S. V. Polyakova, 'К вопросу о византино-французских литературных связях: («Повесть об Исмине и Исминии» Евмафия Макремволита и «Роман о розе» Гийома де Лорриса)", *VizVrem*, 37 (1976) 114–22; Meunier, *Le Roman*, 248–50.

[12] For the fullest discussion of the movements of the characters in space in this novel see Meunier, *Le Roman*, 75–8, 104–9. Her suggestion that the fictional name Daphnepolis is intended to be understood as a reference to Antioch (41, 76), possibly picking up on the allegorising interpretation proposed in K. Plepelits, ed. and trans., *Eustathios Makrembolites, Hysmine und Hysminias* (Stuttgart, 1989), seems to me gratuitous and unsupported by anything in the text.

[13] Makrembolites, *Hysmine and Hysminias*, 78 (VI.16.1).

[14] See M. M. Bakhtin, 'Forms of Time and of the Chronotope in the Novel: Towards a Historical Poetics' in M. M. Bakhtin, *The Dialogic Imagination: Four Essays*, ed. M. Holquist, trans. C. Emerson and M. Holquist (Austin, TX, 1981), 84–110. For a first attempt to apply Bakhtin's

determines the plot and structure of the ancient novels,[15] has been added a new *spatial* symmetry.

It is this element of symmetry that provides an unexpected link with the otherwise very different spatial organisation of *Cligés*. If the spatial distribution of the main action in *Hysmine and Hysminias* can be summed up in two pairs of alternations (from Eurykomis to Aulikomis and back again; from Daphnepolis to Artykomis and back again), in *Cligés* the equivalent alternation takes place between two supposedly historical locations, situated at opposite ends of Christendom: Constantinople and King Arthur's court in southern Britain. *Cligés* is constructed on the 'bipartite' pattern that would become standard in western romance from then on,[16] and there are both thematic and formal symmetries between the two 'halves' (despite their unequal length). In each, a hero sets out from Constantinople for Britain; the second and longer story, that of Cligés himself, also involves adventures roughly midway between the two locations, at Cologne and on the Danube near Ratisbon (Regensburg). Both Alexander and Cligés make a two-way journey, from Constantinople to Britain and back again. Alexander will fall in love at the end of his journey (just as Hysminias did having travelled from Eurykomis to Aulikomis); in addition Alexander will win back Arthur's kingdom for him, from the treacherous Count Angrés. Cligés, already in love with Fenice, leaves Constantinople for Britain when his case seems hopeless; having proved himself there as a knight, he will then return to Constantinople to win her after all. And there is a further symmetry in the action: just as it took the 'Greek' Alexander to defeat the usurper in Britain in the first half, at the end of the second, Arthur prepares his fleet to defend Cligés from the rage of his treacherous uncle, the usurper Alis.

Turning now to the representation of time, this too is organised symmetrically and within self-imposed limits in *Hysmine and Hysminias*.[17] The greater part of the action takes place across a specified number of days and nights, with a gap of just over a year in the middle. The precise extent

---

theory of the chronotope to the twelfth-century Byzantine novels, see R. Beaton, 'The World of Fiction and the World "Out There": the Case of the Byzantine Novel' in D. Smythe, ed., *Strangers to Themselves: The Byzantine Outsider* (Aldershot, 2000), 179–88, reprinted in R. Beaton, *From Byzantium to Modern Greece: Medieval Texts and their Modern Reception* (Aldershot, 2008), no. XII; see also Roilos, *Amphoteroglossia*, 303; MacAlister, *Dreams and Suicides*.

[15] D. Konstan, *Sexual Symmetry: Love in the Ancient Novel and Related Genres* (Princeton, NJ, 1994).
[16] E. Vinaver, *The Rise of Romance* (Oxford, 1971), 33–52.
[17] See Beaton, *Medieval Greek Romance*, 82–7 and Beaton, 'The World of Fiction'; for a slightly different approach, see Alexiou, 'A Critical Reappraisal'. Much the same ground is covered by Meunier, *Le Roman*, 92–4, without apparent reference to these or other studies.

of this displacement is never specified, not least because there are no seasons in the novel – except in the allegorical pictures described in Book 4. Yet although the passage of time within the story is finite and as a rule quite closely specified, the same cannot be said of the temporal distance that separates the world of the story from that of the novel's author and first readers. Nothing is said in the text that would specify the historical period when the action is supposed to be taking place, beyond the fact that it precedes the coming of Christianity. Neither 'new Rome' (Constantinople) nor the old one is ever mentioned in *Hysmine and Hysminias*, or indeed in any of the other Byzantine novels of the twelfth century. It is well known that the ancient Greek novels, before them, kept silence on the subject of Roman rule, under which all of them were written. But Makrembolites goes further, stripping out of his narrative even those traces of real history that do find their way, in varying proportions, into each of the extant ancient novels. So, in *Hysmine and Hysminias*, time as experienced by the characters is very clearly marked in the narrative, while historical time has been abstracted to leave only the sense of yawning distance that separates the fictional world of the characters from the real world of author and readers.

In *Cligés* the main action also takes place over relatively short, and more-or-less defined periods of time, albeit within a much longer span. The story has room for the adventures of two generations and includes a series of journeys, each of which would have taken several months. All of this, however, is considerably distanced in time from the world of the romance's author and first readers, as is made clear at the beginning and end of the text.[18]

Another feature of the way time is represented in *Cligés* can be defined as its *relativity*. The stories of the two Greek protagonists are separated by a gap of approximately fifteen years.[19] But when Cligés follows in his father's footsteps and sets out in his turn for Arthur's court, in order to distract himself from his forbidden love for his uncle's wife, he arrives in Britain to find everything just as the reader remembers it from his father's time.

---

[18] In addition to the narrative assumption, common to all these romances, that Arthur was a historical king who lived long ago, Chrétien at the beginning emphasises his dependence on a source, implied as being rare and perhaps very old (Chrétien, *Cligés*, 1.18–23 and 2.45–6; Chrétien, *Arthurian Romances*, ed. Kibler, 123); the transition to the world of 'today', in which Greek emperors keep their wives shut away, again implies that the events just narrated must have happened a long time before the present time of writing (243.6740–9; *Arthurian Romances*, 205).

[19] Cligés when we first meet him is said to be almost fifteen years old (ibid., 97.2745; Chrétien, *Arthurian Romances*, ed. Kibler, 156). On the distorted chronology of the story see also P. Noble, 'Alis and the Problem of Time in *Cligés*', *Medium Aevum*, 39 (1970), 28–31.

Nothing appears to have changed; nobody is a day older – just as Erich Auerbach famously demonstrated in another romance by Chrétien.[20]

Time is relativised in *Hysmine and Hysminias* too, although in rather different ways. The effect of systematically emptying both time and space of concrete references results in both being filled by the projected consciousness of the narrator. The real sphere of action in *Hysmine and Hysminias* is to be found inside the consciousness of the hero.[21] Hysminias' experiences, as we shall see, are not confined to measurable moments in the waking world, but extend into the subjective territory of dreams. When he and Hysmine flee their parents and embark on the traditional adventures that befall lovers in the Greek novels, they are literally 'at sea', they are lost even to the constructed time and space of their adventures in the four towns. In Book VII, amidst the comic exaggerations of the storm-scene (in which Hysmine is sacrificed to placate the storm), an even greater storm is brewed in the distraught hero's breast,[22] which has the effect of turning the whole *topos* of adventure into a projection of the inner state of mind of the narrator.

Time's passage is presented visually through the *ekphrasis* of the paintings representing the months of the year. In the tendentious and abstruse dialogue that follows, the hero's friend Kratisthenes appears to warn that even love (personified here as Eros) is subject to time, while Hysminias himself asserts the contrary.[23] Love and Time have already been juxtaposed in the paintings that decorate Sosthenes' house.[24] Hysminias submits to Love as his servant or slave (δοῦλος), and the personification of Eros figures largely in the story.[25] Later, at a crucial phase of their adventures, just before they decide to elope, time will appear as the direct adversary of Love and a potent threat to the lovers' hopes. Hysmine implores the hero: 'μή σοι λήθης πόμα κεράσῃ μὴ χρόνος, μὴ πραγμάτων μεταβολαί, μή (τοῦτο δὴ τὸ καὶ θανάτου πικρότερον) παρθένος ἐξ

---

[20] E. Auerbach, *Mimesis: the Representation of Reality in Western Literature*, trans. W. R. Trask (Princeton, 1953), see esp. 128–9, 130, 133, on the opening episode of *Yvain*.

[21] Alexiou, 'Eros and the "Constraints of Desire"'; see Beaton, 'The World of Fiction' and, apparently independently, Meunier, *Le Roman*, 77–80, 88–94.

[22] See Makrembolites, *Hysmine and Hysminias*, 83–5 (VII.9–10), prefigured at 79 (VI.18.1); see also 87–8 (VII.13–14, 15.1 and 16.2)

[23] Ibid., 46–7 (IV.20).

[24] Discussed more fully, and in relation to the novel's ending, from a different point of view, in Beaton, *Medieval Greek Romance*, 84–7.

[25] See especially Makrembolites, *Hysmine and Hysminias* (III.8.2–3), and P. Magdalino, 'Eros the King and the King of Amours: Some Observations on "Hysmine and Hysminias"' *DOP*, 46 (1992), 197–204. On the personification of Amors in *Cligés* (and its predominance in that romance over the others by Chrétien), see Duggan, *The Romances*, 156–8.

Εὐρυκώμιδος [do not let time and changing circumstances mix for you the cup of forgetfulness, nor – and this is more bitter than death – a maiden from Eurykomis]'.[26]

These words are echoed closely at the end of the story, in the prayer which Hysminias addresses to several deities, Eros among them, interrupting his narrative between the wedding and the eagerly awaited wedding-night: 'μὴ βυθὸς ἀμνηστίας κατεπικλύσῃ ταῦτα τὰ καθ' ἡμᾶς, μὴ χρόνος μακρός, μὴ ῥυτίς, μὴ λήθης κρατὴρ ἐν Ἅιδου κιρνώμενος [do not let an abyss of oblivion overwhelm our adventures, nor the passage of time nor decay nor Hades' bowl that pours out forgetfulness]'.[27]

At this point the perspective shifts from time to eternity, as instead of continuing with the story, Hysminias addresses each of the gods in turn, before finally dedicating himself to the art of 'rhetoric' which alone has the power to immortalise 'The adventures of Hysmine and of me, Hysminias'.[28] Love and time are presented as adversaries, but the final victory cannot be won by Love alone, without 'the pen of Hermes which breathes the fire of rhetoric'.[29] It only now becomes clear why time had to be emptied of everything that was not connected with the narrator's subjectivity: the annihilation of time is only possible *within* the subjective consciousness of the hero.

This internalisation and relativisation of time and space on the part of Makrembolites sound remarkably like Bakhtin's diagnosis of how the western chivalric romance most differs from any narrative belonging to the ancient world: 'Time begins to be influenced by dreams; that is, we begin to see the peculiar distortion of temporal perspectives characteristic of dreams . . . In general the chivalric romance exhibits a *subjective playing with time*, an emotional and lyrical stretching and compressing of it . . . Such a subjective playing with time is utterly foreign to antiquity.'[30]

It is hard to think of a convincing model of reception or 'diffusion' that will explain these similarities. Makrembolites' fiction predates the first Arthurian romances by between two and four decades, so older suggestions that the Greek novels might have been influenced by innovations in the west will not stand. But, developing the suggestion of Elizabeth Jeffreys in her article of 1980, we might reasonably suppose that cultural

---

[26] Ibid., 81 (VII.2.2). [27] Ibid., 150 (XI.20.2).
[28] 'κλῆσις δ' ἔσται τῇ βίβλῳ τὸ καθ' Ὑσμίνην δρᾶμα καὶ τὸν Ὑσμινίαν ἐμέ' (ibid., 152 (XI.23.3)). These are the last words of the novel.
[29] 'ἀλλ' ὡς ἐν ἀμαράντοις ξύλοις καὶ λίθοις ἀδάμασιν Ἑρμοῦ γραφίδι καὶ μέλανι καὶ γλώσσῃ πῦρ πνεούσῃ ῥητορικὸν τὰ καθ' ἡμᾶς στηλογραφηθήσεται' (ibid., 151–2 (XI.22.4)).
[30] Bakhtin, 'Forms of Time', 154–5 (original emphasis); Beaton, 'The World of Fiction', 188.

interchanges – dialogue of *some* kind, even if not especially fraternal – *were* going on during the middle decades of the twelfth century. Despite the mutual irritation stirred up by the first two crusades, there was far more possibility for fruitful interchange during the reign of Manuel in Constantinople than there would ever be again after the diversion of the Fourth Crusade in 1204. *Cligés*, in particular, has to be read with a deliberate refusal of hindsight, if we are to realise the significance of an author imagining, even in a work of fiction, an alliance based on shared values between the Byzantine empire and the Britain of King Arthur (for which read: the Anglo-French dominions of the Plantagenet dynasty).

Consciousness, Subjectivity, Relativity

The prominence of dreams in *Hysmine and Hysminias*, particularly in the first half of the novel, has long been noticed, as has the erotic content of many of them. This last has also been linked by Elizabeth and Michael Jeffreys with a wider interest in erotic dreams attested in other Byzantine texts of the mid-twelfth century.[31] Throughout much of the first six books of the novel, the hero's experiences when asleep are rendered more vividly than most of what happens to him awake. Dreaming of Hysmine, Hysminias evidently experiences orgasm in his dream:

> Ἤλγουν, ἠθύμουν, καινόν τινα τρόμον ἔτρεμον, ἠμβλυνόμην τὴν ὄψιν, ἐμαλθακιζόμην τὴν ψυχήν, τὴν ἰσχὺν ἐχαυνούμην, ἐνωθρευόμην τὸ σῶμα, ἐπείχετό μοι τὸ ἆσθμα, πυκνὸν κατεπάλλετό μοι τὸ περικάρδιον, καί τις ὀδύνη γλυκάζουσα κατεπέδραμέ μου τὰ μέλη καὶ οἷον ὑπεγαργάλισε, καὶ ὅλον με κατέσχεν ἄρρητος ἔρως ἀνεκλάλητος, ἄφραστος· καί τι πέπονθα, νὴ τὸν Ἔρωτα, οἷον οὐδέποτε πέπονθα.

> I was in pain, I was in anguish, a strange trembling came over me, my sight was dimmed, my soul softened, my strength weakened, my body grew sluggish, my breath choked, my heart beat faster and a sweet pain poured over my limbs with a kind of tickling sensation and an ineffable, unspeakable, inexpressible passion took possession of me. And I experienced, by Eros, what I had never experienced before.[32]

In words that uncannily seem to anticipate Shakespeare's Caliban, Hysminias then wakes:

---

[31] Noted in the context of their announced edition and commentary of the poems of 'Manganeios' Prodromos, on which see M. J. Jeffreys, 'Rhetorical Texts' in E. M. Jeffreys, ed., *Rhetoric in Byzantium* (Aldershot, 2003), 87–100.

[32] Makrembolites, *Hysmine and Hysminias*, 31 (III.7.6), compare with the sequence of four brief erotic dreams in 51–4 (V.1–4).

καὶ ἡνιώμην νὴ τὸν Ἔρωτα οὕτω καλὸν ἀπολέσας ὄνειρον ... καὶ ἤθελον
πάλιν ὑπνοῦν καί τι πάσχειν ἐρωτικόν, οἷον καθ᾽ ὕπνους ἔπαθον.

and, by Eros, I was disconsolate because I had lost such a beautiful
dream ... and I wanted to go back to sleep again and I wanted to experience the same passionate sensation that I had felt in my sleep.[33]

Erotic dreams, or at least the illusion of erotic possession, also play a part in the plot of *Cligés*. Alexander, taking to bed his beloved's shirt and a lock of her hair,

> A ce ou n'a point de delit
> Se delite an vain et solace:
> Tote nuit la chemise anbrace,
> et quant il le chevol. remire,
> De tot le mont cuide estre sire.
> Bien fet amors de sage fol
> ...
> Mes il changera cest deduit
> Einz l'aube clere et le soloil.[34]

found a vain delight and solace in what could give him no satisfaction. All night long he clasped the shirt in his arms, and when he beheld the hair he thought he was lord of the whole world. Love easily makes the wise man a fool ... but before sunrise and the bright dawn this pleasure will be transformed.[35]

This harmless delusion is only the prelude to the fuller development of the theme of the erotic dream in *Cligés*. Alis is induced by a magic potion to believe that he possesses his wife Fenice while in reality she lies chastely at his side, untouched:

> Il dort et songe et veillier cuide,
> S'est an grant poinne et an estuide
> De la pucele losangier ...
> Tenir la cuide, n'an tient mie,
> Mes de neant est a grant eise:
> Neant anbrace et neant beise,
> Neant tient et neant acole,
> Neant voit, a neant parole,
> A neant tance, a neant luite.[36]

He slept and dreamed and thought he was awake, and in his dream he strove and endeavoured to caress the maiden ... he was convinced he possessed her,

---

[33] Ibid., 31 (III.7.7); see Shakespeare, *The Tempest*, Act III, Sc. 2, lines 140–3.
[34] Chrétien, *Cligés*, 57–8.1628–33, 1636–7.   [35] Chrétien, *Arthurian Romances*, ed. Kibler, 142.
[36] Chrétien, *Cligés*, 119.3329–31, 3336–41,

but he did not. He received his satisfaction from nothing: he embraced nothing, he kissed nothing, he held nothing, contended with nothing.[37]

Thanks to this delusion, Fenice is able to preserve herself for her true beloved, Cligés, with whom she will later steal away to live in a secret tower, after a feigned death that seems to come straight from the plot of an ancient Greek novel.[38] In this way Alis lives with his wife for a considerable time – long enough for Cligés to travel to England, acquit himself in the tournament at Wallingford, and travel through Britain, France and Normandy 'until early summer',[39] before setting sail once more for Constantinople. The lovers do not meet again, to plot the stratagem of the false death that will separate Fenice from her husband, until 'a long while after his return'.[40] No wonder, then, that the emperor will react violently when eventually he learns of the trick that has been played on him:

> Qant l'emperere ot ramentoivre
> La poison qui li plot a boivre,
> Par coi Tessala le deçut,
> Lors primes sot et aparçut
> C'onques de sa fame n'avoit
> Eü joie, bien le savoit,
> Se il ne li avint par songe;
> Mes ce fu joie de mançonge.[41]

> When the emperor was reminded of the potion that was so delightful to drink, with which Thessala deceived him, for the first time he realised and knew that he had never had pleasure with his wife except in dreams, which was a false pleasure.[42]

Hysminias, too, at a bad moment in his fortunes in the real world, turns angrily on the god Eros, who he believes has 'deceived' him in his dreams,[43] and shortly later will be deceived yet again, as he believes, when a subsequent dream Eros appears to restore his beloved to him; but then 'just as I took hold of Hysmine, in my delight [I] woke up from my dream'.[44]

In both texts the subjective experience of dreaming is played off against what is 'really' happening to the characters in the world around them. In *Cligés*, the dream-like delusion that satisfies the emperor for so long turns out to be only

---

[37] Chrétien, *Arthurian Romances*, ed. Kibler, 163. [38] See Doody, *True Story*, 188.
[39] 'Jusqu'au novelemant d'esté' (Chrétien, *Cligés*, 182.5045); Chrétien, *Arthurian Romances*, ed. Kibler, 185.
[40] 'Grant piece aprés ce qu'il revint' (ibid., 185.5137); Chrétien, *Arthurian Romances*, ed. Kibler, 186.
[41] Ibid., 238.6609–16. [42] Chrétien, *Arthurian Romances*, ed. Kibler, 203–4.
[43] Makrembolites, *Hysmine and Hysminias*, 85 (VII.10.3). [44] Ibid., 93 (VII.19).

the most extreme of a whole series of ruses and stratagems by which certain characters are induced to experience, subjectively, something which others know to be false. It is surely no coincidence, either, that all of these ruses are associated with the romance's 'Greek' characters. Here Chrétien was no doubt drawing on a topos that had been revived a generation earlier in the west in the *Roman de Troie*, but had also recently resurfaced in the embittered experience of returning crusaders. Though it is never mentioned explicitly, the author seems to expect that his readers will remember the story of the Trojan Horse.

These ruses include the stratagem by which Alexander and his men discard their own colours to enter Windsor Castle in disguise and defeat the treacherous Count Angrés.[45] Indicatively, an unintended consequence is that Alexander's own men are also deceived into believing that he and his companions have been killed: 'The shields made them take appearance for reality, like a man who *dreams and takes a lie for the truth* '.[46] Later, a similar trick is played by Cligés in the battle by the Danube when he dons his fallen enemy's armour to attack their camp,[47] and again at the tournament in Britain when he changes armour every day so as not to be recognised.[48] More striking examples still are displayed by Fenice's nurse Thessala, the keeper of the potion that deludes Alis. As her name implies, Thessala has explicitly, if improbably, been brought all the way from Thessaly (famous for witchcraft according to Ovid and Apuleius) to Cologne to exercise her profession.[49] Finally the hero's trusted 'serf' John, who is 'known throughout the world for the images he has fashioned with brush and chisel',[50]

---

[45] Chrétien, *Cligés*, 65.1827–61; Chrétien, *Arthurian Romances*, ed. Kibler, 145.
[46]
> De toz fors d'un ont antrepris,
> Mes autres con cil qui *songe*,
> Qui por verité croit *mançonge*,
> Lor feisoient li escu croire
> Que ceste mançonge fust *voire* [= vraie]

Ibid., 73.2084–8; Chrétien, *Arthurian Romances*, ed. Kibler, 148, my emphasis.
[47] ibid., 124–7.3484–3548; Chrétien, *Arthurian Romances*, ed. Kibler, 165–6.
[48] Explicitly described as *guile* (ruse) at ibid., 170.4708 (Chrétien, *Arthurian Romances*, ed. Kibler, 180). The same word is used on one other occasion in *Cligés*, to refer to the machinations of Thessala to make the false death of Fenice appear more convincing (205.5703; *Arthurian Romances*, 193). In the latter passage the synonym *traïson* (glossed as *supercherie*, i.e. 'trick') shows how close this manipulation of appearances by the romance's 'good' characters comes to the treachery of the 'bad' ones: Count Angrés in the first part, Alis in the second.
[49] Ibid., 106.2982–90; Chrétien, *Arthurian Romances*, ed. Kibler, 159 and n. 11.
[50]
> N'est terre ou l'en ne le conoisse
> Par les oevres que il a feites
> Et deboissiees et portreites.
> Jehanz a non et s'est mes sers

Chrétiens, *Cligés*, 193.5360–3; *Arthurian Romances*, ed. Kibler, 188.

will become the architect of the secret tower and garden without visible means of entry, to which Cligés and Fenice retreat – yet another form of subjective reality that until its discovery exists only for the three people in the secret.

Quite apart from trickery, both texts devote a significant proportion of their narratives to representing the inner, often unexpressed, state of mind or thoughts of one or other of their protagonists in the process of falling in love. In the case of Hysminias, this accounts for approximately half the length of the whole text. This contrasts with the nearest equivalent in the ancient novel, *Leukippe and Kleitophon*, in which the more or less 'realistic' falling in love of the protagonists occupies only a fifth of the whole. Chrétien too, in *Cligés*, devotes much more narrative space to the thoughts and emotions, first of Alexander and Soredamors, then of Cligés and Fenice, as they fall in love, than he does in any of his other romances.[51]

Conclusion

This first attempt at a parallel reading of two twelfth-century works of fiction, of which the Byzantine is the earlier by between two and four decades, does not pretend to have discovered the 'holy grail' of romance studies with which we began. But I believe it does go some way towards putting flesh on the bones of the often-invoked Greek or Byzantine substratum of *Cligés*. This in turn may help western medievalists to appreciate why that romance differs in so many respects from the others by Chrétien. The surface differences between the two texts, and the obviously different traditions to which each belongs, would seem to make any direct connection between Makrembolites and Chrétien far-fetched. But if Chrétien did not know *Hysmine and Hysminias*, it seems clear that he had access, most probably through intermediaries, to the fictional world of the ancient novel, and more specifically to its Byzantine revival in his own century. However the fact is to be explained, both writers exert themselves to reinterpret the stories they have separately inherited from antiquity and to rethink them, in the process breaking new ground to explore interior, subjective experience. It is the more striking to find precisely the same preoccupations being explored, within a period of a few decades, in places so widely separated as Constantinople and northern France.

---

[51] Ibid., 20–37.575–1046; Chrétien, *Arthurian Romances*, ed. Kibler, 130–4 (Alexander and Soredamors); 136–40.3795–3892; *Arthurian Romances*, 169–70 (Cligés and Fenice).

An intriguing possibility would be to read *Cligés* as the figurative representation of precisely this relationship: however improbably, the literary imaginations of Komnenian Constantinople and Plantagenet England and northern France meet in the imagined complementarity depicted in the outer episodes of the romance. As we saw, the son of a Greek emperor (Alexander) restores King Arthur to his usurped kingdom; at the end Arthur prepares to restore to power the son of another Greek emperor (Cligés). The two worlds are interdependent but not equal: in both generations the young heir to the greatest empire in the Christian world of the twelfth century swears feudal allegiance to the legendary king of Britain. It is a neat inversion, in fiction, of the actual policy of the Komnenian emperors in their dealings with the crusaders from northern Europe.

Be that as it may, close reading of the two texts suggests that *Cligés* could not have been written without the prior existence of the ancient and/or the Byzantine novels of ideal love, even if the intertextual links are indirect and cannot be proved in detail. When read against the historical background to which Elizabeth Jeffreys first drew attention back in 1980, these two texts together may represent the most tangible link that is now recoverable, in the history of literary fiction, from the ideal novels (or 'romances') of Greek antiquity to the chivalric tradition that would come to dominate the western Middle Ages.

'Reading Byzantium' – in this case, Byzantine fiction – in this way places the Byzantine experience and its reception within the overarching narrative of the 'rise' of what today we call fiction to its dominant position in culture since the mid-eighteenth century.

Further Reading

Translations of the main texts are: E. M. Jeffreys, trans., *Four Byzantine Novels* (Liverpool, 2012) and J. Duggan, *The Romances of Chrétien de Troyes* (New Haven, 2001). For background, see: M. A. Doody, *The True Story of the Novel* (London, 1997), R. Beaton, *The Medieval Greek Romance*, second edition (London, 1996), P. Magdalino, *The Empire of Manuel I Komnenos, 1143–1180* (Cambridge, 1993).

PART IV

Modern Reading as Textual Archaeology

Traces of Authorship

CHAPTER 23

Anonymous Textual Survivals from Late Antiquity
Fiona K. Haarer

This chapter considers the place of an anonymous encomium (P. gr. Vindob. 29788C) on an un-named emperor within the literary milieu of the fifth and sixth centuries. The attempt to tease out the identity of both author and emperor necessarily involves analysis of not just the historical context for the poem, but also of contemporary practice in literary style: the use of metre, word order and vocabulary. If the historical context suggests the reign of Anastasios, as I will propose, as the most plausible period, an examination of the literary context shows just how difficult it is to narrow authorship to one of several poets capable of producing well-written poetry in the Nonnian tradition at the turn of the sixth century.[1]

The Problem and Past Solutions

The identity of the author and honorand of this fragmentary hexameter encomium has been considered a number of times since its first publication in the 1920s. About fifty lines of the poem are preserved on a separate leaf (P. gr. Vindob. 29788C), torn in such a way that the line beginnings on the verso and line endings on the recto are missing, as are the names of the honorand and author. The leaf is thought to have come from the same codex as a binion (P. gr. Vindob. 29788A-B) that contained a hexameter idyll on an autumn or spring day, a hexameter encomium on the patrician, Theagenes of Athens, letters 80 and 90 of Gregory of Nazianzos, and two fragments containing lines from another hexameter poem. Hans Gerstinger, with H. Ibscher, published the *editio princeps* of this Vienna papyrus in 1928, and while his assessment that the hand is the same throughout and that the style of writing belongs to the fifth or sixth

---

[1] I would like to thank Stephen Colvin and Mary Whitby for their help in preparing this chapter for publication.

century is not disputed, his attribution of the hexameter poems to Pamprepios of Panopolis (440–85) has not been universally accepted.[2]

Immediately following the publication of Gerstinger's text, a number of reviews and amendments to the text were published, along with comments on the author and honorand, though one of the most significant advancements to the study of the papyrus was that made by Heitsch, who published photographs of the text along with his edition in the early 1960s.[3] In 1968, Viljamaa discussed the hexameter poems in his monograph, *Studies in Greek Encomiastic Poetry of the Early Byzantine Period*.[4] Against the views expressed by the early reviewers, such as Maas and Keydell, that the works were of differing qualities, thereby suggesting multiple authorship, he accepted Gerstinger's argument of single authorship. However, while agreeing that the poems display the unmistakable influence of the mid-fifth-century Nonnos of Panopolis, he argued that the poet was from a slightly later generation than Pamprepios.[5] Finding thematic similarities with the encomia for Anastasios by Priscian of

---

[2] H. Gerstinger, *Pamprepios von Panopolis. Eidyllion auf die Tageszeiten und Enkomion auf den Archon Theagenes von Athen: Nebst Bruchstücken anderer epischer Dichtungen und zwei Briefe des Gregorios von Nazianz im Pap. Gr. Vindob. 29788 A-C* (Vienna, 1928). For the fragments of the encomium, see section IV, 82–7. On Pamprepios, an Egyptian rhetor, astrologer and senator who played a significant political role under Zeno, see R. Asmus, 'Pamprepios, ein byzantinischer Gelehrter und Staatsmann des 5. Jahrhunderts', *BZ*, 22 (1913), 320–47; H. Grégoire, 'Au Camp d'un Wallenstein byzantin: la vie et les vers de Pamprépios, aventurier païen', *BullBudé*, 24 (1929), 22–38; A. Delatte and P. Stroobant, 'L'horoscope de Pamprépios, professeur et homme politique de Byzance', *BAcBelg*, 9 (1923), 58–76; R. Keydell, 'Die griechische Poesie der Kaiserzeit', *Jahresbericht über die Fortschritte der klassischen Altertumswissenschaft*, 230 (1931), 122–3; A. D. E. Cameron, 'Wandering Poets: a Literary Movement in Byzantine Egypt', *Historia*, 14 (1965), 473, 481, 486, 491, 499–500; R. Kaster, *Guardians of Language: The Grammarian and Society in Late Antiquity* (Berkeley, CA, 1988), esp. 331–2; P. Athanassiadi, 'Persecution and Response in Late Paganism', *JHS*, 113 (1993), 19; L. Miguélez Cavero, *Poems in Context: Greek Poetry in the Egyptian Thebaid, 200–600 AD* (New York, NY, 2008), 83–5.

[3] For example, E. A. Barber, 'Review: Hans Gerstinger, *Pamprepios von Panopolis*', *ClRev*, 43 (1929), 237–8; P. Graindor, 'Pamprépios (?) et Théagénès', *Byzantion*, 4 (1929), 469–75; K. Horna, 'Nachlese zu Pamprepios', *AnzWien*, 66 (1929), 257–63; P. Maas, 'Review: Hans Gerstinger, 'Pamprepios von Panopolis', *Gnomon*, 5 (1929) 250–2; O. Schissel, 'Review: Joannes Gerstinger, *Pamprepios von Panopolis*', *Philologische Wochenschrift*, 49 (1929), 1073–80; R. Keydell, 'Review of Hans Gerstinger, *Pamprepios von Panopolis*', *BZ*, 29 (1929–30), 290–3; Keydell, 'Die griechische Poesie', 122–3; A. Körte, 'Review of Hans Gerstinger, Pamprepios von Panopolis', *Archiv für Papyrusforschung*, 10 (1932), 25–8; P. Bernardini Marzolla, 'A proposito di Pamprepio di Panopoli', *Maia*, 7 (1955), 125–7. On the idyll and Theagenes encomium, see S. Arthur, C. Hunt, C. Edgar and D. L. Page, eds., *Select Papyri*, vol. III: *Poetry* (London, 1932), 560–5. An edition and photographs of the text were published by E. Heitsch, *Die griechischen Dichterfragmente der römischen Kaiserzeit* (Göttingen, 1961–4), vol. I, 108–20, and plates E–F.

[4] T. Viljamaa, *Studies in Greek Encomiastic Poetry of the Early Byzantine Period* (Helsinki, 1968), 55–6, 101–4.

[5] Viljamaa argues (ibid., 55) that the style and metrics differ markedly from the *Hymns* of Pamprepios' contemporary, Proklos.

Caesarea (in Latin verse) and Prokopios of Gaza (in Greek prose) and references in the poem to historical events from the reign of Anastasios, he concluded that all the hexameter poems were the work of Christodoros of Koptos, who we know flourished during the Anastasian years.[6]

In the 1970s, Livrea published several papers on the papyrus texts,[7] and in 1979, having examined the papyrus in Vienna, he published a new edition (which I reproduce for reference at the end of this chapter).[8] His work on the new edition coincided with the publication by McCail in the 1978 *Journal of Hellenic Studies* of another edition of the text (for which he made use of the photographs of Heitsch), a translation and detailed linguistic and literary commentary.[9] McCail, focusing primarily not on the identity of the author but on that of the emperor, argued that, stylistically, the poem fell within the reigns of Leo I to Justinian; but for reasons that will be discussed below, he favoured the years 489–90 just after the suppression of the Isaurian revolt at a time when Zeno was trying to promote the accession to the throne of his brother, Longinos. McCail, therefore, concurred that the honorand was the Emperor Zeno, but such a late date in Zeno's reign certainly rules out the authorship of Pamprepios, who had died in the revolt, and he did not put forward an alternative suggestion. Although McCail rejected Viljamaa's proposal that the honorand was Anastasios, he did accept his suggestions that verso 1–15 refer to an Isaurian war and that the anonymous poet was following the guidelines laid down by Menander Rhetor for the composition of a βασιλικὸς λόγος (*Basilikos Logos*, or imperial oration). Indeed, much of his reconstruction of the poem is based on this assumption.[10]

---

[6] Viljamaa (ibid., 56) notes that since Christodoros wrote a poem about the disciples of the Neoplatonist Proklos, it would not have been out of character to compose a panegyric for the Neoplatonist Theagenes; see L. MacCoull, *Dioscorus of Aphrodito: His Work and His World* (Berkeley, CA, 1988), 60.

[7] E. Livrea, 'Due note a papyiri tardoepici', *ZPE*, 17 (1975), 35–6; E. Livrea, 'Pamprepio ed il P. Vindob. 29788A–C', *ZPE*, 25 (1977), 121–34; E. Livrea, 'Nuovi contributi al testo dei Frr. 1, 2 E 4 di Pamprepio (xxxv Heitsch)', *Rivista di Filologia*, 106 (1978), 281–7; and E. Livrea, 'Per una nuova edizione di Pamprepio di Panopoli (P. Vindob. 29788 A–C)' in J. Bingen and G. Nachtergael, eds., *Actes du xve Congrès International de Papyrologie* (Brussels, 1978–9), vol. III, 69–77.

[8] E. Livrea, ed., *Pamprepii Panopolitani carmina (P. Gr. Vindob. 29788 A-C)* (Leipzig, 1979).

[9] R. C. McCail, 'P. Gr. Vindob. 29788C: Hexameter Encomium on an Un-named Emperor', *JHS*, 98 (1978), 38–63.

[10] Ibid., 40 and 42–3, where McCail reckons that the opening sections, making up between a fifth and a sixth of the total length, would have been written on a separate leaf, now missing. For Menander Rhetor, see D. A. Russell and N. G. Wilson, eds., *Menander Rhetor* (Oxford, 1981), and M. Heath, *Menander: A Rhetor in Context* (Oxford, 2004).

With so much uncertainty remaining, it would be as well to reconsider afresh the arguments concerning both poet and honorand.[11] Further analysis of the historical context and the themes of the fragmentary encomium, alongside the panegyrical works for Anastasios, will strengthen the proposition of Viljamaa and suggest Anastasios as a more realistic candidate than McCail allows. Undoubtedly, as I will argue in the conclusion, another work in praise of an emperor known for his patronage of literary figures and intellectuals would scarcely be out of place. The close comparison with the panegyrics of Priscian and Prokopios also help to vindicate the linking of this encomium with Anastasios.[12] As for the author, the arguments supporting Pamprepios are not conclusive. Although he is a likely suggestion for the author of the idyll (composed by an Egyptian writing in Athens) and even more so for the author of the Theagenes encomium (since Pamprepios benefited from the patronage of a Theagenes in Athens), even these attributions have been disputed.[13] Furthermore, although it would be a neat solution if the fragmentary encomium could be shown to be the lost *Isaurika* of Pamprepios, this does not allow for McCail's interpretation of the historical context. If the author may not be Pamprepios after all and the honorand is more likely to be Anastasios than Zeno, then the options are widened to include, for example, Christodoros, Kollouthos or the anonymous poet(s) of the two *Greek Anthology* epigrams written to honour the emperor.[14]

Historical Context

I begin with an analysis of the historical context of the poem. Essentially, I follow the structure established by McCail, which moves from the section

---

[11] For a bibliography and overview of the scholarship to date, see Miguélez Cavero, *Poems*, 72–4.

[12] The possible references to the Persian War and the insurrection of Vitalian (see below) mean that the fragmentary encomium would belong to the later years of Anastasios' reign and therefore would have been composed after the panegyrics of Priscian and Prokopios even if Priscian was writing in 513 as argued by, for example, A. Chauvot, ed., *Procope de Gaza, Priscien de Césarée, panégyriques de l'empereur Anastase Ier* (Bonn, 1986) and P. Coyne, ed., *Priscian of Caesarea's 'De Laude Anastasii Imperatoris'* (Lampeter, 1991). For a review of the dating, see F. K. Haarer, *Anastasius I: Empire and Politics in the Late Roman World* (Cambridge 2006), 272–8.

[13] Cameron, 'Wandering Poets', 481, n. 64, 502–3; A. D. E., Cameron, 'The Empress and the Poet: Paganism and Politics at the Court of Theodosius II' in J. J. Winkler and G. Williams, eds., *Later Greek Literature* (Cambridge, 1982), 236, believes that it is likely that Pamprepios was the author of the Theagenes panegyric, and (Cameron, 'Wandering Poets', 486) that he was also the author of the idyll. *Contra* see Graindor, 'Pamprépios (?)'; Maas, 'Review'; Page, *Literary Papyri*, 565; Viljamaa, *Studies*, 55, 56; Kaster, *Guardians*, 332.

[14] W. R. Paton, ed. and trans., *The Greek Anthology* (Cambridge, MA, 2014), vol. III, 108–10 (IX.210) and 362–4 (IX.656).

on military affairs (verso 1–15) to the emperor's achievements in peace (verso 17–26, and continuing on the recto with some further references to wars), but make some alternative suggestions for the events he outlines.

According to the βασιλικὸς λόγος, an encomium should begin with references to the emperor's place of birth, family and education. However, this introductory section is missing, and the surviving lines begin in the middle of the section on the emperor's achievements in war (πράξεις κατὰ πόλεμον) which, arguably, are just as appropriate to Anastasios as they are to Zeno. McCail suggests that the description of the conflict (verso 1–15) refers to Zeno's war against Illos and Leontios (484–8) rather than to the later Isaurian revolt that flared up soon after Anastasios' accession, since it is

> odd that the part of the encomium traditionally allotted to the emperor's achievements in war should be devoted to the earlier war [Isaurian War 491–8] while the more recent campaign [Persian War 502–6] is relegated to the part of the scheme reserved for administrative achievement ... Further, some fifteen lines are devoted to the suppression of the Isaurians, but only five (perhaps even fewer) to the Persian war.[15]

However, it is the Isaurian War, rather than the Persian, that forms a major focus of the other panegyrical works in Anastasios' honour,[16] and I cannot see any details in the account of the war which are particular only to that fought by Zeno.[17] There is no reason why the pursuer of the enemy (verso 3, 5 and 9), named as John the Scythian by McCail, should be assumed to be acting here under Zeno's command, for he was also Anastasios' general. McCail argued that the dismissal of Theoderic, Zeno's other general, under suspicion of colluding with Illos, explains why John is described here as acting alone (μόνος, verso 6). However, while Anastasios had two generals, John the Scythian and John the Hunchback, the former was enjoying his consulship in 498 after capturing two of the rebels, Athenodorus and Longinos of Kardala, while his colleague was outwitting Longinos of Selinos, Indes and others. In this respect, each could be described as working 'alone'. Indeed, for that matter, there is no reason why John the Hunchback should not be the general indicated here.

---

[15] McCail, 'P. Gr. Vindob. 29788C', 39; 43–5 for his linguistic commentary, and 54–5 for his narrative of Zeno's Isaurian War and his justification that these lines can be matched exclusively to this war rather than the later Anastasian conflict. He singles out the punitive aspect of the campaign, the general 'acting alone' who drove the enemy to take refuge in some sort of cave, the suffering of the defeated and, finally, the clemency of the emperor.
[16] Priscian, De Laude, ed. Coyne, 40–5, lines 10–139 (out of 312) deal with the Isaurian War, and it is also highlighted in Prokopios, Panégyrique, ed. Chauvot, 12–13 (9–10); Greek Anthology, ed. Paton, vol. I, 88–90 (II.398–406); vol. III, 210 (IX.210.10) and 364 (IX.656.19).
[17] For an account of the Isaurian wars fought by Zeno and Anastasios, see Haarer, Anastasius, 11–28.

Similarly, the vocabulary used, such as ἀ]νιχνεύειν ('to track down', verso 4), ἴχνια θήρης ('the footprints of his quarry', verso 6) and ἐλάσσας ('having driven', verso 7), could equally apply to the imperial army's pursuit of Illos, or to its pursuit of those rebelling against Anastasios.[18] The accounts of the latter's war stress the tactics of guerrilla warfare adopted by the enemy and the difficulty of the terrain for the imperial troops, entirely consistent with the idea of an army tracking down its prey.[19] Verso 5, λέων δ'ἀλάπαξε καλιάς ('and like a lion he plundered their lair') could allude either to the investing of the castle of Papirios and subsequent execution of Illos and Leontios who were dragged from the chapel, or to Anastasios' destruction of the same fortress, as described by John of Antioch.[20] There is also a lion simile in Priscian's panegyric:

> Ut leo . . .
> . . . si commoveat clamor, si turba coronae,
> Infremit horrendum simul et distendit hiatus
> Sanguineis torquens ardentia lumina flammis
> Et ruit in medium, prosternens arma virosque
> Nec vis ulla potest venienti obsistere contra. . .
> Viribus Augustus sic saevos perculit hostes
> Per varios sternens casus non fanda furentes.

However, McCail rejects the possible link between the two similes on the grounds that in the fragmentary encomium it is the general who is the subject of the comparison not the emperor, though it is worth making the association between the two similes since they both pertain to Anastasios' conduct of the war against the rebels.[21] Verso 9 and 10 concerning the

---

[18] All English translations, unless otherwise indicated, are those of McCail, 'P. Gr. Vindob. 29788C'. For detailed discussion on the restoration of l.7, see Livrea, 'Nuovi contributi', 282, in which he draws attention to Paton, ed., *Greek Anthology*, vol. III, 262 (IX.210.1): δέρκεό μοι κρατερῶν καμάτων ἐγκύμονα βίβλον ('Look on me, the book pregnant with vigorous toil').

[19] Compare the descriptions by John of Antioch, S. Mariev, ed., *Ioannis Antiocheni Fragmenta quae supersunt omnia* (Berlin, 2008), 386 (fr. 214b); I. Thurn, ed., *Ioannis Malalae. Chronographia* (Berlin, 2000), 320–1; W. Wright, ed. and trans, *The Chronicle of Joshua the Stylite, Composed in Syriac A.D. 507* (Cambridge, 1882); F. W. Trombley and J. W Watt, eds., trans., *The Chronicle of Pseudo-Joshua the Stylite* (Liverpool, 2000), 2; T., Mommsen, ed., *Marcellini V. C. comitis chronicon, MGH AA* 11 (Berlin, 1894), 94ff. (494ff.), www.mgh.de (accessed 3 February 2018); B. Croke, trans. *The Chronicle of Marcellinus* (Sydney, 1995), 30ff.; G. C. Hansen, ed., *Theodoros Anagnostes, Kirchengeschichte* (Berlin, 1971), 449; J. Bidez and L. Parmentier, eds., *The Ecclesiastical History of Evagrius with the Scholia* (London 1898), 129 and 134–5 (III.29 and 35), trans. M. Whitby, *The Ecclesiastical History of Evagrius Scholasticus* (Liverpool, 2000), 164–6, 179–81; C. de Boor, ed., *Theophanis Chronographia* (Leipzig, 1883), 212–17 (AM 5985–88).

[20] John of Antioch, *Fragmenta*, ed. Mariev, 386 (fr. 214b).

[21] Priscian, *De Laude*, ed. Coyne, 43.67–79 (trans. 54–5): 'Just as a lion … if some clamour or a crowd of encircling men should provoke him, he roars ferociously, opens wide his jaws, and rolls his eyes burning with blood-red flames. He charges into their midst laying low men and arms; no force

woes of the captives are equally relevant for the defeated of both wars, as is the comment in verso 11 on the loss of their ancestral possessions. Sources for the Anastasian war recount how the emperor expelled the Isaurians from Constantinople, confiscated their property, and eventually drove them from their homeland.[22] Finally, verso 13 to 15 allude to the mercy of the emperor towards his defeated foe. McCail suggests that this is a reference to Zeno's clemency towards Illos' wife and daughter and his scheming mother-in-law, Verina, but as he admits, imperial clemency towards the defeated is a rhetorical cliché.[23] Anastasios, too, showed the quality of mercy as celebrated by Priscian:

> Sed tamen Augusti superat clementia cuncta,
> Qui stratos relevant, domuit quos Marte superbos,
> Hostibus et pacis concedit munera pacis.[24]

Later in his panegyric, Priscian also used the image of 'ears' (cf. στε]ρεῆσιν ἀκουαῖς, verso 14) to conjure up the idea of sympathetic listening, this time from God himself:

> Iustitiamque iubet descendere rursus ab axe
> Et faciles precibus populorum praebuit aures.[25]

Lines 16–17 serve as the prooemium to the next section of the encomium, the achievements of the emperor in peace (πράξεις κατ' εἰρήνην).[26] Verso

---

can withstand his rage ... Thus the Emperor with his might has struck down his savage enemies despite their rage for unspeakable deeds and has overthrown them with a succession of various catastrophes.' McCail, 'P. Gr. Vindob. 29788C', 43–4, and Viljamaa, *Studies*, 101–2. On this simile, see Coyne, *Priscian*, 104–5, and F. K. Nicks, 'Literary Culture in the Reign of Anastasios' in S. Mitchell and G. Greatrex, eds., *Ethnicity and Culture in Late Antiquity* (Swansea, 2000), 191. On another occasion, E. W. Brooks, ed., *Zacharias of Mytilene, Historia Ecclesiastica Zachariae Rhetori vulgo adscripta* (Louvain, 1954–67), vol. II, 28–33 (VII.5); G. Greatrex, ed., *The Chronicle of Pseudo-Zachariah Rhetor: Church and War in Late Antiquity*, trans., R. Phenix and C. Horn (Liverpool, 2011), 228–9, quoting a letter from Simeon of Amida to the monophysite Archimandrite Samuel, compared Anastasios to a lion: 'God stirred up the spirit of this believing king like a lion to the prey, and he roared, and made the whole faction of the enemies of truth to tremble.'

[22] Malalas, *Chronographia*, ed. Thurn, 320–1; Joshua, *Chronicle*, ed. Wright, 23; *MGH AA* 11, 95 (498); Marcellinus Comes, *Chronicle*, trans. Croke, 31–2 (498); Theophanes, *Chronographia*, ed. de Boor, 216–7 (AM 5988); see Haarer, *Anastasius*, 27, n. 85.

[23] Menander, ed. Russell and Wilson, 88–9 (374.25ff.), and see note 25. Compare to Viljamaa, *Studies*, 102; McCail, 'P. Gr. Vindob. 29788C', 45.

[24] Priscian, *De Laude*, ed. Coyne, 45.130–2 (trans. 56–7): 'But yet the mercy of the emperor prevails over all. He raises up the conquered, whose pride he has subdued in war, and grants to the enemies of peace the gifts of peace.' See further Viljamaa, *Studies*, 102.

[25] Priscian, *De Laude*, ed. Coyne, 46–7.182–3 (trans. 58): 'He commands justice to descend again from heaven and He has lent His ears to the prayers of the people'; see Livrea, 'Nuovi contributi', 283; Livrea, *Pamprepii Panopolitani carmina*, 38.

[26] Menander, ed. Russell and Wilson, 88–9 (375.6ff.); Viljamaa, *Studies*, 102; McCail, 'P. Gr. Vindob. 29788C', 45 and 56. The πράξεις κατ' εἰρήνην section was to be subdivided into three:

18–20 refer to the championing of refugees and petitioners, among those ἀνδράσιν Αὐσονιήων ('the men of the Ausonians', verso 20).[27] In 475, Zeno ransomed captives in Africa from the Vandal king, Genseric, and in 483, he helped the African Catholics persecuted by the Arian Huneric by offering them asylum in Constantinople. But Anastasios, too, was praised for his hospitality to exiles from Old Rome:

> Omnia sed superat, princeps, praeconia vestra
> Propositum, sapiens quo fidos eligis aulae
> Custodes, per quos Romana potentia crescat,
> Et quo, Roma vetus misit quoscumque, benigne
> Sustentas omni penitus ratione fovendo,
> Provehis et gradibus praeclaris laetus honorum,
> Ne damni patriae sensus fiantve dolores.[28]

There are a number of suggestions for the identity of these immigrants: exiles from Vandalic North Africa, supporters of the anti-pope Laurentius, dissidents banished by Theoderic, or aristocratic families, such as the Anicii, who sought the political and cultural stability of the West. The latter, especially, would be ideal candidates for distinguished positions at the imperial court.

The πολλοὶ δέ τε παῖδες ἀοιδῶν ('many sons-of-poets', verso 21) arguably refers to the poets favoured by Zeno: Pamprepios, awarded a professorship after a public recitation, subsequently became a quaestor, honorary consul and patrician; Pelagius, an epic poet and distinguished ambassador; Panolbius and Aetherius, so-called poet journalists.[29] However, by the time this poem was written, 489/90 by McCail's own reckoning, Pamprepios was already dead. A protégé of Illos, rather than of Zeno, Pamprepios went to Alexandria to drum up support for his patron and later became Illos' *magister officiorum*, but in slightly murky

---

σωφροσύνη, δικαιοσύνη and φρόνησις. The poet begins here with δικαιοσύνη, gentleness towards subjects and mercy to petitioners, the justness of the governors and officials, moderation of imperial taxes, justness of imperial legislation (recto 3–14).

[27] 'Ausonian' usually refers to Old Rome.
[28] Priscian, *De Laude*, ed. Coyne, 48–9.239–45 (trans. 60): 'But, o Princeps, your wise plan of choosing loyal guardians of the royal court, to increase through them the power of Rome, and of generously supporting those sent by old Rome by favouring them in every conceivable way, surpasses all your praiseworthy deeds. You gladly promote them through the ranks of distinguished appointments so that they may not feel pain at the loss of their homeland.' See further, A. Momigliano, 'Gli Anicii e la storiografia latina del VI sec. D.C.' in A. Momigliano, *Secondo contributo alla storia degli studi classici*, second edition (Rome, 1984), 231–53; Viljamaa, *Studies*, 56, 102; Coyne, *Priscian*, 167–9; Nicks, 'Literary Culture', 189–90; Haarer, *Anastasius*, 102–3.
[29] Cameron, 'Wandering Poets', 505–7; A. H. M. Jones, J. R. Martindale and J. Morris, *The Prosopography of the Later Roman Empire* (Cambridge, 1980), vol. II, 857; compare to Livrea, *Pamprepii Panopolitani carmina*, 40.

circumstances seems to have been executed for treason during the siege of the castle of Papirios, and his body thrown over the ramparts.[30] Meanwhile, Pelagius, rewarded with the title patrician for his services as an ambassador, was strangled on Zeno's orders in c. 490, on suspicion of plotting his overthrow.[31] On the whole, the atmosphere at the somewhat unstable court of Zeno could hardly be said to encourage a flourishing of literary culture, while Anastasios was known to reward men of letters and to inspire literary and intellectual endeavour.[32] His appointment to imperial posts of learned and cultured figures who brought with them a wealth of practical experience was praised not only by Priscian –

> Nec non eloquio decoratos, maxime princeps,
> Quos doctrina potens et sudor musicus auget,
> Quorum Romanas munit sapientia leges,
> Adsumis socios iusto moderamine rerum.[33]

– but also by John Lydos:

> τῶν γ' οὖν δικανικῶν ῥητόρων τοὺς ἀρίστους ἐπὶ τὴν ἀρχὴν προῦφερεν. καί ποτε, πρὸς τῆς γαμετῆς Ἀριάδνης ὀχλούμενος Ἀνθεμίῳ Ἀνθεμίου τοῦ Ῥώμης βεβασιλευκότος παιδὶ τὴν ἀρχὴν ἐγχειρίσαι, ἠγανάκτησεν, εἰπὼν δέ, μηδενὸς ἢ μόνων λογικῶν ἀξίαν εἶναι τὴν ἐπαρχότητα.[34]

> Ἦν μὲν οὖν τοιοῦτος ὁ βασιλεύς, τὰ δὲ ἄλλα συνετὸς καὶ πεπαιδευμένος, ἐπιεικής τε ἅμα καὶ δραστήριος, μεγαλόδωρός τε καὶ κρείττων ὀργῆς, ἐρυθριῶν τε τοὺς λόγους, ὡς καὶ πλήρωμα χρόνου καὶ βαθμὸν τοῖς τῶν λόγων διδασκάλοις βουληθέντα παρασχεῖν ταῖς αὐτῶν διχονοίαις ἐμποδισθῆναι.[35]

---

[30] Asmus, 'Pamprepios'; Grégoire, 'Au Camp'; Delatte and Stroobant, 'L'horoscope'; Kaster, *Guardians*, 129–32, 329–32; Athanassiadi, 'Persecution', 19.
[31] Malalas, *Chronographia*, ed. Thurn, 317–18; L. Dindorf, ed., *Chronicon Paschale* (Bonn, 1832), 490; Theophanes, *Chronographia*, ed. de Boor, 206–9 (AM 5982); see Cameron, 'Wandering Poets', 507.
[32] See Nicks, 'Literary Culture', 183–4; Haarer, *Anastasius*, 190–3; see Viljamaa, *Studies*, 56, 102.
[33] Priscian, *De Laude*, ed. Coyne, 49.248–51 (trans. 60): 'Mighty Princeps, you also choose as your associates in just government those distinguished for their eloquence who are embellished by the power of learning and the exercise of poetry, those whose wisdom protects the Roman laws.'
[34] T. F. Carney, trans., *John Lydos. De Magistratibus*, in T. F. Carney, *Bureaucracy in Traditional Society: Romano-Byzantine Bureaucracies Viewed from Within* (Lawrence, KS, 1971), 100 (III.50): 'The cream of barristers, that is, were advanced by him to that magistracy; and on one occasion when he was being importuned by his lady wife Ariadne to entrust the office to Anthemius, the son of the Anthemius who had been Emperor in Rome, he expressed displeasure, and did so with the remark that no one but men of literary training could fitly hold the office of prefect.'
[35] Ibid., 98–9 (III.47): 'And in other matters [Anastasius] was wise and well-educated, fair and active too, with it; lavish with his generosity and with his temper well under control, he showed due respect for literature. So much so that, when he wanted to provide teachers of literature with a career stage to round off their time in the service with an elevated grade, it was their inability to agree that prevented the move.'

It is apparent, then, that Anastasios was known (and arguably rather more appropriately than Zeno) for looking after two categories: exiles from the West and poets, thus fitting McCail's argument that the two groups must not be conflated on grounds of syntax.[36]

The poem continues on the recto, though the first few lines are missing or mutilated beyond restoration. McCail suggests that recto 3–14 deal with aspects of civil administration that may be summed up: εὐνομίης ἀνύσας ἔαρ ('having achieved for all a springtime of good government', recto 9).[37] He rejects Gerstinger's restoration of ἀ[ρ]γυρέη[(recto 4), which could have been a hint at Anastasios' popular abolition of the *chrysargyron* and certainly a reference to the restructuring of the tax system would fit the δικαιοσύνη section (which included such topics as the moderation of taxes, the good conduct of officials, and justice). McCail sees the omission of reference to the *chrysargyron* as a major flaw in the argument for Anastasios as the honorand, but it is significant that the restoration is accepted in Livrea's edition.[38]

Continuing to the next line, McCail suggests that σοὶ γὰρ (recto 5ff.) initiates a list of the emperor's officials and their services to him. Such allusions, apart from being typical of panegyric, are particularly reminiscent of Priscian's lines on Anastasios beginning:

Nunc hominum generi laetissima saecula currunt,

and Prokopios of Gaza:

ἀλλὰ γὰρ ἡμῖν τὸ χρυσοῦν ἐκεῖνο γένος τὸ μέχρι λόγων ἀδόμενον μόλις ἀπέδειξε τοῖς ἔργοις ὁ χρόνος.[39]

Livrea restores Αἴγυ[πτον at the end of line 8 and refers in his commentary to possible connections with Zeno.[40] However, Anastasios also had

---

[36] McCail, 'P. Gr. Vindob. 29788C', 56 argues that the particles δέ τε (verso 21) differentiate the Italians and poets, rather than a reference to Italian poets, which is surely correct. However, his suggestion that Priscian 239–53 is referring to Anastasios' hospitality to Latin poets and scholars is misguided; Priscian is also surely referring to two separate groups, as discussed above. See also Coyne, *Priscian*, 167–75.

[37] McCail, 'P. Gr. Vindob. 29788C', 47–8. Viljamaa, *Studies*, 103 discusses recto 9–14 with reference to the emperor's moderation and morality, alongside Priscian, *De Laude*, ed. Coyne, 47.191–2 and 49.252–5 and Prokopios, *Panégyrique*, ed. Chauvot, 20–1 (22–3); compare with Livrea, *Pamprepii Panopolitani carmina*, 40.

[38] Menander, ed. Russell and Wilson, 88–9 (375.8ff.), and see the references by Priscian, *De Laude*, ed. Coyne, 45–6.149–66 and Prokopios, *Panégyrique*, ed. Chauvot, 15–16 (13). McCail, 'P. Gr. Vindob. 29788C', 39, 47; Livrea, *Pamprepii Panopolitani carmina*, 13, 40.

[39] Priscian, *De Laude*, ed. Coyne, 45.149ff (trans. 57): 'Now there is passing a most prosperous age for the race of men', Prokopios, *Panégyrique*, ed. Chauvot, 21 (23): 'But our time has shown us as a reality the golden age that previously could scarcely be sung in words.'

[40] Livrea, *Pamprepii Panopolitani carmina*, 13, 40.

connections with Egypt. His concern to secure the grain supply led to his restoration of the lighthouse at Alexandria or, as an alternative and perhaps even more appropriate theory, his introduction of the office of *vindex* (a tax collector) seems to have been closely based on the Egyptian office of *pagarch*.[41]

McCail proposes that recto 10–12 refer to the campaign in the country of the Tzani led by Longinos, Zeno's brother, referred to as αὐτοκασ[ιγνητ (recto 6).[42] Longinos established a camp there in 488 or 489 on the border between the Tzani and Lazi, from which region eunuchs were imported. These lines, therefore, refer to the suppression of the Tzani's trade in children, billed here as an act of enlightenment in this section on πράξεις κατ' εἰρήνην.[43] About the same time, Zeno reduced the autonomy of the Armenian satraps who had sided with Illos and Leontios against him, and decreed that the four most powerful satraps would be appointed by the emperor. When Prokopios introduces Justinian's further step of simply replacing the Armenian satraps with Roman *duces*, he makes particular mention of the use of gold on their regalia that would have fitted the description χρυσοχίτωνος (recto 13) very appropriately.[44]

However, it is equally possible that αὐτοκασ[ιγνητ may be an allusion to Anastasios' own brother, Paul, who held the consulship in 496.[45] If διογενη[ς (recto 7) is not the Homeric epithet, but does refer to Diogenes the *comes scholarum*, these lines may refer to his activity as commander of Anastasios' army in 493–4, rather than his activity with Longinos during Zeno's reign.[46] As for recto 10–11, these lines may

---

[41] Haarer, *Anastasius*, 232, 207ff.

[42] Longinos became *magister militum praesentalis* after his release from captivity in 485, and held the consulship in 486 and 490.

[43] See J. Haury and G. Wirth, eds., *Procopii Caesariensis. Opera omnia* (Leipzig, 1962), vol. II, 497 (*De Bello Gothico* IV.3.15–17) and vol. IV, 98–9 (*De aedificiis* III.6.23). McCail, 'P. Gr. Vindob. 29788C', 48, 57–8.

[44] McCail, 'P. Gr. Vindob. 29788C', 48, 58–9.

[45] Paul is singled out for praise in the closing lines of Priscian, *De Laude*, ed. Coyne, 50.290–3 (trans. 62):

> Nam quid commemorem Pauli mitissima corda
> Quem tibi coniungit munimen laudis honestas,
> Non solum generis venerandi vincula sacra;
> Nam mores sequitur mediocres pectore casto.

'For what am I to say of the most merciful heart of Paulus? His integrity, the bulwark of his reputation, not merely the sacred bond of venerable kinship, unites him to you. He pursues modest habits with a chaste heart.' The possibility of a reference to Paul is also admitted by Livrea, *Pamprepii Panopolitani carmina*, 40.

[46] McCail, 'P. Gr. Vindob. 29788C', 47, 57. He is perhaps a kinsman of Ariadne; compare to Haarer, *Anastasius*, 24, n. 72.

instead be a reference to Anastasios' legislation on family matters designed to improve integrity and morality in the state. Prokopios makes a similar reference in his panegyric:

καὶ διὰ τὸν σὸν ἔννομον φόβον δίκαια μὲν τὰ συμβόλαια, σώφρονες δὲ τοῖς ὑπηκόοις οἱ γάμοι, γνήσια δὲ τὰ γένη καὶ οὐκ ἀμφίβολοι τοῖς πατράσι διὰ τὴν ὑποψίαν οἱ παῖδες.[47]

These lines suggest that the reference to θαλάμοιο ('the bed-chamber', recto 11) in this context and an allusion to Anastasios' legislation would be more fitting to the πράξεις κατ' εἰρήνην section, rather than McCail's justification of these lines on military operations as an 'act of enlightenment'.

All this notwithstanding, the following lines (recto 12–14) certainly allude to matters of war, concluding with a reference to a victory over the Persians.[48] The phraseology αὐχένα γαῦρον ('the proud neck') reminds us of Prokopios' use of the phrase, but even without this reminiscence, it is clear that an allusion to a Persian war is rather more fitting with reference to Anastasios, who concluded a five-year war in 506, than Zeno, under whom no military offensive was undertaken on either side.[49] There were also a number of theatres of war during Anastasios' reign to account for the ἔνθα μὲν ... ἔνθα δὲ construction (recto 12–13).[50] Apart from the Isaurian conflict, the imperial troops were involved in resisting the advances of the Bulgars in Thrace and, in the East, Anastasios sought alliances with the Arab tribes, the Kindites and Ghassanids, after fighting between the Roman *doux*, Romanos, and the Ghassanids. The latter's loyalty to Anastasios made them an effective bulwark against the Persians'

---

[47] Prokopios, *Panégyrique*, ed. Chauvot, 21 (22): 'And through lawful fear of you, contracts are just, marriages among the subjects are marked by self-restraint, the succession in families is legitimate, and children do not suspiciously doubt the identity of their fathers.' On Anastasios' legislation, Haarer, *Anastasius*, 222–3. On the reconstruction of these lines, see Livrea, 'Nuovi contributi', 284. He also draws attention to the similar use of θρέπτειραν (r.10) by Kollouthos, *Rape of Helen*, 323, in A. W., Mair, ed., *Oppian, Colluthus, Tryphiodorus* (Cambridge, MA, 1963): τὴν δὲ δολοφροσύνης, κενεῶν θρέπτειραν ὀνείρων ('the [gate] of deception, nurse of empty dreams'); see Livrea, *Pamprepii Panopolitani carmina*, 564, l.41.

[48] These lines would, of course, be equally out of place whether the panegyric concerns Zeno or Anastasios, and McCail does not problematise them. It may be remembered that Priscian (254–60) also refers to Anastasios' dealings with the Arabs in the second half of his panegyric.

[49] Prokopios, *Panégyric*, ed. Chauvot, 24 (30); Viljamaa, *Studies*, 56, although this is a common Nonnian phrase (see McCail, 'P. Gr. Vindob. 29788C', 49). On relations between Rome and Persia in the fifth century and Anastasios' Persian War, see G. Greatrex, *Rome and Persia at War, 502–532* (Leeds, 1998); Haarer, *Anastasius*, 29–72.

[50] See Kollouthos, *Rape of Helen*, ed. Mair, 558, ll.238–40 for use of the same construction; Livrea, *Pamprepii Panopolitani carmina*, 41.

Arab allies, the Lakhmids, prior to the outbreak of war. There was also activity in Ethiopia, and even an uprising of the Tzani in 506 that was swiftly put down.⁵¹

Different reconstructions of the following lines (recto 16ff.) have led to different interpretations. Viljamaa read:

σ]ῇσι σαοφροσύνῃσι τεὴν παρακάτθ[εο
πατρίδι τ[ο]ῖος ἐὼν ἐπιδευέα κηδεμονή[ων
τοῖς [..........ἐπι]δήμιον ἴχνος ἐρ<ε>ίσας.

And in these lines he saw a reference to Anastasios' noble deeds to individual cities, citing comparative references in Prokopios' *Panegyric* 17–21 and Priscian, lines 184–92.⁵² McCail, however, restored the lines thus:

σ]ῇσι σαοφροσύνῃσι τεὴν παρακάτθ[εο νύμφην
           ]εων ἐπιδευέα κηδεμονή[ων
τοῖγ [........ ἐπι]δήμιον ἴχνος ἐρ<ε>ίσας

which he translated: 'to your chastity did you entrust your bride (?) / ... lacking kinsmen to care for her. / Therefore having planted thy (?) footstep ... at home.' McCail refers to similar references to Ariadne in Priscian (l.304) and Prokopios (section 23).⁵³ Livrea's reconstruction is closer to Gerstinger's, as follows:

σ]ῇσι σαοφροσύνῃσι τεὴν παρακάτθ[εο 'Ρώμην
πατρίδα το]ῖος ἐὼν ἐπιδευέα κηδεμονή[ων
τοῖς [...... ἐπι]δήμιον ἴχνος ἐρ<ε>ίσας.

---

⁵¹ On Anastasios and the Bulgars, Haarer, *Anastasius*, 104–6. Priscian, *De Laude*, ed. Coyne, 50.298–300 (trans. 62) notes the actions of Hypatios, one of Anastasios' nephews, in dealing with them, and also refers to the future Persian threat:

> Hypatii vestri referam fortissima facta
> Qui Scythicas gentes ripis depellit ab Histri
> Quem vidit validum Parthus sensitque timendum?

'Shall I mention the most intrepid deeds of your Hypatios who is driving the Scythian tribes from the banks of the Hister? The Parthian has seen that he is strong and knows that he is to be feared.' On the alliance with the Arab tribes, see I. Shahîd, *Byzantium and the Arabs in the Fifth Century* (Washington, D. C., 1989); I. Shahîd, *Byzantium and the Arabs in the Sixth Century* (Washington, D. C., 1995); and on the Arabs, Ethiopians and Tzani, see Haarer, *Anastasius*, 29–47, 70. Admittedly, it is difficult to find an exact reference for 'gold-tunicked', but otherwise the arguments in favour of Anastasios (rather than Zeno) as the honorand in this section of the panegyric (recto 3–14) are equally convincing; see Viljamaa, *Studies*, 56.

⁵² Viljamaa, *Studies*, 103.

⁵³ McCail, 'P. Gr. Vindob. 29788C', 43, 49–50, 59–60. In his configuration, the σωφροσύνη section starts only at l.15 and, omitting the usual themes of morality and order, includes, solely, praise of the Augusta.

This reading does not allow McCail's introduction of the Augusta here. Livrea argues instead that these lines belong with the preceding section concerning good administration and war.[54] I favour the interpretation of Livrea (and Viljamaa) over that of McCail. An allusion to Anastasios as a guardian to Rome and the fatherland fits rather better than a passing mention of the empress in this section, situated as it is between the references to the Persian War and civic insurrection. Recto 19 contains a reference to Odysseus, the first of the comparative figures required by Menander, and it may also be an allusion to one of the other three virtues, φρόνησις, with reference to his patient endurance.[55]

The last lines (recto 21–32) refer to an internal conflict, which, after detailed consideration, McCail identifies as the revolt of Markianos in 479.[56] He was about twenty-four years old, thus fitting the description τις ἀγηνορέων αἰζήιος ('an arrogant young man', recto 26), he and his rebels had Zeno cornered in his palace, and the populace of Constantinople provided support for Markianos by hurling missiles from their houses and roofs onto Zeno's troops, δήμου ξεῖνον ἄθυρμα ('a sport strange to the populace', recto 31). McCail proposes that this last section forms the section in praise of the emperor's good fortune.[57] He does admit, however, that 'the τύχη λαμπρά of Zeno did not present an easy subject' given Zeno's unpopularity, and he has to make the very narrowness of Zeno's escape a virtue.[58] He also has to explain away the use of χθιζόν ('yesterday', recto 22) by citing examples of the use of χθές to refer to the distant, rather than recent, past.[59]

---

[54] Livrea, 'Nuovi contributi', 284–5.
[55] Menander, ed. Russell and Wilson, 92–3 (377.2ff.); Viljamaa, *Studies*, 103–4, 116; McCail, 'P. Gr. Vindob. 29788C', 50; Livrea, 'Nuovi contributi', 285–6.
[56] McCail, 'P. Gr. Vindob. 29788C', 50–2, 60–2 for detailed discussion on the events of the rebellion of Markianos and how they fit with these lines. Viljamaa, *Studies*, 56 suggests, unconvincingly, that these lines (22ff.) refer to the dangers of the sea and possibly its pacification, perhaps alluding to the work on the harbours of Constantinople and Alexandria. He sees the end of the fragment as containing a reference to a faction riot, picking up on the mention of the 'hurling of stones', 'the usual weapons in these riots', without seeming to note the negative (οὐ) or the notion that it was a 'sport strange to the populace'. Later, Viljamaa, *Studies*, 104 again refers to the circus faction riots, but also, somewhat confusingly, the Trojan War and horse, going back to the Odysseus reference above. Cameron, 'Empress', 237, n. 82 would restore πτολίεθρον Ἀμ[ιδαίων...] (recto 22) referring to the 505 capture of Amida during Anastasios' Persian War. He suggests that this poem may be the lost *Persika* of Kollouthos, since there is another reference to the Persians (recto 14) and he sees no evidence for an Isaurian war; contra his earlier proposal, Cameron, 'Wandering Poets', 481, n. 64 that this is indeed the lost *Isaurika* of Pamprepios.
[57] Menander, ed. Russell and Wilson, 92–3 (376.24ff.).
[58] McCail, 'P. Gr. Vindob. 29788C', 60.
[59] See Kollouthos' use of χθιζόν and χθιζός, *Rape of Helen*, ed. Mair, 568, ll.374 and 380; see Livrea, *Pamprepii Panopolitani carmina*, 42.

However, if the poem was composed in the later years of Anastasios' reign, this section arguably concerns the rebellion of Vitalian, which began in 514.[60] The description τις ἀγηνορέων αἰζήιος is equally fitting for Vitalian, and Anastasios' ἐλπωρή ('every hope', recto 25) may well have been shaken as Vitalian threatened the imperial city itself no less than three times. His demands (apart from the usurpation of the throne, which he was careful to deny) included the restoration of the *annona* owed to the federal troops (*foederati*) in Thrace, the healing of the schism with the Church of Rome, and the re-instatement of the deposed Chalcedonian patriarchs, Makedonios and Flavius.

Prior to Vitalian's rebellion there had been a 'hurling of stones' in the 512 Trishagion, described by Marcellinus *comes*: 'Celerem et Patricium senatores ad se supplicandi sibi vel satisfaciendi gratia missos iactis pluviae instar lapidibus reppulerunt.'[61] In this case, however, instead of the usual hurling of stones, there was a 'sport strange to the populace', perhaps a reference to the use of elemental sulphur (θεῖον ἄπυρον), hurled by the imperial forces onto the rebel ships, which immediately caught fire and sank.[62] This explanation fits far better with ἀμάθυνεν in the following line, the basic meaning of which is 'to reduce to dust, by fire'.[63] There are also plenty of candidates for εἰρήνης ἀδίδακτον ὀμήλικα ('[his] equal-in-age uninstructed in peace', recto 29) if McCail is right that ὀμήλικα is the subject of ἔπαλλεν (recto 30). The commander in the sea battle was the praetorian prefect and financial minister, Marinos the Syrian, while John of Antioch's account credits the future emperor Justin with a pivotal role. Perhaps the most notable aid to the emperor's cause came from the celebrated charioteer, Porphyrius, whose achievements were recorded for posterity in a number of epigrams inscribed on the base of a statue dedicated to him.[64]

---

[60] For an account of this rebellion, see Haarer, *Anastasius*, 164–79; also A. Laniado, 'Jean d'Antioche et les débuts de la révolte de Vitalien' in P. Blaudeau and P. Van Nuffelen, eds., *L'historiographie tardo-antique et la transmission des savoirs* (Berlin, 2015), 349–70.

[61] *MGH AA* 11, 97–8 (512); Marcellinus *Comes*, *Chronicle*, trans. Croke, 36 (512: 'They drove back with a storm of stones the senators Celer and Patricius, who had been sent to placate and satisfy them.')

[62] Malalas, *Chronographia*, ed. Thurn, 332; Evagrius, *Ecclesiastical History*, ed. Bidez and Parmentier, 145–6 (III.43); R. H. Charles, ed. and trans., *Chronicle of John, Bishop of Nikiu* (London, 1916), 131 (LXXXIX.81–4); see also David Gwynn's chapter in the present volume.

[63] McCail himself ('P. Gr. Vindob. 29788C', 52) gives comparable references with this meaning from Homer, *Iliad*, IX.589, and adds that it is frequently used with this meaning in Nonnos' *Dionysiaka*.

[64] Paton, ed., *Greek Anthology*, vol. v, 154 (XV.50) and 366–8 (XVI.347–50), with A. Cameron, *Porphyrius the Charioteer* (Oxford, 1973), 126–30.

The last lines (recto 33–4) are too fragmentary to make sense of.[65] There is also the detached top of folio 29788B, the first page of the binion, to consider. On its recto are lines 28–33 of the autumn/spring idyll. On its verso are the remains of six lines that include a comparison with a Constantine, followed by a lacuna with space for about seven lines, followed by the beginnings of three lines. It is unclear, however, whether they form part of the comparative section and epilogue of this hexameter encomium, or if they come from a separate poem.[66] They provide little help with the identification of poet or honorand.[67]

Metre and Literary Style

It should be apparent from this analysis of the historical context that the proposal of Anastasios as the honorand is equally plausible, if not more so, than that of Zeno. As for the poet, all are agreed that he was a proficient exponent of the style of Nonnos, but it is hard to find particular identifying features, since so many poets right up to the seventh century strove to emulate the strict rules of Nonnos' hexameters, especially in maintaining his high standards in achieving almost perfect correctness in his quantities.[68] The level of success of Nonnos' disciples means that it is

---

[65] McCail, 'P. Gr. Vindob. 29788C', 52, 62.
[66] McCail (ibid., 63) believes that it is possible that these lines may contain the expected comparative element (Menander, ed. Russell and Wilson, 92–3 (376.31)) and epilogue containing prayers for the prosperity and continuity of the reign (Menander, 94–5 (377.28ff)), but tends to agree (52–4) with Heitsch and Gerstinger that they come from a separate poem.
[67] Viljamaa, *Studies*, 57 suggests that the Constantine mentioned was the praetorian prefect of 502–5 who had the defensive wall construction of the harbour of Constantinople completed. McCail, 'P. Gr. Vindob. 29788C', 63 suggests a reference to Constantine the Great (rather than Constantine, the consul of 457); Livrea, *Pamprepii Panopolitani carmina*, 43. If these lines did form the comparative element, a reference to Constantine the Great would not be out of place as *Anthologia Palatina* in H. Beckby, ed., *Anthologia Graeca* (Munich, 1957–8), vol. I, 110 (I.10.43) also includes a comparison between Constantine and Anicia Juliana. (I would like to thank Mary Whitby for this reference.)
[68] From the extensive bibliography on Nonnos and metre, see, for example, A. Wifstrand, *Von Kallimachos zu Nonnos* (Lund, 1933); R. Keydell, *Nonni Panopolitani Dionysiaca* (Berlin, 1959); P. Maas, *Greek Metre*, trans. H. Lloyd-Jones (Oxford, 1962); F. Vian, ed., *Nonnos de Panopolis. Les Dionysiaques* (Paris, 1976); M. J. Jeffreys, 'Byzantine Metrics: Non-literary Strata', *JÖB*, 31 (1981), 313–34; M. L. West, *Greek Metre* (Oxford, 1982); M. Whitby, 'From Moschus to Nonnus: the Evolution of the Nonnian Style' in N. Hopkinson, ed., *Studies in the Dionysiaca of Nonnus* (Cambridge, 1994), 99–155; M. Whitby, 'The St Polyeuktos Epigram: a Literary Perspective' in S. F. Johnson, ed., *Greek Literature in Late Antiquity: Dynamism, Didacticism, Classicism* (Aldershot, 2006), 159–87; D. Accorinti, ed., *Brill's Companion to Nonnus of Panopolis* (Leiden, 2016). See also the introductions to the Italian edition of the *Dionysiaka* (D. Gigli Piccardi, F. Gonnelli, G. Agosti and D. Accorinti, eds. and trans., *Le Dionisiache* (Milan, 2003–4)), and Miguélez Cavero, *Poems*, chapters 2 and 5.

often difficult to identify individual authors, though the valuable studies carried out by Mary Whitby, building on the work of Agosti and Gonnelli, show that analysis of particular metrical practices can help to bring out distinguishing features to a certain extent.[69]

One of the key features of Nonnos' metrical style was his preference for dactyls over spondees: he never allowed more than two spondees in a line and rarely in succession; he avoided ending with a double spondee; and he used a double spondee at the beginning of the line only once. Further, he limited the permutations of dactyl and spondee in the line. From Homer's thirty-two variations, Nonnos has nine and Paul Silentiarios six.[70] From the fragmentary encomium, forty-seven of the lines may (usefully) be scanned and of these, only the ends of twenty-five, only the beginnings of fourteen, and the middle section of two.[71] The lines are predominantly dactylic, and there are no cases of a double spondee in any of the parts of the line it is possible to scan. It is impossible to know the total number of different patterns, but there must be a minimum of six (compare eleven in Christodoros' 416-line *ekphrasis*,[72] eight in the twenty-one-line *Greek Anthology* IX.656 and six in the twelve-line IX.210,[73] as well as fifteen in Kollouthos' 394-line *Rape of Helen*).[74]

The anonymous poet follows Nonnos' preference for the third-foot feminine caesura (twenty) over the masculine (ten),[75] and so far as it is possible to tell, he followed Nonnos in regulating the placement of

---

[69] See especially Whitby, 'St Polyeuktos Epigram', and G. Agosti and F. Gonnelli, 'Materiali per la storia dell'esametro nei poeta Cristiani greci' in M. Fantuzzi and R. Pretagostini, eds., *Struttura e storia dell'esametro Greco* (Rome, 1955), vol. 1, 289–434.

[70] Whitby, 'St Polyeuktos Epigram', 169; Miguélez Cavero, *Poems*, 106.

[71] Verso 1–11, 13–25, recto 18 (ends): -ds (2), -dds (8), -ddds (5), -sds (4), -sdds (2), -dsds (1), -dsdds (1), -sddds (1) and –sdsds (1). Recto 8–10, 12–14, 22–7, 30–1 (beginnings): ds- (1), dddd- (4), dsdd- (1), ddsd- (1), dsds- (3), sddd- (3), sdds- (1). Verso 12, recto 11 (middle sections): both dactylic. Of the full lines (recto 15–17, 19, 28–9), there are two patterns: ddddd (4) and sdddd (2). It is important to emphasise that analysis of such a small sample of lines cannot be conclusive.

[72] Figures from F. Tissoni, *Cristodoro: Un' introduzione e un commento* (Alessandria, 2000), 70–1 (and also quoted by Whitby, 'St Polyeuktos Epigram', 172).

[73] Figures from Whitby, 'St Polyeuktos Epigram', 172.

[74] M. L. Nardelli, 'L'esametro di Colluto', *JÖB*, 32 (1982), 324.

[75] This gives a percentage of 66.66 for the third-foot feminine caesura, incidentally the same as in Paton, ed., *Greek Anthology*, vol. III, 362–4 (IX.656), higher than the 50 per cent in ibid., 108–10 (IX.210), lower than Christodoros' 73.79 per cent (ibid., vol. I, 58–90 (II)II), and lower than Kollouthos' 77 per cent. There is a bucolic caesura in twenty-one of the thirty lines (in which it is possible to tell), giving a percentage of 52.5 per cent, compared with Nonnos' 57 per cent in the *Paraphrase of St John*, 42.8 per cent in *Greek Anthology*, vol. III, 362–4 (IX.656), 20 per cent in ibid., 108–10 (IX.210), 64.33 per cent in Christodoros, *Greek Anthology*, vol. I, 58–90 (II), and 42 per cent in Kollouthos. For these figures for Nonnos, Christodoros and *Greek Anthology*, vol. III, 362–4 (IX.656), see Whitby, 'St Polyeuktos Epigram', 172.

word-end: there are no infringements of Hermann's Bridge (no word-end after the fourth trochee), Naeke's law (no word-end after a second-foot spondee), or Hilberg's law (no word-end after a fourth-foot spondee). Nonnos also regulated word accent both at the end of the line and at the caesura. Before a masculine caesura, he used only paroxytone words, which is not always the case in the ten examples in P. gr. Vindob. 29788C. The anonymous poet does, however, follow Nonnos in avoiding proparoxytone words at line-ends,[76] and he also follows Nonnos' concern to achieve a strong line-end, usually a two- or three-syllable noun or verb.[77]

Regarding metre, therefore, it is clear that the anonymous poet seeks to follow Nonnos in his preference for dactyls, his care over the placement of word-ends, and his attention to line-ends. In addition, the detailed linguistic commentary conducted by McCail reveals the poet's close adherence to the vocabulary and word order of Nonnos in almost every line.[78] There are a couple of words (ἀγηνορέων, recto 26 and ἐθήμον[α]ς, recto 30) whose earliest dated attestation is in Nonnos, but the anonymous poet, like other later writers, also uses forms that do not appear in Nonnos' works. For example, θέσπιν (verso 3) was used in the accusative in Homer, *Odyssey*, I.328 (θέσπιν ἀοιδήν), and πο]ινήτειραν (verso 10) is found only in Oppian, *Halieutika*, II.421 and Tzetzes, *Posthomerica*, III.5. Finally, Αὐσονιήων (verso 20) is found at verse-end in Nonnos, *Dionysiaka*, IV.199; Dionysios Periegetes, 78, 333, 467; *Encomium Heraclii Ducis* I (Heitsch I.xxxiv); and Christodoros, *Greek Anthology*, II.398. There are a number of rare forms, such as the singular form ἐλώριον (recto 12), which is found only in *Greek Anthology*, II.264 and *Greek Anthology*, IX.154.3; the rare plural form σαοφροσύνῃσι (recto 16) that occurs in this place only in Homer, *Odyssey*, XXIII.30 and Oppian, *Halieutika*, III.359; and οἰζύας

---

[76] Where it is possible to tell, 65.5 per cent are paroxytone (a little lower than Nonnos' 72 per cent but similar to Kollouthos' 63 per cent).
[77] Whitby, 'St Polyeuktos Epigram', 174.
[78] The instances are too numerous to quote but see, for example, McCail, 'P. Gr. Vindob. 29788C', 45: the line-end: ἀπελύσαο δεσμῶν (verso 15). See Homer, *Iliad*, I.401; Nonnos, *Dionysiaka*, ed. Vian, vol. v, 135 (XIII.27), vol. VIII, 62 (XXI.66) and vol. IX, 103 (XXVI.140); McCail, 'P. Gr. Vindob. 29788C', 46:]ν ἔσω βασιληΐδος αὐλῆς (verso 19) where the vocabulary and rhythm at the line-end are very close to Nonnos, *Dionysiaka*, vol. IV, 40 (IX.162), vol. VIII, 66 (XXI.171) and vol. VI, 33 (XIV.247), A. Scheindler, ed., *Nonni Panopolitani Paraphrasis S. Evangelii Joannei* (Lipsiae, 1881), I.148, XVIII.77; and McCail, 'P. Gr. Vindob. 29788C', 49: αὐχένα γαῦρον (recto 14), a frequent line beginning in Nonnos, *Dionysiaka*, vol. II, 26 (III.125), vol. VII, 46 (XVIII.62). The placing of δεδόνητο (recto 25) is familiar from Nonnos, who uses it fifteen times in this place in the line, and the καί τις (recto 26) is a classic Nonnian line opening used to illustrate and amplify a narrative twenty-six times in the *Dionysiaka* (see McCail, 'P. Gr. Vindob. 29788C', 51).

Anonymous Textual Survivals from Late Antiquity 537

(verso 9) for which the plural is found nowhere else. He also uses several rare adjectives, such as ἀδερκέος (verso 2), which is found only in Agathias, *Greek Anthology*, XI.372.1: ἀδερκέι σύμπνοον αὔρῃ.[79]

Along with this rare vocabulary (or at least forms) is some fairly strong and rich language and imagery. The fragment (verso 4ff.) opens with the evocative, if not uncommon, metaphor of pursuit suggested by the verb ἀ]νιχνεύειν, followed by the familiar comparison of a warrior likened to a lion. Later (recto 9), the poet uses the idea of spring (ἔαρ) metaphorically in the context of the emperor's good government (εὐνομίης). Strong language is found with the verb κατέθλασε[(recto 11), meaning 'to crush' or 'to trample underfoot', only found in the Septuagint and Christian authors, and it is much stronger than the usual θλάω, while the compound χρυσοχίτωνος (recto 13) is a good example of the colourful vocabulary employed by the poet.[80]

Conclusions: the Poetic Landscape of the Fifth and Sixth Centuries

The analysis of metre and language reveals a poet working in the Nonnian tradition, and at pains to produce a vivid portrayal of his subject. Although there are a number of similarities in metre and choice of language, the fragmentary nature of the text, which makes it difficult to produce a full metrical study and to show a clear comparison with any one poet, means that the question of authorship remains unresolved.[81] To assume Zeno incapable of finding a poet willing to celebrate his achievements is to fall into the trap of believing the bad press generated by the Greek historians (and probably encouraged by Anastasios) about Zeno.[82] It is true, however, that if the poem did celebrate Zeno's triumph over Illos in 488, it would be hard to name one of the recognised Zenonian poets as the author, since all had perished in one way or another.[83] It is also true that,

---

[79] 'Made of breadth like the invisible wind.' Paton, ed., *The Greek Anthology*. For the above examples, see McCail, 'P. Gr. Vindob. 29788C', 43–52.
[80] For references, see McCail, 'P. Gr. Vindob. 29788C', 43–8.
[81] For example, Viljamaa, *Studies*, 57–8 points out a number of similarities between Christodoros' *ekphrasis* and the hexameter poems, especially the idyll and Theagenes encomium, but he admits that these are predominantly common Nonnian features.
[82] R. C. Blockley, ed. and trans., *Malchus. Fragments*, in *The Fragmentary Classicising Historians of the Later Roman Empire: Eunapius, Olympiodorus, Priscus and Malchus* (Liverpool, 1981–3), vol. II, 410–11 (fr. 5), 412–15 (7), 422–5 (16.2), 450–3 (22); Evagrius, *Ecclesiastical History*, ed. Bidez n Parmentier, 99–100 (III.1–2); Joshua, *Chronicle*, ed. Wright, 12; Prokopios, *Anekdota*, ed. J. Haury et al., *Procopius Caesariensis. Opera omnia* (Munich, 2001), vol. III, 149 (XXIV.17).
[83] For example, Pelagius, Panolbius, Aetherius and Pamprepios himself, as discussed above.

on the whole, the adjacent reigns (those of Zeno and Justin) reveal much less literary activity than the Anastasian years, during which relative stability and economic prosperity allowed for a high level of cultural activity in provincial centres, such as Gaza, and Constantinople, where imperial patronage of intellectuals and literary figures encouraged several panegyrical works.[84]

The most well-known examples are, of course, the Latin verse encomium of Priscian of Caesarea, written at the imperial court in Constantinople, and the Greek prose encomium composed by Prokopios of Gaza and delivered before a statue of the emperor in Gaza.[85] There is also Kollouthos of Lykopolis who, from his native Egypt, composed a *Persika* celebrating Anastasios' Persian War victory, in addition to the *Kalydoniaka* (a mythical work in six books about the hunting of the Kalydonian boar) and the extant *Rape of Helen*.[86] It has been argued that this work drew on the poem *Hero and Leander*, the only extant work of the poet Musaeus, also believed to have flourished at the end of the fifth and beginning of the sixth century.[87] Shared stylistic features as well as hints of Neoplatonic thinking familiar from, for example, the *Hymns* of Proklos, suggest a close relationship with the School of Gaza, a link made more probable if this

---

[84] E. M. Jeffreys, 'Writers and Audiences in the Early Sixth Century' in Johnson, ed., *Greek Literature in Late Antiquity*, 137. The so-called School of Gaza flourished at the turn of the century, providing a home to numerous scholars, including Zosimos of Askalon, Eutocius (also from Askalon) and Timothy of Gaza. From the extensive bibliography on the Gazan school, see most recently, for example, B. Bitton-Ashkelony and A. Kofsky, eds., *Christian Gaza in Late Antiquity* (Leiden, 2004); C. Saliou, ed., *Gaza dans l'antiquité tardive: archéologie, rhétorique et histoire. Actes du colloque international de Poitiers, 6–7 Mai 2004* (Salerno, 2005); T. Derda, T. Markiewicz and E. Wipszycka, eds., *Alexandria: Auditoria of Kom el-Dikka and Late Antique Education* (Warsaw, 2007).

[85] Chauvot, *Procope*; Coyne, *Priscian*; Nicks, 'Literary Culture'.

[86] Suda K.1951; ed. I. Bekker, ed., *Suidae Lexicon* (Berlin, 1854), p. 614; Viljamaa, *Studies*, 31; E. Livrea, *Colluthus, Il ratto di Elena* (Bologna, 1968); P. Orsini, *Collouthos: L'enlèvement d'Hélène* (Paris, 1972); M. Minniti Colonna, 'Sul testo e la lingua di Colluto', *Vichiana*, 8 (1979), 70–93; O. Schönberger, ed., *Kollouthos: Raub der Helena* (Würzburg, 1993); Nardelli, 'L'esametro'; Miguélez Cavero, *Poems*, 28–9.

[87] For a summary of views and bibliography, see Miguélez Cavero, *Poems*, 25–7. See especially A. Ludwich, ed., *Musaios. Hero und Leandros* (Bonn, 1912); E. Malcovati, *Museo, Ero e Leandro* (Milan, 1946); H. Färber, ed., *Hero und Leander: Musaios und die weiteren antiken Zeugnisse gesammelt und übersetzt* (Munich, 1961); T. Gelzer, 'Bemerkungen zur Sprache und Text des Epikers Musaios', *MusHelv*, 24 (1967) 129–48; T. Gelzer, 'Bemerkungen zur Sprache und Text des Epikers Musaios', *MusHelv*, 25 (1968) 11–47; P. Orsini, *Musée: Héro et Léandre* (Paris, 1968); K. Kost, ed., *Musaios, Hero und Leander* (Bonn, 1971); C. A. Trypanis, T. Gelzer and C. H. Whitman, eds. and trans., *Callimachus, Aetia, Iambi, Lyric Poems, Hecale, Minor Epic and Elegiac Poems and Other Fragments* (Cambridge, MA, 1975); M. Minniti Colonna, 'De Musaeo', *Vichiana*, 5 (1976), 65–86; E. Livrea and P. Eleuteri, *Musaeus, Hero et Leander* (Leipzig, 1982); H. Morales, 'Gender and Identity in Musaeus' *Hero and Leander*' in R. Miles, ed., *Constructing Identities in Late Antiquity* (New York, NY, 1999), 41–69.

Musaeus could be identified as the Musaeus who was the recipient of two letters from Prokopios of Gaza.[88]

There is more evidence for a number of literary circles in Constantinople. Intellectuals, such as the court prefect, Turcius Rufius Apronianus Asterius (known for his verses and work in editing and publishing), the praetorian prefects, Leontios (a previous professor of law at Beirut) and Sergios (also a lawyer as well as a writer and sophist), all add substance to John Lydos' claims that Anastasios promoted men of literary talent. In the literary circle that no doubt evolved around the celebrated grammarian, Priscian, it is possible to tease out some probable members.[89] His treatise, the *Grammatical Institutions*, was commissioned by the patrician and honorary consul, Julian, whom Priscian describes as excelling in every branch of learning, both Greek and Latin. It is possible, though not proven, that this Julian was the praetorian prefect of 530–1, Julian the Egyptian, who contributed a number of epigrams to the *Greek Anthology*. Two of these poems commemorate the death of Theodore, a collector of poems, who may be identified with Theodore, the grammarian and pupil of Priscian who edited the *Ars grammatica* in 526/7.[90] Julian also composed two ἐπιτύμβια for Anastasios' nephew, Hypatios, who had been the unwilling choice of the mob to replace Justinian as emperor during the *Nika* riot, and for Hypatios' grandson, John.[91] Theodore was a *memorialis* of the *scrinium epistularum* and an auditor of the *quaestor sacri palatiii*, and along with Julian the Egyptian, he would have started his career during the reign of Anastasios and benefited from his patronage.

Finally, I come to Christodoros of Koptos to whom the Suda attributes an *Isaurika* in six books, six *patria* (Constantinople, Thessalonike, Nakle, Miletos, Tralles and Aphrodisias), the *Lydiaka* of which a couple of verses survive in a scholium (*Schol.* A *ad Hom. Il.*, 2.461), and elusively 'καὶ ἄλλα πολλά'. He also wrote a poem, *On the Disciples of the Great Proklos* of which a hexameter verse remains in John Lydos' *On the Magistricies* 3.26.[92]

---

[88] A. Garzya and R. Loenertz, eds., *Procopii Gazaei Epistolae et declamationes* (Ettal, 1963), 165 and 177; see K. Seitz, *Die Schule von Gaza* (Heidelberg, 1982), 37ff.; Gelzer, 'Bemerkungen' (1967), 138–41; Gelzer, 'Bemerkungen' (1968), 11, 17, 21; Kost, *Musaios*, 17; T. Gelzer, 'Musaeus: Hero and Leander', in Trypanis, Gelzer and Whitman, eds., *Callimachus, Aetia, Iambi*, 12–22; Miguélez Cavero, *Poems*, 26.
[89] See M. Salamon, 'Priscianus und sein schülerkreis in Konstantinopel', *Philologus*, 123 (1979), 91–6; Nicks, 'Literary Culture', 184–5.
[90] Paton, ed., *Greek Anthology*, vol. II, 318 (VII.594–5).   [91] Ibid., 316 (VII.590–2).
[92] A. Adler, ed., *Suidae Lexicon* (Leipzig, 1928–38), x.525 (and arguably x.526, although this second entry, a *vir illustris* from the Thebaid, credited with a hexameter *Ixeutica* and a work on the *Miracles of the Saints Anargyros, Cosmas and Damian*, is likely to refer to another Christodoros). For general

These works are, in addition to the extant epigrams, composed in honour of the prefect of Illyricum, John of Epidamnos (*Greek Anthology*, VII.697, 698), and the ekphrasis on the statues of the baths of Zeuxippos preserved in the second book of the *Greek Anthology*. This work contains the panegyrical lines to Anastasios (II.398–406) suggesting that Christodoros enjoyed imperial patronage and composed the poem in Anastasios' honour.[93] It is possible that an introductory iambic prologue including explicit praise of Anastasios, rather like Paul Silentiarios' prologue to his *Description of St Sophia*, may have been lost when the poem was incorporated into the *Greek Anthology*.[94] Work has also been done to try to establish whether Christodoros was responsible for one or both of two anonymous poems in the *Greek Anthology*, IX.210, a preface to a work by Urbicius on military tactics that lists Anastasios' various campaigns; and IX.656, a description of the Chalkē Gate, restored by Anastasios and said to surpass all other wonders. Although the results are somewhat inconclusive as yet, it is true that IX.656 shares many stylistic and metrical similarities with the hexameters of Christodoros, including the use of the –φόνος compounds ('Ισαυροφόνος and τυραννοφόνος).[95] But there are also similarities between the epigrams composed in honour of the charioteer Porphyrius (*Greek Anthology*, XV.50, XVI.347, 348, 349, 350), and the epigram composed for Anicia Juliana's church of St Polyeuktos (*Greek Anthology* I.10).[96]

---

works and comments on Christodoros, see F. Baumgarten, *De Christodoro poeta Thebano* (Bonn, 1881); F. Baumgarten, 'Christodoros', *RE*, 3 (1899), 2450–2; Cameron, 'Wandering Poets', 475, 489; Cameron, *Porphyrius*, 154; Viljamaa, *Studies*, 31; Nicks, 'Literary Culture', 185; Tissoni, *Cristodoro*; F. Tissoni, 'Cristodoro e Callimaco', *Acme*, 53 (2000), 213–18; Jeffreys, 'Writers'; Miguélez Cavero, *Poems*, 31–3.

[93] A number of recent studies have considered Christodoros' ekphrasis from various perspectives, including the archaeological, literary and Neoplatonist; see C. Mango, *The Brazen House: A Study of the Vestibule of the Imperial Palace of Constantinople* (Copenhagen, 1959), 37–42; R. Stupperich, 'Das Statuenprogramm in den Zeuxippos-Thermen', *IstMitt*, 32 (1982), 210–35; H. D. Saffrey, 'Théologie et anthropologie d'après quelques préfaces de Proclus' in C. Laga, ed., *Images of Man in Ancient and Medieval Thought, Mélanges Gérard Verbeke* (Leuven, 1976), 199–212; S. Guberti Bassett, 'Historiae Custos: Sculpture and Tradition in the Baths of Zeuxippos', *AJA*, 100 (1996), 491–506; Tissoni, *Cristodoro*, 20–2, 37–44; M. Whitby, 'The Vocabulary of Praise in Verse-celebrations of 6th-century Building Achievements: Anthologia Palatina, AP 2.398–406, AP 9.656, AP 1.10, and Paul the Silentiary's Description of St. Sophia' in D. Accorinti and P. Chuvin, eds., *Des Géants à Dionysos. Mélanges offerts à F. Vian* (Alexandria, 2003), 593–606; S. Bassett, *The Urban Image of Late Antique Constantinople* (Cambridge, 2004); A. Kaldellis, 'Christodoros on the Statues of the Xeuxippos Baths: a New Reading of the *Ekphrasis*', *GRBS*, 47 (2007), 361–83.

[94] Tissoni, *Cristodoro*, 50, 63; followed by Whitby, 'Vocabulary', 595–6.

[95] Paton, ed., *Greek Anthology*, vol. I, 88 (II.399); vol. III, 362–4 (IX.656.1, 19); see Baumgarten, *De Christodoro*, 60; Viljamaa, *Studies*; Tissoni, *Cristodoro*; Whitby, 'Vocabulary', 597ff.

[96] See the arguments presented by Cameron, *Porphyrius*; Tissoni, *Cristodoro*, 21–3; Whitby, 'Vocabulary'; and Whitby, 'St Polyeuktos Epigram'.

That it is impossible to prove Christodoran authorship of any or all of these poems is indicative of the problem in trying to pinpoint one poet among the known (and indeed anonymous) exponents of the Nonnian tradition. Interestingly, it is this difficulty that underlines the general point that poetry of a high quality in both metrical and literary style was still being produced in sixth-century Constantinople, as is evident, for example, from many of the contributions to the *Greek Anthology*. As to the investigation of the authorship and recipient of P. gr. Vindob. 29788C, I conclude that, alongside the further elucidation of its historical context, fleshing out the lively literary scene in the first decades of the sixth century at least strengthens the argument for Anastasios as the honorand.

Further Reading

The main sources are: A. Chauvot, ed., *Procope de Gaza, Priscien de Césarée, panégyriques de l'empereur Anastase Ier* (Bonn, 1986); E. Livrea, ed., *Pamprepii Panopolitani carmina (P. Gr. Vindob. 19788 A-C)* (Leipzig, 1979). For background, see: F. K. Haarer, *Anastasius I: Empire and Politics in the Late Roman World* (Cambridge, 2006); T. Viljamaa, *Studies in Greek Encomiastic Poetry of the Early Byzantine Period* (Helsinki, 1968); R. C. McCail, 'P. Gr. Vindob. 29788C: Hexameter Encomium on an Unnamed Emperor', *JHS*, 98 (1978), 38–63.

Appendix

E. Livrea, *Pamprepii Panopolitani carmina* (P. Gr. Vindob. 29788 A–C) (Leipzig 1979).

[1 verso]

]βασι[λῆο]ς [ἐφετμ]άς
    ]ν ἀδερκέος ἐλ[π]ίδι φήμης
    ]ρτεν, ἔδεκτο δὲ θέσπιν ἀνωγήν
    ἀ]νιχνεύειν βασιλήων·
5   ]ο· λέων ἀλάπαξε καλιάς
    ]τάτῃ μόνος ἴχνια θήρης
    ]ων ἐγκύμονας ἄνδρας ἐλάσσας
    ἔδυ]σαν ὑπὸ σπήλυγγα μελάθρων
    ]ς ἐδίδα[σκ]εν ὀιζύας· οἱ δὲ πεσόντες
10   πο]ινήτειραν ἀναστενάχοντες ἀνάγκην
    ]πατρῴων κτεάνων ῥίψα[ντε]ς ἀέ[λλαις
    ]γεγά[ασ]ιν ἑλώριον αλλα[.].θεον[
    ]υ.. [. . . . . .]. .[. . . . .] . [. .]. τρον ἐλέγξας
    στε]ρεῇσιν ἀκουαῖς
15   ]. ἀπελύσαο δεσμῶν
    ] . . .ς ἔργον ἀνάπτων
    ὑπέ]ρτερα μᾶλλον ἀείσω
    ]ηκαο πᾶσιν ἀρήγων
    ]ν ἔσω βασιληίδος αὐλῆς
20   ]σι σὺν ἀνδράσιν Αὐσονιήων
    ]πολλοὶ δέ τε παῖδες ἀοιδῶν
    μι]ῆς ἥπτοντο τραπέζης
    φ]ερέσβιος ἦσθα πορείη
    ]χης πάντεσσι τιταίνων
25   ]υκες εὖχ[ο]ς ἀοιδαῖς
    ].τι.[. . . . . . .ε]λθών
    ]ος

[1 recto]

τ]οιο[
τ]οσσα[
...].[
ἀ[ρ]γυρέη[
σοὶ γὰρ[
αὐτοκασ[ιγνητ
διογενη[ς
ἐς πυμάτην πιπ[τ . . . .] Αἴγυ[πτον
πᾶσι μὲν εὐνομίης ἀνύσας ἔαρ ε[
ἀ[μπ]λακίης θρέπτειραν ἀτασθάλο[υ
. . . . . .]. . . θαλάμοιο κατέθλασε[
ἔνθα μὲν εὐνήσας ὑπερήνορα .[
ἔνθα δὲ χρυσοχίτωνος ὑπόπτερ[ος
αὐχένα γαῦρον Ἄρηος Ἀχαιμενί[δ
τοῖς ἐὼν βασιλεύς τ' ἀγαθὸς κρατε[ρός τε μαχητῆς
σῆσι σαοφροσύνησι τεὴν παρακάτθ[εο Ῥώμην·
πατρίδα τ[ο]ῖος ἐὼν ἐπιδευέα κηδεμονή[ων
τοῖς [. . . . . . . ἐπι]δήμιον ἴχνος ἐρ<ε>ίσας
ημ . .[. . . . ἐτέλεσσα]ς ὃ μὴ κάμε δῖος Ὀδυσσεύς
                    ] .[.] . . [   ] . . .
εἰ καὶ ιρ. . . σ .ν . οισ[. .] . . [.] . . [
χθιζὸν γὰρ πτολίεθρον ἀμ[ηχανέον
ἵμερος ὠλεσίπατρις ἐρύκ[ακε
πᾶσα δὲ λωβητῆρι περιζως[θεῖσα
ἐλπωρὴ δεδόνητο γαληναίῳ[
καί τις ἀγηνορέων αἰζήιος ε . .[
θαρσαλέ[ως] σῴζων· φονίη δ' οἰστρ[
ἐμφύ[λο]υ στονόεσσαν ἐδύσατο λ[ύσσαν ἐνυοῦς
εἰρήνης ἀδίδακτον ὁμήλικα λάε[σι τύψας·
οὐ μὲν λᾶας ἔπαλλεν ἐθήμον[α]ς .[
δήμου ξεῖνον ἄθυρμα φονοσ[ταγέος
. . .] υ[.]λαν ἀμάθυνεν αχειρ[
. . . .]χατ[.] . [
. . . . . .] . σ . [. . . . .] . [

2

]ε δίκης κοσμήτορι[
σ]αόφρονι Κωστα[ντίνῳ
]τόσσον φίλος ὅσσο[ν
] ὅσσον Διὶ Φοῖβος [Ἀπόλλων
]ωσι ταν[ὑπ]τερο[
]νε[. . . .]νω[

(septem fere versus desunt)

αμ[
παν[   ]λ.[
εισ[   ]κε[

Translation[97]

1 Verso

... the commands of the emperor
... by the hope of invisible rumour
... and he received the divine command
... to track down ... of the rulers;
5   ... and like a lion he plundered their lair
... alone the footprints of (his) quarry
... having driven men swollen with ...
... they entered beneath the caves of (their) dwelling
... he taught them woes; and they, having fallen
10 ... bewailing avenging necessity
... having cast away in a whirlwind ... of ancestral possessions
... (they) are become a prey; but ...
... having put to shame(?) ...
... with stern ears
15 ... you did release from bonds
... kindling ... to(?) the task
... I shall rather sing of things more elevated than these
... you did ... bringing help to all
... inside the royal palace
20 ... together with men of the Ausonians
... while many sons-of-poets
... were touching ... table
... you were a life-giving way
... proffering to all ...
25 ... glory in songs
... having come
...

[97] This translation is based closely on that given by McCail, 'P. Gr. Vindob. 29788C', 42, except where his text differs from Livrea's edition.

1 Recto

      ...
      so many(?) ...
      ...
      silver ...
5   since for you ...
      own-brother ...
      Diogenes ...
      to farthest ... Egpyt
      having achieved for all a spring-time of good government ...
10   the wicked nurturer of sin ...
      ... he crushed ... of the bed-chamber.
      In one place having stilled the overweening ...
      and in another place with swift wing. .. of the gold-tunicked ...
15   ... the proud neck of Persian Ares.
      Being such a man, both a good king and a strong warrior,
      to your moderation did you entrust your Rome;
      being such a guardian to the fatherland in need
      therefore having planted your(?) footstep ... at home
20   ... you accomplished ... which goodly Odysseus did not
      accomplish by toil
      ...
      Even although ...
      for yesterday the city lacking resources ...
      lust to destroy the fatherland restrained ...
25   and every hope of the peaceful emperor had been shaken, beset
      by destructive ...
      and an arrogant young man ...
      boldly saving; and driven madly on(?) by murderous ...
      entered the lamentable frenzy of internecine war
      having beaten with stones (his) unequal-in-age uninstructed in
      peace.
30   But it was not the customary stones that they(?) were hurling
      (but?) ...
      a sport strange to the populace dripping blood
      ... reduced to dust, ... hand(?) ...
      ...
      ...

2
```
        ... orderer of justice ...
        ... to sober Constantine ...
        ... as dear as ...
        ... as Phoebus Apollo to Zeus ...
5       ... with extended wings ...
        ...
        (septem fere versus desunt)
        ...
        ...
        ...
```

CHAPTER 24

Authorship and the Letters *of Theodore Daphnopates*
John Duffy

Among the surviving writings attributed to Theodore Daphnopates, the high imperial official of the tenth century,[1] is a series of letters preserved mainly in a single manuscript from Patmos and numbering thirty-five pieces.[2] The first complete critical edition of these texts, with French translation, was published more than thirty years ago by J. Darrouzès and L. G. Westerink.[3] In addition, their work included an important appendix in which were edited and translated, with equal care, a further five letters from a Vienna manuscript, transmitted anonymously, but for which Darrouzès and Westerink had one or two reasons for believing that they might belong to Daphnopates.[4] The linchpin was the fact that a sixth item in the same Vienna group was also partially preserved in the Patmos collection. The presence, then, of the one identifiable letter in the Vindobonensis group led the editors to suspect that the other five might have been written by the same author. In the end, however, they decided to treat the matter conservatively and opted to confine those five pieces (nos. 36–40) to an appendix, because attribution remained somewhat problematic.

In the course of their further discussion of the problem, Darrouzès and Westerink remark that the five unassigned Vienna letters contain nothing,

---

[1] Daphnopates (see *ODB*, vol. 1, 588), whose dates are not fully known, died sometime after 961; in the course of his career in Constantinople he held the titles of *protasekretis, patrikios* and *magistros*. There is a general account of his various writings in the introduction to J. Darrouzès and L. G. Westerink, eds., *Théodore Daphnopatès. Correspondance* (Paris, 1978), and A. Kazhdan in *A History of Byzantine Literature, 850-1000*, ed. C. Angelidi (Athens, 2006) devotes several pages (153–5) to a discussion of the correspondence, though without touching on any of the issues treated in the present essay.
  The present contribution was originally submitted before the appearance of D. Chernoglazov, 'Beobachtungen zu den Briefen des Theodoros Daphnopates. Neue Tendenzen in der byzantinischen Literatur des zehnten Jahrhunderts,' *BZ*, 106 (2013), 623–44. Happily, on the question of authorship, both of us are 'on the same page' and our different approaches to the issue nicely complement each other.

[2] MS Patmensis 706, 289v–366r.   [3] See n. 1.   [4] Vindobonensis Phil. gr. 342, 91v–111r.

from the point of view of either content or style, that would definitely rule out their composition by Daphnopates.[5] Further, in a slightly more positive vein, they venture to suggest that, whatever obstacles might otherwise stand in the way, objections would be less serious in the case of two of them, numbers 36 and 37 of the appendix, which, because of their descriptive character, shared a similar style with numbers 12 and 14 from the Patmos copy. This was about as far as the two editors were prepared to go in making an argument in favour of Daphnopates as author of the anonymous items in the Vienna manuscript.

The purpose of the present chapter is to focus on those four letters now in question (12, 14, 36, 37), to explore in more detail the nature of the comparable style hinted at by Darrouzès and Westerink, and to highlight some elements in them that, while not individually conclusive, might help in a cumulative way to bolster the case for assigning them with more confidence to Daphnopates.

The correspondence, as found in the Patmos copy, contains a variety of letter types that may be divided loosely in the first instance into official (nos. 1–16) and private (17–35). Each of these broad categories in turn contains different kinds of writing, varying from documents composed in the name of the emperor (by Daphnopates in his role as *protasekretis*), to correspondence with church prelates on issues of orthodox dogma, to ostensibly more private communications with emperors, officials and friends, and on topics as different as gratitude for a gift, good wishes for a happy event or salutations to accompany a present. But over and above those distinctions one can point to two letters in particular (12 and 14) in which Daphnopates moves beyond the ordinary, in thought and expression, and clearly makes a special effort to compose vivid descriptions. Letter 12, truncated in the Patmensis, but complete (as mentioned already) in the Vindobonensis, is addressed to Constantine VII Porphyrogennetos. Written as a report on the state of a funerary encomium that Daphnopates was preparing in the countryside at the request of the emperor, it turns into more of an evocation of pleasant activities associated with the harvesting of the vine, and above all a depiction of the writer idyllically completing his assignment on the grass, under a shady oak, and surrounded by the charming sights and sounds of flowers, birds and gentle breezes. Letter

---

[5] 'Les Lettres 36–40 ne contiennent rien, ni quant au contenu, ni quant au style, qui exclurait absolument la paternité de Daphnopatès', followed by a note of caution, 'Ce n'est pas à dire qu'il n'y ait pas de difficultés' (Theodore Daphnopates, *Correspondance*, eds. Darrouzès and Westerink, 26).

14 is a letter of thanks to Emperor Romanos II, who had sent the author some of the game from a recent hunt, a goat, a hare and a partridge; based on how they looked on arrival, Daphnopates comments on the individual qualities of these animals and speculates in imaginative detail on the manner of their capture in the wild. Then, in the second half, he explains in concrete but still vivid terms how the imperial hunt symbolises the rout of his enemies by Romanos.

Of the two letters in the Vienna collection that are being used for comparison, number 36, written to a friend, a certain Eugenios *koubikoularios*, contains quite an extraordinary account of two storms in which the author was caught while making a round trip by sea between the capital and Pylai, the important seaport on the eastern coast of the Propontis. It is a *tour de force* of dramatic narrative and obviously the work of a consummate rhetorician and talented writer. Letter 37 also has a connection with Pylai, being addressed to Nikephoros the *xenodochos*, no doubt the director of the imperial inn in that port town. The letter is an extended idealised portrayal of the recipient's life amid the charms and pleasures of the countryside and the nearby sea: the seasons of grape-growing and wine-making, of wheat sown, harvested and carted to the storehouse, of hunting parties scouring the wooded hills and valleys, and not forgetting the calms and storms of the sea, as well as the delights of sailing and fishing. By contrast, the writer tells his friend, his own life in the city is bereft of all joys of this sort. It does, however, have the comforts that come with learning, thinking and writing.

Apart from the considerable powers of lively and acute description on display in these four letters, are there other shared elements in them that might be judged to be marks of one and the same writer?

We may begin by drawing attention again to the symbolic twist in letter 14. Having detailed in the first part in turn the physical traits of the dead goat, hare and partridge, and the manner in which each one was successfully hunted down by the emperor and his party, Daphnopates goes on to use the same animals and their characteristics to represent a series of barbarian enemies of Romanos, fierce mountain types who likewise, despite their natural instincts to hide and escape, in the end are no match for the imperial might and experience. This writerly strategy, it seems to me, is very close in spirit to the twist in the latter part of letter 37. In the body of that letter, as we have seen, the author re-creates in succession the pleasurable activities that Nikephoros the *xenodochos* enjoys on land and sea, involving grapes, wine, wheat, the hunt, sailing and fishing. Towards the end, however, despite his drawing a stark contrast between

Nikephoros' situation and his own, he makes a *volte-face* to admit that his life in the city is not without its share of pleasure. He goes on to spell out the nature of his compensations by taking in order a number of those same elements (grape, wine, etc.) and making them stand for the various aspects of his intellectual and literary existence. The passage is an attractive and interesting *apologia* of a committed literary man and deserves to be quoted in full:

> Οὐ μὴν διὰ τοῦτο καὶ χάριτος ὁ βίος ἁπάσης ἡμῖν ἄμοιρος, ἀλλὰ τρυγᾶται μὲν καὶ ἡμῖν ὁ τῆς σοφίας καὶ ἀποθλίβεται βότρυς, οἶνον ἀποστάζων ἀκήρατόν τε καὶ ἥδιστον καὶ ὅλῳ βίῳ τὴν εὐφροσύνην συμπαρατείνοντα· σῖτος δὲ συγκομίζεται λέξεών τε καθαρῶν ἐκλογὴ καὶ δοκίμων καὶ τὸ τῆς Ἑλληνικῆς καλλιεπείας εἰλικρινέστερον· θηρεύεται δὲ νοημάτων ὅσον κεκρυμμένον καὶ ὑποβρύχιον, ὅσον τε γὰρ ἐν τοῖς φύσει θεωρουμένον συνεστῶσιν φιλοσοφία αἱρεῖν ἐπαγγέλλεται. Πρὸς ἓν οὖν ἡμῖν τὸ τῶν λόγων τὸ πᾶν τῆς σπουδῆς ἀναλίσκεται. Ἐντεῦθεν οὖν ἀναπνέομεν λόγους, σιτούμεθα λόγους, πίνομεν λόγους.[6]

> For all that, our own life is not entirely bereft of charm, because we too harvest and press the grapes of learning, and these produce a pure wine of the sweetest variety that affords pleasure lasting a lifetime; we gather in the wheat, namely, our collection of pure and approved words, the very essence of refined Greek speech; we hunt down and ferret out hidden, deep-seated thoughts, because the goal of philosophy is to grasp everything contemplated in the natural world. All our efforts, then, are expended on one pursuit, literature. Hence we breathe words, we eat words, we drink words.

We will consider next a feature of all four letters that, one could argue, points in the direction of a single author. It is a fact that of all the direct and indirect allusions to secular literature in the forty letters published by Darrouzès and Westerink, some 90 per cent of them are found in letters 12, 14, 36 and 37, a state of affairs presumably to be explained in part by the type of subject-matter involved. Perhaps we can say that the writer in these instances changes his style to a more descriptive or ekphrastic mode, one in which a special charge of energy is imparted by the 'fossil fuel', as it were, of ancient literature. The great majority of these instances have their

---

[6] Ibid., 123–30 (xxxvii). This is the translation of Darrouzès and Westerink: 'Toutefois, ce n'est pas à dire que notre vie est totalement dépourvue d'attrait, car nous aussi, nous cueillons et nous pressons notre grappe, celle de l'érudition, qui distille un vin très doux et dont la jouissance dure toute une vie; le blé que nous moissonnons, c'est un recueil de mots purs et approuvés et la fleur de l'éloquence grecque; notre chasse poursuit les pensées abstruses et enfoncées dans les profondeurs, puisque la philosophie se propose de saisir tout ce qui existe dans le monde physique. Tous nos efforts se dépensent donc dans une seule occupation, la littérature. Ainsi les belles-lettres sont l'air que nous respirons, notre pain, notre boisson.'

source in Homer, but other authors detected are Herodotus, Heliodoros and Achilles Tatius. What is also noteworthy is that, except for three cases where Homer's words are flagged in a common oblique way,[7] all the other passages in question either draw no attention whatever to a literary echo or provide only a very general pointer.[8] This consistent mode of operation may be best illustrated by the ways in which allusions and echoes actually function in the text, and we should look at some instances, placing side by side the relevant extracts, with key words from the letters underlined.

Daph. 14, 14–15	Hel. *Aithiopika* 5, 14
ἔκειτο τῶν ἀερίων <u>ἁλμάτων</u> πεπαυμένος καὶ τῶν ἐπ᾽ ἀκροτόμοις <u>ἀκρωνύχων</u> ἐπιξεσμάτων	<u>ἅλμασιν ἀκρωνύχοις</u> τὴν πέτραν ἐπέξεον

'Daph.' 36, 83	Herod. VIII 74, 1
τὴν <u>περὶ τοῦ παντὸς</u> πρόφασιν, τὸ ᾀδόμενον, <u>θέοντας</u>	τὸν <u>περὶ τοῦ παντὸς</u> ἤδη δρόμον <u>θέοντες</u>

'Daph.' 37, 64–5	Hom. *Il.* 17, 676–7
Ἤδη δέ που καὶ λαγωός, <u>ὑπ᾽ ἀμφικόμῳ τῇ θάμνῳ</u> προσλιπαρῶν	πτώξ | θάμνῳ ὑπ᾽ ἀμφικόμῳ ὑποκείμενος

Daph. 12, 12–13	Hom. *Il.* 2, 307
ὑπὸ δρυῒ <u>καλῇ</u> τε καὶ σκιερᾷ, <u>ἔνθεν ῥέεν</u>, ποιητικῶς, <u>ἀγλαὸν ὕδωρ</u>	καλῇ ὑπὸ πλατανίστῳ ὅθεν ῥέεν ἀγλαὸν ὕδωρ

What these examples show is that the ancient authors are not being called into use for their own sakes nor does the letter-writer seem to be drawing on them simply as a demonstration of his personal sophistication. Rather, he is intent on borrowing appropriate ideas and artistically apt words and phrases that he then weaves seamlessly into the fabric of his text. These are carefully chosen tesserae lifted, as often as not silently, from the stock of Hellenic literature and serving to add occasional dashes of colour to the picture or (as already suggested) to impart a special charge of energy.

---

[7] Ibid., 13 (XII) ποιητικῶς; 17 (XIV) κατὰ τὴν ποίησιν; 99 (XXXVI) ποιητικῶς φάναι.
[8] Ibid., 16 (XII) φασίν; 87 (XXXVI) τὸ τοῦ λόγου; 90 (XXXVII) ὡς ἡ παροιμία φησί, all referring to Homer. Ibid., 83 (XXXVI) τὸ ᾀδόμενον points back to Herodotus, but the text is in fact anything but hackneyed, being cited (according to the TLG) only once elsewhere before the twelfth century.

The method is particularly highlighted by a series of echoes in letter 36 that went undetected by the editors. They occur in the dramatic storm scenes of that document and are unmistakably inspired by Achilles Tatius, whose novel *Leukippe* also contains an extended and animated account of a violent storm narrated by the book's hero, Kleitophon.[9] As before, the passages will be presented in parallel and marked as needed.

'Daph.' 36, 19–20
τῶν μὲν καμάτων ... ὄρεσί τε καὶ χάσμασιν ἐοικότα

Ach. Tat. 3.2.5
ἐῴκει δὲ τῶν καμάτων τὰ μὲν ὄρεσι, τὰ δὲ χάσμασιν

'Daph.' 36, 41–2 + 62–3
ὅ τε ἄνεμος, ἐμπίπτων ... συνεπαταγεῖτο τῇ ὀθόνῃ + Συνετετρίγεσαν δὲ τοῖς κάλωσιν ὅ τε ἱστός

Ach. Tat. 3.2.3
οἱ δὲ κάλοι περὶ τὴν ὀθόνην πίπτουσιν, ἀντιπαταγοῦντες δὲ ἐτετρίγεσαν

'Daph.' 36, 46–7
τὸ δὲ κῦμα πρὸς ὕψος κυρτούμενον ἔψαυε μικροῦ τῶν νεφῶν

Ach. Tat. 3.2.7
τὸ γὰρ κῦμα αἰρόμενον ὑψοῦ, ψαῦον αὐτῶν τῶν νεφῶν

'Daph.' 36, 57
ἀντεβόμβει δὲ κάτωθεν τὸ πλῆθος ... ναυτικόν

Ach. Tat. 3.2.2
ἀντεβόμβει δὲ κάτωθεν τῶν κυμάτων ἡ στάσις

'Daph.' 36, 64–5
Ἐπέφλαζε τὸ πνεῦμα, ἐπέκλυζε τὸ κῦμα ... Πάντα θρήνων, πάντα κωκυτοῦ πλήρη

Ach. Tat. 3.2.8
ἐρρόχθει τὸ κῦμα, ἐπέφλαζε τὸ πνεῦμα ... πάντα θρήνων καὶ κωκυτῶν ἀνάμεστα

[9] It may be better known nowadays as *Leucippe and Cleitophon*, but the well-educated Byzantines referred to it by the shorter title; in all periods this novel appeared on their reading lists. It is a little surprising, therefore, to see in an important study by A. Littlewood that Achilles Tatius is quoted or alluded to only five times in the letters of the twenty-three epistolographers that he examined, ranging from the fourth to the fifteenth century. The study in question is A. Littlewood, 'A Statistical Survey of the Incidence of Repeated Quotations in Selected Byzantine Letter-writers' in J. Duffy and J. Peradotto, eds., *Gonimos: Neoplatonic and Byzantine Studies Presented to Leendert G. Westerink at 75* (Buffalo, 1988), 137–54 (point at issue, 151). Incidentally, Heliodoros emerges from the survey with the same tally.

There can be no doubt about the writer's debt to Achilles Tatius, whether he is calling on lexical pieces from memory or is going back to the novel directly. It is worth stressing that, as in the case of Heliodoros in letter 14, the author of letter 36 borrows from the novelist without any hint that he is doing so, and he sometimes reuses and rearranges the older material in ways that can be strikingly different from the original.

For a final point we will consider another element of style common to the letters in both the Patmos and Vienna collections, namely, prose rhythm. It is a subject to which Darrouzès and Westerink paid little overt attention in their work,[10] but W. Hörandner was able to take advantage of the new edition and included Daphnopates in the classic study that he produced a few years later.[11]

As a representative sample, for full clausula analysis, he chose a certain number from each of the three categories of letter: nos. 1 and 2 from the official set, 22–30 from the private, and 38–40 from the anonymous batch transmitted in the Vindobonensis; he labelled these groups A, B and C respectively. The main global results of the examination may be expressed succinctly in the following terms. While all three groups conform, to a not insignificant extent, to the clausula regulations, there are appreciable differences between them. The percentage of clausulae showing either the '2' or '4' form of rhythm is (in round figures) 66 for group A, 72 for B, and 85 for C. The frequency of the 'double dactyl' rhythm, calculated separately by me using the numbers recorded in Hörandner's detailed tables, and expressed as a percentage of the total number of

---

[10] It is mentioned in a note on page 213 in Theodore Daphnopates, *Correspondance*, eds. Darrouzès and Westerink, where an emendation of Lampros is glossed by the comment 'cette forme viole la règle des clausules observée par l'auteur (nombre pair de syllabes entre les deux accents derniers)'.
[11] W. Hörander, *Der Prosarhythmus in der rhetorischen Literatur der Byzantiner* (Vienna, 1981). This monograph constitutes the most complete study of Byzantine prose rhythm in the last eighty years and it includes a short history of the scholarly development of the topic. Also see V. Valiavitcharska, *Rhetoric and Rhythm in Byzantium: The Sound of Persuasion* (Oxford, 2013). A simple formulation of the clausula 'law' would be: 'between the last two primary accents of each sentence part there should be an interval of 2 or 4 or 6 unaccented syllables.' The intervals of 0, 1, 3, 5, 7 syllables are strenuously avoided by some writers, but others are not averse to admitting them to a greater or lesser degree (and for this reason some texts can be deemed more or less 'rhythmical' than others). The most common are intervals of 2 and 4 unaccented syllables ('form 2' and 'form 4', in Hörandner's terminology), while those of 6 are found less frequently. When two unaccented syllables follow a 'form 2' (e.g. γενόμενος ὄψεως or βοτρύων ἐσπούδαστο, etc.), it produces an accentual rhythm analogous to a double dactyl in quantitative metre and hence has been given that name. The 'double dactyl' was a particular favourite with Byzantine authors, as is amply in evidence in the tables assembled by Hörandner.

It is also important to draw attention to another central fact of prose rhythm: certain 'secondary' or 'helping' words (most notably articles, conjunctions, negative particles, prepositions and some pronouns) are ambiguous in the matter of accent; normally they are regarded, for rhythm purposes, as having no accent of their own, but sometimes it happens otherwise.

clausulae in each case, is 18 (A), 20 (B) and 21 (C). The general conclusion of Hörandner, taking into account his extensive set of data, was that group A exhibits the least rhythmical prose of the three, while C shows a considerably stronger penchant to conform to the clausula 'law' than the others. He follows up these observations with a discussion of the surprising fact that of all the letters in the edition, it is the official set that turns out to be the least rhythmical. Two possible explanations are offered, and both of them are very plausible; namely, that in his chancery role Daphnopates placed more emphasis on other components of style, and that an official document by its nature will contain administrative terms, formulaic expressions and special form of address, the presence of which will give rise to clause endings that violate the rhythmical requirements. And as for the difference between groups B and C, he makes the reasonable suggestion that it may have been brought about by a difference of character.[12]

Since Hörandner did not include in his study any of the four letters on which we have been concentrating our attention, it seemed like a good idea to subject these also to a similar analysis, in order to see if this 'descriptive' subgroup could throw any interesting or instructive light on the clausula issue. Each of the four has been examined according to the standard criteria, as exemplified in the work of Hörandner; and in view of its centrality to the discussion we print here letter 12 in its entirety, with all of the clausulae marked, employing a double bar for strong pauses and a single bar for weak pauses. For the most part the marks coincide with the punctuation of the printed edition, but going further I have taken smaller units into account as well.

Κατ' ἀγροὺς ἐξιὼν τῇ κελεύσει σου, | πολυέραστε καὶ ἀγαθέ δέσποτα, | τοῖς ἀνηλίοις Κιμμερίοις ἐῴκειν εὐθύς, | μακρὰν τῆς πολυφαοῦς σου γενόμενος ὄψεως· || τοῦτο γὰρ ἀναντιρρήτως πάσχειν ἐπάναγκες | τοὺς ὅσοι τῶν σῶν δεσποτικῶν ἀκτίνων μακρόθεν ἐστήκασιν. || Ἀλλὰ τοῖς μὲν ἄλλοις ἡ συλλογὴ τῶν βοτρύων ἐσπούδαστο | καὶ ληνοβατεῖν ἐφροντίζετο | καὶ ᾄδειν ὄρεια μεμελέτητο | καὶ Διονύσῳ σπένδειν τὰ ἐπιλήνια μεμερίμνητο. || τό τε ἀποθλιβόμενον ἐκεῖνο γλεῦκος ποταμηδὸν προχεόμενον, | ᾠδικωτέρους τεττίγων τοὺς ληνοβάτας εἰργάζετο. || Ἐγὼ δ' ὡς εἶχον καὶ τάχους καὶ λογισμοῦ, | ἐτραπόμην αὐτίκα πρὸς λόγους, | ἐκεῖνα συγγράφων καὶ διασκεπτόμενος | ὅσα τε νοῦς ἀπεγέννησε | καὶ τὸ κοινὸν ἄλγος ἐπέτρεψε

---

[12] 'Mögen auch die unterschiedlichen 2+4-Werte in B einer- und C andererseits durch den verschiedenen Charakter der Stücke erklärbar sein: In den Trostbriefen 38–40 mag kunstreiche Rhythmisierung eher angestrebt sein als in den lockeren, leicht scherzhaften Briefen 22–30' (Hörandner, *Der Prosarhythmus*, 140).

| καὶ πίστις ἀκίβδηλος ἀπηνάγκασεν· || ἅ καὶ τολμηρῶς τῇ φιλαγάθῳ σου ἔστειλα βασιλείᾳ. ||
Ἀλλ' ὅρα καὶ τὸν τρόπον τῆς σκέψεως· || ὑπὸ δρυῖ καλῇ τε καὶ σκιερᾷ, | 'ἔνθεν ῥέεν' ποιητικῶς 'ἀγλαὸν ὕδωρ', | τὴν στιβάδα πηξάμενος, | τῆς γραφῆς ἀπηρχόμην. || Ἡ δὲ ἦν φύλλοις καὶ κλάδοις συνηρεφὴς καὶ κατάκομος | καὶ τἄλλα χαρίεσσά τε καὶ ἡδυτάτη. || Ὑπὸ γὰρ ῥίζαν αὐτὴν ἄνθη ἐβεβλαστήκει, | οὐχ οἷα τὰ πολλὰ καὶ πᾶσι δρεπόμενα, | ἀλλ' οἷα τῷ Διῒ φασιν ἀναδοῦναι τὴν γῆν τῇ Ἥρᾳ ἐπιμιγνυμένῳ· || αὖραι δέ τινες ὑπὲρ κεφαλῆς διαπνέουσαι | τῇ τῶν φύλλων κινήσει | πολυμελῆ τινα ἦχον ἀπετέλουν καὶ ἥδιστον. || Ἀλλὰ καὶ ὄρνιθες ὕπερθεν ἐπικλαγγάζοντες καὶ περιϊπτάμενοι | καὶ ἄλλος ἄλλο τι μέλος ἀποσυρίττων καὶ προιέμενος, | τοσοῦτον τῇ ποικίλῃ μελῳδίᾳ τὸ ἐπίχαρι καὶ μουσικὸν ἐναπέσταζον, | ὡς μικροῦ με πρὸς ὕπνον ἡδέως κατολισθήσαντα | κἄν τοῖς ὀνείροις τὸ τῆς ἡδονῆς ἀκόρεστον ἐνοπτρίζεσθαι | καὶ μὴ ἄν ποτε θέλειν τηλικούτου θεάματος ἀποστῆναι. ||
Ἀλλά μοι, τὸ μέγα θαῦμα τῆς οἰκουμένης | καὶ βασιλέων ἡ καλλονή, | καὶ ζώοις ἐπὶ μακρὸν | καὶ εὐεκτοίης ἐπὶ πολὺ | καὶ ἀνάσσοις διὰ παντός, | ἐπὶ πολλῶν μὲν καὶ ἄλλων σωτηρίᾳ, | μάλιστα δὲ ⟨τῶν⟩ τὸ γνήσιον τῆς δουλώσεως ἀκραιφνὲς διασωσάντων, | ἀλλὰ καὶ εἰς ἔτι διασωσόντων. || Αἱ δὲ μεγάλαι δωρεαὶ τῆς πλουτοποιοῦ σου βασιλείας, | ἀποδοθεῖσαι ἡμῖν διὰ τοῦ συνδούλου ἡμῶν, | τὸ περὶ πάντα σου προνοητικὸν ὑπηνίξαντο, | καὶ πλειόνως εὔχεσθαι ὑπὲρ τοῦ θείου σου κράτους διήγειραν. ||

In presenting the results below I have decided to forgo the depth of detail pursued by Hörandner in *Der Prosarhythmus*.[13] I have chosen instead to concentrate on the two most important indicators of Byzantine prose rhythm, that is to say, the '2' and '4' forms combined and the 'double dactyl', and can report the outcome in a table (Fig. 24.1) giving for both categories the percentage share of the total number of clausulae in each letter.

The numbers are indeed informative. For a start it is to be noted that within each pair, from the Patmos and Vienna copies respectively, there is a considerable variance in concentration of conforming clausulae. That is to say, the prose of letter 12 is quite a bit more rhythmical, in terms of 2+4 forms and 'double dactyl', than letter 14; and the difference is more or less

---

[13] Among other refinements he distinguishes the different types of 2 and 4 forms depending on the positions of the accents on the two primary words involved in the clausula (i.e. oxytone, paroxytone or proparoxytone), and he also calculates percentages for the occurrences for each of the other possible non-conforming (0, 1, 3 etc.) or less common intervals (6 and 8). On the latter refinement, we can say that letter 12 shows the following 'unrhythmical' clausulae: line 1 ἀγαθὲ δέσποτα (zero interval); l. 9 συγγράφων καὶ διασκεπτόμενος (5); l. 13 ἀγλαὸν ὕδωρ (0); l. 17 Ἥρᾳ ἐπιμιγνυμένῳ (5); l. 26 ἄλλων σωτηρίᾳ (3); l. 27 ἀκραιφνὲς διασωσάντων (3). There is also one instance of form 6: l. 15 ἐπικλαγγάζοντες καὶ περιϊπτάμενοι. These seven cases make up the 14 per cent of the clausulae that are outside the 2 and 4 forms in the letter.

	Patmos		Vienna	
	12	14	36	37
% 2+4	86	72	77	86
% 'dd'	38	24	22	24

Fig. 24.1 Table showing the percentage share of the total number of clausulae (© John Duffy)

the same as that between 12 and the equivalent group B (i.e. 'private' letters) in Hörandner's analysis. It is also to be observed that the clausula quotient of letter 37 is not only higher that than of 36, but is even slightly above the figures for group C.

Two general remarks for present purposes may be made. First, it can be stated with full conviction in the case of Daphnopates that the rhythmical quality of his letters varies and sometimes even dramatically, as is borne out by the figures for letters 1–2 (Hörandner's A group) in contrast to letter 12. Second, that fact itself is enough to allay any concern that, on the basis of the clausula, the letters in the Vindobonensis could not have been composed by Daphnopates.

Now as to why such variation may occur, one likely reason was suggested, as we saw, by Hörandner, who pointed to the different character of the pieces. But what about letters of a similar character, such as the four we have been examining in particular? Here other possible explanations come to mind. For instance, in the case of letter 12, one factor in favour of more pronounced rhythm could be the length of the letter. It may be supposed that it would be easier to sustain compliance with the clausula regulations over the course of a single-page document (letter 12) than over one three times that length (letter 14) or four times longer (letter 36).[14] Then again, the difference may be occasioned by the subject-matter of even a descriptive piece. Perhaps the account of an actual storm in highly dramatic language (letter 36) posed more challenges than an idyllic description of peaceful pursuits in unthreatening conditions (letter 37)?[15] Finally, it can hardly be ruled out that the intended recipient of a letter

---

[14] This is not a point that can be pushed far, but it is perhaps worth making all the same.

[15] In response to this idea an anonymous reader raises the interesting possibility of 'deliberate disruption of the clausula for dramatic effect in the account of the storm'.

This also gives me the opportunity to thank both anonymous readers for a number of helpful comments and suggestions.

might have an important bearing on its literary qualities, influencing the whole gamut of stylistic touches down to the level of rhythmical density.

In summary, we can state that the closer inspection of four of the letters edited by Darrouzès and Westerink, two from those firmly identified as belonging to Daphnopates and two whose pedigree is less secure, has revealed some shared features in manner and style of writing that may have value for helping the case in support of common authorship. In addition to the observation that letters 12, 14, 36 and 37 show a general affinity as 'descriptive' pieces, as put on record by Darrouzès and Westerink, we have picked out and emphasised still other potentially corroborative features, namely, the similarity of the symbolic 'twist' in 14 and 37, the comparable mode of employing Classical allusions in all four, and the entirely compatible results in the matter of prose rhythm. None of these elements on its own is worth much as supporting evidence, nor can one claim that the cumulative effect brings with it any measure of certainty. At the same time it can be reasonably asserted that those elements, combined with the fact that one clearly genuine letter (12) appears in both manuscripts, enhance the likelihood that letters 36 and 37 (and therefore 38–40 as well) owe their origin to Theodore Daphnopates.

Further Reading

The main source is: J. Darrouzès and L. G. Westerink, eds., *Théodore Daphnopatès. Correspondance* (Paris, 1978). Background can be found in: W. Hörandner, *Der Prosarhythmus in der rhetorischen Literatur der Byzantiner* (Vienna, 1981) and A. P. Kazhdan, *A History of Byzantine Literature, 850–1000*, ed. C. Angelidi (Athens, 2006).

CHAPTER 25

Authorship Revisited: Language and Metre in the Ptochoprodromika

Marjolijne C. Janssen and Marc D. Lauxtermann[1]

It is noticeable that the poet [of the *Ptochoprodromika*] seems in control of the linguistic medium he is using, at one moment producing lines which are purer reflections of contemporary Greek than many of the poems which were to follow, at the next, and particularly when addressing a powerful, usually imperial, patron, he raises the language level to a respectful formality ... These poems seem to us the work of a court poet, who is writing to exploit the vernacular tastes of the Comnenian aristocracy ... The poet may well have been expert in the writing of learned fifteen-syllables for ceremonial purposes; here he added personal themes and vernacular Greek, imitating contemporary oral tradition from the outside without being seriously touched by any of its formal constraints.

Thus wrote the Jeffreys in a fundamental study of Byzantine popular poetry and its oral background.[2] Reading in Byzantium is reading aloud, either in private or in public; it is by definition performative, as Elizabeth and Michael Jeffreys have argued with force and clarity in various papers dedicated to the presence of oral and formulaic elements in vernacular poetry written in the later Middle Ages, particularly in the *Chronicle of Morea* and the *War of Troy*.[3] In the above quotation they rightly emphasise

---

[1] This chapter is divided into three parts: MDL wrote the introduction and the section on metre, and MCJ the section on language. We revised the text together and the end result is very much a joint effort. Please note that the abbreviations E and HP before verse numbers refer to the editions of Eideneier and Hesseling-Pernot: H. Eideneier, ed., *Ptochoprodromos: Einführung, kritische Ausgabe, deutsche Übersetzung, Glossar* (Cologne, 1991); D. C. Hesseling and H. Pernot, eds., *Poèmes Prodromiques en grec vulgaire* (Amsterdam, 1910). The abbreviations G, H, S and other capital letters placed after verse numbers refer to the various manuscripts. We are indebted to the Grammar of Medieval Greek project at Cambridge for allowing us to make use of their extensive database and other materials. We are grateful to the two anonymous peer reviewers for their useful comments.

[2] E. M. Jeffreys and M. J. Jeffreys, 'The Oral Background of Byzantine Popular Poetry', *Oral Tradition*, 1 (1986), 517 (repr. in G. Nagy, ed., *Greek Literature in the Byzantine Period* (New York, NY, 2001), 147).

[3] See E. M. Jeffreys and M. J. Jeffreys, *Popular Literature in Late Byzantium* (London, 1983); M. J. Jeffreys, 'Proposals for the Debate on the Question of Oral Influence in Early Modern Greek Poetry'

that the *Ptochoprodromika* allude to the oral tradition, but are not part of it. This is the view of Margaret Alexiou as well, who in a seminal paper in 1986, provided ample evidence that the *Ptochoprodromika* are cleverly constructed and subtle masterpieces of rhetoric which play with the literary conventions of various genres, including those of popular ballads.[4] The latest editor of the *Ptochoprodromika*, Hans Eideneier, may not believe in oral composition, but he leaves much room for oral transmission,[5] despite the fact that, had these poems entered the oral tradition, one surely would expect traces of them to surface in the popular songs of Greece.[6]

In the case of the *Ptochoprodromika*, residues of the oral tradition, if any, are not directly related to orality as such, but are rather the result of the performative nature of the genre of begging poetry to which the texts belong. It is clear that these poems are intended for performance and lose much of their force and effectiveness on paper. The poet (or poets?) of the *Ptochoprodromika* presents himself (present themselves?) in the guise of different characters who narrate in the first person about their petty problems and their little adventures, posing as a henpecked husband, a hungry *paterfamilias*, a poor grammarian, and a lowly and abused monk. This impersonation (*ethopoeia*) needs an audience to be successful: this multitude of voices begs to be heard.[7] It is therefore reasonable to assume that these poems were performed and staged by their poet (poets) who read them aloud with varied modulations of the voice, gesticulations and appropriate facial expressions. The poems of 'Poor Prodromos' are brilliant satires in which the lives of ordinary citizens in a big city are

---

in N. M. Panayotakis, ed., *Αρχές της νεοελληνικής λογοτεχνίας* (Venice, 1993), vol. 1, 251–66. See also R. Beaton, *The Medieval Greek Romance*, second edition (London, 1996), 177–80 and 223.

[4] M. Alexiou, 'The Poverty of Ecriture and the Craft of Writing: Towards a Reappraisal of the Prodromic Poems', *BMGS*, 10 (1986), 21–5 and 32–3.

[5] Eideneier, ed., *Ptochoprodromos*, 23–8, 38–9 and 41–68; modern Greek translation: H. Eideneier, ed., *Πτωχοπρόδρομος: κριτική έκδοση* (Irakleio, 2012). Eideneier has written extensively on Ptochoprodromos, both before and after the critical edition; for a recent summary of his views, see H. Eideneier, 'Tou Ptochoprodromou' in M. Hinterberger and E. Schiffer, eds., *Byzantinische Sprachkunst: Studien zur byzantinischen Literatur gewidmet Wolfram Hörandner zum 65. Geburtstag* (Berlin, 2007), 56–76; and H. Eideneier, 'Νέα (και παλαιά) για το (Πτωχο)προδρομικό ζήτημα' in J. Alonso Aldama and O. Omatos Sáenz, eds., *Cultura neogriega, tradición y modernidad* (Bilbao, 2007), 135–41.

[6] As rightly pointed out by S. Alexiou, 'Η έκδοση του Πτωχοπροδρόμου από τον Hans Eideneier' in S. Alexiou, ed., *Δημώδη Βυζαντινά* (Athens, 1997), 116 (originally published in *Ελληνικά*, 42 (1991–2), 220–6).

[7] See R. Beaton, 'Πτωχοπροδρομικά Γ': η ηθοποιία του άτακτου μοναχού' in A. Kechagia-Lypourli and T. Petridis, eds., *Μνήμη Σταμάτη Καρατζά: ερευνητικά προβλήματα νεοελληνικής φιλολογίας και γλωσσολογίας* (Thessalonike, 1990), 101–7 (repr. in R. Beaton, *From Byzantium to Modern Greece: Medieval Texts and Their Reception* (Aldershot, 2008), no. x).

described – the way they act, the way they move, the way they talk.[8] The poet uses the vernacular as a vehicle of social criticism and colourful realism. He also creates a slapstick effect because of the contrast between the lowly characters he impersonates and the dignified figure of the court poet who declaims these poems before the emperor and his entourage.

In his edition, Eideneier has omitted the poem discovered by Maiuri,[9] even though the poem, like the other four *Ptochoprodromika*, is attributed to Theodore Prodromos, falls into the category of begging poetry and makes use of the vernacular. In his introduction he justifies this decision by dismissing Maiuri's idea that the *Ptochoprodromika* are a form of Byzantine mime theatre, and by denying any connection with Prodromos' historical poem LXXI (an open letter to Theodore Styppeiotes), as has been suggested by Maiuri and Hörandner.[10] But questions such as 'are the *Ptochoprodromika* mime texts?' or 'does the "Maiuri" poem deal with the same subject as poem LXXI?' are, of course, a matter of interpretation. And interpretative quibbles do not, by any means, justify the decision to exclude a clearly Ptochoprodromic text from the corpus. We will refer to the 'Maiuri' poem as poem no. v. It should be noted that the only manuscript to preserve this text (Vat. gr. 1823) offers the beginning, not the whole, of another Ptochoprodromic poem.

Before entering into the vexed question of the authorship of these poems, let us ask ourselves what the name 'Ptochoprodromos' actually means. Of course, the literal interpretation of this name is 'Poor Prodromos', and it obviously refers to the kind of begging poetry in which Ptochoprodromos excels. But there is more to it. The so-called *Chronicle of the Logothete* recounts how one day Michael III, mighty proud of his new stables, exclaimed that the world would remember him for building

---

[8] For an excellent literary analysis of these poems, see Alexiou, 'Poverty of Ecriture', 6–25; see also, M. Alexiou, 'Ploys of Performance: Games and Play in the Ptochoprodromic Poems', *DOP*, 53 (1999), 91–109, and M. Alexiou, *After Antiquity: Greek Language, Myth, and Metaphor* (London, 2002), 127–48. See also L. Garland, 'The Rhetoric of Gluttony and Hunger in Twelfth-century Byzantium' in W. Mayer and S. Trzcionka, eds., *Feast, Fast or Famine: Food and Drinks in Byzantium* (Brisbane, 2005), 43–55, esp. 51–5; and M. C. Janssen and M. D. Lauxtermann, 'Το παράπονο του δασκάλου: ο *Πτωχοπρόδρομος* και η βυζαντινή γραμματική παράδ' in I. García Gálvez and O. Omatos Sáenz, eds., *Tolmiros Skapaneas. Homenaje al Profesor K. A. Dimadis* (Vitoria-Gasteiz, 2012), 25–41.
[9] A. Maiuri, 'Una nuova poesia di Teodoro Prodromo in greco volgare', *BZ*, 23 (1920), 397–407.
[10] Mime: A. Maiuri, 'Un poeta mimografo bizantino', *Atene e Roma*, 13 (1910), 17–26. Poem LXXI: Maiuri, 'Una nuova poesia', 400–1; W. Hörandner, ed., *Theodoros Prodromos. Historische Gedichte* (Vienna, 1974), 65–6. Eideneier's justification: *Ptochoprodromos*, 34–7. See Hörandner's reply: W. Hörandner, 'Autor oder Genus? Diskussionsbeiträge zur "Prodromischen Frage" aus gegebenem Anlaß', *BSl*, 54 (1993), 320–2.

such a marvel of infrastructure – upon which a certain Peter the 'Poor Magistros' (Πτωχομάγιστρος) reacted as follows: 'Justinian once built the Great Church and adorned it with gold and silver and precious stones, and now his memory has faded. And you think, Emperor, that you will be remembered for this pile of muck (κοπροθέσιον), the place where you keep your horses?' Of course, when he heard this jocular remark, the emperor flew into a rage, started to hit him hard and had him thrown out.[11] As it is out of the question that a *magistros*, one of the highest titularies in ninth-century Byzantium, would be poor, Peter's nickname is a contradiction in itself, and, as such, arouses instinctive laughter. In his discussion of the passage in the *Odyssey* in which Odysseus returns to his own palace disguised as a beggar, Eustathios of Thessalonike calls this beggar Πτωχοοδυσσέα, 'Poor Odysseus'.[12] Here, too, the prefix '*ptocho-*' attached to the name does not indicate poverty, but something else. In letter 156, addressed to the abbot of the Kaisariane monastery, Michael Choniates writes from the island of Keos on behalf of another abbot, whom he refers to as Πτωχοηγούμενος: this 'Poor Abbot' had not been given his share of the revenues from beekeeping, and had filed an official complaint.[13] The *Tale of Ptocholeon* (Πτωχολέων) recounts how a rich man suddenly loses all his possessions and tells his children to sell him on the slave market; the king, having heard that a very wise man is for sale, decides to purchase him and test his knowledge – and wouldn't you know it, every time 'Poor Leo' is put to the test he comes up with a clever solution; in the end, when 'Poor Leo' has become a nuisance because he knows too much, the king is forced to set him free and pay him off with a large amount of money.[14]

So, what do these four 'poor' persons have in common? First of all, apart from Ptocholeon, none of these allegedly 'poor' people are actually poor; Peter the *magistros* is not, Odysseus is not, the abbot on Keos is not. And even Ptocholeon is not really one of the poor: he is a rich man who has lost

---

[11] I. Bekker, ed., *Theophanes Continuatus, Ioannes Cameniata, Symeon Magister, Georgius Monachus* (Bonn, 1838), 666–7 (Ps. Symeon), and 825–6 (George the Monk); I. Bekker, ed., *Leonis Grammatici. Chronographia* (Bonn, 1842), 239–40. In the last two sources Peter is nicknamed Πτωχομάγιστρος, in the first one Πτωχομάχης; the former nickname is the correct one: see S. Lampros, 'Πτωχομάγιστρος, όχι Πτωχομάχης', *NE*, 1 (1904), 237–8.
[12] G. Stallbaum, ed., *Eustathii Archiepiscopi Thessalonicensis, Commentarii ad Homeri Odysseam* (Leipzig, 1825–6, repr. Hildesheim, 1970), vol. II, 151.32.
[13] F. Kolovou, ed., *Michaelis Choniatae epistulae* (Berlin, 2001), 251.9 (no. 156).
[14] The name 'Ptocholeon' can be found in one version only; the other versions do not provide a name. See G. Kechagioglou, ed., Κριτική έκδοση τῆς Ἱστορίας Πτωχολέοντος (Thessalonike, 1978), 133–5, who suggests that the name might derive from the (as far as we know, unattested) adjective πτωχαλέος.

his wealth. Second, the prefix '*ptocho-*' ('poor') seems to serve as a generic marker and to indicate that something funny is being said: Peter the *magistros* is cracking jokes, Odysseus is pretending to be a beggar, Ptocholeon is making a fool of the king.[15] And third, the 'Poor Abbot', 'Poor Odysseus', and Ptocholeon (and even the 'Poor Magistros' who is about to lose everything because of his insolence) find themselves in an inferior situation: the abbot is begging to get what is rightfully his, Odysseus gains access to his own palace in the disguise of a beggar and Ptocholeon has to sell himself as an ordinary slave. In all these instances, the prefix '*ptocho-*' points to a (temporary) reversal of fortune and indicates to the reader/listener that the story unfolds in a topsy-turvy world where nothing is what it seems. In short, this is Byzantium's answer to the Bakhtinian concept of the carnivalesque.

The name 'Ptochoprodromos', then, does not necessarily mean that Prodromos is poor, but simply indicates that the poems that go under his name are hilarious because the reader/listener would not expect such a person to be begging for financial support and to do it in the way that he does.

Furthermore, just as the scruffy persons called Ptocholeon, Ptochoodysseus, Ptochomagistros or Ptochoigoumenos do not stand for an entire category of people nor are typical of an entire literary genre, but present individual characters, so, too, does 'Ptochoprodromos' not stand for the average begging poet. He is not a type but an individual. As Wolfram Hörandner has convincingly shown, whenever the Byzantines refer to Ptochoprodromos, they mean the well-known author of the twelfth century, Theodore Prodromos.[16] The oldest attestations of the name 'Ptochoprodromos' date from the early fourteenth century, but Hörandner rightly surmised that the nickname must be much older than that. One could argue that the 'Ptochoodysseus' of Eustathios of Thessalonike and the 'Ptochoigoumenos' of Michael Choniates indicate that the prefix

---

[15] Likewise, Michael Choniates is trying to make light of a serious situation by calling the abbot a 'ptochoigoumenos'. When he wrote this letter, Michael Choniates was living in exile and was no longer in a position to impose his will on the abbot of the Kaisariane monastery in Athens, the city of which he used to be the archbishop. So, instead of asserting his episcopal authority, he resorted to humour.

[16] See Hörandner, 'Autor oder Genus?' In MSS SAC (one of the manuscript branches), poem IV is ascribed to a certain 'Hilarion Ptochoprodromos', but as scholars have pointed out, including Hörandner, 'Autor oder Genus?', 319, and P. Vasileiou, 'Για το τρίτο "Πτωχοπροδρομικό" ποίημα (μικρό σημείωμα για την άρση ενός μεθοδολογικού λάθους)', Ελληνικά, 53 (2003), 171–9, this ascription is based on a misinterpretation of Eideneier, ed., *Ptochoprodromos*, 167 (IV.506) (= Hesseling and Pernot, eds., *Poèmes Prodromiques*, 66 (III.387)).

ptocho- enjoyed particular notoriety in the later twelfth century, and one might even see a possible connection to the nickname 'Ptochoprodromos' here.

The question, then, is not whether the *Ptochoprodromika* are attributed to Theodore Prodromos in the manuscript tradition — they are, beyond a reasonable doubt — but whether this ascription is correct for all five, for some or for none of the poems that go under his name. As Margaret Alexiou has rightly argued, numismatic evidence in poems III and IV points to a date between *c*. 1160 and 1200, and the historical references in the proem to poem III strongly suggest a date around 1175.[17] As Theodore Prodromos died in 1156 or shortly afterwards,[18] he clearly cannot be the poet of poems III and IV — unless we resort to *ad hoc* arguments; for instance, that the traditional date of death is incorrect,[19] or that anything that does not agree with Theodore Prodromos' biography is a later interpolation.[20] We see no reason to challenge the biographical dates of Prodromos' life, as established by Papadimitriou and Hörandner,[21] nor to obelise passages in the *Ptochoprodromika* simply because they cannot have been written by the historical Theodore Prodromos. There are no chronological reasons, however, to reject the attribution of poems I, II and V (the 'Maiuri' poem) to Theodore Prodromos: poem I dates from the reign of John II Komnenos, poem V can

---

[17] Alexiou, 'Poverty of Ecriture', 25–8.
[18] Apart from the fact that none of the texts that can be safely attributed to Theodore Prodromos date from after *c*. 1155–6, this date of death is based on a poem written by Manganeios Prodromos in *c*. 1156–8, in which he says that Prodromos is reminding him from beyond the grave (in nocturnal visions?) that he should retire to a monastery before it is too late and he dies without having repented. Manganeios refers to Prodromos as his 'dear friend' and his 'fellow poet'. For the text of the poem, see S. Papadimitriou, 'Θεοδώρου τοῦ Πτωχοπροδρόμου τὰ Μαγγάνεια. Феодора Продрома Манганские стихотворения', *Letopis'*, 7 (1899), 10–11 (II.27–50); and S. Bernardinello, ed., *Theodori Prodromi de Manganis* (Padua, 1972), 71 (X.27–50).
[19] Thus A. Kazhdan and S. Franklin, *Studies on Byzantine Literature in the Eleventh and Twelfth Centuries* (Berkeley, CA, 1985), 87–93 ('Manganeios' is in fact Theodore Prodromos and he refers to his father in the poem discussed in the previous footnote); R. Beaton, 'The Rhetoric of Poverty: the Lives and Opinions of Theodore Prodromos', *BMGS*, 11 (1987), 12–25 ('Manganeios' is in fact Theodore Prodromos and he refers to John the Baptist (the Forerunner) in the poem discussed in the previous footnote); Alexiou, 'Ploys of Performance', 105–6 ('Manganeios' is in fact Theodore Prodromos and he refers to himself in the poem discussed in the previous footnote. So he is not dead after all!); Manganeios and Theodore Prodromos served different masters, retired to different philanthropic institutions and lived different lives, and yet we are supposed to believe that they are actually one and the same person.
[20] Thus Alexiou, 'Ἡ ἔκδοση του Πτωχοπροδρόμου', 118.
[21] S. Papadimitriou, 'Οἱ Πρόδρομοι', *VizVrem*, 5 (1898), 91–130; S. Papadimitriou, "Ο Πρόδρομος τοῦ Μαρκιανοῦ κώδικος xi. 22', *VizVrem*, 10 (1903), 102–63; and S. Papadimitriou, *Иоанн II, митрополит Киевский и Феодор Продром* (Odessa, 1902); Hörandner, *Theodoros Prodromos*, 21–35. See also P. Magdalino, *The Empire of Manuel I Komnenos, 1143–1180* (Cambridge, 1993), 440–1 and 494; and M. D. J. Op de Coul, 'Théodore Prodrome, lettres et discours: édition, traduction, commentaire', unpublished PhD thesis, Université Paris IV-Sorbonne (2007), vol. I, 7–9.

be dated to the early years of Manuel I's reign, and poem II is addressed to a certain *sebastokrator*, who might, or might not, be Andronikos Komnenos, the husband of the nowadays (thanks to the Jeffreys)[22] more famous *Sebastokratorissa* Eirene. But it cannot be excluded that the attribution of these three poems to Theodore Prodromos is as erroneous as that of poems III and IV.[23]

In order to reach a proper assessment of the problems involved, what is needed above all is good old-fashioned philology. In his review of the critical edition of the *Ptochoprodromika* by Eideneier (1991), Martin Hinterberger rightly deplores the lack of information on language and metre: 'A discussion of their language would have been highly desirable... Investigations into morphology and syntax that take into account the different versions/manuscripts, could shed light on the origins of vernacular literature and its language. Closely related to the linguistic form is the metre, which is the usual decapentasyllable, but which nonetheless should have been treated.'[24] The earlier edition by Hesseling and Pernot (1910)[25] is not much better in this respect; there, too, we find hardly any information on these matters. In fact, it is the *editio princeps* of poems III and IV by Korais in his *Atakta* (1828)[26] that is by far the most informative of the existing editions. Whereas scholarship is usually seen as the accumulation of knowledge, in the case of the *Ptochoprodromika* we see the opposite phenomenon; as time progresses, scholars seem less and less inclined to delve into the basics of grammar and metre.[27]

---

[22] M. J. Jeffreys and E. M. Jeffreys, 'Who Was Eirene the *Sevastokratorissa?*', *Byzantion*, 64 (1994), 40–68; E. M. Jeffreys and M. J. Jeffreys, eds., *Iacobi Monachi, Epistulae* (Turnhout, 2009), xxiv–xxix.

[23] At IV.605 Eideneier changes διέβη τον Οκτάριον/Νεκτάριον, διέβη τον Κανίκλην into διέβη τον Ακτάριον (= Ακτουάριον with synizesis), διέβη τον Καλλίκλην, and in the introduction to his edition (Eideneier, *Ptochoprodromos*, 38–9) he identifies these two doctors with Nicholas Kallikles (late eleventh to mid-twelfth century) and John Zacharias Aktouarios (*c*. 1275–after 1328). Even if this emendation is correct, there is no reason to assume that Ptochoprodromos refers to John Zacharias rather than any other court physician: for instance, Kallikles' colleague at the court of Alexios I, Michael Pantechnes, who was an *aktouarios* (see *PBW*, 'Michael 135').

[24] M. Hinterberger, 'Review of H. Eideneier, *Ptochoprodromos*', *JÖB*, 43 (1993), at 452.

[25] Hesseling and Pernot, eds., *Poèmes Prodromiques*.

[26] A. Korais, Άτακτα, ήγουν παντοδαπῶν εἰς τὴν ἀρχαίαν καὶ τὴν νέαν ἑλληνικήν γλῶσσαν αὐτοσχεδίων σημειώσεων, καὶ τινῶν ἄλλων ὑπομνημάτων, αὐτοσχέδιος συναγωγή (Paris, 1828), vol. I, 1–339. See N. Giakovaki, 'Τα Πτωχοπροδρομικά του Κοραή: μεσαιωνικές αναζητήσεις' in *Μνήμη Άλκη Αγγέλου: τα άφθονα σχήματα του παρελθόντος* (Thessalonike, 2004), 361–76.

[27] The post-Eideneier period saw a number of publications on lexicological problems: N. Oikonomides, 'Ματζουκίνη - Ματζουκάτος in Ptochoprodromos' in C. N. Constantinides et al., eds., *Φιλέλλην: Studies in Honour of R. Browning* (Venice, 1996), 315–19; C. Diamanti, 'Ο ασκοθυράριος', *Σύμμεικτα*, 12 (1998), 57–62; A. I. Thavoris, 'Το προδρομικό:... και ωσάν εσέναν έχει' in G. Papantonakis, ed., *Άνθη φιλίας: Τιμητικό αφιέρωμα στον καθηγητή Κωνσταντίνο Μηνά*

As the manuscripts offer divergent readings and add or omit individual verses or even whole passages,[28] it is obvious that language and metre can be studied only at the level of manuscripts (as Hinterberger rightly pointed out). But as we hope to show below, each of the five *Ptochoprodromika*, irrespective of the manuscripts that transmit them, sometimes do show peculiarities of their own. As it would be impossible to look at all the variant readings in detail, we have restricted ourselves to the oldest manuscripts that contain the poems: G (Par. gr. 396, s. xiv: poems I–III), H (Hieros. Sab. 415, s. xiv: poems II and IV), S (Par. Suppl. gr. 1034, a. 1364: poems III–IV), and Va (Vat. gr. 1823, s. xv: poem v).[29] In addition to Eideneier's edition, we also consulted previous editions, in particular those of Hesseling-Pernot and Legrand.[30] However, not to make things more complicated than they already are, in the following account verse numbers of poems I–IV refer to Eideneier's edition; for poem v we used the only existing edition, that of Maiuri.

∴

There are very few studies of the language of the *Ptochoprodromika*.[31] Arguably the best one is by Geoffrey Horrocks, who offers an insightful

---

(Athens, 2005), 355–68; H. Eideneier, 'Ο κοσκινάς και οι ματσούκες του' in Papantonakis, ed., Ἄνθη φιλίας, 349–53; H. Eideneier, 'Ein Zeugnis für Wagenrennen in Konstantinopel im 12. Jahrhundert', *Nikephoros: Zeitschrift für Sport und Kultur im Altertum*, 18 (2005), 185–90. S. Alexiou suggested some textual emendations in S. Alexiou 'Διορθωτικά στον Πτωχοπρόδρομο' in C. Maltezou, T. Detorakes and C. Charalambakes, eds., *Ροδωνιά: τιμή στον Μ.Ι. Μανούσακα* (Rethymno, 1994), vol. I, 1–5 (repr. in S. Alexiou, ed., *Δημώδη Βυζαντινά*, 165–71). Arguably the most fundamental contribution of the 1990s and 2000s is D. R. Reinsch, 'Zu den Prooimia von (Ptocho-)Prodromos III und IV', *JÖB*, 51 (2001), 215–23. P. A. Agapitos, 'Grammar, Genre and Patronage in the Twelfth Century: a Scientific Paradigm and its Implications', *JÖB*, 64 (2014), 14–22, sees a connection with schedography: we do not.
[28] Hesseling and Pernot, however, exaggerate when they write on pp. 14–17 of Hesseling and Pernot, eds., *Poèmes Prodromiques* and elsewhere, that the manuscripts offer a totally corrupted and interpolated text: this is simply not true. The same goes for P. Speck, '"Interpolations et non-sens indiscutables": the first poem of the Ptochoprodromika' in S. A. Takács, ed., *Understanding Byzantium: Studies in Byzantine Historical Sources* (Aldershot, 2003), 84–103.
[29] Occasionally we refer to the other manuscripts as well: C (Par. Coisl. 382, s. xv), A (Athen. Benaki 48, s. xvi), V (Vat. gr. 579, s. xiv–xv), P (Par. gr. 1310, s. xv), K (Const. Serail 35, a. 1461), M (Monac. gr. 525, s. xiv).
[30] E. Legrand, ed., *Bibliothèque grecque vulgaire* (Paris, 1880–1902), vol. I, 38–124.
[31] See G. Chatzidakis, 'Περὶ τῶν Προδρόμων Θεοδώρου καὶ Ἰλαρίωνος', *VizVrem*, 4 (1897), 100–27, esp. 117–27 (repr. in G. Chatzidakis, *Μεσαιωνικὰ καὶ Νέα Ἑλληνικά* [Athens, 1905–7], vol. II, 361–95, esp. 381–95). J. M. Egea, 'El griego de los poemas Prodrómicos', *Veleia*, 1 (1984), 177–91; J. M. Egea, 'La lengua de la ciudad en el s. XII', *Erytheia*, 8 (1987), 241–62; J. M. Egea, 'El griego de los poemas Prodrómicos (II)', *Veleia*, 5 (1988), 257–74.

analysis of various syntactical and morphological features in III.56–88.[32] He points out that the *Ptochoprodromika* contain both conservative and innovative linguistic elements, and rightly stresses that this mixed language should not be regarded as a *Kunstsprache*, but rather as 'a wickedly contrived mixture' used for satirical purposes, which, to a certain degree, reflects the spoken idiom of the upper classes in twelfth-century Constantinople.

In studying the language of the *Ptochoprodromika*, one needs to distinguish between linguistic features that are shared by all or at least most manuscripts, and linguistic features that can be found in only one or two manuscripts or a particular manuscript branch. The former are likely to go back to the archetype of the manuscript tradition, the latter are probably later accretions and, therefore, not necessarily representative of twelfth-century vernacular. See, for instance, prothetic ε– in MSS SAC: λουτρόν ουδέν εβλέπεις in IV.91 (where the other MSS offer other readings), MS K: κομμάτια εβλέπω in IV.114 (where the other MSS have κομμάτιν βλέπω) and MS Va, the only manuscript to preserve poem V: πλην καν αυτός ελησμονή in V.10 and ουκ εγνωρίζεις in V.41. As prothetic ε– is found nowhere else, it is most probably not an original feature of the *Ptochoprodromika*.

On the other hand, sometimes a reading of a single manuscript can actually preserve genuine earlier features, as appears to be the case with the following rather unusual word order: σαλοκρανιοκέφαλον πάντως να με ονειδίζη, / εάν τον ουκ είπω μάθε το τσαγγάρην το παιδίν σου (III.111–12SAC) (surely he'll forever be accusing me of being a fool if I don't tell him: let your son become a cobbler). As is sufficiently known from recent studies on weak pronoun placement in late medieval Greek,[33] as a rule, the pronoun is found in post-verbal position when the verb is directly preceded by ου. However, when ου + verb is preceded by αν, the pronoun is typically placed before the verb and after ου; compare the reading of MS

---

[32] G. C. Horrocks, *Greek: A History of the Language and its Speakers*, second edition (New York, NY, 2010), 337–42.

[33] See P. Mackridge, 'An Editorial Problem in Medieval Greek Texts: the Position of the Object Clitic Pronoun in the Escorial Digenes Akrites' in N. M. Panayiotakis, ed., Αρχές της νεοελληνικής λογοτεχνίας (Venice, 1993), vol. II, 329, and P. Mackridge, 'The Position of the Weak Object Pronoun in Medieval and Modern Greek', Язык и речевая деятельность, 3 (2000), 139. See also P. Pappas, 'Unus Testis, Nullus Testis? The Significance of a Single Token in a Problem of Later Medieval Greek Syntax', *Ohio State University Working Papers in Linguistics*, 54 (2000), 171–6, reprinted (with minor changes) in P. Pappas, *Variation and Morphosyntactic Change in Greek: from Clitics to Affixes* (New York, NY, 2004), 44–50. On the development from Ancient to Medieval Greek, see G. C. Horrocks, 'Clitics in Greek: a Diachronic Review' in M. Roussou and S. Panteli, eds., *Greek Outside Greece* (Athens, 1990), vol. II, 35–52, and Horrocks, *Greek*, 208–12.

G: ἐάν ου τον εἴπω. But there are some exceptions to this rule in early vernacular texts, where we see that the pronoun is placed before ου + verb.[34] This rare word order is not restricted to environments in which ου is preceded by αν: it can also be triggered by a preceding interrogative,[35] a relative pronoun (το, τα),[36] or a subordinating conjunction (διατί).[37] All examples come from early texts, such as Michael Glykas, Ptochoprodromos, the Grottaferrata version of *Digenes Akrites*, a twelfth- or thirteenth-century collection of proverbs, and *Livistros and Rodamne*,[38] whereas this particular word order is not encountered in fourteenth-century works, such as the *Chronicle of Morea*, the *War of Troy* or *Kallimachos*, to name just a few. This word order therefore probably reflects an earlier transitional phase, in which the placement of clitic pronouns, especially in combination with certain triggers causing them to move, was still in a state of flux. As it would be unlikely that later scribes would add such an obsolete feature to the text, this word order is very likely to be genuinely twelfth-century.

---

[34] IV.514H: αν το ουκ επάρῃ, εξάφες τον (if he doesn't take [his meagre meal], let him be); E. T. Tsolakes, ed., *Μιχαὴλ Γλυκᾶ στίχοι οὓς ἔγραψε καθ' ὃν κατεσχέθη καιρόν* (Thessalonike, 1959), 10.229: γοργόν αν σε ουκ εκβάλουσιν, εκεί να εξεψυχήσῃς (if they don't get you out [of the bath house] quickly, you might die on the spot); this example is discussed by Pappas, *Variation*, 48–9. E. M. Jeffreys, ed., *Digenis Akritis: The Grottaferrata and Escorial Versions* (Cambridge, 1998), 8 (G 1.112): αν την ουχ υποστρέψωμεν, και οι πάντες να σφαγώμεν (if we do not recover her, we shall all be slaughtered).

[35] In II.26.9–11H: και αν θέλουν τρώγειν οι δεκατρείς τους δώδεκα μοδίους ... τι τους ου θάπτω (but if thirteen have to live on twelve modii [of wheat] ... why don't I just bury them?).

[36] See K. Krumbacher, ed., *Mittelgriechische Sprichwörter* (Munich, 1893, repr. Hildesheim, 1969): F 60 μέλος το σε ου προκόπτει, κόψε και ρίψε το (if a limb is of no use to you, cut it off and throw it away); I 60 μέλος το σε ου προσκολλάται, κόψε και ρίψε το (if a limb will not attach to [your body], cut it off and throw it away); I 85 εποίησες, γυνή, το σε είπον; γυνή λέγει· αληθώς, και το με ουκ είπες (did you do, woman, what I told you to do? the wife answers: indeed, and also what you didn't tell me to do). A similar case of the headless relative pronoun pulling the pronoun forward, even though after ουδέν the 'normal' word order is for the pronoun immediately to precede the verb, in Tsolakes, ed., *Μιχαὴλ Γλυκᾶ στίχοι*, 13.293–4: ἔδε και τι χολομανώ και τι βαρεά στριγγίζω,/και λέγω τα ουκ ενδέχονται και τα με ουδέν αρμόζουν; (oh, but why do I get upset and why do I moan, and say things that I shouldn't and that are inappropriate?).

[37] T. Lendari, ed., *Livistros and Rodamne: The Vatican Version: Critical Edition with Introduction, Commentary and Index-Glossary* (Athens, 2007), 154.398–400: την καταδίκην την πολλήν την έχω και την πάσχω,/την υπομένω δια έρωταν, την εκατεδικάστην,/διατί τον ουκ εγνώριζα και ουδέν τον εφοβούμην (this terrible suffering that I endure for love, to which I have been condemned because I didn't know [love] and wasn't afraid of it).

[38] The fact that it is found in *Livistros* may be a small argument in favour of a rather early dating. P. A. Agapitos, ed., *Ἀφήγησις Λιβίστρου καὶ Ροδάμνης. Κριτικὴ ἔκδοση τῆς διασκευῆς α* (Athens, 2006), 48–67, dates the composition of the work to the middle of the thirteenth century, whereas Lendari, *Livistros and Rodamne*, 65–71, tentatively proposes a late thirteenth- to early fourteenth-century dating.

Neither time nor space permits us here to make a full study of the language of the *Ptochoprodromika*, however desirable such a venture would be. We have therefore decided to limit ourselves to a case study of conditional sentences.[39] This choice is to a certain degree an arbitrary one; any phenomenon with a pragmatic dimension that leaves room for an author's personal preference of usage would have been suitable to our aim. The following description is loosely based on the framework used by Gerry Wakker for her excellent study on conditionals in ancient Greek;[40] loosely because our aim is not to construct a theoretical framework for conditional sentences in twelfth-century vernacular Greek, but to describe their usage and pinpoint differences and similarities in five specific texts; loosely also because her framework is at times too fine-grained for the material offered in the *Ptochoprodromika*. Also, medieval Greek differs considerably from ancient Greek: the conjunction εἰ had been replaced by ἐάν/ἄν long before the medieval period,[41] and the monolectic future, no longer a feature of the spoken language, is largely interchangeable with – and often replaced by – the aorist subjunctive.[42] Likewise, there is no real distinction, apart from a graphematic one, between the present indicative and the present subjunctive. For these reasons, in the following classification no distinction will be made between the present indicative and subjunctive, nor between

---

[39] In the following account, we limit ourselves to conditional clauses, but of course the conjunction αν/εάν can introduce other clauses as well, such as concessive-conditional clauses and causal clauses. Concessive-conditional sentences do not express a condition that needs to be met, but rather, contrary to expectation, the apodosis will be in effect if the protasis is: εάν γαρ ουκ εγυρεύετο ράψιμον εις τον κόσμον,/οκάποιας καν γειτόνισσας ρούχον να επαρελύθην/και παρευθύς να με έκραξαν (III.161–3) (even if there were no demand for tailor-made clothes, some neighbour's dress might rip, and they would immediately call me over). For examples of καν (και αν) introducing concessive-conditional clauses, see I.119–20 and V.10–11). For causal αν, see III.232G: αν γαρ ουκ έχω τι φορείν, μεγάλως τουρτουρίζω (since I have nothing to wear, I shiver tremendously), and III.235G: αν γαρ ουκ έχω τι φαγείν, σκοτίζομαι και πίπτω (since I have nothing to eat, I faint and fall down); note that MS S has a participle here: και γαρ μη έχων τι φορείν/φαγείν.

[40] G. Wakker, *Conditions and Conditionals: An Investigation of Ancient Greek* (Amsterdam, 1994), esp. 125–87. Wakker's investigation is carried out within the framework of Functional Grammar, as developed by Simon Dik. For a historical overview of conditional clauses in Greek, see G. C. Horrocks, 'On Condition ...: Aspect and Modality in the History of Greek', *Proceedings of the Cambridge Philological Society*, 41 (1995), 153–73.

[41] A. N. Jannaris, *An Historical Greek Grammar Chiefly of the Attic Dialect* (London, 1897, repr. Hildesheim, 1968), 463.

[42] Not only when the future and subjunctive of a verb are homophonous, e.g. fut. ind. γράψεις, aor. subj. γράψῃς, but even when they are morphologically distinct. Consider the following example, in which, for metrical reasons, the future of προσφέρω is used in the first verse, and the aorist subjunctive of the same verb in the second, in two coordinate main clauses: τι σοι προσοίσω, δέσποτα, δέσποτα στεφηφόρε,/ανταμοιβήν οποίαν δε ή χάριν προσενέγκω 1.1–2 (what shall I offer you, lord, my crowned lord, what reward or favour shall I offer?). For details, see M. C. Janssen, 'Verb Morphology', in D. Holton, G. Horrocks et al., *The Cambridge Grammar of Medieval and Early Modern Greek* (forthcoming).

the aorist subjunctive and the monolectic future, because in most cases the differences in spelling are purely graphematic and simply reflect the choice of the modern editor.[43]

In her book Wakker distinguishes three main categories of conditionals, the first of which proved suitable to describe the phenomenon in the *Ptochoprodromika*:[44] predicational conditionals, which, simply said,[45] are conditional sentences in which the realisation of the action of the main clause (apodosis) is dependent on the condition set out in the subordinate clause (protasis). Depending on the context, these conditionals can be specific (with future, present or past reference), generic (habitual/iterative), or counterfactual (with present or past reference). The *Ptochoprodromika* use ει and αν/εάν to introduce the protasis. Both the protasis and the apodosis are marked for aspect through the use of imperfective and perfective verb forms. The aspectual choice is dictated by the actions/events expressed by the verbs, and the ways in which these are perceived and relate to each other: as completed actions/events that follow each other in time, as ongoing situations, or as repeated/habitual actions/events.[46]

A first observation concerns the choice of conditional conjunctions: the archaic conjunction ει, which, as noted, had long been superseded by αν, is used with some regularity in poems I and IV, and not only in the slightly higher-register addresses to the emperor. Poems II and III, on the other hand, have one isolated instance each, but only in single manuscripts (II.70G and III.47SAC), and poem V has none (apart from one instance

---

[43] Consider the following passage: ει δε πολλάκις δόξει την και φθάσει ο καρκατσάς της/και ορίσει τα ψυχάρια της και την πρωτοβαβάν της/και πιάσουν και ταυρίσουν με και σύρουν με εις την μέστην,/ και δώσουν με τα τρίκωλα και τα χαρακτικά μου,/τις έλθη και εκδικήση με και εκβάλη με απ' εκείνης: (I.35–9) (if, for instance, she gets it in her head and decides to order her servants and the nurse to grab me, to pull me and drag me in their midst and to give me a good thrashing, who will come to vindicate me and rescue me?). Here δόξει, φθάσει and ορίσει are spelled as future indicatives because, according to the rules of ancient Greek syntax, a subjunctive is impossible after ει, whereas έλθη, εκδικήση and εκβάλη in the main clause are spelled as aorist subjunctives because, according to ancient Greek morphology, the first and the third cannot possibly be future indicatives.
[44] The other two main categories she distinguishes are propositional conditionals, in which the protasis expresses a condition for the truth of the proposition rather than for its realisation; and illocutionary conditionals, in which the protasis forms a condition for the appropriateness/validity/relevance of the speech act expressed in the main clause. In the small corpus of Ptochoprodromic poems these conditionals are so few and far between that a classification seems superfluous. We have therefore decided to treat the non-predicational conditionals under the heading 'rhetorical uses of conditionals'.
[45] For an extensive overview of the theoretical discussion concerning the exact nature of conditionals, see Wakker, *Conditions and Conditionals*, 21–42.
[46] For verbal aspect in general, the classic study is B. Comrie, *Aspect: an Introduction to the Study of Verbal Aspect and Related Problems* (Cambridge, 1976). For a diachronic overview of aspect and tense in Greek, see A. Moser, *Άποψη και χρόνος στην ιστορία της ελληνικής* (Athens, 2009).

of the fossilised phrase ει δε και μη in 58). It should be stressed that, although ει is an archaism,[47] its use does not adhere to ancient Greek rules,[48] as it is interchangeable with αν. Where the choice for αν or its more formal variant εάν is concerned, we may observe that εάν is used only in poems III and IV. However, the critical apparatuses of Eideneier's and Hesseling-Pernot's editions show that in the majority of cases εάν is the reading of SAC, while G and H write αν or have different readings altogether. In fact, G has only one case of εάν (III.112), and H three (IV.45, 138, 563). In all cases but two the use of εάν is purely graphematic, as it should clearly be read as one syllable (in other words, as αν: see the section on metre below).

Another sign of conservatism, which is shared by all five poems, is the fact that Ptochoprodromos hardly ever makes use of periphrastic constructions with auxiliary έχω or θέλω in conditional clauses. In fact, there is only one example (1).[49] Two things are especially interesting here: first, the είχα-periphrasis is used in a present-referring counterfactual context, not a past-referring one;[50] second, the infinitive following είχα is a present, not an aorist infinitive:[51]

(1) ει γαρ και λέξων ήρχομουν μυθοπλαστών τους λόγους,/ευλύτως είχες, βασιλεύ, πάντων εκ τούτων λύειν (III.47–8SC; changed to λύσιν in ms. A) (even if I were to tell fabulous tales, you, emperor, would have no problem solving them all [i.e. finding the right allegorical interpretation because you are so wise, etc.])

---

[47] The use of the particle αν in the apodosis of counterfactuals in poems I and IV in (16) and (25) may also be viewed as an archaism, and again appears in certain manuscripts only (GH). Note that Ptochoprodromos' contemporary Glykas does not use this particle at all.

[48] See A. Rijksbaron, *The Syntax and Semantics of the Verb in Classical Greek: an Introduction* (Amsterdam, 1984), 68–74.

[49] Outside the conditional context there are two more examples: έχω + infinitive in IV.499SAC, and θέλω + infinitive in IV.509. For έχω + infinitive and other future periphrases, see T. Markopoulos, *The Future in Greek: From Ancient to Medieval* (New York, NY, 2009). Both constructions had been available for centuries: a first attestation of έχω + infinitive in a future-referring apodosis is found in a sixth-century papyrus, and θέλω + infinitive in the protasis of a future-referring conditional sentence is found in a ninth-century legislative text (Markopoulos, *Future*, 96 and 107–8).

[50] As Markopoulos, *Future*, treats the counterfactual είχα-construction in the context of its later development into the modern Greek pluperfect, he makes no mention of present-referring counterfactuals with είχα + infinitive, even though they can (sporadically) be found as early as late antiquity. See, for instance, the *Apophthegmata patrum* (PG 65, col. 176) (example quoted in Jannaris, *Historical Greek Grammar*, 554): ει ής εν τη χώρα σου, και επίσκοπος πολλάκις και κεφαλή πολλών είχες είναι· νυν δε ως ξένος καθέζη ώδε (if you were in your country, you would for instance be a bishop, a leader of many people, but now you are staying here, as a foreigner).

[51] Present infinitive in είχα-constructions can be found in various texts until as late as the seventeenth century. Further study is needed to establish which contexts trigger present infinitives. A nice eleventh-century example is the following from Kekaumenos' *Strategikon* (G. G. Litavrin, ed., *Советы и рассказы Кекавмена* (Moscow, 1972), 296.13–14): και πάντως ει περιώρισέ σε τις εν μιᾷ πόλει, αγωνιάν είχες και αδημονείν τούτο παθών (and surely, if somebody had confined you to a city, you would be in agony and in anguish over what had happened to you).

Predicational Conditionals – Future Reference

All poems have conditionals that refer to the future, with ει or εάν/αν + future indicative/aorist subjunctive in the protasis. These clauses represent the classic hypothetical construction 'If X happens, then Y will happen'. The apodosis usually has a future, either monolectic or να + subjunctive: perfective in (2),[52] presenting the event as completed, and imperfective in (3),[53] describing an ongoing situation. An imperative in the apodosis (4) expresses what must happen if the condition is fulfilled (mostly in IV).[54] A present/perfect in the apodosis gives extra immediacy to the cause–effect relation between protasis and apodosis (5):

(2) (προφητεύομαι . . .) ως, ει θελήσης, δέσποτα, τα τούτων ερευνήσαι/και δώσης την εκδίκησιν τοις νυν ηδικημένοις,/τοις αλλοφύλοις καθαρώς βαρβάροις θράσος παύσεις (IV.281–3S) ([I predict . . .] that if you, o lord, decide to investigate these matters and vindicate those who have been wronged, you will surely put an end to the impudence of the barbarian tribes) (see (25) for discussion)

(3) ή να αποθάνη σύντομον και να τον λυτρωθούμεν/ή αν υγιάνη και εγερθή, καν πάλιν να δουλεύη (IV.602–3) (he'll either die soon and we'll be rid of him, or, if he gets well and gets back on his feet, at least he'll be working again)

(4) εάν έλθη ο δείνα πώποτε εις την πόρταν να καθίση,/ραβδέας πολλάς κατάραχα, και διώξε τον απέκει (IV.517–18); ραβδέας καλάς τον δος in H) (if so-and-so ever comes to sit outside the door, [give him] a stiff beating and chase him away)

(5) αν συ παράσχης μοι τροφήν, αν χορηγήσης πόσιν,/έχω καρδίας στηριγμόν, έχω ζωής ελπίδα'/αν δ' ου παράσχης, τέθνηκα (V.33–5) (if you provide me with food, if you give me to drink, then I take courage, then I have hope to live, but if you don't provide [food], I'm dead)

In I.271–3 and II.98–100G we find apparently similar instances, but in fact they function quite differently from the ones in (5), because the condition in the protasis does not apply to the main verbs in the apodosis

---

[52] With perfective apodosis in I.35–9, 148–54, 160–2, 163; II.25.2–3H, 108; III.29–32, 74–5; IV.281–3, 611–13; V.37–9. Elliptical in the following: αλήθεια, δίδεις με πολλά, πλην αν τα συμψηφίσης,/τετράμηνον ου σώζουν με (II.24–5) (it is true, you give me a lot, but if you add it all up, [you'll see that] it is barely enough for four months).
[53] With imperfective apodosis in III.111–12G; IV.602–3.
[54] This construction in IV.514, 517–18, 519–20S, 599. Present imperative (repeated action/ongoing situation) in II.67–8G: τότε με κατονείδιζε (then you may be blaming me [as I suspect you are doing now], or perhaps: then you may blame me as often as you like) and in IV.520H: την πόρτα σου ρωμάνιζε (keep your door locked).

(τρέμω, πτοοῦμαι, δέδοικα), but to the dependent clause (μὴ φονευθῶ), in other words not to the act of fearing, but to what is feared will happen:

> (6) αν ουν μη φθάση με το σον φιλεύσπλαγχνον, αυτάναξ, ... τρέμω, πτοοῦμαι, δέδοικα μη φονευθώ προ ώρας (I.271–3) (if your generosity doesn't reach me in time, o emperor, ... I shudder, shake and tremble lest I should find an untimely death)

Finally, poem V has one more instance of αν + aorist subjunctive with a present in the apodosis, with a quite different interpretation; in this rather reproachful utterance, a hypothetical action that is situated in the future ('if you tell him'), will confirm what the speaker already suspects to be the case now ('you don't know me'). It could be viewed as elliptical: 'if you replace me, [that will prove to me that] you don't know me':

> (7) αν τύχη αν είπης τον ζουγλόν να ποίση αντίσηκόν μου ... ουκ εγνωρίζεις, δέσποτα, τον Πρόδρομον τον έχεις (v.40–2) (if you were to tell the cripple to replace me ... then, O lord, you don't know your Prodromos at all)

Present Reference

All poems but V have conditionals with present reference, with ει or εάν/αν + present indicative/subjunctive in the protasis. The apodosis may be expressed in various moods or tenses: a present indicative expresses that the condition is simultaneous to the action in the apodosis: 'If X is the case, then Y is the case.' With this meaning, this construction was found only once in poem II (8); with a perfective future in the apodosis, the sentence is of the type 'If X happens repeatedly/is happening, then Y will happen' (9);[55] with a perfective imperative in the apodosis, the sentence is of the type 'If X is the case, then Y must happen' (10).[56] Finally, with an interrogative apodosis, the protasis poses a hypothesis, 'Say X is the case, should then Y?' (11):

> (8) ει δ' ούτως κατακρίνεις με δίχα τινός αιτίας ... ένι και κρίμα και κακόν, εικάζω, και αμαρτάνεις (II.70–2G; not in H) (if you condemn me in such a way for no reason at all ... it's a gross error, I say, and it's a sin against heaven)

---

[55] This construction also in: πάντως αν το μυρίζωνται, μόλις να τους αρκέση (II.28) (even if they smell [the food], that will barely suffice to satisfy them, or perhaps: that should be enough for them).

[56] This construction in I.164–7; III 249; IV.480–1, 531–3S.

(9) μυρίας γαρ ει λέγω το[ν] καθ' ώραν αληθείας/ου καν να πείσω πώποτε τον νουν του κύρι εγκλείστου (IV.433–4H; 433S corrupt) (if I tell [him] the truth a thousand times, still I will not convince Mr Recluse)

(10) αν δε πεινάς, γραμματικέ, αγόρασον και φάγε (III.249) (if you're hungry, grammarian, buy food)

(11) αν έχω γείτονα τινά και έχη παιδίν αγόριν,/να τον είπω ότι μάθε το γραμματικά να ζήση; (III.109–10G) (if I have a neighbour who has a son, should I say to him: 'teach the boy letters so that he can make a living'?)

Counterfactual conditionals with present reference have ει or εάν/αν + imperfect in the protasis, denoting that something could have happened/been happening (now), if only the condition of the protasis had been met (which it hasn't). The apodosis is να + imperfect for a repeated/habitual action or an ongoing situation (12), or να + aorist indicative for an event/action that would take place if the situation of the condition were in force at the same time (13). These counterfactuals are largely limited to poems III and IV:[57]

(12) εάν ήμουν παραζυμωτής ή δουλευτής μαγκίπου,/προφούρνια να εχόρταινα και ωσάν εμέναν είχεν (III.165–6) (if I were an assistant dough-maker or an apprentice baker, I'd have my fill of fresh bread, and be the luckiest man on earth)

(13) εδάρτε εάν ήσαν κέφαλοι, ψησσία, φιλομήλαι,/αυτίκα να το ενέτυχα (IV.415–16) (if only [the dish] were mullet, brill, or gurnard, then I'd immediately remember [the word for it])[58]

Past Reference

Counterfactual conditions with past reference have ει or εάν/αν + aorist indicative in the protasis. They express that something would be the case, if only the condition of the protasis had been met (which it hasn't). The apodosis consists of a verb in the past tense, usually accompanied by the particle να,[59]

---

[57] This construction in III.165–6, 176–8, 181–2; IV.146–7S. An elliptical example, from which the apodosis is omitted: και καν εάν ήσαν περισσά θρύμματα να χορτάσω,/αμή και εκείνα ολιγοστά (IV.391–2S) (but if at least there were lots of chunks to eat my fill ... [I'd not be hungry], but there is not much of that either).

[58] For the translation of the names of fishes and other foods in the *Ptochoprodromika*, see the useful phrasebook of Byzantine foods and aromas in A. Dalby, *Flavours of Byzantium* (Totnes, 2003), 185–237.

[59] For να as a marker of hypothetical consequentiality, equivalent to the ancient Greek particle ἄν and the Modern Greek particle θα, see Horrocks, 'On Condition', 170–1. Early examples of counterfactuals with να + aorist indicative in the apodosis can be found in Philippos Monotropos' *Dioptra*; see E. Afentoulidou-Leitgeb, 'Language and Style of the Dioptra', *BSl*, 70 (2012), 120.

but sometimes we even find the obsolete particle αν (16); see also (25). The apodosis with να + imperfect denotes a state: a quality/capacity (14) or a habitual action/daily activity (15).⁶⁰ An aorist indicative in the apodosis refers to a completed action/event (16 and 17):

(14) εάν έμαθον την ραπτικήν εντέχνως επιστήμην ... να ήμουν οικοδεσπότης (III.158–60) (if I'd learnt the intricacies of the tailor's craft ... I'd be master of the house)

(15) κεντήκλας καν αν έμαθα και τους πιπεροτρίπτας,/οδοιπορών να εστρίγγιζα, περιπατών να ελάλουν (III.188–9G)⁶¹ (if only I'd learnt to make felt or grind pepper, I'd be going around peddling my wares and shouting in the streets)

(16) ει γαρ ηθέλησα ποτέ τα πάντα σοι συγγράψαι,/ηρώων αν κατάλογον άλλον συνεγραψάμην (I.115–16) (if I had ever decided to write down everything for you, I would have written another catalogue of heroes)

(17) εδάρε και τα γράμματα αν με έποισαν τεχνίτην,/απ' αύτους οπού κάμνουσιν τα κλαπωτά και ζώσιν,/να έμαθα τέχνην κλαπωτήν (III.89–91S) (now then, if those letters had made me into a craftsman, one of those who work gold filigree and make a living, I'd have learnt to be a filigree-maker)

The following two examples, both from poem 1, look like counterfactuals, but are, in fact, not, or not quite. The protasis, with ει or εάν/αν + imperfect, is neutral in the sense that the speaker makes no claim regarding the truth of the proposition: 'If (it is true that) X was the case, then Y.' The apodoses, however, do have a counterfactual element to them, expressing something that in the opinion of the speaker should have happened in the past, but clearly did not: μη + aorist indicative (μη εγένου) and ας + aorist indicative (ας έλαβες). The apodosis of (18) starts with an aorist (μη εγένου), and then continues with ας + imperfect, denoting iterative/habitual actions in the past (ας εκάθου, ας έκνηθες, ας ήφηνες). The aspectual difference between ας ήφηνες εμένα (18) and ας έλαβες ομοίαν σου in (19), is a subtle one: (19) simply denotes a one-time action, a choice Ptochoprodromos did not make; in (18), the fact that he did not leave her but stayed with her triggers the use of the imperfect; therefore it is perhaps best paraphrased as 'you shouldn't have stayed with me':

---

⁶⁰ This type of sentence only in III: 89–92, 158–60, 181–2, 188–9G.
⁶¹ MS S has a present-referring counterfactual, which in the context is less suitable: κεντούκλας εάν εμάνθανα και τους πεπεροτρίπτας,/οδοιπορών να εστρίγγιζα, περιπατών να ελάλουν (if I were learning to make felt or grind pepper, I'd be going around peddling my wares and shouting in the streets).

(18) αν ουκ εθάρρεις κολυμβάν, κολυμβητής μη εγένου,/αλλ' ας εκάθου σιγηρός και απομεριμνημένος,/και ας εκνηθες την λέπραν σου, και ας ήφηνες εμέναν (I.103–5) (if you were afraid to swim, you shouldn't have become a swimmer, but you should have sat quietly and without a care in the world, scratching your leprous limbs, and you should have let me be)

(19) ει δε κομπώσειν ήθελες και λάβειν και πλανήσειν,/ας έλαβες ομοίαν σου, καπήλου θυγατέραν (I.106–7) (if your aim was to deceive, to profit and to swindle, you should have married someone of your own kind, an inn-keeper's daughter)

Habituality

Habitual conditionals usually have ει or εάν/αν + aorist subjunctive in the protasis, and the apodosis typically has a present indicative. These conditionals differ from other conditionals in that they do not express a hypothesis with respect to the future, the present or the past, but state that certain events/actions/situations are sometimes realised. In a way, they are similar to temporal clauses, but instead of specifying the moment(s) in time when these events/actions/situations occur, they specify the conditions under which they occur: 'Whenever X happens, then Y happens' (20). This construction occurs frequently, but only in poem IV.[62] With a present subjunctive in the protasis, the condition is presented as ongoing and the action/event of the apodosis occurs simultaneously. Only one example of this type has been found, in poem II (21):

(20) στιγμήν εάν λείψω ο ελεεινός από την εκκλησίαν,/το κρασοβόλιν μου κρατούν το νεροκοπτημένον (IV.132–3) (whenever I, poor sod, am away from church, if only for a moment, they deprive me of my watered-down allowance of wine)

(21) αν περπατούν, νυστάζουσιν· αν κάθηνται, κοιμώνται (II.90) (whenever they walk, they become sleepy; whenever they sit, they fall asleep)

Rhetorical Uses of Conditionals

There are a few conditionals that we think can most fruitfully be described as rhetorical, since they do not express true conditions, but rather are

---

[62] This construction in IV.132–3, 136–7, 138–9, 140–1, 142–3, 144–5, 155–8, 243S, 249–52, 257–8S, 305H, 311–14, 539–50S, 563–4, 588–9.

rhetorical devices used to make a request more polite or to get a point firmly across.

There are several examples in the *Ptochoprodromika* of requests for attention or money that are cast as conditional clauses (they belong to the 'illocutionary conditionals' in Wakker's classification).[63] These sentences typically have an imperative in the apodosis, and ει, εάν/αν or ως[64] + present in the protasis, expressing 'if you wish', which is added to tone down the directness of the imperative:

(22) αν δε κελεύεις, άκουσον και την οικονομίαν (II.19.4H) (if you wish, let me also tell you about my household)

(23) όμως, ει βούλει, μάνθανε και τα του μονοκύθρου· (IV.204) (but, if you wish, please learn as well what goes on with the stew) (imperfective μάνθανε is used to indicate that the emperor is already listening to the young monk's list of complaints, and would he be so kind as to continue doing so?)

(24) τετράμηνον ου σώζουσιν· ως θέλεις, ψήφισέ το (II.25H; not in G) ([the money] is barely enough for four months; if you wish, take notice why this is so)

Another way of making a request more polite is by using a counterfactual. There is one example in poem IV, with ει + aorist in the protasis and aorist + αν/καν in the apodosis:

(25) ει δε μικρόν ηθέλησας τα τούτων ερευνήσαι,/επέγνως αν εξ ακοής ψιλής και μόνης πάντα,/και του υιού και του πατρός ημίν τας αδικίας,/και ταύτας εξεμίσησας και τας παρανομίας (IV.270–3H; S has the same construction, but with καν for αν) (if you would decide to look into these matters only briefly, you would immediately, at first hearing, understand everything, the wrongdoings of both son and father towards us, and you would spurn these along with their [other] offences)

Example (25) is similar to (2), in that it constitutes a request cast as a conditional sentence; but it differs in the way the request is made. In (2), a typical future-referring conditional, the unhappy monk asks the emperor to investigate the evil acts of the abbot and his son and predicts that if the emperor does so, God will surely reward him by granting him a victory

---

[63] Wakker, *Conditions and Conditionals*, 236–67, esp. 263–6.
[64] Whereas ως θέλεις is usually interpreted as a manner clause, meaning 'as you wish', in (24) it can mean only 'if you wish', a standard expression equivalent to 'please'. This use is not uncommon in post-classical Greek; see, for instance, the *Apophthegmata patrum*: ως θέλεις οὖν, Ἀββᾶ, ἐλέησόν με (please, Abba, have pity on me) (*PG* 65, col. 321). For more examples, see the online *TLG*, http://stephanus.tlg.uci.edu/ (accessed 15 January 2018).

over the 'barbarian tribes'. In (25), on the other hand, the emperor will receive nothing in return: whereas in (2), victory will surely be his, all the emperor stands to gain in (25) is an insight into the wicked character of the abbot and his son. That is why the monk phrases his request in more polite terms, using a classic counterfactual construction, comparable to Modern Greek θα + imperfect (as in θα μπορούσες ... 'could you please ...').

There is one example of the type 'I'll be damned if ...' (pseudo-self-damnation in Wakker's terminology),[65] in which the protasis does not form a condition for the apodosis, but rather stresses the veracity of the utterance:

(26) ἀνάθεμάν με, βασιλεῦ, καὶ τρισανάθεμάν με,/ἐὰν οὐ ζηλεύω πάντοτε τοὺς χεροτεχναρίους (III.156–7S) (I'll be damned, O King, if I'm not always envious of workmen)

Another example of a rhetorical conditional is (27), in which, again, the protasis does not form a condition for the realisation of the apodosis, as it is obvious that the condition (if there isn't enough food) already applies. The apodosis consists of a rhetorical question, and the whole sentence serves to underline the seriousness of the protagonist's condition:

(27) καὶ ἂν θέλουν τρώγειν οἱ δεκατρεῖς τοὺς δώδεκα μοδίους ... τί τοὺς οὐ θάπτω ὡς ὅτε ζῶ καὶ φεύγω ἀπὸ τὴν Πόλιν (II.26.9–11H) (but if thirteen have to live on twelve modii [of wheat] ... why don't I just bury them while I'm still alive, and leave the city?)

The manner in which conditional sentences are constructed in the five poems may seem alike, but there are subtle differences in the ways that they are stylistically employed. Poem IV in particular seems to differ from the rest in certain respects.

Only in poem IV do we find direct requests to the emperor to act on the protagonist's behalf, in the form of conditional sentences (2 and 25), one rather straightforward ('if you help me, you'll be rewarded' (2)), the other made more polite through the use of a counterfactual conditional ('if you would investigate, surely you'd see ...' (25)). Poems I, II and V resort to emotional blackmail in their requests for money, with conditional sentences of the type 'if you don't help me, I'm dead' (5). Poem III does not use conditionals to make requests to the emperor, but rather prefers imperatives laced with flattery and lavish praise (274–86), as does poem IV when asking for financial support (654–65).

---

[65] Wakker, *Conditions and Conditionals*, 189–90.

A second difference is habituality. As noted, habitual conditional sentences are found only in poem IV, in which there are no fewer than fifteen of them. Whenever the young monk complains about the abuse he and his fellow-monks suffer at the hands of the abbot and his son, he invariably presents it in terms of situations/events that repeat themselves over and over again. One could maintain that this is content-related, rather than a deliberate choice by the author, but compare, for instance, poem I. In this poem, the protagonist, the poor husband, recounts how he gets nagged into oblivion by his bossy wife and suffers constant abuse from her. The situation is very similar to that in poem IV, but in contrast to the young monk's repetitive denunciation of abuses, Ptochoprodromos-the-husband gives specific examples of abuse and understands the art of showing, not telling. Instead of enumerating his wife's wrongdoings in the manner of poem IV (whenever I do X, they do Y), he makes his story infinitely more lively by introducing her as a character and letting her speak. The wife's constant scolding is often rendered in direct speech, and in her long diatribes she expresses her indignation by using, for instance, the past-referring conditional that is unique to poem I, which consists of an imperfect in the protasis and an admonition/prohibition in the apodosis (examples 18 and 19).

Of course, no firm conclusions can be drawn on the basis of one small case study. The above data provide empirical evidence of similarities and differences between the five poems. If one were to study every linguistic aspect of these poems and their manuscripts, pinpointing similarities and differences, the accumulation of all these facts surely would shed light on this corpus of poems and the ways in which they relate to each other.

∴

Let us turn now to metre. In his review of Hörandner's edition of the historical poems of Prodromos,[66] Michael Jeffreys rightly pointed out that whereas metre is used as an argument against identifying 'Manganeios' with Theodore Prodromos, this argument is strangely ignored in assessing the equally disputed attribution of the *Ptochoprodromika* to the same Theodore Prodromos. As Jeffreys explained, the accentual patterns before the caesura differ strongly, between 40 per cent on the sixth syllable in Theodore Prodromos to no less than 60 per cent on the sixth syllable in Manganeios Prodromos, and even 63–72 per cent on the sixth syllable in

---

[66] M. J. Jeffreys, 'Review of W. Hörandner, *Theodoros Prodromos: Historische Gedichte*', BZ, 70 (1977), 106.

Ptochoprodromos I–IV (but 53 per cent on the sixth syllable in 'Maiuri', no. V). And he asked a fundamental question: 'Can (Hörandner) prove that the demotic experiments changed Prodromos' metre?' In a paper that deals with this problem,[67] Hans and Niki Eideneier provided the answer: the rhythm of the political verse is indeed *sprachimmanent*; in the 'learned' passages there are fewer stressed sixth syllables, and in the 'vernacular' ones there are more. But as they were quick to point out, even the 'learned' passages never have the absurdly low percentage of stressed sixth syllable that we find in Theodore Prodromos: in other words, he cannot be the poet of the *Ptochoprodromika*. Their findings were then confirmed by the great Prodromos expert, Wolfram Hörandner, who, however, tried to exempt the 'Maiuri' poem from the general deprodromisation of the *Ptochoprodromika* by maintaining that this one at least showed metrical similarities to the historical poems of Theodore Prodromos.[68]

We are not so certain that metre can prove, or disprove, the paternity of the *Ptochoprodromika*. First of all, as Stylianos Alexiou demonstrated beyond doubt,[69] highbrow Byzantine Greek has many more oxytone word endings than vernacular Greek – so the answer to Michael Jeffreys' question should be affirmative: yes, the metrical differences between Prodromos and Ptochoprodromos are intimately related to language. Second, although the Eideneiers and Hörandner recognise that the metrical differences are '*sprachimmanent*', they are keen to emphasise that this does not mean that the 'learned' passages in the *Ptochoprodromika* display the same percentage of oxytone verse endings as the historical poems of Prodromos; if the *Ptochoprodromika* are the work of a 'learned' poet, one might think of Manganeios or Michael Glykas, but emphatically not of the historical Prodromos. The flaw in this argument is that the 'learned' passages in the *Ptochoprodromika* are considerably more 'vulgar' than anything written by Prodromos. In fact, the 'learned' passages often show linguistic anomalies and vernacular forms that are normally not allowed in twelfth-century court poetry, and the reason for this is simple: the satire does not start only after the 'learned' introductory passages, but permeates the poems from beginning to end.

---

[67] H. Eideneier and N. Eideneier, 'Zum Fünfzehnsilber der Ptochoprodromika' in Ἀφιέρωμα στὸν καθηγητὴ Λίνο Πολίτη (Thessalonike, 1979), 1–7.
[68] W. Hörandner, 'Zur Frage der Metrik früher volkssprachlicher Texte: Kann Theodoros Prodromos der Verfasser volkssprachlicher Gedichte sein?', *JÖB*, 32 (1982), 375–81.
[69] S. Alexiou, 'Bemerkungen zu den *Ptochoprodromika*' in H. Eideneier, ed., *Neograeca Medii Aevi 1: Text und Ausgabe. Akten zum Symposium Köln 1986* (Cologne, 1987), 19–23 (repr. in Alexiou, Δημώδη Βυζαντινά, 71–6, in Greek: 'Παρατηρήσεις στα Πτωχοπροδρομικά').

Instead of comparing apples and oranges, a much more fruitful approach is to compare apples with apples: and these 'apples' are the individual *Ptochoprodromika*. Are they all the same, or do they exhibit significant differences? Looking at the data provided by the Eideneiers,[70] the answer to this question can only be that there are indeed differences: poems I and IV have a stressed oxytone syllable before the caesura (on the eighth metrical position) in 28.5 per cent of cases, whereas II and III have a higher percentage, namely, 35.5 per cent and 36.5 per cent. And according to Jeffreys and Hörandner, in poem V the values are 47 per cent and 48.5 per cent, respectively.[71] The important thing to note is that these metrical differences are recognisable in each and every single witness to the textual tradition: in other words, it is not the scribes who impose their own metrical predilections on the texts, but it is the archetypes of these five texts themselves that display different rhythmical patterns.[72] But if the five 'original' *Ptochoprodromika* have variant metrical values, does this necessarily mean that they are by different authors? Here some caution is required. First, the differences between I and IV, on the one hand, and II and III, on the other, are not so great that it can be excluded with absolute certainty that these four poems were written by one and the same poet. Poem V looks like the work of a different author, but as the text has come down to us as a fragment of a longer text, we do not know whether the poet, after his 'learned' introduction, would have continued writing verses with such a high percentage of stressed eighth syllables. Second, metre is intimately connected with content. In poem I, for instance, in the passages in which the wife is nagging about all sorts of things, she inveighs against Ptochoprodromos in repetitive sentences, all of them with the same rhythmical pattern: accent on the sixth syllable before the caesura. It cannot be excluded, therefore, that the poet of poem I, had he been writing on a different subject, would have varied the rhythmical pattern of his verses to a larger degree.

In the following we will discuss synizesis and hiatus in the *Ptochoprodromika*, for which we used a sample of a hundred verses of each of the five poems.[73] The number of cases of synizesis and hiatus in these hundred verses can be seen in the table (Fig. 25.1).

---

[70] Eideneier and Eideneier, 'Zum Fünfzehnsilber', 4.
[71] Jeffreys, 'Review', 105; Hörandner, 'Zur Frage der Metrik', 376.
[72] For the figures, see Eideneier and Eideneier, 'Zum Fünfzehnsilber', 3–4, nn. 13–14.
[73] We looked at Hesseling and Pernot, eds., *Poèmes Prodromiques*, ed., 30–2 (I.1–100G); 39, 41, 43, 45, 47 (II.15–114G); 38, 40, 42, 44, 46 (II.15–105H) (including 19a–p, 24a, 25a–e, 26a–q); Legrand, ed., *Bibliothèque*, 32–5 (III.1–100G); Eideneier, ed., *Ptochoprodromos*, 119–24 (III.56–65,

Poem	Synizesis			Hiatus
	Between words	Within words	Total	
I	56	8	64	11
II G	46	15	61	7
II H	42	29	71	15
II G+H average	44	22	66	11
III G	41	18	59	5
III S	41	22	63	8
III G+S average	41	20	61	6.5
IV S	63	33	96	0
IV H	58	33	91	2
IV S+H average	60.5	33	93.5	1
V	61.5	16.5	78	4.5

Fig. 25.1 Table showing instances of synizesis and hiatus in samples of one hundred lines from the five poems (© Marjolijne C. Janssen and Marc D. Lauxtermann)

As for synizesis, what do these figures show? First of all, that the differences in frequency are not related to individual scribal practices, but reflect a reality that clearly transcends the level of the manuscripts and comes quite close to the archetype. Take, for instance, poem III: although MSS G and S belong to different branches of the manuscript tradition, they have more or less the same number of cases of synizesis: 59 and 63, respectively. Compare this with poem IV: the same MS S that had only 63 cases of synizesis, now has no fewer than 96. Is this the work of a scribe who, having copied poem III, thinks: next time around, let's use more synizesis? The answer is a firm no. MS S has more synizesis in IV than III, for the simple reason that poem IV has more synizesis than poem III in *all* manuscripts of the *Ptochoprodromika*.

Second, if we compare these figures, it is obvious that certain poems have more synizesis than others: whereas poem IV has an average of 93.5 cases in a hundred verses, and poem V an average of 78, the numbers for I, II and III are considerably lower: 64, 66 and 61 respectively. These figures may be seen as an indication that poem IV (and possibly V) cannot have been written by the same poet as poems I–III.

Synizesis within the word falls into the following categories:

1. [i] → [j]: for instance, βραχιόλιν, ψιαθίν, ομμάτια, άγιε, κύριε, δυό, διά, ποιόν (= ποίον), εδιάβασα, εδιέβαινα, επιάσα/επίασα, εδίωκες

70–3, 80–2, 84–98, 101–22, 124–37, and 140–71S); 141–6 (IV.38–142H). As for poem V, see the explanatory note accompanying Fig 25.1.

(εδιώκες), λογαριάσε, ποιήσον, ποιήση, ομοιάζουν, οκάποιας, αιγειομέταξα, μαγειρείαν (μαγειρειάν), τρία (τρια), αφίημι, μανοηλάτα, τοιούτος, Ευλάλιος, λογιούτζικον;

2. [ε] → [j]: for instance, απαλαρέα, σουγλεάν/σουβλέαν, βαθέα, μακρέας, τραχηλεά, all of them (regardless of spelling) oxytone, χαμωμηλέλαιον, and also τέως (III.149GS and 162G; v.63), cf. IV.422 τια;[74]

3. deletion of a vowel: διπλοεντέληνος (διπλεντέληνος?), χρυσοχόος (in the ms.: χρυσοχοός – pronounced: χρυσοχός), λοετρού (λουτρού), εάν (αν), κρούω (κρω), τρώγειν ([trojn]?).[75]

Whereas synizesis is common to all the manuscripts that contain a certain poem, and should, therefore, be studied as a feature of the textual tradition and possibly even of the archetype, hiatus is located at the level of the individual manuscripts and cannot be viewed as typical of the archetype.[76] In poem II, G has seven hiatuses, H fifteen – but they have only one hiatus in common: να έχει θρύμματα πολλά (II.105). In poem III, G has five hiatuses, S eight – but they have not a single hiatus in common. The high number of hiatus in poem IIH is caused by the many interpolations in this particular version; it does not go back to the original. The same is probably true for poem I, which has come down to us in a single manuscript, the readings of which are not always reliable. Poem IV, on the other hand, has remarkably few instances of hiatus: S none and H two; this clearly indicates that it has suffered less in transmission. As hiatus is fairly restricted and is found only in isolated manuscripts, it is very unlikely that the original *Ptochoprodromika* had much hiatus. This means that an editor,

---

[74] In the α version of *Livistros*, monosyllabic τέως is very common (Agapitos, Ἀφήγησις Λιβίστρου καὶ Ροδάμνης, vv. 57, 313, 353, 372, 648, 1280, 1679, 3587 and 3595), whereas the Vatican version avoids synizesis in this word. Sachlikis has at least one example of τέως with synizesis: G. Wagner, ed., *Carmina graeca medii aevi* (Leipzig, 1874), 87.262. Dellaportas has many examples: M. I. Manousakas, ed., Λεονάρδου Ντελλαπόρτα ποιήματα (Athens, 1995), for which see the index, s.v. τέως and το τέως. The Chiot playwrights Vestarches and Kontaratos have four examples: M. I. Manousakas and W. Puchner, eds., Ανέκδοτα στιχουργήματα του θρησκευτικού θεάτρου του ιζ΄ αιώνα: έργα των ορθόδοξων Χίων κληρικών Μιχ. Βεστάρχη, Γρηγ. Κονταράτου, Γαβρ. Προσοψά (Athens, 2000), 168.771, 226.537, 237.768 and 239.808; the editors print τιός, but one should read τιως: on τιως, see H. Pernot, *Études de linguistique néo-hellénique*, vol. II, *Morphologie des parlers de Chio* (Paris, 1946), 377–8. G. S. Henrich, Εμμανουήλ/Μανόλης Λιμενίτης, Το Θανατικόν της Ρόδου (Thessalonike, 2015), 92.491 offers τιόσι (= τιώσι): see Korais, Ἄτακτα, vol. II, 115.

[75] The form θεωρής may belong to the second category, but it is more likely that it has already evolved into θωρής (which would make it an example of the third category). There are also some words that should clearly be read with syncope in order to make the verse scan: εις το etc., after words ending in a consonant (στο etc.), ένι followed by consonant-initial words (εν), περιπατούν (περπατούν), να τους ικανώση (να τους κανώση), έπαρ' το.

[76] As hiatus is allowed at the caesura, we have not counted such cases.

when faced with two different readings, should choose the one without hiatus. Take for instance III.56–7GMPK: ἀπό μικρόθεν με ἔλεγεν ὁ γέρων ὁ πατήρ μου, τέκνον/παιδίν μου, μάθε γράμματα και ωσάν εσέναν έχει,[77] where SAC offer ἀπό μικρού με ἔλεγεν, etc. (ever since I was a child, my old father used to say, 'learn your letters, son, and you'll be king of the hill'). Not only does the reading of SAC introduce a ghastly hiatus, it also spoils the joke right at the beginning of this famous passage, for a Byzantine who had 'learnt letters' (i.e. ancient Greek), would not have dared write the pleonastic ἀπό μικρόθεν[78] – he would not have chosen the vulgar μικρόθεν in the first place (even without ἀπό), but have gone for the more elevated παιδόθεν or νηπιόθεν.

At the end of this chapter, after a long and winding trail through the deserts of Ptochoprodromic scholarship, is there a conclusion in sight? No – unless the platitude that much research is still needed to solve all the unanswered questions counts as one. Scholarship is chasing a fata morgana, a vision of Prodromos, a glimpse of his alter egos, a fleeting presence. There is Theodore, there is Manganeios, there is Ptocho, there is Hilarion, and there may even be more out there. To distinguish all these Prodromoi, we need thorough and detailed studies of all the linguistic and metrical aspects of the five surviving poems both at the level of the individual manuscripts and at the level of their common archetypes. The use of conditional constructions and of synizesis in the *Ptochoprodromika* seems to suggest that poem IV differs from the rest, but it is too early to tell. One thing is certain, though: as long as editors and scholars plod on without any real understanding of language and metre, progress is clearly impossible. To return to the quote from the Jeffreys with which we began, we would like to rewrite it as follows: 'It is noticeable that the poets [addidimus –s] seem [delevimus –s] in control of the linguistic medium they are [in ms. jeffreyano: he is] using', and add, in our learned commentary, '*linguistic medium* anglice: quid sibi velit, nescimus'.

---

[77] For the enigmatic ωσάν εσέναν έχει, which is the equivalent of χαρά σ' εσένα, see, in addition to the parallels from *Livistros* and *Logos parigoritikos* adduced by H. Eideneier, 'Zu den Προδρομικά', *BZ*, 57 (1964), 336, and L. Politis, 'Φιλολογικά σὲ παλαιότερα κείμενα', *Ἑλληνικά*, 19 (1966), 358–61, the following example from a catanyctic alphabet (F. K. Bouboulidis, ed., 'Δημώδεις μεταβυζαντινοί ἀλφάβητοι', *ΕΕΒΣ*, 25 (1955), 298, 1.48 app.crit.): ωσάν τον εύρη εις το καλόν· χαρά σ' εκείνον έχει (blessed is he whom [death] finds prepared; fortunate is he indeed).

[78] The use of the prepositions ἀπό or ἐκ before adverbs ending in –θεν is common in Koine and lowbrow Byzantine Greek, but not in the kind of highbrow Atticistic Greek favoured by Constantinopolitan intellectuals and court dignitaries.

Further Reading

The main edition: H. Eideneier, ed., *Ptochoprodromos: Einführung, kritische Ausgabe, deutsche Übersetzung, Glossa* (Cologne, 1991). Studies include: H. Eideneier and N. Eideneier, 'Zum Fünfzehnsilber der Ptochoprodromika' in Ἀφιέρωμα στὸν καθηγητὴ Λίνο Πολίτη (Thessalonike, 1979), 1–7; M. C. Janssen and M. D. Lauxtermann, 'Το παράπονο του δασκάλου: ο *Πτωχοπρόδρομος* και η βυζαντινή γραμματική παράδοση' in I. García Gálvez and O. Omatos Sáenz, eds., *Tolmiros Skapaneas: Homenaje al Profesor K. A. Dimadis* (Vitoria-Gasteiz, 2012), 25–41; M. C. Janssen, 'Verb Morphology' in D. Holton, G. Horrocks et al., eds., *The Cambridge Grammar of Medieval and Early Modern Greek*, forthcoming; G. Wakker, *Conditions and Conditionals: An Investigation of Ancient Greek* (Amsterdam, 1994).

Recovered Languages

CHAPTER 26

The Lexicon of Horses' Colours in Learned and Vernacular Texts

Erich Trapp

In its broadest sense, philology is concerned with every kind of written text, from the famous to the obscure. Within philology, lexicography especially cannot afford to be restricted to only certain fields of literature. The lexicographer who wishes, for instance, to trace the equine vocabulary used by the Byzantines may study a range of texts in different registers; in doing so, he or she will be able to see the extent to which these texts make distinctions between different kinds of horses with reference to a shared terminology. While preparing the *Lexikon zur byzantinischen Gräzität*, I have seen that rather disparate texts employ the same kinds of specialist terms – mainly those dealing with the identification of a horse by the colour of its coat. Particularly rich in examples are: first, the well-known Byzantine epic of *Digenes Akrites*;[1] second, a collection of veterinary medical writings revised in the tenth century, but based on fourth-century sources, the *Hippiatrika*;[2] and, third, a Coptic or Greek–Arabic *Glossary*, dated between the eleventh and fourteenth centuries, which seems to be nearly unknown to the majority of those working in Byzantine and Near Eastern Studies.[3] Some other examples can be taken from dream-books and several other texts.[4] As we shall see, despite their variety, these texts display almost full agreement in the meaning of their vocabulary. This fact raises interesting questions regarding the pathways by which seemingly technical vocabulary of this type was transmitted in the medieval period.

---

[1] Both for practical and personal reasons I use this edition: E. M. Jeffreys, ed. and trans., *Digenis Akritis: The Grottaferrata and Escorial Versions* (Cambridge, 1998). For a very limited number of quotations I shall refer to my own edition: E. Trapp, ed., *Digenes Akrites. Synoptische Ausgabe der ältesten Versionen* (Vienna, 1971).
[2] E. Oder and C. Hoppe, ed., *Corpus hippiatricorum graecorum* (Leipzig, 1924–7); A. McCabe, *A Byzantine Encyclopaedia of Horse Medicine: The Sources, Compilation, and Transmission of the Hippiatrica* (Oxford, 2007).
[3] H. Munier, ed., *La Scala Copte 44 de la Bibliothèque Nationale de Paris: transcription et vocabulaire*, vol. 1 (Cairo, 1930).
[4] E. Trapp et al., *Lexikon zur byzantinischen Gräzität. Fasc. 1–7: Α-ταριχευτικός* (Vienna, 1994–2011).

If our knowledge of these words is dependent on textual survival – in order to help us understand and translate with greater certainty, we compare written passages – what role, if any, did the reading practices of people such as the authors of our sources play in their selection of words? Did they derive the descriptive language they used from literary or scientific works of reference that were preserved in writing, from compositions that were handed down orally, or from the knowledge that was acquired more generally through lived experience? Here, careful analysis can provide one with a glimpse, however imperfect, of the origin of the words and patterns of circulation.

Before dealing with the Byzantine texts that mention horses' colours, it seems useful to look at the earlier, Roman, tradition on the subject. The most exhaustive discussion in Latin can be found in the *Etymologies* of Isidore of Seville (c. 560–636), which expounds older texts, especially that of Palladios in the fifth century:

> Color hic praecipue spectandus: badius, aureus, roseus, myrteus, ceruinus, giluus, glaucus, scutulatus, canus, candidus, albus, guttatus, niger. Sequenti autem ordine, uarius ex nigro badio que distinctus; reliquus uarius color uel cinereus deterrimus.
>
> These colours in particular should be noted: chestnut, golden, ruddy, myrtle-coloured, fawn, pale yellow, bright grey, piebald, grey-white, shining-white, flat white, spotted, and black. But in the following list 'variegated' as a mixture of black and chestnut is a special case, but other variegations and ash-colour are the least good.[5]

Is there a comparable passage in Greek literature distinguishing different kinds of horses according to their colour?[6] The *Hippiatrika* consists of excerpts of anonymous or little-known authors from the fourth century onward (Apsyrtos, Hierokles and others) that were collected together in the early Byzantine period and revised during the reign of Constantine VII Porphyrogennetos (905–59).[7] But only in one late manuscript, which has so far been published in part, do we find material that concerns our

---

[5] The passage in the original and the translation have been quoted from: S. A. Barney et al., eds. and trans., *The Etymologies of Isidore of Seville* (Cambridge, 2006), 250. For Palladios, see R. Rodgers, ed., *Palladii Rutilii Tauri Aemiliani viri inlustris opus agriculturae, de veterinaria medicina, de insitione* (Leipzig, 1975) 135–8 (IV.13).

[6] As to post-classical Greek literature, it may be sufficient to hint to quote the passage in the Septuagint (Zach. 1:8): ἵπποι πυρροὶ καὶ ψαροὶ καὶ ποικίλοι καὶ λευκοί.

[7] S. Hornblower and A. Spawforth, eds., *The Oxford Classical Dictionary* (Oxford, 1996), 1592–3; H. Cancik and H. Schneider, eds., *Der Neue Pauly, Enzyklopädie der Antike* (Stuttgart, 1998), vol. v, 578–9; A.-M. Doyen-Higuet, ed., *L'Epitomé de la Collection d'hippiatrie grecque*, vol. 1 (Louvaine-la-Neuve, 2006).

subject. The material in question is found in two chapters, the first of which reads as follows:

> Περὶ ἵππων χροῶν. τὸ ποταπαί εἰσιν αἱ διαφοραὶ τῶν ἵππων, καὶ τί τὸ ἐνεργηματι [sic] τῆς διαφορᾶς τῶν τοιούτων. Ὁ βάδεος ἵππος ἐν πολέμῳ. ὁ μαυροβάδεος εὔτονος. ὁ σοῦρτος κάτοχος καὶ ὀξύς. ὁ γρίβας ἵππος καλός. ὁ σιδηρέας ἀρκετὸν καὶ τὸ ὄνομα. ὁ βλάγκας καλὸς καὶ εὔτονος. ὁ δάγαλις ἵππος ἄτονος. ὁ ἀρτουκοῦρος δάγαλος πολλὰ διώκει. ὁ βάλας καλὸς καὶ εὔτονος, ἀηδὴς δέ. ὁ βόρχας καλὸς καὶ εὔτονος. ὁ φάλβας (τῶν ἑκατὸν εἷς ἂν εὑρεθείη) πολλάκις καλός ἐστιν.[8]

About the colours of horses, or concerning where the differences between the horses can be found, and what the nature of their difference is. The bay is the horse to have in war; the black-bay is vigorous; the σοῦρτος is retentive and quick, the grey is a good horse; the iron-coloured, whose name suffices [to indicate his mettle]; the white is good and vigorous; the ruddy is a slack horse; the ἀρτουκοῦρος (?) ruddy pursues well; the one with a blaze is good and vigorous, but unpleasant; the βόρχας good and vigorous, the dun-coloured, if one among hundred could be found, is mostly good.

In an earlier chapter of the same manuscript, dealing with animal sores, we come across the following words: βάδεον ἢ μαῦρον ... ὀφείλεις δὲ λέγειν τὸν ἵππον τὴν χροίαν, ἤ ἐστιν· ᾧ ἵππε μαῦρε, σιδερέα, ἢ βάδε[λτ]ε ἢ δάγαλε (chestnut or black ... you have to tell a horse from its colour. O, black, iron-coloured horse, or chestnut or ruddy).[9] In these passages, the only point of commonality with Isidore is in the use of the Greek term 'βάδιος' or 'βάδεος', which is identical to the Latin 'badius'.

Among other prose texts, of special interest to our subject is the chapter concerning animals in the Coptic or Greek–Arabic glossary (Chapter xix, f.83v–86r), as it mentions the following kinds of horses categorised by their colours: δακάλιν ('ruddy'), ξανθός ('yellowish'), πυρρός ('tawny'), ἄσπρον, λευκόν ('white'), χλωρόν, βλάγκιν, ὠχρός ('pale'), βόρχιν ('fox-coloured'), αἴολος, φιτιλίν, ποικίλος ('spotted, dappled'), σιδεραῖον ('iron-colored'), βοῦρχος, μαῦρον, μέλας ('black'), βάδιος ('bay'), ῥινοφάλαιος ('with a white nose').[10] Additional texts with similar information on the colour of horses include several anonymous dream-books, from which we may give the following passage as an example: Ἵππου **λευκοῦ** ἐπικαθέζεσθαι ἐνθήκης

---

[8] *Corpus hippiatricorum graecorum*, ed. Oder and Hoppe, vol. II, 312.14–23 (c. 201). If we look at the apparatus criticus, we find that the editors have made an unnecessary correction by changing the text of the manuscript σιδερέας ἀρκήτον, which doubtlessly has to be read as ὁ σιδερέας (vernacular form), ἀρκεῖ τον (acc. instead of dat. or gen.) καὶ τὸ ὄνομα.
[9] Ibid., II 289.26–90.3 (61).
[10] Munier, *La Scala Copte 44*, 169.63–170.24. With regard to the replacement of λευκός by ἄσπρος, see the recent study by W. Voigt, *Die Leiden der alten Wörter* (Frankfurt, 2006), 533–67.

προσθήκην σημαίνει· ἵππου δὲ **ψαροῦ**, ἀγγελίαν μετὰ ζημίας δηλοῖ· ἵππου **βαδίου**, ὁδὸν ἐπικερδῆ σημαίνει ... ἵππου **μαύρου** ... (To sit on a white horse, means increase of store; but on a pale, reveals a message with loss; on a chestnut, means a profitable way ... on a black ...'[11] A further passage of similar tenor can be read in the dream-book attributed to Achmet:

Ἐκ τῶν Περσῶν καὶ Αἰγυπτίων περὶ χρωμάτων ἵππων καὶ σελλαρίων βασιλικῶν. Ὁ **λευκότατος** ἵππος ἐν θεωρίᾳ βασιλέως εἰς πρόσωπον αὐγούστης κρίνεται. ὁ λευκὸς **σιδηραῖος**, εἴ ἐστιν βασιλέως σελλάριον, εἰς ἐλάττονα τῆς αὐγούστης γυναῖκα κρίνεται ... σελλάριον δὲ βασιλικὸν ἐὰν ἐστι **ῥοδόχρουν**, εἰς γυναῖκα ἐπίχαριν κρίνεται· καὶ ὁ **μέλας** ἵππος ὁ βασιλικὸς εἰς γυναῖκα πλουσίαν καὶ θλιβερὰν κρίνεται διὰ τὸ μέλαν.

According to the Persians and Egyptians on the colours of horses and the saddle horses of the emperors. The very whitest horse in the emperor's dream is interpreted as the person of the empress. The whitish grey, if it is the emperor's saddle horse, is interpreted as a woman inferior to the empress ... but if the emperor's saddle horse is rose-coloured,[12] it is interpreted as a charming lady, and a black horse of the emperor is interpreted as a rich, but afflicting woman because of the black colour.[13]

Turning from prose to verse, we note that the epic of *Digenes Akrites* is especially plentiful in examples. There we find the following kinds of horses: ἀστεράτος ('starred, with a star-shaped spot on the forehead'); βάδιος ('bay, reddish brown, chestnut'); βοῦλχας or βρόχα ('pony, possibly of a certain colour'); γρίβας ('grey'); μοῦντος ('dark brown'); δαγάλος ('ruddy'); λευκός ('white'); μαῦρος ('black'); and φιτυλός ('piebald'). They occur especially in passages of the two main versions G and E. One of these passages describes the young Constantine preparing for single combat with the Emir:

Ὁ δὲ ἐφ' ἵππου ἐπιβὰς μαύρου, γενναιοτάτου

Mounting his horse that was black and most noble.[14]

Other references are in passages where the Emir approaches Constantine:

[11] F. Drexl, 'Das anonyme Traumbuch des Cod. Paris. gr. 2511', *Λαογραφία*, 8 (1921), 347–75 (especially 357, no. 115). The same text, published independently, forms part of A. Delatte, ed., *Anecdota Atheniensia et alia* (Liège, 1939), vol. II, 533. See also S. M. Oberhelman, ed., *Dreambooks in Byzantium: Six Oneirocritica in Translation, with Commentary and Introduction* (Aldershot, 2008).
[12] The reference to a rose-coloured horse is a rare case of equivalence with the list in Isidore's *Etymologies* (*roseus*). See above, n. 5.
[13] F. Drexl, ed., *Achmetis oneirocriticon* (Leipzig, 1925), 182.15ff. (also 111.22 and 26. German translation by K. Brackerts, trans., *Das Traumbuch des Achmet ben Sirin* (Munich, 1986); also M. Mavroudi, trans., *A Byzantine Book on Dream Interpretation, the Oneirocriticon of Achmet and Its Arabic Sources* (Leiden, 2002), 206–7.
[14] *Digenis Akritis*, ed. Jeffreys, 10–11 (G I.146).

Horses' Colours in Learned and Vernacular Texts

Φαρὶν ἐκαβαλίκευσεν **φιτυλὸν** καὶ **ἀστεράτον**

He had mounted a horse that was piebald and starred,[15]

where the Emir's mother writes to her son:

τὴν **βάδεαν** καβαλλίκευε, παράσυρε τὴν **μαύρην**,
ἡ **δαγάλ'** ἃς ἀκολουθῇ, καὶ οὐδεὶς οὐ μή σε φθάσῃ

Mount the chestnut horse, lead the black horse,
let the ruddy horse follow and no one will catch you,[16]

where the Emir returns with his mother from Arabia:

μοῦλαν ἐκαβαλλίκευσε **βάδεαν, ἀστεράτην**

he rode a chestnut mule with a star,[17]

where Digenes approaches the girl:

Τὸν **βοῦλχαν** ἐπελάλησε, πλησιάζει τῇ κόρῃ

He urged his pony on, he approached the girl,[18]

where Digenes gives instructions to his *protostrator*:

Ἀπόστρωσε τὸν **βοῦλχαν** μου, στρῶσον μου δὲ τὸν **μαῦρον**

Unsaddle my pony for me and saddle the black,[19]

where Digenes comes to the girl at night:

Ἦτον δάος ὁ **μαῦρος** του, τὸ φέγγος ὡς ἡμέρα

His black horse was swift, the moonlight like day,[20]

where the girl, fleeing their pursuers, says to Digenes:

καὶ ἴσχυε κατὰ πολὺ τὸν **μαῦρον** ἀποπλήττων

be very strong and urge on your black horse,[21]

---

[15] Ibid., 239 (E l.10); see *Digenes Akrites*, ed. Trapp, 89 (Z II.304) φαρὶν ἐκαβαλλίκευεν φιτυλόν, ἀστεράτον.

[16] Ibid., 30–1 (G II.95f.); see 258–9 (E ll.279f.) Τὸν βάδεον καβαλίκευε καὶ βάλε τὸ λουρίκιν and *Digenes Akrites*, ed. Trapp, 113 (Z III.640) τὸ βάδιον καβαλλίκευε καὶ τὸ δαγάλλιν σύρε.

[17] Ibid., 58–9 (G III.261); see *Digenes Akrites*, ed. Trapp, 149 (Z III.1174) ἵππον ἐκαβαλλίκευεν δαγάλλον, ἀστερᾶτον (he rode a ruddy horse with a star).

[18] Ibid., 86–7 (G IV.314).

[19] Ibid., 88–9 (G IV.376); see *Digenes Akrites*, ed. Trapp, 187 (Z V.1764) Ἀπόστρωσον τὴν βρόχαν μου καὶ στρῶσον μου τὸν μαῦρον. The corresponding passage in *Digenis Akritis*, ed. Jeffreys, 298–9 (E l.798) runs thus: ἀπόστρωσε τὸν γρίβαν μου καὶ στρῶσε μου τὸν μαῦρον (unsaddle my grey and saddle for me the black).

[20] Ibid., 90–1 (G IV.407). [21] Ibid., 102–3 (G IV.627).

where Digenes is on his way to Ankylas to get his revenge:

> σκάλα βαλὼν ἐπέζευσα τὸν θαυμαστόν μου **γρίβαν** ...
> Πηδῶ, ἐκαβαλλίκευσα τὸν θαυμαστὸν τὸν **μοῦντον**
>
> using the stirrup I dismounted from my wonderful grey horse ...
> I mounted and rode the wonderful dark brown horse,[22]

where Digenes is on the lookout for the guerrillas accompanied by the Amazon Maximou:

> εἰς ἵππον **γρίβαν** ἐπιβὰς ἀνῆλθον εἰς τὴν βίγλαν
>
> mounting the grey horse I went up to the guard,[23]

where the Amazon Maximou appears:

> ἐποχουμένη εἰς **λευκὸν βοῦλχαν** καθάπερ γάλα
>
> riding a pony white as milk,[24]

where Digenes is on his way to Maximou:

> Τὸν **γρίβα** μου ἐπιλάλησα τὸν ποταμὸν περάσει ...
> καὶ ἐξέπεσεν ὁ **γρίβας** μου καὶ ἐχώθην ἕως τραχήλου
>
> I urged on my grey horse to cross the river ...
> and my grey horse stumbled and sank up to his neck,[25]

where Digenes fights with Maximou:

> τοῦ δὲ **βοῦλχα** ἀποτεμὼν τὴν κεφαλὴν εὐθέως
>
> he promptly cut off her pony's head,[26]

where Digenes readies himself for single combat with Maximou:

> καὶ ἵππον μετεσέλλισα **δαγάλην, ἀστερᾶτον**
>
> and I saddled my starred ruddy horse,[27]

and where Maximou appears:

> Εἰς φάραν ἐπεκάθητο **μαύρην**, γενναιοτάτην
>
> She was seated on a black, most noble steed.[28]

---

[22] *Digenes Akrites*, ed. Trapp, 273 (Z VII.3011 and 3019); see 275 (Z VII.3037).
[23] Ibid., 295 (Z VII.3358).=   [24] *Digenis Akritis*, ed. Jeffreys, 184–5 (G VI.552).
[25] Ibid., 352–3 (E ll.1534–6).
[26] Ibid., 186–7 (G VI.588); see *Digenes Akrites*, ed. Trapp, 305 (Z VII.3487) τῆς βρόχας δὲ τὴν κεφαλὴν ἀπέτεμον εὐθέως
[27] Ibid., 192–3 (G VI.717); see *Digenes Akrites*, ed. Trapp, 315 (Z VII.3617) εἰς ἵππον μετεσέλλισα δαγάλλον, ἀστερᾶτον
[28] Ibid., 194–5 (G VI.735).

By way of pointing out further analogies with the romance-epic of *Digenes*, a passage from the *Romance of Alexander* can be quoted as an apt point of comparison for the use of equine vocabulary:

ζεύγνυσιν ἐν μὲν τῇ βίγᾳ δύο ἵππους **βαδίους** (coni. pro καλλίους vel βαλίους), τοὺς δὲ ἀκροτήρας (correct ἀκρωτῆρας) **δαγαλλίους**

he yokes a pair of chestnut horses to a chariot, but flanks them with ruddy ones.[29]

The etymologies of the terms for the colour of horses' coats can be traced with variable degrees of success. One case that is relatively straightforward is that of φιτυλός ('piebald'), which has derived from ancient πιτυλός.[30] Among the more difficult cases is that of δαγάλος. Karapotzoglu, who discusses it at length, compares it to the Arabic '*dāyyal*', which indicates a person or animal with a proud, elegant and conceited bearing. The Coptic or Greek–Arabic Glossary, on the other hand, offers as the Arabic equivalent not '*dāyyal*' but rather '*aqšaru*', which means clear red, ruddy or blond, indicating that it is less the temperament of the horse than a specific colour that is implied.[31] Whereas βούλχας or βρόχα, βόρχιν and βούρχος seem to be connected with βούριχος, derived from Latin *burrichus* ('pony') and possibly also *burrus* (fox-coloured'), these terms are translated in Arabic by '*abraš* (spotted), *ashab* (grey) or *adham* (black)', leaving its meaning uncertain. Two different etymologies can be proposed for the term γρίβας ('grey'): although their exact linguistic provenance is not entirely clear, a Gothic origin seems more plausible than a Slavic one.[32] At the moment, no origin can be postulated for the *hapax legomenon* σισθλάκιν, which occurs in a scholion to Aristophanes, and is most likely a synonym for ψαρόν, i.e. 'dapple-grey' (τὸν ψαρὸν ἵππον· τὸ **σισθλάκιν**).[33] Thus, within these limitations, the evidence that has been examined so far suggests not only derivations from Ancient Greek, but also borrowings from Latin, Arabic, Gothic and Slavonic linguistic contexts. This indicates that medieval Greek texts on

---

[29] J. Trumpf, ed., *Vita Alexandri regis Macedonum* (Stuttgart, 1974), 18.5f.
[30] Compare especially ὁ φίτυλλος ('animal with brown and white spots on its face') in K. Giankulles, Θησαυρός Κυπριακῆς διαλέκτου (Leukosia, 2009).
[31] K. Karapotsoglu, 'Παρατηρήσεις σὲ ἑλληνικὰ δυσετυμολόγητα', *Βυζαντινά*, 12 (1983), 399–400. I want to express my warmest thanks to my colleagues Stephan Conermann (Bonn) and Klaus Belke (Vienna) for help with the Arabic.
[32] D. Georgakas, 'Beiträge zur Deutung als slavisch erklärter Ortsnamen', *BZ*, 41 (1941), 397.
[33] W. Koster, ed., *Scholia in Aristophanem* 1 3, 2 (Groningen, 1974), 452.1225c. Also the etymology of μοῦντος has to remain unclear, E. Kriaras, *Λεξικό της μεσαιωνικής ελληνικής δημώδους γραμματείας, τόμος ια'* (Thessalonike, 1990).

equine matters use vocabulary originating from a variety of ethnic groups. Moreover, this vocabulary was not confined only to the pages of the Byzantine manuscripts we study – whether these included medical and other scientific works, or literary works such as epics and romances – but these terms circulated broadly among both male and female Greek-speaking members of society.[34] An indication of its quotidian use is provided by the testament, dated 1098, of a certain nun Mary, who left in her legacy to her eunuch servant Nicholas 'her iron-coloured horse, Daimonitzes' (τὸ ἄλογον τὸ σιδηραῖον, τὸν Δαιμονίτζην).[35] Much more, no doubt, could be said on this subject by a Byzantinist who also moonlights as a horse-trainer or large animal veterinarian, if such exists, or who at the very least is an accomplished equestrian. I have to confess (while fully convinced that philology and knowledge of the broader world should always go hand in hand), my own limitations regarding direct experience of horses; therefore, I consider it best to end my modest contribution here.

Further Reading

The main text: E. M. Jeffreys, ed. and trans., *Digenis Akritis: The Grottaferrata and Escorial Versions* (Cambridge, 1998); E. Trapp, *Digenes Akrites. Synoptische Ausgabe der ältesten Versionen* (Vienna, 1971). See also: E. Trapp, W. Hörandner, J. Diethart et al., *Lexikon zur byzantinischen Gräzität*, 7 Fasc. (Vienna, 1994–2011); and A. McCabe, *A Byzantine Encyclopaedia of Horse Medicine: The Sources, Compilation, and Transmission of the Hippiatrica* (Oxford, 2007).

---

[34] E. Trapp, 'Zur fragmentarischen Überlieferung im Bereich der Sachkultur' in C. Gastgeber et al., eds., *Fragmente: Der Umgang mit lückenhafter Quellenüberlieferung in der Mittelalterforschung*. (Vienna, 2010), 205–8.

[35] See J. Lefort et al., eds., *Actes d'Iviron II: du milieu du XIe s. à 1204. Edition diplomatique* (Paris, 1990), doc. 47.35.

CHAPTER 27

Multilingualism and Translation in the Edition of Vernacular Texts

Manolis Papathomopoulos

This chapter aims to draw attention to the role of multilingualism for Byzantine and post-Byzantine Greek readers, authors and editors. It emphasises the importance of consulting the version of the text in the original language when constructing an edition of a translation or paraphrase. Although Manolis Papathomopoulos had only completed an initial draft of his contribution before he died, it was felt that it should nonetheless be published because it represented his last work on the edition he had planned of the Theseid. *It proved possible to use the notes in his papers in order to insert the relevant Greek passages. The English of the commentary was also corrected and some further interventions made to the content in order to clarify passages.*

Giovanni Boccaccio's *Teseida: delle Nozze d'Emilia*, written around 1340 at the Neapolitan court of Robert d'Anjou, is an epic poem of 10,374 lines that consists of a short prologue in rhymed political verse, followed by twelve books in stanzas of eight lines, of which only the seventh and eighth lines rhyme together.[1] While its ostensible subject is a retelling of the life of the ancient Greek hero Theseus, King of Athens, in fact most of the narrative is devoted to a love story that takes place at his court. The poem begins with Theseus' conquest of the Amazons, his wedding with their queen Hippolyta, and their return to Athens with Hippolyta's younger sister, Emilia. It then narrates Theseus' triumph against Creon, Oedipus' successor, who had denied the Argive kings burial, and also the conquest of Thebes, when Theseus takes prisoner two young Theban princes and close friends named Archytas and Polemone. The princes are brought to Athens and kept in the palace prison, where they both see Emilia from their cell and fall in love with her. Archytas is freed at the intercession of Perithous, Theseus' Thessalian ally, while Polemone eventually escapes from the

---

[1] I dedicate this chapter to Michael and Elizabeth Jeffreys, two generous old friends of mine, as a remembrance of our long collaboration on the edition of the Πόλεμος τῆς Τρωάδος.

prison and challenges his friend and rival to a duel to the death to determine which of the two will have Emilia's love. Theseus intervenes and arranges the substitution of a joust for the mortal combat to which they had agreed. Archytas is the joust's victor but, while making his triumphal round, he receives a mortal wound from his horse. Before he expires, he obtains from Polemone a promise that he will marry Emilia. Then follow Archytas' death and burial, and finally the celebration of Polemone's and Emilia's wedding.

The *Teseida* was translated into Greek (Βιβλίον τοῦ Θησέου, henceforth *Theseid*) in the Duchy of Athens at the beginning of the fifteenth century. At that time, the Duchy was in the possession of the Florentine family of Acciaiuoli, whose most notorious member was Niccolò, Boccaccio's friend. Nerio I, Niccolò's son, expanded his sovereignty over the whole of Attica and Boeotia, and made Athens, instead of Thebes, the capital of his state. The central plot of the original Italian text takes place in both Athens and Thebes, and this may have been relevant to the choice to translate this particular text into Greek.[2] It is very likely that the translator worked under the patronage of Nerio I, the Duke of Athens and conqueror of Thebes, with the intention of providing mythological background to this momentous occasion.

Two versions of this fifteenth-century translation have survived: the first is preserved in a manuscript from the fifteenth/sixteenth century, Parisinus graecus 2898 (= P); the second is that of the *editio princeps* (= ed.), edited in 1529 in Venice by Dimitrios Zenos, who is also the presumed author of this version.[3] In fact, the text of this edition is a reproduction with slight modifications of a Vatican manuscript, Vaticanus Pal. gr. 426, written by Zenos himself. Zenos made important alterations to the text of the hyparchetype which he had at his disposal, mainly in order to smooth out the metrical anomalies of the translation, to clarify obscure passages or simplify others which seemed to be complicated, to replace Italianisms by Greek words, etc. Apart from the extant versions, I hypothesize the existence of two manuscript hyperarchetypes (one for each of the surviving witnesses of the tradition) and of an archetype.[4]

A comparison of both Greek versions with Boccaccio's original, carried out line-for-line and word-for-word, has allowed me to comprehend the

---

[2] See S. Kaklamanis, 'Ἀπό τό χειρόγραφο στό ἔντυπο: Θησέος καί γάμοι τῆς Αἰμίλιας (1529)', Θησαυρίσματα, 27 (1997), 151–2.
[3] The third edition of *Teseida*, published in 1528 in Venice, may have provided an impetus for Zenos' edition.
[4] The theory of a single hyparchetype was proposed by E. Follieri, 'La versione in greco volgare del Teseida del Boccaccio', *SBN*, 7 (1953), 67–77, who gave the *stemma* of the *Theseid*.

translation's text better, which is at times difficult to understand, and to make some discreet interventions, which rely on the idea that the translator knew not only Greek but also Italian well and was able to follow Boccaccio's text closely.⁵ The clumsy errors of the two versions should not be attributed to the translator's ignorance or his inability but to various accidents of transmission: numerous phonetical errors in both extant versions of the translation lead me to believe that it was written under dictation.

This chapter constitutes part of my preparatory work for a critical edition of the Greek translation.⁶ I propose emendations for most of the damaged passages. A close collation of both extant versions of the translation has shown that they contribute equally to the restoration of the text and that they can be used to emend each other. In addition, I have used the Italian original – following the same reasoning and method as we applied to the *editio princeps* of the Πόλεμος τῆς Τρωάδος.⁷ I think that it would be impossible to edit the Greek translation satisfactorily without a detailed comparison with the original Italian text.

Let us now examine the damaged passages:

1.Prol.13

        Καὶ δίκαιον ἔχω πάντοτε *νὰ κλῶ* τὸν στερεμό σου

νὰ κλῶ ed. νὰ κλαίω P

Given that νὰ κλῶ is not attested, νὰ κλαίω as in P should be preferred instead of νὰ κλῶ ed., adopted by Kaklamanis.

2.Prol.32

        λέγοντας· *γίατηνε δεκεῖ αὐτήνη* ἡ κυρά μου

γίατηνε δεκεῖ ed. Διὰ τὴν ἐδεκεῖ P γιατί 'ν' ἐδεκεῖ Kaklamanis αὐτήνη P et ed. | αὐτείνη Kaklamanis

---

⁵ I have used the critical edition of A. Roncaglia, ed., *Teseida: delle nozze d'Emilia* (Bari, 1941). My Greek references are made on the basis of the Italian edition, since there are close parallels between strophes and lines in the Italian and Greek texts.

⁶ Up to now there have been published only the first book of the version P by E. Follieri, ed., *Il Teseida neogreco, Libro 1. Saggio di edizione* (Rome, 1959); the sixth book of the version P by B. Olsen, ed., 'The Greek Translation of Boccaccio's Theseid Book 6', *ClMed*, 41 (1990), 275–301, and the Prologue of the two versions by S. Kaklamanis, "Ὁ Πρόλογος εἰς τὸ βιβλίον τοῦ Θησέου, Ἐκδοτικὴ διερεύνηση" in N. M. Panagiotakes, ed., Ἄνθη Χαρίτων (Venice, 1998), 101–74. My idea to edit *Theseid* emerged during a discussion with the late Stavros Papastavrou, fellow of Peterhouse, Cambridge, in the course of my residence at that college in 1968–9. For her laurea E. Follieri had prepared the critical edition of both versions of *Theseid*, but regrettably she never published it.

⁷ E. M. Jeffreys and M. Papathomopoulos, eds., *The War of Troy* (Athens, 1996).

It seems obvious that in the phrase γίατηνε δεκεῖ there is no space for a causal conjunction, but only for the demonstrative particule διά/γιά plus the pronoun την and the adverb ἐδεκεῖ, provided by P, while αὐτήνη must hide the verb 'ναι (αὐτή 'ναι).

3.Prol.52

βλέποντας *ποῦ* εὑρίσκομαι καὶ *πρῶτα ποῦ* βρισκόμου

ποῦ P πῶς ed. | πρῶτα ποῦ ed. πρώτου P πρῶτον Kaklamanis

Codex P provides the correct reading ποῦ. Under πρώτου we may discern the correct reading, προτοῦ; Kaklamanis' conjecture πρῶτον makes less sense.

4.Prol.146

ἀγάπης τὰ καμώματα, νὰ *τὸν* τ' ἀναθυμίζουν

τὸν P τοὺς ed.

The reading τοὺς of ed. leads to the correct conjecture: νὰ τῶν τ' ἀναθυμίζουν 'to remind them of it'.

5.Prol.158

καὶ πρῶτα πῶς τοὺς ηὕρηκεν *γιεμίλια γιαμαζόνα*

ἡ Αἰμίλια Ἀμαζόνα P γιεμίλια γιαμαζόνα ed. γιΑἰμίλια γιἀμαζόνα Kaklamanis

The reading of ed. γιεμίλια γιαμαζόνα should be changed to γη (= euphonic γ plus ἡ) Αἰμίλια γη Ἀμαζόνα.

6.Prol.239–40

Καὶ μὴν *εἰδῆς* γιατί ἔν' μικρὸ καὶ χάρισμα ὀλίγο,
ἀμὴ ὡς δοῦλος σου μικρός, κυρά μου, 'σὲν τὸ *πεύγω*

239 εἰδῆς ed. εἰπῆς coni. Kaklamanis 240 πεύγω ed. πέβγω coni. Kaklamanis

The reading εἰδῆς is satisfactory with a sense more or less the same as εἰπῆς, and πεύγω should be corrected to πέμπω, which in the context is less odd than Kaklamanis' πέβγω.

7.A4.6–7

νὰ δῆτε πῶς *τοὺς βάφει δὲ* καὶ πῶς τοὺς ἀλλοχροιαίνει
ἐκείνους ποὺ συνακλουθοῦν τοῦ ἔρωτος τὴν στράτα

The reading τοὺς βάφει δὲ does not make sense. Boccaccio wrote *scolora*, which leads us to the correct reading ξεβάφει τους instead of τοὺς βάφει δέ.

8.A6.8

καὶ ηὖραν τρόπον κ' ἔποικαν τήνδε ἐπεθυμίαν

Given that the Ancient Greek pronoun τήνδε is never used by the translator and does not make grammatical sense either, it should be replaced by τὴν τρελὴ (ἐπεθυμία), in accordance with Boccaccio's *lor follia*.

9.A22.8

ἀρχὴ κυρὰ καὶ λέγει τους· 'Κυράδες φουμισμένες!'
ἀρχὴ P et ed.: ἀρχεῖ Follieri

There is no verb ἀρχῶ: ἀρχὴ should be corrected into ἄρχει, active form for ἄρχεται.

10.A24.5–6

Ἐσεῖς, *ἠξεύρετε* καλά, μὲ ἀνδρικὴν καρδίαν,
τὸν ἔρωταν ἀρνήθητε καὶ τ' ἄρματ'ἀγαπᾶτε
ἠξεύρετε P et ed., rec. Follieri

The reading ἠξεύρετε does not make sense. The emendation I suggest is ἠξεύρω το with a comma after Ἐσεῖς.

11.A29.6

ὡσὰν νὰ μήν 'χαμ' *ἔστεναι* σὰν αὔτους γεννημένες
ἔστεναι ed. ἔσται P

P leads us to the correction of ἔστεναι into ἔσταινε, which is produced by the infinitive ἔσται plus the euphonic particle -νε.

12.A34.3–5

καὶ βοηθήσει θέλουσι, ἂν εἶν' δικαιοκρῖτες,
καὶ δὲν μᾶς θέλουν ξεριστῆ εἰς τὰ προπερασμένα.
Ἢ κι ἂν τόσα *ἐξεσυνεριστοῦν* καὶ νὰ μᾶς ἀπελπίσουν
4 θέλουν ξεριστῆ ed. θέλουν ἐξεσινεριστῆ P 5 ἐξεσινεριστοῦν P τὰ συνεριστοῦν ed.

In l.4 the reading of ed. adopted by Follieri alters the stem of the verb. It seems preferable to write ξε<σνε>ριστῆ and put μᾶς between square brackets. In l.5 instead of Follieri's conjecture συνεριστοῦν I suggest the reading ξεσνεριστοῦν with *aphairesis* of the initial ἐ, *syncope* of υ and *apocope* of the final ι.

13.A37tit.

Πῶς Ἱππόλυτα ἡ βασίλισσα *ἀφυέρωσε* τὸν τόπον της καὶ τὰ κάστρη της
ἀφυέρωσε P Follieri

The incorrect form ἀφυέρωσε should be corrected to ἀφύρωσε.

14.A55.7–8

νὰ μηδὲ ἔχῃ λαβωματέα στὴν κεφαλήν, στὲς πλάτες,
εἰς ἄλλον μέλος τίποτες ἐκ τὲς φρικτὲς σαΐττες
P et ed., rec. Follieri

Boccaccio's text (o) allows us to add ἢ before εἰς ἄλλον.

15.A59.1–4 and 7

Δεῖξε εἰς ἐμᾶς τὰ ἔργα σου μὲ κακοσύνη, ὡς θέλεις,
καὶ κατ' ἐμὲ δὸς δύναμιν τῶν γυναικῶν ἀντάμα
μ' ἐκεῖνες ὁποὺ εἰς τὴν Βλεγρὰν τοὺς διαδόχους τοῦ Ἀνθαίου
ἐνίκησες etc.
...
ὅτι θαρρῶ νὰ ὠφεληθῶ *μόνον* κἀγὼ ἀπατός μου

The reading μ' ἐκεῖνες (l.3) makes no sense. The Italian text *con l'arte* must have been translated by a trisyllabic equivalent in Greek with which it would have phonetic resemblance: μὲ τέχνες. In the same way in l.7 the Italian word *sol* leads to the correction of μόνον to μόνος.

16.A60.1–2

κ' ἐσύ, Ἀρτέμη ἄθλια, ποὺ τὸν ψηλὸν τὸν τόπον
μὲ τοὺς θεοὺς κρατεῖς καλὰ στὴν πόλιν μας ἀπέσω

The phrase μὲ τοὺς θεοὺς makes some sense, but comparison with the Italian text, which has *tra l'iddii*, leads to the conjecture μέ<σ' σ>τοὺς θεούς.

17.A65.1 and 7

Καὶ τί *θέλετε ποίσει* γάρ, ἂν ἦλθαν ἔμπροσθέν σας
οἱ Κένταυροι οἱ πολλὰ σκληροὶ μ' ἐσᾶς νὰ πολεμήσουν
...
Πιστεύω εἰς τὴν θάλασσαν ὅλοι *θέλετε πέσει*

Obviously, θέλετε ποίσει and θέλετε πέσει do not express a future tense, but a conditional. The Italian text *avreste fatto* (l.1) and *sareste sommersi* (l.7) leads to the conjectures θέλατε ποίσει and θέλατε πέσει.

18.A79.4–8

Τότε τὸν κάμπον ὥρισε σύντομα νὰ γυρέψουν,
ὅσες νεκρὲς ἐκεῖ νὰ εὑροῦν, ὅλες νὰ τὲς ἐθάψουν·

τὲς λαβωμένες ὅλες τους μὲ καλοσύνη ἀφῆκαν
νὰ πᾶσιν ὅθεν χρήζουσιν χωρὶς καμμία ἀταξίαν,
οὐδὲ καμμίαν ἀπ' ὅλες τους ἐποῖκε ἀνορεξίαν

In l.6 the plural ἀφῆκαν is surprising, because it is clear that this verb has the same subject as ὥρισε (l.4) and ἐποῖκε (l.8). Thus it should be corrected to ἀφῆκεν. The Italian word *lascio* confirms the conjecture. In l.8 the preposition σ' should be added before καμμίαν.

19. A81.8

γιατὶ γιὰ πόλεμον ποτὲ οὐκ ἔβηκαν τὲς πόρτες

Although ἔβηκαν is a correct type, both the sense made by the text and the fact that ἔβην is never used in the poem lead to the correction of ἔβηκαν into ἔβ<γ>ηκαν. For the sense, 'κ (= ἐκ) should be added before τὲς πόρτες.

20. A91.3

εἰς ὀλιγούτζικον καιρὸν ἐφτάσαν εἰς τὴν πόλιν

The plural ἐφτάσαν looks isolated among the other verbal types (l.1 ἐμίσσευσε, l.2 ἔδιωξεν, l.5 ἔμοσεν, l.6 νὰ μὴ μισσεύσῃ ... νικήσῃ) with which it has the same subject, i.e. Theseus, and thus it should be changed to ἐφτάσεν.

21. A120.5 (ed.)

κ' ἐσεῖς καλὰ τὸ βλέπετε, καθάρια τὸ γροικᾶτε,
πῶς γιὰ νηστεία ἢ δέηση οὐδὲ παραμονές μας
οὐδὲ γιὰ δύναμιν κορμίων οἱ πρόβλεψες οἱ τόσες
μποροῦμε νὰ ἐγλύσωμε ... etc.

It is not clear to which verb the nominative οἱ πρόβλεψες serves as a subject. The Italian text (*forza di corpo o atto provveduto*) helps us change the first οἱ to ἢ: γιὰ δύναμιν ἢ (γιὰ) πρόβλεψες, and οἱ τόσες into τὶς τόσες.

22. A136.6

ὥρισε καὶ ἐρωτήσασιν τὸ ποία καὶ πῶς ἀκούει

A verb is missing after ποία. I add 'ν' (τὸ ποία <'ν'> καὶ πῶς ἀκούει) before καὶ πῶς.

23. B Argum. 3

καὶ τῶν Ρωμαίισσων τῶν πικρῶν κλάψιμον ὁπ' ἀρχίσαν

An article is missing before κλάψιμον. Besides, the phrase πικραὶ Ρωμαίισσαι is unexpected. In accordance with the Italian text (*il tristo lagrimare*) τῶν πικρῶν should be changed to τὸ πικρὸν (κλάψιμον).

24. B3.2

Εἰς τὸν καιρὸν τὸν ἔμνοστον, ποὺ οὐρανὸς 'μορφαίνει
τοὺς κάμπους ὅλους καὶ βουνὰ τὰ *ἄνθη* καὶ χορτάρια

Boccaccio's text (*d'erbette e di fiori*) leads to the correction of τὰ ἄνθη to <με>τὰ ἄνθη.

25. B4.4

καὶ λέγει του· 'Πῶς κάθεσαι ὀκνὸς *ἐδ' ἀναμένης*

Boccaccio's text (*Che fai tu ozioso con Ipolita in Scizia dimorando*) allows us to change the reading ἐδ' ἀναμένης to ἐδὰ νὰ μένῃς.

26. B5.1–2

Βλέπ' ἀπ' ἐσένα ἔφυγε ἡ εὐγενία κ' ἡ δόξα,
ὁπ' *ἀκαρτέρειες* νὰ γενῇς ὅμοιος τοῦ Ἡρακλέους

Obviously it is εὐγενία κ' ἡ δόξα which were wanting. Therefore I correct ἀκαρτέρειες to ἀκαρτέρειε, in accordance with Boccaccio's text (*prometteva*).

27. B11.6–8

Ὕστερο ἀπ' ὅλους 'σφάξασιν τὸν πονεμένο Ἀγῶνε,
τὸν Θειοκλὲν ἐσκότωσαν, τότε τὸν Πολυνείκην·
μόν' Ἄδραστος ὁποῦ ἔφυγεν καὶ μέσ' στὸ Ἄργος ἐμπῆκεν

In l.8 the nominative Ἄδραστος is the subject of a verb which is missing. Therefore I write ἔμεινε Ἀδράστος instead of μόν' Ἄδραστος.

28. B13.1–3

Αὐτὸς μὲ ἀγριώτατην καρδίαν *ἐχρίετον* τῶν Ἑλλήνων
καὶ ὅσους ἡμπόρει ἐσκότωνε, καὶ ἀφὸν τοὺς *ἐσκοτῶναν*
ἀκόμη ὀχθρία εἶχεν πρὸς αὐτούς, ἔτζι ὁρισμὸν ἐποῖκε etc.

In l.1 Boccaccio's text (*li Greci odiando . . . in lor l'odio servava*) allows us to correct ἐχρίετον to ἐχθρίετον. In l.2 in accordance with all the other verbs and the sense of the text, ἐσκοτῶναν is wrong and should be replaced by the singular ἐσκοτῶνεν.

29. B20.5–7

Τὰ πρόσωπα τὰ ἔμορφα μὲ παρρησία ἐδεῖχναν·
ἄλλα ἦσαν ἄσπρα, κόκκινα, ἄλλα σιτόχροια, ὡραῖα,
ἄλλα στρογγυλοκόμματα ... etc.

Obviously στρογγυλοκόμματα is a corrupted form of στρογγυλοκάμωτα.

30. B34.1–5

Ἀϊλὶ τὰ δάκρυα τὰ πολλὰ καὶ οἱ φορεσὲς οἱ μαῦρες
οὐδὲ διὰ παρεκαλεσμοὺς οὐδὲ διὰ δικαιοσύνην
θελήσῃς νὰ μπορέσωμεν νὰ ποίσωμεν τὸ πρέπει,
κάνε το διὰ τὴν πολλὴν ἀτυχίαν ποὺ βρίσκονται ἐκεῖνοι
οἱ βασιλεῖς καὶ οἱ ἄρχοντες· ἰδέ μὴν τοὺς ἀφήσῃς etc.

Boccaccio's text helps us correct this difficult passage. Here is the Italian: *Deh, se l'abito nostro e il lagrimare non ti movon, né prieghi, né ragione movati almen la trista condizione* etc. And here is the way I correct ll. 1 and 4:

Ἀϊλὶ <ἂν 'κ>τὰ δάκρυα τὰ πολλὰ κ' ἐκ φορεσὲς τὶς μαῦρες
κάν' το διὰ τὴν etc.

31. B48.7

ἠδὲ θέλεις, αὐθέντη μας, μὲ τὰ καμώματά μας etc.

In accordance with Boccaccio's text, the epic form ἠδὲ obviously makes no sense here and should be corrected to ἰδεῖ (*voi vederette*).

32. B51.7–8

Οἱ ἀποκρισαρέοι ἐδιέβησαν κι' ἀπέσωσαν τοὺς λόγους
καὶ ταῦτα ἀπιλογήθηκεν καὶ δείχνει τους καὶ φόβους.

The reading καὶ φόβους expresses the contrary of what the author means; thus I correct it to ἀφόβως.

33. B60.8

ἐκ τὸ φαρὶ τὸν ἔρριξεν εἰς γῆν ἀπεθαμένον

Given that Creon in the following lines is still alive, ὡς should be added before ἀπεθαμένον: εἰς γῆ <ὡς> ἀπεθαμένον (*per morto*) 'as if he was dead'.

34. B71.7–8

τὴν χώραν γὰρ ἀφήκασι θεοῦ Διονυσίου
κ' εἰς χεῖρας τοῦ καλοῦ Θησίου κ' ἐδῶκαν τοῦ *Φυγίου*

The phrase δίδω τοῦ Φυγίου is incomprehensible nor does there exist a divine epithet Φύγιος. I am inclined to think that there is here an expression δίδω τοῦ φευγίου 'escape' (see Mod. gr. τὸ φευγιό).

35. B82.5–8 (ed.)

χάρι σοῦ *στρέψουν* οἱ θεοὶ κ' ἡ δύναμις ἐκείνων,
ὁπόχουν κ' ἔχει θέλουσι ἀξίως νὰ στ' ἀντιμεύσουν·
ἡμεῖς εἰς ὅ,τι δύνονται γυναῖκες νὰ τὸ ποίσουν,
ἔξω γὰρ ἀπὸ τὴν τιμήν, ὅλες στὸν ὁρισμόν σου.

It is clear that στρέψουν cannot be a future but a concessive subjunctive: <ἂς> σοῦ στρέψουν. Since the principal clause in ll.7–8 is missing its verb, I add μαστ': ἡμεῖς <μαστ'> σ' ὅτι... ὅλες στὸν ὁρισμόν σου.

36. B89.7–8

καὶ μὲ τοὺς *ὅλους* βάνει τους στὴν φυλακὴν ἀπέσω

Boccaccio's text (*con gli altri*) helps us correct the reading ὅλους to ἄλλους.

37. B93.7–8

μ' ἄλλες πολλὲς ἀρχόντισσες καὶ ἄλλους καβαλλάρους·
χρεία δὲν κάμνει νὰ εἰπῶ, νὰ μὴ σᾶς βάνω βάρος

The Italian text (*il quali ora nomar*) allows us to correct l.8: νὰ <τοὺς> πῶ 'to call them by their name'.

38. B94.4

ἀπὲ τὴν πόλιν *ἅπαντες* ἐκεῖ τὸν ἐγυρίσαν

The Italian text (*per tutto*) allows us to correct the Greek: τὴν πόλιν ἅπασαν.

39. Γ1.6–8

νὰ κιλαδήσω καὶ νὰ πῶ τοῦ Ἔρωτος τὰ ἔργα,
νὰ πῶ ἐκ τοὺς πολέμους του, κι' αὐτὸν παρακαλῶ τον
μ' ἐμὲν νὰ ἔν' σωματικῶς, *γιατί* ἐγὼ 'κλουθῶ τον.

The sense of l.8 is not clear: the Italian text *a cio che* gives the solution once again: I correct γιατί to γιά 'τι (γιὰ ὅ,τι).

40. Γ8.2–3

οὐχὶ ἀπ' ἀγάπην τίποτε νὰ ἔναι εἰς τὸν νοῦν της,
μόνον αὐτὸ τὸ φυσικὸν τὴν ἔσυρνε νεότης

The Italian text (*da propria natura*) leads to the correction of αὐτὸ τὸ φυσικὸν to ἀπὸ τὸ φυσικὸν.

41.Γ16.6

καὶ δὲν δοξεύει γὰρ ἀλλοῦ ἢ μὴ τὰ εἰς ἐμένα

The words ἢ μὴ τὰ are an incorrect transcription for εἴμητα.

42.Γ40.7

καὶ τραγουδεῖ ἐμορφότερα περὶ ὅπου *κάμνει* Ἀπόλλος

The Italian (*cantasse*) allows us to correct the reading of P κάμνει to 'κάμνε.

43.Γ57.6

ὁ ἔρωτας γὰρ *πρόσθυμε* πού μ' ἔχει εἰς δύναμίν του

The erroneous reading πρόσθυμε should be corrected to πρώσθει με.

44.Γ83.5

μὲ μία ἐκ τὲς *καμιζιόλες* της πού 'χε στὴν κάμαράν της
καμιζιόλες P: κοράσια ed. (*con una camariera*)

The word καμιζιόλες is an erroneous reading for καμαριέρες.

45.Δ8.5–6

κ' ἐκεῖνο πού μὲ σφάζει πλέον καὶ καίει τὴν καρδίαν μου,
καὶ μέσα διασπορίζει με καὶ *λιόσυν* τ' ἄντερά μου
6 λιόσυν P: λύουσι ed.

I correct this incorrect reading to λειῶσιν.

46.Δ10.1–2

Ἀλλοίμονο, ὤχου ὁ ταπεινός, ἀϊλί, καὶ τί γυρεύω
μόνε τοὺς ἀναστεναγμούς, τοὺς πόνους καὶ τὲς θλῖψες
2 μόνε τους P: μόνον τοὺς ed.

The Italian text (*ne' sospir*) leads to the conjecture μέσα στοὺς ἀναστεναγμούς.

47.Δ10.5–6

Ὦ ἐκ τὸ βάθος βασιλεία *τὸν πλοῦτον* νὰ πειράζῃς
κανενάπες τοῦ ἄτυχου τοὺς πόνους του νὰ παύσῃ
5 τὸν πλοῦτον νὰ P: τοῦ Πλούτωνος ed. 6 κανενάπες P: κἂν νά 'πες ed.

The Italian text (*di Dite, 's alcun tormentando in voi tenete,* ... *dite*) helps us find the correction: ... τοῦ Πλούτων ἂν πειράζῃς | κανένα, πὲς etc.

48.Δ20.3–4

οὐδέποτε ὁ βασιλεὺς δὲν ἔμαθε ποῖος ἦτον,
καλὰ κι ἂν *ἐξεπάτησε* πολλὰ κρυφὰ γιὰ 'κεῖνον.

4 ἐξιπάτησε P: ἐξεπάτησε ed.

The Italian text (*avesse domandato*) leads to the correction ἐξαπαίτησε.

49.Δ22.3–5

.... ἐσέβη εἰς δουλοσύνην
τοῦ βασιλέως τοῦ Πήλεως διχῶς νὰ τὸν ὁρίσουν·
ὑποκλιτὸς ἐγένετον σ' ὅ,τι κι ἂν τὸν ὥριζαν

4 ὁρίσουν P et ed. 5 ὁρίζαν ed.

In l.4 the reading ὁρίσουν is a mistake resulting from dictation. The Italian text (*sanza sospetto*) helps us find the correction: διχῶς νὰ τὸν γνωρίσουν.

50.Δ46.1–2

Ὡσὰν κ' ἐσὲν καμμίαν φορὰν ποὺ σ' ἔσφαξεν ἡ ἀγάπη
νὰ ἐλευθερώσῃς παντελῶς τοὺς οὐρανοὺς ἀπάνου

Boccaccio's text (*Si come te* ... *costrinse* ... *abandonare*) allows us to correct ἔσφαξεν into ἔσφιγξεν.

51.Δ69.1–2

ὀλίγον ἀναπαύθηκε μπροτοῦ νὰ ξημερώσῃ,
καὶ ὅταν τοῦ ἐφάνηκε, ὁλόρθος ἐστηκώθη

2 τοῦ ed.: versum om. P

The Italian text (*e già vegnenti l'ore vicine al giorno*) leads to the correction of the Greek: καὶ ὅταν ἡ αὐγὴ ἐφάνηκε.

52.E30.7–8

καὶ ἂς εἶσαι τώρα πρὸς ἐμὲν ἐλεήμων, ὡς μοῦ φαίνει,
ἔτζι στὸ τέλος νὰ γενῇς σ' ἐμὲν χαριτωμένη

7 ἂς P et ed.

The sense leads to the conclusion that ὡς is needed instead of ἂς. The Italian text (*e come in questo se' vêr me pietosa* | *cosí nell'altro mi sii graziosa*) confirms this correction.

53. E55.4

καὶ ἐναντίους τοὺς ἔχομεν στὴν πεθυμία μας ὅλη

The Italian text (*tutti*) helps us correct ὅλη to ὅλους.

54. E56.1–3

Ὠϊμέ, τὸ πῶς μὲ φαίνεται θαύμασμα νὰ σκοπήσω
τὸ πῶς ἔτζι ἀναπαυθικὰ μᾶς ἄφηνεν ἡ ὥρα
νὰ στέκετον ἡ ζωΐτζα μας σ' ἀνάπαυσιν καὶ εἰρήνη

2 ἡ ὥρα P: ἡ τύχη ed.

The Italian text (*Iunon*) leads to the correction of ὥρα to Ἥρα (compare with 58. 3 ἡ ἀνελεήμων Ἥρα).

55. E60.6–7

καὶ τότες νὰ τὸ ποίσωμεν εἴτι καὶ ἂν *πεθυμάῃς*
ὁ νοῦς ὁ κακορρίζικος ὁποὺ σὲ συμβουλεύει

6 πεθυμάῃς P et ed.

The sense leads to the correction of πεθυμάῃς to πεθυμάῃ.

56. E72.8–73.1–2

ἐθαύμασε καὶ παρευθὺς οὕτως τοῦ λέγει ὁ νέος.
Λέγει· «στρατιώτη, μὴ θαρρῇς ὅτε τέλειωσε ἡ μάχη»,
λέγει, «διατὶ μὲ ἀπόδειρες· οὐκ εἶμαι νικημένος»

The reading Λέγει in 73.1 is erroneous and comes from l.2. The Italian text (*leva su*) helps us correct Λέγει to Σήκω. The correction of ὅτε to ὅτι can also be easily done.

57. E81.3–4

καὶ τόσα ἀπὲ τὸ θάμασμα ἐδείλιασε ἡ ψυχή της,
ὅτι οὐκ ἐσείστη τίποτες, οὐδὲ *ὁμιλία* καθόλου·

4 ὁμιλία P: μηλία ed.

After οὐδὲ one would not expect a noun but a verb: thus I correct ὁμιλία of P and μηλία of the ed. to ὠμίλειε.

58. E82.5

σκοπῶντας καὶ τὲς κοπανὲς *πόκρω* ὁ εἷς τὸν ἄλλον

πόκρω P: ποὺ δίδει ed.

I correct πόκρῳ of P to πὄκρουε.

59. E99.1–6

      Καὶ ὡς καθὼς ἐβλέπομεν τριαντάφυλλο ἢ ρόδο
      ἀπὸ τὴν θέρμην τοῦ ἡλίου ὁλόχλωμο νὰ γένῃ,
      καὶ τότες ἀπὲ τὴν αὐγήν, ὁ δρόσος τοῦ Ζεφύρου
      μεταμορφεῖται κι ἔρχεται στὴν πρόσοψιν τὴν πρώτην
      καὶ δοξασμένο στέκεται ἀπάνου εἰς τ' ἀγκάθι,
      ἔμορφο καὶ μυριστικό, ὡσὰν ἦτον καὶ πρῶτα
3 ὁ δρόσος P et ed.

The nominative ὁ δρόσος in P and ed. is erroneous, since the following verbs μεταμορφεῖται, ἔρχεται etc. take as subjects the words τριαντάφυλλο ἢ ρόδο. The words ὁ δρόσος are part of a corrupted adverbial phrase equivalent to the phrase ἀπὲ τὴν αὐγήν. Therefore ὁ δρόσος should be corrected to 'κ τὸν δρόσον.

60. ΣΤ11.8

      ἐκείνων ποὺ μὲ ἄρματα δι' αὐτοὺς νὰ πολεμήσουν
P et ed.

This relative clause has no verb. The Italian text (*che arme porteranno*) leads us to the missing verb, which I suggest to be ἦλθαν: ἐκείνων ποὺ < ἦλθαν> μὲ ἄρματα δι' αὐτοὺς νὰ πολεμήσουν.

61. ΣΤ18.3

      οὐδὲν ἐχόρταιναν ποσῶς ὅσοι καὶ αὐτὸν ἐβλέπουν
αὐτὸν P: νὰ τὸν ed.

ὅσοι καί, which is a synonym of οἱ πάντες, is always followed by ἄν plus a pronoun. In l.22.7 the same phrase is found complete: ὅσοι καὶ ἄν τὸν ἠβλέπασιν. That is why in l.18.3 I write ὅσοι καὶ ἄν τὸν ἐβλέπουν.

62. ΣΤ20.1–2

      Ἀπὲ τὴν Νῖσαν τὴν φρικτήν, ποὺ γέμει τοὺς δρυμῶνες,
      μὲ τοὺς δύο νίους ἔφθασεν ὁ βασιλεὺς ὁ Νῖσος,

Who are those δύο νιοί we find in P and in ed.? To answer this let us look at Boccaccio's text:

Né Nisa, di gran boschi copiosa,
tra gli urli dionei Niso ritenne

'Nor did Nisa, rich in large forests,
retain Niso among Dione's doves'

The translator, who did not understand the word *dionei*, translated it with δύο νέοι/νίοι. This is how the two mysterious νίοι (or νιοί), who, of course, are irrelevant to the Italian text, were born.

63. ΣΤ23.4–5

ἔμορφος καὶ περίχαρος, εὐγενικῆς θωρίας·
χωρὶς ἁλμέτον τίποτες, μόν' τὰ ξανθὰ μαλλία του
ἀέρας τὰ 'ξανέμιζε, ἔλαμπαν ὡς χρυσάφι.

Comparison with P (χωρὶς ἅρματα) shows that under ἁλμέτον is hidden a piece of armour, here τὸ ἔλμον: χωρὶς ἔλμ' ἦτον.

64. ΣΤ25.6–8

(the poet narrates the birth of the Dioskouroi)

τὸ πῶς καὶ πότε 'σπάρθησαν, μετὰ μεγάλης τέχνης
ἀπὸ μίαν κόρη εὐγενική, Λήδαν τὴν ὠνομάζαν,
ὅταν τὴν εἶχε ὁ πελαργὸς μὲ τὰ τραγούδια 'μάζι.

In l.8 the expression τὴν εἶχε ... 'μάζι does not make sense. Therefore I correct it to τὴν πῆρε ὁ πελαργὸς μὲ τὰ τραγούδια 'μάζι.

65. ΣΤ42.1–3 and 7–8

Οὐκ εἶχε τέτοιαν ἐμορφία ὀκάποτες Ἀδῶνες
τοῦ Κινεράν ὁπού 'τονε τῆς Ἀφροδίτης φίλος,
ὡς ἦτον ὁ νεώτερος αὐτὸς ὁ Περιθέος
...
εἰς τὴν Ἀθήνα ἔφθασεν κ' ἦλθε *συναπαντή του*
καλὸς Θησεὺς ὁ φίλος του etc.

3 ἦτον ὁ P et ed. (*quanto era Peritoo ancor garzone* Bocc.) 7 συναπαντή του P et ed.

In l.3 the Italian text allows us to correct ἦτον ὁ to ἦτονε; in l.7 the preposition εἰς is clearly missing before συναπαντή.

66. ΣΤ45.1–3 et 8

Ἐκ τὴν Σιδώνια ἔφθασεν ὁ μέγας Πυνιαλεόνες
καὶ μετ' αὐτὸν εἰς συντροφία ἀδελφός του ὁ Συκαῖος,
ἀπολογίθη ὕστερα τὴν ἔμορφην Διδῶνεν,
...
κ' εἰς τὸ παλάτι μετ' αὐτοὺς ἐσέβη, ὡς *τοφάνη*.

3 ἀπολογίθη P ἀπηλογήθη ed. 8 τοφάνη P τόφάνη ed.

In l.3 the reading ἀπολογίθη or ἀπηλογήθη is clearly erroneous: the Italian text (*che poi fui sposo*) shows that there is here a dictation mistake and leads to the correction <ὁπού> εὐλογήθη. In l.8 τοφάνη should be corrected to τοῦ 'φάνη.

67.ΣΤ.65.1 and 4–6

Ὁποιος καὶ ἂν ἦτον ἐδεκεῖ εὐγενικὸς αὐθέντης,
...
ὁπού 'λθε εἰς τὴν βασιλείαν τοῦ αὐθέντη τοῦ Θησέου,
ὅλους τοὺς *ἀποδέχθηκε*, καὶ μὲ χαρὲς μεγάλες
πολλὰ τοὺς ἐτιμήσασιν μετὰ πολλὴν τὴν τέχνη.

5 ἀποδέχθηκε P et ed.

The plural form of the verb in l.6 shows that in l.5 the verbal form ἀποδέχθηκε should be put in the plural as well: ἀποδέχθηκαν.

68.Z1.6

καὶ τὸ θεάτρο τὸ λαμπρὸ καὶ μέγα *τὸν* ἐδείχνει

τὸν ἐδείχνει P δείχνει τους ed.

The sense of the Greek and the Italian text show that τὸν should be corrected to τῶν.

69.Z4.6–7

οὐδὲ μεγάλα ἄλογα, οὐδὲ πολλὴ πεζούρα
νάχανάποφασίσουσιν τὴν φλόγα τῆς ἀγάπης,

7 νάχανάποφασίσουσιν P et ed.

It is clear that this reading in l.7 should be written νά 'χαν ν' ἀποφασίσουσιν.

70.Z5.1–3

Οὐδὲν ἐπίστευα ποτὲ πάντες οἱ Λαριμναῖοι
ἀντάμα μὲ τοὺς βασιλεῖς ὅλους τῆς Ἀχαΐας
νὰ *νίκησαν* μὲ τ' ἄρματα διὰ τόσο ὀλίγον πρᾶγμα

3 νὰ νίκησαν P νὰ 'ρμήσουσι ed.

The Italian text (*movesse*) and the sense of the Greek show that the correct reading is not νίκησαν but κίνησαν.

71.Z24.1–2

Θεέ μου παντοδύναμε, *πού* εἰς χιονισμένα ὄρη
πού κατοικοῦν τὰ ὀσπίτια σου ἐκεῖσε στὴν Πιστόνια

2 πού P, non habet recte ed. | κατοικοῦν P et ed.

It is clear that ποὺ in l.1 makes this word in l.2 superfluous and that the verb with the subject ὁ θεὸς should be corrected to κατοικεῖς, whereas τὰ ὀσπίτια should be corrected to <σ>τὰ ὀσπίτια.

72. Z28.7–8

.... τάσσω σέ το,
ἂν ποίσῃς νά 'μαι νικητής, ὡσὰν καὶ *πρῶτασέτω*

πρῶτασέτω P προεῖπα σοῦ το ed.

Based on ed., I correct the reading of P as follows: ὡσὰν καὶ προεῖπα σέ το.

73. Z31.1

κ' ἕνας δρυμώνας ἄκαρπος, ἄγριους ἰδρύους γεμᾶτος,

κ' ἕνας P et ed. (*é una selva* Bocc.)

The verb is missing. I suppose that it is hidden in the word ἕνας and I replace κ' ἕνας with κ' ἔν' εἶς.

74. Z33.3–6

Ἐκεῖ 'δε τὴν βουρκότηταν τῶν Λογισμῶν ἐκείνων,
ὁπὄκ τὴν πόρταν 'βγαίνασι ἄγροι καὶ θυμωμένοι,
καὶ τὴν τυφλὴ τὴν Ἁμαρτίαν, καὶ τ' Ὤχου *κῆτουμένει*
ἐκεῖσε γὰρ ἐφαίνονταν ὅμοιον ὡσὰν καὶ τ' ἄλλα.
5 καὶ τ' Ὤχου κῆτουμένει P καὶ τὸ Οὐαὶ καὶ Ὤχου ed.

Judging from the Italian text (*e ogni Omei*), I correct the erroneous reading κῆτουμένει to καὶ τ' Ὀϊμένα.

75. Z36.3–4 and 6–7

Καὶ εἴτι πρῶτα ἐσκέφθηκεν, ὁπού 'τον *σκιασμένο*,
ἦσαν τὰ κούρση τῆς νυκτὸς κ' ἐκεῖνα τῆς ἡμέρας,
...
κ' ἐστέκονταν οἱ ἄτυχοι ἐκεῖσε ἀπογνωσμένοι·
ἐφαίνονταν *οἱ ἄτυχοι* στὲς ἄλυσες δεμένες
3 σκιασμένο P 'στορισμένο ed. 7 οἱ ἄτυχοι P καὶ οἱ ψυχὲς ed.

In l.3 the Italian text (*disegnato*) allows us to correct σκιασμένο to σχεδιασμένο. In l.7 the reading οἱ ἄτυχοι of P, which repeats the same reading as l.6, is suspect. Compare also the feminine δεμένες in both P and ed. Therefore the more economic solution is to correct οἱ ἄτυχοι into <καὶ> οἱ ψυχές.

76.Z45.7

Καὶ τοῦτο σὲ παρακαλῶ, *μόνοντι* νὰ ἠμπορέσω
μόνοντι P μόνον ed.

I correct μόνοντι to μόνο ὅτι.

77.Z50.7–8 and 51.1

.... ὁλωνομπρὸς ἐσκέφθη
τὴν κυρὰ τὴν Ἀμουριζία πῶς καὶ τὸ ποῦ 'δοξεύθη.
Καὶ *μετ'* αὐτόν ἐκίνησεν καὶ παρεμπρὸς ὑπάει
2 καὶ μετ' αὐτὸν P et ed. (*con la quale* Bocc.)

It is clear that the pronoum in l.1 which replaces Ἀμουριζία should be corrected to μετ' αὐτήν.

78.Z54.4

καὶ αὐτὲς ἡ *θυγατέρες* του ἡ Ὄρεξι ἔπαιρνέ τες
ἡ θυγατέρες του P οἱ θυγατέρες του ed.

The reading θυγατέρες is due to the preceding plural καὶ αὐτές, whereas it is clear that it is the subject of ἔπαιρνε. Therefore I correct ἡ θυγατέρες of P and οἱ θυγατέρες of ed. to ἡ θυγατέρα. Compare also the Italian text (*le quai sua figlia Voluttà selette*).

79.Z56.7

καὶ *τὴν λαλοῦν* Ἀποκοτία εἶδεν ἐκεῖ *μὲ κλάμα*
λαλοῦν P ἔμορφην ed. | μὲ κλάμα P τότε ἄμα ed.

The Italian text (*vide il folle Ardire*) allows us to correct τὴν λαλοῦν to τὴν λωλήν. Furthermore the reading μὲ κλάμα is clearly erroneous and should be replaced by τότε ἄμα of ed.

80.Z58.8

τριγύρου της *τὰ σύματα* καὶ Τέχνες εἶδε πλέα
τὰ σύματα P Τάξες ed. (*dintorno a lei vide Promesse e Arte* Bocc.)

The Italian text allows us to correct the erroneous text of P τὰ σύματα to Ταξίματα.

81.Z59.1–3

Τότες ἀπέσω στὸν ναὸν μὲ Στεναγμοὺς *μεγάλους*
ἐγροίκησεν ποὺ ἐστρίκησαν μὲ ταραχὴν μεγάλην.
πολλὰ πηρὶ καὶ ὁλόκαυτοι ἐβγαῖναν μετὰ δάκρυα.

1 μεγάλους P μεγάλα ed. | 2 ἐστρίκησαν P στρίγγιζαν ed. | μὲ ταραχὴν μεγάλην P μὲ ταραχὴ μεγάλη ed. | 3 πολλὰ πηρὶ P πολλὰ πυροὶ ed.

The Italian text helps us correct these difficult lines in this case as well:

> Poi dentro al tempio entrata, di Sospiri
> vi senti un tumulto che girava
> focoso tutto di caldi Disiri.

I think that μεγάλους in l.1 repeats μεγάλην of l.2 and should be corrected to γεμάτη. In l.2 ἐστρίκησαν should be corrected to ἐστρίγγιζαν, and μὲ ταραχὴν μεγάλην to μία ταραχὴ μεγάλη. In l.3 πολλὰ πηρὶ of P and πολλὰ πυροὶ of ed. should be corrected to πόθοι πυρροί.

82. Z68.4–8

> ὡς ἤτονε συνήθειο εἰς τὸν καιρὸν ἐκεῖνον
> σ' ἐκείνους ποὺ ἐβούλοντο νὰ ποίσουν ἀλλαξίαν,
> ἀπὸ στρατιῶτες *νὰ γενῇ* καὶ χρυσιοκαβαλλάρους,
> *ὡσὰν αὐτός ποὺ ἐδέχετον* τέτοια τιμὴ νὰ λάβῃ,
> νὰ τόνε ζώσουν τὸ σπαθὶ καὶ νὰ τὸ περιλάβῃ.

The only way to correct this difficult text is to compare it with the Italian:

> si come forse in quel tempo era in uso
> a qui doveva far mutazione
> d'abito scuderesco in cavaliere,
> come e' doveva che era scudiere

In l.6 I correct νὰ γενῇ to σ' εὐγενεῖς and in l.7 ὡσὰν αὐτός ποὺ ἐδέχετον to σὰν αὐτοὺς ἀποδέχετον.

83. Z78.1–2 and 7–8

> Ἀφὸν ἐτοῦτο ἐσύντυχεν, ἐστάθηκε καμπόσο,
> τόσοτίδε ποὺ ἀνάψασιν ὁλοτελὶς οἱ ρόγοι
> . . .
> καὶ τότε τὸ κεφάλιν της ὑπόκλινεν καμπόσο
> καὶ τότες ἀνασήκωσε καὶ δὲν ἐβλέπει πίσω.

I correct τόσοτίδε to τόσο ὅτι εἶδε and I add τὸ before ἀνασήκωσε.

84. Z89.1–2 and 8

> Οἱ θεοὶ γὰρ ἐστήσασι στοὺς οὐρανοὺς ἀπάνω
> γυναῖκα ἑνὸς ἀπὸ τοὺς δύο βέβαια ν' ἀπομείνῃς
> . . .
> καὶ θὲς ἰδεῖ τὸ πεθυμᾶς κ' ἔχε το στὴν καρδία σου.

The Italian text (*che tu sii sposa*) allows us to correct ν' ἀπομείνῃς of l.2 to ν' ἀπογίνῃς, and ἔχε of l.8 to ἔχεις (*cio che il tuo cor disira*).

85.Z136.7–8

.... δι' αὐτὸ εἶμαι στερκτέος
ἐκ τοὺς θεοὺς ἀνταμοιβὴν νά 'χω καὶ οὐχὶ ἀλλέως
8 νά 'χω P et ed. (*avrà* Bocc.)

The Italian text shows that the correct reading, with an ironical meaning, is νά 'χῃ and not νά 'χω

86.H Argum.8

καὶ πῶς ἡ κόρη μέσα της τὰ μέλη της τρομάσσαν·

The Italian text (*il favellare*) indicates that τὰ μέλη της is an incorrect reading for ἡ ὁμιλία της, and that τρομάσσαν is a syntactical variation for τρομάσσεν.

87.H1.1–2

Εἰσὲ σιωπὴν ὅλος ὁ λαὸς ἔστεκε ἀκαρτερῶντας,
τὸν τρίτον γὰρ τὸν ἔκτυπον τῶν παιγνιδίων τηραίνουν
2 τηραίνουν P τοῦ παιγνιδίου ἐκείνου ed. (*del sonar tireno* Bocc.)

The Italian text shows that neither of the scribes of the two hyparchetypes understood the reading of the archetype, whatever that was, and each treated this difficulty in a different way. The scribe of the one hyparchetype converted the singular τοῦ παιγνιδίου (*del sonar*) to the plural τῶν παιγνιδίων but kept the ethnic name Τυρρένων for Τυρρηνῶν in the corrupted form τηραίνουν. The scribe of the second hyparchetype kept the singular τοῦ παιγνιδίου, but as he did not understand the ethnic name Τυρρένων he changed it to ἐκείνου.

88.H9.1–3

Οὐδὲν πιστεύω ἡ κάμινος τοῦ Ἡφαίστου ποτέ της
ἡ βασιλεία τῶν Σικανῶν ν' ἄναψε τέτοιαν φλόγαν
οὐδὲ ποτέ της ἔβγαλεν τέτοιους καπνοὺς μεγάλους,
2 ἡ βασιλεία P et ed. ἔβγαλεν P et ed. (*la fucina arse ne'regni sicani ... o maggior fummo sparse* Bocc.)

The Italian text helps us correct ἡ βασιλεία to στὴν βασιλεία and ἔβγαλεν to νά ἔβγαλεν.

89. H24.1–2

> Εἶχε μετ' αὐτόν συντροφία καλὸν τὸν Ἀγελέον,
> ὁπού 'τον στὴν ἀποκοτία τ' **αὐτάδελφον ἀδαμένος**
> 1 αὐτὸν P αὖτον ed. | 2 ὁπού 'τον στὴν P πού 'τον ἐκ τὴν ed. ἀδαμένος P γαμένος ed.

In addition to slight corrections in P based on the text of ed. (μετ' αὖτον and πού 'τον ἐκ τὴν metri causa, and τ' αὐτάδελφου), I correct the erroneous reading ἀδαμένος of P and γαμένος of ed. to the correct one, ἀναμμένος, thanks to the Italian text (*focoso*).

90. H26.1–2 and 7

> Ποῖον λέονα ποίαν λύκαινα στοὺς κάμπους τοὺς Ὑρκάνους
> πού τὰ παιδία της πούπετες στὴν κοίτην δὲν ηὑρίσκει
> ...
> ἔτζι ὁ Διομήδης ἔκαμνεν...

Ποῖον P ποία ed. | ποίαν P ἢ ed.
Given that the Italian text writes *Ma cotal... o*, I introduce Μὰ before ποῖον which I correct to ὁποῖον, and I replace ποίαν with the reading ἢ of ed. The reading λέονα is either the feminine of λέων or a mistake for λέαινα.

91. H38.7

> τέτοια σπαθία τὸν ἔδωκεν, *λέγει*, στὴν κεφαλήν του

Since nobody else is speaking, it is clear that λέγει should be corrected to λέγω, the first person of the poet.

92. H42.1 and 4

> Ἦτον ὁ Φίφιλ ἐδεκεῖ ἐκ τ' ὄρος τὸ *μεγάλον*,
> ...
> ἐκ τὴν *παρθέμο* ὁ Πρίκολας μὲ ἦθος ἀνδρειωμένον·
> 1 μεγάλον P et ed. *Menalo* Bocc. 4 παρθέμο P et ed. *Partenio* Bocc.

The Italian text allows us to correct μεγάλον to Μαινάλον and παρθέμο to Παρθένο.

93. H47.4

> νὰ τὸν γυρίσουν ἤθελαν, ἀλλὰ ὡς ἀποθαμένος

The phrase beginning with ἀλλὰ has no verb corresponding to the Italian *giva*. Therefore ἀλλὰ should be corrected to ὑπᾶ in P and ed.

94.H74.1–5

Ἐτοῦτο βλέποντας λοιπὸν ὁ ἄγριος ὁ Καπένθος
ὅπού 'χε ἐβγάλει ἐκ τὸ δενδρὸν *ἐκείνων τῶν μερμήγκων*
...
καὶ τότε ἐμεταεγίνετον ἐκ τοὺς πολλοὺς μερμήγκους

2 ἐκείνων τῶν μερμήγκων P ἐκεῖνο τὸ μερμήγκι ed. (*da l'alber fatale* Bocc.)

The reading in l.2 is clearly erroneous and derives from l.5 ἐκ τοὺς πολλοὺς μερμήγκους. The Italian text shows that ἐκείνων τῶν μερμήγκων should be corrected to (τὸ δενδρὸν) ἐκεῖνο τὸ μοιραῖον.

95.H75.7–8

διατὶ ἐναντία τους ἔφθασεν ἐκεῖνος ὁ Λαρσαῖος
μ' ἄλλους πολλοὺς καβαλλαρίους *ἀπὸ τοῦ Ἰδωνέως*

ἀπὸ τοῦ Ἰδωνέως P et ed. (*Dodoneo* Bocc.)

The Italian text in this case also shows how to correct the false reading ἀπὸ τοῦ Ἰδωνέως of P and ed.: μ' ἄλλους πολλοὺς καβαλλαρίους ποὺ ἦτον, ὁ Δωδωναῖος.

96.H80.7–8

καὶ περὶ πρῶτα ἐγίνετον ἄγριος καὶ θυμωμένος,
τόσο ἐκεῖνο *τὸ ἔσπρωξαν* ποὺ 'τον πεθυμισμένος.

τόσο ἐκεῖνο τὸ ἔσπρωξαν P τόσο τὸν ἐνδυνάμωνε ed.

The Italian text (*lo sprono*) leads to the correction of the reading τὸ ἔσπρωξαν to τὸν ἔσπρωξεν.

97.H81.1

Ἐστράφη εἰς τὸν πόλεμον κι *ὅπου* μεγάλη πρέσσα
ἐσέβαινε ...

I add 'ν' after ὅπου because the verb of the subordinate clause is missing.

98.H82.7–8

τέτοια σπαθίαν τὸν ἔδωκε στὴν κεφαλήν του ἀπάνου,
ποὺ τὸν κρομή στὰ πόδια του, πέφτει ὡς ἀποθαμένος.

ποὺ τὸν κρομή P 'τι τὸ κορμὶ ed.

Once again Boccaccio's text helps us correct the erroneous reading of P to ποὺ τὸν γκρεμεῖ (*fé cadere*).

99.H83.7-8

Τέτοια φιλήματα πικρὰ ἡ Αἰμίλια νὰ σὲ δώσῃ,
ὡσὰν μὲ τά 'δωκες κ' ἐμέν *ἐδῶ μέσα στὴν μέση*
ἐδῶ μέσα P μέσα ἐδῶ ed.

The reading ἐδῶ μέσα or μέσα ἐδῶ of the two transmitted witnesses looks strange. Boccaccio's text (*E gia ricadde*) points to the correct reading: <Κ'> ἐδὰ ἔπεσεν στὴν μέση. Compare also Θ31.8 ἔπεσεν - *cadde*.

100.H112.1-4

Ἀμὴ ὁ Ἄρης βλέποντας ἀπὸ ψηλὸν τὸν τόπον
καὶ ἡ Ἀφροδίτη μετ' αὐτὸν ὅλους τοὺς πολεμάρχους,
ἐβλέποντας πῶς *ἔκρουεν* ἡ πύρα τῆς φωτίας,
ποὺ τὲς καρδίες ἐξάναφτε ὅλωνομπρὸς στὴν μάχην
ἔκρουεν P et ed.

The reading ἔκρουεν does not make sense. Boccaccio's text (*intiepidire*) helps us to correct ἐβλέποντας πῶς ἔκρουεν to βλέποντας πῶς ἐκρύωνεν.

101.H125.1

Ἔτζι νὰ ποίσῃ ἔποικεν ἡ *ἕτοιμη* θωρία
ἕτοιμη P et ed. (*il subito vedere* Bocc.)

Boccaccio's text allows us to correct ἡ ἕτοιμη θωρία, which does not make sense, to ἡ ἀπότομη θωρία.

102.Θ11.6-8

οὐδ' ἔναι ἠπορούμενον μὲ κόπο τόσα ὀλίγον
τοῦ ἔρωτος τὰ ἔργατα διὰ νὰ τ' ἀποδιαβάσω·
μόνον ὁσὰν τὰ ἐδοκίμασαν πολλοί νὰ τὰ περάσουν.
8 ὁσὰν P ὡς ed.

In l.8 I correct μόνον ὁσὰν to μόνο ὅσοι and πολλοί to πολύ.

103.Θ13.7-8

τόσα τὸ 'μπροστοκούρβι του σφιγκτὰ τὸν εἶχε σφίξει
ὡσπότε *ἀπάνου* ἔστεκεν, διὰ ὀλίγον νὰ τὸν πνίξῃ.

In l.8 ἀπάνου is unexpected. On the other hand, Boccaccio's text (*mentre il cavallo adosso gli era suto*) allows us to correct ἀπάνου to ὁ ἵππος.

104.Θ17.8

τόσο ἡ καρδία του *ἐντρέπετον* ἐκ τὴν πολλὴν ὀδύνην.

Boccaccio's text (*errava*) leads to the correction of ἐντρέπετον to ἐκτρέπετον.

105.Θ23.3-4

μὲ τὲς γιατρ<ει>ές τους ἔποικαν παρευθὺς καὶ ὑποστράφη
ἡ *Αἰμιλία* του πρὸς αὐτόν, πολλὰ 'κριβὸ τὸ εἶχαν
ἡ Αἰμιλία του P et ed.

Boccaccio's text (*e con loro argomenti fer reddire a lui il parlar*) shows that the erroneous reading ἡ Αἰμιλία του should be changed to ἡ ἐμιλία του (= ἡ ὁμιλία του).

106.Θ26.3-4

Ἐδῶ τὴν 'δῶ, καὶ λάβε τὴν σ' ὅλους τοὺς ὁρισμούς σου
καὶ μετ' αὐτὴν θέλεις χαρῇ ἀκόμη τὴν ζωήν σου.
ἐδῶ P ἔδω ed.

Boccaccio's text (*ecco lei*) helps us to correct the erroneous ἐδῶ of P or ἔδω of ed. to Ἰδέ.

107.Θ31.3-4

οὐκ ἦτον ὅμοιον σ' αὐτό· καὶ πάλι σ' ἐκλαμπρότη
ἀπέρνα καὶ τὴν ἄμαξον ἐκείνου τοῦ Φετώνη
3 σ' αὐτό P et ed.

The adjective ὅμοιος is constructed with ὡσὰν/σὰν, not with εἰς/σ'. Therefore I correct σ' αὐτό to σὰν αὐτό.

108.Θ31.6-8

ὄντα ὁ Ζυγὸς ἐκάηκεν μὲ τὸν Σκορπίον ἀντάμα
κι ἀπὲ τοῦ Ζεῦ *τὸν* ποταμὸν τὸν Πὼ πυρφλογισμένος
ἔπεσεν, *κ' ἐκεῖ* ἔδειξεν *τὸν ἐπιτάφιο* ἐκεῖνος.
7 τὸν P et ed. 8 κ' ἐκεῖ ... τὸν ἐπιτάφιο P et ed.

Boccaccio's text gives the solution to the problematic l.8. Here is the Italian text:

> *quando Libra si cosse e Iscorpione,*
> *e e' da Giove nel Po fulminato*
> *cadde, e li l'ha l'epitafio mostrato.*

It is the ἐπιτάφιος, i.e. the inscription on Phaethon's tomb, which points to the identity of the person buried there (= Phaethon). Therefore I correct l.8 as follows: κ' ἐκεῖ ἔδειξεν ὁ ἐπιτάφιος ἐκεῖνον.

109.Θ57.1–2

Διατὶ *οὐδέν* σᾶς ἔδωσαν σήμερο ἐσᾶς τὸ νῖκος,
φανερὸν ἔναι ὅτι ἀπὸ σᾶς οὐδὲν ἦτον τὸ σφάλμα.

1 οὐδὲν P et ed.

Boccaccio's text helps us correct l.1. Here is the Italian text:

*Perché se oggi non vi fu donata
vittoria, cio non fu vostro difetto*

It shows that a conjunction ἂν should be added before οὐδέν.

110.Θ61.1–2

Ἡ συντυχία τοῦ Θησέου ὁλωνῶν ἄρεσέ τους,
κ' εἰς μερτικὸ οὐκ ἔστερξαν ἀληθινοὺς τοὺς λόγους

2 κ' εἰς μερτικὸ P καὶ μέρος ed.

Although the Greek text looks sound, comparison with Boccaccio's text shows that l.2 belongs to a concessive clause beginning with ἂν: <ἂν> κ' εἰς etc.

111.Θ68.5–6

ἀμὴ τὰ κάστρη γέμουσιν κ' οἱ χῶρες τῶν Ἑλλήνων
ἀπ' ἐμορφίες παράξενες καὶ πλέο νὰ τὲς παινέσουν

It is clear that a verb is missing between πλέο and νὰ τὲς παινέσουν: thus I add 'ν' (= εἶναι) after πλέο in P and in ed.

112.Θ70.1–2

Ἀπὸ ἐμὲν ἐλευθερία νὰ σοῦ ἔναι χαρισμένη,
στὸ θέλημά σου ἃς ἔναι γὰρ τὸ *εἶπα* καὶ τὸ *στέκε*

2 εἶπα P et ed. | στέκε P στέκει ed.

Boccaccio's text (*lo stare e il gire*) allows us to correct the erroneous reading of P and ed. εἶπα to ὕπα and adopt the reading of P στέκε instead of στέκει given by ed.

113.Θ73.5–8

τοῦ Ἡφαίστου τοῦ θαυμαστοῦ, τοῦ ἀρίστου τεχνίτη·
κ' ἕνα σκουτάρι ἔμορφον, 'πιτήδεια γεναμένον,

καὶ πεῦκον μὲ τὰ φύλλα του ἤτονε 'στορισμένον
μὲ σίδερο ὁλοξέλαμπρον ἤτονε σκεπασμένον.

L.7 is incomprehensible unless we look at Boccaccio's text (*con un gran pin delle sue frondi orbato*), which allows us to correct it as follows: μὲ πεῦκον ποὺ ἐκ τὰ φύλλα του ἤτονε στερημένον.

114.I10.5–6

τόσο ὅτι ἀπὲ τὸν θάνατον καὶ ἀπὲ πᾶσαν *μερίαν*
σ' ὀλίγες μέρες ἤσασιν ὅλοι ἐλευθερωμένοι
5 μερίαν P φόβον ed.

The Italian text (*d'ogni altro sospetto*) allows us to correct μερίαν to μερίμναν.

115.I48.8

ἀφὸν ἐσὺ παίρνεις 'ξουσία καὶ ἀφήνεις με ἐξοπίσω

The meaning of l.8 is problematic, but Boccaccio's text (*Antropos ora pigli podestate*) helps us to propose for ἀφὸν ἐσὺ the correction ἡ Φόνισσα (ἡ Ἄτροπος, 'the destiny of inevitable death') and for παίρνεις and ἀφήνεις the correction παίρνει and ἀφήνει.

116.I50.3–4

τότε ὄντα τὰ μέλη σου θέλουσιν εἶσται ἄξια
ἀπὸ τὰ ἔτη τὰ πολλὰ νὰ τὰ μετασαλεύσουν,

Boccaccio's text (*d'esser transmutati in cenere*) allows us to change νὰ τὰ μετασαλεύσουν to εἰς τέφραν νὰ σαλεύσουν.

117.I91.1–3

Ὁ Παλαμὼν ὁποὺ 'τονε ἐκεῖ στοὺς λόγους *τούτους*
εἰς αὔτους ποὺ δὲν ἔλειπεν ποτὲ σιμὰ ἀπ' ἐκεῖνον,
ἔποικεν καὶ etc.
1 τούτους ed. om. P 2 εἰς αὔτους P et ed. | ἔλειπεν ed.: ἔλειπαν P

In l.2 the reading εἰς αὔτους is erroneous: instead I propose ὡς αὗτος in accordance with Boccaccio's text (*come quel che da lui mai non partia*).

118.I101.1–6

Τώρα νὰ λείψῃ ἡ ζωή, τώρα ἡ πολλὴ ἀξία
τ' Ἀρκύτα θέλει τελειωθεῖ, καὶ τώρα νὰ τελειώσῃ
ἡ ἀγάπη ἡ ἀσυνείκαστος καὶ ὁ φρικτός του πόθος·

Translation in the Edition of Vernacular Texts

τώρα θέλει ζυγώσει γὰρ ἐκεῖ πρὸς τ' Ἀχερόντε
τοὺς ἄτυχους τοὺς ἐγκρεμνοὺς καὶ τοὺς θυμοὺς *νανάσι*
τοὺς *μαύρους σκίους τοὺς πικρούς, τοὺς ἐλεεινοὺς καὶ ἀθλίους*

Boccaccio's text (*ora saprà 'l furore delle nere ombre, misere, tapine*) helps us replace the erroneous reading νανάσι with νὰ νοιώσῃ and change l.6 as follows: τῶν μαύρων σκιῶν τῶν πικρῶν, τῶν ἐλεεινῶν καὶ ἀθλίων.

119.I105.7-8

ἂν ἐστεκόμουν μὲ τὸν Ζεῦ διχῶς ἐσέν, κυρά μου,
οὐδὲν πιστεύω χάριτα *νά 'χῃ* ποτὲ ἡ καρδία μου
νά 'χῃ P et ed.

It is clear that the subjunctive νά 'χῃ should be replaced with the conditional νά 'χε. Compare Boccaccio's text: *ma se con Giove sanza te istessi | non credo che giammai gioia sentissi.*

120.IA38.5-6

θεοὺς γὰρ τοὺς *ἀνήσιους* καὶ τὸ κακὸν *τὸ σφάλμα*
μετὰ φωνὲς ψηλὲς συχνὰ ὅλοι τους βλασφημοῦσιν
5 ἀνήσιους P ἀνόσιους ed. | τὸ σφάλμα P et ed.

Boccaccio's text (*l'iniqui iddii e li loro errori*) allows us to replace in l.5 τοὺς ἀνήσιους/ἀνόσιους with τοὺς ἀνίσιους and τὸ σφάλμα with των σφάλμα.

121.IA42.6-8

Ὁ πρῶτος πόθος ποῦ 'τονε καὶ πὄναι ἡ μπιστοσύνη
ὁπού 'χετε στοὺς ἄτυχους κόσμου γὰρ τοὺς ἀνθρώπους;
Καὶ τώρα ἐχάθη ἀπ' ἐσᾶς, βρίσκεται *ἀλλοτρόπους*
8 ἀλλοτρόπους P ἄλλους τρόπους ed.

Boccaccio's text (*Ella n'è gita con li venti vani*) helps us correct ἀλλοτρόπους to <σ'> ἄλλους τόπους.

122.IA43.6-8

ὅλοι ἐστέκαν καὶ ἤκουαν τα, τότε ἄρχισε νὰ λέγῃ,
ὡς τό 'χασιν συνήθειον, ἔμορφο μοιρολόγι,
ποὺ ὁ Πελοπὲς τ' ἀνάδειξεν *ἀρχὴ* στ' ἀρχοντολόγι.

It is clear that in l.8 ἀρχὴ has an adverbial meaning and must be replaced with ἀρχῆς.

123.IA44.7-8

> τὸ ὅμοιον ἐκεῖ τοὺς ζωντανοὺς ἔποικε νὰ δειλιάσουν·
> ἐφάνη τους ὅτι ἐξέπνευσεν κ' ἐδράμαν νὰ τὴν πιάσουν

Boccaccio's text (*e semiviva face dubitare | di morte a chi la potea rimirare*) allows us to replace ἐκεῖ τοὺς ζωντανοὺς with ἂν ἦτον ζωντανή, or ἂν 'κεῖτο ζωντανή.

124.IA46.3-4

> ... τὰ ξέλαμπρά της μάτια
> τὸ βλέμμα 'χάσεν παρευθύς, ἐγύρισαν ἀλλόθεν,

In l.46.4 'χάσεν should be corrected to ἐχάσαν in accordance with the sense of the Greek and with Boccaccio's text (*e' belli occhi lucenti | perdér la luce*).

125.IA.49.3-6

> ὁλομπρὸς γὰρ ἐκύκλωσεν τὸν ρόγο εἰς πᾶσαν τόπον·
> πᾶσα ὥρα πλέον πλουσιώτερη ἐγίνετον ἡ πύρα,
> κ' ἔστερξε ὅτι ἀπεδῶ εἰς πολὺν καιρὸν ἀλλὰ οὐδὲ ὀλίγον
> πλέα πλούσια πύρα καὶ λαμπρὰ τινὰς οὐκ ἐθυμᾶτον

3 ὁλομπρὸς P ἡ λάβρα ed. 5 κ' ἔστερξε P aliter ed.

In l.3 ὁλομπρὸς should be corrected to ὁ λαμπρὸς 'the fire', in accordance with ed. (ἡ λάβρα) and Boccaccio's text (*la fiamma*). In l.5 κ' ἔστερξε is an erroneous transcription for καὶ στέρξε (*e certo 'and surely'*).

126.IA59.4-5 and 7-8

> καὶ μέσα σ' ὅλους τὸ δρομίον ὁποὺ τὴν φήμην πῆραν
> ἦσαν ἐτοῦτοι οἱ βασιλεῖς, ὁ Ἴδας καὶ ὁ Κάστωρ,
> ...
> ἐτοῦτοι τὸ λοιπὸν κ' οἱ δύο ἦσαν χαριτωμένοι,
> τόσα τοὺς εὐεργέτησαν, ὁπού 'σαν 'κανωμένοι

7 ἦσαν ed. ὅμοια P

Boccaccio's text in l.4 (*nel corso*) and in l.7 (*equali*) helps us replace τὸ δρομίον with στὸ δρομίον and ἦσαν with ἴσα, compare to ὅμοια P.

127.IA61.7-8

> Λοιπὸν ὁ Κάστωρ βασιλεὺς καὶ ὁ Ἴδας ὁ Σικούντας
> ἔτζι ἐτιμήθησαν καλά, πολλὰ καὶ περιψοῦτε.

7 ὁ Σικούντας P ὡς ἠκοῦτε ed. | περιψοῦτε P ὑπεριψοῦται ed.

In l.7 I suggest that ὁ Σικούντας should be changed to ὡς ἠκοῦντα ('as it was heard') and in l.8 περιψοῦτε to ὑπερυψοῦντα.

128.IA67.1–2

πολλοὶ ἄλλοι γὰρ ἐπαίξασιν θαυμαστικὰ παιγνίδια,
τὰ ὅποια ἤθελεν περισσὸ ὅλα νὰ τὰ ἐξηγήθη
ἤθελεν P ἔναι ed. | ἐξηγήθη P ἐξηγοῦμαι ed.

Once again, Boccaccio's text (*li quai sarebbe lungo il racontare*) helps us replace ἤθελεν with the conditional ἤθελ' ἔν' and ἐξηγήθη with ἐξηγήθην.

129.IA69.4–5

ἔμορφος γὰρ καὶ ὁλόγλυπτος, μετὰ μεγάλης τέχνης,
ὁποῖον ἱερῶσαν τον τῆς Ἥρας τῆς θεᾶς του

Boccaccio's text (*il qual sacro*) allows us to replace ἱερῶσαν with ἱερῶσεν.

130.IA76.1–2

Τότες ἐθώρειες καὶ τοὺς δύο θλιμμένους νὰ 'παγαίνουν
ἐκεῖσε πρὸς τὸν θρίαμβον καὶ ὁπρὸς εἰς τὸν Θησέον

Boccaccio's text (*al carro avanti*) helps us correct πρὸς τὸν to ἐμπρὸς στόν.

131.IB49.4–6

καὶ μετὰ ροῦχο ξέγλαμπρον, πολύτιμον καὶ ὡραῖον,
ἀπ' ὅλους γὰρ ἐπήγαινεν ὁ βασιλεὺς Αἰγέος
μ' ὅλους τοὺς ἄλλους βασιλεῖς εἰς συντροφία μετ' αὖτον
5 ἀπ' ὅλους γὰρ P et ed.

Boccaccio's text (*di dietro sequitando il vecchio Egeo | con tutti gli altri re*) helps us replace the erroneous reading ἀπ' ὅλους γὰρ, which derives from l.6, with ἀπ' ὀπίσω.

132.IB52.5–6

νὰ δείξω γὰρ τὲς ἐμορφίες ὁπὄδειξεν ἡ κόρη
Αἰμίλια, ἥτις ὠρέγετον νὰ 'πᾷ νὰ τὴν ἐβλέπῃ

Once again Boccaccio's text (*Emilia, a cui le piacque di vedere*) allows us to replace the erroneous reading ἥτις with εἴτις.

133.IB67.1-2

Ἀφὸν ὀλίγο ἀπέρασε, εἰς τὸν ναὸν ἐφθάσαν
τῆς Ἀφροδίτης τῆς θεᾶς μὲ παρρησία μεγάλη

In l.1 the reading of P and ed. ἐφθάσαν should be replaced with ἐφθάσεν according to Boccaccio's text: *Ma dopo certo spazio pervenuta | al gran tempio di Vener.*

134.IB86.4-6

λοιπὸν κάτου ἃς τὰ βάλωμεν ἐδῶ τὰ ἄρμενά μας,
τὸ στέμμα ὁπού 'ν' πρεπούμενον ἐδῶ ἃς τὸ ἀκαρτεροῦμεν,
νὰ μένῃ μὲ τὰ σίδερα ὥστε νὰ μᾶς τὸ δώσουν
5 νὰ μένῃ P ραμμένοι ed.

Obviously in l.6 the reading of P and ed. is erroneous. Boccaccio's text (*con l'ancora fermati*) allows us to write instead 'σταμένοι (= ἱστάμενοι, 'σταματημένοι').

135.Ἀπιλογία 1-2

Ἐπήγαμε τοὺς στίχους σου τοὺς ἔμορφους κι ὡραίους,
ὦ ἀκριβέ μας δάσκαλε, τὸν Θησέα τραγουδῶντας

Boccaccio's text (*o caro alumno*) helps us replace ἀκριβέ μας δάσκαλε with ἀκρίβο δασκαλόπουλο (see Prol.l.238, βιβλόπουλο): the poet is not the Muses's maestro but their pupil.

Our examination has confirmed the hypothesis that most of the corrupted passages are due to accidents in the transmission of the text (such as phonetical errors or incorrect word division). One must wonder about the limitations of the translator himself. Even accounting for the potential for inaccuracy within the Italian manuscript from which he was working, certain corrupted passages contain errors apparently due to the translator's ignorance of mythology. He appears to have been embarrassed in the presence of Boccaccio's tremendous and refined mythological and antiquarian erudition, and frequently replaces a mythological name that he does not understand with a conventional epithet, even though his Italian manuscript may well have included some of Boccaccio's *chiose*, which could have helped him understand such references.

In contrast to the original's sophisticated and artful constructions, he uses a simple, paratactical syntax. Converting eleven-syllable into fifteen-syllable lines, our translator has, in order to respect the rhythm, resorted to periphrastic expressions and formal fillers that often add little in the way of information. Elsewhere he employs the reduplication, amplification, or accumulation of epithets in order to create certain poetic effects. He sometimes abandons his model in order to use some genuine Greek expression or to follow his own expressive impulse, enriching his text with the freshness of a living tradition of indigenous vernacular poetry. Sentiments of love, for instance, are rendered with grace and genuine poetic colour. However, generally speaking, his intention is to render his model as faithfully as possible. Inevitably, this faithfulness prevents him from taking significant initiative and departing from his original text in the ways in which Chaucer did in his rendition of the same Italian poem.

Further Reading

For the Italian edition, see: A. Roncaglia, ed., *Teseida: delle nozze d'Emilia* (Bari, 1941). For the Greek: E. Follieri, ed., *Il Teseida neogreco, Libro I. Saggio di edizione* (Rome, 1959); B. Olsen, 'The Greek Translation of Boccaccio's Theseid Book 6', *ClMed*, 41 (1990), 275–301; S. Kaklamanis, "Ο Πρόλογος εἰς τὸ βιβλίον τοῦ Θησέου, Ἐκδοτικὴ διερεύνηση' in N. M. Panagiotakes, ed., Ἄνθη Χαρίτων (Venice, 1998), 101–74. Study: S. Kaklamanis, 'Ἀπὸ τὸ χειρόγραφο στὸ ἔντυπο: Θησέος καὶ γάμοι τῆς Αἰμίλιας (1529)', Θησαυρίσματα, 27 (1997), 151–2.

Afterword
Reading and Hearing in Byzantium
Elizabeth Jeffreys and Michael Jeffreys

The editors of this volume, when work was nearly complete, invited us to read the papers and write a summary chapter on the present situation and possible future developments in Byzantine research, particularly over the study of reading. Our initial reaction was surprise and delight at the number and quality of the articles, and gratitude to the editors and all the distinguished contributors who thought to include their work in a book linked to our names. Then, after some hesitation, we wrote these pages. Rather than summarise what has been well written elsewhere in the volume by others, we offer reflections deriving from our particular interests, before speaking of the future. We have written the text to stand alone unsupported by footnotes.

To any unthinking twenty-first-century scholar, nothing seems less problematic than the idea of reading. The reader, sitting alone at a desk or in an easy chair, silently absorbs standard pages of standard characters printed identically on well-made paper. Variations in font from book to book are soon dealt with. Reading is fast, because spelling is standardised and proofreading good: after practice it is possible to predict the word from a few letters and the phrase from a few words, and race ahead. Alternative electronic media – e-books and material found on-line – are important, but still new enough to be easily disregarded in comparisons with the past.

It is only necessary to set out the process explicitly to realise that in the Byzantine world reading must have been quite different. Let us consider Byzantine Greek, since it was the most common language in the empire. Byzantine Greek letter-forms were subject to sharp changes of fashion. They also varied from writer to writer, and even individuals sometimes used different forms unpredictably. Writing was often untidy, often with abbreviations, frequently at the terminations of words, where meaning is determined. Spelling and orthography, sometimes very good, could also be atrocious, almost random. Changes in the pronunciation of vowels, diphthongs and consonants caused confusion, as writers used new phonetic values in an orthographic system based on the old. The average level of orthography demanded careful attention and did not allow much acceleration by prediction. The layout of the page was set by ruling, but control was sometimes loose and the general appearance could vary. Parchment, pen and ink were natural products, the first providing a surface which might include imperfections, even holes; the pen could itself be inconsistent in its breadth of strokes; ink could vary in tone. Because of all this, and despite the use of headings (often in colour), Byzantine reading must have been much slower than ours. All our instincts are set to the parameters of a print culture, but Byzantium, like all its contemporary societies, used manuscripts.

As well as difficulties caused by the pages to be read, the whole process of reading was different. It is clear from Byzantine descriptions that silent reading was rare. Most people, including the educated, sounded out words as they absorbed them, even when reading alone. Punctuation was rhetorical, to help readers articulate sentences aloud, not punctuation by syntax, aiming at silent and thoughtful comprehension, as in most modern languages. Literary work was often 'published' by reading aloud, even to learned audiences, as in the much-discussed *theatra*. Speeches and sermons plainly designed for popular performance before audiences of mixed education, including at least some without any schooling, leave modern scholars puzzled as to how much would have been comprehended, for the language is often formal and the thought dense. There is evidence that less educated Byzantines absorbed text largely by listening to books being read aloud. Aural comprehension of difficult texts was probably a learnable skill. This extension of the meaning of reading probably applied even to many who would pass tests of literacy, but preferred the ease and sociability of an audience. More Byzantine reading was probably done by ears than by eyes.

Only in the twelfth century and later were secular texts for wide oral distribution better designed for broad comprehension, with the adoption of political verse and later still of the vernacular Greek language. This was not a pure vernacular, but contained many informal features of phonology and morphology previously excluded from writing. Investigation of this language and its attraction to Byzantines at every level of education, whether they were reading or hearing it, should be a major task of future study.

Another strand of research should begin from the two or three centuries of nationalist ferment in Europe from the late eighteenth to the early twentieth century. During this time, there was great impetus in each country for the systematic creation of national identities, national histories, national literatures and national languages. Medieval manuscripts deemed relevant to such projects were collected and published. Histories were compiled and origins examined. But there was no nation ready to pay nationalist attention to Byzantium: not Greece, which shares a culture and language, but since the War of Independence has given priority to Ancient Greece; not Russia, which for some centuries aspired to make Moscow the third Rome, but then was sent by the Bolshevik revolution on a totally different track, from which the current renewal of interest is unlikely to return it; certainly not Turkey, which incorporates the Byzantine capital and much of the heartland of the empire, but has no intention of identifying with Byzantium, for religious reasons confirmed by centuries of wary contempt.

We do not mean to imply that Byzantine texts remained unpublished and Byzantine history ignored. But research on Byzantium has been much less coordinated than that under nationalist motivation. Methodologies were often inappropriate and the conceptual framework was usually that of classical studies, or later those of the modern states established on territory that had once belonged to Byzantium. Byzantine Greek was condemned without discussion as a degenerate prolongation of Ancient Greek; Byzantine literature likewise. Some Byzantine texts were edited by classical rules, with corrections made to remedy the ignorance of the Byzantine scribes. But those scribes were not working on classical texts created a millennium earlier: they were copying literature produced, in some cases, in their own linguistic milieu during their lifetimes. The rules for correction should have been different. The development of Orthodox thought was often discussed by western theologians in ways which were unsympathetic and hostile. Byzantine history was discussed, particularly by historians of the school of Gibbon, through the prism of the values of the ancient world or the Enlightenment. Greek historians immediately after 1821 elided the periods between antiquity and their own lifetimes in constructing the history of their nation, as if the heroes of the War of Independence were born only a few generations after Pericles or Alexander the Great.

The first printed editions of major Byzantine historians were published with introductions recommending them as useful sources on the rise of the Turks, who were currently threatening central Europe. A subsequent French corpus of editions offered help in the conquest of the Eastern Mediterranean, as the French crown planned to reclaim the imperial title of Byzantium. Byzantine twelfth-century literature until recently was divided in Greek academia into two sections, one for texts using formal linguistic patterns, the other focusing on signs of the Modern Greek language and spirit. These two categories met at the Byzantine court, maybe involving the same writers, but, because of antagonisms over language in the nineteenth-century Greek state, they were taught in different university departments. In the twentieth century, discussions of Byzantine rural landholding mirrored disputes involving communist theory.

Many such projects were poorly conceived, if judged as attempts to understand and study Byzantine culture rather than by the alternative motivations indicated. They were also not well coordinated. There was no central language or scholarly tradition, unlike, for example, work on French culture, which was naturally either in French or written to be attractive to French readers. We are anxious not to overemphasise these points: not all work undertaken in non-Byzantine nationalist frameworks was good – in fact nationalism itself was sometimes its besetting sin. Some studies of Byzantium were extremely impressive, especially magisterial surveys made with Germanic thoroughness that are still used to check the completeness of twenty-first-century work on Byzantium. But the most unfortunate feature of early scholarly forays into Byzantium was their lack of a united voice in the competitive matrices of cultural history, from which membership of the community of nations, the modern university and the diversity of its subject offerings emerged. Though Byzantium was marginally present in many European centres, it became an optional part of European consciousness, indeed usually absent at key moments. In the orientalist prism through which the world was inevitably viewed at that time, Byzantium was classed as non-Europe and therefore part of the observed (and subordinate) periphery rather than the observing centre. If research could have been better coordinated, Byzantium might have played an interesting and important role as a bridge between the two spheres.

Thus, at the level of sweeping generalisation characteristic of this chapter, Byzantine studies suffer from belatedness. As well as aspiring to cutting-edge scholarship to win (or keep) a seat at the different high tables of contemporary research, Byzantinists must still go back to provide or improve much of the infrastructure on which that research has to be based. Important texts remain unedited, or half-edited in scraps. Past editors have often only used one manuscript out of several, and often one of the worst. The many volumes of *Patrologia Graeca* include several that are veritable graveyards of mis-edited texts, mainly with theological content – productions over which, in many cases, modern scholars seem only now to be working out the appropriate research questions. Important auxiliary disciplines like sigillography, epigraphy and numismatics are making great strides, but do not always present their results in ways which are useful to non-experts in those subjects, sometimes forcing the latter to read a century or more of bibliography to be confident in the use of a single seal, coin-type or inscription. Of course, it is not only textual scholarship which is affected, for research into the physical remains of Byzantium has also been hampered by a focus on the classical past or modern national interests.

Thus Byzantinists are often now faced with difficult choices. Should they follow and try to match the methodological advances of their colleagues in neighbouring disciplines, or fill gaps in the infrastructure of texts and objects without which the new methods may be seriously undermined? This dilemma is not exclusive to Byzantinists, but the number and importance of weaknesses in the infrastructure seem unusually high in this subject, especially in view of its huge chronological and geographical scope. It is tempting to try to advance on all fronts – to continue the production of basic infrastructure whilst introducing new ideas and approaches; but this may delay publication of results and do little to remedy the discipline's belatedness.

This book is a good example of the operation of these dilemmas. The chapters range from simple reporting of the readings of manuscripts to issues relating to authorship, performativity, literary sociology and the contextualisation of transmitted texts in a variety of different dimensions. Unease is sometimes visible over the quantity and completeness of the evidence available. Often there are marks of innovation in the research questions asked, the methods framing the answers, or both. But all these levels of research, with their different degrees of prestige and scholarly popularity, are essential for the future of our subject. Whatever else one may say about the future of research on Byzantine reading, it is certain that innovation needs to be fed with more and more reliable basic data, which will sometimes send us back to simple methods of collection.

For likely readers of this book, reading will seem almost as straightforward as breathing. But, as we saw in discussing the physiology of the process at the start of the chapter, how we read now was not how medieval people read. Reading manuscript was and is different from reading print. The definition of reading should be extended to cover other ways in which a written page was transmitted to a receptive Byzantine audience, whether it was large, small, even just one person. This usually meant listening to a voice reading aloud: to a performance. Furthermore, Byzantine books were luxury possessions, owned by the rich or the church, much more expensive than modern books, and some (we shall look at the Old and

New Testaments) had different contents and arrangement from their modern equivalents.

As a result, reading (or hearing) a book might have impressed a sensitive Byzantine in ways that are no longer obvious and need reconstruction.

Quotations from past literature will be picked up by well-informed modern readers, but the precise implications to be drawn from them are elusive. Differences in the impacts of prose and verse, of different verse-forms and of the various genres need to be assessed in Byzantine terms: do some styles, say, suggest performance at a rural festival, or before a large urban audience? Modern circumstances have made us all experts in the swift absorption of text. Research on Byzantine reading must alienate us from these skills in a Brechtian or Jaussian way, stopping our automatic construction of explanatory scenarios based on our own experience. We need to learn to read slowly, in part to experience the limitations of Byzantine technology, in part to pick up the contextual hints our modern reading proficiency overlooks.

The Bible is often the most frequent item in the quotations listed in the relevant register of the edition of a Byzantine text, yet the Byzantine Bible was not set out as a modern reader would expect. Biblical material was most commonly available in the form of lectionaries, arranged in various volumes constructed for liturgical purposes, not in continuous narrative as in modern Bibles. This privileged the book of Psalms, which played (and still plays) a major role in services and often formed a separate volume. Congregations would see, but not themselves handle, the books in use by priests and others with active roles in the services – though priests and congregation alike would know prominent parts of the liturgy by heart. The biblical text was far from stable, and the alert hearer was likely to pick up differences in wording from one volume to another. Thus we must disabuse ourselves of the assumption that Byzantine congregations would have consulted their own critical texts of biblical books in regular narrative form. Virtually all Byzantine readers of works containing biblical quotations, and even some of their writers, are likely to have absorbed them only through their ears during services rather than by conventional reading.

Why did Byzantine writers include so many quotations in their work? What messages were they attempting to convey to their readers? Scholarly practice today, apart from the functional quotation of passages from a work being discussed, is to borrow attractive phrases to support an argument. We rely on the prestige of the writer whose words we use, or the impression made by the quotation itself. Some similar quotations may be found in Byzantium. But if we judge all Byzantine quotations by these criteria, we will be disappointed. Many, especially biblical quotations, add very little authority to the points made, and seem flat, uninteresting parallels to ideas already sufficiently expressed – apparently quotation for its own sake. We should probably see such cases as confirming shared experience between the writer and his audience, the regular Orthodox services which all experienced. The writer would be working on his audience's sympathy, aiming at cultivating trust.

When we move on from the Bible to quotations from ancient texts, the shared experience to which reference was usually made changes a little. The modern critic may assume that the writer is attempting to impress his readers with the breadth of his learning, and may be surprised that most of the references are to popular texts in the school curriculum, like early books of the *Iliad*. But it would be easy for a literate person to make more spectacular quotations. Maybe we should examine the possibility that the restricted list of quoted texts was due to the assumed audience, which was obliged to pick up the quotations to participate in the shared experience, for quotations were most often neither marked nor attributed. What was being shared was a common experience of the first stages of education. There is, of course, a wide range of more complex patterns of quotation, where really learned men compete with each other in the breadth of their reading, but the parameters there are probably easier to parallel to modern situations.

When learned men wrote competitively for their peers, other issues arose. Throughout the Byzantine period, the ability to express oneself well was a qualification for administrative office, though proof of that ability was made in different ways. In late antiquity, the writing of good hexameters qualified a whole class of Egyptian poets as administrators all over the empire. Much later, the competition operated mainly through schools: in the tenth and eleventh centuries, schoolmasters competed in writing rhetorical texts, and there were set occasions pitting the students of one master against those of others. The Komnenians prized military more than literary skills, but many twelfth-century writers and poets became professionals, living off imperial and aristocratic commissions. The years after 1204, particularly the Palaiologan period, saw the climax of the prominence of literary men. Several held the highest offices of state, and their children were ennobled by marriage into the imperial family. The typical Byzantine writer, particularly after the eleventh century, was rarely an other-worldly artist but a competitive man of business, a spin-doctor looking for patrons to praise in prose or verse in return for money. His works were not only written for performance on specific occasions; they were also samples of his wares for purposes of advertisement, heard and read by Byzantine audiences in this spirit. This is a blunt description of a complex scenario, which was not without exceptions – but any modern discussion of Byzantine authorship should have these circumstances in mind.

The cases we have listed are far from exhausting the differences, large and small, between the Byzantine and modern practices of reading. Because of the temptations to assume modern situations with regard to books, education, literary art and other parameters of reading, one of the best ways of clarifying the Byzantine situation is to study every dimension of its difference from modern reading, methodically paring away modern misconceptions.

Research on Byzantine reading will use a large and fast-growing range of tools based on the increasing complexity of electronic methods of analysis and internet presentation. In the fifty years of our association with research into Byzantium, the technology has changed very fast, just as that for playing pop music has progressed from vinyl and reel-to-reel tape to the plethora of current alternatives. Students of our generation paid to have theses typed for us, with three carbons to make smudged copies; the Greek for one of our graduate theses was written in by hand, while for the other the pages were transferred singly to a second typewriter to enter the Greek in spaces left by the first. We still have a heavy suitcase of printout in Greek represented by Roman capitals, produced by the biggest computer (then) in London University, made from data we had entered on punched tape. Some years later we typed a Greek paragraph into a Mac and at once generated a perfect printed page with full diacritics – an exciting experience. Important recent reading-based developments are coming thick and fast. A significant part of future research, as we suggest below, will involve integrating these tools in order to find appropriate research questions on which to use them, and to present and document the answers.

We shall look at the best of the modern tools, which, to avoid long-windedness, must stand for them all. The Thesaurus Linguae Graecae (TLG) is owed to Classical Studies and the University of California at Irvine, but it has blessedly expanded into Byzantium and hopes to include all Byzantine (and even some later) texts, provided they are adequately edited. The Thesaurus is based on the full text of the best edition of any writer it includes, making a gigantic database, though the edition's *apparatus criticus* is not included. There are amazing search possibilities, like the ability to set (by century) the date-range of the material searched. Complexity is being added at every level: standard English translations of many works; the parsing of most inflected words; the addition of searchable copies of several dictionaries, including the Viennese *Lexikon zur Byzantinischen Gräzität*, which is now almost complete. The TLG has often been used as a massive dictionary resource in itself, bringing together all Classical and Byzantine examples of the use of Greek words to enable the linking of several more limited dictionaries. A major misuse has been to lengthen the lists of sources and quotations provided in editions, with little attempt to determine the actual pattern of copying and imitation. In the future, the database could serve as a marvellously complete compendium of readings involving particular names, words, phrases and phrase-patterns, transcending the flexibility of any traditional dictionary.

The key to modern reading of manuscript texts from the past is the edition, which controls access to the text and gives direct and indirect hints on reading it. The critical edition is one of the foundations of humanist scholarship, and its traditional form and pervasive coverage of most periods and languages have done much to standardise the publication of texts found in manuscript, so that it is easy for readers of one tradition to understand how works in another tradition have been edited. But there are good reasons to experiment with other editorial methods, as we shall attempt to show in the rest of this chapter.

The first reason, which we have already mentioned, derives from the fact that the methodology of the critical edition is based on finding errors, common errors between the manuscripts, allowing editors to trace the copying history of the text concerned. The system originated in classical and biblical scholarship. The scribes of such manuscripts are usually copying material composed many centuries earlier, in a language of which they cannot count as native speakers. Thus errors are easy to find. However, when the same scribes copy texts composed by Byzantine authors, it is often harder, especially when the differences reflect developments in language use, to say which are "correct" and which are the "errors". How can a modern editor judge? In extreme cases all scribes may date from the same linguistic milieu as the original writer. Most editions involve a text of readings judged "good" accompanied by an *apparatus criticus* below for rejected readings. Some rejections are self-evidently justifiable, others badly need supporting argumentation, which editions rarely provide. Often, in editions of Byzantine works, readings in the apparatus are as good as those in the text. The standard critical edition cannot express these varied situations: one reading has to be right and the rest wrong.

Critical editions usually standardise minor irregularities in spelling and grammatical orthography, indicating the fact by a sentence or two in the introduction. This avoids weighing down the apparatus with hundreds of tiny variations of no importance for understanding the text, where in any case there is little or no reason to accept one variant and reject another. However these variations would often have made a considerable difference in the ways the text would be read aloud. Historians of grammar, particularly phonology, cannot use critical editions, because much of their most important evidence has been tacitly removed. In general, the critical edition is a modern creation, combining distinct manuscripts. This process of combination, together with orthographic standardisation, may sometimes produce results which would have been abhorrent to the original writer or to a medieval reader performing the text before an audience.

A Byzantine reader who saw one manuscript and read it would have been aware of these constant inconsistencies, as well as conscious of the fact that another copy of the same text might well have differences in wording – but, with the exception of rare cases, he would have considered these features normal and not be scandalised in the same way as a modern editor or proof-reader. All modern editions seem designed to impose modernity on something essentially pre-modern. Some editions go further, providing a translation into a modern language, notes to explain choices made in the text and apparatus, on the content of the work, its sources and linguistic peculiarities, together with identification of the names and place-names involved. These notes are sometimes on the same page as the edition, sometimes elsewhere in the book, for example in an index.

Recent developments take modern reading, especially scholarly reading, even further from the Byzantine experience. For more than twenty years there has been intense discussion of digital editions, trying to overcome the rigidity of the standard book, particularly over the black and white choice between 'right' text and 'wrong' apparatus. One common form of digital edition marks the lemmata of the apparatus and/or notes by highlighting them in the text or attaching superscript numbers. Notes then appear when the reader passes the mouse over these markings, or clicks on them. This may bring up a line or two of apparatus with comments over reasons for its rejection. It may take the reader to another site, a geographical gazetteer, grammar or prosopography. The basic page seems often too cluttered to be absorbed by any process resembling reading: it is more a table for the dissection of the text and the explication of its meaning. This information overload is far removed from the non-standard, bare manuscript of an often volatile text to which the Byzantine reader would have had access. We need the dissection, but it must first be contextualised by achieving a reading experience more closely approximating that of the Byzantines.

Fortunately, in the last five years or so large numbers of manuscript facsimiles have begun to appear on the internet sites of many major libraries. Librarians who had preserved their manuscripts from damage by readers, by locking them away and even restricting the circulation of photographs, changed their policy almost overnight. The cost of reproductions has decreased and many are now freely available on the internet for research purposes. As editions, especially digital editions, have moved away from the Byzantine reading experience, available copies of Byzantine original pages have increased exponentially. This suggests that it may now be possible for digital editions to offer richer and more direct access to Byzantine texts. But before that can happen, several other barriers – for example, institutional, financial and technical – need to be overcome. There is limited motivation for research on reading in Byzantium if its results cannot be shown in the edition of Byzantine texts. The exclusivity of the critical edition must be opened up to change and competition on a level playing field.

A digital edition could begin from complete facsimiles of one or more manuscripts, perhaps with the same page or two from all available witnesses. Transcriptions would be needed, unless the manuscripts were very easy to read. Different kinds of punctuation could be tried and compared. Readers not fluent in Greek would require a translation into a modern language (or two), electronically attached to the facsimiles or transcriptions, so that the versions may appear side-by-side. The rest of the edition would vary according to its assumed audience and the importance of the text. Textual apparatus, notes on variations important to linguists, identification of names and all the rest could be included – with links to each of the versions provided, together with the possibility of hiding such facilities where they are unnecessary and hinder the reading experience. Many editors have individual agendas to pursue, appropriate to a restricted number of texts. One could dream of programs with templates of textual spaces to be filled and links to be added by the choices of the editor, tailored to an assumed audience.

The greatest of the problems created by the printed critical edition is the barrier it forms against innovation and experimentation of this kind. Its roots deep in the humanist tradition are supported by the rules of various dominant publishing houses and prestigious series. Though editors do not expect to grow rich through their editions, at least standard critical editions have a better chance to be published without special subventions from the editor than digital editions, which are by definition experimental. We have met several editors, most of them young, keen to innovate digitally but terrified that their labour will be wasted, because there is no standard for the digital edition that even begins to rival the authority of a critical edition in book form. The future of research on Byzantine reading depends to a large extent on the solution of this dilemma. We do not presume to define the future of the edition, or of research on reading in Byzantium. There will still be many printed critical editions in our future. But the way must be opened to try digital alternatives, which may combine greater authenticity in the reading experience with increased flexibility in the provision of aids to understanding and contextual information.

Bibliography

Primary Sources

Abgaryan, G. V., ed., Պատմութիւն Սեբէոսի *[History of Sebēos]* (Erevan, 1979).
Adler, A., ed., *Suidae Lexicon*, 5 vols. (Leipzig, 1928–38).
Adolf, D., ed., *Martianus Capella. De Nuptiis philologiae et Mercurii* (Stuttgart, 1969).
Agapitos, P. A., ed., Ἀφήγησις Λιβίστρου καὶ Ροδάμνης. Κριτικὴ ἔκδοση τῆς διασκευῆς α (Athens, 2006).
Akinean, N. and P. Tēr-Połosean, 'Թուղթ Փոտայ պատրիարքի առ Զաքարիա կաթողիկոս Հայոց Մեծաց' ['Letter of Patriach Photios to Katholikos Zak'aria of Greater Armenia'], *Handēs Amsōreay*, 82 (1968), 65–100 and 129–56.
Albertella, R., M. Amelotti, L. Migliardi and E. Schwartz, eds., *Drei dogmatische Schriften Iustinians*, second edition, reprinted as *Legum Iustiniani imperatoris vocabularium* (Milan, 1973).
Ališan, Ł., ed., Հայապատում: Պատմիչք եւ պատմութիւնք [*Armenian History: Historians and Histories*], 2 vols. (Venice, 1901).
Anastasi, R., ed., *Michele Psello: Encomio per Giovanni, piissimo metropolita di Euchaita e protosincello* (Padua, 1968).
Anon., Պատմութիւն յաղագս գիւտի նշխարաց սրբոյն Գրիգորի Հայոց Մեծաց Լուսաւորչի' ['*History concerning the discovery of the relics of St. Grigor the Illuminator of Greater Armenia*'], *Ararat*, 35 (1902), 1178–83.
Apostolike Diakonia, ed., Πεντηκοστάριον (Athens, 1959).
—— ed., Τριῴδιον (Athens, 1960).
—— ed., Ὡρολόγιον τὸ Μέγα (Athens, 1977).
Arthur, S., C. Hunt, C. Edgar and D. L. Page, eds., *Select Papyri*, 5 vols. (London, 1932).
Aujac, G., ed. and trans., *Géminos. Introduction aux phénomènes* (Paris, 1975).
Bachmann, L., ed., *Anecdota Graeca*, 2 vols. (Leipzig, 1828).
Bakker, W. F. and A. F. van Gemert, Ἱστορία τοῦ Βελισαρίου. Κριτικὴ ἔκδοση τῶν τεσσάρων διασκευῶν μὲ εἰσαγωγή, σχόλια καὶ γλωσσάριο, second edition (Athens, 2007).

Balsamon, T., ed., *Scholion on Canon 100 of the Quinisext Council* in Mango, ed. and trans., *Art of the Byzantine Empire* (1974), 234.
Barbel, J., ed., *Gregor von Nazianz. Die fünf theologischen Reden* (Düsseldorf, 1963).
Barber. C. and S. Papaioannou, eds., *Michael Psellos on Literature and Art: A Byzantine Perspective on Aesthetics* (Notre Dame, IN, 2017).
Barkhuizen, J. H., ed., *Romanos the Melodist: Poet and Preacher. Introduction with Annotated Translation of Selected Poetic Homilies* (Durbanville, 2012).
Barney, S. A., W. J. Lewis, J. A. Beach and O. Berghof, eds. and trans., *The Etymologies of Isidore of Seville* (Cambridge, 2006).
Beckby, H., ed., *Anthologia Graeca*, 4 vols. (Munich, 1957–8).
Bekker, I., ed., *Theophanes Continuatus, Ioannes Cameniata, Symeon Magister, Georgius Monachus* (Bonn, 1838).
 ed., *Leonis Grammatici. Chronographia* (Bonn, 1842).
 ed., *Suidae Lexicon* (Berlin, 1854)
Berger, A., ed. and trans., *Accounts of Medieval Constantinople: The Patria* (Washington, D. C., 2013).
Bernardinello, S., ed., *Theodori Prodromi de Manganis* (Padua, 1972).
Berry, P., trans., *Pomponius Mela. Geography or De situ orbis* (Lewiston, NY, 1997).
Berschin, W., ed., *Greek Letters and the Latin Middle Ages: From Jerome to Nicholas of Cusa*, revised edition, trans. J. C. Frakes (Washington, D. C., 1988).
Bidez, J. and L. Parmentier, eds., *The Ecclesiastical History of Evagrius with the Scholia* (London, 1898).
Blockley, R. C., ed. and trans., *The Fragmentary Classicising Historians of the Later Roman Empire: Eunapius, Olympiodorus, Priscus and Malchus*, 2 vols. (Liverpool, 1981–3).
Bodnar, E. W. and C. Foss, eds., *Cyriac of Ancona. Later Travels* (Cambridge, MA, 2003).
Boissonade, J. F., ed., *Michael Psellus. De operatione daemonum* (Nuremberg, 1838).
 ed., *Anecdota nova* (Paris, 1844).
Bompaire, J., ed., *Actes de Xéropotamou: édition diplomatique* (Paris, 1964).
Borovilou-Genakou, A., 'Baroccianus gr. 50: Ἐπιμερισμοὶ κατὰ στοιχεῖον Γραφικά. Terminus ante quem pour le lexique de Théodose le grammairien (ixe s.)', *Byzantion*, 72 (2002), 250–69.
Bouboulidis, F. K., ed., 'Δημώδεις μεταβυζαντινοὶ ἀλφάβητοι', *ΕΕΒΣ*, 25 (1955), 284–305.
Boulenger, F., ed., *Grégoire de Nazianze. Discours funèbres en l'honneur de son frère Césaire et de Basile de Césarée* (Paris, 1908).
Boulgares, E. and T. Mandakase, eds., Ἰωσὴφ μοναχοῦ τοῦ Βρυεννίου τὰ παραλειπόμενα (Leipzig, 1784).
Bowen, A. and P. Garnsey, trans., *Lactantius. Divine Institutes* (Liverpool, 2003).
Brackerts, K., ed., *Das Traumbuch des Achmet ben Sirin* (Munich, 1986).
Brightman, F. E., ed., *Liturgies, Eastern and Western* (Oxford, 1894).
Brooks, E. W., ed., *Historia Ecclesiastica Zachariae Rhetori vulgo adscripta*, 2 vols. (Louvain, 1954–67).

Bucossi, A., ed., 'George Skylitzes' Dedicatory Verses for the *Sacred Arsenal* by Andronikos Kamateros and the *Codex Marcianus Graecus* 524', *JÖB*, 59 (2009), 37–50.
  ed., *Andronici Camateri Sacrum Armamentarium: Pars prima* (Turnhout, 2014).
Bury, R. G., trans., *Plato. Timaeus* (Cambridge, MA, 1929).
Cameron, A. M. and S. G. Hall, trans., *Eusebius: Life of Constantine* (Oxford, 1999).
Canard, M. and H. Berbérian, trans., *Aristakès de Lastivert. Récit des malheurs de la nation arménienne* (Brussels, 1973).
Canivet, N. and P. Oikonomidès, '(Jean Argyropoulos), *La Comédie de Katablattas*: invective byzantine du xve siècle', *Diptycha*, 3 (1982–3), 1–99.
Carney, T. F., trans., *John Lydos. De Magistratibus*, in Carney, *Bureaucracy in Traditional Society* (1971), Book 3.
Cesaretti, P., ed., 'Eustathios' Commentary on the Pentecostal Hymn Ascribed to St. John Damascene: a New Critical Edition', *Svenska Kommittén för Byzantinska Studier Bulletin*, 5 (1987), 19–22.
Cesaretti, P. and S. Ronchey, eds., *Eustathii Thessalonicensis exegesis in canonem iambicum pentecostalem: recensuerunt indicibusque instruxerunt* (Berlin, 2014).
Chabot, J., ed., *Chronique de Michel le Syrien*, 4 vols. (Paris, 1889–1924).
Charles, R. H., ed. and trans., *Chronicle of John, Bishop of Nikiu* (London, 1916).
Chauvot, A., ed., *Procope de Gaza, Priscien de Césarée, panégyriques de l'empereur Anastase Ier* (Bonn, 1986).
Chibnall, M., ed. and trans., *The Ecclesiastical History of Orderic Vitalis*, 6 vols. (Oxford, 1969–80).
Chiesa, P., ed., *Liudprandi Cremonensis Antapodosis, Homelia paschalis, Historia Ottonis, Relatio de legatione Constantinopolitana* (Turnhout, 1998).
Christ, W. and M. Paranikas, eds., *Anthologia Graeca carminum Christianorum* (Leipzig, 1871).
Cobham, C. D., ed., *Excerpta Cypria: Materials for a History of Cyprus* (Cambridge, 1908).
Constantinides, C. N., ed., Ἡ Διήγησις τῆς θαυματουργῆς εἰκόνας τῆς Θεοτόκου Ἐλεούσας τοῦ Κύκκου (Nicosia, 2002).
Coureas, N. and C. Schabel, eds., *The Cartulary of the Cathedral of Holy Wisdom of Nicosia* (Nicosia, 1997).
Coyne, P., ed., *Priscian of Caesarea's 'De Laude Anastasii Imperatoris'* (Lampeter, 1991).
Cramer, J. A., ed., *Anecdota Graeca e codd. manuscriptis bibliothecarum Oxoniensium*, 4 vols. (Oxford, 1835–7).
  ed., *Anecdota Graeca e codd. manuscriptis bibliothecae regiae Parisiensis*, 4 vols. (Oxford, 1839–41).
Crick, E., ed., *Niccolò Machiavelli: The Discourses* (London, 2003).
Crisafulli, V. S. and J. W. Nesbitt, eds., *The Miracles of St. Artemios* (Leiden, 1997).
Criscuolo, U., ed., *Michele Psello. Autobiografia: encomio per la madre* (Naples, 1989).
Croke, B., ed. and trans., *The Chronicle of Marcellinus* (Sydney, 1995).

Crouzel, H., and M. Simonetti, eds. and trans., *Origen. Traité des principes, Peri Archôn* (Paris 1978–84).
D'Aiuto, F., ed., *Tre canoni di Giovanni Mauropode in onore di santi militari* (Rome, 1994).
Darrouzès, J., ed., *Épistoliers byzantins du xe siècle* (Paris, 1960).
  ed., *Nicétas Stéthatos, Opuscules et Lettres* (Paris, 1961),
  ed., *Documents inédits d'écclésiologie byzantine* (Paris, 1966).
  ed., *Syméon le Nouveau Théologien. Traités théologiques et éthiques*, 2 vols. (Paris, 1966–7).
  ed., *George et Dèmètrios Tornikès: Lettres et discours* (Paris, 1970).
  ed. and trans., *Chapitres théologiques, gnostiques et pratiques* (Paris, 1996).
Darrouzès, J. and L. G. Westerink, eds., *Théodore Daphnopatès. Correspondance* (Paris, 1978).
Database of Byzantine Book Epigrams, www.dbbe.ugent.be/typ/4278 (accessed 17 January 2017).
Dawkins, R. M., ed., *Leontios Makhairas. Recital Concerning the Sweet Land of Cyprus Entitled 'Chronicle'*, 2 vols. (Oxford, 1932).
de Andrés, G., ed., 'Carta de Teodosio el Grammatico (s. ix) sobre el lexico de los canones de san Juan Damasceno, según el codice Complutense "Villamil No 30"', *Emerita*, 41 (1973), 377–95.
de Boor, C., ed., *Theophanis Chronographia*, 2 vols. (Leipzig, 1883–5).
de Groote, M., ed., *Christophori Mitylenaii Versuum Variorum Collectio Cryptensis* (Turnhout, 2012).
de Lagarde, P. and J. Bollig, eds., *Iohannis Euchaitorum Metropolitae quae in Codice Vaticano Graeco 676 supersunt* (Göttingen, 1882).
de Stefani, L., ed., 'Per le fonti dell' Etimologico Gudiano', *BZ*, 16 (1907), 52–68.
  ed., 'Il Lessico ai Canoni giambici di Giovanni Damasceno secondo un ms. Romano', *BZ*, 21 (1912), 431–5.
Dedes, D., ed., 'An Edition of a Medieval Greek Poem on the Trojan War (Διήγησις τῆς Τρωάδος)', unpublished PhD thesis, University of London (1971).
Delatte, A., ed., *Anecdota Atheniensia et alia* (Liège, 1939).
Delehaye, H., ed., *Synaxarium Ecclesiae Constantinopolitanae* (Brussels, 1902).
  ed., *Deux typica byzantins de l'époque des Paléologues* (Brussels, 1921).
Dennis, G. T., ed., *The Letters of Manuel II Palaeologus: Text, Translation and Notes* (Washington, D. C., 1977).
  ed. and trans., *Three Byzantine Military Treatises* (Washington, D. C., 1985).
  ed., *Michaelis Pselli Orationes Panegyricae* (Stuttgart, 1994).
Diehl, E., ed., *Procli Diadochi in Platonis Timaeum commentaria*, 3 vols. (Leipzig, 1903–6).
Diels, H. and W. Kranz, eds., *Die Fragmente der Vorsokratiker: griechisch und deutsch* (Berlin, 1951).
Diethart, J., and Hörandner, W., eds., *Constantinus Stilbes, Poemata* (Munich, 2005).
Dindorf, L., ed., *Ioannis Malalae Chronographia* (Bonn, 1831).
  ed., *Chronicon Paschale* (Bonn, 1832).

Dindorf, L., L. M. and M. Whitby, eds. and trans., *Chronicon Paschale* (Liverpool, 1989).
Doutreleau, L., B. C. Mercier and A. Rousseau, eds., *Irénée de Lyon. Contre les hérésies, livre 5*, 2 vols. (Paris, 1969).
Downey, G., ed., 'Nikolaos Mesarites: description of the church of the Holy Apostles at Constantinople', *TAPhS*, 6 (1957), 855–924.
Doyen-Higuet, A.-M., ed., *L'Epitomé de la collection d'hippiatrie grecque* (Louvain-la Neuve, 2006).
Drexl, F., ed., *Achmetis oneirocriticon* (Leipzig, 1925).
Duff, J. D., trans., *Lucan. The Civil War* (Cambridge, MA, 1958).
Dulaurier, E., ed., *La chronique de Matthieu d'Édesse* (Paris 1858).
Dumortier, J., ed., *Jean Chrysostome. A Théodore* (Paris, 1966).
Dyck, A. R., ed., *Epimerismi Homerici* (Berlin, 1983).
Edgington, S. B., ed. and trans., *Albert of Aachen. Historia Ierosolimitana* (Oxford, 2007).
Eideneier, H., ed., *Ptochoprodromos: Einführung, kritische Ausgabe, deutsche Übersetzung, Glossa* (Cologne, 1991); Greek translation in H. Eideneier, ed., Πτωχοπρόδρομος: κριτική έκδοση (Irakleio, 2012).
Eramo, I., ed., *Siriano. Discorsi di guerra* (Bari, 2010).
Failler, A., ed., *Georges Pachymérès. Relations historiques*, 5 vols. (Paris, 1984–2000).
Fairbanks, A., trans., *Philostratus the Elder and the Younger. Imagines; Callistratus. Descriptions* (New York, NY, 1969).
Färber, H., ed., *Hero und Leander: Musaios und die weiteren antiken Zeugnisse gesammelt und übersetzt* (Munich, 1961).
Flusin, B., ed., *Saint Anastase le Perse et l'histoire de la Palestine au début du VIIe siècle* (Paris, 1992).
Flusin, B. and J.-C. Cheynet, trans., *Jean Skylitzès. Empereurs de Constantinople* (Paris, 2003).
Follieri, E., ed., *Il Teseida neogreco, Libro I. Saggio di edizione* (Rome, 1959).
  ed., 'Giovanni Mauropode metropolita di Euchaita, Otto canoni paracletici a N. S. Gesù Cristo', *Archivio italiano per la storia della pietà*, 5 (1967), 1–200.
Frier, B. W., S. Connolly, S. Corcoran, et al., eds., *The Codex of Justinian: A New Annotated Translation*, trans. F. H. Blume, 3 vols. (Cambridge, 2016),
Garzya, A., ed., *Opere di Sinesio di Cirene: epistole, operette, inni* (Turin, 1999).
Garzya, A. and R. Loenertz, eds., *Procopii Gazaei Epistolae et declamationes* (Ettal, 1963).
Gautier, P., ed., *Michel Italikos. Lettres et discours* (Paris, 1972).
  ed., 'Diatribes de Jean l'Oxite contre Alexis Ier Comnène', *REB*, 28 (1970), 5–55.
  ed., 'L'édit d'Alexis Ier Comnène sur la réforme du clergé', *REB*, 31 (1973), 165–201.
  ed. and trans., *Nicéphore Bryennios. Histoire. Introduction, texte, traduction et notes* (Brussels, 1975).
  ed., *Théophylacte d'Achrida. Discours, traités, poésies, lettres*, 2 vols. (Thessalonike, 1980–6).

ed., 'Éloge inédit du lecteur Jean Kroustoulas par Michel Psellos', *RSBN*, 17–19 (1980-2), 119–47.
ed., 'Le typikon du sébaste Grégoire Pakourianos', *REB*, 42 (1984), 5–145.
ed., *Michaelis Pselli Theologica*, 2 vols. (Leipzig, 1989).
Gerstinger, H., ed., *Pamprepios von Panopolis. Eidyllion auf die Tageszeiten und Enkomion auf den Archon Theagenes von Athen: Nebst Bruchstücken anderer epischer Dichtungen und zwei Briefe des Gregorios von Nazianz im Pap. Gr. Vindob. 29788 A-C* (Vienna, 1928).
Giankulles, K., ed., Θησαυρός Κυπριακής διαλέκτου (Leukosia, 2009).
Gigli Piccardi, D., F. Gonnelli, G. Agosti and D. Accorinti, eds. and trans., *Nonno di Panopoli. Le Dionisiache* (Milan, 2003–4).
Gill, J., ed., *Quae supersunt actorum Graecorum Concilii Florentini*, 2 vols. (Rome, 1953).
Golitzin, A., trans., *St. Symeon the New Theologian. On the Mystical Life: The Ethical Discourses*, vol. 1: *The Church and the Last Things* (Crestwood, NY, 1995).
Gorce, G., ed., *Vie de Sainte Mélanie* (Paris, 1962).
Gouillard, J., ed., 'Le synodikon de l'Orthodoxie: édition et commentaire', *TM*, 2 (1967), 1–316.
Goulet, R., ed. and trans., *Cléomède. De motu circulari* (Paris, 1980).
Grant, R. M., trans., *Theophilus of Antioch. Ad Autolycum* (Oxford, 1970).
Greatrex, G., ed., R. Phenix and C. Horn, trans, *The Chronicle of Pseudo-Zachariah Rhetor: Church and War in Late Antiquity* (Liverpool, 2011).
Greenwood, T., trans., *The Universal History of Stepanos Tarōnec'i* (Oxford, 2017).
Gregory, S. and C. Luttrell, eds., *Chrétien de Troyes. Cligés* (Cambridge, 1993).
Grosdidier de Matons, J., ed., *Romanos le Mélode. Hymnes*, 5 vols. (Paris 1964–81).
Grumel, V. and V. Laurent, eds., *Les Regestes des actes du patriarcat de Constantinople, 1: Les actes des patriarches, fasc. 11 et 111: Les regestes de 715 à 1206*, revised and corrected by J. Darrouzès (Paris, 1989).
Guthrie, W. K. C., trans., *Aristotle. On the Heavens* (Cambridge, MA, 1953).
Halkin, F., ed., 'Deux vies de s. Maxime le kausokalybe, ermite au Mont Athos (XIVe s.)', *AB*, 54 (1936), 38–112.
'La vie de saint Nicéphore fondateur de Médikion en Bithynie (†813)', *AB*, 78 (1960), 396–430.
Hansen, G. C., ed., *Theodoros Anagnostes, Kirchengeschichte* (Berlin, 1971).
Harf-Lancner, L., ed., *Chrétien de Troyes. Cligès* (Paris, 2006).
Hase, C. B., ed., *Leonis Diaconi Caloënsis Historiae libri decem* (Bonn, 1828).
Haury, J. and G. Wirth, eds., *Procopius. Opera omnia*, 4 vols. (Leipzig, 1963–4).
Haury, J., et al., *Procopius Caesariensis. Opera omnia*, 4 vols. (Munich, 2001),
Hausherr, I. and G. Horn, eds. and trans., *Un grand mystique byzantin. Vie de Syméon le Nouveau Théologien (949–1022) par Nicétas Stéthatos* (Rome, 1928).
Heitsch, E., *Die griechischen Dichterfragmente der römischen kaiserzeit* (Göttingen, 1961–4).

Henry, R., ed., *Photius. Bibliothèque*, 8 vols. (Paris, 1959–91).
Hero, A. C., ed., *Letters of Gregory Akindynos* (Washington, D. C., 1983).
Hesseling, D. C. and H. Pernot, eds., *Poèmes Prodromiques en grec vulgaire* (Amsterdam, 1910).
Hicks, R. D., ed. and trans., *Diogenes Laertius. Lives of Eminent Philosophers*, 2 vols. (London, 1975)
Hörandner, W., ed., *Theodoros Prodromos. Historische Gedichte* (Vienna, 1974).
Hunger, H., ed., 'Liudprand von Cremona und die byzantinische Trivialliteratur' in E. Konstantinou, ed., *Byzanz und das Abendland im 10. und 11. Jahrhundert* (Cologne, 1997), 197–206.
Huygens, R. B. C., ed., *Guillaume de Tyr. Chronique*, 2 vols. (Turnhout, 1986).
Jackson, R., K. Lycos and H. Tarrant, eds. and trans., *Olympiodorus: Commentary on Plato's Gorgias* (Leiden, 1998).
James, L, ed., *Constantine of Rhodes: On Constantinople and the Church of the Holy Apostles*, including a Greek edition by I. Vassis (Farnham, 2012).
Jeffreys, E. M., ed. and trans., *Digenis Akritis: The Grottaferrata and Escorial Versions* (Cambridge, 1998).
  trans., *Four Byzantine Novels* (Liverpool, 2012).
Jeffreys, E. M. and M. J. Jeffreys, eds., *Iacobi Monachi. Epistulae* (Turnhout, 2009).
Jeffreys, E. M., M. J. Jeffreys and R. Scott, trans., *The Chronicle of John Malalas* (Melbourne, 1986).
Jeffreys, E. M. and M. Papathomopoulos, eds. Ὁ Πόλεμος τῆς Τρωάδος *(The War of Troy)* (Athens, 1996).
Jeffreys, M. J. and M. Lauxtermann, eds., *The Letters of Michael Psellos: Cultural Networks and Historical Realities* (Oxford, 2017).
Jordanov, I., ed., *Pečatite ot strategijata v Preslav* (Sofia, 1993).
Kaklamanis, S., ed., "Ὁ Πρόλογος εἰς τὸ βιβλίον τοῦ Θησέου, Ἐκδοτικὴ διερεύνηση' in N. M. Panagiotakes, ed., Ἄνθη Χαρίτων (Venice, 1998), 101–74.
Kaldellis, A., trans., *Genesios. On the Reigns of the Emperors. Translation and Commentary* (Canberra, 1998),
  ed., *Byzantine Readings of Ancient History: Texts in Translation, with Introductions and Notes* (London, 2015).
Kambylis, A., ed., *Symeon Neos Theologos. Hymnen* (Berlin, 1976).
Karlin-Hayter, P., ed. and trans., *Vita Euthymii Patriarchae CP* (Brussels, 1970).
Karpozilos, A., ed., *The Letters of Ioannes Mauropous, Metropolitan of Euchaita* (Thessalonike, 1990).
Kechagioglou, G., ed., Κριτικὴ ἔκδοση τῆς Ἱστορίας Πτωχολέοντος (Thessalonike, 1978).
  ed., Ἀπολλώνιος τῆς Τύρου. Υστερομεσαιωνικές και νεότερες ελληνικές μορφές, 2 vols. (Thessalonike, 2004).
Kendall, C. B. and F. Wallis, eds., *Isidore of Seville. On the Nature of Things* (Liverpool, 2016).
Kennedy, G. A., trans., *Progymnasmata: Greek Textbooks of Prose Composition and Rhetoric* (Leiden, 2003).
Keydell, R., ed., *Nonni Panopolitani Dionysiaca*, 2 vols. (Berlin, 1959).

Keyes, C. W., trans., *Cicero. De Re Publica* (Cambridge, MA, 1928).
Kibler, W. W., trans., *Chrétien de Troyes. Arthurian Romances* (London, 1991).
Köchly, H. and W. Rüstow, eds., *Griechische Kriegsschriftsteller*, 2 vols. (Leipzig, 1853–5).
Koder, J., ed., J. Paramelle and L. Neyrand, trans., *Syméon le Nouveau Théologien. Hymnes*, 3 vols. (Paris, 1969–73).
ed., *Romanos Melodos. Die Hymnen, übersetzt und erläutert*, 2 vols. (Stuttgart, 2005–6).
Kolovou, F., ed., *Michaelis Choniatae epistulae* (Berlin, 2001).
Kost, K., ed., *Musaios. Hero und Leander* (Bonn, 1971).
Koster, W., ed., *Scholia in Aristophanem* (Groningen, 1974).
Kotter, B., ed., *Die Schriften des Johannes von Damaskos, IV, Liber de haeresibus. Opera Polemica* (Berlin, 1981).
Koutsas, S. P., ed., Νικήτα τοῦ Στηθάτου βίος καὶ πολιτεία τοῦ ἐν ἁγίοις πατρὸς ἡμῶν Συμεὼν τοῦ Νέου Θεολόγου (Athens, 2005).
Kralides, B. and P. Philippides, eds., *Nikodemos the Hagiorite.* Ἑορτοδρόμιον ἤτοι ἑρμηνεία εἰς τοὺς ἀσματικοὺς κανόνας τῶν δεσποτικῶν καὶ θεομητορικῶν ἑορτῶν (Venice, 1836).
Krivochéine, B., ed., J. Paramelle, trans., *Syméon le Nouveau Théologien. Catéchèses*, 3 vols. (Paris, 1963–5).
Kurtz, E., ed., *Die Gedichte des Christophoros Mitylenaios* (Leipzig, 1903).
Kurtz, E. and F. Drexl, eds., *Michaelis Pselli Scripta minora*, 2 vols. (Milan, 1936–41).
Lampros, S. P., ed., Μιχαὴλ Ἀκομινάτου τοῦ Χωνιάτου τὰ σωζόμενα, 2 vols. (Athens, 1879–80).
ed., "Ὁ Μαρκιανὸς κῶδιξ 524', *NE*, 8 (1911), 3–59, 123–92.
Lampsidis, O., ed., *Constantini Manassis Breviarium chronicum*, 2 vols. (Athens, 1996).
La Porte-du Theil, F. J. G., ed., 'Lettres de Théodôre l'Hyrtacènien', *Notices et Extraits*, 5 (1798), 709–44.
Laurent, V., ed., *Syropoulos. Les 'Mémoires' du Grand Ecclésiarque de l'Église de Constantinople, Sylvestre Syropoulos, sur le concile de Florence (1438–1439)* (Paris, 1971).
Lee, H. D. P., trans., *Aristotle. Meteorologica* (Cambridge, MA, 1952).
Lefort, J., N. Oikonomidès, and D. Papachryssanthou, eds., *Actes d'Iviron II: du milieu du XIe s. à 1204. Édition diplomatique* (Paris, 1990).
Legrand, E., ed., *Bibliothèque grecque vulgaire*, 9 vols. (Paris, 1880–1902).
ed., *Cent-dix lettres grecques de François Filelfe* (Paris, 1892).
Lendari, T., ed., *Livistros and Rodamne. The Vatican Version: Critical Edition with Introduction, Commentary and Index-Glossary* (Athens, 2007).
Lenz, F. W. and C. A. Behr, eds., *P. Aelii Aristidis Opera quae exstant omnia* (Leiden, 1978).
Leone, P. M, ed., *Ioannis Tzetzae Historiae* (Naples, 1968).
ed., 'Nicephori Gregorae ad imperatorem Andronicum II Palaeologum orationes', *Byzantion*, 41 (1971), 497–519.
ed., *Joannis Tzetzae Epistulae* (Leipzig, 1972).

ed., *Niceforo Gregora. Fiorenzo o Intorno alla sapienza* (Naples, 1975).
ed., *Nicephori Gregorae Epistulae*, 2 vols. (Matino, 1982–3).
Le Quien, M., ed., *Johannis Damasceni Opera omnia*, 2 vols. (Paris, 1712); reprinted in J.-P. Migne, *PG* 94 (Paris, 1864).
Lesmüller-Werner, A., ed., *Byzanz am Vorabend neuer Grösse: Die vier Bücher der Kaisergeschichte des Ioseph Genesios. Übersetzt, eingeleitet und erklärt* (Vienna, 1989).
Lesmueller-Werner, A. and I. Thurn, eds., *Iosephi Genesii Regum libri quattuor* (New York, NY, 1978).
Levi, I., ed., 'Cinque lettere inedite di Manuele Moscopulo', *SIFC*, 10 (1902): 55–72.
Litavrin, G. G., ed. and trans., *Советы и рассказы Кекавмена* (Moscow, 1972); second edition (St Petersburg, 2003)
Littlewood, A. ed., *Michaelis Pselli Oratoria minora* (Leipzig, 1985).
Livrea, E., ed., *Colluthus: Il ratto di Elena* (Bologna, 1968).
Pamprepii Panopolitani carmina (P. Gr. Vindob. 19788 A-C) (Leipzig, 1979).
Livrea, E. and P. Eleuteri, eds., *Musaeus, Hero et Leander* (Leipzig, 1982).
'Nikephoros Phokas in Byzantine historical writings', *BSl*, 54 (1993), 245–53.
Long, H. S., ed., *Diogenis Laertii Vitae philosophorum* (Oxford, 1964).
Loredano, G., *Historie de' re' Lusignani, libri undeci, publicate da Henrico Giblet Cavalier* (Venice, 1660).
Ludwich, A., ed., *Musaios. Hero und Leandros* (Bonn, 1912).
Luzzato, M. J., ed., *Tzetzes lettore di Tucidide: note autografe al codice Heidelberg Palatino Greco 252* (Bari, 1999).
Maas, P. and C. A. Trypanis, eds., *Sancti Romani melodi cantica: Cantica genuina* (Oxford, 1963).
eds., *Sancti Romani melodi cantica: Cantica dubia* (Berlin, 1970).
Machiavelli, Niccolò, *Discorsi sopra la prima deca di Tito Livio*, in F. Bausi, ed., *Edizione nazionale delle opere di Niccolò Machiavelli*, 2 vols. (Rome, 2001).
Macrides, R., J. Munitiz and D. Angelov, eds., *Pseudo-Kodinos and the Constantinopolitan Court: Offices and Ceremonies* (Farnham, 2013).
Mai, A., ed., *Spicilegium Romanum*, 10 vols. (Rome, 1839-44).
Mair, A. W., ed., *Oppian, Colluthus, Tryphiodorus* (Cambridge, MA, 1963).
Maisano, R., ed., *Giorgio Sfranze. Cronaca* (Rome, 1990).
ed., *Romano il melode. Cantici*, 2 vols. (Turin, 2002).
Maiuri, A., ed., 'Una nuova poesia di Teodoro Prodromo in greco volgare', *BZ*, 23 (1920), 397–407.
Malcovati, E., ed., *Museo, Ero e Leandro* (Milan, 1946).
Malingrey, A. M. and R. Flacelière, eds. and trans., *Jean Chrysostom. Homélies sur l'incompréhensibilité de Dieu*, 4 vols. (Paris, 1970).
Manaphes, K. and I. Polemis, eds., 'Βασιλείου Πεδιαδίτου ανέκδοτα έργα', *EEBS*, 49 (1994–8), 1–62.
Mango, C. and R. Scott, trans., *The Chronicle of Theophanes Confessor: Byzantine and Near Eastern History, A.D. 284–813* (Oxford, 1997).

Bibliography

Manousakas, M. I., ed., *Λεονάρδου Ντελλαπόρτα ποιήματα* (Athens, 1995).
Manousakas, M. I. and W. Puchner, eds., *Ανέκδοτα στιχουργήματα του θρησκευτικού θεάτρου του ιζ' αιώνα: έργα των ορθόδοξων Χίων κληρικών Μιχ. Βεστάρχη, Γρηγ. Κονταράτου, Γαβρ. Προσοψά* (Athens, 2000).
Manukyan, G., ed., Ստեփանոս Տարաւնեցի Ասողիկ, Պատմութիւն տիեզերական *[Step'anos Tarōnec'i Asołik, Universal History]* (Ant'ilias, 2012).
Manutius, A., ed., *Poetae Christiani veteres (Prudentii Poetae opera)* (Venice, 1501).
Marcovich, M., ed., *Eustathius Macrembolites. De Hysmines et Hysminiae Amoribus Libri XI* (Munich, 2001).
Mariev, S., ed., *Ioannis Antiocheni Fragmenta quae supersunt omnia* (Berlin, 2008).
Marquardt, J., I. Müller and G. Helmreich, eds., *Claudii Galeni Pergameni scripta minora*, 3 vols. (Leipzig, 1884–93).
Martin-Hisard, B., trans., and A. Hakobian, ed., *Łewond Vardapet Discours historique* (Paris, 2015).
Mascialino, ed., L., *Lycophronis Alexandra* (Leipzig, 1964).
Mathieu, M., ed. and trans., *Guillaume de Pouille. La Geste de Robert Guiscard* (Palermo, 1961).
McCracken, G. E., W. M. Green, D. S. Wiesen et al., trans., *Augustine. The City of God Against the Pagans*, 7 vols. (Cambridge, MA, 1957–72).
McGeer, E., ed. and trans., *The Land Legislation of the Macedonian Emperors* (Toronto, 2000).
McGeer, E., J. W. Nesbitt and N. Oikonomides, eds., *Catalogue of Byzantine Seals at Dumbarton Oaks and in the Fogg Museum of Art*, 6 vols. (Washington, D. C., 1991–2009).
McGuckin, P., trans., *Symeon the New Theologian: The Practical and Theological Chapters and the Three Theological Discourses* (Kalamazoo, 1982).
McKee, S., ed., *Wills from Late Medieval Venetian Crete 1312–1420*, 3 vols. (Washington, D. C., 1998).
Meineke, A., ed., *Ioannis Cinnami Epitome rerum ab Ioanne et Alexio Comnenis gestarum* (Bonn, 1836).
Mercati, G., ed., *Notizie di Procoro e Demetrio Cidone, Manuele Caleca e Teodoro Meliteniota ed altri appunti per la storia della teologia e della letteratura bizantina del secolo XIV* (Vatican, 1931).
Mercati, S. G., ed., 'Versi di Niceforo Uranos in morte di Simeone Metafraste' in A. Acconcia Longo, ed., *Collectanea Byzantina*, 2 vols., (Bari, 1970), vol. 1, 565–73.
Miklosich, F. and J. Müller, eds., *Acta et diplomata graeca medii aevi sacra et profana*, 6 vols. (Vienna, 1860–90).
Miller, E., ed., 'Poésies inédites de Théodore Prodrome', *Annuaire de l'Association pour l'encouragement des études grecques*, 17 (1883), 18–64.
Mioni, E., ed. and trans., *Bibliothecae Divi Marci Venetiarum codices graeci manuscripti*, 7 vols. (Rome, 1981–5).
Moennig, U., ed., *Die Erzählung von Alexander und Semiramis. Kritische Ausgabe mit einer Einleitung, Übersetzung und einem Wörterverzeichnis* (Berlin, 2004).
Mommsen, T., ed., *Marcellini V. C. comitis chronicon. MGH AA* 11 (Berlin, 1894).

Montana, F., ed., 'I canoni giambici di Giovanni Damasceno per le feste di Natale, Teofania e Pentecoste nelle esegesi di Gregorio di Corinto', *Koinonia*, 13 (1989), 31–49.
  ed., 'Dal glossario all'esegesi. l'apparato ermeneutico al canone pentecostale attribuito a Giovanni Damasceno nel ms. Ottob. Gr. 248', *Studi classici e orientali*, 42 (1992), 147–64.
  ed., 'Tre parafrasi anonime bizantine del canone giambico pentecostale attribuito a Giovanni Damasceno', *Koinonia*, 17 (1993), 61–79.
  ed., *Gregorio di Corinto. Esegesi al canone giambico per la Pentecoste attribuito a Giovanni Damasceno* (Pisa, 1995).
Moravscik, G., ed., R. J. H. Jenkins, trans., *Constantine VII Porphyrogenitus. De administrando imperio*, second edition (Washington, D. C., 1967).
Mossay, J., ed., *Symposium Nazianzenum* (Paderborn, 1983).
Mother Mary, ed., F. K. Ware, trans., *The Lenten Triodion* (London, 1978).
Mueller, I., trans., *Simplikios. On Aristotle On the Heavens 3.7–4.6* (London, 2009).
Munier, H., ed., *La Scala Copte 44 de la Bibliothèque Nationale de Paris: transcription et vocabulaire*, vol. 1 (Cairo, 1930).
Nauck, A., ed., 'Iohannis Damasceni canones iambici cum commentario et indice verborum', *Mélanges gréco-romains, Bulletin de l'Académie impériale des sciences de Saint-Pétersbourg*, 6 (1893), 199–228.
Nesbitt, J. and J. Wiita, eds., 'A Confraternity of the Comnenian Era', *BZ*, 68 (1975), 360–84.
Nørgaard, L. and O. L. Smith, eds., *A Byzantine Iliad: The Text of Par. Suppl. Gr. 926. Edited with Critical Apparatus, Introduction and Indexes* (Copenhagen, 1975).
Oberhelman, S. M., ed., *Dreambooks in Byzantium: Six Oneirocritica in Translation, with Commentary and Introduction* (Aldershot, 2008).
Oder, E. and C. Hoppe, eds., *Corpus hippiatricorum graecorum*, 2 vols. (Leipzig, 1924–7).
Oikonomidès, N., ed., *Les listes de préséance byzantines des ixe et xe siècles* (Paris, 1972).
Olsen, B., ed., 'The Greek Translation of Boccaccio's Theseid Book 6', *ClMed*, 41 (1990), 275–301.
Op de Coul, M. D. J., 'Théodore Prodrome, lettres et discours: édition, traduction, commentaire', 2 vols, unpublished PhD thesis, Université Paris IV-Sorbonne (2007).
Otto, J. C. T., ed. *Corpus Apologetarum Christianorum* (Jena, 1880).
Orsini, P., ed., *Collouthos. L'enlèvement d'Hélène* (Paris, 1972).
  ed., *Musée. Héro et Léandre* (Paris, 1968).
Page, T. E., ed. and trans., *Virgil. Georgics* (Cambridge, MA, 1907).
Papadopoulos-Kerameus, A., ed., *Varia Graeca sacra* (St Petersburg, 1909; repr. Leipzig, 1975).
Papazoglou, K. N., ed., Τυπικόν Ισαακίου Αλεξίου Κομνηνού της Μονής Θεοτόκου της Κοσμοσώτειρας (1151/52) (Komotene, 1994).

Patkanean, Kʻ, ed., Թովմա Արծրունի եւ Անանուն, Պատմութիւն տանն Արծրունեաց *[Tʻovma Arcruni and Anonymous, History of the House of Arcrunikʻ]* (St Petersburg, 1887); reprinted (Delmar, NY, 1991).
Paton, W. R., ed. and trans., *The Greek Anthology*, 5 vols. (London, 1916–18).
Pérez, M.-A., ed., *Andanças é viajes de Pero Tafur* (Seville, 2009).
Pérez Martín, I., ed. and trans., *Miguel Ataleiates. Historia* (Madrid, 2002).
Petit, L., ed., 'Typikon du monastère de la Kosmosotira près d'Aenos (1152)', *IRAIK*, 13 (1908), 17–75.
Petit, L., K. A. Sideridès and M. Jugie, eds., *Oeuvres complètes de Georges Scholarios*, 8 vols. (Paris, 1928–36).
Pieris, M. and A. Nicolaou-Konnari, eds., *Leontios Makhairas. Χρονικό της Κύπρου. Παράλληλη διπλωματική έκδοση των χειρογράφων* (Nicosia, 2003).
Pietrosanti, P.. ed., *Nicephori Gregorae explicatio in librum Synesii "De Insomnis"* (Bari, 1999).
Pignani, A., ed., *Niceforo Basilace. Progimnasmi e monodie* (Naples, 1983).
Pilavakis, M., 'Markos Eugenikos's First Antirrhetic Against Manuel Calecas's *On Essence and Energy*: Editio Princeps with Introduction and Commentary', unpublished PhD thesis, University of London (1987).
Pinder, M. and Büttner-Wobst, T., eds., *Ioannis Zonarae Annales et Epitomae historiarum*, 3 vols. (Bonn, 1841–97).
Plepelits, K., ed. and trans., *Eustathios Makrembolites. Hysmine und Hysminias* (Stuttgart, 1989).
Polemis, I., ed., *Theodori Metochitae carmina* (Turnhout, 2015).
Powell, J., ed., *Collectanea Alexandrina* (Oxford, 1925).
Powell, O., ed. and trans., *Galen. On the Properties of Foodstuffs* (Cambridge, 2003).
Preger, T., ed., *Scriptores originum Constantinopolitanarum*, 2 vols. (Leipzig, 1901–7).
Prickard, A. O., ed. and trans., *Plutarch. On the Face in the Moon* (Winchester, 1911).
Pruche, B., ed., *Basile de Césarée: Sur le Saint-Esprit*, second edition (Paris, 2002).
Pryor, J. H. and E. M. Jeffreys, eds., *The Age of ΔΡΟΜΩΝ: The Byzantine Navy ca 500–1204* (Leiden, 2006).
Rabe, H., ed., *Syriani in Hermogenem Commentaria*, 2 vols. (Leipzig, 1892–3).
  ed., *Hermogenis Opera* (Leipzig, 1913).
  ed., *Aphthonii Progymnasmata* (Leipzig, 1926).
  ed., *Ioannis Sardiani Commentarium in Aphthonii Progymnasmata* (Leipzig, 1928).
  ed., *Prolegomenon Sylloge* (Leipzig, 1931).
Rackham, H., trans., *Cicero. Academica* (Cambridge, MA, 1979).
  trans., *Pliny. Natural History*, 10 vols. (Cambridge, MA, 1938–63).
Ralles, G. A. and A. Potles, eds., *Σύνταγμα τῶν Θείων καί ἱερῶν κανόνων*, 6 vols. (Athens, 1852–9); reprinted (Athens, 1992).
Rauer, M., ed. *Origenes. Die Homilien zu Lukas in der Übersetzung des Hieronymus und die griechischen Reste der Homilien und des Lukas-Kommentars* (Berlin, 1959).

Reinsch, D. R. and A. Kambylis, eds., *Annae Comnenae. Alexias*, 2 vols. (Berlin, 2001).
Renauld, É., ed. and trans., *Michel Psellos. Chronographie, ou histoire d'un siècle de Byzance (976–1077)*, 2 vols. (Paris, 1926–8).
Rhys Roberts, W., ed., *Dionysius of Halicarnassus. On Literary Composition Being the Greek Text of the De compositione verborum. Edited with Introduction, Translation, Notes, Glossary, and Appendices* (London, 1910).
Riedinger, R., ed., *Pseudo-Kaisarios. Die Erotapokriseis. Die griechischen christlichen Schriftsteller der ersten Jahrhunderte* (Berlin, 1989).
Rodgers, R., ed., *Palladii Rutilii Tauri Aemiliani viri inlustris opus agriculturae, de veterinaria medicina, de insitione* (Leipzig, 1975).
Roller, D. W., ed. and trans., *The Geography of Strabo* (Cambridge, 2014).
Romano, R., ed., *Timarione* (Naples, 1974).
  ed., *Costatino Acropolita: Epistole* (Naples, 1991).
Roncaglia, A., ed., *Teseida: delle nozze d'Emilia* (Bari, 1941).
Rosenqvist, J. O., ed., *The Hagiographic Dossier of St. Eugenios of Trebizond in Codex Athous Dionysiou 154* (Uppsala, 1996).
Roueché, C., ed. and trans., *Kekaumenos, Consilia et Narrationes* (2013), www.ancientwisdoms.ac.uk/library/kekaumenos-consilia-et-narrationes/ (accessed 13 November 2017).
Rouse, W. H. D., ed. and trans., *Lucretius. On the Nature of Things* (Cambridge, MA, 1982).
Russell, D. A. and N. G. Wilson, eds. and trans., *Menander Rhetor* (Oxford, 1981).
Sakellion, I., ed., 'Documents inédits tirés de la bibliothèque de Patmos. 1: décret d'Alexis Comnène portant déposition de Léon, métropolitain de Chalcédoine', *BCH*, 2 (1878), 113.
  ed., Πατμιακὴ βιβλιοθήκη (Athens, 1890).
Sathas, K. N., ed., *Bibliotheca Graeca Medii Aevi*, 8 vols. (Venice, 1872–94); reprint (Hildesheim, 1972).
Schabel, C., ed., *The Synodicum Nicosiense and Other Documents of the Latin Church of Cyprus, 1196–1373* (Nicosia, 2001).
Schabel, C. and J. Richard, eds., *Bullarium Cyprium*, 3 vols. (Nicosia, 2010–12).
Scheindler, A., ed., *Nonni Panopolitani Paraphrasis S. Evangelii Ioannei* (Leipzig, 1881).
Schmitt, J. J., ed., *The Chronicle of Morea: A History in Political Verse* (London, 1904).
Schoell, R., and G. Kroll, eds., *Justinian, Novellae,* in *Corpus Iuris Civilis*, vol. III (Berlin, 1954).
Scholten, C., ed., *Johannes Philoponos. De opificio mundi. Über die Erschaffung der Welt* (Freiburg, 1997).
Schönauer, S., ed., *Untersuchungen zum Steinkatalog des Sophrosyne-Gedichtes des Meliteniotes: mit kritischer Edition der Verse 1107–1247* (Wiesbaden, 1996).
Schönberger, O., ed., *Kolluthos. Raub der Helena* (Würzburg, 1993).
Schopen, L. and I. Bekker, eds., *Nicephori Gregorae Historiae Byzantinae*, 3 vols. (Bonn, 1829–55).
Schreiner, P., *Die byzantinischen Kleinchroniken*, 3 vols. (Vienna, 1975–9).

'Das Herrscherbild in der byzantinischen Literatur des 9. bis 11. Jahrhunderts',
   Saeculum, 35 (1984), 132–51.
Schwartz, E., ed., *Acta conciliorum oecumenicorum* (Strassburg, 1914).
Ševčenko, I., ed., *Chronographiae quae Theophanis Continuati nomine fertur liber
   quo vita Basilii imperatoris amplectitur* (Berlin, 2011).
Ševčenko, I. and M. Featherstone, eds., 'Two Poems by Theodore Metochites',
   GOTR, 26 (1981), 1–46.
Sewter, E. R. A., trans., *The Alexiad of Anna Comnena* (Baltimore, MD, 1969);
   revised by P. Frankopan, *Anna Komnene. The Alexiad* (London, 2009).
Sideras, A., ed., *Eine byzantinische Invektive gegen die Verfasser von Grabreden:
   Ἀνωνύμου μονῳδία εἰς μονοδοῦντας* (Vienna, 2002).
Simelidis, C., ed., *Selected Poems of Gregory of Nazianzus* (Göttingen, 2009).
Skrekas, D., 'Studies in the iambic canons attributed to John of Damascus:
   a critical edition with introduction and commentary', unpublished DPhil
   thesis, University of Oxford (2008).
Spadaro, G., ed., 'L'inedito Polemos tis Troados e l'Achilleide', *BZ*, 71 (1978), 1–9.
Spadaro, M. D., ed., *Kekaumenos. Raccomandazioni e consigli di un galantuomo*
   (Alessandria, 1998).
Squatriti, P., trans., *The Complete Works of Liudprand of Cremona: Translated with
   an Introduction and Notes* (Washington, D. C., 2007).
Staab, K., ed., 'Photios. In epistolam ad Romanos, Fragmenta' in K. Staab, ed.,
   *Pauluskommentar aus der griechischen Kirche aus Katenenhandschriften
   gesammelt* (Münster, 1933), 470–544.
Stahl, W. H., trans., *Macrobius. Commentary on the Dream of Scipio* (New York,
   NY, 1990).
Stählin, O., ed., *Clemens Alexandrinus. Stromata*, 4 vols. (Leipzig, 1905–36).
Stallbaum, G., ed., *Eustathii Archiepiscopi Thessalonicensis, Commentarii ad
   Homeri Odysseam*, 2 vols. (Leipzig, 1825–6); reprinted (Hildesheim, 1970).
Standford, W. B., ed., 'Tzetzes' Farewell to Thucydides', *Greece & Rome*, 11
   (1941), 40–1.
Stavrou, M., ed., 'Le premier traité sur la procession du Saint-Esprit de Nicéphore
   Blemmydès: présentation, édition critique et traduction annotée', *OrChrP*,
   67 (2001), 39–141.
Stevenson, H., ed., *Theodori Prodromi Commentarios in carmina sacra melodorum
   Cosmae Hierosolymitani et Ioannis Damasceni* (Rome, 1888).
Siwnecʻi, S., ed., 'Մեկնութիւն քերականին' ['Commentary on Grammar'], in
   N. Adontz, ed., *Denys de Thrace et les commentateurs arméniens* (Lourain,
   1970), 180–220.
Stephanou, R. P. E. and P. Tannery, eds., *Quadrivium de Georges Pachymère*
   (Vatican, 1940).
Tabbā', 'U., ed., *Dīwān al-Mutanabbī* (Beirut, 1994).
Tafel, G. L. F., ed., *Eustathii metropolitae Thessalonicensis Opuscula* (Frankfurt,
   1832).
Talbot, A.-M., eds., 'Bebaia Elpis: Typikon of Theodora Synadene for the
   Convent of the Mother of God Bebaia Elpis in Constantinople', trans., in
   J. Thomas and A. C. Hero, eds., *Byzantine Monastic Foundation Documents:*

A Complete Translation of the Surviving Founders' Typika and Testaments (Washington, D.C., 2000), vol. IV, 1557, 1563.

Talbot, A.-M. and D. F. Sullivan, eds. and trans., *The History of Leo the Deacon: Byzantine Military Expansion in the Tenth Century* (Washington, D. C., 2005).

Tēr Mkrtč'ean, G. and S. Malxasean, eds., Պատմութիւն Հայոց Ղազարայ Փարպեցւոյ *[Łazar P'arpec'i History of Armenia]* (Tiflis, 1904; reprinted Delmar, NY, 1985).

Thomas, J. and A. C. Hero, eds., *Byzantine Monastic Foundation Documents: A Complete Translation of the Surviving Founders' Typika and Testaments*, 5 vols. (Washington, D. C., 2000).

Thomson, R. W., trans., *Thomas Artsruni. History of the House of the Artsrunik* (Detroit, MI, 1985).

trans., *The History of Łazar P'arpec'i* (Atlanta, GA, 1991).

Thomson, R. W. and J. D. Howard-Johnston, trans., *The Armenian History Attributed to Sebeos*, 2 vols. (Liverpool, 1999).

Thurn, I., ed., *Ioannis Scylitzae Synopsis Historiarum* (Berlin, 1973).

ed., *Ioannis Malalae. Chronographia* (Berlin, 2000).

Tischendorf, C. V., ed., *Evangelia apocrypha*, second edition (Leipzig, 1876).

Thomas, J. P., ed., *Private Religious Foundations in the Byzantine Empire* (Washington, D. C., 1987).

Toomer, G. J., trans., *Ptolemy's Almagest* (London, 1984).

Trapp, E., ed., *Digenes Akrites. Synoptische Ausgabe der ältesten Versionen* (Vienna, 1971).

Tredennick, H., trans., *Aristotle. Metaphysics* (Cambridge, MA, 1961).

Trombley, F. W. and J. W. Watt, eds. and trans., *The Chronicle of Pseudo-Joshua the Stylite* (Liverpool, 2000).

Trumpf, J., ed., *Vita Alexandri regis Macedonum* (Stuttgart, 1974).

Trypanis, C. A., ed., *Fourteen Early Byzantine Cantica* (Vienna, 1968).

Trypanis, C. A., T. Gelzer and C. H. Whitman, eds., *Callimachus. Aetia, Iambi, Lyric Poems, Hecale, Minor Epic and Elegiac Poems and Other Fragments* (Cambridge, MA, 1975).

Tsames, D. G., ed., Φιλοθέου Κωνσταντινουπόλεως τοῦ Κοκκίνου ἁγιολογικὰ ἔργα, Α΄· Θεσσαλονικεῖς ἅγιοι (Thessalonike, 1985).

Tsolakes, E. T., ed., Μιχαὴλ Γλυκᾶ στίχοι οὓς ἔγραψε καθ' ὃν κατεσχέθη καιρόν (Thessalonike, 1959).

ed., Ἡ Συνέχεια τῆς χρονογραφίας τοῦ Ἰωάννου Σκυλίτζη (Thessalonike, 1968).

Turner, H. J. M, ed., *The Epistles of St. Symeon the New Theologian* (Oxford, 2009).

Uhlig, G. and A. Hilgard, eds., *Grammatici Graeci*, 4 vols. (Leipzig, 1883–1901); reprinted (Hildesheim, 1979).

Vaillant, A., ed., *Textes vieux-slaves*, 2 vols. (Paris, 1968).

Van Dieten, J.-L., ed., *Nicetae Choniatae Orationes et epistulae* (Berlin, 1972).

ed., *Nicetae Choniatae Historia* (Berlin, 1975).

Van Opstall, E. M., ed. and trans., *Jean Géomètre. Poèmes en hexamètres et en distiques élégiaques* (Leiden, 2008).

Vassiliev, A., ed., *Anecdota graeco-byzantina* (Moscow, 1893).

Vian, F., ed., *Nonnos de Panopolis. Les Dionysiaques* (Paris, 1976).
Vinson, M. P., ed., *The Correspondence of Leo Metropolitan of Synada and Syncellus* (Washington, D. C., 1985).
Vogt, A. and I. Hausherr, eds. and trans., 'Oraison funèbre de Basil I par son fils Léon le sage', *OrChrP*, 26 (1932), 44–6.
von Dobschütz, E., ed., 'Maria Romaia,' *BZ*, 12 (1903), 173–214.
Vranouse, E. L., ed., 'Πρόσταξις τοῦ αὐτοκράτορος Μανουὴλ Α' Κομνηνοῦ ὑπὲρ τῆς ἐν Πάτμῳ μονῆς Ἰωάννου τοῦ Θεολόγου' in *Χαριστήριον εἰς Ἀναστάσιον Κ. Ὀρλάνδον*, vol. ΙΙ (Athens, 1966).
Wagner, G., ed., *Carmina graeca medii aevi* (Leipzig, 1874).
Wallis, F., trans., *Bede. The Reckoning of Time* (Liverpool, 1999).
Walz, C., ed., *Rhetores graeci ex codicibus Florentinis, Mediolanensibus, Monacensibus, Neapolitanis, Parisiensibus, Romanis, Venetis, Taurinensibus et Vindobonensibus*, 9 vols. (Stuttgart, 1832–6).
Wassiliewsky, B. and V. Jernstedt, eds., *Cecaumeni Strategicon et incerti scriptoris de officiis regiis libellus* (St Petersburg, 1896).
Winkelmann, F., ed., *Eusebius Werke. Über das Leben des Kaisers Konstantin* (Berlin, 1975).
Whitby, M. (Michael) trans., *The Ecclesiastical History of Evagrius Scholasticus* (Liverpool, 2000).
Wolska-Conus, W., ed., *Cosmas Indicopleustès. Topographie Chrétienne*, 3 vols. (Paris, 1968–73).
Wright, W., ed. and trans., *The Chronicle of Joshua the Stylite, Composed in Syriac A.D. 507* (Cambridge, 1882).
Wright, W. C., ed., *Philostratos, Lives of the Sophists* (Cambridge, MA, 1921),

Studies

Accorinti, D., ed., *Brill's Companion to Nonnus of Panopolis* (Leiden, 2016).
Acerbi, J., 'Why Chortasmenos Sent Diophantus to the Devil', *BMGS*, 53 (2013), 379–89.
Adcock, F. E., *Caesar as a Man of Letters* (Cambridge, 1956).
Adontz, N., 'L'âge et l'origine de l'empereur Basile I (867–886)', *Byzantion*, 8 (1933), 475–500, and *Byzantion*, 9 (1934), 223–60; reprinted in N. Adontz, *Études arméno-byzantines* (Lisbon, 1985), 47–109.
Afentoulidou, I., 'Οἱ ὕμνοι του Συμεών του Νέου Θεολόγου. Σχέσεις των επιγραφών με τους ύμνους', *Byzantina*, 22 (2001), 123–47.
Afentoulidou-Leitgeb, E., 'Language and Style of the Dioptra', *BSl*, 70 (2012), 113–30.
Agapitos, P. A., 'SO Debate: Genre, Structure and Poetics in the Byzantine Vernacular Romances of Love', *SOsl*, 79 (2004), 7–101.
  'Writing, Reading and Reciting (in) Byzantine Erotic Fiction', in B. Mondrain, ed., *Lire et écrire à Byzance* (Paris, 2006), 125–76.
  'In Rhomaian, Frankish and Persian Lands: Fiction and Fictionality in Byzantium and Beyond' in P. A. Agapitos and L. B. Mortensen, eds.,

Medieval Narratives between History and Fiction: From the Centre to the Periphery of Europe, c. 1100–1400 (Copenhagen, 2012), 235–367.

'Grammar, Genre and Patronage in the Twelfth Century: a Scientific Paradigm and its Implications', *JÖB*, 64 (2014), 1–22.

'Contesting Conceptual Boundaries', *Interfaces – A Journal of Medieval European Literatures*, 1 (2015), 62–91.

Agosti, G. and F. Gonnelli, 'Materiali per la storia dell'esametro nei poeta Cristiani greci' in M. Fantuzzi and R. Pretagostini, eds., *Struttura e storia dell'esametro Greco*, 2 vols. (Rome, 1955–6), vol. 1, 289–434.

Agusta-Boularot, S., J. Beaucamp, A.-M. Bernardi and E. Caire, eds., *Recherches sur la chronique de Jean Malalas II* (Paris, 2006).

Ahrweiler, H., 'Sur la carrière de Photius avant son patriarcat', *BZ*, 58 (1965), 348–63.

Akentiev, C., ed., *Liturgy, Architecture and Art in the Byzantine World: Papers of the XVIII International Byzantine Congress (Moscow, 8–15 August 1991) and Other Essays Dedicated to the Memory of Fr. John Meyendorff* (St Petersburg, 1995).

Alexakis, A., 'Μορφολογικές παρατηρήσεις στὴν Εὐχὴ Μυστική, δι' ἧς ἐπικαλεῖται τὸ Πνεῦμα τὸ Ἅγιον ὁ αὐτὸ προορῶν τοῦ Συμεὼν τοῦ Νέου Θεολόγου', in A. Markopoulos, ed., *Τέσσερα κείμενα για την τιοίηση του Συμεών του Νέου Θεολόγου* (Athens, 2008), 37–60.

Alexander, J. C., 'Cultural Pragmatics: Social Performance Between Ritual and Strategy' in J. C. Alexander, B. Giesen and J. L. Mast, eds., *Social Performance: Symbolic Action, Cultural Pragmatics, and Ritual* (Cambridge, 2006), 29–90.

Performance and Power (Cambridge, 2011)

Alexiou, M., 'A Critical Reappraisal of Eustathios Makrembolites' *Hysmine and Hysminias*', *BMGS*, 3 (1977), 23–43.

'The Poverty of Ecriture and the Craft of Writing: Towards a Reappraisal of the Prodromic Poems', *BMGS*, 10 (1986), 1–40.

'Ploys of Performance: Games and Play in the Ptochoprodromic Poems', *DOP*, 53 (1999), 91–109.

After Antiquity: Greek Language, Myth, and Metaphor (London, 2002).

Alexiou, S., 'Bemerkungen zu den *Ptochoprodromika*' in H. Eideneier, ed., *Neograeca Medii Aevi I: Text und Ausgabe* (Cologne, 1987), 19–23.

'Διορθωτικά στον Πτωχοπρόδρομο' in C. Maltezou, T. Detorakes and C. Charalambakes, eds., *Ροδωνιά: τιμή στον Μ.Ι. Μανούσακα*, 2 vols. (Rethymno, 1994), vol. 1, 1–5; repr. in S. Alexiou, ed., *Δημώδη Βυζαντινά* (Athens, 1997), 165–71.

'Η έκδοση του *Πτωχοπροδρόμου* από τον Hans Eideneier' in S. Alexiou, ed., *Δημώδη Βυζαντινά* (Athens, 1997), 115–24.

Alfeyev, H., *St. Symeon the New Theologian and Orthodox Tradition* (Oxford, 2000).

Alivizatos, H. S., *Die Oikonomia: Die Oikonomia nach dem kanonischen Recht der Orthodoxen Kirche* (Frankfurt, 1998).

Allatius, L., *De libris ecclesiasticis Graecorum: dissertationes duae* (Paris, 1645); reprinted in L. Allatius, *De libris ecclesiasticis Graecorum: dissertationes et observationes variae* (Paris, 1646 and 1712).

Althoff, G., *Die Macht der Rituale. Symbolik und Herrschaft im Mittelalter*, second edition (Darmstadt, 2012).
Amato, E., and J. Schamp, eds., *Ethopoiia: la représentation de caractères entre fiction scolaire et réalité vivante à l'époque impériale et tardive* (Salerno, 2005).
Amirav, H. and B. ter Haar Romeny, eds., *From Rome to Constantinople: Studies in Honour of Averil Cameron* (Leuven, 2007).
Anastasi, R., 'Il "Canzoniere" di Giovanni di Euchaita', *SicGymn*, 22 (1969), 109–44.
'ΛΟΓΟΙ ΜΗ ΑΝΑΓΙΝΩΣΚΟΜΕΝΟΙ', *SicGymn*, 23 (1970), 202–4.
'Giovanni di Euchaita e gli ΣΚΕΔΙΚΟΙ (sic)', *SicGymn*, 24 (1971), 61–9.
'Note di filologia greca', *SicGymn*, 26 (1973), 97–131.
'Su Giovanni di Euchaita', *SicGymn*, 29 (1976), 19–49.
Anastos, M. V., 'The Alexandrian Origin of the Christian Topography of Cosmas Indicopleustes', *DOP*, 3 (1946), 73–80.
'Aristotle and Cosmas on the Void: a Note on Theology and Science in the Sixth Century' in M. V. Anastos, *Studies in Byzantine Intellectual History* (London, 1979), 36–50.
Andenna, G., 'Effetti della peste nera sul reclutamento monastico e sul patrimonio ecclesiastico' in *La peste nera: dati di una realtà ed elementi di una interpretazione. Atti del XXX convegno storico internazionale, Todi 10–13 ottobre 1993* (Spoleto, 1994), 319–47.
Anderson, J. C., 'Anna Komnene, Learned Women and the Book in Byzantine Art' in T. Gouma-Peterson, ed., *Anna Komnene and Her Times* (New York, 2000), 125–56.
Anderson, J. C. and M. J. Jeffreys, 'The Decoration of the *Sebastokratorissa*'s Tent', *Byzantion*, 64 (1994), 8–18.
Ando, C., 'The Palladium and the Pentateuch: Towards a Sacred Topography of the Later Roman Empire', *Phoenix*, 55 (2001), 369–410.
Angelidi, C. and T. Papamastorakis, 'The Veneration of the Virgin Hodegetria and the Hodegon Monastery' in M. Vasilaki, ed., *Mother of God: Representations of the Virgin in Byzantine Art* (Athens, 2000), 373–87.
Angelou, A. D., 'Who am I? Scholarios's Answers and the Hellenic Identity', in C. N. Constantinides, N. M. Panagiotakis, E. M. Jeffreys, and I. Martin, eds., Φιλέλλην: *Studies in Honour of Robert Browning* (Venice, 1996), 1–19.
Angelov, D. G., *Imperial Ideology and Political Thought in Byzantium 1204–1330* (Cambridge, 2007).
Angold, M. J., ed., *The Byzantine Aristocracy, IX to XIII Centuries* (Oxford, 1984).
Church and Society in Byzantium under the Comneni, 1081–1261 (Cambridge, 1995).
The Byzantine Empire, 1025–1204: A Political History, second edition. (London, 1997).
'The Autobiographical Impulse in Byzantium', *DOP*, 52 (1998), 52–73.
'Autobiography and Identity: the Case of the Later Byzantine Empire', *BSl*, 60 (1999), 36–59.

'Theodore Agallianos: the Last Byzantine Autobiography' in E. Motos Guirao and M. Morphadakis Philaktos, eds., *Constantinopla: 550 años de su caída* (Granada, 2006), 35–44.
Angold, M., and M. Whitby, 'Historiography' in E. M. Jeffreys, J. Haldon and R. Cormack eds., *Oxford Handbook of Byzantine Studies* (Oxford, 2008), 838–52,
Antonopoulou, T., 'On the Reception of Homilies and Hagiography in Byzantium: the Recited Metrical Prefaces' in A. Rhoby and E. Schiffer, eds., *Imitatio – Aemulatio – Variatio* (Vienna, 2010), 57–78.
Arbel, B., 'Cypriot Villages from the Byzantine to the British Period: Observations on a Recent Book', *EKEE*, 26 (2000), 439–56.
Arentzen, J. G., *Imago Mundi Cartografica* (Munich, 1984).
Armstrong, P., 'Alexios I Komnenos, Holy Men and Monasteries' in M. E. Mullett and D. Smythe, eds., *Alexios I Komnenos* (Belfast, 1996), 219–31.
Arnaud, P., 'L'image du globe dans le monde romain: science, iconographique, symbolique', *MEFRA*, 96 (1984), 53–116.
Asmus, R., 'Pamprepios, ein byzantinischer Gelehrter und Staatsmann des 5. Jahrhunderts', *BZ*, 22 (1913), 320–47.
Astruc, C., 'Les listes des prêts figurants au verso de l'inventaire du trésor et de la bibliothèque de Patmos dressé en septembre 1200', *TM*, 12 (1994), 495–500.
Atasoy, N., *The Ottoman Imperial Tent Complex* (Istanbul, 2000).
Athanassiadi, P., 'Persecution and Response in Late Paganism', *JHS*, 113 (1993), 1–29.
Atsalos, B., *La terminologie du livre-manuscrit à l'époque Byzantine* (Thessalonike, 2001).
Auerbach, E., *Mimesis: the Representation of Reality in Western Literature*, W. R. Trask, trans. (Princeton, NJ, 1953).
Aujac, G., 'Poseidonios et les zones terrestres: les raisons d'un échec', *BullBudé*, 1 (1976), 74–8.
Austin, J. L., *How to Do Things With Words* (Cambridge, MA, 1962).
Auzépy, M.-F., 'State of Emergency (700–850)' in J. Shepard, ed., *Cambridge History of the Byzantine Empire c. 500–1492* (Cambridge, 2008), 251–91.
Bakhtin, M. M., 'Forms of Time and of the Chronotope in the Novel: Towards a Historical Poetics' in M. M. Bakhtin, *The Dialogic Imagination: Four Essays*, ed. M. Holquist, trans. C. Emerson and M. Holquist (Austin, TX, 1981), 84–110.
Ballester, L. G., 'Soul and Body: Disease of the Soul and Disease of the Body in Galen's Medical Thought' in P. Manuli and M. Vegetti, eds., *Le opere psicologiche di Galeno* (Naples, 1988),117–52.
Barber, E. A., 'Review of Hans Gerstinger, *Pamprepios von Panopolis*', *ClRev*, 43 (1929), 237–8.
Barber, C., *Contesting the Logic of Painting: Art and Understanding in Eleventh-century Byzantium* (Leiden, 2007).
Barbour, H. C., *The Byzantine Thomism of Gennadios Scholarios and his Translation of the Commentary of Armandus de Bellovisu on the De ente et essentia of Thomas Aquinas* (Vatican, 1993).

Bartsocas, C. S., 'Two Fourteenth-century Greek Descriptions of the "Black Death"', *Journal of the History of Medicine and Allied Sciences*, 21 (1966), 394–400.
Barzos, K., Ἡ γενεαλογία τῶν Κομνηνῶν, 2 vols. (Thessalonike, 1984).
Bassett, S., *The Urban Image of Late Antique Constantinople* (Cambridge, 2004).
Baumgarten, F., *De Christodoro poeta Thebano* (Bonn, 1881).
'Christodoros', *RE*, 3 (1899), 2450–2.
Baun, J., *Tales from Another Byzantium: Celestial Journey and Local Community on the Medieval Greek Apocrypha* (Cambridge, 2007).
Bayer, A., *Spaltung der Christenheit: Das sogennante Morgenländische Schisma von 1054*, second edition (Cologne, 2004).
Bazzani, M., 'Autobiographical Elements in Symeon the New Theologian: Modes and Causes of Self-disclosure in the Writings of the New Theologian', *BSl*, 64 (2006), 221–42.
Beaton, R., 'The Rhetoric of Poverty: the Lives and Opinions of Theodore Prodromos', *BMGS*, 11 (1987), 1–28.
'Πτωχοπροδρομικά Γ΄: η ηθοποιία του άτακτου μοναχού' in A. Kechagia-Lypourli and T. Petridis, eds., Μνήμη Σταμάτη Καρατζά: ερευνητικά προβλήματα νεοελληνικής φιλολογίας και γλωσσολογίας (Thessalonike, 1990), 101–7.
The Medieval Greek Romance, second edition (London, 1996).
'The World of Fiction and the World "Out There": the Case of the Byzantine Novel' in D. Smythe, ed., *Strangers to Themselves: The Byzantine Outsider* (Aldershot, 2000), 179–88.
From Byzantium to Modern Greece: Medieval Texts and Their Reception (Aldershot, 2008).
Beatrice, P. F., *Anonymi Monophysitae Theosophia: An Attempt at Reconstruction* (Leiden, 2001).
Beaucamp, J., ed., *Recherches sur la chronique de Jean Malalas I* (Paris, 2004).
Beck, H.-G., ed., *Geschichte der byzantinischen Volksliteratur* (Munich, 1971).
Becker, A., 'The Dynamic Reception of Theodore of Mopsuestia in the Sixth Century: Greek, Syriac, and Latin' in S. F. Johnson, ed., *Greek Literature in Late Antiquity* (Aldershot, 2006), 29–47.
Beckwith, J., *The Veroli Casket* (London, 1962).
Early Christian and Byzantine Art (London, 1970); second edition (London, 1979).
Bekker-Nielsen, T., *The Roads of Ancient Cyprus* (Copenhagen, 2004).
Belting, H., D. Mouriki and C. Mango, *Mosaics and Frescoes of St. Mary Pammakaristos (Fethiye Cami Istanbul)* (Washington, D. C., 1978).
Benedictow, O. J., *The Black Death, 1346–1353: The Complete History* (Woodbridge, 2004).
Bentein, K., and K. Demoen, 'The Reader in Eleventh-century Epigrams' in F. Bernard and K. Demoen, eds., *Poetry and Its Contexts in Eleventh-century Byzantium* (Fainham, 2012), 69–88.
Berger, A., *Untersuchungen zu den Patria Konstantinupoleos* (Bonn, 1988).
'Zur Topographie der Ufergegend am Goldenen Horn in der byzantinischen Zeit', *IstMitt*, 43 (1995), 149–65.

'Historical topography in the Roman, Byzantine, Latin, and Ottoman periods, 1. Roman, Byzantine and Latin periods', in Striker and Doğan Kuban, eds., *Kalenderhane in Istanbul* (1997–2007), vol. 1, 8-17.

'Imperial and Ecclesiastical Processions in Constantinople' in N. Necipoğlu, ed., *Byzantine Constantinople: Monuments, Topography and Everyday Life* (Leiden, 2001), 73–88.

Bernard, F., 'The Circulation of Poetry in 11th-century Byzantium' in S. Neocleous, ed., *Sailing to Byzantium: Papers from the First and Second Postgraduate Forums in Byzantine Studies* (Newcastle-upon-Tyne, 2009), 145–60.

Writing and Reading Byzantine Secular Poetry, 1025–1081 (Oxford, 2014).

Bernard, F. and K. Demoen, eds., *Poetry and Its Contexts in Eleventh-century Byzantium* (Farnham, 2012).

'Byzantine Book Epigrams from Manuscripts to a Digital Database' in C. Clivaz, J. Meizoz, F. Vallotton et al., eds., *From Ancient Manuscripts to the Digital Era: Readings and Literacies* (Lausanne, 2012), 431–40.

'Book Epigrams', in A. Rhoby and N. Zagklas, eds., *The Brill Companion to Byzantine Poetry* (Leiden, forthcoming)

Bernardi, A.-M., 'Les mystikoi dans la chronique de Jean Malalas' in J. Beaucamp, ed., *Recherches sur la chronique de Jean Malalas I* (Paris, 2004), 53–64.

Bernardini Marzolla, P., 'A proposito di Pamprepio di Panopoli', *Maia*, 7 (1955), 125-7.

Beyer, H.-V., 'Personale Ermittlungen zu einem spätbyzantinischen Pamphlet' in H. Hörandner et al., eds., Βυζάντιος. *Festschrift für Herbert Hunger* (Vienna, 1984), 13–26.

Bianchi, G., 'Sulla cultura astronomica di Giorgio di Pisidia', *Aevum*, 40 (1964), 35–51.

Bianconi, D., 'Eracle e Iolao: aspetti della collaborazione tra copisti nell'età dei Paleologi', *BZ*, 97 (2004), 521–56.

'Libri e mani. Sulla formazione di alcune miscellanee dell'età dei Paleologi', *Segno e testo*, 2 (2004), 311–63.

'La biblioteca di Cora tra Massimo Planude e Niceforo Gregora: una questione di mani', *Segno e testo*, 3 (2005): 41–430.

Tessalonica nell'età dei Paleologi: Le pratiche intellettuali nel riflesso della cultura scritta (Paris, 2005).

'Qualcosa di nuovo su Giovanni Catrario', *Medioevo Greco*, 6 (2006), 69–91.

Biraben, J.-N., *Les hommes et la peste en France et dans les pays européens et méditerranéens*, 2 vols. (Paris, 1975–6).

Bitton-Ashkelony, B. and A. Kofsky, eds., *Christian Gaza in Late Antiquity* (Leiden, 2004).

Blanchet, M.-H., 'L'ambiguïté du statut juridique de Gennadios Scholarios après la chute de Constantinople (1453)' in P. Odorico, ed., *Le Patriarcat oecuménique de Constantinople aux xive–xvie siècles: rupture et continuité* (Paris, 2007), 195–211.

'L'Église byzantine à la suite de l'union de Florence (1439–1445): de la contestation à la scission', *ByzF*, 29 (2007), 79–123.

Georges-Gennadios Scholarios (vers 1400–vers 1472): un intellectuel orthodoxe face à la disparition de l'empire byzantin (Paris, 2008).
Blanchet, M.-H. and T. Ganchou, 'Les fréquentations byzantines de Lodisio de Tabriz, dominicain de Péra (†1453): Géôrgios Scholarios, Iôannes Chrysolôras et Théodore Kalékas', Byzantion, 75 (2005), 70–103.
Boegehold, A. L., When a Gesture Was Expected (Princeton, NJ, 1999).
Boffito, G., Cosmografia primitive classica e patristica (Rome, 1903).
'La leggenda degli antipodi', in A. Della Torre, ed., Miscellanea di studi critici edita in onore di Arturo Graf (Bergamo, 1903), 583–601.
Borovilou-Genakou, A., 'Οἱ ἐπιμερισμοί κατὰ στοιχεῖον Γραφικά: παρατηρήσεις στὴ δομὴ καὶ στὸν τρόπο σύνθεσής τους', Βυζαντινά, 28 (2008), 21–50.
'Ἐπιμερισμοὶ κατὰ στοιχεῖον γραφικὰ καὶ ιαμβικοὶ κανόνες Χριστουγέννων, Φώτων καὶ Πεντηκοστῆς', ByzSym, 19 (2009), 83–97.
Boulhol, P., 'La geste des saints et l'histoire du monde: À propos des sources hagiographiques de Malalas' in J. Beaucamp, Recherches sur la chronique de Jean Malalas I (Paris, 2004) 103–16.
Boulton, M., The Anatomy of Drama (London, 1960).
Bourbouhakis, E. C., 'Rhetoric and Performance' in P. Stephenson, The Byzantine World (London, 2010), 175–87.
'The End of ἐπίδειξις. Authorial Identity and Authorial Intention in Michael Choniates' Πρὸς τοὺς αἰτιωμένους τὸ ἀφιλένδεικτον' in A. Pizzone, ed., The Author in Middle Byzantine Literature. Modes, Functions, Identities (Boston, MA, 2014), 201–24.
Brandes, W., 'Anastasios Ο ΔΙΚΟΡΟΣ: Endzeiterwartung und Kaiserkritik in Byzanz um 500', BZ, 90 (1997), 24–63.
Brenk, B., ed., La Cappella Palatina a Palermo (Modena, 2010).
Brinkmann, A., 'Phoibammon Περὶ μιμήσεως', RhM, 61 (1906), 117–34.
Brooks, S. T., 'Poetry and Female Patronage in Late Byzantine Tomb Decoration: Two Epigrams by Manuel Philes', DOP, 60 (2006), 223–48.
Brousselle, I., 'L'intégration des Arméniens dans l'aristocratie byzantine au ixe siècle' in L'Arménie et Byzance: histoire et culture (Paris, 1996), 43–54.
Brown, P., 'The Gesta Roberti Wiscardi: a 'Byzantine' History?', JMedHist, 37 (2011), 162–79.
Browning, R., 'The Patriarchal School at Constantinople in the Twelfth Century, Byzantion, 32 (1962), 167–202.
'The Patriarchal School at Constantinople in the Twelfth Century (Continuation)', Byzantion, 33 (1963), 11–40.
'Enlightenment and Repression in Byzantium in the Eleventh and Twelfth Centuries', Past and Present, 69 (1975), 3–23.
'Literacy in the Byzantine world', BMGS, 4 (1978), 39–54.
'Further Reflections on Literacy in Byzantium' in J. Landon, S. Reinert and J. Allen, eds., Τὸ ἑλληνικόν: Studies in Honor of Speros Vryonis, Jr., vol. I, Hellenic Antiquity and Byzantium (New Rochelle, NY, 1993), 63–84.
'Teachers' in G. Cavallo, ed., The Byzantines (Chicago, IL, 1997), 95–116.

Brubaker, L., *Vision and Meaning in Ninth-century Byzantium* (Cambridge, 1999).
  'To Legitimize an Emperor: Constantine and Visual Authority in the Eighth and Ninth Centuries' in P. Magdalino, ed., *New Constantines* (Aldershot, 1994), 139–58.
Bryer, A., 'The late Byzantine identity' in K. Fledelius and P. Schreiner, eds., *Byzantium: Identity, Image, Influence. Major Papers. XIX International Congress of Byzantine Studies. University of Copenhagen, 18–24 August, 1996* (Copenhagen, 1996), 49–50.
Bucossi, A., 'Prolegomena to the critical edition of *Hiera Hoplotheke – Sacred Arsenal* by Andronikos Kamateros', unpublished DPhil thesis, University of Oxford (2006).
  'New Historical Evidence for the Dating of the *Sacred Arsenal* by Andronikos Kamateros', *REB*, 67 (2009), 111–30.
  'The *Sacred Arsenal* by Andronikos Kamateros, a Forgotten Treasure' in A. Rigo and P. Ermilov, eds., *Byzantine Theologians. The Systematization of their Own Doctrine and their Perception of Foreign Doctrines* (Rome, 2009), 33–50.
  'Andronico Camatero e la zizzania: sulla politica ecclesiastica bizantina in età comnena' in F. Burgarella, F. D'Aiuto and V. Ruggieri, eds., *Ortodossia ed eresia a Bisanzio (sec. IX–XII): atti della IX Giornata di studio dell'Associazione Italiana di Studi Bizantini, Pontificio Istituto Orientale, Roma, 5–6/12/2008* = *RSBN*, 47 (2010), 357–71.
  'Dialogues and Anthologies of the *Sacred Arsenal* by Andronikos Kamateros: Sources, Arrangements, Purposes' in C. Macé and P. Van Deun, eds., *Encyclopaedic Trends in Byzantium: Proceedings of the International Conference held in Leuven, 6–8 May 2009* (Leuven, 2011), 269–84.
Bühler, W. and C. Theodoridis, 'Johannes von Damaskos *terminus post quem* für Choiroboskos', *BZ*, 69 (1976), 397–401.
Bulović, I., Τὸ μυστήριον τῆς ἐν τῇ ἁγίᾳ Τριάδι διακρίσεως τῆς θείας οὐσίας καὶ ἐνεργείας κατὰ τὸν ἅγιον Μάρκον Ἐφέσου τὸν Εὐγενικόν, Ἀνάλεκτα Βλατάδων 39 (Thessalonike, 1983).
Burke, J. and R. Scott, eds., *Byzantine Macedonia: Identity, Image and History* (Melbourne, 2000).
Cameron, A. D. E., 'Wandering Poets: a Literary Movement in Byzantine Egypt', *Historia*, 14 (1965), 470–509.
  Porphyrius the Charioteer (Oxford, 1973).
  'The Empress and the Poet: Paganism and Politics at the Court of Theodosius II' in J. J. Winkler and G. Williams, eds., *Later Greek Literature*, YCS 27 (Cambridge, 1982), 217–89.
  The Greek Anthology from Meleager to Planudes (Oxford, 1993).
Cameron, A. D. E. and N. Gaul, eds., *Dialogues and Debates from Late Antiquity to Late Byzantium* (London, 2017).
Cameron, A. M., *Agathias* (Oxford, 1970).
  'Sacred and Profane Love: Thoughts on Byzantine Gender' in L. James, ed., *Women, Men and Eunuchs: Gender in Byzantium* (London, 1997), 1–23.

'Desire in Byzantium: the Ought and the Is' in James, ed., *Desire and Denial in Byzantium* (Aldershot, 1999), 205–14.
ed., *Fifty Years of Prosopography: The Later Roman Empire, Byzantium and Beyond* (Oxford, 2003).
Cameron, A. M. and J. Herrin, eds., *Constantinople in the Early Eighth Century: The Parastaseis Syntomoi Chronikai* (Leiden, 1984).
Canard, M., 'Dwin' in P. Bearman, Th. Bianquis, C. E. Bosworth, E. van Donzel, W. P. Heinrichs, eds., *Encyclopaedia of Islam*, second edition (Leiden, 2009); http://dx.doi.org/10.1163/1573-3912_islam_SIM_2165 (accessed 1 December 2017).
Canart, P., 'Gli scriptoria calabresi della conquista normanna alla fine del secolo XIV', *Calabria bizantina. Tradizione di pietà e tradizione scritoria nella Calabria greca medievale* (Reggio Calabria/Rome, 1983), 143–60.
'Quelques exemples de division du travail chez les copistes byzantins' in P. Hoffmann, ed., *Recherches de codicologie comparée. La composition du codex au moyen âge en orient et en occident* (Paris, 1998), 49–67.
Cancik, H. and H. Schneider, eds., *Der Neue Pauly, Enzyklopädie der Antike*, 16 vols. (Stuttgart, 1996–2003).
Canfora, L., 'Le cercle de lecteurs autour de Photios: une source contemporaine', *REB*, 56 (1998), 269–73.
Cantarella, R., 'Basilio minimo II. Scolii inediti con introduzione et note', *BZ*, 26 (1926), 1–34.
Carney, T. F., *Bureaucracy in Traditional Society: Romano-Byzantine Bureaucracies Viewed from Within* (Lawrence, KS, 1971).
Carruthers, M., *The Book of Memory: A Study of Memory in Medieval Culture*, second edition (Cambridge, 2008).
Cataldi Palau, A. C., 'L'*Arsenale Sacro* di Andronico Camatero: il proemio ed il dialogo dell'imperatore con i cardinali latini: originale, imitazioni, arrangiamenti', *REB*, 51 (1993), 5–62.
Catalogue Des Livres De La Bibliotheque De S.A.S. Frédéric-Henri, Prince d'Orange, &c. &c. &c. (The Hague, 1749).
Cavallo, G., 'Il libro come oggetto d'uso nel mondo bizantino', *JÖB*, 31 (1981), 395–423.
'Le rossignol et l'hirondelle: Lire et écrire à byzance, en occident', *Annales*, 56 (2001), 849–61.
'Sodalizi eruditi e pratiche di scrittura a Bisanzio' in J. Hamesse, ed., *Bilan et perspectives des études médiévales (1993–1998)* (Turnhout, 2004), 645–65.
Lire à Byzance, P. Odorico and A. Segonds, trans. (Paris, 2006).
Leggere a Bisanzio (Milan, 2007).
Cavazzana Romanelli, F. and G. Grivaud, *Cyprus 1542: The Great Map of the Island by Leonida Attar* (Nicosia, 2006).
Chalandon, F., *Essai sur le règne d'Alexis I Comnène* (Paris, 1900).
Chamberlain, C., 'The Theory and Practice of Imperial Panegyric in Michael Psellus', *Byzantion*, 56 (1986), 16–27.
Charanis, P., *The Armenians in the Byzantine Empire* (Lisbon, 1963).

Chatterjee, P., 'Viewing and Description in *Hysmine and Hysminias*: the Fresco of the Virtues', *DOP*, 67 (2013), 209–25.
'Vision, Transformation and the Veroli Casket', *Oxford Art Journal*, 36 (2013), 325–44.
Chatzidakis, G., 'Περὶ τῶν Προδρόμων Θεοδώρου καὶ Ἱλαρίωνος', *VizVrem*, 4 (1897), 100–27; reprinted in G. Chatzidakis, Μεσαιωνικά και Νέα Ελληνικά, 2 vols. (Athens 1905–7), vol. II, 361–95.
Chernoglazov, D., 'Beobachtungen zu den Briefen des Theodoros Daphnopates. Neue Tendenzen in der byzantinischen Literatur des zehnten Jahrhunderts,' *BZ*, 106 (2013), 623–44.
Chernousov, E., 'Études sur Malalas', *Byzantion*, 3 (1926), 65–72.
Cheynet, J.-C., *Pouvoir et contestations à Byzance (963–1210)* (Paris, 1990).
'Foi et conjuration à Byzance' in M.-F. Auzépy and G. Saint-Guillain, eds., *Oralité et lien social au Moyen Âge* (Paris, 2008), 265–79.
'Théophile, Théophobe et les Perses' in S. Lampakes, ed., *E Byzantine Mikra Asia, 6os–12os ai. [Byzantine Asia Minor 6th–12th Centuries]* (Athens, 1998), 39–50.
La société Byzantine: l'apport des sceaux, 2 vols. (Paris, 2008).
Cheynet, J.-C., and G. Dédéyan, 'Vocation impériale ou fatalité diasporique: les Arméniens à Byzance (IVe–XIe siècle)' in G. Dédéyan, ed., *Histoire du peuple arménien* (Paris, 2008), 297–326.
Chiesa, P., 'Liutprando', in *Dizionario Biografico degli Italiani* 65 (2005), 298–303.
Chin, C. M., *Grammar and Christianity in the Late Roman World* (Philadelphia, PA, 2008).
Christodoulou, M. N. and K. Konstantinidis, *A Complete Gazetteer of Cyprus*, 2 vols. (Nicosia, 1987).
Ciggaar, K., 'Encore une fois Chrétien de Troyes et la "matière byzantine": la révolution des femmes au palais de Constantinople', *CahCM*, 38 (1995), 267–74.
Clarke, G., ed., *Reading the Past in Late Antiquity* (Canberra, 1990).
Clayton, P. B., *The Christology of Theodoret of Cyrus: Antiochene Christology from the Council of Ephesus (431) to the Council of Chalcedon (451)* (Oxford, 2007).
Cohn, S. K., *The Cult of Remembrance and the Black Death: Six Renaissance Cities in Central Italy* (Baltimore, MD, 1992).
'Piété et commande d'oeuvres d'art après la peste noire', *Annales: Histoire, Sciences Sociales*, 51 (1996), 551–73.
'The Black Death: End of a Paradigm', *AHR*, 107 (2002), 703–38.
The Black Death Transformed: Disease and Culture in Early Renaissance Europe (London, 2002).
Colvin, I., 'Reporting Battles and Understanding Campaigns in Procopius and Agathias: Classicising Historians' Use of Archived Documents as Sources' in A. Sarantis and N. Christie, eds., *War and Warfare in Late Antiquity* (Leiden, 2013), 571–98.
Comrie, B., *Aspect: an Introduction to the Study of Verbal Aspect and Related Problems* (Cambridge, 1976).

Bibliography 663

Conca, F., 'L'inno 17 di Simeone il Nuovo Teologo', *Atti della Accademia Pontaniana*, 49 (2000), 139–50.
Congourdeau, M.-H., 'Pour une étude de la peste noire à Byzance' in M. Balard et al., eds., Εὐψυχία. *Mélanges offerts à Hélène Ahrweiler*, 2 vols. (Paris, 1998), vol. 1, 149–63.
'La Peste Noire à Constantinople de 1348 à 1466', *Medicina nei Secoli*, 11/2 (1999), 377–90.
Conley, T. M., 'Demosthenes Dethroned: Gregory Nazianzus in Sikeliotes' Scholia on Hermogenes' Περὶ Ἰδεῶν', *ICS*, 27/28 (2002–3), 145–52.
Constantinides, C. N., *Higher Education in Byzantium in the Thirteenth and Early Fourteenth Centuries (ca.1204-ca. 1310)* (Nicosia, 1982).
Constantinides, C. N. and R. Browning, *Dated Greek Manuscripts from Cyprus to the Year 1570* (Washington, D. C., 1993).
Constantinides, C. N., N. M. Panagiotakis, E. M. Jeffreys, and I. Martin, eds., Φιλέλλην: *Studies in Honour of Robert Browning* (Venice, 1996).
Constas, N., 'Mark Eugenikos' in C. G. Conticello and V. Conticello, eds., *La théologie byzantine et sa tradition* (Turnhout, 2002–15) vol. II, 411–76.
Conticello, C. G. and V. Conticello, eds., *La théologie byzantine et sa tradition*, 2 vols. (Turnbout, 2002–15).
Cormack, R. and M. Vassiliaki, eds., *Byzantium 330–1453* (London, 2008).
Corrigan, K., *Visual Polemics in the Ninth-century Byzantine Psalters* (Cambridge, 1992).
Cortassa, G., 'Un filologo di Bizanzio e il suo committente: la lettera 88 dell'Anonimo di Londra', *Medioevo greco*, 1 (2001), 97–138.
Coureas, N., 'Economy' in A. Nicolaou-Konnari and C. Schabel, eds., *Cyprus: Society and Culture 1191–1374* (Leiden, 2005), 103–56.
Criterio, E., 'Nicodemo Agiorita' in C. G. Conticello and V. Conticello, eds., *La théologie byzantine et sa tradition* (Turnhout, 2002), vol. II: 905–98.
Croke, B., 'The Early Development of Byzantine Chronicles' in E. M. Jeffreys, B. Croke and R. Scott, *Studies in John Malalas* (Sydney, 1990), 27–38.
'Malalas: The Man and his Work' in E. M. Jeffreys, B. Croke and R. Scott, *Studies in John Malalas* (Sydney, 1990), 6–11.
'Modern Study of Malalas' in E. M. Jeffreys, B. Croke and R. Scott, *Studies in John Malalas* (Sydney, 1990), 325–38.
Cupane, C., '*Eros Basileus*: la figura di Eros nel romanzo bizantino d'amore', *Atti dell' Academia di Scienze, Lettere e Arti di Palermo*, 33 (1973–4), 243–97.
'Leggere e/o ascoltare. Note sulla ricezione primaria e sul pubblico della letteratura greca medievale' in A. Pioletti and F. Rizzo Nervo, eds., *Medioevo romanzo e orientale. Oralità, scrittura, modelli narrativi* (Naples, 1994), 83–105.
'"Let Me Tell You a Wonderful Tale": Audience and Reception of the Vernacular Romances' in C. Cupane and B. Krönung, eds., *Fictional Storytelling in the Medieval Eastern Mediterranean and Beyond (8th–15th Centuries)* (Leiden, 2016), 479–94.
Cupane, C. and B. Krönung, 'Geschichten von der Grenze', in F. Daim, ed., *Das Goldene Byzanz und der Orient* (Schallaburg, 2012), 155–69.

eds., *Fictional Storytelling in the Medieval Eastern Mediterranean and Beyond (8th–15th Centuries)* (Leiden, 2016).

Cutler, A., 'The *De Signis* of Nicetas Choniates: a Reappraisal', *AJA*, 72 (1968), 113–18.

'On Byzantine Boxes', *JWalt*, 42 (1984–5), 32–47.

'"Ehemals Wien": the Pula Casket and the Interpretation of Multiples in Byzantine Bone and Ivory Carving', *RömHistMitt*, 41 (1999), 117–28.

'The Veroli Casket' in H. Evans and W. Wixom, eds., *The Glory of Byzantium: Art and Culture of the Middle Byzantine Era, AD 843–1261* (New York, 1997), 230–1.

Dagron, G., 'L'église et l'état (milieu IXe – fin Xe siècle)' in G. Dagron, P. Riché and A. Vauchez, eds., *Evêques, moines et empereurs (610–1054): Histoire du Christianisme*, 13 vols. (Paris, 1993), vol. IV, 169–83.

Emperor and Priest: The Imperial Office in Byzantium (Cambridge, 2003).

D'Aiuto, F., 'Note ai manoscritti del Menologio imperiale', *RSBN*, 32 (2002), 189–214.

Dalby, A., *Flavours of Byzantium* (Totnes, 2003).

Darrouzès, J., 'Manuscrits originaires de Chypre à la Bibliothèque Nationale de Paris', *REB*, 8 (1950), 162–93.

'Un obituaire chypriote: le Parisinus graecus 1588', Κυπριακαὶ Σπουδαί, 15 (1951), 25–62.

'Notes pour servir à l'histoire de Chypre (premier article)', Κυπριακαὶ Σπουδαί, 17 (1953), 83–102.

'Notes pour servir à l'histoire de Chypre (deuxième article)', Κυπριακαὶ Σπουδαί, 20 (1956), 31–63.

'Autres manuscrits originaires de Chypre', *REB*, 15 (1957), 131–68.

'Notes pour servir à l'histoire de Chypre (troisième article)', Κυπριακαὶ Σπουδαί, 22 (1958), 221–50.

'Notes pour servir à l'histoire de Chypre (quatrième article)', Κυπριακαὶ Σπουδαί, 23 (1959), 25–56.

'Les documents byzantins du XIIe siècle sur la primauté romaine', *REB*, 23 (1965), 72–8.

Da Villa Urbani, M., 'Perfume Brazier in the Form of a Domed Building' in Cormack and Vassilaki, eds., *Byzantium, 330–1453* (2008), 207 and 423.

de Halleux, A., 'Hellénisme et syrianité de Romanos le Mélode: à propos d'un ouvrage récent', *RHE*, 73 (1978), 632–41.

de Vaivre, J.-B. and P. Plagnieux, *L'art gothique en Chypre* (Paris, 2006).

de Vries-van der Velden, E., 'La lune de Psellos', *BSl*, 57 (1996), 239–56.

'Psellos, Romain IV Diogénès et Mantzikert', *BSl*, 58 (1997), 274–310.

Dedes, D., 'Die Handschriften und das Werk des Georgios Gemistos (Plethon): Forschungen und Funde in Venedig', Ἑλληνικά, 33 (1981), 66–83.

Dédéyan, G., 'Mleh le Grand stratège du Lykandos', *REArm*, 15 (1981), 72–102.

ed., *Histoire du peuple arménien* (Paris, 2008).

Delacroix-Besnier, C., 'Conversions constantinopolitaines au XIVe siècle', *MEFRM*, 105 (1993), 715–61.

De Lacy, P., 'The Third Part of the Soul' in P. Manuli and M. Vegetti, ed., *Le opere psichologiche di Galeno* (Naples, 1988), 43–64.
Delatte, A. and P. Stroobant, 'L'horoscope de Pamprépios, professeur et homme politique de Byzance', *BAcBelg*, 9 (1923), 58–76.
Demetracopoulos, P., 'The Exegeses of the Canons in the Twelfth Century as School Texts', *Diptycha*, 1 (1979), 143–57.
Demoen, K., *Pagan and Biblical Exempla in Gregory Nazianzen: a Study in Rhetorics and Hermeneutics* (Turnhout, 1996).
  'Gifts of Friendship That Will Remain for Ever: Personae, Addressed Characters and Intended Audience of Gregory Nazianzen's Epistolary Poems', *JÖB*, 47 (1997), 1–11.
Dempsey, C., *Inventing the Renaissance Putto* (Chapel Hill, NC, 2001).
Deonna, W., 'Eros jouant avec un masque de Silène', *RA*, 3 (1916), 3–256.
der Nersessian, S., *Armenia and the Byzantine Empire* (Cambridge, MA, 1945).
Derda, T., T. Markiewicz and E. Wipszycka, eds., *Alexandria: Auditoria of Kom el-Dikka and Late Antique Education* (Warsaw, 2007).
Destombes, M., *Mappemondes A.D. 1200–1500* (Amsterdam, 1964).
Devreesse, R., *Essai sur Théodore de Mopsueste* (Vatican, 1948).
Diamanti, C., 'Ο ασκοθυράριος', Σύμμεικτα, 12 (1998), 57–62.
Dickey, E., *Ancient Greek Scholarship: A Guide to Finding, Reading, and Understanding Scholia, Commentaries, Lexica, and Grammatical Treatises, from their Beginnings to the Byzantine Period* (Oxford, 2007).
Dicks, D. R., *Early Greek Astronomy to Aristotle* (New York, NY, 1970).
Diddi, C., 'Le "chiavi tematiche bibliche" nel contesto della tradizione retorica e letteraria europea', *Studia Ceranea*, 3 (2013), 11–28.
Diller, A., 'The Autographs of Georgius Gemistus Plethon', *Scriptorium*, 10 (1956), 27–41.
Dincer, A., 'Disease in a Sunny Climate: Effects of the Plague on Family and Wealth in Cyprus in the 1360s' in S. Cavaciocchi, ed., *Le interazioni fra economia e ambiente biologico nell'Europa preindustriale sec. XIII–XVIII* (Florence, 2010), 531–40.
Djurić, I., 'Théophylacte d'Achrida sous la tente d'Aaron', *ZRVI*, 27–8 (1989), 89–91.
Dolezal, M.-L., and M. Mavroudi, 'Theodore Hyrtakenos' Description of the Garden of St. Anna and the Ekphrasis of Gardens' in A. Littlewood, H. Maguire and J. Wolschke-Bulmahn, eds., *Byzantine Garden Culture* (Washington, D. C., 2002), 105–58.
Dols, M. W., *The Black Death in the Middle East* (Princeton, NJ, 1977).
Doody, M. A., *The True Story of the Novel* (London, 1997).
Dorfmann-Lazarev, I., *Arméniens et byzantins à l'époque de Photius: deux débats théologiques après le triomphe de l'orthodoxie* (Louvain, 2004).
Douglas, M., *Thinking in Circles: An Essay on Ring Composition* (New Haven, CT, 2007).
Downey, G., 'Constantine the Rhodian: his Life and Writings' in K. Weitzmann, ed., *Late Classical and Mediaeval Studies in Honor of A. M. Friend, Jr.* (Princeton, NJ, 1955), 212–21.

Dowsett, C. J. F., 'On Eznik's Refutation of the Chaldean Astrologers', *REArm*, 6 (1969), 45–65.
Drancourt, M. et al., 'Yersinia pestis Orientalis in Remains of Ancient Plague Patients', *Emerging Infectious Diseases*, 13 (2007), 332–3.
Drecoll, V. H.. 'Miaphysitische Tendenzen bei Malalas?' in M. Meier, C. Radtki and F. Schulz, eds., *Die Weltchronik des Johannes Malalas* (Stuttgart, 2016), 45–57.
Drexl, F., 'Das anonyme Traumbuch des Cod. Paris. Gr. 2511', Λαογραφία, 8 (1921), 347–75.
Drpić, I., *Epigram, Art, and Devotion in Later Byzantium* (Cambridge, 2016).
Duffy, H., 'Byzantine Medicine in the Sixth and Seventh Centuries: Aspects of Teaching and Practice', *DOP*, 38 (1984), 21–7.
Duggan, J., *The Romances of Chrétien de Troyes* (New Haven, CT, 2001).
Dvornik, F., *The Photian Schism: History and Legend* (Cambridge, 1948; repr. 1970).
Eastmond, A., 'An Intentional Error? Imperial Art and "Mis-interpretation" under Andronikos I Komnenos', *ArtBull*, 76 (1994), 502–10.
'The Veroli Casket' in R. Cormack and M. Vassiliaki, eds., *Byzantium 330–1453* (London, 2008), 124. and 139.
  ed., *Viewing Inscriptions in the Late Antique and Medieval World* (Cambridge, 2015).
Ebbesen, S. and J. Pinborg, 'Gennadios and Western Scholasticism: Radulphus Brito's Ars Vetus in Greek Translation', *ClMed*, 33 (1981–2), 263–319.
Edbury, P. W., "Η πολιτική ἱστορία τοῦ μεσαιωνικοῦ βασιλείου ἀπὸ τὴ βασιλεία τοῦ Οὔγου Δ' μέχρι τὴ βασιλεία τοῦ Ἰανοῦ' in T. Papadopoullos, ed., *Ἱστορία τῆς Κύπρου* 6 vols. (Nicosia, 1995–2005).
'Philip of Novara and the *Livre de forme de plait*' in Πρακτικά τοῦ Τρίτου Διεθνούς Κυπρολογικοῦ Συνεδρίου, 3 vols. (Nicosia, 1996–2001), vol. II, 555–69.
'Some Cultural Implications of the Latin Conquest of Cyprus' in J. A. Koumoulides, ed., *Cyprus: The Legacy. Historic Landmarks that Influenced the Art of Cyprus, Late Bronze Age to CE 1600* (Bethesda, MD, 1999), 99–110.
'The Lusignan Regime in Cyprus and the Indigenous Population' in P. W. Edbury, *Kingdoms of the Crusaders: From Jerusalem to Cyprus* (Aldershot, 1999), 1–9.
Edwards, M. J., 'Simon Magus, the Bad Samaritan' in M. J. Edwards and S. Swain, eds., *Portraits: Biographical Representation in the Greek and Latin Literature of the Roman Empire* (Oxford, 1997), 69–91.
Egea, J. M., 'El griego de los poemas Prodrómicos', *Veleia*, 1 (1984), 177–91.
'La lengua de la ciudad en el s. XII', *Erytheia*, 8 (1987), 241–62.
'El griego de los poemas Prodrómicos (II)', *Veleia*, 5 (1988), 257–74.
Eideneier, H., 'Zu den Προδρομικά', *BZ*, 57 (1964), 329–37.
'Review of E. Trapp, *Digenes Akrites*', *Südost-Forschungen*, 31 (1972), 515–19.
  ed., *Neograeca Medii Aevi I: Text und Ausgabe. Akten zum Symposion Köln 1986* (Cologne, 1987).

'Ein Zeugnis für Wagenrennen in Konstantinopel im 12. Jahrhundert', *Nikephoros: Zeitschrift für Sport und Kultur im Altertum*, 18 (2005), 185–90.
'Ο κοσκινάς και οι ματσούκες του' in G. Papantonakis, ed., Ἄνθη φιλίας: Τιμητικό αφιέρωμα στον καθηγητή Κωνσταντίνο Μηνά (Athens, 2005), 349–53.
'Tou Ptochoprodromou' in M. Hinterberger and E. Schiffer, eds., *Byzantinische Sprachkunst: Studien zur byzantinischen Literatur gewidmet Wolfram Hörandner zum 65. Geburtstag* (Berlin, 2007), 56–76.
'Νέα (και παλαιά) για το (Πτωχο)προδρομικό ζήτημα' in J. Alonso Aldama and O. Omatos Sáenz, eds., *Cultura neogriega, tradición y modernidad* (Bilbao, 2007), 135–41.
Eideneier, H. and N. Eideneier, 'Zum Fünfzehnsilber der Ptochoprodromika' in Ἀφιέρωμα στὸν καθηγητή Λίνο Πολίτη (Thessalonike, 1979), 1–7.
Eisler, W. L., *The Furthest Shore. Images of Terra Australis from the Middle Ages to Capitan Cook* (Cambridge, 1995).
Eleopoulos, N., Ἡ βιβλιοθήκη καὶ τὸ βιβλιογραφικὸν ἐργαστήριον τῆς Μονῆς τῶν Στουδίου (Athens, 1967).
Elweskiöld, B., 'Cosmas Indicopleustes and John Philoponus: a Christian Controversy on the Structure of the World in Sixth-century Alexandria', unpublished doctoral thesis, Lund University (2005).
Erickson, J. H., 'Leavened and Unleavened: Some Theological Implications of the Schism of 1054', *SVThQ*, 14 (1970), 3–24.
Evangelatou, M., 'Pursuing Salvation Through a Body of Parchment: Books and their Significance in the Illustrated Homilies of Iakobos of Kokkinobaphos', *Medieval Studies*, 68 (2006): 239–84.
'Threads of Power: Clothing Symbolism, Human Salvation and Female Identity in the Illustrated Homilies by Iakobos of Kokkinobaphos', *DOP*, 68 (2014), 241–324.
Evangelatou-Notara, F., Χορηγοί, κτήτορες, δωρητές σε σημειώματα κωδίκων. Παλαιολόγειοι χρόνοι (Athens, 2000).
'Χορηγοί και δωρητές χειρογράφων τον 11 αιώνα' in V. N. Vlyssidou, ed., Η αυτοκρατορία σε κρίση; Το Βυζάντιο τον 11ο αιώνα (Athens, 2003).
Ἀδελφᾶτον. Ψυχικόν. Evidence from Notes on Manuscripts', *Byzantion*, 75 (2005), 164–70.
Evans, H. C., 'Digenis Akritis and a Middle Byzantine Rosette Casket in the Metropolitan Museum of Art' in G. Bühl, A. Cutler and A. Effenberger, eds., *Spätantike und byzantinische Elfenbeinwerke im Diskurs* (Wiesbaden, 2008).
Evans, H. and W. Wixom, eds., *The Glory of Byzantium: Art and Culture of the Middle Byzantine Era, AD 843–1261* (New York, NY, 1997).
Evans, J., *The History and Practice of Ancient Astronomy* (Oxford, 1998).
Featherstone, J. M., 'Metochites's Poems and the Chora' in H. A. Klein, R. G. Ousterhout, and B. Pitarakis eds., *The Kariye Camii Reconsidered* (Istanbul, 2011), 215–56.
Federico, A., *Engagements with Close Reading* (London, 2016).

Felix, W., *Byzanz und die islamische Welt im früheren 11. Jahrhundert* (Vienna, 1981).
Fernández Jiménez, F. M., *El humanismo bizantino en San Simeón el Nuevo Teólogo: la renovación de la mística bizantina* (Madrid, 1999).
Feros Ruys, J., ed., *What Nature Does Not Teach: Didactic Literature in the Medieval and Early-Modern Periods* (Turnhout, 2008).
Flint, V. I. J., 'Monsters and Antipodes in the Early Middle Ages and Enlightenment', *Viator*, 15 (1984), 65–80.
Follieri, E., 'La versione in greco volgare del Teseida del Boccaccio', *SBN*, 7 (1953), 67–77.
Förstel, C., 'Metochites and his Books Between the Chora and the Renaissance' in H. A. Klein, R. G. Ousterhout, and B. Pitarakis, eds., *The Kariye Camii Reconsidered* (Istanbul, 2011), 241–66.
Fourrier, A., *Le Courant réaliste dans le roman courtois en France au moyen âge* (Paris, 1960).
Franses, R., 'When All That is Gold Does Not Glitter' in A. Eastmond and L. James, eds., *Icon and Word: The Power of Images in Byzantium* (Aldershot, 2003), 13–24.
Frankopan, P., 'A Victory of Gregory Pakourianos Against the Pechenegs', *BSl*, 57 (1996), 278–81.
 'The Foreign Policy of the Emperor Alexios I Komnenos (1081–c. 1100)', unpublished DPhil thesis, Oxford (1998).
 'Byzantine Trade Privileges to Venice in the Eleventh Century: the Chrysobull of 1092', *JMedHist*, 30 (2004), 135–60.
 'Challenges to Imperial Authority in the Reign of Alexios I Komnenos: the Conspiracy of Nikephoros Diogenes', *BSl*, 64 (2006), 257–74.
 'Kinship and the Distribution of Power in Byzantium', *EHR*, 122 (2007), 1–34.
 'Where Advice Meets Criticism in Eleventh-century Byzantium: Theophylact of Ohrid, John the Oxite and their (Re)presentations to the Emperor', *Al-Masāq*, 20/1 (2008), 71–88.
 'Expeditions Against the Serbs in the 1090s: the *Alexiad* and Byzantium's Northwest Frontier on the Eve of the First Crusade', *Bulgaria Medievalis*, 3 (2012), 385–97.
 'Turning Latin into Greek: Anna Komnene and the *Gesta Roberti Wiscardi*', *JMedHist*, 39 (2013), 80–99.
Friedman, J. B., *The Monstrous Races in Medieval Art and Thought* (Cambridge, MA, 1981).
Frigerio Zeniou, S., *Luxe et humilité: se vêtir à Chypre au XVIe siècle* (Limassol, 2012).
Frye, N., *The Great Code: The Bible and Literature* (London, 1982).
Furley, D., *The Greek Cosmologists* (Cambridge, 1987).
Galavaris, G., *The Illustrations of the Liturgical Homilies of Gregory Nazianzenus* (Princeton, NJ, 1969).
Gallavotti Cavallero, D., *Lo Spedale di Santa Maria della Scala in Siena: vicenda di una committenza artistica* (Pisa, 1985).

Ganchou, T., 'Les *ultimae voluntates* de Manuel et Iôannès Chrysoloras et le séjour de Francesco Filelfo à Constantinople', *Byzantinistica*, 7 (2005), 195–285.
Garitte, G., 'La vision de S. Sahak en grec', *Le Muséon*, 71 (1958), 225–78.
Garland, L., 'The Rhetoric of Gluttony and Hunger in Twelfth-century Byzantium' in W. Mayer and S. Trzcionka, eds., *Feast, Fast or Famine: Food and Drinks in Byzantium* (Brisbane, 2005), 43–55.
Garsoïan, N., 'The Problem of Armenian Integration into the Byzantine Empire' in H. Ahrweiler and A. E. Laiou, eds., *Studies on the Internal Diaspora of the Byzantine Empire* (Washington, D. C., 1998), 53–124.
Garzaniti, M., 'Bible and Liturgy in Church Slavonic Literature. A New Perspective for Research in Medieval Slavonic Studies' in J. A. Álvarez-Pedrosa and S. Torres Prieto, eds., *Medieval Slavonic Studies. New Perspectives for Research* (Paris, 2009), 127–48.
  'Sacre scritture ed esegesi patristica nella Vita di Metodio' in A. Bartolomei Romagnoli, U. Paoli and P. Piatti, eds., *Hagiologica. Studi per Réginald Grégoire* (Fabriano, 2012), 385–92.
Garzaniti, M. and F. Romoli, 'Le funzioni delle citazioni bibliche nella letteratura della Slavia ortodossa' in M. Garzaniti, A. Alberti, M. Perotto and B. Sulpasso, eds., *Contributi italiani al XV Congresso Internazionale degli Slavisti (Minsk, 20–27 settembre 2013)* (Florence, 2013), 121–56.
Garzya, A., *Storia e interpretazione di testi bizantini* (London, 1974).
Gasquet, F. A., *The Great Pestilence (AD 1348–9), Now Commonly Known as the Black Death* (London, 1893).
Gastgeber, C., 'Manuel Meligalas. Eine biographisch-paläographische Studie' in C. Gastgeber, ed., *Miscellanea Codicum Graecorum Vindobonensium, I: Studien zu griechischen Handschriften der Österreichischen Nationalbibliothek* (Vienna, 2009), 51–84.
Gaul, N., 'Review: Alexander Sideras, Eine byzantinische Invektive gegen die Verfasser von Grabreden', *BZ*, 100 (2007), 257–61.
  Thomas Magistros und die spätbyzantinische Sophistik: Studien zum Humanismus urbaner Eliten in der frühen Palaiologenzeit (Wiesbaden, 2011).
  'Rising Elites and Institutionalization – Ethos/Mores – 'Debts' and Drafts' in S. Steckel, N. Gaul and M. Grümbart, eds., *Networks of Learning: Perspectives on Scholars in Byzantine East and Latin West* (Zurich, 2014), 259–69.
  'All the Emperor's Men (and his Nephews): *Paideia* and Networking Strategies at the Court of Andronikos II Palaiologos, 1290–1320', *DOP*, 70 (2016).
  'Embedded Dialogues and Dialogical Voices in Palaiologan Prose and Verse' in Cameron and Gaul, eds., *Dialogues and Debates from Late Antiquity to Late Byzantium* (New York, NY, 2017), 184–202.
  'The Letter in the *Theatron*: Epistolary Voice, Character, Soul and their Audience' in A. Riehle, ed., *A Companion to Byzantine Epistolography* (Leiden, forthcoming).
Gautier, P., 'Jean V l'Oxite, patriarche d'Antioche: notice biographique', *REB*, 22 (1964), 128–57.

'L'obituaire du typikon du Pantocrator', *REB*, 27 (1969), 235.

'Réquisitoire du patriarche Jean d'Antioche contre le charisticariat', *REB*, 33 (1975), 77–132.

Gelzer, T., 'Bemerkungen zur Sprache und Text des Epikers Musaios', *MusHelv*, 24 (1967), 129–48.

'Bemerkungen zur Sprache und Text des Epikers Musaios', *MusHelv*, 25 (1968), 11–47.

'Musaeus: Hero and Leander', in C. A. Trypanis, T. Gelzer, and C. H. Whitman, eds., *Callimachus, Aetia, Iambi: Lyric Poems Hecale, Minor Epic and Elegiac Poems and Other Fragments* (Cambridge, MA 1975), 12–22.

Genette, G., ed., *Palimpsests: Literature in the Second Degree* (Lincoln, NE, 1997).

Georgakas, D., 'Beiträge zur Deutung als slavisch erklärter Ortsnamen', *BZ*, 41 (1941), 351–81.

Giakovaki, N., 'Τα Πτωχοπροδρομικά του Κοραή: Μεσαιωνικές αναζητήσεις' in Μνήμη Άλκη Αγγέλου: Τα άφθονα σχήματα του παρελθόντος (Thessalonike, 2004).

Giannouli, A., *Die beiden byzantinischen Kommentare zum Großen Kanon des Andreas von Kreta* (Vienna, 2007).

'Education and Literary Language in Byzantium' in M. Hinterberger, ed., *The Language of Byzantine Learned Literature* (Turnhout, 2014), 52–71.

Giannouli, A. and E. Schiffer, eds., *From Manuscripts to Books/Vom Codex zur Edition* (Vienna, 2011).

Giardina, A., 'Melania, la santa' in A. Frachetti, ed., *Roma al femminile* (Rome, 1994), 277–83.

Gill, J., *The Council of Florence* (Cambridge, 1959).

Personalities of the Council of Florence and Other Essays (Oxford, 1964).

Gleason, M. W., *Making Men: Sophists and Self-Presentation in Ancient Rome* (Princeton, NJ, 1995).

Gleye, C. E., 'Beiträge zur Johannesfrage', *BZ*, 5 (1896), 422–64.

Gliozzi, G., *Adamo e il Nuovo Mondo. La nascita dell'antropologia come ideologiia coloniale: delle genalogie bibliche alle teorie razziali (1500–1700)* (Florence, 1977).

Glöckner, S., *Über den Kommentar des Johannes Doxopatres zu den Staseis des Hermogenes* (Kirchhain, 1908).

Golden, P. B., 'Khazar Turkic Ghulâms in Caliphal Service', *Journal Asiatique*, 294 (2004), 279–309.

Goldschmidt, A. and K. Weitzmann, *Die byzantinischen Elfenbeinskulpturen des X–XIII. Jahrhunderts, 1 Kästen* (Berlin, 1930).

Gouma-Peterson, T., ed., *Anna Komnene and Her Times* (New York, NY, 2000).

Graindor, P., 'Pamprépios (?) et Théagénès', *Byzantion*, 4 (1929), 469–75.

Gray, P. T. R., 'The Legacy of Chalcedon: Christological Problems and their Significance' in M. Maas, ed., *The Cambridge Companion to the Age of Justinian* (Cambridge, 2005), 215–38,

Greatrex, G., *Rome and Persia at War, 502–532* (Leeds, 1998).

'Malalas and Procopius' in M. Meier, C. Radtki and F. Schulz, eds., *Die Weltchronik des Johannes Malalas* (Stuttgart, 2016), 169–85.

Greenblatt, S., *Shakespearean Negotiations* (Berkeley, CA, 1988).
Greenfield, P. H., *The Life of Saint Symeon the New Theologian* (Cambridge, MA, 2013).
Greenwood, T. W., 'Failure of a Mission? Photios and the Armenian Church', *Le Muséon*, 119 (2006), 115–59.
'The Discovery of the Relics of St. Grigor and the Development of Armenian Tradition in Ninth-century Byzantium' in E. M. Jeffreys, ed., *Byzantine Style, Religion and Civilization: In Honour of Steven Runciman* (Cambridge, 2006), 177–91.
'Armenian Neighbours 600–1045' in J. Shepard, *Cambridge History of the Byzantine Empire* (Cambridge, 2008), 333–64.
'Patterns of Contact and Communication: Constantinople and Armenia, 860–976' in R. G. Hovannisian and S. Payaslian, eds., *Armenian Constantinople* (Costa Mesa, CA, 2010), 73–100.
'A Reassessment of the *History* of Łewond', *Le Muséon*, 125 (2012), 99–167.
Grégoire, H., 'Au Camp d'un Wallenstein byzantin: la vie et les vers de Pamprépios, aventurier païen', *BullBudé*, 24 (1929), 22–38.
Autour de l'épopée Byzantine (London, 1975).
Grillmeier, A., *Jesus der Christus im Glauben der Kirche*, vol. 1, *Von der Apostolischen Zeit bis zum Konzil von Chalcedon* (Vienna, 1979).
Grishin, A. D., *A Pilgrim's Account of Cyprus: Bars'kyj's Travels in Cyprus* (Altamont, NY, 1996).
Grivaud, G., *Villages désertés à Chypre (fin xiie–fin xix siècle)* (Nicosia, 1998).
'Fortunes and Misfortunes of a Small Byzantine Foundation' in A. Weyl Carr, ed., *Asinou Across Time: Studies in the Architecture and Murals of the Panagia Phorbiotissa, Cyprus* (Washington, D. C., 2012), 13–36.
Grosdidier de Matons, J., *Romanos le Mélode et les origines de la poésie réligieuse à Byzance* (Paris, 1977).
Grumel, V., 'Les patriarches grecs d'Antioche du nom de Jean (xie et xiie siècles): étude littéraire, historique et chronologique', *EO*, 32 (1933), 279–99.
'L'affaire de Léon de Chalcédoine. Le chrysobulle d'Alexis Ier sur les objets sacrés', *Études Byzantines*, 2 (1944), 126–33.
La Chronologie (Paris, 1958).
Grünbart, M., 'Byzantium: A Bibliophile Society?', *Basilissa*, 1 (2004), 113–21.
Formen der Anrede im byzantinischen Brief vom 6. bis zum 12. Jahrhundert (Vienna, 2005).
ed., *Theatron: Rhetorische Kultur in Spätantike und Mittelalter* (Berlin, 2007).
Guberti Bassett, S., 'Historiae Custos: Sculpture and Tradition in the Baths of Zeuxippos', *AJA*, 100 (1996), 491–506.
Guillou, A., and Durand, J. eds., *Byzance et les images: cycle de conférences organisé au musée du Louvre par le Service culturel du 5 octobre au 7 décembre 1992* (Paris, 1994).
Gundell, H. G., *Zodiakos. Tierkreisbilder im altertum. Kosmische Bezüge und Jenseitsvorstellungen im antike Alltagsleben* (Mainz, 1992).
Haarer, F. K., *Anastasius I: Empire and Politics in the Late Roman World* (Cambridge 2006).

Halliwell, S., *The Aesthetics of Mimesis: Ancient Texts and Modern Problems* (Princeton, NJ, 2002).
Hamilton, B., *The Latin Church in the Crusader States: The Secular Church* (London, 1980).
Handbook of the Byzantine Collection, Dumbarton Oaks, Washington (Washington, D. C., 1967).
Hanfmann, G. M. A., *The Season Sarcophagus in Dumbarton Oaks*, 2 vols. (Cambridge, MA, 1951).
Hanke, I., *Aristotle and the American Indians: a Study in Race Prejudice in the Modern World* (London, 1959).
Hankinson, R. J., 'Greek Medical Models of Mind' in S. Eversen, ed., *Psychology* (Oxford, 1991), 194–217.
Hansmann, K., *Ein neuentdeckter Kommentar zum Johannesevangelium* (Paderborn, 1930).
Hanson, J., 'Erotic Imagery on Byzantine Ivory Caskets' in L. James, ed., *Desire and Denial in Byzantium* (Aldershot, 1999), 173–84.
'The Rise and Fall of the Macedonian Renaissance' in L. James, ed., *A Companion to Byzantium* (Chichester, 2010), 338–50.
Harley, B. and D. Woodward, 'Greek Cartography in the Early Roman World' in B. Harley and D. Woodward, eds., *The History of Cartography*, 6 vols. (Chicago, IL, 1987–2003), vol. 1, *Cartography in Prehistoric, Ancient, and Medieval Europe and Mediterranean*, 161–76.
Harris, J., ed., *Palgrave Advances in Byzantine History* (Basingstoke, 2005).
Hartnup, K., *'On the Beliefs of the Greeks': Leo Allatios and Popular Orthodoxy* (Leiden, 2004).
Hatzaki, M., *Beauty and the Male Body in Byzantium: Perceptions and Representations in Art and Text* (Basingstoke, 2009).
Haury, J., 'Johannes Malalas identisch mit dem Patriarchen Johannes Scholastikos?', *BZ*, 9 (1900), 337–56.
Haye, T., 'Liutprand von Cremona' in H. L. Arnold, ed., *Kindlers Literatur Lexikon*, third edition, 18 vols. (Stuttgart, 2009), vol. x, 221.
Heath, M., *Menander: A Rhetor in Context* (Oxford, 2004).
Heather, P., *Goths and Romans 332–489* (Oxford, 1991).
Hennessy, C., 'A Child Bride and her Representation in the Vatican Epithalamion, cod. 1851', *BMGS*, 30 (2006), 115–50.
Henrich, G. S., Εμμανουήλ/Μανόλης Λιμενίτης, Το Θανατικόν της Ρόδου (Thessalonike, 2015).
Herrin, J., 'Mathematical Mysteries in Byzantium: the Transmission of Fermat's Last Theorem', *Dialogos*, 6 (1999), 22–42.
'Book Burning as Purification' in P. Rousseau and M. Papoutsakis, eds., *Transformations of Late Antiquity: Essays for Peter Brown* (Farnham, 2009), 205–22.
Margins and Metropolis: Authority across the Byzantine Empire (Princeton, NJ, 2013).

Herlihy, D., *The Black Death and the Transformation of the West*, ed. S. K. Cohn (Cambridge, MA, 1997).
Hewsen, R. H., *The Geography of Ananias of Širak* (Wiesbaden, 1992).
Hiatt, A., *Terra Incognita: Mapping the Antipodes Before 1600* (London, 2008).
Hill, D. K., 'Bacchic Erotes at Tarentum', *Hesperia*, 16 (1947), 248–55.
Hilsdale, C. J., 'Constructing a Byzantine "Augusta": a Greek Book for a French Bride', *ArtBull*, 87 (2005), 458–83.
Hinterberger, M., 'Autobiography and Hagiography in Byzantium', *Symbolae Osloenses*, 75 (2000), 139–64.
  'Review of H. Eideneier, *Ptochoprodromos*', *JÖB*, 43 (1993), 451–4.
  Autobiographische Traditionen in Byzanz (Vienna, 1999).
  'Δημώδης και λόγια λογοτεχνία: διαχωριστικές γραμμές και συνδετικοί κρίκοι' in P. Odorico and P. A. Agapitos, *Pour une "nouvelle" histoire de la littérature byzantine: Problèmes, méthodes, approches, propositions* (Paris, 2002), 153–65.
  Phthonos. Mißgunst, Neid und Eifersucht in der byzantinischen Literatur (Wiesbaden, 2013).
Høgel, C., *Symeon Metaphrastes: Rewriting and Canonization* (Copenhagen, 2002).
Holmes, C., 'Written Culture in Byzantium and Beyond: Contexts, Contents and Interpretations' in C. Holmes and J. Waring, eds., *Literacy, Education and Manuscript Transmission in Byzantium and Beyond* (Leiden, 2002), 1–31.
  'The Rhetorical Structures of John Skylitzes' *Synopsis Historion*' in E. M. Jeffreys, ed., *Rhetoric in Byzantium* (Aldershot, 2003), 187–99.
  Basil II and the Governance of Empire (976–1025) (Oxford, 2005).
  'Political Literacy', in P. Stephenson, ed., *Byzantine World* (London, 2010), 137–48.
Holmes, C. and J. Waring, eds., *Literacy, Education and Manuscript Transmission in Byzantium and Beyond* (Leiden, 2002).
Holtzmann, W., 'Die Unionsverhandlungen zwischen Kaiser Alexios I. und Papst Urban II. im Jahre 1089', *BZ*, 28 (1928), 38–67.
Hörandner, W., *Der Prosarhythmus in der rhetorischen Literatur der Byzantiner* (Vienna, 1981).
  'Zur Frage der Metrik früher volkssprachlicher Texte: Kann Theodoros Prodromos der Verfasser volkssprachlicher Gedichte sein?', *JÖB*, 32 (1982), 375–81.
  'Autor oder Genus? Diskussionsbeiträge zur "Prodromischen Frage" aus gegebenem Anlaß', *BSl*, 54 (1993), 314–24.
  'The Byzantine Didactic Poem – a Neglected Literary Genre? A Survey with Special Reference to the Eleventh Century' in F. Bernard and K. Demoen, eds., *Poetry and Its Contexts in Eleventh Century Byzantium* (Farnham, 2012), 55–68.
Hörling, E., *Mythos und Pisitis: Zur Deutung heidnischer Mythen in der christlichen Weltchronik des Johannes Malalas* (Lund, 1980).
Horna, K., 'Nachlese zu Pamprepios', *AnzWien*, 66 (1929), 257–63.
Hornblower, S., and A. Spawforth, eds., *The Oxford Classical Dictionary* (Oxford, 1996).

Horrocks, G. C., 'Clitics in Greek: a Diachronic Review' in M. Roussou and S. Panteli, eds., *Greek Outside Greece*, 2 vols. (Athens, 1990–1), vol. II, 35–52.
'On Condition ...: Aspect and Modality in the History of Greek', *Proceedings of the Cambridge Philological Society*, 41 (1995), 153–73.
Greek: A History of the Language and its Speakers, second edition (New York, NY, 2010).
Horrox, R., *The Black Death* (New York, NY, 1994).
Howard-Johnston, J., 'Anna Komnene and the *Alexiad*' in M. Mullett and D. Smythe, eds., *Alexios I Komnenos* (Belfast, 1996), 260–302.
'The *De Administrando Imperio*: a Re-examination of the Text and a Re-evaluation of its Evidence about the Rus' in M. Kazanski, A. Nercessian and C. Zuckerman, eds., *Les centres proto-urbains russes entre Scandinavie, Byzance et Orient* (Paris, 2000), 301–36.
Witnesses to a World Crisis: Historians and Histories of the Middle East in the Seventh Century (Oxford, 2010).
Hunger, H., *Katalog der griechischen Handschriften der Österreichischen Nationalbibliothek*, 4 vols. (Vienna, 1961–94).
'Anonymes Pamphlet gegen eine byzantinische Mafia', *RESEE*, 7 (1969), 95–107.
'On the Imitation (μίμησις) of Antiquity in Byzantine Literature', *DOP*, 23–4 (1969–70), 15–38.
Die hochsprachliche profane Literatur der Byzantiner, 2 vols. (Munich, 1978).
'Die Antithese. Zur Verbreitung einer Denkschablone in der byzantinischen Literatur', *ZRVI*, 23 (1984), 9–29.
Schreiben und Lesen in Byzanz: Die byzantinische Buchkultur (Munich, 1989).
'Zum Dynastieproblem in Byzanz', *AnzWien*, 131 (1994), 271–84.
'Das "Enthymem" in der liturgischen Dichtung des frühen Byzanz' in T. Schirren and G. Ueding, eds., *Topik und Rhetorik* (Tübingen, 2000), 93–101.
Hussey, J. M., *The Orthodox Church in the Byzantine Empire* (Oxford, 1990).
Hutter, I., 'Der *despotes* Demetrios Palaiologos und sein "Bildmenologion" in Oxford', *JÖB*, 57 (2007), 188–214.
Imhaus, B., 'Quelques remarques à propos de Dominique Jauna', *EKEE*, 27 (2001), 127–37.
Lacrimae Cypriae: les larmes de Chypre, 2 vols. (Nicosia, 2004).
Inglebert H., *Interpretatio Christiana. Les mutations des savoirs (cosmographie, géographie, etnographie, histoire) dans l'antiquité chrétienne (30–630 après J.C.)* (Paris, 2001).
Irigoin, J., 'Centres de copie et bibliothèques' in W. C. Loerke et al., eds., *Byzantine Books and Bookmen: A Dumburton Oaks Colloquium* (Washington, D. C., 1975),17–27.
Iuzbashian, K. N., 'Скилица о захвате Анийского царства в 1045г.', *VizVrem*, 40 (1979), 76–95.
Jacoby, D., 'The Chrysobull of Alexius I Comnenus to the Venetians: the Date and the Debate', *JMedHist*, 28 (2002), 199–204.
James, L., *Light and Colour in Byzantine Art* (Oxford, 1996).

ed., *Desire and Denial in Byzantium* (Aldershot, 1999).
ed., *Art and Text in Byzantine Culture* (Cambridge, 2007).
ed., *A Companion to Byzantium* (Chichester, 2010).
Janin, R., *Constantinople Byzantine: développement urbain et répertoire topographique* (Paris, 1964).
La géographie ecclésiastique de l'Empire byzantin, vol. 1, *Le siège de Constantinople et le patriarcat œcuménique, part 3, Les églises et les monastères*, second edition (Paris, 1969).
Jannaris, A. N., *An Historical Greek Grammar Chiefly of the Attic Dialect* (London, 1897); reprinted (Hildesheim, 1968).
Janssen, M. C., 'Verb Morphology' in D. Holton, G. Horrocks, et al., eds., *The Cambridge Grammar of Medieval and Early Modern Greek*, forthcoming.
Janssen, M. C. and M. D. Lauxtermann, 'Το παράπονο του δασκάλου: Το τρίτο Πτωχοπροδρομικό και η βυζαντινή γραμματική παράδοση' in I. García Gálvez and O. Omatos Sáenz, eds., *Tolmiros Skapaneas: Homenaje al Profesor K. A. Dimadis* (Vitoria-Gasteiz, 2012), 25–41.
Jauna, D., *Histoire générale des roïaumes de Chypre, de Jerusalem, d'Arménie, et d'Egypte*, 2 vols. (Leiden, 1785).
Jauss, H. R., 'Literary Theory as a Challenge to Literary History', *New Literary History*, 2 (1967), 11–19.
Jeffreys, E. M., 'Constantine Hermoniakos and Byzantine Education', Δωδώνη, 4 (1975), 79–109.
'The Greek Manuscripts of the Saibante Collection' in K. Treu et al., eds., *Studia Codicologica* (Berlin, 1977), 249–62.
'The Judgement of Paris in Later Byzantine Literature', *Byzantium*, 48 (1978), 112–31.
'The Attitudes of Byzantine Chroniclers Towards Ancient History', *Byzantion*, 49 (1979), 199–238.
'The Comnenian Background to the *Romans d'Antiquité*', *Byzantion*, 50 (1980), 112–31.
'The Later Greek Verse Romances: a Survey' in E. M. Jeffreys, M. J. Jeffreys and A. Moffatt, eds., *Byzantine Papers* (Canberra, 1981), 116–27.
'The Sevastokratorissa Eirene as a Literary Patroness: the Monk Iakovos', *JÖB*, 32 (1982), 63–71.
'Chronological Structures in the Chronicle' in E. M. Jeffreys with B. Croke and R. Scott, eds., *Studies in John Malalas* (Sydney 1990), 111–66.
'Malalas in Greek' in E. M. Jeffreys, with B. Croke and R. Scott, eds., *Studies in John Malalas* (Sydney, 1990), 249–54.
'Malalas' Sources' in E. M. Jeffreys, with B. Croke and R. Scott, eds., *Studies in John Malalas* (Sydney, 1990), 167–216.
'Malalas' World View' in E. M. Jeffreys, with B. Croke and R. Scott, eds., *Studies in John Malalas* (Sydney, 1990), 55–66.
'Malalas' Use of the Past' in G. Clarke, ed., *Reading the Past in Late Antiquity* (Canberra, 1990), 121–46,

'Place of Composition as a Factor in the Edition of Early Demotic Texts' in N. M. Panayotakis, ed., *Origini della letteratura neogreca* 2 vols. (Venice, 1993), vol. 1, 310–24.

'The Novels of Mid-twelfth Century Constantinople: the Literary and Social Context' in I. Ševčenko and I. Hutter, eds., *AETOS: Studies in Honour of Cyril Mango* (Stuttgart, 1998), 191–9.

'A Date for Rhodanthe and Dosikles?' in P. A. Agapitos and D. Reinsch, eds., *Der Roman in der Komnenenzeit* (Frankfurt, 2000), 127–36.

'"The Wild Beast from the West": Immediate Literary Reactions in Byzantium to the Second Crusade' in A. Laiou-Thomadakis and R. Mottahedeh, eds., *The Crusades from the Perspective of Byzantium and the Muslim World* (Washington, D. C., 2001), 110–13.

ed., *Rhetoric in Byzantium* (Aldershot, 2003).

'Nikephoros Bryennios Reconsidered' in V. N. Vlysidou, ed., *The Empire in Crisis? Byzantium in the Eleventh Century (1025–1081)* (Athens, 2003), 201–14.

'The Beginning of Byzantine Chronography: John Malalas' in G. Marasco, ed., *Greek and Roman Historiography in Late Antiquity, Fourth to Sixth Century A.D.* (Leiden, 2003), 497–527.

'The Depiction of Female Sensibilities in the Twelfth Century' in C. Angelidi, ed., *Byzantium Matures: Choices, Sensitivities and Modes of Expression (Eleventh to Fifteenth Centuries)* (Athens, 2004), 73–85.

ed., *Byzantine Style, Religion and Civilization: In Honour of Sir Steven Runciman* (Cambridge, 2006).

'Writers and Audiences in the Early Sixth Century' in S. F. Johnson, ed., *Greek Literature in Late Antiquity: Dynamism, Didacticism, Classicism* (Aldershot, 2006), 127–39.

'Rhetoric in Byzantium' in I. Worthington, ed., *A Companion to Greek Rhetoric* (Oxford, 2007), 166–84.

'Review of Ulrich Moennig, *Die Erzählung von Alexander und Semiramis*', *BZ*, 100 (2008), 870–2.

'Rhetoric' in E. M. Jeffreys, J. Haldon and R. Cormack, eds., *The Oxford Handbook of Byzantine Studies* (Oxford, 2008), 827–37.

'Literary Genre or Religious Apathy? The Presence or Absence of Theology and Religious Thought in Secular Writing in the Late Antique East' in D. M. Gwynn and S. Bangert, eds., *Religious Diversity in Late Antiquity* (Leiden, 2010), 511–22.

'Byzantine Romances: Eastern or Western?' in M. Brownlee and D. Gondicas, eds., *Renaissance Encounters: Greek East and Latin West* (Princeton, NJ, 2013), 221–37.

'The *Sebastokratorissa* Irene as Patron' in L. Theis, M. Mullett and M. Grünbart with G. Fingarova and M. Savage, eds., *Female Founders in Byzantium and Beyond* (Vienna, 2014), 177–94.

Jeffreys, E. M., with B. Croke and R. Scott, eds., *Studies in John Malalas* (Sydney, 1990).

Jeffreys, E. M., J. Haldon and R. Cormack, eds., *The Oxford Handbook of Byzantine Studies* (Oxford, 2008).

Jeffreys, E. M. and M. J. Jeffreys, 'The Traditional Style of Early Demotic Verse', *BMGS*, 5 (1979), 113–39.
  Popular Literature in Late Byzantium (London, 1983).
  'The Style of Byzantine Popular Poetry: Recent Work' in C. Mango and O. Pritsak, eds., *Okeanos: Essays Presented to Ihor Ševčenko* (Cambridge, MA, 1984), 309–43.
  'The Oral Background of Byzantine Popular Poetry', *Oral Tradition*, 1 (1986), 504–47.
Jeffreys, E. M., M. J. Jeffreys and A. Moffatt, eds., *Byzantine Papers: Proceedings of the First Australian Studies Conference Canberra, 17–19 May 1978* (Canberra, 1981).
Jeffreys, M. J., 'Formulas in the *Chronicle of the Morea*', *DOP*, 27 (1973), 163–95.
  'Digenis Akritas Manuscript Z', *Dodone*, 4 (1975), 163–201.
  'Review of W. Hörandner, Theodoros Prodromos: Historische Gedichte', *BZ*, 70 (1977), 105–7.
  'Byzantine Metrics: Non-literary Strata', *JÖB*, 31 (1981), 313–34.
  'The Vernacular *Eiseterioi* for Agnes of France' in E. M. Jeffreys, M. J. Jeffreys and A. Moffatt, eds., *Byzantine Papers* (Canberra, 1981), 101–15.
  'Proposals for the Debate on the Question of Oral Influence in Early Modern Greek Poetry' in N. M. Panayotakis, ed., Αρχές της νεοελληνικής λογοτεχνίας, 2 vols. (Venice, 1993), vol. 1, 251–66.
  'Η γλώσσα του Χρονικού του Μορέως – γλώσσα μιας προφορικής παράδοσης;' in H. Eideneier, ed., *Neograeca Medii Aevi* (Cologne, 1987), 139–63.
  'Manuel Komnenos' Macedonian Military Camps: a Glamorous Alternative Court?' in J. Burke and R. Scott, eds., *Byzantine Macedonia: Identity, Image and History* (Melbourne, 2000), 184–91.
  'Rhetorical Texts' in E. M. Jeffreys, ed., *Rhetoric in Byzantium* (Aldershot, 2003), 87–100.
  'Psellos and "His Emperors": Fact, Fiction and Genre' in R. Macrides, ed., *History as Literature in Byzantium* (Farnham, 2010), 73–91.
Jeffreys, M. J., and E. M. Jeffreys, 'Who was Eirene the Sevastokratorissa?', *Byzantion*, 64 (1994), 40–68.
Jenkins, R. J. H., 'The Classical Background of the *Scriptores post Theophanem*', *DOP*, 8 (1954), 13–30.
  'A Note on Nicetas David Paphlago and the Vita Ignatii', *DOP*, 19 (1965), 241–7.
Johnson, S. F., ed., *Greek Literature in Late Antiquity: Dynamism, Didacticism, Classicism* (Aldershot, 2006).
Jolivet-Lévy, C., 'L'image du pouvoir dans l'art byzantin à l'époque de la dynastie macédonienne (867–1056)', *Byzantion*, 57 (1987), 441–70.
Jones, A. H. M., J. R. Martindale and J. Morris, *The Prosopography of the Later Roman Empire*, 3 vols. (Cambridge, 1971–92).
Jouanno, C., 'Shared Spaces: 1 *Digenis Akritis*, the Two-blood Border Lord' in C. Cupane and B. Krönung, eds., *Fictional Storytelling in the Medieval Eastern Mediterranean and Beyond* (Leiden, 2016), 260–84.

Jugie, M., ed., 'Homélies mariales byzantines,' *PO* 16/2 (1922), 425–589.
Kahane, H. and R. Kahane, 'L'énigme du nom de Cligés', *Romania*, 82 (1961), 113–21.
Kaklamanis, S., "Ἀπὸ τὸ χειρόγραφο στὸ ἔντυπο: Θησέος καὶ γάμοι τῆς Αἰμίλιας (1529)', *Θησαυρίσματα*, 27 (1997), 151–2.
Kaldellis, A., *The Argument of Psellos' Chronographia* (Leiden, 1999).
  Mothers and Sons, Fathers and Daughters: The Byzantine Family of Michael Psellos (Notre Dame, IN, 2006).
  'Christodoros on the Statues of the Xeuxippos Baths: a New Reading of the Ekphrasis', *GRBS*, 47 (2007), 361–83.
  Hellenism in Byzantium. The Transformation of Greek Identity and the Reception of the Classical Tradition (Cambridge, 2007).
  The Christian Parthenon: Classicism and Pilgrimage in Byzantine Athens (Cambridge, 2009).
  'The Timarion: Toward a Literary Interpretation' in P. Odorico, ed., *Le face cachée de la littérature byzantine: le texte en tant que message immédiat* (Paris, 2012), 275–88.
  'The Emergence of Literary Fiction in Byzantium and the Paradox of Plausibility' in P. Roilos, ed., *Medieval Greek Storytelling: Fictionality and Narrative in Byzantium* (Wiesbaden, 2014), 115–29.
  A New Herodotus: Laonikos Chalkokondyles on the Ottoman Empire, the Fall of Byzantium, and the Emergence of the West (Washington, D. C., 2014).
  The Byzantine Republic: People and Power in New Rome (Cambridge, MA, 2015).
Karagiorgiou, O., 'On the Way to the Throne: the Career of Nikephoros III Botaneiates Before 1078' in C. Stavrakos, A.-K. Wassiliou and M. K. Krikorian, eds., *Hypermachos. Studien zur Byzantinistik, Armenologie und Georgistik, Festschrift für Werner Seibt zum 65. Geburtstag* (Wiesbaden, 2008), 105–32.
Karapotsoglu, K., 'Παρατηρήσεις σὲ ἑλληνικὰ δυσετυμολόγητα', *Βυζαντινά*, 12 (1983), 399–400.
Kariakis, M. J., 'Student Life in Eleventh-century Constantinople', *Byzantina*, 7 (1975), 375–88.
Karla, G. A., 'Rhetorische Kommunikation in den Kaiserreden des 12. Jhs.: Der Kontakt zum Publikum', *JÖB*, 57 (2007), 83–94.
Karlsson, G., *Idéologie et cérémoniale dans l'épistolographie byzantine. Textes du xe siècle analysés et commentés* (Uppsala, 1962).
Karpf, E., 'L(iutprand) v. Cremona' in *Lexikon des Mittelalters*, 9 vols. (1980–98), vol. v, col. 2041–2.
Karpozilos, A., Συμβολή στή μελέτη τοῦ βίου καὶ τοῦ ἔργου τοῦ Ἰωάννη Μαυρόποδος (Ioannina, 1982).
  'The Correspondence of Theodore Hyrtakenos', *JÖB*, 40 (1990), 275–84.
  'The Biography of John Mauropous Again', *Ἑλληνικά*, 44 (1994), 51–60.

Karpp, H., *Textbuch zur altkirchlichen Christologie: Theologia und Oikonomia* (Neukirchen-Vluyn, 1972).
Kaster, R., *Guardians of Language: The Grammarian and Society in Late Antiquity* (Berkeley, CA, 1988).
Katsaros, B., Ἰωάννης Κασταμονίτης. Συμβολή στη μελέτη του βίου, του έργου και της εποχής του (Thessalonike, 1988).
'Η ρητορική ως "Θεωρία Λογοτεχνίας" των Βυζαντινών' in P. Odorico and P. A. Agapitos, *Pour une "nouvelle" histoire de la littérature byzantine: Problèmes, méthodes, approches, propositions* (Paris, 2002), 95–106.
Kazhdan, A. P., 'Die Liste der Kinder des Alexios I in einer Moskauer Handschrift (GIM 53/147)' in R. Stiehl and H. Stier, eds., *Beiträge zur Alten Geschichte und deren Nachleben*, 2 vols. (Berlin, 1969–70), vol. II, 233–7.
'Das System der Bilder und Metaphern in den Werken Symeons des "Neuen" Theologen' in P. Hauptmann, ed., *Unser ganzes Leben Christus unserem Gott Überantworten* (Göttingen, 1982), 221–39; reprinted in A. P. Kazhdan, *Authors and Texts in Byzantium* (Aldershot, 1993), XIII.
'Some Problems in the Biography of John Mauropous', *JÖB*, 43 (1993), 87–111.
'Some Problems in the Biography of John Mauropous II', *Byzantion*, 65 (1995), 362–87.
A History of Byzantine Literature, 850–1000, ed. C. Angelidi (Athens, 2006).
Kazhdan, A. P. and S. Franklin, *Studies on Byzantine Literature in the Eleventh and Twelfth Centuries* (Berkeley, CA, 1985).
Kazhdan, A. P. and S. Ronchey, *L'aristocrazia bizantina dal principio dell' XI alla fine del XII secolo* (Palermo, 1997).
Kazhdan, A. P. and A. Wharton Epstein, *Change in Byzantine Culture in the Eleventh and Twelfth Centuries* (Berkeley, CA, 1985).
Kazhdan, A. P. et al., eds., *The Oxford Dictionary of Byzantium*, 3 vols. (Oxford, 1991).
Kees, R. J., *Die Lehre von der oikonomia Gottes in der Oratio catechetica Gregors von Nyssa* (Leiden, 1995).
Kepetzi, V., 'Empereur, piété et remission des péchés dans deux *ekphraseis* byzantines. Image et rhétorique', *DChAE*, 20 (1999), 231–44.
Keydell, R., 'Die griechische Poesie der Kaiserzeit', *Jahresbericht über die Fortschritte der klassischen Altertumswissenschaft*, 230 (1931), 41–161.
'Review of Hans Gerstinger, *Pamprepios von Panopolis*', *BZ*, 29 (1929–30), 290–3.
Kianka, F., 'The Apology of Demetrius Cydones', *Études byzantines*, 7 (1980), 57–71.
Kiapidou, E.-S., Η σύνοψη ιστοριών του Ιωάννη Σκυλίτζη και οι πηγές της *(811–1057)* (Athens, 2010).
Kidonopoulos, V., 'The Urban Physiognomy of Constantinople from the Latin Conquest Through the Palaiologan Era' in S. T. Brooks, ed., *Byzantium: Faith and Power (1261–1557)* (New York, NY, 2006), 98–117.
Kinney, D., 'The King, the Horse and the Cuckoo: Medieval Narrations of the Statue of Marcus Aurelius', *Word and Image*, 18 (2004), 372–98.

Kislinger, E., 'Vertauschte Notizen: Anna Komnene und die Chronologie der byzantinisch-normannischen Auseinandersetzung 1081–1085', *JÖB*, 59 (2009), 127–45.

Kitchener, H. H., *Trigonometrical Survey of the Island of Cyprus* (London, 1885).

Klein, H. A., R. G. Ousterhout, B. Pitarakis, eds., *The Kariye Camii Reconsidered* (Istanbul, 2011).

Klostermann, R. A., 'Heortodromion, ein Alterswerk des Nikodemos Hagiorites', *OrChrP*, 46 (1980), 446–62.

Koder, J., 'Liutprand von Cremona und die griechische Sprache' in J. Koder and T. Weber, eds., *Liutprand von Cremona in Konstantinopel* (Vienna, 1980), 1–70.

'Justinians Sieg über Salomon' in L. Bratziotes, ed., Θυμίαμα στη μνήμη της Λασκαρίνας Μπούρα (Athens, 1994), 135–42.

'Climatic Change in the Fifth and Sixth Centuries?' in P. Allen and E. M. Jeffreys, eds., *The Sixth Century: End or Beginning?* (Brisbane, 1996), 270–85.

'Romanos Melodos und sein Publikum: Zur Einbeziehung und Beeinflussung der Zuhörer durch das Kontakion', *AnzWien*, 134 (1999), 63–94.

'Der Titel der Hymnensammlung des Symeon Neos Theologos', *Palaeoslavica*, 10 (2002), 215–21.

'Anmerkungen zu dem Romanos-Papyrus Vindob. G 26225', *JÖB*, 53 (2003), 23–6.

'Romanos der Melode: Der Dichter hymnischer Bibelpredigten in Dokumenten seiner Zeit' in H. Froschauer, ed., *Ein Buch verändert die Welt: Älteste Zeugnisse der Heiligen Schrift aus der Zeit des frühen Christentums in Ägypten* (Vienna, 2003), 59–71.

'Γιατί ὁ Συμεών ὁ Νέος Θεολόγος ἔγραφε τούς ὕμνους του', *Nea Estia*, 160 (2006), 806–19.

'Ὁ Συμεών ὁ Νέος Θεολόγος καὶ οἱ ὕμνοι του' in A. Markopoulos, ed., Τέσσερα κείμενα για την ποίηση του Συμεών του Νέου Θεολόγου (Athens, 2008), 2–7.

'Imperial Propaganda in the Kontakia of Romanos the Melode', *DOP*, 62 (2008), 275–91.

'Positionen der Theologie des Romanos Melodos', *AnzWien*, 143 (2008), 25–56.

'Romanos Melodos' in C. G. Conticello and V. Conticello, eds., *La théologie byzantine et sa tradition* (Turnhout, 2002), vol. 1: 115–96.

Koder, J. and T. Weber, eds., *Liutprand von Cremona in Konstantinopel. Untersuchungen zum griechischen Sprachschatz und zu realienkundlichen Aussagen in seinen Werken* (Vienna, 1980).

Kokkinophtas, K. and I. Theocharides, Μετόχια της Ιεράς Μονής Κύκκου. Μονή των Ιερέων ή Αγία Μονή (Nicosia, 1999).

Kominis, A., Γρηγόριος Πάρδος, Μητροπολίτης Κορίνθου καὶ τὸ ἔργον αὐτοῦ (Athens, 1960).

Kominko, M., *The World of Kosmas: the Byzantine Illustrated Codices of the Christian Topography* (Cambridge, 2013).

Bibliography 681

Komodikes, K., Οι πληροφορίες των Βραχέων Χρονικών για την Κύπρο. Η κατάταξη και ο σχολιασμός τους (Nicosia, 2006).
Konstan, D., *Sexual Symmetry: Love in the Ancient Novel and Related Genres* (Princeton, NJ, 1994).
Korais, A., Άτακτα, ήγουν παντοδαπών εἰς τὴν ἀρχαίαν καὶ τὴν νέαν ἑλληνικήν γλώσσαν αὐτοσχεδίων σημειώσεων, καὶ τινῶν ἄλλων ὑπομνημάτων, αὐτοσχέδιος συναγωγή, 4 vols. (Paris, 1828–35).
Προλεγόμενα στοὺς ἀρχαίους Ἕλληνες συγγραφεῖς, vol. 1 (Athens, 1984).
Korakides, A., Ἡ περί τοῦ λόγου θεολογία τῶν κοντακίων Ρωμανοῦ τοῦ Μελωδοῦ (Athens, 1973).
Korenjak, M., *Publikum und Redner: Ihre Interaktion in der sophistischen Rhetorik der Kaiserzeit* (Munich, 2000).
Körte, A., 'Review of Hans Gerstinger, *Pamprepios von Panopolis*', *Archiv für Papyrusforschung*, 10 (1932), 25–8.
Kostes, K. P., Στον καιρό της πανώλης. Εικόνες από τις κοινωνίες της ελληνικής χερσονήσου, 1405–1905 αιώνας (Herakleion, 1995).
Koutloumousianos, B., ed., Πεντηκοστάριον χαρμόσυνον (Venice, 1837).
Krausmüller, D., 'Religious Instruction for Laypeople in Byzantium: Stephen of Nicomedia, Nicephoros Ouranos, and the Pseudo-Athanasian *Syntagma ad quemdam politicum*', *Byzantion*, 77 (2007), 239–50.
'Making the Most of Mary: the Cult of the Virgin in the Chalkoprateia from Late Antiquity to the Tenth Century' in L. Brubaker and M. Cunningham, eds., *The Cult of the Mother of God in Byzantium: Texts and Images* (Farnham, 2012), 219–45.
Kresten, O., 'Phantomgestalten in der byzantinischen Literaturgeschichte', *JÖB*, 25 (1976), 213–17.
Kresten, O. and A. E. Müller, eds., *Samtherrschaft. Legitimationsprinzip und kaiserlicher Urkundentitel in Byzanz in der ersten Hälfte des 10. Jahrhunderts* (Vienna, 1995).
Kriaras, E., Λεξικό της μεσαιωνικής ελληνικής δημώδους γραμματείας, τόμος ια΄ (Thessalonike, 1990).
Krivocheine, B., *Dans la lumière du Christ: Saint Syméon le nouveau théologien, 949–1022, vie, spiritualité, doctrine* (Chevetogne, 1980).
Krueger, D., 'Diogenes the Cynic among the Fourth Century Fathers', *VigChr*, 47 (1993), 29–49.
Writing and Holiness. The Practice of Authorship in the Early Christian East (Philadelphia, PA, 2004).
'Homoerotic Spectacle and the Monastic Body in Symeon the New Theologian' in V. Burrus and C. Keller, eds., *Toward a Theology of Eros: Transfiguring Passion at the Limits of Discipline* (New York, NY, 2006), 99–118.
Krumbacher, K., ed., *Mittelgriechische Sprichwörter* (Munich, 1893); reprinted (Hildesheim, 1969).
Geschichte der byzantinischen Litteratur von Justinian bis zum Ende des oströmischen Reiches (527–1453), second edition (Munich, 1897).

Kustas, G., *Studies in Byzantine Rhetoric* (Thessalonike, 1973).
Kyriakides, S. P., 'Grégoire Henri. Inscriptions historiques byzantines. Ancyre et les Arabes sous Michel Ie Ivrogne (Byzantion iv 437-468)', Λαογραφία, 10 (1929), 623–62.
Laga, C., 'Entering the Library of Jacobus Monachus. The Exemplar of Jacobus' Quotations from the Commentary on the Song of Songs by Gregory of Nyssa', in K. Demoen and J. Vereecken, eds., *La spiritualité de l'univers byzantin dans le verbe et l'image* (Turnhout, 1997), 151–61,
Laiou, A., 'The Role of Women in Byzantine Society', *JÖB*, 31 (1981), 233–60.
'The Peasant as Donor (13th–14th centuries)' in J.-M. Spieser and E. Yota, eds., *Donation et donateurs dans le monde byzantin. Actes du colloque de l'Université de Fribourg, 13–15 mars 2008* (Paris, 2012), 107–24.
Lakoff, G., *Women, Fire, and Dangerous Things: What Categories Reveal about the Mind* (Chicago, IL, 1987).
Lampakes, S., ed., Γεώργιος Παχυμέρης: Πρωτέκδικος και Δικαιοφύλαξ (Athens, 2004).
Lampe, G. W. H., *A Patristic Greek Lexicon* (Oxford, 1961).
Lampros, S., 'Πτωχομάγιστρος, όχι Πτωχομάχης', *NE*, 1 (1904), 237–8.
Lampsides, O., 'Die Entblössung der Muse Kalliope in einem byzantinischen Epigramm', *JÖB*, 47 (1997), 107–10.
Laniado, A., 'Jean d'Antioche et les débuts de la révolte de Vitalien' in P. Blaudeau and P. Van Nuffelen, eds., *L'historiographie tardo-antique et la transmission des savoirs* (Berlin, 2015), 349–70.
La Porte-du Theil, F. J. G., 'Notices et extraits d'un volume de la Bibliothèque nationale, côté MCCIX parmi les manuscrits grecs, et contentant les opuscules et les lettres anedcotes de Théodore l'Hirtacènien', *Notices et extraits des manuscrits de la Bibliothèque nationale et autres bibliothèques*, 6 (1800), 1–48.
Larkin, M., *Al-Mutanabbi: Voice of the 'Abbasid Poetic Ideal* (Oxford, 2008).
Lascaris, M., 'La prosopographie de l'empire byzantin, Appendix, La famille byzantine des Aaron et les homonymes', *EO*, 33 (1934), 385–95.
Lassus, J., *L'illustration byzantine du livre des rois*, Vaticanus Graecus 333 (Paris, 1973).
Laurent, J., *L'Arménie entre Byzance et l'Islam depuis la conquête arabe jusqu'en 886 (nouvelle édition revue et mise à jour par M. Canard)* (Lisbon, 1980).
Laurent, V., 'Princes bulgares dans la sigillographie byzantine', *EO*, 33 (1934), 413–27.
Lauritzen, F., 'Paraphrasis as Interpretation. Psellos and a Canon of Cosmas the Melodist (Poem 24 Westerink)', *Byzantina*, 33 (2014), 61–74.
Lauxtermann, M., 'John Geometres, Poet and Soldier', *Byzantion*, 68 (1998), 356–80.
'Byzantine Poetry and the Paradox of Basil II's Reign' in P. Magdalino, ed., *Byzantium in the Year 1000* (Leiden, 2003), 233–70.
Byzantine Poetry from Pisides to Geometres: Texts and Contexts (Vienna, 2003).
Lauxtermann, M. and I. Toth, eds., *Inscribing Texts in Byzantium: Continuities and Transformations* (forthcoming).

Lavagnini, R., trans., *I fatti di Troia: L'Iliade bizantina del cod. Paris. Suppl. Gr. 926* (Palermo, 1988).
'Tales of the Trojan War: Achilles and Paris in Medieval Greek Literature' in C. Cupane and B. Krönung, eds., *Fictional Storytelling in the Medieval Eastern Mediterrenian and Beyond* (Leiden, 2016), 234–59.
Leib, B., 'Deux inédits byzantins sur les azymes au début du XIIe siècle', *OrChr* II/3 (1924), 244–63.
Rome, Kiev et Byzance à la fin du XIe siècle: Rapports religieux des Latins et des Gréco-Russes sous le pontificat d'Urbain II (1088–1099) (New York, NY, 1924; reprint 1968).
Lemerle, P., *Cinq études sur le XIe siècle byzantin* (Paris, 1977).
Le premier humanisme byzantin. Notes et remarques sur enseignement et culture à Byzance des origines au Xe siècle (Paris, 1971).
Lenz, F. W., *Aristeidesstudien* (Berlin, 1964).
Leppin, H., *Justinian: das christliche Experiment* (Stuttgart, 2011).
Levy, P. 'Michaelis Pselli de Gregorii Theologi charactere iudicium: accedit eiusdem de Ioannis Chrysostomi charactere iudicium ineditum', unpublished PhD dissertation, Leipzig (1912).
Lilie, R.-J., *Byzantium and the Crusader States, 1096–1204* (Oxford, 1993).
Lilie, R.-J. et al., eds., *Prosopographie der mittelbyzantinischen Zeit (PmbZ): Erste Abteilung (641–867)*, 6 vols. (Berlin, 1999–2002).
et al., eds., *PmbZ: Zweite Abteilung (867–1025). Prolegomena* (Berlin, 2009).
et al., eds., *PmbZ: Zweite Abteilung (867–1025)*, 8 vols. (Berlin, 2013).
Linardou, K., 'Mary and her Books in the Kokkinobaphos Manuscripts: Female Literacy or Visual Strategies of Narration?', *DChAE* 29 (2008), 35–48.
Lingas, A., 'The Liturgical Place of the Kontakion in Constantinople' in C. Akentiev, ed., *Liturgy, Architecture and Art in the Byzantine World* (St Petersburg, 1995), 50–7.
Litavrin, G. G., 'Три письма Михаила Пселла Катакалону Кекавмену', *RESEE*, 7 (1969), 455–68.
Litsas, E. K., 'Palaeographical Researches in the Lavra Library on Mount Athos', Ἑλληνικά, 50 (2000), 217–30.
Littlewood, A. R., 'An "Icon of the Soul": the Byzantine Letter', *Visible Language*, 10 (1976), 197–226.
'A Statistical Survey of the Incidence of Repeated Quotations in Selected Byzantine Letter-writers' in J. Duffy and J. Peradotto, eds., *Gonimos: Neoplatonic and Byzantine Studies Presented to Leendert G. Westerink at 75* (Buffalo, 1988), 137–54.
ed., *Originality in Byzantine Literature, Art and Music* (Oxford, 1995).
'Gardens of the Palaces' in H. Maguire, ed., *Byzantine Court Culture from 829 to 1204* (Washington, D. C., 1997), 13–38.
Liubarskii, I., 'Об источниках "Алексиады" Анны Комниной', *VizVrem*, 25 (1964), 99–120.
'Nikephoros Phokas in Byzantine Historical Writings,' *BSl*, 54 (1993), 245–53.

'Why is the *Alexiad* a Masterpiece of Byzantine Literature?' in J. O. Rosenqvist, ed., Λειμών: *Studies presented to Lennart Rydén on his Sixty-Fifth Birthday* (Uppsala, 1996), 127–41.

Livanos, C., 'Exile and Return in John Mauropus, Poem 47', *BMGS*, 32 (2008), 38–49.

Greek Tradition and Latin Influence in the Work of George Scholarios (Piscataway, NJ, 2006).

Livrea, E., 'Due note a papyiri tardoepici', *ZPE*, 17 (1975), 35–6.

'Pamprepio ed il P. Vindob. 29788A-C', *ZPE*, 25 (1977), 121–34.

'Nuovi contributi al testo dei Frr. 1, 2 E 4 di Pamprepio (xxxv Heitsch)', *Rivista di Filologia*, 106 (1978), 281–7.

'Per una nuova edizione di Pamprepio di Panopoli (P. Vindob. 29788 A–C)' in J. Bingen and G. Nachtergael, eds., *Actes du xve Congrès international de papyrologie (Bruxelles-Louvain, 29 août–3 septembre 1977)*, 4 vols. (Brussels, 1978–9), vol. III, 69–77.

Loerke, W. C., et al., eds., *Byzantine Books and Bookmen: A Dumbarton Oaks Colloquium* (Washington, D. C., 1975).

Loud, G. A., 'Anna Komnena and her Sources for the Normans of Southern Italy' in I. Wood and G. A. Loud, eds., *Church and Chronicle in the Middle Ages: Essays Presented to John Taylor* (London, 1991), 41–57.

The Age of Robert Guiscard: Southern Italy and the Norman Conquest (Harlow, 2000).

Luttrell, A., 'The Hospitallers in Cyprus: 1310–1378', Κυπριακαί Σπουδαί, 50 (1986), 155–84.

Maas, M., ed., *The Cambridge Companion to the Age of Justinian* (Cambridge, 2005).

Maas, P., 'Review: Hans Gerstinger, *Pamprepios von Panopolis*', *Gnomon*, 5 (1929), 250–2.

Greek Metre, trans. H. Lloyd-Jones (Oxford, 1962).

'Sorti della letteratura antica a Bisanzio' in G. Pasquali, ed., *Storia della tradizione e critica del testo*, second edition (Florence, 1962), 487–92.

MacAlister, S., *Dreams and Suicides: The Greek Novel from Antiquity to the Byzantine Empire* (New York, NY, 1996).

MacCoull, L., *Dioscorus of Aphrodito: His Work and His World* (Berkeley, CA, 1988).

Mackridge, P., 'An Editorial Problem in Medieval Greek Texts: the Position of the Object Clitic Pronoun in the Escorial Digenes Akrites' in N. M. Panayiotakis, ed., Αρχές της νεοελληνικής λογοτεχνίας, 2 vols. (Venice, 1993), vol. II, 325–42.

'The Position of the Weak Object Pronoun in Medieval and Modern Greek', Язык и речевая деятельность, 3 (2000), 133–51.

Macrides, R., 'Nomos and Kanon, on Paper and in Court' in R. Morris, ed., *Church and People in Byzantium* (Birmingham, 1990), 61–85.

'The Historian in the History' in C. N. Constantinides, N. M. Panagiotakis, E. M. Jeffreys and I. Martin, eds., Φιλέλλην: *Studies in Honour of Robert Browning* (Venice, 1996), 205–24.

'The Pen and the Sword: Who Wrote the Alexiad?' in T. Gouma-Peterson, ed., *Anna Komnene and Her Times* (New York, 2000), 63–81.
ed., *History as Literature in Byzantium. Papers from the Fortieth Spring Symposium of Byzantine Studies, University of Birmingham, April 2007* (Farnham, 2010).
'Ceremonies and the City: the Court in Fourteenth-century Constantinople' in J. Duindam, T. Artan and M. Kunt, eds., *Royal Courts in Dynastic States and Empires: A Global Perspective* (Leiden, 2011), 217–35.
Madan, F. et al., *A Summary Catalogue of Western Manuscripts in the Bodleian Library at Oxford which have not hitherto been Catalogued in the Quarto Series*, 7 vols. (Oxford, 1895–1953); revised edition (Munich, 1980).
Magdalino, P., 'Byzantine Snobbery' in M. Angold, *The Byzantine Aristocracy, IX–XIII Centuries* (Oxford, 1984), 173–201.
'Basil I, Leo VI and the Feast of the Prophet Elijah', *JÖB*, 38 (1988), 193–6.
'Honour among Romaioi: the Framework of Social Values in the World of Digenis Akrites and Kekaumenos', *BMGS*, 13 (1989), 183–218.
'Eros the King and the King of Amours: Some Observations on "Hysmine and Hysminias"', *DOP*, 46 (1992), 197–204.
The Empire of Manuel I Komnenos, 1143–1180 (Cambridge, 1993).
'*Digenes Akrites* and Byzantine Literature: the Twelfth-century Background to the Grottaferrata version' in R. Beaton and D. Ricks, eds., *Digenes Akrites: New Approaches to Byzantine Heroic Poetry* (Aldershot, 1993), 1–25.
ed., *New Constantines: The Rhythm of Imperial Renewal in Byzantium, 4th–13th Centuries* (Aldershot, 1994).
'The Reform Edict of 1107' in M. Mullett and D. Smythe, eds., *Alexios I Komnenos* (Belfast, 1996) 199–218.
'"What We Heard in the Lives of the Saints We Have Seen with our Own Eyes": the Holy Man as Literary Text in Tenth-century Constantinople' in J. Howard Johnston and P. A. Hayward, eds., *The Cult of Saints in Late Antiquity and the Early Middle Ages: Essays on the Contribution of Peter Brown* (Oxford, 1999), 83–112.
'The Pen of the Aunt: Echoes of the Mid-twelfth Century in the *Alexiad*' in T. Gouma-Peterson, ed., *Anna Komnene and Her Times* (New York, 2000), 15–43.
ed., *Byzantium in the Year 1000* (Leiden, 2003).
'Prosopography and Byzantine Identity' in A. M. Cameron, ed., *Fifty Years of Prosopography: The Later Roman Empire, Byzantium and Beyond* (Oxford, 2003), 41–56.
'Constantinopolitana' in I. Ševčenko and I. Hutter, eds., *AETOS: Studies in honour of Cyril Mango* (Stuttgart, 1998), 220–32; reprinted in P. Magdalino, *Studies on the History and Topography of Byzantine Constantinople* (Aldershot, 2007).
'Pseudo-Kodinos' Constantinople' in P. Magdalino, *Studies on the History and Topography of Byzantine Constantinople* (Aldershot, 2007), Item XII, 1–14.

Studies on the History and Topography of Byzantine Constantinople (Aldershot, 2007).
'Cultural Change? The Context of Byzantine Poetry from Geometres to Prodromos' in F. Bernard and K. Demoen, eds., *Poetry and Its Contexts in Eleventh-Century Byzantium* (Farnham, 2012), 19–36.
'Knowledge in Authority and Authorised History: the Imperial Intellectual Programme of Leo VI and Constantine VII' in P. Armstrong, ed., *Authority in Byzantium* (Farnham, 2013), 200–7.
Magdalino, P. and R. S. Nelson, 'The Emperor in Byzantine Art of the Twelfth Century', *ByzF*, 8 (1982), 123–83.
Magdalino, P. and R. S. Nelson, eds., *The Old Testament in Byzantium* (Washington, D. C., 2013).
Maguire, E. D. and H. Maguire, *Other Icons: Art and Power in Byzantine Secular Culture* (Princeton, NJ, 2007).
Maguire, H., 'Epigrams, Art and the "Macedonian Renaissance"', *DOP*, 48 (1994), 105–15.
'Enamel Plaques and Medallions: "The Crown of Constantine IX Monomachos,"' in H. Evans and W. Wixom, eds., *The Glory of Byzantium: Art and Culture of the Middle Byzantine Era, AD 843–1261* (New York, 1997), 210–12.
'The Profane Aesthetic in Byzantine Art and Literature', *DOP*, 53 (1999), 189–205.
'Other Icons: the Classical Nude in Byzantine Bone and Ivory Carvings', *JWalt*, 62 (2004), 9–20.
'Art and Text' in E. M. Jeffreys, J. Haldon, R. Cormack, eds., *The Oxford Handbook of Byzantine Studies* (Oxford, 2008), 721–30.
'The Philopation as a Setting for Imperial Ceremonial and Display' in C. Bakirtzis, N. Zekos and X. Moniaros, eds., *Byzantine Thrace: Evidence and Remains; Komotini 18–22 April 2007:*, *ByzF*, 30 (2011), 71–82.
Maisano, R., 'La funzione letteraria della Bibbia nei testi bizantini' in *Pré-Actes XXe Congrès International des études byzantines, Collège de France-Sorbonne, 19–25 août 2001*, 3 vols. (Paris, 2001), vol. 1, 38–46.
'Funzione letteraria delle citazioni bibliche nelle preghiere dei contaci di Romano il Melodo' in N. Grisanti, ed., *Ad contemplandam sapientiam: studi di filologia letteratura e storia in memoria di Sandro Leanza* (Rubbettino, 2004), 369–77.
'La funzione letteraria della Bibbia in Niceta Coniata' in A. Garzya, ed., *Spirito e forme nella letteratura bizantina* (Naples, 2006), 47–64.
Maiuri, A., 'Un poeta mimografo bizantino', *Atene e Roma*, 13 (1910), 17–26.
Malamut, E., 'L'image byzantine des Petchénègues', *BZ*, 88 (1995), 105–47.
Maltese, E. V., *École et enseignement à Byzance* (Paris, 1987).
'Donne e letteratura a Bisanzio: per una storia della cultura femminile' in Francesco de Martino, ed., *Rose di Pieria* (Bari, 1991), 339–93.
'Lettura di Cassia' in F. de Martino, ed., *Rose di Pieria* (Bari, 1991), 339–61.
'Michele Psello commentatore di Gregorio di Nazianzo: note per una lettura dei Theologica', *Syndesmos. Studi in onore di Rosario Anastasi* (Catania, 1994), 289–309.

'Una contemporanea di Fozio, Cassia: osservazioni sui versi profani' in M. Salvador, ed., *La poesia tardoantica e medievale* (Alessandria, 2001), 71–83.

Mamone, K., "Ἐπὶ τοῦ βίου καὶ τοῦ ἔργου Μάρκου τοῦ Εὐγενικοῦ', Ἀθηνᾶ, 59 (1955), 198–221.

Μᾶρκος ὁ Εὐγενικός, Βίος καὶ ἔργον (Athens, 1954).

Mango, C., *The Brazen House: A Study of the Vestibule of the Imperial Palace of Constantinople* (Copenhagen, 1959).

'The Conciliar Edict of 1166', *DOP*, 17 (1963), 317–30.

'The Availability of Books in the Byzantine Empire, A.D. 750–850' in W. C. Loerke et al., eds., *Byzantine Books and Bookmen* (Washington, D. C., 1975), 39–43.

Byzantine Literature as a Distorting Mirror: an Inaugural Lecture Delivered Before the University of Oxford on 21 May 1974 (Oxford, 1975).

The Art of the Byzantine Empire, 312–1453 (Toronto, 1986).

'Review of C. L. Striker and Y. Doğan Kuban, eds., *Kalenderhane in Istanbul: The Buildings*', *BZ*, 91 (1998), 586–90.

Mango, C. and M. Mundell Mango, 'Cameos in Byzantium' in M. Henig and M. Vickers, eds., *Cameos in Context* (Oxford, 1993), 57–76.

Manolova, D., 'Nikephoros Gregoras' *Philomathes* and *Phlorentios*' in A. D. E. Cameron and N. Gaul, eds., *Dialogues and Debates from Late Antiquity to Late Byzantium* (London, 2017), 203–19.

Manuli, P. and M. Vegetti, eds., *Le opere psicologiche di Galeno: atti del terzo Colloquio galenico internazionale, Pavia, 10–12 settembre 1986* (Napoli, 1988).

Marangou, L., *Bone Carvings from Egypt* (Tübingen, 1976).

Marciniak, P., 'Byzantine *Theatron* – a Place of Performance?' in M. Grünbart, ed., *Theatron: Rhetorische Kultur in Spätantike und Mittelalter* (Berlin, 2007), 277–85.

Markopoulos, A., 'La critique des textes au xe siècle. Le témoignage du Professeur anonyme', *JÖB*, 32 (1982), 31–7.

'L'épistolaire du "professeur anonyme" de Londres: Contribution prosopographique', Ἀφιέρωμα στον Νίκο Σβορώνο, 2 vols. (Rethymno, 1986), vol. 1, 139–44.

'An Anonymous Laudatory Poem in Honor of Basil I', *DOP*, 46 (1992), 225–32.

'Constantine the Great in Macedonian Historiography: Models and Approaches' in P. Magdalino, ed., *New Constantines: The Rhythm of Imperial Renewal in Byzantium, 4th–13th Centuries* (Aldershot, 1994), 159–70.

'Überlegungen zu Leben und Werk des Alexandros von Nikaia', *JÖB*, 44 (1994), 313–26.

'Byzantine History Writing at the End of the First P. Millenium' in P. Magdalino, ed., *Byzantium in the Year 1000* (Leiden, 2003), 183–93.

History and Literature of Byzantium in the 9th–10th Centuries (Aldershot, 2004).

'De la structure de l'école byzantine: Le maître, les livres et le processus éducatif' in B. Mondrain, ed., *Lire et écrire à Byzance* (Paris, 2006), 85–96

'Vergöttlichung und Erlösung. Versuch einer Lektüre des Hymnos Nr. 13 von Symeon Neos Theologos' in K. Belke, E. Kislinger, A. Külzer and M. A.

Stassinopoulou, eds., *Byzantina Mediterranea, Festschrift für Johannes Koder zum 65. Geburtstag* (Vienna, 2007), 435–44.

'Education' in E. M. Jeffreys, J. Haldon and R. Cormack, eds., *The Oxford Handbook of Byzantine Studies* (Oxford, 2008), 785–95.

ed., Τέσσερα κείμενα για την ποίηση του Συμεών του Νέου Θεολόγου (Athens, 2008).

'From Narrative Historiography to Historical Biography: New Trends in Byzantine Historical Writing in the 10th–11th Centuries', *BZ*, 102 (2009), 697–715.

'Teachers and Textbooks in Byzantium Ninth to Eleventh Centuries' in S. Steckel, N. Gaul, M. Grünbart, eds., *Networks of Learning: Perspectives on Scholars in Byzantine East and Latin West* (Zurich, 2014), 3–15.

Markopoulos, T., *The Future in Greek: From Ancient to Medieval* (New York, NY, 2009).

Martin, A., 'L'histoire ecclésiastique intéresse-t-elle Malalas?' in J. Beaucamp, ed., *Recherches sur la chronique de Jean Malalas I* (Paris, 2004), 85–102.

Martin-Hisard, B., 'Domination arabe et libertés arméniennes (viie–ixe siècle)' in G. Dédéyan, ed., *Histoire du peuple arménien* (Paris, 2008), 213–41.

Martini, A. and D. Bassi, *Catalogus codicum graecorum Bibliothecae Ambrosianae*, 2 vols. (Milan, 1906).

Masaouti, G., Ἀνωνύμου: Λόγος διηγηματικὸς περὶ τῆς ἐν ἀρχῇ παραγωγῆς καὶ οἰκοδομῆς τοῦ πανσέπτου ναοῦ τῆς πανυμνήτου Θεοτόκου τῶν Κύρου (BHG 479i), ἀπὸ τὸ χειρόγραφο, Ἄθως Ἰβήρων 153 (Λάμπρος 4548)', unpublished MA Thesis, University of Ioannina (2017).

Mavroudi, M., *A Byzantine Book on Dream Interpretation: The Oneirocriticon of Achmet and Its Arabic Sources* (Leiden, 2002).

Mayer, A., 'Psellos' Rede über den rhetorischen Charakter des Gregor von Nazianz', *BZ*, 20 (1911), 27–100.

Mazzucchi, C. M., 'Ambrosianus C 222 inf. (Graecus 886): Il codice e il suo autore: parte seconda: l'autore,' *Aevum*, 78 (2004), 411–40.

McCabe, A., *A Byzantine Encyclopaedia of Horse Medicine: The Sources, Compilation and Transmission of the Hippiatrica* (Oxford, 2007).

McCail, R. C., 'P. Gr. Vindob. 29788C: hexameter encomium on an un-named emperor', *JHS*, 98 (1978), 38–63.

McCredy, W. W., 'Isidore, the Antipodeans and the Shape of the Earth', *Isis*, 87 (1996), 108–27.

McCrindle, J. W., *The Christian Topography of Kosmas, an Egyptian Monk* (London, 1897).

McGeer, E., 'Tradition and Reality in the *Taktika* of Nikephoros Ouranos', *DOP*, 45 (1991), 129–40.

'Two Military Orations of Constantine VII' in J. W. Nesbitt, ed., *Byzantine Authors: Literary Activities and Preoccupations* (Leiden, 2003), 111–35.

McGuckin, J. A., 'Symeon the New Theologian (d. 1022) and Byzantine Monasticism' in A. Bryer and M. Cunningham, eds., *Mount Athos and Byzantine Monasticism* (Aldershot, 1996), 17–35.

'The Luminous Vision in Eleventh-century Byzantium: Interpreting the Biblical and Theological Paradigms of St. Symeon the New Theologian' in M. Mullett and A. Kirby, eds., *Work and Worship at the Theotokos Evergetis 1050–1200* (Belfast, 1997), 90–123.

McKeon, R., 'Rhetoric in the Middle Ages' in R. S. Crane, ed., *Critics and Criticism* (Chicago, IL, 1952), 260–96.

Medvedev, I., 'The So-called *Theatra* as a Form of Communication of the Byzantine Intellectuals in the 14th and 15th Centuries' in N. G. Moschonas, ed., Πρακτικά τοῦ Β΄ Διεθνοῦς Συμποσίου «Η ἐπικοινωνία στὸ Βυζάντιο» (Athens, 1993), 227–35.

Meier, M., 'Σταυρωθεὶς δι' ἡμᾶς – Der Aufstand gegen Anastasios im Jahr 512', *Millennium*, 4 (2007), 157–237.

Meier, M., C. Radtki and F. Schulz, eds., *Die Weltchronik des Johannes Malalas: Autor – Werk – Überlieferung* (Stuttgart, 2016).

'Giambi di Giovanni Tzetzes contro una donna schedografa' in A. Acconcia Longo, ed., *Collectanea Byzantina*, 2 vols. (Bari, 1970), vol. 1, 555–6.

Mergiali, S., *L'enseignement et les lettrés pendant l'époque des Paléologues (1261–1453)* (Athens, 1996).

Mette, H. J., *Sphairopolia: Untersuchungen zur Kosmologie der Krates von Pergamon* (Munich, 1936).

Metzler, K., 'Genesiskommentierung bei Origenes und Prokop von Gaza', *Adamantius*, 11 (2005), 114–23.

Meunier, F., *Le Roman byzantin du XIIe siècle: à la découverte d'un nouveau monde?* (Paris, 2007).

Michel, A., *Histoire de l'art depuis les premiers temps chrétiens jusqu'à nos jours*, 8 vols. (Paris, 1905–29).

Migliori, F., 'La figura di Maria Vergine e Madre di Dio negli Inni di Romano il Melode', *Theotokos*, 15 (2007), 37–76.

Miguélez Cavero, L., *Poems in Context: Greek Poetry in the Egyptian Thebaid, 200–600 AD* (New York, NY, 2008).

Miller, T.S., *The Orphans of Byzantium: Child Welfare in the Christian Empire* (Washington, D. C., 2003).

Mineva, E., Το υμνογραφικό έργο του Μάρκου Ευγενικού (Athens, 2004).

Minniti Colonna, M., 'De Musaeo', *Vichiana*, 5 (1976), 65–86.

'Sul testo e la lingua di Coluto', *Vichiana*, 8 (1979), 70–93.

Mitrea, M., 'A Late Byzantine πεπαιδευμένος: Maximos Neamonites and his Letter Collection', *JÖB*, 64 (2014): 197–223.

Moennig, U., "Ἔρως, μοίρα, ιστορία, θάνατος. Διαπλεκόμενοι θεματικοί άξονες στη Βυζαντινή Ιλιάδα' in S. Kaklamanis and M. Paschalis, eds., *Η πρόσληψη της αρχαιότητας στο Βυζαντινό και νεοελληνικό μυθιστόρημα* (Athens, 2005), 73–85.

'Κοινοί τόποι του υστεροβυζαντινού μυθιστορήματος στη Διήγηση Αλεξάνδρου και Σεμίραμης' in E. M. Jeffreys and M. J. Jeffreys, eds., *Neograeca Medii Aevi V: Αναδρομικά και προδρομικά: Approaches to Texts in Early Modern Greek* (Oxford, 2005), 259–69.

'Biographical Arrangement as a Generic Feature and its Multiple Use in Late Byzantine Narratives: an Exploration of the Field', *Phrasis*, 51 (2010), 103–47.

'Literary Genres and Mixture of Generic Features in Late Byzantine Fictional Writing' in P. Roilos, ed., *Medieval Greek Storytelling: Fictionality and Narrative in Byzantium* (Wiesbaden, 2014), 163–82.

'Romeo und Julia in Byzanz. Oder: Worum geht es eigentlich in der Byzantinischen Achilleis' in U. Moennig, ed., *... ὡς ἀθύρματα παῖδας. Festschrift für Hans Eideneier* (Berlin, 2016), 121–33.

Moffatt, A., 'Schooling in the Iconoclast Centuries' in A. Bryer and J. Herrin, eds., *Iconoclasm* (Birmingham, 1977), 85–92.

'A Record of Public Buildings and Monuments' in Jeffreys et al., *Studies in John Malalas* (1990), 87–110.

Mohler, L., *Kardinal Bessarion als Theologe, Humanist und Staatsmann*, 4 vols. (Paderborn, 1923–42).

Momigliano, A., 'Gli Anicii e la storiografia latina del VI sec. D. C.' in A. Momigliano, *Secondo contributo alla storia degli studi classici*, second edition (Rome, 1984), 231-53.

Mondrain, B., ed., *Lire et écrire à Byzance* (Paris, 2006).

Montana, F., 'L'Inizio del lessico di Teodosio Grammatico ai canoni liturgici nel Laur. 57.48', *Rivista di filologia e di instruzione classica*, 123 (1995), 193–200.

Moore, H., 'From the Greek', *TLS* (8 July, 2005), 5–6.

Morales, H., 'Gender and Identity in Musaeus' *Hero and Leander*' in R. Miles, ed., *Constructing Identities in Late Antiquity* (New York, NY, 1999), 41–69.

Moravcsik, G., 'Sagen und Legenden über Kaiser Basileios I', *DOP*, 15 (1961), 59–126.

Byzantinoturcica, second edition, 2 vols. (Berlin, 1958).

Moretti, G., 'The Other World and the Antipodes: the Myth of the Unknown Countries Between Antiquity and the Renaissance' in W. Haase, ed., *The Classical Tradition and the Americas* (Berlin, 1993), 241–84

Morris, R., *Monks and Laymen in Byzantium, 843–1118* (Cambridge, 1995).

Moser, A., Άποψη και χρόνος στην ιστορία της ελληνικής (Athens, 2009).

Mullett, M. E., 'The Classical Tradition in the Byzantine Letter' in M. E. Mullett and R. Scott, eds., *Byzantium and the Classical Tradition* (Birmingham, 1981), 75–93.

'Aristocracy and Patronage in the Literary Circles of Comnenian Constantinople' in M. Angold, ed., *The Byzantine Aristocracy, IX–XIII Centuries* (Oxford, 1984), 173–201.

'The Imperial Vocabulary of Alexios I Komnenos', in M. E. Mullett and D. Smythe, eds., *Alexios I Komnenos* (Belfast, 1996), 367–70.

Theophylact of Ochrid: Reading the Letters of a Byzantine Archbishop (Aldershot, 1997).

'Novelisation in Byzantium: Narrative after the Revival of Fiction' in J. Burke, ed., *Byzantine Narrative: Papers in Honour of Roger Scott* (Melbourne, 2006), 1–28.
'No Drama, No Poetry, No Fiction, No Readership, No Literature' in L. James, ed., *A Companion to Byzantium* (Chichester, 2010), 227–38.
'Whose Muses? Two Advice Poems Attributed to Alexios I Komnenos' in P. Odorico, ed., *La face cachée de la littérature byzantine. Le texte en tant que message immédiat* (Paris, 2012), 195–220.
'Experiencing the Byzantine Text, Experiencing the Byzantine Tent' in M. Jackson and C. Nesbitt, eds., *Experiencing Byzantium* (Farnham, 2013), 269–91.
'Tented Ceremony' in A. Beihammer, S. Constantinou and M. Parani, eds., *Court Ceremonies and Rituals of Power in the Medieval Mediterranean* (Leiden, 2013), 487–513.
'Performing Court Literature in Medieval Byzantium: Tales Told in Tents' in M. A. Pomerantz and E. Birge Vitz, eds., *Courts and Performance in the Pre-Modern Middle East* (New York, NY, 2017).
Mullett, M. E. and R. Scott, eds., *Byzantium and the Classical Tradition* (Birmingham, 1981).
Mullett, M. E. and D. Smythe, eds., *Alexios I Komnenos: Papers of the Second Belfast Byzantine International Colloquium, 14–16 April 1989. 1: Papers* (Belfast, 1996).
Nardelli, M. L., 'L'esametro di Colluto', *JÖB*, 32 (1982), 324–34.
Nathan, G. and L. Garland, eds., *Basileia: Essays on Imperium and Culture in Honour of E. M. and M. J. Jeffreys* (Brisbane, 2011).
Nelson, R., 'Emphatic Vision: Looking at and with a Performative Byzantine Miniature', *Art History*, 30 (2007), 489–502.
Nelson, R. S. and D. Krueger, eds., *The New Testament in Byzantium* (Washington, D. C., 2016).
Nerantze-Barbaze, B., 'Οι βυζαντινοί ταβουλλάριοι', Ελληνικά, 35 (1984), 261–74.
Nesseris, I., 'Η Παιδεία στην Κωνσταντινούπολη κατά τον 12ο αιώνα', unpublished PhD thesis, University of Ioannina (2014).
Neville, L., 'A History of the Caesar John Doukas in Nikephoros Bryennios's *Material for History?*', *BMGS*, 32 (2008) 168–88.
Heroes and Romans in Twelfth-century Byzantium: The Material for History of Nikephoros Bryennios (Cambridge, 2012).
Nicks, F. K., 'Literary Culture in the Reign of Anastasius' in S. Mitchell and G. Greatrex, eds., *Ethnicity and Culture in Late Antiquity* (Swansea, 2000), 183–203.
Nicol, D. M., 'The Confessions of a Bogus Patriarch: Paul Tagaris Palaiologos, Orthodox Patriarch of Jerusalem and Catholic Patriarch of Constantinople in the Fourteenth Century', *JEH*, 21 (1970), 289–99.
'Byzantine Political Thought' in J. H. Burns, ed., *The Cambridge History of Medieval Political Thought c. 350–c. 1450* (Cambridge 1988), 49–80.

Nicolaou-Konnari, A., 'Greeks' in A. Nicolaou-Konnari, and Schabel, eds., *Cyprus: Society and Culture: 1191–1374* (Leiden, 2005).
Nicolaou-Konnari, A. and C. Schabel, eds., *Cyprus: Society and Culture 1191–1374* (Leiden, 2005), 13–62.
Nilsson, I., *Erotic Pathos, Rhetorical Pleasure: Narrative Technique and Mimesis in Eumathios Makrembolites' Hysmine and Hysminias* (Uppsala, 2001).
Nilsson, I., ed., 'Narrating Images in Byzantine Literature: the Ekphraseis of Konstantinos Manasses', *JÖB*, 55 (2005), 121–46.
    ed., *Plotting with Eros: Essays on the Poetics of Love and the Erotics of Reading* (Copenhagen, 2009).
Nilsson, I. and E. Nyström, 'To Compose, Read, and Use a Byzantine Text: Aspects of the Chronicle of Constantine Manasses', *BMGS*, 33 (2009), 42–60.
Noble, P., 'Alis and the Problem of Time in *Cligés*', *Medium Aevum*, 39 (1970), 28–31.
Nunn, V., 'The Encheirion as Adjunct to the Icon in the Middle Byzantine Period', *BMGS*, 10 (1986), 73–102.
Nuttall, P., 'Dancing, Love and the Beautiful Game: a New Interpretation of a Group of Fifteenth-century "Gaming" Boxes', *Renaissance Studies*, 24 (2010), 119–41.
Oakeshott, W., *The Mosaics of Rome* (New York, NY, 1967).
O'Brien, D. O., 'Derived Light and Eclipses in the Fifth Century', *JHS*, 88 (1968), 114–27.
Odorico, P. and P. A. Agapitos, eds., *Pour une 'nouvelle' histoire de la littérature byzantine: problèmes, méthodes, approches, propositions* (Paris, 2002).
Oikonomidès, N., 'Le support matériel des documents byzantins' in J. Glénisson et al., eds., *La paléographie grecque et byzantine* (Paris, 1977), 385–415.
    'L"épopée' de Digénis et la frontière orientale de Byzance aux xe et xie siècles', *TM*, 7 (1979), 375–97.
    'The Usual Lead Seal', *DOP*, 37 (1983), 147–57.
    'La chancellerie impériale de Byzance du 13e au 15e siècle', *REB*, 43 (1985), 167–95.
    'Mount Athos: Levels of Literacy', *DOP*, 42 (1988), 167–78.
    'Literacy in Thirteenth-century Byzantium: an Example from Western Asia Minor' in J. S. Langdon, J. Allens and S. Kyprianides, eds., *Τὸ ἑλληνικόν. Studies in Honor of Speros Vryonis Jr.* (New Rochelle, NY, 1993), 253–65.
    'Ματζουκίνη - Ματζουκάτος in Ptochoprodromos' in C. N. Constantinides, N. M. Panagiotakis, E. M. Jeffreys, and I. Martin, eds., *Φιλέλλην: Studies in Honour of R. Browning* (Venice, 1996), 315–19.
    'Temps des faux', *Αθωνικά σύμμεικτα*, 4 (1997), 69–74.
Oppolzer, T., *Canon of Eclipses* (New York, NY, 1962).
Pagani, F., 'Un nuovo testimone della recensio pletoniana al testo di Platone: il Marc. Gr. 188 (K)', *Res publica literarum*, 29 (2006), 5–125.
    'Damnata verba: censure di Pletone in alcuni codici platonici', *BZ*, 10 (2009), 167–202.

Pahlitzsch, J., *Graeci und Suriani im Palästina der Kreuzfahrerzeit. Beiträge und Quellen zur Geschichte des griechisch-orthodoxen Patriarchats von Jerusalem* (Berlin, 2001).
Paine, T., *The Age of Reason* (London, 1794).
Panayotakis, N. M., ed., *Origini della letteratura neogreca: Atti del secondo Congresso Internazionale 'Neograeca Medii Aevi' (Venezia, 7–10 novembre 1991)*, 2 vols. (Venice, 1993).
Papacostas, T., 'Byzantine Cyprus: the Testimony of its Churches, 650–1200', 3 vols, unpublished DPhil thesis, University of Oxford (1999).
  'Byzantine Rite in a Gothic Setting: Aspects of Cultural Appropriation in Late Medieval Cyprus' in P. Ł. Grotowski and S. Skrzyniarz, eds., *Towards Rewriting? New Approaches to Byzantine Archaeology and Art* (Warsaw, 2010), 117–32.
Papadakis, A., 'Gennadius II and Mehmet the Conqueror', *Byzantion*, 42 (1972), 88–106.
Papadimitriou, S., 'Οἱ Πρόδρομοι', *VizVrem*, 5 (1898), 91–130.
  'Θεοδώρου τοῦ Πτωχοπροδρόμου τὰ Μαγγάνεια. Феодора Продрома Манганские стихотворения', *Letopis'*, 7 (1899), 1–48.
  ''Ο Πρόδρομος τοῦ Μαρκιανοῦ κώδικος XI. 22', *VizVrem*, 10 (1903), 102–63.
  Иоанн II, митрополит Киевский и Федор Продром (Odessa, 1902).
Papadogiannakis, I., 'Dialogical Pedagogy and the Structuring of Emotions in *Liber Asceticus*' in Cameron and Gaul, eds., *Dialogues and Debates from Late Antiquity to Late Byzantium* (2017), 94–104.
Papadopoullos, T., ed., Ἱστορία τῆς Κύπρου, 6 vols. (Nicosia, 1995–2005).
Papagiannaki, A., 'Aphrodite in Late Antique and Medieval Byzantium' in A. C. Smith and S. Pickup, eds., *Brill's Companion to Aphrodite* (Leiden, 2010), 321–46.
Papaioannou, S., *Michael Psellos: Rhetoric and Authorship in Byzantium* (Cambridge, 2013).
Papantonakis, G., ed., Άνθη φιλίας: Τιμητικό αφιέρωμα στον καθηγητή Κωνσταντίνο Μηνά (Athens, 2005).
Pappas, P., 'Unus Testis, Nullus Testis? The Significance of a Single Token in a Problem of Later Medieval Greek Syntax', *Ohio State University Working Papers in Linguistics*, 54 (2000), 171–6. reprinted in P. Pappas, *Variation and Morphosyntactic Change in Greek: from Clitics to Affixes* (New York, NY, 2004).
Parani, M., *Reconstructing the Reality of Images: Byzantine Material Culture and Religious Iconography (11th–15th Centuries)* (Leiden, 2003).
  'Cultural Identity and Dress: the Case of Late Byzantine Ceremonial Costume', *JÖB*, 57 (2007), 95–134.
Paschalis, M., S. Panayotakis and G. Schmeling, eds., *Readers and Writers in the Ancient Novel* (Groningen, 2009).
Patlagean, E., 'De la chasse et du souverain', *DOP*, 46 (1992), 257–63.
Patrinelis, C., Ὁ Θεόδωρος Ἀγαλλιανός ταυτιζόμενος πρὸς τὸν Θεοφάνην Μηδείας καὶ οἱ ἀνέκδοτοι λόγοι του (Athens, 1966).
Patterson, A., *Hermogenes and the Renaissance: Seven Ideas of Style* (Princeton, NJ, 1970).

Patzig, E., 'Die angebliche Monophysitismus des Malalas', *BZ*, 7 (1898), 111–28.
Peden, A., 'The Medieval Antipodes', *History Today*, 45 (1995), 27–33.
Peltomaa, L. M., 'Die berühmteste Marien-Predigt der Antike: Zur chronologischen und mariologischen Einordnung der Predigt des Proklos', *JÖB*, 54 (2004), 77–96.
'Towards the Origins of the History of the Cult of Mary', *StP*, 40 (2006), 75–86.
Penella, R. J., 'The Progymnasmata and Progymnastic Theory in Imperial Education' in W. M. Bloomer, ed., *A Companion to Ancient Education* (Malden, MA, 2015), 160–71.
Penn, S., 'Liutprand of Cremona' in *The Encyclopedia of the Medieval Chronicle* (Leiden, 2010), 1034.
Pentcheva, B. V., *Icons and Power: the Mother of God in Byzantium* (University Park, PA, 2006).
Perdikis, S., 'Le monastère des Hiereôn (des Prêtres) à Paphos. Du paganisme au christianisme', *Cahiers du Centre d'Etudes Chypriotes*, 43 (2013), 227–42.
Pérez Martín, I., 'El scriptorium de Cora: un modelo de acercamiento à los centros de copia bizantinos' in P. Bádenas et al., eds., Ἐπίγειος οὐρανός. *El cielo en la tierra. Estudios sobre el monasterio bizantino* (Madrid, 1997), 203–23.
Pernot, H., *Études de linguistique néo-hellénique*, 3 vols. (Paris, 1907–46).
Pertusi, A., 'Le epistole storiche di Lauro Quirini sulla caduta di Costantinopoli' in K. Krautter, P. O. Kristeller, A. Pertusi et al., eds., *Lauro Quirini umanista* (Florence, 1977), 163–259.
Pettitt, T., 'Before the Gutenberg Parenthesis: Elizabethan–American Compatibilities', plenary: Folk Cultures and Digital Cultures, Media in Transition 5: Creativity, Ownership and Collaboration in the Digital Age, April 1, 2010 www.academia.edu/2946207/Before_the_Gutenberg_Parenthesis_Elizabethan-American_Compatibilities (accessed 5 December 2017).
Phelan, J., 'Narrative Ethics' in P. Hühn et al., eds., *The Living Handbook of Narratology* (Hamburg, 2013), www.lhn.uni-hamburg.de/article/narrative-ethics (accessed 28 January 2017).
Phillips, J., *The Second Crusade: Extending the Frontiers of Christendom* (New Haven, CT, 2007).
Picchio, R., 'The Function of Biblical Thematic Clues in the Literary Code of "Slavia Orthodoxa"', *Slavica Hierosolymitana*, 1 (1977), 1–31.
Pietsch, E., *Die Chronographia des Michael Psellos: Kaisergeschichte, Autobiographie und Apologie* (Wiesbaden, 2005).
Pigeaud, J., 'La psychopathologie de Galien' in Manuli, Vegetti, eds., *Le opere psicologiche di Galeno* (1988), 153–83.
Pizzone, A., ed., *The Author in Middle Byzantine Literature: Modes, Functions, and Identities* (Boston, MA, 2014).
Podskalsky, G., ed., *Byzantinische Reichseschatologie. Die Periodisierung der Weltgeschichte in den vier Großreichen (Daniel 2 und 7) und dem*

Tausendjährigen Friedensreiche (Apok. 20). Eine motivgeschichtliche Untersuchung (Munich, 1972).
Polak, L., 'Tristan and Vis and Ramin', Romania, 95 (1974), 216–34.
Chrétien de Troyes: Cligés (London, 1982).
Polemis, D. I., The Doukai: a Contribution to Byzantine Prosopography (London, 1968).
Polemis, I., 'Προβλήματα τῆς βυζαντινῆς σχεδογραφίας', Ἑλληνικά, 45 (1995), 277–302.
'Γεώργιος μαΐστωρ ἁγιοτεσσαρακοντίτης', Ἑλληνικά, 46 (1996), 301–6.
'Philologische und historische Probleme in der schedographischen Sammlung des Codex Marcianus GR XI, 31', Byzantion, 67 (1997), 252–63.
'The Treatise On Those who Unjustly Accuse Wise Men, of the Past and Present: a New Work by Theodore Metochites?', BZ, 102 (2009), 203–17.
Politis, L., 'Φιλολογικὰ σὲ παλαιότερα κείμενα', Ἑλληνικά, 19 (1966), 351–61.
Polyakova, S. V., 'К вопросу о византино-французских литературных связях: («Повесть об Исмине и Исминии» Евмафия Макремволита и «Роман о розе» Гийома де Лоррис)', VizVrem, 37 (1976) 114–22.
Pratsch, T., Der hagiographische Topos: Griechische Heiligenviten in mittelbyzantinischer Zeit (Berlin, 2005).
Prince, G., 'Reader' in P. Hühn et al., eds., The Living Handbook of Narratology (Hamburg, 2013), www.lhn.uni-hamburg.de/article/reader (accessed 3 November 2017).
Prinzing, G., 'Das Bild Justinians I. in der Überlieferung der Byzantiner vom 7. bis 15. Jahrhundert', Fontes Minores, 7 (1986), 89–92.
'Beobachtungen zu 'integrierten' Fürstenspiegeln der Byzantiner', JÖB, 38 (1986), 1–31.
Prosopography of the Byzantine World (2016), ed. M. J. Jeffreys et al. http://pbw.kdl.kcl.ac.uk (accessed 20 March 2018).
Puchner, W., 'Europäische Ödipustradition und griechisches Schicksalsmärchen', BalkSt, 26 (1987), 321–49.
Studien zum Kulturkontext der liturgischen Szene: Lazarus und Judas als religiöse Volksfiguren in Brauch, Lied und Legende Südosteuropas, 2 vols. (Vienna, 1991).
'Byzantinische und westliche Einflüsse auf die religiöse Dichtung Kretas zur Zeit der venetianischen Herrschaft: Das Beispiel der apokryphen Judasvita in dem Gedicht Altes und Neues Testament' in N. M. Panayotakis, ed., Origini della letteratura neogreca, 2 vols. (Venice, 1993), vol. II, 278–312.
Ramphos, S., Ἡ πολιτεία τοῦ Νέου Θεολόγου: Προϊστορία καὶ ἀγωνία τοῦ Νέου Ἑλληνισμοῦ (Athens, 1981).
'Αἴσθησις ὀξύμωρος. Θεογνωσία ποιητικὴ στὸν τρίτο ὕμνο τοῦ ἁγίου Συμεὼν τοὐπίκλην Νέου Θεολόγου' in A. Markopoulos, ed., Τέσσερα κείμενα για την ποίηση του Συμεών του Νέου Θεολόγου (Athens, 2008), 89–135.
Rance, P., 'The Date of the Military Compendium of Syrianus Magister (Formerly the Sixth-century Anonymus Byzantinus)', BZ, 100 (2008), 701–37.

Rehm, R., *Marriage to Death* (Princeton, NJ, 1994).
Reinsch, D. R., 'Women's Literature in Byzantium? The Case of Anna Komnene' in T. Gouma-Peterson, ed., *Anna Komnene and Her Times* (New York, 2000), 83–105.
'Zu den Prooimia von (Ptocho-)Prodromos III und IV', *JÖB*, 51 (2001), 215–23.
'Historia ancilla litterarum? Zum literarischen Geschmack in der Komnenenzeit: Das Beispiel der *Synopsis chronike* des Konstantinos Manasses' in P. Odorico and P. A. Agapitos, *Pour une 'nouvelle' histoire de la littérature byzantine: Problèmes, méthodes, approches, propositions* (Paris, 2002), 81–94.
'Stixis und Hören' in B. Atsalos and N. Tsironi, eds., Πρακτικά του Ϛ' Διεθνούς Συμποσίου Ελληνικής Παλαιογραφίας, 3 vols. (Athens, 2008), vol. I, 259–69.
'Der Autor ist tot – es lebe der Leser; Zur Neubewertung der *imitatio* in der byzantinischen Geschichtsschreibung' in A. Rhoby and E. Schiffer, eds., *Imitatio – Aemulatio – Variatio* (Vienna, 2010), 23–32.
'Bemerkungen zu einigen byzantinischen Fürstenspiegeln des 11. und 12. Jahrhunderts' in H. Seng and L. M. Hoffmann, eds., *Synesios von Kyrene: Politik – Literatur – Philosophie* (Turnhout, 2013), 404–19.
Rekaya, M., 'Mise au point sur Théophobe et l'alliance de Bābek avec Théophile (833/4–839/40)', *BZ*, 44 (1974), 43–67.
Renting, A. D. and J. T. C. Renting-Kuijpers, eds., with notes on the manuscripts by A. S. Korteweg, *The Seventeenth-century Orange-Nassau Library: The Catalogue Compiled by Anthonie Smets in 1686, the 1749 Auction Catalogue, and Other Contemporary Sources* (Utrecht, 1993).
Resh, D. D., 'Toward a Byzantine Definition of Metaphrasis', *GRBS* 55 (2015), 754–87.
Rhoby, A., 'Zur Identifizierung von bekannten Autoren im Codex Marcianus Graecus 524', *Medioevo Greco*, 10 (2010), 167–204.
Rhoby, A. and E. Schiffer, eds., *Imitatio – Aemulatio – Variatio* (Vienna, 2010).
Richard, J., 'Le casal de Psimilofo et la vie rurale en Chypre au XIVe siècle', *MEFRM*, 59 (1947), 121–53.
'Agriculture in the kingdom of Cyprus' in K. M. Setton, ed., *A History of the Crusades*, 6 vols. (Madison, WI, 1969–89), vol. V, *The Impact of the Crusades on the Near East*, eds. N. P. Zacour and H. W. Hazard, 267–84.
'Les comptes du collecteur de la chambre apostolique dans le royaume de Chypre (1357–1363)', *EKEE*, 13–16 (1984–7), 1–47.
'Οἱ πολιτικοὶ καὶ κοινωνικοὶ θεσμοὶ τοῦ μεσαιωνικοῦ βασιλείου' in T. Papadopoullos, ed., Ἱστορία τῆς Κύπρου, 6 vols. (Nicosia, 1995–2005), vol. I, 333–74
Richard, M. and R. Olivier, eds., *Répertoire des bibliothèques et des catalogues de manuscrits grecs* (Turnhout, 1995).
Richter, G., *Oikonomia: Der Gebrauch des Wortes Oikonomia im Neuen Testament, bei den Kirchenvätern und in der theologischen Literatur bis ins 20. Jahrhundert* (Berlin, 2005).

Riehle, A., 'Literatur, Politik und Gesellschaft unter Andronikos II. Palaiologos: Untersuchungen zu den Briefen des Nikephoros Chumnos', unpublished doctoral thesis, LMU Munich (2011).
'Review: Niels Gaul, *Thomas Magistros und die spätbyzantische Sophistik*', *Bryn Mawr Classical Review*, 2012.05.37 (http://bmcr.brynmawr.edu/2012/2012-05-37.html, accessed 1 December 2017).
Rigo, A., 'Le père spirituel de l'empereur Cosmas Tzintziloukès et son opuscule sur les parties de l'âme, les passions et les pensées (XIe siècle)', in T. F. Antonopoulou, S. Kotzabassi and M. Loukaki, eds., *Myriobiblos: Essays on Byzantine Literature and Culture* (Boston, MA, 2015), 295–316.
Rijksbaron, A., *The Syntax and Semantics of the Verb in Classical Greek: an Introduction* (Amsterdam, 1984).
Rinaud, A., *Le continent austral: hypothèses et découvertes* (Paris, 1983).
Robins, R. H., *The Byzantine Grammarians: Their Place in History* (Berlin, 1993).
Roilos, P., 'The Sacred and the Profane: Re-enacting Ritual in the Medieval Greek Novel' in D. Yatromanolakis and P. Roilos, eds., *Greek Ritual Poetics* (Cambridge, MA, 2004), 210–26.
Amphoteroglossia: A Poetics of the Twelfth-century Medieval Greek Novel (Cambridge, MA, 2005).
'*Unshapely Bodies and Beautifying Embellishments*: the Ancient Epics in Byzantium, Allegorical Hermeneutics, and the Case of Ioannes Diakonos Galenos', *JÖB*, 64 (2014), 231–46.
ed., *Medieval Greek Storytelling: Fictionality and Narrative in Byzantium* (Wiesbaden, 2014).
Romm, J. S., *The Edges of the Earth in Ancient Thought* (Princeton, NJ, 1992).
Romoli, F., 'Le citazioni bibliche nell'omiletica e nella letteratura di direzione spirituale del medioevo slavo orientale (XII–XIII sec.)', *Mediaevistik*, 27 (2014), 119–40.
Ronchey, S., 'Those "whose writings were exchanged": John of Damascus, George Choeroboscus and John "Arklas" According to the Prooimion of Eustathius's *Exegesis in canonem iambicum de Pentecoste*' in C. Sode and S. Takács, eds., *Novum Millennium: Studies on Byzantine History and Culture, dedicated to Paul Speck* (Aldershot, 2001), 327–36.
'An Introduction to Eustathios' "Exegesis in canonem iambicum"', *DOP*, 45 (1991), 149–58.
Ross, S., 'In Praise of Overstating the Case: a Review of Franco Moretti, *Distant Reading* (London: Verso, 2013)', *Digital Humanities Quarterly*, 8 (2014), www.digitalhumanities.org/dhq/vol/8/1/000171/000171.html (accessed 22 January 2018).
Rotman, Y., *Byzantine Slavery and the Mediterranean World* (Cambridge, MA, 2009), 183–8.
Roueché, C., 'Byzantine Writers and Readers: Storytelling in the Eleventh Century' in R. Beaton, ed., *The Greek Novel AD 1–1985* (London, 1988), 123–33.
'The Rhetoric of Kekaumenos' in E. M. Jeffreys, ed., *Rhetoric in Byzantium* (Aldershot, 2003), 23–37.

'The Literary Background of Kekaumenos' in C. Holmes and J. Waring, eds., *Literacy, Education and Manuscript Transmission in Byzantium and Beyond* (Leiden, 2002), 111–38.

Rubenson, S., 'Philosophy and Simplicity: the Problem of Classical Education in Early Christian Biography' in T. Hägg and P. Rousseau, eds., *Greek Biography and Panegyric in Late Antiquity* (Berkeley, CA, 2000), 110–39.

Rudt de Collenberg, W. H., 'Les grâces papales, autres que les dispenses matrimoniales, accordées à Chypre de 1305 à 1378', *EKEE*, 8 (1975–7), 187–252.

'Les dispenses matrimoniales accordées à l'Orient Latin selon les registres du Vatican d'Honorius III à Clément VII (1223–1385)', *MEFRM*, 89/1 (1977), 11–93.

'The Fate of Frankish Noble Families Settled in Cyprus' in P. W. Edbury, ed., *Crusade and Settlement* (Cardiff, 1985), 268–72.

Rudy, K. M., 'Dirty Books: Quantifying Patterns of Use in Medieval Manuscripts Using a Densitometer', *Journal of Historians of Netherlandish Art*, 2 (2010), www.jhna.org/index.php/past-issues/volume-2-issue-1-2/129-dirty-books (accessed 3 November 2017).

Russell, D. A., '*De Imitatione*' in D. West and A. J. Woodman, eds., *Creative Imitation and Latin Literature* (Cambridge, 1979), 1–16.

Russel, J. B., 'Saint Boniface and the Eccentrics', *Church History*, 33 (1964), 235–47.

Inventing the Flat Earth: Columbus and Modern Historians (New York, NY, 1991).

Saenger, P., 'Silent Reading: its Impact on Late Medieval Script and Society,' *Viator*, 13 (1982), 367–414.

Saffrey, H. D., 'Théologie et anthropologie d'après quelques prefaces de Proclus' in C. Laga, ed., *Images of Man in Ancient and Medieval Thought: Studia Gerardo Verbeke ab amicis et collegis dictata* (Leuven, 1976), 199–212.

Sajdak, J., *Historia critica scholiastarum et commentatorum Gregorii Nazianzeni* (Krakow, 1914).

'Spicilegium Geometreum II', *EOS (Commentarii Societatis Philologae Polonorum)*, 33 (1930-1), 530-1.

Sakkos, S. N., Ὁ Πατήρ μου μείζων μού ἐστι: ἔριδες καὶ σύνοδοι κατὰ τὸν ιβ' αἰῶνα, 2 vols. (Thessalonike, 1968).

Salamon, M. 'Priscianus und sein Schülerkreis in Konstantinopel', *Philologus*, 123 (1979), 91–6.

Saliou, C., ed., *Gaza dans l'antiquité tardive: archéologie, rhétorique et histoire. Actes du colloque international de Poitiers, 6–7 Mai 2004* (Salerno, 2005).

Saradi-Mendelovici, H., 'Notes on a Prosopography of the Byzantine Notaries', *Medieval Prosopography*, 9 (1988), 21–49.

Sargologos, E., ed., *La vie de Saint Cyrille le Philéote, moine byzantin* (Brussels, 1964).

Schabel, C., 'A Knight's Tale: Giovan Francesco Loredano's Fantastic *Historie de' re Lusignani*' in B. Arbel, E. Chayes and H. Hendrix, eds., *Cyprus and the Renaissance (1450–1650)* (Turnhout, 2012), 357–90.
Schechner, R., *Performance Theory*, second edition (New York, NY, 1988).
Schissel, O., 'Review of Joannes Gerstinger, *Pamprepios von Panopolis*', *Philologische Wochenschrift*, 49 (1929), 1073–80.
Schminck, A., 'The Beginnings and Origins of the "Macedonian" Dynasty' in J. Burke and R. Scott, eds., *Byzantine Macedonia: Identity, Image and History* (Melbourne, 2000), 61–8.
Schmitz, T., *Bildung und Macht: Zur sozialen und politischen Funktion der zweiten Sophistik in der griechischen Welt der Kaiserzeit* (Munich, 1997).
 'Appendix: Bemerkungen zum Vaticanus gr. 952', *BZ*, 96 (2003), 56–7.
Schuppe, F., *Die pastorale Herausforderung: Orthodoxes Leben zwischen Akribeia und Oikonomia: theologische Grundlagen, Praxis und ökumenische Perspektiven* (Würzburg, 2006).
Scorsone, M., 'Gli Ἔρωτες θεῖοι di Simeone il Nuovo Teologo: ermeneutica di un'intitolazione apocrifa', *Medioevo Greco*, 0 (2000), 191–6.
Scott, R., 'Malalas, the Secret History, and Justinian's Propaganda', *DOP*, 39 (1985), 99–109.
 'Malalas and his Contemporaries' in E. M. Jeffreys with B. Croke and R. Scott, *Studies in John Malalas* (Sydney, 1990), 67–85.
 'Malalas' View of the Classical Past' in G. Clarke, ed., *Reading the Past in Late Antiquity* (Canberra, 1990), 147–64.
 'The Image of Constantine in Malalas and Theophanes' in P. Magdalino, ed., *New Constantines: The Rhythm of Imperial Renewal in Byzantium, 4th–13th Centuries* (Aldershot, 1994), 57–71.
Seibt, W., 'Untersuchungen zur Vor- und Frühgeschichte der "bulgarischen" Kometopulen', *HA*, 89 (1975), 65–100.
 'Ioannes Skylitzes: Zur Person des Chronisten', *JÖB*, 25 (1976), 81–5.
Seitz, K., *Die Schule von Gaza* (Heidelberg, 1982).
Ševčenko, I., *Études sur la polémique entre Théodore Métochite et Nicéphore Choumnos* (Brussels, 1962).
 'Some Autographs of Nicephorus Gregoras', *ZRVI*, 8 (1964), 435–50.
 'La biographie de l'empereur Basile Ier' in *La civiltà bizantina dal IX all'XI secolo: aspetti e problemi* (Bari, 1978), 91–127.
 'Constantinople Viewed from the Eastern Provinces in the Middle Byzantine Period', *Ukrainian Studies*, 3–4 (1979–80), 712–47; reprinted in I. Ševčenko, *Ideology, Letters and Culture in the Byzantine World* (London, 1982).
 'Re-reading Constantine Porphyrogenitus' in J. Shepard and S. Franklin, eds., *Byzantine Diplomacy* (Aldershot, 1992), 167–95.
Ševčenko, I. and I. Hutter, eds., *AETOS: Studies in Honour of Cyril Mango Presented to Him on April 14, 1998* (Stuttgart, 1998).
Shahîd, I., *Byzantium and the Arabs in the Fifth Century*, 2 vols. (Washington, D. C., 1989).

Byzantium and the Arabs in the Sixth Century, 2 vols. (Washington, D. C., 1995).

Shawcross, T., 'In the Name of the True Emperor: Politics of Resistance after the Palaiologan Usurpation', *BSl*, 66 (2008), 203–27.

The Chronicle of Morea: Historiography in Crusader Greece (Oxford, 2009).

'"Listen, All of You, Both Franks and Romans": the Narrator in the Chronicle of Morea' in R. Macrides, ed., *History as Literature in Byzantium* (Farnham, 2010), 91–111.

'Languages, Record-keeping and Collective Memory in an Imperial Eastern Mediterranean' in A. Law, ed., *Mapping the Medieval Mediterranean, c. 300–1550* (Leiden, forthcoming).

Shepard, J., 'Scylitzes on Armenia in the 1040s and the Role of Catacalon Cecaumenos', *REArm*, n.s. 11 (1975–6), 269–71.

'Isaac Comnenus' Coronation Day', *BSl*, 38 (1977), 22–30.

'Byzantium's Last Sicilian Expedition: Scylitzes' Testimony,' *RSBN*, n.s. 14–16 (1977–9), 145–59.

'A Suspected Source of Scylitzes' *Synopsis Historion*: the Great Catacalon Cecaumenus', *BMGS*, 16 (1992), 171–81.

'Cross-purposes: Alexius Comnenus and the First Crusade' in J. Phillips, ed., *The First Crusade: Origins and Impact* (Manchester, 1997), 107–29.

'Constantine VII, Caucasian Openings and the Road to Aleppo' in A. Eastmond, ed., *Eastern Approaches to Byzantium* (Aldershot, 2001), 19–40.

'Equilibrium to Expansion (886–1025)' in J. Shepard, ed., *The Cambridge History of the Byzantine Empire, c. 500–1492* (Cambridge, 2008), 493–536.

'Slavs and Bulgars' in R. McKitterick, ed., *The New Cambridge Medieval History*, vol. II, *c. 700–c. 900* (Cambridge, 2008), 239–46.

'History as Propaganda, Proto-foundation-myth and "Tract for the Times" in the Long Eleventh Century (*c.* 1000–*c.* 1130)' in T. N. Jackson, *Old Rus' and Medieval Europe: The Origin of States* (Moscow, 2016), 332–55.

ed., *The Cambridge History of the Byzantine Empire c. 500–1492* (Cambridge, 2008).

Shirinean, M. E., 'Armenian Elites in Constantinople: Emperor Basil and Patriarch Photius' in R. G. Hovannisian and S. Payaslian, eds., *Armenian Constantinople* (Costa Mesa, CA, 2010), 53–72.

Signes Codoñer, J., *The Emperor Theophilos and the East 829–842: Court and Frontier in Byzantium during the Last Phase of Iconoclasm* (Farnham, 2014).

Simeonova, L., *Diplomacy of the Letter and the Cross: Photios, Bulgaria and the Papacy 860s–880s* (Amsterdam, 1998).

Simon, E., 'Nonnos und das Elfenbeinkästchen aus Veroli', *JDAI*, 79 (1964), 279–336.

Skarveli-Nikolopoulou, A., Τὰ Μαθηματάρια τῶν Ἑλληνικῶν Σχολείων τῆς Τουρκοκρατίας. Διδασκόμενα κείμενα, σχολικὰ προγράμματα, διδακτικὲς μέθοδοι. Συμβολὴ στὴν ἱστορία τῆς νεοελληνικῆς παιδείας (Athens, 1993).

Skoulatos, B., *Les personnages byzantins de l'Alexiade: analyse prosopographique et synthèse* (Louvain, 1980).
Smythe, D., 'Alexios I and the Heretics: The Account of Anna Komnene's Alexiad' in M. E. Mullett and D. Smythe, eds., *Alexios I Komnenos* (Belfast, 1996) 232–59.
Sorabji, R. R. K., *Time, Creation and the Continuum* (London, 1983).
Sourvinou-Inwood, C., 'Review: *Marriage to Death. The Conflation of Wedding and Funeral Rituals in Greek Tragedy* by R. Rehm', *Classical Review*, n.s. 46 (1996), 58–9.
Spatharakis, I., *The Portrait in Byzantine Illuminated Manuscripts* (Leiden, 1976).
  Trésors de Byzance: manuscrits grecs de la Bibliothèque nationale de France (Paris, 2001).
  The Illustrations of the Cynegetica in Venice: Codex Marcianus Graecus Z 139 (Leiden, 2004).
Speck, P., *Die kaiserliche Universität von Konstantinopel* (Munich, 1974).
  '"Interpolations et non-sens indiscutables": the first poem of the Ptochoprodromika' in S. A. Takács, ed., *Understanding Byzantium: Studies in Byzantine Historical Sources* (Aldershot, 2003), 84–103.
Speigl, J., 'Formula Iustiniani, Kircheneinigung mit kaiserlichen Glaubensbekenntnissen (Cod. Iust. I,1,5–8)', *Ostkirchliche Studien*, 44 (1995), 105–34.
Spingou, F., 'Word and Image at the Court of Manuel Komnenos. Epigrams on Works of Art in Marc. gr. 524, Followed by a Description of the Manuscript', unpublished MPhil thesis, Oxford University (2010).
Spiteris, J., *La critica Bizantina del primato romano nel secolo XII* (Rome, 1979), 177–94.
Stadter, P. A., *Arrian of Nicomedia* (Chapel Hill, NC, 1980).
Staikos, K. P., *The History of the Library in Western Civilisation*, 5 vols. (New Castle, DE, 2007).
Stamatios, A. and A. Weckwerth, 'Löwe' in *RAC*, 23 (2010), col. 257–86.
Stanković, V., 'Nikephoros Bryennios, Anna Komnene and Konstantinos Doukas', *BZ*, 100 (2007), 169–75.
Steckel, S., N. Gaul and M. Grünbart, eds., *Networks of Learning: Perspectives on Scholars in Byzantine East and Latin West, c. 1000–1200* (Zurich, 2014).
Stefec, R. S., 'Zwischen Urkundenpaläographie und Handschriftenforschung: Kopisten am Patriarchat von Konstantinopel im späten 15. und frühen 16. Jahrhundert', *RSBN*, 50 (2013), 303–26.
Stegemann, W., 'Phoibammon', *RE*, 39 (1941), 326–43.
Stephenson, P., *Byzantium's Balkan Frontier: A Political Study of the Northern Balkans, 900–1204* (Cambridge, 2000).
  The Legend of Basil the Bulgar-Slayer (Cambridge, 2003).
  ed., *The Byzantine World* (London, 2010).
Stevenson, E. L., *Terrestrial and Celestial Globes: Their History and Construction, Including Consideration of Their Value as Aids in the Study of Geography and Astronomy*, 2 vols. (New Haven, CT, 1921).

Stichel, R., 'Die musizierenden Hirten von Bethlehem: Die Bedeutung der mittelalterlichen slavischen Übersetzungsliteratur für die byzantinische Lexikographie' in W. Hörandner and E. Trapp, eds., *Lexicographica Byzantina* (Vienna, 1991), 249–82.

Stickler, G., *Manuel Philes und seine Psalmenmetaphrase* (Vienna, 1992).

Stratis, D., Βαρθολομαῖος Κουτλουμουσιανός *(1772–1851)* Βιογραφία– Ἐργογραφία (Mt. Athos, 2002).

Striker, C. L. and Y. Doğan Kuban, eds., *Kalenderhane in Istanbul: The Buildings, their History, Architecture, and Decoration. Final Reports on the Archaeological Exploration and Restoration at Kalenderhane Camii, 1966–1978*, 2 vols. (Mainz, 1997–2007).

Stupperich, R., 'Das Statuenprogramm in den Zeuxippos-Thermen', *IstMitt*, 32 (1982), 210–35.

Stuveras, R., *Le putto dans l'art romain* (Brussels, 1969).

Svoronos, N., *Les novelles des empereurs macédoniens concernant la terre et les stratiotes* (Athens, 1994).

'Ζητήματα σχετικά με την οικονομική, κοινωνική και νομική κατάσταση των Ελληνοκυπρίων στη διάρκεια της φραγκικής κυριαρχίας', Σημεῖο, 4 (1996), 29–50.

Talbot, A.-M., *Faith Healing in Late Byzantium* (Brookline, MA, 1983).

'Epigrams in Context: Metrical Inscriptions on Art and Architecture of the Palaiologan Era', *DOP*, 53 (1999), 75–90.

'The *Miracles of Gregory Palamas* by Philotheos Kokkinos' in Stephenson, ed., *Byzantine World* (2010), 236–47.

Tamarkina, I., 'The Date of the Life of the Patriarch Ignatius Reconsidered', *BZ*, 99 (2006), 616–30.

Tannery, P., 'Les manuscrits de Diophante à l'Escorial', *NAMSL*, 1 (1891), 383–94.

Temkin, O., 'Byzantine Medicine: Tradition and Empiricism', *DOP*, 16 (1962), 95–115.

ter Haar Romeny, B., 'Procopius of Gaza and his Library' in H. Amirav and B. ter Haar Romeny, eds., *From Rome to Constantinople: Studies in Honour of Averil Cameron* (Leuven, 2007), 173–90.

Thavoris, A. I., 'Το προδρομικό: ... και ωσάν εσέναν έχει' in G. Papantonakis, ed., Ἄνθη φιλίας: Τιμητικό αφιέρωμα στον καθηγητή Κωνσταντίνο Μηνά (Athens, 2005), 355–68.

Theodoridis, C., 'Die Abfassungszeit der Epimerismen zu Homer', *BZ*, 72 (1979), 1–5.

Thesaurus Linguae Graecae Digital Library, http://stephanus.tlg.uci.edu/ (accessed 16 January 2018).

Thomson, J. O., *History of Ancient Geography* (Cambridge, 1948).

Thurn, H., *Oikonomia von der frühbyzantinischen Zeit bis zum Bilderstreit. Semantologische Untersuchungen zur Wortfamilie* (Munich, 1961).

Tinnefeld, F., 'Der Blachernenpalast in Schriftquellen der Palaiologenzeit' in B. Borkopp and T. Steppan, eds., Λιθόστρωτον. *Studien zur byzantinischen Kunst und Geschichte* (Stuttgart, 2000), 277–85.

'Georgios Gennadios Scholarios' in C. G. Conticello and V. Conticello, eds., *La Théologie Byzantine et sa tradition* 2 vols. (Turnhout, 2002), vol. II, 477–541.

Tieleman, T., *Galen and Chrysippus on the Soul: Argument and Refutation in the De Placitis II–III* (Leiden, 1996).

Tiftixoglu, V., 'Gruppenbildungen innerhalb des konstantinopolitanischen Klerus während der Komnenenzeit', *BZ*, 62 (1969), 25–72.

Tissoni, F., 'Cristodoro e Callimaco', *Acme*, 53 (2000), 213–18.

Cristodoro: un'introduzione e un commento (Alessandria, 2000).

Tobias, N., *Basil I: Founder of the Macedonian Dynasty* (Lewiston, NY, 2007).

Todd, R., 'Galenic Medical Ideas in the Greek Aristotelian Commentators', *SOsl*, 52 (1977), 117–34.

Todt, K.-P., 'Die Frau als Selbstherrscher: Kaiserin Theodora, die letzte Angehörige der Makedonischen Dynastie', *JÖB*, 50 (2000), 139–71.

Toth, I., 'Rhetorical Theatron in Late Byzantium: the Example of Palaiologan Imperial Orations' in M. Grünbart, ed., *Theatron: Rhetorische Kultur in Spätantike und Mittelalter* (Berlin, 2007), 429–48.

'Fighting with Tales: the Byzantine Book of Syntipas the Philosopher' in C. Cupane and B. Krönung, eds., *Fictional Storytelling in the Medieval Eastern Mediterranean and Beyond (8th–15th Centuries)* (Leiden, 2016), 387–94.

Tougher, S., 'After Iconoclasm (850–886)' in J. Shepard, *Cambridge History of the Byzantine Empire c. 500–1492* (Cambridge, 2008), 292–304.

Trahoulia, N. S., 'The Venice Alexander Romance: Pictorial Narrative and the Art of Telling Stories' in R. Macrides, ed., *History as Literature in Byzantium* (Farnham, 2010), 145–65.

Trapp, E., 'Learned and Vernacular Literature in Byzantium: Dichotomy or Symbiosis?', *DOP*, 47 (1993), 115–29.

'Digenēs Akritēs' in H. L. Arnold, ed., *Kindlers Literatur Lexikon*, third edition, 18 vols. (Stuttgart, 2009), vol. VI, 603–4.

'Zur fragmentarischen Überlieferung im Bereich der Sachkultur' in C. Gastgeber and C. Glassner et al., eds., *Fragmente: Der Umgang mit lückenhafter Quellenüberlieferung in der Mittelalterforschung. Akten des internationalen Symposiums des Zentrums Mittelalterforschung der Österreichischen Akademie der Wissenschaften Wien, 19.-21. März 2009* (Vienna, 2010), 205–8.

et al., eds., *Prosopographisches Lexikon der Palaiologenzeit (1261–1453)*, 12 vols. (Vienna, 1979–96, and 2001).

Trapp, E., W. Hörandner, J. Diethart et al., *Lexikon zur byzantinischen Gräzität, besonders des 9.-12. Jahrhunderts. Fasc. 1–8: A-ὤχρωμα*, 8 vols. (Vienna, 1994–2017).

Travis, M. A., *Reading Cultures: The Construction of Readers in the Twentieth Century* (Carbondale, IL, 1998).

Treadgold, W., *The Nature of the Bibliotheca of Photios* (Washington, D. C., 1980).

'The Byzantine World Histories of John Malalas and Eustathius of Epiphania', *International History Review*, 29 (2007), 709–45.

The Early Byzantine Historians (Basingstoke, 2007).
Trélat, P., 'Clio sous le regard d'Hermès: itinéraires et oeuvre de Dominique Jauna, historien de Chypre et des croisades', *Crusades*, 10 (2011), 147–74.
Tsirpanlis, C. N., 'Byzantine Parliaments and Representative Assemblies from 1081 to 1351', *Byzantion*, 43 (1973), 432–81.
Mark Eugenicus and the Council of Florence: A Historical Re-evaluation of his Personality (Thessalonike, 1974).
Turner, C. J. G., 'George-Gennadius Scholarius and the Union of Florence', *JThSt*, n.s. 18 (1967), 83–103.
'Notes on the Works of Theodore Agallianos Contained in Codex Bodleianus Canonicus Graecus 49', *BZ*, 61 (1968), 27–35.
'The Career of George-Gennadius Scholarius', *Byzantion*, 39 (1969), 420–55.
Turner, H. J. M., *St. Symeon the New Theologian and Spiritual Fatherhood* (Leiden, 1990).
Twigg, G., *The Black Death: A Biological Reappraisal* (London, 1984)
Uthemann, H., 'Kaiser Justinian als Kirchenpolitiker und Theologe', *Augustinianum*, 39 (1999), 5–83.
Valiavitcharska, V., *Rhetoric and Rhythm in Byzantium: The Sound of Persuasion* (Cambridge, 2013).
van der Ploeg, K., *Art, Architecture and Liturgy: Siena Cathedral in the Middle Ages* (Groningen, 1993).
van Oort, J. and O. Hesse, eds., *Christentum und Politik in der Alten Kirche* (Leuven, 2009).
Varzos, K., Ἡ γενεαλογία τῶν Κομνηνῶν, 2 vols. (Thessalonike, 1984).
Vasileiou, P., 'Για το τρίτο "Πτωχοπροδρομικό" ποίημα (μικρό σημείωμα για την άρση ενός μεθοδολογικού λάθους)', Ἑλληνικά, 53 (2003), 171–9.
Vassis, I., *Die handschriftliche Überlieferung der sogenannten Psellos-Paraphrase der Ilias* (Hamburg, 1991).
'Graeca Sunt, Non Leguntur', *BZ*, 86/87 (1993–4), 1–19.
'Τῶν νέων φιλολόγων παλαίσματα: Ἡ συλλογὴ σχεδῶν τοῦ κώδικα *Vaticanus Palatinus gr.* 92', Ἑλληνικά, 52 (2002), 37–68.
Vickers, B., *In Defence of Rhetoric* (Oxford, 1988).
Viljamaa, T., *Studies in Greek Encomiastic Poetry of the Early Byzantine Period* (Helsinki, 1968).
Vinaver, E., *The Rise of Romance* (Oxford, 1971).
Violaris, Y., 'Excavations at the Site of Palaion Demarcheion, Lefkosia', *Cahiers du Centre d'Etudes Chypriotes*, 34 (2004), 69–80.
Voigt, W., *Die Leiden der alten Wörter* (Frankfurt, 2006).
Volk, O. O., 'Die byzantinischen Klosterbibliotheken von Konstantinopel, Thessalonika und Kleinasien', unpublished PhD thesis, Munich (1955).
Vollrath, H., 'The Western Empire under the Salians' in D. Luscombe and J. Riley-Smith, eds., *New Cambridge Medieval History*, vol. iv.2, *c. 1024–c. 1198* (Cambridge, 2004), 38–71.
von den Brincken, D., *Fines Terrae. Die Enden der Erde und der vierte Kontinent auf mittelalterlichen Weltkarten* (Hanover, 1992).

von Falkenhausen, V., 'A Provincial Aristocracy: the Byzantine Provinces in Southern Italy (9th–11th Century)', in M. Angold, ed., *The Byzantine Aristocracy, IX to XIII Centuries* (Oxford, 1984), 211–35.
von Staden, H., 'Body, Soul, and Nerves: Epicurus, Herophilus, Erasistratus, the Stoics, and Galen' in J. P. Wright and P. Potter, eds., *Psyche and Soma: Physicians and Metaphysicians on the Mind-Body Problem from Antiquity to Enlightenment* (Oxford, 2000), 105–16.
von Wartburg, M.-L., 'Cypriot Contacts with East and West as Reflected in Medieval Glazed Pottery from the Paphos Region' in C. Bakirtzis, ed., *VIIe congrès international sur la céramique médiévale en Méditerranée, Thessaloniki 11–16 octobre 1999* (Athens, 2003), 153–66.
Voss, A., 'Reformed Orthodoxy in the Netherlands' in H. J. Selderhuis, ed., *A Companion to Reformed Orthodoxy: Brill's Companions to the Christian Tradition* (Leiden, 2013), 121–76.
Wakker, G., *Conditions and Conditionals: An Investigation of Ancient Greek* (Amsterdam, 1994).
Wander, S., *The Joshua Roll* (Wiesbaden, 2011).
Waring, J., 'Literacies of Lists: Reading Byzantine Monastic Inventories' in C. Holmes and J. Waring, eds., *Literacy, Education and Manuscript Transmission in Byzantium and Beyond* (Leiden, 2002), 265–86.
'Byzantine Book Culture' in L. James, ed., *A Companion to Byzantium* (Chichester, 2010), 275–88.
Webb, R., *Demons and Dancers: Performance in Late Antiquity* (Cambridge, MA, 2008).
Weitzmann, K., *Illustrations in Roll and Codex: A Study in the Origin and Method of Text Illustration* (Princeton, NJ, 1947).
'The Selection of Texts for Cyclic Illustration in Byzantine Manuscripts' in W. C. Loerke et al., eds., *Byzantine Books and Bookmen* (Washington, D. C., 1975), 69–109.
Greek Mythology in Byzantine Art (Princeton, NJ, 1984).
Wellesz, E., *A History of Byzantine Music and Hymnography* (Oxford, 1961).
Wenger A., *L'Assomption de la Très-sainte Vierge dans la tradition Byzantine, du VIe au Xe siècle* (Paris, 1955).
Wessel, K., 'Kaiserbild', *RBK*, 3 (1978), col. 722–853.
West, M. L., *Greek Metre* (Oxford, 1982).
Westerink, L. G., 'Philosophy and Medicine in Late Antiquity', *Janus*, 51 (1964), 169–77.
Weyl Carr, A., 'Art' in A. Nicolaou-Konnari and C. Schabel, eds., *Cyprus: Society and Culture 1191–1374* (Leiden, 2005), 285–328.
Whitby, M. (Mary), 'From Moschus to Nonnus: the Evolution of the Nonnian Style' in N. Hopkinson, ed., *Studies in the Dionysiaca of Nonnus* (Cambridge, 1994), 99–155.
'The Vocabulary of Praise in Verse-celebrations of 6th-century Building Achievements: AP 2.398–406, AP 9.656, AP 1.10 and Paul the Silentiary's Description of St. Sophia' in D. Accorinti and P. Chuvin, eds., *Des Géants à Dionysos. Mélanges offerts à F. Vian* (Alexandria, 2003), 593–606.

'The St Polyeuktos Epigram: a Literary Perspective' in S. F. Johnson, ed., *Greek Literature in Late Antiquity: Dynamism, Didacticism, Classicism* (Aldershot, 2006), 159–87.

'The Biblical Past in John Malalas and the Paschal Chronicle' in H. Amirav and B. ter Haar Romeny, eds., *From Rome to Constantinople: Studies in Honour of Averil Cameron* (Leuven, 2007), 279–302.

Whitby, M. (Michael), *The Emperor Maurice and His Historian: Theophylact Simocatta on Persian and Balkan Warfare* (Oxford, 1988).

'*Malalas Continuatus*: Review of E. M. Jeffreys ed. with B. Croke and R. Scott, *Studies in John Malalas* (Sydney 1990)', *ClRev*, 41 (1991), 325–7.

'Religious Views of Procopius and Agathias', *Electrum*, 13 (2007), 73–93.

White, A. W., *Performing Orthodox Ritual in Byzantium* (Cambridge, 2015).

Whittow, M., *The Making of Orthodox Byzantium, 600–1025* (London, 1996).

Wiet, G., 'La grande peste noire en Syrie et en Égypte', *Études d'orientalisme dédiées à la mémoire de Lévi-Provençal*, 2 vols. (Paris, 1962).

Wifstrand, A., *Von Kallimachos zu Nonnos* (Lund, 1933).

Wildberg, C., 'Prolegomena to the Study of Philoponus' *Contra Aristotelem*' in R. Sorabji, ed., *Philoponus and the Rejection of Aristotelian Science* (London, 1987), 197–209

John Philoponus' Criticism of Aristotle's Theory of Aether (Berlin, 1988).

Williams, J., 'Isidore, Orosius and the Beatus Map', *Imago Mundi*, 49 (1997), 7–31.

Wilson, N. G., 'The Libraries of the Byzantine World', *GRBS*, 8 (1967), 53–80.

'Books and Readers in Byzantium' in W. C. Loerke et al., eds., *Byzantine Books and Bookmen* (Washington, D. C., 1975), 1–16.

Scholars of Byzantium (London, 1996).

'Libraries' in E. M. Jeffreys, J. Haldon, and R. Cormack, eds., *Oxford Handbook of Byzantine Studies* (Oxford, 2008), 820–4.

Witakowski, W., 'Malalas in Syriac' in E. M. Jeffreys, B. Croke and R. Scott eds., *Studies in John Malalas* (Sydney, 1990), 299–310.

Wittkower, R., 'Marvels of the East: a Study in the History of Monsters', *JWarb*, 5 (1942), 159–97.

Wolska-Conus, W., *La topographie chrétienne de Cosmas Indicopleustès: théologie et science au VIe siècle* (Paris, 1962).

'Les écoles de Psellos et de Xiphilin sous Constantin IX Monomaque', *TM*, 6 (1976), 223–43.

'L'école de droit et l'enseignement du droit à Byzance au XIe siècle: Xiphilin et Psellos', *TM*, 7 (1979), 1–103.

Woodfin, W., *The Embodied Icon: Liturgical Vestments and Sacramental Power in Byzantium* (Oxford, 2012).

Woodhouse, C. M., *Gemistos Plethon: The Last of the Hellenes* (Oxford, 1986).

Woodruff, R. 'Plato's Early Theory of Knowledge' in S. Everson, ed., *Epistemology* (Cambridge, 1990), 60–84.

Wormald, B. H. G., *Clarendon: Politics, History and Religion, 1640–1660* (Cambridge, 1951).

Wright, J. K., 'Terrae Incognitae: the Place of the Imagination in Geography' in J. K. Wright, *Human Nature in Geography: Fourteen Papers 1925–1965* (Cambridge, MA, 1966), 68–88.
Wright, J. P. and P. Potter, eds., *Psyche and Soma: Physicians and Metaphysicians on the Mind–Body Problem from Antiquity to Enlightenment* (Oxford, 2000).
Yatromanolakis, D., *Sappho in the Making: the Early Reception* (Cambridge, MA, 2007).
 'Genre Categories and Interdiscursivity in Alkaios and Archaic Greece', *Synkrisis/Comparaison*, 19 (2008), 169–87.
 'Symposia, Noses, *Prosôpa*: a Kylix in the Company of Banqueters on the Ground' in D. Yatromanolakis, ed., *An Archaeology of Representations: Ancient Greek Vase-Painting and Contemporary Methodologies* (Athens, 2009), 414–65.
Yatromanolakis, D. and P. Roilos, eds., *Greek Ritual Poetics* (Cambridge, MA, 2004).
Yatromanolakis, D. and P. Roilos, *Towards a Ritual Poetics* (Athens, 2003); Greek edition with an introduction by M. Detienne, Προς μία Τελετουργική Ποιητική (Athens, 2005).
Zeitler, B., '*Ostentatio Genitalium:* Displays of Nudity in Byzantium' in L. James, ed., *Desire and Denial in Byzantium* (Aldershot, 1999), 185–204.
Zeses, T., Άνθρωπος καί κόσμος ἐν τῇ οἰκονομίᾳ τοῦ Θεοῦ κατὰ τὸν ἱερὸν Χρυσόστομον (Thessalonike, 1971).
 Γεννάδιος Β' Σχολάριος: Βίος, συγγράμματα, διδασκαλία (Thessalonike, 1980).
Ziegler, P., *The Black Death* (London, 1969).
Zuckerman, C., 'The Military Compendium of Syrianus Magister', *JÖB*, 40 (1990), 209–24.

Index

Page numbers in italics are figures; with 'n' are notes.

Aaron (general) 201–3, 421–2
Aaron, Rodomir 420–3, 427–8
Abraham (Biblical figure) 421–2
Abul Aswar (emir) 195–6, 203
Acciaiuoli, Nerio I 596
Acciaiuoli, Niccolò 596
Achilleid, *Tale of Achilles* 353–5, 364, 368–70
Achilles see *Tale of Achilles*
actors, in the *theatron* 219–22
Adam (biblical figure) 241, 251, 258, 264–5, 443–4
  in *First Ethical Discourse* (Symeon the New Theologian) 282–5, 288–9
Admonitions and Anecdotes (*Consilia et Narrationes*) (Kekaumenos) 185, 206–7
Aemilius Buca, Lucius 440n53
Aetherius (poet) 526
Africanus, Sextus Julius 240–1
Agallianos, Theodore 68–9, 72, 84
Agathias 32
Agnès-Eirene 24
Aimilianos (patriarch of Antioch) 107
Aithiopika (Heliodoros) 551
Akathistos Hymn 258
Akindynos, Gregory 231n82
Aktouarios, John (Zacharias) 564n22
Albert of Aachen
  on John the Oxite 93
Alexander the Great 249, 456
Alexander Romance 228
Alexiad (Anna Komnene) 317–35, 467–70
  compared to the *Gesta Roberti* 475–85, 489
  sources of 485–9
Alexios I Komnenos 18, 23, 187, 471
  and Anna Komnene 211
  and the church 109–10
  and family relationships 108–9
  and John the Oxite 94–108
Alexios II Komnenos 24

Alexios III Angelos 298
Alexios III Komnenos (emperor of Trebizond) 228
Allatios, Leo 69, 378–80
Allegoriai (Tzetzes) 362
'Allegory of the Cave' (Plato) 290–1
Amadi 136
Amazons 18, 23, 595
Ambron (Prinzing) 341
Ampelites (Cyprus) 140, 146–8
Amphion 478
Anastasios I 245–6, 520–4, 537–41
Andronikos I Komnenos 24, 564
Andronikos II Palaiologos (Anthony) 224, 226–7, 230–2, 385
Anemodoulion 404–9, 413
Ani and Iberia 194–6
Anjou, Robert d' 595
anonymous texts
  19788 A–C 542–6
  29788C 519–22
    historical context 522–34
    metre and style 534–7
Antapodosis (Liudprand of Cremona) 337, 342–8
Antioch 93, 242–3
antipodes 430–44
Apelates 454n30
Aphrodite 241, 365–6, 406
Aphthonios 167–8, 365, 367
Apokaukos, Alexios 227
Apollonios of Tyana 249
apostasy 81–4
Apsyrtos 588
Apuleius 511
Aquinas, Thomas 72, 74
Archytas 595–6
Arcruni, Thomas 448
Ares 249
Arethas of Caesarea (bishop) 9
Argyropoulos, John 75

Ariadne 300, 531
'Arian' Controversy 244–5
Arianites, Constantine 192n25
Aristakes of Lastivert 196
Aristeides, Ailios 163n10, 173, 184n77
aristocrats, and family histories 334–5
Aristotle
  Organon 9
  and Sikeliotes 169, 176–7n56
Arklas, John 379–80n11, 383–4, 386
Armenia 447–66
Armenopoulos, Constantine 385
Arrian 474n20
Ars Grammatica (Theodorus) 539
Aršak 456
Arsinoe (Cyprus) 140, 150
Artabanos (Arsacid) 456–8, 461
Artabasdos (Artavazd) 449–50
Artaxerxes 453–4
Arthur of Britain 502, 504, 513
Asklepios 397
Aspasios 165n15
Atakta (Korais) 564
Athanasios of Alexandria 385
Athanasios I of Constantinople (patriarch) 216n6, 217n12
Athena, statue from Lindos 404–5
Athenodorus 523
Attaleiates, Michael 188, 194
  History 210
audience
  in *theatron* 223–4
Augustine 434, 444
Augustus 251
aurality 23, 275, 627
autobiography
  Mauropous 55–67
  Scholarios 68–89
  see also Katakalon Kekaumenos
Autoreianos, Arsenios (patriarch of Constantinople) 217n12

Bābak 449
Babylon 283–4
Bagratuni, Ašot 448–9
Bagratuni, Smbat 464
Bailleul, Roussel de 97, 320
Bakhtin, Mikhail 503, 507
Balsamon, Theodore 124, 128–9, 307, 385, 411
Baradeus, Jacob 248
Barberini Psalter 441–2
Bardas, Caesar 129
Barlaam of Calabria 229
Basil the Great 165–6, 171
Basil I 24–5, 338–41, 347–50, 453–66

Basil II 120, 162
Basil the Lesser (bishop) 7
Basilakes, Nikephoros 97, 221, 320, 408n47
Basilikos 165n15
Batatzes (*strategos*) 461
Beatus of Liebana 443
beauty (*kallos*) 177–8
Bede 443
begging poetry 560–3
Bekkos, John 298
Berengar II of Ivrea 337
Bessarion 298, 385
  Oratio dogmatica 70, 74–6
Bible 26, 631
  in Andronikos Kamateros 296–314
  books
    Acts 2:4–5 444
    Amos 300
    1 Cor. 304
    2 Cor. 4:7 293
    1 Cor. 12:22–5 279–87
    Daniel 351
    Ephesians 301
      5:16 280
    Exodus 32 267
    Gen 2:25 288–9
    Gen 27:22 232
    Isaiah 1:15 98–9, 104–5
    John 10:1–16 310
    2 Kings 17:32–33 438
    Luke 11:9–13 309
    Matthew
      7:7 309
      13:16–17 309
      25:31–3 311
      28:19 444
    Psalms 42
      19:3–4 306
      101:25 442
      103:5 442
      136.1 284
    1 Samuel 17, 34–7 348
    Song of Songs 3:1–3 285
    2 Timothy 3:13 438
  in Romanos 267
  Symeon the New Theologian 285–9
  Bibliotheca (the 'Library or *Myriobiblos* (the 'Myriad Books')) (Photios) 3
bilingualism
  Paraphrasis 387
  see also Alexias; *Gesta Roberti Wiscardi*; multilingualism
Black Death
  Cyprus 133–40
  and the Par. gr. 136, 140–3, 143–4

Blasteres, Matthew 385
Blemmydes, Nikephoros 68, 298, 382
Boccaccio, Giovanni
　Teseida: delle Nozze d'Emilia 595–7
　　translations 598–600, 602–4, 606, 608–9, 616–25
Bohemund of Antioch 319, 470–3, 484–5, 491–2, 495
Boilas, Eustathios 4
Boris of Bulgaria 463
Borsa, Roger 470–2, 474–5, 482, 484–5, 494
Botaneiates, Nikephoros 188, 210, 471
Boutoumites, Manuel 321
Branas, Theodore 88
Brindisi 474, 482, 493–5
Briseis 361
Bryennios, Nikephoros 97, 188, 197–8, 210–11, 318, 320, 332
　and the *Alexiad* 490–8
Bustron, Florio 136

Calabria 28
Calabrian, marginal notes 27–8
Cappella Palatina 426
caskets
　Troyes 348
　ivory 348–9
　Veroli 397–413
Centuriae (Symeon the New Theologian) 292
Ceprano 477–8
chain, golden 292
Chalcedon, Council of (451) 245–8, 269
Chalke *see* Christ at the Chalke
Chalkomatopoulos 220
Chalkoprateia (church) 129–32
charistike 94
Chelidonion 195
Chiesa, Paolo 343–4
Chiliads (Tzetzes) 297
Choiroboskos, George 380
Choirosphaktes, Leo 385
Choniates, Michael 5, 561
Choniates, Niketas 18, 125, 407–9
Chora Monastery 5
Chorosantes 203
Chortasmenos, John 7
Choumnos, Nikephoros 221, 225, 228
　quarrel with Metochites 230–2
Chrétien de Troyes 499
　Cligés 501–3
Christ at the Chalke (church) 128
Christian Topography (Indikopleustes) 435–41
'Christmas Hymn' (Romanos) 264–6
Christodoros of Koptos 521–2, 535–6, 539–40
Chronicle (Malalas) 237–54
Chronicle of the Logothete 560–1

Chronicle of Morea xix, 23, 558, 567
Chronicon Paschale 240, 248, 474n20
Chronographia (Psellos) 211–13, 330–1
Chronographia (Theophanes) 240, 450
Chryseis 360
Chrysoberges 341
chrysoboullos logos ('golden-sealed word') (golden bull) 27, 349, 486–7, 496–7
Chrysocheir 342
Chrysostom, John 128, 165–6, 172, 275
　homilies 141
　theologia and *oikonomia* 258
citizenship 25–30
classicism 403–4
clausulae 553n12, 556
Clement of Alexandria 172–3
Clement III (anti-pope, prev. known as Guibert) 494
Clement VI (pope) 138
Cligés (Chrétien de Troyes) 501–3, 512–13
　and dreams 509–12
　and time and space 504–8
close reading 9, 39–41, 49, 381
colours of horses 587–94
Commentary on the Apocalypse (Beatus of Liebana) 443
confraternities 116–32
Conrad of Germany 500
Consilia et Narrationes (*Admonitions and Anecdotes*) (Kekaumenos) 185
Consolation Concerning Bad Fortune and Good Fortune 356
Constantine of Constantinople (consul of 457) 534n66
Constantine of Rhodes 404–5, 407
Constantine I 249–50
Constantine V 452
Constantine VI 456
Constantine VII Porphyrogennetos 342, 403, 455, 459–66
　De administrando imperio 459–60, 462–3
　and the *Letters* of Daphnopates 548
Constantine IX 191–2, 194, 196
Constantine X Monomachos 212n128
Constantine XI 83
Constantinople
　Council of (553) 261
　Scholarios on the fall of 79–89
Constantius II 244
Constitution of Man, The (Meletios) 177n59
Continuatus, Theophanes 188
copying books 9–10
costumes, and *theatron* 227
Council of Chalcedon (451) 245–8, 269
Council of Constantinople (553) 261
Council of Ephesus (431) 245, 264, 268–9

Council of Nicaea (318) 244–5
Council of Trullo 128–9, 411
Crates of Malos 431–2
Creon 595, 603
critical editions 634–7
  see also digital editions
Cutler, Anthony 400
Cyprus 18, *23*, 98, 133–43, *143–4*
Cyriacus of Ancona 79
Cyril of Alexandria 258–9
Cyril of Thessalonike 25
Cyrus of Panopolis 130

Dalassene, Anna 108, 318
Dalmatia 472–3, 481–2
Daphnopates, Theodore 188n13, 547–57
David (Biblical figure) 101, 103–4, 286–7, 465
De administrando imperio (Constantine Porphyrogennetos) 459–60, 462–3
De monasteriis (John the Oxite) 106–7
Deguignes, Joseph 137
Deiphobus 360
Demosthenes 160–1, 166
Description of St Sophia (Silentiarios) 540
Diakene 190–4, 211, 213
Diasorenos, Neilos 385
Digenes Akrites 336–50, 364, 367–8
  and horses' colours 587, 590–2
  and love 406
  tent description 426
digital editions 49, 626–37
  see also critical editions
Diodoros 385
Diogenes *comes scholarum* 293, 529
Dionysiaka (Nonnos) 536n77
Dionysios of Halicarnassus, *On Literary Composition* 38–9
Dionysios (mythical figure) 250
Discourses on Aphthonios (Doxapatres) 173
divine providence 242–3
Dogmatic Panoply (*Panoplia dogmatike*) (Zigabenos) 109n65, 301
  with portrait of Alexios Komnenos 18, *23*
Domitian 249
Doukaina, Eirene *see* Eirene (wife of Alexios I)
Doukaina Kamatera, Euphrosyne 297–8
Doukas, Andronikos 342
Doukas, Constantine 385
Doukas, John *caesar* 210–11, 321, 329, 333
dove, symbol of Theotokos 125, 128
Doxapatres, John 163–4, 163n10, 167, 173
Dragaš, Helena 78
dreams 508–12
Dristra 321–2, 331
Drosilla and Charikles (Justinian) 410

Dvin 194–6
Dyrrachion 486–8
  in the *Alexiad* 321, 331, 468, 475–85, 492–5
  in the *Gesta Roberti* 471–3, 475–85

Edict of 1166 300, 313
education
  access to 15–25
  literacy 11–15, 30–4, 467, 627
  the *Paraphrasis* 377–91
  in rhetoric 185
  value of 29–32
  see also *paideia*
Eirene the *Sebastokratorissa* 16, 127–8
  tent poem 409–11, 414–19, *418*, 424–5, 427–8
Eirene (wife of Alexios I) 108, 325–6, 420
Ekphrasis (Kallikles) 110
Eleanor of Aquitaine 499
Elijah (Biblical figure) 266n55, 457n49, 464
Emilia 595–6, 623
emotion 33, 42–3
  in *Cligés* 512
  and Eros 410
  and Mauropous 55–67
  in Sikeliotes 183
  and *theatron* 221–2
  see also Scholarios
Encomium Heraclii Ducis 536
Ephesus, Council of (431) 245, 264, 268–9
epic
  Persian 464
  and the *Vita Basilii* 457
  see also *Digenes Akrites*; *Tale of Achilles*; *Teseida: delle Nozze d'Emilia* (Boccaccio)
Epicurus 65
Epidamnos 478
Eratosthenes 431–2
Eros or erotes
  in *Hysmine and Hysminias* 506–10
  in Manasses' *Synopsis Chronike* 357
  in Manganeios Prodromos' poems 417, 424–5
  and the Veroli casket 401–2, 404–13
Ethiopia 431–2n9, 442–3n66, 531
Etymologies (Isidore of Seville) 443
Eugenikos, John 385
Eugenikos, Mark 77, 298, 378–9, 385–6, 389, 391
Eugenios *cubicularios/koubikoularios* 549
Eulabes, Symeon 274, 288–9
Eulogios 454n30
Euphemios of Constantinople (patriarch) 245
Euphrasios of Antioch (bishop) 246

Euripides 223
Europa 397–402, 412–13
Eusebios of Caesarea 241, 404
Eusebios of Nikomedia 245
Eustathios of Thessalonike 307, 312, 381, 383–4, 390
Euthymios of Constantinople (patriarch) 129–30
Eutocius of Askalon 538n83
Eutyches 262
Eutychios 141
Evagrios 248, 253
Eve (Biblical figure) 264–5, 288–9
expropriation of church property, and Alexios I 103–4, 111–12
Eznik of Kolb 433–4n21

Famagusta (Cyprus) 152–4
family histories 334–5
fictional literature 45–6
Filelfo, Francesco 72, 79
Filioque 71, 75, 301, 308
First Crusade 93
First Ethical Discourse (Symeon the New Theologian) 278
Flavian of Antioch (bishop) 245
Flavius (patriarch) 533
Florence, Council of, and Scholarios 70–9
forgeries 28–9
Forty Martyrs (church) 128–9
France 628–9
Frankopoulos, Hervé 197–8

Gagik II of Ani 195
Galen 175–7, 178–9n61
Genesios 340–1, 347
Gennadios II, Patriarch *see* Scholarios, Gennadios II (George)
Genseric (king of Vandals) 526
Geoffrey of Briel 429n58
geography *see* Antipodes
Geometres, John 116–24, 130
and Sikeliotes 163
George the Cappadocian 335n71
George of Cyprus 221
George the Monk 561n10
George of Pisidia, *Hexaemeron* 434n23
Gerasimos of Hiereon (abbot) 140
Germanos of Hiereon (from Polemi) 143
Gesta Roberti Wiscardi (William of Apulia) 468–70
compared to the *Alexiad* (Anna Komnene) 475–85, 488–9, 495–8
Giblet, Henrico *see* Loredano, Giovanni Francesco
Gideon 97

Gigantomachy 404–5
Gill, Joseph 69
girl reading 18, 23
Gliceus River 474–5, 482, 494
Glossary 587, 589–90, 593
Glykas, John XIII (patriarch of Constantinople) 385
Glykas, Michael 579
golden bull ('golden-sealed word') (*chrysoboullos logos*) 27, 349, 486–7, 496–7
Gorgias (Plato) 174, 182
Gorgonia (sister of Gregory of Nazianzos) 172
grammar
and critical editions 634–5
and education 13, 377–8, 380–1
Grammatical Institutions (Priscian) 539
handbook 38
in the *Ptochoprodromika* 564
in the *theatron* 219, 223–4
Grammatical Institutions (Priscian) 539
Grammatikos, Nicholas III (patriarch of Constantinople) 109
graphiphagy 31–2
Great Lavra monastery (Mount Athos) 4, 119
Great Rebellion 186, 189, 196–204, 207–8
Greek
Byzantine 626–8
vernacular 627
Greek Anthology 522, 535–7, 539–41
Gregoras, Nikephoros 11, 149, 229
on Synesios 181
Gregory III Melissenos 77–8
Gregory the Illuminator 455, 458n55
Gregory of Nazianzos 7–8, 172, 275, 377–8, 385, 519
and poem 29 (Mauropous) 56
Sikeliotes 161, 165–6, 165n15, 168
and Symeon the New Theologian 290–1
Gregory of Nyssa 165–6, 275
Gregory of Paphos (*chartophylax*) 144
Gregory (son of Mosoulakios (Mušel)) (*strategos*) 450
Gregory VII (pope) 471–3, 476–8, 486, 488, 494
Guido of Bellapais (abbot) 137
Guiscard, Robert 321–3, 331, 470–85, 493–5
Guy de Lusignan 141

Hades 13, 251, 262, 264, 507
Hadrian 162
Hagia Sophia 225
Halieutika (Oppian) 536–7
Hasan 'the Deaf' 202
Hecker, Justus Friedrich Karl 137
Hector 360, 367
Hecuba 361

Index

Helen 357, 359–61, 366
Helena 250
Heliodoros 551, 553
Henry II of Cyprus 142
Henry IV of Germany 323, 471, 473, 494–5
Hephaistos 250
Hera 419, 425
Herakleios 456–7
Herakles 397, 405
Hermes 184n77, 507
Hermogenes 365, 367
  Sikeliotes on 159–84
Hermoniakos, Constantine, *Iliad* 362, 372
Herodotus 551
Hesychios of Miletus 252–3
Hexapterygos, Theodore 221
Hiera Synaxis 78
Hiereon (Hagia Mone monastery) 139–54, 140
Hierokles 588
Hippiatrika 587–9
Hippolyta 595
Hippolytos 397–8
History (Attaleiates) 210
History of the House of Arcrunik' (Thomas Arcruni) 448
History of the Hun, Turks and Moguls (Deguignes) 137
History (Łewond) 450
History (Niketas Choniates) 18
History of the Peloponnesian War (Thucydides) 9
History (Sebeos) 464
Hodegetria (church) 128–9
Holofernes 422n31
Holy Spirit, and the dispute between the Latin and Orthodox churches 72–3
Homer
  and Daphnopates 551
  Iliad 292, 361–2, 551
  metrical style 535–6
  Odyssey (Homer) 293, 561–2
Honorius 250
horses, colours of 587–94
Hugh of Italy 346
humanism 110
Huneric 526
hunting 340, 347–50, 406, 538, 549
Hyaleas 220
Hygeia 397
hymns and hymnographers
  Romanos the Melodist 117, 123–7, 130, 255–70
  Symeon 278–94
Hypatios (nephew of Anastasios) 539
Hyrtakenos, Theodore 220, 223

Hysmine and Hysminias (Makrembolites) 410–11, 500–2, 512–13
  dreams in 508–9
  and time and space 503–8

Iasites, Job 307
Ibrahim Inal 203
icons
  Panagiotissa 125
  Virgin Blachernitissa 125
  Virgin Hodegetria 125
  Virgin Kyriotissa 117, 125–6, 130
  Virgin Naupaktiotissa 125
identity 627–8
  and Scholarios 88
Iliad (Homer) 292, 361–2, 551
  Hermoniakos version 362, 372
  see also *War of Troy*
Illos 524, 529, 537
Imagines (Philostratos) 406
imperial ideology 25–9
Imperial School of Law 14
Imperial School of Philosophy 14
In Defense of Rhetoric (Aristides) 173
inconsistencies in texts 634–5
Indikopleustes, Kosmas, *Christian Topography* 435–41
injustice, and Alexios I 104–5, 112
ink 27, 627
inscriptions 630
  and education 24
  and funerary slabs 135, 144
  Phaethon's tomb 619
intensive (*epimeles*) reading 9
intertextuality 40–1
  in *Cligés* 513
  in Sikeliotes 174–9, 181
  in Symeon 278–94
  in the *Tale of Troy* 351–72
  see also quotation
Invective on Paris (George Pachymeres) 369
Iphigeneia 397, 412
Irenaeus 257
Isaac I Komnenos 186, 189, 198–200, 330
Isaiah 104–5
Isaurika (Christodoros of Koptos) 539–40
Isaurika (Pamprepios of Panopolis) 522
Isidore of Seville 442–3
Isocrates 173
Italos, John 111

James I of Cyprus 149–50
Jerusalem 83
  Crusade to 330, 492
John of Antioch 248, 524, 533

John the Baptist 264, 305
John of Caesarea 164–5n14
John of Damascus 377, 379, 386–7
John of Ephesus 248
John of Epidamnos 540
John the Evangelist 232
John the Hunchback 523
John II Komnenos 563
John IV the Nesteutes 385
John of Kitros 385
John of Melitene (bishop) 116
John *ostiarios* 123
John the Oxite 93–6, 106–8
  De monasteriis 106–7
  speeches to Alexios I 96–105, 111–14
John of Sardis 168
John the Scythian 523–4
John the Theologian 232, 305
John tou Boutin 146
John V Katholikos 448
John VIII Palaiologos 46n36, 72–3, 75–8, 86–7
Jordan I of Capua 473
Judas see *Life of Judas*
Judith (Biblical figure) 422
Julian the Apostate 182, 241, 249–50n46
Julian the Egyptian 539
Julian (patrician of Priscian) 539
Juliana, Anicia 534n66, 540
Julius Caesar 474n20
Justin I 246
Justinian I 248, 256, 262, 267–8

Kabasilas, Nicholas 385
Kaisariane monastery 561, 562n14
Kalandion of Antioch (bishop) 245
Kalenderhane Camii 117–18, 125, 130
Kallikles, Nicholas, *Ekphrasis* 110
Kalliope 415, 417, 425
kallos (beauty) 177–8
Kalydoniaka (Kollouthos of Lykopolis) 538
Kamateros, Andronikos 296–314
Kamytzes 321
Kantakouzenos, John 225
Karisterotzes (Varaztiroc') (*strategos*) 450
Kariye Camii 227
Kassia (abbess) 10
Katablattas 75
Katakalon Euphorbenos, Constantine 321
Katakalon Kekaumenos 209–14
  Skylitzes on 186–201, 204–5
Katrarios, John 228
Katsaros, Vasilis 367
Kecharitomene monastery 322n21
Kegen 192–3, 203–4
Kekaumenos 25, 206–7

Kephalas, Leo 323
Keroularios, Michael I (patriarch of Constantinople) 110, 203–4
Kharisian Gate 325
Khludov Psalter 441
Kinnamos, John 306n62
Kleines (Arsacid) 456–8, 461
Klementia (Pseudo-Clementine) 128n43
Klemes of Hiereon 140–1
Klimax (Sinaites) 275
Knighton, Henry 137
knowledge, Sikeliotes on 180–4
Kokkinos, Philotheos 220, 231–2
Kollouthos of Lykopolis 522, 532n55, 535, 538
  Kalydoniaka 538
  Persika 474n20
Komnene, Anna 16, 110, 125, 127, 468, 489–98
  Alexiad 317–35, 467–70
  on Psellos 126
Komnene, Isaac (brother of Alexios I) 107, 326
Komnenos, Manuel, and Kamateros 297, 300–14
Kontaratos 582n73
Korais, A. 500
  Atakta 564
Kosmas II Attikos (patriarch of Constantinople) 307n65
Kosmidion (monastery) 333
Koulinos (Galinos) 192–3
Kourkouas, John 208, 460
Koutloumousianos, Bartholomaios 379
Kroustoulas, John 131–2
Krum 463
Ktesias 442–3n66
Kydones, Demetrios 68, 71
Kynegetika (Pseudo-Oppian) 426
Kyriotai 116–32
Kyros church 118, 127, 130

Laertius, Diogenes 430
Laloutas, Constantine 147n39
Lambros 553n11
Lament (Scholarios) 80, 84–7
Laomedon 369
Laurentius (anti-pope) 526
Leib, Bernard 110
Leo of Chalcedon 104, 329
Leo the Deacon 462, 474n20
Leo I the Great 457–8, 461
Leo III 452
Leo IV 450
Leo *protovestiarios* 120n17
Leo VI 342, 385, 453
Leontios 539
Letters (Theodore Daphnopates) 547–57

Leukippe (Achilles Tatius) 552
Łewond 448, 450
Lexikon zur Byzantinischen Gräzität 634
libraries 4–6, 25
Libya 442
Life of Alexander 356, 364
Life of Anthony 274
Life of Arsenios 274
Life of Euphrosyne 274
Life of Judas 367–8
Life of Mary of Egypt 274
Life of Pelagia 274
Life of Sabbas 274
Life of St Constantine (Nikephoros Gregoras) 231n82
Life of Theodora 274
Life of Xene 274
lighting, and *theatron* 226–7
Liparit 195–6, 202–3
literacy 11–15, 17–23, 30–4, 467, 627
Liudprand of Cremona 216
  Antapodosis 337, 342–8
Longinos (brother of Zeno) 521, 529
Longinos of Kardala 523
Longinos of Selinos 523
Loredano, Giovanni Francesco 134
Love *see* Eros
Lycophron 388
Lydiaka (Christodoros of Koptos) 539
Lydos, John 247, 527, 539–40

Macedonian Renaissance 403
Machairas, Leontios 136–7
Magdalino, Paul 95, 111, 300–1, 312–13, 410
Maiktes (grandfather of Basil I) 456, 461
Makedonios of Constantinople (patriarch) 245, 533
Makrembolites, Eumathios, *Hysmine and Hysminias* 410–11, 500–8
Makres, Makarios 385
al-Makrizi 136–7, 149
Malalas, John, *Chronicle* 237–54
Malaterra, Geoffrey 323
Manasses, Constantine, *Synopsis Chronike* 354, 356–8, 361–3
Maniakes, George 186, 197, 208–10
Manuel (bishop of Adrianople) 463
Manuel I Komnenos 414
Manuel II Palaiologos, on success of performances 230
Manuel (judge and *protospatharios*, author of a book on John Kourdouas) 208, 460
Manutius, Aldus 387
Mar Aba 437n38
Marcellinus *comes* 533

Marcus Aurelius 162n7
marginal notes 6–7, 9–10, 27–8, 30, 140–3
'Maria the Roman' (icon at Chalkoprateia) 125n34
Marinos the Syrian 245–7, 533
Mark the Hermit, *Spiritual Law* 274–5
Markellos of Ankyra 258n17
marriage 411–12
  during the Black Death 138
Mary *see* Virgin Mary
Mathieu, M. 483–4
Maurianus *mystikos* 250
Maurice, Emperor 451
Maurix (admiral) 481
Mauropous, John 23, 55–67, 166n23
Maximos 220
Maximos the Confessor 232, 275
medical discourse, in Sikeliotes 174–80
Megasthenes 442–3n66
Mehmet II 83, 87
Meletios, *Constitution of Man, The* 177n59
Melissenos, Nikephoros (*caesar*) 325–6, 420
Meliteniotes, Theodore 356
Menander Rhetor 365–6, 411, 521
  On Epideictic Speeches 364
Menelaus 359–62, 366, 369
Mesarites, Nicholas 15
Metaphrastes, Symeon 26, 123
Metochites, Theodore 5, 11, 25, 227–8
  quarrel with Choumnos 230–2
  metrical prefaces 128–30
Miaphysites/Monophysites 246–8
Michael of Diabolis 192n27
Michael I (Michael Rangabe) 129
Michael III 454n30, 463–4
  horse episodes 340–1
Michael of Paphos (son of Gregory) 144
Michael tou Lemoneos 144
Michael VI 205–9
  downfall 201–5
  and the Great Rebellion 186, 196–201
Michael VII Doukas 210, 471, 480
Michael VIII Palaiologos 227, 230
Michalou 144
Middle Ages, Greek 159–60
millenarianism 244, 251–4
Miltiades 166
Minucianus 165n15
Miracles of St Artemios 124
mise-en-scène 218, 224–9
Monastras 420, 422
Monomachatos, George 486
Monophysites/Miaphysites 246–8
Moore, Helen 499
Moschopoulos, Manuel 385

Moschopoulos, Nikephoros 4
Moschos, John 406
Moses 267, 364, 435–6
multilingualism see *Teseida: delle Nozze d'Emilia* (Boccaccio)
Musaeus (poet) 538–9
Al-Mutanabbi 425
Mutragon (Omurtag) 463
Myriobiblos (the 'Myriad Books' or *Bibliotheca* (the Library)) (Photios) 3
mysticism 110
mystikoi 250–1
mythology (pagan)
  in Malalas 241, 249–51
  see also *individual mythological figures*
Mytilenaios, Christopher 119

Nabinaud, Léger de 153
nationalism 627–30
Neamonites 220n30, 223
Neoptolemos 358
Nerio I 596
Nestorios 245–6, 248
Nicaea, Council of (318) 244–5
Nicator, Seleucus 249
Nicholas of Myra 141
Nikephoros of Constantinople (patriarch) 385
Nikephoros I 451
Nikephoros II Phokas 186, 208, 464
Nikephoros III Botaneiates 210, 327–30, 332
Nikephoros *raiktor* 193, 201
Nikephoros the *xenodochos* 549–50
Niketas of Ankyra 101n34
Niketas of Herakleia 385
Nikodemos the Hagiorite 379
Nilsson, I. 356–7
Niphon, Patriarch of Constantinople 225n59
nomismata/nomisma 147–8
Nonnos of Panopolis 520, 534–7
  Dionysiaka 536n77
Norman–Byzantine war 496
  according to the *Gesta Roberti* 470–85
  and the *Alexiad* 467–70, 475–89
  see also Dyrrachion
novelisation 355–7

O Heavenly King (Symeon the New Theologian) 281
Odysseus see *Odyssey*
Odyssey (Homer) 293, 561–2
oikonomia 255–70
Olympiodoros 174–5n51
Omurtag (Mutragon) 463
'On the Ascension' (Romanos) 260, 263–4
On Azymes (John the Oxite) 94

'On the Beheading of the Forerunner' (Romanos) 260
'On the Birth of Christ' (Romanos) 269–70
'On the Decapitation of the Forerunner' (Romanos) 264
On the Disciples of the Great Proklos (Christodoros of Koptos) 539
'On Earthquakes and Fires' (Romanos) 260, 266–8
On Epideictic Speeches (Menander) 364
On Ideas (Hermogenes) 161, 164
On Issues (Hermogenes) 164
On Literary Composition (Dionysios of Halicarnassus) 38–9
On the Making of the World (Philoponos) 438
On Monasteries (John the Oxite) 94
'On the Presentation in the Temple' (Romanos) 261
'On the Resurrection' (Romanos) 260–3
'On the Samaritan Woman' (Romanos) 260
On the Use of Parts (Galen) 177
Oppian, *Halieutika* 536–7
oral traditions 37, 46–8, 185, 336–7
  and the *Ptochoprodromika* 558–60
  see also performance
Oratio dogmatica (Bessarion) 70, 74–6
Organon (Aristotle) 9
originality
  and rhetoric 223
  in Sikeliotes 164
  in Symeon 278–94
Orphanotrophos 382n19
Orpheus 251
Otranto 472, 476, 485, 493
Our Lady of Tortosa (abbey) 135
Ouranos, Nikephoros 120–4
Ovid 511
Oxeia 93n2

P. Gr. Vindob. 29788C see anonymous texts
Pachymeres, George 221, 231
  on the antipodes 441
  Invective on Paris 369
  Progymnasmata 369
paideia 220–2
Pakourianos, Gregory 4, 330, 335n71
Palaiologos, Demetrios 73, 78, 228–9n73
Palaiologos, George 319–35, 472, 486–7
Palaiologos, Nikephoros 327–30, 332
Palamas, Gregory 231–2
Palamedes 361
Palatine Anthology 407, 410
Palladion 249–50
Palladios 588
Pammakaristos church 226–7

Index

Pamprepii Panopolitani carmina (P. Gr. Vindob. 19788 A–C) 542–6
Pamprepios of Panopolis 520, 522, 526–7
Panagiotissa (icon) 125
Pankratoukas *strategos* 461
Panolbius 526
Pantechnes, Michael 428n53, 564n22
paper 26, 29, 228, 626
  and performative literature 47, 559
Paphlagon, Niketas David 465
  Vita Ignatii 454–5
Papirios (castle) 524
papyrus 29, 268–9
  Vienna 519–21
Paraphrasis of the Three Iambic Canons 377–94
parchment 26, 29, 228
Pardos, Gregory 179, 381–2, 389–90, 526
Paris see *Tale of Troy*
Paris Psalter 441
Parisinus Graecus (Par.gr.) 100, 120, 136, 140–51
Parmenides 431
'Pastoral Letter' (Scholarios) 80–4
Patmos 547–8
  monastery 6
Patriarchal School 14
Patrikios (Kosmas Indikopleustes' mentor) 437
Patrologia Graeca 629–30
Paul of Antioch (bishop) 246
Paul of Caesarea 164
Paul, St 172, 280, 286–7, 293, 304–7
Paulicians 342, 462
pearl, precious 279–80
Pechenegs
  in the *Alexiad* 321–5
  and Katakalon 190–4
Pegasus 397
Pelagius 526–7
Pentheus 164
performance 23, 46–8, 627
  poetics of Kyriotai 127–32
  see also *theatron*
Periegetes, Dionysios 536
Periplus of the Black Sea (Arrian) 474n20
Perithous 595
Perseus 250
Persika (Kollouthos of Lykopolis) 474n20
Peter the 'Poor Magistros' 561–2
Peter (saint), Manuel Komnenos compared to 300–14
Peter (son of Aliphas) 487
Petros Chartophylax 385
Phaethon 619
Philip of Nicosia 137–8
Philip of Novara 147

Philippopolis 456, 462–3
philology 39n8, 63–6, 564, 587, 594
Philopation 340
Philoponos, John, *On the Making of the World* 438
Philostratos 385, 406, 408, 413
Philotheos (patriarch of Constantiople) 385
Phlorentios (Gregoras) 229
Phoibammon 178n60, 182–3
Photios 3, 385, 441, 454–5, 465
Phournes, John 385
Pikridion (monastery) 162
Planoudes, Maximos 220, 224, 385
Planudean Anthology 406, 410
Plato
  'Allegory of the Cave' 290–1
  cost of producing copy of works 18–23
  Gorgias 174, 182
  politeia 173–4
  Protagoras 182
  and Sikeliotes 169, 182–4
  Timaeus 179, 430
Plethon, George Gemistos 10, 73
Pliny 442–3
Plutarch 178–9n61, 432–3
poem 29 (Mauropous) 56–64, 66–7
poem 142 (Geometres) 117–18
poem 143 (Geometres) 118
Poem to Sophrosyne (Meliteniotes) 356
Polemon 595–6
polis 171–3
politeia, and Plato 173–4
politikos logos 167–73
Polyakova, S. V. 502–3
Polyxene 360–1
Porphyrius the charioteer 533
portraits of important males, showing texts 17–23
Pothos *bestarches* 165
Preslav 191–2
Priam 359–62, 369
print 32, 626–7, 630–1
  and critical editions 636–7
Priscian of Caesarea 520–2, 525–7, 538–9
Prodomos (monastery) 84
Prodromos, Hilarion 562–3n15
Prodromos, Manganeios 127–8, 409–11, 414–29, 578–9
Prodromos, Theodore 381–3, 390, 578–9
  and the *Ptochoprodromika* 560–4
Progymnasmata of Aphthonios 168
Progymnasmata of Pachymeres 369
Proklos 179, 257

Prokopios of Gaza 165n15, 247, 253
  on the antipodes 434, 441
  and P. Gr. Vindob. 29788C 521–2, 528–30, 538–9
Prolegomena (Sikeliotes) 166, 168–73, 182–3
Prometheus 163n10
propaganda, and the speech by John of Oxite 105, 114
Prosopography of the Byzantine World 186
Protagoras (Plato) 182
Psellos, Michael 7–8, 12, 16, 30
  on the antipodes 441
  Chronographia 211–13, 330–1
  and humanism 110
  and Katakalon Kekaumenos 205–6, 208
  Komnene on 126
  and Mauropous 55, 65
  on Michael VI 204–5
  on readings at the church of the Chalkoprateia 129, 131–2
  on Sikeliotes 163–6
Psenas 119–21
Pseudo-Clementine, *Klementia* 128n43
Pseudo-Dionysios, the Areopagite 275, 386
Pseudo-Kodinos 227
Pseudo-Makarios 275
Pseudo-Oppian, *Kynegetika* 426
psogoi 364–9
Ptochoprodromika
  language in 558–78
  metre in 578–83, 581
Ptochoprodromos 560, 564n22, 570, 574, 579–80
punctuation 627
putti *see* erotes
Pyrrhus 478
Pythagoras 430

quotation 10, 631–2, 634
  in the *Alexiad* 483–4, 486, 491
  in Kamateros 296–314
  in Symeon the New Theologian 271–94
  in *Tale of Troy* 362
  in *theatron* 222, 228
  see also Bible

Rangabe *see* Michael I
Raoul 485
Raulaina, Theodora 224
Raymond of Saint-Gilles (Toulouse) 492
Rhakendytes, Joseph 167
rhetoric 364, 367–8
  and Eustathios of Thessalonike 312
  and Menander Rhetor 411
  Sikeliotes on Hermogenes 159–84

and *theatron* 215–33
  see also Kekaumenos; *Ptochoprodromika*
Rhodanthe and Dosikles (Andronikos Kamateros) 410
Richard the Lionheart 141
Richter, Gerhard 257
romance 352–5
  Leukippe (Achilles Tatius) 552
  Tale of Achilles (Achilleid) 353–5, 364, 368–70
  Tale of Achilles (Naples version) 355
  Tale of Alexander and Semiramis 355, 370–1
  Tale of Apollonios 361
  Tale of Belisarius 355, 370–1
  Tale of Ptocholeon 561
  Tale of Troy 351–2, 355, 357–72
  see also Teseida: delle Nozze d'Emilia (Boccaccio)
Romance of Alexander 18, 23, 593
Romanos *doux* 530
Romanos I Lekapenos 337, 341–50
Romanos II, and the *Letters* of Daphnopates 549
Romanos the Melodist 117, 123–7, 130, 255–70
Roucy, Ebles de (Ebalus) 479n30
Rudolf of Rheinfelden 478
Rudt de Collenberg, W. H. 138
Russia 628

Sacred Arsenal (Kamateros) 296–314
St Anne of Nicosia (Benedictine nunnery) 134
St Basil (monastery) 123
St George of the Greeks (cathedral) 153
St George of the Mangana 191
St Germain l'Auxerrois (Paris) 152
St Hilarion 134, 149
St John the Baptist (Oxeia) 124
St John library (Patmos) 4
St Nicholas Mesomphalos 119n13
St Polyeuktos 540
St Protasios (*ta Protasiou*) 119
St Sophia (Constantinople) 266–8
St Theodore at Letymbou 147n39
Salarios, Aspan 203
'salvation history', John the Oxite on Alexios I 101–2
Samuel, Archimandrite 524–5n20
Samuel Kometopoulos of Bulgaria 461–2
Santa Maria della Scala (hospital) (Siena) 151
Sayf al-Dawlah 425
Scholarios, Gennadios II (George) 46n36, 68–70
  apologetic writings 48n44, 70–9, 88–9
  on the fall of Constaninople 79–89
School of Gaza 538n83
School of the Holy Apostles (Constantinople) 15
scripts, in the *theatron* 218–19

scriptural texts 26
  see also Bible
Sebeos, *History* 464
Second Crusade 499–500
Segete of Paphos (sister of Gregory) 144
self-representation 44
Sergios 539
Severos of Antioch (bishop) 246–7
sexuality, and the Veroli casket 399, 410–13
Sichelgaita (wife of Robert Guiscard) 472,
  484–5, 495
Siena 151–2
Sikeliotes, John, on Hermogenes 159–84
Silentiarios, Paul 535, 540
Simeon of Amida 524–5n20
Simokattes, Theophylaktos 474n20
Simon Magus 250–1
Sinaites, John, *Klimax* 275
Sisinios II 385
Skleros, Bardas 188, 208
Skylitzes, John 186–90
  on Armenian generals 461–2
  and Kamateros 298
  on Katakalon Kekaumenos 190–201, 204–5
Socrates, in *Gorgias* 174
Solomon 268, 305
Soultzous 192
Spiritual Law (Mark the Hermit) 274–5
Sta Costanza (Rome) 406
Stepʿanos Siwnecʿi 452–3
Stephen of Antioch (bishop) 245
Stephen (Metropolitan of Nikomedia) 122
Stephen of Nikomedia 123, 276–7
Stephen of Tarōn 448–9
Stethatos, Niketas 110, 271–3, 275–7
Stilbes, Constantine 125, 130
Stoics 175
Stoudios monastery 5
  and Symeon the New Theologian 273–4
Strambali, Diomede 136
Strategikon (Kekaumenos) 185–6n3
Studies in John Malalas (Jeffreys, Croke and
  Scott) 237–41
'Styles of Gregory the Theologian, Basil the
  Great, Chrysostom, and Gregory of
  Nyssa' (Psellos) 165–6
Styliane 17
Stylianos (Zaoutzes) 455, 465
Styppeiotes, Theodore 560
Symeon of Bulgaria 461–2
Symeon *logothetes* and *magistros* 122
Symeon the New Theologian 110, 271–94
symphtharsis 179–80
Synada, Leo 122–3
Synesios of Cyrene 181, 385

Synkellos, Michael 385
synods, in Kamateros 306–7
Synopsis Chronike (Manasses) 354, 356–8, 361–3
Synopsis of the Histories (*Synopsis Historion*)
  (Skylitzes) 186–90
Syrianos 164, 173n46

ta Kyrou (monastery) 116–32
taboullarioi 29
Tačat Anjewacʿi *see* Tatzates (Tačat Anjewacʿi)
Tagaris, Paul Palaiologos 68
Tale of Achilles (*Achilleid*) 353–5, 364, 368–70
Tale of Achilles (Naples version) 355
Tale of Alexander and Semiramis 355, 370–1
Tale of Apollonios 361
Tale of Belisarius 355, 370–1
Tale of Ptocholeon 561
Tale of Troy 351–2, 355, 357–72
talismans 249–50
Tatikios 321
Tatius, Achilles 551–2
Tatzates (Tačat Anjewacʿi) 449–50
Tekfur Saray (Istanbul) 225
tents 414–29, *418*
Tertullian 442
Teseida: delle Nozze d'Emilia (Boccaccio) 595–7
  translations 598–600, 602–4, 606, 608–9,
    616–25
Theagenes of Athens (patrician) 519
theatron 215–18
  actors 219–22, 229–30
  audience 223–4
  felicitous/infelicitous performances 231–3
  means of symbolic production/*mise-en-scène*
    218, 224–9
  scripts and background symbols 218–19
  and social power 229–31
Themistocles 166
Theodora 196, 267–8
Theodore of Mopsuestia 436
Theodore Psalter 441–2
Theodore of Stoudios 385
Theodoret of Cyrrhus 259
Theodorus *memorialis* of the *scrinium epistularum*
  and *quaestor sacri palatii* 539
Theodosios (end of 9th c.) 380
Theodosios I 244–5n27, 250, 404
Theodote 16–17
Theokritos 386n38
theologia 258–9
'Theologian Style' (Psellos) 165
Theophanes the Confessor, *Chronographia* 240,
  450
Theophanes continuatus 340, 342, 455
Theophilos (892–42) 449, 451

Theophobos 449
Theophylaktos (archbishop of Ohrid) 420, 422, 428
Theotokos 264
Thesaurus Linguae Graecae (TLG) 633–4
Theseid 595–7
Theseus see *Theseid*
Thetis 417–19
Thomas Magistros 220
Thrax, Dionysios 38
Three Chapters 248
Thucydides, *History of the Peloponnesian War* 9
Timaeus (Plato) 179, 430
Timarion 411
Timothy of Gaza 538n83
To the Sebastokratorissa (poem) 416–17
Tornikios, Leo 195
Tourkos, Bardanes 451–2
Trisagion 245–6
Trismegistos, Hermes 251
Trojan Legend see *Iliad* (Hermoniakos); *Iliad* (Homer); Odyssey; *War of Troy*; *Tale of Troy*
Trullo, Council of 128–9, 411
Tübingen Theosophy 251
Turcius Rufius Apronianus Asterius 539
Turkey 628
Turner, C. J. G. 69
tyche 249–50
Tyrach 193
Tzetzes, John 536
  Allegoriai 362
  on the antipodes 441
  on education of women 15–16
  and Kamateros 297
  notes in books 6–7, 9
Tzimiskes, John 462, 474n20

Union of churches, and Scholarios 70–9
Urban II 470
Urbicius 540
usurpation, and Alexios I 103–4

Valens 244
Vatopedi (monastery) 84
Venice 323, 471, 486, 496–7
Verina 525
vernacular 352–3, 627
  Old French 499
  in the *Tale of Troy* 352–3, 369
  see also *Digenes Akrites*; *Ptochoprodromika*; *Teseida: delle Nozze d'Emilia* (Boccaccio); *Theseid*
Veroli casket 397–413, *398*
Vienna papyrus 519–21
Vigilius of Rome 248
Virgil of Salzburg 443
Virgin Blachernitissa (icon) 125
Virgin Hodegetria (icon) 125
Virgin Kyriotissa (icon) 117, 125–6, 130
Virgin Mary, in Romanos 257–8, 264–6, 269–70
Virgin Naupaktiotissa (icon) 125
Vision of Sahak 458
visual representations of texts 24
Vita Basilii 340, 347, 453, 455–66
Vita Euthymii 455, 465
Vita Ignatii (Niketas David Paphlagon) 454–5
Vitalian 533
Vitalis, Orderic 93, 485
Vladislav, John 420
voice 44

War of Troy 354–5, 361–2
  see also *Iliad* (Hermoniakos); *Iliad* (Homer)
Welf IV 478
William of Apulia 323
  Gesta Roberti Wiscardi 468–70
William of Malmesbury 485
William of Tyre, on John the Oxite 93
women
  and education 15–17
  see also Kassia; Komnene, Anna

Xenos family 146–9

Zacharias of Mytilene 524–5n20
Zacharius (pope) 443–4
Zeno 523–32
  and P. Gr. Vindob. 29788C 521, 537–8
Zenos, Dimitrios 596
Zeses, Theodore 69
Zetas 478
Zeus 241, 292, 546
Zigabenos, Euthymios, *Dogmatic Panoply* 18, 23, 109n65, 301
Zonaras, John 102
Zosimos of Askalon 538n83